Rus' Restored:
Selected Writings of Meletij Smotryc'kyj
1610–1630

HARVARD LIBRARY OF EARLY UKRAINIAN LITERATURE
ENGLISH TRANSLATIONS VOLUME VII

Cambridge, Massachusetts

ГАРВАРДСЬКА БІБЛІОТЕКА ДАВНЬОГО УКРАЇНСЬКОГО ПИСЬМЕНСТВА
КОРПУС АНГЛІЙСЬКИХ ПЕРЕКЛАДІВ ТОМ VII

Rus' Restored:
Selected Writings of Meletij Smotryc'kyj
1610–1630

Translated and Annotated

with an Introduction by

David Frick

Distributed by Harvard University Press
for the Harvard Ukrainian Research Institute

The Harvard Ukrainian Research Institute was established in 1973 as an integral part of Harvard University. It supports research associates and visiting scholars who are engaged in projects concerned with all aspects of Ukrainian studies. The Institute also works in close cooperation with the Committee on Ukrainian Studies, which supervises and coordinates the teaching of Ukrainian history, language, and literature at Harvard University.

The preparation of this volume was made possible in part by a grant from the National Endowment for the Humanities, an independent federal agency.

Smotryts'kyĭ, Meletiĭ, 1578–1633.
   [Selections. English. 2004]
   Rus' restored : selected writings of Meletij Smotryc'kyj, (1610–1630) / translated and annotated by David Frick.
      p. cm. -- (Harvard library of early Ukrainian literature. English translations ; v. 7)
   Includes bibliographical references.
   ISBN 0-916458-64-4 (alk. paper)
  1. Apologetics--Early works to 1800. I. Frick, David A. II. Title. III. Series.
  BX4711.695.S6A25 2004
  274.77'06--dc22
                       2004020150

Jacket Illustration: Motto and printer's mark from Meletij Smotryc'kyj, *Exęthesis abo Expostulatia* (Lviv, 1629), fol. 102r. Taken from the facsimile edition: *Collected Works of Meletij Smotryc'kyj,* intro. David A. Frick (Cambridge, Mass., 1987), p. 804.

Jacket Concept: Jennie Bush, Designworks, Inc.

Jacket Design: Marika L. Whaley

Publication of this volume has been made possible
by the generous support of
Dr. Alexander Gudziak and Mrs. Jaroslawa Gudziak

Цей том появляється завдяки
щедрій підтримці
д-ра Олександра Ґудзяка й пані Ярослави Ґудзяк

Editorial Statement

The *Harvard Library of Early Ukrainian Literature* is one portion of the Harvard Project in Commemoration of the Millennium of Christianity in Rus'-Ukraine, which is being carried out by the Ukrainian Research Institute of Harvard University with the financial support of the Ukrainian community.

The *Library* encompasses literary activity in Rus'-Ukraine from its beginning in the mid-eleventh century through the end of the eighteenth century, and primarily contains original works. Included are ecclesiastical and secular works written in a variety of languages, such as Church Slavonic, Old Rus', Ruthenian (Middle Ukrainian), Polish, and Latin. This linguistic diversity reflects the cultural pluralism of Ukrainian intellectual activity in the medieval and early-modern periods.

The *Library* consists of a *Texts* series and an *English Translations* series. The *Texts* series publishes the original works, in facsimile whenever appropriate. Texts from the medieval period are offered either in the best available scholarly edition or in one specially prepared for the *Library*, whereas those from the later periods are reproduced from manuscripts or early printed editions. The *English Translations* series comprises translations of the original works and extensive analytical introductions, notes, and indices.

For much of the period covered by the *Library*, Ukrainian and Belarusian cultural figures were active in a shared social, intellectual, and religious milieu. Since the *Library* selects authors and works important to the Ukrainian part of this sphere, their names are rendered in Ukrainian form, even though at times they may also have been of significance in Belarusian territory. Appellations such as Rus', Rusija, Rossija, Mala Rossija, Malaja Rossija, Malorussija, Ruthenia, Malorussijskaja Ukrajina, Ukrajina, and so on, are presented according to their actual use in the given text. All of these terms have historically been used to designate Ukraine or its parts. In addition, the word "Ruthenian" is employed to translate early-modern nomenclature for "Ukrainian" and early-modern terminology describing common Ukrainian and Belarusian culture, language, and identity. Except for toponyms with already established English forms, place-names are given in accordance with the official language of the state; premodern or alternative modern forms are indicated in the indices.

For Smotryc'kyj and his contemporaries in the early decades of the seventeenth century, the term "Rus'" (Lat. Ruthenia) and its derivatives had a number of meanings. In the territorial sense, Rus' referred to specific lands within the Polish-Lithuanian Commonwealth, areas today largely within Ukraine and Belarus. Muscovy was not covered by the term. In a narrower territorial meaning the term denoted the palatinate of Rus' (Pol. Województwo Ruskie), roughly coterminous with historic Galicia. As a collective noun signifying a people or ethnos, Rus' ("the Rus'" or "Ruthenians") referred to the East Slavic population of Poland-Lithuania, the ancestors of modern-day Ukrainians and Belarusians. Additionally, the term Rus' was linked inextricably with Eastern (Greek) Christianity (that is, both Orthodoxy and the Uniate Church), the Slavonic language and its Cyrillic alphabet, and their cultural expression. Often, however, there was no clear-cut distinction among these meanings and connotations, thus permitting a nuanced stylistic fluidity. In the phrase "Let there be Rus' in Rus'," for example, individual notions of territory, people, religion, and culture are merged in such a way as to preclude a single interpretation.

Contents

Illustrations x
Abbreviations xi
Introduction xv
Translator's Note lxvii
Acknowledgments lxix

The Works of Meletij Smotryc'kyj

Thrēnos (1610) 1
Homiliary Gospel (1616) 83
Church Slavonic Grammar (1618–1619) 95
A Funeral Sermon (1621) 101
A Verification of Innocence (1621) 111
A Defense of the "Verification" (1621) 239
A Refutation of Acrimonious Writings (1622) 281
A Justification of Innocence (1623) 325
Five Letters (1627–1628) 351
Apology (1628) 369
A Revocation (1628) 567
A Protestation (1628) 571
Paraenesis (1629) 601
Exaethesis (1629) 685
A Final Letter (1630) 749

Glossary 763
Works Cited 767
Index of Biblical References 775
Index 787

Illustrations

Plate 1. Vilnius, from Georg Braun and Franz Hogenberg,   82
Civitates Orbis Terrarum, vol. 3 (Cologne, 1581), 59.

Plate 2. Vilnius, by Tomasz Makowski, *Panorama miasta*   100
Wilna, 1600.

Plate 3. Woodcut of Vilnius by an unknown seventeenth-   110
century Dutch artist.

Plate 4. Poland and surrounding areas, from *Kozmograffia*   324
czeská (Prague, 1554), 1006. Reprint: *Specimina Philologiae
Slavicae* 78 (Munich, 1988), 100.

Plate 5. Kyiv, from Afanasij Kaľnofojsʹkyj, *Teraturgēma*   350
(Kyiv, 1638). Reprint: *HLEULT 4,* 139.

Plate 6. Lviv, from Georg Braun and Franz Hogenberg,   368
Civitates Orbis Terrarum, vol. 6 (Cologne, 1617), 49.
Courtesy of Volodymyr Peleshak.

Plate 7. Constantinople, from G. F. Camocio, *Isole famose,*   570
porti, fortezze, e terre maritime (Venice, 1572).

Plate 8. Cracow, from Hartmann Schedel, *Liber chronicarum*   600
(Nuremberg, 1493).

Plate 9. Jerusalem, from Stefano Du Perac, *Hierusalem*   762
(Rome, 1570?).

Abbreviations

AJuZR	*Arxiv Jugo-Zapadnoj Rossii,* 35 vols. in 8 pts. (Kyiv, 1859–1914).
ANF	*Ante-Nicene Fathers,* vols. 1–9 (Buffalo and New York, 1886–1887); vol. 10 (Grand Rapids, Mich., 1951).
Arthaber	Augusto Arthaber, *Dizionario comparato di proverbi e modi proverbiali italiani, latini, francesi, spagnoli, tedeschi, inglesi e greci antichi* (Milan, 1929).
AVAK	*Akty, izdavaemye Vilenskoj arxeografičeskoj kommissieju,* 39 vols. (Vilnius, 1865–1915).
AZR	*Akty, otnosjaščiesja k istorii Zapadnoj Rossii, sobrannye i izdannye Arxeografičeskoju kommissieju,* 5 vols. (St. Petersburg, 1846–1853).
ChrKS	John Chrysostom, *Knyha o svjaščenstve* (Lviv, 1614).
CPG	*Clavis Patrum Graecorum,* ed. M. Geerard, 5 vols. (Turnhout, 1974–1987).
DługEng	*The Annals of Jan Długosz,* trans. Maurice Michael (West Sussex, 1997).
Ephr.	S. Ephraemus Syrus, *Opera omnia quae exstant,* 6 vols. (Rome, 1732–1746).
Erasmus *Ad.*	Desiderius Erasmus, *Adagia,* in his *Opera omnia,* vol. 2, ed. Jean Le Clerc (Leiden, 1703; Hildesheim, 1961).
FC	*The Fathers of the Church. A New Translation*, vols. 1– (Washington and New York, 1947–).
Gibbs	Laura Gibbs, trans. and ed., *Aesop's Fables* (Oxford, 2002).
HC	Theodoret and Evagrius, *A History of the Church* (London, 1854).

HLEUL 3   *Lev Krevza's* A Defense of Church Unity *and Zaxarija Kopystens'kyj's* Palinodia, trans. Bohdan Strumiński, 2 pts. [=Harvard Library of Early Ukrainian Literature, English Translations 3] (Cambridge, Mass., 1995).

HLEULT 1   *Collected Works of Meletij Smotryc'kyj,* intro. David A. Frick [=Harvard Library of Early Ukrainian Literature, Texts 1] (Cambridge, Mass., 1987).

HLEULT 2   *The* Jevanhelije učytelnoje *of Meletij Smotryc'kyj,* intro. David A. Frick [=Harvard Library of Early Ukrainian Literature, Texts 2] (Cambridge, Mass., 1987).

HLEULT 3   *Lev Krevza's* Obrona iednosci cerkiewney *and Zaxarija Kopystens'kyj's* Palinodija, intro. Omeljan Pritsak and Bohdan Struminsky [=Harvard Library of Early Ukrainian Literature, Texts 3] (Cambridge, Mass., 1987).

HLEULT 4   *Seventeenth-Century Writings on the Kievan Caves Monastery,* intro. Paulina Lewin [=Harvard Library of Early Ukrainian Literature, Texts 4] (Cambridge, Mass., 1987).

LF   *A Library of Fathers of the Holy Catholic Church Anterior to the Division of the East and West,* 48 vols. (Oxford, 1840–1885).

LVIA   Lietuvos Valstybės Istorijos Archyvas (Lithuanian State Historical Archive, Vilnius).

Mansi   *Sacrorum Conciliorum Nova et amplissima collectio,* ed. Giovan Domenico Mansi, 53 vols. (Paris, 1901– 1927).

Mar   St. John Chrysostom, *Margarit* (Ostroh, 1595).

MarEph   Marcus Eugenicus Metropolita Ephesi, *Opera anti-unionistica* [Concilium Florentinum, Documenta et scriptores, ser. A, vol. 10, fasc. 2] (Rome, 1977).

MUH   *Monumenta Ucrainae historica,* vol. 1, *1075–1623* (Rome, 1964).

NKPP   Julian Krzyżanowski, ed., *Nowa księga przysłów i wyrażeń przysłowiowych polskich,* 4 vols. (Warsaw, 1969–1978).

NPNF1   *A Select Library of the Nicene and Post-Nicene Fathers of the Christian Church,* 1st ser., 14 vols. (Buffalo and New York, 1886–1890).

NPNF2   *A Select Library of the Nicene and Post-Nicene Fathers of the Christian Church,* 2nd ser., 14 vols. (New York, 1890–1900).

Oct   *Octoechos or The Book of Eight Tones, a Primer Containing the Sunday Service in Eight Tones* (London, 1898).

OktB   *Oktoichos oder Parakletike,* ed. A. von Maltzew, 2 pts. (Berlin, 1904).

OktD   *Oktoix* (Derman', 1604).

PG   *Patrologiae cursus completus, bibliotheca omnium SS. patrum, doctorum, scriptorumque ecclesiasticorum sive Latinorum, sive Graecorum,* series graeca, ed. J.-P. Migne, 161 vols. (Paris, 1857–1866).

PL   *Patrologiae cursus completus, bibliotheca omnium SS. patrum, doctorum, scriptorumque ecclesiasticorum sive Latinorum, sive Graecorum,* series latina, ed. J.-P. Migne, 221 vols. (Paris, 1844–1880).

PP   *Prawa y Przywileie od naiaśnieyszych Krolow Ich Mci Polskich y W. Xięstwa Litewskiego nadane obywatelom Korony Polskiey y W. X. Litewskiego religiey Greckiey w iedności z ś. Kościołem Rzymskim będącym* (Vilnius, 1632).

RIB   *Russkaja istoričeskaja biblioteka.*

Tanner   Norman P. Tanner, ed., *Decrees of the Ecumenical Councils,* vol. 1, *Nicaea I to Lateran V* (London and Washington, 1990).

Tosi   Renzo Tosi, *Dizionario delle sentenze latine e greche* (Milan, 1991).

Introduction

Ruthenia restituta, Ruthenia restaurata. The title is borrowed from a passage, published in 1629, in which Meletij Smotryc'kyj urged Cyril Lukaris, then Patriarch of Constantinople, to place his see in union with Rome and transfer its seat from Constantinople to Kyiv. By doing so, Smotryc'kyj argued, Lukaris would end the enmity between Uniate and Orthodox in Rus' and become known as "the *restitutor* [restorer] of peace in the Church of Christ the Lord, which He has in this most noble Polish kingdom, and as the *restaurator* [renovator] of the freedom that is already almost lost in the Ruthenian nation."[1]

Smotryc'kyj was likely serious about the creation of a Ruthenian patriarchate, but his plea to Lukaris was motivated by a more nuanced agenda. On the surface, Smotryc'kyj was asking for something that would probably never take place. It was not clear that the Roman Church would accept such an innovation in hierarchy among its Ruthenian Uniates, and it was certainly unclear that the Calvinizing Lukaris would be the choice for the job.[2] Before a smaller, less public audience of Uniate and Roman Catholic hierarchs, Smotryc'kyj himself claimed a different purpose in writing to Lukaris—namely, that he intended to pose questions in a public forum in such a way as to force the patriarch to reveal himself to the world as a heretic, and thereby to cause Rus' to turn its back upon him.[3] This claim, too, however, may have been a matter of posturing, and there is no reason to assume that Smotryc'kyj's first approaches to the patriarch were entirely disingenuous.

This ambiguity in Smotryc'kyj's motivations reflects the larger conflict between Uniate and Orthodox in the Polish-Lithuanian Commonwealth of the early seventeenth century, and the weak position

---

1.   Smotryc'kyj 1629a, 51/670, 94/692, and see below, pp. 654, 683. References to Smotryc'kyj's works are double: the number after the slash indicates pages in the facsimile editions (*HLEULT 1* and *HLEULT 2*).
2.   On the Ruthenian patriarchate, see Krajcar 1964, Tanczuk 1949, Andrusiak 1934.
3.   See Velykyj 1972, 128, and below, p. 356.

of Rus' as a member of that Commonwealth. In order to gain credibility
and followers, participants from all sides in the religious debates of the
time claimed that their goal was the restitution and renewal of Rus';
or, as Smotryc'kyj would put it (borrowing here from Jan Szczęsny
Herburt, a quite different kind of Ruthenian), the goal was "that there
be Rus' in Rus'."[4] Even those whose programs seemed to minimize
Ruthenian difference in Polish-Lithuanian society made use of such
slogans. But the real question under debate was the fundamental one of
Ruthenian identities. The restoration of Rus' required taking a position
on the original nature of the Rus' polity, religion, society, and culture,
and it was here that the battle was fought.

As a prominent religious figure and polemicist, and a person caught
up in the struggle between Orthodox and Uniate beliefs, Smotryc'kyj is
a crucial source for understanding the turmoil that gripped Rus' in the
early seventeenth century. The works collected in this volume, written
by Smotryc'kyj over a period of twenty years, offer unusual insight into
the life of the elite of early modern Rus' and their place in the Polish-
Lithuanian Commonwealth.

Maksym (Maksentij) Smotryc'kyj (ca. 1577–1633) was the son of
Herasym Danyjilovyč, a *pisarz* or *notarius* for Palatine of Kyiv
Kostjantyn Vasyl' Ostroz'kyj. Herasym was himself an author of
Orthodox polemical pamphlets, one of the editors of the so-called
Ostroh Bible (Ostroh, 1580–1581), the first printing of Holy Scripture
in Church Slavonic (the liturgical language of the Orthodox Slavs), and
perhaps one of the first Ruthenian versifiers. Smotryc'kyj's grandfather
was a certain "Deacon Danyjil," who copied and signed an anti-Hussite
pamphlet at Smotryč (Podolia) in the second half of the sixteenth
century. Smotryc'kyj was thus the scion of one the first documented
literary families of early modern Rus'.[5]

---

4.   Smotryc'kyj 1621b, 51v/376, and see below, p. 203. For Herburt and
his *Opinion about the Ruthenian Nation,* see Lipiński 1912, 80–97. Later, as
a Uniate, Smotryc'kyj would also use the formula. See Smotryc'kyj 1628a,
194/620, and below, p. 558.
5.   For a discussion in English of the controversies surrounding a Smotryc'kyj
biography, as well as secondary literature in other languages, see Frick 1995.
Among pertinent works that have appeared since, see Thomson 1998, Mycyk

Smotryc'kyj experienced the Union of Brest (1596) as a young man of about nineteen years, and his entire literary and ecclesiastical career would unfold in the context of the confessional, cultural, and political debates that agitated Rus' and the Commonwealth in the first decades of the seventeenth century. In the later sixteenth century, Rus' was increasingly the object of the confessional and cultural propaganda of the Polish-Lithuanian Reformation and Counter-Reformation. Some Ruthenian magnate and noble families, as well as some burghers, were "lost" at this time to conversion to Calvinism or Catholicism. Already before the Union of Brest, a Ruthenian elite was attempting to mount an Orthodox response—something we might call an Orthodox Reform—through the creation of Orthodox schools, printing houses, confraternities, and the reform of the clergy.[6] The Union, which created a Greek-rite Ruthenian Church in communion with Rome, both intensified the reform activities (on all sides) and complicated the competition for Ruthenian hearts and minds. Many participants in the debates—and Smotryc'kyj was something of a master at this—shifted frequently, as the polemical context required, between exclusive definitions of Ruthenianness (e.g., we Orthodox against Uniates and other apostates) and inclusive definitions based on traditions and genealogies appealing to ties of "blood."

Smotryc'kyj was one of those unusual individuals who were at home at the intersection of the Christian East and West and could speak from personal experience of the state of affairs in both Constantinople and Reformation Wittenberg. From 1610 to 1623, he was one of the leading spokesmen for Ruthenian renewal under the Orthodox (or, as the opponents would put it, Dis-Uniate) banner. After his conversion in 1627 and until his death in 1633, he would serve as one of the leading polemicists for the Uniate cause. His life—his goals, successes, and failures—bears witness to the dilemmas facing the burgeoning cultural elite of the Ruthenian clergy and middling gentry during the latter two decades of the reign of Sigismund III.

Even the sources for Smotryc'kyj's biography were influenced by the larger religious conflict. Much of our information about his life

---

1993, Mycyk 1997. On Smotryc'kyj's birth and family, see Frick 1995, 21–9.
6. Among important new works on this topic, with extensive bibliographies, see Gudziak 1998, Plokhy 2001.

comes from reports of local Uniate and Catholic authorities to Rome, polemical pamphlets written by him or by others in response to his writings, and a *vita* by Uniate Bishop of Chełm Jakiv Suša (1666) that was a part of a campaign for the canonization of the martyred Uniate archbishop of Polack Josafat Kuncevyč. Thus the biographical materials were themselves part of the polemic and must be interpreted accordingly.

According to old tradition, Smotryc′kyj received his first education in the Tri-Lingual Academy (Greek, Latin, Slavonic) that Herasym Danyjilovyč had established for Ostroz′kyj at Ostroh, and in which the elder Smotryc′kyj served for a time as rector. It may have been here that Smotryc′kyj first encountered Lukaris, the future patriarch of Constantinople, who visited the Polish-Lithuanian Commonwealth as a patriarchal legate twice (ca. 1596 and ca. 1601), and among whose "pupils" (he used the term *dyscypuł*) Smotryc′kyj would later count himself.[7] Thereafter, Prince Ostroz′kyj sent Smotryc′kyj together with the young Orthodox nobleman Jurij Puzyna to study at the Jesuit Academy in Vilnius. In all likelihood, this took place in the late 1590s. Smotryc′kyj seems not to have completed his program of studies in Vilnius, and the circumstances of his departure from the Academy are a matter of some debate. A brief Uniate biography sent to Rome in 1630 (i.e., after his conversion was made public) stated that he had completed the program of "lesser studies of letters," whereupon, on account of his parents' concerns over the confessional orientation of the education he was receiving, he was sent by them "to Germany, to the heretical schools."[8] A report of the papal nuncio in Warsaw sent to Rome on 1 January 1628 (i.e., after his conversion, but while he was still presenting himself as Orthodox) alleged that he had been expelled (*escluso*) from the Academy "on account of the schism."[9] In any event, Smotryc′kyj did indeed make a subsequent study tour of Protestant German academies and universities and served as *praeceptor* to a young Orthodox nobleman, Prince Bohdan Bohdanovyč Solomerec′kyj. According to a later account of the Uniate Smotryc′kyj, they had visited Leipzig and Wittenberg;[10]

---

7.   Smotryc′kyj 1629a, 68/679, and see below, p. 667. On the Academy, see Myc′ko 1990.
8.   Velykyj 1972, 218.
9.   Velykyj 1960, 298.
10.   Smotryc′kyj 1628a, 95–6/571.

according to Suša, they visited Wrocław, Leipzig, Nürnberg (i.e., Altdorf), "and other cities and academies of non-Catholic Germany."[11] The fact that the name Solomereckyj appears among the matriculants in Leipzig for the year 1606 offers some evidence for the chronology of Smotryckyj's study tour.[12]

Thrēnos

Smotryckyj was back in Lithuania by 1610 when his first polemical work, *Thrēnos, That Is, The Lament of the One, Holy, Universal, Apostolic, Eastern Church,* appeared at the printing house of the Orthodox Brotherhood in Vilnius. Studynskyj (1906, xxxvii–l) argued that a young Smotryckyj hid behind the pseudonym "Clerk of Ostroh" and authored two Ruthenian-language polemical pamphlets in response to then Bishop of Volodymyr and Brest Ipatij Potij in 1598 and 1599, but there is no evidence to support this hypothesis. Studynskyj also argued (1925) that Smotryckyj authored the work *Antigraphē,* which appeared at the Vilnius Brotherhood press in 1608, but there is strong evidence against this.[13]

   Thrēnos was a work of considerable audacity. The anonymous author was then a thirty-year-old layman, "a disciple [*zwolennik*] of Luther," as Smotryckyj himself would later allege, "who, having spent his young years at the Leipzig and Wittenberg Academies by the grave of Luther, arrived in Lithuania sooty from the smoke of the Lutheran heats and, singing his *Lament,* infected Rus′ with those same fumes."[14] The work was a first-person narration by a personification of the Holy Mother Eastern Church and allegedly written down in Greek by a certain Theophil Orthologue, "son of that same Holy Eastern Church." It was allegedly translated at some point from the sacred Greek into the likewise sacred Church Slavonic, and finally translated from Slavonic into Polish "for the easier understanding of all people."[15] *Thrēnos* claimed to speak for all of Orthodoxy before all of Christendom. In fact,

11.   Suša 1666, 16.
12.   On Smotryckyj's education, see Frick 1995, 30–7.
13.   On these questions of attribution, see Frick 1995, 38–44.
14.   Smotryckyj 1628a, 95–6/571, and see below, p. 472.
15.   Smotryckyj 1610, ( )1r/1 and () ( )2r/6, and see below, pp. 3 and 8.

it was a much more local affair. The translation history was a fiction:
Thrēnos was composed and printed in the same Polish that was quickly
becoming the language in which the Ruthenian polemic was conducted,
the language in which Smotryc'kyj wrote all of his printed polemical
works. It spoke to the concerns of members of the Orthodox community
of Poland-Lithuania who had been "abandoned" by their ecclesiastical
and political elite.

Despite the political ramifications of the work's contents, *Thrēnos*
studiously avoided direct involvement in politics. The anonymous author
of the "Preface to the Reader" (also Smotryc'kyj), like other spokesmen
for religious movements eager to prove their loyalty to secular authority,
quoted St. Paul's plea for a "quiet and peaceable life" (1 Tim. 2:1–2),
and he declared that in the Eastern Church "no service, no ceremony of
the Church order begins or ends without offering a prayer to almighty
God for the good health and happy increase (with victory over the
enemies) of the reign of His Majesty the King."[16] Nevertheless, these
reassurances seem not to have calmed the suspicions of King Sigismund
III. Perhaps the king was concerned that the desire for peace and quiet
masked an attempt to create room for Ruthenian maneuverings. In any
event, he treated the work as a challenge to authority. Catholic and Uniate
polemicists attacked it as an act of treason during a time of hostilities
with Muscovy. Encamped near Smolensk, Sigismund III wrote on 1
April 1610 that "we have information that in the Ruthenian printing
house of the Holy Spirit [Brotherhood] they are secretly printing some
sort of pasquils and books against authority." A circular dated 7 May
placed a penalty of 5,000 *złoty*s upon all who "dared to buy or sell such
books, leaflets, and pasquils," which were seen as a threat to "spiritual
and secular authority." Private citizens were commanded not only
not to buy or sell such printings, "but . . . to collect and burn them."
In a decree of the preceding day (6 May) to the secular authorities of
Vilnius, Sigismund III had identified the "corrector" as "Łotwin" (i.e., a
Latvian, but probably a mistake in this text for the given name Lohvyn)
Karpovyč, and he had ordered him imprisoned, "especially if he is not
a member of the *szlachta,* about which Your Graces can easily discover
amongst yourselves."[17]

16.   Smotryc'kyj 1610, () () () () 1r/13, and see below, p. 18.
17.   See Anuškin 1970, 134–6; AVAK 8:93–5.

Sigismund's actions did not prevent *Thrēnos* from becoming a sort of best-seller. Dem'jan Nalyvajko (an Orthodox priest and brother of Cossack insurgent Severyn) allegedly—this according to the Uniate Smotryc'kyj—said of the work that "it is equal in the authority of God's truth described in it to the writings of St. [John] Chrysostom, and it is fitting for us to pour out our blood and to lay down our lives for it."[18] In 1666 Smotryc'kyj's Uniate biographer, Jakiv Suša, wrote this assessment of the work's attractive pull among the Orthodox and the heterodox: "There were here as many severe wounds as words; as many deadly poisons as ideas. And since they were characterized by a remarkable refinement of the Polish language, made pleasant as if by a sweet poisoner, they were all the more harmful. So much so that not only schismatics, but also heretics wore out that *Lament* with eager hands, embraced it in their bosoms, finally fixed it deeply in their hearts. There were those who, as if they were rich people, cunningly left it behind through their last will to be passed on to their descendants as an excellent manifest *cimelium* [heirloom, treasure] . . . . Nor did a certain heretic hold it inglorious to be buried with it for eternity in lamentable fashion."[19]

One of the reasons for the work's impact lay in the rhetorical strategy Smotryc'kyj had chosen. The first chapter was a *querela* or complaint, a device that belonged to the realm of forensic rhetoric. This was a piece of legal oratory in which the Eastern Church, personified as a mother, brought charges against her "degenerate sons," that is to say all "apostate" Ruthenians, but especially the Uniate Church hierarchy, before God their Father, who was the impartial but severe judge. The first chapter, the lament proper, contained the six clearly marked sections of a forensic oration as prescribed by the reigning treatments of the art of oratory. Here we find an *exordium* (which wins the goodwill of the audience), a *narratio* (which presents the events that are alleged to have occurred), a *partitio* (which lays out the structure of the further oration), a *confirmatio* (which lends credit and authority to the case through the use of arguments), a *refutatio* (which seeks to weaken the arguments of the opponent), and a *peroratio* (which provides the conclusion to the speech). Moreover, Smotryc'kyj's prose had a certain rhythm to it, which

18. Smotryc'kyj 1629a, 7/648, and see below, p. 610.
19. Suša 1666, 18–19.

may also have owed something to classical rhetorical models. Perhaps it was a Polish imitation of something akin to the *cursus* of Latin prose rhythm. In any event, the rhythm of Smotryc'kyj's prose was one aspect of the *ornatus* that contributed to the work's highly affective style.

Smotryc'kyj, of course, had not invented the literary *querela*. His work continued a long tradition of personifications, usually personifications of secular polities, most often of the Mother Republic bringing her complaint against her degenerate children in a public forum. The device had enjoyed considerable popularity in the recent polemic over the Zebrzydowski Rebellion (1606–1607). In its anti-Jesuit rhetoric, Smotryc'kyj's work shared one aspect with that polemical literature, and there is reason to suspect that he may have been a reader of the Rebellion's pamphleteers.[20]

Smotryc'kyj equated apostasy from Orthodoxy (including acceptance of the Union) with the abandonment of the "Ruthenian nation." Perhaps most frequently cited by Orthodox supporters was a passage from chapter 1 in which the Church lamented the loss of Ruthenian noble houses,[21] although Henryk Litwin has shown that, in one sense, Smotryc'kyj exaggerated here: many of these families were still at least partially Orthodox, even on the eve of the Xmel'nyc'kyj Uprising.[22] The exaggeration was effective, however. Through his list of family names Smotryc'kyj was both lamenting the loss of noble houses and making a claim for a continuing "Ruthenian" presence in Polish-Lithuanian politics, in the hope of attracting some of the apostates back to the national cause.

But the true audacity of the work lay in Smotryc'kyj's treatment of the Uniate clergy, especially the metropolitan of Kyiv and founder of the Union, the then nearly seventy-year-old Ipatij Potij. Speaking for the entire Eastern Church, Smotryc'kyj labeled Potij the chief offender against the Ruthenian religion and nation in his first-chapter juridical speech. And in his second chapter, Smotryc'kyj directly and strongly admonished the chief apostate.

The remainder of the work contained, still as a first-person narration, an exposition of Orthodox faith: chapter 3, "Against the

20.   On the rhetorical models for *Thrēnos,* see Frick 1987.
21.   Smotryc'kyj 1610, 15r–v/31–2, and see below, pp. 44–5.
22.   See Litwin 1987.

Autocratic Authority of the Bishop of Rome"; chapter 4, "On the Present-Day Roman Church"; chapter 5, "On the Procession of the Holy Spirit"; chapter 6, "On the Unleavened and Leavened Bread of the Sacrament of the Lord's Supper"; chapter 7, "On Purgatory"; chapter 8, "On the Rejection of the Chalice of the New Testament by the Roman Church"; chapter 9, "On the Invocation of the Saints"; and chapter 10, a "Catechism" of Orthodox faith.

By the early 1620s, the Uniate and Roman Catholic sides knew who had authored *Thrēnos*. But even then, Smotryc'kyj seems to have been reluctant to take public credit for the book. His first printed work after he had been made archbishop of Polack was a funeral sermon for Leontij Karpovyč, his predecessor as archimandrite of the Vilnius Orthodox Holy Spirit Monastery. In that work, Smotryc'kyj wrote that Karpovyč had become

> a confessor in essence and a martyr by will, when he had to die harshly every day for the Gospel truth for two entire years, tortured through harsh and cruel imprisonment in the dungeon. You, Orthodox Christians, are aware of the course of this matter; you are aware of the cause, aware also of the effect.[23]

This seems to have been a reference to the punishment meted out to Karpovyč for his role in the *Thrēnos* affair. If so, it is worth noting how cautious Smotryc'kyj was in his remarks ten years later, saying to his audience little more than "you all know what I am talking about here." Smotryc'kyj himself seems to have escaped punishment.

The king may have been informed of some of the details by the Vilnius Jesuits. In any event, they perceived *Thrēnos* as a threat requiring an immediate reply. The man chosen to craft that response was no less a figure than the seventy-four-year-old Jesuit Piotr Skarga. As a member of the first Polish generation in the Order, as the author of saints' lives in Polish, of sermons, and of polemical tracts, including the pro-Uniate manifesto *On the Unity of God's Church* (Vilnius, 1577), and as educator and royal preacher and confessor, Skarga had been one of the chief architects of the Polish Counter-Reformation. One of Skarga's last works (he died in 1612) was a response to the young Smotryc'kyj:

23. Smotryc'kyj 1621a, D3r–v/250–1.

A Warning to Rus' of the Greek Rite against the Threnodies and Lament of Theophil Orthologue (Cracow, 1610). Skarga devoted much of his effort to linking *Thrēnos,* its author, and, by extension, its readers, with acts of treason. In a dedicatory epistle to Bishop of Vilnius Benedykt Wojna, dated 1 September 1610, he set the stage:

> Having arrived in Vilnius last year with His Majesty the King, Our Lord, we found the Ruthenian rite divided in two: some standing by the community of the Holy Universal Church, but others remaining with a certain church that is called that of Nalyvajko. From that church and from its printing house, quietly and without knowledge of the authorities, just at the time of His Majesty the King's departure for, and campaign against, Muscovy, there appeared a writing and a book under the name of a certain Theophil Orthologue.[24]

Although the king had ordered the printing seized, he was too late: the work had already spread "here in the town, and to Volhynia, and to Rus'."[25] Therefore, Wojna had asked Skarga to write a refutation. Skarga portrayed the conflict with the Orthodox as part of the larger campaign of the Polish Counter-Reformation. In the conclusion to his dedicatory epistle, he wrote:

> Be strong, O Most Reverend Pastor, even in these difficulties more burdensome than all temporal fires and destructions, in that you have not only many and various heretics, Lutherans, Calvinists, Arians, Anabaptists, who have been sown throughout this city and this diocese of the Grand Duchy of Lithuania, and lay waste the Church of God with the infernal fire of wrong teaching, but also those heretical Schismatics, who dare, shamelessly and fearlessly, to attack with such

---

24.   Skarga 1610, A2r. "Nalyvajko" refers here to Severyn Nalyvajko, the leader of a Cossack revolt in 1594–1596. Nalyvajko was seized and executed in Warsaw in 1597. The name became a term of abuse for the Ruthenian people and faith, and it was employed as an easy way to link Orthodoxy with treason.

25.   Skarga 1610, A2v.

blasphemies the Holy Catholic Church, the foundation and
pillar of saving truth.[26]

In one passage of *Thrēnos*, Smotryc'kyj compared the servitude
of the Orthodox under Catholic liberty with the freedom that was
perceived to exist under Turkish tyranny. His conclusion—"that it is
a far more beneficial thing [for the Church of God] to live externally
enslaved but free with respect to the soul under Turkish masters, than to
serve the Roman pope with body and soul"[27]—was actually a variant of
a paradoxical commonplace used by Protestants under Catholic rule in
sixteenth- and seventeenth-century Europe. Skarga certainly recognized
this, but he also knew that, in the Eastern lands of the Polish-Lithuanian
Commonwealth, Turkish commonplaces were not simply rhetorical. By
returning to Smotryc'kyj's statement with some frequency, Skarga was
able to represent the Orthodox as either traitors or fools:

> Those Christians who live under the Turk would stone that
> *krzywolog*,[28] saying, "Just live with us a little, and bear that
> cross: you will see whether it is good under the Turk." Ask
> our Ruthenians whether they wish to move to that cross with
> you. Go there yourselves to teach them to blaspheme the
> popes whom they honor better than you, and who know you
> self-willed and new heretics well.[29]

Skarga ended his work by printing in Latin and in Polish translation
a letter written in 1601 to Archbishop of Lviv Jan Dymitr Solikowski by
the future patriarch of Constantinople, Cyril Lukaris. In it was a passage
that the Uniate Smotryc'kyj would later claim had contributed to his
conversion, and which he would cite against his former co-religionists.
Lukaris wrote:

> And although heretics from Europe, out of hatred toward the
> Roman Church and the see of Peter, attempted an agreement

26.   Skarga 1610,)(3v.
27.   Smotryc'kyj 1610, 83v–84r/100.
28.   This was Skarga's Polish-Greek neologism—a "twister of words," the
opposite of an "Orthologue."
29.   Skarga 1610, 68.

with the Easterners, nonetheless they were never received.
For they only agree with us to the extent that the Jews
and the Mohammedans do. As for example in saying that
God is one, the creator and ruler of the world, righteous,
good, punishing the evil and rewarding the good, and in
other such [articles of] confession. But in the foremost
articles of the Christian faith they do not agree with us.
Concerning the antiquity of orders or Church consecration,
concerning apostolic traditions or those things handed down,
concerning the authority of the holy fathers and doctors of
both Churches, which either all of them, or some of their
sects, reject, and concerning the number and canon of the
books of Holy Scripture, and concerning Church customs,
and concerning justification, and concerning the holy liturgy
and the offering, concerning the honoring and relics of the
saints, concerning the Mother of God, concerning the Most
Holy Trinity—in all this, they do not have agreement with
us, but they wrench new understanding of Holy Scripture
from their heads. Reason itself testifies that this matter is
most dangerous. Since, then, they have been planted so far
from us, they cannot grow together with us. And whatever is
a matter of controversy between the Eastern and the Western
Church can give offense to the unlearned; but learned
people will easily deduce one understanding in the love of
Christ.[30]

Although Skarga had argued, correctly, that *Thrēnos* was a local
product, a work of the Orthodox Brotherhood Monastery of the Holy
Spirit, he was unable to identify the author. Two years later a second
refutation of the work appeared: *Parēgoria [a Consolation] or, Relief
from the Acrimonious Lament of the Supposed Holy Eastern Church by
the Invented Theophil Orthologue* (Vilnius, 1612). Its author was Illja
Moroxovs'kyj, royal secretary and future Uniate bishop of Volodymyr
and Brest. Moroxovs'kyj's point of departure was similar to that of
Skarga. *Thrēnos* was a suspect product of local conditions, and not a
work of authority on the Eastern Church:

30.   Skarga 1610, 122.

For this work never existed in Greek (unless *dialecto Cretensi* [in the Cretan dialect], which it uses), nor was it in Slavonic—this is the first point. Second, that into this lament and complaint he introduces some sort of woman dressed up in the crude customs of the heretical school, having given her the authoritative name of the Holy, Universal, Apostolic, Eastern Church.[31]

Also like Skarga, Moroxovskyj devoted considerable attention to the discussion of religious freedom under Turkish rule and in Poland-Lithuania. Moroxovskyj found Orthologue's (he said "Pseudologue's") masters in Luther and Calvin, and he traced to Luther a central argument in Smotryckyj's view of the true Church:

> ... practically with every third word you are wont to say: that our Church is subordinate to the cross, being constantly in trials, in troubles, in persecution; and Christ the Lord says: Blessed are ye, when men shall revile you, and persecute you [Mt. 5:11]. And thus [you say], since this persecution is with us, so also is the blessing, wherefore also His true congregation is found nowhere else but with us. I see that in this too you do not depart from Luther, the dear friend of your doctrine, who likewise considered superficial persecution . . . a mark of the true Church of God.[32]

Against the religious tolerance of Polish-Lithuanian society, and in favor of confessional compulsion, Moroxovskyj cited Calvinist authorities, Beza and Calvin, the first of whom had written that

> to allow freedom in conscience, to leave it to each one's will whether he would perish, is an entirely Satanic dogma. And this is precisely the diabolic freedom that today has filled the Polish and the Transylvanian land with so many plagues . . . .[33]

31. Moroxovskyj 1612, A2v.
32. Moroxovskyj 1612, 4–5.
33. Moroxovskyj 1612, 7.

And he cited St. Augustine in arguing that the recalcitrant must be "compelled by fear" (*timore cogi*).[34] By the end of his life, the Uniate Smotryc'kyj would make use of similar arguments about the licitness of compulsion in the conversion of the obstinate.[35]

For this volume, I have translated most of the front matter (including a dedicatory epistle to Mixajil Korybut Vyšnevec'kyj and a "Preface to the Reader") and chapters 1, 2, and 10 (Smotryc'kyj 1610, ()1r–()()()()3r/1–15, 1r–30r/17–46, and 208r–218v/224–35).

Homiliary Gospel

Smotryc'kyj spent the early 1610s, as he would later write, engaged for a few years "in courtly amusements . . . as a sort of rest from the dust of the schools."[36] Probably he was still a client of the Solomerec'kyjs at this time. Around the middle of the decade he returned to Vilnius and, as a lay collaborator of the Orthodox Brotherhood, began to work on two larger projects. The first was the first Ruthenian translation of the old *Homiliary Gospel,* or *Jevanhelije učytelnoje* (falsely attributed to Patriarch of Constantinople Callistus I, 1350–1353 and 1355–1363/64). The second was a grammar of Church Slavonic.[37]

A Church Slavonic *editio princeps* of the *Homiliary Gospel* had been published in Zabłudów in 1569 with the funds of Lithuanian Hetman and *starosta* of Hrodna and Mahilëü Hryhorij Oleksandrovyč Xodkevyč (Chodkiewicz) and was reprinted three times thereafter, in 1580, 1595, and 1606—a measure of the work's widespread use, in spite of the fact that it appeared in the not so widely understood Slavonic. Smotryc'kyj's Ruthenian translation appeared in 1616 at the printing house of the Vilnius Brotherhood, which had moved to Vievis (Jewie, a town near Trakai [Troki] owned by Orthodox patron and chamberlain of Trakai, Bohdan Ohins'kyj) after the legal battles over *Thrēnos* in 1610. In 1637, Metropolitan Peter Mohyla issued a revised edition of the 1616 printing in Kyiv, making no mention of the original translator,

---

34. Moroxovs'kyj 1612, 8.
35. See below, pp. 391, 563, 660, 681, 754.
36. Smotryc'kyj 1621c, 104–5/451, and see below, p. 261.
37. On Smotryc'kyj's philological projects of the 1610s, see Frick 1995, 56–74.

perhaps because of the scandal to which Smotryc'kyj's conversion had given rise.

The Gospel pericopes, which constituted the first printing of large amounts of biblical texts in Ruthenian, were not so much an original translation as a transliteration and adaptation of the Bible (Zaslaŭe, 1572) and New Testament (Losk, 1574) of radical Antitrinitarian Szymon Budny—a fact to which Smotryc'kyj naturally did not call his readers' attention. (Mohyla's "corrected" version of Smotryc'kyj's text drew in similar fashion on the Polish Calvinist Gdańsk Bible of 1633.)[38] Smotryc'kyj's major innovation, which Mohyla maintained in his edition, was to adapt to the requirements of Reformation and Counter-Reformation confessional propaganda a work whose content and form strongly reflected its medieval origins. In Smotryc'kyj's reworking, the *Homiliary Gospel* became an Orthodox response to Catholic and Protestant Polish postils, an answer to what Smotryc'kyj called the "infectious pastures of heretical teaching," from which many Orthodox parish priests preached to their flocks.[39]

Kasijan Sakovyč, Smotryc'kyj's future Uniate collaborator and a man whose confessional path would take him from Orthodoxy to the Uniate Church and ultimately to Roman Catholicism, printed the following anecdote in 1642 as an example of Ruthenian "simplicity":

> And sometimes another *pop* [i.e., simple Orthodox priest] will babble any old thing, and there is nothing to listen to. And others tell their sermons to the people from heretical postils. As was the case with one *pop* outside of Lviv, who said: "Listen, Christians, to the sermon of St. Rej." Having noticed this, the Franciscan Father Koropatnicki, who was then still a layman, took from the *pop* as a punishment for this two oxen and that postil of Rej.[40]

The Orthodox were reading not only the sixteenth-century Calvinist Mikołaj Rej (who was hardly a saint), but also the work of that other first-generation Polish Jesuit, Jakub Wujek, as well as his late-sixteenth- and early-seventeenth-century Calvinist and Lutheran competitors.

38.   On the Smotryc'kyj/Mohyla *Homiliary Gospel,* see Frick 1988.
39.   Smotryc'kyj 1616, 4r/21, and see below, p. 91.
40.   Sakovyč 1642, 105. See also Frick 1994.

Sakovyč's poor *pop* was probably happy to have any printed book from which to instruct his flock, and Orthodox and Uniate hierarchs alike frequently complained of the difficulty in removing the books of the opposition from the hands of parish priests. (Often it was necessary to arrange an exchange of volumes.) In the later sixteenth century the participants in the wars of the postils placed more and more emphasis on form: they polished their Polish, added interesting woodcut illustrations, and employed all sorts of graphic innovations in order to encourage their flocks (and those of their opponents) to use their product in their private devotion and, in the case of simple priests, in their own sermonizing.

Smotryc'kyj's *Homiliary Gospel* adopted many of these formal novelties. In addition to ornaments and a few woodcuts, the first Ruthenian version reflected a major graphic innovation over the printed Slavonic versions, one that was modelled directly on the Polish competition. The old version had presented the Gospel pericopes analytically—a verse at a time followed by a paragraph of explication. In the new version, as in the Polish postils, the pericopes were presented synthetically—in one continuous passage at the head of each sermon, and in a typeface that clearly set Holy Writ apart from its exegesis.

These works fulfilled a double function. In addition to offering explanations of Gospel readings, they also provided a sizable lectionary of Scripture in the vulgar tongue. For Ruthenian readers, Smotryc'kyj's version was a first. Holy Writ had not been available to Ruthenian readers/listeners in any widely accessible form. In one section of the dedicatory epistles that preface the various printings of the *Homiliary Gospel,* the translator explained why he was using not "the more noble, the more beautiful, the more concise, the subtler, and richer Slavonic language," but rather "the baser and more vulgar tongue." The reason was the need for intelligibility in private devotion and in confessional propaganda that had led the Reformers to make extensive use of the vulgar tongues for certain types of writings, and that had forced the Catholics grudgingly to follow suit. And Smotryc'kyj drew here on one of the favorite proof texts for the need to use an intelligible tongue: "The alert and wise preacher should seek not glory among his listeners on account of the quickness of his wit, but only the benefit of their salvation, and he should remember that saying of God's chosen vessel: that it is a more useful thing to speak five words in an intelligible tongue, than ten thousand in an unknown tongue [1 Cor. 14:19] (especially in instruction for the people)."[41]

Smotryc'kyj's version exists with several title pages and dedicatory epistles, all of which contain a certain amount of common textual material. The translation in this volume presents one such letter in its entirety, that to Chamberlain of Trakai Bohdan Ohins'kyj and his wife Rajina Volovyčivna; as well as the conclusion of the letter to Prince Bohdan Bohdanovyč Solomerec'kyj, by that time a royal courtier and the young nobleman who was in Smotryc'kyj's charge during his study tour of German academies in the early 1600s.[42] This was the only version in which the translator stepped forward out of anonymity to claim credit for his work. Here he signed his given name as "Maksentij."

Grammar of Church Slavonic

If the Ruthenian vulgar tongue, in Smotryc'kyj's view, was suited for use in certain contexts, it was still to be excluded from many others. As his next philological project, he published in 1618–1619 (again at the Vilnius Brotherhood press in Vievis) a grammar of Church Slavonic. Over the years, the work would become the basis for study of the liturgical language of the Orthodox Slavs in an area that reached from Poland-Lithuania and Muscovy in the north to Bulgaria in the south, and included the Roman-rite Glagolitic monasteries of the Dalmatian coast and their printing house in Rome. It remained a standard for nearly two centuries, supplanted only by Josef Dobrovský's *Institutiones linguae slavicae dialecti veteris* (Vienna, 1822).[43]

In his Ruthenian-language preface to the *Grammar* (itself written in Church Slavonic), Smotryc'kyj addressed the "teachers of the schools." Here he provided a kind of brief Orthodox *ratio studiorum,* including the stricture that "the Slavonic dialect will be maintained in usual school conversation among the pupils under threat of punishment."[44] This was an attempt to put Church Slavonic on an equal footing in a

41. Smotryc'kyj 1616, 3v–4r/19–20; and below, pp. 91–2. On Smotryc'kyj's linguistic program, see Frick 1985.
42. Smotryc'kyj 1616, 1r–4r/25–6 and 5r/13.
43. See the bibliography in Frick 1995, 1, 261.
44. Smotryc'kyj 1618,)(3r.

new Orthodox trinity of languages of cult and culture that comprised
Greek, Latin, and Slavonic. As such, it was an answer to the challenge
mounted by the Jesuit Piotr Skarga, who had denied Slavonic the status
of a language of learning in his pro-Union manifesto *On the Unity of
God's Church under One Pastor and on the Greek Apostasy from That
Unity* (Vilnius, 1577; reprinted Cracow, 1590 and 1610). Skarga had
written:

> Furthermore, the Greeks greatly cheated you, O Ruthenian
> nation, that in giving you the holy faith, they did not give
> you their Greek language. Rather, they ordered you to stay
> by this Slavonic language, so that you might never attain
> true understanding and learning. For only these two, Greek
> and Latin, are languages by means of which the holy faith
> has been propagated and disseminated throughout the
> whole world, without which no one can attain complete
> competence in any field of learning, least of all in the
> spiritual doctrine of the holy faith. Not only because other
> languages change continuously and are unable to be stable
> within their framework of human usage (for they do not have
> their grammars and lexicons; only those two are always the
> same and never change), but also because only in those two
> languages have learned disciplines been established, and
> those disciplines cannot be translated adequately into other
> languages. And there has not been in this world, nor will there
> ever be, any academy or college where theology, philosophy,
> and other liberal arts could be studied and understood in any
> other language. No one can ever become learned through the
> Slavonic tongue.[45]

In writing a grammar of Slavonic, Smotryc'kyj was demonstrating that
Slavonic did indeed possess a fixed norm.

Although students of the history of Slavic philology agree that
this *Grammar* represents a step toward describing Slavic grammatical
categories, rather than making a Slavic language fit well-established
Greek and Latin prescriptive models, it is also clear that this work
would have been unthinkable—and is sometimes incomprehensible—
without recourse to the humanistic grammars on which Smotryc'kyj

45.   *RIB* 7:485–6.

and his contemporaries were raised. This is most obviously the case in the fourth section of the *Grammar*, where Smotryc'kyj provided a groundbreaking description of the rules for a Church Slavonic poetry. This was, however, an entirely prescriptive affair, since Slavonic possessed no tradition of secular or religious poetry similar to that of the Latin West. Further, no one had ever written verse according to the Greek-inspired system Smotryc'kyj laid out for Slavonic poetry, in which syllables were divided arbitrarily into long and short, and meter was marked accordingly. Smotryc'kyj's justification for embarking upon this uncharted path tells us much about his way of thinking. This treatise was both highly innovative and remarkably traditional, an expression of Orthodox Slavic cultural patriotism couched in the rhetoric of the Polish-Lithuanian elite. He wrote by way of introduction and defense of this new step that he had "judged possible the art of poetry in the Slavonic language" because—as contemporary readers of Maciej Stryjkowski's *Kronika* of 1582 knew well—Ovid, in his Black Sea exile, had learned the local, "Sarmatian" language and had deemed it a suitable medium for writing poetry. Here Smotryc'kyj followed in the footsteps of his Polish competitors (and fellow Sarmatists) by adding a Church Slavonic claim to Sarmatism.[46]

The current volume presents a translation of Smotryc'kyj's preface to the school teachers (Smotryc'kyj 1618,)(1r–4v). Both the *Grammar* and the *Homiliary Gospel* before it were central to a program for the spiritual and cultural renewal of the Ruthenian nation and can be characterized as expressions of the Orthodox Reform that arose in direct response to the Polish Reformation and Counter-Reformation.

Funeral Sermon

Smotryc'kyj became a monk sometime between 1616, when he signed a preface to his translation of the *Homiliary Gospel* still with his given name Maksentij, and 1618–1619, when he published his grammar under the name of the "most sinful monk Meletij."[47] Smotryc'kyj had been connected with the Vilnius Brotherhood Monastery at least since

46.   Smotryc'kyj 1618, Ъ3v. On Ovid as a Sarmatian authority, see Otwinowska 1974, 160.
47.   See below, pp. 94 and 97.

1610, when he published his *Thrēnos* at the Brotherhood press. Perhaps he had some contacts even earlier, during his stay in the city as a student of the Jesuit Academy sometime most likely in the late 1590s. From ca. 1616 (the year he published his Ruthenian *Homiliary Gospel*) he had resided there, and he continued to do so after 1620.

In the fall of 1620, the Brotherhood delegated Smotryc´kyj to Kyiv to meet with Patriarch of Jerusalem Theophanes, who was spending a few months in the Commonwealth on his return from a trip to Moscow, where he had consecrated Fedor Nikityč Romanov (father of Tsar Mixail) as Patriarch Filaret. Smotryc´kyj was sent as representative for the then archimandrite of the Vilnius Brotherhood Monastery, Leontij Karpovyč, who was too weak to make the trip in person. Smotryc´kyj received ordination and consecration as archbishop of Polack and bishop of Vicebsk and Mscislaŭ from Theophanes.

After the Union of Brest, only two Ruthenian bishops—Hedeon Balaban of Lviv and Mixajil Kopystens´kyj of Przemyśl—had remained loyal to the Orthodox Church. Kopystens´kyj died in 1609 and was replaced by the arch-Uniate and much disliked (among his largely Orthodox parishioners) Oleksandr (Atanazy) Krupec´kyj. Thus in 1620 the Orthodox had only one bishop—that of Lviv (which see was occupied after Balaban's death in 1607 by the Orthodox Jarema Tysarivs´kyj); the other sees were occupied by Uniates. Theophanes consecrated seven new Orthodox bishops to the "vacant" sees, including those given to Smotryc´kyj.

Karpovyč died either while Smotryc´kyj was still in Kyiv or shortly after he returned to Vilnius. Smotryc´kyj was chosen to replace him as archimandrite of the Vilnius Brotherhood Monastery. The new archbishop and archimandrite-elect gave the funeral sermon for Karpovyč, titled *Sermon on the Illustrious Funeral of the Most Noble and Most Reverend Man, Lord, and Father, Leontij Karpovyč* on 2/12 November 1620. The work was also published, in both Ruthenian (with a preface dated 8/18 November 1620) and Polish (with a preface dated 17/27 February 1621). The present volume contains a translation of the dedicatory epistle to Metropolitan Jov Borec´kyj found in the Polish version.[48] Here again, as in *Thrēnos,* a personification of the Ruthenian Orthodox Church speaks in the first person (at least at the beginning),

---

48.   Smotryc´kyj 1621a, 1r–4v/236–40.

now not in complaint but in rejoicing that she, who, as Sarah and Elizabeth, had been thought barren, had now given birth to new sons, the newly established hierarchy.

With the death of Karpovyč, Smotryc'kyj occupied the second most important position in the newly reestablished Orthodox hierarchy (after Metropolitan of Kyiv Jov Borec'kyj), and the *Sermon* positioned him as the chief defender of the Orthodox in a polemic over the legality of the new consecrations.[49] According to the Roman Catholic and Uniate sides, the consecrations were illegal for a number of reasons: Theophanes was, they alleged, not patriarch of Jerusalem but rather a layman and a Turkish spy; the new bishops had no bishoprics to occupy, since all but that of Lviv were occupied by legally consecrated Uniates; and the king's presentation had not preceded the consecrations.[50] Moreover, these acts had occurred almost precisely at the same time that troops led by Chancellor and Great Crown Hetman Stanisław Żółkiewski were suffering defeat at the hands of Turkish forces at Ţuţora (Cecora); they thus represented an act of treason against the Commonwealth.

Smotryc'kyj defended the legality of the new hierarchy in four printed works from this period: *A Verification of Innocence* (Vilnius, 1621; two editions); *A Defense of the "Verification"* (Vilnius, 1621); *A Refutation of Acrimonious Writings* (Vilnius, 1622); and *A Justification of Innocence* (n.p., 1623). Like *Thrēnos,* all these works belong to the realm of forensic rhetoric. Their titles often refer in loosely generic terms to the kinds of protestations and re-protestations in which the books of the Magdeburg, Castle, and Land courts of Poland-Lithuania abounded. And their rhetorical strategies, as is typical in these sorts of documents, alleged slander and "boasts" (*pochwałki*) against health and reputation on the part of the opponent and defended one's own wronged honor against "dishonoring words" (*słowa uszczypliwe*).[51] The guilt from which Smotryc'kyj (who wrote anonymously, or at least semi-anonymously, in all these works) sought to free his side stemmed from

49.   On the events surrounding Smotryc'kyj's consecration as archbishop of Polack, see Frick 1995, 75–88.

50.   On the secular *jus patronatus* in the Eastern Church, see Vladimirskij-Budanov 1907, Chodynicki 1931, Florja 1992.

51.   On the Ruthenian polemic and the language of litigation, see Frick 2002.

allegations of *lèse majesté* and treasonous acts committed in conspiracy with the Ottoman Empire. The wrongfully accused defendants were Patriarch Theophanes (who was portrayed by the Uniates and Catholics as a Turkish spy), the hierarchy in general and Borec'kyj and Smotryc'kyj in particular (who were guilty of *lèse majesté* in accepting illegal consecrations), and, by extension, the entire (Orthodox) Ruthenian nation (which was accused of disloyalty to the Polish-Lithuanian Commonwealth). A charter of King Sigismund III of 1 February 1621 and a letter from the king to Chamberlain of Trakai Bohdan Ohins'kyj (the same who was the dedicatee of Smotryc'kyj's grammar and of one printing of the *Homiliary Gospel*), dated 7 February 1621, alleged that Smotryc'kyj and Borec'kyj were Turkish spies, that Borec'kyj was protected by a Cossack guard in Kyiv, and that Smotryc'kyj had amassed his own force in Lithuania.

The spring of 1621 saw a series of legal actions. On 12 March 1621—at the complaints of Josafat Kuncevyč (Smotryc'kyj's Uniate competitor as archbishop of Polack) and of Lev Krevza (his competitor as archimandrite of the Uniate Holy Trinity Monastery across the street from the Orthodox in Vilnius)—Uniate Metropolitan Josyf Ruts'kyj summoned Smotryc'kyj (under Smotryc'kyj's secular name Maksym Herasymovyč) to appear before his ecclesiastical court no later than 19 March. When Smotryc'kyj did not appear, he was given until 27 March to manifest his repentance. (An open letter containing all this information was nailed to the doors of the Holy Spirit Monastery.) Smotryc'kyj did not respond to the Uniate demands, and Ruts'kyj declared him excommunicated on 28 March and made this known through a solemn public ceremony and through publication of the decree of excommunication.

From this point on, the battle was fought in the courts and in the public forum through polemical pamphlets and attempts to control the rumor mill. On 3 April, four Orthodox city officials and twelve Orthodox burghers of Vilnius were arrested and charged with *lèse majesté* and treason for their financial support of the new hierarchy (and of Smotryc'kyj in particular).[52]

---

52. On Smotryc'kyj and the events of 1620–1621, see Frick 1995, 75–88 and the literature cited there.

Verification

A Verification of Innocence, and a Christian Removal of the Erroneous Accounts Sown throughout All of Lithuania and Belarus, Which Were Aimed at Causing the Demise of the Life and Honor of the Noble Ruthenian Nation was published in Vilnius in 1621, sometime after 5 April (but perhaps this was Old Style—if so, then after 15 April). A second, expanded edition was published after 16/26 June. These works contained a thorough defense of the legality of the new Ruthenian hierarchy. Smotryc'kyj answered the Uniate and Catholic objections by citing letters of safe conduct from Sigismund III and various senators in "proof" that the authorities considered Theophanes the patriarch of Jerusalem; by denying the Uniate bishops, who had abandoned obedience to the patriarch of Constantinople, jurisdiction over souls in Rus'; and by arguing that promises made at various Sejms for the "pacification" (*uspokojenie*) of the Ruthenian religion (e.g., the constitution of 1607) gave Rus' the right to present bishops for consecration when the opportunity offered itself. In general, Smotryc'kyj attempted to reclaim for Orthodox Rus' the noble and burgher rights, freedoms, and liberties that had been granted to the Ruthenian nation before the Union of Brest, and to exclude Uniate Rus' from participation in those rights. A governing myth here was that the Commonwealth had been created through the voluntary union of three equal nations: Poland, Lithuania, and Rus'.

In addition to providing a fundamental legal defense, Smotryc'kyj offered some interesting observations on the nature of calumny, on the difficulties of defending oneself against slander, and on the functioning of the rumor mill. At the same time, Smotryc'kyj would show himself adept at similar kinds of manipulation of opinion, fraudulently—so his opponents would soon claim—making his own personal transgression and shame into a matter of the honor of the entire Ruthenian nation. The current volume contains a translation of the entirety (with a few minor—and noted—omissions) of the second edition of *A Verification of Innocence* (Smotryc'kyj 1621,)(1r–73v/313–98).

A Verification drew several immediate responses, the most comprehensive of which was a work produced by "the fathers of the Vilnius Monastery of the Holy Trinity" (some have alleged the author was actually Metropolitan Ruts'kyj) entitled *Twofold Guilt* (Vilnius,

1621). The basic contention of this work was that "it is wrong to sin; but to remain in sin, to defend it, to seek to prove that it is not sin— this is twofold guilt."[53] The work was written in response to the first edition of *A Verification,* but it contained a brief discussion of some points of the second edition in an addendum. It would thus seem to have appeared in print shortly after that second edition (dated 16/26 June 1621) and before Smotryc'kyj's reply, *A Defense of the "Verification,"* and the Uniate response to that new work, both of which appeared in the course of 1621. As we see, the works for and against the new Orthodox hierarchy were appearing in rapid succession.

The author of *Twofold Guilt* (in his response, Smotryc'kyj would call him the *Redargutor,* or Refuter) argued with Smotryc'kyj in part over the rules of the encounter. Whereas Smotryc'kyj drew from printed Polish historians, the author of *Twofold Guilt* drew upon "not only Ruthenian, but also Muscovite chronicles, whence the truth will be proved, for writers of two nations that are in such disagreement and have been in enmity for so long are here in unanimous agreement."[54] The strategy was, of course, the same for both sides: to enlist the authorities of the other side in one's own defense. Further, the Verificator (i.e., Smotryc'kyj as the author of *A Verification*) had compounded the crimes of his side by publishing the private letters of the king and certain senators:

> Every closed letter is in secret, and a sign of this is the fact
> that they are sealed and the name of the addressee is written
> on the outside . . . . Ought not His Majesty the King properly
> be offended that his private letters not only fly through the
> hands of many, but are read aloud in the squares and streets,
> are interpreted as the reader sees fit, and what is more, are
> brought to the knowledge of the entire world through their
> printing?[55]

An important thread of the further polemic began here with certain allegations about Smotryc'kyj himself, most importantly that he had

---

53.   *Sowita* 1621, A1v/443.
54.   *Sowita* 1621, 11/451.
55.   *Sowita* 1621, 23/460.

been close to joining the Uniate cause in the years 1616–1617, about the same time he decided to become a monk in the Orthodox monastery:

> Concerning your Smotryc'kyj I can no longer keep silent about what, until now, has not come out from our side in public as a public declaration. And even now, not all will be told; a little something will remain secret. But it is absolutely necessary to mention what properly belongs to this matter.[56]

According to the Uniates, Smotryc'kyj negotiated for some time in the mid-1610s "to see how he himself might come to union with us and might bring his group along with him."[57] Smotryc'kyj had claimed he believed (at least in this Uniate account) all the same articles of faith as the Romans. "Proof" of this was the fact that some of the Orthodox had allegedly reported to the Uniates that Smotryc'kyj had asserted to his own side that "the Romans will be saved in their religion."[58] Throughout this period, Smotryc'kyj

> did not cease to negotiate with us, and he even attached to himself certain laymen, until he was found out. Thereupon everything was made public, and the poor fellow was in some trouble with those of little understanding. That man—if he is now of that same faith of which he was at that time—is our brother. If he is of a different faith, then he is a proper and true apostate, for he betrayed the faith that he had recognized and had already professed before people (and there were several of them there, both clergy and laity).[59]

A second polemical response, dated 7 August 1621, appeared in the form of a printed *Letter to the Monks of the Vilnius Monastery of the Church of the Holy Spirit* (Vilnius, 1621), written in direct response to the preface to the second edition of *A Verification*. Smotryc'kyj had dedicated that version to four Ruthenian noblemen: Notary of the Grand

56. *Sowita* 1621, 69/492.
57. *Sowita* 1621, 69/492.
58. *Sowita* 1621, 69–70/492.
59. *Sowita* 1621, 71/493.

Duchy of Lithuania and *Starosta* of Braslav Janusz Skumin Tyszkiewicz
(Tyškevyč), Adam Chreptowicz (Xrebtovyč), Chamberlain of Slonim
Mikołaj Tryzna, and Standard-Bearer of Slonim Jerzy Mieleszko
(Meleško). The *Letter* was presented as the response of those four
noblemen, and it was signed in their names. An epigram taken from
St. Basil set the tone and theme for the work: "It is seemly for a monk
to understand much, speak little, not be audacious or injudicious in his
speech, to be humble toward all, and to avoid arrogance."[60] The main
argument was one that defined the Ruthenian nation as the collectivity
of the Ruthenian *szlachta*—actually, the Uniate *szlachta* alone, but
this distinction was hidden in the argument. It derided the audacity
of Smotryc′kyj and others, who, as plebeians, had no reason to see
in the royal and other decrees against them an attack on the *honor* of
the Ruthenian nation. Those who had been attacked had no honor to
lose: "For in what way is our noble blood one *cum plebeiis* [with the
commonality]? What consanguinity with peasants? You unite in blood,
and you set yourselves equal in birth, with ancient Ruthenian families,
on the grounds that you too, with your common birth, are Rus′. This is
your foolish presumption, not befitting monastic humility."[61]

Two other themes raised here were then taken up by the
further polemic. First, Smotryc′kyj himself, his actions and personal
motivations, became more and more a part of the debate. He was now
unmasked as the author of the Orthodox pamphlets: "[The second
edition of *A Verification of Innocence* was dedicated to us] by your
side, or rather by you alone, Smotryc′kyj, who . . . clearly gave yourself
away in it by your affected style, by the childish-stupid phrasing, and by
the confounded sense from the interwoven words (through which you
pass yourself off as a wise one with the simpler people)."[62] The authors
of the *Letter* would return frequently to ridicule Smotryc′kyj's "most
wanton style and language,"[63] his love of neologisms or, as the *Letter*
put it, his "invented morosophic words."[64] (The words "childish-stupid

---

60. *List* 1621, A1v/732.
61. *List* 1621, 7/737–8. For the controversies over the quality of Smotryc′kyj's
birth, see Frick 1995, 25–9.
62. *List* 1621, 1/733.
63. *List* 1621, 36/760.
64. *List* 1621, 8/738.

[*dziecinogłupi*]" and "morosophic [*głupiomądry*]" may themselves
have been intended as a parody of Smotryc'kyj's style.) Moreover,
according to the Uniates, Smotryc'kyj reveled in the artful complexities
of his rhetoric:

> We looked even further in that book of yours, and we were
> amazed at the duplicity of the words and at their mass, at the
> incomprehensible confusion *sensus insensati* [of insensate
> sense], from which even the author himself would not be
> able to extricate himself and which is comprehensible only
> when he sharply assaults and attacks someone.[65]

Further, the authors of the *Letter* mocked the unfitting arrogance of the
monk and plebeian:

> Did you stray far from monastic poverty, from humility, and
> monastic modesty when you became apostate? Seized by
> disgusting ambition, you force your way, against God and
> man, upon the thrones of the metropolitanate and bishoprics.
> And that of Polack appeals to you most of all: already
> Reverend Melentij [*sic*] usurps for himself the insignia and
> episcopal power of the archbishopric of Polack, against the
> power (pitiful thing) of His Majesty the King, since he did
> not submit or nominate him. He borrows the titles, submits
> them to print himself, revering himself (truly a ludicrous
> thing), celebrates not just in the episcopal garments but
> perhaps even in those of the metropolitan. He has episcopal
> seals cut for himself, he makes inscriptions on the chalices.
> He allows himself to be led by the hand of the aristocracy
> (*ne quid ambitionis et arrogantiae desit* [lest there be
> anything lacking in ambition and arrogance]), he himself
> being of the condition of which he is, and he glories in this.
> He appropriates the bishopric of Polack, and he does not see
> that in that same constitution of 1607 it was written that such
> dignities are to be given to noblemen.[66]

---

65. *List* 1621, 28/753.
66. *List* 1621, 26–7/752. For the constitution of 1607, see *VL* 2:438–9.

A second thread of the argument concerned the relationship between the new hierarchy and the Cossacks, which, to the noble authors of the *Letter,* smelled of treason and plebeian rebellion:

> What sort of tumult, sedition, rousing of the people against the bishop in Polack [i.e., against the Uniate bishop Josafat Kuncevyč], who had been established according to canon and according to the laws and authority of His Royal Majesty, and against the local palatine, were worked by means of the letters and patents and emissaries of the intruder upon that bishopric, the Reverend (as he titles himself) Miolentij [*sic*]? But that knightly people [i.e., the Cossacks] (that we return to this), brought by you to sedition, was convinced to undertake negotiations with Their Lord Graces, the Hetmans, concerning these bishops and the metropolitan and to undertake a legation to His Royal Majesty.[67]

A final Uniate response to *A Verification* was the *Proof of the Unheard-of Audacity of the Monks and of the Like-Minded of the Vilnius Brotherhood,* published in Zamość in 1621 by Tymoteusz Symanowicz sometime after 10 August 1621. An interesting *novum* of the work was the more direct assertion of an allegation at which the *Letter* had hinted: that Smotryćkyj had been the author of *Thrēnos.* (Symanowicz wrote of the "acrimonious Laments of Harasymowicz [i.e., the son of Herasym].")[68] This served, of course, to further link the new Orthodox archbishop of Polack and his followers with treason.

Defense

Smotryćkyj (again anonymously) responded with *A Defense of the "Verification"* sometime in the late summer or fall of 1621. (The Uniates still had time in 1621 to print a response to this work.) The main collocutor here was the author of the *Twofold Guilt.* Presented in this volume are translations of the front matter and several passages dealing with such topics as historical arguments for the spiritual jurisdiction of the patriarch of Constantinople over Rus′ (and—so Smotryćkyj

67.   *List* 1621, 14/742.
68.   Symanowicz 1621, B2r.

would argue, employing the "outdoing" *topos*[69]—over all of "barbary,"
including Poland and Lithuania); further political arguments that
the new bishops were free to accept consecration; a discussion of
allegations about Smotryc'kyj's previous Uniate leanings; reasons why
the Orthodox side was unable to enter into a public disputation; and
further considerations of the relations between power and rhetoric.[70]

In an attempt to explain why, as the Refuter had alleged, he
could claim that the Romans could be saved in their faith, Smotryc'kyj
initiated in *A Defense* a discussion of orthodoxy, heterodoxy, and
heresy, couched in terms of excesses and defects. He who believed all
that belonged to true faith and a few things more (i.e., the "excesses,"
or what others would have termed *adiaphora,* or indifferent things) was
a member of the universal Church; he whose faith lacked some article
of faith suffered a defect and was outside the Church. Smotryc'kyj had
taken this definition of correct faith, without citing the source, from
the *De Republica Ecclesiastica* (London and Hanover, 1617–1622) of
the pre-irenicist, pre-ecumenicist and two-time convert Marcantonio de
Dominis. This former archbishop of Split and veteran of the Venetian
pamphlet wars with the pope resided in London in 1621 and was in
communion with the Church of England. He was infamous throughout
Europe and was not the sort of authority Smotryc'kyj could introduce
overtly into the discussion. De Dominis stated some of his beliefs,
motivations, and goals, in an autobiographical passage:

> From the earliest years of my priesthood I had an almost
> innate desire to see the union of all Christ's Churches: I
> could not regard the separation of West from East, South
> from North, with equanimity, and I anxiously desired to
> discover the cause of such great and frequent schisms and
> to see if it were possible to find out some way to bring all
> Christ's Churches to their true and ancient unity.[71]

69. Curtius 1973, 162–5.
70. Smotryc'kyj 1621c, A1r–3/399–400, 38/418, 50–5/424–6, 61/429, 62–5/430–1, 76–81/437–9, 86–91/442–4, 100/449, 104–12/451–5, 112–27/455–62.
71. English translation from Malcolm 1984, 39; De Dominis 1618, a4r.

This was a unionizing view of a universal Church too loosely situated under the banner of any one of the organized Churches to please people on either side of the Ruthenian debate. De Dominis converted back to Roman Catholicism in 1623, but he ended his days in the prison of the Holy Office in Castel Sant'Angelo, where he died in 1624. Later that year, he and his works were put on trial—*praesente cadavere*—in the Church of Santa Maria sopra Minerva before the Supreme Tribunal of the Inquisition; he was declared a heretic, and his books and bodily remains were burned on 21 December at Campo dei Fiori and the ashes thrown into the Tiber. Representative of the perplexities many felt about de Dominis's beliefs was the statement of Sir Dudley Carleton, viscount of Dorchester and English legate in Venice at the time of the archbishop's move to London: "I cannot say he is so much a Protestant as his writings shew he is not a Papist."[72]

De Dominis would become an important influence on Smotryc'kyj's work, and he was to resurface at crucial moments throughout the archbishop's career. In the course of the Orthodox works of 1621–1622, we find Smotryc'kyj tacitly employing de Dominis to explain how it was possible to accept the Roman Catholics while excluding the Uniates. But in the course of the polemic we find a certain backing away on Smotryc'kyj's part from de Dominis's inclusive definition of correct faith, perhaps indirect evidence that the archbishop was caught in a difficult situation between Uniate and Orthodox extremes.[73]

Refutation

Before the end of 1621—a busy year in the pamphlet wars—a response to Smotryc'kyj's *Defense of the "Verification"* appeared, again from the monks of the Holy Trinity Monastery just across the street in Vilnius. It was entitled *An Examination of the "Defense"; That Is, A Reply to the Writing Called "Defense of the 'Verification.'"* It too was anonymous.

Here, again, Smotryc'kyj himself became a central target of the attack, and he responded with his *Refutation of Acrimonious Writings*

---

72. See Malcolm 1984, 61.
73. On the controversies of 1621–1629 over Smotryc'kyj's allegiances ca. 1617 (i.e., just before he became an Orthodox monk), see Frick 1995, 61–74. On Smotryc'kyj and de Dominis, see Frick 1995, 206–26.

(Vilnius, 1622), which appeared after 4/14 February. Although the authors did not unmask Smotryc'kyj directly as their polemical opponent, they winked at their readers on this issue frequently. The Latin phrase *stultorum plena sunt omnia* or "the world is full of fools," was glossed, using Smotryc'kyj's secular name, as "the world is full of Maksyms."[74] The author's scholarly apparatus was further ridiculed, an apparent attempt to neutralize the considerable erudition of the opponent—"He would do better to read that entire history, of which there are ten to twenty sheets, if he won't be too lazy";[75] and fun was made of his "schoolboy's Polish."[76]

More important—and potentially damaging to Smotryc'kyj's standing among the Orthodox—were further revelations concerning his negotiations with the Uniates ca. 1617:

> We mentioned the reason in *Twofold Guilt* why we did not write out everything there concerning Smotryc'kyj's negotiations with us, believing that this was sufficient at that time for an admonition to Smotryc'kyj. And now the [author of] *A Defense* denies what we wrote there truly and without any exaggeration. We must say more—and the genuine pure truth—for the affirmation of this, even if it will not be to Smotryc'kyj's liking, obliging him in the fear of God to acknowledge, having consulted his memory (and he can remember, for it was not four years ago), whether it was not as we write here.[77]

Chief among the new pieces of incriminating evidence was the allegation that Smotryc'kyj had soon regretted writing *Thrēnos*—something he had supposedly repeated to the Uniates "about three times." This was no minor charge: the Orthodox treated *Thrēnos* as a priceless jewel, an heirloom, a work equal to those of Chrysostom, a book worth taking to the grave; and yet, according to the Uniates, the new leader of the Orthodox had soon changed his mind. The Uniate account cited Smotryc'kyj's alleged words to them: "I have disgusted many . . . with

74. *Examen* 1621, 19/574.
75. *Examen* 1621, 8/566.
76. *Examen* 1621, 11/568.
77. *Examen* 1621, 43/590–1.

this book. I wish to make it good to the Church of God through some significant service, by which as much would be corrected as was ruined." Further, the Uniates contended that the response to *Thrēnos* by Illja Moroxovs'kyj, bishop of Volodymyr, had convinced him: "I wished [Smotryc'kyj says in this Uniate allegation] to respond to it, but I could never bring myself to this in any way. There was an occasion, when I wished to respond, that a fear fell upon me; I cast my pen upon the table, and I myself broke into tears."[78]

The "significant service" that Smotryc'kyj had in mind, according to the Uniates, was the reunification of Rus'. In this Uniate portrayal, many of his actions in this period were directed toward this end. First, he allegedly converted one person in Volhynia to the Union who later went over to the Roman Catholic Church, for which a certain priest in Vilnius chastised him. (The Uniates withheld the name but offered to make it known to the skeptical.)[79] "He had contracted with us that he was to travel throughout all the Ruthenian lands so that he might arrange their hearts for mutual harmony and Church unity"—this is how the Uniates began their account of Smotryc'kyj's life as a sort of double agent. His activities in Vilnius were conducted in an atmosphere of deceit and mistrust. He met secretly with the other side many times (and not just the three times, as Smotryc'kyj now claimed), until he was eventually "caught" by a "nosy" Orthodox shopkeeper at a meeting with the Uniates at the Bernardine friars, after which the Orthodox Brotherhood "vented its anger upon him," and he received a "solemn fraternal admonishment" from the entire Brotherhood, including Leontij Karpovyč, with whose blessing (in Smotryc'kyj's version) he had begun to meet with the Uniates. Things finally came to a head when an Orthodox spy ("who, having cunningly inclined to us, found out about everything we had discussed among ourselves—and this is an important person among them") reported on Smotryc'kyj's dealings with the Uniates, and the Brotherhood demanded that he "either take the habit or depart from them."[80]

Thus, in this Uniate picture, Smotryc'kyj was on the verge of converting ca. 1617, and he would have done so were it not for two

78.   *Examen* 1621, 43–4/591.
79.   *Examen* 1621, 44/591.
80.   *Examen* 1621, 45/591–2.

things. The first was his innate (according to the Uniates) timorousness. The second was something more specific:

> And at that time he was given the books from the conventicle of Marcantonio de Dominis, archbishop of Split, the apostate. And having embraced them, he became what he is now. Such is the constancy of this man that one book of one apostate—who introduced a new, unknown sect, one that had not existed previously, and which sect the English Kingdom (to which he had gone) did not wish to receive—so altered him in every regard that *ab equis descendit ad asinos* [he descended from the horses to the asses]. And if, in all this, he should wish to be so shameless, we will convince him, and we will name the individuals.[81]

As late as 1624, in a report to Rome dated after 6 May of that year, Uniate authorities wrote that "the pseudo-bishop of Polack [i.e., Smotryc'kyj] constantly reads and recites well-nigh from memory" the works of de Dominis.[82]

Yet no one connected Smotryc'kyj's discussion of excesses and defects of faith with the *De Republica Ecclesiastica,* and they treated the ideas as his own. The authors of the *Examination* rejected the discussion outright, since both excesses and defects caused heretical beliefs:

> And he [i.e., the author of *Defense of the "Verification,"* Smotryc'kyj] gave us his *axiomata* [axioms] as if *ex communi sensu Theologorum* [from the common understanding of theologians]: *Defectus fide non utitur, Excessus fide abutitur* [a defect does not make use of the faith, an excess uses the faith entirely]. Both the *axiomata* and the *distinctio fidei* [definition of faith] are new and unheard of among theologians. And they were invented by a new theologian and an old grammarian.[83]

According to the authors of the *Examination,* both the extremes of

---

81. *Examen* 1621, 46/592.
82. Šmurlo 1928, 35.
83. *Examen* 1621, 26/579.

excess and defect should be avoided since "virtue is always contained in the mean."[84]

One final point: Smotryc'kyj had attempted to prove that the faith had come from the East to all of "barbary," in which he included, in addition to the Orthodox Slavs, the Poles, Czechs, Lithuanians, and Hungarians. The authors of the *Examination* countered by claiming the apostles to the Slavs, SS. Constantine/Cyril and Methodius, for Rome. Thus all those peoples of barbary enumerated by Smotryc'kyj were actually "old Uniates":

> Cyril and Methodius, the apostles to the Slavs, were under the obedience of the Roman popes, and they did not begin to celebrate the liturgy and other Church sacraments in Slavonic until they went to the pope for permission and received it. Some of them [i.e., followers of Cyril and Methodius] were consecrated there, and one of them [St. Constantine/Cyril] died in Rome, and to this day everyone can read his gravestone as one enters the Church of St. Clement.[85]

This volume contains a translation of the title page and of several extended excerpts of *A Refutation of Acrimonious Writings* (Smotryc'kyj 1622, A1r/463, 14v–16r/477–8, 28r–32v/490–5, 32v–50v/495–513). Smotryc'kyj apparently received two responses to his *Verification*—the *Letter* (*List* 1621) and Symanowicz's *Proof* (1621) with some delay. The first half of *Refutation* was directed against them; the second half against the *Examination*.

Justification

Once Smotryc'kyj had published *Refutation (Elenchus)*, a Uniate *Counter-Refutation (Antelenchus)* was not far behind. The author of the *Counter-Refutation, That Is, A Reply to the Acrimonious Writings of the Monks of the Apostate Church of the Holy Spirit* (Vilnius, 1622) was the archimandrite of the neighboring Uniate Holy Trinity Monastery, Antonij Seljava. The attacks on Smotryc'kyj's learning continued:

84.   *Examen* 1621, 27/579.
85.   *Examen* 1621, 23/577.

> We have to grant you in this that you are *multae lectionis homines* [men of much reading], and you can boast of your reading as excellently as once one similar to you boasted, saying that he had read the entire Bible, but when he was asked where in the Bible were written the words "In the beginning God created heaven and earth," he answered that he hadn't gotten that far yet.[86]

Or, more pithily: "You know dialectics like a pig knows pepper."[87]

And Seljava continued the discussion on Smotryc'kyj's (and de Dominis's) definition of faith with an entire seventh chapter devoted to the topic: "Whether an Excess in the Faith Damns [Souls]." Here again, the Uniates rejected the definition of correct faith given by Smotryc'kyj (and ultimately de Dominis), stressing that correct faith meant to believe each and every thing revealed by God, neither more nor less. If God revealed one hundred things, then both he who believed ninety-nine of them, and he who believed all of them plus some new thing of his own invention, sinned against the faith.[88]

Once again the Uniate side sought to connect the Orthodox with the Cossacks, and thus with crimes against order. Seljava argued that "whatever occurs in this matter on the part of the Cossacks, occurs through your causing it."[89] More specifically, Seljava alleged that certain Cossacks (he knew their names but withheld them) had drowned a Uniate monk in Kyiv.[90]

The *Counter-Refutation* received no *Counter-Counter-Refutation,* although Smotryc'kyj did author one more work from the Orthodox side. This was the *Justification of Innocence,* signed by Metropolitan Borec'kyj on 6/16 December 1622 and directed first and foremost to King Sigismund III at the Sejm that was held in Warsaw from 24 January to 5 March 1623. Borec'kyj signed the work from Kyiv, and its title page bore a date of 1623 but no place of publication. Smotryc'kyj acknowledged authorship of the work in Uniate pamphlets of 1628 and

---

86. *Antelenchus* 1622, 26/697.
87. To "know something like a pig knows pepper" is a Polish expression meaning "not well at all." *NKPP* 3:910–1, "Znać," 21.
88. *Antelenchus* 1622, 35–6/705–6.
89. *Antelenchus* 1622, 53/720.
90. *Antelenchus* 1622, 54/721.

1629.[91] In *Justification,* Smotryc'kyj sought one last time to defend the actions of Theophanes and the new Ruthenian hierarchs and to gain the king's blessing from them. The translation presented in this volume is of the entire work (the title page is from the reproduction in Prokošina 1966, 124; the text is from Smotryc'kyj 1623 as reprinted in *AJuZR* 1:7:511–32).

Pilgrimage and Conversion

In the years 1623–1625, Smotryc'kyj made a pilgrimage to the Holy Land, during which time he visited Jerusalem and Constantinople and encountered his former teacher Cyril Lukaris, now patriarch of Constantinople. He left for the East late in the fall of 1623. In any case, we know that Smotryc'kyj was in Constantinople for some part of 1623, and that the journey there, according to a statement he made after his return, took about six weeks.[92] He seems to have followed the normal route through Moldavia and onto the Black Sea at the mouth of the Danube, thence toward the Bosporus and Constantinople. Smotryc'kyj remained there until 17/27 August 1624, when he departed for Jerusalem, arriving at the Lord's Sepulcher twelve days later (29 August/8 September). He stayed there until Easter of 1625, when he departed for Rus', again via Constantinople and Iași. He did not remain long in Constantinople on this second occasion, however, as the plague was raging there at that time; he probably returned to the Commonwealth by the summer or fall of 1625. Smotryc'kyj's account of his trip offers a kind of pilgrim's guide to the sites of the Holy Land: he visited Zion, Jerusalem, Bethlehem, the river Jordan, Golgotha, the Mount of Olives, the grave of the Virgin Mary in Gethsemane, and

91. Smotryc'kyj 1628a, 105/576 and 1629a, 22/656. See below, pp. 480 and 626.
92. Tomasz Kempa has recently (2004) published two little-known letters by Smotryc'kyj: one to Andrij Mužylovs'kyj in 1623, the second to Adam Chreptowicz in 1626. The first is dated 20/30 November 1623 from Kyiv. If the date is correct, it would indicate that Smotryc'kyj left for the East on 1 December at the earliest. This conflicts with the archbishop's own statement that he was in Constantinople for some portion of 1623. See Frick 1995, 94, and below, p. 494.

other places where Christ taught and preached, in each place kissing the ground and offering a bloodless offering in the Slavonic language "for the intention of the Ruthenian nation and all the nations that praise God in that tongue."[93]

Directly connected with his conversion to the Uniate Church, Smotryc'kyj's pilgrimage—its motivations and goals—became a subject of considerable controversy. Smotryc'kyj himself would later claim that he had made his trip to the East in an effort to discover whether "we drink the same soul-saving water from the evangelical source that flowed from them to us, which our fathers, the founders and builders of the Ruthenian Church, drank."[94] (He was to answer this question in the negative, finding Calvinist and other heretical elements not only in the works of Ruthenian Orthodox theologians, but also in those of Lukaris.) Smotryc'kyj alleged later that he had sought out the patriarch, with the knowledge and blessing of the Ruthenian hierarchy, in order to present his Ruthenian catechism of the Orthodox faith for Lukaris's approval; he also claimed that the leaders of the Orthodox side were well aware of his questions about the state of the Ruthenian Church from at least 1618. According to later allegations of the Orthodox side, Smotryc'kyj returned to Rus' a patriarchal exarch and with documents removing the stauropegial rights of the major brotherhoods (which had placed them directly under the jurisdiction of the patriarch of Constantinople and not under that of the local bishop); thus the goal of his trip had been one of personal aggrandizement.

A later Uniate tradition would connect Smotryc'kyj's pilgrimage and his conversion with the responsibility he felt for the martyrdom of Josafat Kuncevyč at the hands of burghers of Vicebsk on 12 November 1623; Smotryc'kyj's conversion—which, in this tradition, had come through the intercession of the martyred archbishop—would then become one of the miracles cited by Uniate authorities in their campaign for Kuncevyč's beatification. (Kuncevyč was beatified in 1642 and canonized in 1867.) In the rhetoric of the time, it was through St. Josafat's intercession that Smotryc'kyj, the Saul of the Dis-Union, saw the light and became the Union's St. Paul.[95]

93.   See Smotryc'kyj 1628a, 67/526, and below, p. 389.
94.   Smotryc'kyj 1628a, 2/524, and see below, pp. 385–6.
95.   On Smotryc'kyj and Josafat, see Frick 1995, 102–9.

The Uniates extended this metaphor of binary opposition in order to strengthen their claims of a connection between Smotryc′kyj's pilgrimage to Constantinople and the martyrdom of Kuncevyč. Wojciech Kortycki, Smotryc′kyj's Jesuit confessor in his last days and author of his funeral sermon, added a fictitious trip to Rome as a counterbalance to Constantinople in the itinerary of Smotryc′kyj's pilgrimage; in other words, when Smotryc′kyj didn't find what he was looking for in the East, he went west.[96] This was pure fantasy, a result of a scheme of thought that required a purely either/or world.

These false claims are an example of the propagandistic use of Smotryc′kyj's life by Uniate and Catholic authorities. Smotryc′kyj did not go to Rome, and, in all likelihood, he was already in Constantinople at the time of Kuncevyč's murder. Although he might certainly have felt some indirect responsibility for the events, his own published writings and letters do not indicate that the archbishop's death played any role in his decisions.[97] Somewhat different versions of Smotryc′kyj's spiritual path arise from his own post-conversion writings, but all these versions agree that the process was a lengthy one and that it had begun sometime around 1617, around the time he was engaged in discussions with Vilnius Uniates and became a monk with the Orthodox Brotherhood Monastery. With one notable exception, Josafat the martyr was absent from Smotryc′kyj's writings; and even this passage points rather in the opposite direction from the Uniate versions of the relationship between the two bishops of Polack.[98] Moreover, if Smotryc′kyj's statements about the chronology of his pilgrimage to the East are accurate, if we accept his statement that he spent some portion of 1623 in Constantinople, it is highly likely that he had departed for Constantinople before the day of Josafat's death.[99] This does not mean he did not feel any responsibility or remorse for the events; it simply calls into question the role of the martyr's death in Smotryc′kyj's spiritual path to the Uniate Church.

In a letter of 19 February 1627 we first encounter the Saulus-Paulus formula employed by the Uniates. The palatine of Braclav,

96.   Kortycki 1634, B3r–v, E3v, and see Frick 1995, 97.
97.   On Smotryc′kyj's pilgrimage, and the controversies surrounding it, see Frick 1995, 89–101.
98.   Smotryc′kyj 1629b, 3v/704. See also below, p. 702; Frick 1995, 103–4.
99.   For the chronology of Smotryc′kyj's pilgrimage, see Frick 1995, 90–7; see also Kempa 2004, who cites contradictory evidence.

Aleksander Zasławski, wrote to Smotryc'kyj, stating the terms under
which he would give Smotryc'kyj control of the monastery at Derman';
the letter was printed in the *vita* by Bishop of Chełm Jakiv Suša, and it
was he who popularized the formula in the course of his campaign for
the canonization of Kuncevyč. Zasławski wrote:

> Who here does not remark Your Most Reverend Paternity's
> most forceful calling? I might truly dare to set it equal, not
> to say to place it above, the calling of St. Paul, that most
> illustrious torch in the Church of God. For in the latter case,
> it confounded and bound the feet of the horse and cast down
> the rider himself; whereas in the other case, it bound Your
> Paternity's very sharp intellect, darkened your illustrious
> wit, restrained entirely your contrary will. And so, with
> external means did the Lord deal with the latter, and with
> Your Eminence he dealt with internal means.[100]

To the extent that the schema implied a sudden illumination leading to a
change of faith, it was, again, at odds with Smotryc'kyj's own account of
a long-term struggle with the issues at the core of the Ruthenian debate.
In the period after his return to Rus' and before his public espousal of
the union, we find him again conducting discussions with both sides,
much as he apparently had done ca. 1617.

Letters

Smotryc'kyj seems not to have returned to Vilnius. By the summer
of 1627 we find him residing in Derman' as archimandrite over the
local monastery, which at that time must have been at least nominally
Orthodox, but which was located on the estates of Zasławski, himself
a recent convert to Catholicism. Zasławski (husband of Eufrozyna
Ostroz'ka, who was the daughter of Januš and the granddaughter of
Kostjantyn Vasyl' Ostroz'kyj), together with Uniate Metropolitan
Ruts'kyj, presided over Smotryc'kyj's move toward the Uniate Church.
Our first witness to what would be the culmination of a long process
of conversion comes in the letter from Zasławski to Smotryc'kyj dated
19 February 1627, in which the palatine outlined the conditions under

100. Suša 1666, 42–3.

which he would give Smotryc'kyj control over the Derman' Monastery
and likened Smotryc'kyj's calling to that of St. Paul.[101] The next step
was taken on 6 July 1627, when Smotryc'kyj officially converted, on
Zasławski's estate and in the presence of Ruts'kyj.[102] That day he wrote
three letters in Latin to Rome, translated below. The first is his petition
to Pope Urban VIII asking for forgiveness and reception in the Church
(*Letter 1* in this volume; Velykyj 1972, 125–6). The second is a similar
letter of introduction to Cardinal Ottavio Bandini, the man most directly
responsible at the *Congregatio de Propaganda fide* [Congregation for
the Propagation of the Faith] for Polish-Lithuanian affairs in those days
(*Letter 2* in this volume; Velykyj 1972, 126–7). The third, of which we
have only a third-person summary (*Letter 3* in this volume; Velykyj
1972, 127–9), was a letter to the Holy Office of the Inquisition, in
which Smotryc'kyj asked for permission to remain for a time a covert
Uniate, arguing that the model of the Jesuits on missions and in other
adverse situations allowed the use of mental reservation for the good of
the cause. He also announced here his intention to produce two crucial
programmatic works: a letter to Patriarch Cyril Lukaris and a series of
"Considerations" of the six key differences between the Eastern and
Western Churches. (Translations from contemporary Polish printings of
these works appear below; see pp. 664–83 and 501–63.)

Thus, in the period between his return to Rus' sometime in 1625–
1626 and the Kyiv Council of the Orthodox Church in August 1628
when he was discovered as a Uniate, Smotryc'kyj was operating in some
middle ground between the two camps, and he portrayed his activities
to both sides as attempts to bring about the reunification of Rus' under
the appropriate banner. We have two letters that are illustrative of this
situation. The first, in Ruthenian (written 20/30 October 1627; printed
in *AJuZR* 1:6:605–7 [*Letter 4* in this volume]), was directed to the
Orthodox Brotherhood of Vilnius, over which he was still nominally
archimandrite. In it he sought to put to rest rumors that he had gone
over to the Uniate side. In a Polish letter of 2/12 April 1628 (edited,
badly enough to make it incomprehensible in places, in Kojalovič 1861,
366–73 [*Letter 5* in this volume]), he wrote to Ruts'kyj—who was
serving as doctrinal censor for his Ruthenian catechism—informing the

---

101. Printed in Suša 1666, 42–3.
102. For more on Smotryc'kyj's conversion, see Frick 1995, 110–46.

metropolitan of his progress on that work and telling of his troubles with some of the Orthodox, who had recently spread the rumor "throughout all of Volhynia" that he had been meeting with the Uniate hierarch.

It is crucial to an understanding of subsequent events to note that Smotryc'kyj, drawing on the model of Jesuits in India and the Far East, asked for permission to dissimulate for a time; by "hiding under the cover of the schism," as he put it in his letter to the Holy Office, he would have access otherwise closed for Uniates both to Patriarch of Constantinople Cyril Lukaris and to the Orthodox hierarchy of Rus'. His plan was twofold. First, he wrote his letter to Lukaris asking him to state his beliefs on the articles of the Orthodox faith, the result of which, in Smotryc'kyj's argument, "would surely be this: that . . . he might show him to be a heretic and lead the schismatics to the absurdities in the letter of the patriarch, whom they venerate as their head."[103] This suggestion from Smotryc'kyj fit nicely with a long-term effort on the part of *Congregatio de Propaganda fide* to represent Lukaris to the world as a crypto-Calvinist. Second, Smotryc'kyj's "Considerations" would be presented at a council of the Ruthenian Orthodox Church, thereby leading them to union with Rome.

This, at least, was the picture Smotryc'kyj offered to Uniate and Catholic authorities. There are certain indications, however, that Smotryc'kyj may have been pursuing a plan for a unified particular Ruthenian Church in somewhat looser union with Rome, perhaps under the immediate jurisdiction of a Ruthenian patriarch in Kyiv (a motif that would resurface under the Orthodox Metropolitan of Kyiv Peter Mohyla).[104] Smotryc'kyj continued to read de Dominis in this period, and the ideas of the Dalmatian heretic—who envisioned a *Respublica ecclesiastica* comprising a rather loose confederation of particular churches—as well as his unhappy end, may have been on his mind. In any event, the documents of the years 1627 and 1628, a period when Smotryc'kyj was covertly Uniate and overtly Orthodox, paint a picture of a man in the middle, and perhaps that was where he wished to be.

There are indications that Uniate and Catholic religious authorities were, perhaps on account of mistrust, slow to decide what official status to accord Smotryc'kyj. The question had come up already in the spring

103. See Velykyj 1972, 128; and below, p. 356.
104. On these discussions, see Plokhy 2001, 93–9, and the literature cited there.

of 1628 (while Smotryc'kyj was still a covert Uniate): on 8 April of that year the *Congregatio de Propaganda fide* had written to Ruts'kyj stating that they would wait for the metropolitan to certify that the convert had shown "in words and in deeds" that he was indeed sincere.[105] For the time being, he would be the *nuncupowany* or *rzeczony*—i.e., "called" or "so-called" (without the negative connotations of the latter term in English)—archbishop of Polack (which see was occupied, after all, by the successor to Josafat Kuncevyč, Antonij Seljava). Ruts'kyj gave his certification of Smotryc'kyj's *bona fides* in a letter to Rome dated 9 January 1629 (by which time Smotryc'kyj had confessed to the metropolitan his "re-apostasy" in Kyiv and had reaffirmed his allegiance to Rome), suggesting that it was now "necessary to see about his episcopal title."[106] Various possibilities were discussed: Smotryc'kyj might be given a vacant Ruthenian bishopric, he might be made suffragan of someone else's cathedra, or he might be given some title *in partibus*. The third option was chosen, but not without considerable delay and much discussion in Rome: only on 5 June 1631 did Pope Urban VIII write to Smotryc'kyj making him archbishop of the "Church of Hierapolis, which is *in partibus infidelium,* under the patriarchate of Antioch."[107]

Apology

Smotryc'kyj wrote his long letter to Lukaris on 21/31 August 1627. It was probably in Latin, the language in which a copy would also be deposited in Rome;[108] it would appear in Polish translation as an appendix to Smotryc'kyj's *Paraenesis* of 1629. Smotryc'kyj's few extant letters from the period reveal that he was in close, but semi-secret, contact with Ruts'kyj, who was serving as censor for his dogmatic statements. These contacts raised suspicions about Smotryc'kyj's allegiance, as did, we can assume, his absence from Vilnius; and he wrote letters to both sides explaining his contacts with the other as necessary for his ultimate

---

105. Šeptyc'kyj 1971, 657.
106. Velykyj 1956, 223–5.
107. Velykyj 1953, 482. On the controversies surrounding the granting of a new episcopal title to the Uniate Smotryc'kyj, see Frick 1995, 147–57.
108. A Latin version is printed in Velykyj 1972, 130–45.

goal of reuniting Rus′ (under the appropriate banner, and he allowed the addressee to think what he would on that issue).

Around 8/18 September 1627 Smotryc′kyj met with other Orthodox hierarchs, including Borec′kyj and Peter Mohyla, then still a layman, in Kyiv. He was commissioned by his fellow Orthodox hierarchs at this time to write his "Considerations." Smotryc′kyj was summoned half a year later, on Palm Sunday in 1628 (6/16 April), to a gathering in Horodok (in Volhynia) that included Borec′kyj, Mohyla (by now archimandrite of the Kyivan Caves Monastery), and Bishops Isakij Boryskovyč of Luc′k and Ostroh and Pajisij Ippolytovyč of Chełm and Belz. Here a council of the entire Ruthenian Orthodox Church was called for August 1628 in Kyiv. Smotryc′kyj was asked to write a call to the council and permitted to publish his "Considerations" along with it. This general appeal became Smotryc′kyj's *Apology . . . for the Peregrination to the Eastern Lands,* which he claimed he began writing immediately after Easter (13/23 April 1628) and which he had finished by Pentecost (1/11 June 1628). He then had it recopied and sent early during the Apostles' Fast (i.e., sometime after 9/19 June, although the Apostles' Fast ended only on 29 June/9 July 1628) to Borec′kyj and Mohyla, together with letters he would later publish in his *Protestation.* Smotryc′kyj told Borec′kyj in the accompanying letter that the work could be printed in the course of about three weeks if two presses were employed. The two churchmen replied through Smotryc′kyj's messenger that they would read the work and give him their reactions. When Smotryc′kyj had heard nothing from Borec′kyj and Mohyla after three weeks (i.e., earlier rather than later in the period between 30 June/10 July and 20/30 July), he decided to move forward with the printing, which he entrusted to Kasijan Sakovyč, by now the Uniate archimandrite of the nearby Dubno Monastery.[109] This tight schedule for the composing, copying, and printing of such a long work, while perhaps not unfeasible, raises a few questions. Smotryc′kyj's goal here was to portray his actions as in accord with, indeed sponsored by, the Orthodox hierarchy. We might wonder, nonetheless, whether he had not begun his work on the project before he received the official blessing from the Orthodox side, especially since he had already envisaged something like these "Considerations" in his first letters to Rome on 6 July 1627.

---

109. Smotryc′kyj 1628b, A3r–4v/628–30, and see below, pp. 576–8.

In any event, over the spring and early summer of 1628, Smotryc′kyj was in contact with the metropolitans and other hierarchs of both sides, conferring with the Uniate metropolitan on the orthodoxy of his doctrinal statements and with the Orthodox metropolitan on plans to present his thoughts at a local Church council. And he was surprised—as we will see later in his *Protestation*—by the violence of the reaction on the Orthodox side to his unionizing vision. This miscalculation seems to have arisen from a belief in the influence of hierarchy in such matters and a trust that if Borec′kyj and Mohyla believed the same things he did—as far as Smotryc′kyj had been able to ascertain—and thus were "uniate" in their core beliefs, then the three of them would be able to convince the other bishops, and the flock would follow its chief shepherds. He may also have been hoping that a discussion of his "Considerations" at the Kyiv Council would have led to a discussion of the possible varieties of a united Rus′, including a vision of an independent patriarchate. No such discussion took place, and as a result, Smotryc′kyj's room for maneuvering soon became much more circumscribed.

Presented in this volume is a translation of the entirety of *Apology*, including the "Considerations." The work appeared with one of at least two dedicatory epistles, one to Aleksander Zasławski, by now palatine of Kyiv, a second to Tomasz Zamoyski, crown vice chancellor (and son of Jan Zamoyski, the old great crown hetman). Both prefaces (and the title page) were dated 25 August and at Derman′ (although the work was issued from a Lviv printing house). In other words, the finishing touches to the printed version of *Apology* (perhaps nothing more than the prefaces and the title page) were added after Smotryc′kyj's return from the Orthodox council, for which he had arrived in Kyiv on 13/23 August. (Smotryc′kyj left Kyiv to return to Derman′ on 15/25 August, at the earliest. This would seem good evidence that, at least on this occasion, he had dated a printed work using the old calendar, but without marking the usage as such.)

Revocation and *Protestation*

Smotryc′kyj arrived for the council in Kyiv on 13/23 August 1628. In a description of the council taken from his *Protestation* written the following month, Smotryc′kyj painted a picture of a world turned upside down, in which Cossacks, other laymen, and lesser clergy told the bishops what to believe. Borec'kyj refused to see him in private, and "the father archimandrite of the Monastery of the Caves [i.e., Mohyla] attacked me harshly with dishonorable words."[110] The culmination of the council occurred at services on the night of 14/24 August in the Monastery of the Caves, when each of the bishops solemly anathematized Smotryc'kyj's *Apologia,* tearing pages of the work and casting them under foot. Sakovyč was singled out and condemned for his role in printing the work. In order to avoid violence, and perhaps in fear for his safety, Smotryc'kyj, before going to vespers, signed a prepared revocation of his *Apology,* thinking that this—which he viewed as a stalling maneuver—would suffice and (so he claimed) not expecting to witness or play an active role in the anathema placed upon his work.

The Orthodox side was quick to publish Smotryc'kyj's revocation both in Ruthenian (*Apolleia* 1628, Б2v–3r/308–9) and in Polish (Mužylovs'kyj 1629, 41r–v), the Ruthenian version being included in an account of the same events entitled *Apolleia [Destruction] of the Book "Apology"* (Kyiv, 1628).[111] This document, dated 14 August 1628, appears in this volume in English translation. In his *Protestation against the Council Held in This Year, 1628, in the Days of the Month of August, in Kyiv, in the Monastery of the Caves, Made by Him Who Was Wronged at It,* dated 7/17 September 1628 at Derman', Smotryc'kyj narrated his own version of events. The "protestation" was a genre well known in the acts of the various courts of Poland-Lithuania. Smotryc'kyj had his printed, so he would argue, because the courts, in control of Orthodox officials, refused to receive it. It is translated in its entirety here.

Paraenesis

Although the Orthodox hierarchy had forbidden Smotryc'kyj to leave Kyiv after the Council of August 1628, it seems he left immediately for Derman', and from that monastery on Aleksander Zasławski's lands he continued to agitate for the Union among the Orthodox, much as if nothing had changed since he was revealed as a Uniate. He made

110. Smotryc'kyj 1628b, C3r/636, and see below, p. 590.
111. On Smotryc'kyj's conversion and on the Kyiv council of 1628, see Frick 1995, 102–46.

his case now through his printed *Protestation* and through private and public letters. In a letter of 28 October/6 November 1628 to Orthodox Cupbearer of Volhynia Lavrentij Drevyns'kyj, Smotryc'kyj mentioned in passing that he planned to meet his Vilnius representative Josyf Bobryc'kyj in Kyiv at Epiphany (6/16 January 1629).[112] This offhand comment is difficult to interpret, coming so soon from a man who appears to have left Kyiv under some fear for his safety. In any event, it reveals a Uniate who still felt he had direct access to the Orthodox, and Smotryc'kyj would continue to write as "one of them/us."

Smotryc'kyj's *Paraenesis, or Admonition* appeared in early 1629. (The title page bore a date of 12 December 1628 together with the information that the work was printed in Cracow in 1629. The imprimatur of the Roman Catholic censor was dated 19 January 1629.) The work took the form of an open letter to the Orthodox Brotherhood of Vilnius, of which Smotryc'kyj was still at least nominally archimandrite. In it he sought to answer concerns expressed in a letter handed to him in Kyiv by his Vilnius representative, Bobrykovyč. In that letter the Vilnius Brotherhood had asked Smotryc'kyj

> . . . for a clear response: that I remove the suspicion that has risen about me in Your Graces' hearts due to the repute carried in the mouths of men, some alleging that I am a Uniate, and others that I am inventing something new and thus attempt to tear Rus' into a third part, whence there would finally arise a deception worse than the first.[113]

In a lengthy appendix, Smotryc'kyj printed a Polish version of the letter he had written to Patriarch Cyril Lukaris on 21 August 1627, in which he asked for Lukaris's opinion on the doctrinal questions at the center of the Ruthenian debates and urged him to adopt a unionizing stance. This was the letter that Smotryc'kyj had promised to write in his first communication with the Holy Office at the time of his official conversion on 6 July 1627.

The work also contained some passages that refuted claims made in the Orthodox *Apolleia*. The Orthodox side did its best to distance the hierarchs from Smotryc'kyj's version of the preparations for the Kyiv

112. Golubev 1883b, 322.
113. Smotryc'kyj 1629a, 3/646, and see below, p. 607.

Council, apparently fearful of any hint that Borec'kyj and Mohyla might have shared in the apostate archbishop's unionizing vision. According to the *Apolleia,* the purpose of the council was quite different. The work began with an extract from a constitution of the recent Sejm, which served to prove that the council was called not to discuss Smotryc'kyj's agenda, but to address a much more immediate, secular need:

> And as to the Ruthenian clergy and non-Uniates, they are to confer amongst themselves before the coming Sejm so that, following the example of our clergy and of the Uniates, they too, according to their obligation, might contribute to the present salvation of the Commonwealth.[114]

Thus the Orthodox—as good citizens—were answering the call to rally to the defense of the Commonwealth against the constant Turkish threat (and not coming together to discuss the Union).

The Orthodox side was also beginning to understand the danger of continuing to allow the Uniates to tie it to "its authorities," whom Smotryc'kyj would call the Ruthenian "new Theologians"—Philalethes, the Clerk of Ostroh, Zizanij, and Orthologue. The new Orthodox strategy was to characterize these authors as lacking authorization from the Church hierarchy. Smotryc'kyj's transgression was that he had "dared and made bold to charge the entire Eastern Church, his mother, in the person of three writers not approved by the Church, with errors and heresies."[115] For his part, Smotryc'kyj would point to the unusual authority that the Vilnius Brotherhood of the Descent of the Holy Spirit held for the Orthodox throughout Rus'. For him, the name of the Brotherhood printing house on the title page of Orthologue's *Thrēnos,* for example, was tantamount to official approval by the Orthodox Church of Rus'.

The present volume contains a translation of *Paraenesis* in its entirety (with the exception of a neo-Greek encomiastic poem on Smotryc'kyj that appears on the last leaf, the author of which was professor of Greek at the Cracow Academy, Mikołaj Żórawski).[116]

---

114. *Apolleia* 1628, A1v/303.
115. *Apolleia* 1628, B2r/308.
116. Reprinted in Czerniatowicz 1991, 184.

Exaethesis

One of the main architects of Smotryc'kyj's defeat at Kyiv in August 1628 was the Orthodox protopope of Sluck, Andrij Mužylovs'kyj. At least this was the way Smotryc'kyj portrayed the events in his *Protestation,* although we should remember that his goal throughout this period was to prove that authority had been upended, that archpriests were telling metropolitans, bishops, and archimandrites what to believe, and that Borec'kyj and Mohyla were, in fact, fearful crypto-Uniates. In any event, in 1629 Mužylovs'kyj published a work entitled *Antidotum [Antidote] for the Most Noble Ruthenian Nation; or, A Guard against the "Apology" Full of Poison, Which Meletij Smotryc'kyj Published, Unrightfully Ascribing Heresy and Schism to the Orthodox Ruthenian Church on Account of a Few Writers.* The "few writers" were, again, Smotryc'kyj's Ruthenian "new theologians"—Philalethes, the Clerk of Ostroh, Zizanij, and above all Orthologue—who had been the direct object of his criticisms in *Apology* and *Paraenesis.*

Mužylovs'kyj took up and expanded here some of the new threads of arguments touched upon briefly in the Orthodox *Apolleia* of 1628. The question was one of order and censorship of books. The Orthodox side was beginning to realize that this was a weak point in its polemical stance with respect to the Uniates and Catholics and that some of the writers who had passed for Orthodox authorities were indeed liable to criticism for heterodox views. One of Mohyla's projects, upon coming into power in the Ruthenian Orthodox Church, would be the imposition of a centralized control that included the censorship and approval of books printed at Orthodox presses—a kind of imprimatur system. Mužylovs'kyj made two contributions to this discussion. The first was the continued attempt on the part of the Orthodox to distance themselves from their former authorities. In short, Mužylovs'kyj argued that since the Church had not specifically approved these works, Smotryc'kyj could not accuse the Orthodox side of heretical views. For example, in his chapter 7 ("That the Eastern Church Never Defends Its Truth with Heretical Writings, Nor Does It Base Itself upon Them"), Mužylovs'kyj argued that Philalethes was an historian, not a theologian; that, as long as he wrote as an historian, the Eastern Church could draw on his authority; and that the fact that he committed heretical errors the moment he strayed into the field of theology had nothing to do with the

Church, since in this matter "our Orthodox Ruthenian Church under the obedience of the patriarch of Constantinople does not receive him and does not approve him as an authority."[117]

Mužylovs'kyj's second contribution had to do with the status of his own *Antidotum*. Since he had not submitted his work for the censorship and approval of the hierarchs, he was in a sense writing as a private, concerned citizen:

> Seeing all of which [i.e., Smtoryc'kyj's actions], I was unable to restrain myself, and against the synodal prohibition [mentioned in *Apolleia*] I made bold, without censorship, from my own person, to enter into a conversation with this Apologist.[118]

If his work found favor with the authorities, so much the better. If not, he could withdraw it, and the Church could in effect disown it.

Mužylovs'kyj thus made a very easy target of himself on these issues and others, and Smotryc'kyj's *Exaethesis,* which was written sometime after 3/13 April 1629, devoted to the protopope some of his most offensive and least witty invective. For his part, all of Smotryc'kyj's Uniate works, beginning with *Apology,* carried the title-page advertisement *"Cum licentia superiorum"* ("with the permission of the superiors"), and both *Paraenesis* and *Exaethesis* bore an additional signed imprimatur.

In an attempt to diminish Smotryc'kyj's authority, Mužylovs'kyj revisited the period 1617 to 1622 and claimed that there were at that time three omens of the archbishop's future apostasy: first, at the time of his monastic tonsure, when the common people had raised the objection that he would disturb the peace of the Church; second, when he was to receive his consecration from Patriarch Theophanes and, lacking proper priestly vestments—lest it be said of him, "Friend, how camest thou in hither not having a wedding garment?" [Mt. 22:12]—he had to put on Mužylovs'kyj's own robes; and third, when, on the occasion of his farewell to Vilnius before leaving for the East, a column had fallen from

117. Mužylovs'kyj 1629, 25r.
118. Mužylovs'kyj 1629, A2r.

the church.[119] Smotryc′kyj answers these objections in the fragments translated below.

This volume presents translations of the title page, the dedicatory epistle (again to Aleksander Zasławski, by now palatine of Kyiv), the "Preface to the Orthodox Reader," and two extended excerpts from *Exaethesis*. Among the topics discussed are the relationship between the Orthodox Church and its "new theologians"; Orthodoxy and heresy; the circumstances of Smotryc′kyj's tonsure and ordination; Smotryc′kyj's pilgrimage to the East; the Orthodox Church and the Council of Florence (Smotryc′kyj 1629b,)(1r–17v/695–718, 89v–102r/792–804). The work can be seen as a kind of call to the All-Rus′ Council that had been scheduled for October 1629 in Lviv, and it ends with a survey of the remaining topics for discussion.

Letter to Pope Urban VIII

The last years of Smotryc′kyj's life must have been a time of disappointment, since his hopes for a joint council of the Ruthenian Uniate and Orthodox Churches in Lviv in October 1629 went unrealized.[120] The archbishop took part in a meeting of Uniate hierarchs at that time, but the Orthodox side failed to appear. There is some evidence that faith in Smotryc′kyj's *bona fides,* which may never have been absolute, was shaken in Rome by his revocation of his *Apology* at the Kyiv Council of August 1628. After these events, he seems to have entered what one scholar has called a "three-year quarantine" as far as Roman authorities were concerned.[121] During this period, as is outlined above, Uniate Metropolitan Ruts′kyj was charged with attesting to the sincerity of Smotryc′kyj's conversion, and a decision was finally reached on 5 June 1631 to grant Smotryc′kyj the archbishopric of Hierapolis *in partibus.*[122]

---

119. Mužylovs′kyj 1629, 11–12r.
120. On the Council of 1629, see Žukovič 1911; Hruševs′kyj 2002, 65–75; Kryp'jakevyč 1913; Sysyn 1979–1980; Sysyn 1985, 54–63; Plokhy 2001, 127–9.
121. Šmurlo 1932, 517.
122. On Smotryc′kyj's last years and the controversies surrounding his new title, see Frick 1995, 147–57.

During this "quarantine," on 16 February 1630, Smotryćkyj wrote a final, lengthy letter to Urban VIII in which he outlined a plan for the reunification of Rus´. Two points are important here. First, the entire project was to be based on force: "compel them to come in" (*compelle intrare;* Lk. 14:23)—the classic proof text on the licitness of, even the necessity for, the use of compulsion in bringing heretics and schismatics in from the highways and the hedges to sit at the Lord's costly supper. Second, a similar kind of compulsion should be employed to keep Ruthenians from converting to Roman Catholicism, since a Ruthenian can help another Ruthenian from the position of a Uniate, but not from the position of a Roman Catholic: "For he offers greater help to him who is in danger of losing his life, who helps with living voice with laid-on hand, than he who helps from far away only by shouting."[123]

This volume contains a translation of the entire Latin letter to Urban VIII (printed in Velykyj 1972, 186–97, with omission of a few Greek phrases, and, more completely but with a few other textual problems, in Theiner 1863).

Postscript

Smotryćkyj died in December 1633, and the Uniate and Catholic side immediately proclaimed that a miracle had taken place in which the dying archbishop had made clear his exclusive confessional allegiance. The central source for these events is the funeral sermon—*A View of the Fight Well Fought, the Course Finished, the Faith Kept* (Vilnius, 1634)—delivered on 29 January 1634 by Smotryćkyj's confessor in his last days, the Jesuit Wojciech Kortycki. According to this account, when Smotryćkyj knew he was about to die, he asked that he be given to hold in death the papal *bulla* that had made him archbishop of Hierapolis. In the confusion of the moment the monks forgot the request, and only five hours after Smotryćkyj's death, "when the limbs had already stiffened," did the monks remember. Then, in imitation of St. Alexis, Smotryćkyj's "cadaverous [right] hand so grasped the letter with all its fingers that the parchment was wrinkled."[124] Smotryćkyj gripped the letter and would not release it, despite several publicly staged attempts over the next few

123. Velykyj 1972, 210; Theiner 1863, 386; and see below, p. 759.
124. Kortycki 1634, F4r–v.

days, until Uniate Metropolitan Ruts'kyj arrived to receive it from him. Over the same period all attempts to place a letter from the patriarch of Jerusalem (other accounts say the patriarch of Constantinople) in the left hand came to naught. (The best known iconography, including the picture of Smotryc'kyj found in Suša's *vita,* depicts this posthumous miracle.)[125]

Scholarly treatments of Smotryc'kyj have tended to focus on his conversion. Most assessments have been shaped by the confessions and nationalities of the investigators, who have told the story either as one of betrayal or as one of a long—and finally successful—search for the truth. As such, they have drawn on and continued the polemic of the early seventeenth century; they have also simplified its terms considerably. For Orthodox scholars of various nationalities, Smotryc'kyj's conversion represented an abandonment of Ruthenian difference and an assimilation to Polish and Western cultural and political values. For Polish Catholic scholars, Smotryc'kyj's conversion represented a recognition of the superiority of those values. The course of Smotryc'kyj's life, however, does not easily fit either of these binary schemes, and there is evidence that each side mistrusted him to a certain extent, even when he was a spokesman for that side.

One constant in Smotryc'kyj's life and work was a concern for the well-being of a Ruthenian Church, culture, and nation, which, in his view, should be led by an elite of bishops and nobles. This defense of Ruthenian difference made itself felt at all levels of his work, ranging from concerns over the loss of Ruthenian noble families to Catholicism and Polonization, on the one hand, to a highly creative use of the Polish language, on the other. On this topic, it is worth noting that throughout his career, Orthodox and Uniate, Smotryc'kyj was engaged in an effort to create a Ruthenian-Polish rhetoric by silently "correcting" according to the Greek text the Catholic Leopolita and Wujek translations of Holy Writ that he cited in his polemical works; and by introducing conscious "orthodoxisms" into his Polish (e.g., a highly artificial genitive of surprise or remorse in imitation of Greek and Slavonic: "O nieporządnego, o

---

125. On the controversies surrounding Smotryc'kyj's death and posthumous miracles, see Frick 1995, 158–69.

przewrotnego, o niezbożnego rąk wkładania obyczaju" or "O skarania bożego").[126]

Smotryc'kyj pursued goals similar to those of Orthodox Metropolitan of Kyiv Peter Mohyla, and with similar means (though the younger Mohyla had the fortune to rise to power in the Ruthenian Church during the reign of Władysław IV and at the time of the re-legalization of the Ruthenian Orthodox hierarchy).[127] In both cases we see an attempt—using what were quite clearly the methods and materials of the Western, and specifically Polish, Reformation and Counter-Reformation—to build and defend a Ruthenian "national" Church and culture that could participate as an equal in the life of the Polish-Lithuanian Commonwealth. Such a program necessarily brought both men into moments of greater and lesser conflict, both with the Polish and Catholic authorities and elite, who increasingly viewed Ruthenian difference with condescension or alarm, and with the Orthodox—especially with the lesser clergy, the brotherhoods, and the Cossacks—for whom their programs looked too much like the Polish Catholic norm.

Translator's Note

The works collected here are representative of the entire range of Smotryc'kyj's career and concerns. They appear in chronological order. I have kept annotations to a minimum. Information about historical figures (dates, titles, etc.) can be found in the main index. Other appendices provide an index of the biblical passages cited by Smotryc'kyj and a glossary of heresies, heresiarchs, and technical terms from the political and ecclesiastical cultures of early modern Poland-Lithuania.

Throughout the texts, the information provided in square brackets has been supplied by me. These interventions in the text are almost all either translations of phrases in a language other than the basic language of the given work or additional information identifying citations from the Bible and other authorities. I have based my translations of biblical citations on the King James Version.

126. On Smotryc'kyj's adaptation of Ruthenian linguistic and rhetorical usages in his Polish, see Frick 1995, 181–205, 363–7.
127. On Mohyla, see Ševčenko 1984; Plokhy 2001, 237–46; and the literature cited in those works.

The Gregorian, or new-style, calendar was implemented in Catholic Europe in 1582 and advanced the date ten days ahead of the older Julian calendar. Smotryc'kyj and other Ruthenian writers used primarily old-style dates. Where old-style dates are used in the book, I have provided the new style equivalents; e.g., "6/16 January 1629" means 6 January 1629 old style, 16 January 1629 new style. Elsewhere, dates are given in the new style.

Personal names have been rendered in Ukrainian orthography when the individual's Ruthenian affiliation is known. For persons given only a passing reference in the text, or whose exact affiliations are unknown, I have used Smotryc'kyj's Polish spelling.

Smotryc'kyj placed all his own annotations in the margin next to the text in the original editions. Removing this material to footnotes required distinguishing between identifications of sources for biblical and other authorities, on the one hand, and Smotryc'kyj's own marginal comments on his text, on the other. References to authorities permitted the use of normal note style, with a numbered marker at the end of the passage in question. For marginal commentary, it was necessary to place a symbol, usually a dagger (†), at the beginning of the passage annotated, since there was rarely any clear final cutoff point for the content of the comment in question.

References containing a date (e.g., Anuškin 1970) are listed at the end of the volume under the heading "Works Cited." References without a date (e.g., *AJuZR*) are found at the beginning of the volume in the list of abbreviations. References to handbooks on proverbs (*NKPP,* Erasmus *Ad.,* Gibbs, Arthaber, Tosi) are to entry numbers. References to the classics adhere to the standard rules (e.g., Cicero, *Book of Offices* 1.7.23).

In annotations in the text, glossary, and index, I have silently borrowed dates, biographical information, and definitions of heresies and other concepts from a host of standard reference works. These include the *Polski Słownik Biograficzny,* volumes of *Urzędnicy dawnej Rzeczypospolitej XII–XVIII wieku,* the *Oxford Dictionary of the Christian Church,* the *Catholic Encyclopedia,* the *Oxford Dictionary of Byzantium,* and David Christie-Murray's *History of Heresy* (Oxford, 1989).

Acknowledgments

I have been working on this project, on and off, for about twenty years, so the ineffability *topos* is not merely a *topos* in this case. But I will try. Warmest words of gratitude go first of all to my dissertation adviser, Riccardo Picchio, who suggested I write a dissertation on Smotryc′kyj and was always an ideal mentor, as well as to the other members of my committee, Alexander Schenker and Harvey Goldblatt. All of them helped me complete that work and have continued to respond to my many questions. Ihor Ševčenko, serving that year (1986?) as acting director of the Harvard Ukrainian Research Institute while Omeljan Pritsak was on sabbatical, wrote the letter asking me to undertake this project. I hope I have not disappointed either of them. Professor Pritsak has furthered my work over the years, as has Professor Ševčenko, who helped clear up some remaining questions in the last stages of annotations. Thanks, and all respect, to all of them.

Many friends have tried to help me understand Smotryc′kyj's world over the years—Frank Sysyn, Borys Gudziak, Serhii Plokhy, and Roman Koropeckyj chief among them. If I still don't get it, it wasn't for lack of effort on their part.

In the last stages, thanks to email, East European specialists around the world have been flooded with requests for help in clearing up issues of chronology and identity. Above all, thanks and warm words of gratitude to Andrzej Rachuba and Andrzej Zakrzewski, professors at the Polish Academy of Sciences and at Warsaw University, respectively, who have shared of their expertise generously and tirelessly.

I benefited greatly from the help of my research assistant, Michelle Viise, who cast her eagle eye over the manuscript and generally helped the project along in its middle stages.

I have had wonderful readers and editors at the Harvard Ukrainian Research Institute. Thanks to Robert De Lossa, who first received the work, and to Matthew Kay, who gave it its first editing. Thanks also to Lubomyr Hajda and to G. Patton Wright, who gave the whole manuscript one more reading in the later stages. Pat Wright's untimely death kept him from seeing the project to completion. We all miss him.

The final words of gratitude go to my editor at HURI, Marika Whaley. I wish all scholarly projects could be the object of such attentive care.

Thrēnos
(1610)

ΘΡΗΝΟΣ
[Thrēnos]

That Is,

The Lament of the One, Holy, Universal, Apostolic, Eastern Church, with an Explanation of the Dogmas of the Faith.

First Translated from Greek into Slavonic, and Now from Slavonic into Polish.

By Theophil Orthologue, a Son of that Same Holy Eastern Church.

In Vilnius, The Year of Our Lord 1610.

[...]¹

> To the Most Illustrious Lord, His Grace, Lord Mixajil
> Korybut, Prince Vyšnevec̆kyj, *Starosta* of Ovruč, etc.
> etc., Lord, Lord, My Gracious Lord:
>
> Theophil Orthologue W[ishes] the S[oul's] S[alvation].²

ALTHOUGH, MY NOBLE AND GRACIOUS LORD, those ancient pagan philosophers conducted great and rather subtle arguments and controversies *de summo bono*, that is, about the highest good and the greatest happiness and blessing of human life, they could not quite hit the target of the truth they desired. Those came closest to this, however, who asserted that the highest happiness is located in virtue itself and in the honorable glory that derives therefrom. "For virtue itself," says Seneca, "works eternal and sure happiness in man. Bearing the burdens even of sometimes opposing things, it does not fall under them, nor does it bend; rather it stands upright and thoroughly unmoved." Such a wise and excellent disquisition about virtue could not bring them any benefit but remained dead and useless. And why was this? Because the very source from which the currents of all virtues always flow in an abundant stream—that is, the knowledge of the true triune God, and the knowledge of His most holy will—was entirely unknown to them. For whenever the true and saving light illumines the eyes of a person's heart, immediately (so says the voice of the Lord in the Gospel) he becomes like the man who, having built his house not on sand but on a hard, rocky foundation, fears no destruction of it from the opposing winds and the rains so violently poured forth.³

Your Princely Grace's ancestors, noble and worthy of eternal glory and renown, did precisely this, in that, having first established a strong and unmovable foundation—that is, the true and in naught suspect faith in the triune God, which they received from their mother, the Holy

---

1.   [I have omitted the page containing the Vyšnevec̆kyj coat of arms and Smotryc̆kyj's verses devoted to them; Smotryc̆kyj 1610, ()1v/2.]

2.   [My solution for "Z(bawienia) D(uszy) Ż(yczy)."]

3.   Mt. 7[:24–7; Lk. 6:48–9].

Eastern Church, by rebirth through the water and the spirit[4]—they built
the house of their great and excellent virtues and gallantry not on sand,
not on clay, nor on any other material subject to decay and corruption,[5]
but on the very faith and confession, the foundation and the cornerstone
of which is the King of eternal glory Himself,[6] without whom, says
St. Paul, no one can lay another foundation.[7] Wherefore, the state of
events itself—which is described not only in the books of old and new
historians, but is also part of the common knowledge of all people that
has been gained *successu temporis* [in the succession of time]—bears
witness how He who dwells in Zion blessed that building of theirs,
and what kind of strengthening and multiplying[8] He deigned to bestow
upon it.

For since they were a branch grafted to the true Vine, Christ the
Lord,[9] they could direct their affairs and deeds to no other goal but
first to the honor and glory of almighty God, and then to the benefit
and support of their dear fatherland. Thus they successfully waged
such frequent battles and individual combat with the enemies of the
Holy Cross, at the risk not only of their wealth, but even of their very
health, for no other reason but so that not only they themselves, but also
other citizens of their paternal land, might be able to enjoy in peace
not only the other ornaments and the benefits of this Commonwealth
guaranteed by rights and freedoms, but especially the voluntary praise
of the name of the Lord, and that they might be able to enjoy this in
the normal fashion. And in brief, having kept faith toward God, faith
toward the fatherland, faith toward the kings their lords, absolutely and
inviolably until the final term of their life, they could not die even after
death. For here on earth they live in the constant memory of all people
and in immortal glory; and there (about which there is no doubt) they
expect, with certain and sure hope in the joy and delights not subject
to opposing changes, the perfect remuneration of eternal goods and the
unfading crown of life.[10]

4.   [Jn. 3:5.]
5.   [Mt. 7:26–7.]
6.   [Eph. 2:20.]
7.   1 Cor. 3[:11].
8.   [Gen. 1:22, 28; 8:17; 9:1, 7.]
9.   Jn. 15[:1].
10.   [Jas. 1:12; Rev. 2:10.]

Surrounded by opposing tempests, the Holy Eastern Church takes no small joy, in its present affliction, from the fact that Your Princely Grace, Our Gracious Lord, deigns, with a heart burning in love for God, to imitate your holy ancestors not only in brave and courageous acts of service to the fatherland (which are not only well known to the citizens of the broad domains of His Majesty the King, but also have been declared to almost the entire circumference of the earth), but also and no less in the constant use of the ancient faith and of the patrimonial rite, which was left by them as their most precious jewel. Likewise do all her faithful sons take joy, and they are glad in their hearts, incessantly begging the Giver and Multiplier of every good that He deign to give Your Princely Grace ever more of the spirit of counsel, the spirit of wisdom, the spirit of courage, the spirit of fear of Him, and, having fully strengthened you in the truth that you received at baptism and came to know and love, that He deign to cause that you leave here on earth for your descendants a wreath woven from virtue and glory in long life, and that there you might receive the crown of life with His elect;[11] for no one will lose it who—in these lamentable final days, in such great love for God of many people, in this corrupt age of coldness, in such a significant increase of iniquity,[12] and in such various and marvelous manners of deceivableness[13]—does not abandon the poor fold of a poor pastor and flee to the costly buildings, beloved of this world (in which false prophets claim Christ resides).[14] He will rather cry out with the psalmist: "I had rather be despised in the house of my God than live in the dwellings of sinful people."[15]

For I know well, I know that maxim of the golden-tongued theologian: "Do not tell me," he says, "that the city of Rome is great, but show me there such diligent hearkening to the word of God; for even the city of Sodom had great columns, whereas Abraham had a little tent, but the angels bypassed Sodom and came to that little hut,[16] for they had their sight not on the building but on the internal adornment

11.   [Jas. 1:12; Rev. 2:10.]
12.   Mt. 24[:12].
13.   [2 Th. 2:10.]
14.   Mt. 24[:11].
15.   Ps. 83 [84:10].
16.   [Gen. 18:1.]

of virtues."[17] Here end the words of St. John Chrysostom, which, if ever there was a time, then now most of all, should be in everyone's thoughts. For the final state of the Church is supposed to correspond to the first. As it was then under Annas and Caiaphas, the Jewish high priests[18]—a very small group of God's chosen and, what is more, poor and despised by the world—precisely thus is it supposed to be in the final times as well, in which (says Holy Writ) the enemy of the soul will attempt to deceive, were it possible, even the very elect.[19] But whoever escapes that subtle temptation, supported and defended by the wondrous mercy of almighty God, will not be harmed in any way by the second death; he will hold to what he has, and no one will wrest the crown from his hands.

It will be sufficiently expounded below in the "Preface to the Reader," the Lord God granting, that (after the grace of God) diligent examination of Holy Scripture gives no minor sustenance to constancy in faith; for there it will be demonstrated clearly and convincingly that in the final days the true Church of God cannot be recognized by any other means than by Holy Writ, which promises it, in the bearing of the cross, the maintenance of the integrity and the purity of the teaching of the Gospel. To which the excellent maxim of Basil the Great also testifies: "Let Scripture inspired by God (he says) be established by us as a judge; and let his opinion be recognized as true, whose teaching is in accord with the word of God."[20] Finally, Probus, a certain worthy senator, who was charged by the emperor with listening to the dispute between St. Athanasius and Arius, makes the following admonition to them, even though he was a pagan: *Si hoc totum est in quo a vobis invicem dissentire videmini, id nunc disputationis ratio poscit, ut assertiones vestras non subtilitate argumentorum, sed simplicibus et puris divinae scripturae documentis robustius fulciatis;* "If this," he says, "is all in which you disagree among yourselves, then I require that you carry on your disputation in this manner: that you firmly support

---

17.   *Chrysostom. de verb. Esaiae Prophet. vidi Dominum sedentem* [Chrystostom, *On the words of the Prophet Isaiah "I saw the Lord sitting"* (Is. 6:1); *PG* 56:120].

18.   [Lk. 3:2; Jn. 18:24.]

19.   [Mt. 24:24.]

20.   *Basil. Epist. 80* [*Letter 80* (alternate numbering 189); *PG* 32:688].

your proofs not by the subtlety of arguments, but by simple and true teachings of divine Writ."[21]

This entire book is composed of those mighty and unassailable proofs of Holy Scripture; for in it, the Holy Eastern Church, after making a mournful lament, truly appropriate to this age, gives a certain and thorough account about herself and about her genuine doctrine, which is unsoiled by the least addition in the confession of its faith and in the use of its ceremonies. And I, the least and unworthy servant of the Church of God, having translated this book into the Polish language for the easier understanding of all people, decided to dedicate it to Your Princely Grace as a true and faithful son of this Holy Eastern Church and no minor pillar of it in these lamentable times, and to publish it under the protection of Your Princely Grace's noble name. When Your Princely Grace, My Gracious Lord, having graciously received it (which I humbly beg and which I do not doubt in the least), will deign to read it diligently and carefully, I am certain that you will receive from this no small benefit and heart's delight, and that you will deign to present yourself all the more willingly and eagerly to bear the present burdens of your afflicted Mother (to your immortal glory and certain hope of eternal reward). Once again, humbly wishing you, along with Your Princely Grace's entire noble and most glorious family, a long and fortunate reign in God's abundant grace and blessing, I submit myself most urgently to the merciful kindness of Your Princely Grace, My Gracious Lord.

Preface to the Reader

According to the common opinion of wise people, one is supposed to consider the manner and nature of whatever matter one undertakes: that is, for what reason, purpose, and occasion, to what goal and end, and by what manners and *media* [means], something happens or happened. Thus it befits you, too, Gracious Reader, to do this upon your first

---

21.   In the book of Athanasius. [*Vigilii Tapsensis contra Arianos Dialogus. Athanasius, Ario et Probo judice interlocutoribus.* (Dialogue of Vigilius, Bishop of Thapsus against the Arians. Conversation between Athanasius, Arius, and Probus); *PL* 62:160.]

glance at this book and to weigh and consider these aforementioned things with care.

For as far as the first point of this consideration is concerned, I do not know which of the true sons of the Church of Christ would have the eyes of his reason so blinded that he could not see clearly that the cause of this is none other than the Ruler of heaven and earth Himself; that, at this time when, most of all, the adversaries attempt to darken it by various means with fogs, directed by wondrous industry toward leading human souls astray and toward oppressing and defaming the Innocent Lamb's innocent sheep in the Holy Eastern Church—that at this time, the light of His holy truth shines with all the brighter rays of its immaculate purity in faith, hope, and charity[22] (which commands us to bear everything patiently and eagerly for the Beloved) upon truly all the world and shows more and more the essence of its Orthodox faith, which is hidden before the ignorant. And opening the jewel box of those precious stones (with which she is excellently adorned within by her most mighty Bridegroom—*gloria enim filiae Regis [ab] intus* ["for the glory of the king's daughter is within"][23]—before those who, according to Solomon, despise her external black figure),[24] she boasts of them and speaks in these words:

"Do not despise me, sons of man, looking upon the blackened aspect of my face; do not despise me, but examine my inner beauty and the adornment of heavenly goods that my King and my God deigned to bestow abundantly upon me through His ineffable grace. Black is my countenance (I grant it), for it is not speckled with the paints of the riches, pomp, and artifice of this world; rather it is afflicted with the fasting, labor, vituperation, and persecution that I suffer constantly in the days of my pilgrimage; and going to the higher Jerusalem along the narrow road, full of sharp thorns, I bear the burden of the cross of pain and afflictions for my poor Bridegroom, who is despised by this world.

"Black is my countenance, for I do not partake of bodily pleasure and comfort on this wandering, or rather exile, of temporal life; but, nourishing myself with the fundamental hope of those infinite goods,

22.   [1 Cor. 13:13.]
23.   [Ps. 45:13.]
24.   S. of S. 1[:5] *Nigra sum sed formosa* [I am black, but comely].

and enclosing my heart and all my senses in that eternal fatherland, where also my Immortal Head resides, I constantly mortify myself with such great desire and longing for it and with the yearning of this temporal life; and I say these words along with blessed Augustine: 'O our gracious and peaceful fatherland: having glimpsed thee from afar, while sailing on this stormy ocean, we greet thee; lifting our eyes from this vale, we sigh to thee; and with tears we strive to come to thee. O hope of human kind, Christ, God of God: illumine our eyes with Thy light in the thick fogs and darknesses of temporal life that we might sail into port; govern and direct our ship with Thy right hand; draw us out of those dangerous storms at sea unto Thee our comfort, whom, with our tearful eyes, we barely see now as the morning star from afar, waiting for us on the shore of our heavenly fatherland.'

"Black is my countenance (that I say it for the third time), for it can never be comforted for its heartfelt pain and bloody lament, as it looks and sees that there are such great and truly innumerable numbers of people, redeemed by the most precious blood of the Immaculate Lamb, who—having exchanged such abundant gifts, such precious jewels, and such priceless goods, which the generous hand of the generous Lord deigns to give them *gratis* [freely], for the bauble of the wealth of gleaming glass, the luxury, pomp, and the short and uncertain peace of this world—run along the wide and spacious road that leads to eternal destruction,[25] overtaking one another gladly and eagerly. And what is even more marvelous, the very people who should lead them away and stop them from this unfortunate intent (since they have been entrusted with government and pastorship over them) have become the authors of their demise and guides on their road to perdition. 'Who will grant,' I say with the Prophet, 'waters unto my head and a fountain of tears unto my eyes, that I might weep day and night for the slain of the daughter of my people?'[26]

"In these respects, then, black and unadorned seems my countenance to the sons of this world. For in truth, my exterior adornment is somewhat changed by the malice, the persecution, and (before their apostasy) by the crude and harmful carelessness for the flock entrusted to them, not only of the others, but even of my own sons, who, although born of me,

25. [Mt. 7:13.]
26. [Jer. 9:1.]

constantly fight against me. But just look with the eyes of your heart at what I have within me, and straight away, marveling, you will say with the psalmist: 'O how great is the greatness of your sweetness, O Lord, which you have laid up for those who fear you.'[27] For do I not still retain in unviolated integrity the adornments and jewels that I received from the immortal and invincible King as a token and remembrance of my betrothal and eternal union with Him? Do I not wear on my body even until today that garment not made by human hand,[28] but woven of the highest theology, which none of the murderers of Christ my Lord, though crucifying his members, could tear into the rags of heretical teachings; nor can they now, nor will they be able to do so in the future (since the Lord's invariable promise must be fulfilled)?[29] Have I ever removed it from me or stained it with the spots of human inventions and alterations? No one, in truth, no one can cast this in my teeth; no one, I say, can declare of me in good conscience, what the Roman doctor Cassander wrote of his mother: *Praesens haec Ecclesia (Romana) non parum in morum et disciplinae integritate, adde etiam in doctrinae synceritate, ab antiqua illa unde orta et derivata est, dissidet.* That is: 'The present-day (Roman) Church differs not a little in its customs, and discipline, and, what is more, in the genuineness of its doctrine from the ancient Church out of which it grew.'[30]

"But I remain, with the help of my Lord, constant and unmovable even until today in what I once learned from Him. I adhere to and maintain in its proper integrity what I once received from Him, without any deletion, addition, or change, according to apostolic doctrine, the interpretation of the holy doctors, and the explanation of the seven main councils convened by the Holy Spirit. And, repeating it time and again, I call to my sons' memory the dictum of the Council of Chalcedon: 'If anyone retracts, let him be anathema, if anyone inquires, let him be

27. Ps. 30 [31:19].
28. [2 Cor. 5:1–4; Mk. 14:58.]
29. [Probably a reference to Mt. 16:18: "Upon this rock I will build my Church, and the gates of hell shall not prevail against it."]
30. *Cassand. in Consult.* [Georg Cassander, *Consultatio de Articulis Religionis inter Catholicos et Protestantes Controversis (A Consideration of the Articles of Dispute between Catholics and Protestants,* 1564)], art. 7, p. 43. [Cassander 1616, 929. The parenthetical insertion "(*Romana*)" was Smotryćkyj's.]

anathema, anathema is he who adds, anathema who deletes, anathema who innovates.'"[31]

With these and similar words the Holy Oriental Church renders account of herself to everyone who errs in ignorance; and this account, with God's help, is treated here, in the books written under her name, quite sufficiently and clearly, as far as time and other circumstances permitted. And the unvarying and unsuspect purity of her faith and rituals shines more brightly than the noonday light.

It is not necessary to expend many words concerning the goal or end to which this is done, or what sort of benefit the wise reader can receive from the diligent and careful reading of these books: after all, he knows well how important it is for every man to recognize the true and not invented Church, the one pure and immaculate bride of the Heavenly Bridegroom. For who will not recognize her, if he remains in her and by her (especially in such great tribulation)? And who will not remain by her, and will not stay in her, when he can become an heir to the eternal and blessed life after this temporal abode? Who, further, will not become a partaker of that future blessing and of the happiness and luxuries prepared for the Lord's chosen? What worse unhappiness can meet him, and what harm greater than this inestimable loss: "For what," cries the voice of God, "will it profit a man, if he gains the whole world and forfeits his soul?"[32] If you, Gracious Reader, would protect yourself against such a great and inexpressible loss and against an unhappiness complete in every regard, then, having set aside all your pride in temporal peace and luxuries, strive for this alone, ponder it day and night, cry out to God about it with tears and a humble heart, saying: "Show me, my Lord, the true way, following which I will not err but come to eternal life and communion with you, my Lord; show the genuine and uncounterfeit coin (of faith in You), without which nothing pertaining to salvation can be bought; show Noah's secret ark, in which, with your help, I can take shelter from that fiery flood."

For happy is the man, and exceedingly happy, whom the Lord of heaven and earth summons to the vineyard planted by God's right hand and, having summoned him, causes to work faithfully in it and to bear

31.   *Synod. Chalcedo. arti. 1* [Council of Chalcedon, AD 451, First Session; Mansi 6:653A–654A].
32.   Mt. 16[:26].

gladly the heaviness of the day's labor and the heat of the sun; for He comes quickly and has His reward with him.[33] He will give unto him that is athirst of the fountain of the water of life freely.[34] And him who hungers will He nourish with the fruit of the tree of life, which is in paradise.[35] Happy is the man—I say it for the second time—who, in these latter and lamentable times, when almost all the signs that were to precede the judgment day and the laudable coming of the righteous Judge on the clouds of heaven are clearly being fulfilled, and who, in such marvelous and varied manners of deceivableness,[36] will truly recognize God's truth and, having recognized it, will stand by it constantly until the final goal of life. For he is to expect without fail those exceedingly comforting promises of the Lord: "He who conquers shall be clad in white garments, and I will not blot his name out of the book of life; and I will confess his name before my Father."[37] And again: "Be faithful unto death, and I will give you the crown of life."[38]

Does there appear now only one path to lead astray and tear away the lambs from Christ's fold? Are not these words of the Lord now fulfilled?—"And then many will fall away, and betray one another, and hate one another. And many false prophets will arise and lead many astray. And because wickedness is multiplied, the love of many will grow cold. But he who endures to the end will be saved."[39] Are not false Christs and false prophets found today? Do they not say that Christ is here and is there? Do they not display the title of the true Church in costly buildings, in excellent dress, in the abundance of temporal riches and luxuries? Finally, do not predacious wolves come to mangle and drive asunder Christ's little flock; for, covered in the clothing of the humble exterior of a sheep,[40] they allegedly maintain the same rites as the Orthodox, boast of the same clerical estate, invent for themselves the same aspect of monastic life and dress? And what is more, are they not

33. [Mt. 20:1–16.]
34. Rev. 21[:6].
35. Rev. 2[:7].
36. [2 Th. 2:10.]
37. Rev. 3[:5].
38. Rev. 2[:10].
39. Mt. 24[:10–13].
40. [Mt. 7:15.]

ashamed, in such great variance of confession, to usurp for themselves the title of the Holy Eastern Church?

How, then, can a man protect himself against such an artful temptation? How can he recognize the true fold of the Highest Pastor in such a great confusion of all things? He should recall often the Lord's warning and admonition; for, speaking of the final times, He adds these words: "Then let those who are in Judaea flee into the mountains."[41] St. Chrysostom interprets this Gospel passage with these words: "Let those who are in Christianity have recourse to Scripture. For since that time when heresies began to trouble the Church, those who wish to know the righteousness of faith can have no other test or recourse for true Christianity but Holy Scripture itself. For previously there were many means to know the true Church of Christ and the pagan synagogue; but now we cannot know which is the true Church of Christ through any other means than by Scripture. And why is this? Because the heretics, too, in their separation have all those things that are properly and truly of Christ: they have similar churches, likewise Holy Scriptures, similar bishops and other clergy in the spiritual order, similar baptism, similar sacraments, and all the other things—even Christ Himself. Thus if anyone wishes to know which is the true Church of Christ, how can he know in such a confusion of similarity except by Scripture? Moreover, previously the Church of Christ was recognizable through customs and actions, when it was the case that behavior was holy among all or many Christians, but not among the impious; but now the Christians have become just like the heretics and the pagans, or even worse. Nay, even though they are in separation, the heretics show greater restraint than the Christians. Therefore if anyone wishes to know which is the true Church of Christ, whence can he know it if not from Holy Scripture? Knowing that such will be the confusion in the latter days, the Lord commands that those who are Christians, and who wish to strengthen themselves in true Christian faith, have recourse to nothing but Scripture. For if they look to anything else, they will be led astray and perish, not understanding which is the true Church."[42] Here end the words of St. John Chrysostom, with which, having portrayed truly *ad visum* [unto

41.   Mt. 24[:16].
42.   *Chrysosto. in Matt. homil. 49* [St. John Chrysostom, *Homily on Matthew,* 49].

the sight] a mirror of these present times, he makes it clearly known that the Lord's elect can have, after His grace, no greater comfort and support than that which comes from Holy Scripture and the diligent investigation of it.

This very thing also incited the author of these books, so that, wishing to know certainly and thoroughly which faith or religion is deserving of the title of the genuine Church of Christ, he had recourse, according to the Savior's counsel, to those strong and high mountains of Holy Writ. And having spent no little time on them not without diligence, he brought forth this great and excellent monument, which is presented to you, gracious reader, in this book. Receive it gratefully, and read it; and read it not *perfunctorie* [perfunctorily], as though hurrying to something else, but with diligent and good consideration and attention. I assure you that you will receive a benefit from this, and no insignificant benefit, but the greatest there can be in the world. For here, truly as in a mirror, you will see an image of Christ's true Church, where all the members of its Orthodox confession are represented; and they are represented with the certain and well-founded explanation and the thorough affirmation of Holy Scripture. Here you will learn what you previously did not know; and you will receive certain and sufficient resolution about what you knew imperfectly. You will eradicate from your heart every doubt (if you ever had any doubt about any article of the faith); and you will be strengthened in your undertaking even more greatly and more perfectly about what you have adhered to with a constant heart, doubting it not in the least. You will learn, moreover, how terribly erroneous and unjust is the account and allegation of those who are wont to speak and write of us, alleging that we, for no valid reason, but only on account of malicious stubbornness, not being well-disposed toward the revered union with the Roman Church that was patched together by our apostate pastors, did not wish to render obedience to their visible head and the Church autocrat, against our customary pastors, the oriental patriarchs.

Therefore, take into your hands, read, judge, and compare the works published by this side and by that, and you will understand easily and sufficiently which side here is deficient in certain and well-founded supports for its opinion, such that what it cannot fashion from truth and the Writ, it must fashion with stubborness and perfidy. A certain and infallible testimony to which is the current behavior of anonymous authors who recently published to the world in print some works full of marvelous and truly unheard-of shamelessness under the title *A Certain Nalyvajko* and also *A Relation or a Consideration of the Events that Occurred in Vilnius in the Year 1609*.[43] They placed here so many hideous accounts composed of manifest calumny, that whoever glances at them must ascribe to these anonymous authors the exceeding of absolutely all bounds of fear of God, innate virtue, and human shame. They did not omit there any man, from the higher to the lower condition of the clerical and lay estates; rather they smeared and slandered all in general in their manifest innocence before God and man, having christened with obscene names the congregations that gather in the house established to the praise of God. They charged them with rebellions, seditions, license coupled with crude impiety, disobedience to the authority given by God, and what is more, with harmful conspiracies against the Commonwealth, conceived with the manifest enemies of our fatherland and of His Majesty the King, who happily reigns over us; and in general, they bring against the innocent lambs of Christ, who do not have the least stain on the honorable glory they have gained from virtuous actions, whatever poisonous thing comes to their foul minds. And truly as He Himself deigns to say: *"Omne verbum malum,"* that is, they "speak all manner of evil *against them* falsely on account of His holy name,"[44] so that not even the very author and father of every lie,[45] the soul's enemy, could invent greater and more harmful calumnies against innocent people than this, his chosen vessel, devised in his addled pate for the heaping of disgust and slander upon God's faithful.

---

43.   [Smotryc'kyj refers here to two works sometimes attributed to the Uniate metropolitan, Ipatij Potij (1541–1613): *Zmartwychwstały Nalewayko* (*Nalyvajko Resurrected,* 1607) and *Relacja i uważenie postępków niektórych około cerkwi ruskich wileńskich roku 1608 i 1609 Wilnu wszystkiemu świadomych* (*A Report and a Consideration of the Actions of Certain People Concerning the Ruthenian Churches of Vilnius in the Year 1608 and 1609, Which are Known to All in Vilnius,* Vilnius[?], 1609). The title of the first work refers to Severyn Nalyvajko, who led a rebellion of Ukrainian Cossacks and peasants and was executed in Warsaw in 1597. The second work is published in Studyns'kyj 1906.]
44.   [Mt. 5:11.]
45.   [Jn. 8:44.]

O impious and in every way shameless man: how did you not fear that the earth would swallow you alive like Dathan and Abiram[46] when you invented and wrote such manifest and crudely mendacious calumnies? Did He not truly suffer, who deigned to suffer it of impious ones similar to you, when they called Him a Samaritan and one who has devils,[47] and shamelessly brought calumny against Him (as you do now against His members), alleging that He would destroy the Church[48] and forbid to give Caesar his due?[49] But do not let His great patience give you false comfort. He suffers long, but He punishes severely those who misuse His patience. It is a fearful thing, says the Apostle, to fall into the hands of the living God,[50] who hates all who do evil, and promises to destroy those who speak lies.[51] For He Himself is truth; He delights in truth, and the righteous will see His countenance.[52] What can he who whet his tongue like a razor[53] expect here, pouring out the poison of vipers upon the virtuous,[54] whose mouth is full of cursing and bitterness and deceit, and under his tongue is toil and pain,[55] and whose words are arrows imbued with poison, which he shoots at the innocent?[56] But those arrows (may God grant it) will enter his own heart, when that infernal tongue will be stopped by the infernal fire (if he does not repent).[57] And the salvation of the righteous is from the Lord; He is their defense in their times of troubles. The Lord helps them and will deliver them; He will tear them away; He will bring forth their vindication as the light, and their innocence as the noonday.[58]

Therefore God's elect, enjoying their justification and innocence through these promises, cannot be harmed by your infernal poison.

46. [Num. 16:31–3; Ps. 106:17.]
47. [Jn. 8:48.]
48. [Mk. 14:58.]
49. [Lk. 23:2.]
50. Heb. 10[:31].
51. Ps. 5[:5–6].
52. [Ps. 11:7.]
53. [Ps. 64:3.]
54. [Ps. 140:3.]
55. Ps. 9 [10:7].
56. Ps. 119 [120:4; Jer. 9:8].
57. [Ps. 37:15.]
58. Ps. 36 [37:6].

Rather they cry confidently to you: if there yet remains in you some little spark of the fear of God, virtue, and natural shame, come out into the open, cast down that mask from your face, reveal your name, and you will see whether you do not experience this with shame and eternal disgrace. A clear conscience—their innocence united with the truth—gives them good hope that He who always stands by the truth, who knows (as St. Peter says)[59] how to deliver the godly out of temptation, knows how to guard and protect them like the apple of his eye, who deigned miraculously to deliver the innocent Susanna (who was calumniated by elders equal to you in virtue) from evident and (in their opinion) certain death, and deigned to cast the perfidious calumniators themselves into the hole prepared for her,[60] that He deigns even now to cause (one must not doubt His mercy and righteousness) that the words of the psalmist be fulfilled upon you: "Behold he conceives evil, and is pregnant with mischief, and brings forth injustice; he has made a pit, and he has digged it out, and he himself has fallen into the hole which he has made; his mischief will return upon his own head, and on his own pate his injustice descends."[61]

For it will be made known, as it is even now manifest to God and to all people, that Christ's faithful flock, having first maintained its conscience clean and its faith unsuspect for that King of Kings, and Lord of Lords, also maintains whole and inviolate and always truly renders virtue, faith, submission, and obedience, along with everything that pertains to it, to the authority established by Him, that is, to His Majesty the King, Our Merciful Lord, who happily rules over us. Since we also bear well in mind these words of the holy Apostle: "First of all, then, I urge that supplications, intercessions, and thanksgivings be made for all men, for the King, and for all who are in high positions, that we may lead a quiet and peaceable life."[62] For which religion so often fulfills these apostolic words as the Holy Eastern Church, where no service, no ceremony of the Church order begins or ends without offering a prayer to almighty God for the good health and happy increase (with victory over the enemies) of the reign of His Majesty the

59.　2 Pet. 2[:9].
60.　[Sus. 42–60.]
61.　Ps. 7[:14–16].
62.　1 Tim. 2[:1–2].

King? Therefore it is not the faithful sons of the Holy Eastern Church, but rather you yourself, O shameless tongue, who transgresses the boundaries of these two obligations: you transgress, I say, against God, in that you impiously oppose the truth and innocence manifest to all, and you also transgress against His Majesty the King, Our Gracious Lord, in that you shamelessly attack the noble glory, acquired through virtuous actions, of his faithful subjects who are suspect in naught, and you defame them before the entire world through the calumny you have published in print.

And in what other matters? In those that the common law saw fit to guarantee so well: that if anyone should charge someone with offending the majesty of His Majesty the King, and should not prove it, he himself should be punished thereby, so that thus the other man's honor (about which it is fitting for no one but His Majesty the King himself to make a decision, and that at a general Sejm) be recompensed.[63] Do you not know that even His Majesty the King himself, God's anointed, promises to punish no one on the basis of anonymous accusations, brought with paltry and weak proofs? And who made you such a shameless and unrighteous judge, that you should deprive honorable people of their honor (when, if God grants it, you can lose your own first), revile them, abominate and christen them with exceedingly obscene names, not only the common burgher, but also the clergy and many worthy individuals of the noble estate, who in this Church use their ancient rite in the usual manner appropriate and dear to God, whereby you also did not omit their gracious lords, the judges of the main tribunal? And knowing that you deserve special praise and thanks for this, you did not wish in any way to reveal yourself to the world in connection with that shameless work of yours, rather you veiled yourself so that no one could recognize you. Although conscience was much assaulted by you, it did not allow you to achieve such manifest shamelessness that you would step out into the open with your false account; rather, as cunning and well trained bandits do, standing hidden behind a wall, you shoot the poisonous arrows of your furious words at virtuous people. But tell

63. [The so-called *lex talionis* or punishment in kind applied to those who brought calumnious charges against anyone and were unable to prove them. On crimes against honor in the law codes of Poland-Lithuania, see Bardach 1964, 524; Kaczmarczyk and Leśnodorski 1966, 336.]

me, to what end do you do this? So that unity with the Roman Church (of which you show yourself an adherent) might be patched together and established? But consider how in this very manner you declare yourself impious, since you wish that God's praise (as you understand it) might be increased by your lie. Did truth ever need falsehood and lie to explain it? It is easier indeed for water and fire, darkness and light, than for these two mutually opposing things to be brought into harmony. Do you not rather in this very manner cause greater shame and unprofitableness to your Church, in that, not being able to triumph in any way over Christ's sheep with the truth and Scripture, you had recourse to those obscene fables and impious calumnies? Do you not show by this very thing that you are not of God, who, being Himself the truth, calls those who delight in the truth His sons, and promises to make them to rejoice and to fill them with the light of His countenance for all time?

But listen to what He says about those who resort to untruth: "Ye are," He says, "of your father the devil." And that is because, as He later adds there: "For he abode not in the truth, because there is no truth in him; when he speaketh a lie, he speaketh of his own: for he is a liar and the father of it."[64] In this way, you show yourself his faithful son and highly deserving servant, and, moreover, the follower of those old pagans and of the accursed Arian sect of heretics, who invented wondrous and various slanders and libels (very similar to those you make today) against Christ's innocent and immaculate flock.

Witness to this, among other things, is the golden defense (as Father Skarga himself calls it) or *justificatio* of Tertullian, in the name of all Christians, against the calumnies alleged against them in their innocence. Witness, too, is the highly exemplary life of the mighty defender of the true faith and the great pillar of the Church, St. Athanasius. For when the ungodly Arian sectarians were unable to overcome him with writings or disputations, they invented various and repulsive calumnies unto his disgust and abuse, among which were also these: that he had allegedly compelled a certain woman, while he was a guest in her house, to submit to his filthy intent; and that he had allegedly cut off the hand of his clerk Arsenius through black magic (and to support their allegation they obtained somewhere a human hand and showed it to those who wished

64.   Jn. 8[:44].

to see it).[65] That great soldier of Christ and highly exemplary model of patience, suffering in his innocence these and similar calumnies that were forged in the infernal forge itself, comforted himself with these sweet words of his Savior: "Blessed are ye, when men shall revile you, and persecute you, and shall say all manner of evil against you falsely, for my sake. Rejoice, and be glad: for great is your reward in heaven."[66] And he comforts others who helped him to suffer this oppression and affliction with these words: *"Nubecula est transibit."* That is: "It is a little storm, or a little cloud; it will pass."[67] For he knew well that from of old the truth has this privilege granted to it: that it can be oppressed, but it cannot be completely suppressed. Rather by and of itself it will be made manifest (even though it have no supporter in this world). That hope did not disappoint him in the least; for his innocence coupled with the truth, and the falsehood and treachery of his opponents, became well known even during his life and now is famous over the entire circumference of the earth, and will be famous, without a doubt, so long as the world will be.

But enough about this for now. And as far as the order maintained in the writing of these books and the things contained in them is concerned, I do not need to speak much about this; for by looking at the title of each chapter (of which there are ten), everyone can easily understand what is contained in them, since the annotations or notes concerning the more important things that have been placed also offer considerable help in this. It also seemed fitting to mark in the margin the testimonies of our holy Greek Fathers, as well as various Latin authors, and even, in some cases, to cite the very text in the Latin language (since the disputation is with the Latins). It is likewise for this reason that, for the explanation of terms used by theologians that could not be translated properly from Slavonic into Polish, many Latin words are used (especially in that main article on the procession of the holy and life-giving spirit). In all this, however, accommodation was made so that you might grasp and understand as well as possible. Just do not neglect to apply your good

---

65. In the Life of St. Athanasius. [Cf. Sozomenus, *Church History* II, 23; *PG* 67:993–4; *NPNF2* 2:273.]

66. Mt. 5[:11–12].

67. [Cf. Socrates Scholasticus, *Church History* III, 14:1; *PG* 67:415–16; *NPNF2* 2:86.]

diligence in the most careful reading of these books for the sake of your
spiritual benefit. Farewell!

[. . .][68]

Chapter 1

In Which Is Contained the Lament,
or the Complaint of the Holy Eastern Church
against Her Degenerate Sons

Alas, I am wretched, alas, hapless; woe, I am plundered of my goods
from all sides; alas, torn from my garments to the worldly shame of
my body; alack, weighted down with unbearable burdens: my hands
in shackles, a yoke on my neck,[69] fetters on my legs, a chain on my
loins, a double-edged sword over my head, deep water beneath my feet,
inextinguishable fire at my sides; everywhere cries, everywhere fear,
everywhere persecution; woe in the cities and in the villages, woe in
the fields and the forests, woe in the mountains and the abysses of the
earth. There is no peaceful place or safe abode, the day spent in pains
and wounds, the night in groaning and sighing; summer sweltering unto
fainting, winter freezing unto death.[70] For I suffer wretchedly in my
nakedness, and I am persecuted even unto death.[71] Beautiful and rich in
days of old, now I am desecrated and poor; once the queen, beloved of
the entire world, now I am scorned and oppressed by all. Come hither
to me with great haste, all the nations, all citizens of the earth: hear my
voice, know what I was long ago, and marvel.

Now I am the laughingstock of the world, though formerly the
wonder of men and angels. [†]I was adorned before all, graceful and
agreeable, lovely like the morning star in the east, beautiful as the
moon, exquisite as the sun, the only daughter of my mother, the only
chosen pure dove of my parent: I was immaculate, not having spot, or

68.   [A two-page list of "Authors Whose Testimony was Cited in the Book"
has been omitted; Smotryc'kyj 1610, ()()()3v–4r/16.]
69.   [Lam. 1:14.]
70.   2 Cor. 11[:26].
71.   [Lam. 1:8.]
†   The first ornament of the Eastern Church.

wrinkle, or any such thing.[72] My name was ointment poured forth,[73] my surname a well of living waters.[74] Seeing me, the daughters of Zion declared me the most blessed queen. And, in brief, I was among the daughters of Zion what Jerusalem was among all the cities of Judaea;[75] and what a lily is among thorns, that was I among the maidens.[76] For which handsomeness did the King, more handsome than the sons of man, desire my beauty;[77] and having chosen me, He joined me to Him in an eternal matrimonial union.

[†]I bore children and raised them, and they repudiated me; and they became unto me a laughingstock and a mockery. For they pulled me from my garments and drove me naked out of my house; they removed the adornment of my body, and they took the charm of my head. What is more, night and day they seek my poor soul, and they think incessantly of my demise.

O you who stand before me, you who look upon me, listen and consider: where is there pain like my pain; where tribulation and sorrow like my affliction? I bore children and raised them, and they repudiated me, and they became my demise. Wherefore I now sit like one of the lamenting widows, once the mistress of the orient and occident, of the south and the northern lands. I weep night and day,[78] and the tears flow over my cheeks like river streams, and there is no one to comfort me.[79] All have run away from me, all have scorned me. My kinsfolk are far away;[80] my friends have become enemies; my sons, envying the viper breed, cut up my womb with their lashing fangs. Listen to my sorrowful tale, all the nations; receive it into your ears, all who inhabit the circumference of the earth.

My sons and daughters, whom I bore and raised, left me and followed after her who did not suffer the pains of labor with them, that

72. Eph. 5[:27].
73. S. of S. 1[:3]; 2[:2]; [6:4]; 7.
74. S. of S. 4[:15].
75. [S. of S. 6:4.]
76. S. of S. 2[:2].
77. Ps. 44 [45:11].
† The Eastern Church suffers at the hands of her own sons.
78. Lam. 2[:18].
79. Lam. 1[:2, 17, 21].
80. Ps. 37 [38:11].

they might be satiated with the excess of her fat.[81] My priests have gone blind, my pastors (not wishing to know that souls are at stake) have become dumb, my elders have grown stupid,[82] my young men have become wild, my daughters have given themselves up to harlotry,[83] and all with one thought, having ignored God and His truth, have conspired against my soul. They have opened their jaws, and, hissing, they gnash their teeth at me, saying: "Behold the day has come that we have looked for; let us go and destroy her and uproot her memory from the earth."[84] Instead of offering love, they reprimand me; they pay back my goodness with malice, and they reward my love with hatred. They offered me rotten rags in place of my costly garments; and I became a proverb to them.[85]

Oh the pain of my soul; woe, I am assailed, alas, I am scorned. The quickness of my eyes has grown dull from incessant tears. My bowels are troubled; my womb has grown weak in pain, and my years in sighing.[86] My days have ceased like smoke, and my bones have dried up like cracklings. I am mowed like hay, and my heart has withered. From my loud lament my bones have dried to my flesh.[87]

They have torn open their jaws against me, like the jaws of enemies filled with treacherous and perfidious words. They have taken axes in their hands, and they seek my soul that they might destroy it. Everywhere there are snares, everywhere vales, everywhere lashing fangs; there rapacious wolves, and here roaring lions; there poisonous serpents, and here ferocious basilisks. I find nowhere to turn; I know not where I am to go, to whom I should incline my head, into whose protection I should give myself. Is this not, O heaven and earth, a new sorrow and unheard-of grief: that I bore sons and raised them, and they have repudiated me.

Betrothed as a virgin to one husband,[88] given to one in matrimony, from one I conceived, in one womb I bore, with one milk I nurtured;

81.   Ez. 34[:1–10].
82.   Jer. 23[:1–4; Is. 56:10–11].
83.   Lam 1[:18–19; Hos. 4:14].
84.   Lam. 2[:16].
85.   Ps. 68 [69:11].
86.   [Lam. 2:11; 1:20.]
87.   Ps. 111 [102:3–5].
88.   Eph. 5[:23–7].

and yet, alas, I see, to my shame and sorrow, that my sons are of various customs. There is none to emulate the Father, there is none to follow the Mother. What is more, envying the degenerate and suspect, they have sharpened their tongues against their parents.[89] Their Father they disgrace, their Mother they revile. They have scorned their Father's teaching, they have reviled their Mother's efforts; all of them have fallen away and have become useless. There is not one of so many who does good.[90] Woe, I am barren; woe, I am childless. As the Law says: Cursed be the man who leaves no offspring in Israel. Oh, how much greater the woe, and abundant the evil, to leave offspring of evil customs, perfidious and willfully disobedient, who are a disgrace to their Father and an abuse to their Mother. For it is written: thus shall you live, so that people seeing your good works might glorify your Father.[91] Seeing which evil, I say that they disgraced their Father and Mother according to the saying: A wise and obedient son is an honor to a father, but a foolish and intractable son causes his mother shame.[92]

Many times in my life have I borne various afflictions from my sons; many manners of disrespect before the Law and in the Law have I suffered from my daughters; but in no way can they be compared with my present affliction and shame. †For living under the Law of sin, they bore veils on their hearts, because of which they could neither know sufficiently the will of God, nor could they fulfill it perfectly. And now—with the advent of Grace, which removed those veils from them,[93] and which took upon itself all their iniquities,[94] bore them, and rendered satisfaction for them to God the Father, chose them, summoned, justified, and sanctified them—now no thanks are rendered to the Giver of such great blessings, and no gratitude is demonstrated. Rather what? Instead of gratitude and thanks, ingratitude and scorn. What can I do in this matter? What am I to say of this? What else but that, in truth, it had been better for me to die without offspring than to see my children undisciplined and impious. For the greater the gifts they became worthy

89. [Ps. 140:3.]
90. Ps. 13 [14:1].
91. Mt. 5[:16]; 1 Pet. 2[:12].
92. Prov. 10[:1].
†   The difference between the Church of the Old Law and that of the New.
93. 1 Cor. 3 [2 Cor. 3:13–18].
94. Jer. 24[14:7], 31[33:8].

of, the greater the gratitude they should have displayed to the world; and the more perfect the covenant created for them, the more constantly they should have abided in it.

What happened then? Whither did they turn? On what road did they set out? They preferred to fulfill the will of Baal than that of God. They deigned to go the way of Balaam rather than that of the faithful prophet of God.[95] They have again taken upon themselves the veils that had been removed from their hearts.[96] They have chosen unrighteousness, and from that time they have entered into worse iniquities. They heed not the call, they scorn the election, they reject the justification and the sanctification; and, to be brief, they render evil for good. I nurtured sons of such virtue in my house, I nursed children of such humanity at my breast, but throughout all this present time they gnaw at my reins and strive to bring me to my death.

Though once under the care of tutors and governors,[97] they took no care for the commandment; and it is no wonder, for their heart had hardened, so that seeing, they did not see, and hearing, they did not hear.[98] Now the very Giver of those tutors stands, makes effort, summons, and offers the hand of help, opens ears to hear, and illumines eyes to see. Not only, however, are they disobedient and insubordinate to Him, but, having voluntarily averted their eyes and stopped up their ears,[99] they guard against the goodness of their Lord, and they flee into bottomless abysses. Woe, I truly labor with this unrepentant progeny, labor with this venomous generation of vipers.[100] And who will not take up this sorrow equally with me; who will not help me to lament? I gave birth to sons and raised them, and they have repudiated me; they have cast the venomous fangs of their tongues at me.

First they did not wish to heed the messengers and servants. And now the Lord Himself has come. He Himself summons and teaches that those weighted down with the burden of sins might seek relief in Him and might abide in Him.[101] The more authoritative the voice of the

95.   [Jer. 7:9, 9:14; 2 Pet. 2:15.]
96.   2 Cor. 3[:13–18].
97.   Gal. 3 [4:2].
98.   Jer. 5[:21].
99.   Is. 6[:10].
100. Mt. 23[:33].
101. Mt. 11[:28–30].

Lord is over his servants, the more gladly should obedience have been rendered to Him. What do the degenerates say to this? They preferred to chase after Egyptian caldrons and garlic[102] than to appear at the costly supper of their Lord who summons them.

†Where now are those times in which I bore martyrs? Where those years in which I sheltered the righteous and the godly in my house? Where are those blessed doctors and apostles of the entire world? Where are their unerring followers, the pastors and teachers? It is you I need now, my dear and faithful sons. You I praise. Of you I boast, lovers of your Father. In you I take comfort, who have given your souls for me. You came to the Father righteously, and you remained by him constantly. You recognized that the branch cannot bear fruit of itself, except it abide in the vine.[103] Neither death, nor life, nor angels, nor principalities, nor powers, nor the sword, nor fire, nor things present, nor things to come, nor height, nor depth, nor any other creature, was able to separate you from the love of God.[104] You, were it possible, would show Elijan zeal against the ministers of Baal, who serve their belly, God, and Mammon,[105] and against the wolves who have been set in the place of pastors over the sheep. You would check the wild sheep; you would separate the mangy rams from the sheep; you, like the Samaritan, would take care of the wounds of the wounded, pouring in oil and wine.[106] You pay no regard to estates and principalities in your admonishment. You hold slave and freeman in Christ the Redeemer in one esteem[107] with respect to teaching, correction, and instruction in righteousness.[108] In your lifetime, the Church of the living God, the chosen people, the royal priesthood[109] remained unblemished and inviolate. Even today, your writings inspired by God, the unwithered lily of spiritual wisdom, are a reminder of what you were and whither you departed. You drove out the heresiarchs from among God's faithful; you weeded out the tares of

---

102. [Num. 11:5.]
† The first-born sons of the Eastern Church.
103. Jn. 15[:4].
104. Rom 8[:38–9].
105. [2 Kg. 11:18; Mt. 6:24; Lk. 16:13.]
106. Lk. 10[:34].
107. Col. 3[:11].
108. [2 Tim. 3:16.]
109. 1 Pet. 2[:9].

errors from among the wheat;[110] you conquered this world and all that is in it: you, exemplary teachers of pious life; you, zealous punishers of impious living; you, pastors in word and deed, who know that earthly men are exhorted to the good not so much through words as through the deeds of their superior authorities. For, as St. Luke says, Christ began to do and to teach,[111] following in whose footsteps you, too, did and taught, since it was for this reason that Christ came to you, that you might follow his footsteps.

Oh, your praiseworthy faith; oh, heart magnanimous in love! Where now is Basil, called the Great on account of his special effort and diligence on behalf of Christ's flock? Where is Ambrose, the Bishop of Milan, and St. John, called Chrysostom for the golden-flowing streams of his heavenly teaching of penance? Where is Jerome, the excellent translator of the God-given Scriptures? Where is Cyprian, where Augustine, the zealous scatterers of heretical tares? For the former gave the impious Novatian over to damnation, and the latter the false Pelagius, heretics both, pierced with the arrows of Holy Writ. Where are Athanasius and Cyril, Patriarchs of Alexandria, and Bishop Gregory of Nazianzus, brave knights of their Father and my vigilant deputies, the brightly shining lamps of those first three ecumenical councils, who felled with their evangelical sword those perfidious heresiarchs condemned for their heretical blasphemy—Arius, Macedonius, and Nestorius, together with their sectarians—and gave them over to Satan's power? So that each of them, not fearing the face of man, and without any regard for persons and estates, would boldly restrain the present-day heretics, who trouble their Mother day and night, for whom they courageously gave their souls, and each would say: "The Holy Ghost commands of you, accursed Arian Anabaptist sectarians, that you cease disparaging the glory of the eternal consubstantiality of the Son of God, who sits at the right hand of God the Father, mendaciously saying of Him that there was a time when He was not, lest you come, according to your merits, together with Arius, your patron, to a terrible effluence of your bowels, and lest, in the temporal stench of your body, you immediately cast your ungodly souls into everlasting stench.[112]

110. [Mt. 13:24–40.]
111. Acts 1[:1].
112. [It was Athanasius who related that Arius had died shamefully in a latrine. See Letter 54, "To Serapion," *PG* 25:688C; *NPNF2* 4:565.]

Christ the Lord orders you, too, followers of Cerinthus, and deputies of Macedonius, who, willfully and openly opposing the Spirit of God, take away all His power in Holy Scripture; and having removed the authority of faith, you submit His constant and everlasting doctrine to doubtfulness and indignity; for by calling Holy Scripture a nose of wax, you place the traditions and mortal mandates of the head of your Church above it."[113]

Where, in addition to these, is that other army of Christ, which, standing guard at all the ecumenical and particular synods, always placed their souls on the side of holy truth—the true interpreters of true Divine Writ—so that, with the sword of the Gospel,[114] they might block the path to the sheep of Christ against the present-day sophists, full of their own spirit, that is, the followers of the Nestorian heresy, as well as those who introduce into the Church of God the *stoicam fatalem eventuum necessitatem* [fatal Stoic inevitability of events], and those who blasphemously assert that God is the cause of sin and of human perdition? Where, further, are those brightly burning lamps of the Western Church, Gelasius and Leo, holy bishops of Rome, so that, revered for the height of their majesty in ecclesiastical matters, they might rebuke and charge the present-day bishops, who, having occupied their sees, break the laws and commandments of Christ because of their pompous pride?

May Lord Jesus close your mouths, people of sin, sons of perdition, who oppose God and exalt yourselves above all that is called God or worshipped as God, and who, sitting in the Church of God as gods[115] and wickedly assailing the sacrament of the Lord's mystical supper, remove the chalice of His most precious blood, and thus the inheritance of eternal life, from the innocent souls of men.[116] And with the spirit of

113. [Cf. Calvin's commentary on Jeremiah 17 and 18 (Calvin 1950, 171): "For when the Papists feel themselves driven to an extremity, when they prevail nothing by clamour and falsehood, they run to this sort of evasion, 'Ho! if we must determine everything in religion by the Law, the Prophets, and the Gospel, what certainty can be found? The Scripture is like a nose of wax, for it can be turned to anything, and no meaning can with certainty be elicited; thus all things will remain doubtful, if authority belongs to Scripture alone.'"]
114. [Eph. 6:17.]
115. 1 Th. 2 [2 Th. 2:3–4].
116. Jn. 6[:53–8].

your quibbling Aristotelian intellect you oppose Christ the Lord, who
in giving the bread said, "This is my body," and in giving the cup, "This
is my blood,"[117] as if He had done unwisely, when it is you yourselves
who are foolish, who, taking only the bread into your hands, preach in
the opposite manner, saying, "This is my body and my blood." Do you
not know that in this matter not your paltry understanding but Christ's
unchangeable commandments are to be maintained, and that the
rending of one and the same sacrament cannot occur without a great and
significant sacrilege?[118] And that heretics and seducers are distinguished
from God's faithful by this sign? And that if you do not repent in this,
the punishment of eternal fire will bring you to repentance?

Where, finally, are my sons of the latter age, who equally with the
others gave up their souls for me unto death: blessed Maximus, John of
Damascus, and Bishop of Bulgaria Theophylactus, Mark of Ephesus,
and Nilus of Thessalonica, so that, standing with the entire authoritative
choir of those old, noble theologians, they might close the jaws of the
present-day matheologians,[119] which were opened against the truth,
saying: "May God the Father enjoin you by His only-begotten Son,
you sowers of the accursed Sabellian blasphemy and propagators of
Manichean impiety, who, against the doctrine of Holy Scripture, teach
that the Holy Spirit proceeds from the persons of the Father and of the
Son, as from one person, and thence, introducing one cause for the Holy
Ghost, ὑποστατικῶς [hypostatically], from the Father and the Son, you
violently cause the fusion in one person of two persons separated from
each other in essence. Or else, maintaining whole the personal division
of the persons (knowing that the Father Himself is the one cause of
divinity, who has in Himself his own property *sine communicatione*
[without communication] to the other persons), you introduce two
causes into the Divinity."[120] And if you remain henceforth without

---

117. Mt. 26[:26–8]; 1 Cor. 11[:24–5].

118. *Gelasius Papa de consecr. distinct. 2 cap. Comperimus: Leo Papa
serm. 4 de quadragesima* [Pope Gelasius, *On Distinction of Consecration* (?),
chap. 2. Cf. Pope Leo, *Sermon 4 On Lent* (*Sermon 42, On Lent IV,* chap. 5; *PL*
54:279–80; *NPNF2* 12:158)].

119. [*Mataiologoi, vaniloqui,* "vain-talkers." Cf. Tit. 1:10. I have inserted the
"h"—"mat(h)eologians"—required for the pun: theologians vs. matheologians.]

120. [Smotryc'kyj alludes here, of course, to the controversies over the *filioque,*
the Western doctrine that the Holy Spirit proceeds "from the Father *and from*

rebuke for this blasphemy from me your Mother, the Eastern Church, you will be given up to cleansing for eternity in the coming age, through the purging fire prepared by the devil and his angels.

†In the present age I need the sort of sons who, without any regard for persons, would rebuke those who wickedly blaspheme God; and who, having turned their authoritative countenances upon their brethren, would boldly punish their disorderly life, saying: "It does not befit you, O pastors and teachers of Christ's spiritual flock, to whose vigilance and fidelity the beloved of the Son of God has been entrusted, to be pastors in name, but predators in deed; for you yourselves lead an evil life and allow those entrusted to you to live wantonly. Having flourished and grown fat on the patrimony of Him who was crucified, you do not regret the unhappy dispersal of the sons of God among all the sects, wherefore you are wolves and not pastors. You take your title from Christ, but in actual fact you carry out the office of the Antichrist on earth. God grant that you stop at milk, for you desire blood."

Such sons do I need today, I say to you, such children do I require in this time of affliction, who not only would close the obscene mouths of the blasphemers, but would also admonish, punish, and correct even their own people, sufficiently and according to their merits, from the highest to the lowest, from the archpriests to all the priests who are under their power, together with the people entrusted to their rule.

But where will I find such sons? Shall I call down from heaven those who are already triumphant? This is an impossibility. Or shall I search the lands of the fatherland? There is no one. All have risen against me, as against one who had never suffered the pains of labor with them. All have rebelled, armed as if against the main enemy, and they seek to drive out my soul. I am an unhappy mother. What have I done that I suffer unbearable persecution from my own sons? What have I committed worthy of death that I am uncertain of my health? Some, through their carelessness, are useless to me. Others, through their abuse, are burdensome. Some, on account of their persecution, are unbearable, whereas others, on account of their repudiation, are inhospitable. For, when they reached the depth of malice (as is the nature of malice), they were careless.

---

the Son."]
†   The Eastern Church requires sons like these.

†But since the word is the beginning of every cause, and counsel precedes before anything else begins, it behooves me indeed to proceed carefully in the complaint that I have begun. It is proper that I not treat rashly the case at hand against my sons. Justice exacts, and my very complaint requires, that I examine the matter diligently and that I consider judiciously: Whence come such great increases in bad morals among my sons? For what reason has such an unmitigated hatred toward their mother overcome the children? It certainly behooves me first to think of this before either repudiating them entirely, possessed by maternal sorrow in heartfelt grief, I curse them in the bitterness of my heart and give them up to paternal punishment, or I again approach a few of the leaders whom the younger brethren respect and speak with them about conversion: Will they not feel shame at their mother's visage and feel pain at the pain of the one who suffered the pains of labor with them; and, having softened their hearts in humility on account of her tears, will they not embrace her feet, knowing that it had been better for them not to be born than to come to the powerful hand of eternal punishment of the almighty Father? For although He knows my afflictions, He waits, held back by compassion, in the hope that they sometime repent and offer penance. But as soon as I release the slightest word from my lips, or as soon as I decide to bring a complaint against them in any way, in the twinkling of an eye He will miserably destroy the wicked men, and with a gust scatter their memory in the winds, so that even the place where they dwelled will not be known.[121] For it is a fearful thing, says the holy apostle, to fall into the hands of the living God.[122]

Let me examine the cause of their unhumbled malice. Did they take it from the Father by right of birth, or from the Mother through nurturing? For, as good fruit testifies to a good tree,[123] thus also the good morals of the children tell of the good life of the parents. Likewise in the opposite manner, what is censured in the offspring is sometimes ascribed to the malice of the parents. ‡But in no manner can this be found in the parents: for the Father is good, quiet, modest, gentle, gracious, humble,

†   The Eastern Church seeks the reason for her sons' malice.
121.   [Mt. 21:41.]
122.   Heb. 10[:31].
123.   [Mt. 7:16–20; Lk. 6:43–5.]
‡   Not by right of birth are the parents of the sons of the Church the cause of their malice.

and obedient unto death; and the Mother is pure, holy, immaculate, kind-hearted, and virtuous. The Father is wise, just, generous, compassionate, slow to anger, quick to forgive, not harsh to the end, nor angry for all time. The Mother loves her children, teaches them, gives thought for her own, is obedient unto death, and adorned and enriched with every sort of virtue by Him to whom she is betrothed. Therefore neither paternal birthright nor the Mother's milk was the cause of such great malice on the part of our children.

Let us accept that we parents are not the cause of their malice by right of birth. †Shall we yet be considered the cause by lack of attention to good upbringing? In no manner. For the Father summons them, calling without cease:[124] "Come to me, follow me, do my will, wash and purify yourselves, remove the malice from your souls, and be holy, as I am holy, and you will find peace, you will receive blessing, you will receive the crown of life."[125] ‡And what does the Mother say? "Listen, children, to your Father's voice; receive the words of your Mother in your ears. Remain with us, and you will abound in the bounty of all goods. And you who have already fallen away from us, wounded by sin: return to the Father, and He will receive you. Make fruits meet for repentance, for the ax has already been laid unto the root of the tree, so that every tree that does not bring forth good fruit be hewn down and cast into the fire.[126] The Father, too, is already coming, who carries a fan in His hand, and He will thoroughly purge His floor and gather His wheat to the garner; and He will burn up the chaff with unquenchable fire."[127] Such are the words of constant training with which we teach all our children; such is the upbringing we give to their proud youth. Their deceitful hearts, however, do not wish to be moved to this in the least. And this is the common teaching for all in general.

On the other hand, we make special admonition day and night to each estate individually. *You, princes and authorities, judge the subjects entrusted to you by divine judgment, bearing in mind that you

---

† Nor by right of upbringing and training.
124. 2 Pet. 1[:3].
125. [1 Pet. 3:9; Jas 1:12; Rev. 2:10.]
‡ The teaching of the Eastern Church to all in general.
126. Mt. 3[:8, 10].
127. Mt. 3[:12].
* The teaching to the temporal authorities.

may be judged by the same judgment.[128] Do not place upon them a great tax, knowing that your Lord remitted you your entire debt and paid your tribute for you.[129] And whatever you do in secret, do not say, "Who sees us?"—for your Father who is in heaven sees everything and does everything He wishes.[130]

[†]You, archpriests and priests, pastors and teachers of the sheep of Christ's spiritual flock: stand unwavering in the faith given you by God; keep watch diligently over the lambs entrusted to you; courageously oppose those who attempt to destroy the truth; punish the unruly, comfort the fearful,[131] teach the ignorant, restrain and check the dissolute and disobedient, heal the infirm, rebuke the contrary; be an example for the faithful in speech, communion, love, faith, and purity.[132] Take care for reading, admonition, teaching; preach the word, be instant in season and out of season; reprove, rebuke, exhort with all long-suffering and doctrine;[133] defend the weak, and correct the disorderly. For you are the salt of the earth and the light of the world.[134] The Holy Ghost established you that you tend Christ's flock, which He has purchased with His own blood.[135] Be, therefore, blameless, sober, wise, honest, pure, given to hospitality, apt to teach, not given to drink, not strikers, but humble, not brawlers, not covetous, those who rule well in your own house.[136] You are the eye for the blind, the leg for the lame, the arm for those needing a guide. You are the doorkeepers and stewards of the heavenly kingdom. The power of loosing and binding has been entrusted to your hands.[137] You are the priests of God the Most High, having the gift of consecrating each other and others. And therefore, keep diligent watch lest, plunged into the blindness of carelessness and the sleep of laziness, you cast yourselves and those entrusted to you into the bottomless abyss

128. Eph. 6[:9]; Col. 4[:1].
129. [Mt. 18:33–4.]
130. [Sir. 23:18–19.]
†   The teaching of the Eastern Church to the spiritual authorities.
131. 1 Th. 5[:14].
132. 1 Pet. 5[:1–4].
133. 2 Tim. 4[:2].
134. Mt. 5[:13–14].
135. Acts 20[:28].
136. 1 Tim. 3[:2–4].
137. Mt. 18[:18; 16:19].

and disfigure with the eternal stench of the infernal mud those whose innocent blood will be required at your hands.[138]

†And to the common people we make admonition and teaching in these terms: Let every soul be subject to the higher powers. For the superiors are not a terror to the good deed, but to the evil.[139] Will you, then, not be afraid of the higher power? Do that which is good, and you shall have praise from him, for he is the minister of God for your good. But if you will do that which is evil, have fear; for he bears not the sword in vain. Render therefore unto all their dues: the things that are God's unto God, and the things that are the King's unto the King, etc.,[140] tribute to whom tribute is due; custom to whom custom; fear to whom fear; honor to whom honor; owe no man anything, but love one another.[141] Be liked in everything by your superiors, do not slander, do not cheat, but show your good fidelity in all matters. Obey your spiritual superiors, who, sitting in Christ's seat, teach you the same thing as Christ; for they are watchful, as they that must give account of you, that they may do it with joy, and not with grief.[142] Know and esteem them all the more in love for their work's sake.[143] For so is the will of God, that with well-doing you might put to silence the ignorance of foolish men, as free, and not using your liberty for a cloak of maliciousness, but as the servants of God. Honor all men; love brotherhood; fear God; honor the King. Servants, be subject to your masters with all fear; not only to the good and gentle, but also to the forward. For this, too, is thankworthy, if a man for conscience toward God endure grief, suffering innocently. For what glory is it, if when you sin and are guilty, you suffer patiently; but if, when you do well, you patiently bear persecution—this is acceptable with God. For even hereunto were you called: because Christ suffered for us, leaving you an example, that you might follow in His steps, who did no sin, neither was guile found in His mouth.[144]

138. [Ez. 3:18, 20; 33:6, 8; 34:10.]
† The teaching of the Eastern Church to the common people.
139. Rom. 13[:3–4].
140. Mt. 22[:21].
141. Rom. 13[:7–8].
142. Heb. 13[:17].
143. 1 Th. 5[:13].
144. 1 Pet. 2[:15–22].

Such are our general and incessant instructions and admonitions to our sons, from which everyone can see clearly that, as we parents were not the cause of our progeny's evil by right of birth, so we are not the reason for this through lack of training and good upbringing. For we reprimand, punish, admonish, and teach all in general, without any regard for the person, and each in particular, without any flattery. But as one can see, they indeed closed their ears in order not to hear our voice.[145] Whom, then, does this trouble more? Whom does this give more pain? Whom does this torment more severely? And whom does this offer a more dangerous life? I am afflicted, I am miserable, and more unhappy than all mothers. Wherever I turn, I find my sons betraying me. Here they are digging impenetrable caverns; there they are casting wire snares. There they are releasing venomous fangs, and here they are pouring deadly poisons, some openly, others in secret, some through flattery, and some through threat. All, however, to a one, seek my life; all hold one mother in hatred.

So ought I to be afraid? Ought I to fear? Not in the least. Here I stand; let one of them come and thrust a sharp iron into my faint heart. Let him approach and open the aching womb of his mother. Let him work his malice upon the body of his afflicted mother. For death is better than a miserable life, and it is more pleasant for me to die once suddenly than to die a little in tribulation every day through the ungodliness of my sons. Oh, woe is my pitiful life; alas, the unbearable pains of my body. But so that I still might seek out the filthy source from which the infectious malice of my sons has flowed, it befits me to halt my complaint for a moment, lest in my vehemence, before receiving certain knowledge, I utter a curse upon them. But that neither birth nor the parents' upbringing of their children is the cause, this I have ascertained.

†It is fitting that I place the blame on their own despicable carelessness in following the road shown them by the Father and on their immoral disobedience in heeding the command given them in their Mother's teaching. Which I understand to be nothing other than spiritual as well as bodily decay, on account of which neither is the soul capable of obedience, nor is the body free to fulfill. Because to hear

---

145. Is. 6[:9–10].
†   Carelessness is the cause of the evil.

and yet not to hear is spiritual decay, and to hear and yet not to fulfill is bodily decay.[146] For on account of carelessness in obedience there arose indolence in training, and thence was born the stubborn indiscipline, whence there flowed sloth in fulfillment. This was the reason for the disgusting contempt; from this root grew up enmity; this was the source of the persecution I now suffer incessantly day and night. And persecution was the reason for their so great malice, which, the higher it was exalted, the lower it was to fall. Indeed, it is not necessary to seek any reasons other than these, since carelessness and indiscipline are the mother of intractability, sloth, indolence, coldness, and every crude ignorance, whence flows every malice as from a spring. Oh, the putrid source of listless water; oh, the venomous spring of waters filled with poison!

Now that I have determined this, it certainly behooves me to know at the outset: which one of my sons did this hideous guest first visit? Which one did he first recruit to his obedience? In which one did he take up residence and change the house of the Spirit of God into the house of the spirit of this world? Did he conquer them all at once, or did he subjugate them to his power one at a time? Did he place his yoke on the necks of the princes and superiors first? Or did he make his beginning with their subjects? But it is not proper for any superior authority to imitate the simplicity in which they see their subjects, since their birth and upbringing avoid every carelessness; nor is it proper that those who feel themselves the leaders, representatives, and defenders of the commonality, and who became used in childhood to every sort of elegance, sensitivity, and eminence, should imitate the life and customs of their subjects.

And since it was not the subjects, then it must have been the superiors whom this cruel fury first possessed. And it is to some extent likely that, in addition to them, she also seized those who protected themselves with their power. But I see yet another obstacle, and a no lesser one, since the princes and superiors are not of such power that they can direct both external and internal, that is, worldly and spiritual, matters according to their will. For as far as worldly power is concerned, they are lords and they command; but as far as spiritual power is concerned, they are sons, and they are obliged to listen. But

---

146. [Jer. 5:21.]

this injury caused by carelessness is not bodily (as I see) but spiritual; therefore, it must be sought not with them but elsewhere.

Who, then, remains upon whom that unassuaged ill was first founded? Whom have I yet overlooked? Certainly, whoever is at the scene (as they say)[147] is the enemy. Perhaps he, about whom there is the least suspicion, harbors the criminal? Where I expect it the least, there I find the snake in the grass.[148] †Apparently, for the disease to have spread through the whole body like a cancer, those who boast of being the leaders of the entire community first allowed themselves to be ensnared by this infernal snare, those to whom power over the souls of men is given, to whom master and lord, freeman and slave ought to render obedience, and to whom the keys of the kingdom of heaven have been entrusted,[149] of whom, some are priests and others archpriests, all equally the pastors of the spiritual sheep of the Father and the teachers of their younger brothers, the leaders of my sons, and their guardians. For to them—after the Lord God—the princes and superiors, rich and poor, young and old are required to render their first obedience in spiritual matters. They are the ones to whom it was said: "Whatever you shall bind on earth shall be bound in heaven."[150] They, as it is obvious to see, through careless use of the keys of power, first bound not only others, but also themselves, and having closed heaven to the younger brethren, themselves remained in the courtyard: so that, having bound heavy burdens and grievous to be borne, they laid them on men's shoulders; but they themselves did not wish to lift even a finger to move them.[151] Seeing this, the lambs who were entrusted to them entered upon a carelessness equal to theirs; and having shed the burdens that had been placed upon their shoulders, they became enamored of sloth in which they now shamefully rot along with their pastors, and they persecute and seek to destroy me, their mother, who leads them to their former effort and diligence.

Therefore, woe to them that they shut up the kingdom of heaven against men, for neither do they go in themselves, nor do they suffer

---

147. [Cf. *NKPP* 2:607, "Nieprzyjaciel," 2.]
148. [*NKPP* 3:630–1, "Wąż," 6; Arthaber 1272.]
†   The clergy are the cause of the evil.
149. [Mt. 16:19.]
150. Mt. 18[:18].
151. Mt. 23[:4].

others to go in.[152] Woe to them that they devour the souls of the sheep of
their Father, and make broad their phylacteries, and enlarge the borders
of their garments,[153] and, straining at gnats, swallow camels:[154] these
are the blind guides, and those who, sitting in the seat of Moses,[155]
teach evil and do evil, and yet desire that they be called rabbis. Is this
not, by God, a strange and lamentable thing, that they themselves, who
have been handed the medicine, and whose sheep have become mangy,
and to whom the keep and care of others has been entrusted—that they
themselves should first have been overcome by carelessness?

[†]O lamps of the Church, O pillars of the house of God, O pastors
of Christ's sheep, O teachers and masters of your younger brethren: how
you have put on flesh and grown fat; how you have forgotten God your
Savior! Woe to you, pastors, who have frightened away and scattered
the flock of my sheep, and who have infected them with the sickness of
carelessness, since you will receive a harsher judgment and an abundant
punishment.[156] For if the salt have lost its savor, wherewith shall it be
salted? It is thenceforth good for nothing but to be cast out and to be
trodden under foot of men.[157] Salt, you have gone stale; light, you have
grown dark; lamps, you have gone out; teachers, you have become
undisciplined; leaders, you have gone blind, and you have fallen into
the ditch of carelessness, whither you also drag the lambs entrusted to
you.[158] What will you answer when your Father and Lord comes in
order to hear your accounting for his sons and servants? When he asks
about the talents entrusted to you?[159]

Oh, on that day it will be hard for me, your mother, to look on the
destruction of her sons. Woe is me in that hour when my sons and the
sons of God, who voluntarily put out the brightness of the evangelical
light, will be sent away to the infernal fire. Who will comfort me then?
Who will stop the streams of my tears? Woe, I am miserable, that I bore

152. Mt. 23[:13].
153. Mt. 23[:5].
154. Mt. 23[:24].
155. Mt. 23[:2].
†   The complaint against the priests and archpriests.
156. Dt. 22[:1]; Jer. 23[:1–2]; Ez. 34[:5].
157. Mt. 5[:13].
158. [Mt. 15:14; Lk. 6:39.]
159. Mt. 25[:26–30].

sons to give me pain and daughters to wound me. It had been better
for me indeed to live issueless than to look upon such great throngs of
impious sons. And it had in truth been better that they not be born, than
once born to inherit eternal perdition, in which it shall be more tolerable
for Sodom and Gomorrah than for them.[160] For the servant who knows
the will of his Lord and does not act according to it shall be punished
with no small penalty.[161]

O archpriests and priests, teachers and pastors of the sheep of
your Father: how long do you wish to be dumb, how long will you
improvidently consume the sheep? You are not satisfied with the milk
and the wool that you plunder, you also drink the blood, and you cast
out the meat to be eaten by ravens and wolves.[162] You yourselves have
grown silent, but you forbid others to speak. Was there not, not so long
ago, such a great flock of sheep in the Church's fold? And was not
the government and rule of God's people entrusted unto you alone?
You sleep, pastors, but the enemy wakes. You snore, guards, but Satan,
like a lion, snatches the sheep;[163] and some he leads astray to eternal
destruction, whereas others he gives up to shameful passions, so that
they do those things that are unfitting. Your folds have fallen into decay,
but those of the enemies of God and of you are expanding. You close
your ears not wishing to hear the Father who says: "Son of man, I have
set thee a watchman unto the house of Israel: and hearing what I say,
thou shalt warn them from me. When I say unto the wicked, O wicked
man, thou shalt surely die; and if thou shouldst not speak to him, that
the wicked give up his ways, that wicked man shall die in his iniquity;
but his blood will I require at thine hand."[164] Truly a harsh speech and
a fearful judgment. Do you not fear or dread that terrible day in which
you are to give account of the flock entrusted to you? Does not that
speech of the righteous Lord terrify you: "Thou wicked and slothful
servant, thou hadst my money; thou oughtest to have put it to those
who deal in money, and then at my coming I should have received mine
own with usury. Take therefore the talent from him, and cast ye the

160. Mt. 10[:15].
161. Lk. 12[:47].
162. [Ez. 34:2–3.]
163. [Ez. 34:5–6.]
164. Ez. 33[:7–8].

unprofitable servant into outer darkness: there shall be weeping and gnashing of teeth."[165]

Where now are the priests without blame who would gratify not themselves, but would have the kind of concern and care for the flock entrusted to them that the Highest Archpriest demands of them, and which I mentioned above in instruction to them. These now are the teachers, whom, according to their lusts, my sons adopted for themselves: they have itching ears, have turned their hearing away from the truth, and have inclined unto fables,[166] loving themselves, the world, glory, riches, and luxuries more than God and the salvation of man, having to some degree the model of piety, but closing themselves to its power and opposing the truth, people of corrupt judgment and suspect faith. But they will not accomplish more, for their madness will be manifest to all, that they rested not on heavenly but on earthly thoughts. Because of them, I have come to experience not hunger for bread, but hunger for the word of God; not thirst for water, but craving for evangelical preaching. Prophet and teacher have been taken away from me, leader and pastor. There are now many pastors in name but few in deed.

†For some of the present-day pastors of Christ's spiritual flock would barely be worthy of being pastors over a flock of senseless asses. What is more, they are not pastors but rapacious wolves, not leaders but hungry lions who themselves mercilessly devour some of the sheep, and others they mercilessly stuff into the jaws of the dragon. O unhappy flock. Can he be pastor and teacher who himself has never studied, who knows not what is owed to God, nor what to his neighbors, to say nothing of what is owed to the lambs entrusted to him, who from childhood occupied himself not with the study of the teaching of Holy Scripture, but with some other occupation unnecessary to the spiritual estate, or who wasted his fleeting time in idleness? And when he was pressed by lack of food and clothing, and when poverty began to bend his miserable neck, he undertook to preach, neither knowing what preaching is, nor understanding how it should be done. But some from taverns, others from a court, some from armies, and a few from conscriptions without any election, and without any good witness, stole into the house of God

---

165. Mt. 25[:26–30; Lk. 19:12–27].
166. 2 Tim. 4[:3–4].
†   The life and customs of present-day priests.

for the sake of gold and silver. Therefore it is no wonder that, since you are unworthy of it, you shamefully abandoned it and became apostates from divine truth and traitors of the flock entrusted to you.

Woe to the poor lambs who have such pastors. Woe to those who follow such guides, who, themselves being blind, strive to shove them into that vale of the abyss.[167] Woe to you, too, on account of whose carelessness they entered the house of God. Woe to you, too, who lay waste to the houses of God, for you yourselves will be sent to perdition by Him. Woe to you, fathers, who, without having learned to be sons, lead my children astray by your paternal title. Woe to you, fathers, who, without having raised your own offspring well, give examples of evil living to the sons of God. And woe to your accursed Simons, from whom you have received consecration for these spiritual offices, who, I know, laid their hands upon you not on account of your worthiness, nor through the effort of your brothers' request, but on account of disgusting greed, because of the grasping love of money, desiring which they strayed from the true faith and entangled themselves in many tribulations.[168]

†The holy apostles, wishing, on account of the murmuring of the Greeks against the Jews, to establish deacons in the everyday service of tables and not in the teaching of God's word, say: "Brethren, look ye out among you men having good report, full of the Holy Ghost and wisdom, whom we may appoint over this business."[169] And now, without any election, or proving, and without any good report (to say nothing of being filled with the Holy Ghost and wisdom), they are being received for prayer, for divine office, for dispensing the life-giving sacraments, and they are being sent to preach the word of God.

These are the pastors and teachers I have. These are my leaders and masters. They themselves are dying of hunger, and yet they undertake to nourish others. They themselves have gone blind, and yet they attempt to be the leaders of others. They themselves limp on both legs, and yet they offer themselves as a support for others. They are themselves unlearned, and yet they dare to teach others.

Alas the disorderly, alas the perfidious, alas the wicked custom of

---

167. Mt. 23[:16, 24; 15:14].
168. 1 Tim. 1.
†   The ancient election of priests.
169. Acts 6[:2–3].

laying on of hands. "Lay hands suddenly on no man," says the apostle, "neither be partaker of other men's sins."[170] And in another place: "For this cause left I thee in Crete, Titus, that thou shouldst set in order the things that are wanting and ordain priests in the cities, as I had appointed thee: If any be blameless, the husband of one wife, having faithful children, not accused nor given to excess."[171] For a bishop must be blameless, as the shepherd of God; not haughty, nor rancorous, not given to drink, no striker, not greedy for filthy lucre; but a lover of hospitality, kind, sober, just, holy, temperate; holding fast to the faithful words, which are according to doctrine, that he may be able by sound doctrine to exhort and to convince the gainsayers.[172]

But my present-day bishops and archbishops, having rejected all apostolic teaching and blinded by the greed for silver, trampled it with the feet of disorder. [†]Would that the wise and intelligent priest of these times, who has something to impart even to his bishop, although he has been removed from Church affairs, might again be returned to them. Woe is me, entrusted to careless workers; woe is me, given to the care of insatiable gluttons; woe, also, is you who sell, and you who buy, the gift of the Holy Ghost: your silver will be your demise.[173] You do not wish to know the truth, nor do you wish to see the untruth. You do not wish to understand whence those who give it to you get it, with what industry they grow rich. They draw the milk from the sheep, they shear the wool, they flay the skins and sell them, and they feed themselves with the meat and give themselves to drink of the blood. And they give to you of the abundance of those meats and of the excess of innocent blood. O transgressors and not instructors, O lumps and not lamps, *impostores* [impostors] and not *pastores* [pastors], *epi-scoti* [over-cattle] and not *episcopi* [over-seers, i.e., bishops]: you have transgressed the law of God's will; you have beguiled your souls with that accursed, worldly mammon; you have deceived Christ's innocent lambs with the mask you have assumed; you have darkened the brightness of the evangelical light with your infectious carelessness. What will you do when the vineyard

170. 1 Tim. 5[:22].
171. Tit. 1[:5–9].
172. 1 Tim. 3[:2–10].
† The custom of the laying on of hands of the present-day bishops.
173. Acts 8[:18–24].

will be taken away from you and given over to other husbandmen, and you evil ones shall be miserably destroyed?[174] What will you say when it is answered unto you: you are the sons of your father the devil;[175] go, condemned, from me, I do not know you. What will you answer when it will be said: Bind them hand and foot, and cast them into outer darkness; there shall be weeping and gnashing of teeth.[176] At that time, woe will be you, O my sons, and woe me: you, suffering unbearable tortures, and me, looking at your eternal demise. O bishops, bishops, O sons who have scorned your Father and Mother, children born and raised in royal palaces and now of their own will lured into taverns and stables: how long will you sleep the sleep of idleness? How long before you wipe the shame of carelessness from the eyes of your hearts? Come to the quadrifluous waters of the evangelical streams, and wash the mud of simplicity from your understanding.

Are you not yet satisfied with the inestimable loss that I bear on account of your carelessness, such a great loss of the gold, silver, pearls, and precious stones, with which I, as the most noble queen, was adorned by your Father several decades ago? Where now is the priceless jewel, the carbuncle shining like a lamp, which I wore among the other pearls in the crown of my head as a sun among stars: the house of the princes of Ostroh, which shined before others with the radiance of the light of its ancient faith? Where, too, are the other costly and equally precious stones of that crown, the noble houses of Ruthenian princes, invaluable sapphires and priceless diamonds: the princes Sluc'kyj, Zaslavs'kyj, Zbaraz'kyj, Vyšnevec'kyj, Sanhuško, Čartoryjs'kyj, Prons'kyj, Ružyns'kyj, Solomerec'kyj, Holovčyns'kyj, Krošyns'kyj, Masal's'kyj, Hors'kyj, Sokolins'kyj, Lukoms'kyj, Puzyna, and others without number who, if I were to name them individually, would make for a long oration? Where, in addition to these, are my other priceless gems, that is, those wellborn houses, glorious, proud, strong, and ancient, in good report throughout all the world, houses of the Ruthenian nation, renowned for its might and courage: the Xodkevyč, Hlibovyč, Kiška, Sapiha, Dorohostajs'kyj, Vojna, Volovyč, Zenovyč, Pac, Xalec'kyj, Tyškevyč, Korsak, Xrebtovyč, Tryzna,

174. Mt. 21[:40–1].
175. Jn. 8[:44].
176. Mt. 22[:13].

Hornostaj, Bokij, Myško, Hojs'kyj, Semaško, Hulevyč, Jarmolyns'kyj, Čolhans'kyj, Kalinovs'kyj, Kyrdej, Zahorovs'kyj, Meleško, Bohovytyny, Pavlovyč, Sosnovs'kyj, Skumin, Potij, and others? I do not mention here the principalities and counties of the Ruthenian land, broad in its bounds—my costly garment, strewn with countless pearls and stones of various colors, with which I constantly adorned myself.

And so you malefactors plundered me of my so luxurious garment, and you wreak your malice in derision and abuse over my miserable body, whence you all came. But damned is he who uncovers the nakedness of his mother to scorn;[177] and damned are you who deride and rejoice in my nakedness. There will come a time when you will be ashamed of all this. It were better indeed that you had not known the light of truth, than to reject, extinguish, and suppress it, once you had come to know it. And are you the pastor who boasts of his shepherding, when you revile God through the loss of his sheep?[178] Are you the priest who boasts of his consecration, when you renounce God through the blemishing of the sacrament? Neither your life, nor morals, nor behavior, nor dress show you to be teachers. [†]Neither wisdom, nor training, nor conversation testify to your consecration and shepherding. In life you are tavern keepers and merchants, in your morals layabouts, in conversation ignoramuses, in behavior crafty foxes, and in your dress predatory wolves. What, then, shall I say about the qualities of your understanding? Your wisdom, knowledge, and conversation are foolish, vain, and obscene, and your entertainments lewd, in which both you yourselves and those who follow you are perishing. Why, then, by God, are you a priest? Why a pastor? You were sent to consecrate others, but you yourself lie desecrated from head to foot. Care for shepherding has been entrusted to you, but you yourself die faint from hunger.

O consecrator, everywhere desecrated. O pastor made cowardly from hunger. Is it you who are a lamp to those in the darkness of simplicity? Are you the eye to those blind through ignorance of the evangelical light? Are you the hand to lift up those who have fallen into the abyss of Satan's power? If you, unwise sons, do not fear God, then at least feel shame before men. Prick your heart, and show your

---

177. [Lev. 18:7.]
178. Ez. 34[:1–10].
†   What sort of priests the present-day apostate pastors have.

knowledge, and come to vigilance, and having come to your senses, repent.[179] For it is fitting of human weakness to fall; but to fall and not to get up is characteristic of satanic obduracy itself. At least serve worthily in the vineyard of your Lord in the eleventh hour, so that you might take your payment along with those who began to work from the first hour and bore the heat of the sun all day.[180] Halt the heartfelt sighs at least at the end of your mother's life. Wipe your mother's crying eyes, lest her bloody tears ever fall on you and your mother's lament destroy you. Deign to be priests not in name but in actual fact. Seek to be teachers not by word but by deed.

To whom do I say this? To whom are these words of mine addressed? Do I cast them against an iron wall, or rather to the wind? For when I say this to them, it is as if I converse with sleeping people who ask what you said at the end of the tale.[181] It were easier indeed for me to bear salt and a mass of iron in my breast[182] than to converse with shameless, malicious, and unruly sons. Who cries woe from this? I do. Who alas? I do. Who alack? I do. Who pity? I do. I am scorned. I am abused. I am driven out. I am insulted. But you too will cry woe who scorned me. You too alas, who abused me. You too alack, who drove me out. You too pity, who insulted me. For the impiety of the sons is dishonor to the parents. And a mother's curse is perdition to the sons. Once a sagacious son hears a wise word, he praises and accepts it. But you, stupid ones, listen to my words constantly; and since they do not please you, you cast them behind you. I tell you a wise word every day in the Prophets, I tell it to you in the Epistles of the Apostles. Finally, I also always offer unto you the salvatory evangelical teaching of our Lord and God, the very wisdom that turned the intellects of this world into foolishness,[183] and without which no one ever was, nor could call himself, wise, the gain of which is better than the merchandise of gold and silver.[184] For it is more precious than pearls, than precious stones, and all the fortunes of this world. The length of days is on its right hand,

---

179. Sir. 22[:19].
180. Mt. 20[:1–16].
181. [Cf. Erasmus *Ad.* 1.4.87.]
182. Sir. 22[:15].
183. [1 Cor. 1:20.]
184. Prov. 3[:13–14].

and on the left side, wealth and glory. Its ways are beautiful ways, and all its paths peaceful. To those who will grasp it, it is the tree of life, and whoever attains it shall be blessed. This I say to you every day. Night and day I call to you about this. Whoever among you is small, let him come to me. And you who wish understanding, come hither; eat of my bread, and drink of the wine which I have mingled for you. Leave childhood behind, and live; go in the way of understanding, and you shall reign forever.[185]

But one of my sons will say: "Why did our mother's heart become inflamed with cruel anger? Why does she rebuke her children so vehemently? Why does she burden herself and us, her sons, with such a harsh curse? This does not befit maternal love, since it knows well that it is impossible to find among men a man without sin. We all suffer this defect, we all bear the yoke of this slavery. And since no one is without sin, except for God Himself, she should have treated her children more leniently, and she could have found a more gentle method for admonishing her sons. For she is not a stepmother, but a mother; and we are not stepsons, but sons. A rod should have been used for punishment, and not an iron backsword; punishment at home, and not a curse announced to the entire world. What mother ever removed her children's honor? What mother cursed her sons and gave them up to Satan for the damnation of soul and body? For this is unfitting not only for a mother, but even for a stepmother."

What shall I answer to this? Whence shall I summon the words? If God would only grant that I had no response. Indeed, I would rather be found mendacious than truthful in what I have spoken here. But it pains me that everything I say is true, that it is an infallible account I have cited here. Even if I had kept silent about it, their own conscience, conquered by the truth, would have to testify.

And as to the statement that God alone is without sin, and all men are subject to sin: who does not know this? For they were created in the image and likeness of Adam,[186] who stumbled; and they were conceived in transgression and born in sin.[187] But you, who were dead in your trespasses and sins, in which in time past you walked according

185. Prov. 9[:4–6].
186. Gen. 5[:3].
187. Ps. 50 [51:5].

to the age of this world and according to the prince of the power of the
air, the spirit that now works his power in the children of disobedience:
among whom also you all had your conversation in times past in the
lusts of your flesh, doing the will of your body and of your mind, and
were by nature the children of wrath, even as others; but God, who is
rich in mercy, through his great love wherewith He loved you when you
had died in sins, has quickened you together in Christ (by Whose grace
you are saved), and has raised you up together with them, and made
you sit together in heaven in Jesus Christ.[188] And therefore, it no longer
befitted you to walk as the pagans walk, in the vanity of their mind,
having their understanding entangled in darkness, being alienated from
the life of God through the ignorance that is in them, and because of the
blindness of their heart; for, despairing, they have given themselves over
unto lasciviousness to work uncleanness and greediness. But you have
not so learned from Christ; if so be that you have heard Him, and have
been taught by Him, that you put off concerning the former action the
old man, which is corrupt according to deceitful lusts, and be renewed
in the spirit of your mind, and that you put on the new man, which after
God is created in righteousness and in the holiness of truth.[189] For, as
through the transgression of one man, Adam, there came to all men
the judgment of death, so also, through the righteousness of one man,
Jesus, there came to all men the justification of life.[190]

I thus bore you in the image and likeness of the second Adam,
Jesus, who chose me for His bride, and gave Himself for me, that, having
cleansed me through the washing of water in the word of life, He might
sanctify me.[191] And therefore how did I, being pure and holy, give birth
to you who are defiled and damned? Purifying and sanctifying you in
the same manner in which I myself was purified and sanctified, that is,
by water and the Spirit, through which if any not be born again, he is
not my son, and he will not enter into the kingdom of God the Father,[192]
but he will pass from the first death to the second death, which is worse
than the first. You are no longer under the Law, but under Grace.[193]

188. Eph. 2[:1–6].
189. Eph. 4[:17–24].
190. 1 Cor. 15[:22].
191. Eph. 5[:25–6].
192. Jn. 4 [3:5].
193. Rom. 6[:14].

Those who are born under the Law draw the sin of their fathers with them, but those who are born under Grace are no longer encumbered with the yoke of sin. I bore you under Grace, and not under the Law. I raised you in freedom and not in slavery. I enlightened you with the light rather than leave you in darkness. And therefore, it was fitting for you to conduct yourselves as sons of the light, in all goodness, in righteousness, and in truth, proving what is acceptable unto God, and to have no fellowship with the improper works of darkness, but rather to reprove them.[194]

You say further: "There can be no man without sin, except for Him alone, who redeemed the sins of the world, since even a righteous man, to say nothing of a sinful man, falls seven times a day." Good. I too accept this. But I answer this as well: that the righteous man jumps to his feet from a slip quickly, whereas you have only begun to think of lifting your head, and of standing up—not at all. Sin has come to reign in your mortal body, that you should be obedient to its demands and yield your members as an instrument unto sin of unrighteousness,[195] whereas you should live according to the spirit and not according to the flesh. For if you live in the flesh, you shall die. And they that are Christ's, and have crucified their flesh with affections and lusts, living in the Spirit, should also walk in the Spirit.[196] Do you not know that so many of you as were baptized in Jesus Christ were baptized in His death? For you are buried with Him by His baptism unto death: that like as Christ arose from the dead by the glory of the Father, even so you also should walk in newness of life, knowing thus that our old man is crucified with Him, that the body of sin might be destroyed, that henceforth we should not serve sin.[197] And if it should happen that any of you fall into sin, if you confess your sins, the Lord is faithful and just to forgive you your sins, and to cleanse you from all unrighteousness.[198] Whence it is made known that not sin, but the constant abiding in it, is the cause of second death. Since, for those who sin willfully, after having received the knowledge of truth, there remains no more sacrifice for sins but a

---

194. Eph. 5[:9–11].
195. [Rom. 6:12–13.]
196. Gal. 5[:24–5].
197. Rom. 6[:3–6].
198. [1 Jn. 1:9.]

certain fearful looking for of judgment and fiery indignation, which shall devour the adversaries.[199] And therefore it was not your sins that moved me in my wretchedness to such a manner of rebuke but your constant abiding in sins, and not so much the abiding in sins as the daily entering upon worse iniquities, for which you deserve not the iron rod of punishment but the staff of repudiation and condemnation unto loss of soul and body.

I know that I am your mother, and you were my children. But when, on account of your repudiation and rejection of me, I shall be moved in the bitterness of my heart, shall despise you, repudiate and curse you, and give you up to the abuse of all the nations, then neither shall I wish to be called, nor yet to be, your mother. And what is more, when I call to my Betrothed, and your Father, He too will reject you, repudiate you, and give you up to the eternal death of outer darkness, where there will be eternal torments and constant gnashing of teeth.[200] Then you will say: "Woe is her who gave us birth, woe is her who nourished us; it had been better for us not to have been born, than to come to this place of eternal torment. Alack the day in which we were born; woe the earth over which we walked, the heaven that lighted us. Woe to us too that we deserted our mother. Alas for us too that we ignored the commandments of our Father and walked in the lust of our will."

You will cry, and no one will hear you out; you will summon, and no one will answer; you will shout, and no one will come down to you.[201] For as you deserted your Father and Mother, so also will you be deserted by them and cast into the void of eternal oblivion. Did I only once admonish you privately at home and not *publice* [publicly] in the market place? Did I only once beg you myself in person that you return to me? Did I not also send your brethren to you not many years ago so that you might beg my forgiveness and, having compensated my losses with your diligence, that you might remain by me and not think any more about my harm? Did I not recount to you your transgressions, with which you desecrated both me and yourselves, and did I not tell you that you attack me in vain with sharpened tongues,[202] knowing of my invincibility?

199. Heb. 10[:26–7].
200. [Mt. 8:12; 22:13; 25:30.]
201. Prov. 1[:28]; Jer. 7[:27].
202. [Ps. 140:3; 64:3.]

What happened to me at your hands for my constant effort on your behalf? What? Certainly that which the wise man uttered somewhere: He that teaches a scorner gets to himself wrong: and he that rebukes with words a wicked man gets to himself a blot.[203] For you said, "We have sinned, and what harm has happened unto us because of this? For the Lord is long-suffering." But I said, "Do not say: 'Great is the mercy of the Lord; He has mercy upon the greatness of our sins.' For He has love, but also wrath and vehemence against the sinners, which, if it should come of a sudden, will certainly scatter you in the day of vengeance. Therefore, add not sin to sin, but aid goodness with goodness."[204]

What have I achieved through my reproving? What have I built in you with my verbal rebuke? I see that not only do you not think of improvement, but you fall into ever worse iniquities. How far will you incline the walls of your souls? For you believe that after their unhappy fall you will erect them. But your belief is vain, miserable your designs, since a great abyss will be established immediately between you who fall and those who stand, so that passage will be possible neither for them to you, nor for you to them. And at that time your work will be crowned with a reward. But I believe Him who loved me and who gave Himself up for me, that He Himself will lift me up with His mighty right hand and will entrust His vineyard to more diligent workers.[205] Grant it, almighty God, before whose most holy majesty I fall in fear, and I summon with a contrite heart and a lamenting voice thine ineffable goodness:

†Thou King of eternal praise, Ruler of heaven and earth, whose throne is inestimable and whose glory may not be comprehended, before whom the hosts of angels and of all the higher powers stand in fear and trembling, whose word is true and sayings constant, whose commandment is strong and ordinance fearful, whose look dries up the depths, and indignation makes the mountains to melt away, and whose truth witnesseth;[206] Thou, I say, who of every wood of the earth, and of all its trees, hast chosen one only vine, and of all the flowers of

203. Prov. 9[:7].
204. Sir. 5[:3–7].
205. [Mt. 21:41; Mk. 12:9; Lk. 20:16.]
†   Prayer to God.
206. 3 Esdr. 8 [2 Esdr. 8:21–3].

the world hast chosen Thee one lily, and of all the depths of the sea hast filled Thee one river, and of all builded cities hast hallowed unto Thyself Zion alone, and of all the fowls of the air hast named Thee one dove, and of all creatures hast chosen Thee one sheep, and among all the multitude of peoples hast gotten Thee the people of the New Israel,[207] that is, me, Thy Church, which from the beginning and until today, through Thy miraculous providence and the unfathomable depth of Thy judgments, Thou wert accustomed to maintain safe and inviolate among enemies open and hidden, internal and external, and thereby hast deigned long ago and for all time to bestow upon me a privilege—that I grow in persecution, multiply in oppression, rise in the poverty and disdain of this world, that I conquer while suffering, triumph bearing wrongs and abuse, grow and flourish abundantly through the sprinkling of martyr's blood, and that I be strengthened most through Thine help when the sons of this world were wont to threaten me with the surest fall through external conjectures: Thou Thyself look even now with a merciful eye upon my ineffable sorrow, oppression, and affliction, and deign to lighten, if such is Thy will, the cross that has been placed upon me; assuage my lament, soothe the pain of my heart, of which my own sons are the cause. Come from Lebanon, come to my aid, let them be ashamed, and let them turn back who seek after my soul[208] and who shamelessly whet their tongues against me.[209] For I place my trust and hope in Thee alone, to Thee alone have I recourse in all my sorrows and tribulations. And although I have suffered, and I suffer to this day much oppression and persecution, not only from foreigners, but even from those who come from my womb, nonetheless I have not abandoned Thee, nor have I raised my hands to a foreign god. Through Thy help I stood and I stand inviolate upon that mighty rock, upon which Thou hast deigned to found me.[210] I have not lost, nor have I stained with the blot of any error or heresy the garment that Thou Thyself hast deigned to bestow upon me, woven of the highest theology of faith in Thee, in naught suspect; nor have I stained it with the blemishes of the inventions of man or with new and ever changing statutes and traditions.

207. 3 Esdr. 5 [2 Esdr. 5:23–7].
208. Ps. 69 [70:1–2].
209. Ps. 63 [64:3].
210. Mt. 16[:18].

And although many of my impious and degenerate children seek after this, it is not of my doing. Rather it comes from their perfidious design, from their unbelief, from their pride, from their ambition, from their heart inclined to wealth and to the delights of this world; for, not wishing to go to eternal life along the narrow road filled with sharp thorns,[211] they set out on the wide and commodious road (along which many of them go). And having set out, they would gladly draw all behind them; and they have caused me, their mother, shame, disgrace, and eternal ruin. Do not allow the wicked sons to rejoice in the fall of me, their mother. And yet, almighty Lord, do not immediately visit their unrighteousness with the rod of demise, but, for my sake, hold back for a short time Thy right hand stretched out for vengeance,[212] that I go to them once more, and admonish them to repent at the end of their life, and to come and render unto me the requisite bow; and being in harmony and mutual love with them, I shall stand before Thy countenance, and again in joy and gladness I shall honor and worship Thy holy name together with them. Behold I am coming now, and I ask Thine ineffable goodness: send down upon them the gift of Thy grace and mercy, and fill their hearts with true understanding. Kindle in them the fire of Thy love, so that hearing they might understand, having understood they might accept, and having accepted they might repent, and through repentance that they might cause rejoicing and gladness for Thy citizens of heaven.[213]

And since I have resolved to go to them, I must consider to whom I shall go first, that I not undertake a labor in vain. For if I go to the common crowd, I fear that, through their simplicity and mean understanding, when they see me, they would attack me and wet their hands in their mother's blood. For the heart of the servant is hard, and it cannot be instructed by words; though it understand anything, it will in no manner accept it.[214] And if I go to the princes, the superiors, and the lords, even if they should wish to listen to me and to remain by me, it does not depend entirely on them, since their subordinates are to be obedient to them not in spiritual matters but only in temporal. It befits

211. Mt. 7[:13–14].
212. Ps. 88 [89:32–3].
213. Lk. 15[:7].
214. Prov. 29[:19].

me (as I see) to go to those who govern the soul, since the very matter that concerns me is a spiritual matter. It is proper that I do this for this reason: that the correction might come from him through whom the harm came; and that those who were the beginning and the cause of evil for others—that through them all might be returned to the good. For they are the ones to whose care the souls of all have been entrusted. They are the ones who undertook to bear the path of truth on their tongue and promised to guard the eyes of their sheep. It befits me to go to them, it is proper that I converse with them. Deign, then, Comforter Holy Spirit, to visit them first and to soften their hardened hearts, that they might receive me gratefully and listen to me diligently. But I will appear before them who call themselves the bishops of my paternal heritage, the Ruthenian land, and to the elder of them will I speak.[215]

Chapter 2

In Which Is Contained the Admonition of the Eastern Church to the Son Who, along with Others, Deserted Her

Son, behold: I, your Mother, appear before you with every wish of God's blessing. Here I stand before your countenance, and with humility I ask permission for gentle conversation with you. Lift up your reverend head, and look with a happy eye upon your mother; look, my son, and recognize me; show the humanity befitting children. Let me approach you, and, having stretched out your hands, receive me. Let your heart not become hardened. Lift up your eyes upon your suffering mother, and with gracious glance deign once again calmly to converse with me, since I have come to you not to rebuke you, but to teach you. I did not come to arouse you into angry vehemence, but to make you well disposed and humble. I did not come to rend a son's love for his mother, but rather for reconciliation. Marvel, my son, looking upon the unheard-of degradation of your mother, and have pity on my immeasurable lament, remorse, pain, and affliction, of which you yourself, along with your other brethren, my younger sons, are the cause.

215. [The immediate addressee of chapter 2 will be the Uniate Metropolitan of Kyiv, Ipatij Potij.]

For I brought you up with gladness, but with sorrow and heaviness have I lost you.[216] I gave birth to you for the consolation and support of my old age, but I experienced at your hands worse enmity, more fervent hatred, harsher oppression, persecution more cruel, and a more harmful demise than at the hands of my manifest opponents. For you and on account of you, I, your unhappy mother, became wretched, afflicted, bereaved, and truly scorned by the entire world. And sitting now, alas, at the miserable edge of the salty Babylonian water, and seeing you yourselves and, because of you, many others of my sons drowning miserably in it, I cry bitter and disconsolate tears,[217] and I lift up to the very clouds the mournful tones of my painful laments, so that the words of the prophet can now properly be said of me: A voice was heard in Ramah, a very great lamentation and weeping, Rachel weeping for her children; and she would not be comforted, because they were not.[218]

Let filial affection for your mother move you. Let my so bitter and heaven-piercing lament, my sighing and weeping penetrate your heart. Console me, by God, I beg you, my son; console me in this my tribulation, for I have not ceased to console you since your youth. Wipe the tears from my eyes through your repentance and conversion, for I did not allow you to cry in the years of your childhood. Remain, my son, by your mother in her old age, for everyone who deserts her in deed and in word is cursed by the Lord. Deign to honor me, and you will be blessed by the Most High. Do not give reason for your mother to curse you, since the curse of the mother rooteth out the foundations of her children's houses.[219] For what glory do you receive from my abuse? And what joy from my disgrace? Therefore listen carefully, my son, to my teaching, and accept my admonition; deign to adapt your will to the thought of your Father, and it will be well with you. Listen to me, my son, and do not reject my words. I give you a good present; do not scorn it. Seek after study rather than silver; strive for wisdom, not gold; search for knowledge of God's will, and not pearls and precious stones.[220] For wisdom surpasses all these things, and there is nothing

---

216. 3 Esdr. 2 [2 Esdr. 2:3].
217. Ps. 136 [137:1].
218. Jer. 31[:15].
219. Sir. 3[:9].
220. Prov. 3[:13–15].

on earth equal to it.[221] When you have it, you will be blessed, and you will gain eternal glory.

Keep my commandments, and you will attain wisdom. Fear God, and do not oppose Him, since all people are in the hands of Him who created them as clay in the potter's hands.[222] Look, my son, at the generations of old, and judge who of them trusted in the Lord and was confounded, who abided in His fear and was forsaken, or who called upon Him and was not heard. You, too, my son, prepare your soul for service unto your Lord; prepare your heart for the receiving of wisdom, which will not enter the perfidious soul.[223] Emulate your holy ancestors, the first pastors and teachers, and wipe from your heart the rust of carelessness; cast off the stone of laziness, wash the eyes of your understanding.[224] Acquire the fear of God, and touch your conscience, and know yourself. Take care of those who have been entrusted to you.

With the same diligence look upon the carelessness of your fellow pastors, whose leader you are. And with them, with one thought of watchfulness, look also upon the priests sent by you, whom you ordered to walk before the flock of your sheep, so that you might determine whether they behave fittingly, whether they keep diligent watch over the flock entrusted them. You yourself, arise as quickly as possible and act according to my will, and according to the will of my Father. Converse with your fellow pastors. Ask them whether they conduct themselves in the office of authority given to them as it is proper to do so. Ask them also whether they keep diligently the evangelical preaching that has been entrusted to them; whether they are pastors who are watchful over their sheep, and not careless hired husbandmen; whether they are servants faithful to the Church of Christ, and not unfaithful hirelings.[225] Discover whether they rule in orderly fashion the Church of God, whose superiors they are; whether they are the genuine followers of the holy apostles and their blessed representatives; whether there is not among them a Simon, or a Judas, who would not build, but destroy

---

221. Prov. 4[:7].
222. Sir. 2[:7–17; Is. 64:8; Jer. 18:6; Job 10:9].
223. Sir. 2[:17].
224. [Eph. 1:18.]
225. [Jn. 10:12–13.]

and betray the Church of God. And having acquired certain knowledge, striving with one thought for the good and benefit of your mother, come together all, and, having taken your conscience alone as a witness, give yourselves up to discussion in brotherly love, and deign to consider your insufficiencies diligently. Come to know what you yourselves are, and having understood what is your calling, reprove each other, that you all be corrected without insult.

Be moved, my son, in God's love; acquire zealous boldness, and speak to your brethren: "Brethren, we are the pastors of the spiritual flock of Christ's sheep. We are the guardians of the house of God. It is fitting that we pass judgment on ourselves from the pasture entrusted to us (knowing that we must give account to the Lord on Judgment Day) as to whether we have conducted ourselves worthily and without rebuke in the office entrusted to us, whether we give unto our little sheep from the abundance of the food and drink of the evangelical bread and water, whether we maintain whole and without diminishment the flocks entrusted to us. Let us also look, moreover, upon the priests consecrated by us, let us also look upon the little sheep entrusted to them. Let us converse among ourselves and with them, while we still have time, lest later on we receive shame from the Father for our carelessness and, denied the crown of life, be given up to eternal perdition."

And since it befits every faithful and just judge among the brethren to take stock first of his own conscience before he approaches others, lest it be said to him, "Physician, heal thyself;[226] master, teach thyself," therefore you, too, my son, bring yourself unto the beginning of reproving; make inquiry first of yourself; judge yourself first; arise boldly, and without any hypocrisy beg pardon of your Father; open before Him the wounds of your heart, and He will heal you.

Move immediately, and say to your brethren with gentle countenance and with fervent heart: "I am not ashamed, brethren, to make known before you everything in which I have proved unfaithful to my God. I am not ashamed, my fellow pastors, to confess before you the transgressions with which I have angered my Father, knowing that it is better for me to be shamed before a few of you than before the entire world and before the angels of God and to be removed from eternal life.

226. Lk. 4[:23].

I am the salt that has lost its savor, I am the light that has been put out,[227] a careless teacher, a hired laborer and not a shepherd, the betrayer of the sheep of my Father to an unwonted fold and not the watchful defender against predatory wolves.[228] Through my carelessness, I allowed the hedge around the Lord's vineyard to be destroyed and the winepress to be dug up from it; I overturned its tower through untimely silence, and I sold it to unfaithful husbandmen for silver.[229] I buried the talent entrusted to me in the earth,[230] I lost the countless flocks of sheep, for which my King and God died. Where are my spiritual foods gathered from the evangelical field and given to the flock entrusted to me so that all the sheep might be fed with one food, and be strengthened by one drink, and not walk in various foreign pastures? Where are the doctrines by which the hearers might be instructed in the fear of God and in the love of their neighbor? Where too are the other works of mercy coming from my office and authority, the holy ruling of monasteries, the fitting adornment of churches? For what should have been given out and expended for that purpose from my pastoral obligation, I turned only to my own benefit, or rather luxury (not serving the spiritual benefit of the flock entrusted to me, but only filling my own caskets, chests, and cellars), having gathered for myself several spiritual offices, contrary to custom and the canons of the holy Fathers, and extorting from the churches and monasteries their ancient charters. And so that there be no one to admonish me in this, I appointed unworthy men—unlearned, and what is more, twice-married, thrice-married,[231] and those led into strange errors concerning faith and morals—to bishoprics and other ecclesiastical offices, upon the testimony of a liberal offering. Therefore, I am the scatterer of my Lord's treasure, I am the pillager of my Father's goods, I am the hedonist in the abundance of Christ's church, I am the prodigal in the paternal inheritance of my King. What shall I yet say of the monasteries subject to my power, in which the monks wantonly

---

227. Mt. 5[:13–16].
228. Jn. 16 [10:12].
229. Mt. 21[:33; Mk. 12:1; Lk. 20:9; Is. 5:2; Jer. 2:21].
230. Mt. 25[:18].
231. [On the problem of twice- and thrice-married men among the Ruthenian clergy and on the 1589 reforms of Patriarch of Constantinople Jeremiah II Tranos, see Gudziak 1998, 196–9.]

broke, trampled, and destroyed the holy statutes of their ancestors, so that there did not remain in them even a trace of that ancient pious abiding in prayers and fasting, in work and study of Holy Scripture? Woe is me, who, calling myself a shepherd, must give account of all this disorder to my Lord on Judgment Day."

Having judged yourself in this manner, my dear son, and having humbly confessed your iniquities before the righteous Judge, reprove your brethren boldly and without any regard for persons,[232] and ask them, saying: "You, too, fathers and brethren, confess: does it not go with you exactly as with me? Have you not come to dishonor through the same evil deeds in the office entrusted to you? Which of you will bring doubled to his Lord the talent given to Him?[233] We have all equally confined our necks in the same yoke of carelessness. We have all sunk into the same mud. Let us punish ourselves, brethren, and reprove ourselves before we are called to judgment. Let us first entreat the Judge, before, by His just decree, we receive eternal shame according to our deeds. And having judged ourselves, let us also look upon the priests who were sent by our placing on of hands, whom we sowed throughout the Ruthenian land like a worm that gnaws at souls: immature boys and unlearned men, interlopers, ill-mannered boors, disgusting gluttons, shameless liars, self-important sophists, immodest bacchants, obstinate clerks, restive profligates, fractious gadabouts, fearful bumblebees, conceited chatterers, indifferent flatterers, wicked buyers of holy offices, accursed sellers of holy offices, insatiable gluttons, blind leaders, careless fathers, unwatchful pastors, licentious priests, incompetent teachers, suspect preachers, unrighteous judges, hypocritical Pharisees, cunning Judases, infernal blasphemers, who, in the inconstancy of their young years, are more attracted to childish games and other frivolities than to the reading of divine Writ, more given to licentiousness than to study, more eager to drain tavern mugs and to play cards than for the orderly conducting of ecclesiastical affairs. The statutes of the blessed Fathers do not accept those under thirty among the number of God's priests, but we licentious Simons accept those barely fifteen.[234] Everyone knows that the mother's milk has not even

232. [Mt. 22:16; Mk. 12:14.]
233. [Mt. 25:14–30; Lk. 19:12–27.]
234. [Perhaps the reference is to the *Ancient Statutes of the Church,* which

dried on the mouths of some, and we have already made them fathers
in unseemly fashion. They themselves have not yet learned to make out
syllables, and we have sent them to preach the word of God. They have
not yet ruled their own houses, and we have charged them with the rule
of the Church. And are we not here, brethren, on account of miserable
gold, participants in the sins of others through our unwise laying on of
hands? Without a doubt.

"O hideous gluttony, how you reign over those who undertook to
follow poverty. O invincible silver, how you settle upon the necks even
of the clergy. Through the inevitable greed for you, we have brought
our mother to such a great risk of great danger; we have led Christ's
bride to such a great dishonor and temporal shame, entrusting her to the
charge of frivolous boys, and handing her over to the care of inconstant
children, who, through the insufficiency of their understanding, do not
know what they owe to themselves, or to their mother, to say nothing of
the office entrusted to them.

"But in order to acquire more certain knowledge about this, let us
order these immature shepherd boys to show us the fields in which they
graze Christ's sheep. Let them place before us the food and drink with
which they feed them and give them to drink. I am certain, brethren,
that as are the lords, so are the servants; as are we, those who lay on
hands, so are those who receive the laying on of hands from us. And
if we doze in the shade of carelessness, then they have fallen asleep
through sloth. If we, who are the light of the sun, have grown dark
through the fog of incompetence, so that some of us do not even know
how to read writings well in our own language, what will be the light of
the moon, since our light was to shine both in them and in the spiritual
flock entrusted to them? Where is there not gloom, where not darkness,
on account of which there arose the great errors of many, the great
scandals, the great and unchecked apostasies from the Church of God?
For where is there one preacher among them who would feed his sheep
with his own customary spiritual bread of evangelical teaching, and not
with that of another?"

These, my son, are my words to you. This is my conversation
with you. Having heard it from your mother, gratefully accept it, and

---

were the result of the Fourth Council of Carthage, AD 398. Cf. the canons of
the Council of Carthage, AD 419, canon 19; *PL* 56:868C.]

keep it diligently in your heart for all time, and having moved yourself, make fruits meet for repentance[235] along with those who followed you. Be mindful of God's law, O pastors and teachers. Return to me, your mother, whom you impiously abandoned and betrayed. Feed your own soul and those of others with the nourishing bread of good tidings and give them to drink of the wine of salvatory doctrines. Stand steadfastly by your mother, and take care for her honor and glory in every way. Open the eyes of your hearts, and know yourselves, know your Father and Mother, know in whose house and in what kind of house, you were born. You were a chosen generation, a holy nation, a royal priesthood, and sons of God the Most High.[236] Know yourselves, I say, and me, your mother, against whom you now have arisen wrongly and storm with all your might.

Did I not just a few years ago, at the hands of manifest adversaries, suffer slander and calumny, which they, in seeking to render abhorrent to the whole world the holy and unsuspect faith in the triune God that is held by myself and by my true sons of the glorious Ruthenian nation, give to the entire world to read instead of the canons or rules or articles of the religion of the Ruthenian Church? Witness to this are the *scripta* [writings] published in print in the Latin language by a certain Joannes Sacranus, canon of the Church of Cracow, and by Father Piotr Skarga, and the letter *incerti authoris ad Davidem Chytreum* [of an unknown author to David Chytraeus], allegedly about the faith, morals, and ceremonies of the people of the Ruthenian religion, where, among other calumnies worthy of ineffable amazement, they also allege the following things, gathered here *summatim* [briefly]: that my sons, the priests and teachers of the Ruthenian Church, along with the entire people entrusted to their care, have not yet come to know the truth of the heavenly word; that the salvatory light of the Gospel has not yet illumined them; that the Holy Gospel was never read among them; that they supposedly tell pure fables in the churches instead of the Gospel, thus leading astray the simple people; that they would give great indulgences for sins to whoever would kill an enemy or a Roman Catholic; that they order people to commit perjury; that they supposedly teach that a living man cannot commit mortal sin; that they assert that Church prayers and *oblationes*

235. [Mt. 3:8.]
236. 1 Pet. 2[:9].

[oblations] help those who are in hell and no one else; that they say that adultery and usury are not mortal sins; that they allow one man to have two wives at the same time; †that they teach that adultery is not a sin; that they, according to their pleasure, allow divorces without any proper reason; that they, a crude and stupid nation, used many impious ceremonies during the performance of marriage blessings and the burial of the bodies of the dead; that they give to the dead letters of attestation to be brought to the apostle Peter; that they hold holy confession in contempt; that they allow no unmarried man to the priestly office; that they do not hold simony a sin; that they baptize not *in* the name, but *through* the name of the Father, and the Son, and the Holy Ghost; ‡that they consecrate the mysteries of the Lord's Supper in kvass and mead instead of wine; that they are permitted to partake of the body and the blood of the Lord immorally like swine, after dinner or drunk in the morning; that they give one mystery of the body and blood of the Lord to the healthy to eat and another to the sick, and that they say that the one is without benefit to the others and vice versa.[237]

Having invented against me these and similar calumnies, these obscene fables, these blasphemies loathsome to God, my adversaries were not ashamed to publish them to the entire world and to present them to the ignorant as a true account, adding to these ever new calumnies, and abominable abuses, not only orally but also in various writings, which people of the same *farina* [grain, i.e., ilk] not long ago did not hesitate to print as a testimony to their malice and enmity, full of mortal poison against God's faithful, and no less a testimony to their stupidity

---

†   Worthless calumny.

‡   Look what a calumny!

237. *Joannis Sacrani, Canonici Cracoviensis, cap. 2* [chapter 2 of the work of Joannes Sacranus, canon of Cracow; either *Elucidarius errorum ritus ruthenici,* 1500; or *Errores atrocissimorum ruthenorum,* 1500; probably the former, which was published in Gwagnin 1584, 347–91]; *Skarga c. 2 partis 3 lib. Pol. Anno 1577. de uno pastore et de verit. Ecclesiae* [(Piotr) Skarga, chapter 2 of part 3 of a Polish book of the year 1577, *On the One Pastor and of the True Church* (i.e., *O jedności kościoła Bożego i o greckim od tej jedności odstąpieniu* [(On the Unity of God's Church and on the Greek Apostasy from That Union*), Vilnius, 1577]. *Et Epist. incerti authoris ad Davidem Chytreum* [and *The Letter of a Certain Author to David Chytraeus;* also published in Gwagnin 1584, 392–417].

and madness; shamelessly inventing against my innocent and in naught suspect sons things that not only never were *in rerum natura* [in the nature of things], but were not even possible, but rather truly arisen from the father of every lie (who, as the Scripture says, never abides in truth).[238] But we refer those who wish more sufficient knowledge of these things to those same writings.

Addressing my oration to those of you, O glorious Ruthenian nation, who have not yet abandoned me, your mother, and have not blemished yourselves with the blot of apostasy, I ask why you are silent at such great and unheard-of calumnies? Why do you not defend yourself when you are so abused? Why do you not care that you are insulted? [†]The calumniators came within a hair's breadth of leaving you no honor and faith, but you did not lift even a glib tongue in opposition to such a contagious evil. The wolves howl at the sheep, and having scattered them with their wild and terrifying voice in the wilderness of various thoughts, they snatch them little by little, and having dragged them to their lairs, they devour them without any hindrance. And what do you do? Hearing, you do not hear; seeing, you do not see;[239] and, as if that did not trouble you in the least, you pay no attention. You have indeed become unfaithful husbandmen of the Lord's vineyard, dumb shepherds of spiritual sheep, and the deaf watchmen over the house of God.

O abuse worse than all other shames, to see the glory (without which the life of man is not life) changed into unglory and to keep silent; to hear the faith (without which a man is not a man) abused as unfaith and not to answer. Tell me, I ask you: why did nature give you a tongue? Why did it provide you with reason and adorn you with speech above other creatures? A senseless and dumb beast, when wronged and angered, drives away as best it can the one who wrongs and angers it, and it shows watchfulness. Fire came down from heaven and burned those who destroy truth.[240] The earth opened its mouth and swallowed those who suppress the truth.[241] The waters came together and enveloped those

---

238. [Jn. 8:44.]
†   Digression to the non-apostate sons.
239. [Mt. 13:13; Mk. 4:12; Lk. 8:10; Acts 28:26.]
240. [Gen. 19:24.]
241. [Num. 16:32–3.]

who persecute the truth. The air dissolved into poison and infected those who blaspheme against the truth. The walls, bastions, mountains, rocks, and trees fell on those who overthrew God's truth. But you, endowed with reason and speech, created in the image and likeness of God, see and hear holy truth slandered, abused, blasphemed, and insulted, and yet you remain silent, showing yourselves more careless in your duty than dumb and senseless creatures and more thankless toward God your Creator, before whom every abuse of the truth is repelled as before the independent truth itself.

Deign, then, not to suffer any longer such terrible disgrace. Deign not to bear on yourselves the abuse of the entire world. Show yourselves, make yourselves known, that you are God's chosen people, His illumined Church. Let them, one and all, know of you and your true faith. Show to all the nations the purity of your confession. Stop the mouths of the calumniators who seek to suppress the loveliness of your pure faith, so that they might no longer be able to caw about you and about your faith, and so that those who, through their untrue allegation, submitted you to suspicion of impiety, might consider you God's faithful. For on account of this allegation about you to the entire world, all nations that boast of the name of Christ believe thus and not otherwise about you; thus and not otherwise do the Spanish, Italians, French, Navarrese, English, Norwegians, Danish, Irish, Scots, and all the principalities of the Roman Empire believe about you; even some of your fellow citizens—Poles and Lithuanians—believe thus about you. I beg you by the living God, my dear children, give way to reason and judge wisely.

What do their words tell you? It is in truth, so they say, a pitiful thing that the light of the Gospel has not yet illumined Rus' to this day. Have you not yet come to know the triune God, the unborn Father, the born Son, and the proceeding Holy Ghost? Have you not yet come to know God's only begotten Son (who descended from heaven for man and his salvation, and was made incarnate through the Holy Ghost and the Virgin Mary), the true and perfect God, and the true and perfect man, glorified in a twofold essence [istność] and one person? Have you not yet been baptized in the name of the Father, and the Son, and the Holy Ghost, for the remittance of sins? Have you not yet become partakers of the life-giving mysteries of the body and blood of the Son of God, poured out on the tree of the cross for the sins of the entire world?

Have you not yet believed in the one holy universal apostolic Church, in which, through the death of the Son of God, free remittance of sins is given, and the resurrection with eternal life, through the resurrection of Christ who lives for all time, is taught? Have you not come to know, I say, the salvatory heavenly doctrine, such that these ungodly messengers seek to darken your light of the Gospel truth with the wretched fogs of their vain talk?

I see in you, my sons, incompetence but not blasphemy. I see sloth, but I expect diligence. I see carelessness but expect effort. I see frigidity but not final despair. And therefore, I infer without a doubt that those rumormongers observed such accursed heresies and impious idolatries not in Vilnius, not in Lviv, not in Ostroh, nor in any orthodox and non-apostate Ruthenian church, but in the Crimea, Očakiv, or in Perekop,[242] that they accuse you without shame and without any fear of God. For what have simplicity and incompetence to do with impiety? What has an unjudicious and wanton life to do with the rectitude of faith? Let them recall that not long ago their priests of the Roman court walked in not many hundreds with your priests in all the same qualities of birth and morals. Let them remember that they too were foolish almost until today in a simplicity that was not of the spirit. Testimony to this is the debate of the Bishop of Salzburg and the Archbishop of Mainz, which arose over the formula of holy baptism on account of the simplicity and incompetence of a certain priest from Bavaria, who always performed holy baptism with these words: *in nomine Patria, et Filia, et Spiritus Sancta,* that is, "in the name, the fatherland, and the daughter, and the Holy Ghost."[243] There remain even today in certain parts a significant trace of such crude priestly incompetence. Witness to this account are the French, Italian, Spanish, Austrian, Bavarian, Styrian, and Croatian lands, where even now preaching is a mortal sin, and many not only do not understand what they read, but they barely even know how to read.

And look how quickly they have managed something better in your own homeland, how quickly crude drones have transformed themselves into hard-working spiders. Arise, then, from mortal sleep, my sons, I

242. [Cities in the Crimea. The point, I suppose, is that they are provincial, not centers of Orthodox learning or spirituality.]
243. *Aventinus* [Johannes Thurmair], *lib. 3 Annalium* [*Annales Boiorum,* Ingolstadt, 1554, bk. 3].

ask a second time, arise; and having looked with your internal eyes upon the proposed account, shake the dust of abuse from your raiment upon the heads of those who abused you with slander.[244] Close their lips with a proper response, so that they might no longer speak untruth about your unsuspect faith. Only move your lips and lift your tongue, and the very Spirit of your Father will guide them. For your part is only to wish to stand by God, and God's part will be to bring that which was begun according to His will to a successful result. And I, your afflicted mother, wishing this for myself and for you, again return in my accusation to the son who abandoned me.

[. . .][245]

Chapter 10

In Which Is a Catechism, That Is, a Summary, or a Short Collection of the Faith and the Ceremonies of the Holy Eastern Church

[†]I believe in One God the Father Almighty, Creator of heaven and earth, of all things visible and invisible. I also believe in the only begotten Son of God, Our Lord Jesus Christ, begotten from the Father before all time. I also believe in the life-giving Holy Spirit, who proceeds from the Father, and who rests essentially in the Son (as the Son in the Father, and the Father in the Son and in the Holy Spirit). I confess the unmixed unity in three persons and the indivisible Trinity in one essence of God the Father, God the Son, God the Holy Spirit, but one God and not three, the unbegotten Father, the begotten Son, and the proceeding Holy Spirit, the Father and the Son and the Holy Spirit, all together and each individually, one uncreated, one uncaused, one eternal, one almighty, one Lord, one Spirit, one holy, one inconceivable, one ineffable, one incomprehensible. All three of which have one essence, one divinity, one birth, one will, one rule, one power, one kingdom, one form, one praise, one honor, and one adoration. [I believe in] the Father [who

---

244. [Mt. 10:14; Mk. 6:11; Lk. 9:5.]
245. [Chapters 3 to 9 omitted; Smotryc'kyj 1610, 30r–208r/46–224.]
†   *De Symbolo fidei* [On the symbol of the faith].

is] from no one, both according to His essential and according to His personal being; in the Son and the Holy Spirit, [who are] also from no one with respect to the essence of being; but with respect to the manner of personal being, in the Son [who is] from the Father by birth and in the Holy Spirit [who is] by procession. In the Father, who has two sorts of internal properties: toward Himself, [and] toward the Son and the Holy Spirit. In the Son and the Holy Spirit, who each have one property, both of them toward the Father. In the Father toward Himself, in that He is without beginning, without cause, and unbegotten; and toward the Son and the Holy Spirit, in that He begets and releases them. In the Son toward the Father, in that He was begotten; and in the Holy Spirit toward that same Father, in that He proceeds. In the Son and the Holy Spirit, who have a *relationem* or a relationship toward the one and only Father, who Himself is the indivisible and unmediating, but special and closest, *causa* or cause or their personal being. And in each, having their relationship of one cause in equality with the other, divided from each other by their different manners as of being; and [divided] from the Father, in that I acknowledge the divine essence from Him incomprehensible and ineffable. And I declare it divided from the persons, as the common is divided from the proper. Thus do I believe concerning the one essence of the three persons, and confess concerning the three persons of the one unattainable divinity, and I seal it with the undoubting faith of my baptism.

†And concerning the mystery of the incarnation of the only-begotten Son of God, I believe thus and confess that the true, uni-essential and always-existing Son and Word of God, who was begotten before all time at the will of the Father for us people and for our salvation, descended, in time, from the heavens; [and] through the causing of the Holy Spirit, He took a body upon Himself from the immaculate and most pure Virgin Mary; being a perfect God, He became a perfect man, God from the essence of God the Father, man from the essence of Mary the human being, equal to the Father according to divinity, less than Him according to humanity; also equal to man according to humanity, and greater than him, for, together with God, He himself alone is without sin. Although He is God and man, nonetheless one Christ and not two; one, not through the changing of divinity into humanity or of humanity

---

†   *De incarnatione Christi* [On the incarnation of Christ].

into divinity, but through the receiving of man in God; one, not through the mixing or the fusion of nature, but through the unity of the person, for which unity of person the difference of nature does not perish in the least; rather it maintains the property of both natures composed in one person, not so that the one person of nature should divide into two, but so that, for the unity of the person, one and the same only-begotten Son of God might be confessed as God the Word and Our Lord Jesus Christ, who for the sins of man suffered death on the cross, died, and rose up from the dead on the third day, and after forty days ascended to heaven and sat at the right hand of God the Father. That is, He ascended higher than all the heavens and sat with the Father in divine majesty; that is, in the glory and reverence of God the Father, on the right hand, that is, in equal power and in equal praiseworthiness, on account of the God-Man person. Whom I expect to come at the common resurrection to judge the quick and the dead and to render unto each according to his merits, eternal life to the righteous in untold joys, and eternal death to the sinners in unbearable torments.

And I condemn and I curse those who are not ashamed to say that Christ the man is θεόφορος, *Deifer* [God-bearing], and not truly God, and that the Word of God the Father is God and Christ the Lord, who as if not by Himself, but with the help of the causing Word of God did everything he did, rendering the glory of the only-begotten to anyone else but Him.

Likewise [I condemn and curse] those who blaspheme that the received man is to be praised with God the Word, glorified with Him, called even God with Him, as if one with another, and not rather that Emmanuel, praised, glorified, and honored with one praise and with one reverence.

I curse those who do not confess that the only-begotten Son of God, who was crucified in the body, also suffered in the body, died in the body, and was buried in the body; and arose from the dead on the third day through the power of His divinity as God, and returned life to Himself as the Giver of Life.

I also curse the thrice-cursed heretics, Ebion, Cerinthus, Photinus, Arius, Servetus, and their present-day impious sectarians, the Anabaptists, who deny divine nature to Christ the Lord.

I curse Cerdo, Valentinus, Marcion, Mani, and all their followers, who do not acknowledge true human nature in Christ but ascribe to him a *phantasticum corpus* [imaginary body].

I curse [Paul] the Samosatene and Nestorius, disgusting heretics, who improperly rend the two natures personally united, and impiously make two persons in the one Christ.

With them Eutyches and the Monophysites, Monothelites, and others without number, whom our blessed fathers and the God-inspired bishops cursed at the fourth and fifth universal synods, having placed upon them an *anathemae edictum* [edict of anathema]. I end the genuine confession of my Orthodox faith about the mystery of the incarnation of the Son of God, and I urge you to continue to listen to me with the same diligence, for the mutual good, both yours and mine.

Mundi creatio et providentia.
[The Creation of the World and Providence.]

I believe that the world and everything in it is made, protected, and ruled by God.

Prudentia vel praecognitio.
[Providence or Foreknowledge.]

I declare that God's providence in the matters that depend only upon the will of God is constant and unchanging.

Contingentia.
[Contingency.]

I acknowledge that natural matters and the matters that depend upon human will occur by chance. But I reject and I curse the opinion and the teaching of those who introduce the *stoicam eventuum necessitatem* [stoic necessity of occurrences] and blasphemously assert that God is the cause of sin and of man's perdition.

Praedestinatio.
[Predestination.]

I pass judgment concerning predestination not according to human understanding, but, together with blessed Hilarius, according to Scripture given by God; having rendered to which one and the same good end (since it is general or universal), I call it the unaltered and eternal decree of God's will. By which God, on account of His great mercy, before the founding of the world, in His Son, who was to come to the world, elected for Himself to the eternal life of the heavenly kingdom all those who would believe in His Son who was to come, and who would remain in the recognized truth, so that they would be holy and immaculate before Him, praising and adoring His goodness and mercy that are beyond glorying, in this temporal life and in the coming eternal one. Which predestination by divine will I divide with blessed John of Damascus *in antecedentem et consequentem* [into antecedent and consequent], and the latter *in agentem et permittentem* [into causing and allowing], of which the first is about the good and the second is about bad people. And with the same Damascene I teach that the abandonment with which God abandons man is of two sorts, *eruditiva* [instructional], unto salvation, *et desperativa* [and despairing], unto eternal perdition, both of which remove one from the spirit of God, the first temporarily, that is, until repentance, whereas the second [does so] for all time.

Fides, Faith.

I teach that faith is a gift of God that seals the certainty of the Evangelical teaching together with all of the mercies of Christ the Lord, through undoubting trust in them, by constant hope in eternal life.

Charitas, Love.

From which good deeds come, as the good fruit from a good tree, which it rules, and arouses, and without which it is dead and useless.

Spes, Hope.

Commands that whosoever has this living faith be strengthened with the undoubting hope of eternal life.

Justificatio, Justification.

By which we obtain remission of sins and, reconciled with God, are found righteous before Him: I teach that it comes through faith in the Son of God.

Lex, Law.

Lex moralis [moral law]. I confess that it is eternal, standing in faith and love, given in the ten commandments by God to Moses; that through it no one was, is, or will be saved without faith in the Messiah who was to come.

I maintain the Mosaic laws or judicial rights in the courts of the common secular and spiritual law.

And I adhere to those same ceremonial laws as subject to mutability and time (through the transformation of the shadow into the very essence) in the Church order.

Evangelium.
[Gospel.]

I teach that the Gospel, that mystery hidden in God from before all time, is the good tiding of penance, remission of sins, and the inheritance of the heavenly kingdom, for those who wish to believe in the present Messiah, in which the free and certain promise of every good for every man, of both the temporal and eternal life, is told.

Peccatum.
[Sin.]

Together with John the Evangelist, I call sin a transgression that, according to Basil the Great, does not have its own essence, but attacks the blindness of the human soul, rules over the will, and causes death.

Peccatum originale.
[Original Sin.]

This sin is divided into the original sin that is innate in every human being, which sin is subject to the washing of holy baptism.

Peccatum actuale.
[Active Sin.]

And into *peccatum actuale* [active sin], separate for every human being, which I confess to be of two sorts: mortal, which repels grace and faith and the Holy Spirit; and venal, which does not lose any of that. I confess with Basil, however, that both are removed by the free mercy of Christ the Lord, in those who genuinely and truly repent.

Liberum arbitrium.
[Free Will.]

I declare, together with that same theologian, that free will is a cause of the external good deeds of human nature and common to all people, reborn and not reborn. And although I know that human nature is entirely free of internal good deeds, and although, together with the blessed Paul, I teach that it is the sort of cause that can neither begin nor end without the grace of the Holy Spirit, nonetheless, such that, according to Chrysostom, God, who causes, causes in those who will, and not in those who oppose.

Bona opera.
[Good Works.]

Together with blessed Augustine, I declare that the good deeds of the holy in this life are gifts of God and not the goodnesses of human nature, which of themselves are neither good nor worthy of eternal reward, but they are pleasant to God, and they await reward, on account of the faith that works in love. In this manner, however: that the Lord God crowns not some good of ours, but His own good in us; not our good deeds, but His gifts.

Gratia, Grace.

Which I declare to be, according to Basil the Great, God's grace to humankind, and I teach, together with St. Augustine, that it is given by God for the fulfillment of the law, for without it no one can be saved, since it is given not according to merits but as a gift, wherefore it is called grace. But to the extent that, although it is indeed grace, nonetheless God grants it, as Chrysostom says, not to those who do not wish it, but to those who wish and seek it.

Homo, Man.

Together with Moses I declare that, after the creation of the entire world and everything in it, man was created from the dust of the earth by God, animated through the divine spiration of a reasoning soul, and a companion or a helpmate was derived from a rib of his side. And together with blessed Chrysostom I teach that all the things in the world were created for him and that he himself was made for God; and I declare that the state of his life and that of his descendants is fourfold:

†before transgression, after transgression, after renewal, and after the coming general resurrection.

In the first state, then, was the perfect divine image in Adam of free and perfect understanding, by the powers of which, as a free-willed and free person, he could have chosen not to fall into transgression, if he had wished it so.

The second state, through which the aforementioned first state of free understanding was made subject, and free will made servile, so that already having lost freedom they became slaves. Although understanding in earthly matters remained judicious, and the will remained free, nonetheless in spiritual matters they were insipid and infirm, understanding blind and will perfidious.

The third struggles, possessed by the enslavement of the second, in which, through evangelical tidings, conversion is made available and is sealed through consecrations. But partially, renewed through the grace, understanding, and will of a kindly God, and battling with the body in the name of the fear of God and the love of one's neighbor (so that, like pieces of wood or stones, according to Chrysostom the Theologian, the slothful and indolent not receive salvation), they begin to have watchful zeal according to the grace granted to everyone.

The fourth state will be the perfect divine image of free reason, in which both reason and will shall receive such great perfection through the grace of Him who made them that they will no longer be able to succumb in any way to transgression.

Anima, Soul.

I declare that divine human souls, an inspired creation in the first man, Adam, are spiritual and immortal. And with blessed Gregory of Nyssa, I teach that seed, separated from the living body, entrusted to the workbench of life-giving generation and nature, is not soulless; which forces, conceived with the bodily organ in its first formation, with the progression of time, according to the *subjecti capacitatem* [capacity of the subject], both grow and are magnified. In it I understand the image and likeness of God, immortality, before the fall perfect in reason and will, now partially subject to renewal, and according to blessed

---

†   The Fourfold state of man.

Chrysostom, causing wholeness, and I expect it perfect in the coming age.

And with Bernard, I confess that there are three states in every soul. The first in the body, which is subject to decay, the second beyond the body, the third in the body revered. That is, the first at war, the second at peace, the third in perfect blessedness.

Ecclesia, Church.

I confess that the Church is the visible congregation of those who listen to the uncorrupted teaching of the Gospel and who truly partake of the mysteries of Christ, the cornerstone of the foundation of which I acknowledge to be Christ the Lord himself and alone, upon whom build the prophets, apostles, evangelists, doctors, and other men of the Church, and all the faithful, which, being one, holy, universal, apostolic, receives *indifferenter* [indiscriminately], as blessed Chrysostom says, the good and the bad.

Angeli et Daemones.
[Angels and Demons.]

I declare that angels, good and sentient spirits, were created, sent, and ordered by God for His glory unto the serving of people and for eternal delight. And I acknowledge that after his casting down, Lucifer (whom I call the angel of the abyss with his hordes) is kept in eternal torments with the impossibility of conversion.

Magistratus.
[Civil Office.]

I praise and receive the magistracy, or the authority in the temporal Christian republic, that behaves righteously according to the rights and decrees.

Crux piorum.
[The Cross of the Pious.]

I teach that we are to suffer and to bear humbly the cross in the Church of Christ that was placed upon us by God for our sins, which, in patience, through prayers, by the grace of the angered and once again appeased God, is removed from us. And I acknowledge that it is appropriate to the universal Church of Christ, so that through it God's chosen might be made known.

Antichristus.
[Antichrist.]

I make known, with the blessed apostle Paul, that before the glorious second coming of Christ, that chief Antichrist is to come, by Satan's cause, and settle in the Church of God.

Confidentia.
[Confidence.]

I declare with St. Augustine the confidence of blessedness: I do not say I am holy from myself alone, lest I be considered haughty; nor do I say I am not holy, lest I be counted in the number of the ungrateful; rather, so that I might maintain both humility and gratitude, I say boldly and in confidence to my God: I am holy, in that You have consecrated me, in that I have received and not that I have had, in that You gave to me and not that I merited.

Sacramenta.
[The Sacraments.]

The name of sacrament, which signifies many various things, is sometimes taken *latissime* [most broadly], concerning all matters, I say, of the incarnation of the Lord, up to the Ascension and the coming Judgment Day.

Sometimes *minus late* [less broadly], that is about the seven different accounts in Holy Scripture, with regard to which, with distinction, I also affirm that there are seven mysteries.

And sometimes *stricte* [narrowly], concerning the two mysteries given by Christ the Lord, having rendered to which the καταξίαν [esteem] and the name of holiness, I define them thus: the *sacramenta* [sacraments] of the holiness of the new covenant, established through Christ the Lord, composed of word and element, eternal, remaining not in voluntary will but in commanded use, common to all in general and to each of the faithful in particular, which, having joined to them the remission of sins and the promise of indubitable righteousness, renew those who use them with faith. I confess baptism and the Eucharist—

that is, the communion of the most holy body and the most precious blood of our Lord and Savior Jesus Christ.

Baptismus.
[Baptism.]

And so, through the mystery of holy baptism, by threefold immersion in water in the name of the Father and of the Son and of the Holy Spirit, we wash away original sin, and we become sons of God by His holy grace.

Eucharistia.
[Eucharist.]

And through worthy receiving of these most precious mysteries, that is of the body and the blood of the Son of God, commemorating the death of the Lord, we also declare our faith, sealing and confirming it in the free grace of the remission of sins, and seizing the impulse for a better and more holy life in this world, we gain the enlightenment of our souls and bodies and eternal union with God.

Paedobaptismus.
[Baptism of Children.]

I praise the baptism of children. I do not repeat holy baptism.

Communio sub utraque specie.
[Communion under Both Species.]

Together with blessed Pope Gelasius, I call it sacrilege to violate the final will and the eternal testament of our Lord Jesus Christ, which occurred in the rejection and the withdrawal of the chalice of the New Testament by the Roman Church. And I believe and confess that under the species of the bread the true life-giving body of Christ, which was received from the Virgin Mary and crucified, and under the species of the wine the true and life-giving blood of Christ, which flowed from His side on the Cross, are truly and essentially received. But as to how this is—I revere this as a mystery in faith, and I do not investigate in words the incomprehensible. He himself knows, that True Giver, with whom nothing is impossible, who said: *This is my body, and this is my blood*.[246] I do not ask whether we consume all of Christ the Lord, or which part of His body, but I simply believe that He is broken although indivisible, and is taken although unconsumed, and is drunk although inexhaustible, whose body I consume in faith with my mouth, and whose blood I drink not in natural and earthly fashion, but in supernatural and heavenly manner, truly, as I said, and essentially, and not figuratively nor in thought, and yet spiritually (that is, in a manner unfathomable and removed from all bodily reason); knowing that this is not a human matter, but of Him himself, who promised to live with us for ever, Christ the Lord.

Liturgia.
[Liturgy.]

I acknowledge that the liturgy, that is the divine service, in which the mystery of the Lord's Supper is celebrated, is a sacred matter, and I call it the bloodless sacrifice of prayers and offerings of thanks, in which *mystice* [mystically] the Lamb of God is sacrificed; and I praise and receive its pure, orderly, and pious celebration transmitted by the apostle James, the brother of the Lord in the body, the bishop of Jerusalem, by Basil the Great, and by John Chrysostom, and I say that it is urgently necessary that it be every day.

Poenitentia.
[Penance.]

I declare that penance is the unhypocritical conversion to God of him who repents, and I teach with blessed Chrysostom that it is true and beneficial at that time when he who repents has contrition in his heart, confession in his mouth, and humility in all deeds, that is, proper regret for sins in the heart, both conceived and sealed through faith in the remission of sins; accusation and imputation of oneself before God in one's mouth; renewal in deeds, which is new obedience to God, through which confessed penance, so that it might be shown manifestly before God and man, orders not only to cease doing evil (since this is not sufficient), but also to do good.

246. [Mt. 26:26–7; Mk. 14:22–4; Lk. 22:19–20; 1 Cor. 11:24–5.]

Contritio.
[Contrition.]

I teach that contrition is the unhypocritical heartfelt regret, for the punishment of sins, and the proper gnawing of conscience in the recognition of God's anger, which is mitigated and pacified by the grace of Christ the Lord through the remission of sins.

Confessio.
[Confession.]

I receive the confession of sins, both the confession that is everyday *immediate* [without mediation] to God Himself, as also that which, *mediante sacerdote* [through the mediation of the priest], is before the communion of the Lord's Supper to that same God Himself; and I teach that it is a holy matter and appropriate to penance, to which I also link the Church keys given to the office of priest by Christ the Lord (Who said: "Whatsoever thou shalt bind on earth shall be bound in heaven: and whatsoever thou shalt loose on earth shall be loosed in heaven");[247] and I praise *epitimiae* [acts of penance].

Jejunium vel abstinentia.
[Fasting or Abstinence.]

And, for the easier incentive to penance and the mortification of the body, I commend and praise fasting or abstinence from more exquisite food and drink, together with prayer and alms. And I especially command all to maintain properly the four general fasts by which every part of the year is crowned.

Ordo Sacer.
[Holy Order.]

I acknowledge that the priestly estate is honorable in every way, established for Church order in seven degrees. I esteem and honor priests, archpriests, and other clerics, chosen and sent according to Church decree; from the poorest priest up to the highest degree in the spiritual estate, I declare that the power of the priestly office of binding and loosing is equal. But that the power of blessing, or of laying on of

247. [Mt. 16:19.]

hands, is not equal, but different for the sake of Church order, that is, that some both give and receive blessing, whereas others receive but do not give.

Matrimonium.
[Marriage.]

I teach that marriage, both in secular as well as in spiritual people, is a good, honorable, and immaculate bed. However, I place virginity (according to the apostle Paul) above it, and I praise the pious living of monks in it. And I do not allow those who already once took an oath to serve God in the virgin state to pass over to the married state. In addition, for the authority of priestly dignity, I remove from priestly power and I count among the secular remarried widowers, whom I no longer find in Christian law, but whom I find as the husbands of a second wife, whom I call twice-married men.[248]

Chrysma, vel unctio.
[Chrism or Anointing.]

[†]I teach that the chrism, from which not only Christ is called Anointed with the oil of joy, anointed more than His partakers, but from which also we Christians are called anointed ones, is the holy incorporated anointing of the mystery of holy baptism, by which Christendom reborn is sealed in baptism through the Holy Spirit.

Communio seu obsignatio infantulorum.
[Communion or Sealing of Infants.]

I teach that the old communion of the body and the blood of the Son of God, of which immediately after holy baptism in perfect years the baptized were wont to become partakers, in the infants of today's times, on account of the inability of innate disposition, is the sealing of Christianity through the life-giving blood alone of the Son of God, poured out for our salvation and redemption, through the anointing of the lips of the baptized, as the anointing of oil is the seal of the holy baptism.

---

248. [See above, p. 58, n. 231.]
† The anointing during baptism with holy myrrh.

Unctio infirmorum.
[The Anointing of the Sick.]

I declare that the anointing of the sick with oil is a holy matter, with which the living and not the dead are anointed. And the prayer of faith, according to blessed James the Apostle, both heals the sick and remits his sins in the free grace of God.

Adoratio in Orientem.
[Worship toward the East.]

I command to bow down to Christ, to the East, toward the rising of the sun.

Crucis signum.
[The Sign of the Cross.]

I praise and receive, before the performance of every matter and labor and before prayers, the sealing of honorable foreheads with the sign of the cross for the eternal commemoration of Christ's passion on the cross, with the appropriate summoning of the name of God for help.

Ecclesia et Scriptura Sacra.
[Church and Holy Scripture.]

I believe in one holy universal apostolic Church, and in it in the God-given writings of the Old and New Testament and Covenant.

Sancti eorumque honoratio.
[The Saints and Their Revering.]

I also believe in the communion of saints, in this and in the coming age, whom I praise, glorify, and revere, as the representatives of the truth and those who constantly pray for their brethren, as the dear company of Christ, who gave up their souls for Him unto death.

I confess one baptism for the remission of sins.

I await the resurrection and the coming judgment.

I await also eternal life in glorious delights.

I say that the fire of Purgatory is a fable.

I also acknowledge eternal torments, prepared for the devil, in which unbelievers, and the impious, and perfidious Christians will, for eternal times, be oppressed, tormented, and tortured with those angels who did not maintain their estate.

Finally, I receive with humility all that, either for the good of the Church order or for the consolation of the faithful, was decreed and transmitted by our holy and God-thinking fathers, and especially at the seven universal synods gathered by the grace of the Holy Spirit. And I reject, condemn, and curse everything all together that was turned upside down and contaminated by the disorder and the sycophancy of the present times, or was invented for miserable this-worldly glory and hideous benefit, newly, unnecessarily and against the old apostolic and synodal decrees and canons, and partially received, partially approved by the present-day apostates.

Thus, then, and in no other way, do I believe with my heart unto righteousness and confess and teach with my mouth unto salvation.[249] In this and by this faith, teaching, and confession, from the beginning and until today, fortified by the mighty right hand of my immortal Head, constantly and unmoved by any storms of opposing winds,[250] I stood, stand, and will stand upon this cornerstone placed in Zion, upon my Savior, through His grace, help, and wondrous providence, until His glorious second coming upon the clouds of heaven, where I expect to attain the unwithering crown of life and the perfect inheritance of the eternally lasting goods and delights in that heavenly fatherland, by the ineffable grace and goodness of my Lord; and constantly consoling and strengthening myself with this hope, I humbly and patiently bear the cross of pain, oppressions, and persecution, to which I am constantly subject, always having in good memory these apostolic words: *The sufferings of the present time are not worthy to be compared with the glory which shall be revealed in us.*[251] *For we have died, and our life is hid with Christ the Lord. And when Christ, who is our life, shall appear, then will we also appear with him in glory.*[252] Unto Him be honor, glory, and benediction together with God the Father and with His Holy and Life-Giving Spirit, today, always, and for ever and ever. Amen.

249. [Rom. 10:10.]
250. [Cf. Mt. 7:25, 27.]
251. Rom. 8[:18].
252. Col. 3[:3–4].

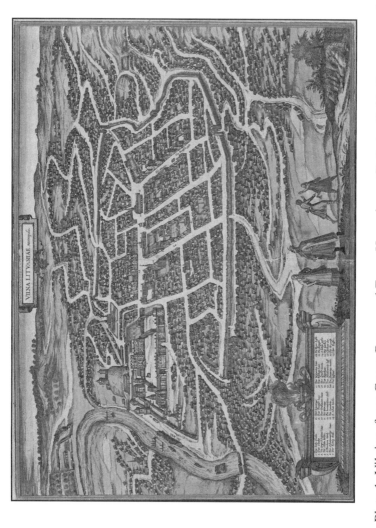

Plate 1. Vilnius, from Georg Braun and Franz Hogenberg, *Civitates Orbis Terrarum*, vol. 3 (Cologne, 1581), 59. Courtesy of Historic Cities Research Project, Hebrew University of Jerusalem, The Jewish National and University Library (historic-cities.huji.ac.il).

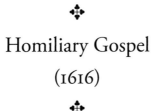

Homiliary Gospel
(1616)

Homiliary
Gospel,

or

Sermons for Every Sunday
and Holy Days

by

Our Holy Father Callistus,
the Constantinopolitan and Ecumenical Patriarch,
Written in Greek Two Hundred Years Ago,

and Now Newly

Translated from the Greek and the Slavonic Languages
into Ruthenian

at the Expense of His Gracious Lord, His Grace Prince
Bohdan Ohins'kyj, Chamberlain of Troki [Trakai], Thane of
Dorsuniszki [Darsuniškis] and Kormiałów [Karmėlava];
and of His Grace's spouse,
Her Grace, Lady Rajina Volovyčivna,

and Printed through the Labor and Effort
of the Monks of the Common Life of the Vilnius
Brotherhood Monastery of the Descent of the Holy Spirit.

In Jewie [Vievis],
the year 1616.

[. . .]¹

For
His Gracious Lord,
His Grace, Lord Bohdan
Prince Ohins'kyj of Kozielsk, Chamberlain
of Troki [Trakai], Thane of Dorsuniszki [Darsuniški] and
Kormiałów [Karmėlava], etc., Our Gracious Lord,
and
Her Gracious Lady, Her Grace,
Lady Bohdanova Ohins'ka, Chamberlainess
of Troki [Trakai], Lady Rajina Volovyčivna, etc., Our Gracious Lady,

May They Rejoice in the Lord.

OUR GRACIOUS AND MERCIFUL LORD and Gracious and Merciful
Lady! Through various and marvelous means, people of all
nations since the creation of the world, seeking the glory by
which they might live even after death in the memory of future people,
sought to establish it on the sort of foundation that would not suffer any
blemish either in this temporal age or in that to come. There were many
from among the pagans who, believing it more proper to become rich
in glory than in treasures, risked their belongings and all their temporal
wealth for glory. There were those who gave up health and life itself in
exchange for death, just so that their glory not die in the coming ages,
although they knew either nothing or very little (and that without any
benefit) about the eternal life prepared for man.

In the nations more illustrious than practically all the others, the
Greek and Roman, there were, among many who sought such glory,
the Lycurguses, Codruses, Themistocleses, Fabiuses, Deciuses, and
innumerable like them, who—though in various fashion—purchased
the supposed immortality of glory at the risk not only of wealth and
possessions, but also of health and life. There were in the foremost
nation of those times, the Jewish nation, Abraham, Lot, Joseph, Moses,

1.   [I have omitted the Ohins'kyj and Volovyč coats of arms and Smotryc'kyj's
verses on them; Smotryc'kyj 1616, 1r/23.]

Samuel, Elijah, Daniel, the three youths in Babylon, and the seven
brothers with their mother and teacher, the Maccabees, and many
others.

And in the New Grace there were by far more people, of both
sexes and every estate and stature, who, although not having—and
not wishing to have—any place to live here on earth, rather seeking
that higher and eternally lasting city in the future eternal life, or rather
the Master and Architect Himself, not only despised, but were even
disgusted by the earthly glory brought to them, albeit willingly, by
dwellers of the earth, and they fled from it. They did not place all their
effort and zeal upon what they were to be in the eyes of creation, but on
what they were in the eyes of the Creator Himself, gladly and zealously
seizing every reason and occasion (not only those brought to them from
somewhere, or offered by chance, but also those discovered through
great and long labor and effort) so that they might be able to serve and
please no one else but Him Himself as well as possible; and they also
paid dearly, that is through the risk of fortune, health, and temporal life
itself, through many trials, oppressions, and cruel tortures, that they
might earn true and unchanging glory from God Himself. And when
they had found it, then the one they had despised—the glory that comes
from people—also necessarily had to chase all the more quickly after
them, just as they fled from it, and had to follow constantly their brave
deeds and actions, worthy of undying praise and memory, as a shadow
after a body, such that they live in it and through it, both now with us
and with all the citizens of the entire world.

And their memory, which is carried forth from generation to
generation, will not allow them to experience any change in their
glory for all times, since it is founded upon the strong and eternally
immovable foundation that is the knowledge of the true God glorified
in the Trinity. For glory is the unerring and inseparable companion of
virtue. But virtue without God is not virtue; and without virtue, a man
is not a man, one of those ancient wise men says. As if he had said:
whoever delights in virtues, but does not know God, for him, virtue is
not virtue, since although it itself is eternal, it does not bring unto him
eternal reward, but barely a temporal one, and that only unto his shade.
For by not knowing the true God, after the virtues flee, the soul together
with the body receives eternal torment. And this is what the virtue of
pagan people brings with it, with which a man is barely a man, since he

does not come to the end for which he is created; rather he lives from glory only as long as this temporal age runs its course.

If anyone both knows God and delights in virtues, virtue—both with regard to itself and with regard to that man—is eternally glorious and life-giving, is virtue. It is the virtue of God-fearing people that causes a man to live eternally and adorns him with eternal glory, and with which a man is a man, since he comes to the goal of eternal life for which he is created. But whoever should both not know God and tread upon virtues, that man is not a man, but a beast. He is a monster, composed of a rational soul and irrational deeds, living unhappily, dying miserably, wretchedly subject for all times to cruel torments. Therefore that most excellent philosopher calls a malicious man the worst of animals, as if the cruelest of beasts. Therefore also Chrysostom the theologian calls man the worst evil, above all evils.

So, then, that the more excellent people of those pagan nations might avoid this profanity by which a man is deprived of being a man—not knowing God, but supposing that they knew him—they both themselves delighted in virtues, and they recommended them to other of their people, so that with regard to the supposed knowledge of God they might be able to live eternally, on account of the glory of virtues they had acquired; although with regard to God, whom they did not truly know, they lived only temporally through the life and the glory of virtues. Did it not rather befit those who knew God, and knew Him truly, and knew that He is the source of all virtues, avoiding that profanity, so that they might be able to arrive even with temporal glory at the goal at which they were to be adorned by the God whom they knew and by whom they were created—did it not rather befit them to allow themselves to be deprived of their goods and belongings, of their health and life, than, having been deprived of their virtues, to lose the God they had come to know? From whom, as the Father of lights, and the source of all goods and happiness, comes every good gift and every perfect gift from above.[2]

For whoever wishes to submit some act of bravery for glory in the coming ages ought to lay the sort of foundation for it upon which is founded first the glory of eternal life: the true (as I said) knowledge of the true God, so that both his deeds and he himself might be judged

2.   [Jas. 1:17.]

to be from God. Whatever is founded and built on such a foundation of virtue is not subject to even the most gusting winds, to even the most stormy tempests. And that is because that foundation does not suffer a building upon it of hay, stubble, wood,[3] and it does not mix with anything of mud, rather it receives and it fuses with the sort of material that is purified of the impurities of the earth by the heat of the sun, as are gold, silver, and precious stones; with these acts of gallantry, I say, virtue fuses into one material, which, poured into man by God, does not suffer the impurities of sin. For virtue does not suffer sin, nor does it mix with it. As then virtue is a foundation that is not subject to any blemish, so also the building that is fused into one with it cannot be subject to the least corruption, having been founded as deeply as is virtue in the foundation of its source, the Giver and Cause of all goods.

Having chosen to found the glory of their deeds of gallantry upon such a foundation of virtues, Your Graces' ancestors, worthy of undying memory, of both highly glorious families joined in one, live on, not dying after death, and will live the true life for all coming times. For if the most excellent men of the pagan nations, who had a supposed knowledge of God and only sought after the shadow of virtues, live for such a long age in the people's memory (although without any benefit for the soul), how much more generous is and will be the reward for those who, having followed the essence of virtues in the unerring knowledge of the true God, not only live gloriously in this temporal world in the people's memory, but also already triumph in that eternal one in the hope of the resurrection from the dead into the heavenly kingdom? To which the faith contained in the true knowledge of the true God gave them an unerring reason and showed them the sure road. For faith is the ornament of all virtues. Whoever glories in the true faith is truly glorious. And whatever anyone builds upon the foundation of faith will enjoy the benefits of his labor forever. For to know God is to believe in God, and, having become a son of God through the faith, to remain an heir to the eternal heavenly kingdom.

There is certainly no happier man under the heavens than that man who truly knows his Creator, and truly, through true faith, glorifies His highly honorable name. But that faith is recognized as not dead, but alive, by the deeds and actions that proceed from the unerring love for

3.   [Cf. 1 Cor. 3:12.]

God and for one's neighbor, as is a tree by its fruit.[4] For what is the benefit of believing in God in words, and opposing Him in deeds? What is the praise and honor in commanding that a naked and hungry brother be given to eat, drink, and warm himself, not having given in addition the necessities that pertain to that?[5]

Your Graces, Our Gracious Lords, well mindful of that warning of divine Writ, and having laid as your powerful and immovable ground and foundation the true knowledge of the true God and the constant and undoubting faith in Him and unto Him, which was left by your holy ancestors as a most precious jewel, seek to show yourselves not fruitless vines in His vineyard.[6] But in addition to your other pious and illustrious deeds and actions, of which the unwithering crown of eternal praise and memory is woven, you especially delight in the virtue that is called the queen of other virtues, that is, charity or alms.

And since that is twofold, that is, the one corporeal, and the other spiritual, the corporeal serves the corporeal and superficial needs (without which our nature and temporal life cannot survive), and the spiritual concerns the supply of spiritual things (which the soul and the superessential or supernatural life of our inner man requires). Of these, one surpasses the other, that is, the second surpasses the first in its weight and nobility as far as heaven surpasses the earth. Both of them, however—when they flow forth from that source from which they should do, that is, from the genuine and true love for God, and are directed to that goal and end to which they ought to be, that is, to the spreading and magnification of the honor and glory of His most holy and highly honorable name—acquire great and truly ineffable honor and weight.

Your Graces, Our Gracious Lord and Lady, do not lack in the least for the bounteous rendering of either of these alms. Since you graciously and generously provide God's servants (although little worthy) and the shepherds of His mysteries, who voluntarily choose poverty in the monastic estate (for the easier following in the footsteps of their Lord and Creator, who voluntarily became impoverished, and for the more capable serving of Him without hindrances), with this first alm; and

4.   [Mt. 7:17, 18; 12:33; Lk. 6:43–4.]
5.   [Prov. 25:21; Lk. 10:30–7.]
6.   [Jn. 15:1.]

through this provision for corporeal needs—in order to maintain the temporal life of those who serve people's spiritual benefit, and who strive to achieve the eternal good, and who arouse others to this—you give a spiritual alm to many.

And so that it not be afflicted with any limitation of place or time, you did not begrudge great cost or expense that the weekly (and nearly daily) ecumenical, that is, universal, preacher and teacher of the Church, who occupied the throne of the universal pastorship and patriarchate of Constantinople two hundred years ago, and watered the field of the Church with the streams of his golden-flowing words not only during his lifetime, but, never dying after his death, through leaving the teaching of his sermons in writing, first taught his Greek nation in the Greek language, and then, through the translation of his writings into the Slavonic language, almost as if having come alive for a second time unto our Slavic nation, and having come to these our lands (during the more learned age of our ancestors), was very necessary and beneficial; but now (through the ignorance and lack of knowledge of the Slavonic language on the part of many), having become for many not very necessary and beneficial, again through his translation into our vulgar Ruthenian language, as if resurrected from the dead, and through the edition in print being sent out unto all the broad lands of the glorious and ancient Ruthenian nation, might teach all, for all future ages, no matter how simple and incapable of understanding the Slavonic language, and who, consequently, were wont sometimes to have recourse to the infectious pastures of heretical teaching (which is offered in words and published in writing).

And therefore, if anyone in these days, on account of the inability of the listeners, was not beneficial to many when he used the more noble, the more beautiful, the more concise, the subtler, and richer Slavonic language, now, though he use the baser and more vulgar tongue, he can be necessary and beneficial to many, or rather even to all of the Ruthenian tongue, whatever their abilities; since this is the duty of every Christian preacher—not to compose discourses on the unintelligible secrets of the mysteries of the faith, but to teach simple and ignorant people God's will and commandments—the alert and wise preacher should seek not glory among his listeners on account of the quickness of his wit, but only the benefit of their salvation, and he should remember that saying of God's chosen vessel: that it is a more useful thing to speak five words in an intelligible tongue, than ten thousand in an unknown tongue (especially for the instruction of the people).[7]

For although even the most costly jewel, which has been buried in the ground, moves one to try to find it, nonetheless, through its secret hiddenness, it does not yield any benefit. This most costly and sure jewel, which had been buried through the secretiveness of the Slavonic language in the *Homiliary Gospel,* is now (through God's grace and help), unearthed through the intelligibility of the Ruthenian tongue and returned and submitted to its former benefit and use; and having appeared under the title of Your Graces' noble name, it will not cease to spread and declare the glory of Your Graces' most glorious house on all sides and for all times. And that it also have a nest in Your Graces' noble descendants, made of noble and pious deeds, and founded on the hard and immovable ground of the true faith in God the One in the Trinity and of the paternal piety, we do not cease constantly to beg the Giver and the Perfector of all goods in our unworthy prayers; and courteously wishing a long and fortunate reign in this world in good health and joyful and salvatory consolations from His generous mercy and holy blessing for Our Merciful Graces, Our Lord and Lady, we submit ourselves most urgently to Your Graces' grace.

> Your Graces', Our Merciful Lord's
> and Our Merciful Lady's,
> Constant servants and suppliants of God,
> The monks of the Common Life of the
> Monastery of the Church of the Holy and
> Life-Giving Spirit, of the Vilnius Church
> Brotherhood of Greek Orthodoxy.

7.   [1 Cor. 14:19.]

[From the end of a preface to the *Homiliary Gospel* dedicated to Prince Bohdan Solomerec'kyj.]

Although the breadth of the glory that the pure lineage and piety introduced and made to grow in the house of Your Princely Grace required further and broader words so that what can in no way be diminished not seem to be diminished by me, nonetheless since both these things are in themselves both glorious and illustrious, my intention too on this occasion is not to enumerate the gallant acts of glory, but to show gratitude for the acts of kindness I received from the house of the Solomerec'kyjs, and especially from the highborn and pious Lady, Her Lady, Eva Borkolabivna Korsakivna, the Lady Mother of Your Princely Grace, and from Your Princely Grace himself. For I find that I must ascribe all that I am capable in the way of reason (if I am at all capable)—after the grace of God and after the grace of Their Illustrious Graces, the Princes of Ostroh—to the grace and acts of kindness of the house of Your Princely Grace, at whose side the Lord God caused me to experience the charms of the liberal arts of local and foreign academies, according to my meager wit. Wherefore, together with the act of kindness I have received, it is not only the most proper, but even the most obligatory thing that I present myself, according to my ability, to the service of the praise of the name of the all-giving God, and to the glorifying of the important acts of kindness that Your Princely Grace has rendered me (which are never to experience old age, to say nothing of death). So that, therefore, Your Princely Grace's grace might be repaid in the coming ages with my gratitude, if not in equal weight of acts of kindness, then at least in equal measure of courtesy, I bring the *Homiliary Gospel,* or Sermons on the Gospels of Sundays and Holy Days, translated from the Slavonic language by my labor (through the grace and help of God) into the Ruthenian language as an ἀντιπελάργωσιν [a "return of benefits"] for Your Princely Grace, confident that both with respect to my entire courtesy and with respect to the importance of the matter and of the author, on account of the piety of the man and his life, and on account of the dignity of the office of the illustrious Callistus, patriarch of Constantinople, this my respectful offering, will be received by Your Princely Grace with a merciful eye.

Your Princely Grace's

Courteously well-wishing, subservient
      servant,
Maksentij Smotryc′kyj

Church Slavonic Grammar

(1618–1619)

A Collection of Rules

of Slavonic

Grammar

Sought and Obtained through the Effort of the
Most Sinful Monk Meletij Smotryc'kyj, Pilgrim in the
Monastery of the Church Brotherhood of Vilnius, at the
Bricked Church of the Descent of the

Most Holy and Life-Giving Spirit.

In the Year 1619 from the Incarnation of God's Word,

Lord Father Timothy, the Ecumenical Patriarch, Ruling
the Apostolic Throne of the Great Church of God of
Constantinople,

and Lord Father Leontij Karpovyč, Archimandrite,
Superior of the Vilnius Monastery.

In Vievis.

[. . .]¹

For the Teachers of the Schools

The Author W[ishes] S[piritual] S[alvation] and B[odily] H[ealth]²

I T WILL DEPEND ON YOUR dutiful zeal, diligent teachers, that the benefit of grammar, which, in the Greek and Latin languages, has been shown through experience itself to be clearly significant, be perceived in the Slavonic language as well and, in time, through a similar experience, be demonstrated clearly. For you who have studied the art of Greek or Latin grammar know what it brings to an understanding of the purity of the language, as well as of correct and fine speaking, writing, and understanding of written works according to the characteristics of the dialects. Every benefit that the grammars of the above-mentioned languages commonly bring, the Slavonic grammar is indubitably capable of bringing to its Slavonic language.

It will teach the recognition in expressions of the difference of the grammatical parts of the word. It will teach the declension of nouns and the conjugation of verbs, according to the property of the endings of the purely Slavonic language (a thing we have sorely lacked). It will teach the order and the succession of words: which are to be placed after which according to the syntax for the easier understanding of the sense that is found in them. It will indicate the incorrectly placed word; it will indicate the excessive; it will also indicate whatever is lacking.

1. [The coat of arms of Bohdan Ohins'kyj appears on the reverse side of the title page. It is accompanied by the letters B O P T at the corners (beginning in the upper left and proceeding clockwise). The letters are Latin (not Cyrillic), and they stand for the Polish phrase B[ohdan] O[giński], P[odkomorzy] T[rocki]—that is, B[ohdan] O[hins'kyj], C[hamberlain] of T[rakai]. It is worth noting that the title page, as well as the description of grammar itself is written in Slavonic, but the preface to the teachers is in Ruthenian.]

2. [In Ruthenian: Учителемъ школнꙑмъ Авторъ Д[ушꙑ] С[пасенъꙗ] и Т[ѣла] З[доровъꙗ] З[ꙑчитъ]. Nimčuk's hypothesis (1979, 27)—Учителемъ школнꙑмъ Авторъ Д[идаскаломъ] С[ловенскимъ] и Т[щателемъ] З[доровъꙗ] З[ꙑчитъ]—makes less sense, above all because it repeats the dative of the person to whom health is wished: why duplicate Учителемъ with Д[идаскаломъ]? Also cf. the similar formulae used above and below, pp. 4 and 104.]

It will teach, I say, both to read and to write in Slavonic distinctly and to understand easily what is read, when, in addition to it, through your dutiful diligence, Slavonic lessons will be read in the common manner of the schools and translated into the Ruthenian language, as for example from the Proverbs of Solomon, or from his Wisdom, or from that of Sirach, or something else translated from the Greek in the pure Slavonic language. In addition, the lexicon will be treated, arguments given, and the Slavonic dialect will be maintained in usual school conversation among the pupils under threat of punishment.

Through your diligent striving, in the hope of God's help, I promise, in short order, the elevation of the Slavonic language in our nation, its understanding, use, and benefit, through the neglect of which, inasmuch as it is native to our Church, our nation grew quite cold in piety. It will depend then, as I said, only on this, so that the children and youths entrusted to your supervision, care, and industry not lose in vain their years and time, neither of which can return, and for both of which you will have to give account on the day of Christ's terrible judgment.

Let the children beginning to study be given for study a primer, commonly called an Alphabet Book, drawn from this very grammar, so that they might become used to the grammatical inflections from their childhood years right along with speech. And after learning the Book of the Hours and the Psalter (which are not to be omitted), there follows this grammar, together with an explanation, that is, with the demonstration and the use of its benefits. And if someone should himself not have studied the art of grammar, he too must give it to the children and youths to study who already know how to read Slavonic; for once it is easily and quickly entrusted to memory, on the occasion of their passage to a more illustrious school, they will understand it, and they will come to a beneficial use of its art.

Whatever this grammar might be lacking is not so greatly essential to it: for example, the collection that you teachers have of anomalous nouns and verbs, which you will bring to the attention of the students. With which I am certain, through your dutiful effort, time itself (should the Lord God grant it to us in health) will quickly reward us, with the help of the same merciful God, without long difficulty.

Hail, beloved, and pray for the lover of labor.

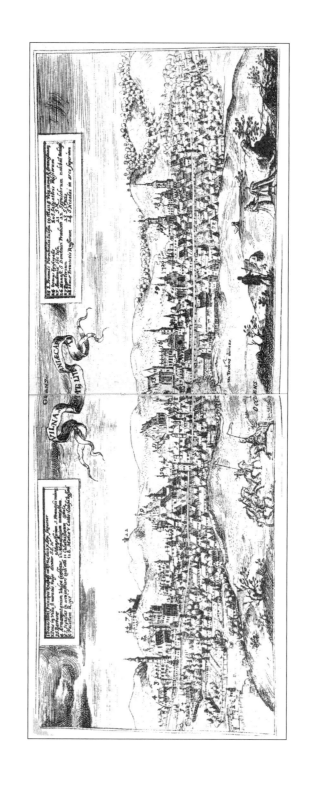

Plate 2. Vilnius, by Tomasz Makowski, *Panorama miasta Wilna*, 1600.

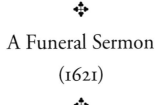

A Funeral Sermon

(1621)

Sermon

on the Illustrious Funeral of the Most Worthy
and Most Reverend Man, Lord,
and Father:

LEONTIJ

KARPOVYČ,

Nominated Bishop of Volodymer and Brest,

Archimandrite of Vilnius;

Delivered in Vilnius by

MELETIJ
SMOTRYC'KYJ,

Humble Archbishop of Polack,
Bishop of Vicebsk and Mscislaŭ,
Archimandrite Elect of Vilnius.

In the Year from the Incarnation of the Word of God
1620, November, the 2nd Day.

For the Most Noble and the Most Reverend
Lord and Father,

Lord Father Jov
Borec'kyj,

by the Grace of God Metropolitan
of Kyiv and Halyč
and of All Rus', Archimandrite
of the Monastery of the Holy Archangel Michael
in Kyiv, Beloved Fellow Servant and Brother
in Christ,

Meletij Smotryc'kyj
by the Grace of God, the Humble Archbishop
of Polack, Bishop of Vicebsk and Mscislaŭ,
Archimandrite of Vilnius,

Asks, desires, and wishes grace, peace, health, and all prosperity
in spiritual and bodily goods from God the Father and from our
Lord Jesus Christ, and from the Holy and vivifying Spirit, for
many years.

I T IS THE PROPER TIME, so it seems to me, for me to cry out in amazement, having come, through unfathomable divine judgments, with the blessed apostle of the pagans (in view of this not unpropitious occurrence, by the grace of God, which has arisen through God and through the reason arranged by God unto salvation in spiritual matters)[1] to that amazement: O the depth of the riches both of the wisdom and knowledge of God! How unsearchable are his judgments, and his ways past finding out.[2] For who hath known the mind of the Lord, or who was his counselor?[3] Who of us could descend, climb, or enter so far, so deep, so high in the thought, not to say in the deed or the counsel, to that which almighty Lord God, through the unsearchable counsel, judgment, and sentence of His eternal will over our thought, industry, and effort, in deed, in action, and in effect, ordered, caused, and effected that we and our entire pious nation, that is, our holy Ruthenian Church, might quickly, easily, and piously achieve, receive, and acquire?[4]

Who will tell Abraham that Sarah is giving a son to suck? That in her old age she gave birth to a son?[5] Who will make known, tell, and declare throughout all the Ruthenian lands, counties, and cities, that, in the face of degenerate stupidity, through these good tidings there will be born in me the bridegroom who has friends,[6] that somehow I, the barren Ruthenian Church, bear the loins of conception and a womb heavy with birth. The Lord has made me to laugh, so that all that hear of this will take pleasure with me from this.[7]

Elizabeth conceived and hid herself for five months, saying, "Thus hath the Lord dealt with me in the days wherein he looked on me, to take away my reproach among men."[8] Having come to conceive, by the grace of the Holy and vivifying Spirit, I hid: for thus did the Lord God see fit to deal with me in the days wherein he looked on me to take away

---

1. [Smotryc'kyj refers here to the recent consecration of a new Orthodox hierarchy by Patriarch Theophanes of Jersusalem.]
2. Rom. 11[:33].
3. 1 Cor. 2[:16].
4. Wis. 9[:13, 17]; Is. 40[:12–13].
5. Gen. 21.
6. [Jn. 3:29.]
7. Gen. 18[:1–15].
8. Lk. 1[:24–5].

my reproach among men. But when the time to give birth had already come, when I became fruitful through divine birth, according to the apostolic tidings of the annunciation,[9] I am glorified, I am praised, I am glad, and I take comfort. And my neighbors and kin, having heard that the Lord God worked His great mercy over me, rejoice, are glad, and take comfort together with me.[10]

This almighty Ruler of unsearchable judgments, who, not summoning anyone to His counsel,[11] does what He pleases in heaven and in earth, through the unsearchable counsel of His inconceivable will,[12] having seen fit that each one be a participant in our present joy not in the same way, but one nearer, the other farther: having, I say, established that some being closer to Him should enjoy greater joy, others being far from Him should have less, He deigned to leave us to the labor of that joy, but to transfer my Lord and Father, Your Reverence's fellow and brother, Father Leontij Karpovyč, archimandrite of Vilnius, to the pure delight of that joy, precisely at that time, wishing to have him nearer Himself and that joy, through death's passage from earth to heaven. For he, through the human counsel of our thoughts, which sees before it either nothing or little, was chosen by the first unanimous choice of all to be the first after that in which, by the grace of Christ the Lord, Your Reverence finds yourself.[13]

Since his dormition, which, sad for us as human beings, but comforting for us as Orthodox (for it is a great comfort for those who are afflicted to have a fellow, brother, father always present before the countenance of the King as a mediator in their needs), required of me among other things a final service, according to Christian custom, I presented myself to offer it, as I was both obliged, and, by the grace of Christ my Lord, as I was able. And inasmuch as the righteous is to remain in everlasting remembrance, according to the blessed David,[14]

9.   1 Cor. 4[:15].
10.   Lk. 1[:58].
11.   Rom. 11[:33–5].
12.   Ps. 134 [135:6]; Wis. 9[:13].
13.   [Smotryc´kyj refers here to the fact that Patriarch of Jerusalem Theophanes had consecrated Borec´kyj (the addressee of these words) metropolitan of Kyiv and Karpovyč (still among the living in October of 1620) bishop of Volodymer and Brest.]
14.   Ps. 111 [112:6].

therefore, considering it a holy thing that also the remembrance of this noble and righteous man might remain in everlasting remembrance according to the manner in which he caused it to be everlasting before God,[15] through His almighty help, I deemed it fitting that the words of his immortal virtue that were pronounced by me faithfully and righteously during his illustrious funeral—words that are wont to pass quickly into forgetfulness—be expressed in writing and submitted to the protection of Your Reverence as a man of all virtues and now, by the grace of the most Holy and vivifying Spirit, the eye, or that I speak more clearly, the head (to which belongs knowledge of its members, men of virtues and piety) of the body of the holy Ruthenian Church. And in addition to my fraternal obligations, I offer and surrender it with an everlasting remembrance by us of this transfigured holy man. That Your Reverence will deign to show it a happy and gracious face, through your innate inclination to virtues and through your entire fatherly love for us both, and that you will deign to accept it under your pastorly protection both he and I are certain.

Coeterum [further], I cordially ask God, from whom is every good gift, and every perfect gift,[16] that He might deign to grant to His holy Church that is in our Ruthenian land Your Reverence in good health for many years in peace, noble, hale, of many days, and directing well the word of Christ's truth, unto the thorough trodding underfoot and destruction of the apostasy, which is hateful to God and which rages in beastly fashion in it until today. For thus will the golden peace be restored to our Ruthenian nation and to the entire Crown and Lithuanian Commonwealth, when the apostate spirit, which hatches all the evil, is removed from it; for without any remembrance of the fear of God and of shame before man, from the cathedral pulpits it alleges and it declares us and all our Ruthenian nation (itself having been born from it) before the entire Commonwealth, our dear fatherland, to be godless, blasphemers, disobedient and ill-disposed toward the king, God's anointed, Our Merciful Lord, and traitors and Turkish spies. But he will never demonstrate even the least iota of this against our noble Ruthenian

15.   [Smotryc'kyj refers here to Karpovyč's abilities as an author of homilies, examples of which were printed in Vievis in 1615 under the title *Two Sermons (Kazan'e dvoe)*.]

16.   Jas. 1[:17].

nation, honorable in birth, Orthodox in faith, fervent in love for the fatherland, always submissive and honest in obedience and loyalty to Their Lords the Kings.

Alas, one unhappy person, together with six like him, brewed that drunken beer[17] for one year, and the entire Republic has been walking about drunk from it for twenty-six years now,[18] and will have to walk in this way until it pours this stinking yeast beyond its borders. Throughout all those years all the dietines were in commotion and turmoil, all the courts in confusion and uproar. Innocent people in court litigation, and subject to the burdens of penalties, banishments, imprisonments, murders; whence there were cries, complaints, enmities, pourings of blood, homicides, and other intolerable miseries in the fatherland. The Sejms are always belabored, the king our lord is often molested. And for whom? For seven apostates, who are so rich in followers that not one of them in his entire diocese will find as many followers of his apostasy as is their own number.

Here our city, the capital of your metropolitan diocese, and allegedly the richest in that deceit, does not have so many followers of genuine heart (with the exception of those, whom the town hall bench, which is rich in bread, maintains *actu* [in actuality] or *spe* [in expectation], as if in rent, and feeds those hungry ones with its little bits, *qui* [who] must, as they say, *alienas quadras sequi* [attend other people's tables]). And as is readily apparent, our apostates will not find for themselves, beyond this exception, in all the Ruthenian land, as many followers of their heart as the number of years this apostate evil has been brewing in them. And if the offices and bread should be taken away from them, even those few would immediately flee them. Elsewhere they strive to bring people to their deception even so, without offices and bread (for it is difficult to bestow these things upon all of Rus'), as today in Mahilëŭ and in Orša, in both of which excellent cities of my diocese of Polack, the Orthodox churches have already been sealed for two years, such that the miserable Christian people must live without Church services on Sundays and on the most important feast days, as on weekdays. Verily I say unto you, Reverend Father, that in this above-mentioned diocese

17. [*NKPP* 2:946–7, "Piwo," 24.]
18. [This is a reference to Ipatij Potij and the other Ruthenian hierarchs who agreed to the Union of Brest.]

that has been allotted, by God's will and through the choice of the Holy
Spirit, to my spiritual oversight and rule, and which is three palatinates
and five counties wide, there are not even seven (which I have already
discovered by the grace of God), who would follow the apostasy, with
the exception, as I said, of those desirous of the bench or hungry for
bread; and even those are with them only in body. All the others, by
the grace of God, are entirely piously submissive and obedient as sons
to their father and sheep to their shepherd. From all the greater and
from many of the lesser cities of this diocese they devoutly rendered
me their bow and obedience before they were summoned by me for
that, crying for joy and praising the Lord God that He deemed them
worthy to see raised up the hierarchy in the holy Ruthenian Church,
which had been oppressed by the apostates. Thus deign, Lord of Zion,
to bless it foremost. And so, may the God of peace and love be with
Your Reverence. From Vilnius. The Year of the Incarnation of the Lord
and Savior, 1621, the 17th day of the Month of February.

Plate 3. Woodcut of Vilnius by an unknown seventeenth-century artist.

A Verification of Innocence
(1621)

A Verification
of Innocence,

and a Christian
Removal

of the Erroneous Accounts Sown Throughout All of Lithuania
and Belorussia, Which Were Aimed at Causing the Demise of
the Life and Honor of the Noble Ruthenian Nation.
Submitted unto the Gracious, Lordly, and Paternal Defense
of the Highest and the First Authority, after the Lord God,
of This Worthy Nation, and the Safe Haven of All
Righteousness.

Lipsius.

*Nihil quidquam tam probe aut provide dici potest, quod non
vellicare malignitas possit.*

Nothing can be said so carefully and thoroughly that malice
could not pick at it.[1]

---

1.   [Lipsius 1589. The quotation appears in Lipsius 1610, 80.]

Levit. cap. 19[:13]
Non facies calumniam proximo tuo, nec vi opprimes eum.
Thou shalt not place calumny upon thy neighbor, nor shalt
thou oppress him forcefully.

Ibid. [:16]
Non eris criminator, nec susurro in populo.
Thou shalt not be an accuser nor a tale-bearer among the people.

Jer. cap. 22[:3]
Haec dicit Dominus: Facite judicium et justitiam, et liberate vi
oppressum de manu calumniatoris.
Thus saith the Lord: Execute ye judgment and righteousness,
and deliver those oppressed by force out of the hand of the
calumniator.

D. Chrysost. Hom. 43 in Matth.
[Chrysostom, Homily 43 (42) on Matthew][2]
Non injuriam pati, sed injuriam facere, malum est.
Not to suffer wrong, but to do wrong is the evil thing.

2.   *PG* 57:453; *NPNF1* 10:270.

Verification
of Innocence:
Published for the Second Time.

For Their Gracious Lords, Their Graces
Lord Janusz Skumin Tyszkiewicz,
Notary of the Grand Duchy of Lithuania, Starosta of Braslav,
Jurborz, and Novovola;

Lord Adam Chreptowicz;

Lord Mikołaj Tryzna,
Chamberlain of Slonim;

Lord Jerzy Mieleszko,
Standard-bearer of Slonim:

May they enjoy the grace of God, the salvation of their souls,
and the health of their bodies with all blessed prosperity from
the Lord God for many years to come.

H AVING HAD A PROPER CAUSE for a second edition of our
Verification, since several letters pertaining to it—about which
we had heard, but which, due to the great distance involved,
we were nonetheless unable to obtain—were sent to us only after its
first publication: to wit, a second letter of His Majesty the King, Our
Gracious Lord; also, a letter of the most reverend in God, father bishop
of Cracow, written to the holy father patriarch of Jerusalem; as well
as a letter from that holy man written to the Zaporozhian army of His
Majesty the King, all of which make our *Verification* clearer, since they
prove that that most worthy and holy man, the patriarch of Jerusalem,
and in addition to him other honorable persons, on account of whom
reflexive [by reflection] the entire noble Ruthenian nation innocently
bears and suffers a blot that strikes, stifles, and destroys simultaneously
its health and honor, as one could hear and as one can now discover
from the voices of the magistracy of Vilnius and from the pulpits of our
apostates, as well as from the protestations made in several castles—
inflicted especially by our neighbors and brethren, to whom one
fatherland, one and the same Ruthenian blood and Church gave birth to
many; through which proper cause, as we said, of the second edition of
our *Verification* it came to our attention that in the first edition published
during Your Graces' presence here in Vilnius, something was declared
as if in Your Graces' persons, that worked to Your Graces' dislike and
gave *ansam* [an opportunity] for further enmity toward us, your fellow
citizens, fellows in blood, and brothers, who were born in the Spirit,
along with Your Graces in one fatherland, from one blood, from one
mother, by one God the Father. To which we could not properly plead
guilty, since we had natural law and written law on our side, of which
the one forbids us to do to our neighbors what we would not wish done
by him and commands us to do unto others what we would wish them to
do unto us;[3] and the second allows one to pay back in the same measure
in which one is paid, an eye for an eye, a tooth for a tooth.[4] That is,
neither forbids us to render tit for tat, or to answer force with force.
Moreover, in answering the blows inflicted upon us, we were much
more modest, which we will show clearly in the proper places in our
Verification, which is somewhat expanded in this regard. But the Law

3.   Mt. 7[:1–5]; Tob. 4[:7]; Lk. 6[:31].
4.   Ex. 21[:24]; Mt. 5[:38]; Lev. 24[:19–22]; Dt. 19[:16–21].

of Grace, in which by God's mercy we now live, teaches us rather to suffer than to wrong, rather to bear than to inflict, rather to be wronged than to cause harm, so that we might love our enemies, do good to those who hate us, pray for our persecutors and calumniators, speak well to those who speak badly to us;[5] and if we should bring our gift to the altar and there remember that our brother has something against us, that we should leave our gift there before the altar and return and be reconciled first with our brother and then come to offer our gift.[6]

Taught by the Law of Grace (to which, although all are required to be subject equally, yet especially those *voto obstricti* [bound by vow]), we abandoned retributions and retaliations, trusting that as further blows will not be inflicted upon us by those who oppress us, so will the first ones be buried in oblivion. But in our retaliations and retributions, as we said, there is nothing of what was declared there, what the enemy strove to bring to our abomination, by which he sought to submit us to the dislike and enmity of many others, but especially of Your Graces, Our Gracious Lords. It is certainly characteristic of the base man to seek a flaw in a healthy eye, of yet a baser man to seek a spot on the clear sun, but of a most base man to seek a stain in pure honor. In what regard do the honor and the sublimity of Your Graces' noble birth—which have received the great rewards of the brave deeds of your ancestors and of Your Graces yourselves—yield to anyone? In what regard can the honor earned with praise through zealous chivalrous labor in the service of the Commonwealth, the honor of the great virtues and services of men who worked and work illustriously by the example of their noble ancestors for the glory of their worthy houses and for the good of the fatherland, throughout all those years spent in this service—in what regard can this honor be suspect to anyone? Our temperament, well disposed toward Your Graces, Our Gracious Lords, sees that invaluable jewel in Your Graces' worthy houses; and not only does it not envy or suppress it, but rather, to the contrary, it delights in it and adorns itself with it as if with its own. For as there is a natural access for the members of one body to delight mutually in its adornment, so also is it natural for those born of one most noble Ruthenian blood, for each one of them to delight in the most valuable jewels of the other. We thus

5.   Mt. 5[:38–48].
6.   Mt. 5[:23–4].

knew and know what we owed and what we owe before God and before
God's anointed, His Majesty the King, Our Gracious Lord, to the high
virtues of Your Graces, on the one hand, and to our monastic humility,
on the other, in our *Verification* of ourselves and of our entire nation, of
which Your Graces are an illustrious part.

Thus in our work (to which, in the image of the walls of the city
of God built by Nehemiah,[7] as if in some arduous and cruel siege, our
wounded heart gave birth in troubled loins) you will not find what
our enemy, in enmity toward us, alleges to great people, what would
blemish anyone's adornment, what would touch, as we said, anyone's
jewel purchased at great price. Rather you will find in it this alone:
what carefully guards all that, what does not allow all that to suffer any
injury, what urges one to maintain all that in its proper value and weight.
And in addition, you will find that at which the *immediatus* [immediate]
ancestor of the author of our present-day trials and tribulations[8] was
wont often to cry out aloud: "We led conscience astray, we lost faith;
what we set as a goal we did not achieve, what we had we lost." And
when he was once commanded to be content and to be satisfied with
the fact that he and others with him had learned good faith,[9] the event
itself testified what a cry, what a shriek, what a pulling of his hairs,
what words, what anathemas he then made, for soon the Vilnius
priests, together with their churches, witnesses to that strange tragedy
in him himself, abandoned him for the time being. In their hearing,
with an invocation of the name of God and with a declaration of his
conscience, he lamented his inconstancy in these words: "Did we ever
need to be taught the faith away from home, always having it pure and
immaculate through the gift of the Holy Spirit from our ancestors?
Did our Ruthenian Church ever seek from abroad any correction in its
Orthodox confession of the faith, which, by the grace of God, it had
never lacked at home, from eternal antiquity, in complete form and in
all ways perfect?" And even our apostates themselves are well aware of

7.   2 Es. 4 [1 Esdr. 4:47–61? Ez. 4; Neh. 2–6].
8.   [Here and elsewhere Smotryc'kyj appears—without naming names—to
ascribe second thoughts to Uniate Metropolitan Ipatij Potij. In any event, this
is how the Uniate side would interpret this passage. See *Sowita* 1621, 93.]
9.   [And had not been allowed, as Uniate bishops, to take up senatorial seats
next to their Roman Catholic counterparts.]

all this and of his further statements at that time, since they were well known and only barely, and with difficulty, to be quieted; nor can they hide them in good conscience, especially those who were present for all this and from whose fresh memory this could not have faded.

This then, Your Lord Graces, is what is found in our *Verification,* what even our apostates themselves feel biting at their consciences like a gnawing worm, what they see for themselves, and when the time comes, whether they like it or not, must acknowledge; but we, who do not imitate them in this fruitless labor, we are afflicted terribly and oppressed by them and persecuted in what we may call an un-Christian manner. We suffered at their hands various miseries and oppressions in various cities; much abjection and difficulty in many counties. There were law cases, there were banishments. Testimony that all of this was both against the law and holy justice, as well as against good conscience, is the very fact that the righteous judgment of His Majesty the King, Our Gracious Lord, voided and annihilated all their crooked court victories. Not satisfied with this, they now dared what would disturb the domestic peace in the Commonwealth and to cast even the final *infortunium* [misfortune] upon the fatherland. They attacked that for which an honorable man is supposed to die: they laid violent hands upon honor, which is supposed to be dearer to every man than health, and they did it so crudely and harmfully that, in the persons of several chosen individuals, they proceeded to deprive our entire Ruthenian nation at once of that invaluable jewel. For what sort of vulgar protestations were there, not only against entire cities of people of the burgher condition, but also against entire counties of people of the noble vocation, of highly illustrious houses?

In the not too distant times of our age, our holy and most worthy Vilnius Brotherhood, founded and protected for all future times by, we can say, the adamantine laws by His Majesty the King, Our Gracious Lord, who now rules fortunately over us, had among those who had inscribed themselves in it with heart and hand estates of all dignities— princes, palatines, castellans, *starostas*—and other superiors of the court dignities of His Majesty the King and of the land dignities, people of most worthy houses, as we said: Their Graces Lords Sapiha, Volovyč, Skumin, Tyškevyč, Xrebtovyč, Vojna, Tryzna, Meleško, Kmita, and many others; likewise the princely families, Vyšnevec'kyj, Košyrs'kyj, Ohins'kyj, Solomyrec'kyj, Sokolins'kyj, Hors'kyj, Polubens'kyj, Masal's'kyj, and others. It has even now countless numbers of those same most worthy houses and of many other houses and families, citizens of both the Crown and of the Grand Duchy of Lithuania.

Deign, Your Graces, Our Gracious Lords—nay even all the other most high houses inscribed in that holy and most worthy Brotherhood—to see what sort of protestations are made against you in the castles, how you and your honor have been assailed. And you will see how our *Verification* insults Your Graces; for it protects your honor and the honor of the entire Ruthenian nation, struggles for it, and calls upon you not to allow this evil to spread further, that the evil might perish miserably at the spot where it burst into flames. It is a fortunate evil that, noticed early, can be opposed in time.

Thus, opposing this evil and protecting the irreproachable glory of our nation and the glory of Your Graces and of other worthy families and verifying the innocence of persons who were erroneously and anonymously charged before His Royal Majesty, Our Gracious Lord, we published our *Verification* to the world; and now for the above-mentioned proper reason, we publish it a second time, having removed in this for the sake of the Law of Grace what would disgust one's neighbor and what would offend a brother. We believe that Your Graces, Our Gracious Lords, admonished by the importance of the matter and *aequissimis rationibus* [by most just reasons], will deign to turn to us your love instead of the dislike that our opponents seek to cause toward us in Your Graces. *Amantium enim iras, amoris esse redintegrationem* [for hatreds of lovers are the renewal of love], someone said.[10]

Nor is it a secret to anyone that *Qui nec defendit nec obsistit injuriae, si potest, tam est in vitio, quam si parentes, aut amicos, aut patriam deserat:* Whoever is able to oppose lawlessness and wrong, and does not do so, is as guilty as if he had abandoned his parents, or friends, or fatherland in time of need.[11] Thus we had to do this. We also believe this to be well known, that *Nemo malus est, qui peccaverit invitus:* if anyone transgresses in any matter, but under constraint, he is not judged an evil man.[12] *Saepe enim laesa Patientia fit furor* [for when

---

10.   *Terentius.* [Terence *Andria*, 555; cf. Erasmus *Ad.* 3.1.89.]
11.   *Cicer. lib. officior.* [Cicero, *De Officiis (On Duties),* 1.7.23].
12.   *Sophocles.* [The exact source of Smotryc′kyj's reference remains unclear.]

patience is mistreated again and again, it turns into rage].[13] We suffered and we suffer: so grant us, Lord Christ, strength in further suffering, for now the current trials are almost beyond our strength. For in an aching body, every injury is painful—even the smallest one, to say nothing of such a ferocious one.

We believe, then, that Your Graces, Our Gracious Lords will deign to preside over these certain just matters and will wish to turn a kind face toward us, who pray to God for you, and a happy eye toward our *Verification,* which we urgently beg of you. Your Graces will find in us open hearts toward yourselves, pure love, humble submission, and well-disposed friendship. And in our *Verification,* Your Graces, Our Gracious Lords will find that which in our good is concealed against the evil.

What voices do we always hear? "God forbid that, by reason of apostasy, the faith, the *ritus* [rite], and the morals of the Holy Eastern Church should ever come to their demise." But "God forbid" is said at that very time when that demise is occurring; and when this is said, that demise is already occurring. If only those would be willing to see, who, in our nation, are supposed to see. The wolf lies down before the lamb,[14] but in order to eat it. Certainly what they do to us today they would not have done for too long to themselves, if it had been as it was for all those years. Who of healthy sight does not see this childish confusion? Turn where you will: on all sides you find horrid pyres, on all sides shameful slaps in the face, on all sides a harmful demise. For it has almost come to the state where, as is commonly said, what's yours is mine, and what's mine is none of your business; where soon it would be said, what's yours is also none of your business.[15] This is happening *in meditullio* [in the middle] now of almost every Ruthenian land. But those who are allegedly ours, who were supposed to be watchful, sleep absolutely soundly. Everywhere our internal and external good is already, to a large extent, no longer ours. They see (if they are able to see)—those who worked for this dishonor at home—what sort of respect they have gained abroad. It has happened to many of them and rather frequently (just let them take stock among themselves) to stand

13. *Labetus.* [The exact source of Smotryćkyj's reference remains unclear.]
14. [Is. 11:6; 65:25.]
15. [Cf. *NKPP* 3:554, "Twoje," 1.]

before the door, and in shame at that, where and when even the lowest clerk ought not to stand; and sometimes even to be dismissed with "His Grace is busy," or "the Master is not at home." We do not mention other disgraces, taunts, nay even insults.

For the metropolitan of such a large, densely populated, and innumerable Christian people, of Volhynians, Podgorians, Podlasians, Polesians, Podolians, Nizovians, Ukrainians, Lithuanians, Rus' White and Black, from the Beskid Tatras to the Baltic Sea, in the east and the south, in the Crown and in the Grand Duchy of Lithuania, of the widely spreading Christian Ruthenian peoples, in sixteen populous episcopal dioceses, who has six bishops, and the seventh an archbishop, under the power of his jurisdiction—for him to stand at the private consultations behind the backs of the bishops who are under one and the same pastor; for him in the performance of ecclesiastical affairs and in episcopal inaugurations to suffer wrong from them; for him in many cases to yield all authority of the metropolitan dignity even to a chorepiscopus, where he ought not to have yielded even to a bishop himself: Is this not disgrace? Is this not shame? Is this not insult?

At some point during the improper suffering of these slights, when the current metropolitan[16] was asked about the reason for this (he can remember by whom and when), when he heard the claimed senatorial dignity decisively rejected in the performance of private consultations and Church matters (where it is not the senator, but the bishop, who has authority), he answered *simpliciter* [simply]: "Speak against this if you will; we can no longer avoid this." There you see, worthy Ruthenian nation, the honor you have from the Union and the elevation of your clergy. Let them consider whether they did not also introduce that unwonted burden upon their liberty, which, as one hears, never was before: that they allowed the Church benefits that were to come to them from the Church brotherhoods to be encumbered contrary to custom. For wherever you turn, you see that their unwise apostasy brings demise to our holy faith, damage to our laws, harm to our freedoms, dishonor to our dignities, shame to our entire nation, and destruction to our Ruthenian Church. Where finally are their senatorial seats? Who grew in stature, even among those, who, in our opinion, were supposed

16.   [Josyf Veljamin Ruts'kyj was Uniate metropolitan of Kyiv in the years 1613–1637.]

to do so? Both were thus (as we see) directed to be content with the fact that they have been taught good faith.

Already now in our days, and during the fortunate reign of His Majesty the King, Our Gracious Lord, we saw with our own eyes senators of the ancient religion of the Eastern obedience at the side of His Majesty the King: Their Graces, Lord Kostjantyn, prince of Ostroh, palatine of Kyiv; Lord Aleksander, prince of Ostroh, palatine of Volhynia; Lord Bogdan Sapieha, palatine of Minsk; Lord Fedor Skumin, palatine of Naŭharadok, the father of blessed memory of Your Grace, Our Gracious Lord *Starosta;* Lord Martyn Tyškevyč, palatine of Brest; Lord Fylon Kmita, palatine of Smolensk; Lord Symeon Vojna, castellan of Brest; Prince Ivan Solomerecʹkyj, castellan of Mscislaŭ; Lord Petro Haraburda, castellan of Minsk; not to mention many others who lived at that time and shortly before them: Lord Vasyl Tyškevyč, palatine of Podlasie; Lord Ivan Sapiha, palatine of Vicebsk; Lord Symeon, prince of Pronsk, palatine of Kyiv; Lord Hleb Vjaževyč, palatine of Smolensk; Lord Ivan, prince of Dubrovyč, palatine of Kyiv; and especially those three most bold Ruthenian Hercules, Hannibals, and Scipios, the Highest Hetmans of the Grand Duchy of Lithuania, men of holy memory and of a bravery difficult to praise sufficiently: Prince Roman Sanhuško, palatine of Braclav, field hetman of the Grand Duchy of Lithuania; Lord Hryhorij Oleksandrovyč Xodkevyč, castellan of Vilnius; and shortly before him, Lord Kostjantyn, prince of Ostroh, palatine of Trakai, who, being confessors of the ancient Greek religion under the obedience of the holy see of Constantinople, were adorned with such highly illustrious senatorial dignities and bore in their trust the invaluable jewel of the fatherland—the mace. For in our fatherland in these three worthy nations—the Polish, Lithuanian, and Ruthenian—lordly honor was not customarily consequent to faith but to bravery. By changing faith no one of our Ruthenian nation ever purchased it. As long as our spiritual authorities remained under the obedience of their natural pastor, then also their followers themselves were held in greater value and consequence at home and abroad; then also was the access for all estates of our faith freer to every sort of ornament in the fatherland.

To what end, Your Gracious Lords, did we mention this? The reason is obvious: so that what was broken might be repaired; so that, we say, the false oath might return whence it mendaciously came forth against divine and human law, with offense to conscience, with the constant troubling of the fatherland, with the rending of one Church, with the variation of one faith, with the mutual quarreling of the brethren of one and the same nation. For which they have a proper time, not troubling further either themselves or the entire fatherland and not engendering a greater disorder for our Ruthenian Church, which finds itself in a lack of learning and in crude simplicity. And they have the years and reason to know what they ought to do. We say from the excess of our heart what we desire with all our heart: Grant, O God, that we see them in their proper home, their proper home in which their own Father lives. How can it not be with joy, since some of us are their brothers, others their sons? And it is well that it occur now, at the time when we gladly await them with a loving heart with outstretched arms. Which grant, O holy Lord, as quickly as possible. Meanwhile, may the God of peace and love remain with Your Graces, Our Gracious Lords, to whose kind mercy we urgently commend ourselves.

> The Servants of Your Graces, Our Gracious
>   Lords,
> Who wish you every good thing
>   and constantly pray to God for you:
> The monks of the Vilnius Brotherhood
>   Monastery of the Church of the Descent
>   of the Holy Spirit.

Kind and Gracious Reader:

Calumny, which is a false and anonymous allegation made out of hatred, has the property that it causes a diminishment in the honor of a good and in no wise suspect man, and, having presented falsehood as truth to people, it assures them that this and nothing else is the case about the calumniated person (not giving him the necessary place and time to demonstrate his innocence). It is also part of its nature that it is wont to trouble even the wisest and most innocent man; wherefore, even if it were the most hypocritical, it should not be taken lightly, since there is nothing that is more poisonous, nothing that abuses, disgraces, and stains a person's honor more than it does and arouses greater hatred among people toward a man who is in no wise guilty.[17] One who is struck by a stone, says St. Athanasius, seeks a doctor; but calumny inflicts worse wounds than stones.[18] For calumny is an incurable blow inflicted by an arrow, as it were. But truth itself can put a stop to all that and heal those wounds. The longer it is ignored, however, the more those wounds spread, and the more painful they become. For calumniators, who know how to make allegations and spread calumny, exalt it above all truth; and in despite of God, who permits the existence of the father of lying, a murderer from the beginning, whose name is the Devil[19] (that is, Calumniator), they allow themselves purposefully to run rampant against innocence. Wherefore, on account of the obligation to watch over oneself, everyone who has been calumniated—even, as we said, in a most hypocritical manner—is obliged to take care for his innocence, so that when his innocence is placed before everyone's eyes, and when it has drawn over to its side the opinion of at least the wise people, it might be able to repulse the evil asserted by them. For it has often occurred that he who has the truth on his side and remains silent loses; while he who speaks much, even if it is a manifest falsehood, wins.

And we had intended to ignore this matter as manifestly false, not wishing to publish it from our side, since already during the Moscow expedition we met the same false allegations from those people who take heed of nothing good, and since we passed over it in silence, it disappeared as if it had never existed.[20] For we know well that the evil thing is not to suffer calumny but, according to St. John Chrysostom, to work calumny and not know how to suffer it.[21] For just as, if someone were to call a poor man rich and were to praise him because of it, that

17. Eccl. 4.
18. *Apologia I* [*Defense before Emperor Constantius,* I, 12; *PG* 25:609C–610C; *NPNF2* 4:242].
19. Jn. 8[:44].
20. [Perhaps a reference to the campaign of 1610, during which Smotryc'kyj's *Thrēnos* appeared. See above, p. xx. A more recent campaign occurred in 1618.]
21. *Homil 43 in Matth.* [St. John Chrysostom, *Homily 43 (42) on Mt.; PG* 57:453; *NPNF1* 10:270]. *Homi. 12 in Ioann.* [St. John Chrysostom, *Homily 12 on Jn.*].

praise does not belong to him in the least and only causes laughter, so also when someone is erroneously calumniated, he ought not to think that the calumny belongs to him.

But since that evil has already been spread so exceedingly widely and has been raised so very highly upon our entire noble Ruthenian nation, especially here in Vilnius, where the town hall authorities and the apostates, from their positions and their cathedras, are already forbidding people to associate, do business, and speak with Rus' of the ancient religion; and with every third word they abuse us and dishonor us as traitors to the fatherland and as Turkish spies; and already, without any *delator* (since every calumny must necessarily have these three: *delatorem, delatum, et auditorem* [accuser, accused, and auditor], that is, calumniator, calumniated, and the one who hears it), without any legal defense and without any proof, through a harsh, sudden, and unheard-of inquisition of a dozen or so honest citizens of Vilnius of that identical ancient religion, people never and in no way suspect have been locked up, some in the town hall, others cast into the cruel, dark, underground prison under the town hall. They have suspended from the bench the gentlemen of the town hall council, and others they have forbidden to leave the town hall. They have taken away from artisans the keys to their privileges and treasuries; and they have tortured by drawing on the wheel those who did not wish to give them up, and they have excluded them as traitors from the meetings of their guilds. So since, we say, that evil had already arisen and become aggravated so excessively, it did not seem proper to us to ignore it in silence (not opposing it with our speech, as Basil the Great says, so that we might wish to take revenge on the calumniator, but so that, to the extent of our abilities, we not permit a lie erroneously imposed on innocent people to spread);[22] and so that we save from loss of their souls those who believed this lie that has been alleged against us (for with one and the same action a calumniator harms three types of persons: he wrongs the calumniated, deceives the hearers, and offends his own conscience),[23] it seemed necessary to us to submit briefly to the attention of each citizen of the domains of His Majesty the King, Our Merciful Lord, what follows.

22. *Epist. 65* [actually, Letter 63, new numbering 207; *PG* 32:759–60; *NPNF2* 8:246].
23. Eccl. 4.

Having forgotten the fear of God, which says *Non facies calumniam proximo tuo, nec vi opprimes eum,* "Thou shalt not place calumny upon thy neighbor, nor shalt thou oppress him forcefully,"[24] someone (we call him "someone," since he is concealing himself), against good conscience, with the most frivolous of intentions, unto the confounding of internal peace in the Commonwealth, during the military expedition against the Christian enemy, the pagan Turkish emperor, was not ashamed, nor did he fear to report and allege to His Majesty the King, Our Gracious Lord, to whose honorable ears, says the wise man, nothing false is to be reported,[25] around the seventh day of February in the present year 1621 (for thus does His Majesty the King, on account of this fallacious and anonymous allegation, deign to write under the date of the year, month, and day we have mentioned, in his private letters to certain offices and persons: "It has come to our knowledge") that the most blessed father, Patriarch of Jerusalem, who was in the domains of His Royal Majesty throughout almost the entire preceding year of 1620 and remained in them and then departed from them, with the knowledge of His Royal Majesty, was an impostor, sent as a spy to the domains of His Royal Majesty by the Turkish emperor, and that Borec'kyj and Smotryc'kyj, having entered into an agreement with the Turkish emperor through that Impostor-Patriarch of Jerusalem, under the pretext of religion and piety, caused and spread harmful rebellions and disagreements among the people. On account of which fallacious allegation to His Royal Majesty, putting a timely end to this evil, as one is wont to do in such sudden enthusiasms, by virtue of his royal authority and obligation, His Royal Majesty wishes and orders that the offices to whom His Royal Majesty had written, knowing about such traitors and rebels sent on behalf of the Turkish impostor, capture them as traitors and send them to the castle and Magdeburg offices of the cities of the domains of His Majesty the King. But here you have a fallacious allegation, erroneous and false calumny against innocent people.

Against this, Kind and Gracious Reader, concerning all three persons portrayed unjustly and improperly to His Majesty the King, Our

24. Lev. 29 [actually, 19:13]; Ez. 18[:7]; Lk. 3[:14]; 1 Cor. 9; Zech. 7[:10]; Prov. 24 [actually, 22:22].
25. [Sir. 51:6.]

Gracious Lord, as impostors, spies, and traitors, we bring the following to your attention briefly and truly: that, having received word of the arrival in the domains of His Majesty the King of a certain cleric by the name of Theophanes, who was declared the patriarch of Jerusalem, the gentry, nobility, and citizens of the Polish Crown and of the Grand Duchy of Lithuania and Rus', of both the clerical and the lay estates of the ancient Greek religion, who remain constantly and faithfully under the blessing of the Most Holy Father, the patriarch of Constantinople, and amazed at the announcement of such unheard-of fame in our lands, at the arrival of such a distant and illustrious guest, dear and pleasing to all Christendom on account of those holy places where our salvation took place, and of which, by the grace of God, he is the guardian and Christian authority and in whose hands the life-giving grave of Jesus Christ our Lord and God works miracles every year to the consolation of all Christendom and to the amazement of the local pagans through the fire that descends from Heaven every Easter Sunday, and especially to us on account of our unanimity in faith, although we could not hold him, as a patriarch who draws his title from such an illustrious holy apostolic see, in suspicion of anything evil, nonetheless, on account of the accusation made during the enmity and military expedition with the Islamic emperor, we had decided among ourselves not to see him or to write to him until we were informed who he was from that source whence recognition is wont to come in our fatherland about such individuals arriving from foreign lands to the domains of the Crown and the Grand Duchy of Lithuania. And this is how it happened: beginning about Mid-Lent Sunday of the preceding year, 1620, at which time that man arrived in the domains of His Royal Majesty, almost up to the feast of the Dormition of the Most Holy Virgin in that same year,[26] we adhered to the decision we had made.

For just before this time, first of all, two letters were written by His Excellency, Stanisław Żółkiewski, crown chancellor and hetman of

26.   [Orthodox Mid-Lent Sunday—the fourth Sunday in Lent—came in 1620 on 26 March according to the old calendar, or 5 April *stylo novo*. The Feast of the Dormition of the Most Holy Virgin is celebrated on 15 August. As Smotryc'kyj was thinking in terms of the old calendar here, the date would have been 25 August 1620 according to the new calendar.]

blessed memory,[27] concerning the man who was declared the patriarch of Jerusalem: one to all the citizens of the Ukraine in general, a second to the *wójt,* mayors, and councilors of the city of Kyiv, in both of which letters, when he mentions the arrival of the man in question in the domains of His Royal Majesty, he calls him the patriarch of Jerusalem, a great man, a noble guest, honorable, free, and worthy of safe passage through the domains of His Royal Majesty. And shortly thereafter two letters were written by His Majesty the King himself, Our Gracious Lord: one private, to the identical above-mentioned man; and a second, universal, to all the citizens of the Volhynian palatinate and of the Ukraine, in both of which letters His Majesty the King deigns with honorable respect, worthy of both persons, to call the above-mentioned man "blessed father in Christ," "piously dear," "patriarch of Jerusalem and all Palestine," to invite him to appear at the court of His Majesty (if that should seem to him a proper thing), and to order the dignitaries, officials, *starosta*s, and all the citizens in general of all the above-mentioned palatinates to conduct that man, as a worthy and unsuspect person, in the appropriate respect, safely and without any molestation, through the domains of His Royal Majesty, requesting this of them by his grace. In addition to these letters from His Royal Majesty and from the hetman, there went out letters to that man, written honorably with great respect by other worthy people: by the blessed in God, His Grace the bishop of Luc'k; the Underchancellor, at that time the Crown Chancellor, Andrzej Lipski; and by His Grace, Prince Krzysztof Zbaraski, crown equerry, *starosta* of Pinsk.

And so, we say, having thus received certain knowledge from all these letters that His Majesty the King and Their Graces, the above-mentioned lord senators, call this man noble, honorable, unsuspect, worthy of every respect and honor, and at the same time they also give him the title "blessed and devoutly dear father in Christ," and, "by the grace of God, Most Reverend Patriarch of Jerusalem," we found reason to write to him, as the patriarch of Jerusalem, to send, and to travel to him, as a noble man who had arrived to visit us from the holy land of Jerusalem, from the grave of God, and as the guardian of the holy places, an Orthodox teacher, the brother in spirit, fellow pastor, and

27.   [He led the Polish-Lithuanian forces in the defeat in the First Turkish War at Țuțora on 6–7 October 1620, where he also lost his life.]

fellow patriarch of our most holy patriarch of Constantinople, since the doors to him were opened for us by the letters of His Royal Majesty and Their Graces the lord senators. And for that reason many of us felt free to travel to him personally, and many called on him, through our letters and emissaries, as a noble and honorable man and the patriarch of Jerusalem. And when we saw in person from his letters of testimony, or when, from afar, we had received sure information that he was who he was declared to be by many and what he was titled by His Royal Majesty, and Their Graces, lord senators, and that he was the true patriarch of Jerusalem, we also recognized him as such, and as a pastor of our faith, a successor to the blessed James, brother of the Lord in the body, the first archpriest consecrated by Christ the Lord Himself to the bishopric of Jerusalem;[28] we rendered him our spiritual greeting; and we asked him for his paternal and pastorly blessing, which we received from the power given him by the Holy Spirit and from the personal grace that was upon him from the life-giving grave of Christ the Lord, through the many letters of blessing he wrote to many persons, brotherhoods, and cities among us.

And since just at that time we also received sure knowledge that an honorable letter from the most holy father Timothy, our patriarch of Constantinople, with the signature (in addition to his own hand) of some fifteen metropolitans, had been given to him for the complete oversight and rule in his dioceses over all spiritual matters and insufficiencies that should happen to present themselves on his trip; and since, in addition to this worthy patriarch of such high dignity, our father patriarch of Constantinople also sent a legate or exarch, a man of great virtues and dignity, Arsenius, the great archimandrite of the great Church, therefore, by the grace and the inspiration of the most holy and life-giving Spirit, we decided to seek from him, as a man who had arrived in our lands by divine dispensation in a propitious time, what we clerics had been lacking in our holy Ruthenian Church, and what he could give *canonice* [according to Church law], by virtue of the permission of the father patriarch of Constantinople, given through his letter and his exarch, as well as through his spirit, which was present. For we had the promise of His Majesty the King, Our Gracious Lord, that had already been

28.   *Chrys. Hom. 38 in Epist. 1 ad Cor.* [St. John Chrysostom, *Homily 38 on 1 Cor.*, PG 61:327; *NPNF1* 12:229].

brought into effect, since it was made at the General Sejm in the year 1607 and reaccepted and confirmed at the most recent, equally General Sejm, and inserted into the constitution at both those Sejms, whereby he deigned to allow us, according to our laws and liberties, to have a metropolitan and bishops under our customary patriarchal spiritual obedience and to promise graciously to return to them all the goods that pertained to those dignities.

And seeing that the Lord God Himself deigned, through His divine providence, to send to us at home—without any exertions, expenses, or difficulties on our part—what we would have had to acquire with difficulty abroad, that is, the restoration of the hierarchy that had fallen on account of a metropolitan and some bishops who had become apostates from their customary obedience to the holy see of Constantinople, through which they were born in spirit, and raised, and adorned with every spiritual good; seeing this, we say, we decided to seek the restoration of the hierarchy that had fallen in our Ruthenian Church.

Thus we decided among ourselves, secure in the above-mentioned promise of His Majesty the King, Our Gracious Lord, to ask the patriarch, according to the laws, freedoms, and privileges given to us and to our ancestors by Their Majesties the Kings of Poland of blessed memory, the ancestors of His Majesty the King, confirmed by oath and by new privileges from His Majesty the King, the Lord who happily reigns over us, and likewise according to the eternal Church laws, discussed, by the power of the Holy Spirit, who was pleased to have it so happen, many years ago at the holy universal councils, and submitted to the eternal, inviolate maintenance of all of Orthodox Christendom throughout all the world—that is, we say, of the entire Holy Catholic Apostolic Church, and guaranteed under pain of excommunication from the Church and anathema against the transgressors and violators of those laws; we decided, we say, to ask that he ordain and consecrate, according to the authority of those laws, a metropolitan and bishops to replace those who had abandoned our holy Ruthenian Church. But we imposed this order and guarantee on the matter: that, as far as the spiritual investiture is concerned, which, as the canon laws teach, creates a bishop by divine law,[29] we entrusted, gave, and left the election of persons to

---

29.   *Juret. ad Ivonem. Carno. Epist. 229* [Fr. Juretus, *Observations on the Letters of Ivo of Chartres, PL* 162].

those illustrious, lofty, and holy metropolitan and episcopal offices, as
well as the reporting of our request to the most holy father, patriarch of
Jerusalem, in the complete power of those noble men of both estates,
clerical and lay, of every dignity and vocation, who were at that time
with the father patriarch of Jerusalem, in the name of all of us who were
present in spirit with them. We believed there would be many of them at
that time for two reasons: partially on account of the fact that that holy
man was present there at that time; and partially on account of the fact
that there fell at that very time the illustrious Feast of the Assumption of
the Most Holy Virgin, the Most Blessed Mother of God, for the solemn
celebration of which many people of our faith and rite, of both estates,
clerical and lay, by an ancient pious custom, were accustomed *ex voto*
[by solemn promise] to visit the Monastery of the Caves in Kyiv and in
it the Church of the Dormition of the Most Holy Virgin.

As far as the temporal investiture is concerned, which, as canon
laws also teach, grants, defends, and feeds a bishop by human law,[30]
with respect to all those persons concerned with the restoration of that
Church, that is, with regard to the electors, the elected, and the spiritual
investitor [investor], we left it entirely, wholly, and absolutely inviolate
in the power of His Majesty the King, Our Gracious Lord, who is its
proper granter and defender; for we all wished, as at all the past Sejms
for the last twenty-six years, so also at this most recent Sejm, to ask
His Royal Majesty that, having preserved us in the laws, freedoms, and
privileges given to us and confirmed by oath by His Royal Majesty
himself and by the ancestors of His Royal Majesty, he might deign
graciously to fulfill and to carry out his gracious lordly promise—made
at all Sejms, and specifically vouchsafed, guaranteed, and declared
in the year 1607, reaccepted, renewed, and confirmed in the previous
year 1620—upon these persons consecrated for these dignities, so
that, through this gracious treatment of our Ruthenian nation by His
Majesty the King in the promise made to us, all the internal enmities
and unrest, hatreds and legal burdens regarding our Ruthenian religion
might give way, the Sejms might cease to be troubled, and His Majesty
the King himself, Our Gracious Lord, might no longer be troubled in
this matter.

Having thus presented our defense against that calumny, so that

---

30.   *Juretus ibid.*

we might truly show what was said to everyone who wishes to know, and especially to whoever ought to know about this, we cite word for word the letters of His Majesty the King, Our Gracious Lord, and of Their Graces, the lord senators, written to that holy man, Father Theophanes, the patriarch of Jerusalem, and in addition the letters of Their Graces, the lord senators. We cite, moreover, the letter of the Most Reverend Father Timothy, patriarch of Constantinople, which makes clearly known that the holy patriarch of Jerusalem is a genuine patriarch and not an invented one; and that our father the patriarch of Constantinople has granted to the holy patriarch of Jerusalem power to exercise complete jurisdiction in spiritual matters throughout all the dioceses subject to the see of Constantinople. Finally, we also cite the apologia of the beloved of God, Father Meletij Smotryc'kyj, archbishop of Polack, etc., our archimandrite of Vilnius, made to His Grace, Prince Ohins'kyj, chamberlain of Trakai, on the occasion of the letters written to him by His Majesty the King and His Grace, the Lord Chancellor of the Grand Duchy of Lithuania. From all of which every person of sound reason can easily see with what justice those above-mentioned, worthy, honorable, and in no wise suspect men, who were portrayed to His Majesty the King, Our Gracious Lord, as Turkish spies and traitors, suffer a blot on their honor.

And since (as I noted above) letters were first written to this holy man, patriarch of Jerusalem, by His Grace, Lord Chancellor and Crown Hetman, Stanisław Żółkiewski, of blessed memory, before those from His Majesty the King, we cite the former first.

A Copy of the Letter of His Excellency Stanisław Żółkiewski, Chancellor and Grand Crown Hetman of Blessed Memory, Written to Their Lords, the Citizens of Kyiv

Glorious Lord *Wójt*, and Lord Councilors of Kyiv:

I wrote to His Royal Majesty, Our Gracious Lord (about which I had told you previously), informing him of the arrival in Kyiv of the holy patriarch of Jerusalem. You did well to receive such a great man and worthy guest with the appropriate respect. And so, for his even safer transit and that he be respected all the more in every place along the way, His Royal Majesty deigns to send Lord Paczanowski, his courtier, to accompany him on the way to Kam'janec' as far as Xotyn; and Your

Graces can send whomever you wish of your own to travel with him as far as the Wallachian border. I commend myself herewith to Your Graces' gracious, long-standing amity. From Żółkiew, the 5th day of May, in the year 1620.

Wishing Your Graces every good thing,
Stanisław Żółkiewski,
Crown Chancellor and Hetman.

A Copy of the Open Letter of That Identical His Grace, Hetman, Written to Their Lord Graces, the Citizens of the Ukraine, Volhynia, and Podole

Stanisław Żółkiewski, Grand Crown Chancellor and Hetman, *Starosta* of Bar, Javoriv, Kam'janec', etc.

I inform whomever it befits to know that His Royal Majesty deigns to send Lord Paczanowski, his courtier, to accompany the patriarch of Jerusalem, in order to conduct him to Kam'janec' or wherever. Therefore, knowing about this, may Your Graces be helpful in his timely conduct, wherever he should lead the patriarch, and may you always hold him in the appropriate respect as an honorable and worthy man, since it is quite important for the Commonwealth, especially at this time when some are waging war against the domains of the Commonwealth, that the patriarch, this worthy man, have a free and safe transit through the domains of the Commonwealth. Given in Żółkiew, the 5th day of May, in the year 1620.

Stanisław Żółkiewski, Crown Chancellor and Hetman.

A Copy of a Letter of His Majesty the King Written to the Holy Father, Patriarch of Jerusalem.[31]
Which, Translated into the Polish Language, Reads as Follows.

Sigismund III, by the grace of God, King of Poland, Grand Duke of Lithuania, Ruthenia, Prussia, Mazovia, Livonia; and the hereditary King of the Swedes, Goths, Vandals, etc.

---

31.   [Latin version of letter omitted; Smotryc'kyj 1621b, 8v–9r/327.]

Reverend Father in Christ, devoutly beloved of us: When we received word of Your Reverence's arrival in the domains of our Kingdom, we understood that Your Reverence arrived here with no other purpose but to carry out modestly and peacefully that which was Your purpose. Although various opinions of various people about Your Reverence's arrival were reported to us, they nonetheless did not carry such weight with us that they could give rise to any suspicion against Your Reverence; but rather we decided to wait until we could learn something more certain about Your Reverence's purpose. Since, just as we supposed, this is made clearly known by Your Reverence's letter, we suffer it gladly that Your Reverence sojourn during that time in our domains. And we believe that all of Your Reverence's deeds, which Your very vocation seems to demand, lead to nothing other than to tranquility and peace. Wherefore, whatever Your Reverence asks of us, we benignly concede to Your Reverence, and we command our chamberlain by letter that, for safety's sake, he accompany Your Reverence through those places where you are to make your way. Although it would seem not inappropriate if Your Reverence were also to stop by our court and visit us in person, nonetheless, you must consider carefully whether it should seem appropriate for Your Reverence to do this. And so, may Your Reverence fare well and be fortunate. Given in Warsaw, the 1st day of the month of August, in the year 1620. The 33rd year of our reign in Poland, the 27th in Sweden.

Sigismundus Rex [Sigismund the King].

The inscription of this letter.

To the Reverend Father in Christ, Theophanes, Patriarch of Jerusalem and all Palestine, devoutly beloved of us, etc.

A Copy of a Second Letter of His Majesty the King Written to Lord Paczanowski, the Courtier of His Majesty the King, Who Was Sent to Accompany the Holy Father Patriarch

Sigismund III, by the grace of God, King of Poland, Grand Duke of Lithuania, Ruthenia, Prussia, Mazovia, Samogitia, Livonia, and the hereditary King of the Swedes, Goths, and Vandals, etc.

We send to the hands of Your Honor an open circular letter or passport for the safer conduct of the Patriarch of Jerusalem, whom we have ordered Your Honor to conduct from Kyiv to Kam'janec', and from there further, wherever it should be necessary. Therefore we urgently admonish Your Honor that Your Honor accompany the above-mentioned patriarch of Jerusalem without delay from Kyiv to Kam'janec', taking special care that he not suffer any unpleasantness in Your Honor's presence along the way; rather to the contrary, that, as a worthy man, he enjoy everywhere the appropriate respect. Which Your Honor will do, fulfilling our will. Given in Warsaw, the 31st day of July, in the Year of the Lord 1620, the 33rd year of our reign in Poland, the 27th year of our reign in Sweden.

Sigismundus Rex [Sigismund the King].

Copy of a Third Letter or Open Circular of His Majesty the King Written to the Citizens of the Ukraine and Volhynia

Sigismund III, by the grace of God, King of Poland, Grand Duke of Lithuania, Ruthenia, Prussia, Mazovia, Samogitia, Livonia, and the hereditary King of the Swedes, Goths, and Vandals, etc.

To all in general and to each in particular whom it befits to know, and namely, to the dignitaries, *starosta*s, officials, and to all the citizens of the palatinates of Volhynia and the Ukraine. We inform you that we are sending the noble Szczęsny Paczanowski, our courtier, that he might conduct the patriarch of Jerusalem and Palestine, the reverend Theophanes, from Kyiv to Kam'janec' and thence further, wherever it should be necessary. Wherefore we urgently admonish Your Honors and Worships to aid our above-mentioned chamberlain for the quicker and orderly conduct of the above-mentioned reverend patriarch; and that you hold him, as a worthy man, in the appropriate respect and not allow that any unpleasantness be done to him along the way. For much depends upon this for the Commonwealth, especially in this time of dangers arising from the pagans, that the patriarch, a worthy man, be conducted through our domains. Which Your Honors and Worships will do for the sake of our grace and on account of your obligation. Given in Warsaw, on the 30th day of the month of July, in the year of our Lord

1620; the 33rd year of our reign in Poland, the 27th year of our reign in Sweden.

> *Sigismundus Rex* [Sigismund the King].
> *Petrus Gembicki Secretarius* [Piotr Gembicki, Secretary].

Copy of the Letter of the Most Reverend, His Excellency, Bishop of Luc'k, Crown Vice Chancellor, Written to the Holy Father Patriarch

Most reverend father in God, Patriarch of Jerusalem.

Having received news from an epistle given to me concerning the presence of Your Reverence in the domains of His Royal Majesty, I am pleased, and I desire that this might be unto the good of all Christendom. I gained a benignant admission to and a quick dismissal from His Royal Majesty for the monks that Your Reverence sent to His Majesty the King, as Your Reverence will learn from them themselves. And since sufficient information in this matter has been given to the courtier of His Majesty the King, Lord Paczanowski, by His Royal Majesty himself, referring to it for the present, I commend myself to Your Reverence's prayers and friendly wishes, asking the Lord God moreover that He Himself support with His grace and blessing Your Reverence's *pias intentiones* [pious intentions] and strengthen you with good health. From Warsaw, the 1st day of August, 1620.

Your Reverence's well-wishing friend.

> *Andreas Lipski Episc. Luceoriensis, Vicecancellarius Regn. etc.* [Andrzej Lipski, Bishop of Luc'k, Royal Vice Chancellor, etc.].

The inscription of this letter is this:

For the Most Reverend Father in God, Theophanes, Patriarch of Jerusalem and all Palestine.

*A Copy of a Letter Written to the Holy Father Patriarch of
Jerusalem from His Excellency, Prince Zbaraski,* Starosta *of
Pinsk, Crown Equerry, etc.*

Illustrissime et Reverendissime Domine [Most Illustrious and Reverend
Lord].

I did gladly what Your Reverence, My Gracious Lord, deigned to
command by letter through Your emissaries. If they receive permission
from His Royal Majesty for Your Reverence's departure, and if they
send someone to me, I will give my officials a letter telling them to
allow Your Reverence to pass everywhere freely and to offer you every
respect. Moreover, I offer my services to the grace of Your Reverence,
My Gracious Lord. Given in Końska Wola. 22nd of July.

The well-wishing friend of Your Reverence,
My Gracious Lord,
Krzysztof Zbaraski, Equerry.

The inscription of this letter is such:

*Illustrissimo et Reverendissimo D[omin]o Theophano, Dei Gratia,
Patriarchae Hierosolymitano, D[omin]o et amico observantissimo.*
[To the Illustrious and Most Reverend Lord Theophanes, by the Grace
of God, Patriarch of Constantinople, Most Esteemed Lord and Friend.]

*The Explanation that the Reverend Father in God, Meletij,
Archbishop of Polack, etc.,
Made to His Gracious Lord, the Chamberlain of Trakai,
in Response to the Letter of His Majesty the King*

Having declared before God that I am an entirely faithful subject and
not in the least—either in that with which I have been slandered or in
anything else—a suspect subject of His Royal Majesty, I say that if we
had not received the letter of His Majesty the King written to that man
with sufficient respect, according to the dignity with which he titles
himself, our meeting with him would not have come about. But in view
of the fact that this letter was sent to us, and of the assurances we took
from it, and, moreover, in view of a second letter written to the citizens
of Volhynia and the Ukraine, I was sent by my elder, as his servant,

in order to visit him, holding and believing him to be what His Royal Majesty deigns to title him in his letters. And we—not just the two of us, but also others of the Volhynian and Ruthenian lands—were assured in our belief that it was not an offense to the majesty of His Majesty the King to receive consecration from him by the fact that many other foreign bishops and archbishops sojourned freely in the domains of His Royal Majesty and served in our Church throughout all that time. For never were they—neither they themselves, nor those who had and have them on their estates—charged with even one iota of anything that would bring offense to the majesty of His Royal Majesty. Once we had received *nuda officia* [the mere offices], we decided to wait peacefully in all other matters for the grace of His Majesty the King, to whom the *jus patronatus* [right of patronage] belongs, as the defender and giver of these sees and goods, to see whether this were the will of God and the will of His Royal Majesty, before we allowed ourselves to be consecrated. Wherefore I do not find that it was from our persons that the alleged evil arose that was mentioned in the letter of His Majesty the King, Our Gracious Lord.

The Second Explanation of the Same in Response to the Letter of His Excellency, His Gracious Lord, Chancellor of the Grand Duchy of Lithuania Written to the Same Prince, His Gracious Lord, Chamberlain of Trakai

The elder of our monastery, my piously departed predecessor, the archimandrite of Vilnius, urged us his brethren in a closed council not to write to, nor for any of us to meet with, the man who was announced as the patriarch of Jerusalem until it became known who he was from that source whence recognition about such people customarily comes in our fatherland. And that is how it happened that from Mid-Lent of the preceding year, at which time that man arrived in the domains of His Majesty the King, almost until the Feast of the Virgin Mary of the Herbs,[32] the matter remained determined as we had discussed it.

32. [*Panna Maria Zielna*—i.e., what is known in the Western Church as the Assumption (Polish: *Wniebowzięcie*) and in the East as the Dormition (Polish: *Zaśnienie*). Smotryc′kyj uses all three Polish terms to identify the date, which

But at this time there reached us the letters of His Majesty the King that were written to that man and to the citizens of Volhynia and the Ukraine, which had been entered into the court acts. And since they were respectful, containing the express title of the Patriarchate of Jerusalem, they made it safe for us to travel to him and they gave us a reason to do so. (I understand that the autographs remain even now with Father Borec´kyj.) There, on account of the large presence of many clerics and lay people who had arrived in Kyiv from all parts for the illustrious Feast of the Dormition of the Virgin Mary, we made bold to receive consecration. We did this since, as far as his person was concerned, we believed that he was what His Majesty the King, Our Gracious Lord, and many other Crown senators, clerical and lay, gave us to understand him to be in their letters; and as far as our persons were concerned, we were assured by the example of clerical persons—bishops and archbishops—who came to the domains of His Majesty the King from foreign countries and performed in our Church, securely throughout all those times, what their dignity allowed, without any accusations of any offense to the majesty of His Majesty the King committed by them or by those on whose estates they lived and continue to live until this very day.

For we only received from the father patriarch what he could give to us, having determined among ourselves and having promised neither in word nor in deed to make bold to abrogate the *jus patronatus* [right of patronage], the giving of benefices, which remains in the complete power of His Majesty the King, wishing to wait patiently—living openly and not surreptitiously in the domains of His Royal Majesty, in peace and without any rebellions or seditions—for the grace of God the Almighty and for the kindly grace and the promise that His Majesty the King made at the Sejm in the year 1607 and which was reaffirmed at this most recent Sejm. And as far as the laws of the Church are concerned, they too were maintained in their integrity, since they would suffer violence and transgression if this had been done without the knowledge and will of our highest pastor, the patriarch of Constantinople. But he purposefully entrusted complete power in this matter to the patriarch of Jerusalem, and he also sent with him his legate or exarch, a great man, so that in his person, here in the Ruthenian diocese that belongs to him

---

is 15 August—here old style; which means 25 August 1620, new style.]

by Church canons (as Your Grace, My Gracious Lord, also deigns to acknowledge in your letter to me), by the ancient laws and privileges given by Their Majesties the Kings of Poland, the ancestors of His Royal Majesty, as well as by the King himself, Our Gracious Lord, who now reigns fortunately over us, he might do whatever belonged to his office—as far as ecclesiastical laws are concerned—more securely, more freely, and with greater faith in him on our part. The consecration of the present reverend father in God, the bishop of Lviv, is a recent example that this could take place lawfully, through the office of the patriarch of Jerusalem with such a permission from the patriarch of Constantinople; for, having received consecration, with the permission of the patriarch of Constantinople, from the metropolitan of Wallachia (who has as much right to the local domains as the patriarch of Jerusalem), he remains the lawfully established bishop.[33]

Letter of the Most Reverend Father, Timothy, Patriarch of Constantinople, Given to the Most Reverend Father, Theophanes, Patriarch of Jerusalem, When he Travelled to Moscow.[34] *Which, Translated into the Polish Language, Reads as Follows:*

Timothy, by the mercy of God, Archbishop of Constantinople, the New Rome, and the Ecumenical Patriarch.

To the most enlightened metropolitans and *hypertimoi* [supremely honorable],[35] God-loving archbishops and bishops, and to the brethren beloved in the Holy Spirit, whom this our letter reaches: grace be unto you, peace, and the love of God the Almighty.

The most blessed and most holy patriarch of Jerusalem, Lord Theophanes, beloved brother in the Holy Spirit, and the co-servant of our humility, travels with good reason to the Muscovite land; wherefore, wherever among you Orthodox he should arrive on his trip, you will summon His Reverence and have him celebrate the divine liturgy, bless and consecrate you, since you are obliged to receive His Reverence with good will and respect and to provide him without fail with every

33. [Jarema Tysarivs'kyj, Orthodox bishop of Lviv from 1602 to 1641.]
34. [Greek version of letter omitted; Smotryc'kyj 1621b, 15v–16r/334.]
35. [Smotryc'kyj polonizes the Greek term: "metropolitom i *hipertymom.*"]

means, as the one whom we allowed to carry out the Church sacraments
and all archpriestly matters in our eparchies, as the Church canons and
propriety itself wished us to do. And if anyone should prove contrary
and disobedient to him in any way, let every such person be subject to
the appropriate Church punishment. We thus inform you in order that it
not happen otherwise. And so, may the grace of our Lord, Jesus Christ,
be with you. Amen. From Constantinople, the year from the creation of
the world 7126 [AD 1618], the 1st indiction, in the month of April.

Once you have read and considered all this, kind and gracious reader,
we believe that you will easily be able to determine with how good a
conscience that anonymous and mendacious *delator* [accuser] stained
and dishonored the honor of these persons, accused before God's
anointed, to whose honorable ears, as we said, nothing false is to
come.[36] Who would have avoided meeting this man, who had arrived
here from foreign lands, not only since we did not have any prohibition,
rather we had seen such honorable letters written to him by His Majesty
the King and many illustrious senators? His Majesty the King and his
most illustrious senate consider him a noble man, honorable, unsuspect,
worthy of every honor and respect, a father in Christ, devoutly beloved,
and the most reverend in God, patriarch of Jerusalem and all Palestine,
and he summons him to his court for a visit. Which he certainly would
have done, had he not been obliged during that time of expedition to
take into account the suspicion of the Mussulmans, for among them
there is no righteousness and mercy, only violence and cruelty, and the
will itself is the law. Perhaps His Majesty the King, Our Gracious Lord,
was taking this into account and was saving such a great man from
falling into the suspicion of the tormentor (if he had visited the court of
His Royal Majesty) when he deigned to place in his letter of invitation
to him the following words, which are wise and worthy of a Christian
lord: *Sed num id rationes ipsius permittant, secum ipsa accuratius
considerabit;* "but You must consider carefully whether it should seem
appropriate for Your Reverence to do this."

Thus, as we said, His Majesty the King and his most illustrious

36.   [Sir. 51:6.]

senators consider him a noble, great, and unsuspect man, worthy of every honor. Were we, then, supposed to consider him a spy and a traitor? We ourselves, according to both divine and human law, would certainly have to become just like that shameless *delator* [accuser]. If all of those who, on the strength of such letters of His Majesty the King and Their Graces, the lord senators, visited that holy man, either in their own persons or by means of letters and their emissaries, rendered him their spiritual obeisance and asked for blessing, were supposed to be Turkish spies and traitors, not only all Rus', but also many noble people of Poland and Lithuania would have to be spattered with that dishonorable stain. Moreover, at the time of the very departure of that holy man from these domains, after the consecration of the priests had already been completed (which took place during the time when the courtier of His Royal Majesty, Lord Paczanowski, was present with the holy father patriarch), when Lord Paczanowski had returned to His Royal Majesty, His Majesty the King, Our Gracious Lord, deigned to send a second letter to that holy man, similar to the first in its respectfulness. And in addition to the letter of His Majesty the King, the most reverend in God, His Excellency, Bishop of Cracow, Marcin Szyszkowski, also wrote at the same time to that same holy man with equal respectfulness. Already at the time of the departure of that holy man from the domains of His Majesty the King, His Excellency, Prince Zbaraski and the most reverend in God, His Excellency, Bishop of Cracow, furnished and supported him with abundant provisions, and they graciously received him on their estates and honored and respected him as a great and worthy man, and many others of the noble and illustrious gentry did the same. What does that shameless *delator* [accuser] say about these senators, who are worthy of every honor, and about other honorable people? Did only Borec'kyj and Smotryc'kyj, as opposed to countless other clerical and lay persons, give rise to dishonor and suspicion through their conversation with that honorable and unsuspect man? If he is honorable and unsuspect—as His Majesty the King, Our Gracious Lord, and Their Graces, the lord senators, hold him to be—in what way could he make them dishonorable and suspect? Was that holy man adorned with such high titles just in order to mislead Borec'kyj and Smotryc'kyj, who, deceived by them, could then be condemned and punished as traitors?

If that holy man had been criticized even in the least and declared to be what they now allege he is by one who could appropriately do so, or if conversation with him had been forbidden, who would have made bold to converse with him against that prohibition or that characterization? But the Lord God Himself sees the innocent conscience of those who were accused and the calumnious intent of that shameless *delator* [accuser], who in his campaign made bold, without fear of God, to stain so shamefully that holy man, the patriarch of Jerusalem, and those worthy persons who were with him. This is the thing, as the common fable has it, that flows from such an unpleasant height: the ram muddies the water for the wolf, even though he stands downstream.[37] If he wished to support his own cause through that calumny, as is the case, then he testified in that very manner that he is not in the right: for no good person defends the truth with falsehood, and no honorable person defends righteous things with calumny. If he defends God's work, why did he begin its defense not with the Lord God, but with the opponent of God, whose name is the Devil, that is, Calumny? If he trusts in his righteousness, why does he dust the eyes of the judges with calumny? For what has darkness to do with the light, and Belial with Christ?[38] "Ye," says Christ the Lord, "are of your father the devil." And why does he say this? He says this, because "ye will do the lusts of your father. He was a murderer from the beginning, abode not in the truth, because there is no truth in him. When he speaketh a lie, he speaketh of his own, for he is a liar, and the father of lying."[39] If he conceived a desire for that little bit of the blood of Borec̆kyj and Smotryc̆kyj, why did he not proceed to drink it in its pure form rather than muddied with the dirt of calumny? He did not wish to be satisfied with killing an innocent man's body, if he did not simultaneously kill his honor;[40] that spiteful man would perhaps have made an attempt on the soul as well, if he could have had even the least access to it. But God, the defender of innocence,[41] will judge between him and those innocent men, and will Himself decide this case. He will deliver them from men of blood, who have conceived unrighteousness in their hearts,[42] have sharpened their

---

37.   [*NKPP* 3:728, "Woda," 2.]
38.   [2 Cor. 6:14–15.]
39.   Jn. 8[:44].
40.   Ps. 9 [10:7–8].
41.   Ps. 63 [64].
42.   Ps. 42 [43:1].

tongues like vipers, and under whose lips is snake's poison.[43] He will give his judgment to the King, and his righteousness to the King's son, that he judge his people in righteousness and his poor in judgment.[44]

Concerning Church Dignities and Benefices

But the rumor is spread forth that they make bold to be named—the one metropolitan, the other bishop—without the granting of His Majesty the King, granter of these dignities, and without the blessing of the metropolitan; and that they succeeded to dignities that have living pastors, who were established by a lawful consecration for their positions and by the granting of His Majesty the King; and that thereby they fell into disrespect for the majesty of His Majesty the King.

If this is the case, why does this frivolous man tack calumny onto that? Why does he abuse the good fame and honor of honest people before presenting proof and before the sentence of the judge? Of the above-mentioned reasons, was not the disrespect (as he alleges) for the majesty of His Majesty the King sufficient in itself, without the falsely invented treason? In truth, dear reader, that *calumniator* schemes in his intent not what he pretends in his words: since, from the reasons mentioned by him, an intended disrespect for the majesty of His Majesty the King could not be drawn, he tacked calumny onto them so that, through the striking of one against that other, he might strike in the fatherland the sparks of the conflagration that he had himself invented; so that he might set innocent people on fire through seizure, imprisonment, and murder; so that he might spread the flames throughout all the domains of the Crown, Lithuania, and Rus´; and then, so that he might quell and extinguish the fire with innocent blood.

For in this matter, by the grace of God, nothing occurred that should properly have concerned His Majesty the King. As *indigenae* [natives], as citizens of the Crown, well aware of the spiritual and temporal laws (by which our fatherland is governed and ruled), they knew what, with respect to the *juris patronatus Regii* [the right of patronage of the king], they should leave inviolate and completely untouched in the power of His Majesty the King, as the giver *beneficorum* [of benefices] and of

43. [Ps. 140:2–3].
44. Ps. 71 [72:1–2].

the Church prelature, and what they could take from the spiritual power without disrespect for the majesty of His Majesty the King.

They found that two things in this matter were to be taken upon their persons: the first and foremost thing, the spiritual dignity; the second, which necessarily follows upon the first, the *beneficia* [benefices] of those dignities. For it is not the dignity that is created, granted, and established for the benefices, but the benefices for the dignity. The dignity that they found in this matter was metropolitan, archepiscopal, and episcopal; the *beneficia* [benefices] that belonged to those dignities were the wealth from which the metropolitan, archbishop, and bishops live and maintain themselves together with their clergy. According to both laws, spiritual and temporal, they saw that the first thing in this matter, that is, the dignity, was in the hands of the spiritual authorities, namely, for the metropolitan, in the hands of the patriarch of Constantinople, and for the bishops, in the hands of that same patriarch and in the hands of the metropolitan of all Rus'. According to the temporal law of the Crown and Lithuania, they saw that the second thing in that same matter, that is, the benefices, were in the hands of His Majesty the King, Our Gracious Lord, as the proper granter and defender of those benefices.

That the metropolitan and episcopal dignities in the domains of Our Lord the King are in the hands of the spiritual authorities, that is, for the metropolitan, in the hands, as we said, of the patriarch of Constantinople, and for the bishops, in the hands of the same patriarch and in the hands of the metropolitan of all Rus'—this they saw from the twenty-eighth canon of the spiritual laws of the fourth universal synod, which adjudges Thrace, Pont, Asia, and Barbary to the rule and power of the patriarch of Constantinople,[45] as well as from the eighth canon of the third universal council, which leaves spiritual rule and power in each land to the patriarch by whom it was led to the faith of Christ the Lord and baptized.[46] From temporal laws they saw the constant custom and the privileges of Their Graces the Kings of Poland, who grant and

45.   Canon 28 of the 4th Universal Synod [of Chalcedon, AD 451; Mansi 7:369–70].
46.   Canon 8 of the 3rd Universal Synod [of Ephesus, AD 431; Mansi 4:1470].

permit spiritual rule and power in their domains in our Ruthenian nation to the patriarch of Constantinople.

And that the Church benefices are in the hands and in the power of His Majesty the King—this they saw from the right *juris patronatus* [of right of patronage], which properly belongs to His Majesty the King.

Which two things, that is, the dignity and the benefices, canonists commonly call spiritual and temporal *investitura* [investiture]. They say that it is the property of spiritual investiture to establish a bishop by divine law and the property of temporal investiture to feed the bishop by temporal law. It is one investiture, so they say, that makes the bishop, and another that feeds the bishop: the former is acquired by divine law, and the latter by human law. Take away the divine law, and the bishop ceases to exist in spiritual terms; take away the human law, and he loses the possessions by which he is physically fed. For the Church would not have possessions, were it not granted them by the kings, by whom it is endowed not with divine mysteries, but with earthly property.[47]

Of these two things, Their Majesties the Kings of Poland, Our Lords, were accustomed to confirm in their oath the first, that is the law concerning spiritual dignities, with the authority of these words: "We promise and will be obliged neither to diminish, nor to suppress, but rather to maintain whole, the greater and lesser spiritual dignities of the Greek order."[48] They confirm in that same oath the second thing, that is, the benefices that belong to those dignities, with the authority of these words: "We are to give the *beneficia juris patronatus Regii praelaturarum ecclesiasticarum* [benefices of the right of patronage of the king for ecclesiastical prelatures] in Greek Churches to people of the Greek faith."[49]

Of these laws, the former makes abundantly clear that Their Majesties the Kings of Poland promise not to diminish or to suppress the spiritual dignities, but rather to maintain them whole; and since they have the *beneficia* [benefices] of those dignities in their power *jure*

---

47.   *Juret. ad Ivonem. Carna. Epist. 239* [Fr. Juretus, *Commentary on the Letters of St. Ivo of Chartres*, 233 (?), *PL* 162:398–9].

48.   From the Privilege of His Majesty the King, Sigismund August, given at the General Sejm in Lublin in the Year 1569.

49.   From the Confederation made in the year 1575 at the General Sejm in Warsaw during the interregnum.

patronatus [by right of patronage], they promise to give them to people of the Greek religion. Whence, as also from all that has been cited, it is made known indeed that since the above-mentioned persons received their dignities, the one metropolitan, the other episcopal, from the appropriate spiritual authority, according to the ancient Church laws, they are obliged to await the *beneficia* [benefices] that, *jure patronatus* [by right of patronage], are in the hands of His Majesty the King, from the hands of His Majesty the King, Their Gracious Lord.

†They raise the objection of the questionable presentation, which, so they say, usually precedes the consecration. But we do not find that it should come *necessario* [necessarily] before the consecration in our Greek religion (which contents itself with the apostolic see alone);[50] to the contrary, in some scores of metropolitanates, if not in all of them, we find this law left as an example: that first, in their times, the Ruthenian princes (whose spiritual customs and laws are sworn by oath to our Ruthenian nation), and then Their Majesties themselves, the Kings of Poland and the Grand Dukes of Lithuania, graciously received the metropolitans sent by the patriarch, even though they had already been consecrated without any presentation before their consecration, and they graciously conferred upon them their *beneficia* [benefices]—of necessity, as it were—not finding in this any disrespect for their majesty, to say nothing of offense.

Canon lawyers say in this matter: "Priests are, by human law, indebted to kings to the extent that they love the possessions by which the Church is acknowledged to have been enriched and adorned by them or by their parents."[51] Therefore, after a lawful election and after a free consecration, kings can give, without offense to themselves, permission, aid, and defense to the bishop through royal investiture in Church goods. By the custom of which usual, ancient manner of spiritual investiture, in this case too the current Orthodox metropolitan, as well as other bishops, were consecrated before they were presented to His Majesty the King.

Which, however, Their Majesties the Kings of Poland did not

---

†   Concerning presentation.
50.   [That is, which does not lay claim to senatorial seats for its bishops.]
51.   *Juret. ad Ivonem. Carna. Episto. 239* [Fr. Juretus, *Commentary on the Letters of St. Ivo of Chartres*, 239; *PL* 162].

allow among the Roman archbishops and bishops who were consecrated without their knowledge and will; and that was for this reason: because the bishops of the Roman religion (which is not contented with the apostolic see alone) occupy not only the episcopal seat in the domains of Their Majesties the Kings of Poland, but also the senatorial. Of which, upon the first alone, that is, on the episcopal seat, he is seated by the bishop of Rome, and he does not lose his dignity even if His Majesty the King should not wish to confer upon him his benefices. He can be punished, however, *privatione bonorum,* that is, by not granting goods and by not permitting the extension of episcopal power. But no bishop can occupy the senatorial seat and take over the benefices without the knowledge and will of His Majesty the King. For the first, that is, the consecration, the bishop of Rome has in his complete power as the *absolutus* [absolute] spiritual *investitor* [investor]; and the second, that is, the elevation to senatorial rank and the conferral of benefices, the King of Poland has in his complete power as the *absolutus* [absolute] temporal *investitor* [investor].

Wherefore (since the metropolitan and the bishops of the Greek religion do not occupy the senatorial seat) even without the presentation made before the consecration, the metropolitans, already consecrated and presented by the patriarch of Constantinople, were always kindly received by Their Majesties the Kings and graciously admitted to benefices, as consecrated to the metropolitanate *ab absoluto investitore spirituali* [by the absolute spiritual investor], the patriarch of Constantinople.

It follows from this difference between dignities and benefices that in some palatinates the freedom of choosing one's spiritual authorities is guaranteed by privilege, and that the *beneficia* [benefices] that are not *juris patronatus regii* [of the right of patronage of the king] can be taken away from those dignities, as, for example, the *beneficia* [benefices] that princes, lords, and gentry create from their own goods under the care of themselves and their descendants.

It was for this reason that it could happen that, after the apostasy of Ruthenian priests, the possessions given them by princes were taken away from them. With respect to such benefices created by princes, lords, and gentry, Their Majesties the Kings did not exercise power in the increase or diminution of the dignities; rather, this remains in the power of the founders and lords of those benefices, as their patrons.

Therefore Their Majesties the Kings leave the archimandritehoods on the estates of the Sluc'kyj and Ostroz'kyj princes, as well as on the estates of other princes, lords, and gentry, as the grants of their spiritual and temporal founders—as, for example, the Vilnius archimandritehood of the Church Brotherhood of Vilnius and others like it, founded by the princes, lords, and gentry on their benefices, with the blessing of the spiritual power of the metropolitan or patriarch.

It is for this reason too that princes, lords, and gentry have it in their power, without any disrespect for the majesty of His Majesty the King, that on their goods, which are called *beneficia,* they keep and sustain bishops and metropolitans, which, throughout the entire time of the apostasy of our Ruthenian priests, the princes Ostroz'kyj, Vyšnevec'kyj, Korec'kyj, and other lords and gentry did and do even now.

Wherefore also the present-day spiritual authorities, the metropolitan and bishops consecrated *legitime* [legitimately] and *canonice* [according to canon law] by the most reverend father, the patriarch of Jerusalem, knowing that His Majesty the King is the giver and defender of those benefices, which lawfully belong to their dignities in the Ruthenian Church, do not intrude upon them, do not have recourse to any violence, as the calumniators impiously allege against them. They do not steal those possessions away, they do not push the present-day possessors out of those benefices; rather they live on the benefices of their other dignities and on the benefices provided by the gentry, lords, and princes, and they peacefully await the grace and the promise of His Majesty the King, Their Gracious Lord.

And the citizens, both of the Crown and of the Grand Duchy of Lithuania, people *mere* [wholly] of the Greek religion, ask His Majesty the King, as the giver of those benefices and as (after the Lord God) the highest defender of our laws and freedoms, and they beg of him with lamentation—for them and for themselves—that, according to the privileges given long ago to the Ruthenian and Lithuanian nation by the ancestors of His Majesty the King and confirmed by the oath and privileges of His Royal Majesty himself, having taken the *beneficia* of the dignities of the Ruthenian Church from our manifest apostates, to whom they do not belong, he might deign to give them to us. Through all of which we not only do not do anything against the authority of His Majesty the King, Our Gracious Lord, but rather we maintain, with due propriety, respect for the majesty of His Majesty the King, as befits faithful subjects who love their Lord.

If anyone should fault us on the grounds that the dignities for those benefices were taken before the request was made and reported to His Majesty the King, then he would fault us in this improperly as well, as was shown above. For witness to the fact that throughout all the years of the apostasy of our clergy we asked and we continue to ask His Majesty the King for this, and that, as we said, we begged and we beg with lamentation, is that *solennis* [solemn] promise of His Majesty the King made on the occasion of our request concerning this at the Sejm in the year 1607 with the unanimous decision of all estates and reaccepted and renewed at the present, most recent Sejm, which states that His Majesty the King deigns to promise to us, according to the foundations and the ancient custom given to us by his ancestors, to confer and to give the dignities and the *beneficia* of those dignities to people of our rite, *mere* [wholly] of the Greek religion. Assured and protected by which promise of His Majesty the King, as though by a word similar to divine judgment, we presented worthy persons for those dignities and *beneficia,* chosen and consecrated on the occasion of the arrival of the most reverend father patriarch of Jerusalem, to His Majesty the King at this recent Sejm through a letter written by us to the circle of the deputies, submitted, and read aloud *publice* [publicly] on the order of His Grace, the Lord Marshal of that meeting, and we asked and do now ask that the benefices that properly belong to them be granted to them.[52]

For if, with that certain promise of His Majesty the King, it was proper for us to send those persons abroad in order to receive consecration, it was immeasurably more appropriate to seek it when we could have it at home. And if His Majesty the King, Our Gracious Lord, in fulfilling his royal promise to us, had the will to allow those persons to go abroad to our patriarch in order to receive consecration (for otherwise the promise of His Majesty the King, Our Gracious Lord, could not be kept and brought into effect), why could it not be received within the borders of the domains of His Majesty the King and thus be

52. [This was the Sejm held in Warsaw from 3 November to 11 December 1620. For the constitutions of 1607 and 1620, see below, pp. 176–82.]

completely dependent upon the power and the grace of His Majesty the King?

But even safely established upon our immediate and soul-saving need and upon the promise of His Majesty the King, Our Gracious Lord, which is certain and unchanging, and, as we said, similar in its certainty to divine judgment, let us grant, as you say, that our Ruthenian nation transgressed in having wished that the metropolitan and bishops be consecrated in the Ruthenian Church under the obedience of the father patriarch of Constantinople; it did not, however (if anyone will judge with a pure heart according to God), transgress more than David, who, when he hungered, together with all who were with him, entered the house of God and ate the shewbread, which it was not proper for him to eat, nor for those who were with him, but only for the priests alone.[53] Those persons who received the blessing of consecration from the most reverend patriarch of Jerusalem also transgressed, but less, according to the judgment of truth, than the great Patriarch Jacob transgressed when he stole the blessing of his father from his older brother.[54] In that instance, although there was divine dispensation, there was not the will of the father, not to mention the promise; but in this instance there is divine dispensation, for that is how it pleased the Holy Spirit and the holy universal councils; there is also the will and the promise of His Majesty the King, *solenniter* [solemnly] made and declared at two general Sejms.

Thus trusting in holy righteousness and in the paternal mercy of His Majesty the King to his faithful subjects, we see clearly that the consecrated persons did not transgress before God's anointed, the King, Their Gracious Lord; nor did our entire Ruthenian nation transgress, which wished harmoniously, as with one heart and one mouth, to obtain that for them. But shall we grant *simpliciter* [simply] that our Ruthenian nation transgressed by not having presented to His Majesty the King, Our Gracious Lord, those it had elected before their consecration? Alas, to be able to dare to speak freely what the heart desires; but everyone can easily divine what I would say. Everyone who is acquainted with this matter can easily conjecture that if the apostates strive so maliciously that a refusal be given to the matter already completed that they practically

53.   1 Kg. 21 [1 Sam. 21:6]; Mt. 12[:4]; Lev. 24[:5–9]; [Mk. 2:26; Lk. 6:4].
54.   Gen. 27[:1–29].

seek to swallow those persons alive, what sort of assent do you think they would give to the matter if it had only been presented? Oh, the times; oh, the customs! They saw in their dioceses that, just as they despised the Church celebrations of our priests, so we despised theirs. Wherefore the one did not wish to receive, and did not receive, anything from the other—not Holy Baptism, not the blessing of marriage, not confession, not the salvatory mysteries of the body and the blood of the Son of God, not the burial of the bodies of the dead; rather, not without bitterness in their soul and in them who looked and now look upon this, they had to, and still have to, live and die as non-people.

To what, therefore, did it have to come? To ruin. Wherefore *sacra necessitas* [sacred necessity] compelled what was done to be done, having counselled us to cast beneath the most illustrious feet of His Royal Majesty, Our Gracious Lord, the assent or the refusal of the presentation of consecration, both before consecration or after consecration. Compulsion is such an unyielding thing that, while defending one's head, the hand, moved by nature itself, often lifts itself unto harm and ruin in place of the head. Why, they say, did you not receive all that from the Uniates? Before we say anything further, we say: Why did the Uniates forbid their followers to receive all that from us? What then? All of us, both the clerical and the lay citizens, gentry, nobility, and all the common people of the Crown and of the Grand Duchy of Lithuania, having prostrated ourselves subserviently beneath the most illustrious feet of His Majesty the King, Our Gracious Lord, bathe them with our tears; and we ask him as Lord and Father for paternal forgiveness for this transgression, and as the protector, guardian, and defender of the holy righteousness of our rights and freedoms, with a humble heart, in words of all humility, fidelity, and submissiveness, that, having treated us kindly and graciously, in lordly and paternal fashion, he might deign, according to the royal promise he made to us, to maintain for us the form of our clergy among the spiritual authorities of our Ruthenian nation that he found in these his domains at the time of his felicitous coronation and that he confirmed with his lordly will and oath; that he might deign to allow us to have our metropolitans and bishops under the spiritual blessing and obedience of that authority whom he himself— during his fortunate reign, by means of his circular letter, according to our ancient laws and freedoms, in the person of Jeremiah of blessed memory, patriarch of Constantinople, who was here in Vilnius in the year 1589, having acknowledged to him the power and supervision among the clergy that belonged to him from ancient times—deigns to allow to celebrate all the spiritual matters that pertain to his clergy, to judge, govern, rule, command, punish transgressors, and to have all the priests of the Greek order, from the eldest to the lowest estates, in his power and obedience; and that he might deign to establish and bring to fruition this pacification in our Greek religion, which he deigns to promise in the granting of dignities and spiritual goods according to our foundation and the ancient custom given to us and to our ancestors by his ancestors and to assure us through his lordly promise made in two general Sejms, not wishing to cause us *praejudicium* [damage] in conscience and in our laws.

Nor can anyone properly say that the patriarch did this contrary to Church law—that, with a living metropolitan and bishops elevated to those positions through a proper consecration, he elevated and consecrated other persons for those dignities. For who else can judge people as worthy of those dignities? Or who has the right to elevate and consecrate spiritual authorities to the Ruthenian metropolitanate and bishoprics other than the patriarch of Constantinople himself, who is the *absolutus* [absolute] spiritual *investitor* [investor] in our Ruthenian lands since the time of the baptism of all Rus', on account of ancient customs, guaranteed by spiritual and temporal law and by privileges from Their Majesties the Kings of Poland and the Grand Dukes of Lithuania and confirmed by oaths? He judged them as unworthy of those dignities, he excommunicated them; and the holy eastern Church, to which, as sons reborn in it through water and the spirit[55] they were supposed to have been obedient, considers them, on account of the malice of their apostasy, as apostates, as excommunicate, and as not living. Who, other than their proper pastor, other than, we say, the patriarch of Constantinople, is to pass judgment on their worthiness and unworthiness? He and no one else is to recognize them as worthy and as unworthy of that dignity. He and no one else was to elevate and consecrate them to those dignities. He has complete power to pass judgment about their lawful and unlawful accession to those sees. He and no one else. What sort of authority in the Roman Church would an archbishop of Gniezno or a bishop of Vilnius have who was consecrated

55. [Jn. 3:5; Acts 1:5, 11:16.]

by the patriarch of Constantinople without the knowledge and will of the bishop of Rome? The Ruthenian metropolitan and all the other bishops consecrated by the bishop of Rome without the knowledge and will of the patriarch of Constantinople certainly have the same authority in the eastern Church. For the bishop of Rome has as much right to consecrate a Ruthenian metropolitan and bishops as the patriarch of Constantinople has to consecrate the archbishop of Gniezno and other bishops.

Let anyone snatch from musty chroniclers whatever he wishes and present it for the deception of the ignorant. We show and cite the constant custom, the laws, privileges, letters—circular and private—of Their Majesties the Kings of Poland, and the Grand Dukes of Lithuania, and chronicles not produced out of thin air, but the writings of people worthy by birth, skilled in learning, honorable in dignity, who, in addition to all that has been mentioned, make known in express words that Rus' was never, from the time of its very baptism by the patriarch of Constantinople, under any other spiritual obedience, but remained and continues to remain under his power, jurisdiction, and spiritual rule throughout all the past ages of its Christianity; from him and from no one else did it have and does it have its authorities, the metropolitans, and through them the bishops.[56] And so, this our proper native pastor, as recognized by spiritual and temporal law, the patriarch of Constantinople, condemned, beginning with Myxajil Rahoza (the first apostate metropolitan), him and all his followers in apostasy, as well as his successors in office, as excommunicate and not living. Wherefore, not being able to consider the present, fictitious metropolitan and all the apostate bishops as anything other than what they are declared to be by our superior pastor in spirit, we did not and we do not recognize him as our proper metropolitan. Therefore, with the permission of the spiritual laws, the spiritual persons presented by the patriarch of Jerusalem acceded to the orphaned dioceses, whereby they did not do any spiritual violence in this respect either, and they were elevated and

---

56. *Strykowsky pagin. 141* [Stryjkowski, *Chronicle*, p. 141. Stryjkowski 1582, 141–2; Stryjkowski 1846, 1:133]; *Gwagnin rerum Polon. Tom 1, pa. 213* [Gwagnin, *History of Poland*, 1:213]; *Kromerus de rebus Polon. lib. 3. pag. 13* [Kromer, *History of Poland*, bk. 3, actually p. 31].

consecrated *legitime* [legitimately] to the dignities of those dioceses *a legitimo pastore et investitore* [by the legitimate pastor and investor].

What sort of authority of spiritual law would there be if it were permitted to the archbishop and the bishops of the Roman Church in Poland and in the Grand Duchy of Lithuania to abandon *impune* [unpunished] their customary pastor, the bishop of Rome (by whom they were baptized and to whose rule and power, by natural law, they are obliged to be subject as sons to their father, as are our Ruthenian metropolitan and bishops to the patriarch of Constantinople)? And to draw forcibly behind them, to trouble unlawfully and to oppress those who would not follow them in their apostasy?

There is certainly no other nation under the sun like the Ruthenian nation that our apostates wish us to be: a nation that would be a slave in faith. What is supposed to be the most free in a wise man they wish to have in us the most servile. If you do not believe as the apostate metropolitan orders, then you are a rebel, a *turbator* [disturber] of the common peace, an offender of the majesty of His Majesty the King, a traitor to the fatherland, though you be the most humble, most peaceful, and most honorable. And if you bow down to Father Ruts'kyj, then you are not a traitor.

A Short Summary of the Previously Mentioned Objections, to Which Is Appended a Second Letter of His Royal Majesty, Our Gracious Lord, Written to the Holy Father Patriarch, and the Letter of the Most Reverend in God, His Excellency, the Bishop of Cracow; as Well as a Letter Written at That Time by the Holy Father Patriarch to the Zaporozhian Army

You must know, Kind and Gracious Reader, that if Borec'kyj were not metropolitan and Smotryc'kyj not archbishop, and if they had conversed even twice as much with that man, then that holy man would not be an *impostor* [impostor], but the proper, genuine patriarch of Jerusalem (as he is), and Borec'kyj and Smotryc'kyj would not be traitors. Nor would it have come to such a cruel imprisonment of honorable citizens of Vilnius, who knew as much about the fact that Father Smotryc'kyj was to return as what he now is, or that he was to go for that purpose, as he himself knew about both things. Our opponents themselves know how inclined his soul was to that illustrious dignity in the Church of God, for he refused many implorings of the Church to receive even the first degrees *sacri ordinis* [of holy order]. Our apostates themselves are also well aware of what kind of taste he had for the *beneficia* of that dignity (which are now ascribed to him by someone as ambition for goods, titles, and honor), which he could very easily have acquired when he was offered *ultro* [in addition], by those to whom it belonged, that same archepiscopal see of Polack; we will not mention the second one offered after that.[57] But he avoided such high dignities in the Church of God, especially those subject to conscience, and he had intended to avoid them until the end of his life, as one who was after all *alienus* [alien] to that harmful intrigue. And had it not been for the counsel of God, to which human counsel yields of necessity, and had it not been for the voice of men, which in such matters is the voice of God, he would never have come to this of his own will. But, at the very time when it fell to him to fulfill in deed the divine and human voice of divine and human counsel, without any knowledge not only of the citizens of Vilnius or of the elder by whom he had been sent, but even without his own knowledge, he had to bend his neck beneath the easy yoke and the light burden of Christ the Lord[58] and offer his shoulders at the will of Him who examines the hearts and reins of men,[59] and to oppose whose will it is *nefandum nefas* [an abominable sin].

But however it happened, it happened, according to them, incorrectly: for by this consecration the power of His Majesty the King was assailed. As a common saying has it, whoever does not know how to speak well must speak badly.[60] A God-fearing man, in the consideration of either an amicable or an inimical matter, does not yield to the private affection of love or hatred when he proceeds to mete out a righteous judgment between the truth and untruth; rather he measures and considers the essence of the matter with a rule or a scale

57. [This seems to imply that the Uniate side had offered the archbishopric of Polack to Smotryc'kyj (as well as some other unmentioned dignity) before they gave it to Josafat Kuncevyč in 1618.]

58. [Mt. 11:30.]

59. [Ps. 26:2.]

60. [Cf. *NKPP* 2:536, "Mówić," 47.]

of holy righteousness. Therefore they do not speak properly who present *sinistre* [as evil] our *dexterum negotium* [good business] to His Majesty the King, Our Gracious Lord. Is it in the power of the royal dignity to consecrate bishops? If the matter of their sudden and lawless attack upon us had received a pure determination and a just judgment even from the apostates themselves, to the extent that spiritual and temporal law allows them to judge—if, we say, our apostates had looked only at the justice of the matter itself and had not been carried away by the affect of hatred in a blind rush, not only would they never have brought us to further lawless difficulties and to such inhuman oppression, but they would certainly also not have leaped to such crude protestations, which sully the unassailable honor of worthy people. Especially the one who ought to have remembered these two things: *ne sutor ultra crepidam* [let the cobbler stick to his last][61] and that the *candor* [purity] of honest people ought not to be sullied by a feverish brain.

For it is not the custom of a good man to be vehement only against someone else's exaltedness and to be stubborn about his own paltriness. It is certainly characteristic of the stupid man to raise a rose to his nose with hands dirtied with birch tar and to wish to smell its scent: for the sweet scent of the rose must smell of the unpleasant stench of the birch tar. Virtue, which in its clarity does not cede its place even to the most beautiful skin, does not call for itself to be poked in a stove with a fire iron. Those who, through the courageous chivalrous deeds of their ancestors and through the praiseworthy wages of glory, purchased the great gem at a great price, keep a more careful eye on it in their honorable, noble heart, than on their health, but in magnificent *munimenta* [fortifications, legal proofs] of eternal memory, in an exalted place where envious eyes do not reach.

If then, as we said, our opponents had wished to decree in the matter of the consecration of the newly erected Church as both laws justly allow them to do, they would never have made bold to say that by this consecration the power of His Majesty the King was assailed, since, as was cited above, the ceremony of spiritual investiture, which the spiritual investitor has in his complete power, is one thing, and that of temporal investiture, which the temporal investitor has in his

---

61.   [Pliny the Elder, *Natural History,* 35.85. Erasmus *Ad.* 1.6.16. Cf. *NKPP* 3:394–5, "Szewc," 23.]

complete power, is another. And the latter comes last, and the former first. For canonically, the spiritual investiture precedes, and the temporal investiture necessarily follows. Just as a man is not baptized before he is born, so a bishop is not fed before he is created. Spiritual authority gives birth to a bishop through consecration, and temporal authority feeds him through the granting of benefices. For Scripture assures the Church of God, as far as its spiritual authorities are concerned, that it is to be fed from the royal breasts: *Suges lac gentium, et mamilla Regum lactaberis* [Thou shalt suck the milk of the Gentiles, and shalt suck the breast of kings].[62] But they were to be born not by the kings, but *a Pastore et Episcopo animarum nostrarum,* by the pastor and bishop of our souls,[63] and especially by His holy and vivifying Spirit, according to the unerring assurance of the same Holy Spirit, who speaks through the Apostle Paul: *Attendite vobis et universo gregi, in quo vos Spiritus s. posuit Episcopos, regere Ecclesiam Dei,* take heed, therefore, unto yourselves, and to all the flock, over which the Holy Ghost hath made you bishops, to govern the Church of God.[64] Thus the Holy Spirit establishes bishops through bishops and not through kings.

They say further: "Let us grant that consecration is in the spiritual power, but the persons chosen for consecration were to be presented to His Majesty the King before they were consecrated." Enough was said above both about this point and about the first. Here we say only that in the matter of the erected Church hierarchy our opponents are concerned with two things: the consecration of persons and their non-presentation. That the first of these—that is, consecration—might occur has been permitted by His Majesty the King, Our Gracious Lord, for these thirteen years already, through the constitution made in the year 1607, in which His Royal Majesty sees fit, not to give us, Rus' of the ancient Greek religion, a metropolitan and bishops, but, presupposing consecrated persons, to promise to grant benefices to the metropolitan and bishops. The second—that is, the presentation (which we have shown to be performed in our Ruthenian Church *indifferenter* [indiscriminately], both before consecration and after consecration)—was omitted by the electors and the elect, that is by the Kyiv chapter, which made that

62.   Is. 60[:16].
63.   1 Pet. 2[:25].
64.   Acts 20[:28].

election, and by the elected persons, who allowed themselves to be consecrated, not in order to show disrespect (as our enemies declare) for the majesty of His Majesty the King, Our Gracious Lord—*absit* [far from it]—beneath whose most illustrious feet they bend their humble and faithful necks, but only on account of the constraints of time connected with the imminent departure from these domains of the most reverend father patriarch, since we wished to present them already consecrated.

For both knew well that both a person who has been presented before his consecration, even if he has received a privilege, but has not received a consecration, and also a person who has been presented after consecration, who has received a consecration, but has not received a privilege, does not rule over his dignity in his diocese. And since it is a much greater thing that was permitted to us by His Majesty the King, Our Gracious Lord, than was omitted by us, we trust that the gracious kindness of His Royal Majesty will deign to grant also the lesser thing to our nation, especially since those consecrated persons testify absolutely before God and His Royal Majesty, Our Gracious Lord, that they did not do this in order to show disrespect for the majesty of His Majesty the King, Our Gracious Lord, to say nothing of entering into any sort of conspiracy with the Turk, or in order to commit treason with some Turkish spy, which they not only could not do, but which never even occurred to them. For both they, as well as our entire nation, were concerned both with seeing that what had been omitted, and what His Royal Majesty, Our Gracious Lord, deigned to allow us to have through the constitution of his lordly will, not be lost to us, since we had at home, through God's special industry for us, that for which His Royal Majesty would have to allow us to go to Constantinople, if he were to realize his lordly promise. For on account of that *defectus* [lack] of consecrated persons, after the departure from this world of Father Potij and of several bishops after him, the provisions of the constitution were not satisfied since there were neither a metropolitan nor bishops upon whom, according to the promise of His Majesty, those vacant metropolitan and episcopal *beneficia* [benefices] might be conferred.

They say further: "Those persons who now enjoy the benefices of those dignities have the grant and the privileges of His Majesty the King." We too know that they have them, and although they have it against the rights, freedoms, and privileges granted to the Ruthenian nation of the ancient Greek religion, the persons of the newly elevated Church do not assail their grant and privileges; rather they peacefully await the grace of His Majesty the King, Our Gracious Lord, not so much in their own persons, but in the person of the entire Ruthenian nation, to whom that promise was made by His Majesty the King, Our Gracious Lord, and to whom, and not to them, the jurisdiction about this properly belongs.

They further say: "They allowed themselves to be consecrated with living bishops and a metropolitan on those sees." Having presented the fact that His Majesty the King, Our Gracious Lord, deigned to confirm for the Ruthenian nation through his royal oath what he found in the domains of His Royal Majesty—and His Royal Majesty found our whole nation entirely under the obedience of the patriarch of Constantinople and not under the obedience of the bishop of Rome—we say that our apostates, to the extent that they are people, are living, but to the extent that they are priests, they are not living to us. Therefore, we say that they allowed themselves to be consecrated to sees occupied by unliving people, which, God willing, we will show irrefutably a little below.

They finally say also this: "If they had wished to avoid that blemish, then why, during such a difficult time for the fatherland, when the enemy with bloody hand troubled it with the defeat in Wallachia, did they make bold to acquire this, and what is more, from a Turkish spy?" This too we answer: that they were consecrated before that happened;[65] and as before that tribulation of our fatherland, by divine visitation, the man who consecrated them, as far as His Majesty the King, Our Gracious Lord and the most illustrious senate of His Royal Majesty was concerned, was unsuspect, worthy, and holy, as one could learn from the above-cited letter to him of His Royal Majesty and of their graces, the lord senators, so was he also after that tribulation, as one can learn from a second, private letter of His Majesty the King, Our Gracious Lord, and from a letter of the most reverend in God, his excellency, the bishop of Cracow, written to that same holy man a dozen or so weeks after the consecration of those persons, already almost at the time of his very departure from the domains of His Majesty the King. Which we cite here in this place, bringing them to your attention, Kind and Gracious Reader, so that you might see with your own eyes with what

65.   [On the chronology of the consecrations, see Plokhy 2001, 111–23.]

sort of good conscience our apostates dishonor this holy man calling him a Turkish spy.

A Copy of the Second Letter Written by His Majesty the King to the Most Reverend Father, Patriarch of Jerusalem.[66] *Which, Translated into the Polish Language, Reads as Follows:*

Sigismund III, by the grace of God, King of Poland, Grand Duke of Lithuania, Ruthenia, Prussia, Mazovia, Samogitia, Livonia, and the hereditary King of the Swedes, Goths, and Vandals.

Reverend, devoutly beloved of us: a few months ago we gave our letter to Your Reverence, by which we gladly gave assent to Your Reverence's request. And for that very reason we had sent our chamberlain so that Your Reverence might receive the desired transit through the domains of our kingdom all the more safely. Your Reverence's intentions changed, however, and the result that our army achieved in Wallachia was different from the one we had desired and for which all of Christendom had waited, which we commend to God's will. But against this common foe of all Christendom, so that he not become haughty from the victory, we are gathering such an army, by which, with God's help, his attacks could be repulsed. As even now we order our Zaporozhian army to march against this common foe as quickly as possible and to oppose him. We also commanded our envoy to visit Your Reverence and to present this in our name so that Your Reverence, knowing that it is a matter not only of our Kingdom, but of all of Christendom, might help to cause that army to be submissive and obedient to our will. About which we commanded our envoy, the well-born Bartłomiej Obałkowski to speak with Your Reverence more extensively. Your Reverence will give him complete faith and will incline in all this to our will as kindly as possible. Further, we wish Your Reverence health and every success. Given in Warsaw, the 10th day of the month of November, in the year of our Lord 1620. The 33rd year of our reign in Poland, the 27th in Sweden.

Sigismundus Rex [Sigismund the King].

---

66.   [Latin text omitted; Smotryc'kyj 1621b, 28+1r–v/347–8.]

The inscription of this letter.

To the reverend in Christ, Father Theophanes, patriarch of Jerusalem and all Palestine, devoutly beloved of us, etc.

A Copy of a Letter Written by the Most Reverend in God, His Excellency, the Bishop of Cracow, to the Holy Father Patriarch of Jerusalem

Most reverend, gracious Patriarch of Jerusalem: Having heard from His Majesty the King that Your Reverence deigns to be in this Kingdom for urgent matters of the Church of God, it seemed appropriate to write to Your Reverence with a wish of good health in long life and a happy success in all pious intentions. And further, knowing that Your Reverence has care for the increase of the Christian faith and that you turn all your thoughts toward seeing that Orthodox people not be oppressed by the main foe of all Christians, I can do nothing but be extremely glad, hoping that the Lord God, through His grace, will bless such a righteous cause. I ask Your Reverence only what His Royal Majesty also indicated through his envoy: since Your Reverence has great authority with the people of the Ukraine, the Cossacks, that you might lead and arouse them in such a difficult time for our Commonwealth and for all of Christendom to keep faith steadfastly with His Royal Majesty, Their Gracious Lord, to offer themselves gladly for the present service against the pagans, and to defend both the holy faith and the security of the fatherland. Your Reverence will have from this a great service in the eyes of the Lord God and a commendation in the eyes of this Commonwealth. And since Lord Chalecki, my kinsman, an important nobleman, lives near Your Reverence, I recommend him urgently, asking you to know him and to show him your grace. Meanwhile, I wish Your Reverence good health and every happiness from the Lord God. Given in Warsaw, the 1st day of December, in the year of Our Lord 1620.

Your Reverence's

Well-disposed friend.

Marcin Szyszkowski, Bishop of Cracow,

Prince of Siewierz, in his own hand.

Inscription of this letter.

To the Most Reverend in Christ the Lord, His Grace, the Father Patriarch
of Jerusalem.

This is the second letter of His Majesty the King to the holy father
patriarch of Jerusalem and the letter of the most reverend in God, father
bishop of Cracow. What did the holy man, the father patriarch have to say
in answer to this highly honorable letter, worthy of great respect, from
His Majesty the King, Our Gracious Lord, and to the letter of similar
respectability from the most reverend in God, father bishop of Cracow?
Only that which he was obliged unto the high humanity of His Majesty
the King and the pious heart of a Christian lord: he carried out with great
gladness, a pure heart, and as a well-disposed, faithful servant, what
was instructed him by letter by His Royal Majesty, his great benefactor,
and commanded orally by His Grace, Lord Obałkowski. Immediately,
with the authority that was appropriate to him in a foreign domain,
writing to people who were not his subjects, but were nonetheless well
disposed toward him, interceding in this matter gladly, already almost
at the very time of his departure from the domains of His Majesty the
King, he wrote down the following letter in the Greek language and
had it translated into Ruthenian and sent by the same, His Grace, Lord
Obałkowski, to the Zaporozhian army according to the will and decree
of His Royal Majesty:

> Theophanes, by the grace of God, Patriarch of Jerusalem, of
> God's city of Zion, of Syria, Arabia, Cana, Galilee, Jordan
> of that side, and all Palestine.
> To the hetman, the colonels, the captains, lieutenants, generals,
> and to the entire, most worthy and most excellent Zaporozhian
> army: may there be with you for ever grace and peace
> from almighty God and from Our Lord Jesus Christ,
> and the blessing of the life-giving grave of God, and of Saint James,
> the Lord's brother in the body, the first Christian archpriest, and of our
> humility. Amen.

Most worthy and most glorious lord hetman, army officers, and the entire most courageous army, beloved sons in the spirit of our humility. Even if the command of the most illustrious king, your lord, and our exhortation to you in this matter had not reached you, we would still have to believe that, looking partly at your knightly obligation, partly at the immediate need of your fatherland, you would do gladly whatever your knightly trade—with which alone since ancient times you and your ancestors have been occupied—should demand of you during the bloody attack of the enemy of God and Christendom against the domains of the most illustrious king, your lord. Especially since you see all this before you. The most illustrious king, your lord, commands you as his ever faithful and obedient subjects; and I join in with my own reason and request: the obligation of your chivalrous trade demands of you, and the violence against your fatherland worked by the main enemy of Christendom, whose yoke is unbearable,[67] requires of you, that you present yourselves ready with every desire, in all of your strength, for that service to which your lord, the most illustrious king of Poland urges and commands you through his envoy, who also gave us a letter from the most illustrious king. Whereby you will do much to bring about the lordly grace toward you of the most illustrious king, your lord, and you will know me as a constant suppliant of God for you and for your entire army. You will offer aid to the fatherland in its time of need, and you will add luster to the glory of your army.

We do not doubt in the least that you will do this, both for the reasons mentioned, and so that the most illustrious king of Poland, your lord, and our most generous and most merciful benefactor, might recognize thereby that we are entirely well-disposed friends of this Christian kingdom, which, in our need and oppression at the hands of the pagans, is a refuge for our Greek nation burdened by servitude, and thus that he might recognize that our request had authority with you. Moreover, through your eager and illustrious service, you will easily be granted from the most illustrious king, your lord, that he will strengthen and guarantee through his royal consensus and privileges the hierarchy that we have raised in your holy Church, that is, the metropolitan and bishops consecrated by us to replace those who had abandoned the holy apostolic see of Constantinople; which you must seek most urgently from

67. [Cf. Mt. 11:30].

the most illustrious king, your lord, through your insistent requests. And we will not cease to pray to the Lord God for this most worthy kingdom and also for the most illustrious king of Poland and for the entire senate of this kingdom and for you, the most courageous knighthood, here in every place of his realm and at the grave of God, if the Lord God should return us in health to our see. Meanwhile, let for a second time the grace and peace of God and the blessing of our humility remain with your love. Amen. Given in the Traxtemyriv Monastery. In the year 7129 from the creation of the world and 1621 from the incarnation of the Son of God, in the month of January, the 7th day, the 4th indiction.

> Signature by hand.
> Θεοφάνης ἐλέῳ θεοῦ Πατριάρχης τῆς ἁγίας
> πόλεως Ιερουσαλὴμ.
> [Theophanes, by the grace of God, Patriarch
> of the holy city of Jerusalem.]

With this letter the holy father patriarch of Jerusalem interceded with the Zaporozhian army at the command of His Majesty the King, Our Gracious Lord, and his most generous and most merciful benefactor, as he calls His Royal Majesty in his letter. And he often paternally urged the same thing and nothing else of those colonels and lieutenants who were always in his presence. He especially, however, urged Lord Petro Kunaševyč-Sahajdačnyj (who, according to the permission of His Majesty the King granted by circular letter and according to military command, accompanied him with a chosen regiment of military people as far as the Wallachian border), as well as other lieutenants and adjutants, when he was in the process of taking leave of them at the border and when he had before him those who had arrived to kiss his hand. He urged them with expansive words through a translator (about which we know from the reports of those who were present) zealously to avoid the pagan yoke, which he showed to be heavy and unbearable to Christians, against which he admonished and asked them—to the extent that, with God's grace and help, it is in their power—with the help of other armies of these domains, vigilantly to defend their dear fatherland and, in it, themselves.

This is how His Majesty the King, Our Gracious Lord, treated this holy man throughout the entire time of his presence in these domains; likewise also their graces, the lord senators, as you can clearly understand, Kind and Gracious Reader, from the letters we have cited and from the entire course of events. And likewise did that most worthy and holy man, most reverend in God, father patriarch of Jerusalem, treat His Majesty the King and the entire Commonwealth, our fatherland. When were kings ever wont to treat spies and traitors of their kingdoms in such a manner? Or spies and traitors, the domains and the kings whom they seek to ruin? O omniscient God, You see and know everything: how wrongfully that great, worthy, and holy man, without any fault of his own, must suffer that shameful blemish from some malicious man who portrays him to that holy Lord as a spy and traitor, when he, the king, with his own lips portrayed him to his entire domain through his private and circular letters as a man worthy, great, pious, and unsuspect.

You heard, Gracious and Kind Reader, what the most reverend in God, father bishop of Cracow writes in his letters to that holy man. "Having heard," he says, "from His Majesty the King, that Your Reverence deigns to be in this kingdom on account of urgent matters of the Church of God . . . ." O holy truth, although you can be harshly oppressed, you can never, nonetheless, be suppressed. Even if people should hold their peace, the stones would certainly speak at the innocence of this holy man.[68] The father bishop of Cracow learned from His Majesty the King that the father patriarch of Jerusalem is in the kingdom of His Royal Majesty on account of urgent matters of the Church of God; but some malicious tongue is not ashamed to portray him to His Majesty the King, Our Gracious Lord, not to say not as a patriarch, nor as a bishop, but as a simple monk, and as a spy and a traitor in addition. Alas, the malice. Restrain, O holy Lord, those perverse tongues, lest they be a cause of vengeance from You unto even the innocent.[69] Is it a lesser thing to revile such a worthy man, the great chaplain, the keeper of God's grave, a man of divine miracles, than to deprive him of life? Would that the news had reached him. How eagerly would he present himself before the majesty of His Majesty the King, Our Gracious Lord, even from abroad! We trust that he who opened

68.   Lk. 19[:40].
69.   [Cf. 1 Pet. 3:10.]

that pit upon him and digged, would himself fall into the ditch which he made; his mischief would return upon his own head, and his violent doing would come down upon his own pate.[70]

Thus it remains for those to whom that judgment belongs to have their assiduous eye in healthy wisdom on nothing else now, in view of that holy man's so obvious and manifest innocence, but *ne condemnetur justus,* as the wise man says, that the just man not be condemned.[71] *Haec dicit D[omin]us. Facite judicium et justitiam, et liberate vi oppressum de manu calumniatoris, et advenam, et pupillum et viduam nolite contristare, neque opprimatis inique.* Thus saith the Lord: "Execute ye judgment and righteousness, and deliver him who is oppressed by force out of the hand of the calumniator; and do not afflict the stranger, the fatherless, nor the widow, nor oppress them unjustly."[72] And again in the Law: *Maledictus qui pervertit judicium advenae, pupilli, et viduae: et dicet omnis populus, Amen.* "Cursed be he that perverteth the judgment of the stranger, fatherless, and widow. And all the people shall say, Amen."[73] Terrible indeed is divine judgment in the matter of the stranger and the guest.

The Spiritual Laws That Do Not Allow Us to Consider the Apostate Metropolitan and Bishops as Clergy

We said above that we never acknowledged and considered, nor could we acknowledge and consider, our apostates—the metropolitan and his followers, the bishops—as our bishops, according to the reasons cited above; and we did and do this, assured and instructed by the decrees and judgments of the holy universal synods and the blessed fathers, and admonished by our holy pastors, the patriarch of Constantinople. Which we cite here:

The blessed apostles say in the thirty-sixth canon of their laws that, if a bishop consecrates in a foreign diocese without the knowledge of its proper bishop, both he himself loses his dignity, and those whom he

70.   Ps. 7[:15–16].
71.   Prov. 17[:15].
72.   Jer. 22[:3].
73.   Dt. 27[:19].

consecrates do not achieve their consecration.[74] Therefore, according to the authority of this canon of the blessed apostles, our apostates cannot be acknowledged by us as bishops.

The holy fathers of the first universal synod say in their sixth canon that if anyone should be consecrated by another patriarch without the knowledge of his own patriarch, he should not be considered a bishop.[75] Therefore, according to the authority of this holy synod, we did not consider, do not consider, and cannot consider as bishops our apostates, who were consecrated without the knowledge of their own patriarch of Constantinople by another bishop who does not belong to the Ruthenian diocese.

The holy fathers of the second universal synod, taking up again the sixth canon of the first universal synod, say in their second and fourth canons that no bishop should take possession of a diocese that does not belong to him and is under another bishop, nor cross the boundaries set for him; nor should he confound or trouble the Church contrary to the decreed laws.[76] Therefore, since our apostates, having rendered obedience to the wrong bishop, crossed their allotted boundaries, and confounded and troubled the Church contrary to the synodal decrees, they were not considered and cannot be considered bishops by us.

The holy fathers of the third universal synod say in their eighth canon that if any bishop (or metropolitan or patriarch), puffed up with fractious pride, should confer consecrations in another diocese, the consecration of each such person is not to be valid.[77] And since our apostates have been imposed upon our Church in this manner, their consecration was not valid in our eyes and could not be so.

Further, the same holy fathers of the third universal synod in the same eighth canon say that the laws of every land are to be maintained inviolate; and if anyone should introduce another form of laws, it is not to be valid.[78] And since our apostates violated the laws of our Ruthenian land and introduced into the Ruthenian Church a new form of canon

---

74.   Apostolic Canon 36 [Mansi 1:54].
75.   1 Universal Synod, Canon 6 [Nicaea AD 325; Mansi 2:671–2].
76.   2 Universal Synod, Canons 2 and 4 [Constantinople AD 381; Mansi 3:559–64].
77.   3 Universal Synod, Canon 8 [Ephesus AD 431; Mansi 4:1469–70].
78.   Ibid.

laws, unusual to our nation, therefore, both they themselves and that unusual form were not valid in our eyes and could not be so.

The holy fathers of the same third universal synod also establish in that same eighth canon that lands are to remain eternally with the patriarch by whom, through baptism and preachers, they were brought to the Christian faith and that they are not to suffer any attack from any other bishop. And if any should attack and subject them violently to his power, he must of necessity yield them, lest thereby he work violence upon the decrees of the holy fathers, and lest haughtiness of power reign in the guise of the power of Church order.[79]

Furthermore, the holy fathers of the fourth universal synod, in their twenty-eighth canon, gave spiritual rule and power over Thrace, Pont, Asia, and Barbary, in which part our Ruthenian lands are contained, to the patriarch of Constantinople.[80] And since our clergy obstinately left this power and rule and became apostate from the pastor and father who, through his antecessors, brought them, in the persons of their ancestors, to the Christian faith and baptized them, they were properly abandoned by us as apostates and must be abandoned as not ours but foreign, imposed by force upon the government of the Ruthenian Church.

Wherefore, blessed Cyril, the *praeses* [president] of the third universal synod, in the second canon of his laws, which was accepted by the sixth and seventh universal synods, says: "If anyone should dishonor and violate any of the decrees that the God-bearing fathers decreed and established, that must not be called a *dispensatio* [keeping], but rather a *praevaricatio* [violation], a violation of the decrees and an impiety against God."[81] Therefore, the change wrought by our clergy against the decrees of the God-bearing fathers is, according to the opinion of that blessed teacher, a *praevaricatio* [violation]; it is a transgression of the law, a violation of the decrees, and an impiety against God.

Furthermore, even Zosimus, the bishop of the Roman Church itself, says, "Even the authority of the Roman see cannot establish anything or change anything against the statutes of the holy fathers."[82] Therefore

79.   Ibid.
80.   4 Universal synod, Canon 28 [Chalcedon AD 451; Mansi 7:369–70].
81.   *S. Cyr. Alexan., Canon 2* [St. Cyril of Alexandria, Canon 2; *PG* 137:364–5; *NPNF2* 14:235].
82.   *Zosim. Episcop. Rom. Tomo Conci. 1. pag. 811* [Zosimus Bishop of Rome, in vol. 1 of the Councils, *PG* 811; cf. Mansi 4:369].

we too, considering the deed wrought by our clergy improper since it was against the decrees of the holy fathers, do not and cannot give it authority. And with Zosimus, blessed Leo, the first bishop of Rome, also says: "In no manner can those be considered bishops who are not elected by the clergy, demanded by the nation." And further: "Those who acquire consecration against the canons of the holy Fathers—who will wish to appropriate for them what they have not acquired?"[83] And so, since our apostates were not elected by the clergy of our Eastern Church and were not desired by the common Ruthenian people and acquired their consecration against the canons, therefore, we did not consider them bishops and could not consider them as such; and what they could not acquire, we cannot acknowledge and appropriate for them.

Everything cited is the decree and canons of those four universal councils, which blessed Gregory the Great, bishop of Rome, accepts as the four Gospels.[84] Therefore we, too, following the example of that holy man, accepting as the four Gospels those four universal councils, approved and accepted by the other three that met after them, could not consider our apostates as bishops, and so long as the Church laws shall stand we cannot consider them as such.

Finally, blessed Chrysostom counsels and teaches that we are to observe and to defend the common canonical order of the consecration of bishops as the faith itself. "For otherwise," he says, "if every bishop will be allowed to seize government and rule in a diocese that does not belong to him, and if it will not be forbidden to all to seek another consecrator beyond the borders of his diocese, then everything will become confused. The altar is raised in vain; in vain, too, is the entire establishment of the Church body; in vain, the number of priests. And if anyone of the Orthodox should consider this an insignificant matter and take no heed of it, let him see: I do not count it lightly; rather I will watch and take care for this." Thus St. [John] Chrysostom.[85]

---

83.   *Epist. 95* [Letter 95 (actually 92), alternate numbering 167; *PL* 54:1203; *NPNF2* 12:110].

84.   *S. Greg. lib. 2 (3), ind. 11, Episto. 10* [St. Gregory, bk. 2 (3), ind. 11, letter 10; *PL* 77:613; *NPNF2* 12:127].

85.   *Homil. 11 in cap 4 Episto. Ad Eph.* [*Homily 11 on Eph. 4; PG* 62:86; *NPNF1* 13:106–7].

Considering these Church laws and, in addition to them, the laws of the freedoms and liberties of our Ruthenian nation, Their Majesties, the Kings of Poland, in times past were wont to give judgments about us: that Rus' cannot determine anything in spiritual matters without the permission of their elder, the patriarch of Constantinople, wherefore without his knowledge they are not to be forced to any such matters by anyone in our domains.[86] In proof of the fact that also the present King His Majesty, Our Lord—inclining with his will and judgments to our inviolate ancient matters and to the laws of his ancestors the Kings of Poland, and maintaining us in them inviolately for all times to come, so that we be free from those spiritual authorities who abandoned the obedience of the patriarch of Constantinople and that we not be obliged to be subject to any of their rules, jurisdiction, laws, judgments, or decrees over us—deigned to make us free from them according to both our laws mentioned above, canon and secular, we cite the privileges and tribunal decrees and constitutions, from which every wise guardian of the laws, freedoms, and liberties can easily see with what right our elders are troubled by citations from our apostates, who, if they would wish to look upon their nakedness and see their state in our Church by the lawful judgment of the patriarch of Constantinople, who has jurisdiction over the metropolitan of the Ruthenian diocese, would see clearly that they can do as much in the matters of the Ruthenian Church as one who is dead, since they have been excluded from our Ruthenian Church by their proper lord in spirit, their pastor and father. In which they should blame not us, who do not help them in this malice and do not follow them in this apostasy, but themselves and their ancestors, who, not having informed us or their highest authority in the spirit, the patriarch of Constantinople, about this first, deceitfully abandoned us all of a sudden, believing that they would drive us like cattle wherever they should wish according to their will and that they could do this *impune* [unpunished] by their pastor. But for their careless affront, cast upon us sheep and upon their pastor, they have rightfully been abandoned by us sheep, and they have been lawfully excluded by the pastor through excommunication from the Church of God.

86.   His Majesty the King Stephen, in his circular letter in the year 1584 [Charter of Hrodna, 21 January 1584; printed in *AZR* 3:280–91; *RIB* 7:1101–4].

May you deign to know, our Orthodox co-confessionalists, what sort of pastors you had over you. What sort of priests, what sort of bishops and metropolitan. Whom did you see above you in archpriestly ornament? From whom did you receive your consecrated priests? What could he, who did not have it himself, give to others? Wherever you look in spiritual laws, you find that they have crept in through a hole into the sheepfold of Christ the Lord. You see that, for you and for your Ruthenian Church, they are laymen, simple people, unconsecrated. The holy apostles and the God-bearing fathers, through their decrees at the universal synods, inspired by the Holy Ghost, show you that they are such.

Does someone say that it is a trifle that they are ordered not to be acknowledged and considered as bishops? Does someone believe that it is a joke that consecration is not acknowledged to them? In this manner, then, certainly all the synodal decrees of the holy apostles and the God-bearing fathers will be trifles and jokes; and thereby all the Church ordinations decreed by the holy universal synods, all the dogmas of piety will be cast into disrepute. You heard the honorable doctrine about this by the great doctor of the Church, St. John Chrysostom, and the eternal judgment about the attacking of another diocese by an improper pastor, where he says, "Where do you place the matter of *cheirotonia* or the spiritual laying on of hands, which through such behavior of the apostates falls and is lost? What sort of benefit is there from its ruin and loss, which it is necessary to guard and defend as fervently as faith itself?"[87] And further, as was cited a little while ago from the honorable doctrine of that authoritative Doctor, who—having said that by apostasy the matter of the laying on of hands falls and is lost—thus teaches that we must guard and defend as the faith itself the matter of the laying on of hands, which is ruled by the Holy Spirit and confirmed by Church laws. Forfend then, Lord Christ, that we should believe that the synodal decrees of the holy apostles and God-bearing fathers are jokes and trifles. For thus is it said about all the synodal canons that we have cited: "Thus it pleased the Holy Spirit and us." All our pious ancestors maintained this matter piously in its authority; even now their pious descendants maintain it, and so long as the sun will make

---

87. *Homi. 11 in cap. 4 Episto. Ad Eph.* [St. John Chrysostom, *Homily 11 on Eph. 4; PG* 62:86; *NPNF1* 13:106].

its course, they will maintain it inviolately, strengthened by the grace of the Holy Spirit. And with blessed Chrysostom (when he says, "If anyone of the Orthodox should consider this an insignificant matter and take no heed of it, let him see: I do not count it lightly; rather I will watch and take care for this"),[88] they will not cease to cry out against that lawless deed of our apostates, until, with God's help, they either bring them to repentance, or they will rid themselves of them.

Perhaps someone will say: "But do not the bishops consecrated by the bishop of Rome acquire episcopal dignity and power?" We say: for the present, our concern is not to consider whether the bishops consecrated by the bishop of Rome in his proper diocese are bishops of complete power, but to consider whether layers-on-of-hands introduced by the bishop of Rome without the knowledge and will of our proper bishop in his own diocese, that is, of the patriarch of Constantinople, are bishops of complete power. Assured by the authority of the cited spiritual laws, we do not acknowledge and cannot acknowledge such as bishops (as are ours, who have been placed by him on our necks through force and violence, *pace ejus dixerimus* [that we might say it with his good leave]).

And in what way is the patriarch of Constantinople our proper pastor and father in spirit? If we had nothing else to prove it but the fact that he made us reborn in Christ the Lord, that he led our ancestors through Volodimer the Great out of paganism to the recognition of the true God, baptized us, and provided us with every spiritual good, with books of various psalmody and of the yearly and daily hymns, with the holy liturgy, with postils, and provided us and adorned us with every other salvatory Church facility—this would be sufficient for us to show that he belongs to us. But we have the laws of the universal synods for this, and we have the laws of Our Lords, the Kings of Poland: the former guaranteed against transgressors by anathema; the latter confirmed against violators by oath. Whatever spiritual laws there are have already been cited, if briefly, then nonetheless genuinely and clearly. And so that the temporal laws, which were given to the Ruthenian nation concerning freedom of religion under the obedience of the patriarch of Constantinople, be known to whomever it is fitting to know about them, we offer a summary of them as well.

88.   Ibid.

The Temporal Laws That Remove Us from the Power of the Apostate Metropolitan and Bishops

The first privilege

Of King Stephen of blessed memory, under the date of the year 1585: That people of the ancient Greek religion cannot proceed to any change in their calendar, ceremonies, and rite without the permission of the patriarch of Constantinople.[89]

The second

Privilege of that same King Stephen of blessed memory under the date of the year 1586 concerning the free celebration of the Ruthenian holidays, that we are not to be oppressed or forced to the obedience of the Roman Church against our ancient laws and customs.[90]

The third

Privilege of the present King, Our Lord, under the date of the year 1589 given to the patriarch of Constantinople, the most reverend Jeremiah, for the free spiritual rule, judgments, and punishment of the disobedient in the domains of His Royal Majesty, together with a fundamental confirmation of his jurisdiction.[91]

The fourth

Privilege of His Majesty the King, Our Gracious Lord, under the date of the same year 1589, given to the same holy father patriarch of

89. [*AZR* 3:292–3; *RIB* 7:1103–8.]
90. [Decrees of 29 July 1586 and 8 September 1586. Printed in *Zbiór* 1843, 139–40; Dubiński 1788, 149–51. These decrees were directed to the citizens of Vilnius. In the first, Stephen ordered the Rus' of Vilnius not to open their shops on Roman—new calendar—holy days. In the second, the king ordered that Ruthenian citizens of Vilnius not be forced to engage in the business of the city on Greek, i.e., old calendar, holy days.]
91. [This was a circular letter dated 15 July 1589. Printed in *AZR* 4:20–1; *RIB* 7:1117–22.]

Constantinople, for the orders of our Church Brotherhood of Vilnius, by which he deigns to remove the Brotherhood foundations from the city jurisdiction, fees, taxes, and obligations.[92]

The fifth

Parliamentary privilege of the same Lord King, who reigns over us fortunately, under the date of the year 1592, by which His Royal Majesty, Our Gracious Lord, confirms all Brotherhood regulations established by the patriarch of Constantinople, allowing it to build a church of brick and wood on our lands, to buy buildings, to have schools and a printing house, to maintain, according to need, people of the clergy for the teaching of the Christian people and for the performance of other Church matters, excluding from city taxes and jurisdictions both those buildings and places that have already been purchased as well as those that should be bought later.[93]

The Constitution of the Year of Our Lord 1607 Concerning the Greek Religion[94]

Pacifying the Greek religion, which has its own laws since ancient times, we guarantee: that we are not to distribute dignities and spiritual goods according to any other law, but according to their foundations and the ancient custom of our ancestors given to them, that is, to the noble people of the Ruthenian nation, and *mere* [wholly] of the Greek religion, not causing them any *praejudicium* [damage] in their conscience and law, nor forbidding or hindering them in the free celebration of their Church services, according to their ancient rites. Nor are we to confer two Church benefices upon one person, but the metropolitanate upon the metropolitan, the bishoprics upon the bishops, the archimandritehoods upon the archimandrites, and similarly *subsequenter* [in succession] should it be understood about the others, as the privilege given by us at this Sejm discusses more broadly. And whoever should hold two benefices at this time must leave one of them no later than in a

---

92. [Printed in *AVAK* 9:140–4, dated 21 July 1589.]
93. [There were two privileges for the Holy Trinity Brotherhood, dated 9 October 1592, printed in *AVAK* 9:144–9 and 149–53.]
94. [*VL* 2:438–9.]

year's time, at the cost of paying a fine of a thousand *grzywna*s to the accuser, concerning which the *forum* [proper court] is at the Sejm *ad instantiam* [at the intercession] of the land representatives. And they are to obtain the Church goods alienated from the Church according to the constitution *Anni* [of the year] [15]88 written about that, which we now reconfirm.[95] The lessees, however, of Kwasów, Tarnki, Janiewicze, Liplany, Buremiecz, Woderada, Teremna, are to remain by their right. We also leave the Church brotherhoods of the Greek religion with their laws and privileges. But the churches that do not now have possession of those goods are not to obtain and acquire landed noble goods through inscriptions in Gospels.[96] Further, we annul the court cases and the proceedings of law and banishments that had been declared against persons of the clergy in any court and had been won, both in the Crown and in the Grand Duchy of Lithuania, and we make those cited free from them.

At That Very Same Sejm, for the More Guaranteed Assurance of our Pacification in Religion, His Majesty the King, Our Gracious Lord, Deigned to Give Such a Privilege to Our Ruthenian Nation, to People Mere *[Wholly] of the Greek Religion*

Sigismund III, by the grace of God, King of Poland, Grand Duke of Lithuania, Ruthenia, Prussia, Mazovia, Samogitia, Livonia, and the hereditary King of the Swedes, Goths, and Vandals.

We make known by our letter to all in general and to each in particular, whomever it befits to know about this, for now and for posterity: that at the present General Sejm of Warsaw the representatives of the lands of Kyiv, Volhynia, and Braslav,[97] in the name of their brethren, people of the Greek religion, reported that they had suffered insult against the ancient laws and privileges given by our ancestors

95. [Charter of 28 January 1588. *VOIDR* 19:iii–iv.]
96. [The Gospel books kept on the altar served as a record of important events of the given community. Bishops and other dignitaries could sign their names during solemn visits. Similarly, benefactors could be documented there, on the inside cover, first page, etc.]
97. [*Sic.* Perhaps it should be Braclav.]

of blessed memory, Their Majesties the Kings of Poland and the Grand Dukes of Lithuania and Ruthenia, to their ancestors the citizens of our domains, all estates of the Greek Ruthenian religion and that they had suffered lawlessness in the free enjoyment of their faith; that Ruthenian Churches without appropriate pastors are suffering lack of, and are subject to diminishment in, the praise of God and the customary order; that they did not have wedding services, baptism of infants, and other Christian sacraments and rites according to the Greek custom, order, and rites, and the canons of the holy fathers established at the synods. And they asked us that we not allow them to suffer wrong and oppression and injury in this, but that we rather maintain in their ancient customs, laws, and liberties the churches of the Greek order and the people of this faith in our domains; that we always for all time present their pastors and spiritual authorities, the archbishop metropolitan, bishops, archimandrites, and other priests according to those same laws and privileges; and that we allow, guarantee, and assure that they might enjoy this ancient Christian Greek faith entirely freely, completely, peacefully, and securely.

Having heard out their request in this matter and wishing under our fortunate reign that, as everyone has enjoyed their freedoms, liberties, and law, so also particularly all the estates and people of those of our domains who are of the Catholic Greek Christian religion might not suffer any injury, wrong, or lawlessness, but that they might enjoy peacefully, freely, and securely the faith and religion according to their Greek order and rites; having maintained in entirety—wholly and completely—all people of that faith, citizens of our domains, according to the laws, privileges, and liberties given by our ancestors to the Greek churches and faith, as well as to the estates and people of that religion, clerical and lay, with this present letter of privilege we guarantee that all the estates and persons, people of the Greek religion, clerical and lay, are and will be free to enjoy according to ancient custom their faith, the orders, rites, and ceremonies of the Greek oriental Church freely, securely, and peacefully and to celebrate their religious services. And as from of old that faith has lasted through long years, having the ancient Church orders, the doctrines and writings of the holy Fathers given at synods, so it is now to last and be maintained absolutely inviolate. We are also to grant and to place over people pastors or spiritual authorities—bishops, archimandrites, hegumens, and other

Church teachers and authorities—according to those identical rights, privileges, and liberties given as of old, and we order that they not be forced to any change of the rites; rather, as it was as of old, and as the old canons and privileges describe them, they are not to have any force or compulsion; to the contrary they are to enjoy liberty and good will in all this according to the canons of the holy Fathers and their ancient laws, privileges, freedoms, liberties, and customs. And to this end we gave this our privilege with the signature of our royal hand and the Crown seal. Written in Warsaw at the General Crown Sejm in the year 1607, the month of June, the 18th day; in the twentieth year of our reign in Poland and the fourteenth in Sweden.

Sigismundus Rex [Sigismund the King]
Zachariasz Jełowicki,
Secretary and Scribe

On the Same Greek Religion: The Constitution of the Year 1609 [98]

Since the people of the Greek religion required a more fundamental pacification of their religion and explanation of the article made about this at the most recent Sejm, therefore, being unable to come to this now on account of the multitude of matters before us, we postpone it in the same force until the next Sejm. And *interim* [meanwhile], maintaining completely the constitution of the most recent Sejm, we guarantee that those spiritual authorities who accepted Union with the Roman Church in no manner and under no pretext are to oppress or trouble those who do not wish to remain with them, nor are the latter to do so to those who are in the Union; rather, they are to be maintained in peace in the bishoprics, monasteries, churches, and Church goods, both in the Crown and in the Grand Duchy of Lithuania, under a penalty of ten thousand *złoty*s against whoever should do anything against this, about which we indicate the *forum* [proper court] at the tribunal, not including in this clerical judges. *This is the constitution that was discussed. But after the completion of the Sejm, they removed the point* "not including in this clerical judges," *and they added in its place:* "And we add that if either side, beginning with the last Sejm, should take anything by force

98.   [*VL* 2:465.]

or in any manner, then we leave a free legal action by law before the tribunal *compositi judicii* [of the composite court of justice]." *Protests were made against this change to the decree of the Sejm immediately at that time.*[99]

On the Same Greek Religion: The Constitution of the Year 1618[100]

Since, on account of the multitude of matters facing the Commonwealth, we did not come to a complete pacification of the Greek religion at the present Sejm, therefore we postpone this matter to the next Sejm, during which time we maintain the people of the Greek religion, clerics and lay people, in peace and in the free and customary religion to which they are not to be compelled or drawn away by law.

On the Same Greek Religion: The Constitution of the Year 1620[101]

Pacifying the Greek religion, we reassume the constitution of the year 1607, and we are to act according to it *in futurum* [in the future] in the distribution of Church benefices.

Tribunal Decrees
Reinforcing the Degradation of the Apostate Metropolitan and Bishops by Meletius of Blessed Memory, Patriarch of Alexandria, topoteretes *[representative]* of the Patriarch of Constantinople, Published through Epistolary Decrees

The first decree in the year 1605, in which the main tribunal court does not recognize Potij, the apostate metropolitan, as elder in the extension

99.   [A tribunal *compositi judicii* included secular and clerical (Roman Catholic) judges. This was something against which not only the Orthodox but also the heterodox and some "politic" Catholics objected.]
100. [*VL* 3:158.]
101. [*VL* 3:184.]

of jurisdiction over people of the Greek religion who remain under the blessing of the patriarch of Constantinople and removes him from the metropolitanate of Kyiv and all Rus′ (in agreement with the decree of the exarch).

A second in that same year, in which the same main tribunal court makes our brotherhood of clergy and lay people free for all time from the apostate metropolitan, does not recognize him as our superior and removes us from his jurisdiction and commands him to make his claim that we have committed a wrong against him either with the patriarch of Constantinople, the natural pastor of the Ruthenian Church in this domain, or with his exarch.

A third in the year 1609, in which the main tribunal court recognizes before itself the *forum* [proper court] for Potij, the apostate metropolitan, and removes the phrase *compositi judicii* [of the composite court of justice]; moreover, it adjudges the monastery of the Holy Trinity to our brotherhood for all time.

A fourth in the same year, in which the same main tribunal court likewise recognizes the *forum* [proper court] before itself and cancels the decrees of the clergy's circle and removes all cases of the royal court.

A fifth in the same year, in which the same main tribunal court likewise recognizes before itself a *forum* for the apostate metropolitan Potij, judges him to a loss in the case, adjudges all the Orthodox Churches of Vilnius to the office of the protopope,[102] the Orthodox priests, the Ruthenian bench, and the entire Church brotherhood, people of the Greek religion, and it cancels and annuls citations summoning to the clergy's circle.

A sixth decree in the present year 1621, in which the main tribunal court, having acknowledged that the privileges and letters of Their Majesties the Kings, Our Departed Lords, and of His Royal Majesty, Our Gracious Lord, who now rules fortunately over us, cited by us pertaining to the goods of the Church and the spiritual orders, do not belong to the present-day Uniates, but properly to the people of the ancient Greek religion, the metropolitans and their clergy who are under

102. [A protopope is the first in rank among the priests of a cathedral who administers the eparchy during the absence of the bishop or a vacancy in the see.]

the power and obedience of the patriarch of Constantinople; and, given to us, are confirmed by decrees of the Sejm. Having also recognized, according to the decrees of the Sejm and the decrees of the main court of the great circle cited by us, the *forum* [proper court] before itself so that that matter might receive a fundamental pacification, it referred us, people *mere* [wholly] of the Greek religion, together with the opposing side of the Uniates (having imposed a fine of ten thousand *złotys* so that one side not cause any oppression or *praejudicium* [damage] for the other), to the court at the coming Sejm of His Royal Majesty, Our Gracious Lord, and of all the estates belonging to the Sejm.

That the Titles of the Newly Erected Church Hierarchy Could Be Declared in a Certain Manner without Disrespect for the Majesty of His Majesty the King

Thus having shown clearly, Kind and Gracious Reader, from our secular and canon laws that the newly erected hierarchy of the Ruthenian Church was erected *legitime* [legitimately], by God's grace, and that all those six bishops (for we still had the seventh Orthodox bishop of Lviv) and the eighth hierarch, the metropolitan, consecrated by the most reverend father, the patriarch of Jerusalem, were consecrated for orphaned dioceses (according to the secular and canon laws we cited), we also show that the persons consecrated to those dignities could not be consecrated without the titles of certain episcopal sees and that in this manner their titles could and had to be declared without any disrespect for the majesty of His Majesty the King, Our Gracious Lord.

Therefore, having established as certain according to the eternal canons of the Church that no bishop ought to achieve, nor can he achieve, consecration without a certain diocese (for it is characteristic for the apostolic dignity to be a bishop unlimited with respect to diocese, but not for the episcopal dignity), therefore, we say, when our Ruthenian nation for those twenty-six years asked His Majesty the King, Our Gracious Lord, for a metropolitan and bishops, it did not ask for bishops and a metropolitan bearing the titles of any sees other than those on which from days of old bishops of the Ruthenian Church resided and the metropolitan presided. For although throughout all those years it had and now has many other foreign bishops and metropolitans residing in various places in the domains of His Royal Majesty, nonetheless, it did not wish to be, and could not be, content with them since they were not its own (albeit of one and the same faith); rather, even during the constant presence of such bishops and metropolitans, it constantly asked for its own metropolitan and bishops, who belonged to it by canon and temporal law, with the titles of those sees that were already given privileges by law and by ancient custom itself. Thus when His Majesty the King, Our Gracious Lord, promises to return to our nation *in futurum* [in the future] the clergymen we have mentioned, he deigns to promise not to erect other, new bishoprics and a metropolitanate, but to place them upon those old ones that were granted privileges from days of old. Therefore, just as the patriarch of Constantinople, who is our spiritual investor, could not invest anyone through consecration to episcopal sees unheard of in the domains of His Majesty the King, Our Gracious Lord, so also His Majesty the King, Our Gracious Lord, who is the temporal investor, does not promise to erect new episcopal sees and a metropolitanate, but to restore those customary ancient ones and to give them to the bishops and the metropolitan who had been consecrated by the patriarch of Constantinople according to the eternal custom in the Ruthenian Church.

Thus the patriarch of Constantinople consecrates a metropolitan of Rus' and bishops through his brother and fellow bishop, the patriarch of Jerusalem; and he does not consecrate without specified dioceses, and not new ones at that, but the ancient ones, the spiritual investiture of which is in his hands and the temporal investiture in the hands of His Majesty the King, Our Gracious Lord. For His Majesty the King deigns to promise our nation that he does not wish to diminish or to suppress, but rather to maintain whole the greater and lesser spiritual dignities of the Greek order. And the patriarch, without the *consensus* [consent] and the permission of His Majesty the King, does not have the power to erect new dioceses. Wherefore, consecrating a metropolitan of Rus' according to his spiritual power, the father patriarch had to consecrate him to a certain diocese, which is titled "the metropolitanate of Kyiv and Halyč and all Rus'." Likewise, consecrating all the other bishops of the Ruthenian Church to their certain dioceses, which are customarily titled "of Volodymyr and Brest," "of Polack, Vicebsk, and Mscislaŭ," "of Luc'k and Ostroh," "of Przemyśl and Sambor," "of Chełm and Belz," and "of Pinsk and Turov," he had, we say, to consecrate them to precisely these particular dioceses. Further, when the consecrated persons received the dignity given to them by consecration, they received from the spiritual investiture simultaneously the dioceses and titles, since without certain dioceses, as we said, they could not be consecrated, being obliged to await temporal investiture, which *jure patronatus regii* [by the right of patronage of the King], is in the power of His Majesty the King himself. And that is what happened and continues to happen.

And since that investiture of His Majesty the King, Our Gracious Lord, could not reach them if the spiritual investiture, which contains both the dioceses and titles, was not first declared before His Majesty the King, therefore it was declared at the most recent Sejm[103] through a letter given to the representatives' circle and read aloud *publice* [publicly], which asked that Their Graces the Lord Representatives, through their duty to take care for the good of the Commonwealth, bring this matter to the attention of His Royal Majesty, Our Gracious Lord, and, at the same time, that they ask His Royal Majesty to confirm this spiritual investiture by conferring the temporal investiture, which remained in the power of His Majesty the King. And that is precisely what we were to show and what we do show: that, by their very nature, the titles of the hierarchy newly erected in the consecrated persons could and had to be declared without any disrespect for the majesty of His Majesty the King, Our Gracious Lord.

For if the spiritual investiture of those persons of the newly erected Church hierarchy, the metropolitan and bishops, were not to be declared before His Majesty the King and before the entire Commonwealth, unto what end would they bear that consecration? Was it fitting to hide what ought not to have been hidden and what could never have been hidden; what, if hidden, had to bring dishonor upon those persons and their dignity? Thus the persons were declared in their titles first before the representatives' circle so that, through Their Graces the lord land representatives, it might be brought to the attention of His Majesty the King, Our Lord. Thereafter, it was also declared in writing; and this was so that the entire Ruthenian nation might know that now, by the grace

103. [See above, p. 151, n. 52.]

of God, it had, by spiritual investiture, what His Majesty the King, Our Gracious Lord, deigned to promise to confirm by his lordly investiture, that is, through the bestowing of benefices (having promised to bestow, by his royal word, guaranteed by the constitutions of two General Sejms, the metropolitan's benefice upon the metropolitan, and the episcopal benefices upon the bishops); so that, we say, our Ruthenian nation might know of the restored Church hierarchy and might ask His Majesty the King, Our Gracious Lord, to fulfill upon it the promise of His Royal Majesty, by which he deigns to promise to give to us, as we said, not a metropolitan and bishops, but to bestow the metropolitan benefice upon the metropolitan and the episcopal benefices upon the bishops. Wherefore, for both these reasons, the titles of the newly erected metropolitan and bishops could be and had to be declared without any dishonor to the majesty of His Majesty the King, Our Gracious Lord. In which matter we proceeded purposefully so that the Church hierarchy be presented in its titles to the attention of His Majesty the King, Our Gracious Lord, before it be offered to the world as such, so that, if they were immediately ordered to keep silent about them, they would certainly have kept silent. But alas, where is the candor that is wont to seek, without any hypocrisy, the same good in the heart of one's neighbor that it feels in its own?

The Wrongs and the Afflictions That We Suffer at the Hands of Our Apostates

These, then, are the canon and secular laws, the freedoms and privileges (not citing for the time being the older privileges in this same matter) that pertain to our Ruthenian nation in its religion, to people *mere* [wholly] of the Greek religion. Having read them, Kind and Gracious Reader, deign to consider how properly our apostates draw us—against custom and intolerably—under the yoke of their obedience and seek to harness us; how properly they trouble us with their summonses and citations, deny us our honor through circular letters, sully, abuse, and dishonor honest, worthy, and absolutely unsuspect persons through the calumny of the falsely invented Turkish treason. Like mockingbirds, they disgrace and revile us, the spiritual monks and the entire common people of the city of Vilnius of our religion, with acrimonious words in the houses, in the town hall, from the pulpits, in the square, and in the streets; like some wild beast, they avoid and flee from us; they forbid the discussions and all conversation with us that had been customary until now, as if they were not Christians. They cause us the greatest pains they can, in word and in deed; they shoot stones from a slingshot at our monastery; they fling arrows from bows against the foundations and the buildings, and against the Church they fling arrows lit with a sulfur wick; they cast lit torches over the wall into the courtyards of that same monastery; into the cornerstones of the walls of the Church they stick pieces of smouldering waxed cloth together with other incendiary preparations and wicks; at the town hall and in many castles they refuse to receive protestations from us and to issue to us the cases from the books necessary for the law; they forbid the beadles to serve in our cases, and they penalize and incarcerate those who do serve; along the roads they take away our letters from the couriers, and they invent, write, and send others under our name in order to deceive uninformed people, and they scatter in populous places still other insidious ones, full of falsehood and lies together with perjury.

And thus having darkened the pure gold of our nobility and having altered the beautiful color of the good glory of our entire Ruthenian nation in order to deprive us entirely of our internal consolation, to wrest our holy faith from our breasts, and to remove us from our customary salvatory Eastern obedience, they invented and spread the allegation that three Eastern patriarchs sent Muscovy an absolution for waging war with Lithuania, alleging moreover that the pagan has all his knowledge concerning the domains of His Royal Majesty from those newly consecrated clergymen. Furthermore, they also allege that our most reverend father archimandrite, in order to cause rebellion and confusion among people through various intrigues, spread the word and alleged in Vilnius and in the Polack area that he is archbishop of Polack and that this occurred with the will of His Majesty the King.

Oh, the shamelessness: how do you, shamelessly and ignominiously, attack men worthy of every honor and respect, who love to bear upon themselves in humility and in peace the cross given to them by Christ the Lord, always well disposed toward this kingdom as a Christian kingdom, from which they await, as if from some sort of *chrēmatism*,[104] with God's help, their liberation from this harsh servitude? How do you maliciously assail, without any fear of God, God's faithful servants, who are not wont to absolve anyone when that will cause a sin and who enjoy the peace of Christian domains? Throughout all the years of the servitude of our holy patriarchs did you ever see even the least suspicion of ill will toward our fatherland, to say nothing of treason? How unwisely do you also attack, against all truth, those newly consecrated persons of good conscience, who love their fatherland as their soul itself and who have parents, brothers, sisters, and other relatives and kin in those lands nearer to the Foe—in Volhynia, the Ukraine, Podillja, and Pidhir'ja. And that the person so charged boasted of the will of His Majesty the King in order to cause rebellion among people—this is a mendacious allegation here as in everything else. To the contrary: the opposite is clear. Does the quick pupil of revenge in the never-sleeping eye in God's vengeful might sleep in the presence of such calumniators? Your truth is just like the one with which you suffocated almost all the Lithuanian and Crown domains, alleging that here in Vilnius citizens convicted of treason are poisoning themselves in the houses and prisons; that in Lviv some tens of citizens convicted of the same treason were executed; that great men, noble, high-born, who serve their fatherland and His Majesty the King, Our Gracious Lord, in this present campaign—captains and colonels— through the demonstration of this same treason had their companies taken away from them and that they themselves were punished with death; that we too sent two brothers from our monastery to Muscovy in order to commit treason. Oh, the malice. Where here is conscience? Where piety? If anyone should wish to believe the daily news from your infernal smithy, he would have to give up the ghost on the spot. Now (so you say) letters of treason have been intercepted; now those who were tortured have confessed; now many from Rus' have been caught at spying.

But they speak three sorts of falsehoods (for that is how the apostate theologians, who were rebuked for this malice, defend themselves):

104. [Smotryc'kyj sets the word in italics as a foreign expression. A χρηματισμός is (1) a divine injunction or message; (2) a charter or instrument recording the liberties of a city.]

officiosum, jocosum, perniciosum [helpful, humorous, malicious].[105] Does any one of these three allow you to lie against the honor and the blood of your neighbor? Are humorous and helpful lies of the sort that cause harm? It is about the malicious lie that God says: "Thou shalt not lie."[106] Will we not give account to the Lord on the day of judgment for each idle word, to say nothing of each mendacious and blood-thirsty word?[107] Are we supposed to do evil things that good might come?[108] "Abstain from every thing similar to evil," says the blessed apostle Paul.[109] Further, David, the king and prophet, giving testimony about God who hates lying, says: "Thou hatest all workers of iniquity. Thou shalt destroy them that speak lies: the Lord will abhor the bloody and deceitful man."[110] Let them speak lies in order to earn God's hatred, abhorrence, and extermination (which we do not wish them, but rather repentance), since their theology allows them this. We and the Church of God do not have that custom.

But is that the only evil against us and against our entire nation from this smithy of the abyss? We would certainly run out of paper before we could present the daily, unbearable, and acrimonious vexations that we suffer from our apostates. For with every third word they revile and shame us, calling us schismatics unto the abomination of our immaculate faith and calling us Nalyvajkos unto the shame of the pure honor of our nation. In which a great injustice is done us by them: Their Majesties the Kings, Our Lords, the ancestors of blessed memory of His Majesty the King, Our Gracious Lord, and His Royal Majesty himself, in all of our laws, conditions, oaths, statutes, constitutions, privileges, in their circular letters and in their private letters, deign to call us in no other manner but people of the Greek religion and that is *ad differentiam* [to distinguish us] from people of the Roman religion. Whereas, with respect to our apostates, His Majesty the King, Our Gracious Lord, in

---

105. [This is the tripartite categorization of types of lies that St. Thomas Aquinas provided in the *Summa Theologica, secunda secundaeque* 110, art. 2. See Thomas 1897, 423; cf. Suarez 1859, 682.]
106. Ex. 23[:1]; Job 13[:4]; Lev. 19[:11].
107. Mt. 12[:36].
108. Rom. 3[:8].
109. 1 Th. 5[:22].
110. Ps. 5[:5–6].

the above-cited constitution of the year 1607, deigns to call us people *mere* [wholly] of the Greek religion, and in the cited privilege given to us at that same time he deigns to call us people of the Catholic Greek Christian religion. But that people (that we not use that word, at which, so we hear, they take offense, although wrongly so; for what sort of respectable name for a man of the Eastern confession—of which they boast—is the name "Uniate"?); but, we say, that people—which, as far as its religion itself is concerned, knows its own name—abuses us by calling us apostates, without any justice or proper cause, not wishing to see (mercy, by God, it is holy mercy that we seek even through this work, wherefore we refrain from using here those words that would increase hatred); not wishing, we say, to see that they themselves are neither of the Greek religion nor of the Roman. We Rus' of the Eastern obedience and confession are people *mere* [wholly] of the Catholic Greek religion; their lords the Poles and Lithuanians of the Western obedience and confession are people *mere* [wholly] of the Roman Catholic religion. They [the Uniates] are between us and the Romans something *non merum,* something not pure, but *fictum,* something invented, neither the one nor the other. Therefore it is rather their proper name and not ours, since they, having become apostate from their customary and natural pastor, the patriarch of Constantinople, acquired the name of apostates; having become apostate from the Holy Catholic Apostolic Church that is in the East, they acquired the name apostates.

But deign to consider, Kind and Gracious Reader, whether the name of Nalyvajko does not also properly suit them. For not having kept faith with their proper lord in the Spirit, that is, the patriarch of Constantinople (whom the authorities of our Ruthenian Church are obliged by both canon and temporal law to recognize as their lord in the Spirit and pastor), they broke their oath against all proper reason, not to mention against all law; they withdrew their spiritual obedience; they rendered obedience to another lord in the Spirit; and having declared war against the first, they oppress, tax, impoverish, and persecute unto death in every manner his subjects in the Spirit; and they revile, shame, and deny honor and faith to their former, natural lord himself. Does not the name of Nalyvajko suit rather such people? By what right are we reviled with this name, we who remain with our customary lord in the Spirit and pastor, whom our ancestors acquired when they received Christianity and whom their descendants passed on to us?

If some palatine, having broken his oath to his proper king, should withdraw his obedience from him and offer his obedience to some other foreign king, wage war against the former, and seek to remove the people who belonged to him in his palatinate by right of supervision and to the king by innate right, using compulsion and force through various afflictions and oppressions—if this should happen, what must we then believe? Would it be the people who abandoned the palatine and stand faithfully by their customary, natural king and lord that should be known as and called unfaithful to the king (that we not speak more precisely)? Or would it be the palatine and those who follow him in this? Judge the same in this case. The metropolitan in the Ruthenian land is after the image of the palatine, and the patriarch of Constantinople is after the image of the king. Who is more at fault here? Who is Nalyvajko? We who, keeping complete faith with the patriarch our natural lord in Spirit, do not abandon him? Or the metropolitan who, not having kept faith with him, both abandoned him and led away some of his subjects in the Spirit and, seeking to lead others away, oppresses, taxes, wrongs, and by various difficulties seeks to convince them to abandon their proper lord in Spirit and offer obedience to the one to whom, against all law, he falsely offered his oath?

Therefore consider, Kind and Gracious Reader, and judge, we ask, as your God and conscience are dear to you: whom do both things suit properly and justly, to be called a renegade and a Nalyvajko?

The Tragedy That Happened to the Faithful in the City of Vilnius at the Importunity of the Apostates

Our apostates did and do treat us this way during this and all other times, presenting us as a spectacle for the abuse of the world, not fearing in this either the fear of God, nor having regard for human shame, nor respecting even the obligation of nature itself, not to say of humanity (we do not even mention the severity of common law). For they did this (if we may briefly present to you the lamentable tragedy that happened to us recently in Vilnius) just at that time when it fell to all of Christendom to celebrate the salvatory memory of the death on the cross of Christ our Lord during the week that we call *strastny* [Ruthenian: "passion"], that is, *hebdomadam passionis* [week of passion], the week of the passion of the Lord, in which Judas, Caiaphas, and Annas, scheming treason with the like-minded, thought up the calumny by which they would bring the innocent, calumniated Christ the Lord to his death; during that time, when every Christian, conforming externally and internally to the crucified Christ the Lord, endeavors, in a humbled and contrite heart, to crucify himself entirely with Him unto the world and the body and all their lusts;[111] during this week, we say, in which pious people of our religion in the city of Vilnius, humbling their hearts before the Lord God, prepared for fervent penance and the lamentatious remembrance of the passion of Christ the Lord and, righting their consciences, prepared themselves for a confession of their sins, thinking to make themselves ready to receive the life-giving mysteries of the body and the blood of the Son of God.

But on Flower Saturday[112] all their pious intentions were confounded. For wherever the city servants met one of them, they gave him the order on the spot to appear at the town hall, where, without any accuser, at the instigation of the city procurator, not allowed access to any defenses or benefits of the law and given to the procurator for defense almost in the last instance, they were taken from the court of arraignment to the Councilor's Court. Immediately thereupon, on one and the same day, questioned individually at an inquisition under threat of the torture chamber, they were given over to the town hall prison.[113] And from among them, three—their belts and knives taken away from them—were separated out on Monday of Holy Week and brought to the underground prison, where the most dishonorable, manifest criminals are usually placed.[114] Others remained in the first prison. On Wednesday of the same week a councilor of the same city of Vilnius was ordered not to leave the town hall because he asked the city scribe for extracts from

111. [1 Jn 2:16–17; Gal. 5:24; Gal. 6:14.]

112. [That is, the Saturday before Palm Sunday; in 1621, 25 March/4 April. That year, Orthodox Easter (1 April, old style) fell on the same day as Western Easter (11 April, new style).]

113. Gentlemen incarcerated in the town hall: Semen Iwanowicz, Jan Kotowicz, Fedor Kuszelicz, Bogdan Borysowicz, Wasyly Baranowicz, Wasyly Kułakowski, Wasyly Druhowina, Krzysztof Wasylewicz, Stefan Zahorski.

114. Gentlemen incarcerated under the town hall: Semen Krasowski, Bogdan Symonowicz, Isaak Wołkowicz.

the books on this case.[115] On Thursday another councilor of the same city of Vilnius was forbidden and was ordered not to leave the town hall because he attended the funeral of his colleague, a mayor of Vilnius, who was buried in our church.[116] In those same days a certain cobbler was thrown into prison because he had gone on the pilgrimage to Kyiv during the feast of the Dormition of the Most Holy Virgin.[117] For other pious faults, others were banned, seized, tormented, and tortured under the town hall without any law and judgment during the entire week of the Lord's passion and during the holy days. At that same time the keys to their guild privilege were taken away from the artisans.

Oh, if only, noble Ruthenian nation, you could have been present to behold our miserable and merciless tragedy! You would have seen honorable matrons, barely alive, running with children across the square, not knowing what was happening so unexpectedly and occurring so suddenly to their dear spouses. Mothers ask about sons, wives about husbands, children about fathers, and they seek to discover where they were and what was happening to them. Crying, clamor, complaint, heartfelt laments pierce the heavens; heavy sighs darken the skies with clouds; tears from eyes that stream with blood drench faces and breasts as with rain. For everywhere in the houses, streets, and on the square, we heard that one un-Christian voice: traitors, traitors—Rus' are godless people, traitors, and spies.

O noble Ruthenian nation, that we say it for the second time! To what sort of dishonor for your faithful and bloody deeds shown in the past and demonstrated even today in the service of the Kings, God's anointed, Our Gracious Lords, to what sort of dishonor, we say, have you come during these your heavy times of the unhappy apostasy that threatens your honor and piety, such that burghers of insignificant condition, a careless town hall court, without any law and proof, without judgment and sentence, at the instigation of a blustery apostate, declares and decrees *publice* [publicly] that you are traitors? You would have heard and seen all this for yourselves if you had been present with us in Vilnius during these several weeks.

---

115. Lord Jerzy Chociejewicz.
116. Lord Filip Sienczyłowicz. [He was a member of the Vilnius annual council in 1620. See LVIA SA 5324:13v.]
117. Lord Łukasz Sobol.

You would have heard in the Church of God hymns about the passion of Christ the Lord, and in the houses, the sobs of pious people at the murders of the chosen people of Christ the Lord. In the Church of God they sang "Today Judas watches to betray Christ,"[118] and in the city hall they hold court that His servants as well be betrayed. It was customary that during that last week of Lent there be no court cases and the city hall be closed; now even this was not kept. Oh, he watched all right; he watched to betray Christ. He watched that in the house of God one stone not stand upon another,[119] that old and young be scattered from it. He tried force, he risked the lives of many for that. But what can a man do against him with whom God is?[120] What are the eyes of man against the sun? Thus passed for us in sorrow the sorrowful week of the Lord's passion.

The glorious day of Easter came. What sort of consolation was this for the poor prisoners who, throughout all the bygone years, had the custom, as on other days, especially on that excellent day of the Lord's resurrection, to nourish their souls with the life-giving mysteries of the body and the blood of the Son of God, and yet at that time, in spite of great requests made to the city magistracy, they could not receive it? They were unable to make themselves capable of the humanity—that we do not say, of the piety—not to deny to these honorable and God-fearing men what no man is denied in his religion by any court: they did not allow them to enjoy that spiritual consolation on that excellent day. Oh, woe to the city where one lives in such a way that the good are not distinguished from the evil, nor the evil from the good! Woe to the city that abhors the peaceful and delights in the rebellious! Woe to the city that makes citizens of ignoramuses and exiles of wise men! And that must occur in every city where frivolous youth governs, and wise old age is in disrepute. Looking at the similar government of some city, the dying Diogenes ordered that, after his death, he be put into the ground and buried there upside down. When one of his comrades raised with him the unusualness of this, he said: "Do not be surprised. Young men, and all of the same condition, now rule in this city. Soon they will turn this city upside down; at that time they will also turn me right

118. [Good Friday matins, Antiphone 6; *VS* 3:1:468.]
119. [Mt. 24:2; Mk. 13:2; Lk. 19:44.]
120. Rom. 8[:31].

side up."[121] God forbid that this happen here. But back to the matter at hand.

There were some of those honorable prisoners who offered that their mothers, wives, and children be put into prison as a surety that they might be allowed to go to church for a few hours, so that, having set themselves right in their consciences before the Lord God through holy confession on such a glorious holy day, they might have been able to become worthy of being partakers of the life-giving mysteries of the body and the blood of the Son of God. But they were not permitted even this in this manner. Alas, for piety. What sort of consolation can there be for the body where the spirit is sorrowful?

Thus these blessed sufferers, covered with the false cloak of treason by malicious calumniators, deprived by the obstinacy of merciless judges of both bodily and spiritual consolations on account of their religion, spent these glorious days in sorrow of their souls in this cruel prison, where, patiently bearing the inconveniences of prison in pleasant gratitude, they praised the Lord God that he deigned to make them worthy to suffer somewhat for His holy truth according to the capacity of their strength.

We commend them themselves and their liberation, kind and gracious reader, unto your prayer to the Lord God and unto your care, to the extent that a man can take care for another man; and especially unto your prayer, our Fellow in Confession, so that bearing one another's burdens we might fulfill the law of Christ the Lord.[122]

A Short Admonition to Our Own People

And in addition to your prayer for them and for us, Fellow in Confession, Beloved of God, O Noble Ruthenian Nation, we also ask of you these two things: that, constantly mindful of the Lord God, your Creator, you might also be mindful of your holy faith and of your noble glory. Serve the Lord your God, loving Him with all the strength of your soul, and guard your faith more carefully than your health, than your life. For you are a follower and lover of the holy faith that, in you, God declared

---

121. *Diogen* [Diogenes Laertius relates this story about Diogenes the Cynic in his *Lives of Eminent Philosophers,* 6:32].
122. Gal. 6[:2].

genuine and Orthodox through illustrious miracles. It was this faith that the Lord God declared genuine and soul-saving through the Gospel that was thrown into the fire but did not burn. It was also this faith that almighty God showed to be immaculate and genuine in the blinded Volodimer, as in a second apostle Paul, through the opening of his eyes and the return of his sight during his reception of holy baptism in your holy Church. It is also this your faith that the incorruptible bodies and the bones flowing with myrrh in the holy monasteries of Kyiv declare to be the faith of Christ the Lord, taught by His holy apostles.[123] Perhaps someone else will boast of a similar good, but which is not his own or which he does not possess; but you have all that here at home. Whoever wishes to receive information about all this with his ears, let him read reliable chronicles; and whoever desires to see it with his eyes, let him go to the Kyiv Caves, and there with his faithful heart he will see clearly the Lord our God worshipped in his saints.[124]

Further, according to your constant and native custom, honor as king, the King, Your Gracious Lord, God's anointed, to whose majesty the hearts that drench you with bile and the unharnessed tongues of raging mouths allege that you are ill disposed, unfaithful, a traitor, an enemy. Respect him as God's anointed, fear Him as the Lord, keep faith with Him as your protector, render obedience to Him as your superior, pray to the Lord God as the guardian of your peace.[125] And mindful of the glory of your worthy ancestors, deign to show in the present instance as well that you are their descendants in prowess and fidelity to their lords.

Let your enemies be ashamed. Let their lying mouths be stopped,[126] and let them swallow in themselves their calumnious words, those who traduce you with calumny before Your Gracious Lord, His Majesty the King, beneath whose most illustrious majesty you always bent, bend, and will bend your humble neck in all fidelity, humility, and goodwill.

---

123. Zon. *lib. 3 in Imperato. Basili Maced* [Zonaras, *Annales,* bk. 16; *PG* 135:59–60]; Długo. *lib 2. in An. 990* [Jan Długosz, *History of Poland,* bk. 2, s.a. 990; Długosz 1962, 272–4; DługEng 6], Stryk. *lib. 4 pagin 143 et 144* [Maciej Stryjkowski, *History,* bk. 4, pp. 143 and 144; Stryjkowski 1846, 125–34].
124. Ps. 150 [149:1].
125. 1 Pet. 2[:17].
126. Ps. 6[:10]; Ps. 62 [63:11].

You can have an important and, by God's grace, illustrious protection in this current successful (may God grant it) expedition against the sworn enemy of Christendom, the Mussulman: in the lieutenants, the captains, the colonels, and the company, in all the army units and regiments, and in the entire Zaporozhian army. Therefore, you must report for duty as a nation of good repute, of all fidelity, humble goodwill, and submissive subservience, in all peace, in harmony, love, fear of God, and in the obedience owed to the highest authority and the superior regiment. And may almighty God bless you; let Him lead you; let Him aid you. By your forces and those of your brethren, the worthy Polish and Lithuanian nations, let the enemy of Christendom—in his haughty neck and all the Christian estates he has gained as plunder—be cast and spread at the most illustrious feet of the King our Lord, whom may the Lord deign to bless out of Zion.[127]

And especially as throughout all those past years of the apostasy you kept a watchful eye on the apostates from your Church, so now keep an even more watchful eye, that you might beware of them and that you not allow yourselves to be led by them any further and to be led astray; for they did not cause for you the unification for which you pray to the Lord God in the daily prayers of the holy liturgy, but some sort of confusion most harmful to your canon and secular laws, and they cast the evil shame of impiety upon the holy eastern faith, upon its faithful sons, and upon its unsuspect faith. "The holy Church of Christ the Lord," says St. John Chrysostom, "is never done such great harm and injury by her manifest enemies as by her own apostate sons. For an injury from her manifest enemies makes her more magnificent and more illustrious, but an injury from apostates brings her shame and disgrace before her enemies, since she is persecuted and destroyed by her own sons to whom she gave birth. For a great sign of scandal unto the enemies must arise from the fact that her own sons suddenly abandon the mother Church in which they were born and raised, and in which they learned the salvatory mysteries, and, having become her betrayers, storm against her, like her main enemies, and beat and do battle against her."[128] Thus St. John Chrysostom.

---

127. Ps. 127 [128:5].
128. *Homil. 11 in cap. 4 ad Eph.* [St. John Chrysostom, *Homily 11 on Eph. 4; PG* 62:85–6; *NPNF1* 13:106].

You yourself now learn, noble Ruthenian nation, that it is so and no other way when you see that your apostates, who were born of your own mother and raised in her soul-saving goods, place both your holy Catholic Church and your Orthodox faith in some sort of suspicion and dishonor through their careless apostasy; for they cast into hell their ancestors and yours as if they were heterodox and impious, and they declare that the patriarchs of the Holy Eastern Church are convicted heretics. And in short, they subject your entire salvatory spiritual good to the disgust and abhorrence of all of Christendom. Is that then a characteristic of unification: to criticize even the best of one's own and to prefer even the basest of someone else's to the most important of one's own? Certainly he who has lost his head, but imagines that he has eyes in his body, must see just as much. For what sort of happy success can be expected in this matter without the head of our Ruthenian Church? Without, we say, the patriarch of Constantinople, our superior pastor, who is the head of the body of our Ruthenian Church? For he was not approached with even one iota or any word to discover whether this could have happened *with* his knowledge, permission, and blessing, and not without him himself.

But (you say) Jeremiah, the patriarch of Constantinople of blessed memory, was present here—and soon after his stay the man he himself consecrated caused this apostasy at the provocation of worthless people.[129] Was he informed of this? Were the need and proper reason for this presented to him? Was he asked for the means? Nothing of the sort. Rather, having transgressed against the Church canons, escaping lawful punishment—since for some it was a matter of the entire dignity—they determined to, and did, abandon him rather than justify themselves before him for any transgressions. And with what fortune they did this, not only do you experience yourself, worthy Ruthenian nation, but all the citizens of the dual Commonwealth experience and see what sort of tumults, what tortures, what legal cases, what deprivation of goods

---

129. [On his return from Muscovy in 1589 (where he had helped create the patriarchate of Moscow), Jeremiah stopped in Rus'. Among his reforming interventions in Ruthenian Church life, he deposed Metropolitan Onysyfor Divočka on the grounds that he had been twice married and replaced him with Myxajil Rahoza, one of the eventual proponents of the Union of Brest. See Gudziak 1998, 189–207.]

and health of many people there have been for a long time in many cities, Brzeście Wielkie, Pinsk, Lviv, Przemyśl, Luc'ko, Krasnystav, Bużko, Chełm, Sokal, and other cities and towns of those lands testify; and nowadays and earlier in Vilnius, Minsk, Naŭharadok, Polack, Vicebsk, Orša, Mahilëŭ, and many others, where, without any mercy, our apostates torment, beat, calumniate, imprison, torture, and charge with blood crimes the poor people of our ancient religion.

But if it were permitted that all this reach, in our bloody tears, His Majesty the King, Our Gracious Lord, the merciful, paternal heart of His Royal Majesty would already take mercy upon our unbearable miseries; he would already have saved us, the humble and well-disposed subjects of Our Gracious Lord, from those cruel oppressions. May almighty God deign to cause it to happen that, this time at least, in the case of the harsh, mendacious allegation about us to His Royal Majesty, Our Gracious Lord, our honest *Verification* might be allowed to reach the hands of His Royal Majesty. If he directs just one glance of his lofty understanding toward it, we trust that he will deign to see our innocence and, moreover, will order that we, his faithful subjects, be left in peace, for which we ask His Royal Majesty, Our Gracious Lord, with a humble heart and without which we cannot live. May the holy Lord grant it unto the eternal peace of our dear fatherland.

The heat was so hot and sudden, so tempestuously blustering the gale, so terrifying the storm as if it had been that Terrible Day; nor does it storm so in the cruelest siege when defeat hangs just over one's neck. The poor people, stupefied and unaware of what was happening to them, run here and there as if unconscious and ask what this is, whence such unheard-of voices, whence that unprecedented outrage, whence such unusual mockings and abuse, truly inimical, from neighbors and fellow merchants and fellow artisans. So sudden and harsh was the persecution and un-Christian the oppression that they could properly have declared about themselves in their heavy days in the bitterness of their hearts these words of the prophet.

The Consolation of the Innocence of the Noble Ruthenian Nation[130]

We weep sore, and our tears are on our cheeks. There is no sorrow like unto our sorrow,[131] and we do not have a comforter.[132] Our brothers have despised us and become our un-brothers, and they wish to roll the yoke of their transgressions and to place it upon our necks.[133] We live among Christians, and yet we find no rest for our great affliction in body and heavy servitude in conscience.[134] We sob, oppressed in bitterness[135] by the apostate brethren, who have removed from us all our beauty;[136] they have turned our heart within us,[137] and we are full of bitterness from them. We sigh, and there is none to comfort us.[138] We cry, and there is none to wipe the tears from our eyes. Many are our sighs, and our heart is pitiful,[139] for our apostates have begun to burn, like a burning and devouring flame; they have drawn out their treacherous bows, and they have placed us as a mark for the arrows.[140] They stretched out and strengthened their right arms in order to slay all they saw that was pleasant to the eye in our holy Ruthenian Church.[141] They have opened their calumnious mouths against us,[142] they have given out false and stupid things. They feed us with the ashes of bad glory, and they give us to drink of the wormwood of dead treason.[143] They clap their hands above us, they whistle, and they wag their heads; they hiss at us, they gnash their teeth, and they say:[144] "We will swallow

130. Jeremiah in *Lamentations*.
131. [Lam. 1:2, 12.]
132. [Lam. 1:9; 1:2, 17, 21.]
133. [Lam. 1:14.]
134. [Lam. 1:3.]
135. [Lam. 1:4, 3:15.]
136. [Lam. 1:6; 2:1.]
137. [Lam. 1:20.]
138. [Lam. 1:21.]
139. [Lam. 1:22.]
140. [Lam. 2:3–4; 3:12.]
141. [Lam. 2:4.]
142. [Lam. 2:16; 3:46.]
143. [Lam. 3:15.]
144. [Lam. 2:15.]

them up, we will devour them. Certainly this is the day that we looked for; we have found it, we have seen it, we have done what we intended, we have carried out what we schemed in our hearts.[145] Therefore, let us corrupt them, and let us not allow their good to pass. Let us rejoice at the evil that we have cast upon their heads, and let us raise up the horn of our pride,[146] and let us shout out in the strength of our falsehood, 'Hah, now we reign over them.'"

Struck by this from them, our heart cries out to the Lord, pours out tears like a river; it gives itself no rest, and the apple of our eyes does not cease.[147] We pour out our heart like water before the face of the Lord; we lift up our hands toward him,[148] and in the bitterness of our heart we cry out: Remember, O Lord, what has happened to us;[149] look upon us and see our abuse. Our apostates wish to turn our inheritance over to strangers, our churches to aliens.[150] We eat our own bread in their house for a fee; we must drink our own water for money.[151] They imprison us, press and drive us after them that we lose our way; they give no rest to the weary. They themselves have sinned, and yet they command us to bear their iniquities; they wish to rule over us at risk to our souls, believing that there is no one to liberate us from their hands.

See, therefore, O Lord, see—we ask urgently—and behold our sorrow.[152] Behold how our apostates have summoned as for a solemn day those who will frighten us round about, so that one of us would betray unto them or do what makes a guilty man of an innocent man; behold how they build around us and compass us with their gall.[153] They have become for us, alas (but even here, pure charity, which does not seek its own benefit in this holy matter, which thinks no evil, rejoices in the truth, and expects all things;[154] even here, we say, pure charity gives way to the words of the wailing we have heard); they have become for

145. [Lam. 2:16–17.]
146. [Lam. 2:17.]
147. [Lam. 2:18.]
148. [Lam. 2:19.]
149. [Lam. 2:20.]
150. [Lam. 5:2.]
151. [Lam. 5:4.]
152. [Lam. 1:18.]
153. [Lam. 3:5.]
154. 1 Cor. 13[:5–7].

us, alack, [bears lying in wait to betray us, lions in secret places,[155] snakes in the cracks of the earth, vipers on the road, dragons along the paths];[156] and they seek to break us with the poison of their vehemence and to make us desolate. Sensing in our misery and considering in our hearts what has been inflicted by them, we have our hope in You, our God, whose mercies have not ceased and whose compassions are whole.[157] You are our portion, our oppressed soul awaits You.[158] For You are good to those who have their hope in You. You are good to the soul that seeks You.[159] We are already filled with abuse, but You have compassion, O Lord, according to the multitude of Your mercies.[160] Malicious people incline their judgment according to their lust that they might overturn innocent people in their judgment. But who could say for something to happen when God does not command it? Our apostates have torn open their mouths with fear, a snare,[161] and false hourly reports. But our Lord God will allow Himself to be entreated. He will look and see from heaven, and He will shield us with a cloud that their snares and terrors might not reach us.[162] They have chased us sore, like a bird;[163] they dig dungeons against our life, and they prepare the stones that they would place upon us;[164] and they cry out: "They have already perished, they have already perished."

But You, Lord of heaven and earth, whose holy name we summon: hear our voice; do not turn Your ear from our sigh and cry.[165] Look upon our affliction, for our enemies have tormented us; look upon the entire people sighing and seeking peace. Draw near in the day that we

---

155. [Lam. 3:10.]
156. [The text in brackets, from "bears" to "paths," is supplied from the first edition (Smotryc'kyj 1621a, K2v/303). In reworking the text for the second edition, the typesetter seems to have omitted it.]
157. [Lam. 3:22.]
158. [Lam. 3:24.]
159. [Lam. 3:25–6.]
160. [Lam. 3:32.]
161. [Lam. 3:46–7.]
162. [Lam. 3:44.]
163. [Lam. 3:52.]
164. [Lam. 3:53.]
165. [Lam. 3:56.]

call upon You; say unto us, "Fear not."[166] You Yourself judge the cause
of our soul, O Redeemer of our life.[167] See the wrong of our opponents
against us, and judge our cause.[168] See all their vehemence, all their
imaginations against us.[169] You hear, O Lord, their reproaches, and You
see all their imaginations against us.[170] We are their song, to whom You
will render a recompense, O Lord, according to the deeds of their lips
and their hearts.[171]

They could properly have declared about themselves, that we say
it again, in their heavy days in the bitterness of their hearts these words
of the prophet; and they did declare them: they roared in the sad sorrow
of their soul.

Epilogue to the Calumniator

But now at the conclusion of our undertaking to prove our innocence
we would ask him who mercilessly caused this malice, blustering over
us: to what end did he attack our honorable Ruthenian nation with
such a crude calumny? With what intent does he seek to smear our
face, pure in its glory, with this ugly blot? It is certainly unheard of
that anything should be more oppressive for a good man than violence
to his conscience and a blot on his honor. For one of them prevents a
man from living his temporal life, and the other wrests away his eternal
life. And were it possible, a person would prefer to die many times
a most difficult death than to be enslaved or blotted by either one of
these. But only he can know this who loves and takes delight in his
honor more than his health, and in his conscience more than his life.
Good conscience has given birth to so many martyrs that almost every
day of the year it abounds in fifty thousand souls laid down for the
faith. The defense of honor, which often sacrificed health and life itself,
has left illustrious examples both among the pagan nations and among
God's people. Swords, fires, saws, beasts, wheels, and various similar

166. [Lam. 3:57.]
167. [Lam. 3:58.]
168. [Lam. 3:59.]
169. [Lam. 3:60.]
170. [Lam. 3:61.]
171. [Lam. 3:63–4.]

instruments of torture would seem as nothing if only conscience had remained pure and honor unblotted. For it is by far a dearer thing to a good man to die well than to live badly or to have bad fame. Hence the blessed apostle Paul says, "Our glory is this, the testimony of our conscience."[172] And again: "It were far better for me to die, than that any man should make my glorying void."[173] Thus what can be more oppressive for the conscience than this "Believe as *I* wish?" And what can be more hideous for honor than calumny?

We would ask, then, the worker of this malice, who breathes calumny and threatens death: to what end does he do this? Whether under the pretext of calumny to spread his evil and to suppress our good? And to cause that there be no Rus' in Rus'?[174] That sort of intent may be in his hands, but the outcome is with God's will. But if it is to leave Rus' in Rus' and to display the Ruthenian good that arrived from the East by God's providence, then why does he do it with such malice? But this is already the twenty-sixth year, and there has been nothing good for the Church of God, nor beneficial for our nation, not to mention salvatory for human souls.

What sort of spiritual benefit have we received from this disorderly and most harmful undertaking? The Ruthenian Orthodox churches on the estates of their lords, the Romans, have been turned into Catholic churches, Uniates into Romans, altar places in the cities into kitchens, taverns, and Mussulman mosques. The Church rites are in a shameful disorder, the clergy in boorish crudeness. The schools have been neglected, the Slavonic language despised, the Ruthenian ridiculed; monastic discipline is disrespected, canon laws trampled, the faith made heretical, conscience stupefied, and love destroyed. Hatred has conquered, falsehood reigns, calumny has come to rule. Innocent blood abounds for the pouring. What sort of strange spiritual good is this?

172. 2 Cor. 1[:12].
173. 1 Cor. 9[:15].
174. [A silent borrowing from Jan Szczęsny Herburt's "Statement about the Ruthenian Nation," first presented as a speech to the dietine in Sudova Vyšnja in November 1613. The text circulated in manuscript, and Zaxarija Kopystens′kyj translated it into Ruthenian in his *Palinodia*. For an English translation, see *HLEULT* 3:708–15.]

Certainly undeliberated action in eternal, divine matters can provide the answer to this.

Diu delibera, cito fac [deliberate for a long time, act quickly], someone advises.[175] Those who arranged this matter did not deliberate as much as they have been quickly acting. They deliberated barely a year, and they have already been acting for twenty-six years; and yet this is the sum of the internal good from their work. That is, as we say, our apostates are such great enemies of the eastern religion in us that the Slavonic schools in their dioceses are completely abandoned, neglected, and suppressed. The churches in the cities and towns are desolate. In Vilnius, in those same places in which our eyes saw the altars of bloodless sacrifice before the fire of the several years past, they now see built taverns and public kitchens.[176] In Minsk, now that the Tatar mosque has been built on the Orthodox Church square, the would-be metropolitans seek through their letters to oblige the local Mussulmans to serve them. On the lordly estates of the Roman religion they allow their Uniate churches to be transformed into Catholic churches. With the loss of human souls they send boy-priest ignoramuses, by whom, as if on purpose, they submit the most pure piety of Eastern Orthodoxy to the disgust of our people and of others. They allow twice-married and thrice-married men to celebrate the sacrifices of the altar and the sacraments. Throughout all the ages since Rus' was baptized, it was never permitted that Ruthenian bishops and monks eat meat. Now they do not forbid this to either of them. That undeliberated apostasy has brought and caused for our Ruthenian nation so much internal unmitigated harm and in so short a time.

And what about the external harm? On account of the Union, the dietines face uproar and chaos, all the courts face confusion and contention, Sejms face difficulty, God's anointed faces molestations, innocent people face court proceedings, banishments, penalty, prison,

---

175. [Arthaber 1049; cf. Erasmus *Ad.* 4.2.75; Tosi 1584.]

176. [Much of Vilnius burned in 1610. Several of the formerly Orthodox, now Uniate, churches were either abandoned or only slowly rebuilt. In the response to Smotryc'kyj's *Verification* we read: "Ten years ago the Lord God visited Vilnius with such a violent fire that barely anything remained whole in the city. Among other churches (Catholic), five of our bricked churches (Uniate/ Orthodox), and six wooden ones" (*Sowita* 1621, 78).]

torture, calumny. On this account the churches are sealed, Church services forbidden, children leave this world without baptism, adults without the salvatory sacrament of the body and the blood of the Son of God. On this account there are unheard-of excesses, and on this account, we say, there are also acrimonious writings. And, in one word, on this account our Ruthenian Church, both externally and internally—were it not for the fact that the Lord of mercy supports it—is in a conflagration that leads to destruction.

They seek to destroy us, and they themselves are also dying. They have become some sort of unhappy camp, only too harmful to us, set up from us ourselves against the Church of our Ruthenian nation and artfully compassed about us. From behind which whoever wishes to do so attacks us, and we, to say nothing of repelling anyone, are unable to defend ourselves. And it goes quite the same for them. Whence the people of God's Church are scattered like chaff among various sects, although we know for certain that none is lost, but the son of perdition.[177] In Naŭharadok and in many other cities practically all the foremost citizens were forced into this apostasy, and in various palatinates, and especially in the Volhynian palatinate, the *szlachta* preferred, at the risk of losing their soul, rather to cast themselves to the Dunkers[178] than to suffer and bear the apostate compulsion. Whence someone, whether justly or unjustly we do not judge, called them March snow with respect to us: since, as we said, they both drown us and themselves more quickly melt; they destroy us, and they themselves are quickly lost. Which this time, through their inhuman treatment of us, they see clearly, when they reckon how many they gained from this present war; for, as they say, three score rode out to it, but half a score returned. This, as we said, is what undeliberated action in eternal divine matters can do.

Were it not for that undertaking, comprised less of deliberating than of acting, would there be in the world such *Apologies, Parēgorias, Admonitions, Resurrected Nalyvajkos,* such Clerks, *Apocrises, Antigraphēs, Laments,* and other such works? In which, as far as the

---

177. [Jn. 17:12.]
178. [*Nurkowie*—a generic term of abuse in Polish for all Anabaptists, akin in its etymology to the word "Dunker," although the latter refers, at least in the American context, to a one particular Anabaptist group, the Church of the Brethren.]

words are concerned, there often had to be, what the *primi motus* [first passions] in man, as they say, are wont to do. May God have pity on this, which occurs with harm to the conscience in people of the same birth according to the Spirit.

If the current need for the elevation of the Church hierarchy, and a need so drastic that we could not remain alive in the soul any longer without it, was alleged a criminal transgression, would the doer of the current evil deeds have deliberated longer about this rather than acting quickly? Where is the place in this matter for dishonoring publications, improper citations, unlawful anathemas, cruel tortures? Has the work of God become subject to the world? And what do the servants of Christ the Lord care for the dishonor of this world, for calumny? He is a Samaritan, he has a devil in him, he makes himself a king, he wishes to destroy the Church of Solomon. The archpriests dishonor and calumniate Christ the Lord, and thus they bring Him to death. And is the servant to be in any way superior to the master in this?[179] Having removed Father Smotryc'kyj (which God, we trust, and the power in the holy righteousness of God's anointed, Our Gracious Lord, who is equally merciful to us and to them, will not allow him to do, against the law and the truth), does he believe that he has also removed all of Rus'? Not at all. As before, there is the same Uniate handful. Father Smotryc'kyj is in the Church of God, by His holy providence, a servant who is, although not despised, nonetheless the least among God's chosen. His place and dignity will not be vacant. Elijah is not alone in Israel.[180] It did not befit him, then, if he understands this matter, to be a hinderer of this salvatory matter, but rather to be a promoter, if he wished to be known among us *legitime* [legitimately] for what he is known *illegitime* [illegitimately]. *Privata* [private concerns] ought to have given way here to the public good. It is not at all a matter of titles, which also in this newly erected Church are not, by God's grace, in danger of loss, so long as the obligation of the titles, if God would cause it, should remain in the normal authority of the canon and temporal laws of the holy Ruthenian Church. The holy Church has a proper method of portioning out, for the sake of peace, eight from sixteen when the need arises.

---

179. Mk. 14[:11]; Jn. 8[:48]; Mt. 26[:3–4]; Lk. 22[:2]; Jn. 15[:15, 20].
180. 3 Kg. [1 Kg.] 19[:16]; Rom. 11[:2–3].

It certainly seems to us that this causes violence to nature, this thing that occurs today crudely to his dignities, at this sudden and unmeditated importunity, to which, as one hears, there occurs dishonor and no little harm to our common Church good. "Thou shalt not calumniate; and thou shalt not stand against the neck of thy neighbor," says God's Law.[181] Especially because we find this to be presented for the good, by God and by the mother Church of all Christian Churches of the entire world. In which matter, was it a question of satisfying his disorderly lust and the undeliberated counsel against the healthy one? We say: that holy Church hierarchy erected with God's will and providence (with which, as also with our entire nation, he, without any fear of God and without any justice strives to do what in his day Haman had proceeded to do to Mordecai and to the entire Jewish nation,[182] and what Ahithophel did to David and to the entire people of God);[183] the newly erected Church hierarchy, we say, and all of us too, with the help of God's grace, are ready to bear patiently and gracefully from his disgusting calumny what Christ the Lord wishes us to be worthy to bear for the sake of His holy truth.

He should consider to what confusion he has brought the entire fatherland through his present undeliberated (undeliberated, because quick) action. For sown throughout all the corners thereof, the calumny invented by him everywhere confuses heaven and earth, as if there no longer existed the God of Susan, David, the three youths, Mordecai, Daniel, and others like them. He ought to consider carefully that, if through the former artificial mysteries he achieved little in his undertaking, through this present cruel oppression he has managed much less. And even if it were to remain, as he strives for it to remain (which, we trust, the Lord God and holy righteousness in His Majesty the King, Our Gracious Lord, will not allow him); but even if it should remain as he strives, through God's wrath upon him, as that proverb of eternal shame has it—"Let them divide the child; let it be neither mine nor yours"[184]—he will receive the benefit of dispersing from the Church of God poor innocent souls among various sects, and he himself will not

181. Lev. 19[:16]; Zech. 8:[16–17]; Eph. 4[:25].
182. Es. 7 [Esther 7:9–10].
183. 2 Kg. [2 Sam.] 17[:1–23].
184. 3 Kg. 3 [1 Kg. 3:26].

delight in them. For violence brings one to desperation, and desperation (as wise people understand it) is not always wont to consider even God Himself, to say nothing of any seemliness.

Looking upon this so unbearable violence, the most illustrious Orthodox metropolitan of all Rus', the most reverend father in God, Jov Borec'kyj, in the protestation he submitted to many castles in the name of the entire clergy and all estates, princes, lords, gentry, and knighthood of the ancient Greek religion, who are and immovably remain under the obedience of the most holy father patriarch of Constantinople, declares *solenniter* [solemnly] and protests in these words: "If, on account of the lawless action on the part of our apostates, which is difficult to refute and which brings a dishonorable blot against the honor of several mendaciously accused persons, and in addition to them, of our entire Ruthenian nation; and if, under the pretext of an imaginary Turkish treason, on account of the violent attack against our faith, it should, or would, have to come to some confusion in the fatherland (from which, God protect us), then this would have to come and occur from no one else, nor for any other reason, but for the reason of our apostates and from them themselves on account of their so violent attack against us, against our faith, and against our honor and that of the entire Ruthenian nation." Thus the most reverend in God, the father metropolitan.

Thus it is incumbent upon the doer of this malicious deed, as we said, to consider to what confusion, through his present undeliberated, sudden, and harsh action he has brought, and does not cease to bring, the entire fatherland. In which, as also in the very apostasy from his proper pastor (which irreconcilably offends us in his person), may the holy Lord grant him timely repentance. The Holy Eastern Church, and in it our Ruthenian one, would know, on account of this sort of action on his part, how unapproachable and significant is the abyss of so many centuries' duration that separates the East and the West. *Vexatio dat intellectum* [vexation gives understanding], says God's prophet.[185] And he himself would not be heard as he is now heard by us, unto our own sorrow, according to the obligation upon us of both our laws, but as he is heard by his own people: *Qui intrat per ostium, pastor est ovium, et oves vocem ejus audiunt* [He that entereth in by the door is the shepherd

---

185. [Cf. Is. 28:19.]

of the sheep (. . .) and the sheep hear his voice],[186] as the Son of God, our Lord and Pastor speaks.

Concerning the Genuine Good Will of the Eastern Patriarchs toward the Noble Polish Kingdom

But is this fitting, too, what he alleges through his people: should the fact that our elder in the Spirit (that is, the patriarch of Constantinople) is in servitude under the cruel Ottoman have caused the most illustrious majesty of the King, Our Gracious Lord, to be offended toward us? We do not believe so. For how can something that does not offend God offend a Christian king? Throughout the entire first three hundred years, all of Christendom was under harsh pagan tormentors; and yet this did not offend the Lord God with respect to the Christians. Throughout another three hundred years, shortly thereafter, the entire western Church moaned in the harsh servitude of cruel Goths, Heruli, and Longobards; neither did this cause the pious Christian emperors, who reigned in their majesty in Constantinople, to be offended toward the Christians.[187]

Charged with the suspicion of having betrayed the city of Rome to the Goths, Bishop of Rome Silverius nonetheless receives this gentle sentence from Emperor Justinian: "If it is shown that Silverius wrote this letter, let him lose his see, and let him become the bishop of some other city. If it is not shown, let him remain with his Roman see."[188]

But when the patriarchs of Constantinople are accused of some ill will toward the domains of His Majesty the King, Our Gracious Lord, should they be condemned and removed by the judgment of His Majesty the King, Our Gracious Lord, from their own diocese, given and adjudged to them by the cause and the power of the Holy Spirit? Never, by God's grace. Wherefore, since all our eastern patriarchs have

---

186. Jn. 10[:2–3].

187. *Diaco.* [Paul the Deacon?] *Jornand.* [Jornandes or Jordanis, *De Getarum sive Gotharum Origine et rebus gestis* (Jornans or Jordan, *History of the Goths*), PL 69:1251–96.] *Onuph. Baron. Anno 324, pagin. 389* [Baronius, s.a. 324, p. 389].

188. *Liberatus in Breviario, cap. 22* [Liberatus, Deacon of Carthage, *Breviary,* chap. 22; *PL* 68:1040].

a clear eye and a free access to the domains of His Majesty the King, in the year 1586 Joachim, patriarch of Antioch, was in the Polish Crown and in the Grand Duchy of Lithuania; in the year 1589, Jeremiah, patriarch of Constantinople; in the year 1596, the current patriarch of Alexandria, Cyril, at that time the exarch of that same apostolic see; and in the past year 1620, Theophanes, patriarch of Jerusalem. On account of his entirely humble good will toward these domains, the patriarch of Alexandria of blessed memory, Meletius, who is of honest heart toward His Royal Majesty, Our Gracious Lord, in his letters written to His Majesty the King, also names His Royal Majesty "beloved son in the Spirit"; and His Majesty the King, out of his Christian inclination to him, deigns to call the most reverend Theophanes, patriarch of Jerusalem, "reverend father in Christ."

Is this wrong? No God-loving soul will say so. All patriarchs of the four eastern holy apostolic sees are the cordial friends and constant beseechers of God on behalf of the domains of His Majesty the King, Our Gracious Lord. And the Lord God listens to them, for they are His servants and His disciples in shackles. They are not schismatics (as worthless people worthlessly allege they are), still less heretics; rather they are Catholics, pastors of the Holy Catholic Church, who night and day bless Christian kingdoms, and especially this one of ours, to which, in all the miseries that have fallen upon them from the tormentor, they have safe refuge. They wish much more of every happiness to this domain, our fatherland, than to their own fatherland, which suffers want under the tyrant. Military successes of this domain over their own tyrant are always dearer to them than when that tormentor comes away the victor.

With what sort of heartfelt groans on this occasion, too, did the holy patriarch of Jerusalem ask the Lord God for fortunate successes for this domain, when, at the time of his arrival in the domains of His Majesty the King, Our Gracious Lord, he blessed the Zaporozhian army in its campaign against the tormentor? And when, together with several thousands, the then hetman of the Zaporozhian army, Petro Kunaševyč-Sahajdačnyj, stood before him, and in the name of the entire army asked for absolution from the confessed sin of pouring Christian blood in Moscow, he answered paternally with a face drenched in tears:

"Whatever you did on that Muscovite expedition[189] on account of your subordination and at the command of your lord the King, you had to do on account of the obligation of obedience; and the propriety and impropriety of your action was not in your power, but in the power of him, to whose rule, by God's will, you are subject; wherefore also the offense, if there is any, concerns you the less. But in whatever things you were cruel and malicious out of an embittered and bloodthirsty heart (which often occurs in a soldier through some sort of habit), in torturing people and in tormenting the weaker sex and children, against order and against propriety—that is your own evil. Have regret for this, praying to the Lord God, whose mercy surpasses even all the heaviest sins; humble yourselves before Him; but do not lose heart in His grace and do not despair of your salvation. And turn that weapon, with which you—following your ancestors—faithfully (as we have heard) and mightily serve your fatherland, against the Mussulman, the sworn enemy of Christendom. In which may God's almighty right hand help you to the effective service of the most worthy and most illustrious King, your lord. And may the blessing of my humility and my prayers from the miracle-working grave of God aid you, that our eyes, enslaved by the pagan force, might become worthy of seeing His Most Illustrious Magnificence in His Majesty upon the great throne of Constantine the Great." Thus, we say, are the holy eastern patriarchs well *affecti* [disposed] toward the noble Polish Crown and our fatherland.

With what heart, by the living God, did the incautious and, in this regard, not very pious *delator* [accuser] make bold to attack with such a dishonorable stain and shame this holy man, who is entirely well disposed to our fatherland, this Christian kingdom? If the holy words of the honorable letters of His Majesty the King, Our Gracious Lord, and of the most illustrious senate of His Royal Majesty were unable to restrain him from this malice, at least his own genuine goodwill toward the domains of His Majesty the King, our dear fatherland, and toward His Majesty the King himself, Our Gracious Lord, ought to have restrained him. When the entire Commonwealth, using this word *paulo latius* [a little more broadly], that is, when Their Graces, the lord

---

189. [Sahajdačnyj led twenty thousand Cossacks on Moscow in 1618, although he did not reach the city itself. This is likely the expedition Smotryc'kyj had in mind, and he was using the term "Moscow" in the sense of "Muscovy."]

land representatives, came from all the counties of both domains to
the most recent Sejm, and when it was presented in our letter read in
their circle that the most reverend father patriarch of Jerusalem had
consecrated for Rus' of the ancient Greek religion, under the obedience
of the most reverend father patriarch of Constantinople, a metropolitan
and bishops, no one was found from that so great gathering of men of
(we might say) divine wits and supernatural quickness of intellect who
said against this holy man even one word of the sort that this incautious
delator [accuser] sowed by the mouthful throughout the entire Crown
and the Grand Duchy of Lithuania. For who would wish to make
bold to bring to the most esteemed ears of His Majesty the King, Our
Gracious Lord,[190] the allegation that this servant of God, the guardian
of the grave of Christ the Lord, a truly holy man, is dishonorable and
ignominious—who, if not a man reviled and disgraced before God and
before men? Who made bold to invent falsehoods and calumny against
that great priest, who for fourteen years now yearly illumines his hands
with the fire that descends to God's grave from heaven—who, if not a
man worse in attributes than an infidel?

For the Mussulmans themselves—on account of that yearly,
most wonderful divine miracle that is celebrated through his hands
at the grave of God every Easter Saturday toward evening—honor,
respect, and esteem the patriarch of Jerusalem and speak well of him.
Only the merciless *delator* [accuser] attacked him more cruelly than
the Mussulman, since he reviles and disgraces him with his fallacious
allegation to His Majesty the King, Our Gracious Lord. He should,
however, have remembered these words of the wise man: *Oculum qui
subsannat Patrem, etc. et linguam dolosam, etc.* The eye that mocketh
at his father, etc.[191] and a deceitful tongue, etc.[192] That is his father;
for he boasts of the law that went out from Zion and of the word of
the Lord that went out from Jerusalem. That is the pastor of God's city
of Jerusalem and of holy Zion, the successor to the brother, according

190. [Sir. 51:6.]
191. Prov. 30[:17, which reads in its entirety: "The eye that mocketh at his
father, and despiseth to obey his mother, the ravens of the valley shall pick it
out, and the young eagles shall eat it"].
192. Mic. 6[:12, which reads in its entirety: "For the rich men thereof are full
of violence, and the inhabitants thereof have spoken lies, and their tongue is
deceitful in their mouth"].

to the body, of Christ the Lord, the apostle James, whom Christ the Lord Himself consecrated to the bishopric of Jerusalem, as blessed John Chrysostom and other doctors of the Church make known about this.[193] He is the foremost defender of the mother of all Churches, as he himself often sings about this when he sings, "Hail thou, holy Zion, mother of Churches, God's abode,"[194] the mother, we say, of all Christian Catholic Churches and the first custodian of God's abode. He could not have seen, nor could it come to his mind, not only in deed or in word, but not even in a dream or in imagination, what that scoffer invented against his innocence and published to the world.

If that man, little mindful of his salvation, had wished to see that holy man (who, not leaving his cell at the grave of God for seven years on end, was a constant contemplator of God, and from which he was elevated to that high Apostolic throne); if, we say, he had wished to see in person that holy man's respectable figure, honorable customs, polite humility, his life exemplary in every respect, he would have to be of almost an iron Pharaoh's neck,[195] if he did not bow down to kiss the traces of those feet that tread the traces of the earth trodden by the most holy feet of our Savior and God, Jesus Christ the Lord. But envy does not know how to esteem even the most beneficial things; it is blind to even the most salvatory good.

You, however, our Beloved of God, Fellows in Confession, fret not yourselves because of the evildoer, neither be you envious against the workers of iniquity.[196] For his tongue, according to Solomon, does not love the truth, and his mouth works ruin.[197] For us, that holy man is truly holy and in no way suspect, truly the patriarch of Jerusalem, a successor to the blessed apostle James, brother of the Lord according to the body, a God-sent renovator of the temple of our Ruthenian Church, which had fallen through apostasy, our genuine father in the Spirit; and we desire, and we beseech the Lord God for him, that the Lord God might deign to establish him preserved in health from all dangers and

193. *Chrys. Hom 38 in Epist. 1 ad Corin* [Chrysostom, *Homily 38 on 1 Cor.;* *PG* 61:327; *NPNF1* 12:229].
194. *Damascen. S.* [St. John of Damascus; from the *Oktoechos* attributed to John of Damascus, *Par.* 318; *OktD* 76, 2d pag.; *OktB* 2:846; *Oct* 125].
195. Ex. 10.
196. Ps. 36 [37:1].
197. Prov. 26[:28]; Sir. 27[:11, 13, 14, 23].

from this impious calumny and to establish him upright that he might set right the word of God's truth upon his holy see. But if that incautious *delator* [accuser] does not repent and does not cease spreading further his vulgar malice, let him be certain of the ready vengeance of God over him, which we do not wish him; rather, to the contrary, we beseech the Lord God for him that He deign to straighten his mouth and tongue to holy truth. For he touched what, among other things, almighty God deigns to speak of: He that touches you touches the apple of His eye;[198] my vengeance in your wrong;[199] I will repay those who harm you.[200]

†In vain, then, does that malicious *delator* [accuser] strive to bring down this repulsive stain of unbearable shame upon that holy man; and he wrongfully alleges that he is guilty of introducing unrest into the domains of His Majesty the King, Our Gracious Lord, on account of the fact that he consecrated an Orthodox metropolitan and bishops in Rus', when, to the contrary, he thereby brought the desired peace into these domains. For what, through these twenty-six years, during all the times of this apostasy, more frequently and more greatly encumbered all the affairs of the Commonwealth? What more frequently and more greatly oppressed the entire senate? What more frequently and more greatly molested His Majesty the King, Our Gracious Lord, than this constant, lamentatious request of the Ruthenian nation that our apostates be removed from our necks and that an Orthodox metropolitan and bishops be returned to us? That which has introduced complete peace into the domains of His Majesty the King, Our Gracious Lord, they judge to be unrest.

It is certainly peace that has arrived, by God's grace, in our fatherland, and not unrest. For as soon as, through the happy establishment of this peace, both the churches and Church goods will be returned to the persons consecrated by this holy man, the metropolitan and the bishops (for which our entire Ruthenian nation asks His Majesty the King, Our Gracious Lord, and will not cease to ask until it finds mercy in his lordly eyes), then the unrest kindled by the apostasy, blown into flames by oppression and burning wildly through this abominable calumny,

---

198. Zech. 2[:8].
199. Dt. 32[:35, 41, 43].
200. Rom. 12[:19].
†   On peace from the place of peace.

will immediately be extinguished in our fatherland. Immediately our entire Ruthenian nation will be pacified in its conscience. Thereupon the attacks, assaults, oppressions, tortures, pouring of blood, and unheard-of excesses arising from the apostasy will cease; then will cease the calumnies, deceits, and all the enmities of one toward the other that comes from hatred, since each one will delight in his own good; then will cease complaints, protestations, interdictions, bringing of charges, the convening of courts, and thereby will cease citations, summonses, and banishments; all courts will grow silent in the matters of the Ruthenian religion.

God's anointed will no longer be molested in this matter; nor will the affairs of the Commonwealth be encumbered. Everything will go peacefully, everything will remain in peace. A brother will cease to be a wolf to his brother. Peace in the churches, peace in the homes, peace in the town halls, peace in the castles, in the lands, in the tribunals, in the Chancellor's and Commissioner's courts, in the dietines, and in the Sejms: for each and every unnecessary lawsuit that is brought by our apostates against our entire nation, to the detriment of our internal and external goods, will cease. And thereby the domains of His Royal Majesty will be adorned with complete peace and will stand truly crowned with the desired peace. And that peace will cause a much greater harmony and love toward us on the part of their lords, the Romans, with respect to religion itself, not to mention the friendship of fellow citizens and neighbors, than the revered Union of our apostates, whom we have come to hate irreconcilably, as we said, on account of their apostasy from the obedience of the patriarch of the holy apostolic see of Constantinople, their natural pastor.

Since they adhered to the Union throughout all the past times, and we opposed it, often even an honorable tongue, in the decorous speeches and writings to and about each other, had on both sides to be carried beyond the bounds of humility, touching whom and what it ought not to have done. May Christ the Lord grant us this in our days: may the heart of God's anointed, His Majesty the King, and of his most illustrious senate, which You have in Your divine hands, pour out like water according to Your holy will, and deign to return, through Your and his righteous judgment, peace to Your holy Church in our days, as we ask it, from east to west. And having consecrated that day as an eternal memorial, we will sing to You, our Lord and God, forever, from generation to generation, triumphal songs to your inexpressible goodness toward us.

Unrest then—by God's grace, O Orthodox Ruthenian Nation and every Kind and Gracious Reader—unrest has no place in this matter. Peace has conquered. Internal peace has entered into our fatherland from the place of peace. Grant, O God, that it be nested in it, established and propagated in it, for all future years. For Jerusalem is interpreted "the vision of peace." Thus that holy man came to us with peace from the place of peace, through God's industry toward us. For our Ruthenian nation, protected through this peace (after God's grace) by the grace of His Majesty the King, Our Gracious Lord, and always faithful to its lords, always submissive, always obedient to every order, presented, presents, and will present itself ready to risk, lay down, and pour out its possessions, its health, and its blood, for his honor, for his health, and for his safety, asking the Lord God—small and great, day and night, publicly in our Churches and privately in our homes—for the good health and the happy reign of His Royal Majesty.

Our apostates snatched our heart from us when, employing upon us the strange mysteries that are their wont, for twenty-six years now they have been cruelly snatching our faith from our breasts. But even in such dire straits has not the integrity in the fidelity, humility, obedience, and goodwill of our nation been unvarying? For just as, throughout all those past years of its unbearable miseries, it did not have any other demand but that there be returned to it justly what was taken away from it by the apostates unjustly—that, we say, we be maintained in peace and in possession of what is ours—so even now there is no other demand from the entire Ruthenian nation to God's anointed, the King, Our Lord, and until it be heard successfully, it must continue to be so. It is certainly difficult, nay even unbearable, for a free nation, a nation equal in rights and liberties to all the citizens of the Crown and the Grand Duchy of Lithuania, which no other surpasses in nobility of birth, none in goodwill to the fatherland, to be deprived of its rights and liberties and finally even of its faith by the force of a few persons; to be so heavily enslaved in freedom of conscience that we are not permitted to believe as God's Law teaches us, but have to believe as our apostates order us to do. Whom from our Ruthenian nation, by the living God, would that not hurt? Whom even of its fellow citizens will that not move to commiseration? In this regard, even all of the non-Christian sectarians, who do not have any access to the enjoyment of the liberties of these domains, are freer than are we, a free nation, as we said, an independent nation, a nation born in one fatherland with the two others and that bears equally with them all its burdens, a nation genuinely faithful to God's anointed, the Kings, Their Gracious Lords, and that eagerly pours out its blood at their every command. All of which the righteous eye sees from heaven, sees our submissiveness and fidelity. Likewise every God-fearing eye of our fellow citizens that takes delight in the truth sees this. Only the eyes of the apostates, which run with bile and are clouded against the truth by the smoke of hatred, are closed to this. For they seek to disgrace our and their noble Ruthenian nation with the stain of treason, depriving it of every liberty.

What sort of unhappy bird is this that so hideously fouls the pure nest of the virtue of its ancestors?[201] They grumble and they breathe forth flame because we called them "neither the one nor the other," or "both the one and the other," in the bitterness of our hearts; but they take delight and rejoice when they slander us as traitors, and they do not consider this an unbearable burden for us. If they would contemplate and consider both names with the scales of righteous deliberation, without a doubt they would prefer to be both "neither one" or "both," than to be disgraced as traitors to the fatherland. Let them believe the same thing about us as well. Our honor is our life; and whoever snatches at it, snatches our soul from our breasts. Our honor, wounded by the shame of treason, hurts us and will not cease to hurt us until, cleansed of that shameful stain, it will be healed of its injury.

If they are truly Rus', as they ought to be and must be (for whoever changes his faith does not immediately also degenerate from his blood; whoever from the Ruthenian nation becomes of the Roman faith does not become immediately a Spaniard or an Italian by birth; rather he remains a noble Ruthenian as before; for it is not the faith that makes a Ruthenian a Ruthenian, a Pole a Pole, or a Lithuanian a Lithuanian, but Ruthenian, Polish, and Lithuanian blood and birth); if, then, they are truly Rus', as they are (of which nation and blood there is, by the grace of almighty God, no smaller a number than from the other two member nations honored with the senatorial dignity at the side of God's anointed, the King Our Gracious Lord; most noble Ruthenian

201. [*NKPP* 2:1152, "Ptak," 77; Arthaber 1379.]

blood excels in these times in the spiritual and temporal Lithuanian senate; most noble Ruthenian blood has in these days entrusted to it the priceless jewels of the Lithuanian Republic: the seal and the staff);[202] if, then, they are truly Rus', that we say for yet a third time, as they are, then, by God, with what heart can they bear such a hideous stain upon their nation, which has always been faithful, pure, and never in any way suspect to Their Majesties the Kings of Poland and the Grand Dukes of Lithuania, Their Gracious Lords? With what ears can they bear to hear this horrible shame, which infects unto ruin the health as well as the honor of its worthy nation?

O most noble Ruthenian blood: let this pain you; let this move you. What do you have more valuable than honor? What dearer than glory? Already someone makes bold to strike the ground with both your glory and your honor and to tread on them with their calumnious feet. According to all the chronicles, never did you, noble Ruthenian nation, lift bloody hand against your head, against the crown of your glory and honor. So will you now in your innocence allow that dishonorable shame to insult you? Christ the Lord keep you from this. Your ancestors maintained both things for you in complete integrity; may you too maintain both things for your descendants in the same untouched integrity. For as far as all your brave acts of illustrious virtue are concerned, you do maintain them; but someone under some pretext creeps up (a snake, as they say, in the grass)[203] to approach you when you are not looking. Thus those born of most worthy Ruthenian blood ought not to have snorted and breathed fire against this; rather, they ought to have protected these invaluable jewels in their worthy Ruthenian nation, that is honor and glory, and to have snorted and breathed fire against whatever submits those two to dishonor. It is a lean year, so they say, when a wolf eats a wolf;[204] it is certainly leaner yet, when

202. [The "greater seal" was wielded by the chancellor, the lesser by the under-chancellor. Smotryc'kyj had the former in mind: Lew Sapieha (Sapiha) converted from Orthodoxy to Calvinism to Catholicism. The "staffs—great and field" were accorded to the great and field hetmans. Smotryc'kyj meant the former, Jan Karol Chodkiewicz (Xodkevyč), the scion of an old Orthodox noble family.]

203. [NKPP 3:630–1, "Wąż," 6; Arthaber 1272.]

204. [NKPP 3:690, "Wilk," 32; Arthaber 722.]

a Ruthenian swallows a Ruthenian, and it is entirely famished when one Ruthenian eats all of Rus'. In which we warn you to be cautious, O worthy Ruthenian nation, asking you in the name of the integrity of your glory and honor.

It was not bad enough that a few years ago, during the war with Moscow, in their work entitled *Resurrected Nalyvajko,*[205] having first called all of Rus' that remains under the ancient obedience of the patriarch of Constantinople bears, basilisks, lizards, crocodiles, they finally called them spies and Turkish secretaries. But now along with the honor of all of Rus' that did not and does not know the Union, they are cited in the books in acrimonious protests, and namely, against the Vilnius Brotherhood, which is formed from the nation, adorned by the costly jewel of the noble prerogative, full of illustrious people born of noble families, of all estates of the citizens of the Crown and of the Grand Duchy of Lithuania. †And in addition to it, against the *szlachta,* citizens of the palatinates and counties of Polack, Vicebsk, Mscislaŭ, and Orša, alleging that, having come to terms with some Turkish spy, they made some sort of conspiracies by letter for rebellions and for the demise of the fatherland. Such are already the writings and protestations against you, O Noble Ruthenian Nation, wherefore let them judge for themselves how properly they snort against us, since we speak about our wrong in the bitterness of our heart not as an allegation but as a response. Is it only their censured *tumor* that is supposed to hurt, and not our insulted *honor?* Is the only insult what we say against them in our defense? And what they say against us in order to cause a blemish, is that not supposed to be painful to us? What sort of separate law is this? Whence this exclusivity with regard to the same freedoms? Has a nobleman an advantage over another nobleman in such a case? Everyone has one honor, just as everyone has one life.

But, our faithful co-confessionalists, having returned to our first topic, we would ask yet at this point our apostates, whose hearts run over with bile: with the removal of the spiritual power of the patriarch of Constantinople and of our obedience to him, what do they see remaining for us in our laws and freedoms, which are given, protected, sworn to

---

205. [Potij? 1607.]
†   The protest of His Grace, the Palatine of Polack [Prince Michał Drucki-Sokoliński], entered into the books of the Braslav castle.

us through constitutions and privileges by Their Majesties the Kings, Our Gracious Lords of Poland, and of the Grand Duchy of Lithuania, and of Rus'? We do not find anything at all remaining, rather we see quite everything falling. For where is there even one law, even one constitution, even one privilege that pertains to the Ruthenian nation of the Western obedience and to the defense of the Roman religion in us? There is none; rather all pertain to people of the Greek religion of the Eastern obedience. Wherefore, through the change of the Greek religion into the Roman, and of the Eastern obedience into the Western, we would have to lose not only the spiritual laws and liberties, but also the temporal. And rightly so, for with the change of religion and obedience, our laws would also have to be subject to change.

If anyone pretends or believes that the remaining Greek *ritus* [rites] and ceremonies of the apostates are the entirety of the Greek religion, he believes just as wisely, and he pretends just as knowledgeably, as if he were to believe and pretend that the bell tower, the baptistery, the censer, and similar things are Church sacraments. Wherefore we ourselves would have to become the violators of our laws and liberties if we were to abandon the Eastern obedience. If we ourselves were to violate what Their Majesties the Kings, Our Gracious Lords, confirm for us under their oath, we would remain without absolutely anything; we would ourselves have deprived ourselves of all our liberties.

†They remind us about the Union of Florence. But what has that one to do with the present-day Union? If that previous Union (leaving alone for the time being its other circumstances as well as the council itself) were reestablished, a confessor of the Greek religion would never have allowed himself to be called by the unsuitable name *Unit* or *Uniat,* which name is a non-name, as we said. Certainly now they have to and must be called thus. But on the basis of the Union of Florence, both a Roman could be called a Uniate with respect to a Greek, as also a Greek with respect to a Roman, each side remaining with its own pastors and with its own articles of the faith, since that council was not celebrated for the detriment of the integrity and the authority of either side (as the name Uniate necessarily brings with it). They were not convened so that the Greek faith should suffer any sort of change or so that it would unite itself to the Roman faith as to the better one, with the change of

†   The difference between the Union of Florence and the present one.

anything in itself, but so that from both sides, between the two local Churches of one (as they were known) faith and the one Universal Church, there might be removed those things that the Eastern objected to in the Western and not the Western in the Eastern. And so that the one (having removed that addition to the Niceno-Constantinopolitan Creed "and from the Son," which was the greatest objection that the Eastern Church made to the Western) unite with the other in such a way that there not be the least detriment to the integrity and authority of the one or the other. And that is what happened. The Greeks remained by all that was theirs, and the Romans by theirs, having removed the difference concerning the procession of the Holy Spirit, for which very thing the Greeks appeared at that council (since, with the exception of the matter of the procession of the Holy Spirit, there was neither a general discussion—only a private one—nor was there a general decree concerning other articles of faith); having removed the difference, we say, according to many proofs from both sides drawn from divine Writ and from the writings of the doctors of the Church, concerning the procession of the Holy Spirit, in the words "through the Son" and "and from the Son," of which the first belongs to the Eastern Church and the second to the Western.

†Since the creed was never read in the Greek Church with that addition, therefore it should not be so read; rather it should be submitted to use without the addition "and from the Son," as it was first created at the second universal council of Constantinople.

As the *sacra* [consecration] and the obedience of the metropolitan and of the entire clergy of the Ruthenian Church remained before the Council of Florence in the hands of our customary pastor, the patriarch of Constantinople, so they also remained in his hands after the council.

As the fire of purgatory was never known in the Greek Church, so also after the Council of Florence it was not to be known.

The place of the souls of righteous people who passed away is heaven; and that of the sinful is *ad*[206] or hell. And as the Eastern Church confessed before the Council of Florence that their blessing and tortures were not completely perfect until the Day of Judgment, so it was also to confess and confesses after it.

---

† The *contenta* [assertions] of the Union of Florence.
206. [Smotryc'kyj gives the Slavonic word first, then glosses it in Polish.]

As the leavened bread was in use in the Eastern Church in the celebration of the mysteries of the salvatory Eucharist before the Council of Florence, so it, and not unleavened bread, remained and remains in use also after the council.

As the Eastern Church now receives the mysteries of the body and the blood of the Son of God under two species, so it always received them under two species also before the Council of Florence.

As before the Council of Florence the bishop of Rome and the Eastern patriarchs remained by their rights of universal conciliar decree, so each of them was to remain by them in precisely the same manner also after this council.

†But now, after the present Union, only apostate Rus' are Uniates to the Romans, and properly so; for they united with the Romans without their highest pastor to the detriment of the integrity and authority of the Holy Eastern Church. Now each bishop and the metropolitan himself at his inauguration to the diginity *publice* [publicly] reads the Niceno-Constantinopolitan Creed with the addition "and from the Son." And that is a great slap in the face to the Union of Florence. A much greater one is the fact that they secretly abandoned their own proper patriarch and rendered obedience to the bishop of Rome. Wherefore it followed that not only in other differences, which were somehow effaced through private discussions at this council, they became and they must be more inclined to the Roman Church; for they do not have anyone who would draw them away from this and keep them with their customary ancient usage. For more certain knowledge of all of which, we cite for you, Kind and Gracious Reader, and for you, Orthodox Fellow in Religion, after the conclusion of our *Verification,* the oath by which our apostates bound themselves to the bishop of Rome in obedience and in faith.

They also show us some patriarchal letters that permit us to maintain harmony and love with their lords, the Romans; but for the change of the Greek religion into the Roman, and of the Eastern obedience into the Western, no letter can ever be shown. No patriarch ever allowed us, the Ruthenian nation, to abandon our Eastern faith and his obedience, and, so long as he will be the guardian (as he is, by God's grace, eternally) of synodal laws and of our temporal and canon laws, he cannot allow it, knowing that the harmony and love of these two or three nations, that is,

---

†   The defects of the present Union.

of the Eastern and Western Churches in the domains of our fatherland, can be maintained suitably and honorably even without change of religion and obedience. But although all four patriarchs (since more is demanded of them, in some sort of extraordinary obedience, than their canon laws allow them) do not allow themselves to bend beyond certain limits to the detriment of the eternal Church laws, to the dishonor of the dignity that they bear and against the obligation of their authority, nonetheless, that they should not have Christian Catholic love for all Catholics, as Catholics and pastors of the holy Catholic Church, or that they should forbid us, their sons in the Spirit, the lawful and appropriate union with their lords, the Romans, according to the eternal synodal decrees—whoever would believe this of them would do them a great wrong unto the harm of his soul.

Oh, would the Lord God grant that those five senses of the body of Christ the Lord, that is, the five pastors of the holy Catholic Church of God, the bishops of the foremost apostolic sees, those of Rome, Constantinople, Alexandria, Antioch, and Jerusalem, walk so fittingly, according to the blessed apostle Paul, in the election in which they were called, with all lowliness, meekness, and with long-suffering, forbearing one another in love, endeavoring to keep the unity of the Spirit in the bond of peace,[207] lest the sight say to the hearing, you are not of the body, wherefore you are not necessary; nor the hearing to the smell, nor the smell to the taste, nor the taste to the touch. For if the whole body were an eye, where were the hearing? And if the whole were hearing, where were the smelling? And if the whole were smelling, where were the tasting? And finally where were the touching, if the whole body were tasting? But now hath God set the senses every one of them in the body, as it hath pleased Him. And if they were all one sense, where were the body? But now there are five senses, yet but one body. One sense is nothing without the others, and nothing in place of the others; for thus there were no body. Since the eye ought not say to the hearing, you are not of the body, and you are of no need; nor can the whole body be one eye, but five senses and one body.[208]

Oh, would the Lord God grant, we say it yet a second time with all our heart, that those five senses of the body of Christ the Lord, that

207. Eph. 4[:2–3]; 1 Th. 1[:3]; Col. 1[:11].
208. 1 Cor. 12[:12–27]; Rom. 12[:4–6].

is, His holy Church, maintain such a unity one to the other in the bond of peace, so that one not chase after anything of his own before another, that one not do anything to the dishonor of another, but that all five be pleasant, graceful, and agreeable, in the form of the five pleasant, graceful, and salvatory wounds of the body of Christ the Lord.[209] But alas, alack for the lawless particularity of separateness! Is this variance in faith of the Christian nations in one domain pleasant to us? Do we delight in this disharmony? Is this harmful rending of the Church of God pleasant to us?

We read blessed John Chrysostom, who says (and we believe) that: "as nothing was more wont to rend the Church than the great desire for rule, so there is nothing that offends the Lord God more than the rending of the Church. For although (he says) we do innumerable good works, we will not suffer lesser punishments than those who impiously whipped, spat upon, and crucified the body of Christ the Lord, if we rend the wholeness and integrity of the Church. And if we (he says), the clergy, will do this, who are established to build others from us, if we make bold to tear apart the body of the Church, what will be the wonder if those who should desire to follow us in this will do the same? A certain holy man says of such apostates, although boldly, nonetheless he says, that their sin cannot be erased even by martyr's blood. Tell me (he says), I ask you, why you submit yourself to martyrdom? Is it not for the glory of Christ the Lord? Why then do you, who wish to lay down your life for Christ the Lord, strive against the Church, for which Christ the Lord laid down his life? Listen to Paul when he says, 'I am not meet to be called an apostle, for I persecuted the Church and destroyed it.'"[210] Thus St. John Chrysostom, whom we read and whose words we believe. Wherefore we say yet a second time that everyone who believes about our holy patriarchs that they do not have Christian Catholic love toward all Catholics, as Catholics and pastors of the Holy Catholic Church, or that they forbid us, their sons in the Spirit, to unite suitably with the Roman Church according to the Church laws and synodal decrees, does them a great wrong, and not without harm to his soul.

Let us ask, therefore, O noble Ruthenian nation, Our Gracious

---

209. 1 Cor. 1[:10].
210. *Homi. 11 in cap. 4 Epist. ad Eph.* [St. John Chrysostom, *Homily 11 on Eph. 4; PG* 62:85; *NPNF1* 13:106]. 1 Cor. 15[:9].

Lord, the King, God's anointed, that, in these years of his reign over us and in the future, he deign to bear in us graciously and paternally what he deigned graciously and paternally to bear in the first years, after his happy accession to these domains, for eight years, and what the ancestors of His Royal Majesty, the Kings of Poland, Our Gracious Lords, deigned for our Ruthenian nation, for one hundred fifty years and more, without any insult to themselves: not only gently to bear in those eastern lands and toward the patriarchs of Constantinople who were in servitude, but also, in addition, together with persons chosen for the metropolitanate of Rus', to send his courtiers with his letters of recommendation for their consecration to Constantinople. He is the father of our Ruthenian nation in the domains of His Royal Majesty, Our Gracious Lord, by whom we were born again of the water and the Spirit.[211] Does it befit a virtuous son to abandon his father? He is also our benefactor, who endowed us with every spiritual good. Is it proper for an honorable man to repay his benefactor with evil for good? It is degenerates and ingrates who are wont to do both.

Whence our Ruthenian nation is adorned with the title of the ancient religion by all Christian sects and by Their Majesties the Kings, Our Gracious Lords, in the laws given to us by Their Graces, such that we consider it a sin to deviate in even the least degree from the Church decrees and the articles of the faith of holy antiquity. This our ancient jewel also separates us from our apostates in the mutual discussion of today. For what else is the antiquity of religion than the invariability of the faith preached by Christ the Lord and by the apostles? And what in the world can be more illustrious, splendid, and noble than the invaluable jewel of our nation?

That People of the Ancient Greek Religion Suffer Unbearable Praejudicia *[Damages] in the Faith from the Apostates*

Although even today there are many voices and there is much allegation that we, Rus' of the ancient Greek religion, have not suffered any *praejudicium* [damage] with respect to faith from our apostates and that our cries to His Majesty the King, Our Gracious Lord, are in vain and

211. [Jn. 3:5.]

are needless vexations of His Majesty the King, Our Gracious Lord, consider, we ask you, our cordial co-confessionalist, and every Kind and Gracious Reader, to judge according to God and His holy truth: what can be a greater *praejudicium* [damage] than that which snatches our souls living from our breasts and casts them under the feet of the apostate will? Can a man live without a soul? Or a Church without bishops? Either they consider us bereft of reason, or they who say this consider themselves as such. Having deprived us of eyes, they say to us, "We do not forbid you to see"; not allowing us to have, according to our law, our spiritual authorities, bishops and a metropolitan, still they command us to be pious. Our apostates direct our attention to themselves and command us to listen to them by means of citations. Alas the unbearable *praejudicium* [damage]. Not long ago the bishop of Kyiv abandoned his bishop of Rome. Why were the citizens of his diocese not directed to him? Why were they not ordered to listen to him? To the contrary, they were forbidden to do so.[212] A few years ago the archbishop of Split abandoned his bishop of Rome. Did the bishop of Rome order the people entrusted to his spiritual care to follow him?[213] We do not believe so.

Let everyone who is wont to say of us that we cry in vain, that we needlessly vex His Majesty the King, Our Gracious Lord—let them litigate with us by natural law. Natural law says: *Quod tibi fieri non vis, alteri ne feceris;* do not do to others what you would not wish done to you by others.[214] Would it be in vain that they cry, and needlessly that they vex, if it had been their archbishops and bishops that had abandoned the bishop of Rome, and they had thus remained without their spiritual authorities? It seems to us that the pipes with which they now deride us would play a different tune, especially if their apostates,

212. [A reference to the "Protestant" (Roman Catholic) bishop of Kyiv, Mikołaj Pac, who, although he was prevented from fulfilling his ecclesiastical functions, held a seat in the senate in accordance with his episcopal title. He was bishop from 1555 to 1582, in spite of the fact that he converted to Calvinism in 1564.]

213. [This is a reference to Marcantonio de Dominis, whose pre-ecumenicist *De Republica Christiana* had, as we will soon see, a large influence on Smotryc'kyj's thought about orthodoxy and heresy. See above, pp. xliii–xliv, xlvii, and below, 252, 308–12.]

214. Tob. 4[:15]; Lk. 6[:31].

attacking their justice, *impune per fas et nefas* [with impunity, right or wrong], would oppress and torment both their souls and their bodies. It seems to us that willy-nilly they would have to cry and scream and to vex their highest authority after the Lord God in their so unbearable *praejudicium* [damage]. Is it not *praejudicium* [damage] that many more Christian children from our side die without baptism than there are all Uniates? And although that holy mystery is performed not without validity both by them and by every man *de necessitate* [out of the necessity] that obliges one *leges frangere* [to break the laws], what will we do? Our apostates are so kind to the Ruthenian nation that, practically like a figure of Zipporah,[215] they prefer in reality to treat their children in that manner than to unite with their apostates in religion. *Perfecto odio oderunt eos, inimici facti sunt eis.* They hated them, as the king and prophet of God says, with perfect hatred, and they became their enemies.[216] *Nec immerito* [and not without cause], but according to their deeds. The Lord God rendered to them according to their deserts, according to their deeds.[217] They improperly abandoned their elder, and we properly removed respect from them as our elders. And this proceeds according to God and according to His righteousness. For as soon as the first man withdrew his obedience from the Lord God, immediately he experienced the disobedience of the beasts, fish, and birds that had been subject to him.[218] He was paid back in the same little measure with which he had meted out,[219] so that now miserable little fleas bite him vexatiously, showing him thereby the way of turning back to the first road of obedience, which he had abandoned. And we do the same thing to our clergy *divino instinctu* [by the divine impulse] and *favore* [by the favor] of holy righteousness: we bite them like mean nits so that we might drive them to climb again to that degree of the obedience from which they had fallen away, with the amelioration of them and of us and of their very cause.

During one of the Sejms, a certain senator of high authority said aloud with a free—and, we can say, holy—tongue, from his senatorial

215. Ex. 4[:25].
216. Ps. 138 [139:22].
217. Ps. 27 [28:4].
218. Gen. 3.
219. [Mt. 7:2; Mk. 4:24; Lk. 6:38.]

place to the entire Commonwealth: "four persons consented to the Union and *praejudicium* [damage] occurs to some fifteen hundred thousand who did not consent to it." Did that senator of high virtues and splendid bravery speak properly? Does not that little group of the Union, which can be counted by name on the fingers, work *praejudicium* [damage] upon the countless multitude of the ancient religion when it forbids them every salvatory work? Christian children die, as we said, without baptism; adults, and their parents, without the salvatory mysteries of the holy Eucharist; burials of Christian bodies are done without the usual Church ceremonies; in many cities, with the sealing of the church, people live without Church services. We do not mention here in this place many other wants, burdens, and oppressions since we mentioned them elsewhere. And even if we were not lacking any of the things that we mentioned, even if we had maintained in us the integrity of all we have named, the very fact that they do not allow us to have our spiritual authorities—a metropolitan and bishops—according to our temporal and canon laws (since our apostates have occupied the places of these dignities unduly and against the law), by this very fact, we say, they unbearably work *praejudicium* [damage] upon us.

Where, without bishops, would we find presbyters? Are we supposed to go to the Garamant and the further Indies for them?[220] Or deprived of them, are we ourselves supposed to go in the name of perdition into dispersion among the wildernesses of innovations. There remains for us no third refuge. We have here already both check and mate. *Actum esset* [let it be done], it would have to mark the end of us and of our holy ancient faith. And perhaps someone will say that this is still a small *praejudicium* [harm] to our nation from our apostates? We certainly do not find a greater one. For who can take away from us something that takes from us a greater thing? He takes away our faith; and whoever takes away our faith seeks to take away and to wrench our soul from our breasts. Who, by God, does not see this unbearable *praejudicium* [damage]? Only he who mocks our entire spiritual good and ignores it; only the main enemy of our nation and faith.

---

220. [The Garamantian Empire existed in central Libya from 400 BC to AD 600, offering resistance to the expansion of the Roman Empire. The "further Indies" likely refers to the West Indies. In any event, Smotryc'kyj means "a long way."]

Thus having deprived us, as we said, of eyes, they allow us to look and to see; having wrenched our souls from us, they command us to be living. Is that not a manifest derision of us? Is that not an obvious ridicule of us? They offer us to eat, not only not having put anything before us on the table or into our hands, but even having torn from our hands that little bit that we had for the nourishment of our souls in our religion. We did not manage to prepare again the eyes we had lost out of the incomprehensible industry of that lord who orders us imperiously, "I command that you see"—when, immediately those who pretend that no *praejudicium* [harm] occurred to us with respect to the faith, these same apostates of ours, who burden us in various manners, then jump up to pluck them out again for us. And they call out to their helpers so that, having helped them out with some sort of most harmful barbs, in addition to the eyes, the entire body might be thoroughly beaten; they once again deprive our nation, or rather our Ruthenian Church, of eyes, that they might blind it again and cast it under their ill-willed apostate feet, which they, according to the outburst of their harsh lust, might tread under foot and crush. Which they do allegedly with some sort of subtle, artful, foreign piece of cunning, as if no one from here could see and perceive it. But not having been able to bury such a shameful Jew in these ashes,[221] which, though glowing, are nonetheless fine, they had to make it visible to the entire world of the Crown and Lithuania and to declare that the fable—well known even to children—has come into being, which concluded an eternal peace between the wolves and the sheep so long as the sheep gave up the dogs to the wolves as hostages; but when they agreed to this, they learned what sort of peace they had incautiously acquired, for they paid for it with their own blood and that of their dogs.[222] Only he does not see—with his living reason—this palpable subtlety and the unbearable *praejudicium* [damage] that lies in it, who does not see the sun with healthy eyes in the middle of day. Let anyone believe and allege concerning our constant cries, moans, and vexations as he wishes; we declare before God and God's anointed, His Majesty the King, Our Gracious Lord, and before the illustrious senate of His Royal Majesty, entirely in the bitterness of our heart, that we

221. [*NKPP* 3:989, "Żyd," 239. "To bury a Jew" means to plot something in secret.]
222. [A fable in the Aesopian tradition. See Gibbs 32.]

suffer cruel *praejudicium* [damage] from our apostates in our spiritual good and in our consciences.

We do not find anything else that our Orthodox fellows in confession should do to us during such a time and in such a matter other than to render daily and hourly thanks and praise to the good Lord God with all the strength of our souls for our internal goods, which He deigned to bestow upon us through the erection of the Church hierarchy. And enjoying this spiritual good if not in external, then at least in the desired internal peace, we all remain equally obliged to ask His Majesty the King, Our Gracious Lord, that he deign to have mercy upon our poor nation, afflicted mercilessly without compassion by our apostates through these and through other *praejudicia* [damages] and to show compassion for our internal and external unrest of such long standing, and that he allow us to enjoy the power and the dignity of the jurisdiction of the Church hierarchy erected according to our Church laws; for we have no one else to whom to turn with our lamentatious request, other than to this highest authority (after the Lord God).

We have been asking for twenty-six years, and, by God's grace, we received a promise made by His Royal Majesty in the year 1607 and repeated by the most recent Sejm, and it is proper for us to ask that it be brought fortunately into effect. Our apostates have the favor of many, by which they have been afflicting us and have been troubling and molesting the entire Commonwealth for so long now. But we, by God's grace, have justice. God's anointed himself sees this, wherefore he deigns to promise us the return of our good, which was unjustly torn from our hands by our apostates; and he assures us that he wishes, together with all the estates, with the senate and the Commonwealth, to return it to us. This worthy domain was not lacking in holy righteousness; we are certain that also in our case, which is as clear as the sun, it will not be lacking either. For this is the end of holy righteousness: that each might enjoy his own property. And the entire world of the Crown and Lithuania sees that we seek our property; all the general Sejms, and all the main courts acknowledge it; His Majesty the King, Our Gracious Lord, promises us its return; and we are certain of it from His Royal Majesty, as this is the word of the King. We and our ancestors lived in these our rights and freedoms for several hundred years during the reigns of the ancestors of His Majesty the King; we trust that also during his fortunate reign over us, His Majesty the King, Our Gracious

Lord—as it was in the first eight years of his reign over us—will not permit that *praejudicium* [damage] in them be committed against us and that he will command that what is our property, according to our ancient laws, be returned to us.

That this might happen soon, let us seek, with lamentatious pleading, to gain the mercy over us (after the mercy of God) of His Majesty the King, Our Gracious Lord, trusting that our so frequently repeated request to His Royal Majesty will not receive a rejection. And the Lord God, in whom is all our trust, who has in his hands both the divisions of the waters[223] and the heart of the king,[224] and inclines it whither He wishes, will cause in the heart of His anointed that he will appear with a kindly, paternal face to us who are afflicted, that he will not deny his ear to those who express their sorrow, that he will open his heart to those who ask, that he will condone the offense, if there is any, *violentae necessitati* [by necessity of force], and having embraced us with his lordly mercy, that he will not allow our anxious request to fade without his bringing it to effect. That the Lord God might deign to grant him a long, fortunate, painless, and entirely successful and blessed reign over us—the entire newly erected temple of our Church, together with the entire Ruthenian nation, asks, prays, desires, and wishes. Amen. In Vilnius, 1621, the 16th day of June.

> Our Kind Graces' and Gracious Lords',
> Servants and Suppliants of God,
> Wishers of every good thing.
> The monks of the Monastery of the Vilnius
> Brotherhood of the Church of the Descent
> of the Holy Spirit.
> Μία ζωῆς ἡμῶν ἐλπὶς Ιησοῦς ὁ χριστόΣ.
> [My life's only hope, Christ JesuS.][225]

---

223. [Ex. 14; Neh. 9:11; Ps. 74:13.]

224. [Ex. 14:8; Dt. 2:30.]

225. [Actually, "Our life's only hope . . . ." This motto, which begins and ends with Smotryc'kyj's initials, had already appeared at the end of Smotryc'kyj's grammar of Church Slavonic (which was *not* an anonymous work; Smotryc'kyj 1618–1619, Ы8v). He would use it to "sign" the anonymous Orthodox works of 1620–1622, and he would continue to use it, in Latin and in Polish, in the signed Uniate works of 1628–1629. See below, pp. 280, 323, 371, 564, 573, 599, 687, and 748.]

We promised at the end of our *Verification* to cite the oath of our apostates by which they bound themselves, in the rendering of obedience and in the acceptance of the confession of faith, to the bishop and the Church of Rome. And we do this, Kind and Gracious Reader, and especially you, O Orthodox Fellow in Confession, so that you might see clearly how their confession, in all the articles of faith mentioned in this oath, greatly differs from our present confession and from that of the entire Eastern Church and from the decision made between the Eastern and the Western Churches at the Council of Florence. Whereby you will also see how far the present Union is from that of Florence, when you compare and consider the points of this oath with the points that were discussed at the Union of Florence, which we have cited on folio 61 of our *Verification*,[226] and foremost among them the creed itself, which was supposed to be confessed for all time by Greeks and in the entire Eastern Church, without any addition, just as it was made at the second universal synod in Constantinople and submitted for the eternal use of the entire holy apostolic Catholic Church. That oath, extracted from the books of Baronius's *Annales* and translated from the Latin language into Polish, reads as follows (*Ad finem Tomi 7. Annal. Eccles. Baron. Impressum Moguntiae, Anno 1601* [at the end of Volume 7 of the Annales of the Church of Baronio, printed in Mainz, in the year 1601]):

Most Holy and Most Blessed Father:

I, humble Ipatij Potij, by God's grace the *protothronos* of Volodymyr and the bishop of Brest in Ruthenia, of the Ruthenian nation, one of the emissaries of the reverend fathers in Christ, their lords, the prelates of this same nation—namely, Myxajil Rahoza, archbishop, metropolitan of Kyiv, Galicia, and all Rus', Hryhorij [Xrebtovyč], archbishop-nominate, bishop-elect of Polack and Vicebsk, and Jona Hohol', bishop-elect of Pinsk and Turov, and Myxajil Kopystens'kyj, bishop of Przemyśl and Samborz, and Hedeon Balaban, bishop of Lviv, and Dionisij Zbirujs'kyj, bishop of Chełm—chosen and sent by them specially, together with the

---

226. [Actually, fols. 61v–63r/386–7. See above, pp. 220–2.]

reverend father in Christ, Lord Kyryl Terlec'kyj, exarch, bishop of Luc'k and Ostroh, the second emissary of that same nation, of the named lord prelates, my colleague, for the establishment and acceptance of Union with Your Holiness and with the holy Roman Church and for the rendering of the proper obedience in the name of them themselves and of their entire Church estate, and of the sheep entrusted to them, to the holy see of blessed Peter and to Your Holiness as the highest pastor of the universal Church, having fallen to Your Holiness's feet, do make and confess the below-described confession of holy Orthodox faith, according to the form established for Greeks converting to the aforementioned Union. I promise and pledge, both in the name of the aforementioned lords, the Ruthenian archbishop and bishops, my principles by whom I was sent, and in my own name, together with the aforementioned Lord Kyryl, exarch, bishop of Luc'k and Ostroh, envoy and my colleague, that the lords archbishop and bishops will consent to it, gladly and thankfully declare it, and will adhere to it, and in due time they will strengthen and confirm it, and that they will render it again according to the form given, word for word, and will publish it; and they will send it, signed by their own hands, and sealed with a seal, to Your Holiness and this holy apostolic see, in these words:

I believe in one God, the almighty Father, maker of heaven and earth, of all things visible and invisible. And in one Lord Jesus Christ, the only-begotten Son of God, and born of the Father before all time, God from God, light from light, true God from true God, born and not created, of one essence with the Father, through Whom all things came into being. Who for us people and for our salvation descended from heaven and was made incarnate through the Holy Spirit from the Virgin Mary and became man. He was crucified for us under Pontius Pilate, tortured, and buried. On the third day, He arose from the dead, according to the Scriptures, and He ascended into heaven. He sits at the right hand of God. And He will come again in glory to judge the quick and the dead; His kingdom will have no end. And in the Holy Spirit, Lord, and life-giver, who proceeds from the Father and the Son, who is worshipped and glorified together with the Father and the Son, who spoke through the prophets. And in one holy, catholic, and apostolic Church. I confess one baptism for the remission of sins. And I await the resurrection of the dead and the life of the age to come. Amen.

I also believe, accept, and confess all that the holy universal Council of Florence decreed and explained concerning the union of the Western with the Eastern Church: that is, that the Holy Spirit is from the Father and the Son eternally; and has His personal essence and being from the Father as also from the Son; and He proceeds from both eternally, as from one beginning and one spiration. For what the doctors and the holy Fathers say about the Holy Spirit proceeding from the Father through the Son, draws us to the understanding that it be signified thereby that the Son is, according to the Greeks, the *causa* or cause, and according to the Latins, the beginning of the being of the Holy Spirit, as also is the Father. And since all that is of the Father, with the exception of being the Father, the Father Himself gave to his only-begotten Son in begetting Him, therefore the Son has it before the ages from the Father, from Whom He was born before the ages, that the Holy Spirit proceeds from the Son. Therefore the interpretation found in the words "and from the Son" was added properly and *licite* [rightfully] to the *symbolum* [creed] for the explanation of the truth and on account of a need that arose at that time.

Moreover, I believe, accept, and confess that the body of Christ is truly celebrated in unleavened or leavened wheaten bread; and priests are to consecrate the same body of the Lord in one of those—that is, each according to the custom of his Church, whether Western or Eastern.

Furthermore, I believe, accept, and confess that the souls of those people who truly repent and depart from this world in the love of God, before rendering satisfaction in fruits meet for repentance[227] for transgressions of commission and omission, are cleansed after death through purgatorial punishment. And that the aid of living people of faith is helpful to them that such punishments be relieved for them: that is, the offerings of the Mass, prayers, and alms, and other pious deeds that the faithful were accustomed to make for other faithful according to the establishment of the Church.

And I believe, accept, and confess that the souls of those who, after the reception of baptism, were not stained with any sin, and those souls that, after sinning in the body, or after separation from the body (as was said above), became cleansed, are received immediately into heaven, and clearly see God Himself, the One in the Trinity, as He is;

227. [Mt. 3:8.]

one is more perfect than the other, however, according to the difference of merits. But that the souls of those who depart from this world in a mortal sin of commission, or only in original sin, descend immediately to hell, but suffer various tortures.

Moreover, I believe, accept, and confess that the holy apostolic see and the bishop of Rome hold primacy throughout the entire world and that the bishop of Rome is the *successor* of blessed Peter, prince of apostles, and true vicar of Christ, the head of the entire Church, and the father and teacher of all Christians. And that the complete power to shepherd, govern, and rule the universal Church was given to him in blessed Peter by our Lord Jesus Christ, as is contained in the history of the universal councils and the holy canons.

Further, I acknowledge and accept all the other things that, through the decrees of the holy universal general Council of Trent, the holy Roman and apostolic Church commanded us to confess and to accept above and beyond the *contenta* [assertions] in the Niceno-Constantinopolitan Creed, and which it submitted in writing, namely these:

I approve and accept most firmly the apostolic and Church traditions and other rites and determinations of that same Church.

I accept Holy Scripture according to the sense that holy mother Church held and holds, to whom alone belongs judgment concerning the true understanding and interpretation of Holy Scripture; and I will never understand and interpret it other than according to the unanimous agreement of the holy Fathers.

I also confess that there are seven genuine and proper *sacramenta* [sacraments] of the new Law, established by Jesus Christ our Lord and necessary for the salvation of human kind, although not all of them for everyone, that is: baptism, confirmation, Eucharist, penance, extreme unction, order, and matrimony, all of which give grace. And I confess that the repetition of baptism, confirmation, and order is sacrilege.

I also approve and accept the accepted and approved rites of the Catholic Church in the honorable celebration of all the above-mentioned sacraments.

I approve and accept everything in general and each thing in particular that was decreed and explained concerning original sin and justification at the holy Council of Trent.

I likewise confess that in the Mass a true and proper offering of atonement for the quick and the dead is offered to God and that in the most holy sacrament there is truly, really, and essentially the body and the blood of our Lord Jesus Christ together with the soul and the divinity; and that the entire essence of the bread is transformed into the body and the entire essence of the wine into the blood, which transformation the Catholic Church calls *transubstantiatio,* that is transubstantiation.

I also acknowledge that Christ and the true sacrament is received wholly and entirely under one species.

I hold steadfastly that purgatory exists; that the souls kept in it are aided by the help of the faithful; that it is necessary to venerate and to invoke the saints who reign together with Christ; that they bring prayers for us to the Lord God and that their *reliquiae* [relics] are to be held in veneration.

I assert firmly that images of Christ the Lord, of the Most Holy Virgin, and of other saints are to be held and maintained, and that due honor and respect is to be rendered to them.

I assert that the power of indulgences was left by Christ in the Church and that their use is most salvatory for the Christian nation.

I acknowledge that the holy catholic and apostolic Roman Church is the mother and teacher of all Churches, and I promise and swear true obedience to the bishop of Rome, the successor to blessed Peter, the prince of apostles and the vicar of Jesus Christ.

In like manner I accept and confess without doubt also all the other things given, decreed, and explained in the holy canons at the universal councils, and especially at the holy Council of Trent. And all the contrary things, the schisms and the heresies, whichever the Church condemned, rejected, and excommunicated, I also condemn, reject, and excommunicate.

And that I will strive to the best of my ability, with the help of God, to hold and confess complete and unchanged, until the last breath of my life, the true Catholic faith, without which no one can be saved, which I here voluntarily confess and to which I truly adhere, and that it be held, taught, and preached by those subject to me or those whose care will belong to me through my office, I, that same Ipatij Potij, *protothronos,* bishop of Volodymer and Brest, envoy of the above-mentioned lords, the Ruthenian archbishop and bishops, at their commendation and in my own name, do promise, pledge, and swear as above. May God and the holy divine Gospel help me.

Having touched the holy Gospel, Ipatij, the Ruthenian envoy, confirmed earnestly with an oath and the signature of his hand this confession of the Catholic faith made by himself. And he also confirmed with this sort of oath the version that was translated correctly into Ruthenian, guaranteed by his *cheirograph* [signature by hand, written bond], and read *publice* [publicly].

Then at the same time, the same confession offered by the second envoy Kyryl, read *publice* [publicly] in the same Ruthenian language and also in Latin by a translator according to custom, was affirmed with the renewal of the oaths and the signatures. And after the completion and conclusion of all this through the customary ceremony described in the holy canons, they again fell to the feet of the Most Holy and kissed them (as public *monumenta* [legal documents] make clear, which the office of the holy inquisition sent forth through public servants *publice* [publicly]).

This then, Kind and Gracious Reader and Orthodox Fellow in Confession, is the oath made by our apostates to the bishop of Rome in rendering the obedience that made this reverend Union. And you see what the Union brought into our fatherland. For so long as it did not exist, our Ruthenian nation was well known as faithful to the Kings, God's anointed, Their Gracious Lords, as always well disposed; but you hear and see what through all those years we suffered and what we now suffer on account of its erection. Which the Lord God made as sweet and pleasant to us as it is sweet and pleasant to Him. And how sweet it was to the Lord God, the Lord God, who is Himself miraculous in His deeds, deigned to show clearly and to declare indeed through a great and wonderful miracle. There was certainly a great miracle at the conclusion of the Union of Florence when patriarch Joseph, a man *alias* [otherwise], as the history declares about him, modest and pious, sealed the things discussed at this council with his own life—instead of with a signature—through his sudden farewell to this world.[228] But a much

228. [Joseph II (ca. 1360–1439), metropolitan of Ephesus from ca. 1393, patriarch of Constantinople from 1416. He died of dropsy on 10 June 1439 and was buried in the church of Maria Novella in Florence.]

greater miracle occurred at the conclusion of the present Union at the Council of Brest, in that, when our apostates celebrated the first liturgy or divine service during the declaration of the Union—at which we Orthodox who remained with holy antiquity and with the obedience to the holy apostolic see of Constantinople were excommunicated—unto the eternal opprobrium of their apostasy and unto the manifest disgrace of their perjurious hypocrisy, God, who does everything according to His will unto the end of saving human souls, deigned to transform the wine into water in the bloodless offering, so that through this very thing He might show that as far as the taste of water is from the taste of wine, so far is the piety of the Union, which was made without the knowledge of our father in the Spirit and pastor, from ancient piety. And although an important man in his time in the Roman Church explains this miracle as the mistake of a second pouring of water instead of wine,[229] nonetheless everyone can see how well this explanation removes the shame from our apostates, to whom the Lord God allowed this mistake at no other time than during the bringing of the first bloodless offering in this Union: for the righteous Lord God judged them to be unworthy through this very mistake, that, from the time of this apostasy from their natural pastor, they brought this bloodless offering which He wished to be brought to Himself in wine and in water, and not in water alone. Although we could amplify, we do not do so; for this matter itself calls out loudly of itself against the perjury of our apostates. Having left which, along with our entire *Verification* (of which, as we hear, the hater of holy justice and peace in our fatherland forbids the reading) to your careful attention, Kind and Gracious Reader and Orthodox Fellow in Confession, we entrust you and ourselves to God's love and to His holy care.

Psalm 118 [119:137]
Justus es Domine, et rectum judicium tuum.
Righteous art thou, O Lord, and upright are thy judgments.

---

229. Father Skarga in defense of the Council of Brest; look in his *Occasional Books*, p. 404. [Piotr Skarga's *Synod of Brest* (Cracow, 1597; Ruthenian version Vilnius, 1597) was reprinted in Polish in his *Occasional Sermons* (*Kazania przygodne*, Cracow, 1610). Page 404 is a reference to the 1610 edition. See *RIB* 19:328.]

A Defense of the *Verification*
(1621)

A Defense
of the *Verification,*

Which Maintains the Honor and Reputation of Noble People,
Clerical and Lay,
Innocent of the Offense
against the Majesty of His Majesty the King

That Has Been Alleged by the Work
Entitled
Twofold Guilt,

Which was Published by the Congregation of the Church
of the Holy Trinity unto the Offense of the Majesty of
His Majesty the King and of the
Honor and Reputation of Noble
People, Clerical and
Lay.

Published by the Monks of the Monastery of the Vilnius
Brotherhood of the Church of the Holy Spirit.

In Vilnius: The Year of Our Lord 1621.

Kind and Gracious Reader:

HAVING GIVEN YOUR GRACE certain knowledge, in brief, a few weeks ago through our *Verification*—as much as could be given at such a hurried and pressed time—about the unheard-of abuse and about the unbearable harm caused us by the calumny and oppression against us and against our entire Ruthenian nation, which was raised and wrought against us a dozen or so weeks ago by our apostates, and after verifying our innocence of the crime alleged against us before the entire Commonwealth and especially before His Majesty the King, Our Gracious Lord, as far as that violent and sudden attack of our apostates against us allowed, our intention was to refrain from further difficulties and labors in this matter, if it is a labor to defend one's innocence. But the fretful man, who seeks quarrels (as they say) in voids,[1] having beaten us up, does not allow us to cry;[2] having brought charges against us, does not give us an opportunity to justify ourselves; having calumniated us, forbids us to verify ourselves; having abused us, does not permit us to give account of ourselves and to remove the calumny and abuse. What is more, in all his wrongs against us, he seeks to be right.

Such are our apostates (although they unjustly chafe at that name), who, having torn our spiritual good away from us, against temporal and spiritual law, having harmed us severely with regard to our conscience, oppressed us harshly with regard to our freedoms, dishonored our honor shamefully in order further to wrong and oppress us according to their custom, made use in this matter of some incautious person, entirely unaware of the laws and customs of the Holy Eastern Church, who, *redargutorem agens* [acting as a refuter] in their name (wherefore we will call this writer thus in our *Defense*), adding *afflictionem afflicto* [affliction to the afflicted], alleged the opposite about true things. And having made this his intent, he published a work full of falsehood, cavil, illusions, and similar taunts and sophistic tricks, to use which *in re seria* [in a serious matter] is the mark of a worthless man. Having had of necessity to oppose this man to the extent that the time would bear, lest

1.   [*NKPP* 2:609, "Niespokojny," 1.]
2.   [*NKPP* 1:87, "Bić," 29.]

it seem to anyone that he spoke the truth in his work, we submit in haste this our defense of the *Verification* for Your Grace's reading. [. . .]³

The Inscription of the Refuter's Fourth Chapter:⁴
That, after seeing the Royal and Senatorial letters to him, they could not safely be consecrated by that foreigner.

Reply:
That, having seen the Royal and Senatorial letters, they could safely travel to the patriarch of Jerusalem; and they could be consecrated by him according to the laws of the Eastern Church.

[. . .]⁵

As to what you say concerning the promises made to us by His Majesty the King and confirmed by the general Sejms—our dispute with you now about this is pointless. Holy righteousness will demonstrate this, if it does not allow violence to be done to itself. But even now I will not allow the following to pass by untouched. You say to us, you perfidious deceiver (I will not apply a different name to you): "How do you dare to urge this so securely, that is to say, you as subjects upon your lord? Where is it promised to you? In the constitution, you say, of 1607, and in the most recent Sejm. But is mention made there about patriarchal obedience? And is mention made there about the reception of dignities and of the goods that belong to those dignities? Neither does His Majesty the King acknowledge such a promise, nor does the

3.   [Smotryc'kyj 1621c, 3–38/400–18 omitted.]
4.   [Smotryc'kyj uses a late Latin word *redargutor* (from *redarguo* 'disprove, refute') and makes it function as a Polish word. This is how he refers to the anonymous author of *Twofold Guilt (Sowita Wina),* the refutation of his *Verification of Innocence.* The Uniate side had referred to the author of that work as the "Verificator" *(Weryfikator),* a somewhat jarring form in Polish and English, which I will keep.]
5.   [Smotryc'kyj 1621c, 38–50/418–24 omitted.]

letter of the constitution have that in it. To the contrary it will show you something precisely contrary to that assertion."[6]

Thus the Refuter to us. To whom we respond that we do not urge this upon our lord, but our lord voluntarily deigned to make to us his lordly promise, and he acknowledges it. For both these constitutions were published at the personal command of His Majesty the King and confirmed by a privilege from His Majesty the King given to us together with the first constitution. To speak against which is to touch God's anointed, whose word is his word.

You ask whether there is a mention in that constitution of the patriarchal obedience? We say that there is. First, where His Majesty the King deigns to say "pacifying the Greek religion, which has its rights from of old." The Greek religion has, then, as its first and native right among our rights, the patriarchal obedience, given to it by the holy universal councils, as the Verificator thoroughly demonstrated. Second, where he deigns to say that "we are not to distribute spiritual dignities and goods by any other right than according to their foundation and the ancient custom of our ancestors that were given to them." And what sort of law of foundation that was, and what sort of ancient custom that was, he expresses in that same passage, where he says: "To distribute the spiritual dignities and goods to noble people of the Ruthenian nation is the first law of foundation and ancient custom." He says further, "and to those *mere* [wholly] of the Greek religion."[7] And this is the second right and ancient custom.

But the law of foundation of the Ruthenian religion is none other than for Rus′ to have its religion from the patriarch of Constantinople and to be obedient to him. For it is the ancient custom of Rus′ to be under the patriarchal obedience. And when he deigns to say ancient custom, he expresses the same thing, for although it can be shown that, on account of a great turmoil in the fatherland, some one metropolitan was raised to his see without the knowledge of the patriarch of Constantinople, as Ilarion was raised around the year of our Lord 1051 on account of the war that Rus′ was waging at that time with the Greeks (about which, see what the Kyivan Caves Monastery *Paterikon* says, and even more

---

6.   [*Sowita* 1621, 29; *AJuZR* 1:7:464. See above, pp. 176–82.]
7.   [*VL* 2:438.]

clearly Zonaras the Greek historian);[8] and as around the year of our Lord 1146 Metropolitan Klimentij was raised on account of the internal war of the Ruthenian princes among themselves, of Izjaslav, prince of Kyiv and Perejaslav with other princes, against whom Izjaslav employed the Polish King Bolesław the Curly and Henryk, the royal brother, prince of Sandomierz (about which, see Miechowita, Kromer, and Stryjkowski);[9] for although, we say, it can be shown that, for highly important reasons, some one metropolitan was raised without the knowledge of the patriarch of Constantinople, nonetheless, it can never be shown that any one of them was not under his obedience or that any one of them, bypassing the patriarch, rendered obedience to the bishop of Rome, as Krevza says pointlessly, without any proof, from out of his dreams.[10]

This is attested by the very fact that, even after Ilarion, Greek metropolitans were sent by the patriarchs, as right after him, George, John II, and Ephrem, about whom Krevza *stolide* [stupidly] conjectures something.[11] For also immediately after him there were the Greeks, Nicholas, Nicephorus, Nicetas, and Michael, after whom followed the above-mentioned Klimentij. All of these were sent by the patriarch.[12] Who will doubt that they were also obedient to him? Likewise after Klimentij there followed—sent by the patriarch—the Greek Theodore, John III, Constantine, Nicephorus II, Matthew, and others. Whereby, when Krevza babbles about Kirill the Ruthenian, who followed this Matthew, he babbles nonsense.[13] After him, following a second Ruthenian Kirill, there came the Greek Joseph, who was sent by the patriarch, and others after him, in this manner up to our times, before whose eyes Father Jeremiah, patriarch of Constantinople of blessed

---

8. *Serm. 7, tom. 3, fol. 169, col. 4 in Imp. Const. monomachi.* [Cf. Kosov 1635, 18–19; *HLEULT* 4:18.]

9. *Lib. 3, cap. 21, fol. 96; lib. 6, fol. 99; lib. 6, pag. 221.* [Miechowita 1521, 96; Kromer 1558, 99; Stryjkowski 1582, 221–2; cf. Stryjkowski 1846, 198. Here as elsewhere Smotryc´kyj could have drawn his page references to the other Polish historians from Stryjkowski, who seems to have been his main source.]

10. [Krevza 1617, 55–68; *HLEUL* 3:1:109–11; *HLEULT* 3:31–8.]

11. [Krevza 1617, 57; *HLEUL* 3:1:97; *HLEULT* 3:32.]

12. *Stryk. lib. 5, pag. 179* [Stryjkowski 1582, 179; Stryjkowski 1846, 1:163.

13. [Krevza 1617, 58; *HLEUL* 3:1:99; *HLEULT* 3:33.]

memory, deposed Metropolitan Onysyfor Divočka, whom he had also
consecrated, and he consecrated in his place Myxajil Rahoza.[14]

Testimony to this, as well, is the fact that none of the Polish
historians, great men, all of them of the Roman religion, such as
Kadłubek, Długosz, Miechowita, Wapowski, Kromer, Herburt, and
Stryjkowski, who in writing his *Chronicle* collected information
faithfully from all the historians who had lived before him (and he makes
known about himself that, in addition to the above-mentioned historians
and others, whom he himself enumerates, he had the history of Jan
Tarnowski, Sigmund Herberstein, Bielski, two chronicles of the history
of the emperors of Constantinople, old Ruthenian chronicles, Slavonic
chronicles, Muscovite histories, four old Kyivan chronicles, twelve
Lithuanian chroniclers)—and still, not one of all the above-mentioned
writes that the metropolitans of Rus′ were ever under the obedience of the
bishop of Rome or that the pope was supposed to have consecrated any
metropolitan of Rus′ and have submitted him to the Ruthenian Church.
But that Rus′ from the very time when it received holy baptism from the
patriarch of Constantinople never had metropolitans from anyone else
but from the patriarch, and the Ruthenian metropolitans never offered
obedience to anyone other than to the patriarch of Constantinople—this
is asserted in express words, after all the others, by Bishop Kromer and
by Canon Stryjkowski, a diligent historian of the Ruthenian past, and
by Guagninus. Only Krevza, a crafty person, crafted some Metropolitan
Grigorij or other, a hegumen of Constantinople, who was consecrated
by Pope Pius II and submitted to Rus′. And yet, that injudicious man
ought to have considered the fact that, if it was only on account of the
Union that Rus′ chased away Isidore, who, consecrated by Patriarch
Joseph, remained firmly under the obedience of the patriarch, how
would it have tolerated that Grigorij, who was brought to the Ruthenian
land (as Krevza says) by that same Isidore with the Union and with
a papal consecration and placed upon the Kyivan metropolitanate?[15]
Who could wish, having abandoned such worthy and ancient historians
worthy of credence, to give credence to Krevza, who is not in the least
worthy of credence in this matter, since he is without proof? Only one
like him.

14.   [See above, p. 197.]
15.   [Krevza 1617, 62–3; *HLEUL* 3:1:104–5; *HLEULT* 3:35.]

And so, having said how things are in their essence, that when
His Majesty the King deigns to promise in a constitution to distribute
the dignities and spiritual goods according to our foundation and
according to ancient custom, he means *this* foundation and *this* ancient
custom. Which he expresses in that same passage with the immediately
following words: "to the people *mere* [wholly] of the Greek religion."
And His Majesty the King deigns to understand as people *mere* [wholly]
of the Greek religion those whom he names in that same passage as
those who ask His Majesty the King that no *praejudicium* [damage]
be done to them in their conscience and rights, that is, that they not be
drawn and compelled by you forcibly to the obedience of the bishop
of Rome and that the free celebration of the liturgy according to their
old rites not be forbidden or hindered, that is, that they remain by
their customary spiritual obedience of the patriarch of Constantinople.
Which His Majesty the King deigns to promise to them. Whereas
those who asked His Majesty the King for this and who were and are
oppressed are we, who for twenty-six years now have been suffering
unbearable *praejudicium* [harm] in our conscience and rights from you
our apostates through apostasy from the patriarch of Constantinople,
for you forbid and hinder our free celebration of the liturgy under the
patriarchal obedience.

His Majesty the King, Our Gracious Lord, deigned to guarantee
and to confirm his royal promise with his lordly privilege granted to
us at that very same time at that very Sejm, which was mentioned in
the same Constitutions, and to assure us that we were supposed from
that time forth to enjoy our faith in peace, according to the ancient
custom of the Oriental Greek Church, freely, safely, and peacefully, and
to celebrate our liturgy. And it is the custom of our ancient faith to
be under the obedience of the patriarch of Constantinople. Paying no
attention to which, even today you make disturbances in our Ruthenian
Church that is under the obedience of the patriarch for the very reason
that it is under his obedience; you work *praejudicium* [damage] to our
conscience, you forbid us to use our customary rite. A visible witness
to all of which are the churches sealed in many cities for two years and
sometimes for three, as in Orša and in Mahilëŭ, where Christian people
have been living for so many years without any liturgy, children dying
without christening, older people without the salvatory mysteries of the
Eucharist, Christian bodies without the burials customary to Christians.

Thus, then, do we answer your question in which you ask us whether a mention is made of the patriarchal obedience in the constitution that was passed in the year 1607.

[. . .]¹⁶

The Inscription of the Refuter's Fifth Chapter:
The privileges, constitutions, and tribunal decrees that they cite were not such that they could safely be consecrated without the presentation of His Majesty the King.

Reply:
The privileges, constitutions, and tribunal decrees that were cited by the Verificator
make known that the apostates have no right over all of us who are under the obedience of the patriarch.

[. . .]¹⁷

Having presented this briefly, we say: There were two types of laws in our fatherland for the Ruthenian nation even from the beginning of the Christian faith among us—secular and ecclesiastical. The secular ones were established by Their Graces the Princes of Rus' and submitted in writing, as by Volodimer himself, by his son Jaroslav, and by others. All the spiritual laws were received at once from the Eastern Church together with the faith and were submitted for use to the Ruthenian Church. Thus when our Ruthenian nation was first partially joined to the Grand Duchy of Lithuania and to the Crown and then when it became completely incorporated into the Polish Kingdom, it was immediately admitted to absolutely all the secular laws, freedoms, and liberties of the Crown and of Lithuania that it was to enjoy, as it also enjoys them, having entirely relinquished the secular laws given to it by Their Graces the Princes of Rus'. But it was left absolutely and completely in possession of its own spiritual laws, and not those of any others, namely those that it had, given to it precisely at the time of baptism by

16.   [Smotryc′kyj 1621c, 55–60/426–9 omitted.]
17.   [Smotryc′kyj 1621c, 61–2/429–30 omitted.]

the Holy Eastern Church, with the guarantee from Their Majesties the Kings that Rus′ was to enjoy the same sort of freedom in its spiritual laws as the freedom the Roman Church enjoys in its laws in the Crown states. Which is made known from the privileges given to the Ruthenian nation at its incorporation into the Crown and in many others given at various times, some of which we mentioned in our answer to the first chapter of the Refuter.

And since this Ruthenian spiritual law is eternal, decreed by canons of the universal councils, submitted to Rus′ by the Eastern Church at baptism, and received by Rus′ at that very time, and permitted by Their Majesties the Kings of Poland, confirmed by privileges and oath, we are required to be under the obedience of that spiritual pastor by whom we were taught the Christian faith and baptized. Why then would you ask us what right we have to remain under the obedience of the patriarch of Constantinople? Custom alone bears witness, since at the very time when that incorporation took place the clergy of the Ruthenian Church and all Rus′ were under the obedience of the patriarch of Constantinople, as even our adversaries acknowledge in Krevza. Why do they ask us needlessly about our spiritual laws? Or why also about the secular ones? For during the reign of King Sigismund I of blessed memory, by whose will and effort this incorporation of the Ruthenian states into the Crown took place, the metropolitan of all Rus′ was Jona [III] Protasovyč, who was consecrated by Metrophanes [III], patriarch of Constantinople.[18] After him there followed Ilija Kuča. Both of them, and all those after, up to Rahoza, were under the obedience of the patriarch. Rahoza was the first to change, and even he was consecrated by the patriarch.

And that our nation was left in possession of the spiritual laws customary in the Holy Eastern Church—after the aforementioned custom (which is as if natural law), after the synodal laws cited by

18.   [There is something wrong here. Smotryc′kyj writes out "Sigismund the First," so this is not likely a typo. He reigned 1506–1548. But Jona III occupied his see from 1568 to 1577; his successor Ilija, 1577–1579; and Patriarch of Constantinople Metrophanes III, 1565–1572. Thus the Sigismund in question must have been Sigismund II August, who reigned 1548–1572. And the "incorporation of the Ruthenian states into the Crown" was of course that which occurred with the 1569 Union of Lublin. Smotryc′kyj makes the same mistake below (see p. 276).]

the Verificator and by us in the answer to Chapter Three and after the aforementioned privileges granted to us at the time of incorporation— this too testifies in practice: the fact that our Church was never governed by the spiritual laws of the Roman Church, nor was it judged by them; and that the spiritual laws of the Greek religion were confirmed by many privileges both after the incorporation and before the incorporation of the Ruthenian principalities into the Crown. Which laws, having recorded in them the decrees and canons of the universal councils, have this canon: that the laws of every land be maintained inviolate. It also has this decree: that that patriarch judge and rule in spiritual matters the nations that he brought to the Christian faith and baptized. Since the patriarch of Constantinople caused both these things in our Ruthenian nation, by God's will and His holy providence, therefore our Ruthenian nation belongs to his spiritual power and jurisdiction by divine and human law. Thus, when Their Majesties the Kings acknowledge, confirm, and swear under oath to the spiritual laws of the Greek religion, they deign to acknowledge, confirm, and swear to these and no others. No exception in this oath can occur without perjury. And none was made and none is made, since His Majesty the King does not deign to forbid our Ruthenian nation to remain even now under our customary obedience to the patriarch of Constantinople. To the contrary, he deigns to promise, according to our ancient customs and foundations, laws and privileges, not to allow you our apostates to work *praejudicium* [damage] against us. Which is made manifest by the privileges, constitutions, and tribunal decrees that were cited by the Verificator, in which our spiritual obedience belonging to the patriarch of Constantinople was expressed in deed, without whose will and permission we cannot establish anything in spiritual matters, nor can any of our spiritual superiors of the Ruthenian Church.

[. . .][19]

But the Refuter argues further, waxing enthusiastic: "Who," he says, "would be so incautious as to dare to assert that His Majesty the King, a Catholic lord, would acknowledge that those are of the Catholic faith who do not hold the Roman pope as the head of all Christendom? For thereby he would have to judge that he himself is not of the Catholic

19.   [Smotryc'kyj 1621c, 65–76/431–7 omitted.]

faith."[20] O our dear Refuter, you are truly to be pitied. Why do you, a self-taught man, why do you think that you reach the heavens with your head and that you are as one of them? Know that the Lord God is wont to have the heart of kings more in His providence than that of even the wisest in the kingdom, to say nothing of your boorish heart; and that his spirit is governed by a more special grace of God than that of the most industrious scribes and Pharisees, to say nothing of yours, you wretched scribbler. Leading His Majesty the King, Our Gracious Lord, by the path of his ancestors, the spirit of God, which is in him and with him, directs him to call us as his ancestors called us, and as we are properly to be called.

Look into all the laws and privileges that we have from Their Majesties the Kings that were given to us and to our ancestors who were under the obedience of the patriarch before your apostasy, and you will see that wherever mention is made of people of the Roman and the Greek religion they deign to mention both in the same manner everywhere. "People of the Roman religion, people of the Greek religion; churches of the Roman order, churches of the Greek order; Church matters of the Christian order of the Roman obedience, Church matters of the Christian order of the Greek obedience. We, the highest defender of the Catholic and the Orthodox Churches of God." Hearing Their Majesties the Kings speak about our Orthodox Church of God that is under the obedience of the patriarch in the same manner as about the Catholic Church of God that is under the obedience of the pope, why are you surprised, Refuter, that His Majesty the King, in calling the people of the Roman religion Christians and Catholics, likewise adorning us, the people of the Greek religion, with the same title, calls us Christians and Catholics?

Is not the Church of God the name of the Christian and Catholic Church? This you cannot deny. But His Majesty the King, Our Gracious Lord, in a circular letter given to Patriarch Jeremiah (whom we have mentioned here) calls our Ruthenian churches, which are under the obedience of the patriarch, churches of God. Why do you wonder then that in the privilege he gave us he sees fit to call us people of the Christian Catholic religion? For if so, you say, he would have been denying that he himself is of the Catholic faith. You are mistaken, Mr. Refuter. I

20.   [*Sowita* 1621, 36; *AJuZR* 1:7:469.]

would say that His Majesty the King is better able to define what the One Holy Catholic and Apostolic Church is than you are. But I do not dare to compare your stupidity to such a high intellect. His Majesty the King is pleased to know that the Holy Catholic Church—which is one in its reins and in which the particular Churches were conceived and to which both have the same right—bears both our sides, the Eastern particular Church and the Western. And since they are united by the unity of mutual love, both sides beg the Lord God that He paternally remove and eliminate what separates them, that is, whatever has come between them as a difference *non per defectum* [not by defect], but *per excessum* [by excess]. And since, as they say, *defectus fide non utitur, excessu[s] fide abutitur* [a defect does not make use of the faith, an excess uses the faith entirely], therefore His Majesty the King finds no defect in our Holy Greek faith, nor in his own Roman faith. Wherefore, when he is pleased to call us people of the Greek Catholic Christian religion, he does not deny himself the same Catholic Christian title. Therefore the Refuter is much mistaken in arguing the opposite, not wishing to know that *neque in excessu, neque in defectu* [neither in excess nor in defect] (if he can also say this of his own Church) has the Holy Eastern Church left the Catholic Church.[21]

And so you see, dear Refuter, that we knew by the grace of God what we were arguing. The understanding that the apostasy took away from you remained with the Church of God, with the result that you are unable to understand this. It must befall you, we see, as it does a drowning man who must hold on for dear life. Do not frighten us with the notion that "His Majesty the King remains the faithful *interpres* [interpreter] of his privileges."[22] We have the same sort of Lord, His Majesty the King, Our Gracious Lord, as do you; ours is the same sort of defender as also yours; we trust in Our Gracious Lord, and we yield to his holy judgment.

But now as to the constitutions, removing which the Refuter says: "As far as the Sejm constitutions are concerned, everyone scoffs at your stupidity, how you make yourselves interpreters of them, wrenching

21.   [This definition of correct faith stems from Smotryc'kyj's reading of Marcantonio de Dominis's *De Republica Christiana*. See Frick 1995, 206–26 and above, pp. xliii–xliv, xlvii.]
22.   [*Sowita* 1621, 36; *AJuZR* 1:7:469.]

them by force to your side. And you believe that the intent of His Majesty the King and of the entire senate was to destroy the Union. But this would be against their conscience, if they were to allow this and to decree this for your sake. You truly do them a great wrong in this."[23]

We too acknowledge, Refuter, that "everyone" scoffs, but only idiots similar to you, who are wont to celebrate their triumphs before victory. What are you laughing at, derisive scoffer? That we supposedly did not interpret these constitutions according to the intent of His Majesty the King and the twofold senate of His Majesty the King and of the entire knighthood? And that we supposedly drew them by force to our side? You certainly do us wrong in both of these things, both with your laughter and with your speech. We do not touch the intent of His Majesty the King, Our Gracious Lord, in the passing of these constitutions. We leave it in the position in which we left it in the citing of privileges a little above. On the other hand, as far as our interpretation of these constitutions and our forceful pulling of them to our side is concerned, we refer you and the gracious Reader to our answer to your fourth article, where we thoroughly proved our point concerning those constitutions and the promises made to us through them by His Majesty the King—with their proper interpretation, without any forceful pulling of them to our side. Which you yourself must acknowledge, whether you will or not.

But you claim amazement in your meddlesomeness, and you allege that removing the Union is a thing against conscience. I, on the other hand, am not amazed at your speech; for everyone who wishes unrest for the fatherland says this. You have been arranging this Union for twenty-six years now. Tell us, we ask you, how much—through citations, summonses, various punishments, beating, and imprisonment, murder, banishment, the sealing of churches, and the forbidding of services (for this is your teaching in the Union, and this is how you spread it)—how much, we say, did you spread it? Is your Union of ten-some people comparable to the great troubles, miseries, disturbances, and dangers that come from it for the fatherland? When you seek salvation, you point to the Union. Why do you not pass straight over to the Roman rite itself, rather than sow quarrels and storms between the lord and subjects? If you should wish to compare your revered Union with the harms and

23. [*Sowita* 1621, 36–7; *AJuZR* 1:7:469.]

difficulties of the fatherland of which it is the cause, once you had come to your senses, you would abandon it to the garbage heap.

What has set us, Rus', more at odds with the Romans than that perfidious Union? Such that they shun our Orthodox churches and we their Catholic churches; such that they condemn our rite and we theirs, even though it is almost one and the same. What has given birth to the acrimonious writings that lead to the little-needed internal discord between us and the Romans, if not the Union? What molests His Majesty the King more frequently, what disturbs the Commonwealth more, what makes greater laments and cries in the fatherland, if not the Union? What is the cause both of the unheard-of excesses and of the unprecedented audacities that occur today in the fatherland, if not the Union? If you say that it is against conscience to allow the Union to be removed because souls are at stake, you ought to know that no one but the son of perdition will die.[24] And if, as we see is your intent, you wish to preach this Union by fire and to spread it by the sword[25]—which may Christ the Lord deign to forbid—this already goes beyond the bounds of the property of the Gospel teaching.

You say, then, that to allow and to decree the removal of the Union is against the conscience of His Majesty the King and of the entire senate, spiritual and lay, and of the knightly estate. We do not insist upon this, nor are we so insistent that the Union be removed, since in these domains it is permitted to each to believe as he will. Rather, our Ruthenian nation asks His Majesty the King, Our Gracious Lord, that His Royal Majesty might deign to leave us in possession of our rights and freedoms, both temporal and spiritual; that the spiritual dignities, together with the benefices that belong to them, be returned to us; that the churches be given over to us; that we remain under our usual obedience; that our rite be permitted to us: this is what our Ruthenian nation asks of His Majesty the King. And you do as you see fit. Once you have relinquished to us our proper spiritual and temporal goods, even if you were in the thousands, we will not envy you.

We ask you, dear Refuter, what law allows you, our apostates, to ride upon our souls even unto Charon? Why are we in your eyes a nation so despised that you attempt to yoke us as oxen to the plow of your

24.   Jn. 17[:12].
25.   [Is. 66:16.]

will? You wonder at our forced actions, but you do not wish to wonder whether we are obliged to bear such unbearable oppression from you. We would never bring ourselves to inflict upon our greatest enemy what we suffer at your hands, waiting either for your repentance, or—more likely—for the merciful grace of His Majesty the King, Our Gracious Lord, that he finally see fit to save us from your heavy servitude by his lordly decree. You certainly ought to consider what you are doing, whether you are attempting a possible thing or not. It seems to us an impossible thing. For if, in proceeding gently for so many years, you have not accomplished anything, you have accomplished still less through the tyranny you have undertaken. For in what way, by God, is it proper that, for the sake of the apostate who is today learning to make out syllables in Ruthenian,[26] we ought to abandon our faith, which has been declared before all the world with excellent miracles? Where here is wisdom? Where understanding? You spill blood, and do you think that thereby you will acquire love from the Ruthenian nation so that it would consider you a metropolitan or bishop? We do not think so. If then, as you say, Refuter, conscience does not allow His Majesty the King to allow that the Union be removed, does conscience allow you to inflict your excesses upon us? Let, then, the will of His Majesty the King, Our Gracious Lord, be done in the removing of your Union. We ask this of His Majesty the King, Our Gracious Lord, for the perfect pacification of us in our religion.

[. . .][27]

The Inscription of the Refuter's Sixth Chapter:
That it was not to vacant bishoprics that those newly consecrated sought to succeed;
and that the patriarch of Constantinople
does not have a right to the Ruthenian lands.

26.   [A reference to Uniate Metropolitan Josyf Ruts'kyj?]
27.   [Smotryc'kyj 1621c, 81–6/439–42 omitted.]

Reply:

That the newly consecrated metropolitan and bishops
allowed themselves to be consecrated to the vacant sees of
the metropolitanate and bishoprics and that the patriarch of
Constantinople has a natural right to the Ruthenian lands,
confirmed by the canons of the universal synods.

In this sixth chapter the Refuter undertakes to destroy three of the
Verificator's paragraphs. I will place before your eyes, Kind and
Gracious Reader, with what sort of weapon he outfitted himself, from
which you will easily see just how ready he is for combating, to say
nothing of destroying the Verificator's first paragraph: that the patriarch
of Constantinople is the natural pastor in the Ruthenian lands by spiritual
and secular law and by custom. The second paragraph: that the patriarch
of Constantinople condemned, degraded, and excommunicated the
apostate metropolitan Rahoza and his followers, the bishops. Third
paragraph: that with such a degradation, the episcopal sees became
vacant, to which orphaned sees the newly consecrated were raised.

In destroying and removing the first paragraph, the Refuter,
founded upon and strengthened by the canons of the universal councils,
begins with the twenty-eighth canon of the fourth universal council, by
which Pont, Asia, Thrace, and the barbarian nations are appointed to
the spiritual rule of the patriarch of Constantinople, where, discoursing
about the barbarian nations, he wasted an entire sheet. Together with
Balsamon, the interpreter of these canons, we tell him that the intention of
the holy fathers in the interpretation of this twenty-eighth canon was that
through it all the barbarian nations, such as the Bulgarian, Slavonian,[28]
Serbian, Rascian, Bosnian, Croatian, Dalmatian, Illryian, Multanian,
Wallachian, Hungarian, Czech, Polish, Ruthenian, Muscovite, and others
of this name of Barbary, who were called barbarians both with regard
to their crudeness at that time as well as with regard to their paganism,
were submitted to rule and government.[29] And they submit to him these
pagan nations for such rule so that, in consecrating bishops, he might
send them unto those nations for the teaching of the Holy Gospel.

28.   [Smotryc'kyj wrote "sławackie," by which he seems to have meant some
specific Slavic people. It is not clear to me which one.]
29.   [Theodore Balsamon, *Commentaries on Canons, PG* 137:485.]

And why should it be to him and not to someone else? For no other reason but on account of propinquity itself. Wherefore what that Refuter blabbers here has no validity: that "laws are written only for the subordinate."[30] For those nations were submitted to him so that he might gain them for Christ the Lord and, sending to them teachers, bishops, make them subordinate to him, to whom consequently those laws would apply. Thus it is a paltry argument of the Refuter, where he says that "if in the Ruthenian lands in those times there were not even the beginnings of the Christian faith, then the patriarch of Constantinople did not have anyone to consecrate."[31] He ought to have inferred that it was the patriarch of Constantinople who was to send teachers of the Gospel there and that, by bringing them through them to the Christian faith, he was supposed to consecrate bishops for them and to give them Church laws.

This argument too is worthless, where he alleges that "this law would be unjust"; and he gives as a reason for this the fact that "by the cause of this decree a great multitude of human souls would have to perish, if, on account of some sort of confusion or through some incapacity for some other reason, teachers of the Gospel could not be sent from Constantinople, and others were not allowed to do so."[32] We say that the holy fathers did not pay any attention to those confusions, for all states are equally subject to this; rather they paid attention partially to the fact that, even if there should have been confusions, the word of God is not subject to binding[33] and confusion, and partially—and that, the greater part—because no one could send teachers of the Gospel more quickly to those nations on account of their propinquity to the see of Constantinople, and no one could rule them in spiritual matters more ably and more adroitly than the patriarch of Constantinople, as the one nearest to all those nations. For in fulfilling that canon, he gained all those above-mentioned barbarian nations for Christ the Lord.

And when I say all, I do not except any one of them. But perhaps the Refuter will say: we will grant the teaching of the Gospel by the patriarch of Constantinople in those nations in which even now the faith

---

30.   [*Sowita* 1621, 42; *AJuZR* 1:7:473.]
31.   [*Sowita* 1621, 42; *AJuZR* 1:7:473.]
32.   [*Sowita* 1621, 42; *AJuZR* 1:7:473.]
33.   [2 Tim. 2:9.]

of the Eastern Church and the obedience to the see of Constantinople remains, as in the Bulgarian, the Serbian, the Slavonian, the Ruthenian, the Muscovite, and others. But where in Poland is the Gospel teaching from the patriarch of Constantinople? Where in Hungary? Where in Bohemia? Where in Lithuania? For those nations too were barbarian, pagan. Let the Refuter and his *complices* [confederates] know that in all these nations there was the Gospel teaching of the Holy Eastern Church by the patriarch of Constantinople. There are *munimenta* [defenses, legal proofs] that are certain and imposing, against which no one can properly speak. There are also the teachers of the Gospel, Methodius and Cyril, bishops from Patriarch Methodius of Constantinople, a holy man, who were sent to those nations for teaching, as we can read about Methodius on 11 May and about Cyril on 14 February in the lives of the saints in the Slavonic language. Whence Stryjkowski says, "And Cyril and Methodius, holy bishops, labored most of all toward the training and instruction in the new faith of these newly baptized Slavic nations."[34]

And so, among other Slavic nations, these holy bishops brought Świętopług, or rather Światopołk, the king of Moravia, to the Christian faith in the year of Our Lord eight hundred eighty-five, as Stryjkowski writes, drawing on Kromer and on Venceslas Hájek, the Czech chronicler. For which reason our Slavonic *menologia* call this Methodius the bishop of Moravia. Five[35] years after his baptism, that is, in the year nine hundred, the King of Moravia, Świętopług, brought the Czech prince Bořivoj and his wife Ludmila to that same Christian faith.[36] Sixty-five years after that, the Polish prince Mieczsław[37] received that same Christian faith that had come from the East to Moravia, and from Moravia to Bohemia, for the sake of the Czech princess Dubravka, the sister of the Czech princes Vaclav and Boleslav, when he wished to take her for his wife. The proof of the fact that Świętopług or Światopołk, the King of Moravia, received the Christian faith from the East, from the Greeks, is first this one from Długosz, who says the following about him and about two other princes of the Slavic nation: "Three Slavic

---

34.   *Lib. 4, p. 148* [bk. 4, p. 148. Stryjkowski 1582, 148–9; Stryjkowski 1846, 1:138–9].
35.   [A mistake. It should be fifteen.]
36.   Ibid.
37.   [That is, Mieszko I.]

princes received the Christian faith and ceremonies from the Greeks—
Rastislav, Svjatopolk, and Kocel."[38] The second proof of this is the
fact that the Eastern Church and our Ruthenian one considers as a saint
Ludmila, Queen of Moravia, who was the wife of Svjatopolk, King of
Moravia, their first Christian; and it celebrates her martyr's memory on
the sixteenth day of September. Likewise, the Eastern Church and our
Ruthenian one also considers as a saint—having consecrated a day for
his memory on 29 September—Vaclav (Vjačeslav in Ruthenian), the
brother of Princess Dubravka, the wife of the Polish prince Mieczsław,
on account of whom he received the same Christian faith that was hers.
Having cited these two clear proofs, we conclude that the Polish prince
Mieczsław received the faith that was Dubravka's; Dubravka was of
the same faith as her grandmother Ludmila; Ludmila was of the same
faith as was Svjatopolk, King of Moravia; Svjatopolk was of the faith
that he learned from Methodius and Cyril; Methodius and Cyril taught
Svjatopolk the faith they had been taught by Patriarch Methodius of
Constantinople, who sent them. Therefore, the Poles, having received
the same faith of which were the Polish prince Mieczsław and his
wife, Princess Dubravka, received the Greek Christian faith that
had come fortunately from the East, from the holy apostolic see of
Constantinople.

And the Greek historian Zonaras makes known that the Hungarians
too received the Christian faith from the patriarch of Constantinople
when he writes that the Hungarian prince Bologudes and another one,
Gylas, who was prince over some part of that same state, received the
Christian faith through baptism in Constantinople during the reign of
Emperor Constantine of Constantinople, son of Leo, and during the
time of Patriarch Theophylactus. For they took with them to Hungary
a bishop who was given to them by that same Patriarch Theophylactus
for teaching the doctrine of the Gospel.[39]

Concerning Lithuania, there is no doubt that it first received the
Christian faith from the East, from the see of Constantinople, and on
this occasion: Algirdas the prince of Lithuania, who had two wives

38. *Lib. 1, tom. 1* [bk. 1, vol. 1; Długosz 1962, 232–3].
39. *Zon. tom. 3, fol. 158 in Im. Constantin: Filii Leonis* [John Zonaras, vol.
3, fol. 158, on Emperor Constantinus, son of Leo; *Annales,* bk. 16, chap. 21;
PG 135:103–4].

one after the other, the first princess Uliana, daughter of the prince of Vicebsk, and the second princess Maria, daughter of the prince of Tver', both of the Greek religion, for whose sake Algirdas himself took the Greek faith and erected two Orthodox churches in Vicebsk, one in the lower castle and the other beyond the Ručaj. And he baptized all the sons he had—six with Uliana and another six with Maria—in the Greek religion.[40] Perhaps the astounded Refuter will ask whence the Roman faith came in these states now? If he wishes to know, we refer him to the third book of Kromer[41] and to the twelfth book of Stryjkowski.[42]

Thus, with the help of God, we have shown the Refuter that even in Moravia, Bohemia, Hungary, Poland, and Lithuania, the teaching of the holy Gospel received its bounteous sowing from the holy Eastern Church, from the see of Constantinople, to which was assigned teaching, even though today someone else sends his sickle into them (I leave it to others to consider by what right). It was thus for this reason that the holy fathers of the fourth universal council, through this twenty-eighth canon, gave these nations to the spiritual rule of the patriarch of Constantinople, and, as has been demonstrated, it was he who happily exercised it in them with the passing of time.

[. . .][43]

The Inscriptions of the Refuter's Seventh and Eighth Chapters:
Concerning the wrongs that the Verificator supposes
they have suffered from us in words and in deed.

---

40.   *Stryjkowski, lib. 12, pag. 424. Idem. lib. eo. pa. 46.* [Stryjkowski 1582, 424, 461; Stryjkowski 1846, 2:13–14, 57. *Ruczaj* is a generic Polish term for a small stream, but here it seems to be a proper noun. In the first cited passage, Stryjkowski wrote that Algirdas had built two Orthodox churches, "one in the lower castle, and the other in the field beyond the Ruczaj"—he capitalized it—"or the castle rampart."]

41.   *Pag. 33 and 34* [Kromer 1568, 33–4].

42.   *Pag. 461* [Stryjkowski 1582, 461; Stryjkowski 1846, 2:57].

43.   [Smotryc'kyj 1621c, 91–100/444–9 omitted.]

The Inscriptions of the Refuter's Ninth and Tenth Chapters:
Concerning the wrongs that we suffer from you
in words and in deed.

[. . .][44]

"The cause of all that uproar," you say, "was the evil man Smotryc'kyj: he brought the citizens of Vilnius to such difficulties, and he will yet bring them to greater ones." But, dear Refuter, these are empty words and false ones. Smotryc'kyj sits not with an army in the Vilnius Brotherhood Monastery, but only with a dozen or so brother monks, not with some sort of cannon but only with a crozier. What kinds of uproar did he cause? You say: "Read the ninth chapter and you will discover how I charge this uproar to Smotryc'kyj."[45]

To which Father Smotryc'kyj answers your allegations thus: if you had not mixed falsehood in with the truth, he would accept everything with which you filled your ninth chapter concerning him. But since some of this is said by you so deviously that, if it were not refuted by a proper answer, it could harm his reputation, especially with those who are concerned only with the glory of his honorable deeds and of his salvatory labors in the Church of God, and not also with his earnest constancy in affairs—therefore, in view of these very people, we record this account in his favor against yours.

Father Smotryc'kyj, who spent his young years up to manhood on liberal arts, both here in the fatherland and in foreign countries, when, after courtly amusements of several years as a sort of rest from the dust of the schools, it came time for him to order his life and to employ, for his own benefit and that of his neighbors, the tool of the studies that he had spent so many years acquiring, had always planned not to enter the monastic order (for which he had an eager soul almost since the days of his childhood) until he had obtained certain knowledge of the intended goal of both sides among the confounded brethren (for this had troubled him for a long time). He was not ignorant of the goal of his own side. He was ignorant of that of the other side. And when it had already become his intent to bring into effect the holy undertaking

44.   [Smotryc'kyj 1621c, 100–4/449–51 omitted.]
45.   [*Sowita* 1621, 66–7; *AJuZR* 1:7:489–90.]

of the monastic state he came to Vilnius, and he entered our Vilnius monastery, so that present in it he might examine for some time without taking on monastic vestments (as the monastic custom has it) both his own suitability for this order and our way of life. Living here, freed from all the distractions of this world, he directed his thought toward receiving knowledge from the other side concerning the goal they intended in their undertaking, wherefore he sought such means that his elder[46] (to whose will and power he was subject as an servant) might permit them to come to him, and him to go to them, in order to conduct mutual conversations.

Once he had easily received this, they know well themselves how many times he was visited by the youth of the other side, where they had frequent spiritual conversations both with him and with his predecessor, the archimandrite of blessed memory. But since his goal in this undertaking was not the youth, who could not offer him certain knowledge in what he needed, he met with Father Ruts′kyj two times, and since Father Ruts′kyj did not appear for the third *condictamen* [appointment], he met with Father Josafat and with Krevza. Through these three meetings with these individuals he discussed with them not, as the Refutor alleges, how he himself might come and bring his group with him to agreement with them, but what goal the Union had, and how, if it should come to a total [union] of our entire Ruthenian nation, the faith of our eastern confession could remain whole in it, since without the patriarch, whichever direction that Union turns, we face an obstacle. And they can remember well for what reasons. He demonstrated to them the indignity [we suffer], from both their side and from ours; he demonstrated to them the loss of those who confess their faith, both by them and by their Union: that entire houses of Uniates transfer from the Union to the Roman Church; that the [Orthodox/Uniate] churches on the estates of Their Lords, the Romans, are transformed into [Catholic] churches;[47] that it is permitted to come from the Ruthenian to the Roman religion, but that it is forbidden to go from the Roman to the Ruthenian; that they force you out of the Ruthenian cities, establishing

---

46.   [That is, Leontij Karpovyč, archimandrite of the Vilnius Orthodox Brotherhood Monastery.]

47.   [Smotryc′kyj distinguishes here between Ruthenian—both Uniate and Orthodox—churches (*cerkwie*) and Roman Catholic (*kościoły*).]

their schools where your Uniate schools were supposed to have been, and such things. This is what the conversation of Father Smotryc'kyj was about with them during his thrice-held meetings with the superiors.

As far as the salvation of confessors of the Roman faith is concerned, he could safely say that *defectus fidei non excessus condemnat* [it is the defect in the faith, not the excess, that condemns];[48] and therefore, whoever heard this from him could infer what he wished, according to his desire. As to the disputation, the discussion was about the public one of our entire side with the opposing one, without any participation of the Lord Romans; but when it came to the judge of that disputation, and a healthy counsel was not found among ourselves, and when an *instantia* [insistence] was made about it, such a response was given to them in writing.

Reasons Why We Cannot Enter into a Disputation for the Present.

The first is that which St. Ambrose used *in simili causa* [in a similar case]: that we do not see appropriate and capable judges on our side. For, as far as the laymen are concerned, they, as St. Ambrose writes in that same passage, cannot judge concerning the mysteries of the faith and cannot be the masters of spiritual people.[49] And as far as the spiritual authorities are concerned, that is, the metropolitan and the bishops, not only we, but also the entire Commonwealth have been asking His Majesty the King and the estates that belong to the Sejm for this for twenty years, that we might receive them according to the ancient laws, liberties, and customs.

Second, because we cannot see a happy conclusion to this matter, and this not because of any deficiency of the truth on our side, but only partially because of the greater power of the opposing side in secular matters, with regard to which the Orthodox wrote in their turn to Leo [V] the Armenian, Emperor of Constantinople, saying: "We do not wish to engage in disputation about this and to consider as doubtful what we have from the tradition of the Church and what is confirmed at the universal councils. And we also know, O Emperor, that those whom you

48.   [See above, p. 252.]
49.   [Ambrose, *Letters,* no. 8; *PL* 16:932A.]

wish to bring together with us will win, if you will help them in this, and if you will oppress us by force. For if you wish, you will order us to be silent";[50] and partially because of their usual manner of dealing with us in such a case, whereby not only do they not present themselves eager to receive the truth shown to them, but they are apt to find in this a cause for greater hatred and disputes.

Moreover, even without the considerations that have been mentioned, we could not do this without the knowledge and permission of our elders in the clergy, that is, the patriarchs. For that was how also in bygone times our holy ancestors were wont to excuse themselves in such instances before the opposing side. As Theodore the Studite says, in writing to Emperor Michael III, who sought to draw the Orthodox side into disputation with the heterodox: "The Lord God ordered the apostles, prophets, evangelists, pastors, and teachers, but not kings, to rule His Church."[51] Such then was the response that was given by us to the opposing side in the matter of the disputation.

As far as the theses about the procession of the Holy Spirit are concerned, they were and are an *exercitium scholasticum* [school exercise] of Father Smotryc'kyj, collected and written not for disputation, but for their consideration. He has much of this sort of thing from his constant lucubrations. If the opposing side used something from them, it was free to do so. For Father Smotryc'kyj saw that they were powerful and appropriate to the opposing side; but he also simultaneously saw that they were used very *corrupte* [perversely], against the will and understanding of the holy fathers, first in words, then in the punctuations, then in the translation from Greek into Latin, so that thus the truth might become all the more manifestly clear if these theses were to become known and be destroyed on account of their *corruptela* [corruption].[52]

[. . .][53]

And in recalling the honorable men of our Ruthenian nation who left in our Ruthenian Church, according to their strengths, the *munimenta*

---

50.   *Bar. in Anno 513. Nice. lib. 16. cap. 31* [Baronius, *Annales,* s.a. 513; Nicephorus Callistus Xanthopulus, *Church History,* bk. 16, chap. 31; *PG* 147:177–80].

51.   *Bar. in Anno 823* [Baronius, *Annales,* s.a. 823].

52.   [On these theses, see *HLEUL* 3:xlix–l.]

53.   [Smotryc'kyj 1621c, 108–9/453 omitted.]

[defenses, legal proofs] of their love for God and His holy faith for the opposing of various sectarians, you mention Herasym the priest, and you call him Father Smotryc'kyj's father. O hypocritical Ruthenian! Do you think that this would shame and insult Smotryc'kyj, having said that he was the son of a priest, when thereby you rather rebuke the presbyter's marriage? Father Smotryc'kyj would consider it one good among the other goods of his honorable birth if he had been born of a man assigned to the service of God. But since you said it unto his dishonoring, it is not inappropriate that we charge you with erring from the truth in this. If someone sits in a hole, can he properly say that the sun does not shine because he does not see it? Because that man of high virtues is unknown to you, you hole-and-corner man, is this supposed to harm in any way his noble dignity? Herasym Danyjilovyč Smotryc'kyj was known to Podolia, which bore and raised him, and had him as castle notary of Kam'janec' under three Kam'janec' *starostas*. He was known to Volhynia, where he lived in the Konstantyn tract, provided with no small estate on his little field of land in Podolia by the Illustrious Grace, Prince of Ostroh, Palatine, of blessed memory, of Kyiv.[54] That man [i.e., Herasym], great in his time in the Ruthenian nation, seeing our Ruthenian nation inclining unto ruin on account of the simplicity and crudeness of those who ought to have been wise and learned, left his *munimentum* [defense] worthy of eternal memory, having dedicated it to all the superiors in the Ruthenian Church in actual fact, although one of them by name, and then a second, and a third.[55] Nothing *haeretice* [heretically], by the grace of God, only *pie, Orthodoxe, Catholice* [piously, in Orthodox manner, in Catholic manner]. So much in this place about our Smotryc'kyj, through the occasion given by the Refuter.

And why does the Refuter, wishing to get rid of the name of apostate that he has properly acquired, twist and turn like a piece of old leather on the fire?[56] He says: "Apostasy from the faith cannot be ascribed to us, for we always declare *publice et privatim* [publicly and

---

54. [Kostjantyn Vasyl' Ostroz'kyj.]
55. [Extant works of Herasym Smotryc'kyj: preface to the *Ostroh Bible* of 1580–1581; *Key to the Kingdom of Heaven* (*Ključ carstva nebesnoho*, Ostroh, 1587; *AJuZR* 1:7:232–49); *The New Roman Calendar* (*Kalendar rymsky novy,* Ostroh, 1587, *AJuZR* 1:7:250–65).]
56. [*NKPP* 2:258, "Kurczyć się," 3.]

privately] that we receive the universal and local councils. We listen to
the teaching of the holy Greek fathers, and we believe as they taught,
etc."[57] The prodigal son, as long as he gallivanted about as he saw fit,
was a son to his father, but a prodigal one. You also receive the councils,
but only as long as they suit you. Do you not protest against the second,
fourth, and sixth? If not, then we are all one, by the grace of God, and
we differ in vain. But if you protest, then you say hypocritically that
you receive all the councils, and thus you are apostates. You listen
to the teaching of the holy Eastern fathers, but only once you have
refashioned them according to your own mold through *expurgatoriae
indices* [expurgatorial indexes].[58] You believe as they taught, but only
once you have made unheard of spectacles from their pure and unified
faith.

You confess, practice, and teach one way *publice* [publicly] and
another way *privatim* [privately]. For *publice,* during every liturgy you
confess that the Holy Spirit proceeds from the Father, but *privatim,*
"and from the Son." *Publice,* you yourselves use leavened bread in
the sacrament of the Holy Eucharist, but *privatim,* you use unleavened
bread. *Publice,* you receive the mystery of the body and the blood of
the Lord under two species, but *privatim,* under one species. *Publice,*
you ask for the comfort of the departed souls when the Lord will come
to judge the quick and the dead, but *privatim,* you cleanse them through
fire *in instanti* [in the present]. *Publice,* you confess that everyone will
be completely repaid according to his deeds when the Son of man will
come in the glory of His Father with the holy angels, but *privatim,* you
confess that the heavenly kingdom is given right away to the pious and
hell to the sinful. *Publice,* you baptize through threefold immersion in
water, but *privatim,* through a single immersion. *Publice,* you administer
the holy chrism immediately after baptism, but *privatim,* you put it
off until they are grown up. *Publice,* you monks do not eat meat, but
privatim—ha! *Publice,* you celebrate according to the old calendar, but
privatim, according to the new one. *Publice,* you sing "Rejoice, holy

---

57.   [*Sowita* 1621, 68/491.]
58.   [An *Index expurgatorius* was issued in addition to the *Index librorum
prohibitorum* by the Holy Office of the Index. Its purpose was to list books that
might be freely read after certain passages had been deleted from them.]

Zion, mother of the Churches,"[59] but *privatim,* you confess that Rome
is the mother of the Churches.

Thus do you listen to the teaching of the holy Eastern fathers,
having made such and similar spectacles for your Church. In which
regard, it is not we, as the Refuter alleges, but you Uniates who have
made for yourselves as many faiths as there are heads.[60] There are
many who confess with the Romans, but despise their sacrament of the
Eucharist, holding it as incomplete. Some praise everything Roman,
but do not receive the procession of the Holy Spirit "and from the Son."
Some are with the Romans with all their soul, but in the Union only with
their body *pro forma.* There are even those who criticize everything
Roman, only the obedience do they praise. If you ask us who they are,
we will point them out to you. Therefore, on account of these and similar
monsters, never before heard of in the Ruthenian Church, which were
spawned by you through apostasy from the holy see of Constantinople,
apostasy is appropriately ascribed to you, and you are known to all as
apostates.

[. . .][61]

And where the Refuter speaks in the ninth chapter toward the
end, and in the tenth at the beginning, concerning our spreading of
mendacious pieces of news, we too certainly call them mendacious, for
they are mendaciously ascribed to us. The Refuter will never prove that
the arrival of Father Borec'kyj in Vilnius was announced by us from the
cathedra.[62] You yourselves, without us, know how to forge bad news
(although this is allegedly pleasing to us), so that it might hurt us all the
more later on. For thus did you invent and allege that Father Borec'kyj
and Father Smotryc'kyj, having acquired for themselves bands of
rogues, supposedly attacked Vilnius for the metropolitanate and Polack
for the archbishopric;[63] and thus you allegedly did something pleasing

59.   [See above, p. 213.]
60.   [Derived from the saying *Quot capita, tot sensus* ("As many
understandings as there are heads"), paraphrased in Horace (*Satires* 2.1.27).
Cf. Terence (*Phormio* 454): *Quot homines, tot sententiae,* with the same
meaning. It became a favorite taunt in the age of confessional controversy,
used by members of all confessions against their opponents.]
61.   [Smotryc'kyj 1621c, 112/455 omitted.]
62.   [*Sowita* 1621, 74/495.]
63.   [*Sowita* 1621, 75–6/496.]

for our simple people, but something very harmful to those individuals; for it was through your spreading and alleging of this mendacious piece of news that it came to such circular letters against them. You do the same thing even now, when no longer only verbally, but also in writing, you allege mendaciously in print that we had announced the *concessus* [permission] given to us in writing for the bishoprics by His Majesty the King.[64] Nor will you ever prove this: these are your vain *commenta* [fabrications], and done to this end: so that you might harm us more with regard to the grace of His Majesty the King, Our Gracious Lord. Who does not know of your malicious tricks? You can excellently ascribe to yourselves here that saying: the fox can always be outfoxed.[65]

You also make up stories against us, alleging that we spread the news, if it was ever spread, when you write about the outfitting of your superiors after the recent Sejm and about the intention of transferring a great part of their people to the Roman rite.[66] Let us suppose that as you say, these pieces of news (not spread by us, however, if they did exist) had moved a large number of you to transfer themselves from you. We ask you: now, when it is your victory, your win, your triumphs, why is it that they flow away from you in waves, so that almost only the Mazurians and the Prussians (whom you had maligned) have remained by you? So is it our news that now frightens them away from you? The love of the Eastern Church, love of orderly rite, love of their native obedience move their hearts that they return whence they had departed. For they were never able to have free conscience among you, where there are no more urgent deliberations than how you might oppress us and overturn our ancient usage.

You write in your tenth chapter (I now use the plural so that, together with the Refuter, I might speak with all of you) that: "In Polack, by the grace of God, and through the striving of the local pastor, it had already come to such perfection of external and internal matters that nothing was lacking any more, etc. But Smotryc′kyj sent out throughout the entire diocese his circular letters full of poison toward us, full of rebellion against our superiors, having also enlisted the monks who delivered those universals. And after settling in Vilnius,

64. [*Sowita* 1621, 74/495.]
65. [*NKPP* 1:304, "Chytry," 15.]
66. [*Sowita* 1621, 74/495.]

in the Brotherhood Monastery, he himself set to work so haughtily, as if there were neither God in heaven nor king or any spiritual and secular authority on earth. He announced to the world that he was bishop, the other the metropolitan, etc. He consecrated priests and deacons not only to the bishopric of Polack, but also to the metropolitanate, as a *universalis pastor* [universal pastor], etc. After the publication of his universals, Smotryc'kyj celebrated *omnia episcopalia* [all things belonging to the bishop], as also before, etc. And in Kyiv what did your pseudo-metropolitan Borec'kyj stir up? The office of His Majesty the King posts circular letters of His Majesty the King throughout all the cities, commanding that he be seized, but he posts in the same place his own threatening circular letters commanding that the priests travel to him for a council. He has already convened one council of the priests in Kyiv, a second of the *szlachta* in Żytomyr. And is this not rebellion?"[67] Thus far your side, or rather you, Refuter.

As far as Father Borec'kyj is concerned, we cannot answer. We are far away; we do not know what was happening at this time in Kyiv. But we do know that this man of high wisdom does not do anything that would lead to even the least confusion in the fatherland, to say nothing of anything (as you vainly allege) that would lead to *rebellio* [rebellion]. We are certain he is able, by the grace of God, to render account of himself before whomever it will be fitting.

As to the peace, and then the non-peace, in Polack, of which you ascribe the former to the local pastor[68] and the non-peace to Smotryc'kyj: the discussion about this is not with us. Their lords, the citizens of Polack are of age; they will answer for themselves. They had peace under Herman, for he was only slightly in the Union.[69] He did not force the priests into anything. To the contrary, when he ordered them to sign their names to the Union, and a protopope of that city by the name of Solomon and a second with him did not wish to do this, he grabbed the document where the others had already signed their names, shed tears, admonished those priests who had signed their names to the Union, and, having praised the constancy of those two, he took the protopope

67. [*Sowita* 1621, 75–7/496–7.]
68. [That is, Josafat Kuncevyč.]
69. [Does he mean Hryhorij Xrebtovyč, who was archbishop of Polack 1594–1600?]

unto himself for his confessor, and thus he remained, as those who know about this relate, until his death. There are letters in which he was admonished by many to remain in the Union, but he always declared before people that he regretted what he had done. They also had peace under Hedeon Brolnyc'kyj:[70] he announced *publice* [publicly] that the Union disgusted him, and through letters he allowed the cities of his diocese to be under the obedience of the patriarch.

On the other hand, what sort of peace (which you exalt so much) they had under your holy, as you call him, pastor—the words with which their lords, the citizens of Polack, greeted him make clear, when, among other things, they said this to him aloud: "If you come to us not with the Union, then we receive you like the angel of God. If you come with the Union, then we shun you like him from the abyss." Such was the beginning of the peace that lasted throughout those three years in no other manner but in constant taunts and squabbles from the burghers, since he hid from them [his allegiance to] the Union through all that time; and he did not openly renounce obedience to the patriarch until the moment came for that gold of yours to be rubbed *ad lydium lapidem* [against the touchstone];[71] then the lord citizens of Polack discovered he was brass. Not from the allegation of some nonexistent universals sent by Smotryc'kyj, as the Refuter falsely alleges, but for the following reason. When, after frequent conversations and investigations with their bishop, their lords, the citizens of Polack, could not understand for certain what he was, a Uniate or Orthodox, they were given an occasion to test him by the arrival of the Father Patriarch of Jerusalem. For having heard about this, the foremost not only of their lords, the citizens of Polack, but also their lords, the citizens of Mahilëŭ, went to the bishop, informed him of the arrival of the patriarch, asked him whether he is their Orthodox bishop, which he pretends to be, and asked that he visit the father patriarch at their expense. He praised it, promised, gave them his hand on this. He gladdened all of them with his promise. News of the departure of the bishop to visit the father patriarch was spread throughout the entire city. All the common people were joyful that they had not been deceived by the Orthodox pastor. Those who were supposed to travel with him directed their thoughts to the streams

70.   [Archbishop of Polack, 1601–1618.]
71.   [Erasmus *Ad.* 1.5.87.]

(for they had determined from their discussion to set off for Kyiv along the Dnepr) and to the needs of the trip.

But ha! When it came to realizing the word affirmed by the giving of his hand, my bishop put away his aforementioned boasts; flies attacked him from somewhere else, such that they buzzed around his head and scattered the plans. Thus it was not Smotryc'kyj through some sort of circular letters (as you allege in your fairy tales) who submitted the pastor (as you call him) of Polack to disgust and to the manifest demonstration of what he is to their lords the citizens of Polack and to his entire diocese, but rather that deceitful action of his. The entire city is still living; also living are those to whom he had promised and confirmed by his giving of the hand: they acknowledge and confess. Do not cast your incautious actions (not to say deceits) upon innocent people, and do not wish to harm their grace with the Lord through your false *commenta* [fabrications]. You yourselves commit the crimes, and then you charge the innocent.[72]

Father Smotryc'kyj did not send out any of his circular letters. He wrote to their lords, the citizens of Polack, but he wrote in answer, not to initiate the correspondence. That letter of Father Smotryc'kyj was shown to His Grace, the Lord Palatine of Polack;[73] it was carried further to show others, in which there was nothing of the sort, by the grace of God, as you, Refuter, falsely allege. It was written from that place upon which he is the superior even before these letters to the nobility and to the burghers of all the counties who presented themselves to them first with their letters and asked for some spiritual counsel and teaching. But these letters were not termed circular letters, nor was their teaching that of turmoil. Concerning the monks you mention who were sent about: did you not torture nearly unto death in his diocese one monk until he confessed that he had been sent by Father Smotryc'kyj? The Lord God will seek his blood at your hands.[74] And when you allege concerning Father Smotryc'kyj that he consecrated priests not only for the bishopric of Polack but also for the metropolitanate—with the exception of those, as well as the monks, who are on Brotherhood foundations—you allege a falsehood.

72.   [Cf. *NKPP* 1:87, "Bić," 29.]
73.   [Prince Michał Drucki-Sokoliński.]
74.   [Ez. 3:18, 20; 33:6, 8; 34:10.]

In response to the allegation that even after the publication of the circular letters of His Majesty the King, Father Smotryc'kyj celebrated divine services and other *episcopalia* [things belonging to the bishop], we say—and honestly, as our conscience is dear to us—that we gave no credence to these circular letters, and for these reasons: because no legal proceeding preceded them, and we were not informed of these in the least by anyone. And because they had a different form in every city. For although Their Graces, the Lord Senators (as the Refuter says) were sent for this purpose by His Majesty the King, Our Gracious Lord, we heard about the presence of Their Graces in Vilnius, but we were not able to learn to what end they were here. What is more, at that very time a letter was delivered to our monastery bearing inside at the very top the name and title of His Grace the Most Illustrious Lord Chancellor of Lithuania,[75] written in the form of a universal to Father Smotryc'kyj, telling him not to dare to consecrate priests on the land holdings and estates of His Grace. But when we examined this together with many noble people who had come to the tribunal at that time, we noticed the recent writing, we became aware of the *stylum* [style] and of the draft book of the monks from the Holy Trinity. Third, we noticed the seal of His Grace, which had been torn out of another letter and glued to the inside of this one in a rectangle. We sent this letter to the steward of the house of His Grace the Lord Chancellor, who had delivered that letter to our monastery into the hands of one of the presbyters. He admitted before the beadle and the gentry that "I delivered the fascicle of letters sent to me by His Gracious Lord, the Lord Chancellor, to the Monastery of the Holy Trinity, where it belonged, whence thereupon the letter in question was sent to me, and I was commanded to deliver it to the Monastery of the Holy Spirit. Which I in fact did." These then were the little tricks of our apostates, which they did during this difficult time of our affliction, such that we also did not give credence to the circular letters of His Majesty the King, Our Gracious Lord. Thus having you, our foremost enemies, attacking us both from the left and the right, *per fas et nefas* [by right and wrong], who had taken away from us all our joy and had frightened us even unto death—if we had also relinquished

75.   [Lew Sapieha was chancellor of Lithuania from April 1589 to 6 February 1623, when he became palatine of Vilnius.]

the spiritual joy in the service of God, which you envy us, we would have had to allow ourselves to be buried alive.

Before you, Refuter, had submitted this to the world in order to bring disgust upon honorable men, you ought first to have read this saying of Phalereus[76] that: *Mendaces tantum lucri habere, quod eis ne vera quidem dicentibus deinceps fides adhibeatur* [Liars have such an advantage, because when they are in fact telling the truth, faith should be placed in them accordingly]. Nor should credence be granted to what you say toward the end of the tenth chapter, that "children die without christening, and adults without the sacrament of the body and the blood of the Lord, that they live without matrimony, thus did your Smotryc'kyj order it to be in Polack, etc."[77] This is calumny against Smotryc'kyj. Their lords the citizens of Polack do this by the example of other cities, which, not wishing to receive the sacraments from your priests, have been asking His Majesty the King for a long time, together with citizens of these domains of the gentry estate, that it be permitted to them to do this according to their religion. And in the year 1607 they received an assurance of this from His Majesty the King Our Gracious Lord, guaranteed by a constitution. Similar to this is what you also say there, that there is no city without open churches and the rite. There are indeed open Catholic churches in these cities, but we ask for the opening of the churches of our rite, which stand sealed even until this very day in Mahilëŭ and in Orša.

Titles of the Eleventh and Twelfth Chapters of the Refuter:
Apostrophe to the Ruthenian Nation: That the present action of Smotryc'kyj is bad, but the action of the Uniates is good.

Reply:
Apostrophe to the Ruthenian Nation: That the action of its antiquity is good, but the action of the Uniates is bad.

We will consider now whether we ought to choose you, noble Ruthenian nation, or the Refuter as the collocutor in this apostrophe. The title is

76. [Likely Demetrius of Phalerum, sometimes referred to as Phalareus.]
77. [*Sowita* 1621, 81/500.]

directed to you, wherefore our address ought also to be to you. But
since our conversation is with the Refuter in your person, we will rather
leave you a listener, and we judge it proper to finish with whom we also
began to converse.

We marvel, Refuter, that, having ascribed to Smotryc'kyj the matter
that is now pending, as if he had some special power over people among
us and our elders, you show yourself such a great boor, as if, being
unaware of the laws in the fatherland and ignorant of the obligation
of a good man, you do not feel the power of the highest authority over
us and you. *Vix enim,* in this chapter, *aut ne vix quidem vel nobile, vel
honestum, sapis* [for you have sense for hardly anything at all (in this
chapter) that is noble or honorable].

You must certainly know that what is happening today in the
Church of our Ruthenian nation of the eastern obedience is not to be
ascribed to human industry, but to God Himself alone. Who led the
patriarch here from Jerusalem, if not God? Who caused him to find
grace, as long as he was here, before the countenance of God's anointed,
His Majesty the King, Our Gracious Lord, and with the most illustrious
senate of His Royal Majesty, and especially the spiritual one, if not the
Lord God Himself? Smotryc'kyj was still in Vilnius, and he had not yet
heard of the arrival of the patriarch (for he received certain knowledge
only ten weeks after his arrival), and the voice of men, and therefore also
the voice of God, had already nominated a metropolitan and bishops.
Smotryc'kyj had no thought of going there until, at the command of his
elder (who himself was not capable because of a severe illness), it fell to
him to visit the father patriarch; then he did what he had to do because
of that command. Thus all of this must rather be ascribed, as we said, to
God and not to Smotryc'kyj, not to man. Wherever He wishes, natural
order gives way, human counsel gives way. No malice, either of man
or of Satan, can hinder this. He Himself deigned to cause, through His
industry (which is unfathomable to us), a salvatory thing, without which
we could no longer live—not for the disruption of our fatherland, but
for the introduction into it of the desired peace, and through the holy
and authoritative means through which that dear peace lasted in our
fatherland for six hundred years.

For the pacification of the Greek religion no more authoritative
means could ever have been found than to have a spiritual hierarchy of
the Greek religion. A capon can indeed cackle at the chicks when, while

leading them, he finds a grain; but he does not know how to gather them under him and to embrace them with his wings, for he did not spread them over them, as a hen does when she hatches them. Wherefore, when they jump upon their leaders, they seek peace and safety on their backs. You are Ruthenian priests, as you call yourselves, but you did not labor with these chicks (the human souls that you lead), wherefore when you do not gather them in with your wings, they jump upon your backs and become prey for the birds of the sky.[78]

We do not expect tumults from this divine matter, since holy righteousness will make a judgment that everyone be content with his own. We both have one law, we are subject to one power: if it does not allow our clergy to advance, we will bear it patiently; if it orders you to retreat, you will have to do so, even unwillingly, without any tumult, without any pouring of blood, which you threaten. Our side does not think of using force; it entrusts this matter to the Lord God and to the righteous decree of His Majesty the King, Our Gracious Lord. We learned in the Church of God to suffer force, and not to work it.

We are not afraid of your lion cubs and lions. We have Daniels against them, by the grace of God; they will shut their mouths.[79] We also have the citizens of Jordan, who will pick out the thorns stuck by you into their paws, and, with the help of God, will make them obedient to themselves and fit to tend our donkeys.

The law does not allow the eviction of our people from the city council and from the guilds and from their liberties. For you ought not to think that, with the fall of your Union, the laws and holy righteousness ought also to fall in our fatherland. Terence's fool, Thraso, thought that with his fall, the heavens ought also to fall.[80] Just examine the laws of our local city of Vilnius, whether they do not serve equally the people of the Greek and the Roman religions in everything, both for the magistracy and for merchant and guild liberties. But they were given when all Rus' was under the patriarchal obedience. And if it should happen as you say, this would not be to pacify Rus', but to unpacify it, to make them outcasts and exiles from the fatherland. Lithuania would render unto the

---

78.   [*NKPP* 2:253, "Kur," 13.]

79.   [Dan. 6. Is the reference to "lion cubs and lions" (*lwięta i lwy*) an allusion to Chancellor of Lithuania Lew (Leo) Sapieha? See above, p. 272.]

80.   [Thraso is a character in Terence's comedy *The Eunuch*.]

Ruthenian nation, and Poland unto the Greek (from whom, by the grace of God, they were first enlightened with the light of the Christian faith, as was thoroughly proved in the answer to the sixth chapter),[81] as the evil son to the good mother for an honorable upbringing: by thrusting a knife into her heart. Wherefore what you said can be properly recalled in this place—*non sunt facienda mala, ut eveniant bona* [let not evil be done that good may come]—for we too understand thus with St. Paul.[82] That would be a poor pacification of Rus': to return to them their religion according to their laws, but then to take away the laws.

But who would listen to you, such a wretched counselor? Do you think it is the same in the senate as in the monastery? They guard their rights and liberties there—I was going to say like their eye, but rather like their soul. Is this not a Ruthenian law, where the Polish king deigns to say: "We receive the Ruthenian nations, as equals to equals, free people to free people. We find and we cause that they enjoy, just like all the other citizens of the Polish Crown, the dignity and the custom, all the privileges, liberties, and freedoms of all the estates, of each estate according to its calling."[83] Thus our Ruthenian law, and it was given when all of Rus' was under the obedience of the patriarch of Constantinople, when we had Metropolitan Jona Protasovyč, who was consecrated by Patriarch Metrophanes of Constantinople.

To whom does that town hall bench properly belong? Show that it belongs to you with just one word, and we will show you where the Polish King and the Grand Duke of Lithuania say thus: "We, the Sovereign King of Poland and Grand Duke of Lithuania, establish in our city of Vilnius twenty-four councilors and twelve burgomasters, half of those councilors and burgomasters of the Roman rite and half of the Greek rite, as the Magdeburg Law has been given to both rites. And in every year there are to be sitting two burgomasters, one of the Roman rite and the other of the Greek, and four councilors, two of the Greek and two of the Roman." And this is our Ruthenian burgher law, which we prove to be ours since it was given to Rus' when all of Rus' was under the obedience of the patriarch of Constantinople.[84] Show us

81. [See above, pp. 255–60.]
82. [Rom. 3:8. Cf. *Sowita* 1621, 84/502.]
83. Privilege of Sigismund I in the Constitution, p. 164. [Actually, it was Sigismund II August; see Kutrzeba and Semkowicz 1932, 379.]
84. [Smotryc'kyj was quoting a royal decree of 9 September 1536, in which

your law, by which you believe that our Ruthenian nation that is under the patriarchal obedience can be removed from this law. By force? This is not law, nor will the authority allow you this that is the guardian of our laws, freedoms, and liberties. Wherefore that *diu* [long] deliberated matter in our nation, and *cito* [quickly] realized, vainly aspires to draw upon the eternity of its laws and to use them freely, both secular and spiritual, since they rather indicate who should suffer degradation. If your hope is in might, ours is in right. Moreover, that ought to be understood not as degradation (for it is crude to understand so), but as a voluntary withdrawal.

Having divided the twelfth chapter, in which you speak of your good action, into two parts, to remove the first would be nothing other than to contend with the Roman Church, which has wronged us either little or not at all, about which we would be glad of nothing more than a good word. In the second part we do not find anything to criticize in you, with the exception of the fact that, in whatever you expend your strength, you do to the destruction of the name and the glory of the Ruthenian nation. We say, however—and we think to end our account with this most important point—that if your antecessors had deliberated long and had acted *cito* [quickly], they would have summoned to their deliberation him who, by righteous judgment according to divine and human law, ought not to have been excluded from it. If even the best sons of the worst father—if they had caught him in some sort of evil doing, and if they did not admonish him first humbly in filial manner, did not inform him that "we will leave you if you do not cease to do this, for you do us shame, if you do not see this or take care for it, we both see and take care"—should simply leave him, scoff at him to his greater disrespect and disdain, through announcing his transgression and abusing him, would they not have transgressed the obligation of good sons? No good person will say otherwise. Did your antecessors inform their father patriarch of Constantinople with even one letter about their three-year (as you say) deliberation? Did they summon him in filial manner to it? Did they present to him the reason why they could not be with him? Did they ask that he cease whatever evil doing that they saw

---

Sigismund I established parity between "Greeks" and "Romans" in all levels of the Vilnius magistracy: benchers, councilors, and burgomasters. See Dubiński 1788, 54.]

in him? Did they inform him that they did not wish to have him as their father if he would not cease the evil that they criticized in him? That they were going to leave him, abandon him, and not recognize him as their father? Not in the least. Wherefore, although they deliberated for a long time and acted quickly, they deliberated badly and acted badly.

We know that the Bulgarian, the Serbian, the Illyrian, and the Iberian [Georgian] are patriarchs *sui juris* [of their own jurisdiction]. And the Muscovite makes five. But the first four have their special rights from of old. And Patriarch Jeremiah of Constantinople of blessed memory permitted and gave the right to the Muscovite to be such.[85] We do not deny that this could happen here, but *cum licentia, cum venia* [with a license, with permission], with an honoring of the father, with respect for the benefactor; *aequivalens* [of equal weight] to whom, you could never more fittingly render anything more important, than if, not having removed him from you, through yourselves you would join him to whom you saw it a salvatory thing for him to be joined. You cannot say that he would not have allowed this, for you did not make even the least attempt to try this. Lay clerks are of weight when it is a matter of some private thing; publicly they go their own way. Our great domain, wide bishoprics—a perspicacious man has here something to marvel at. It remains in our power to disdain the non-perspicacious. And in this way the gates of recourse to our dear fatherland would not be closed to our dear enslaved father as they are not closed to Muscovy, although he allowed them to have their own patriarch. Our Greek *ritus* [rite] requires this of you as if *naturaliter* [naturally]—that you not be separate from the Greeks.

If it had happened thus, even if you had deliberated as briefly as can be, you would have deliberated long, and you would have acted well, even if not quickly. There would not be these storms in our dear fatherland. There would not be in one and the same Ruthenian nation such quarrels. The rites would have remained the same. The praise of God would have been magnified in our Ruthenian churches. Schools would flourish. The Church books would be corrected. *Heirmologia*[86] would be brought *ad concinnitatem textus simul et vocis* [to proper

---

85. [On the autocephalous churches, see below, pp. 633–5.]

86. [From εἱρμός, a liturgical term signifying "original strophe on pattern of which other strophes of same ode were fashioned."]

harmony of text and tone]. We would have our own catechism. We would also have our own postils. And it would not be as today, when our poor Ruthenian nation has poisoned itself and continues to poison itself from various postils that are not our own. *Coenobia* [the monasteries], which have degenerated from their property, would be returned to their proper order. Now all of this is in the dust and in great neglect. And it must be so. We before you; you cannot before us. From experience, we see that both hands are clean when one washes the other,[87] when priests help laymen, and laymen help priests in the spreading of the praise of the name of God. Either of them can wet and immerse itself in water separately, but it does not become clean; to the contrary, it becomes dirtier. Forfend, Christ the Lord, that this should happen to us as well. For as to that hundred you mention, whom you are educating against us, or rather against your own nation—this is not settled yet. Ten or so of them will die before they get to work. Ten or so may be of the inconstant sort that will harm you more than help you. Ten or so will be incapable of teaching others. Ten or so will be dissolute. And how do you know that ten or so will not come to us? All of this is still just straw, not bread. But our Ruthenian nation is already dying of hunger. It is already being poisoned, reaching for poison instead of nourishment. That will not come about there quickly, but our Ruthenian nation requires this today.

All the greater is the necessity that we look in this instance with great diligence to Christ the Lord, who is just when He says: *Omnis domus divisa contra se non stabit;* A house divided against itself cannot stand.[88] It is both necessary, we say, to see to it that we not bring our house divided and sundered against itself to demise. We seem to glow, but whoever knows how to examine this more closely will see that we are burning out. And we must fear that these lamps will both extinguish together, that, with great shame and with the final harm of our souls, we will come from both sides together with the entire house to our demise. Consider now as well, our cordial Refuter, Smotryc̆kyj's action (since it pleased you to ascribe this to him) and your own, and you will see that you will sooner bring our and your noble Ruthenian nation to demise than to an arising by the sort of action with which you proceed. Force and necessity will not cause a union, to say nothing of multiplying it.

87. [*NKPP* 3:36–7, "Ręka," 95; Arthaber 752; Erasmus *Ad.* 1.1.33.]
88. Mt. 12[:25].

And since we sincerely wish for the peace of the Church of Christ the Lord and cordially desire fraternal love with you—as a sign of this we end our *Defense of the Verification* with the same words with which you ended your *Twofold Guilt:* Deign to help both our sides to what we sincerely wish and to what we demand with all our hearts, Christ the Lord, Our Redeemer, who reigns with the Father and the Holy Spirit in eternal and perfect unity for ever and ever. Amen.[89]

> Your Merciful Graces' and Gracious Lords'
> Servants and Suppliants of God,
> Who Wish You Every Good.
> Monks of the Vilnius Brotherhood Monastery
> of the Church of the Descent of the Holy
> Spirit.
> Μία ζωῆς ἡμῶν ἐλπὶς Ιησοῦς ὁ χριστόΣ.
> [My life's one hope Christ JesuS][90]

89.   [*Sowita* 1621, 91/507.]
90.   [See above, p. 231.]

A Refutation of Acrimonious Writings
(1622)

A Refutation
of the Acrimonious Writings

That were Published by the Monks of the Vilnius
Congregation of the Holy Trinity.

Written
by the Monks
of the Monastery of the Vilnius Church Brotherhood
of the Church of the Descent
of the Holy Spirit.

In Vilnius, in the Year of Our Lord 1622.

Proverbs of Solomon Chap. 18[:23]

Cum observationibus loquitur pauper, et dives
effabitur rigide.
The poor man speaks humbly, and the rich man
answereth roughly.

[...][1]

WE HAVE RESPONDED SUFFICIENTLY just a little above concerning the Cossacks and the ambition of our spiritual superiors (to both of which topics you return *ultra modum* [beyond measure] as frequently as you can).[2] Nonetheless, we answer here as well that although the Cossacks are a knightly people, they are nonetheless Christians, and *orthodoxi*—Orthodox Christians—at that. Who will judge that they have no part in matters of the faith? For our Ruthenian Church considers them as members of Christ the Lord and as its sons. Is it a novelty in the Church of God for soldiers—for the sake of the faith, for the name of Christ the Lord—to offer themselves for the pouring of their blood and for their own deaths in single combat, by battalions, and by regiments? And so, the Cossack soldiers are a people well trained in the school of the faith and in the school of the knight's work, such that one cannot properly say about them: *quid* [what] do they hold *pensi, quid considerati* [of weight, what of consideration]? For the fear of God is more magnificent in them, liveliness in faith more ardent, *disciplina militaris* [military discipline] more circumspect. There are to be found in this knighthood many who do not yield in their piety even to the most pious! And they surpass in gallantry those Roman Scipios and Carthaginian Hannibals. For like the Maltese in the Italian land, this Zaporozhian soldier is unto the most noble Polish Kingdom a defense against its neighboring pagan enemy, stands in his good order, and gives birth to gallant cavaliers for the fatherland. Thus it is a shame, looking upon the integrity of their faith and their illustrious feats of gallantry on the sea and in various lands, and having before your eyes their most recent acts of prowess in Wallachia, to abuse them with *nil penses* and to submit them to people as *nil considerati*.[3]

1.   [Smotryc'kyj 1622a, A1r–14v/464–77 omitted.]
2.   [For the Uniate allegations, see *List* 1621, 8–12, 14, 17–18, 20–1; *AJuZR* 1:8:738–41, 742, 745, 747–8.]
3.   [Smotryc'kyj was playing here with the notions he had introduced above, that the Cossacks were allegedly people who held nothing in regard: "nothing-weighters" and "nothing-considerers." He was responding to *List* 1621, 20; *AJuZR* 1:8:747.]

We have already said unto what end our spiritual superiors dared to undertake the salvatory matter of their consecration: because our Ruthenian nation could no longer remain, and ought not to have remained, without priests. For no Polish king, as long as the Ruthenian nations have been incorporated into the Polish Kingdom, has demanded of our ancestors that they live without the priests of their religion. And we, their descendants, hold the same of His Majesty the King, our present Gracious Lord. You, however, had already led our Ruthenian nation to this through your apostasy, such that we had left only the one bishop[4] and not the seven plus the eighth one, the metropolitan. Throughout all the past twenty-six years we made it known to His Majesty the King, Our Gracious Lord, that we did not consider you—and could not consider you, the apostates—our spiritual superiors. In this domain, in our own fatherland, we, the Ruthenian nation, are of lesser condition than are Armenians, Jews, and Musulmans, newcomers to these domains, and than are Lutherans, Calvinists, and Anabaptists. For they are allowed to have their superintendents, ministers, bishops, preachers, rabbis, mullahs, but we are not allowed to have our metropolitan and bishop. If these nations are not compelled to any unwonted obedience, by what lawlessness ought we to suffer this compulsion from you? Are we the only ones in this domain without rights, such that anyone who wishes might wrong us and, having stepped upon our necks, might compel us to his obedience? In truth, you will sooner, by the grace of God, provide us with the crown of martyrdom than you will force the Ruthenian nation to lose its priests. You have already sufficiently and freely exercised your brutality upon our poor nation. It is time to stop and no longer trouble the fatherland with your perfidies.

You charge our spiritual superiors with ambition, but they, having *victum et amictum* [food and raiment],[5] by God's providence for them, are satisfied with this. If your wings were clipped, you would not fly so high; if, we say, those Church *beneficia* [benefices], which you unjustly enjoy, were justly taken away from you, you would not be very eager to risk your health and blood for that revered Union of yours. It is the fat prebends that resound in you, and not love for the Union. If our seniors

---

4.　[That is, Jarema Tysarivs'kyj, the Orthodox bishop of Lviv.]

5.　1 Tim. 6[:8. But this technical phrase is not from the Vulgate, which has *alimenta et quibus tegamus*].

are supposedly *ambiciosi* [ambitious], to whom those *beneficia* belong *jure* [by law], how is it that your seniors are not *ambiciosi,* who possess them *injuste* [against the law]. *Pungite cor, proferetis sensum* [Prick the heart, make it to show her knowledge].[6] Only prick your heart, and you will feel pain, and you will acknowledge that, after all, you did not sing the same song when you were hungry that you now sing satiated.

But since in this matter between you and us it is not a matter of ambition for us, but of the demise of our Ruthenian Church and the corruption of our Orthodox faith (to both of which, through your apostasy, it is coming in our nation), pious men from among our priests—not looking upon your fat prebends, nor enticed by desire for benefices, but through love of the faith and of their Holy Church—have taken that sweet yoke of Christ the Lord upon themselves,[7] pulling which, they do not look back (that is to say, upon your prebends), just so long as they might feed their souls, which have been starved by you unto death, and might establish them in the usual state in the Holy Eastern Church. In which may the Lord God, who loves the salvation of mankind, illustriously come to their aid, such that, by the grace of God, surrounded from all sides like wolves who have been roused out, you hold onto nothing but the prebends (for they are not inconsiderable), through nothing but ambition.

[. . .][8]

That Our Apostates Are Apostates from Monastic Religion

You say in the third place: "Our elders did not become apostate *a statu relligionis, quam professi sunt* [from the state of religion that they professed], they did not leave the order; they are monks as of old," etc. But having turned to us, you say: "You, Brotherhood monks, by your monastic humility *et voto obstricti* [and bound by vow], are our apostates from religion and profession, and the rule, and your oath and monasticism."[9] We answer: the wise man says, *laudat te alienus, et non*

6.   Sir. 22[:19].
7.   [Mt. 11:30.]
8.   [Smotryc'kyj 1622a, 16r–28r/478–90 omitted.]
9.   [*List* 1621, 25–6; *AJuZR* 1:8:751–2.]

os tuum, extraneus, et non labia tua [let another man praise thee, and not thine own mouth; a stranger, and not thine own lips].[10] Or

> *Cur maculas alios maculosior omnibus, Albi?*
> *Et carpi dignus, carpere non metuis.*
> [Why, Albius, do you defile others, when you are most
> defiled of all?
> And worthy of calumny, you are not afraid to calumniate.][11]

Wherefore we are content with this very thing in the life of monastic perfection, without any boasting, but not without consolation; and we constantly offer thanks to God that every day we see the affairs of our monastery progressing toward betterment, through which good order and progress we also expect a good end. By the grace of God we do not leave behind us any excesses of the sort that would be announced in any public places causing dishonor to our order. We labor in our monastery unto the glory and honor of the name of God. We strive among ourselves for an orderly life, and we maintain it, with God's help, according to our strengths. We maintain in dignity the celebration of the things of the Church. The pulpit, by the grace of God, is not vacant on our side; schools have been organized by us for the training of children in the Greek, Latin, Slavonic, Ruthenian, and Polish languages. We support a *bursa* for impoverished paupers by our labor. And in brief, we rejoice, in just seven years in our monastery, to the adornment of the Church of the Ruthenian nation, in what you, our apostates, in more than ten years have not rejoiced. We also rejoice, and we render undying thanks to God, that in our monastery are found men of that piety, whom almighty God judged worthy of, and deigned to be honored with, the archpriestly dignity. Which, as we see, is as pleasing to you as salt in the eye. But it is difficult to oppose God's counsels: it must necessarily be precisely as He ordained and will have.[12]

In addition to all this: we render every obedience to those to whom it is fitting to do so, to our spiritual and secular superiors. By the grace and help of God we satisfy our monastic *vota* or vows so vigilantly

10. Prov. 27[:2].
11. *Martia., lib. 1., cap. 1.* [Martial, bk. 1, chap. 1. Actually, it is "Pseudo-Martial," Godefridus Prior or Godfrey of Winchester (d. 1107), epigram 161.]
12. Is. 40 [46:10]; Wis. 9[:13–17]; Rom. 11[:33–4].

that we can be charged with *recessus a statu relligionis* [departure from the state of religion] by no one, except by the envious one, *qui alienae laudi inhiat, et putat sibi demi, quod tribuitur alii* [who regards with longing someone else's glory, and thinks that what is granted to another ought to be taken away for himself]. This same thing bears witness that you (not entering into it further) have committed a *recessus a statu relligionis* [departure from the state of religion], that you have strayed from abstinence, having sworn *in voto* [in a vow] of purity to be a *comes perpetua sanctitatis* [perpetual partaker of sanctity]. For the Christian faith in the Ruthenian nation has come to a halt. Greek and Ruthenian monks or bishops never ate meat, but you now eat whole mouthfuls. *Regula fundatoria etiam a vobis observanda erat* [For the foundation rules should have been observed by you]. Wherefore, you are also apostates *ex recessu a statu relligionis* [through departure from the state of religion], and it is necessarily improper that you are insulted by us when we call you what you are and must call you according to your faith and works. *Convenit enim operantibus secundum merita remunerationis optata concedere* [For it is proper to grant the desires of those working according to the merits of recompense].[13]

That Our Apostates Are Apostates from Monastic Humility and Innocence

You say further: "You have become apostate, Brotherhood monks, from monastic humility and innocence when you stir up tumults and seditions in the fatherland and when you slander without reason, when you disgrace, call sordid names, and condemn as orderless our elders and all of us who are in the Union."[14] We answer: We have already sufficiently answered you in this regard, that this is calumny against us on your part and that those are your own affairs, who, founding that Union of yours with nothing other than oppression and calumny, arouse and lead the common people to rebellions and seditions. When you infringe upon our rights and freedoms, when you torment us with unheard-of inquisitions, when you imprison us, when you stretch us

---

13.   *Cassiodorus* [Flavius Magnus Aurelius Cassiodorus Senator, *Variae,* bk. 11, 25; *PL* 69:844B].
14.   [*List* 1621, 27; *AJuZR* 1:8:752–3.]

upon the wheel, when you oust us from offices, when you remove us
from the guilds, when you seal the churches, when you do not allow us
free religion: do you not arouse rebellions and seditions in the common
people? And were it not for the constant providence of almighty God,
you would gladly look upon our shed blood.

But when you make us defectors, deserters, and traitors, do
you not attack our honor without reason? Do you not condemn us as
orderless when you shamelessly say of us that we have removed the co-
essence of the only-begotten Son of God with God the Father? Do you
not slander us when you call us *lenonum pueri* [children of panders] and
incerto patre nati, vulgo quaesiti, quocunque in fornice fati [born of an
uncertain father, illegitimate children, begotten in any brothel]? Do you
not speak of us sordidly when you seek *androgynaeos* [hermaphrodites]
among us?[15] So it is with your own cloak that you dress us in all these
things you have charged against us. Whom does the apostasy from the
aforementioned virtues of humility and innocence more befit—we leave
this to you yourselves to answer—than you, such that you also remain
apostates from those things, for you revile and abuse and disgrace and
torment, and yet you wish to be righteous and to have us for guilty. But
this is not to be: *homines enim frugi* [for honest men], as one commonly
says, *omnia juste faciunt* [do everything justly].[16]

And charging our superiors with excessive curiosity, you also add
at the end what would have to leave you yourselves with barely one
bishop, when you say of Father Smotryckyj: that "he strives for the
Polack bishopric, but he does not see that in that same constitution of
1607 it was written that those dignities are to be given to noble people."[17]
If, we say, you wished to sift your bishops on that sieve, just see how
many of them would remain in the sieve. And you spoke well a little
below: *carere debet omni vitio, qui in alterum paratus dicere* [whoever
is prepared to speak of the fault in another ought to be free of every
fault].[18] No one can properly take from Father Smotryckyj, even with
his bishopric, what his honorable noble birth gave him properly without

---

15.   [*List* 1621, 12–13, 34–5; *AJuZR* 1:8:741, 758–9. The phrase *lenonum
pueri quocumque ex fornice nati* comes from Juvenal (*Satires* 3.156).]
16.   [Cf. Erasmus *Ad.* 2.2.62.]
17.   [*List* 1621, 27; *AJuZR* 1:8:752.]
18.   [A saying. Attributed to Cicero in *PL* 49:334B.]

the bishopric. And although in these present times the Church of God needed pastors and teachers, bishops and a metropolitan, which it had not had for twenty-six years now, those it acquired were nonetheless honored with the noble calling through God's special providence for the Church.

After all this you ask us at the end, "Is it not about you or about such apostates that the Holy Spirit speaks through Solomon: *Homo Apostata, vir inutilis, graditur ore perverso, annuit oculis, terit pede, digito loquitur, pravo corde machinatur malum, et omni tempore jurgia seminat* [An apostate man, a useless man, walketh with a perverse mouth, he winketh with his eyes, he scrapeth with his feet, he speaketh with his finger, with a perverse heart he deviseth evil, and he soweth contentions continually]?"[19] We answer: not about us, but about you and about those like you, who are in the Ruthenian nation, between it and the Lach nation, what the foe of God and man is between God and man. For you do nothing more between them than to embitter the one against the other. You embitter the Ruthenian nation toward the Polish when, by the means cited in our last point, you draw us to the Lach faith (as we in Rus′ commonly call it). And you embitter the Polish nation against the Ruthenian when you allege of us to it that we have been commanded by the patriarch to treat you Uniates with all violence and force, but to behave graciously toward the Lachs if they should not obstruct us in this in any way; otherwise, to proceed against them in the same manner as against the Uniates.[20] This is certainly calumny against the Father Patriarch, but even worse, it is a harmful means to embitter the Polish nation toward the Ruthenian. And your Symonovyč, or rather the apostate Stec′kovyč, was not ashamed to publish this in print.

It is through your industry and effort that the Ukraine is filled with people driven out of the cities and towns on account of the Union. Not to mention Polack, Vicebsk, Orša, Mahilëŭ, our Vilnius, Pinsk, Grodno, Brest, Luc′k, Krasnystav, Sokal, Przemyśl, Busko, and other cities of His Majesty the King, this is also happening in the Grand Ducal and lordly cities and towns such as Bychow, Szklow, Bielica, Dąbrowna, Kleck, Grodek Dawidowy, Jarosław, Rivno, Ołyca, Olesk, Berdyczów, and in many others, where, on account of your Union, at your *instantia*

---

19.   [Prov. 6:12–14. *List* 1621, 27–8; *AJuZR* 1:8:753.]
20.   In the *Trial,* chap. 1 [Symanowicz 1621, B4v].

[importunity], poor people, harassed with both imprisonment and whippings, oppressed with monetary penalties, suffer oppression and persecution. Whereby you deservedly earned what the wise man wrote about those like you, as we had said: *Huic ex templo veniet perditio sua, et subito corruet, nec habebit ultra medicinam* [Therefore shall his calamity come suddenly; suddenly shall he be broken without remedy].[21] But may the Lord God grant you (we wish this with a Christian heart) *medicinam* [remedy], repentance.

Above all, you say: "From your apostasy flow poison and embitterment and disdain, which you show to our elders and to all of us who are in the Union."[22] Do you believe we will not repay you in kind? For after abandoning us and wishing to see us where you yourselves are, you trouble, embitter, and abuse us ceaselessly. That in all this, to the extent that the law of God and of man allows us, we take care for ourselves, defend ourselves, and do not allow you to take possession of us, and you understand our defense to be poison, embitterment, and disdain. Only return to us, and you will see what sort of respect and love you will experience from us. Or at least leave us in peace. Why are we not embittered toward the Roman priests? Because we have pure peace from them. And we would have even purer peace if they too were not incited against us by you. Against all justice you dub us schismatics, heretics, disturbers, traitors. Having right on our side, we measure out unto you with the measures you measured for us, according to the Scripture: *Qua mensura mensi fueritis, remetietur vobis* [With what measure ye mete, it shall be measured unto you again].[23] But you must know from us, by the witness of God's love toward us, without which we neither can nor wish to live, that we do not do this out of malice, but through the very love of our faith, which we have even today as pure as it was purely made for us and given unto us. Not having anything added or deleted in the confession of our faith concerning God, the One in the Trinity, nor in the confession of our faith concerning the incarnation of the only begotten Son of God, but as the holy ecumenical councils—of which we have seven—taught us, so even today we believe and confess

21.   Prov. 6[:15].
22.   [*List* 1621, 28; *AJuZR* 1:8:753.]
23.   Mt. 7[:2].

concerning both these things and concerning the Church mysteries, and we defend this, and we die for this.

You ask us why we would not add that the Holy Spirit proceeds "and from the Son" in the *symbolum* [creed] of the faith?[24] We answer you that the holy fathers, who discussed and wrote that *symbolum* at the second ecumenical council, did not add this. And the Roman Church itself taught this *symbolum* for a thousand years without this addition. But you are angered at us for this truth. You ask us again why we do not use unleavened bread in the salvatory mystery of the Eucharist? We answer you that Christ the Lord celebrated it in leavened bread, to which the Roman Church itself bears witness since it used leavened bread in this sacrament for almost one thousand years. But when we answer you, you are angered against us on account of this truth. You ask us why we celebrate these soul-saving mysteries of the Eucharist under two species rather than under one? We answer you that Christ the Lord transmitted it to His disciples to be celebrated under two species, as we celebrate it, and He commanded us to celebrate in no other fashion. But that the *primitiva ecclesia* [early Church] celebrated these mysteries in this way, as also the Roman Church for more than a thousand years— even for this truth you are angered against us.

You ask us, after citing yet a few more differences between us and you, why we do not acknowledge the Roman bishop as the ecumenical bishop of all Christendom?[25] We answer you that the ecumenical Church, through all the seven ecumenical councils, did not acknowledge him as such, and it did not make the slightest mention of such authority for him in its synodal canons. And we cited a little earlier from St. Gregory, bishop of Rome, for what reasons the Holy Church did not do this. For he, among many other important things, says about this name "ecumenical" the following as well: that *in isto scelesto vocabulo consentire, nihil est aliud quam fidem perdere;* that is, "to assent to this most abominable name is nothing other than to lose the faith."[26] But you take offense and are angered against us that we too

---

24. [*List* 1621, 23–4; *AJuZR* 1:8:750.]
25. [*List* 1621, 29; *AJuZR* 1:8:754.]
26.   *Gregor. lib. 4, epi. 39* [Gregory the Great, bk. 4, letter 39 (actually letter 29); and in the newer numbering bk. 5, letter 19; *PL* 77:744D; *NPNF2* 12:169].

do not agree to it, according to the salvatory teaching of this holy pope. Thus, as we said, you should know for certain that we do what we do out of piety alone for the maintenance of our ancient holy faith, which has been passed down to our ancestors from the East and to us from our ancestors, whole and inviolate, so that we too might pass it down unchanged in the same integrity and inviolateness, from hand to hand, to the inheritors of this faith who come after us. For standing on such an unchanging foundation of the faith, we cannot be asked by anyone who is knowledgeable of the dogmas of the faith and of things of the Church why we believe this way, why we celebrate this way, why we do things this way. For they see clearly our true recourse to holy antiquity. But we ought rather to ask why you confess, why you celebrate, why you do as the holy ancient Church did not confess, did not celebrate, did not do for a thousand and more years. And we would ask, as our ancestors asked; but the hearts of both our sides, embittered by the harsh, crude, and useless words of one side to the other, have caused in us and in you that if we speak without offending ears and tongue, without the derision by one side of the other, it seems to you as if we either had not said anything or had not spoken convincingly, if we do not abuse each other. If anything like this should be found on our side, we regret it before God as a harmful thing, knowing that each one can say what he has to say honorably and without evil words and that the truth, as an honorable thing, ought to be defended with honorable words. And cause, Holy Lord, who causes all good, that from now on this frivolity of words not be found in the mouths of either of our sides, since it does not build anything good between us and cannot build anything but enmity and quarrels.[27]

Proceeding then further, however much we wish to be more modest in words, nonetheless we cannot bear this, nor is it fitting that we should say to the bitter that it is sweet and to the sweet that it is bitter.[28] We will acknowledge the truth if we should receive any from you; but we will call vain and erroneous words by their proper names. And you ought not to search in vain for hypocrisy in our words since there is absolutely none of it in our words, by the grace of God. Nor be surprised at their

27.   2 Tim. 2[:14–15, 23].
28.   Is. 5[:20].

abundance: Time does not serve time, as they commonly say.[29] The time required this, wherefore *tempori obsecundare visum est* [it seemed proper to fall in with the time]. Concerning the incomprehensibility of the mixture *sensus insensati* [of insensate sense] we do not argue, especially not with one who is not entirely in possession of his senses.[30] Let him come and ask; we are certain that the author will explain it to him.

[…][31]

You say yet again: "You attack the Roman popes with such venom and, slandering the superiority of the Roman popes, you charge Pope Silverius with treachery."[32] We answer that it is not so. For this is the most difficult thing between us: that, often intentionally turning our words well-nigh upside down just so that there would be more to say and so that we would be made disgusting to those who are at issue here, you twist them against their proper meaning according to your liking. You said somewhere that the pope cannot err. In answering you that he can, we cited, among others, the example of Pope Marcellinus, who made offerings to idols, and of Liberius, who subscribed to the Arian heresy—to this very end: in order to show that if these popes erred in the faith, others can err too. Nonetheless, we considered them holy men who, as human beings, had slipped, but, once they had stood up again, one of them came to the crown of martyrdom, and the other died piously in the Orthodox faith.[33] But although you probably knew to what end we said that, you alleged that we had disparaged the honor that belongs to these holy bishops. You do the same with Silverius as well, whom we cited only as an example, so that we might demonstrate that even great people do not escape treachery, defamation; and thus, even if something of this sort were ever raised against our patriarchs, that it be understood as just this sort of calumny. But you broadcast and allege that we had attacked the glory of this innocent bishop.

29.   [Cf. *NKPP* 1:355, "Czas," 7.]
30.   [For the Uniate complaint about the quantity and the comprehensibility of Smotryc'kyj's writings, see *List* 1621, 28; *AJuZR* 1:8:753.]
31.   [Smotryc'kyj 1622a, 32v/495 omitted.]
32.   [*List* 1621, 29; *AJuZR* 1:8:754.]
33.   *Bar. in Anno 302, num. 6* [Baronius, *Annales*, s.a. 302, no. 6].

Undertaking to bring under suspicion of ungenuineness the genuine goodwill of which we have written, which our patriarchs hold for the Christian dominions and especially for this Commonwealth, you say: "It is a weak proof of their goodwill since they come here for their *quaestus* [gain, seeking of alms]. Their good desire for the acquisition of money draws them to this, whereby they might pay for their patriarchates, which they must buy from the pagan and pay for through simony."[34] If you had examined what you owe benefactors, or rather, what you owe love of your neighbor, you would not have said this against your benefactors, the Eastern patriarchs, and you would not have mocked your fathers in the spirit. If you would have given them anything, you would have given them an alm, which is regardless of the person. But we know that you did not give out much for the *quaestus* that you charge against them. If it were the *quaestus*, as you allege against them, that brought them here, they would be more frequent guests here. And yet, through the more than one hundred and fifty years that they are under the pagans, four patriarchs were in our fatherland, one time each.[35] And did they depart from it with great treasures? With incomparably lesser ones than those with which they came; for here, too, no one fed them for nothing, no one gave anything for nothing. But let us suppose (which you say not without sin) that they came for the *quaestus:* that *quaestus* would not be gathered by them for any other goal than for redeeming themselves from the calumnies with which they are frequently charged by the pagans and are beset with monetary *poenae* [penalties] from which they must redeem themselves.

You say that they gather the *quaestus* so that, through simony with the pagan, they might buy and pay for their patriarchates. It is the case that every patriarch pays a certain annual tribute, and he gives a certain gift at the time of his ascent to the patriarchate, and especially to that of Constantinople. But is this simony, what they must do involuntarily and not of free will? St. Luke the Evangelist described what simony is in the Acts of the Apostles when he wrote: "And when Simon saw that through laying on of the apostles' hands the Holy Ghost was given, he offered

---

34. [*List* 1621, 31; *AJuZR* 1:8:756.]
35. [Actually, three patriarchs and one future patriarch: Joachim V of Antioch (1585–1586), Jeremiah II of Constantinople (1588–1589), Cyril Lukaris (1596 and 1601), and Theophanes of Jerusalem (1620–1621).]

them money, saying, 'Give me also this power, that on whomsoever I lay hands, he may receive the Holy Ghost.' But Peter said unto him, 'Thy money perish with thee, because thou hast thought that the gifts of God may be purchased with money.'"[36] This is the description of simony, from which it is made known that a simple man comes to him who has in his control the gifts of God and wishes to buy them from him, that he too might have them from him. Simon buys from the Apostle Paul, who has them; but he could not buy them from Herod, who did not have them, no matter how much he might wish to do so, for the former had nothing to sell and the latter, nothing to buy.

Who then, according to this description of simony, will count the Turkish emperor as the controller of the gifts of God, who, being the enemy of God and of Christians, does not have them and cannot have them? And how will he sell that to others what he himself does not have? Or how can one buy that from him? To the contrary, we consider this to their good, and we praise them for the fact that, in whatever manner they can, in spite of their poverty, they make efforts to maintain the praise of the name of Christ the Lord under this tyrant. What then? Would it be better if the Christians there did not have pastors at all? If the tyrant did not allow the Christians to make any order among themselves? If he forbade them all practice of the Christian religion? And if, in this manner, he were to destroy entirely the Christian faith and to turn it completely upside down? Of course not. Let them buy peace from this tyrant in the name of God, if they can have it in no other way. Let them strive for the good of the Christian faith as they can with tribute, and with payment, and with presents, without which they cannot get by.

Often even here at home they seal the churches of poor presbyters who do not have the wherewithal to pay the payments, and they, poor folk, having gotten the money together, must redeem their altars, which they serve and from which they live. Is this to be reckoned simony? Nor is this simony, then, in the case of our patriarchs; this is not the buying of sacred things, for they do not buy holy things from the accursed pagan, rather they buy peace for themselves, they buy the freedom of the Church, they buy the freedom of their rite.[37] It is truly not a matter

36.   Acts. 8[:18–20].
37.   1 Cor. 9[:13–18].

of surprise that not everything goes as the Christians living in servitude would wish, but it is a matter of surprise that you allege this as simony on the part of enslaved Christians, in which not only are they innocent, but these poor folk, with great lament, through constraint and servitude, suffer, living in the Christian religion as they are able, when it does not go as they would gladly have it. But this is a mote in the eye of our patriarchs; you will find a beam in yours, and a shameful one at that, if you will only wish to examine it in the mirror of good conscience.[38]

You say in this same point: "We respect the Greek patriarchs."[39] To which we answer you: If you were respected in the same way that last year you respected the patriarch of Jerusalem in this kingdom, you would all together be labeled as impostors, for that is how you respected him.

You say in that place: "And we would be under the rule of the patriarch of Constantinople if he would return to the obedience of the see of Rome and rule Rus' from it." This is in truth a wondrous thing you say here. We have read the apostolic canons; we have also read all seven ecumenical and the local councils between them, and we did not read anything that gave the see of Constantinople unto the obedience of the see of Rome. Rather, in three ecumenical councils we find a thing contrary to your account, that is, that the holy fathers make it equal with the Roman—in all its prerogatives, and preeminences—and not subordinate. For the holy fathers of the second ecumenical council say in their third canon: *Constantinopolitanus episcopus habeat priores honoris partes post Romanum episcopum, eo quod sit ipsa nova Roma.* That is, "Let the bishop of Constantinople have primacy of honor after the bishop of Rome, and for this reason: because Constantinople is the new Rome."[40] And this is the first equating of the see of Constantinople with that of Rome.

Also, the holy fathers of the fourth ecumenical council say in their twenty-eighth canon: *Sanctorum Patrum decreta ubique sequentes et canonem qui nuper lectus est centum et viginti Dei amantissimorum episcoporum agnoscentes, eadem quoque et nos decernimus et statuimus de privilegiis sanctissimae ecclesiae Constantinopolis novae Romae.*

38. Mt. 7[:3–5].
39. [*List* 1621, 31; *AJuZR* 1:8:756.]
40. [Constantinople, AD 381; Mansi 3:559.]

Et enim antiquae Romae throno, quod urbs illa imperaret, jure Patres privilegia tribuere. Et eadem consideratione moti centum quinquaginta Dei amantissimi episcopi, sanctissimo novae Romae throno aequalia privilegia tribuere: recte judicantes, urbem, quae et imperio et senatu honorata fit, et aequalibus cum antiquissima regina Roma privilegiis fruatur, etiam in rebus ecclesiasticis, non secus acilla extolli ac magnifieri, secundam post illam existentem, etc. That is, "Adhering throughout to the decrees of the holy fathers, and acknowledging the canon now read of the one hundred and fifty God-loving bishops, we too decree and establish the same concerning the privileges of the most holy Church of Constantinople of new Rome. For the fathers properly granted privileges to the see of old Rome, since that city had been honored with the imperial majesty, and moved by this same consideration the hundred and fifty God-loving fathers granted equal privileges to the most Holy See of new Rome, properly judging that the city that is honored with both the imperial majesty and the senate should enjoy equal privileges with the old imperial Rome and that it should also like it be elevated and revered in Church matters, being the second after it, etc."[41] And this is the second equating of the see of Constantinople with that of Rome.

Further, we cite the thirty-sixth canon of the sixth holy ecumenical synod, which reads as follows: *Renovantes, quae a Sanctis centum et quinquaginta patribus in hac Dei observatrice et regia urbe convenerunt: et sexcentorum triginta, qui Chalcedone conventere, constituta sunt; decernimus, ut thronus Constantinopolitanus aequalia privilegia cum antiquae Romae throno obtineat, et in ecclesiasticis negociis, ut illa magnifiat, ut qui sit secundus post illum: post quem magnae Alexandrinorum civitatis numeratur thronus: deinde Antiochiae: et post eum Hierosolymitanae civitatis.* That is, "Renewing what was established by the holy one hundred and fifty fathers gathered in this regnant city protected by God, and by the six hundred and thirty gathered in Chalcedon, we decree that the see of Constantinople should hold equal privileges with the see of the old Rome, and that it be revered in Church matters just like the latter, as the one that is second after it, after

---

41.   [Chalcedon, AD 451; Tanner 99–100. This was a resolution of the sixteenth act, which was not accepted by the Roman legates. It is found in a different text in Mansi 7:427.]

which let the see of the city of great Alexandria be counted, after which that of Antioch, and after that, that of the city of Jerusalem."[42] This is the third equating of the see of Constantinople with that of Rome.

And so we cited these canons of the holy ecumencial councils, from which one can see clearly what we said: that the see of Constantinople is equal in everything to that of Rome and not subordinate. Wherefore, to say and to allege that the patriarch of Constantinople was ever under the obedience of the bishop of Rome and ruled Rus′ from it is an account similar to the truth of those decretal letters of yours and of the Arabian canons.[43] For the Holy Spirit, which worked in the holy fathers at these holy councils, could not be contradictory to Himself. Having equated the see of Constantinople here with that of Rome, He could not have made it subordinate to it elsewhere. For the Holy Spirit is the spirit of truth.[44] Wherefore, when you spoke here about the obedience of the see of Constantinople to that of Rome, you said a thing deviant from the truth. But we demonstrated that it was equal to it in everything; and being equal to it, it could not be obedient to it, rather just as [the see] of Rome is to it. Thus, not having been obedient to it, it could not have fallen away from its obedience. And thus, it does not have an obedience to which it ought to return. Therefore you, who, having thought thus concerning the obedience of the see of Constantinople, became apostate from it to the see of Rome until the former return again to the latter, ought to return again to that of Constantinople, which did not become apostate from the obedience of the Roman one, for it was never under it, and never ruled Rus′ from it. Rather it rules her as a mother, as the one that gave birth to it; the see of Constantinople rules Rus′, we say, *jure haereditario* [by right of inheritance].

42.   [Constantinople, In Trullo or Quinisext AD 680–681; Mansi 11:959.]
43.   [The first is a reference to the so-called *False Decretals,* a collection of documents falsely attributed to St. Isidore of Seville and containing forgeries of papal letters. They were frequently employed in defense of the papacy, and their debunking came with the great Lutheran historiographic project known as the Magdeburg Centuries. (*Historia Ecclesiae Christi,* Basle, 1559–1574.) The second refers to the spurious eighty canons of the Council of Nicaea discovered in an Arabic manuscript in the Vatican and made a part of Jesuit historiography in the late sixteenth century.]
44.   Jn. 15[:26].

APPENDIX
against the Examination
of the Defense of the "Verification"

From the First Chapter

Since you charge us in all your writings with a certain excessive wantonness of words, and you exhort us to their moderation and modesty, although you yourselves are just the same in your own writings, we were nonetheless certain that you ought to have given us first from yourselves what you wished to have of us. But as they say, *fontes ipsi sitiunt* [the springs themselves are thirsty].[45] Thus if you are the doctors who teach us moderation and modesty in words, you are *immoderati* [immoderate] and *immodesti* [immodest] in them. Nor should you properly have held it against us if we had to be in them similar to you in some places, since we are examining your *Examen [Examination]* of our *Defense of the "Verification."* Although even if we had left alone your *Examen* that has already appeared and ours that was about to do so, we would not have sinned much, but as you yourselves said well from Solomon, that although we are not to answer the fool according to his folly, lest we seem like unto him, nonetheless we ought to answer the fools according to their folly, lest they be wise unto their own conceit.[46] But when we do this, we take under our *Examen* only those points for now from that of yours in which you fly high in pompous words, so that you might see and recognize that you are Icaruses and not Daedaluses.

And so, leaving alone all the twigs and shrubs, dried up thorns and thistles, which a springtime fire—which, we say, our very silence—can burn up without our labor, we undertake a few unhewn logs, having hurled which upon us, you thought that they could be neither consumed by the fire of truth nor removed by us. For as far as the violation of the law of submission, or the *jus patronatus* [right of patronage], is concerned, fidget as you like, this stands *immobile* [immovable] in our *Verification*

45.   [Cf. Erasmus *Ad.* 1.7.59.]
46.   Prov. 26[:5–6; *Examen* 1621, 2; *AJuZR* 1:8:562].

and in its *Defense*. The law of both presentations, overturned by your elders (as we said and demonstrated earlier), also overturned the law of submission through those same persons, who were presented neither by those, nor in that place, by whom and where, for those dignities, it was fitting for them to be so presented. What happened for six hundred years and longer, that was the law and is; what happened against that for something more than ten years was and is a violation of the law. Thus as soon as your elders place the law of both presentations in their proper order, the *jus patronatus haerebit* [right of patronage will stand fast] also from your side, as it today *haeret immobile* [stands fast immovably] from our side. When one sick member of a body is healed, the entire body is freed from pain; and when the law of presentation that had been violated by your elders is set in its proper order, this will set all the laws in their place. Wherefore all of that with which you stuffed the first chapter of your *Examen,* you stuffed unto your own humiliation and shame; for by breaking the law of presentation you have also overturned the *jus patronatus* [right of patronage], which your elders use, contrary to the law given to the Ruthenian nation and Church, which is under the Eastern obedience. You believe that so long as you have words enough according to the power of this world, these words are in the defense of the truth. But when you look upon the authority of the laws by which the Ruthenian Church was ruled until your age, you will see, even without our demonstration, that these words were purposefully ordered unto the breaking of the laws of the Ruthenian Church.

Your elder broke the ancient law of the Ruthenian Church, since he was neither chosen by the Kyivan chapter, nor presented unto the Kyivan metropolitanate. He broke a second law, not having been presented for consecration unto him, to whom all the Ruthenian metropolitans, however many of them there have been in the Ruthenian land, have been and ought to be presented. And yet he wishes to be in the right also toward the Ruthenian Church and nation, and he tries to avoid being understood as the violator of our spiritual laws, against which, for this reason, you twist and turn in those *Twofold Guilts, Tests,* and *Examinations* of yours like an old piece of leather on the fire.[47] Show us one metropolitan upon the Ruthenian see through such a presentation, and we will not charge you with the breaking and the violation of the

47.   [*NKPP* 2:258, "Kurczyć się," 3.]

laws of the Ruthenian Church. But as long as first Potij, and now your current, second one are upon the Ruthenian metropolitanate through such presentation, they will have to be known as and called corrupters and violators of the laws of the Ruthenian Church by us and by the entire Ruthenian nation, those of us who are in the Ruthenian Church and whom that law properly serves and to whom it belongs.

At the end of that first chapter, where you say that it is not our affair, but yours, to interpret the intentions of the ancient founders, for they cannot be known to us; but *ater an albus* [a black man or a white one] (you know which)[48] whispered them to you, proving which knowledge, you say: "We know this from our Ruthenian books, and we know this from old people, worthy of credence, who are still alive; they saw it themselves; they did it, and they heard it from their elders that they also did it: to wit, that old Rus' considered Orthodox and Catholic churches one and the same." And you prove your account thus: "In Vilnius, having heard the morning divine service at the [Church of the] Holy Most Pure, the entire people used to go to the Bernardines for the sermon."[49]

We answer: With such knowledge of the intention of the founders, even the Calvinist ministers could always now demand union with us and thus Church benefices as well; for they know this not from old people, but even now from the young and from what they themselves saw with their own eyes and reckoned, that when their Calvinist church took up its place alongside the Holy Church of the Most Pure in Vilnius, the Rus' of Vilnius, after hearing the morning divine service, almost all of them (for you too, after gathering all you could, were the cause of empty churches during the great Liturgy) used to go to the Calvinist church for the sermon, whereby many of them even remained there.[50]

48.   [Erasmus *Ad.* 1.6.99.]
49.   [*Examen* 1621, 13–14; *AJuZR* 1:8:569–70. This was the Orthodox, later the Uniate, Cathedral Church of Vilnius. The Bernardines were a stone's throw away.]
50.   [*Zbór,* "Protestant church," refers here to the congregation of the Calvinists (and not the Lutherans) of Vilnius, whose place of worship was established in the 1560s in the neighborhood of the Bernardine churches, monastery, and convent, and of the Orthodox Cathedral Church of the Most Pure Virgin. It functioned there until 1640, when it was removed just beyond the city walls.]

And thence, from this sort of action of the Ruthenian people in Vilnius, they could seek to prove, as could you, the intention of the founders of the Holy Most Pure in its benefices; and they could cite: If the Calvinist Church and the evangelical sermon (for you too ought to have cited this same thing) were in such respect in Rus', then, in founding the churches, how could they not to have had even if *non expressam, saltem virtualem intentionem* [not the express, then at the least the virtual intent] that those who are going to serve in the Ruthenian churches should never be in union with the Evangelical Church. So then, with this interpretation of the intention of our founders, will you bring us to the Union, and will you take the laws and the benefices of our Church? And are we simply supposed to look upon this and to allow ourselves to be led with our own good wherever they would lead us, like reasonless creatures? Let them not, nor ought you, expect from us, following this interpretation of the intention of the founders, that we be deprived of our laws so long as holy righteousness will have a place in this Kingdom of Poland.

Rus' used to go to the Roman Church in Vilnius; it used to go even to the Calvinist Church. It goes even now in many cities, but not led astray by the love of the rite, only partially for the spectacle, partially *curiositatis gratia* [for the sake of curiosity], and no less for the organ, which the commonality, the simple folk, are wont to do. But what wonder is it that the simple people did this. For even your antecessors, our apostates, through their apostasy and lack of care, after scattering the Ruthenian people among the Catholic and Protestant Churches and allowing them to be poisoned with the teaching of the heterodox (witness to which is, in the Grand Duchy of Lithuania, the city of Naŭharadok, in which, at the advent of your Union, almost all the people of ancient Rus' converted to the Anabaptists), themselves also came to their own demise. When, through their carelessness, there fell upon them the *crassa ignorantia dogmatum* [crass ignorance of the dogmas] of the Holy Eastern Church, and it subjected them to the ridicule and abuse of the various sects that are found in the Kingdom of Poland, unable to take care of themselves since they were unlearned, they did not betake themselves to their own correction and to that of their people; rather they blindly rushed into apostasy, where they saw not salvation, but the favor of the great estates, the baubles of this world, hopes for haughtiness, and where the final lure enticed them. Such that, all together, after treading upon all that was their own, they grabbed for what was not theirs, whereby they themselves, as we said, came unto demise, and they misled the poor people. Thus it was not love of the rite that drew Rus' to the Catholic and Protestant Churches, but novelties, spectacles, *comoediae* [comedies], organs, swings, little rattles, driving out Judas, casting him down from the heavens, and other similar frivolities. *Vulgus enim* [for the commonality], as someone said, *novitatum est cupidum* [is desirous of novelties].[51]

From the Second Chapter

We promised to exercise modesty in words. Mindful of which, although we are offended by your rather harsh words, as if that did not distress us, we do not take offense. And having left in its authority, unassailed, what was said in our *Defense of the "Verification"* from the spiritual laws concerning the non-violation of the law of submission when someone is consecrated *canonice* [according to Church law] although he has not yet received presentation, we proceed to consider your amazement; for in your astonishment, thinking that you have won, you triumph injudiciously. Just remain a little, and listen to us diligently: you will see clearly that the Defender of the *Verification* is an ass (since that was how it pleased you), but of Balaam, for he tells the truth;[52] but you yourselves will remain a mule, *cui non est intellectus* [which has no understanding].[53] You are amazed at the fact that in our *Defense of the "Verification"* we called a certain council that was gathered in Constantinople under Patriarch Ignatius and under Emperor Theophilus a general council. But we are yet more amazed at your lack of sincerity in citing our writings, that you charge us with untruth. Where did you read in our *Defense of the "Verification"* what you are triumphing over? Where do you find mentioned with even one word Patriarch Ignatius or Emperor Theophilus, under whom you claim that council was gathered?

---

51.   *Tacitus, Histori., lib. 1.* [Tacitus, *Histories* 1.80. Brückner (1990, 303) sheds light on the "little rattles": "On the last three days of Holy Week the candles were extinguished on the altars, the bells fell silent . . . . They were replaced in church by larger rattles . . . . And boys, as soon as (the rattles sounded) ran along the street with their own little rattles . . . ."]
52.   Num. 22[:21–33; *Examen* 1621, 16; *AJuZR* 1:8:571].
53.   Ps. 31[32:9].

So that you might see, then, that you treat us insincerely, we cite for you our words from the *Defense of the "Verification,"* where we say: "And that even from the Western Church we are not lacking for the right in this matter, we cite Canon 22 of the Eighth General (as it claims) Council gathered in Constantinople." Where is there anything like the truth in your account of our words? But in order also to demonstrate your insincerity toward us in this account, to those who listen to us speaking we say: that during the time of the difference between Patriarch Ignatius and Photius there were three councils gathered in Constantinople, and a fourth after the death of Ignatius, already during the time of Patriarch Photius. The first did not come to pass because it was interrupted by the disagreement of the bishops, as Balsamon makes known in the preface to this council. Soon thereafter a second one took place, which was gathered for this same matter, and it decreed seventeen canons in the matters that pertained to the Church at that time. And this council is called First-Second, since the matters proposed at the first council came into effect at the second.[54] The third council was gathered in the matter of Ignatius against Photius, the acts and canons of which are found described in the books *Conciliorum* [of the Councils].[55] The fourth council was gathered after the death of Ignatius, when Photius had already become patriarch. And on account of the seriousness of the matter that was discussed at it, we call this last, fourth council, the Eighth General Council.

The Romans, however, receive as the Eighth General Council the third in this number. But it is no wonder that you do not acknowledge (although you must) this fourth council gathered under Patriarch Photius and Pope John VIII. For at this council the addition in the *symbolum* [creed] of the *filioque* ["and from the Son"] was censured, and whoever should add it, or use it with the addition, was subjected to anathema. And we know that the fourth one under Pope John and Patriarch Photius, and not that third council gathered under Hadrian and Ignatius, was general, and is to be called such from the fact that it is the general matter that customarily gives the title "general" to a council. At

---

54. [Balsamon, Foreword to the First-Second Photian Council at Constantinople (861), *CSA* 283; *PG* 137:1003–4.]
55. Vol. 4 of the Councils [Fourth Council of Constantinople, AD 869–70; Tanner 155–86; Mansi 16:1–534].

the council that you titled general, a private matter was discussed that concerned the see of Constantinople alone, and not concerning a matter of the faith, but concerning one wronged individual. But at the one that we call general, there was discussed a matter that concerned the entire Eastern Church, that concerned, we say, all of Christendom. For it was concerned with a matter of the faith decreed by the seven ecumenical councils, with the matter of the violation and the profanation of the ecumenical *symbolum* [creed] and with the schism that arose on this account between the Eastern and the Western Church. Wherefore, this council is truly general and was for all times held and acknowledged as such by all of Christendom. It is no wonder, then, as we said, that you do not acknowledge this council, since even until this very day you are under its anathema, and so long as you will use that addition in the Church, you must bear upon you the anathema of this council. For it passed such a decree against you: If anyone should remove anything from the holy Niceno-Constantinopolitan Creed, or add anything to it, and would call this a creed—let him be condemned, deposed from his dignity, and expelled from every Christian community, and anathema.[56] It is therefore not without reason that you did not see fit to introduce this council into the books *conciliorum* [of the councils].[57]

Whence, then, did you come to understand that it was in the bitterness of our souls that we called it a general council, when we come to speak of that council? About which we say *libere* [freely] and with an eager soul that it is general, although it is not from the number of the seven universal. We called it the eighth and general on account of the very importance of the matter decided at it; that at it all seven ecumenical councils were affirmed, heresies and schisms were trampled and destroyed. But we called that canon the law of the Western Church not in order to remove authority from the Eastern Church and to acknowledge some sort of weight thereby to the Western. Rather

56.   [Mansi 17:520E–521A.]

57.   [The third council in Smotryc'kyj's list was held in 869–870. It deposed Photius and reinstated Ignatius as the patriarch of Constantinople. His fourth council, held in 879–880 after the death of Ignatius, again recognized Photius and annulled the council of 869–870. The fourth council is still accepted as the "Eighth Ecumenical Council" by the Orthodox. It was viewed similarly by Rome until the Gregorian reforms, since which time the West has accepted the council of 869–870 as the Eighth Ecumenical.]

because you consider that third one in the number of councils to be general, at which this canon cited by us was passed, and therefore we added this parenthesis—("as it claims")—that is, as the Roman Church calls this council the Eighth General Council. Thus you triumphed in vain in your insincerity toward us since the rights cited by us stand inviolate.

We have already said at the beginning who the universal pastor of the Church of God is and whom we consider him to be. With the blessed Apostle Peter, we too say here that it is Christ the Lord, whom he calls *principem pastorum*, ἀρχιποιμένα, that is, the chief shepherd,[58] about whom the prophet of God, Ezekiel, also says in the person of God: *Et suscitabo super oves meas pastorem unum;* and I will set up, he says, one shepherd over my sheep.[59] And Christ the Lord says of Himself: *Ego sum pastor bonus;* I (He says) am the good shepherd.[60] And again: And other sheep I have, which are not of this fold; them must I also bring, for they shall hear my voice; and there shall be one fold and one shepherd.[61] And so, we acknowledge, consider, and confess Christ the Lord Himself as the universal pastor, who is the ruler and the universal shepherd of His Church,[62] who has all the pastors under Him as His servants and workers, to whom He did not commend rule over His sheep, for He left that to Himself alone; rather he commended to them only the labor of shepherding.

But not tarrying over this, which is well known to the entire world, we proceed to those words of yours in this same chapter, where you say: "The Defender of the *Verification* acknowledges to the people of the Roman rite that they are in the Holy Catholic Church. He acknowledges that it is one; and he also acknowledges that the Romans are of the sort of faith in which they can be saved."[63] To which we answer you together with the Defender of the *Verification* that, of the three things you have cited here, the first is your own testimony concerning yourselves, and not ours nor that of the Defender of the *Verification,*

58. 1 Pet. 5[:4].
59. Ez. 34[:23].
60. Jn. 10[:14].
61. Jn. 10[:16].
62. Ez. 37[:24].
63. [*Examen* 1621, 25; *AJuZR* 1:8:578.]

who cites these words from the privileges not as his own, but as those of him who gave these privileges. For the Defender says to the Refuter on page 77: "Why are you amazed, Refuter, that His Majesty the King, calling people of the Roman religion Catholics, adorning us, people of the Greek religion, equally with the same title, calls us Christians and Catholics?" And again on page 78: "Wherefore, if His Majesty the King deigns to call us people of the Christian religion, he does not abjure for himself that same title of Christian Catholic."[64]

The third of these three is also your own, and neither ours nor that of the Defender of the *Verification,* who says the following on page 106: "And as far as the salvation of the confessors of the Roman faith is concerned, he could safely say that *defectus fidei non excessus condemnat* [it is the defect in the faith, not the excess, that condemns], and thus whoever heard that from him could infer what he wished according to his own desire."[65] And so you heard this from the Defender (that, for the sake of agreement in this, we grant this to you), and you inferred at that time, and you infer even today, according to your desire, what you wished, and not what he wished.

The second of these three, where on page 77 the Defender of the *Verification* says: "His Majesty the King is pleased to know that the Holy Catholic Church—which is one in its reins and in which the particular Churches were conceived and to which both have the same right—bears both our sides, the Eastern particular Church and the Western. And since they are united by the unity of mutual love, both sides beg the Lord God that He paternally remove and eliminate what separates them, that is, whatever has come between them as a difference *non per defectum* [not by defect], but *per excessum* [by excess]."[66] This second is [the opinion] of the Defender of the *Verification* and of us. For as one holy Ecumenical Church carried in its reins the four particular Eastern Churches of the four highest patriarchal sees and all the Catholic Churches that are under them, likewise also the fifth Western Roman see, and all the local Churches that were, and are now, under its rule; that is the one that also gave birth to them, and that is the one that raised them to adulthood, whence both the Defender of the *Verification* and we

64. [See above, pp. 251–2; Smotryc'kyj 1621c, 77–8/437–8.]
65. [See above, p. 263; Smotryc'kyj 1621c, 106/452.]
66. [See above, p. 252; Smotryc'kyj 1621c, 77/437.]

can safely say that the Holy Catholic Church, which is one, bears us, both sides, both the Eastern local Church and the Western, in its reins, in which they were conceived.

For St. Augustine says: *Ecce Roma, ecce Carthago, ecce aliae et aliae civitates, filiae regum sunt, et delectaverunt regem suum in honore ipsius, et ex omnibus fit una quaedam regina.*[67] "Behold Rome," he says, "behold Carthage, other and still other cities are the daughters of kings, and they delighted their king in his honor, and from all of them is made one queen." Likewise *Venerabilis Beda* [Venerable Bede]: *Non latet, inquit, rabies haereticorum de angulo: toto terrarum orbe ecclesia diffusa est, omnes gentes habent ecclesiam, nemo nos fallat: ipsa est vera, ipsa est Catholica, coepit ab Hierusalem, pervenit ad nos: et ibi est, et hic: non enim ut huc veniret, inde discessit: crevit, non migravit.* "Let," he says, "the heretical anger not rage from the corner. The Church has been diffused throughout all the world. All the nations have the Church. Let no one deceive us: this is the genuine one, as it is universal. It began from Jerusalem; it came to us. It is both there and here—not that it left from there in order to come here. It grew; it did not transfer."[68]

Looking then upon these times, and upon almost the thousandth year since the birth of Christ the Lord, the Defender of the *Verification* and we too safely use this word *in praesenti* [in the present]: "it bears." But looking at the further years after the thousandth, in which the unity of the Church became rent, that word said *in praesenti* [in the present], "it bears," *per Grammaticum zeugma* [by grammatical zeugma] (for you too are familiar with old grammarians and with new theologians),[69] we inflect *in praeteritum* [in the past]: "it bore." And therefore we immediately add "to which both have the same right," since they were born from it and raised by it, although both of them did not remain in its reins. But, as we have demonstrated thoroughly, set at variance by the submission from the Western side of a cause for their division, they ask from both sides, through the unity of love of the Lord God,

67. *S. Aug. in Ps. 44* [St. Augustine on Ps. 44 (45); *PL* 36:509. *NPNF1* 8:152].
68. *Libro. 6 in Luc., cap. 93* [Bede, in bk. 6 on Lk., chap. 93; *PL* 92:632A].
69. [Cf. the allegation in *Examen 1621*, 26; *AJuZR* 1:8:579; cited above, p. xlvii.]

that He might paternally remove and destroy what separates them. And we assert that whatever variance and separation there is comes from *excessus fidei, et non defectus* [an excess of the faith, and not a defect]. And this is not with regard to us, who acknowledge in you not only *excessus* [an excess] but also *defectus fidei* [a defect in the faith]— both with regard to the man, the universal bishop, and with regard to *Katholika* or *Orthodoxia* corrupted through excesses and defects—but with regard to the Romans alone, who are wont to speak of us thus: that we are lacking only the obedience to the bishop of Rome, wherefore they call us schismatics, although, nonetheless, they acknowledge that our faith is the Orthodox Catholic one.

Father Skarga says about our Ruthenian faith in the preface to his *Warning:* "Through my great inclination to the holy Greek rite and to the Church ceremonies full of God's honor, I have through my writing for thirty-five years now been summoning our Ruthenian nations to Church union so that the ancient love of their holy Eastern fathers might return to them and that it might vivify their Catholic faith, which is dying without the love and unity of the Church of Christ."[70] Thus the words of Skarga.

Orzechowski, on the other hand, canon of Przemyśl, is even more authoritative concerning us, Rus', and the entire Eastern Church of the peoples who are subordinate to the four patriarchs; for after he said that the Greeks and Rus' are Christians and are in the Church of God, he concludes: "We who live nearer to Thrace know that the see of Constantinople, with the other sees that all the people of old called apostolic, is intact, which God granted to find favor in the eyes of Süleyman, the Turkish tyrant, like a second captive Joseph, so that the promise might always be true, that the gates of hell should not prevail against the Church, nor against its apostolic sees."[71]

And Lyranus [Nicholas of Lyra], the Roman doctor, who lived already three hundred years ago in this separation, beautifully interprets these four patriarchal sees in the East as the mystery of those four animals in the prophet Ezekiel, whereby, comparing them to the four

---

70.   [Skarga 1610,)(4r.]

71.   *Stanisl. Orze, in Diatr. contra calumn. anno 1540 edita.* [Stanisław Orzechowski in *A Diatribe against Calumny,* published 1540 (actually, 1548); Orzechowski 1548, B2v; cf. Gen. 41:40–5; Mt. 16:18.]

Evangelists: (1) in the lion he understands the see of Jerusalem on account of the bold preaching of the Gospel there by the Apostles;[72] (2) in the ox, that of Antioch on account of the obedience of the faithful who come under the apostolic yoke; (3) in the face of a man, that of Alexandria on account of the most learned men there, Athanasius, Clement, Cyril, etc.; (4) in the eagle, that of Constantinople on account of the men who contemplated God there, Chrysostom, Gregory of Nazianzus, and others.[73]

It is with regard, then, to the Romans alone, who charge us only with non-obedience to the Roman pope as an excess, but acknowledge that our faith is the true Catholic faith. The more judicious, however, acknowledge that even without the obedience to the pope we are in the Church of God, and they accord us salvation, as does the above-mentioned Stanisław Orzechowski. With regard to us, however, neither we nor the Defender of the *Verification* acknowledges to you, our apostates, that, finding yourselves *in excessu fidei* [in an excess in the faith], you do not also find yourselves *in defectu* [in a defect] in it. Which we have already thoroughly demonstrated to you many times; and it can be demonstrated, God willing, on another occasion.

Wherefore, for the time being forbear with your syllogism, and solve it for yourselves, as if it had been charged by us against you. For the Romans themselves—as we demonstrated with these four testimonies of people of high estates and dignities, with the royal privileges, with the writings of Lyranus the Roman doctor, of Father Orzechowski, priest and canon, of Father Skarga, priest and preacher— call us Christians of the Catholic faith, and they acknowledge that we are in the Church of God, which is one, and they do not doubt that we are certain of the salvation of our souls. For Orzechowski says in the same place: "The Greeks and Rus' are not to be counted on the side of the impious, or in the number of God's enemies. To the contrary, I believe that they are Christians and that they are in the Church of God."[74] When you do this, when, we say, you solve this syllogism for yourselves, you will see indeed that you find yourselves with Esau, you

72.   Acts 4.
73.   *In 3 par Lyra. Comme. Ezechi. cap. 1* [In part 3 of Lyranus's commentary on Ezekiel. Nicholas 1:10].
74.   [Orzechowski 1548, A8r.]

who persecute Jacob unto death.[75] And you do not belong to the inside of the Holy Church, which is one, and outside of which no one can be saved, since you abound in both excesses and in defects. Having one Church, we believe that the Holy Eastern Church, which is subordinate to the obedience of the four apostolic sees of the patriarchs, is of one mind in faith with the Church throughout the various nations in various parts of the world. Whichever Churches do not communicate in faith with this holy Church must find themselves both in excesses and in defects.

And what you concluded after a long discourse from moral philosophy and from ancient theology concerning what an *excessus in fide* [excess in the faith] might be, and the fact that Nestorius was condemned *propter excessum in fide* [on account of an excess in the faith]—this you concluded senselessly, since you ought to have known that *una quaeque haeresis non excessus est in fide, sed defectus* [every heresy is not an excess in the faith, but a defect]. Sabellius fuses the three divine persons into one person, *defectum fidei patitur* [he suffers a defect in the faith]. Arius divides the three persons into three different natures: *defectum et is patitur* [he too suffers a defect]. Nestorius divides Christ the Lord into two persons and two natures: he suffers a defect of faith. Eutyches fuses two natures in one nature of one person: he too suffers a defect of faith. Therefore, having labored in such a matter, you sweated so *laboriose* [laboriously] in vain, since it does not release you either from excess or from defect. For according to your ancient (as you call it) theology, it would be *ex defectu fidei* [by defect in the faith] to celebrate the mystery of the Holy Eucharist under one species, and *ex excessu* [by excess] to confess that the Holy Spirit proceeds "and from the Son." We, on the other hand, say that if both these things *excessus est, non est de essentia fidei* [are an excess, they are not of the essence of the faith]; if the one and the other *est essentiale fidei* [is essential to the faith], as they are, *defectus est* [each is a defect].[76]

We wonder, indeed, that you did not also cite these words of the Defender, where, on page 79, he says: "What embittered us more toward the Romans than this hypocritical Union, such that they avoid our churches and we their churches? Such that they criticize our rites,

75.   Gen. 32.
76.   [*Examen* 1621, 26–8; *AJuZR* 1:8:579–80.]

and we theirs, although they are almost one and the same thing?"[77] We wonder, we say, that you did not cite these words, and did not form such an argument from them: "The Defender of the *Verification* does not wish to flee from the Roman churches, and he does not criticize their rite; rather he says that the Roman and the Greek rites are nearly one and the same. Therefore, as well, the Roman and the Greek faiths are nearly one and the same, *et per consequens* [and as a consequence], by the opinion of the Defender, the Union is good." But perhaps you thought that this particle "nearly" would have to hinder you greatly from this consequence, nay even from the conclusion itself. For if the rite, that is, the ceremonies, which the Defender of the *Verification* understands by the word "rite," are "nearly" one and the same, as if having said, "they are not the same but they are similar to the same thing," to what greater extent is the faith not one and the same, but similar to one and the same?

For although in ceremonies and in rites the Roman Church seems, in appearances, to be somehow one and the same with our Eastern Church, nonetheless in actual fact the difference is great. Since it is entirely caught up in mutations, that is, in variations, how much more so is it not one and the same thing in faith, since it is ἐν καινοτομίαις, *in innovationibus,* that is, in innovations? Leaving aside the variation in the Roman rite—that it rejected the Wednesday fast, which was in custom in the ancient Roman Church;[78] that it received the Saturday fast, which at first the ancient Church did not hold;[79] that it received organs, trumpets, drums, and other instrumental music, which the ancient Church did not use; that it received the practice of cutting or shaving the beards and mustaches of priests, which neither the holy Apostles nor the ancient Roman Church did;[80] that on Sundays, on quinquigesimal days, and on all holy days, it allows the faithful to pray, kneeling in public congregations, which the ancient Church did

77. [See above, p. 254; Smotryc'kyj 1621c, 79–80/438–9.]
78. *Can. Apo. 68* [*Apostolic Canons* 68 (actually 69); *PG* 137:175D–176D; *NPNF2* 14:598].
79. *Can. 65* [*Apostolic Canons* 65 (actually 66); *PG* 137:169A–170A; *NPNF2* 14:598].
80. *Cleme. Constit. Apost. 1, 1 Cap. 3* [St. Clement of Rome, *Apostolic Constitutions,* bk. 1, chap. 3; *PG* 1:565–6].

not allow;[81] that it does not maintain those three fasts, the apostolic one (which is commonly called Petrine), that of the most holy Virgin, before her Dormition, and the fast before the birth of Christ the Lord, which the ancient Church maintained[82]—leaving aside, we say, these and many other similar variations of the present-day Roman Church, after looking only at the variation of the calendar, this is sufficient to demonstrate that the present-day rite of the Roman Church and that of the Eastern Church are not one and the same thing. In this year the Roman Church will celebrate their *Pascha* [Easter] together with the Jews, for whom the *Pascha* [Passover] falls on that same day of Sunday as for the Roman Church, if the Jews will celebrate their *Phase* [Passover] according to the new calendar. But if they would celebrate it according to the old calendar, as they are supposed to celebrate it, then the Roman Church will precede them by four weeks. But the Eastern Church will celebrate its Easter six days after them since the Jewish *Phase* [Passover] must not go beyond the *Strastna Niedziela* [Ruthenian: Passion Week], that is, of the seventh week of Lent. And when the Eastern Church commemorates the passion of the Lord, the Roman then commemorates the Resurrection. The latter rejoices, but the Eastern one is saddened. This is truly unharmonious for one and the same rite, and it is against the canons of the holy Apostles and the constant decrees and customs of the Church.[83]

We say, then, that this very variation of the calendar is sufficient to demonstrate that the rite of the Roman Church is not one and the same with the rite of the Eastern Church. In which matter the Lord God Himself judges between us and passes sentence which rite is pleasing to Him and which is not. And He passes sentence in that holy place in which He will pass righteous sentence when He comes to judge the quick and the dead, that is, in Jerusalem, at His holy grave, where every Easter eve, that is, on Great Saturday, He deigns to cause fire to descend to His holy grave. He waters it as if with a fiery water, within the grave,

---

81.   *1 Syno. Nic. Vn. Can. 20* [*Canon 20 of the First Universal Council of Nicaea;* Mansi 2:677B; Tanner 16; *NPNF2* 14:42].

82.   *Nicola. PP. in respon: ad cons. Bulgar. cap. 4* [*Pope Nicholas (I) in the Replies to the Inquiries of the Bulgars, PL* 119:981A].

83.   *Cano. Apost. 7* [Apostolic Canons 7 (actually 8); *PG* 137:47B–48B; *NPNF2* 14:594].

against the background upon which His most holy body lay.[84] And He fills the entire internal chapel of His holy grave with this fire and lights the lamps, where every year on Great Saturday, toward evening, with great piety, our patriarch of Jerusalem makes a procession around the chapel of the grave of God, going around it three times while singing this hymn: "O Christ the Savior, the angels in heaven praise your resurrection; make us, too, on earth, worthy to praise and to glorify you with a pure heart."[85]

So when for the third time the *clerus* [clergy] (at which time there are gathered *ex voto* [by vow], or simply on account of piety, deacons, archimandrites, presbyters, bishops, metropolitans from various lands of various nations, all the dioceses subordinate to the four patriarchs; there are often even patriarchs, each of these people in the spiritual garment that befits him, and they celebrate this procession in the presence of the patriarch of Jerusalem); when, then, for the third time the Church *clerus* [clergy] goes around the grave of God, the patriarch of Jerusalem enters into the internal chapel of this holy grave (and if some other patriarch is there, he too enters), and he lights from this fire a candle of glowing white wax; and having made his bow befitting this holy place, he leaves. When he leaves the vestibule of the internal chapel with the lit candles, he sings this hymn, which is customary in our Church: "Christ has arisen from the dead, having conquered death with His death, and having granted life to those who are in the grave."[86] At the sound of which the entire *clerus* [clergy] sings the same thing, and all of Christendom that is gathered at that time from various lands. And the patriarch is led with this miraculous fire and is placed at the elevated place of marble between the church and the chapel; and he remains upon it until all light their candles from him. Not only the Orthodox do this, but also various sectarians, even the Turks themselves. And as soon as this is completed, the father patriarch enters into the Church of the Lord's Resurrection, which is in the control of the patriarch, and every day a service is celebrated in it by the Greek monks who permanently reside there. And when the candles and lamps that are inside the Church are lit with this fire, and the fire in the coal for the censer is made to

84.   *Baro. in Anno 1101, num. 2* [Baronius, *Annales,* s.a. 1101, no. 2].
85.   [*VS* 3:1:5, Stichera, voice 5; Easter service.]
86.   [*VS* 3:2:6, Troparion, voice 6; Easter service.]

glow, after stopping in front of the open doors of the altar, which we commonly call the royal doors, the patriarch censes; and after raising up his voice that it be heard by the entire people, he says: "Praise to the holy, uni-essential, life-giving and indivisible Trinity, the Father and the Son and the Holy Ghost, now and always and forever and ever." And when the *clerus* [clergy] has said Amen to this, they begin the vespers, that is, the Easter vespers.

And so, we say, almighty God Himself judges between us concerning the rite and demonstrates miraculously which one He receives and which He does not receive, when, during the commemoration of the celebration of His glorious resurrection He causes this excellent miracle according to the old calendar and not according to the new. If, then, there were no other variations in the rite of the Roman Church from the rite of the Eastern Church, this alone suffices to demonstrate that the Roman and the Greek rite are not one and the same. Looking upon this, the Defender of the *Verification* said it is nearly one and the same, as if he had also said it is one and the same, but either it is not celebrated at the same time, or it is celebrated differently. But as it was easily corrupted, so it can more easily be corrected. For it was a great work to corrupt the calendar, but one edict can correct it. All of Christendom demands this with all its soul, as if aroused by some sort of internal yearning of praise, desiring to sing "Christ has arisen from the dead" at that very time when the Lord God Himself demands that this be sung by them and miraculously demonstrates the time. But for this occasion this will suffice about this.

Thinking, then, that you should succeed in this according to your intent—what you pronounced from your old theology—and jumping for joy, you seek to remove from yourselves the mantle that fell upon you, put upon you by us through God's punishment and the patriarch's anathema, and to give it to us; but what we once gave you (we keep our word), we will not take back:[87] *semel valeat pro semper* [let once serve for always]. For it fits you like no other: sewn for you according to size, it has come to fit your bones as if you had been born with it.

And since we monks find ourselves, the one in Church work,

---

87.   [Is this a kind of ethno-confessional self-stereotyping? Cf. *NKPP* 3:101, "Ruś," 16: "The Ruthenian gift: given today, taken back tomorrow" ("Ruski dar: dzisiaj dał, jutro odebrał").]

another in school occupations, yet another in the labors of the printing house (with which charge you vituperate us),[88] another in housekeeping toils, each according to his ability and strength, we strive to imitate the bees in this, so that we not become similar to drones lulled to sleep by the humming in the honey and by the lure of the hives. And further wishing to censure us for our wisdom by alleging communion with the Protestants, you employed a not inelegant saying, which testifies that you are sagacious men: "The birch tar boasted," you say, "that, together with the pitch, it makes a good grease,"—as if you found yourselves more frequently around grease boxes than around the ink pot, that you are able to give shape to such shapely sayings of your own knowledge.[89]

After you did this, you set off on further exaggerations and absurdities against us, but since we disposed of them by answering them for ourselves with silence, we pass them by without touching upon them. We will touch a little, however, upon the exaggeration that you employed in the example of Sienieński. You say: "The example of Sienieński cited by the Defender from Kromer not only did not defend the Verificator in that in which it was used as defense, but it fundamentally destroyed all his other defenses in one blow." And after finishing the story you argue: "Look how he cited Sienieński against himself here."[90] We answer: We look and we see, by the grace of God, that in citing [the case of] Sienieński, which we did intentionally and by design, we said nothing against our superiors.[91]

Who does not see that there is not the slightest equality between the transgression of Sienieński and the progression of our spiritual superiors? The motivation of Sienieński's transgression was free will, its cause was wealth, and its goal was the senatorial eminence. But the motivation of our superiors' progression was the need for salvation, its cause was the oppressed hierarchy, and its goal was the raising of the affairs of piety in the Church of the Ruthenian nation. The rights that Sienieński violated with his action remained intact for him; but our

88. [Cf. *Examen* 1621, 29; *AJuZR* 1:8:580.]

89. [*Examen* 1621, 29; *AJuZR* 1:8:581.]

90. [*Examen* 1621, 31–3; *AJuZR* 1:8:582–3.]

91. [The account of this chapter in the life of Jakub of Sienno (Sienieński) is found in Kromer (Latin, 1568, 370–1; Polish, 1611, 492–3).]

rights have been violated, which you our apostates violated with your action. Sienieński was not lacking spiritual superiors, and the Cracow church would not have been lacking a bishop even if he had not been consecrated; but we, our superiors, and our entire Ruthenian nation of the Greek religion lacked spiritual superiors. And if they had not allowed themselves to be consecrated, we would have been lacking an Orthodox metropolitan and bishops, and thereby we would have had to live like dumb animals. For Sienieński it was a matter of the principality of Siewierz and other goods of the bishopric of Cracow, and of the senatorial seat. But for our superiors it was a matter of the faith, since we were running out of presbyters. Since in many counties and cities, the people, oppressed by you apostates, had already begun to disperse among various sects; children were dying without holy baptism and adults without the mysteries of the salvatory Eucharist. And in a word: Sienieński did what the law did not allow him to do, for he had the right of presentation in the hands of the king, complete, whole, inviolate. But our superiors did what the law did not forbid them, for they had the right of presentation that had been violated by you our apostates and overturned there, where our faith, through the change of pastor, would have had to suffer a change.

If Sienieński had dared to do this in the face of the sort of violence in which our superiors had to dare to do this, he would certainly not have received such disfavor for himself from King Kazimierz, on account of the protection of the right that would have shown him to be innocent; if, we say, all the bishops in the Kingdom of Poland had turned for their presentation to some other pastor that did not belong to them, against the bishop of Rome, they would have caused a change of faith through the change of pastor. And if at such a time, wishing to save the confessors of the obedience of the bishop of Rome from such apostates from his proper pastor, Sienieński had gone—without the knowledge of the king, who had not allowed him this—to his customary pastor, the bishop of Rome, and if he had received consecration from him, and if, in this matter, he had awaited peacefully from the hands of the king whatever belonged *ad jus patronatus* [to the right of patronage], would he have suffered such disfavor from His Majesty, King Kazimierz? We do not think so. And if he had suffered it, this would have happened to him against the law, since the law of the presentation of bishops of the Roman rite belongs to no one else but to the bishop of Rome.

Alias [otherwise], through the change of pastor, the right of presentation would have had to be violated. Forced *in tali casu, tali necessitate* [in such an event, in such necessity], saving the confessors of the Eastern obedience from you apostates, our spiritual superiors proceeded, having allowed themselves to be consecrated by their pastor, to whom rule in the Ruthenian Church properly belongs, and to whom the right of presentation for Ruthenian clerics pertains, whom you, our apostates, licentiously abandoned.

Thus for Sienieński it was a matter of temporal good; but for us it is a matter of the Orthodox faith. Wherefore, as Sienieński thereafter (although his transgression against King Kazimierz was immeasurably more serious) came to the King's grace and received the episcopal see from him, our superiors are certain, by the grace of God, of that same grace from His Royal Majesty, Their Gracious Lord. Calm yourselves, we ask, and, convinced by the righteousness of the thing that has been carried out, cease your injustice. For you know who said this: *Mea est ultio, ego retribuam eis in tempore, ut labatur pes eorum* [to me belongeth vengeance; I shall requite them in due time, that their foot shall slide].[92]

From the Third Chapter

There is nothing in this chapter over which we would tarry, for, as far as disputation is concerned, *injuriam sane faceremus sanctis synodis, si semel judicata et recte disposita revolvere, et iterum disputare contenderemus* [we would certainly do harm to the holy councils if we were to strive to reflect upon things once judged and properly ordered and to discuss them again].[93] That was a wise man, nay also a holy man, who in his day said what we say today: that we do not wish to dispute, nor do we wish to hold as doubtful what we have from the tradition of the Church and what was confirmed at ecumenical councils. And where you say that "if the secular magistrate were to use his power (and were to do this righteously), there would long ago have been peace

---

92. Dt. 32[:35].
93. *Niceph. lib. 16, cap. 31* [Nicephorus Callistus Xanthopulus, *Church History,* bk. 16, chap. 31; *PG* 147:177–80]. *Baro. in Anno 513* [Baronius, *Annales,* s.a. 513].

between you and us,"[94] thus certainly *norunt aristarchi cornicum oculos configere*,[95] *et Deo leges ponere* [the Aristarchs—i.e., "critics"—know how to delude the most wary, and to establish laws for God].

Looking upon such a disputation in their day with the opponents of the Church of God, for which you are so eager, the Orthodox said: "We know, oh emperor, that those whom you wish to bring together with us will win when you help them, and you oppress us by force, by fist, and by club; and if sword and fire were added to that, you would nearly have won your disputation, but against the sons of perdition and not the sons of God."[96] But do you say that this was in the Turkish domain? And yet, even there, almighty God does not allow this to be. And even if, according to His holy will, He were to allow it there or even here, you would not have any other joy than the pouring of Christian martyrs' blood. Thus we are not concerned about the might of you, our opponents, but we are concerned about submitting to doubt what we have from Church tradition and what was confirmed at the ecumenical councils. We are concerned neither with your wisdom, nor with your *crassa ignorantia et diffidentia causae* [crass ignorance and the diffidence of the cause][97] (as you deign to understand about yourselves and about us). For untaught God-thinking Spyridons dispute about the dogmas of the faith and not the philosophical most wise Coridons. Rather we are concerned *semel judicata et recte disposit revolvere, et iterum disputare: quod etiam legibus cautum est et prohibitum* [about reflecting upon things once judged and properly ordered and to discuss them again: which is decreed and prohibited by the laws].[98]

We do not deny Father Smotryc′kyj's discussions with you: it is not customary to criticize in anyone *pium intentum ad optimum finem* [the pious striving toward the best end], by whatever *media* [means], so long as it proceed *honesta* [honorably]. If he had conferred with you in order to remain with you, he would have done that. But since he conferred

94.   [*Examen* 1621, 39; AJuZR 1:8:587.]
95.   [Erasmus *Ad.* 1.3.75.]
96.   *Theodorus Studites* [Theodore the Studite]. Jn. 17[:12].
97.   [*Examen* 1621, 43; AJuZR 1:8:590.]
98.   *Concil. Chalce. Act. 6* [Council of Chalcedon, Session 6; *Edict of Emperors Velentinianus and Marcianus, by Which Disputations concerning the Faith in the Presence of the Common People Are Forbidden;* Mansi 7:475C–476C] *et apud Bernar. epistol. 194* [St. Bernard, Letter 194; *PL* 182:360D].

with you so that he might understand from you whether there would ever be the hope of your return whence you fell away, and since he did not see this in you, he left you. And he himself did what befitted him. As to the *Lament* (since you wish to have him as the author), neither he nor any of us regret its publication. To the contrary, we take delight in it, and we recommend it for the reading of all Orthodox and heterodox.

And where you say that he converted someone in Volhynia to the Union, who thereupon passed over to the Roman rite—as other things, this, too, you say against him in error.

And finally, that having feared some sort of harsh attack upon himself from the Brotherhood, he took upon himself the monastic habit—these are your customary rumors. For not only the Vilnius Brotherhood, but even all the others could not have driven him by force to that for which he himself did not have a good heart and a good will. Did he lack for anything? Was he not a free man, having the freedom to live here and elsewhere? Both as a monk and as a layman? After conferring with you for a long time, he did voluntarily what he judged, by the grace of God, to be salvatory for his soul. And he finds himself today in the Church of God, by a sincere undertaking, in that which contributes in seemly fashion to magnifying the honor and glory of the name of God, to fraternal union, to Christian love, and to Orthodox unanimity in our Ruthenian nation. May almighty God, by His holy right hand, deign to protect him from all adversities.[99]

Concluding your *Examination,* you complain against us pitifully before the Lord God and all Christendom: that a great wrong is done you by us and that we have generally despised fraternal love. Arguing both things, you simply turn the wheels of your own mill, having poured all the water of your insincerity upon them, believing that it would turn your wheels for a long time—well, at least until the truth made a dam for it. That we generally despised fraternal love or that some sort of wrong was done you by us—you do us a great harm in both these allegations through this insincerity of yours. So it is we who do not love you, we who do you wrong, when we are deprived of our own churches and of our goods, when we look upon our rights, freedoms, and liberties violated by you? So it is we who do not love you and do you wrong, when, tearing from our breasts our ancient holy

99. [For the allegations against Smotryc'kyj, see *Examen* 1621, 43–6/590–2.]

faith, you trouble, torture, and bring us to harm and dishonor through mandates, banishments, inquisitions, commissions, decrees of the lesser court circle? So it is we who do not love you and do you wrong, when you revile, with the calumny of treason, innocent people from among us, unseat honorable citizens from the town council magistracy, turn artisans out of the guilds, and bring the entire Ruthenian nation into disfavor? So it is we who do not love you, and it is we who do you wrong, when you take away from us by force the freedom of religion, seal our churches, seize our presbyters, dispossess them of their goods, and take their churches away from them? What is more, when, through your writings such as these and others similar, you represent us to God's anointed, His Majesty the King, Our Gracious Lord, and to the entire Commonwealth, as disturbers of the public peace, and as traitors of the Fatherland, do you then love us? That is what you call love?

If you were to suffer all this from someone, so it seems to us, you would call this the opposite of love. Yet you find us guilty that we, so ferociously oppressed and wronged by you, seek recourse for holy justice from the tribunals, from the dietines and the Sejms; and you charge that in this way we deserve embitterment rather than peace. But having, after the Lord God, no other recourse in our innocence than the tribunals, dietines, and Sejms, what else are we supposed to do? We constantly beg for justice at them, we ask for peace and for our liberation from you who harm us. And we must do this until the righteous judgment of God and the decree of His Majesty the King, Our Gracious Lord, removes from our necks you, our persecutors, who have sat upon them by force. And this—does this come from your love toward us?—that, distorting our writings with a perfidious tongue, with a wrong-headed interpretation, as your venomous heart counsels you, you turn them inside out and you represent them as criminal acts. You impute of us that in them we showed disrespect for His Majesty the King, Our Gracious Lord. And you focus upon such words that are never found in our writings.

Finally, you charge against our Brotherhood that it is somehow organized not for the honor and the glory of the name of God and not for the pious residence of those who are inscribed into it, to which you say: "The *szlachta* is received only as protectors."[100] We answer you

---

100. [*Examen* 1621, 50; *AJuZR* 1:8:595.]

and that love of yours, that our Brotherhood is permitted, guaranteed by privileges of the Sejm, and is *primario* [principally] a noble Brotherhood. Wherefore, whoever incorporates himself into it in ancient faith through his piety, grants to it the unity of its faith and rite. For it is organized and established not for what you allege against it out of your love toward us; rather almighty God Himself deigned to raise, organize, and establish it for acts of piety, in which, through the grace and help of God, it has magnificent results. This is attested by the monastery in which we live, the church, hospitals, schools, and other *munimenta* [bulwarks] of piety here in Vilnius and elsewhere, raised and outfitted by the industry and cost of this Brotherhood, in all of which is praised and worshipped the most laudable name of God the One in the Trinity, the Father and the Son and the Holy Ghost, who reigns for ever and ever, Amen.

And ending this our conversation with you, falling at His most holy feet, we ask that, ruling us through His divine industry, if such be His holy will, He deign to keep us in this cross even longer, but that He not deign to remove from us the hand of His help and consolation. But if He wishes now to make an end with this experience, in this too we submit to His holy will. And for you, who by His divine permission are given to us as a goad to the body, whichever of you have smitten us on the face,[101] we wish, in sincere heart of Christian love, repentance and the conversion whence you fell away.

From Vilnius, the 4th day of February.

Your Grace's well-wishing servants and suppliants of God
The Monks of the Monastery of the
Brotherhood of Vilnius, of the Church
of the Descent of the Holy Spirit.
Μία ζωῆς ἡμῶν ἐλπὶς Ἰησοῦς ὁ χριστόΣ.
[My life's only hope, Christ JesuS.][102]

---

101. 2 Cor. 12[11:20].
102. [See above, p. 231.]

Plate 4. Poland and surrounding areas, from *Kozmograffia czeská* (Prague, 1554), 1006. Reprint: *Specimina Philologiae Slavicae* 78 (Munich, 1988), 100.

A Justification of Innocence
(1623)

A Justification of Innocence,
Submitted
by the Newly and Legitimately Erected Hierarchy
of the Holy Ruthenian Church
That is Obedient to the Patriarchs
of the Holy See of Constantinople
to Its Highest and
First (After the Lord God) Authority.

David, Ps. 102 [103:4–5]

Let the Lord God crown you with loving-kindness and tender
mercies, and let him satisfy your demand with good things.

The Year of Our Lord 1623.

For the Most Excellent Sigismund III, by the grace of God, King
of Poland, Grand Duke of Lithuania, Ruthenia, Prussia, Samogitia,
Mazovia, Livonia, and Sweden; hereditary King of the Goths and
Vandals, Lord, Lord, Our Gracious Lord:

The hierarchy of the Ruthenian Church of the ancient Greek religion
wishes and desires grace, peace, the soul's salvation, the body's health,
and all blessed prosperity in fortunate reign.

Most Excellent, Gracious King, Lord, Lord, Our Gracious Lord:

T HE BLESSED APOSTLE OF THE NATIONS, God's chosen vessel, who
was to proclaim and did proclaim the name of Christ the
Lord before the nations and the kings and the sons of Israel,
in describing the obligation of subjects to superiors and the power of
superiors over subjects—and for both, of what compliance the former,
and of what authority the superiors are supposed to be—establishes
this pious law: *Omnis anima potestatibus sublimioribus subdita fit.
Non est enim potestas nisi a Deo: quae autem sunt, a Deo ordinata
sunt. Itaque, qui resistit potestati, Dei ordinationi resistit; qui autem
resistunt, ipsi sibi damnationem acquirunt. Nam principes non sunt
timori boni operis, sed mali. Vis autem non timere potestatem? bonum
fac et habebis laudem ex illa. Dei enim minister est tibi in bonum;* "Let
every soul," says that holy apostle, "be subject unto the higher powers.
For there is no power but of God: the powers that be are ordained of
God. Whosoever therefore resisteth the power resisteth the ordinance
of God: and they that resist shall receive to themselves damnation. For
rulers are not a terror to good works, but to the evil. Wilt thou then not
be afraid of the power? do that which is good, and thou shalt have praise
of the same: For he is the minister of God to thee for good."[1] Thus this
blessed apostle.
    At the time when, six hundred years ago, the salvatory name of
Christ the Lord made its happy arrival in the Ruthenian lands, when
at the same time along with it, through God's cause, our Ruthenian
nation became enlightened from the East through the mystery of holy
baptism and was granted from that place the divinely inspired writings

---

1.   Rom. 13[:1–4].

of both laws, whence it also received holy baptism—at that very time it also learned the apostolic teaching of evangelical annunciation that we cited above, having in constant memory and daily practice in no way to resist, in no way to oppose, the power that it knew was established over it by the Lord God, but to be unto it submissive, obedient in everything, and to do that which is good, to render gladly all that is owed to it in benefit: tribute and duty, and in addition to that fear and honor. It rendered all we have mentioned first to the princes of Rus', then to their Graces the Kings of Poland and the Grand Dukes of Lithuania (in the process, laying down and pouring out its health and its blood for the health and honor of them, of their domains, and of its fatherland). And it rendered this in the fear of God, with all its soul, in good conscience, with genuine goodwill, humble fidelity, eager submissiveness, watchful readiness, so that through it the divine dispensation and the salvatory apostolic judgment might not be diminished in even the smallest point, but that it be satisfied in absolutely everything. Our Ruthenian nation observed all this through all the past ages of its Christianity; it observes it diligently even in these present times; and it will strive to observe it, with God's help, even in the coming times.

For its fidelity, submissiveness, humility, and goodwill, it received glory from them, as from servants of God, given to His good: it received from them that *quod et maximum et optimum inter homines est* [that which is greatest and best among men]. It received from them what man desires by nature. It received from them the good that among all the goods of this world is the greatest, and best, and dearest, and most desired. It received from them, we say, the glory of its good deeds; that is, it received liberty from them, endowed with laws, protected with privileges, confirmed with constitutions, and transmitted by oaths unchanged to future ages, so long as they shall be. And that golden or rather invaluable, if we may so call it, freedom—what, and of what weight, is it? Only he does not know and does not see this who has not placed it on the scale of virtue and weighed it with every good of this world. That good, as Sallust said—"*Nemo bonus nisi cum anima simul amittit* [no one good gives it up except together with his own soul]."[2] A good man guards that good like his own soul and does not give it up until he also gives up his soul.

2.   *Salust. De conjur. Catil.* [Sallust, *The War with Catiline,* 33].

For the above-mentioned honorable deeds and bold acts of
courage that the noble Ruthenian nation rendered to the Grand Dukes,
Their Lords, Their Majesties the Kings of Poland, it has been given
the freedom by them to sit next to their Graces in senatorial dignity
equally with the two Polish and Lithuanian nations, to give counsel
concerning the good of their domains and of their own fatherland, and
to enjoy all the dignities, prerogatives, the call to offices, freedoms,
rights, and liberties of the Polish Kingdom. This is granted to it as a
nation united and incorporated in community of honor and in unity of
body, as equal with equal, as a free nation with the free Polish nation, to
the princes, lords, nobility, and knighthood, to the priestly and the lay
estates. Likewise at the same time the appropriate rights and liberties
are given to the people of the burgher condition of that nation for its
fidelity of obedience and humility of goodwill.

Which inestimable freedom we commonly call our jewel purchased
by blood. Which is in temporal, worldly use more pleasant to us than
the greatest possessions, dearer than health, more important than life;
for it is that which is founded on the life of all temporality, that is, on
the honor gained through the virtue of piety and courage. The loss of
which makes a man unworthy of any dignities, dishonorable, ignoble,
and an exile; as, to the contrary, its acquisition makes even the basest
man exalted, splendid, noble, glorious, with access to all dignities, and
capable of every honor and calling. Whence Diogenes, when asked what
is best in human life, answered: *"Libertas: haec enim semel amissa non
facile recuperatur"*—"liberty, which once lost is not easily regained."
He preferred rather to lick Athenian salt with his liberty intact than to
live with it diminished on the abundant wealth of Craterus.[3] For what
is freedom for us if not the power of living in freedom, that is, to live
not at the nod of the powers but according to laws voluntarily accepted?
And what is heavier, more unbearable in human life than slavery? In
view of which, what else does that free Lacedaemonian nation say to
King Philip of Macedonia, who was threatening them with death and
asking what they thought at that time of their sudden danger and death:

---

3.   *Laer. lib. 6* [Diogenes Laertius, "Life of Diogenes the Cynic," in *Lives
of Eminent Philosophers,* 6.2; the story about Athenian salt at the sumptuous
fare of Craterus's table is at 6.2.57; at 6.2.69, Diogenes declares that *freedom
of speech* is the most important thing in life].

"*Nisi quod fortiter, moriemur* [Only that we might die valiantly]"? And Plutarch concludes just there: "*Quam dulce bonum est libertas, quae morte emitur; quam misera res est servitus, cui mors anteponitur* [What a sweet good is liberty, which is surrendered with death; what a miserable thing is slavery, to which death is preferred]."[4]

Sweet, sweet indeed is liberty, since in exchange for it not only property, not only health, but even life itself is gladly risked. The risk of life, as we see, gains liberty, risk of the same protects it once acquired, and it is not lost except with the risk of life. *Nemo servire cogitur, qui mori paratus est* [No one is thought a slave who is ready to die]. He can never be subjugated who risks his neck for liberty. Whence that illustrious Brutus, giving advice to his enslaved fellow citizens, says, "We must choose one of two: *aut vitam liberam, aut mortem gloriosam* [either a free life or a glorious death]. For it is an incomparably more useful thing to die honorably than to live ignobly."[5] And in this matter that blessed apostle, whose teaching we placed as the foundation of our of our oration, also subscribes to this when he says: *Satius est mihi mori, quam quis gloriam meam evacuet;* "it were better for me to die, than that any man should make my glorying void."[6] Such is the risk of glorious death.

Our Ruthenian nation acquired that liberty under its princes; with it, it was incorporated into the most noble Polish Kingdom; it possesses it, confirmed by privileges and the oath of their Majesties the Polish Kings; it maintained it, untouched throughout all preceding centuries, and it is supposed to maintain it even today, to pass it on to its descendants, and to continue to pass it on so long as it and its Grand Dukes exist, that is, with God's help, until the end of the world. With that freedom the Ruthenian nation was united in one body, was joined, and had its support in one head, together with the free Polish and Lithuanian nations. To which King Sigismund August of blessed memory, in the matters granted to it, deigns to give to such testimony: "The entire Ruthenian land from old times, among other leading members, is joined to the Polish Crown by our ancestors the Kings of

4.   *Plut. in Lac.* [The source of Smotryc̆kyj's reference remains unclear.]
5.   *Bruson. lib. 3, cap. 33 ex. Liv.* [The source of Smotryc̆kyj's reference remains unclear.]
6.   1 Cor. 9[:15].

Poland; and we restore and join its citizens, all in general and each one in particular, to the Kingdom of Poland, as equal to equal, free people to free, as a proper and genuine member, to its proper body and head, unto community, unto honor, unto propriety, and we make them equal with other citizens of the Crown, and we make them and find them to be participants in all the liberties, freedoms, and calling of the Polish Crown; and we promise and will be obliged to appoint each according to his virtue and dignity and according to our pleasure to the offices of our castles, holdings, and courts, and to allow to the bench of our councils princes, lords, gentry, and knighthood, both of the Roman and of the Greek order."[7]

What then? Is it a matter of glory for the free nation simply to be known to be free? Is it only for its adornment that it is adorned with this invaluable jewel of freedom? Nothing of the sort. The first and the foremost member of this body, the head, has its first ornament and pleasure from the fact that it, to the greatest degree, enjoys and takes pleasure in all the ornaments of the body as in its own. The ornament of liberty upon the subjects is their own ornament; it adorns and makes to rejoice above all, however, their superiors, the princes and kings. For as the jewel of liberty is pleasant and sweet to every noble nation, so their jewel of liberty is also pleasant and sweet to the superiors of such magnificent spirit, the kings and princes: to rule in freedom over a free nation. Since, as a healthy man does not wish that sick men serve him, does not desire that his close friends be ill, but both wishes that they be healthy and rejoices and delights in their health as in his own, so also the magnificent lord does not desire that slaves serve him and does not wish to look upon the slavery of his dear friends; but reigning as a free man over a free nation, he rejoices and takes delight in their freedom as in his own.

It is true that it would be fitting for us who, having acquired freedom in Christ the Lord, are supposed to be dead to the world and live only to Christ the Lord,[8] to recommend not the freedom that is of this world, which is only temporal, and often the cause of dissoluteness and license, but that which the Spirit of God causes, about which it is

7.   In the Privilege of Incorporation. [Here Smotryc'kyj got it right— Sigismund II August, and not Sigismund I. See above, pp. 249 and 276.]
8.   [Gal. 2:19.]

said: *Ubi Spiritus Domini, ibi libertas,* "where the Spirit of the Lord is, there is liberty."[9] Which the Son of God brought to us through His death on the cross, as He Himself deigns to speak to us about this: *Si vos Filius liberaverit vere liberi eritis,* "if the Son shall make you free, ye shall be free indeed."[10] That is, it would be fitting for us to criticize the liberty of the world in its dissoluteness, the liberty of the body in its desires, and the liberty of Satan in his temptations; and to recommend the servitude of Christ the Lord in not loving the world or those things that are in the world, as the lust of the flesh, the lust of the eyes, and the pride of life.[11] "For he that is called, being free," says the blessed apostle, "is Christ's servant."[12] And whoever is a servant of Christ the Lord is granted liberty in the Lord, the liberty that teaches us to speak well and to do well, that is, to live well and to die well.[13] So that we recommend the freedom that teaches us to yield our members as instruments of righteousness unto holiness,[14] that admonishes us to be free of sin and to be servants of righteousness, so that being free of sin, whose end is death, and having become servants of God, we might have our fruit unto holiness and our end everlasting life.[15] Thus it would be fitting for us, who are dead to the world, to recommend rather the servitude of Christ the Lord than the freedom of the world, as the blessed apostle says: *Servus vocatus es, non sit tibi curae, sed etsi fieri liber, magis utere;* "art thou called being a servant," he says, "care not for it, but if thou mayest be made free, enslave yourself more."[16]

How can we manage to satisfy both recommendations, that is, of liberty and of servitude, without offense to conscience, since those things—liberty and servitude—are *e diametro* [diametrically] opposed? It can be done, and easily, if we examine the foundation of both of these things internally and not superficially. The foundation of the liberty about which we are speaking is virtue, without which liberty can neither be acquired nor made lasting. The foundation of the servitude of Christ

9.   2 Cor. 3[:17].
10.   Jn. 8[:36].
11.   1 Jn. 2[:16].
12.   1 Cor. 7[:22].
13.   Jas. 2[:12].
14.   Rom. 6[:13].
15.   Rom. 6[:22].
16.   1 Cor. 7[:21].

the Lord is virtue, which in the enslaved body makes the soul free. Therefore, to extol the freedom of subjection and the spiritual servitude of the body is to extol virtue. Thus without harm to the conscience, both of these things—liberty, as we said, and servitude—can, through such a mutual exchange, be extolled even by us who are dead to the world: just as the extolling of our liberty bears in itself, of necessity, the servitude of the body in its desires and passions, so the extolling of servitude bears the liberty of the spirit in its righteousness unto holiness.[17] So that, thus prepared, redeemed at the price of the invaluable blood of Christ the Lord, we not wish to be slaves of man, but that we enjoy the liberty that the will of God wishes to have us enjoy, that with well doing you may put to silence the ignorance of foolish men, as free, and not using your liberty for a cloak of maliciousness, but as the servants of God[18] being subservient to God in the hidden places of our hearts and in our reins, which he searches out in lordly fashion as their creator;[19] being subservient to every human office for the Lord, whether to the king as the foremost, or to the powers, as to those who are sent by him, both as punishment of evildoers and for the praise of them that do well.[20]

Thus enjoying both of them freely, the above-mentioned liberty and servitude, we and our entire Ruthenian nation were always submissive and faithful subjects, are now, and, to the extent that, through His holy help, it is in our power, we will continue to be so unto our Lord God, as the Creator, the Giver of all good things, and the Caretaker for the good of our souls and bodies. We were submissive and faithful subjects, are now, and will be, with God's help—in our ancestors, ourselves, and our descendants—to our lords, the Grand Dukes of Rus', their Majesties the Kings of Poland, as the rulers, the guardians of the common peace, and our defenders from every injustice. We were, we say, submissive and faithful subjects of our lords, we are, and, God granting, we will be, not having allowed, not allowing, and, God granting, not intending to allow ourselves to be charged with even the least insubordination and infidelity.

The past centuries are trustworthy witnesses to what we say; the

---

17.   1 Cor. 7.
18.   1 Pet. 2[:15–16].
19.   [Jer. 11:20, 17:10, 20:12; Ps. 7:9, 26:2, 44:21; Rev. 2:23.]
20.   1 Pet. 2[:14].

present years are as well; God granting, the coming ones will be too. For so long as virtue is renowned as such for its property, it suffers no change, and although *dente mordaci roditur* [it is gnawed at with the biting tooth] of envious Theons, *non tamen arroditur* [nonetheless, it is not gnawed through].[21] Past centuries testify, we say, to the virtue of our Ruthenian nation, that is, to its submissiveness and absolute fidelity to the Grand Dukes of Rus', their lords, their Majesties the Kings of Poland. Annals and chronicles are a witness; a witness, too, is the fresh memory passed down by subsequent ages from one to another, from ancestors to descendants, that, having learned the Christian faith, our Ruthenian nation learned at the same time the apostolic teaching that we placed at the foundation of our oration, having it established in itself and given for use by the very law of nature: not to hinder or to oppose in any way the powers given to it by God, but to be submissive and faithful to them in everything. There are eternal *munimenta* [bulwarks, legal proofs] where one sees how faithfully, with what strengths, with what risk of property, health, and life our Ruthenian nation declared its submissiveness and fidelity to their Majesties, the Kings of Poland, the Princes their lords. There are fields strewn with the corpses of enemies; there are rivers covered with bloody streams in their times through their courage, here in the fatherland and in foreign kingdoms and principalities. Both of which are a sure sign and an eternal *munimentum* of the fidelity of the Ruthenian nation to the princes, their lords, their Majesties the Kings of Poland.

Some unhappy man, unmindful of all severity of common law, of any obligation of natural law, and of all responsibility of commanded law, in spite of the fear of God and the good reputation of good people, after attempting to submit to suspicion the well-disposed submissiveness of our Ruthenian nation to its superior authority and its genuine fidelity toward him in the present times, during the happy reign over us of Your Royal Majesty, the King, Lord, Lord, Our Gracious Lord, made bold to insult almost the entire nation (almost the entire, we say, for we mean the entire nation that is under the ancient eastern spiritual obedience) with ignominious calumny, since he was not able to find even the least shadow of a proper occasion to do so. He made bold to dare to dishonor its fidelity with the stain of treason and to submit untruth about it in

---

21. [Cf. Horace, *Ep.* 1.18.82. "Theon's tooth" is proverbial for calumny.]

place of the truth to the entirely honorable ears of Your Royal Grace, which nothing vain is to reach,[22] lest, as the wise man says, something vain come out of the mouth of the king.[23] And at what time? Under what condition of the domains of Your Royal Majesty? When the enemy of the Holy Cross lay in wait for the Christians with fire and sword; when the Mussulman marched in person with countless armies to the domains of Your Royal Majesty, our dear fatherland—at that time that unhappy man submitted us and our entire faithful Ruthenian nation of the ancient Greek religion to Your Royal Majesty's most excellent ears as traitors of the fatherland who had entered into a conspiracy with the pagan. With what propriety? With what shadow of a pretext?

In the year 1620 there arrived in the domains of Your Royal Majesty, Our Gracious Lord (by what providence, God alone knows) a pious man, Theophanes, patriarch of Jerusalem, having certain testimony about himself from three fellow patriarchs, his brothers, and from the Jesuits who live in Constantinople, that he is who he was said to be. At whose request, with respect for his so high dignity, he received from Your Royal Majesty permission to stay in the domains of Your Royal Majesty and for free passage through them. Living some length of time in Kyiv with Your Royal Majesty's permission and the demonstration of Your Gracious Royal kindness toward him, partially through his pastoral duty, partially at the request of those whose concern it was to take care for the spiritual deficiencies in our nation, he substituted *legitimos pastores in locum illegitimorum pastorum* [legitimate pastors in place of illegitimate pastors], in place of those spiritual authorities of the Ruthenian Church, who, against the spiritual laws, had abandoned the patriarch of Constantinople, the highest pastor given to the Ruthenian nation through divine providence: he consecrated a metropolitan and bishops. After which act of consecration he remained in Your Royal Majesty's domains almost a half year without any disrespectful opinions about him, without any suspicion of any sort of enmity toward the domains of Your Royal Majesty.

He had barely left the state (*en subitam metamorphosin* [behold the sudden transformation!]) when some unchecked tongue represented him—such a great archpriest who had arrived happily from the grave of

22.   [Sir. 51:6.]
23.   Prov. 24.

God through divine dispensation to the domains of Your Royal Majesty, the highest pastor of the holy see of Jerusalem, a man of high virtues, highly honored by Your Royal Majesty—to the Majesty of Your Royal Majesty, Our Gracious Lord, as a Turkish spy, as a common man, a layman, a main enemy of the domains of Your Royal Majesty; and the persons of the hierarchy restored by him, the metropolitan and the bishops, as traitors to their fatherland, who undertook, through that spy, in a conspiracy with the Turk, to betray the domains of Your Royal Majesty, Our Gracious Lord, and their dear fatherland, to the hands of the pagans. Through which mendacious allegation, in universals of Your Royal Majesty published from both chancelleries, that of the Crown and that of the Grand Duchy of Lithuania, that pious patriarch, suspected of no evil toward the domains of Your Royal Majesty, was represented to the public as an impostor; and from our hierarchy restored by him, honorable men, faithful subjects in every respect to Your Royal Majesty, Their Gracious Lord, Metropolitan Borec'kyj and two bishops, Kurcevyč and Smotryc'kyj, were represented as traitors.

Having leapt at Your Royal Majesty's public pronouncement against those three persons from among us because of what they desired with all their hearts to have, apostates from the Holy Eastern Church, surmising more—and improperly—than what was found in Your Royal Majesty's circular letter, not only ordered that those circular letters published in Your Royal Majesty's chancellery be posted in every city throughout almost all of Lithuania and White Russia, having revised them to include other persons in addition to those three mentioned *specialiter* [specifically]; rather, having made bold to target absolutely all of Rus' who remain under our normal obedience to the patriarch of Constantinople with those circular letters concerning treason published at the order of Your Royal Majesty, they cited entire cities, entire palatinates, entire brotherhoods, as *complices* [confederates] in that same treason, under their own name and that of others, in the castle books of Braclav,[24] if not also elsewhere in the Grand Duchy of Lithuania. This belonged to the secular authority—although the

24. [This is the reading—Bracław—found in the nineteenth-century edition. I used (*AJuZR* 1:7:521), as I was unable to find a copy of the original printing. Perhaps Braslav (Brasław) would be more likely here, since Smotryc'kyj goes on to say "if not elsewhere in the Grand Duchy of Lithuania."]

allegation was incorrect—for the keeping of the common peace (even though, by the grace of God, matters were not tending in the least toward unrest), and not to those who try to pass themselves off as clerics *per nefas* [impiously].

And they declared these two things as arguments for imposture and treason. First, that that holy patriarch was supposed to have caused the Zaporozhian army of Your Majesty the King to rebel so that it would refuse to serve Your Royal Majesty, Our Gracious Lord, against the pagan Turk, effecting all that through those above-mentioned persons, Borec'kyj, Kurcevyč, and Smotryc'kyj, who, supposedly having taken a dislike to Your Royal Majesty and developed a taste for Turkish rule, dedicated themselves to the goal of giving up the fatherland all the more quickly and easily to destruction at the hands of the pagan. Second, that above-mentioned father patriarch consecrated a metropolitan and bishops allegedly for the destruction and dishonor of the authority of the majesty of Your Royal Majesty without the will, knowledge, submission, and permission of Your Royal Majesty. These two arguments were also announced as somehow in the circular letter published from the chancellery of Your Royal Majesty. The result itself has clearly shown Your Royal Majesty of what weight both are.

For as to the first, the very fact of the eager presentation for that expedition of Your Royal Majesty's Zaporozhian army, and of its illustrious service, destroys it and testifies that as nothing ever came from that holy archpriest of God, the patriarch of Jerusalem, for disturbing the customary submissiveness and constant readiness of the soldier to serve Your Royal Majesty, His Grace, so also nothing came from us, the persons who have been unjustly accused. Not with empty words, nor with a vain voice, but with its knightly heart did that army of Your Royal Majesty—with the help of almighty God, with the blessing of that holy man, and with the prayers to God of the hierarchy that was erected by him, having waded high in pagan blood next to the forces of Polish and Lithuanian knighthood—remove that calumny from those calumniated persons; and it stands ready foremost, with God's help, to remove it against every enemy of Your Royal Majesty.

As to the second argument—that the patriarch of Jerusalem restored in our Church the hierarchy overthrown by the apostates unto the destruction and dishonor of the authority of the majesty of Your Royal Majesty—we honestly report to Your Royal Majesty how the matter stands: that it was never in the humble intention or in the pious heart of that holy patriarch that any dishonor to the most excellent majesty of Your Royal Majesty should have had a place in him. He went the way, as they say, of divine laws; he followed the laws of the Holy Eastern Church, which were submitted by the holy universal councils through canonical decrees and confirmed by eternal custom. For the Holy Eastern Church was accustomed first to consecrate the elected person and then to present him. Assured by the decree of conciliar laws and by the constant Church custom in all times, he restored the hierarchy that had been oppressed in the Ruthenian Church, and he consecrated for it a metropolitan and bishops, not unto any dishonor, to say nothing of destruction, of the authority of the majesty of Your Royal Majesty, but for the care of the obligation of his archpriest's office; and although this was done without presentation, it was not done without the will and the permission of Your Royal Majesty, Our Gracious Lord. For at the time when Your Royal Majesty deigned to guarantee and affirm our rights, freedoms, and liberties, Your Royal Majesty, Our Gracious Lord also deigned to grant your will and permission *libere* [freely] and *deliberate* [deliberately] to the fact that no one else but the patriarch of Constantinople, either himself or through an exarch or some plenipotentiary of his spiritual eminence, should consecrate a Ruthenian metropolitan.

For that is the eternal right of the Ruthenian nation and its foremost liberty, with which it was incorporated into the Polish Kingdom and which all Your Royal Majesty's ancestors, Their Majesties the Kings of Poland, left intact when they acceded to that noble domain and which, having maintained it as *sacrosanctum* [a most holy thing] untouched throughout their entire age, they left it in its integrity when they departed for that other world. Your Royal Majesty deigned to leave for the coming ages an important *specimen* [token] of your will and permission of the right sworn to the Ruthenian nation in your special circular letter given to Father Jeremiah of blessed memory, Patriarch of Constantinople, after he guaranteed and made known through it that in the Polish Kingdom the patriarchs of Constantinople have had since ancient times the power of jurisdiction over the Ruthenian priesthood. Thus if consecration took place without submission or presentation to Your Royal Majesty, it was not unto any dishonor of the majesty of Your Royal Majesty, Our Gracious Lord, that this occurred; rather our very right, violated by our apostates, caused this. Some wise man said: *Quemadmodum in aedificio ruunt omnia uno aliquo ligno exempto: sic unius legis mutatio, ruinam trahit omnium;* "just as in a building everything falls down when only one beam is removed, so also the change of one law draws after it the downfall of all laws," and thence countless confusions must arise *necessarie* [of necessity].

For where the foundations of the house fall down, the walls must also fall down. The presentation that usually came from Your Royal Majesty, Our Gracious Lord, had built upon it a presentation that usually went to Your Royal Majesty; since the former, as the foundation, suffered a change, to the violation of our laws, it also brought down the second one that was to go to Your Royal Majesty, which was built upon it. So long as the former remained whole, the latter also of necessity had to remain in the same integrity. With the downfall of the former, the latter too had to fall of necessity.

For it is known that where His Majesty, King Sigismund August of blessed memory, in the privilege he gave to the Ruthenian nation, takes an oath for himself and for his descendants, the Kings of Poland, he deigns to promise "neither to diminish nor to suppress the spiritual diginities of the Greek order that are in his domains, but rather to maintain them whole." Likewise, where Your Royal Majesty, Our Gracious Lord, in the privilege given by you to our Ruthenian nation, also promising for yourself, deigns to guarantee that Your Royal Majesty is not to give out the spiritual dignities and goods of the Greek religion according to any other law but according to the foundation of the Ruthenian nation and its ancient custom. It is also known, we say, that His Majesty the King, Sigismund August of blessed memory, and Your Royal Majesty, Our Gracious Lord, do not deign to give to the Ruthenian nation some new, previously nonexistent law, but to confirm and to guarantee their old law and ancient custom, with which it was incorporated into the Polish Crown.

In addition to this, it is also known that the privilege was given by His Majesty, King Sigismund August of blessed memory, at a time when the spiritual authorities of the Ruthenian Church and the entire Ruthenian nation of the Greek religion, according to the laws and customs of our Greek order, were under the obedience of the patriarch of Constantinople. But the privilege was given by Your Royal Majesty at a time when the spiritual authorities of the Ruthenian Church, against the laws and customs of our Greek order, had abandoned the obedience to their proper pastor, the patriarch of Constantinople. Wishing to return to its proper order that apostasy of the spiritual authorities from obedience to the patriarch on the grounds that it was illegal, done against the law of foundation and the ancient custom, Your Royal Majesty, Our Gracious Lord, as the guardian and defender of our laws, deigns to guarantee to submit to us, the Ruthenian nation, our spiritual authorities according to the foundation and the ancient custom *in posterum* [in posterity]. Which promise of Your Royal Majesty, Our Gracious Lord, to submit in the future the spiritual authorities according to the foundation and our ancient laws, also shows that the right of presentation that usually came from Your Royal Majesty has been violated; and it promises to restore that violated law. Which could not come to its order and restoration otherwise except that, according to the merciful promise of Your Royal Majesty, the spiritual authorities, who were, according to its foundation and ancient custom, under the obedience of the patriarch of Constantinople and consecrated by him, be returned to our Ruthenian Church.

For that reason, then, Most Excellent Merciful King, Our Gracious Lord, the presentation that usually went to Your Royal Majesty had to be omitted at the time when that consecration was received, since it had fallen into disuse: for the apostate Ruthenian clergy had overturned by force the presentation that usually came from Your Royal Majesty. Through the restoration of the Ruthenian hierarchy, the latter will also be restored. For to present the elected of the Ruthenian Church to the [in]appropriate pastor is not to gain spiritual authorities for it, but to lose them; it is not to maintain its law of foundation and its ancient custom, but to suppress it. Since Your Royal Majesty, Our Gracious Lord, deigns to promise in the aforementioned privilege and in last year's constitution to restore and to place in its proper order that law of foundation and ancient custom, so that Your Royal Majesty's gracious promise might achieve its desired effect all the more quickly and easily, the father patriarch of Jerusalem consecrated a metropolitan and bishops to those spiritual authorities; not for any dishonor to the majesty of Your Royal Majesty, either from his person or from those consecrated, but unto the care of the obligation of his pastoral office, considering as the presentation Your Royal Majesty's certain and unchanging promise, which was made known to him, with this order urgently instilled in us—that we wait for affirmation of what belonged to us from Your Royal Majesty *ratione juris patronatus Regii* [by reason of the right of patronage of the King], which we do.

Father Josyf Kurcevyč, the bishop consecrated to the bishoprics of Volodymer and Brest, appeared from among us—sent by us before the majesty of Your Majesty the King, Our Gracious Lord—at the most recent Sejm in order to give account of himself and of two others who had been calumniated;[25] and, after receiving sufficient account from him of his innocence and ours and after graciously being permitted access to his lordly grace and hand, Your Royal Majesty, Our Gracious Lord, deigned to release him from Your Royal Majesty with these words: "You have our favor. Tell others as well to do the same, they will also receive favor." And then, in addition, there came to our attention other similar words of Your Royal Majesty, Our Gracious Lord, in directives given in writing by Your Royal Majesty to the Zaporozhian army: "But His Majesty the King acts from his innate good nature, that they not hurry with the execution of his orders; he waits so that they themselves acknowledge that they have sinned before His Majesty, as one has already given His Majesty the King an account of himself."

Having heard such words of Your Royal Majesty, Our Gracious Lord, we the accused appeared willingly at the recent Sejm, having undertaken at these words to give account to Your Royal Majesty, Our Gracious Lord, as if from the oral command of Your Royal Majesty. But since during such a great danger to the fatherland it was proper for us to pay attention less to our own honor than to its safety, at our counsel and that of those whom it befitted to give good counsel about this—that we not seem to anyone to impede with our own private matter the public matter of the Commonwealth during such an anxious and dangerous time (since restless heads were accustomed to present our most peaceful matters as disturbances)—we had to abandon for the time being the matter we had undertaken, having commended it to a better time, if the Lord God should deign to lengthen our life and grant us health. With which, through God's help (having first appeared through our *Verification* and through our fellow bishop, who is as guilty in that

25.   [The "most recent Sejm" would have been that which met in Warsaw from 28 August to some time in September 1621.]

calumny as we were), we now appear at this present Sejm[26] before Your Royal Majesty, Our Gracious Lord, through this *Justification* of ours, and in humble submissiveness and complete humility, as faithful subjects of Your Royal Majesty, Our Gracious Lord, we give this account of our innocence.

We recognize that the authority of Your Royal Majesty, Our Gracious Lord, comes from God; and if we should wish to oppose you in any way, we would have to oppose the dispensation of God; and in opposing the dispensation of God, we would ourselves, according to the apostolic teaching we presented, bring punishment upon ourselves, knowing that no power bears the sword in vain, for he is the minister of God, a revenger to execute wrath upon him that doeth evil.[27] Therefore, we prove through God our Creator, to whom nothing is secret, and through the purity of our conscience that we never did anything against the authority of Your Royal Majesty, Our Gracious Lord, either unto its destruction or its dishonor. Not only did we never have any discussions with anyone about betraying our dear fatherland and the domains of Your Royal Majesty, but that impiety, by God's grace, never even came into our minds. We received spiritual dignities, metropolitan and episcopal, without the presentation of Your Royal Majesty for the above-mentioned reasons, but that too was not unto any dishonor of the majesty of Your Royal Majesty, Our Gracious Lord—God forfend—nor was it a reaching for any private gains, but on account of the requirement of the spiritual authority that was extremely oppressed in the Ruthenian Church, without which our Ruthenian nation suffered immeasurable harm to its souls. We do not touch Your Royal Majesty's *jus patronatus* [right of patronage], either in deed or in word; rather we wait in peace for the gracious favor of Your Royal Majesty, Our Gracious Lord.

Our Ruthenian nation, having become accustomed to look to the hands of Their Majesties the Kings of Poland, their lords, for their every spiritual and worldly good, and to await from them their every benefit, presented itself, and was to present itself in eternal memory not otherwise toward Your Royal Majesty, Our Gracious Lord, with the

26. [The work was signed on 6 December 1622, and the title page bears a date of 1623. The work seems to have been addressed to the king at the Sejm that was to meet from 24 January to 5 March 1623.]
27. Rom. 13[:4].

happy accession of Your Royal Majesty to these domains, than it was accustomed to present itself toward the ancestors of blessed memory of Your Royal Majesty, Their Majesties the Kings of Poland, their Gracious Lords, throughout all the ages of their subjection to them: to look for and to await that twofold good mentioned by us, spiritual and temporal, and every benefit from them from the hands of Your Royal Majesty, Our Gracious Lord. And it happened that, in the year of Your Royal Majesty's coming to rule, in the presentation of the metropolitan to the governance and direction of the Ruthenian Church, to which at its request it presented to Your Royal Majesty the person chosen for that dignity, Myxajil Rahoza, Your Royal Majesty, through the required dignity of your superior authority, deigned, according to the eternal custom and the laws of our foundation, to present for consecration the person that had been presented to you to Jeremiah, patriarch of Constantinople of blessed memory, who was in Vilnius then during the presence of Your Royal Majesty in the same city.[28] The presentation that was usually made by Your Royal Majesty, Our Gracious Lord, as also by the ancestors of Your Royal Majesty, was supposed to be made in the future by none other of the highest spiritual authorities (so long as our rights of the ancient foundation, guaranteed by privileges and constitutions, remain whole) than by the natural highest pastor of our Ruthenian Church, the patriarch of Constantinople.

The presentation from Their Majesties, the Kings of Poland, that was usually made, according to our laws, by the patriarch, is the foundation, as we said, of the presentation that is customarily made by the clergy of the Ruthenian Church to Their Majesties the Kings, at the change of which the latter must also undergo change, since the change of the former breaks our laws, destroys the freedom of the Greek rite, and separates the holy faith of the Eastern Church from the Ruthenian Church. For wherever anyone acquires his spiritual authorities, he also thence, through them, acquires his faith. Therefore at that very time when our Ruthenian nation first inclined to political union with the Polish nation and when thereafter it allowed itself to be incorporated with the Polish Crown in one body under one head, it did not do that before the integrity of its faith was promised by Their Majesties the Kings of Poland, guaranteed by laws and privileges and confirmed

28.   [This was in July 1589. See Gudziak 1998, 199–200.]

by oath.[29] Your Royal Majesty, at your happy accession, by divine providence, to the Kingdom of Poland, deigned to leave that integrity of faith and the spiritual authorities of our Ruthenian Church consecrated from Constantinople, to guarantee them by privileges, and to declare the presentation made to the patriarch of Constantinople its custom and law of foundation.

So, as we said, when the presentation that was usually made by Your Royal Majesty to the patriarch of Constantinople, our superior pastor in spirit, suffered a change, it also caused an omission of the presentation that was supposed to be made to Your Royal Majesty. For through the change of the presentation to the bishop of Rome and through the submission of spiritual authorities from him to the Ruthenian Church, Church doctrine and therewith also faith would have to undergo change especially in those points in which the Western Church has differed from the Eastern without its knowledge (which was not supposed to occur according to the authority that belongs to Church laws). Through such a change of the presentation that usually came from Your Royal Majesty, Our Gracious Lord, our so broad and populous Ruthenian nation, which previously could barely make do with seven bishops and the eighth the metropolitan, now was directed to make do with only the bishop of Lviv (to come to whom for consecration the journey from Belorussia was one of around two hundred miles).

Wherefore, looking at the harmful demise of all spiritual matters in our Ruthenian Church, and at the sullying of all its ornaments, and especially at the pitiful scattering into various sects, and at the unbearable oppression in souls (that in many cities children had to depart this world without baptism, adults without the life-giving mysteries of the Holy Eucharist and without the customary ceremonies for the burial of Christian bodies), on account of the disturbing of people of the Greek rite by the Union our Ruthenian nation has made for twenty-seven years and continues to make constant molestations to the point of weariness at every Sejm to Your Royal Majesty, Our Gracious Lord, through our

29.   *Crom. lib. 12, pag. 263–264, lib. 15, pag. 313, lib. 20, pag. 399.* [Kromer, bk. 12, pp. 263–4, bk. 15, p. 313, bk. 20, p. 399. Page references here are apparently to Marcin Błażewski's Polish translation of Kromer's *De origine*, published in Cracow in 1611. An earlier reference was to an original Latin edition. See above, p. 245.]

lamentatious requests that, having left it with its laws, freedoms, and liberties (without which it would have to feel oppressed by the yoke of servitude, for if one is a slave in faith, in what is one free?), Your Royal Majesty might deign to allow it to have its spiritual authorities under its customary obedience.

Through its requests, it received the promises of Your Royal Majesty and the assurance, guaranteed by constitutions and privileges, that it should be thus *in posterum* [for posterity] from Your Royal Majesty and that the spiritual authorities should be submitted *in futurum* [in the future] by our customary pastor.[30] In view of which gracious promises of Your Royal Majesty, Our Gracious Lord, almighty God, through his incomprehensible providence for us,[31] brought *tempestive* [at the right time] to the domains of Your Royal Majesty the above-mentioned father, the patriarch of Jerusalem, and through him restored to the Ruthenian nation the hierarchy in our persons. Since our progression was presented to Your Royal Majesty, Our Gracious Lord, as a transgression and an offense, having been obliged through the obligation of our faithful subordination to be alert in this matter, we immediately gave Your Royal Majesty, Our Gracious Lord, an account of ourselves in writing through our *Verification;* we gave oral account shortly thereafter through our fellow bishop, Father Josyf Kurcevyč, one of the three of us who was accused of treason and offense against Your Royal Majesty; we also give account now through our *Justification.*

And we ask Your Royal Majesty, Our Gracious Lord, humbly and submissively, with our faithful heart, which never suffers change in subjection, that Your Royal Majesty not deign to permit into your royal heart the suspicion about us either of treason or of offense toward Your Lordly Majesty. For we trust in holy righteousness that the spiritual law of the Church of the Greek order will be in our favor with Your Royal Majesty, Our Gracious Lord, the maintenance of which Your Royal Majesty deigns to guarantee to the Ruthenian nation with your royal oath and privileges. Our secular law will be in our favor, which directs the presentation by Your Royal Majesty to the patriarch of Constantinople. Also in our favor will be the violation by our apostates

---

30.   In the Constitution of 1607; in the Constitution of 1620 [*VL* 2:438–9; *VL* 3:184].

31.   Rom. 11[:33].

of the presentation that usually comes from Your Royal Majesty, which has become the reason for our omitting the presentation that usually went to Your Royal Majesty. Finally, this will also be in our favor: that we did this out of necessity and out of a necessity that could not have fallen any other way since our Ruthenian nation, which is under the obedience of the patriarch, could in no way make do without its own clergy.

It was not possible for the father patriarch of Jerusalem to remain long in the domains of Your Royal Majesty. And if we had let him go, we would have been judged ungrateful for the grace of God, through which that holy man's happy arrival in the domains of Your Royal Majesty had been effected; but Your Royal Majesty, Our Gracious Lord, was not easily accessible to us for such a presentation. Wherefore in such an anxious and ambiguous matter we had the fear of God in mind and also the fear of Your Royal Majesty. For if we had not done what we did, the Lord God would have punished us as being ungrateful for His manifest grace toward us; but through our doing it, there would have to be those who made bold to portray our good matter in a bad light to Your Royal Majesty. Which is precisely what happened. For seeing that the matter was not to their liking, our apostates tacked onto it calumny, so that it might seem great and worthy of harsh punishment. If we were what we have been falsely alleged to be, we would ask for forgiveness in vain. But by the grace of a beneficent God, our conscience does not shame us in this; no impiety, not in thought, to say nothing of deed, punishes us,[32] who love the safety of the fatherland more than our own health, and consider as nothing our own honor before the honor of Your Royal Majesty.

Therefore, trusting in our spiritual and secular laws, in our salvatory matter and innocence, in God's grace above all, and in Your Royal Majesty's innate beneficence, we decided to do that which God wished to have from us, having maintained *sartum rectumque* [in order and proper] what is in the hands of Your Royal Majesty, Our Gracious Lord. For God is the witness to our conscience that we seek nothing in this matter that is our own, but only what is God's, nothing for ourselves, but only for our neighbors, nothing temporal, but only what is eternal. By the grace of God, in this matter we are free of ambition, free of

32.   1 Jn. 3[:19–21].

evil intent, free too of striving after private gain; and *libere* [freely] and *sancte* [solemnly], as faithful subjects before the majesty of Your Royal Majesty, Our Gracious Lord, we call on the testimony of the fact that, if Your Royal Majesty deigns to order us to relinquish our consecration to other persons from among us worthy of that dignity, according to our spiritual and secular laws and the ancient customs of our Holy Ruthenian Church, having eagerly submitted to the will and order of Your Royal Majesty, Our Gracious Lord, we will gladly agree to those whom Your Royal Majesty deigns to place on the Ruthenian metropolitan and episcopal sees.

Wherefore we trust that Your Royal Majesty, Our Gracious Lord, will deign to treat us, your faithful subjects, and our entire Ruthenian nation of the ancient Greek religion, according to the law of God and of man. We have the law of man of our fatherland that prescribes for us the presentation by Your Royal Majesty to the patriarch. We also have the law of God that commands us to render unto Caesar in all humility that which is Caesar's and to render unto God in all piety that which is God's.[33] But here, making good what was omitted among us, we present ourselves to Your Royal Majesty, Our Gracious Lord, with consecration, and with it we submit to the grace, will, and consideration of Your Royal Majesty, Our Gracious Lord, asking humbly that the *infamia* [ill repute] that was brought upon our innocence *per calumniam* [through calumny] might be removed by the order of Your Royal Majesty, Our Gracious Lord, and that our honor might remain inviolate with us. When our apostates do this along with us and when they put down from themselves that in which they violated our ancient laws, then immediately the law of both presentations will return to its proper order, and the desired peace will come into being in the Ruthenian nation and in the domains of Your Royal Majesty. Which may Christ the Lord grant us to live to experience in the days of Your Royal Majesty, Our Gracious Lord.

It was truly fitting for me[34] to appear in person, along with Father Meletij Smotryc'kyj, archbishop, before the majesty of Your Royal Majesty, Our Gracious Lord, and, through the merciful grace of the Lord, humbly to thank Your Royal Majesty, Our Gracious Lord, for the letter of safe conduct sent to us from Your Royal Majesty. But our

---

33. Lk. 20[:25]; Rom. 13[:7].
34. [Smotryc'kyj wrote the work, but in metropolitan Jov Borec'kyj's name.]

insufficiency and the great incapacity of my health did not allow this to happen. We trust, however, in the consideration and innate beneficence of Your Royal Majesty, that Your Royal Majesty will deign to receive the subject words of thanks that we humbly offer together with this *Justification* of ours to Your Royal Majesty, Our Gracious Lord, as if they were oral and made in person, along with this *Justification* submitted in writing, to allow us who have been portrayed incorrectly to Your Royal Majesty, Our Gracious Lord, into your lordly grace, to remove the infamy that was published against us through circular letters of Your Royal Majesty, and to return our honor to us as faithful and in no way suspect subjects of Your Royal Majesty, Our Gracious Lord. For which we ask humbly and subjectly of Your Royal Majesty, Our Gracious Lord, falling to the most excellent feet of the majesty of Your Royal Majesty.

From Kyiv, Monastery of St. Michael the Archangel. The year 1622. *Decembris* [of December] the sixth day.[35]

> The faithful subject of Your Royal Majesty,
> Our Gracious Lord,
> Your lowest servant, who constantly
> beseeches God for you,
> Metropolitan Jov Borec'kyj,
> together with all the Ruthenian bishops,
> humbly requests.

35. [Perhaps a new-calendar date, since the work was addressed to the king. If it were an old-calendar date (certainly a possibility), the date would have been 16 December 1622.]

Plate 5. Kyiv, from Afanasij Kaľnofojsʹkyj, *Teraturgēma* (Kyiv, 1638).
Reprint: *HLEULT 4,* 139.

Five Letters

(1627–1628)

Letter 1

[To Pope Urban VIII, Dubno, 6 July 1627.]

Most Holy and Blessed Father:

THE LIGHT OF THE SUN that illumines the entire mass of the earth with its rays seems in these most lamentable times to be Your Holiness's fortunate pontificate of the Church of God, and it is all the more brilliant the more it is obscured by the clouds of so many heresies and schisms. Such that, as I ought to say of it, there is no one who can hide from its warmth. Behold, situated in the most remote appendage of the sinful world, born in the schism as out of necessity, having rolled along in it for fifty years out of ignorance, extracted from the pit of miseries by the rays of Your Holiness's benefices and compassion toward the Ruthenian Church, I am moved, my feet and hands bound, to throw myself in tears at the knees of Your Holiness and to kiss Your feet most humbly. And thus, all ambiguity of words set aside and the schismatic heresy abjured, rendering obedience to You, I am able to say nothing besides: "Father, I have sinned against heaven, and before thee, and am no more worthy to be called Thy son."[1]

But you, indeed, Most Holy Father, forgive me everything I have sinned, with mind, mouth, and pen, against You and Your Holy See, as well as against the Holy Roman Catholic Faith; and I wish to retract all those things, without shame, God helping, so that, by slaying the sin in me that was mine, I might obtain grace in You, Most Blessed Father, and the life which is of God. May You deign to make me as one of your servants. I wish for this one thing, that, as I say from my heart with the holy sinner, "I have sinned against the Lord," thus, together with him, I might hear from You, Most Blessed Father: "And the Lord also has put away thy sin."[2]

I believe that my most illustrious father and pastor[3] has written a rather copious account to Your Holiness about all of this. Meanwhile, I

1. [Lk. 15:18–19.]
2. [2 Sam. 12:13.]
3. [That is, Uniate Metropolitan of Kyiv Josyf Ruts'kyj.]

have expressed in my other letter sent to the Holy Congregation of the Holy Office the things that occurred to me in these initiations of the Union that should be proposed to them, subjecting myself absolutely to the paternal will of Your Paternal Holiness. May glorious God make me to do what you command; and may you, Most Blessed Father, command me to do what you wish.

With another casting of myself at the feet of Your Beatitude, I most humbly beg Your Beatitude's benediction for me. May the God of His holy Church and of the Christian republic preserve You in good health as long as possible. Dubno, the sixth day of July, the year MDCXXVII.

Your Beatitude's unworthy son,

Meletij Smotryc'kyj, called Archbishop of Polack, etc., Archimandrite of Vilnius and Derman' *m[anu] pr[opria]* [in his own hand].

Letter 2

[To Cardinal Ottavio Bandini, Dubno, 6 July 1627.]

Blessed be our God, the God of mercy, who wishes mercy and not a sacrifice.[4] Indeed, I know His will in myself as certainly as I experience it sweetly. For on account of many years of schism, yea, rather as the leader of the schismatic host, who called forth others to the infernal regions through his teaching, writings, and example, there awaited me nothing else but the punishments of this age and of that to come. But to be sure, with the help of His grace, who chooses His own from the mother's womb, with the cooperation of my Most Illustrious Pastor, the Metropolitan of All Rus', who for many years attended eagerly to my salvation, and finally with the labor of the Most Excellent Prince, Lord Aleksander Zasławski, palatine of Braclav, who from his first acquaintance with me deemed it worthwhile to seek methods and means for my salvation, today for the first time, the schism foresworn, I have

4.   [Hos. 6:6; Mt. 9:13, 12:7.]

written to the pope, rendering obedience to Our Most Holy Lord, the father of the entire world and the successor to Peter, and entrusting to the hands of the Most Illustrious Metropolitan my oath and declaration.

And since I know that Your Domination is a most illustrious protector of our Ruthenian Church, I most humbly kiss your hand. I beseech you to consider it meet to have me from now on under your patronage, and I solemnly promise through you to the Holy Apostolic See that, God helping, I will make good, with all the zeal I command, the damages inflicted by me upon the Church of God. Would that by the pouring forth of my blood I might be able to commit some sort of seed to it.

Thus, I beg Your Eminence that you deem it worthwhile to consider paternally what I have written to the Holy Congregation of the Holy Office; and then, to write to me willingly at length, instructing me what it will behoove me to do. For this one thing is already in my vows: not to depart by a hair's breadth from the will of Our Most Holy Lord and of Your Domination.

Die 6 Julii, Anno 1627 [The sixth day of July, in the year 1627].

Letter 3

[Summary of requests to the Congregation of the Holy Office, Dubno, 6 July 1627.]

The sixth day of July, the year 1627.

The request of Meletij the Ruthenian, nuncupate archbishop of Polack, converted from the schismatic heresy to the Catholic faith, which was rendered to the Holy Office.

After offering obedience to the Most Reverend Lord Josyf, metropolitan of all Rus', and receiving absolution from the same on 6 July of the present year 1627 from ecclesiastical judgments, and after carrying out a profession of faith according to the Gregorian usage, he made some more requests. Not wishing to respond to them, the most reverend metropolitan has sent them on to Rome to the Holy Office.

And so, he first requests that he might be able to remain a secret Uniate until necessity should require that he be made known as a Catholic.

Second, he requests that he might use the archiepiscopal title that he had wrongly acquired for himself, consecrated to the position of another who had been legitimately elected and was then still living.

Third, he requests that he might consecrate schismatic priests for three bishoprics of the Uniates, that is to say, for those of Volodymer, Luc'k, and Polack, having received the power, nonetheless, from the *ordinarius*.

Finally, he asks that he might commemorate the name of the patriarch of Constantinople in the sacrifice of the Mass, but with an altered intent, to wit, that he might not so much recognize him as a pastor but might pray to God for his conversion.

Further, the reasons that moved him to conceal his Catholicism for the time being are the following:

When the aforementioned Meletij was in Constantinople a few years ago, he approached Patriarch Cyril, from conversation with whom he learned that he was a heretic; and since, on account of the subsequent plague, he was not able to receive from him [i.e., Lukaris] his profession of faith in writing, now finally, on account of the acquaintance he had made with him and the confidence [he enjoys] in the schism, he would write to him, hoping for and awaiting a response concerning dogma and his profession of faith, which he supposes he will obtain from him more easily hiding under the cover of the schism. The result of his response would surely be this: that once it was acquired, in his book of refutations he might show him to be a heretic and lead the schismatics to the absurdities in the letter of the patriarch, whom they venerate as their head.

He dwelled for many years in the midst of the schismatics, both religious and secular, among whom he indeed obtained for himself a great and commanding love. Thus he would now like to instruct those who trust him in the articles of the faith, the understanding of which— otherwise subject to agreement by council—separates many from the Holy Roman Church, and thereby to demonstrate that the opinion about them of the holy fathers, both Greek and Latin, was one and the same.

In which none of them has so far acquired even the least experience. And this is the reason: the ignorance that is a part of the schism.

For some time now it has been Meletij's intention that some council be convened, in common for Uniates and schismatics, so that, in a mutual disputation of souls, just as fire from the contact of flint stones, an ardent love might be elicited from mutual promises. But since the schismatics do not wish to have anything to do with the Uniates, even at a council, he intends indeed to persuade some of the noblemen and members of the brotherhoods of the schismatics that the schismatics might convene some council for themselves alone, since in this way the light of faith is spread in the minds of many. At this council Meletij himself, received as a schismatic, would be able to set forth and to explain the twofold causes of the present discord of the Church, which was once one, and to cause doubt for them in the schismatic faith (through the reasons that had taught him himself that there is no contradiction in thing, only in words, between the holy Greek and Latin fathers) and to demonstrate that anything that could be found for preserving the discord is nothing but a misinterpretation of the true sense of the writings of the old holy fathers produced by the audacious venture of more recent writers.

But granted that he ought to be an open Catholic for the benefit of those he destroyed in the schism—how should this come about? Certainly in no other way but by writing in answer to those works he had written, as he already has prepared for publication the *Considerations*,[5] which had convinced him to make his regress [to the Union]. If his writings are about to make him known as a Catholic, it seems appropriate that before their publication he might bear the appearance of sins, without sin. Since it has not yet been determined by the Holy Apostolic See, and consequently by the most reverend metropolitan, what title Meletij should use, it seems proper in the meantime that he conceal himself under the mantle of the archiepiscopate, so that, by suffering the judgment of the Church as required, he might be considered to be converting properly.

Finally, if any reason should urge Meletij to overt Catholicism it would be this—that his adherence to the schism not be a stumbling block to others. But this would urge the opposite: for all know that he

5. [Printed as the second part of Smotryckyj's *Apology* of 1628. See below, pp. 501–63.]

was a schismatic up to now, but none (with the exception of some who have been privy to this matter) that he has now come back to the bosom of the Church. Wherefore, indeed, if the fathers of the Society of Jesus and other priests in India can live with the heathens in secular habit, this should cause no one scandal, especially since, with God's help, we will hope for the much greater fruit of holy Union from his hidden Catholicism for the time being than if he were now known by all.

Further, the Roman practice over many years in this matter gives one courage, in accordance with which freedom is given to many in the Greek Catholic rite to take orders in Greece from schismatic bishops and to remain in their dioceses. Otherwise they would be kept out of the borders of Greece, and thus the future crop would be reaped in the seed; and so, if someone should co-celebrate while a schismatic bishop is consecrating, he would be bound to commemorate him [the patriarch of Constantinople] and consequently to conceal himself under the mantle of the schism. This reason, too, prompts indulgence for commemorating the patriarch of Constantinople according to the Greek custom, about which see the end of the second point above.

Nonetheless, Meletij subjects all this to the censure of the Holy Roman Church as fully as he sincerely awaits eternal salvation.

The petitions of Meletij Smotryc'kyj, archbishop of Polack, to be converted to the Catholic faith, remitted to the Holy Office.

Letter 4

[Letter to the Vilnius Orthodox Brotherhood of the Descent of the Holy Spirit, Derman', after 20/30 October 1627.]

My Most honorable Lords and Brethren beloved in Christ!

What I write here briefly I report only for the knowledge of those of you who can keep this to yourselves and take counsel in this, both religious and lay. Let God's grace be with you, and the blessing of my humility and my prayer. On the twentieth day of October, a Uniate monk, Ivan

Dubovyč, arrived here in Kyiv, saying he had been sent by Father Ruts′kyj Josafat [*sic*] in the name of all their spiritual superiors, to His Grace our Lord Father Metropolitan and to all his co-bishops, desiring that our Lord Father Metropolitan and I, together with His Grace, might agree to meet with Father Rutskyj Josafat, who, together with all their cohort, wishes to leave the pope, having undertaken to submit themselves again to the obedience of the patriarch of Constantinople, so that we might discuss from both sides how this could come to pass most gravely and most surely, with the protection of spiritual and secular rights.

Hearing from the mouth of the envoy a thing so pleasing to us, unable to contain our joy, we sent Dubovyč back, informing them orally that "we sincerely delight in what we hear with our ears, and we ask the Lord God that He might grant us to see the result with our eyes, but that, nonetheless, we cannot meet with them, in addition to many other important reasons, also because they are suspect to us in their sincerity. But if they genuinely have in their hearts what they report to us through your mouth, ask them, if they should not wish to write to us (on account of the titles, as you say), that they give you points of instruction with their own signature, outlining what they promise us in this matter and what they wish from us. We, in the meantime—since this concerns the entire Ruthenian Church—will make this known to those of us who ought to know about it, and we will discuss it."

He departed from us with this after promising us that he would return to us either before Christmas, or soon thereafter. What happened here in those times I thus inform Your Graces, and by command of His Grace, our lord father and father,[6] [I ask you that] if there, at Your Graces', something similar should repeat itself with you as well, not allowing such an important thing to pass your attention unalertly, you might send us your opinion in this matter as to what Your Graces think about this. For if this is genuine, we ought not to shun it since we never required of them anything more than that they return whence they fell away. And if it is not genuine, they will see: this cannot harm us, since it is not we who rebuke them for obedience to the pope, but they who rebuke us for obedience to the patriarch. If in addition it should come to Your Graces' knowledge that His Majesty the King and the entire senate wish that we, in the manner of the land of Muscovy, had our own

6.   [Presumably Jov Borec′kyj.]

patriarch (which we cannot oppose, not being able to have any reason to object to this), let Your Graces consider this carefully as well, since just as throughout all the times of this apostasy you did not neglect to take counsel for the good of our Ruthenian Church, even now it befits you to do the same thing, testing whether it is God's spirit in this, as far as this matter is concerned, or that of the deceiver.

Hail in the Lord, Beloved.

Meletij Smotryc'kyj, Archimandrite of
Derman' and Vilnius,
by his own hand.

Letter 5

[Letter to Uniate Metropolitan of Kyiv, Josyf Ruts'kyj, Derman', 2/12 March 1628.]

Inlustrissime ac Reverendissime Pater et Pastor meus Dignissime.
[My Most Illustrious and Most Reverend Father, Most Worthy Pastor.]

On the 29th day of February, the letters from Your Reverence, sent by His Grace, the Prince,[7] together with eight sexterns of the catechism, reached me. Together with them also the *annotationes censoriae* [critical annotations], in which Your Reverence refers me to the works *R. Thomae Aqu.* [of reverend Thomas Aquinas]; unfortunately, I do not have them. I am writing to His Grace the Prince that he order that they be lent to me for that purpose, if they [are to be found] in the Dubno library. I corrected the *Dialogum de processione Spiritus S. secundum mentem annotationum* [dialogue on the procession of the Holy Spirit according to the intent of the annotations] of Your Reverence. I now send to Your Reverence seven sexterns of that same catechism. There remain with me twelve still uncorrected; these too I will send when a sure occasion offers itself. Your Reverence must hurry with the censoring of them— not without great labor, but in the hope of heavenly reward.

7.   [I.e., Aleksander Zasławski.]

The letters written from Rome to Your Reverence delighted me thoroughly. May almighty God deign to help Your Grace, to add strength and desire, so that this soul-saving work—in which Your Reverence finds yourself entirely, through which He deigned to gain me as well, the sinner, for Your Reverence—might receive their salvatory effects from day to day, from hour to hour, with the magnification of His holy glory in the souls of men led astray by the unhappy schism. Your Reverence may rest assured that, as long as, by the will of God, my soul remains in my body, *ultro citroque* [this way and that] I wish to be ready to present myself at the least nod of the head, *etiam ad impossibile* [even unto the impossible] for me, trusting in almighty God that through the holy prayers and paternal blessing of Your Reverence this will become *possibile* [possible] for me by His grace. I also leave to the will of the Holy Father, *s. congregationis de propaganda fide* [of the Holy Congregation for the Propagation of the Faith], and of Your Reverence, how long You will wish for me to remain covert; not for my sake, but for the sake of this holy matter, undertaken more effectively by Your Reverence. For only recently I was in great troubles from the brother monks of my monastery of Derman', who, having received knowledge that I met with Your Reverence in Dubno (Your Reverence's servants told my Heliasz Ilkowski, and he the other brethren), almost all of them had abandoned me and had spread the news throughout all Volhynia. I have curbed that evil now already by the grace of God, in that, having alleged to them that this was an uncertain thing, I caused them not to believe it. And they returned to me again from Luc'k (for five of them had made their way there), among whom was also that cantor Heliasz. And that is what occurred here in Volhynia through their return to me. Thus, Reverend Father, it is most necessary to take care for this; and this holy work, in which You labor for so long, depends very much that I be covert. For as soon as I had been conclusively announced to them, I was reviled and abandoned, and I was deserted by all, as were others of the spiritual superiors of our side, or even more so.

Nothing can make me known to our entire Ruthenian nation with more reason than my catechism. Before which the *Apology of My Peregrination* together with the *consideratio dissensionis dogmatum inter Ecclesiam orientalem et occidentalem* [consideration of the dissent of dogmas between the Eastern and the Western Church] will make a *celibanem* [?], if the Lord God will aid me to complete what I have already begun through the holy prayers of Your Reverence. And in the meantime, that I might have *integram existimationem* [unimpaired reputation] and unsuspect confidence with that side, which I have in the Vilnius Brotherhood, with Father Borec'kyj, with the father archimandrite of the Caves Monastery,[8] and with others, with the exception of certain people of the least weight, who are not given credence. Wherefore it is also very difficult for me to meet with Your Reverence a second time in these days leading up to Easter, or even soon thereafter, especially *secreto* [secretly], at a table or in such a place where I would be seen or heard speaking with Your Reverence; [and so I will] take care of my affairs, if any should come up, either through His Grace the Prince himself or through His Grace Lord Bojarski.

I send to Your Reverence to read what *homo iste superbus* [that haughty man] Izajas[9] sent about in writing and dispersed in these recent days throughout all Rus' concerning my first meeting with Your Reverence (although from hearsay without real proof); until his horns are scraped down to the bone by taking away those monasteries and the one that he gained from Muscovy, he will not cease raging. His Grace Prince Vyšnevec'kyj has a very proper access to remove him from those monasteries of his, which I will show to Your Reverence. Father Borec'kyj writes to me *de data Februarij* [dated February] 9th that he wrote to Prince Vyšnevec'kyj, complaining to him about those circular letters of his. Whereas the access of Your Reverence to His Grace the Prince and to His Princely Grace to moving him can be greater.

I had two writings this winter from Lord Izaak Wołkowicz, who announces to me his vocation to the office of notary of Vilnius. I answered him both times that he should do this *sine ullo conscientiae scrupulo* [without any scruple of conscience]. His Grace the Father Archimandrite of the Caves Monastery was with me in Derman' for two days two weeks before Shrovetide[10] on the way to his estate in the county of Przemyśl. From him there is good hope of Church peace. He is a man pure, pious, obedient, intelligent, being with whom in his

---

8.   [I.e., Peter Mohyla.]
9.   [That is, Isaija Kopyns'kyj, who was then archbishop of Smolensk and Černihiv.]
10.   [That is, before 24 February/5 March 1628.]

house last summer around St. Peter's,[11] while he was still a layman, we conversed about this freely, and I expounded for him the *coincidentia sensus in controversis dogmatibus quae intersunt inter orientalem et occidentalem Ecclesiam* [coincidences of sense in the dogmas that are a matter of controversy between the Eastern and the Western Church]. I stayed with him ten days. He remained very obdurate for several days, not, however, from any stubbornness (as one can see already from the conversation and the following uncertainties); for, when he had them brought together and the heart of the matter elaborated by me,[12] he said: *quid est propter summum Deum, quod nos in tantum a Romanis disterminat* [what is it, by God the Most High, that so divides us from the Romans]? (For he was a man versed in both Latin and Greek.) And from that time he has been much more gentle in his speech concerning the Roman Church and about this difference *dogmatum* [of dogmas]. He promised me, however, not to pass me by on his way back. For he is still at home. If this comes to pass, I will not forsake, with God's help, aided by Your Reverence's holy prayers, to make a purposeful introduction to conversation with him about this face to face. He had intended to visit His Grace the Prince in Dubno, but His Grace the Prince had gone away at that time to the Lokaszes, to His Grace the Prince Palatine of Volhynia. His Grace the Prince could do a great thing in this matter with him and with Father Borec'kyj, through his authority and wisdom, if means could be discovered such that they could come to see His Princely Grace. For both men are well wishing and understanding of the Roman religion.

And that Your Reverence deigned to confer with His Grace Lord Standard-Bearer of Słonim concerning the foundation of the Boskołoboski Monastery, this too is a sign of Your Reverence's ardent heart in the magnification of the glory of the name of almighty God in the Church of our Ruthenian nation. The progress of this will be immeasurably quicker and more successful when the protestation concerning the disturbance of the peace and the non-reception of the protestation at the castle office of Orša is registered. In which His Grace

11. [St. Peter's is 29 June, but since this date is certainly according to the old calendar, this would have been 9 July 1627, n.s.]
12. ["Brought together . . . elaborated": I am guessing here. Kojalovič's reading is corrupt; he has "colrovaną" and "envolvowaną."]

the Father coadjutor of Your Reverence[13] had promised to help me; and I understand he has done it. For Their Graces the Lord founders must thus be more amenable.

As to what Your Reverence deigns to suggest to me *ex literis Romani sedis de querendi modis et rationibus quibus juvari possit misera Graecia. Utinam per s. preces Illustrissimi Beatitudinis Vestrae tanto de me in s. Curia Romana habito conspectui respondeam: ad quod si vires defuerint: alias Deo juvante nunc fuerant defuturos* [from the letter of the Roman see on the need to seek means and reasons by which it would be possible to aid miserable Greece—would that by the holy prayers of Your Most Illustrious Beatitude I might respond to such regard had for me in the Holy Roman Curia: for which if strength were lacking, for another time, God helping, they had been lacking (?)]. For the time being I offer what I know about the matter, as much as the quickly approaching hour of the dismissal of the envoy allowed, and I submit it to Your Reverence's judgment.

I know that the Greek nation, partially through an incorrect understanding about the Roman faith, partially yet on account of those old military incursions *Latinorum* [of the Latins] or rather *Francorum* [of the Franks] against their ancestors,[14] is so very embittered and angered toward the Romans that a means cannot easily be found for the harmony of the Greek and Roman nations set so at variance in heart and, as they suppose, in faith. Which those same noble men discovered who sought, in their times, the harmony of those two nations. One thinks immediately of Michael and John Palaeologus, emperors of Constantinople, who, among their own people at home, and even having the patriarchs on their sides, the latter Joseph [II] and the former John Beccus, nonetheless were unable to accomplish anything. If anyone were to attempt that now, it seems that he attempts a thing already absolutely impossible. And this is also in addition for these three reasons: first, because the Turks interpret *unionem Graecorum cum Romanis* [a union of the Greeks with the Romans] as a *conjurationem omnium Christianorum contra Turcam* [a conspiracy of all Christians against the Turks]; second, because the current patriarch is *dissensissimus* [most in disagreement] with the Lord

13.   [Rafajil Korsak, bishop of Pinsk and Halyč.]
14.   [A reference to the Crusades, especially the Fourth Crusade (1202–1204), in which the "Franks" conquered and looted Constantinople.]

Romans, *imo haereticus est, nisi resipuerit* [nay, he is even a heretic, unless he should have returned to his senses]; third, because the entire Greek people, spiritual and lay, consider the Romans disgusting heretics and especially (of which I am well aware) those on Mt. Athos.

And although *virtus rei in infirmitate humana perficitur* [the strength of a thing is made perfect in human weakness],[15] nonetheless, to the extent that I would not gladly despair in God's grace even there as far as this matter is concerned, I would not gladly persuade anyone else to despair in this. For one hour, by God's will, frequently gives what long years deny. As my God by His holy grace, through whatever means He Himself knows, deigned to draw me, a sinful man and a severe schismatic and an obdurate enemy of the Romans, to holy Church unity, why should I despair that by His same holy grace, by His same limitless mercy He will draw entire nations to love, harmony, and holy unity? Nonetheless—speaking and proceeding according to human possibilities—until through us, by God's help, our Ruthenian Church is drawn to holy unity, it will be vain for us, Rus′, to make an attempt to gain the Greek nation, the Holy Mountain,[16] Muscovy, and other nations of the Greek rite. For it is not only that we halve our strength, and weaken, and will not accomplish anything this time, either here or there; but what is more, we will only make a sort of warning to the Athonites (if we wish to make a beginning with them), such that later on we will make the approach, both to them and to all of Greece, all the more difficult.

Thus it is the paltry opinion of my insignificant wit that we labor and work first entirely at home with all our strength, not dividing ourselves here and there (since we are not doing so very well even in one fatherland, on account of the above-mentioned reason that even our Ruthenian nation considers the Romans disgusting heretics of five heresies), summoning the Lord God for help. Then, when the Lord God causes for us that the Ruthenian nation should stand in holy unity it will be easier, since we will have an already tested method for gaining other nations of the Greek rite. And without Rus′ no other nation can accomplish anything toward the end of unity in the Holy Mountain. For in their monasteries they offer as proof great miracles that occur against

15. [Cf. 2 Cor. 12:9.]
16. [Mt. Athos.]

the Union, and they are similar to the Muscovites in that they scorch
the place in Church upon which a Latin sat.[17] Until their miracles are
criticized and until it be soundly and conclusively demonstrated that the
Romans are not heretics and never were, it will be a difficult matter to
come to agreement with them. They would rather become Turks than
Latins. Which we experience even in our very Rus', which says that
they always prefer to be [. . .] heretics than papists. Wherefore it does
not seem right to me to burden Your Reverence with this labor during
this difficult time for us in our very own nation.

I wrote recently to the father patriarch of Constantinople. (His
Grace the Prince has a copy of this letter. If Your Reverence should
deem it worthy of the ears of people who are [. . .] and wise, having
ordered it to be copied, I entrust it to Your Reverence's will to send it
to Rome.)[18] He did not write anything in response through that courier,
having said that "these things require a longer time for consideration
than the time of your departure allows"; he did, however, promise to
respond.

When, with God's help, the *Considerationes* and this catechism
appear in print, and what we desire comes to be, by God's will, in the
Ruthenian nation, it will be published also in Slavonic for the Russians[19]
and in Greek for the Greeks. At that time a means can be found for
sending the brethren to the monasteries of the Holy Mountain with
these writings, as a ready material for discussion, and not one sought
and found by them.

Ending my writing with this, having entrusted the care of the

17.   [Cf. the radical Antitrinitarian Szymon Budny, who wrote in the preface
to his Polish New Testament of 1574 (fols. b1r–v) that the Ruthenians and all
who use the Church Slavonic Bible "hold the 'Latins' not only for heretics,
but truly as pagans, and especially the Muscovites, who go so far as to plane
down the place where a *Latinin* (that is what they call them) sat, or to scrub it
thoroughly, so that they not be defiled by him."]
18.   [A reference to the letter appended, in a Polish version, to Smotryc'kyj's
Paraenesis of 1629, which was in fact sent to Rome in its presumably original
Latin form. See below, pp. 664–83.]
19.   ["Dla Russian": this would be an *unicum* for Smotryc'kyj *if* the text is
correct here. The context seems to suggest that he means the Muscovites, but
Smotryc'kyj and his contemporaries normally referred to them as "Moskwa,"
"naród moskiewski," etc.]

matter of Your Reverence to the Lord God, I submit myself and my humble obedience to the grace, love, and blessing of Your Reverence, asking God Almighty that He might deign to keep Your Reverence in good health for many years unto the right effecting of the word of His truth in our Ruthenian Church. From Derman', Anni 1628, the second day *Martii* [of March].

Your Reverence's brother, who wishes him
every good thing,
And his most lowly servant.
M. Smotryc'kyj

Plate 6. Lviv, from Georg Braun and Franz Hogenberg, *Civitates Orbis Terrarum*, vol. 6 (Cologne, 1617), 49. Courtesy of Volodymyr Peleshak.

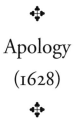

Apology

(1628)

Apology,

Prepared and submitted to the most noble Ruthenian nation
of both estates, clerical and lay, by me, Meletij Smotryc'kyj,
M[isericordia] D[ei] [by the Grace of God] Archbishop of
Polack, Bishop of Vicebsk and Mscislaŭ, Archimandrite of
Vilnius and Derman',
for the Peregrination to the Eastern Lands
That I made AD 1623 and 1624, and which had been
calumniated orally and in writing by the false brethren.

A[nno] 1628, the 25th day of August,
in the Monastery of Derman'.

Ecce quam bonum, et quam jucundum, habitare fratres in unum.
Psal. 132.
[Ps. 133:1: Behold, how good and how pleasant it is for brethren
to dwell together in unity!]

*Pater Sancte, serva eos in nomine tuo quos dedisti mihi, ut sint
UNUM, sicut et nos UNUM sumus. Ioan. 17.*
[Jn. 17:11: Holy Father, keep through thine own name those
whom thou hast given me, that they may be ONE, as we are
ONE.]

Meae vitae unica Spes, IEsus ChristuS
[My life's one hope, Christ JesuS][1]

Cum Licentia Superiorum.
[With the permission of the superiors.]

1.   [See above, p. 231.]

[. . .]²

For the Illustrious Lord,
His Lord Grace,

TOMASZ
ZAMOYSKI
At Zamość,

Vice Chancellor of the Crown, *Starosta* of Cracow, Knyszyń, Goniądz,
etc., etc., His Gracious Lord,
Meletij Smotryćkyj, *M[isericordia] D[ei]* [by the grace of
God], Archbishop of Polack, Bishop of Vicebsk and Mscislaŭ,
Archimandrite of Vilnius and Derman',
Wishes and begs, with his humble bow, the grace of almighty God.

I N THE YEAR 1597 A CERTAIN obscure author, Christopher Philalethes
(I call him obscure because, having hidden his own name, he had
invented for himself the name Philalethes)³ made bold to strike
against two great and hard things, believing—but unwisely—that he
would survive them or even overcome them: for only a stupid man
attacks the sun with a hoe,⁴ and only a raving man attempts to crush
a rock with his head. The first thing is the Holy Eastern Church; the
second thing is Jan Zamoyski of blessed memory, chancellor and
grand hetman of the Crown, Your Grace's father. He made bold to
strike against the first thing, in that, being a heretic in faith, he dared to
hide behind the mask of a confessor of the Orthodox faith of the Holy
Eastern Church; and against the second thing, in that he submitted his
heretical blasphemies to the protection of a pure Catholic, a man of high
virtues and illustrious piety. To whom it happened as it often happens

2.   [The coat of arms of the Zamoyski family and a short poem on that coat
of arms have been omitted; Smotryćkyj 1628a, *1v/515.]
3.   [I.e., "lover of truth." Usually identified as the pseudonym of a Protestant
polemicist from Great Poland named Marcin Broniewski. Smotryćkyj identifies
Philalethes as a non-Ruthenian and a Protestant but does not decipher the
pseudonym.]
4.   [*NKPP* 2:526–7, "Motyka," 3.]

to him who strikes *in lapidem offensionis, et petram scandali* [against the stone of stumbling and the rock of offence].[5] For Your Grace's Lord Father of blessed memory also knew that he was a fictitious Ruthenian and a true heretic, and neither the Ruthenian Church nor the Eastern Church acknowledged him as her son, but considered and considers him a foundling. Wherefore, just as he did not receive protection from the summoned protector, neither did he receive thanks from her whom he allegedly defended; rather he received from both of them what he merited: disgrace and shame. For pure Catholic conscience does not allow one to defend heresies, and the Catholic Church does not arise to thank sowers of blasphemies. A benumbed conscience does not sense even the millstone that has fallen upon it, whereas a conscience that has been caressed by the grace of God does not bear even the least little speck of dust.

The heretic wished to make himself pleasing to the Catholic through what the latter calls impiety and to the Catholic Church through what it censures with anathema. And no wonder: for it commonly happens to him who covers his eyes too much with a mask that not only can he not see a yard before himself, but not even an inch. As the heretic bears a heart that is frozen unto piety—for he is devoid of the grace of the Holy Spirit—so he believes the same concerning the fervor of the heart of the Catholic; and therefore he makes an assault upon it, and he believes that he can overcome it and draw it unto the defense of his blasphemies against the majesty of God. But the Catholic both senses his own fervor, for he is full of the spirit of God, and knows the frigidity of the heretic; and he both regrets his downfall, as that of a neighbor, and he scoffs at his stupidity for attempting what his strength will in no manner allow him to manage. For a true Catholic knows that a confessor of heresies, as also their defender, are held in one esteem and are marked with the same quality—that of a heretic and not a Catholic. If anyone confesses *haeresim* [heresy], he is a heretic; if anyone defends a heresy, he is a heretic. Thus were Eutyches and Dioscorus condemned at the Fourth Ecumenical Synod: the latter as a heretic and the former as his defender.

That this Philalethes was of the heretical error, and not of the Ruthenian faith, I prove from his own writing entitled *Apokrisis;* and I

5.   [Is. 8:14; Rom. 9:32–3.]

clearly demonstrate his foul heretical errors, lest anyone believe that it is the faith of the Ruthenian or, rather, of the Eastern Church, that this heretic describes and that he ascribes as dogmas to that Holy Church, whence she would have to bear shame from people and punishment from God. And with a Catholic heart I decided to submit to the protection and defense of Your Grace, My Gracious Lord, Lord Vice Chancellor, this my work, which was conceived and undertaken against him and against similar writers from our Rus' who wield a heretical tongue: a Catholic writing unto a Catholic; a defense of the truth unto a defender of the truth; unto a born descendant—a correct confession of the faith of the Ruthenian Church from the correct confession of the faith of the Ruthenian Church of the ancestors; unto a pious son of a pious father, so that what that heretic submitted hypocritically unto the defense of the father, the son might demonstrate to the world in his defense as something that never was.

That heretic says to Your Grace's father of blessed memory: "Your Grace once criticized the fact that we people of the Greek religion are troubled in our rite."[6] What he describes in this most disgusting writing of his he calls our Ruthenian rite. But can one find a Ruthenian of the Greek religion of so blind a soul that he would call and acknowledge as the Ruthenian rite what that one wrote and pretended to be Ruthenian? Can a Catholic be found of such paltry understanding that he would not trouble people of such a rite? He would have to be deaf to these words of the apostle: *Fratres mei, Si quis ex vobis erraverit a veritate, et converterit quis eum: Scire debet, quoniam qui converti fecerit peccatorem ab errore viae suae, Salvabit animam ejus a morte, et operiet multitudinem peccatorum* [Brethren, if any of you do err from the truth, and one convert him; Let him know, that he who converteth the sinner from the error of his way, shall save a soul from death, and shall hide a multitude of sins].[7]

If that Philalethes, and before him Zizanij, and after him Orthologue, had not led the Ruthenian nation astray from the path of Catholic teaching through heretical teaching, our people would not have suffered, nor have required "troubling," that is, conversion to the path of truth from the path of errors. Only love would be sought from them, not

6.   [Broniewski 1994, 6; *RIB* 7:1007–8.]
7.   Jas. 5[:19–20].

faith as well, in which action what Catholics call conversion and consider a salvatory thing, the heretics call a hostile thing and entitle "troubling." But let the heretics turn upside down in words, however they see fit, the holy Catholic actions in this matter. I dedicate to the most noble name and protection of Your Grace what I wrote *orthodoxe* [in orthodox fashion] and *catholice* [in catholic fashion] for the demonstration and destruction of the errors and heresies of that Philalethes, and in addition to him of the other two cited by name just a little above, believing that Your Grace, thoroughly and properly informed from this short writing about the holy faith of your holy ancestors,[8] will deign to wish to delight in it and to love these genuine confessors as brethren and co-confessors of one and the same faith; to overcome the adversaries and urge them to repent and to defend against those who, having arisen against the Western Church, strive to overturn also the Eastern Church in one and the same confession of the dogmas of the faith of both; and to be for me a Gracious Lord, benefactor, and defender. I commend myself urgently with my humble priestly services to Your Grace's mercy and protection, and I ask almighty God that He, maintaining Your Grace in good health for many years unto the honor and glory of your holy name and to the faithful counsel of the most illustrious Polish Kingdom, might deign to grant and to bless you with the blessed prosperity that Your Grace wishes and asks of Him for yourself and for all of your noble house in the hope of eternal heavenly delights. From the Monastery of Derman', the 25th day of August, *Anno Domini* 1628.

[. . .][9]

8.   [An odd statement, since Tomasz Zamoyski's ancestors were Catholic. Either Smotryc'kyj meant to say he was describing the holy faith common to the Eastern and Western Churches, or he was thinking of Zamoyski's wife, Katarzyna Ostroz'ka, who certainly did have Orthodox ancestors.]
9.   [A different dedication is found in some copies. The coat of arms of the Zasławski family and a short poem on that coat of arms have been omitted; Smotryc'kyj 1628a, *1r/518.]

Unto the Illustrious Prince,
His Grace, Prince

ALEKSANDER
Zasławski of Ostroh,
Palatine of Kyiv, etc.,
My Gracious Lord
and Benefactor,
Meletij Smotryc'kyj, *M[isericordia] D[ei]*
[by the grace of God]
Archbishop of Polack, Bishop of Vicebsk
and Mscislaŭ, Archimandrite of Vilnius
and Derman',
Wishes and requests the grace of almighty God
with his humble bow.

The glory that enticed me to take refuge under the wings of the protection
of Your Princely Grace and to seek lifelong lodging in it (should the
will of God be such)—at first from afar through third persons and now
heard with my own ears and seen with my own eyes—brought me
gladly to the point where I find myself in actual fact a part of the matter
that for several years I have borne in my mind. Your Princely Grace
was famous, and is famous, in our Ruthenian nation because you take
delight in the Greek rite of your holy ancestors,[10] speaking about it
gravely, and often being piously present at its celebrations. What I had
heard about Your Princely Grace from afar, I have now seen from close
by, and I have come to know that Your Princely Grace values equally
the holy ceremonies and the celebration of the salvatory mysteries in
the Eastern Church and the Western. For you deign to know well that
it was one and the same Holy Spirit in both Churches that ordained
and ruled this matter through holy men. Through which love of both
the holy Greek and the Roman rites, Your Princely Grace would gladly
see, with all your heart, one and the same Church of God, which had
been miserably divided into two, once again made one and the same

---

10.   [Zasławski himself converted from Orthodoxy to Roman Catholicism.
His wife, Eufrozyna Ostroz'ka, was the daughter of Januš and granddaughter
of Kostjantyn Vasyl' Ostroz'kyj.]

and united in one body, both through the unity of the faith, which the Eastern Church has been lacking, and through one love, which is denied to the Western by a great part of the Eastern. And you desire to see progress toward the conjoining in one body in the beginning that has already been made by the Ruthenian nation, employing serious means on your part, which would not cause offense on the part of the Roman Church toward Your Princely Grace and which would not seem irksome to the Eastern Church, going *medio tutissimus* [along the middle, most safely].

In Your Princely Grace's mouth are often the words: "Oh, if only the Lord God would grant unto the Ruthenian nation unification with itself. With His holy aid, through that one nation, the Eastern and Western Churches would soon have holy unity with each other." True words born of pure reason. For Your Princely Grace sees the nations of the Greek religion divided, by God's unfathomable judgments, into three conditions: into the slave condition, into the free but ignorant condition, and into the free and learned condition. Your Princely Grace does not expect this salvatory good either from slaves or from the unlearned, but rather from learning itself, and from that which is in freedom. And Your Princely Grace judges that our Ruthenian nation, by the grace of God, is in the third dispensation. For a slave walks about as if not his own person, an unlearned person as if blind, but a wise and free man can be good unto both himself and unto his neighbor.

After I heard these words from Your Princely Grace's mouth at the time when I was often a guest at Your Princely Grace's estate, I marveled at the marvelous divine judgments: that I should hear from Your Princely Grace's mouth what I had been bearing for some considerable time established upon my heart, and I became certain of the hope that almighty God would make Your Princely Grace the sponsor of my plans. For you perspicaciously deign to judge that the Eastern Church, *sic stantibus ejus rebus* [so long as her affairs stand thus], can never in any manner come to the point where it would return its innate love to the Western Church unless it be through the Ruthenian Church. And this is for this important reason: that all those nations that are under the four patriarchs of the Eastern Church, being from of old in dissension with the Latins through hatred and now also oppressed by pagan servitude and overcome by crude ignorance, cannot of their own accord see that good and demand it. For once they had alleged to themselves that the Western Church was infected with many heresies (such as the Manichaean, Sabellian, Macedonian, Apollinarian, and the Origenist), they did not wish, led astray by such an opinion, to bring themselves to love for it or to think of unity with it, nor can they do so, oppressed and overcome by servitude and ignorance. They neither know nor ask whether what they charge against it is truth or lie; and they either do not read those books that are published by the Latins, which destroy such disgusting calumnies against them [i.e., the Latins], or if they read them, they give greater status to their own stubbornness than to the account in defense of their innocence. In which regard, the Muscovite nation takes the palm, for although it is free it is nonetheless ignorant, entirely unaware of this matter, and hardened in its opinion concerning the Romans.

But our Ruthenian nation—which, on account of its frequent conversation with the Romans and the nearly daily discussions that clearly show the truth concerning these differences in faith between the Eastern and the Western Churches, began to come to itself and partially to cease to believe so crudely concerning the Romans, having in it, by God's grace, men who are well trained in human and divine philosophy, versed in ancient histories and in Church history, who are wise, who know and love God and His holy truth—can sooner manage to become accustomed to thinking well of the Romans and to allow itself easily to be attracted to love the Western Church. And by this action it will become the cause of dear unity for others. For that holy matter was set in motion forty years ago and made no small progress, by God's grace, and makes significant progress daily. For as soon as the entire Ruthenian nation should conclude holy unity, through its authoritative writings and especially through the edition of an orderly catechism of the holy dogmas of the faith of the Eastern Church in the Greek, Slavonic, Ruthenian, and Wallachian languages, it could easily bring to recognition of the truth and to holy unity all the nations of the Eastern obedience and bring about what flourished in the days of our ancestors in the Church of God. Which may the Lord Jesus Christ grant in our days.

Looking upon this, Your Princely Grace deigns to desire the unification of the Ruthenian nation with itself. For now, divided in two, it bites at itself, and it brings itself to its demise, although it could be, with God's help, the cause for so many nations' arising from their fall in faith and in love. Other pious people from our Ruthenian nation see this, as well. I too see it. But since they who see this remain silent, I made bold to speak out and, according to my strength, to demonstrate this to my nation through this writing of mine for the awakening of others, fearing that terrible judgment of the Lord: *Serve male et piger, sciebas quia meto, ubi non seminavi, et congrego, ubi non sparsi: oportuit ergo te committere pecuniam meam numulariis, et veniens ego recepissem utique quod meum est, cum usura. Tollite itaque ab eo Talentum, et inutilem servum ejicite in tenebras exteriores: illis erit fletus et stridor dentium* [Thou wicked and slothful servant, thou knewest that I reap where I sowed not, and gather where I have not strawed: Thou oughtest therefore to have put my money to the exchangers, and then at my coming I should have received mine own with usury. Take therefore the talent from him, and cast ye the unprofitable servant into outer darkness: there shall be weeping and gnashing of teeth].[11]

In addition to the above-mentioned, memorable words of Your Princely Grace, I also remember well, on the topic of this desired Church peace—may the Lord God grant it through the unification of the Eastern Church with the Western Church—a frequent speech in addition to the many Catholic discourses of Your pious soul at that hour in which I presented myself in person to make Your Princely Grace's acquaintance: that "the Roman Church, in seeking unity with the Eastern Church, does not desire to gain for itself any other benefit than eternal reward in heaven; rather it seeks to return to the Eastern Church the original internal and external ornament that it lost through its departure from the Western Church. The Eastern Church has declined in freedom and learning, through which two things there have fallen upon it in its disorderliness anarchy among the spiritual authorities and hunger for the word of God. It has lost love, and it has harmed the faith, and through these two things it has fallen into the punishment that it bears and into the unmercifulness that it experiences. For once it had lost love, it became unworthy of love; and having harmed the faith, it fell from God's grace, and it fell into His wrath, which remains manifest upon it in that it no longer gives birth or nourishes: for it does not have the living and efficacious word of God, which pierces even to the dividing asunder of soul and spirit, by which it would give birth

11. Mt. 25[:26–8, 30].

and which discerns the thoughts and intents of the heart by which it would nourish.[12] Striving that He return to the Eastern Church all this and other lost goods in addition and that He remove the evils that had befallen it, the Western Church takes care that it be united with it, and not for any other reasons."

After I considered these and other important discourses of Your Princely Grace and found them concordant with my heart, I gave praise inwardly to almighty God that He deigned in this salvatory matter, by His holy grace, to cause me to see what He also caused high estates, full of human and divine wisdom, to see before me: for in truth the Western Church does not seek any temporal gain for itself in this when it draws the Eastern Church to unity with it, but only the common honor and praise of God and the mutual love of the brethren. Witness to this are: the school in Rome for the Greeks, or rather for the sons and confessors of the Eastern Church and faith from every nation, set up at great cost and provided with every abundance and need;[13] witness, as well, the college in Constantinople at Galata, where Greek children study Greek and Latin with the fathers *Societatis Jesu* [of the Society of Jesus] without any payment and remuneration;[14] but the most remarkable witness to this is that populous Council of Florence, at which for fourteen months the highest bishop of Rome sustained at his cost the emperor of Constantinople and his brother the despot, with both courts, and the patriarch of Constantinople, with the legates of the other three eastern patriarchs and with his entire clergy, which had come for that council. Whence it is clear that he did not seek any sort of temporal gain, having taken upon himself such great expense throughout an entire year and a half (for he also saw them off at his cost as far as Venice), but rather he purchased so dearly only the love of the brethren and the unity in the praise of God—not paying attention to his loss of gold or other riches that serve this world—so that he not be lacking

12.   Heb. 4[:12].
13.   [Pope Gregory XIII founded the College of St. Athanasius for Greek boys in Rome on 13 January 1577.]
14.   [Galata or Pera was a settlement occupying the promontory on the north side of the Golden Horn facing Constantinople. It was granted to the Genoese in 1267, and it retained some of its privileges after the fall of Constantinople in 1453. The Jesuits had established a school there by the late sixteenth century.]

for them. Finally, witness too the pious, excellent action of the present holy father, *quem amoris et honoris causa nomino* [whom I name for the sake of love and honor], Urban VIII, worthy of eternal praise from people and of heavenly reward from the Lord God in the same sort of beneficence toward the Eastern Church, who (as we hear for certain), through his special love toward the Ruthenian nation, which is also a part of the Eastern Church, is erecting a new school in Rome for Rus' itself at a considerable cost, having assigned all sorts of funds for it for all times to come in perpetuity from certain incomes so that in it the rite be celebrated by monks of the Order of St. Basil the Great in the Slavonic tongue, properly, without any alteration, just as it is celebrated here among us in the Ruthenian monasteries and that the pupils sent from Rus' might be trained in it in the disciplines of both philosophies and that, leaving that place, they might serve the Ruthenian nation in this matter. Neither does this pious father seek his temporal gain through these his salvatory expenditures, worthy of undying gratitude from us (for Rus' did not bring him anything for this, but it receives his significant expense, and, God granting, will continue to do so), rather he seeks only the benefit in heaven of the praise of God alone and the love of the brethren through his holy deed.

Whence is demonstrated thoroughly and made clearly known what Your Princely Grace deigned to say to me during that hour: that, in summoning the Eastern Church to holy unity, the Western Church does not seek its own temporal benefit, rather it desires to bring both a temporal and an eternal benefit to the Eastern Church. For which our Ruthenian nation (*si sapere vellet* [if it should wish to be prudent]) ought to grasp with both hands and thank the one [i.e., Urban VIII] who is so lovingly solicitous toward it and toward its holy rite, and it ought to go to kiss his feet, together with its father [i.e., the patriarch of Constantinople], who would kiss his countenance.

For my part, showing it the path already worn and the means already undertaken, I drew up this my *Apology,* together with "Considerations" of the six differences that arise from us and the Greeks in the division of those two Churches, the Eastern and the Western, asking almighty God in my unworthy prayers that He Himself might deign to cause the internal eyes of our Ruthenian nation to open and to see its salvatory good so that we might rid ourselves of the heretical taunt, together with the schismatic; and, acknowledged by the Catholics as brethren and co-

confessors, that we might enjoy in common with them those spiritual and worldly goods, rights, freedoms, and liberties according to God; so that we ourselves, since God wishes to have us in freedom, maintaining upon ourselves those adornments with which almighty God adorned us through true faith, and our ancestors through their bloody acts of service, might not voluntarily be cast into peasant servitude. For through our own fault we have clearly headed in that direction, and this will meet us without delay if we do not take care for our own salvation in time.

Which, for the greater authority among all Orthodox people, I publish to the world in print under Your Princely Grace's most noble name as a lover of the holy faith and rite of your holy ancestors and as my merciful benefactor, certain that Your Princely Grace—conferring in this matter *oportune et importune* [in season and out of season][15] with those of our side whom it concerns, from both the spiritual and the secular noble estate (as Your Princely Grace does not omit to do whenever the occasion presents itself)—will deign, through your princely and senatorial dignity, in the hope of reward from heaven, to be a more eager enticement and incentive for undertaking the means offered for help and for avoidance of such a great downfall with respect to the spirit and the body. In which matter, may almighty God, the insatiable lover of the salvation of man, be of aid to Your Princely Grace. And I beg Him in my unworthy prayers that, maintaining Your Princely Grace for many years, to the honor and glory of your holy name and to the faithful counsel of the most illustrious Polish crown, bestowing upon you good health and every blessed prosperity, according to His will and according to Your Princely Grace's own will, He might deign to cause you to enjoy soon the unification that Your Princely Grace deigns to wish and to demand for the Ruthenian nation. Amen. Whereby, I commit myself with my humble priestly services to the merciful grace of Your Princely Grace and my merciful benefactor. From the Monastery of Derman'. *Anno Domini* 1628, the 25th day of August.

15.   [2 Tim. 4:2.]

For the Gracious Reader:
The Grace of God.

In accordance with the opinion, blessing, and command of my father and brethren in the spirit, my highly revered lords, I give to Your Grace, Gracious Reader, to read in this my *Apology* what my understanding counseled me, what my will permitted, what my conscience allowed, and what desire of salvation necessarily required of me, having named my work *Apology* because I publish it in part to stop the mouths of the false brethren, who have now for three years been gnawing at my pilgrimage to the eastern lands with a jealous Theon's tooth[16] (not that I should give account of myself before these calumniators, for they are not *tanti* [of such importance], but so that I, obliged by the requirement of my priestly dignity, might make known to every pious person whose ears this reaches that I did this on account of the lamentable state of our Ruthenian Church); and in part to demonstrate and destroy the errors and heresies with which our new writers have made bold for more than thirty years to besmirch our Ruthenian Church and with which they have subjected our entire Ruthenian nation to the suspicion of foul heretical blasphemies against the majesty of God before the entire world. To which *Apology* I have also added "Considerations" that properly pertain to the present state of our Ruthenian Church in accordance with the opinion, blessing, and command of those same highly honored lords of mine, my father and brethren, who, seeing that the house of our Ruthenian nation (for whose salvation they would suffer anathema from Christ their Lord) is pitifully sundered into two parts, moreover, in parts that stand hostilely opposed to each other and that these words of the Savior are coming true in actual fact upon it—*Omnis Domus divisa contra se, non stabit* [every house divided against itself shall not stand][17]—first, before it should come to that downfall (which Christ the Lord forfend), by their pastoral obligation they proceeded to move, with God's help, to avoid that evil, and they commanded me, the least brother from among them and their servant, to announce this. Which I do both *ex debito* [by the obligation] of obedience, as well as *ex officio* [by the office]

16.   [Cf. Horace, *Ep.* 1.18.82. See above, p. 335.]
17.   Mt. 12[:25].

of my dignity, through the means described in this *Apology* and in the "Considerations" added to it.

Wherefore I diligently beg every gracious reader, and especially Your Graces, whom, from the Ruthenian nation, which first and most urgently ought to know of this, almighty God honored with high birth, understanding, and priesthood, and who alone are supposed to take counsel about this, that Your Graces (having from me, as God is my witness, this announcement—that we do not seek any private gain from this, only the salvatory peace of our Ruthenian Church itself; and this declaration—that we wish to be content with mutual, healthy counsel about this), having received what I say as a fraternal opinion with a loving heart, each according to the obligation of your calling, might not allow yourselves to be lacking in this. A paltry person, who measures the gifts of God with his own span,[18] or an intruder, who sticks his nose into other people's business,[19] can have a paltry understanding and speech about this; but from Your Graces I expect that, having heard this from me with a gracious ear, you will wish with all your heart to give thought to rapid aid for our already declining affairs. I commend Your Graces to the Lord God.

Meletij Smotryc'kyj
by the Grace of God Archbishop of Polack,
Bishop of Vicebsk and Mscislaŭ,
Archimandrite of Vilnius and Derman':

Humbly prays in the Holy Spirit, desires, and requests

Grace, peace, and love from God the Father
And Jesus Christ our Lord

for the most noble Ruthenian nation
of the eastern obedience,

18.   [*NKPP* 2:463–4, "Mierzyć," 12. Cf. Mt. 7:2; Mk. 4:24; Lk. 6:38.]
19.   [*NKPP* 2:750, "Ostrowidz."]

for all in general, clerical and lay,
of every estate,
Highly revered and greatly beloved lords, fathers, and brethren.

[†]It has already been three years, most noble Ruthenian nation, since I returned to the fatherland from the peregrination I undertook to the eastern lands, where, by the grace of God, I spent two years with great consolation, not without my spiritual and bodily benefit. And I held with good memory in my undertaking this thing: that I not seek only a change of scenery, having set off for such distant, dangerous, and (for my advanced years and fickle health) difficult lands, nor that I measure the distance of the place in my own person, but rather that I seek in them to strive for myself, but more for you, for what would win for me grace from God, love from you, and would gain for you—before God and before the entire Christian world—salvation and immortal glory. I set off for those parts for the same reason the wise son of Sirach advises us to wound ourselves and to wear out the doorsteps of wise men with our feet.[20] Having listened to Moses the God-seer,[21] I went to ask my father and yours to make known to me and to ask our elders to tell us about the word of life that was brought down from heaven by the eternal Word of God, declared by the prophetic, evangelical, and apostolic writings, confirmed by the traditions that were passed on from hand to hand from the fathers to the sons and given to our ancestors, explained by the holy conciliar decrees of our God-bearing fathers, received by them, and maintained and preserved until our ages in simplicity of heart, purely and immaculately.

I went, I say, to our father and to our elders of the Eastern Church so that I might discover and learn from them about the dogmas of piety, about the faith of our hope, in which we understand and believe that both our temporal happiness and our eternal blessing is established and founded. That is, I went to ask whether our faith is now the same as it was in the time of our ancestors, the faith that had come to us from them by the will of God, and which, not having departed from them, had reached us in our ancestors. Do we drink the same soul-saving water

†   The author gives the reason for his pilgrimage to the eastern lands.
20.   Sir. 6[:36].
21.   Dt. 32[:44–52].

from the evangelical source that flowed from them to us, which our fathers, the founders and builders of the Ruthenian Church, drank? Is it the same pure, light, transparent water? Of the same taste, the same sweetness and healthfulness? So that I, having been informed by them truthfully about this, might inform you, most noble Ruthenian nation, about the same in my peaceful conscience. And I did not do this out of any sort of frivolity, or seeking vainglory in this, God forbid, for my years no longer allowed me to make jokes in serious matters; nor did my dignity (in which, beyond my worthiness, my God deigned to have me) allow me to play games in divine matters; rather I did it, having been attracted and moved by that same serious and salvatory reason that was mentioned above.

†For what can be dearer to man in this temporal life than this invaluable jewel? Faith is the health, consolation, ornament, wealth, and temporal and eternal life of our souls and bodies. He who walks without faith, walks in darkness, walks without understanding, walks without life, walks as the living dead. Faith is in man the power of God that vivifies, fortifies, and maintains him. A man without faith is like unto a beast and is the most unhappy and the most wretched of creatures: *Quid enim prodest homini, si mundum universum lucretur, animae vero suae detrimentum pariatur? Aut quam dabit homo commutationem pro anima sua?* [For what is a man profited, if he shall gain the whole world, and lose his own soul? or what shall a man give in exchange for his soul?], says our Savior Jesus Christ.[22] A man who does not have the faith of God, suffers harm in his soul. With what can he recompense that harm? According to the judgment of the Savior, not even by gaining the entire world. For even if someone were to receive the entire world for his own, nonetheless his end is death, and after death, perdition, that is, the eternal fire prepared for the devil and his angels. His only benefit is from gaining the entire world, and his only gain, the loss of his soul, so that he must suffer eternal torment in hell with the devil and his angels; and what is more, with this addition: *Quantum glorificavit se et in deliciis fuit tantum date illi tormentum et luctum* [How much

†   The effects and fruits of true faith.
22.   Mt. 9 [Mt. 16:26. Cf. Mk. 8:36; Lk. 9:25].

she hath glorified herself, and lived deliciously, so much torment and sorrow give her].[23]

†Therefore, having been moved and prompted by such a serious and excellent reason, I went to our father, as I said, and to the elders of the Eastern Church, seeking for you, most noble Ruthenian nation, as well as for my own soul, the salvatory benefit that would remain for our use unchanged for all time, both in this world and in the next. Guaranteed and assured by which, we would lose our souls here in this world for Christ the Lord, our Savior, and for His salvatory Gospel, and in the next world we would find them saved: *Qui enim voluerit animam suam salvam facere, perdet eam: qui autem perdiderit animam suam, propter me et Evangelium, salvam faciet eam* [For whosoever will save his soul shall lose it; but whosoever shall lose his soul for my sake and the gospel's, the same shall save it].[24] And since the pure and immaculate faith of Christ the Lord causes men's souls to be lost in this world and makes them saved in the other, since here on earth it kills them, and there in heaven it finds them alive, therefore, I did not go to seek the faith, for it had already been found, by the grace of God, by our ancestors. Rather I went to find out whether the one we have now is the same and identical with the one that our ancestors had before. And it was there I went to find out, where it was found by our ancestors, and nowhere else; at that source whence it flowed out and at no other. I went east to the Constantinopolitan see of the patriarch from which you, most noble Ruthenian nation, accepted the faith and holy baptism, the celebration and use of the holy mysteries, and the entire Church ornament in rites and ceremonies, to the patriarch of Constantinople, who these days is the Most Reverend in God Cyril—he who was sent here to you twice on Church matters as a legate from Patriarchs Matthew of Constantinople, of blessed memory, and Meletius of Alexandria, and who is well known to you.[25] And after I offered him my bow and yours and had done a certain part of what I was supposed to do, I postponed

23.　Rev. 18[:7].
†　The goal of the author's peregrination.
24.　Mk. 8[:35].
25.　[Lukaris was indeed twice in the Commonwealth as a legate of the patriarchs, in 1596 and 1601.]

pursuing this further for a time freer than, for many reasons, he had then.

†But meanwhile, having commended myself to the Lord God, I set off further east, and I was in those holy places where our Savior, Jesus Christ, deigned to cause salvation for the nation of man. I was in holy Zion, whence the law of God went forth, and in the city of Jerusalem, whence the word of the Lord went forth. I made my bow in that holy place unto God, my creator, where His most holy feet had stood. I fell to those holy places with my soul and body, where the invisible God deigned to be visible in the body of a man, and I kissed them with my unworthy lips. I was there where the only begotten Son of God, God the Word, was born from the most pure Virgin, where He was baptized, where He preached His salvatory Gospel, where He taught and worked miracles, where He suffered and died, and on the third day arose from the dead, and whence He ascended into heaven and sat at the right hand of God, His Father. I visited those holy places, and, having removed the spiritual shoes from the feet of my soul, I kissed them with a holy kiss, as righteousness and peace kiss at the meeting of mercy and truth. I kissed that cave in which the eternal Son of God was born in the body, and the manger in which, wrapped in swaddling cloths, He was laid down. I sprinkled myself with the water of the Jordan in which He was baptized, and I drank it unto my spiritual joy. I kissed the place of His crucifixion, His deposition from the cross, burial, and ascent into heaven, that is, holy Golgotha, His most holy grave, and the Holy Mount of Olives. And in addition I also kissed other places that had been trodden by my Savior, who proclaimed peace. I also kissed the grave of our most pure holy Lady, the Mother of God, the eternal Virgin Mary in Gethsemane. ‡And in all those places I offered prayers for you and for myself, most noble Ruthenian nation, to our Lord and God, Jesus Christ, that He might deign to grant to us, through His grace, what He himself asked of merciful God, His Father, on our behalf.

I asked that our Ruthenian nation, which is divided in two, might be entirely one, as He is one with His heavenly Father[26] and that we

---

†   Description of the author's departure from Constantinople for the Holy Lands.

‡   The pious affection of the author for his nation.

26.   Jn. 17[:11, 21].

might all be where He is. I brought, for the remission of my sins and yours, a bloodless offering unto the Lord our God at the altar of the Church of the Nativity of Lord Jesus in Bethlehem; at the altar of the Church of the Life-Giving Grave of the Lord in the Garden; at the altar of the Crucifixion of Christ the Lord in Golgotha. If only I could express with my words with what joy my soul was filled then, in what happiness all the senses of my soul and body were plunged there and then, when I, who am wretched, brought a bloodless offering for the beseeching of merciful God for the remission of my sins and those of the entire Ruthenian nation at that very holy place where the only-begotten Son of God, that immaculate lamb, offered Himself as a bloody offering for the beseeching of God His Father for the sins of the entire world. There was not within me any internal or external sense that did not take comfort, did not rejoice, was not glad, that did not feel itself present at the place of the crucifixion of my Savior. My thoughts, with all my soul, were entirely joy and comfort. Holy Golgotha was then for me paradise. I was to experience there how amiable and sweet are the tabernacles of the Lord of Hosts, how beautiful and ornamented the palaces of the Lord for which the soul of the righteous longs and faints.[27]

And it was in the Slavonic language that I brought a bloodless offering in that place of our salvation and in others, when I could have made an offering in the Greek language which is customary there. Which I did to this end: that I, through my special intention, might bring for you, my most dear Ruthenian nation, and for all those nations that praise, glorify, and worship their Creator in the Slavonic language, a bloodless offering that beseeches and cleanses of sin. I did this purposefully to this good end: [†]that I, through my priestly obligation, might submit and commend to the Lord my God, unto His paternal industry, all the Slavonic nations at once, asking His goodness that we all, through whatever judgments He alone knows, might be that ONE requested by Him from God His Father and that He might deign to grant that within His Holy Church the most praised and most adored name of the Father and the Son and the Holy Spirit might be praised and glorified as if with one mouth and one heart. Where immediately, having subjected myself with all my soul and with my pure heart unto

27.   Ps. 83 [84:1–2].
†   Commendation of holy unity.

that ONE requested by Him from His Father, I offered, pledged, and committed myself unto Him, as my Lord and God, for that service in His Holy Church, that I might declare His salvatory ONE in my nation and that I might gain its love for it, as that thing without which there is no salvation according to the strength granted me by Him Himself, with His holy aid, †not doubting in the least that the merciful Lord God will have mercy upon us and that He will give us that ONE we desire if we ourselves will but strive with a true heart and with all our soul, helped by His holy grace. For He is not mendacious, who says: *Petite et dabitur vobis, quaerite et invenietis: pulsate et aperietur vobis* [Ask, and it shall be given you; seek, and ye shall find; knock, and it shall be opened unto you];[28] and further: *Si quid petieritis Patrem in nomine meo, dabit vobis* [Whatsoever ye shall ask the Father in my name, he will give it you].[29]

He will give, He will certainly give, if we will ask Him for this with our fervent prayers in fasting and in alms. When, having lit the candles of love, we will seek from Him in humility and in tranquillity that drachma we have lost;[30] when we will hasten to the doors of the peace of His Holy Church, which is given by Him in harmony and in unanimity, before we knock unto Him, we will already find Him standing at the doors, awaiting us as we knock, and saying: *Ecce sto ad ostium et pulso: si quis audivet vocem meam, et aperuerit mihi januam, intrabo ad illum, et cenabo cum illo: et ipse mecum* [Behold, I stand at the door, and knock: if any man hear my voice, and open the door, I will come in to him, and will sup with him, and he with me].[31] He will give us that ONE, so that we might believe one thing in His Holy Church as with one heart unto righteousness, so that we might confess one thing as with one mouth unto salvation.[32] For if He stands at the doors of our hearts and knocks unto us that we open unto Him and permit Him to enter the house of our hearts and allow Him to sup with us and us with Him, how much quicker, gentler, more merciful, and more eager to

---

†   There can be no salvation without holy unity.
28.   Mt. 7[:7].
29.   Jn. 16[:23].
30.   [Lk. 15:8–9.]
31.   Rev. 3[:20].
32.   [Rom. 10:9–10.]

give will we find Him when we seek Him, knock at His merciful doors, ask Him for what He himself wishes us to have, and for what He asks God His Father to give us, saying: *Pater Sancte serva eos in nomine tuo, quos dedisti mihi: ut sint UNUM, sicut et nos UNUM sumus* [Holy Father, keep through thine own name those whom thou hast given me, that they may be ONE, as we are ONE].[33]

Let us only ask Him for this without cease, let us only knock at the doors of His mercy without departing, let us seek diligently, and let us seek with the candle of love lit, as I said, in the illumined light of peace, for without such a candle we will in no way find that ONE. But He will grant it to us and grant in abundance. He will grant that we Rus′ and all the nations of the Slavonic tongue will find the ONE we seek, and He will grant in abundance that, through our so diligent and humble prayer to Him, the same ONE we seek and find will be found by all the nations that are of the same faith with us. For God desires the salvation of all the people of all the world, seeks all, summons all, and asks, once that He sup with us and another time that we dine and sup with Him. *Beatus qui manducabit panem in regno Dei,* blessed is he that shall eat bread in the kingdom of God.[34]

Oh happy, and most happy, most noble Ruthenian nation, blessed, and most blessed will we be too if we do not refuse to accept from God, who summons us, this His most costly dinner either on account of purchased villages or unproved oxen or taken wives.[35] We will be blessed, in that we will be permitted, through His holy grace, to eat the dinner of His heavenly kingdom. And if we wish to receive this from Him indeed and if we desire to assure ourselves of this indubitably, let us ask Him that He give us as members of His household one mouth and one heart to glorify His holy name in one faith and one love. *Vir enim duplex animo inconstans est in omnibus viis suis,* a double-minded man is unstable in all his ways.[36] The song of a man whose mouth

---

33.   Jn. 17[:11, 21].

34.   Lk. 14[:15].

35.   [Lk. 14:18–20. These excuses for refusing the "most costly dinner" are from the parable of the banquet, which ends with the classic proof text for the use of compulsion in the conversion of heretics and schismatics—*compelle intrare,* "compel them to come in" (Lk. 14:23).]

36.   Jas. 1[:8].

is torn open is not pleasant, as is now disagreeable and unpleasant to God and His saints (unfortunately) the song of the divided heart and the torn open mouth of our one Ruthenian nation, among those who hearing with their ears do not hear, seeing with their eyes do not see, understanding with their heart do not understand.[37] It is the part of the base mouth of those upended and torn from their place, of an ugly heart frozen with hatred and surrounded with enmity.

[†]This, then, was the intent of my peregrination, this its goal, this also its cause. For which reason, as I see and experience, the hater of good attacked me harshly. He did not find my pilgrimage to his liking, and I had barely made it beyond the threshold of the fatherland when he caused such a confusion through them in our Church, in our (I say) Ruthenian nation, already having found vessels suitable for his cause, who even today, day in and day out, boil and roar as in hell, and thereby he pretends that he could confound heaven and earth. The salvatory matter of my peregrination, which I have presented here, grasped the ancient hater of brotherly love by his hateful heart. The unanimity and harmony of the brethren in faith and in love, which is agreeable to God, became disagreeable to him. Wherefore, when I had returned to the fatherland, having acquired for himself a greater and more capable vessel, he shook the entire Church, such that all people stood still as in a daze, all became as if they had taken leave of themselves, and even today he does not cease to shake it. Whence some, and these of little understanding, are only amazed at this; others, and these careless, yawn at this; a third group, and these pious, go about as if scalded, unable to do anything in this matter, unable to understand this clever, Satanic perfidy or to see that he was concerned with the ultimate thing in our Ruthenian nation, wherefore he had to move all of hell against the good that was being done at God's dispensation, had to raise his heel, and to threaten with his horns. Nonetheless, even if he were to move all the infernal forces and powers with all their craft, he will not manage anything. *Durum est contra stimulum calcitrare* [it is hard to kick against the pricks].[38] Satan does not hasten to enter into contest with the Lord God.

37.   [Dt. 29:4; Prov. 20:12; Is. 6:10, 32:3; Ez. 12:2; Jer. 5:21; Mt. 13:13–15; Mk. 8:18; Rom. 11:8; Acts 28:27.]
†   The soul's enemy always envies the good.
38.   Acts 9[:5; 26:14].

For what beneath heaven is as powerful as the truth is powerful? This is a stone against him such that when he should stumble against it, he will be broken, but if it should fall upon him, it will grind him to powder.[39]

†Someone from that fretful rabble will say to me, as they indeed do say: "What troubled you that you went, that you made a pilgrimage to the eastern lands, that you visited the father and the elders? For, by the grace of God, as far as the faith is concerned, we have everything intact; and as far as the confession is concerned, everything at home is complete. You did this without any proper reason as far as the Ruthenian Church is concerned. You did this for your own harm or benefit; and we could have done without that so difficult and laborious peregrination." ‡I answer him as follows before all of you, noble Ruthenian nation: of course, you must feel some amazement in this; and until you examine and consider this matter and cause well, this thing will seem more unlikely than likely, and not without reason. For as long as the sea is a sea, and a spring is a spring, it is not possible that they be without water. Likewise, so long as the sun is the sun, and as long as fire is fire, it is impossible that they not give light. This troubled me, I will answer him, that I, a bishop, nay even an archbishop, in the Church of our Ruthenian nation, did not know what I believed. *Will it seem an impossible thing to you that a bishop not know what he believes? That a master himself not know what he ought to teach—nay even does teach—others? This will seem just as impossible a thing as if someone should assert that a man without a soul is alive, or to the contrary, that a living man is dead. But I will demonstrate to you clearly and thoroughly that what I say is both a possible thing and true, for I will demonstrate that I believed errors and heresies more than the true faith of Christ the Lord that had come to us from the East, that this was what I taught, and this was what I preached. And I fear, most noble nation, that you too are entirely (forgive me) stricken from head to foot with that same sickness together with me. If only the Lord God would grant that this was an invented and impossible thing: that I, a bishop, a man of such high office in the

---

39.   [Mt. 21:44.]
†   Objection against the peregrination.
‡   Solution to the objection.
*   It is difficult for one to teach the faith to another if one has not learned it oneself or if one has learned it badly.

Ruthenian Church, did not know what I believed, or if I knew, then I knew incorrectly and I believed incorrectly. Was this not supposed to trouble me, a bishop? And was this not a proper reason for my so laborious peregrination? Was I supposed to remain deaf to those words of the blessed apostle Paul, when he says: *Oportet Episcopum esse doctorem* [a bishop must be apt to teach].[40] How, then, was I supposed to teach others if I myself did not know what I was supposed to teach them? If I was supposed to teach them to be good and pious, then first I had to teach them that they be faithful and true believing.

†For faith is the foundation, hope the walls of that foundation, and love the covering over both.[41] Thus, as the covering or roof cannot remain standing without the foundation and without the walls, so neither can love without hope or faith. Wherefore, for someone to be good and pious, he must first be faithful. But I could not teach this, for I myself did not know what I should rightly believe, and therefore I could not teach them to be good and pious, and they could not truly become such. For as I would proceed to erect the covering without the foundation and without the walls, so they would seek to raise the roof without both those things, which is an improper and an impossible thing. For who can speak without a tongue? Or see without eyes? Nor can he put up a covering without a foundation and walls. It is not a proper thing, nor is it possible, that someone should first love something before he had somehow come to know it, that he should desire it before he had any knowledge of it. Nor, truly, is this proper, nor was it possible, that I should teach anyone to be good and pious, not having taught him first to be faithful and Orthodox, for without faith—and the Orthodox Catholic faith—every goodness and piety is invented goodness and piety, and not true; and it is rewarded only in this world, but in the other world it will be subject to eternal tortures. *Sine fide enim impossibile est placere Deo* [without faith it is impossible to please God].[42]

Will he yet say to me that I did not have a proper reason for my pilgrimage? That there was nothing that troubled me and compelled me to make such a laborious journey? Both as far as I myself was

---

40.   1 Tim. 3[:2].
†   No one can be truly good if he is not truly faithful.
41.   [1 Cor. 13:13; 1 Th. 1:3; 1 Th. 5:8.]
42.   Heb. 11[:6].

concerned and as far as the entire Ruthenian Church was concerned? Whoever does not see the proper need in this matter—and a great need at that—sees as much of the light of the spiritual sun as a mole sees of the light of the sun that is subject to the senses. I had, therefore, a reason, and a proper reason. I had something that was troubling me. I had something that had sent me almost by force to the East, to the father and to the elders.

†He will say again: "By saying this you disgrace not only yourself and us, but also all our holy ancestors and the blessed fathers of the Ruthenian Church. For it is a disgrace above all disgraces for us not to know what we believe. Moreover you yourself are in disagreement with yourself since you said a little above that the pure and immaculate faith had been transmitted from the East unto our ancestors and received by them and maintained and preserved until our days pure and immaculate." ‡I will answer him that what I said at the outset is also true, since that pure and immaculate faith was preserved pure and immaculate right up until our days, and in our unfortunate times it became impure and besmirched. And also the second thing is true: that in saying this I disgrace both myself, most noble Ruthenian nation (forgive me for speaking the truth), and you. But I do not disgrace either the Holy Ruthenian Church or the holy and blessed fathers of the Ruthenian Church: to the contrary, I bear them honorably upon my head, since they maintained and preserved pure and immaculate the pure and immaculate faith of Christ that had been transmitted to them, and they bid farewell to this world in that pure and immaculate faith. And we received the truly pure and immaculate faith from these, our holy ancestors, but we ourselves, only in our own days, dirtied it and allowed it to be besmirched, which will be demonstrated thoroughly a little below.

And if we should not prevent this in time, we will find our Church left in great danger. For we must fear that this harmful cancerous ulcer will in time attack the pure body of the pure Ruthenian Church. For once it is infected with this (from which Christ preserve us), it will then have to be rendered soulless, to fall, and be destroyed. The most pure bridegroom, the only-begotten son of God, says of his most pure body:

†   Objection.
‡   Solution.

Tota pulchra es amica mea et macula non est in te [Thou art all fair, my love; there is no spot in thee].[43] And the blessed apostle Paul: *Christus dilexit Ecclesiam, et se ipsum tradidit pro ea, ut illam sanctificaret, mundans lavacro aquae, in verbo vitae, ut exhiberet ipse sibi gloriosam Ecclesiam, non habentem maculam aut rugam aut aliquod huismodi, sed ut sit Sancta et immaculata* [Christ loved the Church, and gave Himself for it; that He might sanctify and cleanse it with the washing of water by the word, that He might present it to himself a glorious Church, not having spot, or wrinkle, or any such thing; but that it should be holy and without blemish].[44] A mouth dumb to the truth and a dried up tongue could move and speak out, given such a need, set in motion by the greatness of the matter, since it is a matter of God's honor and of the salvation of human souls, of the infection and downfall, to no small extent, of His holy Church. Otherwise, if especially we, the clergy, should not wish to be vigilant and alert in this matter and were to allow, as if purposefully, this matter that threatens the downfall of our entire Church to pass us by, by this alone we would show that we are hirelings in it.[45] For to see that the soul-destroying infernal wolf seeks not just to snatch away and to smother some one of the sheep of our flock, but to swallow the entire body of our Ruthenian Church, striving to infect it with that infernal ulcer, which, as our holy ancestors were disgusted by it, so also in striving to give us the faith of the blessed fathers of our Ruthenian Church, they rejected and trod upon it; to see this, I say, and to turn one's back upon it in silence is not only the work of a hireling, but also of a thief and a robber. For what can be a more infectious ulcer upon the human soul, and more harmful to the soul, than *haeresis* [heresy]? What can give the human soul over to perdition unto the teeth of the infernal wolf more capably and more easily than blasphemy against God? This thousandfold clever infernal wolf has prepared both these things for the infection of the body of our Ruthenian Church that he might dirty it and render it Godless thereby, that he might turn all of us away from God, and that he might deprive us of His grace. Which we already see manifestly and openly, and we feel and experience it becoming rooted in us ourselves more and more deeply.

43.   S. of S. 4[:7].
44.   Eph. 5[:25–7].
45.   [Jn. 10:12–13.]

Thus to see this, and to remain silent, is more than to be a mute stone.[46] It will certainly be more tolerable for the land of the Sodomites at the day of judgment[47] than it would be for us, the pastors of the Ruthenian Church, on account of such a great and manifest perdition of many souls redeemed by the invaluable blood of the Son of God. When *haeresis* gains dominion over any man, it deprives him of Orthodox faith, and it removes him from God. A soul infected with heresy is living-dead. We can say of each and every heresy what the blessed apostle James said of the nonkeeping of any one of God's commandments, when he said: *Quicunque totam legem servaverit, offendat autem in uno, factus est omnium reus* [For whosoever shall keep the whole law, and yet offend in one point, he is guilty of all].[48] For one heresy suffices for perdition; two, three, and so on, for greater perdition, and it is immeasurably more harmful for a man than the heaviest mortal sin. For *haeresis* not only removes man from God, which mortal sin also does, but it also deprives him of faith, which sin—even the most grievous—does not do. And what I say about one man—understand the same as well about the local Church: that one heresy suffices for it to fall away from the body of the Universal Church and to become a heretical conventicle, since it, having deprived it of its faith, deprives it also at the same time of the presence of the grace of God, removes it from God, and makes it entirely unfaithful and impious.

Consider, most noble Ruthenian nation, what a great reason I had for my pilgrimage to the East. In what way, then, do I disgrace myself and you. Consider in addition this as well: what a most harmful fall it is to fall into *haeresis,* which is all the more harmful the deeper it is. From which sort of fall it is as difficult for a man to rise up as it is a difficult thing for a dead man to walk, if he be not moved by the special grace of God. *Voluntarie peccantibus nobis,* says the blessed apostle Paul, *post acceptam notitiam veritatis, jam non relinquitur pro peccatis Hostia, terribilis autem quoddam expectatio Judicii, et ignis aemulatio, quae consumptura est adversarios. Irritam quis faciens legem Moysi, sine ulla miseratione, duobus vel tribus testibus moritur: quanto magis, putatis, deteriora mereri supplicia, qui Filium*

46. [Lk. 19:40.]
47. Mt. 55 [Mt. 10:15; 11:24].
48. Jas. 2[:10].

Dei conculcaverit, et sanguinem Testamenti pollutum duxerit, in quo sanctificatus est, et spiritui gratiae contumeliam fecerit? Scimus enim qui dixit: Mihi vindicta, et ego retribuam. Et iterum, Quia judicabit Dominus populum suum. Horrendum est incidere in manus Dei viventis [For if we sin willfully after that we have received the knowledge of the truth, there remaineth no more sacrifice for sins, but a certain fearful looking for of judgment and fiery indignation, which shall devour the adversaries. He that despised Moses's law died without mercy under two or three witnesses: Of how much sorer punishment, suppose ye, shall he be thought worthy, who hath trodden under foot the Son of God, and hath counted the blood of the covenant, wherewith he was sanctified, an unholy thing, and hath done despite unto the Spirit of grace? For we know Him that hath said, Vengeance belongeth unto me, I will recompense, saith the Lord. And again, The Lord shall judge His people. It is a fearful thing to fall into the hands of the living God].[49] For through receiving heresies in oneself and abandoning the Orthodox faith, both one man and the entire local Church fall victim to that terrible judgment of the Holy Spirit, that a certain fearful looking for of judgment and a zealousness of the fire awaits it, which must swallow it as an adversary of God, if it should not wish to take care for itself and guard itself, if it should not repent before it suffers upon itself the vengeance of God, before it falls into the hands of the living God. For thereafter it will not find any offering for itself.

[†]And although it is true that heretics are wont to say: "We do not tread upon the Son of God, rather we bear Him on our heads, and we do not consider besmirched His holy blood, through which we are consecrated, rather we drink it with fear and terror as most holy and salvatory for the salvation of our souls; and we do not revile the acts of grace of the Holy Spirit, rather we constantly ask the Lord God for them, and we acknowledge that we cannot live without them," nonetheless, the Lord God will answer them: *Populus hic labiis me honorat: cor autem eorum longe est a me* [this people honors me with their lips, but their heart is far from me];[50] they have the appearance of piety, but they have opposed its might. For although every heretic speaks thus, nonetheless

49.   Heb. 10[:26–31].
†   The excuse of the heretics.
50.   [Is. 29:13.]

each one treads upon the Son of God, has Him under his feet. He [i.e., the heretic] holds His holy blood, by which he was consecrated, as besmirched, and he reviles the acts of grace of the Holy Spirit since he rejected and he trod under foot the accepted knowledge of the truth and the usual confession of the true faith, since he excluded himself from among those who bear the Son of God on their heads and who know and confess that the blood of the Testament is pure and who hold in honor the acts of grace of the Holy Spirit: unto these he has become an opponent, and in them, unto God Himself. The same blessed apostle Paul orders the faithful to reject a man that is a heretic after the first and second admonition.[51] But how to reject him, Christ the Lord Himself teaches: as a heathen man and a publican.[52] Who more than a heathen man treads upon the Son of God, dirties His holy blood, and reviles the acts of grace of the Holy Spirit? And the Son of God Himself considers a heretic similar to such an opponent of God and His holy truth. That same blessed apostle calls the heretics servants of Satan when he says of them: "Satan himself is transformed into an angel of light; therefore it is no great thing if his ministers also be transformed as the ministers of righteousness."[53] Do the servants of Satan bear Jesus Christ, the Son of God, upon their heads? Do they believe that His blood was poured out for the cleansing of the sins of the entire world? And do they hold the acts of grace of the Holy Spirit in honor? Not at all. A man that is a heretic is a servant of Satan, a son of the Devil, according to what was said by Christ the Lord: "Ye are of your father, the Devil."[54] Therefore, that defense will not work for any heretic; it will not work. But rather every such person ought to strive to avoid such a harsh decree of God through conversion back to the straight way of true faith from which he had harmfully fallen away, having desecrated and trodden upon the true faith he had once come to know. "For it is impossible for those who were once enlightened, and have tasted of the heavenly gift, and were made partakers of the Holy Ghost, and have tasted the good word of God, and the powers of the age to come, if they shall fall away, to renew them again unto repentance; seeing they crucify to themselves the Son

51.   Tit. 3[:10].
52.   Mt. 18[:17].
53.   2 Cor. 11[:14–15].
54.   Jn. 8[:44].

of God afresh, and put him to an open shame."[55] It is not possible, dearly beloved, that the Son of God should die a second time for a heretic; but it is possible that a heretic might from his fall arise again in the Son of God, who died once for him, and might revert to the former righteousness of truth.

It is not necessary to demonstrate to a wise man why I have presented all this; for every such person can see clearly even without a demonstration, and he can understand that the obligation to save souls requires of us that we not only order people from the pulpits of the churches to avoid the false heretical doctrine newly arisen among us, sown by our new theologians, with which nowadays certain eloquent heralds smear their lips and abominate our ears and souls, but that we throw them out of our houses and bury them in oblivion, if we wish to acknowledge that we have the true faith of Christ the Lord and to be known as such, and if we do not wish to suffer the heretical demise upon our souls and upon the entire Ruthenian Church. For these theologizers impiously assailed the majesty of God; they blasphemously attacked the mysteries of the incarnation of the Son of God; they heretically abused the sacraments given to His Church by our Lord Jesus Christ; and they declared that all of this was our faith. Having lost the Catholic confession concerning these three things, what could remain that was soul saving for them or for us? If this is part of the confession for all true theologians—that the true faith about these three things, that is, about God, the incarnation of the Son of God, and the salvatory mysteries, makes a man Orthodox and Catholic—and if they have disturbed these three things, believing and teaching in un-Catholic fashion about each of these three things and about many other dogmas of the Catholic faith, how then will they be able to be known as, and called, Catholics?

They assailed the majesty of God when, dividing the divine essence *realiter* [in reality] from the divine person, they caused each divine person, indivisible in itself, to be divided in reality; when they destroyed the natural order of the divine persons with respect to their being; and when they blasphemed that the Son of God, the Word of God, was not born of the essence of God the Father. They attacked the unalterable mystery of the incarnation of the Son of God when they teach that Christ the Lord is not a priest and mediator and when they

55. Heb. 6[:4–6].

tore from him the priestly and mediatorial dignity that had rested upon Him for all times, and which had remained unchanged for ages. They also abused the salvatory Church sacraments, confessing that there are only two given by Christ the Lord, and not seven. If these three things, most noble Ruthenian nation, are blasphemy and heresy, then what salvatory thing, on account of them, do we still have intact? Having become infected with one heresy, they would have to bear the shame of the heretical name that had been placed upon them by the Church; but since they had become infected and abominated by so many manifest heresies (for this is not the only evil here), what are they to expect from the Church of God, which condemns them even after death?

†They do not acknowledge that the souls of the righteous are in heaven with Christ the Lord. They believe that the particular judgment is a fable. They judge the priestly and episcopal dignities to be one and the same. They tear away from St. Peter his authority over the entire Church. They say that the essential transformation of the bread and the wine in the sacrament of the Eucharist into the body and blood of Christ is an invented thing. They mock transubstantiation, and they carry about other similar blasphemies, hidden in the bosom of their souls and brought into the open through their writings. Are these not heresies? Are they not blasphemies against the majesty of God and against the Orthodox faith given by Him, which could not be greater, worse, and more harmful? Arius, Sabellius, Eunomius, Nestorius, Eutyches, and other similar heretics, each one of them for only one heresy, was named a heretic by the God-bearing fathers and driven from the Church. In blaspheming that the Son of God was not born of the essence of the Father, how do they blaspheme less than Arius? In not acknowledging the natural order among the divine persons, how do they cede place to Eunomius in this heresy? In equating a priest and a bishop in the level of dignity and in the prerogative of jurisdiction, how do they err less than the heretic Arius?

But so that we might examine with our own eyes in what way they strayed from the faith of our holy fathers, I cite the false doctrine of the three foremost and first, having noted the places and folia in the printed editions of their writings, so that no one, either from the greater or from the lesser people, believe that what I say are words without

†   He names the blasphemies of the Ruthenian writers.

proof. *Visus enim* [for sight], as they commonly say, *certior est auditu* [is more certain than hearing].[56]

The First Such Ruthenian Theologian
Stefan Zizanij

†The doctrine of that matheologian,[57] Stefan Zizanij, was published in print, in Ruthenian and in Polish in the same book, *anno* [in the year] 1596. In his doctrine against purgatory, he calls it a heretical error to acknowledge particular judgment. In the same place he does not acknowledge that righteous souls that have departed this world are with Christ the Lord; rather he says that they are in an earthly paradise. In the same place he also does not acknowledge that ᾅδης in Greek, or *infernus* in Latin, is hell and that the sinful and the devils already suffer in hell. On folio 32 [88–9],[58] he says that Christ the Lord is even now the visible head of His Church. On folio 56 [123], he calls a holy man, Bishop Celestine of Rome, an accursed heretic. On folio 40 [actually, 44/106], he does not acknowledge that unleavened bread is simply called bread. On folio 101 [189], he blasphemes about Christ the Lord, saying that he is no longer a priest or a mediator since, he says, the priesthood of Christ did not remain in Christ, but flowed out from Him to the priests and came to rest upon them. I omit his other blasphemies against the procession of the Holy Spirit and against the bishop of Rome and his other errors and heresies. I proceed to the second theologian, Christopher Philalethes.

The Second Ruthenian Theologian
Christopher Philalethes

This Philalethes published his doctrine in print, called Ἀπόκρισις, *anno* [in the year] 1597. *Pagina* [on page] 66 [1165],[59] he fabricates and

---

56.   [Cf. Erasmus *Ad.* 1.1.100.]
†   The errors and heresies of Zizanij.
57.   [See above, p. 30, n. 119.]
58.   [Page numbers in brackets from Zizanij refer to Studyns'kyj 1906.]
59.   [Page numbers in brackets from Philalethes refer to *RIB* 7.]

calumniates against the Greeks, alleging that they do not acknowledge transubstantiation, that is, the transformation of the bread and the wine into the body and blood of Christ the Lord in the sacrament of the Eucharist.

P. 298 [1711]: he mocks such a transubstantiation and says that it is an invented thing.

P. 87 [1215]: he believes that the office of the bishop and the priest are one and the same.

P. 88 [1215] and 90 [1221]: he asserts that lay people have the right *suffragii decisivi* [of decisive suffrage], to make and establish decrees about the faith.

P. 93 [1227]: he does not acknowledge that the God-seer Moses is a priest, rather he calls him a layman.

P. 94 [1229]: he confuses spiritual priesthood with sacramental priesthood, and he does not acknowledge the second.

P. 111 [1271]: he appropriates for lay people the power of election to the spiritual estate *jure divino* [by divine law].

P. 114 [1277] and 124 [1299]: he asserts that bishops are greater than priests in their dignity *non jure divino* [not by divine law], but by human custom.

P. 142 [1337]: he does not acknowledge that the holy apostle Peter was established the pastor of the Universal Church by Christ the Lord.

P. 147 [1349]: he does not acknowledge that Christ the Lord called St. Peter a rock.

Ibid. [1349]: he does not acknowledge that Christ the Lord built His Church upon the holy apostle Peter or that the Eastern Church ever confessed this.

P. 151 [1359]: he does not acknowledge that when Christ the Lord said to St. Peter the words "feed my sheep,"[60] he entrusted all His sheep to his feeding.

Ibid. [1359]: he does not acknowledge that two types of keys were given to the apostles by Christ the Lord, that is, *ordinis* [of order] and *jurisdictionis* [of jurisdiction].

Ibid. [1359]: he confuses archpriestly pastorhood with priestly pastorhood.

P. 206 [1489]: he does not acknowledge that from ancient custom

60. [Jn. 21:17.]

and from the decree of Church laws, the appeal of decrees of Church laws was to be made to the bishop of Rome.

P. 216 [1513]: he asserts that, for the bishops, appeal in spiritual matters is to be made to the emperors.

P. 219 [1521]: he appropriates for the emperors the power to convene councils.

P. 223 [1529]: he does not acknowledge that at universal councils the bishops of Rome occupied the first place.

These and others like them are the errors and heresies of our second theologian, Philalethes.

The Errors and Heresies of Orthologue

There follows the third such theologian of our Ruthenian Church, Theophil Orthologue, who in his work called *Lament,* published in print in the year 1610, founded and built the entire treatise on the procession of the Holy Spirit upon the real division of the divine essence from the person.

Folio 111v [128]:[61] in express words he does not acknowledge that the Holy Spirit is from the essence of the Father. And on folio 113v [130] he says that the Son is born, and the Holy Spirit proceeds, not from the essence of the Father, but rather from the person of the Father, all of which is heretical blasphemy against the Son of God and against the Holy Spirit, the first who was born, and the second who proceeded from the essence of God the Father.

Folio 99v [116]: he considers the Holy Spirit, as also the Son, to be second according to the order of the divine persons.

Ibid. [116] and folio 101 [117] and 122v [139]: he disrupts and tears apart the natural order among the divine persons.

The entire treatise against purgatory is heretical, not Greek, for in it, on folio 161 [177–8] and 163 [179–80], he heretically rebukes the holy teachers of the Church—Ambrose, Augustine, and especially Gregory of Nyssa, Gregory the Great, bishop of Rome, and, on folio 162r [178], Irenaeus and Dionysius of Alexandria—which the entire Eastern Church, to whom Orthologue ascribes that treatise, is not wont to do.

61. [Page numbers in brackets from Orthologue refer to *HLEULT* 1.]

Folio 151r: he says that the place of the holy souls that have departed from this world is an earthly paradise.

Folio 164 and 165 [180–2]: the reasons put forth remove the necessity that anyone, after departure from this world, would need remission from sins.

Folio 166r [182]: he says that generous God remits sins through His most ineffable grace, by grace, as a gift, and without any merits.

Folio 157 [173–4] and 176 [192–3]: he asserts that venial sins are remitted for the souls departing this world *gratis* [freely] through the generous mercy of a merciful God.

Folio 177r [193]: he does not acknowledge particular judgment.

Folio 212r [228]: he says that mortal sin also removes faith from a faithful man.

Folio 213 [229–30]: he establishes that the rational soul comes from the seed of man.

Folio 214v [231]: he asserts that only two sacraments were given by Christ the Lord, baptism and the Eucharist.

Folio 206v [223] and folio 5r [21]: he mocks the traditions.

I omit other errors, heresies, and blasphemies of this dear Crookologue of our Church.

Examine, most noble Ruthenian nation, what sort of errors and heresies have been introduced into our Church by these our newly arisen theologians and submitted to us as if they were the genuine dogmas of the faith and received and approved by us. Let us look and see how we have allowed ourselves to be infected with blasphemous doctrine, and so incautiously that before the Zizanijs, Philaletheses, Orthologues, Antigraphists, Clerks, Suraz'kyjs, Azarijs, and other similar matheologians,[62] our seducers from the genuine faith—that before them our holy teachers of the Church, the Athanasiuses, Cyrils, Basils, Gregorys, Chrysostoms, Damascenes, and other holy doctors have become of little significance for us. And if anyone were to say to us, Rus', on account of that reason and occasion, what once the blessed apostle Paul said, writing to the Galatians—"O foolish Galatians, who hath bewitched you, that ye should not obey the truth," and below, "Are ye so foolish? having begun in the Spirit, are ye now made perfect by

62.   [See above, p. 30, n. 119.]

the flesh?"[63]—we ought not to be offended at him for that since we too, not being obedient to the truth, followed false theologians.

For what, by the living God, brought us to such a great simplicity that we—as if in the whole Church, since it was in the entire nation— accepted such obvious errors and manifest heresies and that we boast of them as our own without any consideration? Were we not warned of this by the blessed apostles Paul and John: that we prove all things, that we hold fast that which is good,[64] and that we believe not every spirit, but try which one is of God, since, he says, many false prophets are gone out into the world.[65] If nothing else, this alone ought to have submitted the doctrine and writings of those obscure authors to suspicion of untruth: that none of them signed his own name to those deceptions of theirs, but only an invented one. What parent was ever ashamed of his honorable generation as these were ashamed of their offspring, such that they did not wish to acknowledge them? In this manner, they made clearly known about themselves and about them, that they had released to the world the generation of a dishonorable bed. But as that evil has already come into being through our incaution, God grant that it now cease through our admonition. For not that which can be corrected is evil, but that which will never tend to good. As soon as we compare their doctrine, which is disgusting to God, with the doctrine of the ancient theologians of the Church, immediately, through their very difference from the holy doctors in the doctrine of dogmas of the faith, the Lord God will grant that we come to our senses and recognize ourselves, since a man is sure of his salvation not from the supposition of good faith, but from truly good faith, and, moreover, in love, without which a man can be faithful and of true faith, but dead in faith, having no hope of salvation. He can even be tormented, lashed, beaten, but he cannot be saved. If faith without love[66] is of such weakness, what will be the futility where there is neither faith nor love? What shall we say about him where, beneath the cloak of faith, there are errors, heresies, and blasphemies?

Was that not blasphemy—and profane, heretical blasphemy at that—which Stefan Zizanij sowed in our Ruthenian Church, telling

63.   Gal. 3[:1, 3].
64.   1 Th. 5[:21].
65.   1 Jn. 4[:1].
66.   [1 Cor. 13:2.]

us not to acknowledge particular judgment?[67] To cast down from heaven the souls justified by divine merits and to remove them from communion with Christ the Lord?[68] To tear from Christ the Lord His eternal priestly and mediatorial dignity?[69] What more profane thing could indeed arise in our days? What shall we say to the fact that in that same work of his he calls Christ the Lord the visible head of His Church?[70] That he locates holy souls in an earthly paradise?[71] That he removes the blessed apostle Paul from the presence of Christ?[72] That he does not acknowledge that *infernus* is hell?[73] That he denies that unleavened bread is called bread?[74] That he invented the words "there unleavened bread, and here bread" and added them to the text of St. John Chrysostom?[75] That he unfaithfully cited the witness of the same St. John Chrysostom concerning the priest and mediator Jesus Christ?[76] That he interpreted in Arian fashion the mystery that occurred during the baptism of the Lord in the voice, in the dove, and in Christ the Lord, who was being baptized?[77] That he condemned as a heretic, denied the priestly dignity, and removed from the Church Bishop Celestine of Rome, the ruler of the Third Universal Council,[78] representing whose person at this council, St. Cyril, patriarch of Alexandria, condemned Nestorius, patriarch of Constantinople, and thence acquired the title by which all his successors as patriarchs of Alexandria are titled popes and universal judges and serve more than other patriarchs *in Trigio*?[79] The patriarchs of Alexandria have both these things from St. Celestine, and our wise Zizanij calumniated him as a heretic who was condemned at the third Universal Council. It is a strange thing indeed to be ignorant

67. Fol. 5 [46].
68. Fol. 13 [58].
69. Fols. 101 [189], 103 [191].
70. Fol. 31 [87–8].
71. Fol. 14 [60].
72. Ibid. [60].
73. Fol. in his doctrine on purgatory. [Fol. 11 (55).]
74. Fol. 44 [106].
75. Fol. 47 [111].
76. Fols. 101 and 102 [188–90].
77. Fols. 31 [86–7] and 55 [121–2].
78. Fol. 56 [123].
79. *Theod. Bals. addecr. Const. in Photii nomocanon Tit. 8 c.1* [Theodore

of Church history, to say nothing of Holy Scripture and of its profound hidden meanings, and to make bold to theologize. What sort of concord in all this does our Ruthenian Church have with this new theologian? What does our pure, soul-saving wheat have to do with his impure, soul-destroying chaff,[80] through which he presented us as heretics to the entire Catholic world, as if our Ruthenian Church both believed and confessed according to his new theology? But he himself is as far from the evangelical truth and from our Orthodox confession in all the articles of the faith he described as is falsehood from the truth, or as is Belial from Christ the Lord.[81]

Concerning Particular Judgment

Although it is a strange thing, most noble Ruthenian nation, that this man dared to hazard so fearlessly what he could in no manner manage, it is an incomparably stranger thing that we did not notice his so manifest errors and heresies, that we could not see such simple things that offer themselves to be seen by natural reason itself. For as far as particular judgment is concerned, each of us having established for ourselves as certain that, after the separation from the body, some souls depart for a light and peaceful place,[82] and others for a dark and unpeaceful place, we ought to ask ourselves who orders the souls such that some go to happy places and others to sad places? And if we were to grasp this, then we would understand that this does not happen to them by chance, or of their own will, or through any sort of Satanic or angelic power over them, or through their evil or good deeds, without a judgment made over them. For both an angel and a devil can know of the downfall of a man, but they cannot always know of his rise, for they cannot know of the heart's contrition, without which penance, even if it should exist superficially, has no weight. For the Lord God, as the One who sees

---

Balsamon, *Commentaries on Photius's Nomocanon, PG* 137:1003A–1004A], and *Niceph. Callistus eccl. Hist. lib. 14, c. 34* [Nicephorus Callistus Xanthopulus, *Church History*, bk. 14, chap. 34; *PG* 146:1169–70].
80.   [Mt. 3:12; Lk. 3:17.]
81.   [2 Cor. 6:15.]
82.   Fol. 52.

into hearts,[83] has left this for Himself alone. We would certainly, with this sort of consideration of the matter, necessarily have to come to the conclusion that this happens to them through a certain special divine judgment made upon them according to their deeds, that the righteous reach the hands of the angels, by whom they are borne to the light and happy places, and the sinful reach the hands of the devils, by whom they are borne to dark and sad places.

And we would call such a divine judgment particular or individual judgment. [†]For if we did not confess this, we would of necessity have to believe that both righteous and sinful souls are gathered in one place. But it is not a pious thing to locate Abel with Cain, Lot with the Sodomites, the apostle Peter with the traitor Judas, and others like them. Thus natural human reason ought to have shown us that there is a particular judgment of souls and that we ought not to grasp at that heretical opinion of Zizanij. With that sort of particular judgment Christ the Lord judged the wise malefactor when he said to him, "Today shalt thou be with me in paradise."[84] With the same sort of judgment He also judged Judas when He said of him, "Woe unto that man by whom the Son of man is betrayed."[85]

Concerning such a judgment, St. Augustine says: "It is properly and highly salutarily believed about this, that when the souls leave the body, they are judged before they come to that terrible judgment at which they are to be judged with the received bodies."[86] But let us listen concerning such a judgment, dearly beloved, to a doctor of the Church closer to our times, our own St. John of Damascus, to whom either Zizanij did not listen, or he listened with deaf ears, who, *sermone de iis qui obdormierunt in fide* [in the sermon on those who have fallen asleep in death in the faith], which is often read in our Church, says this about it: "Men inspired by God say that, at the death of every man, all human affairs and deeds are weighed as if on a scale, where the benign Lord God"—let us listen, most beloved, with open ears to what

83. [1 Sam. 16:7; Acts 1:24; etc.]
†   It is a great error not to recognize particular judgment.
84. Lk. 23[:43].
85. Mt. 26[:24].
86. *Lib. 2 de propagatione anima, c. 4* [St. Augustine, *On the Soul and Its Origin*, bk. 2, chap. 4; *PL* 44:498–9].

this holy doctor says, where he says "the benign Lord God"—"places Himself in the grandeur of His power, for He is righteous, wise, good, and powerful, or, to put it more truthfully, righteousness itself, wisdom, goodness, and the hypostatic power. As the righteous one, then, He gives of His riches to the abandoned man; as the wise one, He fills in the insufficiencies of the poor man; as the good one, He saves the creature of His hands; as the powerful one, He overcomes the strong man, and He strengthens the weak man, with the exception of the man who is manifestly condemned and who has fallen away from the true faith, whose pan departs too far from balance. Thus when the right pan outweighs the left on the scales, it is manifest that the one being weighed is located with God's saints. If both weigh the same, God's mercy conquers. If the left even weighs just a little bit more, even then, according to the doctrine of the God-bearing fathers, divine compassion fills in the lack. There are three divine judgments of the Lord: the first righteous, the second merciful, and the third compassionate. I will add to these yet a fourth: when evil deeds predominate by far, even then He righteously decrees with His righteous judgment against the guilty one."[87] Thus St. John of Damascus.

Clearly, then, this holy doctor speaks of particular judgment; and he took his doctrine not from himself, but, as he himself makes clear there, from that of the holy doctors who lived before him. Thus our Ruthenian Church, instructed about this by the Eastern Church, always knew and acknowledged such a judgment of each individual soul; and it knows it now, believes and confesses it, and it tramples and suppresses Zizanij's, which was heresy borrowed from the heretics.

Concerning the Blessing of the Righteous Souls That Have Departed from This World

But as to the righteous souls that have departed from this world, which Zizanij does not acknowledge as being with Christ the Lord, and as to the blessed apostle Paul, whom he removes from the presence of Christ the Lord, and as to the fact that he says that all the holy souls are in an

---

87.   *S. Damascenus in Sermone de iis qui in fide obdormierunt.* [St. John of Damascus, *Sermon on Those Who Have Fallen Asleep in Death in the Faith;* PG 95:271B–C].

earthly paradise[88]—as to this doctrine of Zizanij, I say, not venturing into further investigation of this from the holy doctors of the Church, the daily Church hymns themselves ought to have taught us that this opinion of Zizanij is *haeresis* [a heresy] and not Church doctrine. Can we really in good conscience believe that our Ruthenian Church, or rather that the entire Eastern Church, teaches and confesses one thing and believes another? Not in the least. For whatever the Church of Christ the Lord believes unto righteousness, with its mouth it confesses all that unto salvation. And conversely: whatever it confesses with its mouth unto salvation, it believes the same with its heart unto righteousness.[89] And since our Ruthenian Church confesses this truth—that the saints are in heaven where Christ the Lord is in the body and not in an earthly paradise, and that the blessed apostle Paul, as also all the saints, is already with Christ—then it is a falsehood and *haeresis* that Zizanij teaches our Ruthenian Church to believe, and to which we incautiously gave our consent.

And it is clear from all its hymns and homilies written down in the Church books that our Ruthenian Church teaches as I cited about the righteous souls that have departed from this world: in the Oktoechoi, the Triodia, the Menaia, the Anthologies, and finally in all the doctors of the Church who happened to write about this matter. To make convincing what I say, I cite the witnesses of the holy hymnographers of the Church, in which the Ruthenian Church is accustomed to confess every day that the holy souls of God are in heaven and are crowned with perfect crowns, that they stand before the majesty of God, are with Christ the Lord, are with the Lord God, see Christ the Lord, see God face to face.[90] And they see not through a likeness, not as if through some veil, nor through a glass, nor as if in some sort of portrait, but face to face, as He himself is. They see Him as the angels see Him. For innumerable in our Church are the hymns that contain this understanding, as, for example: "Seeing Christ now face to face, you saints enjoy ineffable lightness in delight."[91] And again: "Behold the kingdom of heaven is

---

88.   Fol. 14 [60].
89.   Rom. 10[:10].
90.   1 Cor. 13[:12].
91.   From the common canon for the hieromartyrs, ode 5 [troparion 2; *VS* 1:460].

opened before you, where, after you have finished your course, you see God as the angels see Him, who gives crowns to you as the reward for your labors."[92] And again: "Your martyrs, O Christ Jesus, who suffered great torments for You, have received perfect crowns in heaven."[93] And especially it confesses about the holy apostles Peter and Paul thus: "Now you see Christ the Lord not through a likeness, or through a glass, but face to face, who reveals unto you His perfect knowledge of His divinity."[94]

Hearing this, most noble Ruthenian nation, it remains for us to lend our faith either to our immaculate Ruthenian Church or to Zizanij, who has been rendered abominable through heresy. For one of these two must be the case: that either our Church errs in this, or Zizanij has erred, who, not wishing to listen to her, has attempted to have her listen to him. Which he has also achieved to a great extent in hearts that are unwatchful for God's truth. For, as can be clearly seen, Zizanij, with that heresy of his, has remained on our lips, and the doctrine of the truth of God has remained in neglect.

And I demonstrate that what I assert is God's truth from the doctrine of other doctors of the Church as well, which is concordant with the daily teaching of the Church. [†]For blessed Chrysostom teaches in express words *sermone de omnibus sanctis Paraenetico* [in the admonitory sermon on all saints] that the saints have gone from earth to heaven and, having been led there by the angels of God, stand before the throne of God. St. Basil the Great, *serm. Paraen. in 40 Martyres* [in the admonitory sermon on the forty martyrs], says of them that the earth did not hide them, rather heaven received them, before whom the doors of paradise were opened.[95] And having added to these words of the saint the words "and being within, take delight in the tree of

---

92.   From the common canon for the saints, ode 9, 1 [troparion 1; *VS* 1:407].

93.   In the Oktoechos on Friday for the stichos of voice 6.

94.   From the canon [2] for the holy apostles Peter and Paul, ode 9 [troparion 3; *VS* 2:2:101].

†   *Sermo iste* [this sermon] is read in our Church every year on the Sunday of All Saints.

95.   [St. Basil the Great, *Sermon 19 on the Holy Forty Martyrs; PG* 31:523C.]

life," the Church often sings and confesses this. That saint calls heaven the paradise in which the saints delight in the tree of life, which is the Lord God Himself. St. Athanasius says in the *Life of Anthony* that he saw the soul of St. Ammon being borne unto heaven.[96] St. Gregory of Nyssa says *serm. Paraen.* [in the admonitory sermon] on St. Ephrem that His soul has taken up its abode in the heavenly palaces, where reside the angelic hosts, the nations of patriarchs, the choirs of prophets, the thrones of the apostles, the joys of the martyrs, the happiness of the pious, the brilliance of the doctors, the illustrious gathering of firstborn, the pure voices of those in delight.[97] We hear, dearly beloved, that that holy doctor locates St. Ephrem, as St. Athanasius also locates St. Ammon, not in an earthly paradise, but in heavenly palaces, where the angels, patriarchs, prophets, apostles, martyrs, and all the saints dwell. In the life of St. Basil the Great, having said of him that he is in heaven, St. Gregory the Theologian acknowledges that he sees the Holy Trinity as it is.[98] The doctors of the Church, East and West, the Cyrils of Jerusalem and of Alexandria, Epiphanius, Ambrose, Jerome, Augustine, and others say and teach the same.[99] St. John of Damascus says of Prince Josaphat in his *History of Barlaam* that he came to the presence of the countenance of the Lord without fear and naked and that he is adorned with that praise by the crown that had been promised him before.[100] Theophylactus says *in exegesi* [in exegesis] of the words

96.   [St. Athanasius, *Life of St. Anthony; PG* 26:929–30; *NPNF2* 4:212.]

97.   [St. Gregory of Nyssa, *Life of Our Holy Father Ephrem of Syria; PG* 46:847B.]

98.   [St. Gregory of Nazianzus, *Oration in Praise of Basil the Great; PG* 36:605–6; *FC* 22:99.]

99.   *Cyr. Hieros. Katech. 13* [Cyril of Jerusalem, *Catechetical Lectures,* 13; *PG* 33:809–12; *NPNF2* 7:90–1]; Alex. *lib. 1, c. 36 in Ioannem* [Cyril of Alexandria, *On the Gospel of St. John,* bk. 1, chap. 36; *PG* 73 (there is no chap. 36 in the edition in *PG*)]; *Epiph. Her.* 78 [Epiphanius, Against Heresies, *Heresy 78; PG* 42:699–740, perhaps 705–6]; *Ambr. lib. 7, Epist. 19. ad Thessal.* [Ambrose, *Commentaries on the First Epistle to the Thessalonicans,* chap. 2, verses 19, 20; *PL* 17:446D]; *Hier. Epist. ad Marcellam de obitu Leae* [St. Jerome, *Letter 23, To Marcella on the Death of Lea; PL* 22:426; *NPNF2* 6:42]; *Aug. lib. medit. c. 22* [Augustine (uncertain attribution), *One Book of Meditations,* chap. 22; *PL* 40:917–18].

100. [John of Damascus (spurious), *Barlaam and Ioasaph,* 40.360–1; *PG*

of Christ the Lord—*hodie mecum eris in paradiso* [Today shalt thou be with me in paradise]:[101] "One must say (he says) that paradise and the heavenly kingdom are one and the same thing. Otherwise he (the thief) would not enjoy perfect happiness."[102]

This is the doctrine of the holy doctors of the Church, which is concordant with the doctrine of the hymns of the Church; and either Zizanij did not listen to it and erred, or he listened and purposefully did not wish to understand. An example is also found in the witnesses of Holy Writ about this Orthodox confession in our Ruthenian Church, assured by which the holy doctors of the Church gave us this doctrine concerning the state of the holy souls that have departed this world. The blessed apostle Paul says: "For we know that if our earthly house of this tabernacle were dissolved, we have a building of God, a house not made with hands, eternal in the heavens."[103] And further: "Therefore we are always confident, knowing that, whilst we are in the body, we are absent from the Lord (for we walk by faith, not by sight): and we are confident and willing rather to be absent from the body, and to be present with the Lord."[104] Both these witnesses teach us the same thing: that after the dissolution of our body, in which the soul resides as in some sort of house and which becomes dissolved after the departure of the soul from it, we immediately attain in our souls another dwelling not made with hands, eternal, which is in the eternal God Himself, who was not made with hands.[105] And having departed from the body, we hasten to go to Him in our souls. And Christ the Lord said to the thief: *hodie mecum eris in paradiso* [today shalt thou be with me in paradise].[106] And the blessed John, Apostle and Evangelist, says: "And I saw the souls of them that were slain for the word of God," etc. And further: "and white robes were given unto every one of them."[107] And again:

96:1233/1234B–1235/1236B.]

101. Lk. 23[:43].

102. [Theophylactus, *Exposition on the Gospel of Luke,* chap. 23; *PG* 123:1105/1106A.]

103. 2 Cor. 5[:1].

104. 2 Cor. 5[:6–8].

105. [Mk. 14:58; Acts 7:48, 17:24; 2 Cor. 5:1; Heb. 9:11, 24.]

106. Lk. 23[:43].

107. Rev. 6[:9, 11].

"After this I beheld a great multitude, which no man could number, of all nations, and kindreds, and people, and tongues, standing before the throne, and before the countenance of the Lamb, clothed with white robes, and palms in their hands."[108] And yet again in the same place: "These are they which came out of great tribulation, and have washed their robes, and made them white in the blood of the Lamb. Therefore are they before the throne of God, and serve him day and night in his temple."[109] Thus already then are their robes given to the holy souls; already are they clothed in them, in which they stand not outside of heaven, but within heaven, before the throne of God and the Lamb. And they serve Him there in heaven day and night. As he was dying, the holy protomartyr Stephen said to Christ the Lord: "Lord Jesus, receive my spirit."[110] And the blessed apostle Paul: "I have a desire to be dissolved and to be with Christ."[111] These are the passages of Holy Writ, assured by which the holy doctors confidently taught that the holy servants of God are in heaven, are with Christ, are in paradise, that is, in the kingdom of heaven, and similar things. In his interpretation of the words of the blessed apostle Paul—"For to me to live is Christ, and to die is gain; but if I live in the flesh, this is the fruit of my labor, yet what I shall choose I know not"[112]—St. John Chrysostom says the following of blessed apostle Paul, before whom Zizanij closed heaven, and whom he did not allow to Christ the Lord: "What do you say, Paul? When departing from here you are to come to heaven and to be with Christ, do you not know what you are to choose?"[113] Let the lips of those who speak untruth be closed in their heretical opinion.

†And when St. John Chrysostom and Theophylactus and some others, interpreting these apostolic words—"And these all, having obtained a good report through faith, received not the promise: that God provided some better thing for us, that they without us should not be

108. Rev. 7[:9].
109. Rev. 7[:14–15].
110. Acts 7[:59].
111. Phil. 1[:23].
112. Phil. 1[:21–2].
113. [St. John Chrysostom, *Sermon 4 on Phil. 1:22–6; PG* 62:205; *NPNF1* 13:198.]
†   Understanding this passage of St. Paul incorrectly, the opponents seek to show that the souls of the righteous do not yet have their reward in heaven.

made perfect"[114]—seem to say that the righteous have not yet received the reward for their services, we are to know that they are speaking not of the crowns and of the perfection of the blessing of souls, but of the crown and blessing of the bodies, about which the blessed apostle Paul also speaks in this passage. For by "promise" one understands the perfect blessing of both souls and bodies, which neither Abel, nor Noah, nor Abraham, nor Paul, nor anyone else, had as yet, nor has now. And that is so that they not have it without us. Which can also be seen from these very words of the apostle: *ut non sine nobis consummarentur* [that they without us should not be made perfect]. "For," as the blessed John Chrysostom says, "he did not say that they not be crowned without us, but that they without us not receive the perfect reward not only in their souls, but also in their bodies."

Thus from the doctrine of divine witnesses, the doctrine of the writings of the holy doctors, and the daily doctrine of the Church, we have seen, most noble Ruthenian nation, and we have learned that the souls of the holy servants of God are in heaven with Christ their Lord and God, and they delight in His presence, awaiting more perfect happiness after the resurrection of their bodies, when, together with their bodies that shine like the sun, they will enjoy that which eye has not seen, ear has not heard, and what has not arisen in the heart of man:[115] when they will cease to look upon the brethren in prayers and upon the resurrection of their bodies, but rather when their entire prospect will be of the Lord God Himself alone, and they will turn to the Lord God Himself alone, and they will reside in Him. Which perfection will occur on the day of the general resurrection when the sown natural body is raised a spiritual body,[116] upon which, then, these prophecies of Holy Writ will be fulfilled, where Christ the Lord says: "If I go and prepare a place for you, I will come again and receive you unto myself; that where I am, there ye may be also."[117] And where the blessed apostle Paul says: "When Christ, who is your life, shall appear, then shall ye also appear with him in glory."[118] Further, these words of the same

114. Heb. 11[:39–40].
115. [Is. 64:4; 1 Cor. 2:9.]
116. 1 Cor. 15[:44].
117. Jn. 14[:3].
118. Col. 3[:4].

blessed apostle cited a little above: *Et hi omnes testimonio fidei probati, non acceperunt repromissionem, etc.* [These all died in faith, not having received the promises, etc.].[119] For then they will come in their bodies unto the perfection of the enjoyment of those heavenly goods, which now before that time they enjoy perfectly without their bodies. Which is for them that white robe given to them by God, in which they are clothed before the majesty of God and serve Him day and night.[120]

Let us believe, most noble nation, with Christ the Lord Himself, with His holy apostles, with the God-inspired fathers, the teachers of the Church, whose doctrine was cited here as a proof of the Orthodox confession of our Ruthenian Church, and with the holy Church hymnographers, Bishop Andrew of Crete, John of Damascus, his fellow student Cosmas, Theodore of Studios, and his brother Joseph, with Theophanes the Stigmatized, Joseph the Hymnographer, and others of that number. And let us not grant Zizanij with his erroneous heretical doctrine access to our Ruthenian Church.

That Infernus *Is Hell*

I will also touch briefly upon that other heretical error of Zizanij in which, in his doctrine against purgatory, he does not acknowledge that *infernus* is hell and that the sinful and the devils are already being tormented. From human experience it has become accepted as certain that a man who has once strayed from the true path and whom error has seized has nothing else in his eyes but error, and his own true path seems to him not to be his path. We see that this same thing also happens to those who set off from the true path of Church doctrine into one heretical error, and stubbornness seizes them such that they no longer wish to see even the well-paved road of genuine faith, nor perhaps, by God's punishment, are they even able to do so. Christ the Lord Himself says in the Gospel: "And in hell he lift up his eyes, being in torments."[121] If that rich man is in *infernus* and in torments, then he is in infernal torments, for other than infernal torments, there are not any other torments of unrepentant souls except the infernal. Therefore, *infernus* is hell. For even if we

119. Heb. 11[:13].
120. Rev. 7[:9–17].
121. Lk. 16[:23].

accept this as something that was said in a parable, nonetheless we cannot believe of the place of torments other than that it is *infernus*. Otherwise, we would have to think that Christ the Lord speaks falsely, whereas it is rather Zizanij who commits this fault. For he ought to have listened in this matter to the blessed king and prophet David when he says: "Not the dead will praise you, O Lord, neither all who go down to hell."[122] For those who went down to the bosom of Abraham, where David later also came, praised the Lord. And again: "Let the wicked be ashamed, and let them be led to hell."[123] The monk Maksim the Greek, who, being *in exilio* [in exile] in Muscovy, wrote *capite* [in chapter] 50 of his writings these words of the blessed psalmist, "Let the wicked be turned into hell,"[124] noting the following: "Let us learn two things from these words: first, that the souls of the wicked and sinful are kept in *infernus* until the second coming of the Judge; and second, that souls also return there, that they might be tormented for eternity." If even now, before the judgment, the wicked go to *ad,* according to the Greek, and to *infern,*[125] according to the Latin, and after the terrible judgment they return for eternity to that same *ad* or *infern,* therefore, *infernus* is hell, according to the Greeks as well.

That Both Sinful People and Devils Are Already in Torments

And if he had consulted that same Maxim the Greek in this matter, if he did not wish to consult others, he would not say that neither sinful people nor devils are in torments yet. For he says on this topic in his letter to Jan Ludwik,[126] *capite* [in chapter] 73 of his writings, that "there is a fire kept under the earth by the Creator for the torments of the wicked, which Holy Writ is accustomed to call *gehenna,* in which that unmerciful rich man (here Zizanij ought to have listened to him), when he complained, asked patriarch Abraham to send the poor Lazarus to him so that he might cool his tongue with water, when he was roasting in the flame of the subterranean, unquenchable fire. Let the fire of Mount

122. Ps. 113 [Ps. 115:17].
123. Ps. 30 [Ps. 31:17].
124. Ps 9[:17].
125. [Smotryc'kyj uses polonized versions of the Greek and Latin words.]
126. [I.e., Joannes Lodovicus Vivis Valentinus, or Juan Luis Vives.]

Etna convince you that this fire is subterranean (since it appears on the surface from beneath the earthly abysses), as well as the terrifying voices and screams of the wicked who are tormented there. For do you not hear the Savior when He says: 'The rich man also died, and was buried; and in hell he lift up his eyes, being in torments'?"[127] Thus writes a true Greek and a rare man these days in Greece; and he confesses in express words that the wicked are already in torments in the fire of *ad,* that is, in the fire of hell. And no wonder: for he learned this in the Eastern Greek Church, which, speaking through its teachers of the martyrs and of their tormentors, is accustomed to end its oration about them in the same fashion as Abraham ended his oration about Lazarus and the rich man when he said, "Now he is comforted, and thou art tormented."[128]

Zizanij too ought certainly to have learned this same thing from his Ruthenian Church, and he ought not to have made bold to introduce into it his mad doctrine in this matter. For it always ends its stories about the martyrs and their tormentors with the same words: that the former are happy and command, and the latter are sad and are tormented. Thus it speaks of SS. Boris and Gleb, princes of Rus', and about their tormentor, the fratricide: that they have received their crowns in heaven, and their murderer is tormented in hell.[129] In such a clear and manifest matter we ought not to have allowed either Zizanij to lead us astray or ourselves to be led astray. In this we ought to have listened to the blessed apostle Peter, when he teaches: "The Lord knoweth how to deliver the godly out of temptations and to reserve the unjust unto the day of judgment to be punished."[130] The Greek has *kolazomenos in presenti* [κολαζομένος, in the present], i.e., "who are already being punished." Thence St. John Chrysostom says of the Sodomites that "four thousand years passed, and the torment of the Sodomites has now begun as if anew."[131] Moreover, if the righteous already delight in the eternal goods in heaven, then it necessarily follows that also the wicked already suffer eternal torments

---

127. Lk. 16[:22–3. See Ivanov 1969, 129].
128. Lk. 16[:25].
129. In the sticheras, glory [Slava of tone 8 after the sticheras of tone 4, 24 July].
130. 2 Pet. 2[:9].
131. *Sermo quod poena inferni est aeterna* [Homily that the punishment of Hell is eternal] in the Slavonic *Margarit* [*Pearl*], *pag. 7, to. 2* [*Mar* O1r].

in hell. "If you receive certain doctrine concerning this matter from Holy Writ," says Pope Gregory the Great, "that the souls of the saints are in heaven, then you must necessarily believe that the souls of the wicked are in hell."[132] But we already received certain doctrine concerning the first thing, and in our Church we confess it freely, as was cited clearly a little above. Therefore we must necessarily accept also the second thing and confess it just as freely.

   [†]And it is clear that devils too are already tormented, among other proofs, also from what St. John Chrysostom says: that there is not, nor will there be any greater torment in hell than to fall away from blessed glory and that the devils have already fallen away from this glory and have been deprived of it, with no hope of returning to that glory, whereby they are already in ceaseless torments, find themselves in ceaseless hell, whether they are in subterranean abysses, whether they are in the waters, whether they are on earth, whether they are in the air, they always carry about such a hell with them. "If anyone were to found for me," says St. John Chrysostom, "ten thousand hells, you would not found anything like what it is to fall away from blessed glory."[133] And since, as I said, the devils have already fallen away from that glory—having been angels of light, but having become angels of darkness—therefore, according to St. John Chrysostom, they are in more severe torments than in a thousand fiery hells.

   Probably Zizanij allowed himself to be drawn to this heresy by the devils, who said: "What have we to do with thee, Jesus, thou Son of God? art thou come hither to torment us before the time?"[134] But he did not wish to know that the devil is the father of lying, who, not having abided in the truth, could not teach the truth to him.[135] Wherefore, our Ruthenian Church, knowing itself to be the Church of Christ the Lord, ought not to listen to him in this matter, having been instructed by the

---

132. *Lib. 4, Moral. cap. 28* [Pope Gregory the Great, *Exposition on the Book of Job, or Twenty-five Books of Morals,* bk. 4, chap. 28; *PL* 75:664–5; *LF* 18:220–1, but I was unable to locate this reading in the chapter indicated].
†   That also devils are already tormented.
133. *Hom. 34 in Matt.* [St. John Chrysostom, *Sermon 34 on Matthew; PG* 57:400; *NPNF1* 10:228; although the reading here is somewhat different.]
134. Mt. 8[:29].
135. [Jn. 8:44.]

blessed evangelists at the same time in that same passage what sort of torment that was, with which the devils ask Christ the Lord not to torment them. St. Matthew says: "The devils besought him, saying, If thou cast us out, suffer us to go away into the herd of swine."[136] St. Mark says: "For Jesus said unto him, Come out of the man, thou unclean spirit. And he (Legion) besought Him much that He would not send them away out of the country."[137] St. Luke says: "Lord Jesus commanded the unclean spirit to come out of the man. And he besought Him that he would not command them to go out into the deep."[138]

It is not difficult to see from this that the torment, with which the devils beseech that they not be tormented, is that they be driven out of the man. [†]And when they say to Christ the Lord, "Do not torment us," it is as if they also said, "Do not drive us out," acknowledging that being driven out of a man constitutes torments for them. For just as the devils consider it their foremost comfort to harm people and especially, with God's permission, to enter into them, to afflict and torment them, so too they consider it a heavy torment when they are driven out of the dwelling they had occupied. And therefore they beseech Christ the Lord, saying, "If you drive us out of this man, do not drive us out from among people, do not order us to leave this country, neither command us to go to the deep," for they would not have anyone to harm there except for those they had already harmed. The devils were concerned with nothing else, as is clear, but that He not command them to go to that place whence they would no longer be able to enter into people and to harm them. This, then, is the torment with which the devils ask that they not be tormented and not the torment that remains in them ever present, which fell upon them from transgression and from their removal from the grace and presence of God, with which they are oppressed and tormented as with the most severe infernal torment, than which, according to blessed John Chrysostom, there is not, nor will there be, any heavier torment in hell. Thus, by the grace of God, our Ruthenian Church remains free from this heresy of Zizanij as well.

---

136. Mt. 8[:31].
137. Mk. 5[:8, 10].
138. Lk. 8[:29, 31].
†   The devils consider it a great torment to be driven out of a man.

That Christ Is Priest and Mediator
for All Time

And who among the Orthodox can bear with a calm heart the fact that that same theologian made bold to deprive and to strip Christ the Lord of His priestly and mediatorial office, which is as eternal for Christ the Lord as His humanity is also eternal for Him?[139] For He is forever priest according to the order of Melchizedek;[140] forever mediator; forever God and man. And although he cited the doctrines of St. John Chrysostom in support of that erroneous opinion of his, he did it dishonestly. For neither in the passage indicated by him, nor anywhere else in the writings of St. John Chrysostom, is there found even one iota of such a profane heretical opinion. He proceeded with the same sort of fidelity here with blessed John Chrysostom, having ascribed to him the deprivation of the eternal office of priest from Christ the Lord, as he did in that same work when he added this to his writings: "there unleavened bread, and here bread," as if it were permitted to him to correct—or rather to corrupt—St. John Chrysostom and to add to his writings, as if he had said what he did not say and did not write.[141] He also discourses with the same fidelity upon the mystery that occurred during the baptism of Christ the Lord; with the same heretical infection, but with greater blasphemy against the Son of God, Christ the Lord. For in proving that the Holy Spirit proceeds from the Father alone, and not also from the Son, he says that the voice of the first person, that of the Father, was heard from heaven; the second person, the Son, stood in the Jordan; the third person, the Holy Spirit, descended in the shape of the dove. And he concludes that it thus descended from the Father alone upon the son. *Ergo* [therefore], the Holy Spirit proceeds from the Father alone.[142]

From this argument we can see Zizanij's heretical belief: that the Son of God did not have anything to do with the voice heard from heaven or with the person of the dove. And in believing this, he also believed that the descent of the Holy Spirit upon the Son of man was not ordered

139. Fols. 101 and 102 [189–90].
140. Ps. 109 [Ps. 110:4].
141. Fol. 47 [111].
142. Fols. 51 and 52 [116–17].

and sent from the Son alone as also from the Father. In addition to these two erroneous things, Zizanij also believed this third blasphemy: that the Holy Spirit descended from the Father not as upon the Son of man, but as upon the Son of God. Since from his argument such a conclusion follows through the transposition *praemissarum* [of the premises] concerning the eternal procession of the Holy Spirit, to the extent that He proceeds in essence from the Father and not to the extent that He is sent and granted to worthy people; whereby, having separated one and the same action of the Father and of the Son in this matter, he separated the Son from the Father as far as their one Divinity is concerned, since *differentia operationis divinarum Personarum essentialis ad extra* [the essential external difference of the divine persons] gives rise to a difference in nature for them. *Quorum enim est una et eadem essentia, una eademque est essentialis operatio* [for whichever have one and the same essence have one and the same essential operation]; likewise to the contrary *quorum est una eademque essentialis operatio, una eademque illorum est et essentia* [whichever have one and the same essential operation have one and the same essence].[143] Whereby, what could and can be said by the wicked Arians that is more blasphemous toward the eternal Son of God than what Zizanij said in this passage? For from his argumentation it necessarily follows that the Son, to the extent He is God, received the Holy Spirit from the Father during His baptism, to the extent that He proceeds eternally from the Father. [†]Therefore the Son, to the extent that He is God, did not have the Holy Spirit eternally with the Father, but He acquired Him during His incarnation at the time of His baptism. Which is a new, unheard-of blasphemy against the Son of God, who is not separated from any essential operation of the Father.

But the Church of Christ the Lord knows that this entire operation is common to the entire Holy Trinity carried out upon the Son of man. The Father sent the Holy Spirit upon the Son of man, sent Him together with Him in one operation of sending; and the Son of God as God upon Himself, not as upon God, but as upon man; and the Holy Spirit descended in the form of a dove by His own power, as if having placed

---

143. *Damsc. sermo qui inscribitur Quoniam ad imaginem Dei facti sumus, pag. 495* [John of Damascus, in a homily that begins "Since we are made in the image of God," p. 495.]

† Zizanij's great blasphemy against the Son of God.

the necessity of sending Himself upon Himself, together with the Father and the Son, for the filling of the Son of man with the entire totality of the Spirit. Whence St. Augustine says, "At the baptism of Christ the Lord, the voice that was heard was formed by the entire Holy Trinity, but for the signifying of the Father alone; in the same manner as the dove was formed by the entire Holy Trinity, but for the signifying of the Holy Spirit alone. Wherefore, this genuine and real *operatio* [operation], through which these things occurred, was in common, and only the signifying was the property of one. There appeared at the Jordan three separate divine persons, but it was one and the same operation of the entire Holy Trinity of those separate three persons, in the voice, in the dove, and in the fact that the Son of God was seen as man."[144] And that is how we are to understand what St. Athanasius says: "Come to the Jordan and see in deed the manifest power of the Holy Trinity, which is in one essence—of the Father, witnessing from on high, of the Son, being baptized on earth, and of the Holy Spirit, descending in the form of a dove." Thus not only Zizanij strayed from the truth through this sort of argumentation, but also a few other of our writers.[145] Which often happens to people of high opinion about themselves through evil, ugly stubbornness itself, for although it sees the truth, it nonetheless blunders along blindly. Which can clearly be seen also from other things in which Zizanij erred.

That Unleavened Bread Is Called, and Is, Bread

It seems impossible to me that Zizanij did not know what even children among us know: that unleavened bread is called bread. But rather, in that work of his, willfully, through blind stubbornness itself, he does not acknowledge that unleavened bread was simply called bread without the addition of that word "unleavened,"[146] as if he had never read or heard the blessed evangelist Luke discoursing and speaking about that supper at Emmaus: "And it came to pass, as he sat at meat with them, he

---

144. *Lib. 2 de Trinitate* [St. Augustine, *On the Trinity,* bk. 2, chap. 11, par. 18; *PL* 42:857; *NPNF1* 3:46; although Smtoryc'kyj's reading seems to be a paraphrase and a compilation].
145. See *Antigrafe,* fols. 24 and 25 [1201–4].
146. Fol. 44 [106].

took bread, and blessed it, and brake, and gave to them."[147] And again: "And how they knew him in breaking of bread."[148] And perhaps he happened upon the same sort of work, which I too had the occasion to read when I was in Jerusalem three years ago, published in Greek under the name of some Leontij, metropolitan of Rus′ (whether he was ours, I do not know),[149] where, discoursing against the Latins on unleavened bread in the very same manner as Zizanij after him, he, writing as if from the Latin side, makes the objection against himself by citing those words from the blessed evangelist Luke—"and how they knew him in breaking of bread." Having ascribed ignorance of the Writ of God to the opposite side, he answers that what the evangelist calls bread is leavened, not unleavened bread, since, he says, that occurred not in Jerusalem, but in Emmaus, and the Law of God commanded the Jews to use unleavened bread for seven days only in Jerusalem and not in cities other than Jerusalem.[150]

I am afraid, most noble Ruthenian nation, that you will say to me that the father's nakedness ought not to be uncovered.[151] I will say: If that nakedness did not touch upon the salvation of all our souls, I would be silent; but that sort of silence causes souls to be lost: "Woe, woe unto the world because of offenses! Woe to that man by whom the offense cometh![152] Woe unto them that call evil good, and good evil; that put darkness for light, and light for darkness; that put bitter for sweet, and sweet for bitter!"[153] If I do not speak, if neither he who is before me, nor he who is behind me, then mute creation will speak, the stones will cry out instead of us,[154] but at least it will be spoken. And we not only will lose our reward, but we will not even escape severe punishment.

I asked one higher than I by a second degree of the hierarchic power

147. Lk. 24[:30].
148. Lk. 24[:35].
149. [On the identity of Metropolitan Leontij of Kyiv, see Podskalsky 1982, 171.]
150. [Ex. 12:15, 13:6.]
151. [Gen. 9:22–3.]
152. Mt. 18[:7].
153. Is. 5[:20].
154. [Lk. 19:40.]

in my first dignity[155] why he wrote in his catechism that offerings and prayers for the dead were unnecessary. He answered that otherwise the Latin purgatory cannot be destroyed. I asked a second, equal to me in my second dignity,[156] why, in confessing that the Holy Spirit proceeds through the Son, he taught by means of that particle "through" that the procession of the Holy Spirit in gifts is to be understood as temporal. He answered that thus the confession of the procession of the Holy Spirit "and from the Son" can be avoided more easily. And are we supposed to do evil things that the good might come to us?[157] Is it proper to defend the truth with falsehood? I do not think so. For by pouring even the purest thing into an impure vessel, it will be made filthy. Likewise, by defending the truth with falsehood even truth is made untrue.

And so, did Zizanij gain anything by the fact that, in addition to his so manifest errors and heresies, he said that a holy man, Bishop Celestine of Rome, was an accursed heretic, and he carelessly alleged to us that he was such?[158] Or by the fact that he invented the idea that Christ the Lord is even now the visible head of His Church?[159] Or that, as has been shown, he corrupted the text of St. John Chrysostom in several places?[160] I do not think so. That is the sort of stone that turns upon the head of him that cast it.[161] What then? Did the truth no longer have enough genuine words and things for its own defense, that, having provided for himself ungenuine words and things, he claims things that never were as true? That is not the work of the truth, which is manifest, clear, pure, and simple; rather, it is the little job of him who did not abide in the truth, the father of lying and of every untruth.[162] Wherefore, to show the father's error in such matters is to cover his nakedness

---

155. *P[atriarcha] C[onstantinopolitanensis]*. [I.e., Cyril Lukaris, as patriarch two "degrees" higher than Smotryc'kyj, the archbishop of Polack, who was subordinate to the metropolitan of Kyiv.]

156. [I.e., Hieromonk Benedict, as archimandrite of the Vatopedi Monastery (about whom, see below, p. 494), equal to Smotryc'kyj in his second dignity as archimandrite of the Vilnius Brotherhood Monastery.]

157. [Rom 3:8.]

158. Fol. 56 [123].

159. Fol. 32 [88–9].

160. Fol. 47 [111; see above, p. 422].

161. [Mt 21:44; Lk. 20:18.]

162. Jn. 8[:44].

and not to uncover it.[163] So long as it remained uncovered, as long as it was taken for the truth, it caused offense to those who unwittingly fell upon it; but once it had been revealed, it became covered, for now none of us can be offended by it any more, only he, who, having closed with stubborn eyelids his eyes running with envy, does not wish to see anything good.

Thus Zizanij, a Ruthenian both by birth and by faith, is so ill informed in our Ruthenian faith.

The Following Errors and Heresies
of Philalethes Are Refuted

What good thing can we expect of Philalethes, who was a heretic both by birth and by faith? As much good, in truth, as is to be found in his heretical faith. A hireling[164] looks no further than to take and, in time of need, to flee. And just so did he take from us well and flee us quickly; and if he had not cheated us, the thing would be more tolerable. But he both took and cheated. †In payment for the heretical book entitled *Apokrisis,* which he published in order to cheat us Rus', he received a little town with several villages deeded to him for life, and in return for this he gave us for our belief the faith cribbed from Calvin's *Institutes.* In truth we paid dearly for this bauble, and I do not know which of us is wiser: he, because he sold it, or we, because we bought a cat in a bag instead of a lynx.[165] Woe is us: what have we, the sheep of Christ the Lord, come to, that we voluntarily give ourselves up to the wolf for his feeding, that we ourselves dearly purchase poverty. We hire someone to cheat us and to lead us astray from the true path; we pay for someone to sneak up to us in our faith, to rob our souls of their salvation, and to bring us unto perdition. That is certainly a severe blindness and the sort that is sent upon man only by a severely angered Lord God, who sends with His righteous judgment the effect of deceivableness[166] upon those

---

163. [Gen. 9:22–3.]
164. [Jn. 10:12–13.]
†   It is a great blindness still to pay him who led me by his writings unto eternal perdition.
165. [*NKPP* 2:165–6, "Kot," 47.]
166. 2 Th. 2[:10–11].

who either do not wish to believe the truth given by Him or who, at the attack of untruth, abandon the truth once received and believed, wishing to believe untruthfully rather than truthfully. Zizanij gave us errors and heresies. And we, having abandoned our truth, received them in place of evangelical doctrine. To punish us for which, God sent us the effect of deceivableness in Philalethes; and we received him as well. In truth, it frequently happens thus to those who walk about yawning in matters of salvation; and where the head follows the feet and not the feet the head, there must be a pitiful order. If we had set on the evangelical scales the chaff of Zizanij and the wheat given us by our fathers, and if, once weighed, we had given it to the pigs to eat, neither would Philalethes have warmed up a spot with us, for we would also have given them his slops for their feed as well. Through our carelessness in divine matters, the evil in us is punished with evil. Wherefore, we ought to complain not against anyone else, but only against ourselves, for the Lord God gave us both eyes to see and ears to hear;[167] but we, having voluntarily both stopped up our ears and closed our eyes, have entrusted ourselves to be led by blind and deaf leaders, who lead us over the stones of stumbling and the rocks of offense.[168] Deign to preserve us from the pit, our good Lord Christ. For this will certainly not pass us by, who follow blind leaders, if we do not repent in time, that is, during our lives, and do not correct ourselves and do not order these our new theologians to withdraw from our Church pulpits and from our internal and external houses. For He is true who said: "If the blind lead the blind, both shall fall into the ditch."[169] I, a man of paltry understanding, noticed so many errors and heresies in this Philalethes that if any one of you of deeper understanding will take him under your censure, you will perhaps not find even one line in all his work which was not a support of falsehood. For if falsehood is at the foundation of the matter, whatever is said in support of it must be falsehood, since only truth defends the truth, as likewise only falsehood, falsehood.

167. [Dt. 29:4; Is. 6:10, 32:3, 33:15; Jer. 5:21; Ez. 12:2; Mt. 13:15; Mk. 8:18; Rom. 11:8.]
168. 1 Pet. 2[:8].
169. Mt. 15[:14].

The Transubstantiation of Bread and Wine into the Body and Blood of Christ the Lord Is in the Confession of the Eastern Church and Is an Article of Faith

Is not everything falsehood that I cited for you a little above, most noble Ruthenian nation, in the foundation of Philalethes's speech? And the sort of falsehood with which, through the attack of many and great heretics, our Eastern Church had never allowed itself to be besmirched before, as it now, for our part (for we are a part of it), has allowed itself to be besmirched, when the Eastern Church did not acknowledge the transubstantiation of the bread and wine into the body and blood of CHRIST? When some heretic in it derided it and said that it was an invention? Because of this false leader, we are the first in it not to acknowledge that during the celebration of the Holy Liturgy the bread and the wine are transformed essentially into the body and the blood of CHRIST the Lord, and we deride such a belief, and we call it a thing invented by someone and not given by God.[170] This heretic has brought us to the sort of shameful blasphemy that in the times of our holy ancestors had never crossed the threshold of our Holy Church. Our doctors of the Church, full of the grace of the Holy Spirit, teach us this freely, that it is the essence of the body and the blood, and not a figure, that is present in the mystery of the Eucharist, the essential, and not the figurative, transubstantiation of the bread and the wine into the body and the blood of Christ the Lord. "The bread and the wine," says St. John of Damascus, "are not a figure of the body and the blood of Christ, God forfend, but the very essential body of the deified Christ, according to the testimony of Christ the Lord Himself, who says 'This is not a figure of my body but my body, not a figure of blood but blood.'"[171] But perfidious Philalethes taught us this piece of wickedness: that we both scoff at this salvatory doctrine of our holy fathers and that we assert that it is an invention. Have pity, O God, on the demise of simple souls. It is no wonder that the common lay people, since they are little learned, did not notice this blasphemy so crude and this heresy hateful to God;

170. *Pag.* 66 [1165] and 298 [1711].
171. *Lib. 4, cap. 14* [St. John of Damascus, *Exposition of the Orthodox Faith,* bk. 4, chap. 14 (actually 13); *PG* 94:1147A–1150A; *NPNF2* 9:83].

it is a wonder that we, the clergy, who ought to be learned, had our eyes closed or were blind to this for so long. And what I said about this first point drawn from his doctrine, I say likewise about all the others I have cited from him: that all of them are either errors or heresies. Wherefore all the pages, lines, and words in his work are the material of errors and heresies built on a foundation of falsehood.

That the Dignity of Bishop and Presbyter Are Not One and the Same

Is it not also heresy—first invented by the accursed Arius and condemned in him—to assert and to teach that the dignities of bishop and presbyter are one and the same?[172] And that by the law of God a bishop is not superior to a presbyter *in gradibus ordinis et in jurisdictione* [in the degrees of order and in jurisdiction]? Then what will we do with these words of the apostle: "For this cause left I thee (Bishop Titus) in Crete, that thou shouldest set in order the things that are wanting and ordain priests in every city."[173] And again: "(*Timothee Episcope* [O Bishop Timothy]) against a presbyter receive not an accusation, but before two or three witnesses."[174] For here, both with regard to the degree *ordinis* [of order] and with regard to jurisdiction, the bishop is declared to be placed above the presbyter. The bishop both consecrates and judges the presbyter, and he executes the decree of his judgment upon him, and not vice versa.

Is it not also an error, and a crude error at that, not to acknowledge that the God-Seer Moses is a priest?[175] About whom the blessed king and prophet David says: "Moses and Aaron among his priests."[176] For he brought offerings, taught, consecrated priestly vestments. And what is more, he anointed Archpriest Aaron himself to the archpriesthood, and he consecrated other priests.

---

172. *Pag.* 88 [1215]. *Dam. lib. de Haeresis* [John of Damascus, *Book on Heresies*].
173. Tit. 1[:5].
174. 1 Tim. 5[:19].
175. *Pag.* 93 [1227].
176. Ps. 98 [Ps. 99:6].

That Lay People Do Not Have the Power
Suffragii Decisivi de Fide
[of Decisive Suffrage concerning the Faith]

And in addition, what divine right do lay people have to make and carry out decrees concerning the dogmas of the faith,[177] whom the Lord God commanded to learn the law from the mouths of the priests?[178] The blessed apostle Paul teaches the priests to take care for the lay persons in salvatory, spiritual matters, and not lay persons for the priests.[179]

Likewise, what divine right do lay people have to choose persons for the spiritual state?[180] †Moses chose Aaron as an archpriest without any counsel or the permission of the people of Israel. And Christ the Lord, choosing apostles and disciples, did not ask the advice of anyone from the common people, nor did he consult them. And He commanded His disciples to do the same thing, saying to them: "As my Father has sent me, even so send I you."[181] Which is also what the apostles did through their power: choosing for themselves disciples without any councils and discussions, they established them bishops and sent them throughout various lands. Our holy and God-bearing fathers, having considered this wisely, first at the local council of Laodicea in canon thirteen,[182] and then at the Seventh Universal Council in canon three,[183] commanded that the common lay people not choose a person who is to enter into the priestly dignity and that with respect to any bishop, or presbyter, or deacon, chosen by the secular power, such an election be invalid. Thus according to this sort of judgment of the holy fathers, what divine right do lay persons have to choose persons for the spiritual estate? And yet we stand in this matter with Philalethes alone and against the fathers, the apostles, and Christ the Lord Himself.

---

177. *Pag.* 88 [1215] and 90 [1225].
178. Mal. 2[:6–7].
179. Acts 20[:28–35].
180. *Pag.* 111 [1269].
†   That lay people do not have the divine right to choose persons for the spiritual state.
181. Jn. 20[:21].
182. [Late fourth century. Mansi 2:566, 578, 586; *NPNF2* 14:131.]
183. [Nicaea II, AD 787; Tanner 140; Mansi 13:748D–749A.]

†And in what way are spiritual priesthood—with regard to which all pious people, men and women, are accustomed to bring an offering of praise to God every day in a humbled spirit—and priesthood, strictly speaking, which consists in the offering of an offering, strictly speaking, and in serving the word of God and the salvatory mysteries and which is proper to bishops and priests one and the same thing? All pious people, men and women, were in the Old Law and are now in the New, a *regale sacerdotium,* a royal priesthood.[184] But only Aaron and his descendants were offerers of superficial offerings, who had in addition the spiritual priesthood, bringing in a contrite heart the calves of their lips[185] in an offering of praise unto God.

That St. Peter Is Established the Universal Pastor by Christ the Lord

Is this not also a crude error, not to say *haeresis,* not to acknowledge that the holy apostle Peter was established as the universal pastor of the Universal Church by Christ the Lord? For whatever Christ the Lord either gave or established or taught in His Church—this is an article of faith. Whereby to acknowledge this in the Church of Christ the Lord is an article of faith; not to acknowledge it is *haeresis.* Therefore, our Holy Eastern Church always knew, believed, and confessed this in its teachers; it knows, believes, and confesses now that the blessed apostle Peter is the universal pastor of the Universal Church. Whence St. John Chrysostom calls him the head and pastor of the Church of Christ.[186] And the Church itself, in its hymns, calls him pastor with regard to itself and archpastor with regard to the other apostles.[187] Where, then, is there room in our Ruthenian Church for yet this heresy of Philalethes?

---

† That spiritual priesthood and sacramental priesthood are not one and the same.

184. 1 Pet. 2[:9].

185. [Hos. 14:2.]

186. *In Matt. Hom. 55* [St. John Chrysostom, *Homily 55 (54) on Matthew; PG* 58:534–5; *NPNF1* 10:334].

187. In *photagogikon* 11 [sung after the canon at matins on Sundays, connected with Jn. 21:15–17 ("Feed my sheep")].

†Nor is it without error to deny that Christ the Lord called St. Peter the Rock. For having said to St. Peter in the Syriac language, *Tu es Cepha, et super hoc Cepha aedificabo ecclesiam meam,* what else did Christ the Lord say but that "Thou art Rock, and upon this rock I will build my Church."[188] Having interpreted these words of Christ the Lord in this manner, St. John Chrysostom speaks of St. Peter with these express words with which Christ the Lord spoke to him: "Thou art Rock, and upon this rock I will build my Church."[189] Having interpreted, along with St. John Chrysostom, these words of Christ the Lord as I say, other holy doctors of the Church also call the holy apostle Peter the Rock without any hesitation. St. Gregory the Theologian says that Peter is called the Rock and has the foundations of the Church entrusted to his faith.[190] St. Epiphanius says, "The Lord established Peter the first strong rock among the apostles, upon which the Church of God is built."[191] St. Jerome says, "Not only Christ is a rock, but He also granted unto the apostle Peter that he be called the Rock."[192] St. Augustine says, "Peter is called the Rock on account of piety, and the Lord is called the Rock on account of strength."[193] St. Ambrose says, "Who does not know this most powerful Rock, who received participation in power and his name from that original Rock?"[194] St. Hilarius says, "O foundation of the Church, happy in its establishment of a new name; o rock worthy of its building."[195] Also the 630 holy fathers of the Fourth Universal Council

† That Christ the Lord called St. Peter the Rock.

188. Mt. 16[:18].

189. *Serm. in festam exaltationis S. Crucis, qui incipit, Quid dicam, quid loquar?* [John Chrysostom, *Homily on the Feast of the Exaltation of the Cross* that begins "What should I say? What should I speak?"]

190. *Serm. de moderat.* [Gregory of Nazianzus, *On the Need to Maintain Moderation in Disputations,* oration 32, chap. 18; *PG* 36:193/194C–195/196B.]

191. *Serm. in disput. in Ancorato.* [Epiphanius of Constantia, *The Well-Anchored; PG* 43:33–4.]

192. *Lib. 3 in cap. 16. Hierem* [St. Jerome, *Bk. 3 on Jer. 16; PL* 24:784C].

193. *Serm. 16 de sanctis* [Uncertain author, *Sermons on the Saints,* 192; *PL* 39:2102].

194. *Lib. 2 de vocatione gentium cap. 28* [Uncertain author, *Two Books on the Calling of the Nations,* bk. 2, chap. 9; *PL* 17:1126B].

195. *In. Matt. c. 16* [*Commentaries on Matthew,* chap. 16; *PL* 9:1009C].

call St. Peter the Rock and Stone of the Universal Church. Whence our Ruthenian Church, taught by the Eastern Church, in *panaegiricis* [panegyric] hymns to the holy apostle Peter, calls him in express words the Rock, and that is the Rock of faith. Wherefore, heresy is far from our Ruthenian Church.

That Christ the Lord Built His Church upon St. Peter

By the testimonies I have cited from the holy doctors, this error too is far from our Ruthenian Church: not to acknowledge that Christ the Lord built His Church on the holy apostle Peter. And the Eastern Church always confessed this. To which I will add St. John Chrysostom, who said: "Thou art Peter, and upon you will I build my Church."[196] And Theophylactus, who taught: "The Lord renders unto Peter gift for gift, giving him a great reward, that He built His Church upon him."[197] And St. Ephrem, who says as if in conversation: "If we remain here, Peter, then how will what I told you be fulfilled? How will the Church be built upon you?"[198] Thus both these errors began to be introduced into our Ruthenian Church recently, for it confesses freely that Christ the Lord built His Church upon St. Peter.[199]

That Christ the Lord Entrusted the Sheep of the Entire World to St. Peter for Feeding

It is also a severe heretical error not to acknowledge that, having said to St. Peter these words—*pasce oves meas* [feed my sheep][200]—he entrusted all His sheep to him for feeding. For in this matter, St. Theophylactus, instructed by St. John Chrysostom, shuts the mouth of Philalethes when

196. *Hom. 55 in Mattheum* [St. John Chrysostom, *Homily 55 (54) on Matthew; PG* 58:534; *NPNF1* 10:333].
197. *In cap. 16 Mat* [Theophylactus, *Sermon on Matthew 16; PG* 123:319AB–320AB].
198. *Serm. in Transfig. Domini* [St. Ephrem the Syrian, *Homily on the Transfiguration of the Lord;* Ephr. 2:426].
199. In our hymns about the apostles Peter and Paul.
200. [Jn. 21:16.]

he says in his interpretation of the words of the Lord, "Feed my sheep": "Once Christ the Lord has finished the supper, he entrusts to Peter authority over the sheep of all the world; He gives it to no one else but him."[201] And St. John Chrysostom, interpreting the same words of Christ the Lord, says: "James received the see of Jerusalem, but Peter was established the teacher of the entire world."[202] And again he says: "(The Lord) commended and entrusted unto him care for the brethren and for the entire world."[203] Likewise St. Theophylactus also says: "He entrusted unto him authority over all the faithful and the brethren of the entire world."[204] In addition, our Ruthenian Church shuts his heretical mouth, for we are taught by the Eastern Church to confess that, having appeared present before His disciples after His resurrection, the Savior entrusted the shepherding of His sheep to Peter.[205]

That Christ the Lord Gave His Apostles
Two Sorts of Keys: Ordinis et Jurisdictionis
[of Order and Jurisdiction]

It is also a heretical error not to acknowledge that two sorts of keys were given to the apostles by Christ the Lord: one set *ordinis,* that is, of order; and the second *jurisdictionis,* of power. For it is part of the undoubtable confession and daily usage of the Eastern Church and, in it, of our Ruthenian one, that bishops—both with regard to order, which is one key, and power, which is the second key—are greater and higher than presbyters. And the bishops themselves recognize some from among themselves who are of greater and higher jurisdiction over themselves. For when Christ the Lord said to His apostles *pax vobis*—"Peace be unto you: as my Father hath sent me, even so send

201. *In cap. 21 Ioan.* [Theophylactus, *Sermon on John 21; PG* 124:309/310A–B].
202. *In cap. 21 Ioan.* [St. John Chrysostom, *Sermon 88 on John 21; PG* 59:480; *NPNF1* 14:332].
203. Ibid. [St. John Chrysostom, *Sermon 88 on John 21; PG* 59:480; *NPNF1* 14:332].
204. Ibid. [Theophylactus, *Sermon on John 21; PG* 124:309A–310A].
205. In *photagogikon* 11 [sung after the canon at matins on Sundays, connected with Jn. 21:15–17 ("Feed my sheep")].

I you"[206]—He gave them one key, that is, *potestatem jurisdictionis,* the power of Church jurisdiction. For through these words He made them His emissaries unto the entire world, and through His power, the rulers of His Church. And by saying immediately thereafter, "Whose soever sins ye remit, they are remitted unto them; and whose soever sins ye retain, they are retained,"[207] He gave them the second key, that is, *potestas ordinis,* the power of order. And in the third place, by saying to St. Peter himself *pasce oves meas,* "feed my sheep,"[208] He gave him the very same key of jurisdiction, with the gathering under his power of those very apostles, established by His power as rulers of the entire world, as we heard a little above St. Theophylactus speaking of this following St. John Chrysostom: that Christ the Lord, through the words He spoke to the apostle Peter—"feed my sheep"—entrusted unto him authority over the faithful and the brethren of the entire world.[209]

That Both by the Law of God and by the Law of the Church, Appeal Belongs to the Bishop of Rome

This too is a heretical error, introduced into our Ruthenian Church by that heretic: not to acknowledge that, both by ancient custom and by the decree of Church laws, appeal was to be made to the bishop of Rome. Before Church law, there are the following examples of this by custom: in Marcion of Pontus, in Fortunatus and Felix of Africa, in St. Athanasius of Egypt, who appealed in legal wrongs to the bishop of Rome. The right of appeal, on the other hand, is described in the third, fourth, and fifth canons of the Council of Sardica,[210] in clear and express words, which was then used in appeals to the Roman popes by St. John Chrysostom and St. Flavian, patriarchs of Constantinople, who were wronged by Theophilus and Dioscorus, patriarchs of Alexandria, and in the appeal of St. Theodoretus, bishop of Cyrrhus, and others. Wherefore, if from ancient custom (which has its beginning in the law

---

206. Jn. 20[:21].
207. Jn. 20[:23].
208. Jn. 21[:16].
209. *In c. 21 Jn.* [St. John Chrysostom, *Homily 88 on Jn. 21:15; PG* 59:478; *NPNF1* 14:331].
210. [Council of Sardica, AD 343–344; Mansi 3:7–10; Mansi 6:1203BC.]

of God) and from Church law, it is clear that in the courts of spiritual matters appeal always was to be made, and is to be made, to the bishop of Rome and not to the Roman emperor, then it follows that this too is a heretical error: to assert that in spiritual matters appeal is to be made to secular authorities, to the kings or the emperors. And Church practice itself, maintained in all these times in the Church, makes it known that this is the case: that in spiritual matters no secular judge or authority, either without appeal or through appeal, judges any clergyman.

That the Power of Convening Universal Synods Belongs to the Bishop of Rome

Furthermore, this too is a severe error urged upon us by that same Philalethes: to appropriate for kings and emperors the power of convening councils. If by Church laws the local episcopal and metropolitan councils are composed, decreed, and convened by bishops and metropolitans, and not by kings and emperors,[211] then certainly for the composition of universal councils the secular power has nothing to say, neither the royal nor the imperial. But the highest spiritual power does have something to say. And during all seven universal councils the bishop of Rome was known as such by the entire Church, to whom belonged both the entire jurisdiction of the Universal Church and the convening of universal councils, which is also the proper obligation of his jurisdiction, according to the law that rested upon him since apostolic times: μὴ δεῖν παρὰ τοῦ Ρώμης ἐπίσκοπου κανον ζειν τὰς ἐκκλησίας, that is, that the church councils are not to be convened or concluded against the opinion of the bishop of Rome.[212] In view of which right, at the Fourth Universal Council the holy and God-bearing fathers did

211. *Can. Apl. 37* [*Apostolic Canons* 37; *PG* 137:113C–114C; *NPNF2* 14:596]. *4 Syn. Can. 19* [Fourth Universal Council, Canon 19, Chalcedon, AD 451; Mansi 7:378D–379A; Tanner 96; *NPNF2* 14:282]. *1 Syn. Ca. 5* [First Universal Council, Canon 5, Nicaea, AD 325; Mansi 2:669D–670D; Tanner 8; *NPNF2* 14:13]. *7 Syn. Ca. 6* [Seventh Universal Council, Canon 6, Nicaea II, AD 787; Mansi 13:750D–751A; Tanner 143–33; *NPNF2* 14:559–60].
212. *Socrat. Hist. Eccle. Lib. 2. c. 5 et 13* [Socrates Scholasticus, *Church History,* bk. 2, chaps. 5, 13; *PG* 67:197–200, 207–10; *NPNF2* 2:39, 41]. *Sozom. lib. 3 c. 9* [Sozomenus Hermias Salaminus, *Church History,* bk. 3, chap. 9; *PG*

not permit Patriarch Dioscorus of Alexandria to sit among the bishops because he made bold to hold a council without the knowledge of the bishop of Rome.[213] For this, they say, was not permitted to anyone to do and was never done by anyone.

This is also made perfectly clear from the words of the new St. Stephen, who said to the iconoclast heretics: "How do you dare to call your council universal when the Roman *praesidens* [president, one who presides] did not allow it, without whom it is invalid to establish anything in Church matters?"[214] Moreover, natural reason itself can show to a man of even limited wit that the universal council is to be convened by him who can compel to be present even those who do not wish to be at it. But there was never a king or an emperor who encompassed the entire Church with his rule such that he could compel even the unwilling to appear at the council. But the spiritual authority does have this, for it extends its complete power uniformly over various kings and monarchs; it orders, compels, and can—and does—punish the disobedient. During the ages of our ancestors, one metropolitan of Kyiv ruled both the Ruthenian and the Muscovite bishops, and all the clergy of both those domains, which neither the prince of Lithuania could ever, or can, accomplish in Moscow, nor the prince of Muscovy in Rus', since they do not have the right for this from God. And the patriarch of Constantinople, throughout almost all the past ages since Rus' was baptized under the Christian emperors, governed the metropolitan of the Ruthenian land and all his clergy. But the secular lord, the emperor of Constantinople, never had this in his power and could not have it. If the patriarch of Constantinople ever convened a local council, the metropolitan was obliged to appear for it; but if the emperor convened it, the metropolitan of Rus' never even gave it a second thought. For he [the emperor] did not have the power to punish him [the metropolitan], nor could he have had in another's domain since his power reaches only as

---

67:1055–6; *NPNF2* 2:288]. *Niceph. Call. lib. 9. c. 5* [Nicephorus Callistus Xanthopulus, *Church History,* bk. 9, chap. 5; *PG* 146:231–8; the Greek quote is close to the passage here].

213. *Act. 1* [Council of Chalcedon, AD 451, First Session; Mansi 6:579D–582A; *NPNF2* 14:247].

214. *Simeon Metaphr[astes] in his [St. Stephen's] Life. [PG* 115:513–24. I was unable to locate this passage here.]

far as the borders of his domain. But the power of the spiritual authority reaches as far as the borders of the Universal Church, that is, throughout the entire world. †The emperor participates in the universal council, as do also the kings, but as defenders of the Church through secular power, its helpers, and the assistants of poor bishops—through providing horse and carriage, provisions for journeys, and all necessities and goods in such matters and in guarding the common peace at it. But just as no king or emperor ever properly participates, or could participate, in the council of bishops and in discussions of spiritual matters, so also they could not take part in convening a council since they could not command or punish the disobedient in another's domain and did not have the power given them by God as is given the Church authority through these words *pasce oves meas,* feed my sheep. By saying "my," He granted, commanded, and ordered that power be extended over all people, both under Catholic and under heretical and pagan lords, wherever His sheep are found.

That the Bishop of Rome Occupies the First Place at the Universal Councils

Finally, this too is an error of Philalethes: not to acknowledge that the bishops of Rome occupied the first places at the Universal Councils. For this was a part of the daily confession in the Church of our holy ancestors, from whom we too have it in our books of rules that in the number of the elders of the councils, at the First Universal Council the Bishop Sylvester of Rome was established as the first elder; at the Second, Damasus; at the Third, Celestine; at the Fourth, Leo; at the Fifth, Vigilius; at the Sixth, Agatho; at the Seventh, Hadrian. And although no bishop of Rome was ever present in person at any universal council, but rather he presided either through his emissaries or through permission and affirmation of decrees, nonetheless the conciliar historians grant to them that they were present as if in person and took first place among the elders of the councils. Of which our Church books are full of evidence, wherever the seven universal councils are found described.

These, among many others, are the heretical errors that the heretic

---

†   In what manner emperors and kings participate in councils.

Philalethes made bold to introduce into our Ruthenian Church. Is this still not enough for us to recognize what we are? How far we are from the truth? And how much we are afflicted with heresies? One error makes a man to stray. One heresy makes him a heretic. And here, through the harmful industry of these our Zizanijs and Philaletheses, several tens of them have been gathered. But perhaps we will still wish to be known as pure and immaculate in the dogmas of the faith? We must be mindful, most beloved fathers and brethren, that it is difficult to heal a sick man who does not recognize and acknowledge that he is sick and that such a one is nearer to death than to life. Here ends my discussion of Philalethes.

The Errors and Heresies of Orthologue
Are Refuted

Let us also yet examine, most noble Ruthenian nation, Orthologue's *Lament*. Does he, with his vexatious tears, make the lids of our eyes that stream with Zizanij and Philalethes to open and to see, and does he awaken us and bring us to see the errors and heresies of both Zizanij and Philalethes, as well as those of his own? For these three saintlets of ours are the Ruthenian lamps of our ages. If only they had never shone forth, for then our Ruthenian Church would never have come to such palpable darkness, to such a hideous blot, and to such a clear fall. These three saintlets deprived us of the true paternal faith; they sowed the tares of errors and heresies into our pure wheat that had been sown by God;[215] they deprived us of noble families; they wrenched from our hands our rights, freedoms, and liberties; they procured our present-day miseries; they set our Ruthenian nation at odds with itself; they divided one house into two, so that it now seeks its own demise. And according to the true words of Christ the Lord, if it does not again reunite through His holy compassion, it will bring itself to a severe and lamentable downfall.[216]

For as soon as the field of our Church began to become overgrown with tares, its wheat immediately began to cheapen; and it became so cheap that not only did no one else buy it, and does not buy it, but many of our own people poured it out from the houses of our hearts and

215. [Mt. 13:25, 40; Mt. 3:12; Lk. 3:17.]
216. [Mt. 12:25; Mk. 3:24–5.]

trod upon it like stale salt.[217] And when thereafter the second sower, Philalethes, and after him the third, Orthologue, joined him and sowed even more the tares of their errors and heresies, it became so cheap that none of the others even wishes to look upon it, since it is now half in tares, nor is it very pleasant for many of our own people.

Take pity upon yourself, O most noble Ruthenian nation, and do not allow yourself to perish both temporally and eternally; do not allow these unwise blind men to lead you blindly. Have your own God-inspired understanding, and do not found your salvation on the error of three people, or even of three more, for souls are at stake. See what I have already cited of those two, and what I will now proceed to cite from the third. Consider whether these are not manifest errors and heresies previously unheard of in your Ruthenian Church. With a loving spirit, free from every hatred, without any stubbornness, examine, in addition to those two already cited, the lamentatious writing as well,[218] and judge its account not with a heart in discord against the brethren, but according to the truth of God, and, by God's grace, you will see, through the enlightenment of your understanding, upon what it is founded, from what it is constructed, and with what it is covered. You will find in its foundation hatred; in its walls falsehood; and in its roof calumny. For having set aside what I cited from him at the beginning, in which he is in error and heretical, let us first examine this alone: †of what does he cry, what does he lament, against whom does he complain, and from whom or in whose person?

Oh, how much more fitting would it have been for him to cry in that person [of the Eastern Church], in that person and in his own, especially after he read the errors and heresies of Zizanij and Philalethes that had already appeared before him; by that time *Antigraphē* had also already appeared, in which Philalethes together with the Clerk of Ostroh, the same sort of blasphemer, are acknowledged and accepted as churchmen of our side. For that Clerk also received and acknowledged

---

217. [Mt. 5:13; Mk. 9:50; Lk. 14:34.]
218. [I.e., *Thrēnos*.]
†   At the beginning of his book, Orthologue laments and complains that the sons of one mother Church, formerly divided and set at variance, are coming to concord and love with each other, that they are abandoning errors and heresies and are taking up the true faith. This is the lament of the devil.

Philalethes as his speaker of truth. They joined together, it is clear, in one spirit of deceit. Thus it would rather have befitted Orthologue to cry for his own person and for that in which he clothed himself than, in their name, to lament against anyone else: for his own person because he allowed himself to abominate his fellow Churchmen with the blot of blasphemies disgusting unto God; and for that other because, although as the Mother she was supposed to do so, she did not warn her daughters of this evil, rather, through her silence for so many years, even until today, she allowed herself to be known as giving assent and approving. That would be a proper and salvatory cry and lament for him, for in lamenting in this fashion he would have alerted and protected himself and his people from these wicked blasphemies of Zizanij, Philalethes, the Clerk, and others like them; and she would not have allowed herself to be lured so easily to this same wickedness. For both have now been given up to drown in them so deeply by their theologians that if they are not protected from this evil through the special grace over them of the compassion of God, human industry cannot protect them from the flood that has been prepared for them.

Let us further examine how acrimonious, vexatious, and unbearable are the words of this Orthologue. For he treats the opposing side, if it is opposing, as if he could not give complete expression to the wrong he has suffered, if it is such, in honorable words. He reviles, shames, abuses, and deprives of faith and honor people of dignities of both estates who are worthy of all honor and respect. I purposefully do not repeat his venomous words lest I seem to break open and to irritate this stinking scab. †For I am sick at this with all my soul, and I ask the Lord my God to be compassionate toward my ignorance. Regret and pain, when they pass measure, make a man as if benumbed: they take his voice, they even stop his tears. I feel both these things occurring in my heart. Nonetheless, I render thanks to the Lord God, who had mercy upon me, who deigned to cause me while still upon this world, through his special grace, to trip upon that rock of offense,[219] to take notice, and to come to myself.

---

†   After acknowledging his errors, the lamentographer laments and regrets in heartfelt fashion that he ever published the *Lament,* as there is reason to regret and to cry, for many lost their souls through his lamentatious writing.
219. [1 Pet. 2:8.]

I said that I do not wish to repeat the irritating and vexatious, lamentatious words, since however many words there are in it, all of them serve untruth. I will recall again from it whatever is untrue to the holy Orthodox faith. I will recall its errors and heresies so that later on they might not be able to harm anyone. I will not repeat them here anew, but for the second and for the third time (*in ore enim duorum vel trium testium stabit omne verbum* [in the mouth of two or three witnesses shall every word be established])[220] I report, most noble Ruthenian nation, that they are proper heretical spawn. And since they are open and manifest by themselves, I will not subject them to examination. For who among the Orthodox does not know that our Eastern Church always confessed and confesses that there were seven sacraments given by Christ the Lord to His Church? Witness to which is the censure of the Lutheran errors and heresies made by Patriarch Jeremiah of Constantinople, of blessed memory, as well as the *syntagma* [collection of writings] on the seven salvatory mysteries published by Archbishop Gabriel of Philadelphia, of blessed memory. But Orthologue, having rejected five of them, accepts and asserts that only two sacraments were given by Christ the Lord.[221] Which is unbearable *haeresis*.

This too is a *haeresis* on the part of Orthologue, one which he holds in common with Zizanij: to establish that an earthly paradise is the place for righteous souls that have departed this world.[222] But in this matter, in addition to the other proofs I have cited against the errors of Zizanij, this thing which we commonly say of deceased people could have instructed us: †for we call those who have departed this world *nieboszczyki* [deceased], wherefore, we understand and confess that they are not on earth but in *niebo* [heaven].[223] For if they have departed this world, then they are not in an earthly paradise, which is in this world, on earth; if they are *nieboszczyki* [deceased], then they are in *niebo* [heaven], as already heavenly citizens and not on earth. ‡Perhaps

---

220. 2 Cor. 12 [2 Cor. 13:1].
221. Fol. 214v [231].
222. Fol. 155r [171].
†   Why we call the dead *nieboszczyki* [deceased].
223. [The etymology is spurious: *nieboszczyk* (i.e., *niebożczyk*) derives from *niebogi*, 'poor.']
‡   The schismatics come forth with this testimony as if from St. Athanasius,

answer number nineteen from the *Questions to Antioch,* which are ascribed to St. Athanasius, misled Orthologue, and before him Zizanij and the author of *Antigraphē,* where it is said that the righteous souls are in paradise?[224] But what is said in this answer is either suspicious, since St. Athanasius writes in the life of St. Anthony the Great that he saw the soul of St. Ammon being carried by angels not to an earthly paradise, but to heaven;[225] or it is incorrectly understood by them, since the author of these answers says that Christ the Lord is also present in this same paradise, in whose presence the holy souls rejoice and are glad as in the presence of their king. But we do not believe that Christ the Lord is in an earthly paradise, but in a heavenly one, wherefore St. Athanasius understood, believed, and confessed that the righteous souls were in the same paradise, and we too must likewise understand, believe, and confess.

That after Departing from This World
the Punishments of Some Sins
Are Remitted

These too are clear heresies of Orthologue: to assert that it is unnecessary that the punishment of sins be remitted after a person's departure from this world[226] and that the sins of those living in this world are remitted *gratis* [for free], without any merits, through the compassionate grace of a benevolent God.[227] The first of these two heresies is destroyed by the Church prayers for the dead in our Church; and the second by the sacrament of penance, the essential part of which is satisfaction. For if what Orthologue teaches us and our Church were true, offerings for the dead, memorials, alms, and other benefactions done by the Church would have to be in vain and unnecessary; and the hairshirts, fasts, alms, early risings, long standings at prayer, and the various mortifications of the body of pious people, and, in short, the mystery

---

asserting that the souls of the righteous remain until the Judgment Day in an earthly paradise and not in a heavenly one.

224. [St. Athanasius, *Questions to Antioch,* no. 19; *PG* 609A–610A.]
225. [St. Athanasius, *Life of St. Anthony; PG* 26:929–30; *NPNF2* 4:212.]
226. Fol. 166r [182].
227. Fol. 157r [173] and 116v [133, but the reference seems incorrect].

of penance, which consists in heartfelt contrition, auricular confession, and the satisfaction of pious corporeal deeds, would have to be in vain and entirely unnecessary in the Church of Christ the Lord. But it is rather the heresies submitted by Orthologue and presented to the world as our own that are vain and unnecessary to our Church.[228]

I pass by that heresy already criticized in Zizanij: not to acknowledge particular judgment.

That Faith Is Not Lost on Account of Sin and That the Soul Is Created by God and Infused into Man, and Does Not Come from the Parents' Seed

And what he says about mortal sin driving faith away from a man—this too is *haeresis*.[229] And this is another: to assert that the soul of man is established *ex traduce* [by transferal, grafting].[230]

For faith, according to the doctrine of Christ the Lord, is not lost through anything other than unfaith, when a faithful person becomes faithless, that is, a heretic or a pagan.[231] For in addition to faith, he also loses at the same time the grace of God, and righteousness, and the presence of the Holy Spirit, according to that which is said: "Now the Spirit speaketh expressly that in the latter times some shall depart from the faith, giving heed to seducing spirits, and doctrines of devils; speaking lies in hypocrisy; having their conscience seared with a hot iron."[232] But when a righteous man falls into mortal sin, he falls out of righteousness, he falls away from the Holy Spirit, and he loses the grace of God until he repents; but he does not lose faith, which keeps him, even with a mortal sin, within the Church, whereas the faithless are not in the Church.

As far as the creation of the soul is concerned, the Church of Christ the Lord, assured by this doctrine of Holy Scripture, teaches that it is created anew for each man by God and not derived by generation from seed: "And the Lord God formed man of the dust of the ground,

228. Fol. 177r [193].
229. Fol. 212r [228].
230. Fol. 213r [229].
231. Lk. 9; 12[:42–8].
232. 1 Tim. 4[:1–2].

and breathed into his nostrils the breath of life; and man became a living soul."[233] "Then let the dust return to the earth as it was: and let the spirit return unto God who gave it."[234] "Furthermore we have had fathers of our flesh which corrected us, and we gave them reverence: shall we not much rather be in subjection unto the Father of spirits, and live?"[235] This, then, is the belief of the Church of Christ the Lord, according to the doctrine I cited from Holy Scripture: that the Lord God creates for each man his soul anew and infuses it, through the blessing He made in paradise, into the body conceived and established from seed in the mother's womb. For as spirit does not give birth to spirit, so certainly the body cannot give birth to spirit. Whence St. John Chrysostom says: "The spirit neither gives birth nor is born, and it knows no father except for Him by whose will it is created."[236] St. Cyril of Alexandria, discoursing gravely from Holy Scripture concerning the incarnation of the Son of God and concerning the name "Mother of God," speaks by way of a parable on the topic we have presented on the establishment of the soul: "This mystery of the incarnation of the Word of God has no little similarity to human birth, for although the mothers of earthly people, serving for birth at birth, carry the body in their womb, which with the passing of time, growing slightly and taking increase little by little according to certain hidden deeds of the Creator, acquires human likeness, nonetheless He infuses the spirit in the manner which He alone knows into the already perfect and living body. For He creates the spirit of man within him, as the prophet says.[237] And although they become the mothers only of the earthly bodies, nonetheless one says of them that they give birth not to some one part of man, but to the whole man, composed of soul and body. For no one (that I explain my argument with an example) will say that Elizabeth is the mother of the body only and not of the soul as well, since she did not give birth only to the body, but to the Baptist, who was made of soul and body."[238] It is manifestly

233. Gen. 2[:7].
234. Eccl. 12[:7].
235. Heb. 12[:9].
236. *Hom. 25 in varia loca Matt.* [Homily 25 on various passages in Matthew].
237. Zech. 12[:1].
238. *Epist. ad Monachos Aegypti tom. Concil. 1 pag. 365* [St. Cyril of

clear from the express and manifest doctrine of that holy doctor that
the Lord God creates every soul anew and infuses the living soul into
the already perfect living body. St. Methodius, bishop of Pamphylia,
says: "We must not believe that the holy apostle wished to teach us
that the birth of the soul was sown together with the mortal body.
For the Creator Himself, who is Himself immortal and the Creator of
incorruptible things, inspires the immortal and unaging things."[239] St.
Augustine says: "The soul is infused when it is created, and it is created
when it is infused."[240] St. Jerome says: "Those are worthy of mockery
who believe that souls are sown from bodies, that they proceed not from
God but from the bodies of their parents."[241] Indeed, Orthologue too is
worthy of mockery, for he attempted to introduce this error worthy of
mockery into our Ruthenian Church.

That the Divine Essence Is Not Divided from the
Divine Person in Reality

This, finally, is Orthologue's error of errors and heresy of heresies: that
he divides the divine essence from the divine person in reality, when
he says that the Son and the Holy Spirit, as far as perfect essence is
concerned (as if there existed some imperfect divine essence), are from
themselves; but with regard to their personal essence, they are from
the Father. And when he asserts that the Holy Spirit is not from the
essence of the Father. And that the Son was not born from the essence
of the Father, but from the person.[242] †From his careless arguments this
blasphemy derives necessarily: that when the Father gave birth to the
Son and brought forth the Holy Spirit, He did not lend to them His
essence, rather He only established their persons; for they had their

---

Alexandria, *Letter to the Monks of Egypt,* in the first volume of the Councils,
p. 365; Letter 1, *PG* 7721/7722BC].

239. *Cap. 16* [Methodius of Pamphylia, chap. 16].

240. *Lib. de Origine animae* [Augustine, *Four Books on the Soul and Its
Origin; PL* 44:475–548; *NPNF1* 5:309–71].

241. *In cap. 12 Eccl.* [Jerome, *On Ecclesiastes,* chap. 12].

242. Fols. 66r [82], 93v [110], 99v [116], 102r [118], 102v [119], 190r [206],
220v [?]. Fols. 101r [117], 122v [139].

†   This is a great blasphemy of Orthologue.

essence from themselves. Whence the following other blasphemies arise: first, that every divine person is divided in itself in reality, with respect to its essence and person; second, that the person is understood *consistere* [to exist] without essence; third, that however many persons there are in one divinity, such is the number of origins. But all this certainly transgresses the bounds of Catholic Orthodox confession.

After he established this unwisely and blasphemously, Orthologue destroys the natural order of the divine persons as far as their being is concerned, and he says that it is the Eunomian *haeresis* to confess that the Holy Spirit is third.[243] But that there is thus an order among the divine persons as far as their originary being is concerned, St. Basil (who received praise from the Fourth Universal Council because he had explained the doctrine of the Holy Spirit) teaches us, saying: "How can we not acknowledge order where there is a first and a second?"[244] And the same great doctor deduces in that same place that that order is natural, saying: "Among them there is a first and a second, not according to our position, but through the consequence that is found in them according to birth."[245] And with respect to this order, the same saint names the Son as the second from the Father and the Holy Spirit sometimes the second from the Son, sometimes the third from the Father and the Son.[246] Wherefore the untruth of Orthologue is manifest, who says that it is the Eunomian heresy to confess that the Holy Spirit is third. For St. Epiphanius also called Him third, saying: "The Holy Spirit is the Spirit of truth, the third light from the Father and the Son."[247] And we commonly confess that among the divine persons the Father is the first person, the Son the second, and the Holy Spirit the third. If anyone were to say, with respect to the natural order of the divine persons in their being, that the Father is the second or the third person, the Son the first or third, the Holy Spirit the first or the second, he would blaspheme just as Orthologue blasphemes in this, not knowing the difference between the number of the divine persons and their order.

243. Fol. 99v [116].
244. *Serm. 1 in Eunomium* [St. Basil the Great, *Against Eunomius, Sermon 1,* chap. 20; *PG* 29:555–8].
245. Ibid.
246. *Serm. 3 in Eunom.* [St. Basil the Great, *Against Eunomius, Sermon 3*; *PG* 29:653–6].
247. *In Anchorato* [St. Epiphanius, *The Well Anchored, PG* 43:147B–148B].

With respect to the number, the counting of the divine persons can be varied, as when one says that one divine person is the Father, a second the Son, a third the Holy Spirit; for one could also say to the contrary, one or the first (having taken the word "first" in the meaning *quantitatis numeri* [of a number of quantity]) person the Holy Spirit or the Son, a second the Father or the Holy Spirit, a third the Father or the Son. But with respect to the natural order of the divine persons as far as their being is concerned, "Without manifest impiety," says St. Basil, "the Son cannot be placed before the Father, nor the Holy Spirit before the Father or the Son. Having said which, the Spirit is counted with the Father and with the Son since He is beyond creation, but He is placed third with respect to order"—let us listen to what this great doctor says: "He is placed third with respect to order"—"as we are taught by the Gospel."[248] Having said this, I say, St. Basil argues that to place the Holy Spirit before the Father or the Son according to time or order is impiety.[249] And again he says: "Whoever places the Holy Spirit before the Son, either according to time or according to order or says that He is older than is the Father, opposes divine disposition and is far from the faith of God."[250] Thus it is rather Orthologue himself who falls into the Eunomian heresy when he does not acknowledge a natural order among the divine persons, not subject to any disturbance or variation, and does not accept that the Holy Spirit is third according to the order of being. Wherefore, according to the testimony of the manifest and clear doctrine about this of the great teacher of the Church, he opposes the divine disposition and establishes an impious thing and is far from the faith of God.

Orthologue's Great Absurdities Are Clearly Demonstrated

Let us see, most beloved fathers and brethren, how we can avoid all this, we who bear upon our heads this lamentatious writing, so thick with ugly blasphemies against the majesty of God, and who allow our

---

248. *Epist. ad canonicas* [St. Basil the Great, *Letter* 52, chap. 4, "To the Canonesses"; *PG* 395/396A–C; *FC* 13:138–9].
249. Ibid.
250. Ibid.

Ruthenian Church to be rendered godless by it. Do not think, most noble nation, that I cited anything unfaithfully from him or that I unjustly destroyed his heretical blasphemies, which are hateful to God. You have before you the pages I noted in it. You have also my narration against him. Read and compare, and you will see that not only is it not worthy of your head, but not even of your hand: it merited being cast under your feet like the first two works of Zizanij and Philalethes and others, spat upon and trodden under foot. For he, having laid the blasphemous foundation for his chapter on the procession of the Holy Spirit, which I cited from him here and a little above, raised and built these blasphemies against Him. First, that the Holy Spirit does not relate to the Father, as to the one spirating.[251] Second, that, with regard to essence, the Son and the Holy Spirit are the same cause unto Themselves as is the Father unto Himself.[252] Third, that, with regard to essence, all the divine persons act of their own accord.[253] Fourth, that as far as their perfect (as he says) essence is concerned, the Son and the Holy Spirit are *sine principio, sine causa* [without beginning, without cause], as is also the Father.[254] Fifth, that the Son and the Holy Spirit are both second according to order.[255] Sixth, that the Holy Spirit relates to the Father, as to His producer, immediately.[256] Seventh, that the Son relates to the Father, as to His producer, mediately.[257] Eighth, that he does not acknowledge that the number—first, second, third—signifies the natural order of the divine persons as far as their originary essence is concerned.[258] Ninth, that the number can properly be applied by turns to each divine person.[259] Tenth, that he establishes that the order between the divine persons is for the Father to the Son and the Holy Spirit, and conversely for the Son and the Holy Spirit to the Father.[260]

251. Fol. 95r [111].
252. Fol. 97v [114].
253. Fol. 98r [114].
254. Fol. 99v [116].
255. Ibid. [116] and fol. 101r [117].
256. Ibid. [117].
257. Fol. 101r [117].
258. Fol. 101r [117].
259. Ibid. [117].
260. Ibid. [117].

Eleventh, that he absolutely denies that the Holy Spirit is third from the Father.[261] Twelfth, that he does not acknowledge that the Holy Spirit is second from the Son.[262] Thirteenth, that he asserts that the Spirit, which the Son promised to send from the Father, is not the person of the Holy Spirit.[263] Fourteenth, that he establishes that the gifts that are now given to God's faithful are not creation but the very spirit of truth.[264] Fifteenth, that he says that the Son is a twofold cause of the creation of the world: first, according to essence; and a mediating cause according to person.[265] Sixteenth, that he does not acknowledge that the Son is born, and the Holy Spirit proceeds, from the essence of the Father, but rather [he asserts] from the person of the Father.[266]

When I write these things, I seem to blaspheme again against the majesty of my God, the Word of God, and His Holy Spirit by repeating these vulgar blasphemies, which heretically take from Them Their divine majesty in divine essence, which They have from the Father, the one through birth and the other through procession. But I do this that I might demonstrate to you clearly, most noble Ruthenian nation, to what sort of blasphemous absurdities and heresies hateful to God Orthologue himself fell victim and caused us to fall victim through his lamentatious writing. For who of us, enlightened by the grace of God, cannot see easily that all the points cited by me from the lamentatious writing concerning the procession of the Holy Spirit are errors and heresies?

For as far as the first absurdity is concerned, does not St. Athanasius call the Holy Spirit the spiration of the Father and of the Son?[267] If the Holy Spirit is their spiration, then it necessarily follows that the Father and the Son, through the identicalness of their power of spiration, are His identical *spirator* [spirator]. And therefore the Holy Spirit relates not only to the Father as to the spirator, but also to the Son. As far as the second absurdity is concerned—if someone can be first with regard

---

261. Ibid. [117].
262. Ibid. [117].
263. Fol. 107v [124].
264. Fol. 108r [124].
265. Fol. 113r [129].
266. Fol. 113v [130].
267. *Epist. ad serap.* [St. Athanasius, *Epistles to Serapion,* sec. 1, p. 20; *PG* 26:577/578C–579/580B].

to himself, then it also properly follows that he can be his own cause; but if the first is *impossibile,* then so too is the second. As far as the third is concerned—can the Son do something of Himself, but what He sees the Father do?[268] As far as the fourth is concerned—is it the usual manner of confession of the holy doctors of the Church to confess that the Son and the Holy Spirit are *sine principio, sine causa* [without beginning, without cause]? But Orthologue mistakenly holds this as common. For although the entire Son is in the entire Father, and all that is of the Father is of the Son, it is as from the Father and not of Himself. Whence St. John of Damascus says: "The Son is not ἄναρχος, *sine principio,* without origin, for He is from the Father. But if you wish to receive the origin according to time, the Son is also without origin."[269] But Orthologue calls the Son and the Holy Spirit ἄναρχον, ἀναίτιον, καὶ αὐτόθεον [without beginning, without cause, and God in His very essence] not with respect to time, but with respect to being from the Father, whereby he blasphemes against God and does not revere Him. As to the fifth—St. Basil teaches with express words that the Son is second from the Father according to the natural order of the divine persons, and the Holy Spirit is second from the Son and third from the Father.[270] As to the sixth and seventh—we also confess that the Son and the Holy Spirit relate to the Father, the former as *ad genitorem immediatem* [to the immediate genitor] and the latter as *ad spiratorem mediatem* [to the mediate spirator], since the Son is from the Father as also the Holy Spirit is from the Father; the Son, however, so *immediate* [immediately] that His birth begins from the Father and ends in Him, whereas the procession of the Holy Spirit begins from the Father, through the Son, and ends in the Holy Spirit. But we do not confess that the Son relates to the Father, called either the Father or the *productor* [producer], *mediate,* that is, mediately, and with St. Basil we call such a confession impiety.[271] For the Holy Spirit, according to the doctrine of

---

268. Jn. 5[:19].

269. *Lib. 1, c. 11* [St. John of Damascus, *Exposition of the Orthodox Faith,* bk. 1, chap. 11 (probably chap. 8); *PG* 94:831A–832A; *NPNF2* 9:11].

270. *Serm. 5 in Eunom.* [St. Basil the Great, *Against Eunomius,* Sermon 5; *PG* 29:709–73.]

271. *Epist. ad Canonicas* [St. Basil the Great, *Letter* 52, chaps. 3–4, "To the Canonesses"; *PG* 393/394C–395/396C; *FC* 13:138–9].

that same great doctor, is not before the Son, does not precede the Son in His being.[272] Rather He is placed below the Son in order and dignity, and He is second after the Son, as the Son is second, according to order, after the Father.[273] And whoever should place the Holy Spirit ahead of the Son according to order (as Orthologue does) would do impiety; and opposing divine disposition in this, he would be far from the faith of God.[274] As to the eighth, ninth, and tenth, it was already shown clearly a little above concerning the order of the divine persons that through that number—first, second, third—as far as the order of their beings is concerned, they cannot be signified *indifferenter* [indifferently], but they can be so signified with regard to the number signifying *quantitatem* [quantity]. As, for example, in speaking of the three sons of Adam, if someone were asked if there are many sons of Adam, and if he answered three and counted them—one, or first, Seth, second Abel, third Cain, after showing their number through that count—he would tell the truth. But if he were asked about the order of their production into being, he could not answer truthfully otherwise but that Cain is the first, Abel the second, and Seth the third. Let us also understand that the same is to be maintained both in the counting *quantitatis,* that is, of the quantity of the divine persons and in the expression of their being of order, with regard to which the Son is from the Father, and the Holy Spirit is from the Father through the Son. But the Son can never be said (except impiously) to be through the Holy Spirit. Finally, the sort of order that Orthologue hypocritically presented to us as if from St. Basil—of the Father to the Son and to the Holy Spirit, and for the Son and the Holy Spirit to the Father—was never known to the holy doctors of the Church, but rather is newly invented.

The holy fathers offer us this order among the divine persons as far as their being is concerned. St. Athanasius says: "The sort of order that the Son has to the Father is the sort of order that the Holy Spirit has

---

272. *Serm. 3 in Eunom.* [St. Basil the Great, *Against Eunomius,* Sermon 3; *PG* 29:655–6].
273. Ibid.
274. *Idem Epist. Eadem* [St. Basil the Great, *Against Eunomius,* Sermon 3; *PG* 29:655–6].

to the Son."[275] And Basil the Great says: "As the Son is second to the Father in order and dignity, so also is the Holy Spirit second to the Son in order and dignity and third to the Father."[276] That—and no other—is the proper, natural order of the divine persons as far as their being is concerned.

As to the eleventh, twelfth, and thirteenth absurdities, it was already stated clearly at the outset that the Holy Spirit both is called, and is, third in the order of the divine persons as far as their originary order is concerned. Perhaps Orthologue was led astray by the fact that, by stopping the mouths of those heretics who, impiously establishing order in one divine essence, divided one divine essence in three and established in one divine essence one thing, a second, and a third, the holy doctors called it blasphemy to know in one divinity one thing, a second, and a third.[277] But none of the holy doctors of the Church denied or denies that one can know, as far as the natural order of the divine persons is concerned, a first, second, and third among them. To the contrary, Basil the Great and St. Epiphanius teach in express words that this is the case, as was cited from their writings a little above. And in his homily on these words of Holy Scripture—"Put thy hand under my thigh"[278]—St. John Chrysostom testifies that it is so, saying: "The holy order that separates the divine persons was known to me, but that which divides the nature in the Holy Trinity is to be rejected absolutely." As to the fourteenth and fifteenth, it is part of the daily confession of the Church of Christ the Lord and of His holy teachers of the Church, from the doctrine of Christ the Lord Himself, that the Holy Spirit descended personally upon the apostles on the day of Pentecost in tongues of fire: not gifts, but the person of the Holy Spirit; not some creature, but the Creator Himself. For we must believe the words of Christ the Lord that He sent Him, whom He promised to send. But He promised to send Him, who proceeds from the Father. Therefore, that is precisely

---

275. *Epist. ad Serap.* [St. Athanasius of Alexandria, *Epistles to Serapion,* 3, chap. 1; *PG* 26:623/624C–627/628A].

276. *Serm. 3 in Eunomium.* [St. Basil the Great; *Against Eunomius,* Sermon 3, chap. 1; *PG* 29:655–6.]

277. *Chrysostom* [?]. *Serm.* ἀνέκδοτον [Chrysostom, in an unpublished homily (?)].

278. Gen. 24[:2].

whom He sent, the Spirit of Truth.[279] But the gifts that were poured out at that time in tongues of fire upon the apostles by the Holy Spirit, who descended in person, and which are poured out and given now and always upon God's faithful are creature. Discoursing about both of which things, through his transition now to one, now to another opinion, Orthologue does not seem to have had his wits about him at that time. As to the sixteenth, that is a self-evident, obvious blasphemy.

And let this now be the end of the lamentatious errors and heresies that I have noted in part in my *Apology*. For the material I intend to narrate does not allow me to speak more broadly about them, and reason itself dictates that by one of his errors, one heresy, to say nothing of so many, he, next to Zizanij and Philalethes, his concurring fellow sowers of untruth, deserved to be reviled and trodden under foot in our Church because of his heretical writings and to be cast out of the hands of the pious and out of Catholic houses, or rather, as I said a little while ago, to be given over to the fire for correction. For each of us holds this for salvation: not to allow blasphemers of Divine Majesty to have communion with us or to allow them to touch the threshold of our Orthodox house. "And what concord hath Christ with Belial? Or what part hath he that believeth with an infidel?"[280] Believe me, my fathers and brethren, that it would already have been immeasurably better for our nation long ago if the mouths of these Zizanijs, Philaletheses, Orthologues, and their like, the heresiarchs in our Ruthenian Church, had been stopped in the manner in which both God's and man's law allow. Certainly then our Church would not have been subject to suspicion of such impious blasphemies against the majesty of God, and our Ruthenian nation would not have come to such a division that leads to its fall. But if they were interested in the faith and if they had God's true faith, they ought to have defended it with God's truth not only by not introducing errors and heresies, but also by not providing themselves with acrimonious words to attack the honor of people worthy of every honor. For the truth can be defended with even the simplest words and explained and made known with the most gentle.

This, then, most noble Ruthenian nation, is what sent me to the East, to the Father and to the elders, on such a far, dangerous, and—for

279. [Jn. 15:26.]
280. 2 Cor. 6[:15].

my advanced years—difficult, journey: the profaning of our Orthodox faith by these our new theologians and others like them and the sowing of their heresies in its place. Which grasped me all the more by the soul to the extent that I had served them diligently for my part.

The Refutation of the Clerk of Ostroh, Who Falsely Described the Council of Florence

Another cause for my pilgrimage was the Clerk of Ostroh, who is as untrue in the mendacious description of his false history of the Council of Florence as any one of those named above. For in what way does he who kills a man with a piece of wood transgress less against the will and command of God than he who kills with iron? And in what regard is the latter's transgression against his neighbor graver than the former's? Certainly both are equally homicides. The Clerk beats and kills with a club, with a cruder club, I say, than the others, and he infects the souls of men with a truly palpable lie, and he brings them to perdition; but in any event, he kills. "For the mouth that belieth," says the wise man, "slayeth the soul."[281] With a cruder one, because his other comrades in this work did not trip over falsehood entirely of their own free will, but led astray for the most part by a misunderstanding of the matter and by a belief that they had found the truth, they themselves accepted falsehood for the truth and submitted it to us as such. But the Clerk purposefully invented—without a credible witness—a falsehood of the sort that neither in the matter itself, nor in an account among us, our ancestors, the foreign nations, or the heretics, is found either described in writing or passed down in words. And he did this for this very reason: that with this wooden instrument of his he might kill the innocent souls of simple people just as well as his other collaborators in this matter do with iron instruments.

Nor was he unsuccessful in this. For we took up his old wives' tales as if they were the Gospel truth. And we do not hold or believe about the Council of Florence otherwise than as this anonymous Clerk made known to us, having thus based ourselves upon his fable, as if by maintaining about this otherwise we would not be sure of our salvation.

---

281. Wis. 1[:11].

Whereby our downfall, which we suffer clearly upon ourselves every day, is for naught. For we allow ourselves to believe a thing, as we see it, that is supposed to serve the salvation of our souls. Is not this as well murderous of our souls? For after believing his lies, we bear our souls dead in us, killed by them. For he, as if an emissary from heaven in this matter, after dispersing the clouds, tearing the stars from heaven, darkening the sun and the moon, fogging in the seas and the rivers, clouding over the heavens, darkening the earth, and filling the entire world with fire and blood, and through all this, after misting our eyes, tells this to us as if he had received it entrusted to him by God for his dealings with us. He dressed himself in such clothes of mourning at the beginning of his story with which he might arouse not only the incautious, but even the most judicious listeners to sorrow and might bring them to believe his account. And so he had little difficulty in bringing about among all of us what he had devised: that we, considering him not the least among other proclaimers of divine mysteries, might believe everything he tells us in his legation, such that God forbid that even one word should be heard against him from anyone. But if, not going any further but only taking counsel among ourselves, we should wish to consider his account among us, we would easily find it to be something that never was. For we would consider among ourselves whence he has the information that he submits for our belief as the truth and especially such a thing that disturbs even the temporal peace among brethren and attacks the eternal peace by deceiving ignorant people. We would first ask Rus' about this, our ancestors, then the Greeks, our parents in the spirit, after them the Romans, our brethren, and finally even the heretics themselves. For if they all answered with the same account and with the account that the Clerk brought to our knowledge, he would have to be found worthy of belief among us and receive our praise. But if he were found different from all the others and opposed to all, he ought then to be driven from us by that same instrument with which he came against us.

He alleges that the Council of Florence not only did not run its course, did not end in peace, and was not concluded in love on both sides, the Greek and the Roman, but rather was broken off with uproar, violence, murder. And supposedly some Greek fathers fled from it; others, captured by the pope, were compelled to sign; and those who did not wish to sign were tormented with imprisonment, dungeons, shackles, wounds, hunger. †He says that sixty bishops and 150 presbyters, syncelli and protosyncelli, and deacons, after being locked in dungeons, were subjected to various tortures. Some were tortured with hunger for fifteen days, others were baked with fire. Still others were suffocated and smothered, their bodies hidden secretly at night, and their hands were brought to sign to the Union after death. ‡Moreover, Patriarch Joseph, who, seeing the cruel tyranny over his people, regretted this not a little, had begun to regret this openly before all and to come to his senses; and he abandoned that Union and did not sign his hand to it. Having sent against him three of their monks (so he says), who, after coming to him at night allegedly in a legation from the pope and cloistering themselves in conversation with him, suffocated him to death; and leaving him, they placed a testament in his hands by which he would appear to have received the Union and all the articles decreed at it, affirmed it, and with his last will, departing this world, given his seal to it. Emperor [John VIII] Palaeologus as well—although he was given great tributes, and won with even greater promises—was no less troubled in his thought and could not have a free and secure conscience. And from the discouraging news that came to him about the sudden incursions of Turks into the Greek domains, he recognized his transgression by which he had offended God, having sold his conscience for gold. And right there in Sylibria, having fallen into despair, he suddenly gave up the ghost.[282]

Thus far the Clerk. I purposefully presented this in his own words so that I might demonstrate to all who wanted to see, for what sort of account he was preparing himself when he presented before us heaven and earth, confounded, at the beginning of his oration. For he certainly presents the sort of thing that could terrify not only a pious heart, arouse it to lament and crying, but that could draw tears from a stone, especially among us who are one in faith with those upon whom this—not to say *unheard-of* tyranny—but even *unwonted* tyranny of Christians against Christians, is said to have been carried out. Having read this and other things described by him with no less incitement to lament, what can one

---

†   If the devil himself had arisen from hell, he could not have told more lies about the Council of Florence than this Clerk.
‡   Look, Reader, at the calumnies of this malicious Clerk.
282. [Clerk 1598, 50v–52v; *RIB* 19:463–7.]

say about this to the heart that easily believes all sorts of accounts but the words of the Psalmist, which that same Clerk alleges were said at that time by the monks of Athos: *Deus venerunt gentes in haereditatem tuam, etc.* [O God, the heathen are come into thine inheritance, etc.]?[283] But having read and considered everything described by the Clerk, the heart that tries every thing and keeps the good thing, but rejects the bad thing, will delight in saying with the same blessed Psalmist: "Let the lying lips be put to silence, which speak grievous things proudly and contemptuously against the righteous."[284] For everything—both in the accounts I have cited and in others written by the Clerk before and after—is a falsehood upon his soul and a lie upon his head. He will not prove his mendacious account with any credible historian—not Greek, not Latin, not our Ruthenian, nor of any other nation. How can I know for certain what happened before my age if not from an oral account or from the description of one during whose age it happened? It is about 200 years since the Council of Florence took place, and not until our age did our Ruthenian nation hear any news about the tyranny that occurred at it; but now it hears it from a Clerk, and an anonymous one at that. And right away, not having known this man either by sight or by his name, it follows him as if someone heaven-sent, believes him, and is assured that this occurred in no other manner, having forgotten the words of the wise man: "He that is hasty to give credit is lightminded."[285]

We are certainly similar in this action to him who, chasing his shadow, believes without a doubt that this is a real man and not a vision. But it is no wonder that we believed him: this came from habit, which grows *in alteram naturam* [into a second nature], for we had already done this before him with others, †having given our faith to an invented Christopher Philalethes, and after him to Theophil Orthologue, since we did not know or ask who they were. Wherefore, it passed from custom to habit for us that whoever he might be, and whatever he would pass off as ours that was not ours—so long as he reviled the pope, criticized him and his Church—he was a good man as far as we were concerned, an

---

283. Ps. 78. [Ps. 79:1. The rest of the verse reads: "thy holy temple have they defiled; they have laid Jerusalem on heaps.]
284. Ps. 101 [Ps. 31:18].
285. Sir. 9 [19:4].
† It is necessary to know whom to believe.

honorable and holy man, wise and glorious. But just as that honor, and glory, and wisdom, and piety were unto his perdition, so his degenerate child was not to our great bodily and spiritual benefit.

†They called themselves Bearers-of-Christ, Lovers-of-truth, Lovers-of-God, and Right-believers, but more truthfully according to their deeds they are Twisters-of-words and Lovers-of-falsehood. Like infants we grabbed at those beautiful names as if they were a toy, not taking care whether it sting, burn, cut, thinking that they were the same inside as they are outside, but the greener their covering, the hotter they burn. Zizanij behaved properly to the extent that he clearly announced to us who he was. ‡But we, not having considered that this work would be according to his name, grasped at those tares[286] as at the purest wheat, and now we shamelessly stuff ourselves with it to the detriment of our souls. If only the Lord God would cause that the palate of our mouths found this taste to be of chaff and not of wheat and thus cause us to have *nauseam* [nausea] toward it, and not allow us any more to take it to our mouths, our souls would soon become healthier. For we would immediately recognize the sickness with which we are severely ill, not recognizing that we are ill, and we would come to a complete cure beyond our expectation.

Concerning the Council of Florence: That It Ran Its Course in the Love and Harmony of Romans and Greeks

I said a little above that the accounts that the Clerk offered us are not found either among the Greeks, among our ancestors, among the Romans, or among the foreigners, but only among us ourselves and come without even the smallest proof, without even the smallest reason, commanding us to be satisfied with the fact that some Clerk said it. But I ought to demonstrate in the opposite manner, from the

---

†   What beautiful names these pseudologians appropriated.
‡   It is a great blindness to buy chaff for wheat.
286. [A pun. Smotryc'kyj derives the name Zizanij from ζιζάνιον 'tares,' a weed that grows in grain fields. See the parable of the wheat and the tares in Mt. 13:24–30.]

testimony of my own ancestors of Rus′, from the Greeks, the Romans, and the foreigners, that the Council of Florence took place without any compulsions and acts of violence, not to mention oppression and tyranny, and was also concluded in peace and in love on both sides, the Greek and the Roman. Having shown which, I will stop the mouth of the Clerk, who speaks untruth. For if it ran its course and was concluded in peace and in love, there could not have been any compulsion and violence there and thus neither any imprisonment nor murder and death. I prove what I say—drawing first on authorities from Rus′—by the fact that no Ruthenian throughout all the times past ever left so much as one iota claiming that the Council of Florence did not run its course; and our Ruthenian nation did not have this, and does not have it, from the traditions that are passed down from hand to hand. †Second, I prove the unification of both Churches, the Eastern and the Western, from the decree of mutual concord that is found written into our books of Church rules in the Slavonic language. But our ancestors would not have suffered this in their books for more than 150 years if that council had not run its course in peace and in love. Although supposedly there were such hasty hands that did tear them out of the books (which our first theologian Zizanij did in our days in the Vilnius Monastery of the Holy Trinity), nonetheless the Lord God Himself halted hands ready to do anything, and He did not allow those to destroy those pages who, not having been able to attack the truth with their tongues, dare to do so with their hands until even our days. Third, I prove this with the letter written as a synod from all of Rus′ to Pope Sixtus IV in the year 1476, which, although it is held by some of us in little esteem, nonetheless, by those who know what is what and who look at those ages with an unjealous eye, is held in the esteem it deserves, as truly written and sent by Rus′. For, after the copy found in Krewo [Belarusian: Kreva], another was found in the church of the village Wielbojn [Wielbojno, Wielbowne/Wielbowna] near Ostroh, of old script, already almost half moth-eaten, about which I was told by him who had found it there by chance, the deceased Aleksander Putjatycki, who is known to many of us. In this letter written by the entire Ruthenian nation, the Council of Florence is acknowledged, approved, and received as having run its

†   Proof from Ruthenian writings about the Council of Florence.

course and concluded peacefully in love.[287] Fourth, I prove this by the privilege given by King Władysław [III] of Poland to the clergy of our Ruthenian nation in the year 1442, within four years after the Council of Florence.[288] This is the first proof from our Rus' authorities against the Clerk's false description of the Council of Florence.

[†]The second proof from the Greeks: first of all, the Greek, Laonicus Chalcocondylas, who lived at just that very time, acknowledges freely at the beginning of his history that the Council of Florence ran its course in peace and that it was concluded in concord of the Greeks with the Romans. But the Greeks, he says, tore asunder the concordant confession of faith that was concluded at it after they had returned home.[289] Second, I prove this from Greek authorities with the letter of Patriarch Nephon of Constantinople, written in the year 7000 from the creation of the earth (according to the Greeks [AD 1498]) to the Metropolitan of Rus', Josyf (Soltan),[290] written in Greek on parchment, which I read in Vilnius in the Monastery of the Holy Trinity, in which the above-mentioned patriarch glorifies and praises the Council of Florence in authoritative words, and he clearly acknowledges (for he was asked about this by Metropolitan Josyf of Rus') that it ended in peace and that it was concluded in love on both sides. Third, I prove this from Greek authorities since even now they maintain [the acts of] this council printed in Greek, word for word as it was translated into Polish here among us. They read it, and the more judicious ones hold it in respect, and none of the more important ones has dared to write even one iota against it since the times of Mark [of Ephesus]. Fourth, I prove this from Greek authorities since Metropolitan Mark of Ephesus, who was the only one who refused to subscribe to this Council, a manifest enemy of the Council of Florence, having written much against it, nonetheless

---

287. [This is the controversial letter from Metropolitan Mysajil. It was printed by Potij in Vilnius in 1605. Reprint: *AJuZR* 1:7:193–231.]

288. [Actually, dated Buda, 22 March 1443. *AJuZR* 1:1:442–4; 1:10:419–21; Harasiewicz 1862, 78–81; Papée 1927, 391–3; *MUH* 1:3–5.]

†   Proof that the Council of Florence ran its course in peace from Greek writers.

289. [*PG* 159:292–3.]

290. [Actually, "Letter to Josyf Bolharynovyč, metropolitan of Kyiv"; *PP* 16–17; *MUH* 1:5–7.]

does not mention in any of his writings even one iota of what the Clerk mendaciously submitted to us. This open enemy of the Council could not manage such a shamelessness as our anonymous councilographer acquired for himself, hidden behind the mask of clerical status. Fifth, I prove this from Greek authorities since many Greeks important in their dignity and illustrious in learning defend this Council of Florence, and they declare that it ran its course in peace and was concluded in harmony. Such are Patriarch George Scholarius of Constantinople, Metropolitan Bessarion of Nicaea, Bishop Joseph of Methone, the hieromonk and great protosyncellus Gregory, George of Trebizond, and others. And this, from Greek authorities, is the second proof that the Council of Florence was conducted, finished, and concluded in peace and in the mutual love of Greeks and Romans.

†The third proof of this from the Romans, who, treating us and themselves honestly, that is, the Eastern and the Western Church, all uniformly acknowledge that this Council of Florence was conducted in peace, that it was ended and concluded in the mutual concord and love of all the Romans and the Greeks.

‡The fourth proof of this is from the foreigners, from Johannes Functius, the chronicler of Nuremberg, who lived around the year 1570. Concerning the Council of Florence, he writes in his chronicle that it was conducted in peace and in love. To the decrees of which the Greek (he says) and the Ruthenian emissaries agreed, as far as the faith is concerned, and both promised the same of their nations.[291] And before him, a chronicler of Nuremberg as well, Hartman Schedel, who lived around the year 1473, soon after the Council of Florence, confesses in express words the same truth about it: that the Council of Florence ran its course, that it was ended and concluded in peace and in love by the Romans and the Greeks, in concord and in unanimity of faith.

This, then, is what I thought to demonstrate against the erroneous accounts of the Clerk—from the testimonies of our Rus', and from the Greeks, and from the Romans, and from the foreigners—that the Council of Florence was conducted and ended in peace and in love

---

† All the Roman writers affirm the concordant conclusion of this Council.

‡ Even the heretical writers testify that the Council of Florence ran its course in concord.

291. Fol. 244v of this Latin chronicle printed on Alexandrian paper.

and that it was concluded and sealed in concord and in unanimity concerning the faith. From which alone it is manifestly clear that all the Clerk's accounts about this council—those cited by me and those not cited—are fables and dreams, falsehoods and calumnies, which are so crude that even a simple man can almost touch them with his hands, not to mention a man firmly established in his reasoning. For who can believe in good conscience that, with so many illustrious people present, the bishop of Rome could employ such a great and truly bestial tyranny over the bishops, priests, hieromonks of the Eastern Church, and over the patriarch himself, in the presence of the Eastern emperor, and in the presence of the despot, the emperor's brother? And if he did employ it, who will allow himself to be convinced that this was not described by some illustrious, pious man, either a Greek, or a Roman, or a German, or finally by one of our Ruthenians, who also became participants in that misery (as the Clerk alleges about it)? If someone from the sons of their father, the devil, from the sons, I say, of lying,[292] invented and released into the world this lie, are we to be the most stupid people in the world who will find ourselves the first to believe that manifest deception?

[†]The main enemies of the pope, Luther and Calvin, and their secretaries, who would gladly snatch anything even out of hell and present it to the whole world in order to bring the bishop of Rome into disrepute, do not mention even one little word about this sort of tyranny or about even the least tyranny at the Council of Florence. To the contrary, the Nurembergers, already having become infected with the Lutheran heresy, give out testimony, through their chronicler, as we heard, that the Council of Florence ran its course in peace, concord, and love. It is only we, Rus', who have as if sworn unwisely to believe anonymous people, liars, or who knows what man, or even a fairy tale, to lead ourselves astray, subject ourselves to the derision of people who are able to judge truth from untruth and thereby to render our souls unto perdition. Are we still going to assert, most noble Ruthenian nation, that this is the truth? Will we still venture forth with the Zizanijs, Philaletheses, Orthologues, Clerks, and others like them? And will we desire to prove our truth with their lies, falsehoods, errors, and

292. [Jn. 8:44.]
†   This is a great proof.

blasphemous heresies? We will truly be in this regard more wretched than all the Christians of the entire world, for we believe any old pieces of gossip without any consideration, and in matters of the salvation of the soul we rely on those who, as they themselves did not know what they believed, so also they sought only through opinion to prove that what they gave for us to believe through their writings was ours. In which they deceived themselves and led us astray.

We Cannot Deny That We Held These
Pseudologians for Our Theologians

We might perhaps say that as we did not know these authors, thus we knew little of their blasphemous writings, whereby the cause of their lies, errors, and heresies cannot touch us. Would the Lord God only have granted it, most noble Ruthenian nation, that we had not known these persons nor acknowledged their writings as our own. But once we glance at the place where they were printed and by whom they were recognized as the teachers and defenders of our side, we have to shut our mouths. And we freely acknowledge them even now as our own defenders of our faith. Who anywhere, even with one word, either from the pulpit or in writing, ever announced that these authors or their writings were not ours? And who revealed to our Church their blasphemies, falsehoods, errors, and heresies, and taught us to beware of them as a heretical infection? No one, not ever, not anywhere. All of us, as one person, considered, and do consider, them as ours. But grant that we did not know about these blasphemies, falsehoods, errors, and heresies in these writings that were edited and published as the dogmas of our faith and that we not only did not wish to believe those who, considering them suspect, warned us in this, but did not even wish to read their writings, whereby we sinned less before the Lord God and we remained less guilty before ourselves. But now, by the grace of God, it is our turn to come to realize what we did not wish to believe, even though we were admonished by the brethren. Were not Zizanij, Philalethes, the *Lament*, and that Clerk answered for us? And were not these lies, blasphemies, errors, and heresies shown to us so clearly that even until today from our side there has been no answer to this, nor in fact could

we give one? For it was hard to kick against the pricks.[293] As is clear
from experience itself, we do not know how to do anything else but to
attack; and to attack not with some serious matter, as is usually done in
matters of salvation, but with vituperation, scolding, shame, acrimony,
falsehoods, lies, calumnies, errors, blasphemies, heresies, and finally
with incorrect interpretation and perversions of the testimonies of the
Writ of God and of the writings of the holy fathers, with the erasure
from the Church books of what does not please us and with the addition
of what does please us. Which certainly did not befit us, nor does it
befit us, who consider ourselves Orthodox. Let us only erase from
our Zizanijs, Philaletheses, Orthologues, Clerks, and others like them
everything that I mentioned here; we will surely find in them nothing
but the letters themselves and blank paper. For whatever mention they
make about God, the faith, the sacraments, the Most Holy Virgin, the
holy servants of God, and other salvatory matters, they have marshaled
to the end that all of it might serve their blasphemy, which they establish
by their errors and heresies, and not the divine truth.

These Errors Compelled Me to Make
a Pilgrimage to the East and, Having Returned,
to Write This Apology

This then grasped me by my soul and sent me to the Eastern lands that I
might seek relief from the evil that had settled upon my soul in that place
whence, in ages past, all the Christian good had come. So that also the
correction for the good that had been harmed by us might come from the
place whence it had come to us whole, holy, and immaculate. For almost
eight years, I struggled at home with myself and with the blasphemies
of those authors; of which Vilnius is well aware, well aware is Kyiv,
well aware the Ostroh chapter, and many of those who seemed to be
of some importance in our nation, with whom I conferred about this,
purposefully convening with them for this very reason. And since I did
not find what I sought at home, I set off to the East to seek this among my
own people; and about what I found there—God willing—later. What
I now do through my *Apology,* I do compelled by conscience, which is

---

293. [Acts 9:5, 26:14.]

for me a heavier goad than a thousand witnesses. I waited for a local council that I might present this orally before those who ought to know about this and offer it for their consideration. But seeing that we were not at all in a hurry for that council for which we have been preparing now already these three years since my return from that peregrination, though somehow we just cannot bring it about; and also being aware that at our previous episcopal councils, throughout those eight years, we could not come to any serious discussion about the matters that pertain to our Church in these present times on account of the private interest of one man among us, not a friend of the good, who even until today digs the earth with Zedekiah's horns of iron[294] and shamelessly smites the prophet of God, seeking to bring his poor Ruthenian nation to a fall similar to the one to which the people of Israel and Judah had come through the evil and wicked hand of that false prophet Zedekiah and his company;[295] moreover, considering the fact that this matter is a matter that concerns our entire Ruthenian Church, clerics and laymen, great and small, men and women, I decided to proceed in this fashion, partly out of the obligation of my dignity as an archiereus, partly out of the obligation of piety itself, which opens the mouth not only of a priest, but even of a layman, and in time of need allows him, and compels him, to speak. All of which I do for you, most noble Ruthenian nation, and I submit it to your careful consideration, and I ask that, after reading it carefully, you not neglect yourself and your salvation, but that you be watchful and hasten as quickly as possible to shake yourselves loose from these impieties. For as long as Zizanij, Philalethes, Orthologue, the Clerk, Azarius, *Elenchus, Antigraphē,* Suraz'kyj, and their ilk are yours, you will remain in the transgression of falsehood, lie, calumny, blasphemies, errors, and heresies.

Let us just examine (I speak to those who have a healthy spiritual understanding), and, having applied our entire soul to this, let us consider diligently so that our consideration might agree genuinely with our will in the unerring testimony of our conscience, saying to ourselves the following: †since we are supposed to give up even unto

---

294. [1 Kg. 22:11; 2 Ch. 18:10. Likely a reference to Isaija Kopyns'kyj, archbishop of Smolensk and Černihiv. See above, p. 362.]
295. 2 Ch. 18[:23].
†   A Christian man must first consider what he must suffer for.

plundering and unto death all that we own and even our very selves, whenever a fitting occasion is presented, for the sake of the Lord God and for His holy truth, that is to say, for our faith, if we were to come to that point, would we or would we not be able to do this safe and secure in certain hope of the salvation of conscience, knowing that if anyone is tormented, but not lawfully, that is, not for God's truth, he is not crowned? You, most noble nation, as God and your salvation are dear to you, make decree according to the witness of your conscience. Under the same obligation of God and my salvation, I, for my part, warn each of you, inform, and assure, that whoever from our Ruthenian nation loses this or dies for the faith that Zizanij, Philalethes, Orthologue, the Clerk, Azarius, *Elenchus,* and others like them have described, loses it to his own detriment and he dies in vain; he loses his soul, rather than saving it. Basil Bogomil went up in flames in Constantinople, burned by the Greeks. Jan Hus was burned in Constance, burned by the Romans. Michael Servetus was burned in Geneva, burned by the Calvinists. Valentine Gentile lost his life, beheaded by the sword by the Zwinglians. The Greek historians Curopalates and Cedrenus write that through the industry of Honorius, the Orthodox Emperor, and that of his wife Theodora, up to one hundred thousand Manichaeans were deprived of their belongings and their lives in various manners. †What did they gain that they lost both property and life for heresy? They received the benefit that they got to hell more quickly than they had expected they would. For every schismatic or heretic can be beheaded or burned, but he cannot be crowned. For royal crowns belong to the sons of the kingdom and not to those banished from the kingdom, as are all schismatics and heretics. Were few in number the heretics, in addition to those named, who died by the sword, by fire, and by other deaths, but in their opinion for faith, since they had judged their heresy to be faith? Nonetheless, not a one of them acquired the crown through their course.[296] For he did not run along the royal road paved by God at the end of which are the crowns, but along the road offered by himmself or by a man similar to himself, at the end of which is eternal torment. As is this road, newly presented by these new theologians; going along it,

---

†   See what benefit schismatics and heretics receive from death for their faiths.

296. [2 Tim. 4:7–8.]

each one, if he does not repent in time, will certainly rest where (from which Christ the Lord deign to protect us) all the heretics came to rest who had been damned by the Church of Christ.

We Ought to Have Ascertained
through Natural Reason and Experience That
These Pseudologians and the Fathers of the Church
Have Different Doctrines about the Faith

The natural light of human reason shows us how to recognize an ox, an ass, a tree, a stone, and other similar things; and whoever would not acknowledge that he knows this would himself have to be an ass or a stump. Natural reason also taught us how to know whose voice to respond to and where to cast ourselves and at what need. None of us responds to the cry of the wolf or that of an owl, nor does anyone pour oil on a fire or bring to his mouth a stone instead of bread. If we go about these everyday matters having drawn on the light of natural reason, why should we not go about salvatory matters as well with the same reason, especially in those things that are granted us to recognize in these matters? Christopher and Theophil are common names among us, but Philalethes, Orthologue, and Clerk are new and unusual names, and the first such in the entire Ruthenian nation; by answering to their voices, we were not acting very much more wisely than if we had answered to an ass's braying and, having acknowledged it as a human voice, had set off after it even though we had already been taught to be wise as serpents and simple as doves.[297] This is certainly an unwise answer: to answer him who asks you "Who taught you this" with "I do not know." If we had established our ignorance on the doctrine of the Gospel and on the faith of our holy fathers, we could use this as a defense before God and His people; for we could answer them that, not understanding the profound dogmas of the faith with our paltry reason, we believe as believed St. John Chrysostom, St. Basil the Great, St. John of Damascus, or some other of the saints or as our holy ancestors, who, from our nation, illumined our Ruthenian Church with sanctity. But we cannot make use of such an answer as our defense, for we had

297. Mt. 10[:16].

already announced and published what our faith was through Zizanij, Philalethes, Orthologue, Clerk, Azarius, and others like them. And that faith is as different from the faith of St. John Chrysostom and other holy doctors of the Church and of our Ruthenian holy fathers as untruth is different from truth, and heresy from faith. Although when someone asks us what we believe, we point to the Eastern Church and to her holy teachers, †nonetheless, when someone asks us for a summary description of our faith to read, we give him these new theologians of ours, whereby we treat ourselves with such care as if we had said to someone that we have balsam, and we pointed to birch tar,[298] and with him we act as sensibly as if someone had asked us for bread and a fish, and we had given him a stone and a serpent.[299] For through the writing we have given him to read, we both declare ourselves heretics, having pretended in our words that we are Orthodox, and we infect him through these blasphemies with a soul-destroying poison. So it necessarily remains for us either to flee these Zizanijs and to adhere to the holy ancient teachers of the Church or to abandon the latter and adhere to the former. For as it is impossible for Christ to be together with Belial,[300] so too the doctrine of the holy doctors, with the doctrine of these teachers of ours. I believe, most noble Ruthenian nation, that, as it seems to me, I have already clearly shown that I had a proper reason for my peregrination to the East, and that I—not to say that you too—did not know what I believed: for if we had known, we would not have yielded here to those corrupters of our Orthodox faith.

Whence That Fall into Errors and Heresies Occurred

Now that I have partially presented with a faithful heart what concerns us ourselves, let us examine, most noble Ruthenian nation, how it happened to these our new theologians that in our times they allowed themselves to be dishonored with blasphemies so hateful to God, and through them allowed themselves to move so far away from the Orthodox faith of our holy ancestors that came to us, by God's will,

---

†   This is the very truth.
298.   [Cf. *NKPP* 1:271–2, "Chłop," 191.]
299.   [Mt. 7:9–10.]
300.   [2 Cor. 6:15.]

from the East. For it was not so, to say nothing of during the time of our more distant ancestors, but not even during the days of our fathers in our Ruthenian Church. They were the first, through all the ages of Christianity in Rus', who made bold to attack our Ruthenian Church with such impious errors and heresies. I, for my part, to the extent that I am able, find no other reason than the contention that has arisen in our days between the Roman Church and us with regard to the unity that has been accepted with it by our spiritual elders. †This has brought this evil upon us, and it has brewed this horrible beer for us, which we have been drinking now for thirty-three years in the bitterness of our souls[301] with no little harm both to the internal and to the external ornament of the Church. By reason of that contention we lost princes, lords, and nobles without number from our Church. We have removed the remaining houses of that eminence from the ornaments of their noble freedom and from the rewards of their services rendered in the shedding of blood. We have made the bench of justice and freedom little accessible to the burghers, and we have lost almost all our bodily and spiritual good. If this is how it is when it is still young, what will happen to us when this evil begins to ferment? Cause, Lord Jesus Christ, that we might act so wisely and pour out the effect together with the cause—the beer, I say, together with the contention—to the infernal depths as a drink for the father of enmity and discord before we have to drink its hops; and that we might crown love and concord among ourselves, without which, and without the Orthodox faith, Christians will receive neither temporal nor eternal happiness.

This contention, then, is the cause of our evil; for having taken on an unequal opponent and not having been able, through our infirmity, to overcome him, we went to his enemies for counsel and aid; and having acquired this from them, in time we made it our own. On account of the unity our spiritual elders had accepted with Rome, I say, after entering into contention both with the Romans and with our own people, whom we did not wish to follow, and, not being able to overcome them, we

---

†   This contention, which is unjustified on our side, has brought upon us all this evil.

301. [*NKPP* 2:946–7, "Piwo," 24. Based on a Polish saying, something like "You've brewed the beer, now drink it," which is a close equivalent to "You've made your bed, now lie in it."]

went for help and aid to the Lutherans and to the Calvinists, and taking errors and heresies from them in loan, we set up camp against the other side, and thereafter we infected ourselves with their errors and heresies. On account of whom we have now forgotten even our native faith, and we believe that what they have offered us is the faith of the holy Eastern Church.

†Who was the Christopher Philalethes who first wrote against that unity of our elders? A Calvinist who knew neither our Greek faith nor our Ruthenian writing, wherefore he wrote and defended us with what he learned from Calvin's *Institutes* and not from our churchmen. Who was Theophil Orthologue? A disciple of Luther who, having spent his young years at the Leipzig and Wittenberg academies by the grave of Luther, arrived in Lithuania sooty from the smoke of the Lutheran heats and, singing his *Lament,* infected Rus' with those same fumes. ‡And who Zizanij? An ignoramus who, thinking that it is as easy to discourse well about the dogmas of the faith as it is not difficult to sermonize indifferently, fell into the errors and heresies he offered to us and made us heretical. And who was the Clerk? A teacher similar to Zizanij and in addition the most foul Anabaptist teacher, whose accursed Arian spirit is clear in the syllogisms cited by the Clerk against the procession of the Holy Spirit "and from the Son."[302] But I treat all of them as *amicus personae* [a friend of the person], but *inimicus causae* [an enemy of the matter], praying with all my soul for myself and for them, and especially for the churchmen, that the Lord God show Himself merciful to us on the Judgment Day.

That by Avoiding Unity with the Romans, We Have Fallen into Errors and Heresies

Thus it was the contention with our elders concerning the unity they effected with the Romans that brought us into such errors and heresies hateful to God and submitted our Ruthenian Church to such suspicion. For it would have been immeasurably more salvatory for the soul and

---

†   Who was the Christopher Philalethes who wrote *Apokrisis*?
‡   Who was Zizanij?
302. On folio 10 [Clerk 1598, 42r–v; *RIB* 19:449–50].

more beneficial for the body if it had crowned unity with the Roman Church in love on both sides, rather than allowing itself to be subjected to the suspicion of those wicked heretical blasphemies. We, that is the Eastern Church, do not contend with the Romans except on six foremost differences among us, of which none is a heresy. But now here, through this avoidance of unity, we have fallen into scores of errors and heresies that present us to God and to all the Orthodox as heretics. And as long as we are in them, they convince us to recognize ourselves and to be known as such even if we do not wish it. Let us ask ourselves whether it would have been more pious for us to consent that it is the Orthodox confession that the Holy Spirit proceeds from the Father and from the Son or to blaspheme with Orthologue that the Holy Spirit does not proceed from the essence of the Father,[303] when we have before us what the First Universal Council of Nicaea says in its creed? For, having said these words "We believe also in Lord Jesus Christ, the only-begotten Son of God, begotten from the Father," it then adds "that is, of the essence of the Father."[304] Which manner of speaking the holy teachers of the Church, Epiphanius and Cyril of Alexandria, later used in their creeds.[305] Whence it is clear that by not acknowledging that the Holy Spirit proceeds from the essence of the Father, Orthologue does not acknowledge that He proceeds from the Father. For to proceed from the Father and to proceed from the essence of the Father is one and the same thing. It will be the same thing not to proceed from the essence of the Father and not to proceed from the Father. What blasphemy can be more wicked than this? St. Basil the Great says: "The Son is born of the essence of the Father." But Orthologue does not acknowledge that the Son is born of the essence of the Father either.[306] What then? Was it better for us to blaspheme thus with Orthologue than to confess "and from the Son" with the Romans?

303. Fol. 113v [130].

304. [Council of Nicaea, AD 325; Mansi 2:665C–668A; Tanner 5; *NPNF1* 14:3.]

305. *Epiph. in Anchorato* [Epiphanius, *The Well Anchored*; PG 43:233B–234B]. *Cyr. Lib. 15. Thesaur. c. 1* [Cyril of Alexandria, *Thesaurus on the Holy and Consubstanial Trinity*, bk. 15, chap. 1; *PG* 75:245/246B].

306. *Lib. adversus Sabellianos et Arium. c. 8* [St. Basil, *Homily against Sabellians, Arius, and Anomeoans; PG* 31:606]. *Fol. eodem* [Smotryc'kyj 1610, 113v/130].

We will say that both are identical blasphemies. The Romans will answer us that our account against them is without proof. And none of the holy teachers of the Church, around the time of the Sixth and the Seventh Universal Councils—although it was made known widely in the East at this time (as we learn from the letter of blessed Maximus written to Marinus, presbyter of Cyprus)—called this Roman confession even an error, to say nothing of blasphemy or heresy. Greeks closer to our times believed that this Roman confession was blasphemy, holding it in suspicion on the grounds that the Romans established from it two origins in one Divinity, or if not that, that they thus fused the two divine persons into one. But the Romans cleansed themselves of these suspicions when, at the Council of Florence, they made a defense against them by raising anathema against those who either establish two origins in one Divinity or fuse two divine persons into one; thus they also cleansed their confession of the slander of blasphemy that came from the Easterners, and they put the Orthodox in a position where now no one even of the Greeks can charge the Romans with blasphemy in this, unless thereby he too will blaspheme at the same time.

Let us further compare Orthologue's doctrine—in which he blasphemes that there are two types of being *realiter* [in reality] in each Divine person, one according to the being, the other according to the person[307]—with the Roman doctrine about either purgatory, or about unleavened bread, or about the disposition of the souls that have departed this world, or about the eldership of the bishop of Rome (for in these articles of faith he differs from the Romans); or his doctrine with all of them together. We will find his incomparable with all those. For Orthologue's doctrine is blasphemous, but among those five Roman doctrines not one is found to be thus. The Romans do not blaspheme in their doctrine concerning purgatory, for with the exception of the material fire, which even for the Romans is not an article of faith, we are in agreement with them in everything as far as the doctrine about purgatory is concerned; and having the thing itself, we only avoid acknowledging the word. The Romans do not blaspheme in their doctrine about unleavened bread, for the Greek fathers of the middle ages, acknowledging their ancient custom in this matter, acknowledge that the consecrated mystery of the Eucharist in unleavened bread is

307. Fol. 101v [118]. *Loci* [passim].

honorable and holy, and honorable and holy the celebration of their liturgy or Mass. They also acknowledge that they offer one and the same Lamb of God, who removed the sins of the entire world, and in unleavened bread they offer Him whom the Eastern Church offers in leavened bread, although the ancient holy fathers call Christ the Lord, on account of his sinlessness, unleavened bread, which does not have the leaven of sin.[308] They do not blaspheme concerning the disposition of the souls that have departed this world. Otherwise our Oktoechoi, Triodia, Menaia would have to blaspheme every third word, as was already treated broadly and thoroughly at the outset. Nor do they seem to blaspheme in receiving the sacrament of the Eucharist under one species, for we too would blaspheme, since we have the custom of receiving this mystery this way. And we have this from the custom of the first centuries. Nor do they blaspheme, finally, in the doctrine about the eldership of the bishop of Rome, for in this too we would find ourselves equal blasphemers with the Romans since we ascribe to the bishop of Rome in our Church doctrine that he is the *protothronos,* that is the first ruler of the Holy Church of Christ the Lord, the head of the Orthodox Church of Christ the Lord, the archbishop of the entire world, the father of the entire world, the archpastor of the Church that is beneath heaven, the bishop of the Church and of the entire Christian flock, and other similar things.[309] Whereby we too in express words confess the eldership of the bishop of Rome, and we acknowledge that his pastoral dignity is foremost, by divine law, above all the other pastorships in the Church of Christ the Lord.

So the Romans, as we have discovered, do not blaspheme in those articles for which we disdain unity with them, but our Zizanijs, Philaletheses, Orthologues, Clerks, and others like them, whom we have acquired as defenders against unity, do blaspheme: when they teach that there are only two mysteries given by Christ the Lord; when they deride the transubstantiation that occurs in the sacrament of the

---

308. *Anast. Sinai. Serm. in Transfig. Dni. qui incipit. Quam terribilis est locus hic* [Anastasius of Sinai, Sermon on the Transfiguration of the Lord that begins "How terrible is this place"].

309. In the life of St. Gregory; in *stichera* 5 on Pope Leo; in the *Anthology* on Pope St. Celestine; in the life of St. Alexis; in the life of St. Theodore of Studios; in the life of the pope St. Sylvester.

Eucharist; when they deprive Christ the Lord of His priestly dignity; when they do not allow God's holy people to go to heaven; when they do not acknowledge particular judgment; when they tear from St. Peter the Apostle his proper pastorly dignity; when they equate a presbyter with a bishop in the dignity *ordinis* [of order] and in the eminence of his jurisdiction; when thus, as was cited, they divide the divine essence from the person in reality; when they establish two beings *realiter* [in reality] for each divine person; when they blaspheme that the Son and the Holy Spirit are not of the essence of the Father, the former born, the latter proceeding; and with similar blasphemies that were cited at the outset from each one of them and noted in their places.

Considering both, that is, the Roman nonblasphemy and our blasphemy, we must see that it would have been immeasurably more salvatory and more beneficial for all of us if, having kept our Church affairs intact, together with our spiritual elders, *servatis,* as they say, *servandis* [keeping (the same) the things that must be kept], †we had entered into unity before we had been infected, together with our entire Church, with these blasphemies that are hateful to God; for we would not have harmed our salvation in the least, nor our benefit, both with regard to this world and the next. We feared terror where it was not; and where it was, we submitted ourselves entirely without fear, whereby we divested ourselves of the internal and external ornament of the Church, and we brought the entire Church to a great fall. Looking upon which and being unable to do anything about it even with their diligent effort, certain pious people of our nation only console the misery within them through sighing, and they await God's mercy, that he will finally have mercy upon us and will grant unification to one house divided in two, which is approaching its inexorable fall.[310] Which division of our one house in two—as I said a little above—and the desire to unite in one the house divided in two, most noble Ruthenian nation, in addition to the reason cited above, sent me to the East so that there I might seek help for it in this matter either from people and from God or from God without people. What I received from people in this matter—about this,

---

† God grant that we be wiser after the harm. [Cf. *NKPP* 3:398–400, "Szkoda," 13.]

310. [Mt. 12:25; Mk. 3:25; Lk. 11:17.]

God willing, on another occasion. But what I received by the grace of a merciful God, this I present to you now.

By my duty as an archiereus, through the love of my salvation and yours, I ask you, the fathers as a son, the brethren as a brother, †and I remind you in love, the sons as a father, the friends as a friend: let us, by the living God, see to saving ourselves, let us seek to help, let us seek to avoid the ever greater evil that awaits us and which is now almost the final one, at the onset of which they will say of us "it was; it is no longer." Let us not say the Church cannot perish. It is true that the gates of hell cannot prevail against the Church,[311] and that Christ the Lord is with His Church until the end of the world.[312] But *hoc opus, hic labor* [that is the task, that the difficulty],[313] to show ourselves and assure ourselves that we are the Church of Christ the Lord, that our heresies have not stripped us of this cloak, and that they have not caused us to be outside the Church. Christ the Lord can have no communion with Belial,[314] nor the Church with heresy. The heretic is inside the Church and is a member of Christ (although a rotten one) until he is condemned for that heresy, cut off from the body of Christ, which is His Church, and cast out of the Church. But all the heresies we have received have already been judged by the Church and recognized as heresies. Wherefore, as long as we are in them and they in us, I leave it to the careful consideration of each one of you how we could wish to be truly known as the Church of Christ.

A Consideration of the Universal and Local Church

But let us grant to ourselves that we are the Church. Let us, however, in addition know also these two things for certain. First, that we are a part of the Church and not the Church, that is, that we are a local Church and not the Universal Church, a part of the Universal and not all of it. Second, that as far as its entirety is concerned, the Church cannot

---

†   The author admonishes [his people] to concord.
311. [Mt. 16:18.]
312. [Mt. 28:20.]
313. [Virgil, *Aeneid* 6.129.]
314. [2 Cor. 6:15.]

fall and perish; but as far as its parts are concerned—now diminishing, now increasing—it does diminish and fall. Examples of which we have before our eyes. There was a time when nearly all the world was Arianizing, and the true Church was rare. The same thing happened with the occurrence of the Monothelite heresy and later during the time of the iconoclasts. But leaving the older examples alone, let us examine examples closer to us: the patriarch of Jerusalem bears the title "of Syria, Arabia, the other side Jordan, *Cana Galileae* [Cana of Galilee], Zion, and all Palestine." But in such great provinces of this broad title, he has barely more than three thousand Christian souls. †The patriarch of Alexandria extends his title over Libya, Pentapolis, Ethiopia, and all of Egypt, but in all his patriarchate, which occupies the Indian and African lands and domains, he has barely one presbyter, to say nothing of a metropolitan or bishop. Wretched Mohammed has swallowed them all; and what part of chewed-up Christendom he did not manage to swallow, the accursed heretics Eutyches, Dioscorus, and their student Jacob Baradeus have in their jaws. What wonder will it be if the same thing also happens to our Church that happened to the local Churches of these patriarchates? And it certainly will happen (for it has already made a good start in that direction), if we will proceed so alertly and take such care for ourselves in the future as we now proceed. Doubtlessly we, the pastors, through such diligent watching over the sheep, will soon have to sing that common song: *"Pasi pasi oweczki do weczora ni iednoi"* [Ruthenian: Watch, watch your sheep, by evening not a one]. And therefore, we can easily guess what sort of reward we the pastors are to expect from Him, who entrusted to us the watching over His sheep.[315]

Horned Zedekiah trumpets in such a miserable state of our Church through circular letters for internal war; he digs at the ground with iron horns unto the downfall of our poor nation.[316] But I, for my part, most noble Ruthenian nation, summon you to peace with this my *Apology,* asking the Lord of the harvest that, although it is almost the

---

†   Consider, Reader, how the Church has diminished under the patriarchs.
315. [Jn. 21:17.]
316. [1 Kg. 22; 2 Ch. 18. He means Isaija Kopyn'skyj, then archbishop of Smolensk and Černihiv. See above, pp. 362 and 467.]

eleventh hour, He might send out His husbandmen for the harvest,[317] who, having no regard for any temporal thing, with all their soul, like good and faithful servants, like alert and proper pastors, might gather together the scattered lambs of Christ and might enclose them in one fold of Christ the Lord.

[†]There was a time when I persecuted the Church of God beyond measure, and wasted it, and profited in Rus' above many of my equals in my own nation, being more exceedingly zealous not of God's law, nor of the decrees of my fathers, which were pure, and are holy and immaculate, but rather of the errors and heresies that were sown by our Zizanijs in our Ruthenian Church when people slept.[318] And my own works themselves, which I had intended for their defense, brought me, by the kind grace of a merciful God, to notice and recognize them such that I could no longer oppose the truth of the Church with my writings unless I had entirely prepared myself for receiving those errors and heresies and did not know myself or call myself a son of the Eastern Church any longer. But my conscience, not without God's special compassion, nonetheless did not allow me to do this, even though I attempted many times as if to struggle with God's calling. For which let eternal thanks be to the living Lord—who does not wish the death of the sinner[319]—from me His miserable creature. Before whom, as also before His holy Church, with all my soul and with all my heart, [‡]I renounce all the little and great errors and heresies of Zizanij, Philalethes, Orthologue, the Clerk, and of other similar writers of ours. And with all of my soul, before my God, and before His Holy Church, I declare that I am a true son of His true Eastern Church, which did not separate from the Western Church, and in it a bishop and an archbishop. With that Holy Catholic Church do I join, in which may my Lord and God Jesus Christ be helpful unto me.

---

317. [Mt. 20:1–16.]

† It is a great penance to confess one's sins before the entire world. This is what St. Paul did.

318. [Gal. 1:13–14. The words of St. Paul about his pre-conversion self.]

319. [2 Pet. 3:9.]

‡ The author's renunciation of all the schismatic errors and heresies.

The Objections that Someone
Might Make to the Author Are Refuted

Perhaps someone will say to me: "You ought to have waited with this until the council." Considering the above-mentioned reason, I ask him whether he could assure me that I was not to die before this council, which is unknown to me and to all of us. He will say again: "Why did you not do this earlier?" And I will answer him this as well: I did this when the Lord God permitted and caused it. And I did this after probing and testing myself greatly. Well aware of this are those who knew of my lucubrations written against the work entitled *Union*,[320] against *The Conversation of the Adherent of Brest and a Member of the Brotherhood*,[321] against *The Resurrected Nalyvajko*,[322] against the *Politics, Ignorance, and Religion of the Members of the Vilnius New Church*,[323] which were already prepared to be released for publication after the publication of the *Lament*.[324] I do not mention *Verification,* its *Defense, Elenchus, Justification,* and others like them, in which, one after the other, the further I proceeded, the less I attacked genuine dogmas, and the more I dealt with the affairs of the moment that had come up suddenly at those times. No doubt even now there is in the library of the monastery of the Church Brotherhood of Vilnius a treatise on the procession of the Holy Spirit written in the Polish language in the manner of the syllogisms that the Greeks are wont to use against the Romans, and the Romans against the Greeks, and which I had submitted for the reading of the archimandrite, my predecessor in that post.

[†]And since, at that time, that place was so agitated that it was headed toward a greater uproar than toward salvatory benefit, I had to consign the matter to silence. In time it even came to the point that I wrote a *Palinode* against the *Lament,* which, after being submitted by me to the hands of the Ostroh chapter in this monastery where I now

320. [Potij 1595.]
321. [Perhaps the work sometimes attributed to Ipatij Potij (1603).]
322. [Potij 1607.]
323. [Potij 1608.]
324. [They seem, however, not to have appeared in print.]
†   Witnesses to this are many from the Vilnius Brotherhood, clerical and lay.

reside and write these words, remained here.[325] Probably on account of
the great affront caused Him by the *Lament,* my God, wishing to keep
me longer in this experience, did not allow me to realize the publication
of the one or the other.

After all this, in the year 1621, having decided to abandon the
lamentatious errors and heresies, I undertook—not without the will of
God, whose special grace in this matter I experienced beyond my worthiness and readiness—a serious means of discovering the truth that we
received in our ancestors from the Holy Eastern Church: that is, I began
to write, in manner of a dialogue, a catechism of the dogmas of the faith,
having called upon the Lord my God for help. Which, organized in this
method in all the dogmas of the faith, with the help of the same merciful
God, I finished in the year 1623. And having immediately given thought
to its correction and censoring when I had been thoroughly informed
about the four books on the dogmas of the faith written by Patriarch
Meletius of Alexandria of worthy memory and wishing to have them,
and especially the very person who ruled at that time the holy throne
of Constantinople,[326] serve as the censor, director, and corrector of my
catechism, I set off for the East.

And when I was informed in Constantinople by the father patriarch
that, when he was departing this world, Patriarch Meletius had ordered
all those four books on the dogmas of the faith to be burned, I saw with
no small regret that I had already lost one censor. I had retained hope,
however, in the second censor, the father patriarch himself, who, when
I asked him, had given me his own catechism to read. †But after reading
in it what I least expected, I did not think it fitting to come forward
with my own catechism, fearing that it would be reformed in that form
in which the catechism recently published in the year 1622 by some
Greek, Zacharias Gerganos, published in print in Greek, is carried about
in all Greece and is found here among us.[327]

Therefore, having conferred orally on some of the more necessary
matters, I returned home with it; and here, after deciding to submit

---

325. [I.e., Derman´.]
326. [I.e., Cyril Lukaris.]
†   You can easily surmise what was written in this catechism.
327. [Gerganos studied in Wittenberg ca. 1619–1621 and published his
catechism there. See Podskalsky 1988, 160–2.]

it for the reading and the censoring of the spiritual authorities of our Ruthenian Church, with the necessary first step of the "Considerations" that belong to this matter of the catechism, and receiving permission for this from Their Graces, with God's help I will not omit to present them after the completion, God willing, of my *Apology*. Proceeding thus in the matter of my catechismal lucubrations, I noted the errors and heresies of our Zizanijs, Philaletheses, Orthologues, Clerks, and the like, and, aided by the grace of God, I wrote a true (as it seems to me) confession of the dogmas of the faith, and I entitled it *Catechism of the Holy Eastern Church*. May the Lord God grant, if it pleases His holy will, that the world soon see it and that it be worn out by the hands of the Orthodox of all nations to the benefit of their souls and by the heretics to the recognition of Catholic faith.[328] All we need, most noble Ruthenian nation, is that we not be lacking for ourselves; that, through carelessness, we not allow to pass us by the proper occasions for correction given to us by God Himself.

I would speak to each of the foremost of Your Graces individually, but this I cannot manage, nor is it my obligation. I will speak, however, in my own name, having offered my submissiveness together with my obedience to the higher parties; I will speak to the clergy as to my lords, fathers, and brethren, having asked for forgiveness for my temerity, offering myself ready to listen with both ears to their exhortations, for the good of the Church, and declaring before them, as God Himself is witness to my conscience, that I do this for no other reason than out of genuine love for the Church of our Ruthenian nation. Seeing that it is nearly in a pitiful fall that seems to bode death, I could not remain silent, remembering the words of my Savior, that He deigned to promise that in such matters He would make the soulless stones to speak.[329]

---

328. [This Ruthenian catechism, which forms a sort of leitmotif of Smotryc'kyj's writings after his return from the East, was never published.]
329. [Lk. 19:40.]

Exhortation to the Clergy of Every Estate

My Lord, most reverend in God, and God-loving fathers, most beloved brethren in Christ the Lord.[330] Having taken your and my consecration to the episcopal state, unawaited and unexpected as it was, as a good and fortunate OMEN for our Ruthenian Church, I remain certain by the grace of God that the law that came from Zion and the word of the Lord that came from Jerusalem, which came in its time to our Ruthenian land pure, holy, and immaculate and became in our times impure, besmirched, and unholy, will cast down from itself through you its impurity, blot, and unholiness and will clothe itself again in its purity, immaculateness, and sanctity. May the Lord Jesus Christ cause this to happen in our times through the prayers of our holy fathers. It does not seem to me, most beloved brethren in Christ, that the Lord God deigned through His marvelous judgments to place us upon this degree of episcopal authority in our Ruthenian Church only so that we might consecrate presbyters in it and that we might have little regard for anything else in His Church, since even without us our Ruthenian Church had enough other bishops who would come from the Eastern lands for the consecration of presbyters, and we never lacked priests anywhere, even though they did not receive consecration from those bishops who considered as holy the unity with the Roman Church, since we had already announced before all people that we did not wish to have Uniate bishops for our bishops.

But perhaps God Almighty deigned to raise us to that dignity from among our nation so that, after undertaking to examine from our side all the differences that divide our Ruthenian Church from the Western Church, we might diligently consider them; and if they are such a chasm, such an abyss between us and the Romans, that we then judge that we could not come to an agreement and unity with each other; but if they are not, as in my opinion they certainly are not, then that, having come together with our brethren the bishops from the other side in the spirit of humility, we might take counsel for the salvation of our Ruthenian Church, which has already begun its fall, and not allow it to fall completely, but rather seek with God's help to bring it to that first

330. [The address is, of course, to the Orthodox hierarchy consecrated in 1620.]

faith and love which blossomed during the time of our holy fathers. For which let us promise ourselves to receive the generous blessing of God, and let us expect that our name will be famous in good memory from nation to nation. For if we will not do this, there is no one else but us, the bishops, who are so much obliged to this. And even if someone else besides us will do this, we will not escape worldly shame from people and eternal punishment from God. For to take the milk and the wool from the sheep and to hand them over to the infernal wolf for slaughter is not the work of a pastor, but of a hireling.[331] And I fear it is that of a thief and a bandit.

Let us only examine, my highly honored lords, this doctrine of Zizanij with both our bodily and our spiritual eyes to see whether there is concord with the doctrine of the holy doctors of the Church. Do we, by drawing from the sowers of chaff, feed the sheep of Christ the Lord entrusted unto our pastoring with the same feed with which their ancestors in turn were fed by our ancestors, those pastors who laid down their lives for the sheep of Christ the Lord and of themselves? For if this food with which we feed them is poison, then we poison them and do not feed them. Wherefore their blood will be sought at our hands.[332] Let us grant that the simple people entrusted to our industry cannot easily see this; will there be anyone from among us bishops of such running internal eyes and so devoid of spiritual understanding that he would not see these manifest blasphemies, unheard of in the Church of our ancestors? It is enough that we were not watchful toward this for those eight years since we became bishops, and we either did not see this, or we purposefully overlooked the food that was being given to the human souls entrusted to us.

It is certainly time for us to take note. God knows what accounting we will make for those as well, who departed this world having been stuffed to their fill with these blasphemies against the Lord God, His holy majesty, and the ancient faith that was given to us by God. If they will be given over to eternal fire for perdition, where will we find ourselves? Is this a joke to us, to lose even one soul entrusted to us, for which the only-begotten Son of God suffered a shameful death and of which this entire world is not worthy? But what will we say when,

331. [Jn. 10:12–13.]
332. [Ez. 3:18, 20; 33:6, 8; 34:10.]

through our carelessness, we find ourselves the cause of the perdition of many of such souls? If we do not wish to take care for them, let us cease to feed ourselves with their milk and to clothe ourselves with their wool. Let us cease using the episcopal title over them. And the spiritual bread that we eat—whatever it is, it belongs to the Church—let us yield it to more watchful pastors to eat. If they should wish to seek upon us their bodily and spiritual losses, having one body and one soul, I do not believe that all of us, who are so many, would have that with which to remit this, to say nothing of returning it fourfold.[333]

Therefore, my fathers and lords, who are worthy of every respect, let us tend toward watchfulness, let us tend toward love and peace and not to the trumpets of internal war among the brethren; let us tend toward common counsel, and let us not each trust only himself. *Ibi salus, ubi multa consilia* [There is safety, where there is much counsel].[334] We are ourselves at stake; and the entire Church is at stake. The eyes of all, of the princes, lords, gentry, knighthood, burghers, and, to be brief, of all our side of Rus', are turned toward us, and all will be led whither we lead them. And with us as guides, they are immediately right at heaven or at the infernal pit, from which Christ the Lord deign to preserve them and us. It is our obligation to see to it both that the faith of our ancestors not suffer any blot and that the flock of the sheep of Christ the Lord, which has been entrusted to our shepherding, not diminish, and especially in this so difficult time for our poor nation, which in every third word is charged with schism and heresies, wherefore we suffer derision and abuse.

Whom of us can this please, that at first meeting us they greet us as schismatics, and in every third word they honor us as apostates? It belongs to no one else in the Church of our nation but to us to determine whether we suffer all this unjustly or justly. For to distinguish between the clean and the unclean, between the leprous and the nonleprous is a priestly function.[335] It is our function to distinguish between schism and nonschism, heresy and nonheresy. And if we are in heresy, then certainly we are also in schism. For there can be schism without heresy, but heresy does not occur without schism.

333. [Ex. 22:1; 2 Sam. 12:6.]
334. Prov. 11[:14; 24:6].
335. Dt. 17 [Dt. 23:10; 24:8].

†Let those customary dodges of heretics not lead us away from the matter that properly belongs to us, those excuses that also Christ the Lord was called a Samaritan, a glutton, a drunkard, and the like.[336] Christ the Lord was calumniated. But we ourselves see well that we bear heresies in our bosom without calumny, we nurse them, and we allow our entire Church to be blotted with them. But let us grant that we will abandon those Zizanijs with their heresies, and we will order their writings out of our Church and our houses: will we then get rid of the appellation of schism in our true faith? I do not expect so. For our ancestors did not know these Philaletheses, Orthologues, Clerks, and their like. They had pure and immaculate faith, and yet they did not avoid the shame of schism. Nor will we avoid it. ‡Having rejected the Zizanijs with their heresies, we will avoid the shame of the heretical name, but not also of the schismatic, in which it belongs to us Church authorities to make a decision. And this is our proper function.

But we have our usual dodge ready in this—that it is not we who are the schismatics but the Romans and that, secure in their secular authority, they shame us with the shame that belongs to them; and that they heap upon us the opprobrium that belongs to them. They themselves, being apostates from the Eastern Church, revile and shame us with this name, by their power and not because of our property. All right. But not even we ourselves are satisfied with our argument, to say nothing of the Romans. For these are mere words, and not also the thing: that is, we only say this, but we do not also prove it. And if we do prove it, we prove it such that we ourselves are not satisfied with these proofs. Our proofs demonstrate to us the disproofs in our very selves. For as long as we do not demonstrate that the Romans are heretics, we cannot hold them as schismatics either. With heresy and without heresy, we can be apostates to the Romans; the Romans can be such to us only with heresy. *But without heresy they cannot properly be known as and called apostates by us. And this is so for these two reasons. First,

---

†   This excuse will not work for us.
336. [Jn. 8:48; Mt. 11:19; Lk. 7:34.]
‡   We will not avoid the appellation of schism even though we cast out of our Church the above-mentioned writers, rather only when we find ourselves in unity with the universal pastor.
*   For what reasons we cannot call the Romans heretics.

because the bishop of Rome is the first ruler of the Church of Christ the Lord and its head pastor, to whom, so long as he does not have heresy, every cleric and layman of every estate and authority who is within the Universal Church is obliged to adhere, love, honor, know and have as the leading pastor of the Church of Christ. Second, because the bishop of Rome summons us every day to Church unity, and we not only do not listen to his summons, but we even scorn him, rail at him, revile him, heap opprobrium upon him, call him Antichrist.

For in the sundering of one Church from another Church, the local Church suffers the sin and shame of schism in that, not having any proper reason, it does not wish to unite with the separated second local Church, although it is summoned to do so. And there can be no other proper reason for this but *haeresis* alone. But for us—having gathered together, by the grace of God, and cast aside the spirit of our Zizanijs, Philaletheses, Orthologues, and the like—for us to see heresy in the Roman Church is to see it, in my opinion, in our own Church, in which, down to the smallest comma, we find and see everything (as far as the dogmas of the faith are concerned, the diminishing of the correctness of which commonly gives birth to heresies) that is found and seen in the Ruthenian Church. Likewise also we find and see in it, right down to the least iota, what is found and seen in the Eastern Church. For who among us does not see that we were given and bequeathed a different manner of belief about the Romans, and not that which was bequeathed to our ancestors and especially the Greeks?

Why the Greeks Did Not Receive the Procession of the Holy Spirit "and from the Son"; and Why We Ought to Receive It

The Greeks could believe with some sort of proper reason that through the addition to the creed of "and from the Son" the Romans introduce two origins into one divinity or that they fuse two divine persons into one person; and thus they charged them with the Manichaean heresy, with regard to the two origins, and with the Sabellian heresy, with regard to the fusing of the two persons into one. But we can no longer believe this about them in good conscience since they themselves at the Council of Florence, as I said a little above, placed anathema upon those who either established two origins in one divinity or fused two divine persons into one. And neither we nor the Greeks could, nor can we now, properly prove against them even one of these two impieties in any manner. For when they, with their holy Western fathers, confess that the Holy Spirit proceeds "from the Father and from the Son," they do not believe anything else but what the Greeks believe when they, with their Eastern fathers, confess that the Holy Spirit proceeds "from the Father through the Son." Wherefore, we now have one belief about the Romans on account of that addition "and from the Son," and the Greeks had another. Before they were informed about this, they could properly find blasphemies in the Romans; but we, having been thoroughly informed by them concerning this, cannot seek blasphemy in this matter without our own manifest blasphemy.

Why the Greeks Did Not Receive Purgatory; and Why We Ought to Receive It

Concerning purgatory, the Greeks believed that the Romans, through their confession of temporary torments in it, destroy the eternal torments of hell and understand as Origen understood that not only all people, but even the devils, will receive God's mercy upon them, and hell will become empty. And thus they charged them with the Origenist heresy. †But when the Romans informed the Greeks that they accord torments—eternal, irrevocable, not at all subject to God's mercy—to all pagans, infidels, heretics, schismatics, devils, and even Catholics who depart this world in mortal sin without penance, ‡and they establish temporary torments for those faithful who depart this world in venial sins or in mortal sins that have been confessed but are unatoned, the Greeks were satisfied with this, and we must be, and ought to be, satisfied with this as with our own confession, with the exception—if it must be excepted—of the material fire, which, as I say here often, is not an article of faith for the Romans either.

---

†   For whom Hell.
‡   See for what kinds of sins is purgatory—not for mortal, unatoned sins, as Azarius printed.

Why the Greeks Criticized the Unleavened Bread in the Roman Church; and Why We Ought Not to Criticize It

†The Greeks alleged of the Romans that, through the use of unleavened bread in the sacrament of the Eucharist, they did not acknowledge the soul in Christ the Lord, whence they ascribed to them the Apollinarian heresy. But when the Romans made known that they have the custom of using unleavened bread in the mystery of the Eucharist even from apostolic times, from the tradition of the blessed apostle Peter, that this is done in their Church as a sign of the unleavenedness—that is, of the sinlessness—of the man, Christ the Lord, who did not have, and does not have in Him, the leaven of sin, the Greeks were satisfied with this, and we ought to be satisfied with this. Even until our age, the Greeks did not raise even the least objection against the Romans' receiving the sacrament of the Eucharist under one species, nor did they criticize them for this, since they had before their own eyes at home such a custom of receiving this mystery under one species in daily use. About which we will speak more thoroughly in "Considerations." Nor ought we to charge against them and to criticize their custom since we cannot do this without allegation and criticism against ourselves. ‡Our very own Church books inform us that the Romans believe in Catholic fashion concerning the disposition of the souls that have departed this world and about the eldership of the bishop of Rome, and they give testimony that we do not believe otherwise about these two things.

Thus, as we can see, one belief about the Roman faith was given to us, and another reached the Greeks. Wherefore, as long as the Greeks were not informed about all this by the Romans, not having been able to grasp the substance of their confession on their own, they could charge them with the Manichaean, Sabellian, Apollinarian, Origenist, and similar heresies. But we, having already been sufficiently informed by them about this and seen that all this, precisely this and nothing else, was sealed in our souls and in our Church by faith and confession—if

† The custom of receiving the mystery of the Eucharist under one species ought not to be criticized by us.
‡ We ought not to criticize the Romans concerning the disposition of the souls that have departed this world, nor about the eldership of the pope.

we should wish to charge them with this, we would shamelessly lie upon our souls.

Thus to seek heresy in the Roman Church is to seek it in the pure Eastern Church, which has one and the same confession of faith in actual fact, although it differs a little in words. But among the Orthodox, according to St. Gregory the Theologian, faith depends not on words but on the thing. Whence St. John Chrysostom says, "It is not necessary to base oneself on the words, but to look to the intention of him who writes. For if we will not grasp the intention of the writer, we can fall victim to much discord, and we will set everything at odds, shaking with fear where terror is not."

This is exactly what is happening now between the Eastern and the Western Church—that, seeking faith in the bare words and not in the thing itself, when we hear that the Romans confess that the Holy Spirit proceeds "and from the Son," we shake with terror where there is none; we fear blasphemy where we do not find it. We do not listen to how they explain their confession, but we invent something of our own, and we charge *calumniose* [calumniously] that it is theirs, whence the discord and hatred among us, and all our temporal and eternal good was upended. It is not the characteristic of a good man to blame his neighbor for that of which he is not guilty. Likewise, not to listen to the justification of the charged, but to charge against him this and that, is the act of lying and calumny.

That the Roman Church Is Not Besmirched with Any Heresy

Seeing before us, then, and knowing for certain that the Roman Church is not infected with any heresy and, moreover, that it summons us every day to holy unity with it, and yet we scorn it—I leave it to your healthy judgment, my fathers and brethren, whether we avoid the shame of schism. Which, as I said a little above, belongs to no one else to know and to put in order, but to us the bishops together with the Church brethren, the archimandrites, the hegumens, and the entire Church in common, according to the dignity of each and his fitness for this matter. Being aware for a certainty, as well, that the Turks consider the union of the Greeks with the Romans to be a conspiracy of all the

Christians against them, †they take care that the patriarchs, especially that of Constantinople, not make any discussions and treaties about this with the pope, as they are wont to take care for the integrity of their domain. Even if, enticed by the righteousness and piety of the matter, the patriarchs desired and wished to do this, they cannot. Especially since the simple people have been embittered against the Romans for a long time for many reasons and are now in these times even more embittered, thanks to sowers of chaff similar to our Zizanijs, thanks to the heretical works that are now being published among the Greeks, similar to those of our Philaletheses and Orthologues, as is the catechism of Zacharias Gerganos the Greek that I mentioned a little above, published in print in the simple Greek tongue, in which, among other things, these errors and heresies are cited in express words and put forth as the Orthodox dogmas of the Greek faith.

The Errors and Heresies of Zacharias Gerganos the Greek, in His Catechism Printed A[nno] 1622

That for the demonstration and for the proofs of faith Holy Scripture is sufficient.[337] That Holy Scripture is in and of itself clear and perspicuous.[338] That the interpreter of Holy Scripture is the very same Scripture.[339] That all the books of Maccabees are apocryphal.[340] That the traditions are unnecessary.[341] That through the killing of Uriah, David had lost faith.[342] That a soul without a body cannot suffer.[343] That the Church is the congregation of the saints.[344] That Christ the

---

† Even if the patriarchs wished concord and unity with the pope, they would not dare on account of the fear of the Turks. But we Rus′ can do this *libere* [freely] and then help the Greeks to come to unity.

337. *Pag.* 4.
338. Ibid.
339. Ibid.
340. *Pag.* 5.
341. *Pag.* 6.
342. [2 Sam. 11.]
343. *Pag.* 54.
344. *Pag.* 122 and 140.

Lord, to the extent that he is the head of the Church, is everywhere.[345] That the bishop of Rome is not the *successor* of St. Peter the Apostle.[346] That the pope scorns the epistles of the holy apostle Paul and rejects them.[347] That the holy doctors of the Church do not say that Christ the Lord built His Church upon Peter.[348] That the holy angels cannot see God.[349] That the pope is the opponent of Christ the Lord, of Peter, and of all the saints.[350] That there are only two places for souls that depart this world.[351] That there are only two sacraments established and given by Christ the Lord.[352] That a priest who is an open sinner cannot effectively celebrate the sacrament of the Eucharist.[353] That Roman priests are not true priests.[354] That they are outside of the Church.[355] That all who are in torments see Christ the Lord.[356]

These are the heretical blasphemies which, having flown in from Germany to our Greece, both lead the Greeks away from the true belief concerning these dogmas of the faith and embitter them against the Roman Church more and more day by day, such that neither the Greeks nor the patriarchs, even if they should desire to do so, can openly strive for Church peace and its internal concord except they were to allow genuine love into their hearts, which drives away all fear from it and, having entrusted themselves and this salvatory matter to the Lord God, they were to enter in these manners into unanimity of faith and into unity of the Church, which the Lord God Himself would give their hearts in His unfathomable judgments.

345. *Pag.* 149.
346. *Pag.* 150.
347. Ibid.
348. *Pag.* 151.
349. Ibid.
350. *Pag.* 152.
351. *Pag.* 166.
352. *Pag.* 179.
353. *Pag.* 197.
354. *Pag.* 223.
355. Ibid.
356. *Pag.* 271.

By What Means the Greeks Could Come to Unity
with the Roman Church

In my opinion, there could be no easier or more serious means to unite the Church that is in the East under all four patriarchs with the Western Church than through us, the Ruthenian nation, who, by the grace of God, enjoy Christian freedom under a pious Christian Catholic lord; than through our Church, by our desire. For which, on our side, it does not belong to anyone else any more intimately to have industry, to strive, and to take care, than to you, Most Illustrious,[357] first of all, and in addition to you, to us the bishops, archimandrites, hegumens, and to the entire Church clergy. And to the princes, lords, gentry, knighthood, and the brotherhoods, with the knowledge and permission of the most illustrious King, Our Gracious Lord, who fortunately rules over us. For as long as we, not having made use of these means, continue to cry out the raven's call *"cras, cras"* [Latin: "tomorrow, tomorrow"], all the evil will be maintained among the Greeks and among us Rus′. Until we, I say, who avoid the light of day, cease opposing the genuine truth of faith and, benighted with the nocturnal darkness of hatred, cease cawing "this and that, the pope's a heretic, the pope's the antichrist" like a raven, although he promises himself he will be white tomorrow, we will never whiten.[358]

Is this, then, such a small beginning toward a more severe servitude for the Greeks than the one they now suffer? †For although they suffered and suffer this servile misery under a human tormentor, nonetheless having pure and immaculate faith, they could take consolation internally and bring other Christian Catholic nations to compassion over them. But once they have become heretic, they will lose their internal consolation, fall away from people's compassion, and they will also subject themselves to that severe tormentor's servitude, to the immeasurably more severe devil's servitude. For every heretic is Satan's slave: he renders homage to him, he suffers misery under him, and he must expect the reward of eternal torments with him.

357. [I.e., Metropolitan of Kyiv Jov Borec′kyj.]
358. [Cf. *NKPP* 2:217, "Kruk," 16.]
†   The schismatic Greeks will suffer a more severe servitude and torment from the devil in hell than they now do from the Turk.

As we can see, it was more than twenty errors and heresies that flew into Greece five years ago on account of that Greek Gerganos; and what is going on there now, the Lord God knows. We do not ask about this, although it belongs to us through our obligation. That catechism was published in print in the year of our Lord 1622. And when I was in Constantinople in the year of our Lord 1623, I heard it preached *publice* [publicly] from the cathedra by some hieromonk Benedict, a teacher of the Great Church of Constantinople, who moreover was titled archimandrite of the Vatopedi Monastery on the Holy Mountain; and so, I heard it preached *publice* [publicly] by that same great teacher of the Great Church of Constantinople that prayers for the dead neither work any benefit for the souls that have departed this world, nor are they necessary in Church. †And when I conferred about this with whom it was proper to do so, not only was that teacher not punished for this, but I received the answer that otherwise it is impossible to destroy the Roman purgatory.

And that is the beginning of the future pains for Greece, if the Lord God will not be with her. These, I say, are the beginnings of the severe Greek servitude. Now we must put away our liturgies for the dead, our memorials, prayers, alms, and other Church benefices for them. But this did not occur through any carelessness of that teacher, rather on purpose, and often. Being acquainted with him, I was often in conversation with him, and I discovered that he had studied together with this Gerganos in Saxon Wittenberg, and it was there they drank of what they breathed here, and in addition to the heretical school doctrines, they also brought with them to Greece the doctrine of heretical theology. If the smoke should rise there, we must keep a watchful eye lest it infect us too with that stinking smoke even more than we have already become sooty from our own new theologians, who are similar to them. For if that wickedness became so sooty from the throne from which we received our Orthodox faith in our ancestors, it could harmfully wound us and our Church. That is certainly an evil wound of mortal infection brought to bear upon unfortunate Greece, presaging a fall more severe for her than the one she is in, in which, through her excessive ignorance, it will be easy to join the final ignorance of salvatory matters to the propounded

†   *Cum P[atriarcha]* [with the patriarch].

heresy, especially by the one in it to whom the key of knowledge has been entrusted.[359]

If only that man,[360] who is accepted in that nation and beloved in our Church, would turn his industry and labor to sewing together the ancient tear between the Eastern and the Western Churches, in my opinion, with God's help from the Western Church, which is ready for this good, he would manage this easily and happily, using our Ruthenian Church as a kind of lime in between those two walls to join them together. If only he would wish to do this today, for what the morrow will bring, God alone knows. No one else could be a cause for this more safely and properly than we, my most reverend fathers in God, than our, I say, Ruthenian nation. For with God's help we can achieve this easily at home. Not seeking any further progress in this matter than to ask God's anointed, His Majesty the King, Our Gracious Lord, that he deign to allow our side to have a council at which we, the clergy, after appearing in our entirety and receiving representatives sent to it from the gentry estate from the brethren of each palatinate and county, from the brotherhoods endowed with privileges, and from the royal, princely, and lordly cities, would treat of nothing else, with God's help, but Church peace. With God's grace we can come to it quickly, after we consider and set in order these differences in the faith at home. For they are the cause of the unfortunate schism between the Eastern and the Western Church. Therefore, let us, all the clergy upon whom this matter depends in our Ruthenian Church and to whom the Lord God gave reason to the head and words to the mouth, renounce all our other occupations at this time, and let us all together take up as with one soul this one matter, which is to serve both the temporal and the eternal happiness of our bodies and souls.

Exhortation to the Noble Estate

Your Graces, most noble, most excellent estate of the Ruthenian nation, princes and lords, gentry and knighthood, citizens of the Crown and of the Grand Duchy of Lithuania, whom nature itself, nurtured and loved in freedom and in liberties, has granted by birth to see what is honorable

359. [Lk. 11:52.]
360. [I.e., Patriarch Cyril Lukaris of Constantinople.]

and to distinguish between that and what is beneficial; who, having received in your noble ancestors the noble holy Christian faith from the Eastern lands, from the Church and see of Constantinople, have served, and do serve, through the pouring out of your noble Christian blood, so that you, comparable to each citizen in these domains of the Crown and the Grand Duchy of Lithuania, through your birth and deeds, might take your place not only in the land offices and castle authorities of His Majesty the King, Your Gracious Lord, but would not be set at a disadvantage to sit at his lordly side and to be honored and adorned with senatorial dignities and the titles of his faithful council—if Your Graces noted to what abasement and disadvantage you have come in a short time among the brethren nobility, that you do not compare to others in this Commonwealth not only in deeds, but also in birth from noble families; if you took note of this (for not to see this is not to see oneself and to be entirely without the eyes of understanding), if you took note of this, I say, and if you sought the cause of this, and if you found what you sought, if you considered what you found, if you pondered what you considered (that this happens to you properly and justly, either according to divine or according to human law); thus if you took note, sought, found, considered, pondered that this is how things are, then by the living God, take pity, you yourselves upon yourselves and upon your descendants; and having become accustomed to know the beneficial and to prefer the honorable to it, take note of both these things in your time lest after your life your ancestors lose both these things, and in addition to these two things they also lose their piety. Our eyes gazed upon most noble senators in our fatherland from our nation and faith, castellans, and palatines, but now we do not see even one of such who is both in our nation and in our faith. And we rarely see anyone of our fellows in religion, not only on those very high places at the side of the lord, but even in the lowest dignities, for this has been happening for some time now.

†What is the reason for your abasement and disadvantage? Do you not serve the dear fatherland as faithfully and laboriously as your ancestors faithfully and laboriously served? Or does His Majesty the King, God's Anointed, Our Gracious Lord, overlook you with his

---

†   What is the reason for the abasement of the noble estate of the Ruthenian religion?

gracious eye, and does he purposefully not wish to remember the faithful services both of your ancestors and of yourselves? Neither one of these. Both the King, Our Gracious Lord, is ready to reward, and does reward, each one according to his merits and his condition; and your faithfulness and labor is not less than the faithfulness and labor of your ancestors. But He causes this, who has in his hands the hearts of kings, and pours them out where He will;[361] who deposes potentates from their majesties, and takes people from the muck and places them with the princes.

But if you did not take note of your significant abasement and seek the cause for it (as must be the case; for if you had noticed your harm and found and considered its cause, certainly, having been compelled by your noble birth itself, you would not have remained until now in such an evil, but you would long ago have raised yourselves out of it); if, then, you did not take note and did not seek the cause, it is certainly time to take note, find and consider the cause, and ask yourselves and us your clergy whether this happens to you properly and justly, both according to divine and according human law.

For my part, having left to those higher than I the higher consideration, examining meagerly according to my meager reason, I do not find any other reason than that expressed by God Himself: "Behold, I set before you this day a blessing and a curse; a blessing, if ye obey the commandments of the Lord your God, which I command you this day: and a curse, if ye will not obey the commandments of the Lord your God, but turn aside out of the way which I command you this day, to go after other gods, which ye have not known."[362] Take note of this reason, most honorable noble estate, and consider whether you did not fall from the true path of our Orthodox faith, which the Lord God Himself had given to you and your ancestors from the East, having been led astray by these Zizanijs, Philaletheses, Orthologues, Clerks, and our other similar Ruthenian writers? And whether you did not go to follow other gods, whom you have not known,[363] that is, whether you did not take up blasphemies, errors, and heresies, which both your ancestors and you yourselves not long before did not know, which our new

361. [Ex. 14:8.]
362. Dt. 11[:26–8].
363. [Dt. 11:28, 13:2, 6, 13; 28:64; Jer. 19:4.]

theologians sowed for us, and gave cause for other gods to be praised in our nation? Judge for yourselves. Do you not find yourselves in what I have mentioned? Do you not find that the cause of your abasement is obvious? If not, then look yourselves for some other cause. I am satisfied with my admonition.

For I know what sort of place these writers have with you: Zizanij, Philalethes, Orthologue, like three new consecrators upon whom you do not allow even a bit of dust to fall; and you believe whatever they say as if you had heard it from God's mouth. I speak of what I know, since it has already befallen me to hear no very good word from many people on account of them. To criticize the *Lament* in any way is like grabbing the listener by his soul, for many declare that it is to be kept for the descendants like an invaluable jewel. And it goes similarly with them as if they were warming up a cold viper in their bosom so that their descendants might die in life bitten by her and thus they might never know temporal and eternal happiness. †This jewel is not dear to me. If only it had not been finished, since it charges me with the transgression of blasphemy before my God, and thereby it also brings to me temporal unhappiness and eternal torment. These unhappy jewels also brought about Your Graces' abasement and caused you to be known as heretics among your fellow citizens. Through the reception of which our paternal Orthodox faith was given up to disrespect and was buried in oblivion, and errors and heresies were declared to be our faith. They earned for us the unblessing of God, which has caused Your Graces' abasement.

A Special Exhortation to the Noble Estate

Just examine for yourselves, most honorable noble estate, the faith that was described by the Zizanijs, Philaletheses, Orthologues, and Clerks, and by other new theologians like them and published to the world in print; and consider in every point of their errors and heresies whether it is concordant with the faith of our ancestors. Doubtless you will find them to be so far from each other as are an Orthodox and a heretic. Someone may say: "This word is a harsh word." I will say: Only a blind man calls the light darkness, and only a liar calls the truth untruth. Whoever

---

†   Whoever founds his faith on the *Lament* will have to lament eternally in hell with Luther. [A rhymed couplet of thirteen-syllable lines in the original.]

would call a heretic a Catholic would have to be blind in reason and a liar in tongue. But what then? Not picking at their words, let us reject their cause, and immediately we will also get rid of the effects of this cause as well. Let us abandon these Zizanijs. Let us cast their errors and heresies beneath our feet, and immediately painful words will depart from us as well. Let us acknowledge the Orthodox faith of our Orthodox ancestors, and we will be known as Orthodox along with them.

And if, furthermore, this word is also harsh—that Your Graces' fellow citizens greet and take leave of you by calling you schismatics or apostates—my advice, and, in my opinion, it is healthy advice: do not suffer this disgrace either. To be known as a heretic in spiritual law is to be known as one banished in secular law, and to be known as an apostate is to be known as a public enemy and as a disturber of the public peace. Both are dishonorable. Thus do not suffer either one upon your faith, which is worthy of every honor; rather crown it with love, pure and immaculate, free from errors and heresies. For, without love for one's brethren, for one's fellows in faith, faith is unfaith, and schism is a just criticism. Either use, Your Graces, the advice I have given you a little above, or find for yourselves a better one—only do something for your salvation. And ask (for it is freer to Your Graces at this time), ask, I say, God's anointed, the King, His Gracious Lord, for the sort of council that was indicated a little above, and we soon, God willing, will be in one house, which we now suffer to be wretchedly divided.[364]

For it is not possible that, unto us who ask, seek, and knock, the Lord God would not give, not open, and not cause us to find the good that it is incumbent upon us to seek by His divine command.[365] If He promised to be with two or three gathered in His name,[366] then who would doubt the presence of our Savior, Christ the Lord, wherever more of us should gather in His holy name? On our side we have the complete hierarchy. In addition to it, we have hegumens, hieromonks, and presbyters. And we have Your Graces of most noble families, princes, lords, gentry, knighthood. We also have the important brotherhoods from the cities so that, God willing, a council gathered in the name

364. [Mt. 12:25; Mk. 3:25; Lk. 11:17.]
365. [Mt. 7:7–8; Lk. 11:9–10; Rev. 3:20.]
366. [Mt. 18:20.]

of the Lord for a salvatory end will be conducted in peace and end according to God's will.

†For all Church disturbances, unrest, and schisms have been pacified throughout all the Christian centuries by nothing other than councils. If Your Graces do not do this, we will be looking in short time, not without the heavy sadness and grief of our souls, at the death of the Ruthenian Church, which is in so much pain on our side. Are there now many of Your Graces of the noble calling on our side? Wish to see, I beg you, and you will easily see that there are thousands less than there were ten years ago. And after you there will be far fewer, for even during your lifetime your children are no longer yours.

Do this, then, most worthy noble estate, and you will soon enjoy, God granting, your entire good, and you will cause the entire Ruthenian nation to enjoy it. For you will do a thing that is dear to God and salvatory for yourselves. What can be dearer to God in a faithful man than love among the brethren and among the fellows in faith? For without it, faith, like a body without a soul, is dead.

‡Let us cleanse the pure faith of your ancestors of the heretical blots, and let us crown it with love through the unanimous in faith: that thus the Lord God will be with us and will return to us all our good according to the body and the soul, which we have not enjoyed for such a long time; He will remove the demise that hangs over our Church; He will establish our Ruthenian nation in its ancient freedom. He will open for you, noble estate, the doors to the land offices and to the senatorial dignities. He will give the burghers access to perform the offices of the town hall bench. He will build us schools. He will adorn the churches. He will organize the monasteries. He will free the presbyters from the burdens of servitude. Finally, for the same reason, He will wipe the daily tears from the eyes of the entire miserably afflicted Ruthenian nation in the cities and in the villages. He will cause us to enjoy that heavenly peace yet on earth. And He will bestow upon us countless other goods. And after the temporal delights, He will render us worthy of those eternal ones in His heavenly kingdom. He will render our names praiseworthy for all ages. For we will do His divine deed, when, through the love and unity of the brethren, we fill in and even out, the

---

† All schisms and heresies have been pacified by councils.
‡ This is the author's healthy and salvatory advice.

uncrossable abyss of the accursed schism that has gaped open for so many centuries. And thus we will cause that, in this most illustrious kingdom, Rus', the Poles, and Lithuania, all of us as with one mouth and one heart will praise and worship the name of God, who is One in the Trinity. Amen. Let it be. Grant it, O God.

And let this be the end of my Apology.
I now proceed to a presentation of the promised "Considerations."

Consideratiae
or
Considerations of the Six Differences That Have Arisen between the Eastern Church and the Western as Regards the Faith

I told you at the outset in the *Apology,* most noble Ruthenian nation, that if the Western Church is without heresy, then the Eastern must of necessity be either in a state of heresy or, even with its correct confession of the faith, in schism. It is an impossibility that both be in heresy since the gates of hell, that is, heresies, cannot prevail against the Church.[367] In view of its Orthodox confession of faith, which it maintains pure, holy, and immaculate in correct understanding, it cannot be shown that the Eastern Church is in a state of heresy. For if someone, having understood its dogmas of the faith incorrectly, speaks and writes about them incorrectly and by his error subjects himself to the suspicion of heresy, he himself suffers shame in his incorrect understanding, but the Church remains without reproof in its correct confession. If the Western is in heresy, it should be in it for no other dogma of the faith than either for all these six, which are taken as a difference between it and the Eastern, or for several, or for one of them. For in all the other dogmas of the faith, with the exception of these six, there is unanimous agreement between them. And since at this time a very urgent necessity requires of us that we lend a little time to the consideration of these differences,

367. [Mt. 16:18.]

that we consider them and discover whether they are such that they properly and justly cause separation between those Churches that are sundered from the one [Church] and that they separate the one from the other and render them inaccessible to each other; for the one that is free from heresy cannot have any communion, agreement, and unity with the one that has been defiled by heresy without its own blemishing by that same heresy; so then, that we might manifestly and clearly see and recognize that the Western Church (which for many years now has been summoning the Eastern Church, and in it especially our Ruthenian Church, to unity along with it) is not in heresy, for this very reason I take these six differences under consideration, and I submit them to your complete consideration, most noble Ruthenian nation: so that, having understood the truth in these differences sufficiently, we might safely allow ourselves to be drawn to unity with the Roman Church in the hope of our salvation, unite with it, and not suffer in vain these miseries, hardships, oppressions, disturbances, and legal battles, to the detriment of our internal and external goods, in the anger of God that rests upon us and in the lack of grace toward us on the part of the brethren.

I mentioned more than once at the outset what sort of differences they were, these six differences between the two Churches; and I will make brief mention of them in this place too, although they are already well known to almost all of us. The first difference comes from the confession by the Romans of the procession of the Holy Spirit "and from the Son." The second from the confession of purgatory. The third from the use of unleavened bread in the sacrament of the Eucharist. The fourth from the confession of the perfect blessing of righteous souls that have departed from this world. The fifth from the confession of the primacy of the bishop of Rome. The sixth difference raised is that which is newly in our times alleged as a heresy by the Greeks and by us, Rus', in the partaking of the mysteries of the Eucharist under the single species of the bread. Proceeding in orderly fashion in the thorough consideration of these six differences, I offer the first consideration concerning the first difference, that is, concerning the procession of the Holy Spirit "and from the Son."

Consideratiae,
or
Considerations of the Difference
Stemming from the Confession of the Procession
of the Holy Ghost "and from the Son"

The holy Eastern doctors teach that the Holy Spirit proceeds from
the Father "through the Son." The holy Western fathers teach that the
same Holy Spirit proceeds from the Father "and from the Son." But
neither of these manners of speaking—neither "through the Son" nor
"from the Son"—is to be found expressed in these clear words in Holy
Scripture. And both these sets of holy doctors, through both manners
of speaking, understand that the Holy Spirit has its being through the
eternal procession of the Holy Spirit, that is, from the Father through the
Son or from the Father and from the Son. Wherefore both confessions
are shown to be of equal validity, both Orthodox and Catholic.

Second consideration. To confess that the Holy Spirit proceeds
through the Son only with regard to the gifts is to confess contrary
to the express teaching of the holy doctors of the Church, who teach
that the Holy Spirit proceeds through the Son *naturaliter* [naturally],
essentialiter [essentially], not by means of birth, etc.

Third consideration. To confess that the Holy Spirit proceeds
through the Son with regard to the one essence, but without regard
for the natural order of the divine persons, suppresses the order of the
divine persons, and it establishes that it can equally be confessed that
the Son is born from the Father through the Holy Spirit. Both of which
are impious.

Fourth consideration. The heretic Nestorius is the first who did not
acknowledge that the Holy Spirit has its being through the Son. Joining
him, Theodoretus did not acknowledge that the Holy Spirit has its being
either from the Son or through the Son. St. Cyril of Alexandria opposed
both of them, confessing with express words that the Holy Spirit is both
from the Son as it is also from the Father. But it is said that the Holy
Spirit is from the Father because it has His being from Him. And by

confessing His being in this manner—"and from the Son"—St. Cyril suppressed the error of Nestorius and of Theodoretus.[368]

Fifth consideration. It is clear that Nestorius and Theodoretus erred in not recognizing that the Holy Spirit has its being from the Son, or through the Son, because of the fact that the holy doctors of the Church opposed their nonrecognition—the Western by teaching that the Holy Spirit has its being "and from the Son," and the Eastern, "through the Son."

Sixth consideration. Through the testimony of St. Maximus the Confessor even before the Sixth Universal Council it came to the knowledge of the Eastern Church that the Western Church confessed that the Holy Spirit proceeded "and from the Son."[369] And yet, neither the Sixth Universal Council nor the Seventh opposed its confession. To the contrary, the Seventh Universal Council confessed in express words that the Holy Spirit proceeds from the Father through the Son, which before this no other council had done.

Seventh consideration. None of the holy Eastern doctors who lived at the time when the confession "and from the Son" had already been proclaimed in the Western Church called it a heresy or an error. But certainly the Holy Spirit that lived in them would not have suffered this if He had judged this confession to be blasphemy against His divine majesty.

St. John of Damascus touches upon this confession when he says *ex Filio Spiritum non dicimus* [we do not say that the Spirit is from the Son], and yet he did not call the manner of speaking "and from the Son" either a heresy or an error.[370] This holy and wise man, who rebukes and destroys every sort of heresy in his writings, would not have suffered this if he had found in this confession any sort of blasphemy against the

---

368. *Lib. 4 ad Pallad.* [bk. 4, *To Palladius* (?); perhaps *On Adoration in the Spirit and in Truth, PG* 68:301–58] and in the interpretation of *Effundam de spiritu meo in Iopilem proph.* ["I will pour out of my spirit" in the prophet Joel (Joel 2:28–9; Acts 2:17–18); Cyril of Alexandria, *Commentary on the Prophet Joel; PG* 71:379/380–381/382].

369. *Epist. ad Marinum Cypris Praesbyterum* [St. Maximus the Confessor, *Letter to Marinus, Presbyter of Cyprus; PG* 91:135/136A].

370. *Lib. 1, c. 13* [St. John of Damascus, *Exposition of the Orthodox Faith*, bk. 1, chap. 13 (actually chap. 8); *PG* 94:831/832B; *NPNF2* 9:11].

Lord God. But it is only with regard to this preposition *ex,* "from," which usually signifies a primary cause in the Greek language, that he says that we do not speak of the procession of the Holy Spirit from the Son; but instead of this preposition *ex,* he applies to the Son the *praepositia* [preposition] *per* [through], which signifies the cause together with the order, saying: "The Holy Spirit is also called of the Son, not because He proceeds from Him but, through Him, from the Father."[371] Whence it is made clear that this manner of speaking of St. John of Damascus does not establish that this matter is not thus, but that, on account of the heretics, one does not speak thus. Thus he says in another place that *Christi param nequaquam dicimus Sanctam Virginem* [we say that the Holy Virgin is in no wise equal to Christ], and yet elsewhere he expresses this with express words, saying: "And therefore we preach that the Mother of God is the Holy Virgin, as the one who properly and truly gave birth to the God who had been made incarnate from her, and we know that she is the *christogenitrix* [Mother of Christ], for she gave birth to Christ. But since the impious Nestorius used this word in order to destroy the name *deogenitrix* [Mother of God], we call her not *christogenitrix,* but, more importantly, *deogenitrix.*"[372] †Likewise, with regard to the heresy of Eunomius, who taught that the Holy Spirit is from the Son alone, this holy man said that we do not speak of the Holy Spirit "from the Son." And therefore in another place, as was cited already above, having said that the Holy Spirit is also called of the Son—not as if from Him (he adds immediately), but as if proceeding through Him from the Father.[373]

371. *Lib. 1, c. 15* [St. John of Damascus, *Exposition of the Orthodox Faith,* bk. 1, chap. 15 (perhaps chap. 8; there is no chap. 15); *PG* 94:831B–834A; *NPNF2* 9:11].

372. *Lib. 3, c. 12* [St. John of Damascus, *Exposition of the Orthodox Faith,* bk. 3, chap. 12; *PG* 94:1031/1032A; *NPNF2* 9:56]; *Serm: qui inscribitur, sermo exactissimus contra Deo invisam Haeresim nestorianorum, Qui incipit, Ad Nestorii sequares* [St. John of Damascus, oration entitled *A Most Accurate Oration against the Heresy of the Nestorians, Hateful to God,* which begins "To the followers of Nestorius"; *PG* 95:223/224B–C].

† See for what reason the St. of Damascus said *Ex Filio Spiritum non dicimus* [We do not say that the Spirit is from the Son].

373. *Lib. 1, c. 15* [St. John of Damascus, *Exposition of the Orthodox Faith,* bk. 1, chap. 15 (perhaps chap. 8; there is no chap. 15); *PG* 94:831B–834A;

Theophylactus also touches upon that same confession "and from the Son," and he ascribes to the Latins a lack of understanding since they established the procession of the Holy Spirit from the Son on the basis of the spiration of Christ the Lord upon the apostles, but he did not dare to call this confession a heresy. Although he warns that from this confession two origins would be introduced, nonetheless he does not prove this with one word. And yet, where Theophylactus ascribes stupidity to the Latins, St. Augustine and St. Cyril of Alexandria before him ascribed wisdom.[374] For both of them make known that through this ceremony of spiration upon the apostles Christ the Lord wished to show that as this spiration came from His bodily lips, so the Holy Spirit, which He gave them to receive, proceeds from His lips, that is, from His divine essence.

That bodily spiration, says St. Augustine, was not the essence of the Holy Spirit, but a demonstration through face to face signifying that the Holy Spirit proceeds not only from the Father but also from the Son.[375] And about this very thing St. Athanasius also says, "That is the reason why, when He had breathed upon the lips of the apostles, the Lord said, 'receive the Holy Ghost,'[376] so that we might understand that the Spirit that had been given to His disciples is from the fullness of His divinity."[377] Moreover it ought to be made known in this matter concerning Theophylactus that in that place he denied what the excellent holy teachers of the Church, such as Epiphanius, Cyril of Alexandria, and others, had confessed before him, who taught clearly and confessed loudly that the Holy Spirit is from the Son, and He is from the Son as He

---

NPNF2 9:11].

374. *Lib. 3. Cont. Maximinum. cap. 14* [St. Augustine, *Against the Heretic Maximus, Bishop of the Arians;* bk. 3 (actually bk. 2), chap. 14; *PL* 42:770]. *Lib. 12 in Ioannem. c. 56* [St. Cyril of Alexandria, *Commentary on St. John,* bk. 12, chap. 56; *PG* 74:709/710D].

375. *Lib. 2. de S. Trinitate* [St. Augustine, *On the Trinity,* bk. 2 (actually bk. 4), chap. 20; *PL* 42:908; *NPNF1* 3:84].

376. [Jn. 20:22.]

377. *Serm. de incarnat. verbi Dei et cont. Arianos. tom. 1. pag. 469* [*Oration on the Incarnation of the Word of God and against the Arians,* vol. 1, p. 469 (*Four Discourses against the Arians,* discourse 1, chap. 12, par. 50); *PG* 26:115–18; *NPNF2* 4:336].

is from God and the Father.[378] But Theophylactus says that no Scripture testifies that the Holy Spirit is from the Son. Which certainly stands in opposition to the writ of the holy fathers.

Eighth consideration. These *praepositiones*—*ex* and *per*—can be used piously in Holy Scripture in each other's place, and one takes on the meaning of the other *indifferenter* [indifferently]. Holy Scripture says: *scientes non justificare hominem ex operibus legis, nisi per fidem Jesu Christi, et nos in Christum Jesum credidimus, ut justificemur ex fide Christi, et non ex operibus legis* [Knowing that a man is not justified by the works of the law, but by the faith of Jesus Christ, even we have believed in Jesus Christ that we might be justified by the faith of Christ and not by the works of the law].[379] *Per fidem et ex fide,* "through faith and by faith" signify one and the same thing to the blessed apostle Paul. The writ of the holy teachers of the Church says that the Holy Spirit is of God the Father and of the Son, essentially from both: that is, by proceeding from the Father through the Son.[380] From the Son and through the Son signify one and the same thing for the holy teachers as well.

Ninth consideration. Omitting two councils, that of Bari convened in the year 1088[381] and the Lateran convened in the year 1215,[382] which were convened to discuss the matter of these differences between the Eastern and the Western Churches and which, with regard to their unity, were not without Greeks present (to the extent that time allowed), I take and submit to consideration two other general councils, and incomparably more important: that of Lyons, convened in the year 1273, and that of Ferrara or Florence, convened in the year 1439. At the first of them the Greek emperor Michael Palaeologus was present

378. *In Ancorato* [In Epiphanius of Constantia, *The Well Anchored; PG* 43:29C–32C]. *Lib. in Ioel. Prophetam in hoc, effundam de Spiritu meo* [Cyril of Alexandria, *Book on the Prophet Joel* on the text "I will pour out of my spirit" (Joel 2:28–9); *PG* 71:379/380–381/382] and *lib. 4. ad Pallad.* [Cyril of Alexandria, *To Palladius,* bk. 4; perhaps *On Adoration in the Spirit and in Truth, PG* 68:301–58].
379. Gal. 2[:16].
380. *Cyril. Alex. lib. ad Pallad.* [Cyril of Alexandria, book *To Palladius;* perhaps *On Adoration in the Spirit and in Truth, PG* 68:301–58].
381. [Actually, AD 1098.]
382. [I.e., the Fourth Lateran Council.]

together with many Greeks, and he concluded unity with the Romans. At first the then patriarch of Constantinople, John [XI] Beccus, opposed that unity very much, and he suffered many miseries from the emperor for this: he preferred rather to be removed from his see and to be put in prison than to agree to the union made by the emperor. †But when he had read diligently the testimonies of the holy doctors of the Church concerning the procession of the Holy Spirit that had been sent to him by the emperor, and when he had carefully considered the teaching of the holy fathers about this matter from the books of the doctors, he received the union and confessed that the Roman confession concerning the procession of the Holy Spirit was Orthodox and Catholic. For the sake of that union and the Orthodox Roman confession in it, he preferred to be deposed from his see by Emperor Andronicus, the son of Michael, and to be put in prison and to die rather than to depart from the truth once he had come to know it.

Present at the second of these synods, that is, at the Council of Florence, was the Greek Emperor John Palaeologus, together with his brother, the despot Demetrius, with Patriarch Joseph of Constantinople, and with the envoys of the other three patriarchs, highly learned and pious men. There, after many public disputations of both sides and many private conferences, the Greeks confessed, received, and put their signatures [to a statement] that the confession of the procession of the Holy Spirit "and from the Son" was Orthodox, and they mutually concluded a union with each other. ‡None of the Greeks present at that council opposed this union, with the single exception of Mark of Ephesus. To Mark, Laonicus Chalcocondylas adds George Scholarius, who was called Gennadius once he had become a monk; Scholarius was patriarch of Constantinople after the taking of Constantinople by the Turks. But the writings of this most excellent man against his own Greeks in support of the Romans make amply clear with which side he remained.

Tenth consideration. There is also a clear sign of the truth of the Roman confession in the fact that many Greeks, once they had come to know the truth, wrote in favor of the Romans against their own Greeks concerning the procession of the Holy Spirit "and from the Son." Such

---

†   Patriarch Beccus was first opposed to the Union, but then he received it.
‡   Likely for the rest he argues in hell.

were: †John [XI] Beccus, Gregory, who succeeded Joseph (who died in Florence), and Gennadius Scholarius, all three of them patriarchs of Constantinople, both pious and learned men; George of Trebizond, Demetrius Cynodius, Hugo Aetherianus, Manuel Caleca, Nicephorus Blemmydes, Joseph bishop of Methone, Bessarion metropolitan of Nicaea, perhaps others, all of them of great glory and illustrious wisdom. But never did any one of the Latins make even a peep in favor of the Greeks against themselves and their own confession.

Eleventh consideration. It is a second, not inconsiderable sign of the truth of the Roman confession concerning the procession of the Holy Ghost "and from the Son" that almost forty years before the Council of Florence many Greek philosophers, such as Manuel Chrysoloras, Constantine Lascaris, Philelphus, Musurus, Theodore Gazes, George of Trebizond, Manuel Moschopulus, Demetrius Chalcocondylas, Marullus of Constantinople, and others, fearing the Turkish cruelty and already envisioning, as if in the present, the enslavement of the Greek state, their fatherland, fled to the Italian land and there (during the schism between the Greeks and the Romans), after receiving unity with the Roman Church, lived the rest of their lives. From among whom George of Trebizond, as was mentioned above, published a work concerning the procession of the Holy Spirit for the monks and presbyters of Crete, in favor of the Latins against his own Greeks. After the departure of which wise men from Greece, the Greek Athens also departed, and after it transferred itself with them to Italy, it established itself there. For these Greeks planted the Greek sciences that bloom even today throughout all the Western lands.

Twelfth consideration. That the Council of Florence ran its course in harmony and was concluded in love, where the Greeks together with the Romans, having considered and judged that these two *praepositiae* [prepositions], *ex* [from] and *per* [through], signify one and the same thing, confessed that it signifies one and the same thing for the Holy Spirit to proceed from the Son and through the Son: authoritative writers testify to this, as was sufficiently presented concerning this point at the outset; and it does not seem to be the mark of a wise man *not* to give credence to them and to depend upon invented tales.

---

† Greek patriarchs and historians believed and wrote about the procession of the Holy Spirit "and from the Son."

Thirteenth consideration. The letter of Nephon [II], patriarch of Constantinople, written to Josyf [I Bolharynovyč], metropolitan of Rus', and the embassy sent from Rus' to Pope Sixtus [IV], about which I made mention at the outset, ought not to be omitted by us frivolously, without serious consideration, since they are means that pertain beneficially and salutarily to the matter at hand. Likewise the letter of the present father patriarch Cyril, written in the year 1601 in Lviv and left in the hands of the archbishop of Lviv, Dymitr Solikowski, published in print in the *Warning* that was edited against the *Lament;*[383] for in it, among many other things worthy of consideration, these two things are cited: [†]first, that even today the Greeks and the Romans have one faith and the same sacraments; and second, that those of us from Rus' who entered into unity with the Romans did so more piously than those who, looking to their patriarchs, do not wish to enter into it.[384]

Fourteenth consideration. St. John of Damascus, after him St. Nikon (who lived already after the times of Michael Cerularius, patriarch of Constantinople, who last rent the Eastern Church from the Western, almost two hundred years after Photius) and Nicephorus Callistus Xanthopulus, an historian of the Church, in describing the heresies that had arisen in the Church up to their age, do not mention any heresy through which the Romans would be rendered heretical. But the first two of them would not have omitted to signify this by reason of piety itself, and the third, who wrote about this already during the time of the schism, would not have remained silent.

Fifteenth consideration. Not its confession, since it is Orthodox, but Photius's own transgression alleged to the Greeks that this teaching about the procession of the Holy Spirit—"and from the Son"—is un-Orthodox. Among other things, this is also made clear from the fact that the Greeks, and Mark of Ephesus himself, confessed at the Council of Florence that this confession "and from the Son" was Orthodox; only with regard to respect for the holy fathers of the Second Universal

---

383. [I.e., Skarga 1610, 108–13.]

†   If that patriarch believes and asserts the same thing even now, he ought to be heeded.

384. [Smotryc'kyj will cite this letter more extensively below. See pp. 551–3, 667–9, and 682.]

Council did they attempt to erase this addition, but elsewhere they allowed it to be written into their creed.[385]

Sixteenth consideration. Disputing *ex professo* [openly] concerning the Holy Trinity *lib. 15 de Trinitate cap. 26* [in bk. 15, chap. 26 of *On the Trinity*], St. Augustine himself believes and confesses with express words that the Holy Spirit proceeds "and from the Son," and he teaches us to believe and to confess thus.[386] And in many other places of his works he proves that this is the case. †Two universal councils, the fifth and the sixth, accept this doctor by name, and they equate him with the holy doctors of the Eastern Church in piety of life and authority of works.

Seventeenth consideration. We are to hold this for a certain and indubitable thing: that it is not forbidden in the Church of Christ the Lord to explain creeds more broadly than they were written. This breadth is to be known and called not an addition but an explanation. Which we can see from the Nicene Creed, which in comparison with the Creed of Constantinople is shorter in many passages, but also broader in many. One can also see the same thing from the answers of St. Maximus the Confessor, who, in answering a Manichaean, acknowledged that the holy fathers of the Second Universal Council had made additions—but not contrary things—to the Nicene Creed: they explained for later times those things that had not come into question previously. Wherefore, when the holy fathers who met at the Third Universal Council forbid any addition to the creed, they mean the sort of addition that is contrary to Orthodox faith. Otherwise, in speaking of the Nicene Creed and of not adding anything to it, they would thereby condemn the holy fathers of the Second Universal Council, for through their creed they both shortened the Nicene Creed in many regards through deletions and broadened it through additions. And they themselves, the holy fathers who made such a decree, would come under the jurisdiction of such a decree, having recognized the personal unity in Christ the Lord at that council, which was not recognized either at the first or at the second

---

385. *Sessione 3. S 8 et 12* [In Session 3. Sessions 8 and 12].

386. [St. Augustine, *On the Trinity*, bk. 15, chap. 26; *PL* 42:1092; *NPNF1* 3:223.]

†   The authority of St. Augustine in the Eastern Church has its recommendation from two councils.

universal councils. But even after that Third Universal Council and after the Fourth, Patriarch Eulogius of Alexandria—in answering the heretics who, in admonishing the Fourth Universal Council for its addition, had cited the decree of prohibition of the Third Council in support of their own position—says that it is heretical stupidity that makes complaint against the definition of the Fourth Council, asserting that the First Council of Ephesus completely forbids this to be.[387] But if this council, as they argue stupidly, ordered that nothing at all be introduced, it certainly made a decree against itself, since it decreed what no other before it decreed. For the phrase "personal union" is received on its authority, which the councils that were before it did not decree.

The great Ephrem makes a similar answer to heretics in this matter when he says that heretics calumniate the Fourth Council by asserting that it was decreed and established that no one be allowed to introduce or to write or to compose or to maintain another faith than the one that was already composed.[388] But that council certainly did not decree or establish this; rather they shamelessly lie. Holding in great honor the faith that was composed by the 318 holy fathers, it commanded that no one dare to introduce any other faith.[389] I cite for a second time in this matter St. Maximus the Confessor, who says to those who sought to overturn the Fourth Universal Council that if it is permitted to express the truth in defense of the truth, then all the holy fathers and every council of orthodox and holy men used their words in no wise to introduce any other definition of faith, as you say so foolishly and quite madly, but to affirm even more the very thing that was decreed by the 318 holy fathers, explaining it and interpreting it as if more openly against those who, through improper interpretation, distort its dogmas according to their impious opinion.

In what manner, then, and with what propriety do you bring charges against the holy Council of Chalcedon, since it used the words of the holy fathers? And how do you calumniate it here and there through

---

387. *Lib.* called *Anthologium rerum selectorum* [Eulogius of Alexandria, in the book (called) *Anthology of Selected Things*].

388. *In eodem lib. Euloii Anthologio* [In the same book of Eulogius *Anthology*].

389. *In compendiosa Apologia pro Synodo Chalcedonensi* [In a compendious apology for the Synod of Chalcedon].

writing and through speech, alleging that it introduced a new definition of the faith? Do not judge according to appearance, says the Lord, but judge according to the righteous judgment.[390] What can we say about the fact that, in one and the same matter, you charge the fathers of the Council of Chalcedon, and you render others free from this charge? For if it is permitted to charge the fathers of the Council of Chalcedon with introducing a new definition of the faith on the grounds that they used words that are not in the definition of the fathers of Nicaea, then it necessarily follows that for that same reason this can also be said against Cyril and against the 150 fathers. If it is not fitting to speak against the latter, then I do not understand how it would be proper to speak against the former.

Eighteenth consideration. After the Council of Florence, when, after the death of John Palaeologus, his brother Constantine had succeeded to the emperorship of Constantinople and had abrogated and sundered the unity concluded at the Council of Florence, †Pope Nicholas, the fifth of that name, wrote to him, reprimanding him for this and threatening him with the sort of punishment that befell the unfruitful fig tree that had been allowed to be dug about for three years and manured; and if it then remained unfruitful, that it be cut out after three years so that it not take up land in vain.[391] A thing worthy of marvel and consideration: the pope wrote this to the Greeks in the year 1451, and the Turk conquered Constantinople in the year 1453.

Nineteenth consideration. One commonly says that in whatever manner anyone sins against God, in that same manner he will also be punished by God.[392] The Greeks contradicted the Roman dogmas of the faith in no point more than that of the procession of the Holy Spirit "and from the Son." And practically through nothing but stubbornness, without any proper reasons. What sort of punishment arose from this? On the very day of the Descent of the Holy Spirit the Turk ordered the storm of Constantinople, and on the next morning, that is, on the day of the Holy Trinity, he took it.

Twentieth consideration. The Romans make certain arguments

---

390. Jn. 7[:24].
†   The prophetic spirit in Pope Nicholas.
391. [The story of the fig tree is in Lk. 13:6–9.]
392. [Cf. Mt. 7:2; Mk. 4:24; Lk. 6:38.]

against us in this matter of the confession of the procession of the Holy
Spirit "and from the Son" that are such that we cannot even open our
mouths against them without manifest blasphemy against God's majesty.
†Such as is this one: the father is the first person in the Trinity, such that
He is the cause, origin, and source of the other persons. The Son is the
second person, such that He is—not according to time but according to
origin—subsequent to the Father but prior to the Holy Spirit. The Holy
Spirit is the third person, such that He is subsequent to both of them
with regard to origin. If this is not granted, there will not be any order at
all between the Son and the Holy Spirit with regard to origin, and there
will be no reason why the Son should be placed, called, and confessed
the second person, and the Holy Spirit the third person, in the Trinity.
But both the Holy Scripture and the teaching of the holy fathers teach
that there is an order among the persons of the Holy Trinity and not
disorder. Having posited this, they argue thus from the words of Christ
the Lord—*Ego et Pater unum sumus* [I and my Father are one][393]—that
since the Father and the Son are one with regard to essence, and with
regard to origin the Son proceeds and the Holy Spirit follows, then the
Holy Spirit cannot proceed from the essence of the Father if He will not
also proceed simultaneously from the Son as well. Thus the Romans.

But if we do not accept this, then we must impiously divide the
Father and the Son in their essence, which is one and the same, and we
must blaspheme that the essence of the Father from which the Holy Spirit
proceeds is one, and that of the Son (separated from that of the Father),
from which the Holy Spirit does not proceed, is another. Answering
this argument of theirs, we are wont to argue: ‡since, on account of the
identity and oneness of the essence of the Father and the Son, the Holy
Spirit is believed to proceed from the Father and the Son, therefore on
account of the identity and oneness of the essence of the Father and
the Holy Spirit, the Son will be believed to be born of the Father and
the Holy Spirit. *The Romans answer our argument that this cannot be
inferred in this manner since the Holy Spirit, being subsequent to the
Son with regard to the originary order, cannot come together with the

†   Read this twentieth consideration diligently.
393.   [Jn. 10:30.]
‡   Our argument based on identity.
*   The response of the Romans.

Father in the birth of the Son. †For in this mystery not only the identity and oneness of essence is to be considered, but in addition the order must also be maintained. Both of which are united through a union not subject to disunion in the divine persons. We rush again with the answer that this brings a division of essence from person, but since our solution introduces a real division of essence from person and establishes the person without the essence, it is impious and blasphemous.

Twenty-first consideration. Not to acknowledge that the Holy Spirit proceeds "and from the Son," but to confess that it proceeds from the Father alone, introduces these two blasphemous absurdities. First: because it sunders in two one and the same divine essence in the Father and the Son, and also because it establishes that the essence of the Father is one thing and the essence of the Son is another. The second absurdity: because it divides the essence from the person in such a way that it divides thing from thing, and it determines that the divine person *consistere* [exists] without essence.

These, then, are the considerations that are submitted to your healthy judgment, most noble Ruthenian nation, as far as concerns the difference of the confession of the Romans on the procession of the Holy Spirit "and from the Son." They can demonstrate to us manifestly whether there is *haeresis* in the confession of the Western Church and whether we can properly avoid unity with it on account of this confession. I proceed to the second difference between the Eastern and the Western Church, which is on account of the confession of purgatory. Concerning which I offer the following first consideration:

Consideratiae
or
Considerations of the Difference
Stemming from the Confession of Purgatory

In their writings many authoritative teachers of the Church expressly cited the fire of purgatory using that very word, and they believed that souls are cleansed by it. Such as, for example, the two Gregorys, the one of Rome, the other of Nyssa, teachers, the one of the Western, the other

---

†　　*Identitas* [Identity].

of the Eastern Church, the former in his dialogues with Peter,[394] and the latter *Sermone de Mortuis* [in the *Sermon on the Dead*],[395] fathers both holy and wise. And of the teachers closer to our time, Anastasius of Sinai *cap. 12* [in chapter 12] of his book and Nikon *cap.* [in chapters] 52 and 56 of his book.

Second consideration. It is the constant, daily opinion of the Eastern Church that souls departing from this world are divided into two states: into the state of the saved and into the state of the damned. [†]The state of the saved includes the further division into those who depart directly for heaven to Christ the Lord, not requiring any prayers for themselves, for whom the Holy Church renders thanks to the Lord God, and those who require prayers, offerings, alms, and other good deeds of the Church to the Lord God from the living, for whom the Holy Church makes prayers to the Lord God. About which St. John of Damascus writes conclusively *sermone de iis qui in fide obdormierunt* [in the sermon about those who have fallen asleep in death in the faith].[396]

Third consideration. The prayers for those who died in the faith, offerings, alms, remembrances or funeral commemorations, triduan, novendial, quadragesimal, annual,[397] and other Church celebrations of blessing make us understand not simply the existence of purgatory, but clearly also of the fire. For in them the Lord God is asked that He remit the sins of those souls that have departed and that He place them in a light place, consecrated, peaceful, cool, where there is no pain, sorrow, and lamentation. Whence it is made clear that the souls for whose saving one prays are in pain, in sorrow, in lamentation, in a dark, listless, unpeaceful, hot place. For the cool place is opposed here to a hot one. Praying to the Lord God for them, the Church is wont to say about those who lament and are in pain and await Christ's comfort that relief may come to them from the great pain and sorrow

---

394. [St. Gregory, *Dialogues,* bk. 4, chap. 39; *PL* 77:393–6; Gregory 1608, 464–6.]

395. [Gregory of Nyssa, *Sermon on the Dead; PG* 46:497–538.]

†   The twofold state of those who die saved.

396. [John of Damascus, Sermon "On Those Who Have Fallen Asleep in Death in the Faith"; *PG* 95:247/248–277/278.]

397. [I.e., the services said for the dead three days, nine days, forty days, and one year after their death.]

and lamentation and that they may be transferred to that place where they will see the light of God's countenance. Pain in the soul signifies its external torment; but sadness and lamentation signify their internal torment in the grave.

Fourth consideration. The *revelatiae* [*sic,* revelations] of souls that suffer torments in the fire and have been liberated from there through the prayers of holy men, which are received by our Eastern Church and are believed to be revealed by God to pious men and written by trustworthy churchmen for eternal memory and teaching—such as about the man seen to burn in the fire of purgatory, first up to the neck, then to the waist; about the man who burned his hand with the fire of purgatory and until his death bore it redolent of that wound; and about others like them—lead us, practically by the hand, to the recognition of the fire of purgatory. Likewise those described by St. John of Damascus *serm. eodem* [in the same sermon], and in St. Sophronius, Patriarch of Jerusalem *in prato spirituali* [in *The Spiritual Meadow*],[398] and in St. Nikon *cap.* [in chapters] 52 and 56.

Fifth consideration. We abhor purgatory only because we understand that the Romans believe that impious souls are cleansed by the fire of purgatory; that those who are burdened with mortal sins and depart from this world without any penance are located with the holy souls; and that the inextinguishable fire of hell is after all removed with time and destroyed, and hell is rendered empty. From our understanding about them we ascribe to them the Origenist heresy, as if they believed that there will be an end to the eternal torments. Which is pure calumny against the Romans.

Sixth consideration. Leaving aside the material fire, which even for the Romans is not an article of faith, the absolute need for salvation demands of us confessors of the Eastern Church that—†in addition to heaven, where we believe the righteous souls to be, and in addition to hell, in which we confess the damned souls to be found—we believe

---

398. [Actually, the *Pratum Spirituale* or *Spiritual Meadow* was the work of John Moschos "Eukratas" (540/550–619 or 634). He dedicated it to his student Sophronius, the future patriarch of Jerusalem and entrusted the manuscript to him on his deathbed. The text is at *PG* 87:3:2851/2852–3111/3112.]

†   It is an article of the faith to acknowledge a third place between heaven and earth.

and confess that there is a third place of purgatory, in which the souls requiring purging obtain the purging of their sins, in which place the souls that are kept bear and suffer not only excessively heavy confinements of sorrow and sighing internally (on account of the distance of the vision of God) and are bitterly worried and troubled, but are also excessively afflicted and tormented by heavy pain externally, and that is because they have come to that place in which the Lord God is entreated on their behalf through the good deeds of the Church, the good actions of the faithful, and through their own suffering, and not through their merits. This is precisely what our elders used to say: that we are in agreement in every regard with the Romans in this article of faith, that is, concerning purgatory, with the exception of the material fire, which, as I said, is not of faith for the Romans either.

It is thus made clear from these considerations that there is purgatory in the Eastern Church as well, not different in words from the Roman one, and one and the same as to the thing itself. Not to recognize this is necessarily both to throw satisfaction out of the Church and to destroy the difference between mortal and venial sins. But the Eastern Church, so long as it is Orthodox, will not allow either one of these to be erased from the dogmas of its faith. I pass now to the third difference, which has arisen between the Eastern and the Western Church through the use by the Romans of unleavened bread in the sacrament of the Eucharist. About which I offer the following first consideration:

Consideratiae,
or
Considerations of the Use
of Unleavened Bread

Unleavened bread is called simply bread, just like leavened bread, without the addition of the word unleavened. Which we can see—as was conclusively argued in the *Apology*—from the words of the blessed evangelist Luke, who says: "and it came to pass, as he sat at table with them, He took bread, and blessed it, and brake, and gave it them,"[399]

---

399. Lk. 24[:30].

and again "and He was known of them in breaking of bread."[400] For that occurred on Sunday, the very day on which Christ the Lord rose from the dead, that is, on the first day of unleavened bread, on which day, as also on others up to the seventh day, leavened bread was not found in the entire land of Judaea, since it was forbidden by law. Wherefore, those broad proofs of ours, by which we seek to prove that unleavened bread is neither bread nor *simpliciter* [simply] called bread, are in vain.

Second consideration. The Roman historians Platina and before him Hartman Schedel, chronicler of Nuremberg, and perhaps someone else, and from our Ruthenian writers, Zizanij, Vasyl' Suraz'kyj, *Antigraphē*, Azarius,[401] write and acknowledge that the custom of consecrating the sacrament of the Eucharist in unleavened bread was introduced into the Roman Church by the decree of Pope Alexander, the first of that name, who lived around the year of Our Lord 111 and who changed the use of leavened for unleavened bread. If this is the case and none of the holy doctors of the Church and not one council, whether universal or particular, criticized this use in the Roman Church throughout all the past seven universal councils and did not charge the Romans with either error or heresy because of this, then we are not correct in criticizing their use of unleavened bread and calling it the Apollinarian heresy.

Third consideration. After so many holy centuries, after almost a thousand years from that change of leavened bread for unleavened in the Roman Church, after so many and such great teachers and God-bearing fathers of the Eastern Church who were entered into the register of the saints, after many local and after all the seven universal councils, only around the year 1053, Michael Cerularius, patriarch of Constantinople, first began to criticize the Romans for their unleavened bread, and after calling their custom of consecrating and taking the sacrament of the Eucharist a heresy, he titled them azymites.[402] Having heard about this, the bishop of Rome, Leo IX, writes to him and to Leo, archbishop of Ohrid, and says: "Oh, your incautious admonishing, when you cause your mouth to ascend to the heavens, but with your tongue crawling upon the ground you attempt to strike down and to overturn the ancient

---

400. Lk. 24[:35; see above, pp. 424–5].
401. Fol. 43 [105], 202, 47, 287.
402. [Or *Infermentarii*, i.e., partakers of unleavened bread (τὰ ἄζυμα).]

faith with human argumentations and conjectures."[403] Almost 1,020 years after the martyrdom of our Savior, only then the Roman Church begins to be taught by us in what manner the memory of His suffering is to be commemorated.

In this same matter, when the same Michael Cerularius wrote to other patriarchs, he received the following response, among others, from Patriarch Peter of Antioch concerning the Roman unleavened bread: "It seems to me," he says, "that I have already answered your question sufficiently well in the letter written to the archbishop of Venice, where I showed that this is done among them not according to Church tradition. For if we defend our usage only by the authority of the canon that says that it was fitting that ancient customs be maintained, they too will say that they have their custom of using the unleavened bread from ancient tradition."[404] Since, then, the custom of using unleavened bread is ancient for the Romans, which, as can be seen from the canon of the First Universal Council cited by Patriarch Peter of Antioch, was in use already before this council, and it never experienced any rebuke from the holy and God-bearing fathers and doctors of the Eastern Church or from any councils, it does not merit that it experience any rebuke from us if, truth be told, following in the footsteps of our holy fathers, we will wish rather to promote fraternal love than our own pride.

Fourth consideration. Already after the times of the above-mentioned Cerularius, at the question posed by Archbishop of Dirach Constantine Cabasilas[405]—namely, in what esteem the unleavened bread consecrated by the Latins is to be held, as holy or as plain; and also their vessel for partaking of it and the priestly vestment, and other similar things—we read the answer given by the Archbishop of Bulgaria, Demetrios Chomatenos, who, among other things, having pointed to the opinions of his predecessor Theophylactus, archbishop of Bulgaria, that those Greeks who carelessly and shamelessly admonish the Latin customs and unbearably ascribe errors to them were roundly

---

403. *Epist. 5* [Pope Leo IX, *Letter 5;* alternate numbering, 100; *PL* 143:747C–D].
404. [Correspondence between Michael Cerularius and Patriarch Peter of Antioch; *PG* 120:807AB–808AB.]
405. *In Jure Graeco Rom., pag. 318* [In *Greco-Roman Law;* Leunclavius 1596, 318].

admonished by him and by others, adds this answer: "We do not believe that either the unleavened bread consecrated by the Latins or the vessels that serve the partaking of the celebration of the mystery of the Eucharist or anything else is impure and repulsive. For in what manner would we do this? Since among them as well the summoning of the name of God seals all of this, and the holy hierurgy of the blessed James, brother of the Lord according to the body, consecrates their offering." If, then, the consecrated Roman unleavened bread is pure and holy, just as is also our consecrated leavened bread, it is manifestly clear that the use of unleavened bread was improperly perceived as a cause of schism.

Fifth consideration. Some cite the opinion of St. Gregory the Great, bishop of Rome, whom we call *Dvoeslovo* [Slavonic: the Dialogist], on the partaking of the sacrament of the Eucharist with leavened bread by the Eastern and with unleavened bread by the Western Church, where he says: "It used to trouble many why some in the Church make offering of leavened and others of unleavened bread. The Roman Church offers unleavened bread because Christ the Lord took the body upon Himself without any admixture; and other Churches offer leavened bread in order to signify that the word of God is covered with a body, and it is true God and true man. But nonetheless, whether this sacrament is celebrated in unleavened or in leavened bread, we receive the body of our Lord and Savior."[406] If for these reasons the Church of Christ the Lord in some places, such as the East, uses leavened bread in the sacrament of the Eucharist and elsewhere, as in the West, uses unleavened bread, and neither one of them is criticized by any of the holy teachers of the Church and God-bearing fathers for this twofold ancient usage, both then are equally praiseworthy, honorable, and holy.

Sixth consideration. St. Anastasius of Sinai, *sermone in transfigurationem Domini* [in the sermon on the transfiguration of the Lord], calls Christ the Lord unleavened bread, saying, "You are *azymus panis,* bread without leaven, not having the leaven of sin. You are the Lamb of the true Passover."[407] And the blessed apostle Paul calls God's faithful—*azymi,* that is, unleavened bread or without leaven.[408]

---

406. *Gennad[ius] Scholarius,* Patr. of Constantinople *lib. 2* [bk. 2].
407. *Serm. qui incipit [in Epit?] Quam terribilis est locus iste, etc.* [St. Anastasius of Sinai, in a sermon that begins "How Terrible is this Place"].
408. 1 Cor. 5[:6–8].

Seventh consideration. There can be no doubt in this that the holy apostles, being in Jerusalem on the days of unleavened bread, took the sacrament of the Eucharist in the sort of bread that was in common usage in those days, since they were not able to have leavened bread, which was not found in the entire land of Judaea for the seven days of unleavened bread.

Eighth consideration. The Romans say that it is not subject to doubt that Christ the Lord maintained and fulfilled the law of God in every regard up to the least point. But the law of God commands that after eating the Passover of the Old Testament, that is, the lamb, the days of the unleavened bread follow immediately, in which leaven was not to be found within all the boundaries of the land of Judaea, to say nothing of Jerusalem. If Christ the Lord maintained the old law in every regard and did not transgress it in the least, who will wish to believe that during the celebration of the Passover of the Law, that is, during the time of the eating of the Passover lamb, He should have had at that supper leavened bread, which even the apostles who were sent to prepare that supper could not prepare or have had during that time of prohibition? For the law of God commands that the lamb be eaten with unleavened bread on the fourteenth day of the first month at eventide. *Tolletis,* says the Lord God, *agnum seu haedum, et servabitis eum usque ad quartam decimam diem mensis huius: immolabitque eum universa multitudo filiorum Israel ad vesperam* [Ye shall take a lamb or a kid, and ye shall keep it until the fourteenth day of the same month, and the whole assembly of the congregation of Israel shall kill it in the evening].[409] And again: *Primo mense, quarta decima die mensis ad vesperam, comedetis azyma, neque ad diem vigesimam primam ejusdem mensis ad vesperam. Septem diebus non invenietur fermentum in domibus vestris: Qui comederit fermentatum, peribit anima ejus de caetu Israel* [In the first month, on the fourteenth day of the month at even, ye shall eat unleavened bread, until the one and twentieth day of the month at even. Seven days shall there be no leaven found in your houses: for whosoever eateth that which is leavened, even that soul shall be cast off from the congregation of Israel].[410] And the Lord God

409. Ex. 12[:5–6].
410. Ex. 12[:18–19].

commands that the lamb and the unleavened bread be eaten together at one and the same supper: *Et edent carnes nocte illa assas igni, et azymos panes cum lactucis agrestibus* [And they shall eat the flesh in that night, roast with fire, and unleavened bread; and with bitter herbs they shall eat it].[411]

Ninth consideration. If Christ the Lord either erred according to time and ate the Passover of the law not on the fourteenth day at eventide, at which time God's law commanded Him to eat it, or if He had leavened bread at His supper, then either in one of these things, or in both, He would have shown himself a transgressor of the law, and He would not have maintained and fulfilled the law of God in its least commandments.[412] But it is impious even to think this, to say nothing of asserting it, since the Savior says of Himself: *Nolite putare quoniam veni solvere legem, aut prophetas: non veni solvere, sed adimplere* [Think not that I am come to destroy the law, or the prophets: I am not come to destroy, but to fulfill].[413] And Holy Scripture says: *Maledictus omnis qui non permanserit in omnibus, quae scripta sunt in libro legis, ut faciat ea* [Cursed is every one that continueth not in all things which are written in the book of the law to do them].[414]

These are the considerations with regard to the third difference between the Eastern and the Western Church. It does not seem proper that they should, with regard to it, give rise to the schism in the Church of Christ the Lord. I offer considerations of the fourth difference, which exists between the Eastern and the Western Church through the confession of perfect blessing for the righteous souls that have departed from this world and of torment for the sinful. In which I offer the following first consideration:

---

411. Ex. 12[:8].
412. [Mt. 5:19.]
413. Mt. 5[:17].
414. Dt. 27[:26] and Gal. 3[:10]. [Smotryc'kyj cites Gal. 3:10, which draws in turn on Dt. 27:26.]

Consideratiae,

or

Considerations of the Difference Stemming from the Confession
of Perfect Happiness for the Righteous Souls in Heaven
and Perfect Torment for the Evil and Unfaithful Souls in Hell

That the souls of God's holy servants are in heaven and already enjoy
perfect happiness—our Church books, which serve our daily public
and private devotions, are full of both these Orthodox confessions,
composed by authoritative and pious men in the Eastern Church, wise
and holy, who have their names entered into the register of God's saints
for annual commemoration, submitted to the Church and received by it.
As, for example, in the *Oktoechoi, Menaia, Triodia,* in which what will
be mentioned here is read by us with express words and confessed, and
thus must be believed if in this matter we should wish that our hearts be
in harmony with our mouths.[415] That is, that the righteous souls are no
longer on earth but are in heaven, for, having entered into that heavenly
paradise through the doors that were opened for them, and living
within it, they delight in the tree of life, Jesus Christ. For *nominatim*
[singly] and *communiter* [jointly] those *elogia* [maxims] and decrees
are often read and sung about the prophets and patriarchs, the apostles
and evangelists, the martyrs and the righteous—that their souls have
been transported to heaven by the angels, that they live on high with
Christ the Lord, that they stand together with the angels before God's
majesty, that they see Christ the Lord face to face, that they see God as
the angels see Him, that they have already acquired completely perfect
joy, that the Lord God has revealed to them the perfect recognition of
His divinity, that they have received perfect reward for their deeds, have
taken perfect crowns from God for their works and labors in heaven. To
submit to suspicion these decrees of the holy churchmen, and others like
them, decrees that are clear and express about the completely perfect
happiness of the righteous souls and are customarily read every day in
our Church, would be to deprive their authors of the authority of their
holiness. I offered at the outset other proofs pertaining to this difference,
where I showed that Zizanij's errors and heresies were contrary to the

415. [Ps. 19:14; Prov. 16:23; Rom. 10:9.]

confession of the Eastern Church. Whence each of us can understand that for us to be opposed to the Romans in this confession will be to introduce either an error or an entire heresy into our pure confession of the faith. I offer the considerations of the fifth difference perceived in the confession of the primacy of the bishop of Rome. About which let the following be the first consideration.

Consideratiae,
or
Considerations of the Difference
Stemming from the Confession of the Primacy of the Bishop of Rome

If among the disciples, apostles of Christ the Lord, the blessed apostle Peter—for the maintenance of order in the Church and for protection against apostasies—was established by Christ the Lord as the first and the head, that is, the most excellent and foremost pastor and ruler, both of that apostolic choir and of the entire Church of Christ the Lord, it was certainly necessary that it be maintained in that same Church of Christ the Lord for all times until the end of the world that some one bishop (since, in the rule and governance of the Church, bishops are the successors to the apostles) be foremost among all the bishops and remain placed both over them and over the entire Church for the maintenance of that same order and for protection against apostasies. For since all of God's creation stands and maintains itself in order, how can the house of God, the Church, I say, of Christ the lord, which is called in Holy Scripture a marshaled army[416]—how can it stand without order?

For what man of even petty understanding will allow himself to be convinced that, when Christ the Lord departed from earth to Heaven and removed Himself from the visible presence of His Church, He would have left it in disorder, that is, without one such superior who, remaining in His place, would be the beginning of that order, both from Him Himself, and from his own self? From Him, that is, from Christ the Lord, in that, with regard to Him, he would be the most excellent member of His body, which is the Church; and from himself, in that,

---

416. S. of S. 6[:10].

with regard to the other members, he would be the head. Christ the Lord, as the sort of head that can say to the feet, you are not necessary to me; and he, as the sort of head that could not say to the feet, you are not necessary to me.[417] So that he might establish the sort of head in His place that would govern His body and order it, Christ the Lord said to St. Peter, *Tu es Petrus, et super hanc Petram aedificabo Ecclesiam meam* [Thou are Peter, and upon this rock I will build my Church].[418] Which passage St. John Chrysostom interprets according to the property of the Syriac language, in which the Savior said to St. Peter, "Thou art Cephas, and upon this cephas," saying: "Thou art Rock, and upon this Rock I will build my Church."[419] And again in addition to this: *Petre, pasce oves meas* [Peter, feed my sheep].[420] About both of these utterances of Christ the Lord, to the extent that the *Apology* presented above could accommodate it, I have already thoroughly presented and demonstrated that, according to the opinion of St. John Chrysostom, who was making an interpretation of the first words of Christ the Lord, St. Peter was made superior over the entire world; and that, from the interpretation of the second passage, care was entrusted to him over the brethren, that is, over the apostles and over the Church of the entire world.[421]

First consideration. That Christ the Lord is, of His very self, the foundation, rock, and foremost head of His Church. But St. Peter is the foundation, rock, and head of that same Church not of his very self, but established a secondary head by Christ the Lord, the foremost head. Thus both Christ the Lord and St. Peter rule and govern the Church—Christ the Lord internally and invisibly and St. Peter externally and

417. 1 Cor. 12[:21].

418. [Mt. 16:18.]

419. *Serm. pro festo exaltationis S. Crucis qui incipit: "Quid dicam? quid loquar?"* [St. John Chrysostom, *Sermon on the Feast of the Exaltation of the Holy Cross,* which begins: "What should I say? What should I speak?" (Cf. Jn. 12:49.)]

420. [Jn 21:17.]

421. In the Slavonic *Anthology. In cap. 16. Matt. Hom. 55* [St. John Chrysostom, *Sermon 55 on Mt. 16; PG* 58:534; *NPNF1* 10:333–4]. *Hom. vit. in Ioan. cap. 12* [St. John Chrysostom, *Sermon on John 12* (*Sermon 88 on John 21:15; PG* 59:477–80; *NPNF1* 14:331); and *Hom 80 ad popul. Anti.* [St. John Chrysostom, *Homily 80 to the People of Antioch* (*Concerning the Statues); PG* 49:15–222; *NPNF1* 9:313–489. The edition in *PG* contains 21 sermons.]

visibly. Christ the Lord is Himself the head of that power and authority such that He infuses internally into His body the gifts of His grace, through which He governs and rules it; but externally and visibly He carries out His rule of authority and governance not by Himself, but through His visible vicar, whom the visible Church requires.

Second consideration. When Christ the Lord said these words to St. Peter, *Pasce oves meas* [feed my sheep],[422] He did not speak them with the limitation that they should be concluded and end with St. Peter alone, or that they should not be applied to His successors, since St. Peter could not always live on earth. For the sheep of Christ the Lord always needed a present and visible pastor. Rather, in saying these words to St. Peter, feed my sheep, Christ the Lord spoke through him immediately to his successors as well. To which Chrysostom also testifies in his writings *lib. 2 de Sacerdotio circa principium* [in bk. 2 of *On the Priesthood*, near the beginning]: "For what reason," he says, "did He (that is, Christ the Lord) pour out His blood? Certainly so that He might redeem those sheep, the care for which he entrusted both to Peter and to Peter's successors."[423]

Third consideration. As long as Christ the Lord was on earth He Himself performed both offices, internal and external, since He Himself both gave internal grace to the faithful and ruled and governed them through superficial governance. And He was the visible head of the Church. But having ascended to heaven and having become invisible to us due to the distance of the place, and thereby having become the invisible head of the Church militant, He carries out the internal office Himself, but He carries out the external one through His vicar.

Fourth consideration. Christ the Lord is the head of the Church as a man. For although He carries out His first office, that is, He infuses His divine grace into His body, the Church, both as God and as man—as God *naturaliter* [naturally], which He has in common with God the Father and with the Holy Spirit, and as a man *meritorie* [by his merits], which is His own property—nonetheless, He is called and is the head of the Church not as God but as man. According to that nature He merited to be exalted, that is, according to His humanity and not

422. [Jn. 21:17.]
423. [St. John Chrysostom, *Book on the Priesthood*, bk. 2, chap. 1; *PG* 48:631–2; *NPNF1* 9:39; *CHrKS* 26–7.]

divinity. "According to the form of God, Christ is the firstborn of every creature," says St. Augustine, "but according to His form of a servant, He is the head of the body, the Church."[424]

Fifth consideration. The Church of Christ the Lord could in no manner be satisfied without a head, such as St. Peter was established to be by Christ the Lord, if it was to remain one and the same Church after the departure of Christ the Lord that it was during His presence in this world, having by necessity become obliged to know, have, and maintain the same form of its rule and governance. Since with the change of the form of rule, by necessity there would have to follow also the change of its very self, just as with the change of the form of monarchal rule into aristocratic or democratic the republic does not remain the same. But so long as Christ the Lord was present in this world, the form of the rule of the Church was monarchal, and it was ruled and governed through the one visible head, Christ the Lord Himself, as far as both rules were concerned, internal and external. Therefore it necessarily had to follow that the same form of rule—that is, the monarchal—was left in the Church and that likewise it was ruled by a visible head in the absence of Christ the Lord, as was its form and with what sort of head it was found to be ruled during His presence, if it was to maintain its integrity unchanged. Otherwise, with the change of the form and the head, it would have had to be changed and to be not one and the same, but another and different. Thus, so it seems, it happened of necessity that St. Peter was established and submitted by Christ the Lord as the sort of head of the Church over which he was made superior. *Chris. Hom. 55. in Cap. 16. Mat* [Chrysostom in *Homily 55 on Matthew 16*]: "Christ made Jeremiah superior over one nation, but Peter over the entire world."[425]

Sixth consideration. Since it is made manifestly known to us through many testimonies of the holy doctors and through the express teaching of Holy Scripture that Christ the Lord, in departing to His Father whence He had come, did not leave His newly founded Church without one ruler more excellent than and superior to others, it seems

---

424. *Lib. 1. de SS. Trinit. c. 12* [St. Augustine, *On the Holy Trinity*, bk. 1, chap. 12; *PL* 42:837; *NPNF1* 3:31; cf. Col. 1:18.].
425. [St. John Chrysostom, *Homily 55 on Mt. 16; PG* 58:534; *NPNF1* 10:334.]

proper that the same Christ the Lord, after His departure hence, would wish to leave such a ruler of the Church, established and left by Him, such that His Church should never be without such a ruler and governor and pastor to whom industry and care for it would belong, both with regard to maintaining order in it and with regard to protecting it from apostasy. Thus the Eastern Church has it in its daily confession that St. Peter the Apostle was the first pastor after Christ the Lord in His Holy Church, which is accustomed to call him, with regard to the other apostles and pastors, the archpastor, chief of the pastors, defender and leader of the Church of Christ the Lord. It is also a part of its confession that St. Peter was the bishop of Rome and that the Roman Church was the see of St. Peter the Apostle. But the bishops of Rome are the successors of St. Peter and successors both in the episcopal dignity and in pastorly authority. Whence our Eastern Church is accustomed to call the bishop of Rome, on account of his eminence of authority in the Church of Christ the Lord, the head of the Orthodox Church of Christ, the father of the entire world, and similar things, acknowledging to him that he will adorn the Divine See of Peter and that he remains enriched with the primacy of St. Peter the Apostle.

Seventh consideration. The preeminence of the prerogatives of the Roman Church and of its bishop has been made known by universal councils, by holy teachers, by authoritative Church historians to be such that no Church compares with it and no bishop with the bishop of Rome. The holy teachers of the Church teach that all the other Churches, that is, all the faithful of the entire world, ought to gather to the Roman Church on account of its more powerful primacy.[426] And that to be of the Roman Church is to be a Catholic.[427] And that to be in communion with the Roman bishop is to be in communion with the Universal Church.[428] And whoever does not gather with the Roman bishop scatters abroad.[429] And other similar things. Moreover, Church

---

426. *Iren. lib. 3. c. 3* [Irenaeus, *Against Heresies,* bk. 3, chap. 3; *PG* 7:848–9; *ANF* 1:415–16].

427. *Hier. in Apolog. cont. Ruff.* [St. Jerome, *Apology against the Books of Rufinus; PL* 23:400B].

428. *Cypr. lib. 4. Epist. 3. ad Antonim* [St. Cyprian, bishop of Carthage, *Letter to Antonianus,* bk. 4, 3 (2); *PL* 4:345B, *PL* 3:768A–775A].

429. *Hier. Epist. ad Damasum: Epist. Rom* [St. Jerome, *Letter* 15, to Pope Damasus, bishop of Rome; *PL* 22:356; *NPNF2* 6:19].

historians are often found to speak in their writings in such manner about this same Roman Church and about its bishop.

SOCRATES: The Roman Church has privileges above other Churches.[430] He also says that Church canon forbids that spiritual decrees be made in the Churches against the will of the bishop of Rome.[431] He also says that Church rule commands that no councils be convened without the will of the bishop of Rome.[432]

THEODORETUS says that the bishops bring complaint against each other to the bishop of Rome, and he commands the charged to appear at a given time.[433] He also says that Emperor Theodosius commands Flavian, patriarch of Antioch, to travel to Rome at the insistence of the bishop of Rome and to give account of himself in an accusation.[434] And on his behalf Theophilus, patriarch of Alexandria, writes to the pope in intercession and asks that he be received into communion and maintained in his see. Flavian then gave account of himself through his bishop-emissaries, with the permission of the pope for such an embassy, and he was received into communion.

SOZOMENUS says that the bishop of Rome judges the Eastern bishops who were charged with various crimes, and he renders decree.[435] He also says that care for all the bishops belongs to the bishop of Rome on account of the authority of his see.[436] He also says that the bishop of Rome commands that certain of the Eastern bishops, against whom charges had been brought, come to Rome at an appointed time for judgment and for rendering account of themselves;[437] the same bishop

---

430. *Lib. 2, c. 11* [Socrates Scholasticus, *Church History,* bk. 2, chap. 11; *PG* 67:205B–207A; *NPNF2* 2:40–1].

431. *Lib. eod c. 13* [Socrates Scholasticus, *Church History,* bk. 2, chap. 13 (actually chap. 12); *PG* 67:207B–208B; *NPNF2* 2:41].

432. *Ibid. c. 5* [Socrates Scholasticus, *Church History,* bk. 2, chap. 5 (actually chap. 8); *PG* 67:195A–198A; *NPNF2* 2:38].

433. *Lib. 2. c. 8* [Theodoretus, *Church History,* bk. 2, chap. 8 (actually chap. 3); *PG* 82:995B–996A; *NPNF2* 3:66].

434. *Lib. 5. cap. 23* [Theodoretus, *Church History,* bk. 5, chap. 23; *PG* 82: 1247C–1248C; *NPNF2* 3:148].

435. *Lib. 3, c. 7* [Sozomenus Hermias Salaminus, *Church History,* bk. 3, chap. 8 (actually chap. 7); *PG* 67:1051C–1052C; *NPNF2* 2:287].

436. Ibid.

437. Ibid.

of Rome threatens the vengeance of his power against the Eastern bishops if they should not cease giving rise to innovations.[438] He also says that the Eastern bishops, in writing to Pope Julius [I], acknowledge that the Church of Rome is foremost among all the Churches even from the beginning, as the one that is the apostolic school and the mother of piety.[439] He also says that there is a law belonging to the priestly dignity that states that those matters are not important and lasting that are established without the opinion of the bishop of Rome.[440] He also says that in the composition of the symbol [i.e., creed] of faith the opinion of the bishop of Rome is above all other bishops.[441]

EVAGRIUS says that, at the Fourth Universal Council, at the command of their bishop Leo [I], the representatives of the bishop of Rome command and are granted that Dioscorus, patriarch of Alexandria, rise up from the circle of bishops and stand before the council and not sit.[442] He also says that Dioscorus is charged and is found guilty because he performed the office of judge at the second council of Ephesus without the permission of the bishop of Rome.[443] He also says that the bishop of Rome forgives the transgression of the bishops who took counsel with Dioscorus at the second council of Ephesus, and he receives them into communion with the Universal Church.[444] He also says that the holy fathers of the Fourth Universal Council judge Dioscorus as malicious and impious because he dared to excommunicate the bishop of Rome.[445] He also says that in every sort of matter from every side the

438. Ibid. [Sozomenus Hermias Salaminus, *Church History*, bk. 3, chap. 8 (actually chap. 7); *PG* 67:1053A–1054A; *NPNF2* 2:287].

439. Ibid. [Sozomenus Hermias Salaminus, *Church History*, bk. 3, chap. 8 (actually chap. 7); *PG* 67:1053AB–1054AB; *NPNF2* 2:287–8].

440. *Lib. eod. c. 4* [Sozomenus Hermias Salaminus, *Church History*, bk. 3, chap. 4 (actually chap. 10); *PG* 67:1057B–1058B; *NPNF2* 2:289].

441. *Lib. 6. c. 23* [Sozomenus Hermias Salaminus, *Church History*, bk. 3, chap. 8 (actually chap. 7); *PG* 67:1451B–1352B; *NPNF2* 2:360].

442. *Lib. 2. c. 18* [Evagrius, *Church History*, bk. 2, chap. 8; *PG* 86:2547B–2548B; *HC* 317].

443. Ibid.

444. Ibid. [Evagrius, *Church History*, bk. 2, chap. 8; *PG* 86:2563C–2564C; *HC* 325].

445. Ibid. [Evagrius, *Church History*, bk. 2, chap. 8; *PG* 86:2583A–2584A; *HC* 336].

clergy referred everything to the judgment of the bishops of Rome, and they rendered account and were judged before him.[446] He also says that whoever the Roman see judged to be a heretic was judged and held by all bishops to be a heretic.[447]

THEODORE Anagnosta, *collector* [compiler] of Church history, says that the patriarch of Constantinople, St. Macedonius, answered Emperor Anastasius, who had urged him to sign the agreement of Emperor Zeno (the Fourth Universal Council of Chalcedon removed that agreement), saying: "I will not give my consent to this agreement without a universal council at which the bishop of great Rome presides."[448]

Cassiodorus says that Church order commands that councils not be convened without the knowledge of the bishop of Rome.[449] He also says that apostolic care for the others belongs to the Church of Rome since it is from of old the mother of piety.[450] He also says that the rules command that nothing be established at councils in Church matters without the bishop of Rome.[451]

Nicephorus Callistus Xanthopoulos, a Church historian who lived already at the time of the schism, around the year 1300, says that the bishop of Rome, Julius [I], on account of the preeminence of his see, considering it certain (on account of an ancient privilege and prerogative) that care and judgment for all bishops everywhere belonged to him, after giving letters to Patriarch Athanasius of Alexandria and Patriarch Paul [I] of Constantinople, and to many other bishops, returned their Churches to them and sent them to the East.[452] He also says that Julius

---

446. *Lib. 3. c. 14 et cap. 20* [Evagrius, *Church History,* bk. 3, chap. 14 and 20; *PG* 86:2619–26 and 2637–40; *HC* 351–4 and 359–60].

447. *Lib. 3. c. 21* [Evagrius, *Church History,* bk. 3, chap. 21; *PG* 86:2639–42; *HC* 360–1].

448. *Lib. 2. collectaneorum* [bk. 2 of *The Collected;* Excerpts from the Church History of Theodorus Lector; *PG* 86:195/196B].

449. *Lib. 4. Hist. tripartite, c. 9* [Flavius Magnus Aurelius Cassiodorus Senator, *Tripartite Church History,* bk. 4, chap. 9; *PL* 69:960A].

450. *Lib. eod. c. 19* [Flavius Magnus Aurelius Cassiodorus Senator, *Tripartite Church History,* bk. 4, chap. 19 (actually chap. 16); *PL* 69:964A].

451. [Flavius Magnus Aurelius Cassiodorus Senator, *Tripartite Church History,* bk. 4, chap. 19; *PL* 69:966A.]

452. *Lib. 9, c. 8.* [Pointing hand in the margin at this point. Nicephorus Callistus

commanded several accused Eastern bishops to come to him and to render account of themselves.[453] And if they should not wish to do this and not cease to give rise to new things, he threatens them with spiritual punishment from himself. He also says that there is a Church rule that removes all authority from spiritual matters that are established against the opinion of the bishop of Rome.[454] That same historian, in many of his books on the history of the Church, makes it known that many bishops from all lands, in their various injustices, had recourse with their petitions and complaints to the bishops of Rome and received justice through their decrees.

These are the noteworthy accounts concerning the primacy of the bishop of Rome from authoritative Church historians, whose words and matter we ought to consider diligently.

From the universal councils I take and submit these two things for consideration for the time being: first, that the 630 holy and God-bearing fathers who had gathered in Chalcedon for the Fourth Universal Council, in writing to Bishop Leo [I] of Rome in the name of the entire council, call him head and themselves his members and sons;[455] second, that those same holy fathers in the same letter acknowledge in express words that protection of the vineyard of Christ the Lord is entrusted by the Savior to the bishop of Rome.[456]

[†]In addition to these considerations presented by me, let us also remember that Hadrian, the second bishop of Rome of that name, judged Patriarch Photius of Constantinople right there in Constantinople and deposed him from his see. Whence the unfortunate present schism

---

Xanthopoulos, *Church History,* bk. 9, chap. 8; *PG* 146:241C–244A].

453. Ibid. [Nicephorus Callistus Xanthopoulos, *Church History,* bk. 9, chap. 8; *PG* 146:243/244B].

454. *Lib. eod. c. 10.* [Pointing hand in the margin at this point. Nicephorus Callistus Xanthopoulos, *Church History,* bk. 9, chap. 10; *PG* 146:247/248B].

455. *Ex. act. 3. Relatio S. Syn. Chalc. ad B. Leonem PP* [From the Third Session. *Letter of the Holy Synod of Chalcedon to Blessed Pope Leo* (I); *PL* 54:951C–952C].

456. Ibid. [From the Third Session. *Letter of the Holy Synod of Chalcedon to Blessed Pope Leo* (I); *PL* 54:953B–954B].

† Photius and Cerularius, patriarchs of Constantinople, great authors of the schism.

began to smoke and was lit by Michael Cerularius, patriarch of that same see, who was condemned by Leo IX, bishop of Rome, and it burns unto this day with no little harm for human souls.

†Let us also note in addition that these above-mentioned patriarchs of Constantinople, Photius and Cerularius, who were the cause of the Eastern Church's sundering of unity with the bishop of Rome and with the Western Church, did not occupy their sees until death, but both, having been shamefully cast down from them, took leave of this world in exile on account of their crimes.

‡Let us also keep in mind this third thing worthy of consideration, that on account of their action neither they nor Mark of Ephesus, the authors of this sundering of the Church, whom we follow as our leaders in this matter, have been entered into the calendar for eternal memory. And perhaps this is how the Lord God wished it to be: that they who sundered into bits that which had consecrated the saints not have communion in memory with them.

After offering all this briefly to your consideration, most noble Ruthenian nation, as far as the primacy of the bishop of Rome is concerned, I offer considerations of the sixth difference stemming from the use in the Roman Church of the sacrament of the Eucharist under the single species of the bread, which was never alleged before by the Greeks against the Romans with even one letter and has now in our days newly begun to be known as a difference, more by us than by the Greeks. With regard to which I take and submit the following first consideration.

Consideratiae,
or
Considerations of the Difference Stemming from the Use of the Sacrament of the Eucharist under the Single Species of the Bread

The Eucharist is used in two manners: as a sacrament and as an offering. As far as the offering is concerned, the Church never made any change

---

†   Their punishment even in this world.

‡   The authors of the schism were not received into the calendar.

in this, nor could it make any change in offering it in either one of these two species, in the bread or in the wine. And this is this case so that thereby the bloody offering of Christ the Lord, brought through death in His crucified body and in His poured out blood, might be expressed in reality. As far as the sacrament is concerned—which is the matter in which the mysterious supper of the Lord, that is, the consecration of the bread and the wine into the body and blood of Christ the Lord—the Church of Christ the Lord sometimes allows the Eucharist to be used only under the species of the bread alone, as for the sick, anchorites, and travelers, and sometimes under the species of the wine alone, as for infants and those in great pain. And for the healthy under both species. And this is because it believes and confesses that he does not receive more who partakes under both species, nor does he less, who partakes under any one species, but rather the entire living Christ Jesus, not with lesser or with greater spiritual benefit, but with one and the same. Wherefore it seems to follow that the celebration of the Eucharist as an offering under two species is according to the law of God, according, I say, to the decree of Christ the Lord; but its celebration as a sacrament, that is, the partaking under both species, is not according to the decree of Christ the Lord, since that, without manifest impiety, could not be disturbed in any manner.

Second consideration. It does not seem to be according to the decree of Christ the Lord that the Eucharist, to the extent that it is a sacrament, be received under both species as a necessity for salvation and for the following reasons. First, because Christ the Lord makes the decree of necessity not after the giving by Himself and not after the taking by the disciples of both species, but after the giving and the taking of the bread alone, saying: "This do in remembrance of me."[457] To which the blessed apostle Paul also seems to testify, for, having come to the mention of the decree made by Christ the Lord of taking the sacrament of the Eucharist and citing these words of the Savior—"Take, eat: this is my body, which will be given up for you"[458]—he adds: "this do in remembrance of me."[459] And after these words of the Savior—"This cup is the new testament in my blood: this do ye as often as you drink it,

457. [Lk. 22:19.]
458. 1 Cor. 11[:24].
459. 1 Cor. 11[:24].

in remembrance of me."[460] By citing the first words, the blessed apostle seems to point out the necessity of partaking on the basis of the decree of Christ the Lord with regard to salvation. But by citing the second words he seems to leave the partaking on the basis of human will alone. That is, that the bread be taken by everyone, but that the cup be taken only by those who wish it. Second, it is made known that the entire Church of Christ the Lord, both in the East and in the West, has the custom of receiving this sacrament under one species. And if it were according to the decree of Christ the Lord and the necessity of salvation not to receive it in any other fashion but under two species, His entire Church would not have done otherwise, nor would it have allowed anyone to do so in it anywhere, since, either in doing this or in allowing it to be done, it would be found a transgressor of the salvatory, inviolable decree of Christ the Lord, and a violator of His eternal testament. And it would then follow that the entire Church of Christ the Lord altogether, having strayed from the true use of the mystery of the Eucharist since apostolic times themselves, if not even in the apostles themselves, would have been overcome by the gates of hell[461] and would remain in this state until today. But this is a thing both improper to say and impossible to believe. Wherefore it seems that it is rather a matter of custom, than of a decree of Christ the Lord, to use the sacrament of the Eucharist under two species.

Third consideration. These words of Christ the Lord—"Except ye eat the flesh of the Son of man, and drink His blood, ye have no life in you," and "whoso eateth My flesh, and drinketh My blood, hath eternal life; he dwelleth in Me, and I in him"[462]—do not seem to make it *necessitatem* [a necessity] to receive under both species by requirement of decree and salvation. Which is made clear from the preceding words of the Savior—"I am the living bread which came down from heaven; if any man eat of this bread, he shall live for ever, and the bread that I will give is my flesh, which I will give for the life of the world."[463] Thereupon, the same is also made known from the words of the Savior that follow: "so he that eateth me, even he shall live by me. This is that

460. 1 Cor. 11[:25].
461. [Mt. 16:18.]
462. Jn. 6[:53–4, 56].
463. Jn. 6[:51].

bread which came down from heaven: not as your fathers did eat bread and are dead. He that eateth of this bread shall live forever."[464] The Savior Himself seems to make clear both through the preceding and through the following words how what He says between those words is to be understood: "Whoso eateth my flesh and drinketh my blood," and "my flesh is meat indeed, and my blood is drink indeed."[465] As if He had said that "to eat my flesh and to drink my blood is to eat the bread that has come down from heaven, is to eat of me. For I am meat indeed and drink indeed, and whosoever eats this bread that has come down from heaven, that is, whosoever eats of me, eats my flesh and drinks my blood and shall not die, but shall live forever and shall live for me, for I am the flesh that he eats and the blood that he drinks." It does not therefore seem to follow that the receiving of the sacrament of the Eucharist under two species was by the decree of Christ the Lord and necessity of salvation, but only from custom alone, since in the eating of the bread alone there is eternal life. And whoever eats of Christ alone will live for Him.

Fourth consideration. These words of Christ the Lord—*nisi manducaveritis carnem Filii hominis, et biberitis ejus sanguinem, non habebitis vitam in vobis* [Except ye eat the flesh of the Son of man, and drink his blood, ye have no life in you][466]—it seems, can also be understood thus: "Except ye eat the flesh of the Son of man or drink His blood," having used "and" instead of "or," as is in the law according to the Hebrew verity: *Qui percusserit Patrem suum et Matrem, morte moriatur* [And he that smiteth his father, and his mother, shall surely be put to death],[467] where *et* [and] is placed instead of *aut* [or], as both the Greek and the Latin translators translated. Thus also does the blessed apostle Paul seem to offer that these words of Christ the Lord be understood when he says: "Whosoever shall eat this bread or drink this cup of the Lord unworthily shall be guilty of the body and blood of the Lord."[468] As if he had said whosoever shall either eat only the flesh of Christ the Lord unworthily or drink only of His blood unworthily—from

---

464. Jn. 6[:57–8].
465. Jn. 6[:54–5].
466. Jn. 6[:53].
467. [Ex. 21:15. The Vulgate has *et* (and). The Septuagint has ἤ (or).]
468. 1 Cor. 11[:27].

each of these separately and individually partaken he is guilty of the body and blood of the Lord. Likewise in contrary manner these words of Christ the Lord—whosoever does not eat the flesh of the Son of man, or does not drink His blood, has not life in him.[469] But whosoever either eats worthily of His body alone, or drinks worthily of His blood alone, that one has life in him, and I live in him and he in me.

Whence the ancient custom of the Eastern Church of offering and receiving the sacrament of the Eucharist in the bread alone is allowed, as was mentioned just a little above, to anchorites, travelers, and the sick, both clerical and lay; and offering and receiving in the blood alone is allowed to infants newly baptized and to adults in great pain, both of whom are unable to swallow the bread. For what the blessed apostle Paul says just there—*Probet autem se ipsum homo: et sic de pane illo edat, et de calice bibat. Qui enim manducat et bibit indigne judicium sibi manducat et bibit* [But let a man examine himself, and so let him eat of that bread, and drink of that cup. For he that eateth and drinketh unworthily, eateth and drinketh damnation to himself][470]—he already explained previously and pointed out that this *et* [and] in those two phrases, *et de calice,* "and of the cup," *et bibit,* "and drinks," can be taken instead of that particle *aut* [or]. And understanding this thus, so it seems, the Church of Christ the Lord safely allowed the division of this mystery and was accustomed to receive it under one species, believing that not less is received under one species, or more under two, but one and the same Christ the Lord, both under either one of them separately or under two of them together, in both ways completely and perfectly. Wherefore it is just as fitting for the Eastern Church to defend against the heretics the use of the sacrament of the Eucharist under one species as it is for the Western Church. For if this is done against the inalterable decree of Christ the Lord, then both have equally transgressed.

Fifth consideration. Our Eastern Church considers the Communion of infants and the sick (that is, either under the species of the wine alone or under the species of the bread alone) to be the perfect Communion of the body and the blood of Christ the Lord, not because in the consecrated wine there is the consecrated bread and in the consecrated bread there was the consecrated wine; and not because in the same cup there is

469. [Jn. 6:53.]
470. 1 Cor. 11[:28–9].

the body under the species of the bread, in which there is blood under the species of the wine; and not because the bread is drenched with the wine. For these are separable matters. The wine is drunk separately from the species of the bread; and the bread is eaten, dried of the matter of the wine. Rather, where in this sacrament the visible matter ends, there the invisible thing ceases to be as well. Where there is not the visible matter in eating, that is, either of the bread or of the wine, neither is there the invisible eating of the body or the blood of Christ the Lord in its manner, that is, with regard to consecration. For when the particle of wine is separated from the cup by means of the spoon, and the piece of bread is dried from the matter of the wine, just there, with regard to these words of Christ the Lord—*hoc est corpus meum* [this is my body][471] and *hic est sanguis meus* [this is my blood][472]—that is, with regard to consecration the body remains in the species of the bread and the blood in the species of the wine. But with regard to ἀλληλουχία [reciprocity], that is, with regard to concomitance, there is in the species of the wine both the blood and the body, and in the species of the bread, both the body and the blood. For after His resurrection, Christ the Lord can no longer be separated and parted for eternity from His soul and from His divinity: *Omnis enim spiritus, qui solvit Iesum, ex Deo non est; et hic est Antichristus* [For every spirit that confesseth not that Jesus is come in the flesh is not of God; and this is Antichrist].[473] Thus, assured by the teaching of the holy doctors of the Church, we confess that in the species of the bread there is inseparably the body and the blood of Christ the Lord, both His soul and His divinity; and in the species of the wine there is together blood and body, both soul and divinity. Wherefore, our Eastern Church believes and confesses that both the Eucharist given to infants in the species of the wine and that given to the sick in the species of the bread are the perfect Communion of the body and the blood of Christ the Lord.

Sixth consideration. Believing in the natural union in Christ the Lord of body and blood and soul, and in the personal union of divinity, we do not therefore believe that their union in the sacrament of the Eucharist came into being from the mixing or the joining of the matter

471. [Mk. 14:22.]
472. [Mk. 14:24.]
473. 1 Jn. 4[:3].

of this sacrament. For these parts, as I said, have this from nature and from personal union. And as the matters are themselves different signs, so do they signify different things, which remain in their signs so long as the *accidentia* [accidents] of these signs remain unchanged. Bread signifies the body, and wine signifies the blood, according to the words of Christ the Lord, but each not without their proper native parts that are not subject to separation. Not, however, with regard to the union of the signs in the things signified by them—which [union], based upon the words of Christ the Lord, did not establish more in this sacrament than the body under the species of the bread and the blood under the species of the wine—but, as I said, with regard to the natural and personal concomitance, which teaches, proves, and demonstrates that as the body is not without blood, soul, and divinity, so the blood is not without the body, soul, and divinity. Whence it is made manifestly clear that in any one of the species, as in both of them together, one living Christ the Lord, who can no longer die or be divided either in His natural or in His personal parts, is taken and eaten in the sacrament of the Eucharist; not more in the two species, nor less in any one of them.

Seventh consideration. It was a custom of the Eastern and the Western Church to take the holy bread into one's hand and to carry it home and to eat of it piously in a free moment.[474] But those who carried away home with them a piece of the consecrated bread could not drink of the cup, since they would not be allowed to drink of the cup before taking and eating of the holy bread; for that would be against the decree of Christ the Lord, who first gave His body to His disciples to eat and then He offered them His blood to drink. Whence it is clear that by eating at home the holy bread that they had taken in Church, they ate it in place of the perfect sacrament of the Eucharist. Or if they were allowed to drink of the cup in Church, then that one species taken by them was for them, in the spiritual eating of the Eucharist, the perfect sacrament.

Eighth consideration. The Eastern Church believes and confesses that in the Communion of the sacrament of the Eucharist the glorious, immortal, and incorruptible body that sits at the right hand of God the Father is given to be eaten; it can no longer be separated or parted from

---

474. *Cyril. Hierosol. Katech. 5 Mistag.* [St. Cyril of Jerusalem, *Catechetical Lectures 23, On the Mysteries 5; PG* 33:1123C–1125A; *NPNF2* 7:156].

its blood, which is in it *per connexionem* [by connection], nor from its soul, which is in it *per conjunctionem* [by conjunction], nor from its divinity, with which it is *per unionem personalem* [by personal union]. Wherefore, in view of such a confession, it believes and confesses that in Communion all of Christ is received by every person, indivisible, entire, living—composed of body, blood, soul, and divinity. For to give, or to take, the body of Christ and His blood without the soul and without the divinity is not to give or to take Christ, who can never be separated from his soul and divinity. Whence it is clear that both under the two species given and taken together and under any one of them separately, the indivisible, whole, entire, living Christ is given and taken. Otherwise neither the *communio* of infants, which is under the one species of the wine, nor the *communio* of the sick, which occurs under the species of the bread alone, nor the *communio* of healthy adults, which is celebrated under both species, would be the Communion of the true Christ. Since the infants would lack the presence of the body, soul, and divinity of the true Christ; the sick would lack the blood, soul, and divinity; and the healthy would lack the soul and divinity.

Ninth consideration. That the *communio* of the Western Church under the single species of the bread was never charged by the Eastern as an error, even though in other matters even its least differences in customs from the Eastern Church were not passed over in silence, as, for example, the unleavened bread itself. What is more, at the Council of Constance, Jan Hus was burned, among other reasons, also because he taught that both species were appropriate for the use of the laity by God's law. Which, however, the Greeks did not charge against the Romans as a transgression, not with even one word, either at the Council of Florence or any time before it, even though they had a fresh memory of this event before them. And this, it seems, was passed over in silence by the Greeks for no other reason but because they saw in the daily use of the Eastern Church the custom of Communion under one species. Thus it does not seem that from such a use of the sacrament of the Eucharist under one species the Western Church differed from the Eastern either through heresy or error. For it is also Christ's ancient apostolic custom of the Eastern Church, celebrated in the breaking of the bread and in Communion.

These, then, are the six differences that are taken as a reason for differing among the Western and the Eastern Churches and for the ancient schism that is hateful to God. And I submit their weighing in this matter to the discriminating consideration, most noble Ruthenian nation, of those among you whom it behooves to consider; and I ask you, by the love of your salvation, that you might deign to look not with a sleepy eye nor with a fearful heart, but with a sober intellect and a robust soul at all that I have offered you, with the permission, or rather with the commandment and blessing, of the elders. For just as the errors and heresies of our new theologians rest upon our souls, whom even until this very day we have not declared with even one word not to be ours—not by even the least person among us, and if not unto all the Orthodox, then at least to our Ruthenian Church itself—so also these differences take us by the soul, whether we feel it or do not feel it; for until this time we have not taken this under our consideration with even one letter, and in this we have not assured or informed ourselves and our entire Church through anyone that we do this piously and salvatorily. We see both these things straining to destroy our souls, but we pretend not to see it. But grant that, through some sort of righteous punishment of God, we do not see and do not notice this: let us see now already, and let us not carelessly permit this unnoticed and unconsidered evil to go unchecked, which seeks to cause the death of our souls. Let us see how, through the errors and heresies of our Zizanijs that I have cited, we have strayed far from the Gospel truth. Let us consider how properly on account of these differences we have separated from our born brethren and suffer from them in every third word the shame of the accursed schism. If there is any reason to lose our wealth, squander our good name, forfeit our offices, suffer miseries, and die, let us adhere to all this as to the means to our salvation. But if there is no reason, it is not even worth a haler.

It is certainly the feeble understanding of a worthless man not to know upon what to establish his good name, honor, wealth, and health, nay even salvation. It has already been about thirty years now since the heresies of our Zizanijs began to spread among us like infernal ulcers, and we then proceeded to lose both our temporal and our eternal good, being doubtlessly of the opinion that we suffered and bore this for God, His truth, and the Orthodox faith of our ancestors. And yet we erred in this as we erred in the truth, in giving through them place and credence among us to falsehood instead of the truth. We already see this manifestly and openly—with how many and with what heavy blasphemies we incautiously allowed those people to stain us. Let us take measure of this, most beloved, and let us consider whether in these differences between the Eastern and the Western Churches with which we have become burdened, the same thing is not occurring with us. Let us no longer trust either the Zizanijs, or the Philaletheses, or the Orthologues, or the Clerks, or any soul embittered toward the truth through unnecessary hatred, but let us test this in ourselves *synodaliter* [in a synod], since we have been punished for so long by our evil. We see all this, if we see, that we are diminished and significantly humbled, but for what—neither do we know this, nor do we investigate it. We must nonetheless know for certain (as was thoroughly presented above) that the Lord God caused this to be upon us through His righteous divine judgment, †as upon those who, on account of the hatred of the brethren, have deserved to succumb to God's hatred. But I leave this for you yourself to see, since you have both years and understanding, and it is already time for you to be knowledgeable in matters of the soul's salvation.

We have taken note of our errors and heresies, which we could not see until this day. Let us now also take note of the differences cited by me between the Eastern and the Western Churches, and let us consider whether the Churches are of such distance from each other that in no manner—without manifest blasphemy against God's majesty—can they be near to each other; which we will, in my opinion, not find them to be when, following God's truth and not setting out after our own desires, with a pure soul in the fear of God and in the love of the brethren, we will wish to examine the truth of both these Churches with the healthy eyes of our heart. When we cast from it, in love with a Catholic heart, and remove from ourselves what the Zizanijs, the Philaletheses, the Orthologues, the Clerks, and our other similar writers have *calumniose* [calumniously] cast upon the Western Church with a heretical tongue, and when we cease to seek in its pure confession of the faith the Manichaean, Sabellian, Macedonian, Apollinarian, Origenist, and other similar heresies. When we will not wish to line up with the Clerk's troops unto evil and soul-destroying things against God's will of constant unity and harmony, carelessly in opposition to the contracted

† Whoever does not love his brethren cannot love God.

harmony and unity according to God's will for good and soul-saving things. †When we will cease to listen to this new sort of faith—written neither in Holy Writ nor in the writ of the holy fathers—of self-taught cabalists who foretell their own dreams, self-wise idols, who, as if *ex oraculo Apollinis* [from an oracle of Apollo], boast in their haughty and exalted pride that they can do everything, know everything, are expert in everything. But both internally and externally they are Janneses and Jambreses, opposed to God's truth, people of corrupt understanding and cast away from the side of faith.[475] When we do these four things we will not only not find any blasphemy against God's majesty in the confession of the Roman Church, but after seeing them to be near, harmonious, of one mind with us in the Orthodox Catholic faith, we will quickly, with the grace and help of a kindly God who wishes the salvation of our souls, become worthy of receiving in actual fact the thing that we all uniformly beg of Him in our daily prayers in the Holy Liturgy: that He will grant us to glorify, praise, and adore, with one mouth and with one heart, His most laudable and most glorious name, of the Father and the Son and the Holy Ghost, today, always, and for ever and ever.

Someone might ask us, most beloved, when we pray to the Lord God so *solenniter* [solemnly], what is it we are praying for? We could not truly answer in any other way but that we pray for unity in love with those with whom we have unity in faith. And if the Eastern and the Western Churches have unity in faith, why should they not also have unity in love, since we pray to the Lord our God so ardently for it during the celebration of the bloodless sacrifice? But from these "Considerations" of the differences offered by me it is a thing clearer than the sun that they have unity in faith. Wherefore, to run away one from the other, when we have mutual unity of faith, is to flee from the hope of our salvation. Since faith without love is not only empty of hope, but is also dead; in love and in unity, it is living and fresh. It was for this unity that our Lord Savior Jesus Christ asked God the Father that we might be one, as He

---

†   *Azarias intelligitur* [Azarius is understood here].
475. 2 Tim. 3[:8, which is a reference to Ex. 7:11. The "sorcerers" and "magicians" are not mentioned by name in Exodus, but they are identified in Jewish tradition and named in 2 Tim.].

was one with His Father.[476] The one that is requested for us and received from God the Father by our Savior in the person of His disciples is Church unity. Our Eastern Church had that holy unity with the Western Church and maintained it for a thousand years. In that holy unity the Eastern Church became glorious through its holy teachers and righteous fathers. That holy unity brought our Ruthenian nation to baptism and made our Church fruitful in pious and holy men, our fathers. That holy unity built for us churches and monasteries, endowed goods upon them, and adorned them with freedoms. As soon as the accursed schism broke off this holy unity, which was caused between the two Churches by the Holy Spirit, the Eastern Church immediately retreated as if behind a wall and began to be stripped of all its internal and external adornments. Immediately secular people, the Greek emperors, took upon themselves power over the clergy and the Churches, establishing laws over them as they saw fit.[477] And immediately it was as if its womb and breasts had become petrified such that from that very time it no longer gave birth to, nor nourished, anyone; that is, I say, that after its separation from the Western Church it did not bring any pagan nation to the faith of Christ the Lord, and it fell into hunger for the word of God. It lost the living and efficacious word of God.[478]

The last patriarch of Constantinople who lived in holy unity, Ignatius, is a saint in our Church, whose memory we celebrate *Octobris 23* [on 23 October]. After his lifetime the disruption of Church unity occurred, and †henceforth no patriarch of this see was entered into the register of God's saints by our churchmen. For without Church unity, even if a man should seem the best and the most pious, he is found empty of God's grace. Are there even now few among the Armenians, the Copts, the Syrians, the Abyssinians, the Nestorites, and other similar heretics, even among the Turks themselves, who labor, fast, depart this world, and live their life in the most extreme humility *ex voto* [by a solemn oath] made to God? And yet without the true faith they are empty of God's grace, and their bodily labors are in vain. We must understand

---

476. Jn. 17[:21].
477. *Choniat. Lib. 6, c. 8* [Nicetas Choniates, *Thesaurus of the Orthodox Faith,* bk. 6, chap. 8; *PG* 140:11–12].
478. Heb. 4[:12].
†　　Look and consider.

this and nothing else concerning the schismatics as well, about whom the blessed apostle Paul says: *Si distribuero in cibos pauperum omnes facultates meas, et si tradidero corpus meum ita ut ardeam, charitatem autem non habuero, nihil mihi prodest* [and though I bestow all my goods to feed the poor, and though I give my body to be burned, and have not charity, it profiteth me nothing].[479] Whence St. Augustine says of these same people that even if they were to give all their wealth to the poor and to yield up their bodies to the fire for the Orthodox faith that they confess, they cannot achieve salvation.[480] And St. Cyprian says that the sin of schism is such that it cannot be redeemed even by a martyr's death; such a blot that it cannot be washed away even by the blood that was poured out by Christ the Lord. He cannot be a martyr (he says) who is not inside the Church; and he cannot become worthy to enter into the Kingdom of Heaven who abandons the one that is to reign. He who does not wish to be of one mind in the Church of God can be killed, but he cannot be crowned.[481] After showing with an example that it is a more cruel thing to tear the king to pieces than to abandon him, St. John Chrysostom adds that the heretic abandons Christ, and the apostate tears His body.[482]

†And so both the heretic and the apostate, even if he should seem *moraliter* [with respect to manners] to be the most pious and the most holy, does not have the grace of God in him since God's anger always remains upon him, and he can never be saved. For both are outside of the Church. The heretic as an exile and the schismatic as a deserter and the one who tears apart the body of Christ the Lord. For they cannot come to any internal Church good, even though they have directed all their strength toward it, since the Lord God does not delight in even their most pious deed. And all the more clearly in that of the schismatic

479. 2 Cor. 19 [1 Cor. 13:3].
480. *Lib. 1 de Baptismo, c. 9* [St. Augustine, *On Baptism, against the Donatists*, bk. 1, chap. 9; *PL* 43:116; *NPNF1* 4:417].
481. *Lib. de unitate* [Cyprian of Carthage, *Book on the Unity of the Church*, chap. 14; *PL* 4:510–11].
482. *Hom. 11 in Epist. ad Ephes.* [St. John Chrysostom, *Homily 11 on Ephesians 4:4; PL* 4:510D; *PG* 62:87; *NPNF1* 13:107].
† Both the heretic and the schismatic have something to fear here.

than in that of the heretic to the extent that the former are nearer to concluding Church unity.

All the other conventicles are far from the Eastern and the Western Churches. Those two are so near and similar to each other that no one who examines this with a healthy eye will not say that they are one, with the exception that the one moves and labors from love, but the other lies indolent and is lazy from hatred. The one is excellent and splendid, but the other has been deprived of every ornament—and not without God's permission, as it seems, and in anger. However many of the *reliquiae* [relics] of the saints there were, the Lord God has taken them all away from it and has sent them to the Western Church. †Whatever there was of the arts in the East, the Lord God has transferred them all to the West. And to whatever extent the East can have a learned man, it acquires him from the West. Even now in Constantinople, on Galata, the *patres Societatis Jesu* [Fathers of the Society of Jesus] teach the Greek children both in Greek and in Latin (if the Calvinist impiety, through the provocation of our elders, did not drive them away from there, as one hears). And if, among the Greeks, there are any teachers taught there at home or in Italian academies, they are in disdain and in scorn among their own. Among the spiritual authorities the disobedience of the lesser to the greater is such that so long as they wish and in whatever they wish, they listen to their superiors: the presbyter to the bishop, the bishop to the metropolitan, the metropolitans to the patriarch, the lesser patriarchs to the fourth, higher patriarch. For some ten years now there have been two patriarchs in the see of Antioch, Ignatius and Cyril. Ignatius was consecrated by Patriarch Timothy of Constantinople, and Cyril was then consecrated by Cyril, the current patriarch of Constantinople, at that time patriarch of Alexandria. But the fallen Church order is not able to come to the point that one of them, if ordered to retreat, would obey. The power of the superiors over the subordinates has fallen, such that they cannot use it *juridice* [in administration of justice], and disobedience toward the superiors has settled on the souls of the subordinates such that they do not wish to offer their obedience to them. Such lack of learning has fallen upon the clergy that through their ignorance of the dogmas of the faith and of the matters of salvation not only secular people do not know what they believe, but not even they themselves.

---

†   Read with consideration and with regret.

We clergy of the Ruthenian Church are a trustworthy witness to this, for if we knew our own faith, we would not permit such heavy errors and the profane heresies of our Zizanijs—as they would not permit those of their Gerganoses—to warm a place with us and to remain in us for such a long time. †In Moscow, Wallachia, Moldavia, the Bulgarian land, and the Serbian, it is a mortal sin to make sermons. This sin has barely been removed from our Ruthenian Church during our times. Testimony to the fact that love for the salvation of one's neighbor has grown cold in our Church are those of ours who die on the streets, in the muck, in the prisons, condemned to death without confession and Communion, and the slaves in Turkey who die without any confession and penance. I do not even wish to mention the further spiritual miseries that have fallen upon us from God's punishment and upon the entire Eastern Church lest it seem to anyone that I do this out of my good will and not obliged by conscience.

‡We must consider all of this, most noble Ruthenian nation: whether these are not the accursed spawn of the accursed schism. For blessed unity bears with it blessed effects as the thing that is from God and is God.

Example of a Secular Union of Two Different States under One King, [Compared] with the Spiritual Union of Two Nations under One Pastor

The unity that is called *Unia* among us seems something strange to our Ruthenian nation, and to be a Uniate is as if to be a Jew; among us it is one and the same, and actually for some it is thought to be something worse. *But this is—let us forgive ourselves—homespun nonsense on the part of some of us and heretical sense on the part of others. Let us take an example from the secular union of the Polish Crown and the Grand Duchy of Lithuania, and let us see what sort of creature this is, the union. It is the foundation of the union of these two states for both of these states to know one lord, to collaborate in counsel and in industry concerning them, and for each of them to enjoy their own proper laws,

---

†   Which nations consider it a sin to listen to a sermon in church.
‡   The evil effects of the schism. And the good ones of unity.
*   The understanding of stupid people concerning the union.

liberties, and freedoms. And it is the foundation of the spiritual union to know one highest pastor of the Church of Christ the Lord, to collaborate with him in faith and in love, and for each of the local Churches to enjoy their own customs, laws, ceremonies, and rites, as far as Church order is concerned.

†In order to conclude Church unity with itself, the Roman Church does not require from the Eastern Church any other condition than unanimity in faith and communion in love. There is already unanimity in faith, as is made clear from the "Considerations" I have offered. Why should there not also be unanimity in love? But the very thing that does not please us is that we be unanimous with the Romans in faith, whom we consider heretics, about whom in every third word we are wont to say that with every pope there is a new faith. Which, however, is an argument of ours against them that is without proof. For, as was made clear from the "Considerations," even the pope holds inviolable the dogmas of the faith, which a man can no more change than establish. The Lord God Himself is the giver of faith, and not some man, for to attack it, through an alteration or some sort of violence, is to make bold against the Lord God Himself. Which the pope certainly does not do. But if he establishes something in the Church, he establishes what belongs to it according to order. Which is not only permitted to the pope, but is permitted even to the Eastern patriarchs and practically to every bishop in his diocese, according to need, so long as it be without scandal.

It was permitted to St. Basil the Great to abandon the manner of celebrating the Holy Liturgy written by the apostles and to write it in his own manner. It was then permitted to St. John Chrysostom to do the same thing. Who, and with what propriety, can forbid the pope to do the same and similar things? For almost one thousand years our Eastern Church did not know the fasts of Peter, *Salvatoris* [of the Savior], and of Philip, which we maintain.[483] But now, by a new decree not heard of at the seven universal councils, it knows them and maintains them. The monks, that is, the black monks of the Eastern Church, were

†   What the Western Church requires from the Eastern.
483. *Balsam. in Respons. ad interrog. 4 Monachorum pag. 119 Graecolat. editionis* [(Theodore) Balsamon in the response to the questions of four monks, p. 119 of the Greco-Latin edition; Leunclavius 1596, 119].

also for almost one thousand years allowed to eat meat, now it is not allowed.[484] This too is by a new decree not heard of at any of the seven universal councils. Bishops in the Eastern Church were allowed to have wives almost until the Sixth Universal Council; now they are no longer allowed to have them.

The Eastern Church likewise for almost one thousand years did not know *Oktoechoi, Menaia, Triodia,* but now from a recent tradition it knows them.[485] For more than one thousand years the Churches of Jerusalem and of Alexandria did not have the liturgies of Basil the Great and of St. John Chrysostom in use, but the latter used the liturgy of the blessed evangelist Mark, and the Church of Jerusalem used that of St. James the Apostle, the Lord's brother.[486] For almost one thousand years the holy bread of the Eucharist was given to the hands of the communicants in the Eastern Church, and they drank from the cup, but now a different custom is maintained.[487] And there are many other similar customs in the Eastern Church that have been changed for others or have been newly received. As are No Fast, Meat Fare, Cheese Fare Sundays, the fast on the day of the Lord's Transfiguration, and others.[488] And yet, we do not ascribe to our elders the creation of a new faith when they do these new things. But since one pope established that the priests not grow their hair, a second that the holy water be mixed with salt, a third that the laity not touch the altar vessel, and others still other things as far as Church order is concerned (but not as far as the

---

484. A Greek chronicle in description of the affairs of Emperor Leo [VI] the Wise and of his wife Theophano.

485. *Blas. in explic. Can. Apostol. 1 et Can. 74 Conc. Cartag.* [Matthew Blastares in the explication of Apostolic Canon 1 and Canon 74 of the Council of Carthage; perhaps a reference to his *Syntagma kata stoicheion* or *Alphabetical Treatise* on canon law, *PG* 144:959–145:212].

486. They were written around the year 840.

487. *Bals.* [Theodore Balsamon] in the interpretation *Can. 32 Syn. in Trullo* [of canon 32 of the Council in Trullo; *PG* 137:616–22], and in the Greco-Latin edition, pag. 119 [Leunclavius 1596, 119].

488. *Dam. lib. 4. b. 14* [St. John of Damascus, *Exposition of the Orthodox Faith,* bk. 4, chap. 14; *PG* 94:1153–62; *NPNF2* 9:84–6, but the reference seems incorrect] and *Nic. Choniates in Imper. Alex. Comn. qui vixit circa A. Dni. 1183* [Nicetas Choniates on Emperor Alexius (II?) Comnenus, who lived ca. 1183; cf. perhaps *PG* 139:573–628].

faith was concerned), the heretics began to make their slander that with every pope there is a new faith. Which the heretics could also say about our patriarchs looking at the recent decrees of our Eastern Church. But only stupidly. Since the decree or change of Church rites and orders does not ruin or harm the constancy of the faith.

Someone will say: In this manner, as you have put it forth, we would have to abandon the patriarch of Constantinople, who is our father in the spirit and highest pastor. I answer: I do not aim directly that this happen. To the contrary, I advise you to adhere to him as to your father so that, by saving ourselves from those errors and heresies that are disgusting to God, which are contrary to our faith, introduced by our Zizanijs into our Ruthenian Church, we also simultaneously save him from precisely the same sort of errors that had been brought by his Gerganoses to cause harm to the Greek Church. I have confidence in his pastorly watchfulness and piety as an archiereus that, having opposed all these heretical writings of the Gerganoses, as also those of our Zizanijs, he will not be an impediment to further progress in the concluding of holy unity. Especially in the manner that was mentioned by me or in some most authoritative sort that either he himself or someone else of the pious will discover. For assured by the gravity and the learning and the dignity of this man, who surpasses the entire East, we can understand of him that as soon as he becomes ardent in this salvatory matter, he will not be able to cool off, since he is able to have the same grace of the Holy Spirit even now governing his soul that had long ago inflamed his heart to that salvatory matter.

A sure witness to this is the letter written in his own hand in our fatherland, in the year 1601, *Januarii 24 die* [on 24 January] in Lviv, and delivered to the hands of Father Dymitr Solikowski, archbishop of Lviv of worthy memory, in which, having made known that he had been sent as an exarch, or a legate, from two patriarchs, Matthew and Meletius of Alexandria, to this most illustrious Polish Kingdom in matters and needs of the Ruthenian Church, he asserted the following about the evangelicals, whom he calls heretics, that "through hatred toward the Roman Church and the see of Peter they had attempted an agreement with the Easterners, but they were never accepted. For they agree with us only to the extent that the Jews and the Mohammedans do. As, for example, in saying that God is one, the creator and ruler of the world, righteous, good, punishing the evil and rewarding the good, and in other such confession. But in the foremost articles of the Christian faith they do not agree with us. Concerning the antiquity of orders or Church consecration, concerning apostolic traditions or those things handed down, concerning the authority of the holy fathers and doctors of both Churches—which either all of them, or some of their sects, reject— and concerning the number and canon of the books of Holy Scripture, and concerning Church customs, and concerning justification, and concerning the Holy Liturgy and the offering, concerning the veneration and the relics of the saints, concerning the Mother of God, concerning the Most Holy Trinity—in all this, they do not have agreement with us; rather they wrench new understanding of Holy Scripture from their heads. That this matter has great danger, experience itself testifies. Since, then, they have been planted so far from us, they cannot grow together with us."

After presenting these two things in his letter, the present patriarch of Constantinople, the most reverend in God, Father Cyril, immediately adds this third thing: that "what is a matter of disagreement between the Eastern and the Western Churches can repulse the unlearned and the simple" (do we hear what our patriarch says about these six differences between the Eastern and the Western Churches that I offered for consideration a little above—that these differences can repulse only unlearned people from unity?), "but learned people easily derive one understanding in the love of Christ. We are not disgusted by the see of St. Peter, but we render it the requisite honor and respect, and we acknowledge it as the first, as the mother. †We have one and the same faith" (let us hear, most noble nation, that our patriarch recognizes the see of St. Peter, that is the Roman Church, as his mother and acknowledges that we Rus' have one faith with the Romans), "one baptism with God the Father, and the Son, and the Holy Spirit, one nature, one omnipotence, one divinity, one hope of vocation, one love, the same prayers and requests in common for kings, rulers, offices, the same sacraments" (if the same, that means seven and not two), "the same holy orders and Church consecrations, lesser and greater, one Gospel, the same prophetic and apostolic writings, one authority of the

---

†   Grant it, O God, that even now this patriarch might understand and believe the same thing.

Holy Orthodox Church fathers, Greek and Latin. What are we supposed
to have in common with other sects?"

Thus our present-day patriarch of Constantinople—if he has, as
I said, the same grace of the Holy Spirit even now in his soul and if
he burns with the same fire of love for holy Church unity with which
he burned when he wrote that letter, holding the Roman Church in the
requisite honor and recognizing it as the mother and acknowledging
the same faith and the same sacraments for the Eastern and the Western
Churches—thus he will easily allow that, by the grace of God, with us
and through us he will enter into Church unity with the Romans. About
which toward the end of that same letter of his he says thus: "I depart
from this kingdom, and I return to my own people, and I declare that I
wished to attempt in this land nothing else but that some sort of peace
and agreement might be established between those who desire unity and
have already entered into it and those who are not in it but suppose that
they do this piously." (Let us open both ears here, most noble Ruthenian
nation, and let us listen to our patriarch, who criticizes us for the fact
that we suppose that we act piously in not wishing to be in the union.)
Proceeding further, he says, "But they themselves, looking to their
foremost heads, do not agree with each other and allow heretical errors.
[In this land I strove for nothing else] but that some sort of peace and
harmony might be established."[489] Thus the patriarch acknowledges for
us that by not wishing to agree with the Uniate fathers and brethren,
we consent to heretical errors. And so this letter, most noble Ruthenian
nation, pious in its entirety, in recommending to us Rus' love, peace,
harmony, and unity with the Roman Church, assures us that what we
see of our Ruthenian Church that is both salvatory according to God and
honorable according to people we will easily receive from Him; only
let us head toward this ourselves, and let us progress in this salvatory
matter not lethargically, for this is a matter of God, and if anyone
performs it carelessly, *maledictus est* [he is cursed].[490] But if he should,

---

489. [Skarga 1610, 113. Smotryc'kyj cited here according to Skarga's Polish
translation. The final clause—"but that . . . "—was dependent upon another
clause ("In this land I strove that . . . "), which came well before the passage
that interested him here, and which he omitted. I have added it in order to give
the whole passage some sense.]
490. Jer. 84 [48:10].

for any of his private concerns, which are harmful to us according to the soul and according to the body, wish to keep us with him in this shame of apostasy with which he himself has been shamed, let him himself judge whether it is a righteous matter before God's countenance to listen to him rather than to God; and you too most noble Ruthenian nation, judge, for it concerns you.

Nonetheless, however it should happen from that side, we must not be careless. Our hope is in our Savior Christ the Lord, that He Himself will rule his heart according to His holy will as the salvation of our soul requires and that He will deign to bring about the fruitful success in our labors. Only let us begin with ourselves; the Lord God has the power to enlighten with the light of truth all the other nations of the Eastern Church through the Ruthenian Church and to bring them to Church unity. Let us clergy show mercy upon ourselves; let us take pity upon our nation that is miserably afflicted not only in wealth, honor, dignities, freedoms, and liberties, but also in the blood of our afflicted nation. For the Lord God will seek it at our hands.[491] We, however, are the cause of its being poured out. For looking upon us as if upon their own faith, everyone everywhere in all the cities and villages, the gentry, common people, and knighthood, cry out that one must die for the faith, and they believe that it is for the faith that some suffer loss of wealth, others loss of health, some honor, and some even life. And yet, to say aright, we suffer loss of all of these things not for the Orthodox faith, but for heretical bad faith. Not for the faith of our ancestors, but for the errors and heresies of the Zizanijs, Philaletheses, Orthologues, Clerks, and other of our masters and doctors like them. For in these days for a wise man to say anything against their blasphemies is as if we were to touch the very apple of the eye of the Church itself.[492] If only those masters and doctors had had healthy sight of the soul and whole spiritual understanding, they would never have attacked the Church that, according to the ancient custom of our holy ancestors, even our current patriarch, as we heard, calls mother. Then they would not cry out so haughtily with Zion, whence the law went forth, or with Jerusalem, whence the word of the Lord went forth. For it happened to us, as we see, alas, both in Zion and in Jerusalem, as it happened to those who

491. [Ez. 3:18, 20; 33:6, 8; 34:10.]
492. [Zech. 2:8.]

sitting there guard the nest, while others delight in the Phoenix that was hatched. Certainly we cannot boast of either Zion or Jerusalem any more than those who hold the tablets, while others preserve the word of God written on them. Which has been demonstrated thoroughly in many ways.

Then they would not blaspheme the holy faith of our holy ancestors. Then they would not flee from the mother's blessing and the love of the brethren. And they would not submit their Church to the disgust of pious people. For having covered its eyes with some sort of scales, it cannot see either the evil in which it finds itself or the good it has lost. And until those unhappy scales are wiped from its pure pupils by the rock of faith, St. Peter, who comes after the rock of faith, Christ the Lord, it will have to wander far from the true faith and from its salvation over the heretical rifts and abysses. Having gotten rid of them and acquired true love, having made peace with the brethren and with the Father, having rendered obedience to the father of fathers and confessed with him as with one mouth the unity of the faith of Christ the Lord, then it can truly boast with its mother, as it now boasts with that anonymous Clerk led astray in bare opinion: that she brought forth her firstborn sons through the sharp scythe of the Saturnian Herod for the meeting and greeting of the King of Kings, who is going to the mangers of Bethlehem from the far and high heavenly palaces. †Now our boast from this is all but in vain; in vain too the joy. And I am afraid that we boast and rejoice in this precisely as the one who, having fallen from the cart into the mud, rejoiced in the fact that he was once sitting in the cart.[493] We boast of this as boast the prodigals who say of themselves again and again, "I had it"; for which "I had it" no one will give them even a haler. Oh, grant it Lord God that our "I HAD IT" might be changed for us into "I HAVE IT." Then we will genuinely be able to boast and to rejoice.

As long as the Eastern Polycarps knew and considered the Western Anicetuses as their fathers and pastors, and the Athanasiuses the Juliuses, the Chrysostoms the Innocents, the Cyrils the Celestines, the Theodoretuses the Leos, the Maximuses the Martins, the Studites

---

† Someone else, but not we apostate Rus′, can now rejoice in the law that went out from Zion and in the word of the Lord from Jerusalem.
493. [A humorous variant of a common Polish saying. Cf. *NKPP* 3:767–8, "Wóz," 5.]

the Leos, the Ignatiuses the Hadrians, they themselves could both boast and rejoice genuinely in all that the Church of Christ the Lord had of adornment, internally and externally. At that time, our Eastern Church gave birth to sons, soldiers of Christ the Lord, not merely in the fourteen thousands but in the forty thousands and more. But as soon as it began to follow the Eastern Photiuses, Sergiuses, Michaels, and others like them who did not consider the Western Nicholases, Johns, Leos, and their successors as their fathers and pastors, immediately— oh, our poor misery—she ceased to give birth to sons, soldiers of Christ the Lord, and she began to give birth to sons, soldiers of the infamous Mohammed. You will no longer hear of a new voluntary martyr in her, a soldier of Christ the Lord; and yet we hear with our ears, and we see with our eyes, that the impious Ottoman selects Christian sons from all of the Greek, Serbian, and Bulgarian lands almost every year for his army, and he turkifies them unto his Mohammedan baseness. Are not every day some from those nations forced into that baseness, not only from the secular people, but even from the clergy?

†These are the sort of unfortunate sons to whom our unfortunate Eastern Church gives birth, having followed its Photiuses, Sergiuses, and Michaels, disturbers of the Church peace who sunder into two pieces the body of Christ the Lord. I say this, most noble Ruthenian nation, not to abuse the one that gave rebirth to our entire Church, and to me in it, from the water and the spirit, but to commiserate with it and to abase our stupidly exalted pride and boasting so that we might sometime see that ALAS, in which we rejoice in the East, and having touched our conscience might come to ourselves and wish to take heathful care for ourselves so that we might be able to move both our senses and, through us and in us, the entire Eastern Church and to unite with that Church, with which, as soon as it began to sunder its entire spiritual peace, immediately it also began to fall into spiritual and bodily non-peace, being punished by the Lord God for what it had sinned.

‡Peter, patriarch of Antioch, a man both glorious for his learning and illustrious for the piety of his life, who lived around the year of our Lord 1150 [actually, 1050], right at the time of the final break of the Eastern Church from the Western, says in his letter on the errors and heresies

---

†   To what sort of sons the Eastern Church now gives birth.
‡   This letter is worthy of consideration.

alleged by the Greeks against the Romans and written in answer to one sent to him by Michael Cerularius, patriarch of Constantinople: "From the time when we began to separate with our holy Church from that great foremost apostolic see, all this evil has begun to befall us during our lifetimes, and misfortune befalls the entire world. Let us take note how the kingdoms of the entire world are in confusion. Everywhere there is lamentation and great suffering, famines and plagues are frequent in every land and in the cities, and our army has not the least fortune in anything."[494] Thus the patriarch of Antioch.

Let us listen on this same topic to Patriarch of Constantinople Gennadius Scholarius, who, writing to his Greeks already after the taking of Constantinople by the Turks, says: "The City of the Emperors has been taken. I must lament and cry and moan at the very mention of this. The altars have been defiled, the Churches destroyed, blood poured, nuns shamed, virgins defiled, children put to the sword, lords, monks, priests, and ladies killed, married couples torn apart, holy vessels broken, most beautiful images trodden upon and disfigured with spittle. Oh, I am unfortunate and miserable. Who can give expression to this demise? Mohammed has swallowed everything. Not only the queen of all cities, but also the lands that pertain to her suffer greater and worse things every day, about which we hear and upon which we look. But what is this for? You say: for our sins. But I: we do not offend God any more than other Christian nations. To the contrary, they have greater sins. Why does the Lord God not punish them as He punishes our unfortunate and miserable nation? Woe is miserable me; I must lament and complain and ask about the reason why we suffer this. I can find no other, for our nation is not inferior to other nations in virtue; to the contrary it is better than others, for it surpasses other nations in virtue and in morals. Thus there is no other reason for our downfall but the schism and apostasy, that we have moved away from obedience and submission to the Roman Church. I find this very thing to be the cause of our demise. For as soon as we separated from it, we received a curse, and we suffer what we suffer. And yet we do not repent, but we become worse, and we curse that same Church." Thus that holy patriarch.[495]

494. [Peter, patriarch of Antioch, *Letter to Cerularius, PG* 120:811C–812C.]
495. *Cap. 15* [in chapter 15] of his book.

Oh, grant that we, most noble Ruthenian nation, grant that we not be punished with the evil of our brethren and that we might mend our ways before the harm,[496] that is, before our demise, which hangs just above us, as vengeance from heaven, having examined in the words of this man, as in a mirror, this very same cause of our miseries and sufferings that was also their demise. This accursed cause forces our miserable Rus' and Muscovy to drink of the same cup with wretched Greece, since countless numbers of them are found in that same Turkish servitude. Since I too can say with this holy patriarch about my own Ruthenian nation that it is not inferior to other nations in virtue; to the contrary, it is better both in modesty and in piety. But it suffers what it suffers for no other reason but the reason of the accursed schism. This is what lowers us every day; this diminishes us every hour. And if we do not save ourselves from it now immediately we will soon experience, even though it seem an impossibility to anyone, that there will no longer be Rus' in Rus', not as far as the people is concerned, but as far as the faith and the rite are concerned. For although some one of us, by God's special grace, can even obtain holy Church unity, nonetheless through obstinate stubbornness Luther will snatch away many, Calvin will snatch some, even the accursed Anabaptist will snatch some. Let us not wish to experience this in ourselves, most beloved, and let us not wait, if we love our faith and salvation. Let us cease to recommend to ourselves non-peace, non-love, enmity; but to the contrary, let us fall in love with love, friendship, harmony, and peace, and let us recommend these virtues to ourselves. Let us not use badly, unto our perdition, the words of the blessed apostle Paul: *cum dixerint pax et securitas: tunc repentinus eis superveniet interitus* [when they shall say, Peace and safety; then sudden destruction cometh upon them].[497] And let us not rejoice in these words of Christ the Lord, which do not serve us: *nolite timere, pusillus grex* [fear not, little flock].[498] For our Anabaptists, looking upon their smallness, use them no less frequently to their own perdition than those tipplers of ours who run from house to house,

---

496. [The Ruthenian, like the Pole, is "wise after the harm" (i.e., too late). Cf. *NKPP* 3:398–400, "Szkoda," 13.]
497. 1 Th. 5[:3].
498. Lk. 12[:32].

homines corrupti mente, reprobi circa fidem [men of corrupt minds, reprobate concerning the faith].[499]

Living in peace and in unity with the Romans, we do not need to fear sudden perdition. For they do not summon us to harmony and peace for impurity, for the lusts of passion, fornication, homicide, extortion, drunkenness, sorcery, and similar evil things, for the workers of which sudden perdition waits, as for sons of night and darkness. [†]Rather they summon us to consecration, to the maintenance of our vessel in sanctity and honor, the keeping of God's will and the decrees of the apostles, brotherly love, compassion, peace, and similar virtues. And those who carry out these things, like the sons of day and light, neither expect nor do they fear sudden perdition, but safety and peace await them with the coming of our Lord, Jesus Christ.[500] This is the Church that summons us, or rather our Church, to unity with it, whose faith began to be preached from the very beginning throughout all the world.[501] Which has been entrusted for teaching and government to St. Peter by Christ the Lord by an exclusive right, and in him to his successors. And throughout all the past Christian ages all the Orthodox emperors and patriarchs had their eyes turned toward it, whose privileges are above the privileges of all other Churches and which is the apostolic school and the mother of piety.

This is the Church that summons us to its unity, that allowed the Slavic nations to celebrate the Holy Liturgy in the Slavonic language and to use the entire rite in it.[502] It is with this Church that holy unity is recommended to us, which not long ago, through the living and efficacious word of God, sharper than every two-edged sword and piercing even to the dividing asunder of soul and spirit, and of the joints and marrow, and a discerner of the thoughts and intents of the heart,[503] gained many Indian nations for its God, Christ the Lord, in countless souls. For it makes industry and takes care maternally for the rising

499. 2 Tim. 3[:8].
†   To what sort of unity the Romans summon us.
500. [1 Th. 5:5.]
501. Rom. 1[:8].
502. *In visita. [?] SS. Cyrili et Methodi* [In the Lives (?) of SS. Cyril and Methodius], the Slavic apostles, 14 February.
503. Heb. 4[:12].

of all Christians everywhere that have fallen into various heresies and apostasies so that it might gain them in a loving soul for the same Christ the Lord, as the Bride for her Bridegroom and Lord, so that not even one soul be lost.

If the licentious life of some of its bishops should repel us from holy unity of the Church, having attributed this to the weakness of human nature, which is inclined to all evil, let us allow ourselves to be attracted *in amorem et amplexum ejus* [into its love and embrace] by this very thing: that even if some Roman bishop was evil and impious in life, nonetheless in faith not one was evil and impious. If Marcellinus slipped, he stood up again, and through a martyr's death he confessed— through love of Him Himself—Him, whom he had denied through fear of temporal torments. If Liberius suffered the same thing, and if he too fell down for His Lord, he also rose up again for his Lord. Honorius, after his death *calumniose* [calumniously] entered into the books by the Monothelite heretics as one in accord with them and a co-confessor, has illustrious defenders against this calumny, holy men: Agatho, bishop of Rome, Maximus the Confessor, and John of Damascus, who lived at that same time. To whom we the faithful ought more properly give credence than to thousands of heretics, who would gladly have stained even the entire world with their stain. These men fell according to their manhood, they were under the rule of sin, they sinned; but this has no propriety and weight that would not allow us communion with the Roman Church. This promise of Christ the Lord, which resides and is realized in this Church—*et portae inferi non praevalebunt adversus eam* [and the gates of hell shall not prevail against it],[504] and *Petre, ego rogavi pro te, ne deficiat fides tua* [Peter, I have prayed for thee, that thy faith fail not][505]—is itself enough, as I said, to attract us and to draw us, if we have spiritual understanding, to embrace it.

Further, if the fact that we should not wish to alter our rite or to take up the use of rites and ceremonies and sacraments that are little known to us and, having abandoned our own, transfer with the Romans to all of theirs—if this fact should render the Roman Church beyond communion for any one of us, or even all of us, this too should not harm our good heart for holy unity. For as the bishop of Rome does not require

504. [Mt. 16:18.]
505. [Lk. 22:32.]

of us that, in entering into unity with him, we leave, abandon our holy paternal faith, which is one and the same with the Roman, and the holy rites, ceremonies, orders, and customs and use of salvatory mysteries in it, and exchange either all in general or some part of them for the Roman ones, so also would it come to us with great difficulty and with no little confusion of the Church to do this. But as we will not do this, so also the pope does not require this of us, for he thinks well of the rites, ceremonies, orders, celebrations, and the use of the divine mysteries that are maintained in the Eastern Church, speaks of them honorably, praises them, loves and receives them as authoritative, honorable, pious, and holy. He calls them the holy Greek religion and rites that are full of the honor of God. And he does not wish it from us that we depart from our patriarch of Constantinople, leave him and abandon him, and that, against him, we receive him [the pope] as our local, particular patriarch and pastor; but he requires of us that, together with our patriarch (if this is a possible thing), nay, even with all four of them, we enter with him into communion of faith and love and into Church unity, as it was in the days of those SS. Athanasiuses, Basils, Gregorys, Chrysostoms, Cyrils, Maxims, Tarasiuses, Methodiuses, Ignatiuses, Damascenes, Studites, and as it had come to be in the days of John [XI] Beccus and Joseph [II], patriarchs of Constantinople, by the decree of the councils of Lyons and Florence, so that the Eastern Church, not disturbing its religion in any respect in the rites and ceremonies and celebrations of the mysteries, nor in the creed, might confess that its faith is one with the Roman faith and so that it might seal it with the communion of love.[506]

The bishop of Rome has not required more, either throughout all the times past from the Greeks, or today from them and from us. He leaves us all that is ours, and he only requires unity of FAITH and LOVE with us—a proper, holy, and salvatory thing for us. For we ourselves already clearly see that without that holy unity we have departed from the true faith both through improper understanding of the teaching of the holy doctors of the Church and through the incautious introduction of heretical teaching into our Church, and we have allowed ourselves and our entire Church to become infected with the errors and heresies that our Ruthenian Zizanijs and the Greek Gerganoses ascribed to the

---

506. Father Skarga in the "Preface to the Reader" of his *Warning* [Skarga 1610,)(4r–v].

belief of the Eastern Church and submitted in print to the knowledge of the entire world. Neither did the Western Church require more from the Eastern at the Council of Florence, nor did the Eastern allow more to the Western than what was a matter of the confession of the true faith for both Churches. Namely, first, that the Roman procession of the Holy Spirit FROM THE SON and the Greek THROUGH THE SON be understood and interpreted unanimously. Second, that the Roman celebration of the sacrament of the Eucharist in unleavened and the Greek in leavened bread be held to be equally valid. Third, that the Roman fire and the Greek chaos or abyss be known as one and the same purgatory. Fourth, that the Roman and the Greek paradise be understood to be one and the same heavenly paradise with the perfect blessing of righteous souls in it. Fifth, that the Roman bishop in the Universal Church, and the Greek patriarchs in their proper Churches, remain in the authority of Church rule and order. This is what the Council of Florence ended with, and nothing else was discussed and established at it. What improper thing here was either required by the Western Church from the Eastern or was allowed to the Western by the Eastern? Nothing. All was of ancient usage, all of the fathers, all holy, all salvatory—only that which shows the faith of Christ the Lord to be pure and immaculate in both Churches and declares the genuine love of brothers for brothers.

We truly have nothing to fear that would hinder us from that salvatory work. Only the soul's enemy, who is wont to allege good for bad, the liar and murderer from the beginning,[507] whose foremost goal it is to be able to tear, rip, wrench, ruin, and destroy the body of Christ the Lord, His holy Church, although he knows that he cannot prevail against it[508] since it is protected by Christ the Lord. Nonetheless, the infernal one attempts to destroy the souls of men so that, after leading them away from Church unity or not allowing them into unity, he would gradually have those who remained outside the Church as his own, and he would take them as his own and swallow them, and thereby cast them where he himself with his dark angels will remain for all times.

Perhaps, finally, the Council of Trent, which was convened already after the Council of Florence, will frighten one of us, or even all of us, from Church unity. But this too would be fear where there is

507. [Jn. 8:44.]
508. [Mt. 16:18.]

none. To the contrary, our Eastern Church ought to be much obliged to the Western for this and render undying thanks that, by defending through this council its pure confession of faith against the Lutheran and Calvinist blasphemies that had recently arisen, it also defended the Orthodox confession of faith of the Eastern Church, and namely in these dogmas of the faith: *de libero arbitrio, de peccato originali et actuali, de originali justitia, de providentia, de praescientia, de praedestinatione, de gratia, de fide, de justificatione, de ecclesia, de sacramentis, de scriptura s. et de ejus canone, de traditionibus* [on free will, original and active sin, original justice, providence, prescience, predestination, grace, faith, justification, the Church, the sacraments, Holy Scripture and its canon, traditions], and in several others, in all of which to whatever extent in these times the Eastern Church has, and can have, manifest, clear, and express knowledge, in harmony with Holy Scripture and with the teaching of the holy doctors of the Church, it ought to be obliged to the Council of Trent. Wherefore, not only should the Council of Trent not be perceived as a cause for avoiding unity with the Western Church, but to the contrary it ought to be perceived as a reason for unanimity in faith and as a cause for harmony and love and Church unity, as that which explained for us these salvatory articles of the faith with a true Orthodox understanding. If we were to understand otherwise about this council, we would have to lutherize and calvinize, that is, to hereticize. Thus even if we seek purposefully, we can find nothing in the Roman Church that would properly repulse us from unity with it. With which we have one God, one faith, the same sacraments, one hope of salvation, one life, one death. Let us wish for ourselves also one Church with it through the means of love and thus also one heavenly kingdom so that the merciful Lord God might deign to cause all of us, the sons of the Eastern and the Western Church, to obtain it through His ineffable mercy. Whom we are obliged to ask with all our heart in all our daily and nightly Church prayers, public and private domestic, so that He might save us whether we will it or not and might deign to compel us to come in to His costly supper[509] by the judgments that He alone knows. Amen. Let it be. Grant it, O God.

509. [Lk. 14:23.]

In Honorem et gloriam unius trini Dei Patris, et Filii,
et Spiritus S. Et in salutem omnium Legentium
*[Unto the honor and glory of the One in Three, God the
Father, and the Son, and the Holy Ghost. And unto the
salvation of all readers].*

My life's one hope Lord Christ JesuS.[510]

Addition to the Considerations.

Since the final sheet remained empty of print, I[511] thought to fill it with
this final consideration and to demonstrate briefly to my Ruthenian
nation that we are nearer to agreement with the Romans than with the
heretics.

Natural reason itself ought to demonstrate to us that we are nearer
to agreement with those with whom we agree in the articles of the faith,
the number of the sacraments, the reception of traditions (although we
differ somewhat in ceremonies among ourselves, which are not taken as
a distinction of faith) than with those who are different and opposite to
us in all this. We agree with the Romans in the articles of the faith. For
we also believe in God, the One in the Trinity, the unbegotten Father, the
Son who was born of the Father before the ages, and—in time—from
the Virgin Mary, His Mother, and the Holy Spirit that proceeds from
the Father and the Son, and according to us through the Son (which is
the same thing). But various heretics believe and teach variously about
the Most Holy Trinity: either they make the Son unequal in divinity of
God to the Father, or they believe in an un-Catholic manner about the
incarnation, passion, resurrection, and His real presence in the sacrament
of the Eucharist, or still others do not believe that the Holy Spirit is true
God. So here already it is difficult for us to agree with the heretics. The
Romans confess seven sacraments in their Church. And we likewise
seven in our Church. But the heretics either two, one, three, or one [*sic*]
of them, and about these two or one they do not believe in a Catholic

---

510. [See above, p. 231.]
511. [This—as we will soon see—was the printer who is speaking here,
Archimandrite of the Dubno Monastery, Kasijan Sakovyč.]

manner. And so in this, as well, we have disagreement with them. The Romans accept the Church traditions or things handed down. And we hold them for holy in our Church. But the heretics call them inventions. The Romans honor *reliquiae,* that is, the bones of the saints; they have images in the Churches and venerate them; they summon the saints for help, they pray for the dead, they teach that eternal purity in monastic orders, and priests, and virgins, is pleasing to the Lord God; they teach and believe that fasting, *mortificatiae* [mortifications], that is various tormentings of the body, pilgrimages to holy places, and auricular confession of sins before the priest are very necessary for salvation. And we have all this in our Church and posit them as certain means that serve our salvation. But the heretics make merry over all these means that serve my salvation, they call them inventions and superstitions, and they even say that some of them are improper to be maintained, as, for example, chastity in consecrated people.

The Romans have matins, hours, masses, vespers, complines, masses for the dead in their Church. And we likewise have matins, hours, liturgies, vespers, *pawieczernice, panachidy* [complines, masses for the dead], etc. in our Church.[512] But if the heretics sing a few psalms and if they ever celebrate their Last Supper, they have nothing more. You will not even see a cross in their Church. They fear it like the devil. When a pious Roman comes to our Church, he will make veneration of the Most Holy Sacrament, kiss the cross, bow before the holy images, sprinkle himself with holy water. And a pious Ruthenian does the same when he enters a Catholic church. But when a heretic comes to an Orthodox church, instead of making any veneration to the Most Holy Sacrament or honoring the Lord's cross and bowing before the image of the Most Holy Mother of God and the images of other Saints, he will laugh at me, deride me, and will call me an artolater, a bread-worshipper, an idolater; he will sneer at all my ceremonies and Church rites; he will say that it is not necessary to light candles unto the Lord God, to burn incense for Him, etc. But the most high bishop of Rome in his writings praises all our ceremonies and rites, calling them holy and worthy of all honor. Consider here, pious reader of the Ruthenian religion, with whom it is fitting to join and unite, whether with the heretics, who are as different

512. [Sakovyč first lists the Roman Catholic services, using the standard Polish terms, and then terms used for the "equivalent" Orthodox/Uniate service.]

from us as heaven is wide and who blaspheme all that is ours, or with the Romans who believe and have in their Church one and the same thing with us. K.S.A.D.[513]

513. [I.e., Kasijan Sakovyč, archimandrite of Dubno.]

A Revocation

(1628)

I, MELETIJ SMOTRYC'KYJ, BY THE GRACE of God Archbishop of Polack, having been charged by our Ruthenian Church with the suspicion of apostasy from the Orthodox Greek faith of the Universal Eastern Church and subjected all the more so to the suspicion of the same apostasy through the appearance in print under my name of the book published under the title *Apology,* through this my announcement to my entire Ruthenian Church, through Your Graces present here at this time in the Holy Monastery of the Caves in this holy Church dedicated to the Dormition of the Most Pure Virgin, Mother of God, report the following: that I myself am partially subject to such a straying from Orthodox dogmas, but that I acknowledge that, to a greater extent, such a straying occurred through the wanton plan of that person to whom the *Apology* was entrusted for publication in print in the Polish language, and namely, through the evil plan of Kasijan Sakovyč, who is the superior in the Dubno Monastery of the Lord's Transfiguration. Having recognized and acknowledged that this incautious behavior—both as far as my own sin is concerned, and as far as the harmful entrusting [of the manuscript to Sakovyč] is concerned—is against the Orthodox dogmas of the Eastern Church, I voluntarily beg the Lord God to be merciful toward my sin, and I voluntarily promise my entire Ruthenian Church of that same merciful God that henceforth I will avoid this with all my heart, providing in this Holy Church knowledge of my desire through this sign that before the eyes of all Your Graces I dishonor, tear, and cast under my feet my work entitled *Apology,* under the oath that I made unto the Lord God at that time when, in the presence of My Most Blessed Lord[1] and the other hierarchs of our Ruthenian Church, I was elected and consecrated to the archpriesthood by the most holy patriarch of Jerusalem, the lord father Theophanes, under obedience to the most holy patriarch of Constantinople.

The 14th day of August of the year 1628.

1.　[I.e., Jov Borec'kyj.]

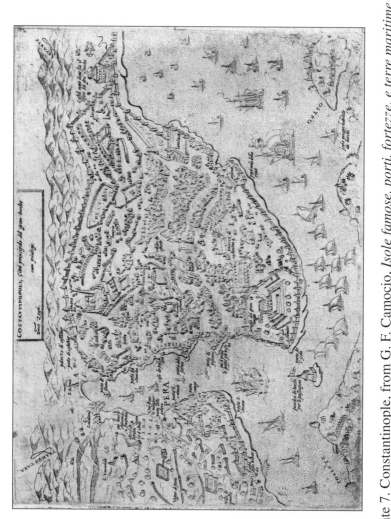

Plate 7. Constantinople, from G. F. Camocio, *Isole famose, porti, fortezze, e terre maritime* (Venice, 1572). Courtesy of Historic Cities Research Project, Hebrew University of Jerusalem, The Jewish National and University Library (historic-cities.huji.ac.il).

A Protestation

(1628)

Protestation
against the Council Held in This Year
1628, in the Days of the Month of August,
in Kyiv in the Monastery of the Caves,
Made by Him Who Was Wronged at It,

Meletij Smotryc'kyj,
Nuncupate Archbishop of Polack,
Bishop of Vicebsk and Mscislaŭ,
Archimandrite of Vilnius and Derman',
to the Most Noble Ruthenian Nation.

Rom. chap. 14, verse 4.
Tu quis es, qui judicas alienum servum? Domino suo stat, aut cadit: stabit autem: potens est enim DEUS statuere illum.
[Who art thou that judgest another man's servant? to his own master he standeth or falleth. Yea, he shall be holden up: for God is able to make him stand.]

Matth. chap. 26[:75]
Et egressus foras, flevit amare.
[And he went out, and wept bitterly.]

Meae vitae unica et sola spes, JESUS CHRISTUS[1]
[My life's one and only hope, JESUS CHRIST];

Cum Licentia Superiorum
[With the Permission of the Superiors].

In Lviv, in the Printing House of Jan Szeliga, Typographer to His Grace, the Prince Archbishop of Lviv, in the Year of Our Lord 1628.

---

1.   [See above, p. 231.]

Meletij Smotryc'kyj,
Nuncupatus [Called] Archbishop of Polack,
Bishop of Vicebsk and Mscislaŭ,
Archimandrite of Vilnius and Derman',
Desires and Wishes
for the Most Noble Ruthenian Nation
of the Eastern Obedience

of Both Estates

Grace, Peace, and Love from the Lord God.

H AVE YOU HEARD, MOST NOBLE Ruthenian nation, that a Church
council was held in Kyiv in this present year of 1628 in the
days of the month of August? Have you also heard—and I
am certain you did—of the anathematizing carried out at it by your
hierarchs in the Church of the Caves? It could not be otherwise. For
a disorderly thing, or that I speak more properly, an impious thing, is
notorious. It is disorderly in that, what two presbyters plotted in their
heads, four bishops brought to execution. And it is impious in that,
through the execution of the thing they plotted, the Catholic Orthodox
confession is cast under foot, and heretical errors and heresies are raised
to the pulpit. And how this happened, just listen: I will relate this to you
in brief.

Last year, in 1627, a council was ordered for us, the bishops, in
Kyiv at the Feast of the Nativity of the Most Holy Virgin.[2] And when
I appeared there through the obligation of my dignity, I was asked
and solicited by those upon whom it was chiefly incumbent there, and
especially by His Grace, Father Jov Borec'kyj (other bishops did not
come to that synod) and by His Grace the present father archimandrite
of the Caves, at that time still a layman,[3] to submit my catechism, with
which I had traveled to the Eastern lands for censure and correction
(since I did not acquire that there), to the censure of the churchmen of our

2.   [Celebrated by both Churches on 8 September, but since this was an old
calendar date it would have been 18 September 1627, n.s.]
3.   [I.e., Peter Mohyla.]

Ruthenian nation so that it might thereby be submitted in print without delay for the use of the Ruthenian Church. Whereupon I answered Their Graces that I was ready to do this thing, but that I ask only that, before I submit it to consideration and censure, I might be allowed to publish *Consideratiae* ["Considerations"] of the six differences that have been introduced between the Eastern and the Western Churches so that this censure might be carried out all the more easily and fortunately. For which I easily received permission from Their Graces and from others present at that time.

With this permission I awaited the appropriate time until, about half a year later, in the sixth week of Lent,[4] both the above-mentioned persons, Father Borec'kyj and the father archimandrite, now in the spiritual estate, having with them two bishops, Father Isakij[5] and Father Pajisij,[6] came here to Volhynia, to Horodok, a holding of the Monastery of the Caves, to which, at their command, I too arrived. Having discussed the spiritual matters of the Church there, we saw a great need for a local council of the entire Ruthenian Church, of both the spiritual and the lay estate, of the noble and the burgher vocation. Father Borec'kyj was to send out private letters for its convocation, and they charged me with writing something whereby everyone could easily be drawn to appear at this conference, which was of most urgent need. And for this end above all: that we might consider and see among ourselves at this council, in love and peace, whether any means might be discovered for uniting Rus' with Rus', that is the non-Uniates with the Uniates, without the infringement of the rights and privileges of our faith. For which reason I was permitted there at the same time by all the four above-mentioned persons to write, in addition to the announcement of the reason for the council, the above-mentioned *Consideratiae* ["Considerations"] of the differences that occur between the Eastern and the Western Churches as well (which we considered among ourselves there and judged to be not great differences), and to publish both of them together. And having determined thus among ourselves, we dispersed in love.

Having wrested some time from my domestic monastery occupa-

---

4. [Orthodox Palm Sunday was 6/16 April 1628.]
5. [I.e., Boryskovyč, bishop of Luc'k and Ostroh.]
6. [I.e., Ippolytovyč, bishop of Chełm and Belz.]

tions right after Easter,[7] I set to work with God's help upon the labor entrusted to me, and around Pentecost,[8] by the grace of the same Lord God, I finished it, and I entitled it *Apologia*. And after immediately ordering that a fair copy be made, I sent it to Kyiv as soon as we had begun the Apostolic fast, having also written to Father Borec'kyj in the following words:

Copy of the Letter to Father Borec'kyj:

What Your Reverence and other brethren deigned to command me to write for the awakening of our nation slumbering in unwatchfulness I send to Your Reverence in manuscript, since I have not been able to obtain a printing house here. And I am certain that in about three weeks it can be printed on two presses and released to the nation so that each of us, before the coming (may God grant it) council, might be able to see clearly with what we as an entire nation are afflicted, and how we can be cured of this illness.

Do not judge this call to wakening, My Most Reverend Lord, according to man's judgment, but judge it with that of God. For woe unto them that call evil good and good evil.[9] Our severe illness—and now nearly mortal—requires diligent care from us the doctors, for souls are at stake, the loss of which will be sought by God the Judge upon our episcopal souls.[10] A more bitter medicine would indeed have been appropriate for such an illness, which, causing our wound to itch, would have brought us to our senses and would have caused us to recognize the fact that we are ill. For the most difficult illness to cure is that which the ill person does not acknowledge he has and in which he does not allow the doctor to come near him.

Let us at least, the doctors, recognize this illness, and let us seek to move and destroy from its very foundations this soul-destroying plague, even if the sick should not wish this. A harmful ulcer is sometimes cut out, sometimes burned out, and the patient must suffer this. And if anyone does not wish to suffer this, but rather prefers to die from this

7.   [13/23 April 1628.]
8.   [1/11 June 1628.]
9.   [Is. 5:20.]
10.   [Ez. 3:18, 20; 33:6, 8; 34:10.]

ulcer, he is bound by those who care for him, and against his will he is briefly afflicted so that through a short suffering, now cured for the rest of his life, he might not suffer that pain any more.

If anything should seem wrong in such a description of our illness and its medicine, I take that upon myself and upon my soul. And before Your Reverence through this letter of mine, with God the Seer of Hearts[11] as my witness, I wash my hands of this, and I declare myself pure of the further destruction of ignorant souls of our nation, which, through this very ignorance of its evil, come to destruction. "Woe unto you, lawyers," says our Lord Jesus Christ, "for ye have taken away the key of knowledge: ye entered not in yourselves, and them that were entering in ye hindered."[12]

Having said briefly to Your Reverence what befitted me, I desire, and I ask my Lord God that He Himself might deign to prepare the future council that has been appointed by Your Reverence, to the honor and glory of His holy name and to the peace that the only-begotten Son of God gave to us in His disciples and to cause and grant our entire Ruthenian nation one mouth and one heart unto His praise. And herewith I submit myself to Y[our] R[everence].

And to His Grace the Father Archimandrite I Wrote in These Words:

Copy of the Letter to His Grace, the Father Archimandrite of the C[aves]:

Having finished, by the grace of God, the work entrusted to me by my Most Reverend Lord and by other of our reverends, I now send it to you. In which I worked as the time itself required of me during our manifest fall and as the very necessity of our salvation required of me. For I am certain of every soul that loves God, its neighbor, and its own salvation that, having had pity upon our so manifest fall, it will desire to see this sickness, without any regard for the person, and will take care for finding a medicine for its prevention with all its soul.

11. [1 Sam. 16:7; Jer. 11:20; Ps. 17:3, 26:2.]
12. [Lk. 11:52.]

Our Lord God deigned to place Your Reverence, who is high born, having endowed you with high understanding, preparing you for higher things, upon a high place in our Ruthenian nation so that Your Reverence might see further from on high than someone who sits lower and might be watchful, take care, have industry, and take counsel for the good not of one part of it, but of the entire Ruthenian nation. Wherefore, Your Reverence, for your part, has done in this matter what your very conscience—which you bear pure in your pure soul through the love of your God—counsels and allows Your Reverence: even if our eyes, which are afflicted in their sight by the antiquity of the disease, should show something else to Your Reverence and tempt you to refrain from moving to save yourself—oppose them and hold back those who would arise as enemies against God and against His truth.

If there is anything in my work that is not genuine, according to my conscience, let it be turned upon my head, under a merciful God. But if everything is true, deign to be its representative and defender, my Most Reverend Lord. If our nation, which is so severely ill, is not cleansed by such a knife of the ulcers that have settled upon its body, it will never come to its senses, but day by day, ruined as if by the infernal fire, it diminishes, and it will be eradicated, overturned in its perversity. For carrying itself about entirely overcome with internal ulcers (the heretical plague of our new theologians) and not only not seeing our profanity, but blindly delighting in it as if in some thing of beauty, it will sooner come to the final inexorable fall, one by one, than it will notice its destruction. Having entrusted all of which to the wise discrimination of Your Reverence's high intellect, I commend myself and my humility to Y[our] R[everence].

In response to these letters, Their Graces wrote back through my messenger that as soon as they had read my work they would inform me of their opinion about it "sufficiently" and "fully" (these are their words). After waiting for Their Graces' opinion about three weeks and not being able to receive it, believing that it pleased Their Graces— as in conversing with me frequently about this, they had seemed to have a good opinion about it—I sent it off to be printed in the Polish language.

I have presented all this, most noble Ruthenian nation, so that you might know the reason why my *Apology* saw the light of day. And when the time for that council had come, I went to it, being persuaded that it was to be held for precisely the goal we had discussed in Horodok, not even having considered the possibility of a change in these persons with regard to this pious undertaking. But when, on the 13th day of August toward noon, I had ventured directly to the Monastery of the Caves, and I sent my servant to His Grace the father archimandrite, who had invited me *solenniter* [solemnly] through his letter to the Feast of the Dormition of the Most Holy Virgin[13] together with his brethren, I was not allowed to go there; I was directed to the Michael Monastery.

Being of the opinion that His Grace the Father Archimandrite was avoiding my presence on account of the suspicion of the people (for this often came up in our discussions), but for the greater part believing that he was wary of doing this in order not to subject himself to the bad graces of His Majesty the King by associating with us (since his predecessor as archimandrite of the Monastery of the Caves had done this before him),[14] I did not even think of any change of his intent in the matter we had discussed. And I went to the Michael Monastery, where I was received in the church by the deputy and the brethren as an archiereus. Then, about a half an hour later, four presbyters sent from the council that was taking place in the Monastery of the Caves came to me. These greeted me not as an archiereus, for they did not kiss my hand.

One of them, the father protopope of Sluck,[15] spoke to me, and the end of all of his words was the following: "The council asks you through us whether you stand by the *Apology* you have published, or not." After my other words, I answered: "But I am just going to the council, and there I will give account in person of myself and of my *Apology*." He says: "You must first answer here before us the question we ask, and then you will be allowed to go to the council, or not." I answered that "I

13. [15 August. The date given above—13 August—was thus certainly an old calendar date; this would have been 23 August, n.s.]
14. [I.e., Zaxarija Kopystens′kyj.]
15. [I.e., Andrij Mužylovs′kyj.]

stand by it as an Orthodox work, since there is nothing in it that is wicked or against the Holy Catholic faith." He says: "The council has judged it from head to foot, from the first page to the last, to be entirely against the doctrine of the Church of God and the Orthodox faith, impure, and wicked." I answered: "May the Lord God forgive you that you speak whatever comes to your mind. Let the council not forbid me to stand before it, and I will, with God's help, defend it [i.e., the *Apology*] from this slander and evil allegation." He says: "So you wish to engage in disputations." I answered: "I do not wish to engage in disputations, but to defend my Orthodox work, which has either been incorrectly understood or calumniated, against this erroneous suspicion." He says: "The council does not need your defenses, for it has already informed itself in this matter well; but it asks you for a response in the matter that we have already presented." I answered: "I give the following response: that I stand absolutely by my work, as far as the dogmas of the faith I have described in it are concerned. And if the fathers took offense to anything in the description of certain defects of the Eastern Church, then we can discuss and avert that." He answers: "But it is already in print." I said: "What of it? This can easily be averted." And therewith, after many other speeches from both sides, they began to speak more gently, showing me what will follow from this: that "in the cities, and especially in Vilnius, there will be oppression from the other side, for they will point to this book written by you, an archbishop of our side, in which the Union is praised." And with these gentle speeches they departed from me with my response that I stand, with God's help, by my Orthodox work.

But then, toward evening, perhaps through persons subordinate to them, they released among my retinue threats, invectives, pointing their fingers at them and calling them Uniates such that they feared to set foot outside the monastery, and they reported to me what was going on around them. Having entrusted myself to the Lord God, I passed the night. On the next day, first thing in the morning, I send to Father Borec'kyj his brother, deacon Porfirij, asking him the reason for the insult I am receiving from them, and I send to him the following letter:

Copy of the Letter to Father Borec'kyj
at the Council:

In the absence of the host, his bread has not taste. If it is by chance that I am deprived of Your Reverence's presence, it is a tolerable thing; if it occurs by design, it is certainly a thing full of disdain. At Your Reverence's command I set off and came to Your Reverence, as to my Father, for common counsel about the good of the Church, so that I might discuss in common with the others who are concerned with this matter, not wishing to dispute in this matter through third persons, but face to face. If such were to be the unfatherly intentions of Your Reverence toward me, I judge it a more tolerable thing to return whence I came than not to attain that for which I came here. My conscience is a pure witness that I did not give Your Reverence any cause for this dishonor toward me. Whether it is because I brought to the attention of our Ruthenian Church the errors and heresies of our writers who strayed from the truth, warning it so that it never trip upon that rock of offense,[16] or perhaps because I show the means for uniting the brethren with the brethren angered against them—I do not know. I do not find a third reason in my work, which, by the grace of Christ the Lord, is free from errors and heresies.

And if I am in any way *excessivus* [excessive], then we should seek a remedy for that not in anger or in hatred, but in the love that builds and perfects every good thing. For in this manner illnesses are not cured, rather they are irritated and lead health to mortal injury. There must be a lawful reason and the appropriate judge for every decree. For without these two things, the defendant and the judged will have a proper excuse. I ask Your Reverence, therefore, that I not be so injured by Your Reverence that later no remedy for that injury could be found.

Having written such a letter to Father Borec'kyj, I sent it on 14 *Augusti* [of August] in the morning through the above-mentioned deacon. After sending it, my retinue brought me various pieces of news that had

16.   [1 Pet. 2:8; Rom. 9:33.]

been disseminated among them, among other things: "On the morrow both your master, and you with him, will be condemned as Uniates, and more than one of you will drink of the Slavuta."[17] And just at the dinner hour, having joined with the father protopope of Dubno,[18] who traveled there with me, and with my deacon Isaja, in addition to several other clergymen, Father Borec'kyj's brother Andrij said to them: "For God's sake, let His Grace, Father Archbishop, take care for himself; for coming now from the monastery village, I encountered a sizable group of Cossacks, who in their counsel, not being cautious before me since I am well known to them, swore not to spare his [Smotryc'kyj's] life if there be anything concerning the Union proved against him by the council." Having heard this reported by my above-mentioned deacon, I summoned the father protopope of Dubno, and after asking him whether he had already heard of this, he answered, "I heard it from the mouth of that very speaker, under his oath." I said: "I have come, as I see, upon anarchy. For in this fashion my fathers and brethren will easily have the better of me in disputation through these people. What should I do in this matter? I would avoid them as people who are unwise and not a party to this matter. But I do not know how and where. I would go to the Castle, but the Lord Vice Palatine is not there. I would return home, but I fear an ambush, for they are already announcing it. I would go to the town, to the monastery, but I would envenom them even more, for already before my arrival they announced I was there. One must also fear that they would not admit me, for there are already everywhere many frivolous people, drunken as if at a fair."

Conversing with myself thus after that piece of news, I said, "I wonder that I have not had any answer to my letter for so long, and it is already toward noon." And having taken up paper, I write again to Father Borec'kyj in the following words:

The Second Letter to Father Borec'kyj
at the Council

I expected a normal conversation in your presence, face to face, with Your Reverence and with other honorable brethren in Christ in these

17.   [I.e., the Dnieper.]
18.   [I.e., Feodor Leontievyč.]

Church matters, and not through third persons, for which very reason I came to this land at the time appointed by Your Reverence, not thinking in the least to establish something of my own in the Church, to say nothing of *against* the Church. For I never desired, nor do I desire, to die in any other but the Church of Christ the Lord in which I was born. And I am certain, with the grace of my God, that I will be wrapped in the shrouds of the grave by the Holy Eastern Church, which gave birth to me by the water and the spirit.[19] Wherefore I ask in filial fashion that I not suffer a harsher fatherly disdain than is my fault either from Your Reverence or from the other reverend fathers and brethren in God. For that will not be to cure the ulcer, if there is one, but to irritate and envenom it. What has already come into being in print cannot be undone; but it is still possible to prevent it from being dispersed throughout this entire realm through our mutual discussion and counsel in this matter: not spreading the things here, to prevent them there whence they can become more widely spread.

Wherefore, admonished by the messengers sent to me by Your Reverence and by the other fathers and brothers, and wishing to prevent all that would be a disturbance unto the Church, I ask Your Reverence and all those who are at Your Reverence's side, My Honorable Lords, brethren in Christ, that I be allowed to the mutual counsel of Your Reverence, and having discussed the means of prevention, that I do this today, not putting off for a later time, on account of the distance of the place in which it is being printed, what ought to be done by me according to the common finding of all those who belong to this counsel, without any disputatious competitions for the present. For if you were to flee from me and to abandon me in this matter, and if you should not wish to allow me to your counsel, I will judge myself the one fled from and abandoned and not the one who flees and abandons; and that would be the sort of injury from Your Reverence that could barely be completely healed later in my injured heart. But it is the work of Your Reverence's vocation to take the injured upon your beast and not to overlook and avoid.[20]

19.   [Jn. 3:5.]
20.   [Lk. 10:30–7.]

I wrote this letter drenched with tears, asking that they admit me to their common counsel. For that was the very reason I had worked on my writing, that was the very reason I went there: so that I might discuss with them the things described in it. Moreover, I was certain with regard to many of the brethren that as soon as I had weakened and removed some tens of the points noted by them in my *Apology*, of which they had one hundred and five in all, they would listen to me more eagerly about everything. After the presentation of which, I trust in my God and in His holy truth that all the evil counsels of the clever Ahithophel,[21] who had already allowed me to catch sight of him, would be turned upon his own pate.[22] But he, along with those who, together with him, had made false allegations concerning my *Apology*, took care as for their health and life that I not be there and that I not be admitted to their common counsel before the execution of the decree discussed by them. Which they managed to do. And when some of them counseled on the basis of my letters that I be admitted and that I give account of myself and that they speak with me about my work as an entire council, Father Borec'kyj (as I have come to know) spoke up in response: "Niechaj z nim Dytko mowit" [Ruthenian: "Let the devil speak with him"]. That is a fine father for you: both succinct and not to the point. But since I was not admitted to speak about this at the proper time, I did not wish to mention it later.

After sending off my letter through my deacon, already around noon, there comes to me a Kyivan Cossack by the name of Solenyk, who, after greeting me, gave me a long lecture, Cossack fashion, as he saw fit, and he concluded it with this: "We acquired this Church by our blood, and we also wish to seal it with our blood, or with that of those who would in any way dishonor it or abandon it." I thought that if the discussion with the clergymen of the preceding day was bad, with him it would be much worse. I did not enter into a long talk with him. He tarried with me, together with another Cossack, about an hour. Just a

---

21.   [2 Sam. 15, 16, and 17 tell of Absalom's conspiracy against David and the help he received from David's former friend Ahithophel. Cf., perhaps, Ps. 54:13–15. It is not entirely clear to me whom Smotryc'kyj meant here— protopopes Zizanij and Mužylovs'kyj, his main opponent among the bishops Kopyns'kyj, or his "collaborators" Mohyla and Borec'kyj.]
22.   [Ps. 7:16.]

little while after his departure, they inform me that Father Borec'kyj had arrived with three bishops and had gone to the church. I too went there, and we greeted each other not fraternally, but as if we were little acquainted.

When all who were in the church were commanded to leave, those two Cossacks who had been at my quarters remained. I asked that they too not be present at our conversation. Having approached them, Father Borec'kyj asked them to do this, and only after a long exchange were they convinced to leave. But upon leaving the church, Solenyk said to me the following words: "Nu bies u waszej matery, machlujte machlujte: dostanet sja tut y Pawłu y Gawłu" [Ruthenian: "The devil take your mother. Just try to cheat us, just try. Both Peter and Paul will get what's coming to them here"]. And then he held forth before the people about some Rail,[23] making known through his account that I was in a trap. And these words were heard and later reported to me by the father protopope of Dubno and others, among many other people, of whom there were very many before the church.

After their withdrawal, after sitting down to conversation, Father Borec'kyj began with a prayer; and then having turned the conversation to me, after an introduction he says to me simply in the following words: "An unclean, haughty spirit spoke through you, Father Archbishop, in the *Apology* that you have published, which is made manifest by the fact that at the very beginning of your writing you boast that in the holy places of Palestine you asked the Lord God for Union for your Ruthenian nation and that for that purpose you brought bloodless offerings in those holy places. You say that throughout all the past time of your life you did not know what you believed." And citing other of the things described in my *Apology,* he elaborated upon them for a long time, which I, yielding to brevity, omit as little necessary. And after everything *pro colophone* [as a conclusion] he concluded that "through your wicked *Apology* you introduce into our Ruthenian Church accursed papal heresies" (I speak in his own words): "Manichaean, Sabellian, Apollinarian, and others." And with this he finished his speech.

23.   [The word *Chruściel* ("rail") is capitalized here in the original, but in Smotryc'kyj's usage this does not necessarily indicate it was a proper name. It could be just the bird (rail), or someone named Chruściel (Rail). In any event, the point seems to be about a bird caught in a trap.]

Hearing this, I nearly grew numb at the newness of the incautious words of this man, who, through the four years of my living with him (I say this about him with God as my witness), criticized the Roman Church, about which we often had conversations among ourselves, in very little; and he found no heretical offense in its faith, and he always spoke well of concord between it and Rus', and he indicated that the method for holy unity was very easy, if only the matter of the calendar could be moderated, which was a stumbling block for the simple people of our nation. Wherefore in the year 1625 he worked on this moderation of the calendar, and he said that he had found an easy method for it, and he presented it on occasions before many people of his side.

Thus having heard at this time the great, unexpected change of this man in his former pious intention, I would have said something else, but I saw from his fervent affections that these words would have been in vain and would have caused worse irritation. I said in amazement: "My most honored fathers and most beloved brethren in Christ the Lord: being, by the grace of God, a son of the Holy Eastern Church and desiring to be throughout all my life, according to the ability of my years, in this its work, through which the elders before me, its sons and our brethren, whom we call our holy fathers on account of the gravity of their merits, served it and are honored in it with eternal memory for that fact, I did not abhor anything more with all my soul than pride, and I did not avoid anything more diligently than haughtiness, which Your Reverence deigns to ascribe to me for this reason: that I asked my Lord God for that salvatory One[24] for the Ruthenian nation in those holy places in which He himself deigned to give that One to His disciples and commanded us to have it for the sake of our salvation. I certainly consider this a great act of humility before my Lord God, since in this I imitated the humble Lord Christ. As I did not have pride in my heart when I did this, neither did I write anything in a haughty spirit in my work. Likewise, as I do not find those heresies mentioned by Your Reverence in the Roman Church, neither do I introduce them into our Ruthenian Church through my writing. And as to what I said—that I did not know throughout those years what I believed—I spoke the truth. Witness to this are my works—*Lament, Elenchus,* and others—in which I wrote what I believed; but I wrote heretically in them, and thus

---

24.   [Jn. 17:22.]

I also believed heretically. Wherefore, I also believed incorrectly, and I supposed that my bad faith was the Orthodox faith of the Holy Eastern Church, and I did not know the truth." And I spoke on this matter and in response to other of his words more broadly.

And at this point they make known that they had brought a deceased man for his funeral, and they bring him into the church. Wherefore we withdrew from the church to his [Borec'kyj's] cell, and there, continuing my speech, I said: "Since my work so displeases you, my fathers, I would like to know from Your Reverences *specifice* [specifically] what you found that was so impious in it that you attack it and—in addition to it—me so forcefully." And just then, having several sheets of my work in his hands that he had acquired from the printing house, the father protopope of Sluck[25] (for he was also with them) began to turn pages in it and to read these titles from it—"On Particular Judgment," "On the Blessing of the Righteous Souls That Have Departed This World," "That *Infernus* Is Hell," "That Sinful People and Devils Are Already Tormented," "That Christ Is Priest for All Times," "That Unleavened Bread Is Called Bread," and after each of these he interjects, "Ho ho." Then, after having turned several sheets, he reads: "That St. Peter was Established the Universal Pastor by Christ the Lord," "That Christ the Lord Built His Church on St. Peter," "That Christ the Lord Entrusted the Sheep of the Entire World to St. Peter for Feeding," "That Both by God's Law and by Church Law Appeal Belongs to the Bishop of Rome," "That the Power of Convening Universal Councils Belongs to the Bishop of Rome." And having closed the book at this point, he says: "Are these small contradictions of our Church and blasphemies against our faith?"

Hearing this and being sick at heart over the intentional stubborn blindness of this man (for it is not possible that he should not see that manifest and clear truth), I said to him: "Read, brother, what is found under these titles, and you will see that all of these are the salvatory dogmas of the Holy Eastern Church and not blasphemies. And I speak because my cause is already going so badly with you that even my truth is not the truth for you, and the proper Orthodox articles of faith of the Holy Eastern Church are judged by you as contrary to it and blasphemies. Please let me speak about this with you either here privately or *publice*

25.   [I.e., Andrij Mužylovs'kyj.]

[publicly] at the council, for this, to put it simply, is not a thing which we could piously allow to pass us by without discussion lest some scruple remain either in my conscience or yours which would later on eat at us, that this divine truth was dishonored and suppressed by you without any examination."

But then that protopope takes from his breast a sheet of paper, and says to me: "The council speaks with you here and now, both privately and *publice* [publicly]; it does not wish or intend to speak any more. If you wish to be a part of the council and to be recognized as one of ours, you must first fulfill these three conditions discussed at the council. First: swear that from this time forth you will not disturb the Ruthenian Church either in speech or in writing, and you will not abandon it. Second: you must revoke your work *Apology publice* [publicly] and read from the pulpit what will be submitted to you by us for its condemnation and for the confession of your sin. Third: you must not return any more to Derman', but remain here in Kyiv."

I responded to this: "That is a greater penance from you, brethren, than my sin toward you." All shout at once: "You offended the entire Church greatly, before all of which you must also confess your grievous sin." I say to them: "My concern with you, fathers, is not to negotiate some conditions with you, but that my cause be heard at the council by you and by all the others and that I be present when judged of my cause. For there, God willing, it will be made manifestly clear whether I offended the Ruthenian Church with my work or you offend it, who, in my opinion, improperly oppose it."

While I was arguing with them about this, His Grace Lord Lityns'kyj, and soon after him His Grace Lord Ivan Stetkevyč, come up, and after a little while the Cossack scribe—for they had been prepared for me, as one could see, in a plan they had discussed. I received from each of them a separate sermon. And although I saw that I ought to have taught them, and not they me, but being aware that already in this Church, as a punishment from God, the clergy had for a long time now been following the will and opinion of lay people and that not the clergy, but lay people, rule in spiritual matters, clergy only *pro forma,* I did not become involved vainly in the tournament of long words with them. Rather I told them not to place these unnecessary conditions upon me and not to submit me, in spite of my transgression, to the disgust of the Ruthenian nation, giving them the method for preventing this matter that I had described in my second letter to Father Borec'kyj, if an *excessus* [excess] had occurred in anything: that I would send in this regard to Lviv and write to Father Kasijan,[26] asking that no copy be given anyone from the printing house. And I know for certain that he will do this once he will have considered the reasons that I would write for him. And meanwhile, we will consider my work here among ourselves *articulatim* [article by article], and wherever we find anything wrong, we will remove it.

But my speech to them was a *surdis* (as they say) *fabula* [a story for the deaf].[27] For insisting upon their intention, listening little to my speech (it had already grown a little late), and after standing up, they left. Having been disturbed by these people's mercilessness—that they improperly denied me a proper thing and did not allow me to be at the council before the execution of the decree that had been discussed by them against me—I was worried that I had unexpectedly fallen into such a situation where I was not allowed (as they say) either to go forward or to go backward.

And then, about an hour later, now at dusk, they sent to me the written instrument of revocation, [asking] whether I would wish to abide by it and to join them. Not wishing, for many important reasons (which I do not express for now),[28] to remain that night in the Michael Monastery and wishing through my presence among them to soothe their hearts, which were irritated toward me, I gave to their messenger the sheet they had sent me, roughly stripped of many of the harsher improprieties, but still bad, and copied but not signed; and I myself rode after him to the Monastery of the Caves for vespers, thinking that there, in a group, and especially since it would be in the church, in a peaceful place, I would beseech them to leave off their childish game with me.

But, as they say, *Aethiopem dealbare difficile* [it is difficult to whiten an Ethiopian]; it is difficult to plow with a wolf.[29] When I was

26.   [I.e., Sakovyč.]
27.   [Erasmus *Ad.* 1.4.87; Arthaber 1111.]
28.   [And did not express later.]
29.   [Here, Smotryc'kyj "translates" a proverb by providing two equivalent versions—Latin and Polish. For the Latin proverb, see Arthaber 122; cf. Erasmus *Ad.* 2.6.28. For Smotryc'kyj's Polish "translation," see *NKPP* 3:697, "Wilk," 96.]

already in the church and in the sanctuary, they sent to me that I sign the sheet, and that I also swear by my conscience that I would no longer go from Kyiv to Derman'. I asked them to stop playing these games with me and said that I could not agree to the signature and their conditions in good conscience. Then immediately, right there in the sanctuary, the father archimandrite of the Monastery of the Caves attacked me harshly with dishonorable words (who not long before had believed and spoken well and piously about the matter that I described in my *Apology* and praised the letter that I had written last year to His Grace the father patriarch of Constantinople,[30] in which is expressed *summatim* [in summary fashion] all that is described in the *Apology,* and then some, for I had read it before him at Derman'; and at our conference in Horodok, when we talked about the six differences between us and the Romans, he mentioned it and praised it before the spiritual authorities who were there); that man, I say, of such good belief about this matter, attacked me venomously with the words that are wont to be used against honorable people somewhere else, but not in the sanctuary, and by the average person at that.

Whereupon there arose such a noise that both those in the sanctuary and those who were rather close to the sanctuary moved as if at some violent act. There went throughout the entire church such a murmur that only those rather near the sanctuary were able to move and to help the clergy along in the tragedy that was occurring around me. Seeing this, some of those who somewhat favored me advised me to agree to this for the time being and thereby to mitigate the tumult before a greater one arose. And seeing that this matter was heading toward an inevitable evil, I signed that sheet according to their will and against my will so that it not come to a greater uproar and to the pouring of guilty and innocent blood (as often occurs in such matters, and especially at night) in the most noble Church of the Caves; and I swore not to go to Derman'. And thus that commotion and murmur quieted down.

And so that I might soothe the hearts of the simple people, embittered against me by the early morning action of the clergy against me, and their own hearts as well, I went with them to the procession and then, not expecting anything more than what had already occurred, to

---

30. [Appended in Polish translation to Smotryc'kyj's *Paraenesis* of 1629. See below, pp. 664–83.]

the liturgy as well. But then, after the reading of the Gospel, beyond my expectation, my Vilnius deputy[31] was sent to the pulpit. And the clergy also went from the sanctuary to the pulpit. The father archimandrite of the Monastery of the Caves distributed to each of the bishops sheets of paper and candles.

Thereupon he who was at the cathedra read the sheet, and then he tore up the sheet from my *Apology* that had been given to him, and he cast it down. Then Father Borec̆kyj, with whom there stood at the pulpit the one who is called of Luc̆k,[32] cast anathema upon the *Apology*, against law and judgment, tore up the sheet, and put out the candle; and along with it, upon Father Kasijan as well, archimandrite of Dubno, a man unsuspect in the Orthodox faith and never convicted or charged with any heresy by even one spiritual law. Following him all the bishops did the same thing.

And thus ended this *intermedium* [sideshow] of a Holy Liturgy, worthy not of laughter but of tears, for it removed the Orthodox faith from the Ruthenian Church of that side, and it clothed it in heretical errors and blasphemies. For it had its beginning in the fact that those to whom my *Apology* had been sent by me for reading and consideration, with the addition of Father Zizanij of Korec and Father Mužylovs̆kyj of Sluck, the main enemies of holy unity (and judging by the heretical judgment they handed out about my *Apology,* one can properly say— great blasphemers against the Orthodox Catholic dogmas of the faith), had treated and discussed this matter with them for four weeks and established what to do with me and my work. And then at one o'clock, on the eve of the Feast of the Dormition of the Most Holy Virgin, they presented this matter in one hundred and five points to three bishops who had been summoned there about this to the Monastery of the Caves. And one of them submitted the opinion of all the bishops, according to his own opinion. And the second, the opinion of all the presbyters, calling to them: "Is it not so, holy fathers; is it not so, *hospodynowie* [Ruthenian: lords]?" But the holy *hospodynowie* did not themselves know to what they were answering: "YES." All this was done by those two to this end: that I be degraded from my dignity. The bishops themselves had not read my *Apology,* nor had they heard it read, not to mention the

31. [Josyf Bobrykovyč.]
32. [I.e., Bishop Isakij Boryskovyč.]

fact that they had not considered the things described in it, and they did not know what was contained in it (for Father Pajisij[33] had come to Kyiv on Tuesday, a day ahead of me; Father Isakij[34] on Wednesday, the same day as I). Father Isaija[35] was not present at the discussion among them. Father Avramij[36] arrived several days in advance, but he too knew as much about this as the others. And yet the council had already announced, through its messengers to me on Wednesday, that it had judged my *Apology* from head to foot as impure.

I say, then, that the bishops had not read my *Apology* and considered the things described in it, for they had not had time for it; rather they were content with the points that were written out in advance from the *Apology* by one of those two, read and interpreted as he believed and wished, *sinistre* [perversely], in the fashion of the Protestant ministers, and they declared that this was sufficient. Wherefore, as the *interpres* [interpreter] wrenched the sense, and as those above-mentioned four persons had agreed among themselves, that impious decree came into being. But it was executed upon a different person,[37] as I said, and upon my *Apology*. By carrying out this execution, the falsehoods, blasphemies, errors, and heresies of these new writers Zizanij, Philalethes, Orthologue, Clerk, and the like, which were noted, enumerated, and expressed in my *Apology,* were acknowledged as the proper articles, rooted in the faith of the Ruthenian Church of that side; and those of Gerganoses, as those of the Greek Church. And those Catholic dogmas of the Orthodox faith, by which the blasphemies, errors, heresies, and falsehoods of these authors are destroyed, are uprooted from it and rejected.

And this happened above all, as one can see, through God's punishment for the disorderly action, unfitting in the Church of God, on the part of those who were holding the council there. For it is unheard of in the Church of Christ the Lord that at an episcopal council presbyters should consider matters of faith against the bishops, judge it [the faith], and establish decrees concerning it, and that the bishops should bring to execution the decrees established by them. This is certainly disorderly

33.   [I.e., Ippolytovyč, bishop of Chełm and Belz.]
34.   [I.e., Boryskovyč, bishop of Luc'k and Ostroh.]
35.   [I.e., Kopyns'kyj, archbishop of Smolensk and Černihiv.]
36.   [I.e., Stahons'kyj, bishop of Pinsk and Turov.]
37.   [I.e., Kasijan Sakovyč.]

order and unruly rule. The canons of the local and universal councils as well as the apostolic canons teach that judgment concerning the dogmas of the faith belongs to the bishops and not to the presbyters. But with them it went in the opposite fashion during that above-mentioned recent council: presbyters, and only two or three of them at that, judged and decreed concerning the dogmas of the faith, and they submitted their decrees to the bishops for execution. And they carried them out, without the examination that properly belongs to them, not only incautiously, but also impiously. Wherefore, as the priests did not know to what they, following Zizanij, were crying YES, so also the bishops did not know to what they, following Father Borecʹkyj, were saying anathema. I can safely say that even to this day none of them knows this.

And if anyone had asked these bishops and priests after their council why Father Smotrycʹkyj's *Apology* had been condemned, I say justly that not one of them would be able to give account of this, for none of them read it. Rare was the one who heard it read, and that only in those brief points. And in good conscience none could answer in any other fashion but that Father Zizanij and Father Mužylovsʹkyj gave such an account concerning it, saying that it is heretical, unclean, and impious. And it happened there that Zizanij after Zizanij, as if gypsy after gypsy, testified and judged. Thus is it wont to happen where the eyes, as they say, go higher than the forehead, where the laymen rule the priests, and the priests the bishops. One heard and saw this with regret at this council, where the priests held sway and disdained the bishops.

I speak of others, not of myself. About myself I say that I was not summoned to any consultation, whatever causes and signatures there were; I believe the same concerning the other bishops. But what the priests somewhere plotted they gave to us the bishops to be signed, and we signed it, whether it was cabala or Mussulman. Which is made clear from the very fact that, against the manifest and clear laws of the Eastern Church, unto the dishonor of the episcopal dignity and the derogation of their jurisdiction, we signed the right of appeal to the archimandrite of the Monastery of the Caves for all the superiors and brethren from all the monasteries of the entire Ruthenian land and with the archimandrite of the Monastery of the Caves to law beyond the sea.[38] It even came to the affront that when the shouting match started, the priests honored

38. [To the patriarch of Constantinople?]

the bishops with the name with which they commonly honor those who chew on bones under the table—and that in the presence of the gathering of the foremost. And they received no punishment for this. For during those days of the council there had been something similar to that Ruthenian saying of ours: "Ne czujesz Korola w zemli" ("You do not feel the King in the land").[39]

But it is the great harm of the Ruthenian Church of that side that through this sort of rule of priests at that council it came to the point that the salvatory dogmas of the true faith were rendered up to anathema, and heretical blasphemies were blessed. The Opponent of Truth caused this through them, for he saw that they would crush their teeth on that hard rock, but that they could not harm it at all with their gnawing; he counseled them to attempt to swallow it whole so that they might remove themselves from answering to this and remove the entire people of their side from the reading and recognition of this truth, and thereby that they might hide from them what it behooves every person to know with regard to his salvation. And so it happened. But I trust in the Defender of Truth, that through His merciful compassion He will deign to cause that, in the good souls that have fallen upon this Satanic counsel on account of ignorance itself, even once it is swallowed it will cause them benefit; but it will be stuck in the throat of the stubborn and those who suppress it purposefully. God Almighty, I say, who hungers and thirsts for the salvation of all people, will cause that this anathema will be a fright unto the sons of perdition, but to the sons of God it will be a means to salvation. For the truth can be oppressed, but it cannot be suppressed. And if Satan has many ploys for the oppression of God's truth, God has immeasurably more means for the suppression of his ploys.

Since my God, by whatever judgments He alone knows, did not judge it proper for me to lay down my soul at that time for the truth, I will not cease to speak about its harm and to struggle, according to the ability of the strengths given me by God, as long as my soul will be in my body. I will ask God's anointed, His Majesty the King, Our Gracious Lord, the defender in this domain of every wronged innocence and whomever in addition it be proper, that he deign to appoint for me a time and a place for the defense of this anathematized truth and command

39.   [Cf. *NKPP* 3:867, "Ziemia," 1.]

those who anathematized it to appear in order to defend their untruth, so that they no longer seduce simple people, ignorant of this matter, nor lead them, through calumny and falsehoods, away from coming to the conclusion of holy unity, alleging before them that the Romans are heretics profane and hateful to God, Manichaeans, Sabellians, Apollinarians, Macedonians, and Origenists (I say this aloud so that the Catholics might know what sort of belief these people have about them), straying from the truth in this upon their souls and upon the pureness and innocence of the Roman Church from these heretical profanities. And so that these heretical errors and heresies of their Zizanijs not be introduced by them into the Ruthenian Church of that side. This very respect and the time granted my life compelled me to be forbearing so that in my time I might place before their eyes in words this my truth and show them indeed that, as it is the genuine truth that Zizanij, Philalethes, Orthologue, and others like them are manifest blasphemers against the true dogmas of the Orthodox faith in their writings, so also it is the genuine untruth that the Roman Church is infected with the Manichaean, Sabellian, Macedonian, Apollinarian, Origenist heresies—all of them or one of them.

Who has the greater power to teach the faith in the Church of God, a bishop or a presbyter? Is it permitted to a priest to lead people away from the path of truth, but not permitted to a bishop to lead them to the path of truth? That is a great lawlessness against the bishop and a great anarchy in the Church. A bishop and his doctrine are subject to the judgment of bishops, and not to the judgment of priests. The bishop has it in his power to judge the doctrine of a priest, and not vice versa. If they were righteous, they ought to have admitted me to the council, and one day, not to say one hour, would have sufficed to judge between us. What is more, it was permitted to simple lay people and heretics by faith to write profane errors, heresies, and ugly blasphemies against the majesty of God and to submit them to print for the infection of ignorant people, instead of the dogmas of the faith of the Eastern Church, for which no one punished them, judged, accused, or asked; and to the contrary, all, almost until this very day, delight in them and make use of them. But to me, an archbishop in the Ruthenian Church, it is forbidden to speak, write, and submit to print the truth that destroys those heresies and thoroughly establishes the Orthodox dogmas of the faith. I was accused of having done something, but in spite of my great appeal and request I was not permitted to speak at that council about myself, my innocence, and the wrong done to the truth that I wrote. Rather I was condemned without law and judgment by improper judges, in my absence, along with the truth that redeemed me from their lawlessness with the harm inflicted upon it.

When I was a secular person, a layman, and I gave them to drink of the Lutheran and Calvinist heresies, they gratefully received from me that cup full of poison in the tears of their lamenting mother; they drank from it, and, alas, they gladly poisoned their souls.[40] They were not angry with me about this, nor did they ask from where I had drawn it for them—from the vineyard of the Church or from the heretical field of poison. But now when I have become, by the grace of God, their archiereus, not the least man in their Church with regard to my archiepiscopal dignity, when I give them to drink of the ἀντίδοτον [antidote] against the poison I had inflicted upon them, they abuse me, revile, and persecute me unto death, not considering that I first wrote as a private individual, and now I write as a priest and an archiereus, nearer than before to the grace of God by that very laying on of priestly hands upon me.

Is this a minor act of lawlessness against a bishop in the Church? In my opinion there can be no greater. For to accuse someone in his absence, and then not to permit him to defend himself, and to pass judgment upon him, is the sort of lawlessness that was never heard of among the pagans. Which brought me to what I did by a great compulsion, hopeful that, against those violators of Church laws and revilers of God's truth, I would be able to beg a time and a place from him,[41] who, both by divine and human law, has it in his power in this domain to defend that wronged Catholic truth, which has been unjustly insulted with anathema, while the heretical blasphemies are blessed.

Thus this recent anarchical council, episcopal by name but priestly in actual fact, which had priests as judges and bishops as executors of their judgment, rendered the Ruthenian Church of that side, as well as the Greek Church, heretical from head to foot. For in what I asked and admonished you through my *Apology,* Ruthenian nation, to be cautious

40.   [Smotryckyj refers here to the *Thrēnos* of 1610, which he wrote as a lay member of the Vilnius Brotherhood.]
41.   [I.e., King Sigismund III.]

lest through your incautiousness your Ruthenian Church be disgraced by the errors and heresies of your new *dogmatographers,* this council, after condemning its Orthodox dogmas described by me and praising heretical errors and heresies in it by this very action, completely turned this disgrace upon its own head.

For which reason, since it is highly important, I *solenniter* [solemnly] protest by the authority of the obligation of my dignity as an archiereus against this disorderly council, which was contrary to the holy Orthodox faith and most harmful to the Catholic Church of God, before all of you, most noble Ruthenian nation, through this my *Protestation* (although I was solicited by them not to protest and to declare before the deputy of the Kyiv castle, whom they had already summoned for this purpose, that no violence had been done me by their action); and I declare that even if I submitted something in writing, even if I signed something, even if I said or did something against my Catholic Orthodox work while I was present with them,[42] unto no little disgust of people who are ignorant of this matter—with all my soul before my Lord God, the Creator of heaven and earth, I renounce all this and I make it as never having occurred.

I confess my sin before my Lord God and before His entire Holy Church as mortally grievous, I regret it, and lament it bitterly. And in the bitterness of my heart I ask God's priests and all the faithful for their prayers for me, having prostrated myself to him for absolution in my contrite heart, who can grant it to me completely by his spiritual power *jure divino* [by divine law].[43] Since I maintained whole during that very time my faith given to my God and promised to him *per obedientiam* [by obedience], and my heart never gave its consent to their anathema cast upon my work with an un-Orthodox heart, nor could it give its consent piously. Whence it was that they condemned my Orthodox Catholic work, which I had written for them with great consideration, and thoroughly and authoritatively supported, explained, and affirmed each thing in it with Holy Scripture and the doctrine of the doctors of the Churches, Eastern and Western. And I cursed the blasphemies,

42.   [Smotryc'kyj refers here, obliquely, to the revocation of the *Apology* that he was forced to sign. It was published in Ruthenian (*Apolleia* 1628, Б2v–3r/308–9) and in Polish (Mužylovs'kyj 1628, 41r–v). See above, p. 569.]

43.   [Perhaps a reference to Uniate Metropolitan of Kyiv Ruts'kyj.]

errors, and heresies of their sowers of tares, the Zizanijs,[44] who were refuted by me in my work; them did I tear; upon them did I put the candles out; and them did I cast under my feet.[45]

I entered upon that grievous scandal not on account of fear of them, who had descended upon me like storm clouds from all sides, for perfect love casts fear aside; nor, as I mentioned a little above, on account of the violent attack of those venomous clergymen, who attacked me with dishonorable words both in my absence and in my presence, everywhere during their discussions, and especially in the sanctuary of the Church of the Caves during the matins, made insulting uproar against me, raised tumult, and aroused with their commotion the simple people against me for vengeance for the affront supposedly caused by me against the Holy Eastern Catholic faith, having first alleged to them that I was a dishonorer of the saints and of the salvatory dogmas of the faith of the Holy Catholic Eastern Church, not justifying this voluntarily, of themselves, upon their souls and my innocence.

It was not, I say, on account of their terrors and insults that I entered upon this scandal, having commended myself to God's compassion, but partially so that this holy place, as I said, not be drenched with innocent and guilty blood. But for the greater part, because they did not wish to hear my account and did not allow me to say anything in the defense of my work; rather, they suddenly proceeded to bring the counsel they had discussed to execution. Thus I have chosen, in my opinion, among two evils the lesser evil. For I am certain that almighty God, not remembering my involuntary sin, which did not reach my heart, but looking upon my future salvatory benefit, which is greater than was the scandal, having pacified through time itself their hearts angered and inflamed against me and against my work, will grant me free time for an oral defense of my Orthodox Catholic work before them and that He will cause them to do what they ought to do in such a situation in the Church of our nation. Through their attack upon me, the crown of a confessor, if not also that of martyrdom, was given into my hands; but alas, my God, in whose hands are my death and life, on account of my

44. [Smotryc'kyj puns again on ζιζάνιον, "tares." Cf. Mt. 13:24–30. See above, p. 460.]

45. [In other words, Smotryc'kyj practiced "mental reservation" when he took part in the anathematizing of his *Apology*.]

respect for the glory of His majesty, which, as I see, was not pleasing, allowed it to fall from my hands for the time being. Which I grievously regret with all my soul; and so long as there is life within me, I will not cease to regret it and to ask for it.

And in addition to the *Protestation* I have made before you, most noble Ruthenian nation, as an archbishop greatly wronged in the Ruthenian Church, I appeal by the truth of God greatly wronged in it to an entire local council of our Ruthenian nation, with the permission of the highest authority of these domains, convened in a safe place, at which my work entitled *Apology* would be examined in the mode of the holy councils prepared by ancient custom and guaranteed by the canons of our holy fathers, decreed according to God and His holy truth.

To the honor of God the One in the Trinity.

At Derman', the Year of God 1628, the 7th day of September.

My life's one Hope, Lord CHRIST JESUS[46]

---

46.   [See above, p. 231.]

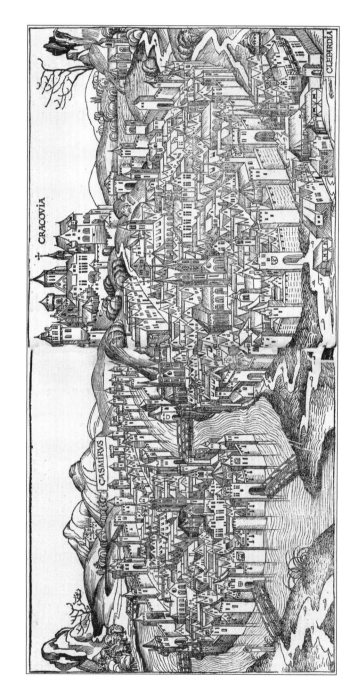

Plate 8. Cracow, from Hartmann Schedel, *Liber chronicarum* (Nuremberg, 1493). Courtesy of Historic Cities Research Project, Hebrew University of Jerusalem, The Jewish National and University Library (historic-cities.huji.ac.il).

Paraenesis

(1629)

Paraenesis,
or

An Admonition,
from
Reverend in God
Meletij Smotryc'kyj,
Called Archbishop of Polack, Bishop
of Vicebsk and Mscislaŭ, Archimandrite
of Vilnius and Derman':

To

the Most Noble Vilnius Brotherhood of the Church
of the Holy Spirit,

And in Its Person, to the Entire
Ruthenian Nation of That Side.

Anno 1628, December 12.

Cum Licentia Superiorum
[With the Permission of the Superiors].

In Cracow, at the Printing House of Andrzej Piotrkowczyk,
Typographer to His Royal Majesty. In the Year 1629.

[...][1]

To the eminent illustrious Prince,
His Grace, Prince
Aleksander
Zasławski
of Ostroh,
Palatine of Kyiv, etc.,
Watchful, pious, and zealous
Catholic, ardent lover
of both the Holy Eastern Church and the Western,
Orthodox follower
of the true dogmas of the holy Catholic faith,
Who prefers, values, and loves
Holy unity,
the harmony, love, and peace of the brethren of the wretchedly
sundered Ruthenian nation above goods, above health, and above his
temporal life:
Patron, promoter, and protector;
in declaration
of his humble good wishes,
and wishing
Help in this salvatory work, blessing in its progress,
the desired consolation from the Lord God in the results,
in certain hope from heaven and in heaven,
and temporal and eternal recompense and reward
for his gracious lord benefactor,
and patron,
the author, in pure heart, in complete humility, and in daily prayers,
this work does
Offer, dedicate, and commit.

1.   [The coat of arms of Aleksander Zasławski and a poem on them by
Cracow professor of rhetoric Grzegorz Goliński have been omitted; Smotryc′kyj
1629a, A1r/644.]

Hoc scriptum Paraenesim legi, approbavi, utile ad conversionem
   Schismaticorum esse judicavi; ac proinde dignum esse ut
   imprimatur, censeo.
         Josephus Velamin Rutski,
            Metropolita Kijoviensis, Haliciensis,
            totiusque Russiae, m[anu] p[ropria].
[I have read this work *Paraenesis,* approved and judged it useful
   for the conversion of schismatics; and I therefore decree
   that it is worthy of being printed.
         Josyf Veljamyn Ruts′kyj,
            Metropolitan of Kyiv, Galicia,
            and of All Russia, with my own hand]

I, Father Sebastian Nuceryn, doctor of Holy Scripture, preacher at the
Cathedral Church of Cracow, censor of books that are to be printed in
the bishopric of Cracow, permitted the printing of this work by the most
reverend Meletij Smotryc′kyj, archbishop of Polack, etc., approved by
his reverence, his grace, Father Josyf Ruts′kyj, etc. The 19th day of
January, 1629.

Palam est, quod in re dubia ad fidem et certitudinem valeat authoritas Ecclesiae Catholicae, quae ab ipsis fundatissimis Apostolorum sedibus, usque ad hodiernum diem succedentium, sibimet, et Episcoporum serie, et tot populorum consensione confirmatur. D. Augustinus contra Manichaeos.

[It is manifest that, in a questionable matter, there should prevail for faith and certitude the authority of the Catholic Church, as supported by a succession of bishops from the original seats of the apostles up to the present time and by the consent of so many nations. St. Augustine against the Manichaeans.][2]

2.　　[St. Augustine, *Against Faustus Manichaeus,* bk. 11, chap. 2; *PL* 42:246; *NPNF1* 4:178.]

Meletij
Smotryc'kyj,
Called Archbishop of Polack, Bishop of Vicebsk and Mscislaŭ,
Archimandrite of Vilnius and Derman', humbly wishes and
desires grace, peace, and mercy from the Lord God
for the brethren of the Church Brotherhood of Vilnius
of the eastern obedience,
for all in general, and each one in particular, religious and lay,
my brothers in Christ and my most beloved sons in the Spirit.

U NABLE, THROUGH LACK OF PLACE and time, to answer sufficiently
Your Graces' letter of the thirteenth day of August of the
present year 1628, when it was handed to me in Kyiv by my
representative, Father Josyf[3] (in which Your Graces ask me for a clear
response: that I remove the suspicion that has risen about me in Your
Graces' hearts due to the repute carried in the mouths of men, some
alleging that I am a Uniate, and others that I am inventing something
new and thus attempt to tear Rus' into a third part, whence there would
finally arise a deception worse than the first)—now, by the grace of
God, having obtained a freer place and time, I answer at greater length
than I had answered previously. And since this is a public matter, I send
my letter *in publicum* [into the public] in print so that not only Your
Graces' Vilnius Brotherhood, but all Rus' of both allegiances, might
have knowledge of this from me personally, not only as archimandrite,
but also as archbishop. Which I do for Your Graces and for everyone
who wishes to know about this, as a response to the question put to me
by Your Graces.

I well remember that in my first letter to Your Graces, among
other things, I answered that question in these few words: "Do not
fear from me, Your Graces, that I would divide Rus' into three, since I
desire and seek with all my soul the unification of the Rus' that has been
divided into two. I lament internally and superficially (let him that hath
understanding . . .)[4] her harmful division into two; I certainly would
not seek her division into three. It does not go well for him who divided

3.   [I.e., Josyf Bobrykovyč (see Golubev 1883b, 194).]
4.   [Cf. Rev. 13:18; Prov. 10:13, 23; 14:33; 15:14; 16:22; 17:24; 19:25.]

her into two; what would console the conscience of him who divided her into three? But we, as I see, will wish to seek and take care for the unification of this Rus' that has been divided into two parts only when, divided into many parts, she will no longer be able to submit to Union. Whereby, we will not lack much to be wise when it is too late.[5] I pray that the Lord God Himself might deign to dispose of, and to order this, according to His holy will for our salvation, etc." This is the answer I have already given to Your Graces' question.

But so that I might respond sufficiently to Your Graces' question in this matter, I add a little more to my first epistle, even though, mindful of that common saying *veritas odium parit* [the truth gives rise to hatred],[6] and wishing to avoid Your Graces' hatred, whose great and devoted love toward me I knew in past times, I should rather remain silent than answer Your Graces' question in any way! But I know that in the face of the truth, hatred falls upon base and thoughtless people, whereas my oration is to great and wise people, moreover, to my brothers (not to say, my sons), and to my younger brothers at that—those people who, wishing to show themselves more ardent in their piety than others in the Ruthenian nation, *et dextris* [both to the right], as they say, *et sinistris* [and to the left], both walking straight and deviating from the true path, believe that they are seeking God's truth and suppose that they follow it. Therefore, commending myself to the defender of truth, I answer clearly what it befits me to answer Your Graces in this matter. And I beg you not to be moved by any affection until you hear out my answer to the end, since it can give spiritual benefit to Your Graces' hearts, if it finds good soil, and it will remove from me the suspicion Your Graces harbor, namely, that I divide Rus' into two or three.

If the matter that concerns me these days in my nation is known to anyone, it is known to Your Graces, since this matter arose among Your Graces in the Vilnius Brotherhood, came from it, and from it mortally infected in body and spirit the entire Ruthenian nation of that side: in body, by wresting from it its freedoms and liberties; in spirit, by wresting from it its faith and love. (Whoever wishes to know how this happened will learn clearly from my *Apology*.) And yet, Your Graces ask me what is the cause of the allegation about me that is carried in many mouths in

5. [Cf. *NKPP* 3:398–400, "Szkoda," 13.]
6. [Erasmus *Ad.* 2.9.53.]

the Ruthenian nation and that caused the anxiety of suspicion in Your Graces' heart, so that it seemed to some that I adhere to the Union, to others that, against the Union, I pull and tear my Ruthenian nation into a third piece. But if Your Graces had called to mind those new theologians of yours, whose writings you have sowed from your Vilnius printing house across the entire Ruthenian nation, and through which you cast blasphemies, errors, and heresies into the Ruthenian Church of your side, Your Graces would not have needed to ask me about this, since the cause would thus have been manifest. When I lived in Your Graces' Vilnius monastery, both as a layman and as a monk, I often spoke about this matter with the man with whom it was appropriate to do so,[7] and I conferred with many other important men in other areas of the Ruthenian land, showing indeed that the writers who were published in print by our Vilnius Brotherhood cause the Ruthenian Church great harm, exchange the true dogmas of the Orthodox faith for Lutheran and Calvinist errors and heresies, and through them kill the souls of the simple people who are unaware of this evil and incapable of noticing it. I also brought to your attention the erroneous accounts of the Clerk of the Ostroh Chapter about the Council of Florence, and I showed that this pestilence was most harmful to our Ruthenian Church.

Although I spoke frequently about all this in those days, I did not speak loudly; and this was because I was a lay person, a simple monk, wherefore, I judged it not my affair to meddle in a matter that was not my immediate concern. But I was not silent before those, as I said, both among you, the Vilnius Brotherhood, and elsewhere, who should know about this. Some of the witnesses to this are dead; others are still alive, both there in Vilnius, and in Kyiv, in Ostroh, and elsewhere. But once I became, through God's will, a bishop in the Ruthenian Church, mindful of my duty and, with God's help, being watchful in it and opposing the evil I mentioned earlier that was sown by you throughout the entire Ruthenian world, in order that it not further harm the salvation of human souls (since I myself had significantly added to that evil through my lamentatious writing, which fact gave me the greatest pain), I began to speak out about this. In the presence of many people I specifically criticized the writings of Zizanij, Philalethes, Orthologue, and the Clerk,

7.   [Most likely a reference to Leontij Karpovyč, Smotryc'kyj's predecessor as archimandrite.]

and I declared them heretical; and where it was necessary, I demonstrated this clearly. This seized the souls of many unlearned people and of some who are allegedly learned, who spread that allegation concerning me about which Your Graces are asking, either because they were blinded by their crude simplicity or because they did not wish to recognize the truth on account of obstinate stubbornness. Which suspicion about me arose in Your Graces' hearts for no other reason than the fact that I criticized the heretical writings of these new theologians, who were some sort of divine *oracula* [oracles], as it were, for the Ruthenian nation of that side, not so much because people knew their writings (for not everyone knows how to read; and there were also many who did not have the opportunity to read them), but rather because they knew that these writings were published in print and commended by such an illustrious brotherhood. Against which neither was it allowed, nor was the possibility even considered that anyone might say anything, to say nothing of writing anything, as if this were to speak against the doctrine of some of those holy doctors of old.

†Last year here in this land there departed from this world a man of no small reputation in the Ruthenian nation, both for the piety of his life and for his knowledge of the dogmas of the faith. Still living, however, are those honorable men, priests of the Ostroh *capitula* [Chapter], in whose presence, at the mention of my lamentatious writing, he said that it is equal to the writings of St. John Chrysostom, as far as the authority of the truth of God described in it is concerned, and that it is fitting for us to pour out our blood and to lay down our lives for it. How many similar opinions were there, before the appearance of that lamentatious writing about the works of Zizanij and Philalethes! ‡I heard from the lips of that same now deceased man that he did not praise the Clerk's work and that it was he who dissuaded the man with whose town the Clerk associated himself from signing his own name to the work[8] (and that is where, through the offices of the author of that work, the matter stood), giving this reason: if some cleric makes injurious reproach to your great and noble name, how will you defend your account? And

---

†   The opinion of the deceased Father Dem'jan Nalyvajko about the lamentatious work.

‡   His opinion about the Clerk's work.

8.   [I.e., Kostjantyn Vasyl' Ostroz'kyj.]

so at his advice, that work appeared under the name of the anonymous Clerk of Ostroh so that if one cleric said something that did not suit another cleric, the harm would not be great. Since I declared, now loudly and at every opportunity, that the writings of such writers were heretical, full of blasphemies against the Orthodox faith and thus also against the Lord God and His holy majesty (and I did this most of all when I had already returned from my peregrination to the Holy Lands, where I offered and promised myself to the Lord God the Creator and my Redeemer, in those holy places, through His holy aid, according to the strength granted me by Him, for their suppression and elimination from the Ruthenian Church), such opinions falsely disseminated by the unlearned brethren carried such an allegation about me throughout the entire land and implanted in Your Graces' hearts that suspicion about which Your Graces ask me, namely, that I would divide Rus′ into two or three.

†My *Apology* makes known what then occurred in this matter. And my public *Protestation* delivered to the Ruthenian nation declares what happened to my *Apology,* from which Your Graces can obtain certain knowledge of that event, about which the ecclesiastical estate *wostocznoho* [Ruthenian/Slavonic: of eastern] Orthodoxy, with the blessing and permission of the elders of the Ruthenian Church, tries to substitute a falsehood for the truth in the apology they printed recently in Kyiv under the Ruthenian title *Pohybel′* [i.e., *Destruction*].[9] And

---

† The hypocrisy of the *Pohybel′*-writing schismatic ecclesiastical estate is demonstrated.

9. [Smotryc′kyj uses here the Ruthenian word *pohibel′* or "destruction," in referring to the Ruthenian polemical tract *APOLLEIA (Destruction) of the Book Apology,* an account published by the Orthodox side in 1628 (and reprinted in Golubev 1883b, 302–16) that relates what happened at the Kyivan Council of that year, at which Smotryc′kyj's *Apology* was condemned. The first word of the title is Greek and should read ἀπώλεια. It appears in the passage from 2 Pet. 2:1–3 that is used as an epigraph for the work (Golubev 1883b, 304): "But there were false prophets also among the people, even as there shall be false teachers among you, who privily shall bring in damnable heresies, even denying the Lord that bought them, and bring upon themselves swift destruction. And many shall follow their pernicious ways; by reason of whom the way of truth shall be evil spoken of. And through covetousness shall they with feigned words make merchandise of you: whose judgment now of a

overlooking the fact that, in the title to its *Pohybel'* that ecclesiastical estate either unwisely deprives the bishops and their superior of the ecclesiastical estate, or it injudiciously ascribes ecclesiastical eldership to lay people,[10] I take as the measure of their erroneous allegation the fact that they do not give as the reason for our congregating in Kyiv for a council the one we had discussed and established in Horodok (a holding of the Monastery of the Caves); and that they allege that I appeared in Kyiv for a reason they mention, about which I neither knew nor had heard.[11] But I am supported in this matter by the very letters of the man who summoned me[12] and other individuals of the Ruthenian nation to this council a few weeks before the end, nay, even before the beginning of the Sejm, not to mention before the publication and appearance of the Constitution.[13]

I mention yet another thing that the ecclesiastical estate says in its *Pohybel':* that on the basis of my *Apology* I was discovered and revealed for one who believes things contrary to Orthodox faith. May God forgive that miserable estate that it does not wish to come to its senses of its own free will in a matter that is so obvious. Here among us, it is he who goes secretly in his affairs that is discovered and revealed, wandering here and there and seeking someone's harm; but that estate will not prove this against me. I proceeded in this matter honestly and openly, communicating this matter not to the commonality (*Vulgus enim cupiditatibus agitur, non ratione* [For the commonality is governed by their passions, not by reason]), but to whom it was fitting. I conferred in this matter with the foremost men of the ecclesiastical estate of the Church of that side, that is, with the bishops and with the archbishop. I

---

long time lingereth not, and their damnation (*pohybel'*, ἀπώλεια) slumbereth not."]

10.   [The title page (Golubev 1883b, 302) ascribes the work to "the spiritual estate of Eastern Orthodoxy." Smotryc'kyj's goal was to separate the true leaders of the Ruthenian Church, Jov Borec'kyj, Peter Mohyla, and himself, from this work and to ascribe it to lesser Church figures or laity who had no business, in his opinion, making statements of this sort.]

11.   [The *Destruction of the Apology* alleges that the Orthodox were to gather at the King's instruction to discuss means for the defense of the fatherland (Golubev 1883b, 305–6).]

12.   [I.e., Jov Borec'kyj.]

13.   [The Sejm met in Warsaw from 12 October to 24 November 1627.]

had from them not only the permission to write those things, but even the request and the blessing. If that estate did not know about this, it must have been the *faex* [dregs] of the ecclesiastical estate and must not have been *legitime* [legitimately] a party to it. And once I had written that *Apology,* I did not wander about with it; rather I sent it immediately to those who permitted me to write it, to those who, in the ecclesiastical estate, I believed were preeminently concerned with this matter. Nor did I seek anyone's harm; rather I sought that I might bring a soul-saving benefit to the Ruthenian nation. I sought that this matter might proceed in orderly fashion according to the laws and customs of the Church, without any quarrel and turmoil; but I see that that estate perverted it as it wished, as he who caused the first brothers to quarrel counseled it to do.[14] In all truth, I could justly accuse of dishonesty, wandering, and hunting for fraternal harm those who gave me permission to write the work, since, once they received the work I sent them, they gave their word to me through their letters to declare to me their opinion about it "sufficiently," as one of them writes to me, and "fully," as the other one writes.[15] But although they had my work for seven weeks, they did not fulfill their promise; rather they secretly and purposefully lay in waiting for my arrival, wishing at that time to attack me, who was unaware of their trap (when I was not expecting or suspecting anything bad from them), and wishing to do what would be not only to my great detriment, but also to that of their entire side of the Ruthenian Church; and they carried this out through evil means that are uncommon among eternal praisers of God and among good men of the Church.

But just as that ecclesiastical estate deigns to allege in its *Pohybel'*, so also did everyone else who makes allegations about the matter of that Kyivan council contrary to the way it proceeded in actual fact. I write to Your Graces because I do not divide the one Rus' into two or three and because, seeing that Your Graces, that is you, the most worthy Vilnius brotherhood, are in such a dire state, in which the soul's perdition is at issue (for from you, as I said, on account of those Zizanijs, Philaletheses, and Orthologues of yours, the Ruthenian Church was stuffed full of

14.   [Gen. 4.]

15.   [Smotryckyj refers here to Metropolitan Jov Boreckyj and Peter Mohyla. The latter had in the meantime been appointed archimandrite of the Kyivan Caves Monastery. See above, p. 574.]

vulgar errors and heresies, and you incurred the woe before the Lord God about which the Son of God says: "Woe to them by whom the offense cometh")[16]—because of this I considered how to remove that from you and how you might be able to free yourself from such a great evil that cries out to the Lord God for vengeance upon you on account of the entire Ruthenian Church. As the head, as the archimandrite of your monastery from which that evil poured forth upon the entire Ruthenian nation of your side, I took it upon myself (having judged it a most fitting thing) to attempt to bring about the end of that evil where it arose.

†Therefore, when the Church elders who convened in the Cave Monastery's Horodok to discuss the coming council permitted me to write something and to send it into the nation to encourage people of both estates to appear more eagerly at the council, unable to find a greater and more appropriate reason than the one presented in the *Apology,* I wrote out *speciatim* [in particular] the most vulgar errors, heresies, and falsehoods found in your three writers, Zizanij, Philalethes, and Orthologue, as well as in the fourth one, the Clerk, demonstrating clearly from Holy Writ and from the doctrine of the doctors of the Church that they are errors, heresies, and falsehoods, and asking and admonishing the Ruthenian nation to gather at the council on account of such a great need. I counseled at the appropriate time that this evil not be introduced into the Ruthenian Church by the daily use of those writers for so many years and by considering and recognizing them as our own, and that in future ages they not be permitted to replace, with the passing of time, the Orthodox dogmas of the Eastern Church. And in the place of their errors and heresies I described the genuine dogmas of the Orthodox faith of the Holy Universal Church; and I appended to that, with their approval and blessing, "Considerations" of the six differences that had arisen between the Eastern and the Western Churches, which were to have been examined at that past council. And I entitled my work *Apology* and sent it into the world in print.

‡So consider carefully, most noble Vilnius Brotherhood, and judge fairly who is crooked and who is straight: I, who freed you from that great evil, or those who poured that evil upon you and upon the entire

---

16.   [Mt. 18:7.]

†   Why the *Apology* was published.

‡   This year's Kyiv Council is most unjust to the Ruthenian nation.

Ruthenian nation of your side and disgraced the Ruthenian Church of your side with the errors and heresies of your Zizanijs, Philaletheses, and Orthologues? It is true that the ecclesiastical estate that I just mentioned excuses itself on the grounds that those writers are *not approved* by the Church;[17] but it ought to have demonstrated that they are *disapproved*—and by whom, where, and when. Otherwise, it is unable to prove what it affirms; for in the matters that are believed with the heart unto righteousness and confessed with the mouth unto salvation,[18] silence stands as approval. Let that estate show me on which bishop's knowledge and hands (however many of them there were in those years in the various Dorohobuzes, Stepan's, Koreces, Brahins, and in other towns) those writers did not base themselves. Did the bishops of Lviv not know of them? Nor can we, the bishops who have been consecrated for these eight years now, deny knowledge of them. Which one of us, or of them, throughout that whole time, managed to stutter out even one word whether *publice* [publicly] from the pulpit in Church or in writing, informing the Ruthenian nation that the Ruthenian Church does not approve and accept the writings of these writers since they are full of errors and heresies; and that it rather rejects and condemns them as heretical and blasphemous, *vel in toto, vel in parte* [either in whole or in part], and forbids their reading so that no one be infected by them to the loss of his soul? No one, not anywhere, not at any time.

Now, when I am the first one to specify, refute, announce, and publicize the errors and heresies, falsehoods and blasphemies of those writers and bring them to the attention of the entire Ruthenian nation in print, that estate excuses itself through its *nonapproval* of them. Can it be that in order to show that they are approved, it is necessary that they be read *publice* [publicly] from the pulpit in church, instead of the Epistles or the *paraemiae?*[19] We never read in church the Revelation

17.   [The *Destruction of the Apology* alleges that Smotryc'kyj "dared and made bold to charge the entire Eastern Church, his mother, in the person of three writers not approved by the Church, with such heresies and errors" (Golubev 1883b, 308).]

18.   [Rom. 10:10.]

19.   [From παροιμία, lessons from Holy Scripture—Old or New Testament— that are read at the evening service on the eve of a holy day and that had some thematic connection with the event to be celebrated.]

of St. John the Apostle or several books of the Old Testament, such as Esther, Ruth, Judith, Song of Songs, and others, and yet I do not suppose that that estate makes bold to charge the Church with nonapproval of those portions of Holy Writ. But let us say that those writings are both not approved and disapproved—I will grant you this. What follows from this? These two things. First, that if that estate is ashamed of its writers (since this is how it declares them nonapproved), it admits to me that I do not believe things that are against the Orthodox faith, even though, contradicting itself, it shamelessly accuses me of this in so many words. Second, that you, the Vilnius Brotherhood, as that estate thus admits in express words, published from your printing house writers who were full of errors and heresies unto the infection of human souls and that for thirty years now you have been harmfully infecting the Ruthenian nation through them.

What will you say here, most noble brotherhood? That for you it is I who am the unrighteous one, I who cleansed and acquitted you before the Lord God and before His faithful of such a great, most harmful, and shameful evil; or is it rather they, those who caused you to remain in this uncleanness and guilt before the Lord God and the entire Ruthenian nation? For you remain, and must remain, guilty in this before the Lord God and all the genuine followers of the genuine holy Eastern faith and Church so long as the works of the writers you have published in print remain, and will remain, in the esteem in which you published them to the nations of the Eastern Church. Then what will you do that you might no longer labor under that evil, to your severe punishment from the Lord God, who has suffered this for so long and who continues to suffer? For although *lento gradu ad vindictam sui divina ira procedit* [divine wrath advances to take its vengeance at a slow pace], but *tarditatem supplicii, gravitate poenae compensat* [it compensates for the lateness of the retribution with the severity of the penalty].[20] You have years and understanding; now it is time for you to be expert in your faith.

This is my advice, and it is healthy advice: read my *Apology* together with its "Considerations," and consider. I am certain that, with God's grace, it will become clear what you should do in this case. Let the

---

20.   [Valerius Maximus, *Memorable Doings and Sayings,* 1.1.3.]

brutum anathema [crude anathema][21] frighten the sons of perdition,[22] rather than the sons of God, from reading it. I hope in the Lord God that by reading it carefully, having examined with the pure regard of your soul both what is happening in unhappy Greece and what is the object of quarrel in our poor Rus', without any hatred and envy and the blind stubbornness that presents the best things as bad, in love of your salvation and in prayer to the Lord God, you will see clearly in both nations what I have presented faithfully in my *Apology*. And thus, with God's help, you will remove the evil you caused unto yourself and the entire Ruthenian Church when you sent out into the Ruthenian nation those sowers of heresies, the Zizanijs,[23] and you will bring peace to the Ruthenian Church (may God grant it, because you are *tanti* [of such importance]). But neither triumph in lamentable matters (for, my brethren, it is broadcast here that your clergy triumph, as it were, in the victory *de suggestu* [by suggestion] of their Vilnius Church; and they portray and publish to the people what happened to me on account of the improper procedure of those who took part in the council in Kyiv differently from the way it took place; but I do not believe that, as reasonable people, people who love me, and people I love, they would triumph in a matter worthy of long and bitter sorrow and lamentation; for to triumph in truth oppressed and in untruth exalted on high is, simply speaking, to be mad); thus, I say, neither triumph in lamentable matters, nor allow just any one, such as your Zizanijs, to continue to lead you and to lead you astray. For through this sort of carelessness you allowed yourselves to be led astray and to be led away from the path of true faith by those writers of yours, of whom even your ecclesiastical estate is now ashamed. And you must bear them to your regret; for certainly of these two things, one must be your lot: either to give up those works and to ask the Lord God for forgiveness for that sin or to be heretics and to be known as such.

†Consider the heavy and severe punishment placed upon us by the

---

21.   [Smotryc'kyj refers here to the ban on reading the *Apology* found at the end of *Apolleia*.]

22.   [Jn. 17:12; 2 Th. 2:3.]

23.   [See above, p. 460.]

†   When schismatic Rus' did not follow its priests into holy union, it immediately began to be infected with heresies as a divine punishment.

Lord God: as soon as we did not wish to follow our spiritual authorities, the Lord God allowed us to go our own way and to fall into the shameful abyss of vulgar errors and heresies. Just then came our first defender against the Union, Zizanij, who introduced new errors and heresies into the Ruthenian Church. Immediately after him there came a second defender against the same thing, Philalethes, who introduced other new errors and heresies into the same Church. Soon thereafter there came our third defender against the same thing, the Clerk of Ostroh, with unheard-of lies and blasphemies. Shortly after all these, yet a fourth defender against that same Union, Orthologue, introduced new calumnies, falsehoods, blasphemies, errors, and heresies into the Ruthenian Church. And after them came other sowers of the new errors and heresies, who simultaneously reviled the pope and taught heresies, like those who simultaneously vituperated Moses and cast the calf.[24] Wondrous indeed is the working of God's quick vengeance! For Rus', now that it is divided in two, sorely chases itself to its death: it bites at itself, oppresses, destroys, reviles, curses itself, and brings itself to the point of its demise. And certainly (if the wrath of God should remain further upon it) the words of the Savior will soon be fulfilled upon it: it will not stand, it will fall.[25]

And as I said in my *Apology,* He will scatter it into heretical congregations because of the ingratitude for God's grace on your stubborn side; and He will incorporate the other side into the Roman Church, and thus He will not allow Rus' to stand on either side. For whenever we most incline our hearts to something, our wishes are fulfilled with God's just permission. Because of the allegation made by Orthologue in his *Lament*—that it is a more beneficial thing to be in Turkish servitude than to be under the power of the pope[26]—people in those lands, when the Union was presented and recommended to them, were wont to say: "We prefer to go to the Tatar mosques than to union with the Roman Church." And that is what the Lord God through his incomprehensible, yet righteous, judgments deigned to cause: He allowed them to be driven into the mosques from Podolia, Pokuttja, Pidhir'ja, and Volhynia in countless numbers (and even, alas, of souls

24.   [Ex. 32.]
25.   [Mt. 12:25; Mk. 3:24–5; Lk. 11:17.]
26.   [See above, p. xxv.]

yet innocent). Everyone sees this who sees Rus′ in the Tatar and Turkish mosques in those lands: slaves, children and adults, young and old, of both sexes, who renounce the Triune God and the incarnate Son of God, Christ the Lord, and, to their eternal destruction, mark their bodies for accursed Mohammed.

It has become common to say here nowadays that we prefer to go to the Calvinist churches, if it should come to that, than unite with the Roman Church; and thus with the demise of your side that will also be your fate. But let the Lord Jesus Christ protect you from that and incline your hearts to holy union with your brethren the Catholics and not with the unbrethren the heretics, and let Him direct you to place anathema upon the heretical errors and cast *them* beneath your feet and not upon Catholic dogmas, as occurred incautiously and impiously at the recent Kyivan council. For it would have been more proper and just for the writings of Zizanij, Philalethes, Orthologue, and the Clerk to have suffered that anathema there, as erroneous and heretical, than for my *Apology,* which demonstrates, refutes, removes, and publishes the errors and heresies of those works. In truth, those judges did to my innocent *Apology* what is said in our Rus′ in a common saying: *Chto wkraw, toy praw* [Whoever stole is in the right], and whoever was robbed, let him be hanged.[27] The *Apology* accuses Zizanij and his helpers of plundering and gathering from their mother her precious inherited jewels and of putting any old thing in their place in her jewel box. And it proves this against them, enlisting evidence and many trustworthy witnesses. But that council frees Zizanij and his gang through its decree, and it condemns the wronged and innocent *Apology* to a shameful death. What am I to say here of these judges, who will only prove the justice of their decree (through which they tore salvation from the hands of their followers and thrust *Pohybel'* [*Destruction*] into their hands, which they even published in print for them) against my *Apology* when, through the anathema, which they are only too eager to use, they have removed the Church books from the Ruthenian Church.

27.   [In the first half of the saying, Smotryc′kyj presents a Ruthenian-Ukrainian phrase, in italics in the original, in a Polish transcription. The second half of the saying is given in Polish, in black letter in the original. See *NKPP* 2:194, "Kraść," 51, although the only source for this saying seems to be precisely this passage from Smotryc′kyj.]

†Just consider, most worthy Brotherhood, the marvelous punishment that has fallen through God's dispensation upon the entire Ruthenian nation of your side: that when I addressed to it pure falsehoods and calumnies against the Roman Church and against its faith and against its superiors and when I submitted for its belief pure Lutheran and Calvinist errors and heresies and new, unheard-of blasphemies against the divine majesty of the Son of God and His Holy Spirit, then they listened to me, loved me, and received me as an angel of God speaking to them; they kissed that work of mine and raised it upon their heads. But now, when I wrote the pure truth, the pure dogmas of the Orthodox faith, pure praise of the divine majesty of the Son of God and of His Holy Spirit, all of them, clerics and lay people, hate me for it, revile me, abuse and heap shame upon me; and they criticize, reject, curse, and trample my work. And this can serve as an indubitable sign: that Satan has not moved even one soul from among the Ruthenian nation of your side against my lamentatious work, whose errors and heresies even your ecclesiastical estate now acknowledges to be contrary to Orthodox faith; but he did do this against the present work, the *Apology,* against which all cry out everywhere *tolle* [away with (it)], although they hear that it has no fault.[28] Recognize, I say, that my *Apology* is Catholic from this alone: that it seized the devil so firmly by the soul that he did not cease until he delivered it unto destruction at his direction by that gathering of priests and archpriests.

But I believe in the Lord my God that He will not allow them to suppress His truth. Nor do I suppose that you would blow on that Satanic cunning, since you have already burned yourself on your heretical writers. To the contrary, I expect from you that, on account of this great and honorable reason, on account, I say, of God's truth, which has been wronged, you will ask God's anointed, His Majesty the King Our Gracious Lord, for a council, at which what is described in the *Apology* might be considered honorably and in orderly fashion, in the fear of God, and might be brought into effect so that this salvatory good might begin with you, and thus that old evil might be suppressed and

---

†   The terrible divine punishment that has fallen upon schismatic Rus' because it despises the true dogmas of the faith and grasps blindly at heresies.
28.   [Cf. Lk. 23:18: "Tolle hunc et dimmitte nobis Barabban" ("Away with this man [Christ], and release unto us Barabbas").]

removed from the Ruthenian nation of your side. Otherwise, you will not free yourself of your grievous sin. And as long as Zizanij, Philalethes, and Orthologue are known as yours, you will be known as the sower, follower, and defender of their errors, heresies, lies, and blasphemies. For if you undertake such expense for the faith that your Zizanijs, Philaletheses, and Orthologues described for you, endure molestations, suffer want, come to great harm, and experience daily difficulties; if for this faith the dignity of your noble estate is not respected according to its calling nor the authority of the burgher estate according to its condition, then consider it certain that you bear that inestimable harm not only in vain (for which may the Lord God have pity), but also to the detriment of your salvation, since you know well that even if one suffers something, but not according to the law, he will not be crowned[29] and that no heretic sees God's countenance.

And you, the sowers throughout the entire Ruthenian nation of so many and such highly blasphemous heresies (forgive me, brethren, for I speak the truth)—what can you expect? †You must indeed know this for certain: you earn eternal tortures through all your sacrifices, expenses, and incomes. It is not enough to say that you are confessors of the Eastern Orthodox Church. You will receive the same answer to that as those who boasted of being the sons of Abraham.[30] They would be sons of Abraham if they would do the works of Abraham; and you would be confessors of the faith of the Holy Eastern Church if you would not join to your faith the Lutheran and Calvinist errors and heresies (which the true Eastern Church does not recognize as other then heretical). ‡Is there not enough for your damnation and destruction in that one blasphemy that, with your Zizanij, you rob the Son of God, Christ the Lord, of his eternal priesthood and intercessorship? Is there not enough in that second one that, with your Philalethes, you mock the transubstantiation of the bread and the wine into the body and blood of the Son of God, into the mystery of the Eucharist? Is there not enough

---

29. [2 Tim. 2:5; 1 Pet. 2:20.]

† That the people of schismatic Rus′ improperly call themselves confessors of the holy Eastern faith.

30. [Jn. 8:33–44.]

‡ Wherein schismatic Rus′ does not agree with, and opposes, the salvatory dogmas of the faith of the Holy Eastern Church.

for your damnation in that third one that, with your Orthologue, you do not acknowledge that the Son was born and that the Holy Spirit proceeded from the essence of the Father? How much more of this is there in your writers, as you can see briefly collected in my *Apology*![31]

I say further that, as long as you claim those sowers of heresies as yours, not only do you claim for yourselves the title of confessors of the faith of the Eastern Church improperly, but you also do it sinfully, since by taking that title for yourself you cause all the Orthodox to suspect errors and heresies in the dogmas of the holy Eastern faith that this faith does not acknowledge as its own. The Holy Eastern Church knows and confesses seven sacraments given by Christ the Lord; but you, with Orthologue, acknowledge only two.[32] She accepts particular judgment; but you, with Orthologue and Zizanij, reject it.[33] She places blessed souls with Christ the Lord in heaven; but you, with Zizanij, lock them in an earthly paradise, and you place them as far from the presence of Christ the Lord as heaven is from the earth.[34] She knows the difference between a bishop and a presbyter according to God's law; but you, with your Philalethes, place them in the very same number.[35] You, with Philalethes again, acknowledge that lay people have power *suffragii decisivi de fide* [to decide by vote concerning the faith]; but she accords that only to the bishops.[36] You, with Philalethes, do not acknowledge that the apostle St. Peter was established as the universal pastor by Christ the Lord; but she does.[37] You, with Philalethes again, do not acknowledge that Christ the Lord built His Church on Peter; but she does.[38] You, with Philalethes, do not acknowledge that two keys were given to the holy apostles, *ordinis, et jurisdictionis* [of order and jurisdiction]; but she does.[39] You, with Philalethes, do not acknowledge that Christ the Lord entrusted all His sheep throughout

---

31. [See above, pp. 422–4, 429–30, and 449–56.]
32. [See above, p. 443.]
33. [See above, pp. 408–10, 443–4.]
34. [See above, pp. 410–17.]
35. [See above, p. 430.]
36. [See above, pp. 431–2.]
37. [See above, pp. 432–4.]
38. [See above, p. 434.]
39. [See above, pp. 435–6.]

the world to St. Peter the apostle for shepherding; but she does.[40] And again, you, with Philalethes, do not acknowledge that appeal belongs to the bishop of Rome according to ancient custom and according to Church decree; but she does.[41] You, along with Philalethes, accord the power to command universal councils to the emperors; but she accords it to the bishop of Rome.[42] You, with Philalethes, do not acknowledge that the bishop of Rome should occupy the first place; but she does.[43] You, with Orthologue, deprive of their faith those who have committed mortal sin; but she grants them faith. You, with Orthologue, divide in actual fact the divine essence from the divine person; but she confesses that they are both *unum idemque* [one and the same], and she divides them *solo intellectu* [only in sense].[44] You, with Orthologue, introduce sixteen other blasphemous absurdities into the mystery of the most Holy Trinity, as I demonstrated clearly in my *Apology;* but she is free of all that.[45]

Because of your differences from the faith of the Holy Eastern Church, you cannot properly call yourselves confessors of the holy and genuine faith: you became apostate from the thing, and so you thereby also became apostate from the title. †For as darkness cannot properly be called light,[46] or falsehood truth, so neither *haeresis* [heresy] can be called Orthodoxy, nor a heretic a Catholic. And you became apostate from the thing as soon as you sent those errors and heresies into the world through your Zizanijs and declared them your own. Therefore you also became apostate from the Orthodox faith and from the title that allows you to be known as confessors of the dogmas of the faith of the Holy Eastern Church. Your allegiance may be Eastern, but your faith is not Eastern. It is not the faith of the holy fathers who flourished in the East, but the heretical one that nowadays sits heavily upon the Eastern

---

40.   [See above, pp. 434–5.]
41.   [See above, pp. 436–7.]
42.   [See above, pp. 437–9.]
43.   [See above, pp. 439–40.]
44.   [See above, pp. 445, 447–9.]
45.   [See above, pp. 449–56.]
†   When schismatic Rus′ began to be infected with heresies and for what reason.
46.   [Is. 5:20; 2 Cor. 6:14.]

Church. And this happened to you as soon as the lay people began to take the rights of the ecclesiastical estate for themselves and to interfere *sacrilege* [sacrilegiously] in spiritual government and in matters that do not belong to them. As soon as you ceased following the opinion of your spiritual elders, the Lord God caused you to follow the opinion of your lay writers and to fall into vulgar errors and heresies. Until you renounce which by name and *specifice* [specifically] before the entire world (which I advise and beg you to do), just as you published them to the entire world in print, you will never be able to call yourselves properly and justly sons of the Eastern Church and confessors of the Orthodox faith. The present-day rabbis take their title from the Old Testament; but they are rather new cabalists, whom that title suits as properly as the title of prophet suits Caiaphas. The Lord God has repaid the Ruthenian nation of your side tit for tat. Its lay people attacked the ecclesiastical estate and its government and office; so God imposed upon it lay leaders who led it away from the true faith. Your leader is Zizanij, it is Philalethes, it is Orthologue. You know whom you harbor in your home and whose work you publish in your printing house. Yours, too, is the Clerk of Ostroh, in whose erroneous account you placed such faith that you do not wish even to glance at a true history of the Council of Florence. And because that evil arose from you (for you published it to the world in print), let it be suppressed by you as well.

[†]And so I, your archimandrite, with God's help, suppressed the deceits of that Clerk at the beginning of [my][47] work. I suppressed the errors and heresies and all the blasphemies of Zizanij, Philalethes, and Orthologue. Give me your assent in this and confess that the dogmas of the Holy Eastern Church described by me are your own and those of your ancestors; acknowledge that the Council of Florence ran its course and was concluded in the harmony and love of Greeks and Romans; and thus you will properly and fittingly be known and called sons of the Holy Eastern Church and confessors of its Orthodox faith. Repent, I ask Your Graces in the name of the living God, repent, you clergy and lay people, elder brethren and younger; for the straying of your Zizanijs from the dogmas of true faith, and of the Clerk from the truth, is obvious. You

---

†   The author's grave admonition to the schismatics.
47.   [The text has "twego" ("your"), but it should probably be "swego" or "mego" ("my"). This is a reference to Smotryc'kyj's *Apology*.]

believed me, a layman, when I told you heretical falsehoods; believe now the archiereus when I tell you the Catholic truth. I spent three years in the place where our Ruthenian nation received the Christian Orthodox faith; but nowadays, unfortunately, the same heresy has come to rule over the ecclesiastical estate even there. As God is my witness, I tell you the truth; for I not only heard it pronounced out loud from the pulpits there, but I also read it in the catechetical work of the highest authority in that place. But about this, God granting, I will have more to say forthwith.

†The entire Ruthenian nation of your side is amazed that I praise the Union and cling to it; and a few worthy individuals from among you write to me that they would sooner expect their own death than this change from me. And some ascribe greed to me, saying that I did this for the sake of Derman'. Others charge me with pride, saying that I did this in order that I might show myself of some importance in my nation. Others invent other reasons and charge that I shamelessly abandoned the Church and faith in my old age and that, having criticized all that was mine, I went off in search of worldly things. Previously, they say, he did not know what he believed; can it be that Derman' has now taught him faith? But I say with a clear conscience before the Lord God, who sees into hearts,[48] that there is nothing evil in me, neither greed (with God's grace) nor pride; and I did not abandon either the Church or the faith. My God deigned to give me Derman' for the consolation of my old age, so long as His holy will should grant it, since for the sake of His holy truth I was despised and driven away by the brethren (for, angry at me because I openly criticized the errors and heresies, lies and calumnies of those Zizanijs, Philaletheses, Orthologues, Clerks, and of my own work on the faith and also because of the letter that I had brought from our father, the patriarch, the former archimandrite of the Monastery of the Caves[49] had insisted that I should not set foot in any Kyivan monastery).

But when I set off for the Eastern lands already an adherent, by God's grace, of the beloved Union, Derman' had its sure resident, who was alive and healthy; and I never thought for a moment, so long as

†   The author gives account of the matter his opponents charge against him.
48.   [1 Sam. 16:7; Ps. 7:9, 26:2; Jer. 11:20, 20:12.]
49.   [I.e., Zaxarija Kopystens'kyj.]

he was alive, that I should ever replace him, since this was for me an impossibility. But haughtiness does not seek what is God's; and the holy Union, which I praise and seek, and which, through God's help, I have already found, is a gift of God. For faith and love are God's gifts. And if I had sought through praising the Union to show myself of some importance in my nation, I would have done that *praepostere* [in reverse order] and in vain: for through my *Lament, Verification,* its *Defense, Elenchus, Justification,* and my other significant works, I had already sufficiently shown myself of some importance in my nation, and for that reason I was exalted, as they say, even unto heaven[50] in the glory, grace, and love of my nation. But I did not expect this from praising the Union, knowing its ability to arouse the affections; to the contrary, more than other Uniates, I awaited hatred, abuse, and shame, which I bear to the consolation of my soul, since I do not care about them. I considered it, however, an unequal trade to lose true heavenly glory for the sake of the supposed glory that I had from my nation through its ignorance as to why it had given this to me. And therefore, for the sake of my salvation, I despised the latter as vain, and I seek the former, in God's grace, as eternal; and I desire, so long as my soul is in my body, with God's help, to work toward it in the Church of my Ruthenian nation.

[†]It was suggested to me at the Kyivan council by several of the leaders of your side that the side I am joining will seat me lower than I now sit with them; that they will make me a bishop from an archbishop and with some dusty title at that; and thus I should be humbled, not exalted, in the Church of the Ruthenian nation. I answered that since I know well that it is a more useful thing to be a lay person in the Catholic Church than an archbishop in the schismatic Church, I do not care about that in the least. For lay people in the Church of God are its *legitimi* [legitimate] sons and the natural heirs to the Kingdom of Heaven; but bishops in the schism are not *legitimi* [legitimate], nor do they have the right of inheritance of the Kingdom of Heaven. *Non potest Deum habere Patrem qui Ecclesiam non habet Matrem* ["He cannot have God as the Father, who does not have the Church as his mother"], says St.

---

50.   [*NKPP* 2:594–5, "Niebo," 60; Arthaber 1313.]
†   As far as the soul is concerned, it is a more beneficial thing to be a layman in the Catholic Church than a bishop in the schismatic conventicle.

Cyprian.[51] And about schismatic bishops he says: *Qui nec unitatem spiritus, nec conjunctionem pacis observat, et se ab ecclesiae vinculo, atque a sacerdotum collegio separat, episcopi nec potestatem potest habere nec honorem* ["Whoever respects neither the unity of spirit nor the union of peace and separates himself from the bond of the Church and the fraternity of the priests can have neither the power nor the honor of a bishop"].[52]

Therefore, since I know about this, I have not the least regard for what you offer me, satisfied as I am with the exaltation I receive from the fact that I am in the Church of God, and therefore I have the Church of Christ the Lord as mother and God as father, which I could not have had in the schism even as an archbishop. In response to other words they addressed to me, I said to them that I am not so deadened that I should not feel the honor, respect, glory, and good name given me by my side; and that I should not be aware that in that side I have already spent my years until my hair is gray, that I wrote much in its defense, that I also worked much toward other ecclesiastical spiritual benefits, whereby I was received by many of my nation in such love that, in order to show their great gratitude toward me for those works and for my services, they were moved to display my image in their homes so that they would always have me before them. I felt all that upon me and I saw it; and seeing it, I accorded it great significance, and I continue to do so. But what of it? I trusted in the Lord my God and in His holy truth, at the defense of which I stand; and I now trust with undiminished strength that by this present action of mine (although it seems disagreeable, for the truth is bitter), not only will I not lose the love of my nation toward me, but, God granting, I will gain a greater love, if it can in any way be increased.

For if I acquired such love from it when I defended its schisms, suppressed God's truth, fought against the Church of Christ the Lord, led people astray unto destruction through heretical doctrine, I expected and I expect to acquire from it considerably greater love now, since I

---

51. *Lib. de simplic. Praelat.* [St. Cyprian, *Book on the Simplicity of the Prelates (Liber de Unitate Ecclesiae: Book on the Unity of the Church),* chap. 6; *PL* 4:503A].

52. *Lib. 4. Epist. 2* [St. Cyprian, bk. 4, letter 2; Alternate numbering, letter 10, *To Antonianus; PL* 3:791A].

work for it in the cause of holy unity, the demonstration of God's truth, the defense of the Church of Christ the Lord, the description of the dogmas of Orthodox faith, and for the salvation of His righteous ones. If that evil could cause so much love toward me in my nation, this good can cause considerably more; for, having allowed God's truth to conquer it in this matter, the common people will gain greater divine gifts and show greater love toward those who work in it. If its fate with regard to holy unity should turn out otherwise (which God forbid), then, since it has offended holy unity, neither will I care about the offense to me, making certain that the temporal glory I have from it not harm my eternal glory with the Lord God, which I will not conquer in myself, nor will anyone else.

†So then, in my old age, in the autumn of my days, when I already stand with one foot in the grave and will have to depart this world at any moment, I underwent a change; and I did this out of love for my God and of desire for my salvation at that time when my God looked upon me in his kind mercy, when the all-seeing eye[53] caused me to see the evil that was bringing me to the loss of my soul. I render everlasting thanks to His kind mercy that He was merciful toward me (although I was already old) that, even in my old age, He granted me time for repentance, which is never late. It is enough for me that, by God's grace, I repented, early or late, young or old; the important thing is that I repented. In my opinion, I repented young enough, since I repented while yet in my temporal life. He repents late and old who, when he has already departed this world, when he has been punished in his misery, sees his evil and repents; but he does not repent in time, since there is no repentance in hell, where even one who goes there while young is old, whereas in heaven even the old is rejuvenated.

‡For since the blasphemies, errors, and heresies against God's majesty that I wrote in my *Lament* and in my other writings threatened me with eternal torture, I had to replace them with the Orthodox dogmas

---

†   The author gives the reasons why he renounces the works he wrote in defense of the schism.

53.   [Ps. 33:13.]

‡   The author declares that by renouncing his works he did not renounce either the Holy Eastern Church or its Orthodox faith and that he has no intention of renouncing either one, since they are holy and salvatory.

of faith. But through this change I did not renounce the Holy Eastern Church; God preserve me from that. My enemies wrongly accuse me of this. Rather I remain in her just as did my first ancestors, to whom she gave birth in the Ruthenian nation: she gave birth to them while in holy unity with the Roman Church; and, united with the Holy Western Church, she keeps and will keep me until she wraps me, God granting, in the shrouds of the grave; nay, even after the grave my hope is to continue to live in her. I did not renounce the faith, and may God not allow me to do so. Only the stupid believe this of me. Rather I remain and I stand by the faith. I separated from myself those who lost faith, and I remained with those who never lost faith. I repudiated the faith—that is, the blasphemies, calumnies, lies, errors, and heresies—of Zizanij, Philalethes, Orthologue, the Clerk, and similar writers, and I adhere to the salvatory Orthodox dogmas of the faith of the Holy Eastern Church of my holy ancestors. I believe and confess them; and I ought to have laid down my life for them at the recent council in Kyiv. But it happened that my life should be spared through no other cause than by God's dispensation (as I see), on account of my long disregard for this salvatory matter, and for paying attention to things that were, in my opinion, great, but in God's judgment, as I came to know, only too small. I regret this, and I ask, through His divine goodness, that He forgive me and that, at the time when He allows me to suffer it, He deign not to deprive me of my crown through death for the sake of His truth, which I have described.

I am of the faith that Rus´ always believed in the past; but Rus´ never believed as Zizanij, Philalethes, and Orthologue teach, nor do I believe thus. And whoever believes as they teach (I speak before the Lord God) is as far from the Kingdom of Heaven as are the vulgar heretics and disgusting blasphemers whom I repudiated for that very reason; and without any shame I renounced them in my old age, not wishing either to believe what they teach nor to defend their doctrine in word or deed, as I had done in those times past to the detriment of my soul. To be evil is shameful; to renounce the true faith is shameful; but to become good from bad, a Catholic from a heretic, is not shameful but great glory before the Lord God and before men. And it is a greater shame if someone is wise in his youth but stupid in his old age, than if someone is stupid in his youth but wise in his old age; for stupidity is natural, as it were, to youth, and wisdom is proper to old age. I blindly followed blind leaders in my youth; but seeing in my old age, I follow seeing leaders. And having repudiated the errors and heresies of Zizanij, Philalethes, and Orthologue, I adhere to the Orthodox faith of my ancestors, the Greeks and Rus'. Since I find no shame in this faith, I do this without shame.

For if shame is born of transgression, and virtue gives birth to glory, then bad faith gives birth to shame, and good faith gives birth to glory, since to believe correctly is virtue, but to believe incorrectly is transgression. Thus I did this without shame and with glory, and this brought me not shame but glory. In the manner in which, in his day, St. Athanasius abandoned the heretical Eastern bishops and with Paul, the bishop of Constantinople, looked to the Roman bishop Julius for his faith, one of the opponents could have alleged against him that he had shamelessly abandoned his faith and Church in his old age; but he would certainly be lying about him.[54] The same thing is now happening with me, since neither did I renounce the Holy Eastern Church; and I exchanged not the faith for heresies, but heresies for the faith. And it was not Derman' that taught me this; rather He whose gift it is taught it to me, and well before I came to live in Derman'.

†Thus let none of Your Graces be amazed at what I said about myself in my *Apology:* that as long as I was in the Ruthenian Church of the side that is not in holy unity, I did not know what I believed; for that is the genuine truth. As I have just said, I followed blind leaders; and since they themselves did not know where they were going, neither did I know where they were leading me. They stumbled over the rock of errors,[55] and I after them. They fell into the pit of heresies, and I after them.[56] What does he think who is amazed at my words? If I had known what I believed, would I have followed Zizanij so far? Would I have listened to Philalethes for so long? Would I have so firmly believed the Clerk? Would I have written blasphemies against God's majesty

---

54.   [This story is recounted, for example, in the *Church Histories* of Sozomen (bk. 3, chaps. 3–13; *PG* 67:1037–68; *NPNF2* 2:284–91) and of Socrates (bk. 2, chaps. 11–22; *PG* 67:205–48; *NPNF2* 2:40–9).]

†   The author demonstrates clearly that as long as he was with schismatic Rus' he did not know what he believed.

55.   [Is. 8:14; 1 Pet. 2:8.]

56.   [Mt. 15:14; Lk. 6:39; Mt. 23:24; Prov. 26:27; 28:10; Eccl. 10:8.]

that were harmful to my soul? Not at all. I was brought to all this only by the fact that I did not know what I believed. For to believe errors and heresies is not to know what one believes, as even today those who believe those errors and heresies, falsehoods and lies, calumnies and blasphemies of their Zizanijs, Philaletheses, Orthologues, Clerks, and the like certainly do not know what they believe. Let him who is surprised by my words prove with the doctrine of Holy Writ and the holy doctors of the Church that the errors and heresies, falsehoods and lies, blasphemies and calumnies that I noted in my *Apology* from Zizanij and his gang cited there are not such. At that time he will properly be surprised by my words; but until he does that, he will be surprised by them like the man who calls Holy Scripture blind.

It was not their name (which I hold in small esteem), but your authority, oh most worthy Brotherhood (which carries great weight with me), that drew me to believe those writers. And I acquiesced in submitting my lamentatious work to the censorship of your authority, trusting you more than myself in this matter when it was a question of the salvatory dogmas of the Orthodox faith. In all this both you and I were in error; and that was because neither you, such an illustrious and leading brotherhood in the Ruthenian nation, nor I, knew what we believed. Otherwise neither I, nor those who wrote before me, would have written such errors and heresies; nor would you have allowed their works and mine, full of blasphemy against the Orthodox faith, to be printed in your printing house or have recognized them as your own. For then your word would have been against the Holy Spirit, which would not have been forgiven you, either in this age or in the next,[57] if you had published them to the world, knowing for certain that they were blasphemies, errors, and heresies and not your Orthodox faith. Thus, by my change, as I said, I exchanged the errors and heresies sent by you into the world for Orthodox faith and not Orthodox faith for heresies and errors. May the Lord Jesus Christ grant that you too, through His holy grace, do this with me and all those who boast of knowing what they believe, but nonetheless are immersed up to their ears in the errors and heresies of their Zizanijs.

†Believe this, most noble Brotherhood: that as you erred when

57. [Mt. 12:32.]
† The frivolity of the recent Kyivan council.

you believed your Zizanijs, so you now err if you do not repent and follow these cursers (may the fathers and brethren forgive me) of God's truth and the true dogmas of the faith. If I were not indebted to you for your great acts of kindness toward me, if I were not the archimandrite of your Vilnius monastery, if I were not an archiereus of the Ruthenian Church, I would remain silent; for it would concern me not at all or very little. But the obligation of all three requires me to admonish and warn you. For that was not the sort of council to convene with deliberation, debate the matter, and examine and consider my *Apology articulatim* [article by article]. It criticized everything according to the opinion of two people, if not of just one, and that of a man esteemed on a daily basis. But I declare upon my dignity as an archiereus that there is nothing there, not even one word, that is worthy of criticism. And I am ready, God granting, to prove and to defend that in any place, on any occasion. Every day, so I am told, they heard from that man there little else but: "Why should we, Orthodox, unite with heretics in faith?" The result was the same as when in recent times Timothy [II], patriarch of Constantinople, sought to bring the Armenian nations into unity with himself and heard the same thing from them: "If the patriarch desires unity with us, let him renounce his heresies, since we cannot unite with heretics in faith."

Thus it is clear that one must speak to even a sober man about these things carefully. It is the custom of people who have become heretics to consider themselves Catholics and their own heresies pure dogmas. Certainly even that hateful *dissuasor* [opponent] of holy unity can believe nothing else about himself and his Zizanijs. Let him place before him a man of any sect—Catholic, schismatic, heretic, Jew, Mohamedan, idolater—and ask him about his faith. Will not every one of them say: "God grant that I might die in the faith in which I was born." Everyone praises his own sect; everyone believes that he and his brethren are saved in their own synagogue, and he condemns the others. But everyone must know that there is one ship of Christ the Lord, and only Catholics sail in it; all the others will of necessity perish in the fiery deluge of the final day.

†We were glad that from the year 1623 there began a movement

---

†   The conferring of the non-Uniates and the Uniates concerning holy unity is salvatory and beneficial for the Ruthenian nation.

toward negotiations, toward an agreement between Rus', of the non-Uniates with the Uniates. And, with God's help, we were certain of quickly achieving the Church peace we desired. But then such *humidi suasores* ["humid," i.e., weak, advocates] (for holy unity would have diminished their licentious humors) thwarted this for us too, and they caused you to ferment in that rotten heretical broth. Would that such people, who are unmindful of their salvation, not find any happiness either with the Lord God or with good people unless they repent and cease to oppress that salvatory matter. In the year 1626 you too, most worthy Brotherhood, applied yourself to that salvatory matter.[58] But what dissuaded you from concluding it I do not know. If it was the resolution of the Uniates that they cannot be under the obedience of the elder of your side, I say from experience itself that you had no proper reason to abandon an agreement with them concerning a mutual understanding on account of their resolution, since you know that no one willingly submits to servitude, except for someone who is desperate or mad. Well then, did you really wish that they submit to the obedience of your hereticized elder? That, freed from the schism, by God's grace, they would again place their necks under its soul-destroying yoke? This they would certainly have done if they did not have a spark of understanding in them and did not care at all about divine or human laws. Therefore, they properly rejected an improper matter. But just listen. In what respect did the Muscovite nation commit an offense that it freed itself from his obedience?[59] In what respect are the Wallachian and Moldavian metropolitans harmful to themselves and to their nations that they do not seek their *pallia* from the patriarch of

58. [King Sigismund III, at the urging of Ruts′kyj, had agreed that there should be a general synod of all Rus', Uniate and non-Uniate, to commence on 26 September 1626 in Kobryn. See Golubev 1883a, 90–2; *AZR* 4:76.]

59. [Moscow declared its Church independent of Constantinople in 1459 after what it saw as Greek apostasy at the Council of Florence-Ferrara and the divine retribution that came in the Turkish conquest of the Byzantine capital. In 1589 its metropolitan see was officially made into the patriarchate of Moscow and All Russia, and it took its place as the sixth after Rome, Constantinople, Alexandria, Antioch, and Jerusalem.]

Constantinople?[60] The archbishop of Cyprus does the same thing;[61] the same the archbishop of Georgia;[62] the same the archbishops of Serbia[63] and Illyria or Achrida,[64] who do not offer obedience to the elder of your side; rather they live, rule, and govern them as independent rulers and governors of their own local churches.

We have here before our very eyes the example of the patriarch of Moscow. But why should I cite foreign examples in this matter? Here, too, around the year of our Lord 1051, after discovering that Michael Cerularius, the patriarch of Constantinople, had severed his union with the Roman pope, our Ruthenian Church did not wish that apostate to consecrate its metropolitan; by itself, not without special divine providence, it consecrated Ilarion to the metropolitanate. Second, around the year of our Lord 1146, the Ruthenian Church itself consecrated its own metropolitan, Klimentij, without sending for it to the patriarch. Third, around the year of our Lord 1407, the Ruthenian Church itself consecrated to the metropolitanate of Kyiv and of all Russia, Grigorij Camblak, whom the patriarch of Constantinople did not wish to consecrate when he was sent to him from Rus'. And this too is a splendid example of this matter: that the Ruthenian Church

60.   [Constantinople established metropolitans in the Wallachian city of Vicina in 1359 and in the Moldavian city of Suceava in 1401. Complete autocephaly came only after political independence in 1856.]

61.   [The independence of the Cypriot Church was established by Canon 8 of the Council of Ephesus (431) and reconfirmed by Canon 39 of the Quinisext or Trullan Council of 692. See Mansi 4:1469–70 and Mansi 11:961–2.]

62.   [Theodore Balsamon wrote in his interpretation of the second canon of the Second Ecumenical Council (Constantinople) that the Bulgarian, Cypriot, and "Iberian" (i.e., Georgian) Churches were autocephalous, and he attributed the status of the Georgian Church to a decision of the Council of Antioch. *PG* 137:317–20.]

63.   [In 1219 the Serbs received an independent archbishopric—the future see of Peć—from Constantinople. In 1346 Stefan Dušan, who had given himself the title "Tsar of the Serbs and the Greeks," elevated Peć to a patriarchate against the objections of Constantinople.]

64.   [*Archiepiskop Illiryski abo achrydoński* refers to the ancient see of Achrida, which is the Macedonian town of Ohrid. Theophylactus testified to the traditional independence of the see from Constantinople in his Epistle 27 (*PG* 126:417–18).]

received Gregorius, the abbot of Constantinople, who was consecrated to the metropolitanate of Kyiv by the Roman Pope Pius II.

What did the Ruthenian Church lose by having these metropolitans consecrated not only not by the patriarch, but even against the will of the patriarchs, and by obeying one who was consecrated by the pope? What harm did it do to the Ruthenian nation, its Orthodox faith, and its rights and freedoms (to which you now pretend)? None at all. What harm can it do now when, for many highly proper and important reasons, it withdraws from that obedience and, following the model of the nations I have mentioned, creates for itself a separate archbishop or even a patriarch? †Not only will this not harm it in the least, but it will bring with it great and salvatory benefits, to wit: it will unite it in faith and love with the Catholic nation, Polish and Lithuanian, and thereby cleanse it of the errors and heresies of your Zizanijs. It will erect schools for it, build seminaries, provide the Church with good preachers and confessors, regulate monasteries, edit a catechism of a concordant confession, put the singing and the melodies in order, revise the Church books and submit them to print in corrected form, correct the bad habits and morals of priests and lay people; and in a short time, in my opinion, it will establish the Ruthenian Church in such internal and external adornment as never before at one time in the Ruthenian nation. I do not mention the rights, freedoms, and liberties for both the ecclesiastical and lay estates, the opening of doors to all sorts of offices and dignities and to the conclusion of eternal peace in the nation. Are these small benefits with respect to both the body and the spirit? In my opinion, they are inestimable.

‡What good did your Ruthenian nation manage to obtain under your present obedience for so many hundreds of years? Once upon a time the Lord God blessed our ancestors under this obedience, but that was when it was obedient to the highest ecclesiastical authority. Now He does not bless it in any way, does not delight in it in any way. It does not flourish, for whatever good is allegedly kindled anywhere

---

† The salvatory benefits that holy unity brings with it for the Ruthenian nation.

‡ That the Ruthenian nation received and receives no spiritual benefit from the obedience it rendered to the patriarch of Constantinople; and that this is due to the schism, which is abhorrent to God.

immediately burns out. Where are those schools of Ostroh, Lviv, Brest, and elsewhere? With what sort of progress for the youth (and at your great expense) does your Vilnius school squeeze through, as if through so narrow a crack, so that from it, as from a rock, over so many years you have neither fire nor water. And that is not because of your insufficiency and carelessness, for we do not lack for the workers' diligence or your expense; rather this is only because of God's nonblessing that has fallen upon the Ruthenian nation of that side. For He does not permit it to have anything good, either internally or externally, certainly for no other reason than the fact that it has lost that in which God delights and acquiesces: faith and love.

Where does it have a good preacher, nay even a mediocre one? Where a wise confessor? Where is there discipline in the monasteries? Where is there obedience among the clergy? Where diligence among the superiors? Where concern for the salvation of souls? Where does anyone work in spiritual matters out of love and not for the belly? Where finally is spiritual nourishment for starving people? Where Christian spiritual consolations? I speak boldly, since the matter is obvious: for a long time now in the entire Eastern Church, in the Greek, Serbian, Bulgarian, Moldavian, Wallachian, Georgian, Karamanian,[65] Arabian, and Muscovite lands, and here in our Ruthenian land, the simple people, in villages, cities, and small towns, have not known what the Christian faith is, what the Church sacraments are, what it is to know "Our Father," "I believe in God," what it is to know God's Ten Commandments and the other things that pertain to every Christian. None of them ever knows the consolations of Christian faith that usually come from listening to the word of God. They live like cattle. If here among us they come to salvatory communion when they are already dying only through fear of penalties, what are we to believe happens in the other lands of this obedience I have named, where these penalties do not exist? And this happens for no other reason but the fact that they do not find either of these things to their liking, and Him they do not know at all; and there is no desire for unknown things.

If, following the example of other nations, the Ruthenian nation would establish a separate archbishop or patriarch, this would not only

65.   [Karamania: the oldest Turkish emirate in Asia Minor; annexed by the Ottomans in 1475.]

not harm it, but it would be very beneficial to it, both for the soul and the body. For with such a local Church ruler, councils would be carried out honorably, insufficiencies in the Church would be remedied, and whatever is useful and salvatory for the Church would be discussed without any obstacles and would be realized; and soon, God granting, it would come to the point where, from the spiritual storehouse of the Ruthenian Church, other nations of the same language and rite would be sufficiently provided. But do we now have a catechism? Do we have postils? Do we have lives of the saints? Do we have any salvatory spiritual *exercitia* [exercises]? We still read the *Anthologies* of that old holy era, we read the *Prologues;* but neither he who reads nor those who listen understand anything; and it is as if the readers wrapped some tasty morsel around a hungry man's mouth—their own and the listeners'—but did not allow either their listeners or themselves to taste and eat it.

†What is more, what should move us to seek a separate patriarch for ourselves is the fact that we find (and often, at that) patriarchs who are simonists, such as the one who, after many others, had deposed the present one from his see and sent him into exile.[66] We find heretics, such as the present one as well, among many others, who is now declared such not only in Constantinople, but everywhere. And finally, this is the most important thing that causes us to seek a separate Church superior: the *schisma* [schism]. For in the Church of God it is *tritum et vulgare, firmum et ratum* [familiar and common, firm and established] that, where it is not a matter of *haeresis* [heresy], a bishop cannot separate himself from another bishop through the division of one Church without causing a schism. Therefore, for the patriarch of Constantinople not to be in union with the nonheretical pope is for him to be in schism. And the characteristic of schism is the same as that of heresy: no one can be saved in it. It severs a man from the body of Christ the Lord and makes of him a member of Satan; it deprives him of sonhood, so that he is no

---

† The two main reasons why the Ruthenian nation should seek a separate patriarch in its nation.
66. [Cyril Lukaris was deposed in 1620 and replaced first by Gregory of Amosea and then by Anthimus, metropolitan of Adrianople. He returned from exile in Rhodes to reoccupy the patriarchal see by October 1623.]

longer a son of God, but remains a son of his father, the devil.[67] And, in brief, although a schismatic can be tortured for the Orthodox faith that he confesses, he cannot be saved.[68] And this is the very thing that moved me to holy union, by God's grace, and established me in it: that my conscience no longer allowed me to invent heresies and to slander the Roman Church with them.

For these reasons (since they are most important), most worthy Brotherhood, enter into the discussion concerning an agreement that has begun among our brethren. Do not consider sinful or shameful what other nations have done without sin and without shame. To the extent that you alone could draw the Ruthenian nation to believe those new writers and to stand in the way of the Union, you alone can likewise draw them away from that and draw them to holy unity.

†Consider what I have just said, which is not in error: that, without the censure of schism, an Orthodox bishop cannot separate himself and his local church from the communion and mutual love of another equally Orthodox bishop and from his local church. Consider, moreover, this as well: that the heresies—Manichaean, Sabellian, Macedonian, Apollinarian, and Origenist—with which you and your writers charge the Romans are pure calumny.

‡For the Romans place anathema upon those who establish two beginnings in one divinity and upon those who fuse the persons of the Most Holy Trinity. They know and confess one beginning for the Son and the Holy Spirit in the Father: for the former through birth and for the latter through procession. And although they confess that the Holy Spirit also proceeds from the Son, nonetheless they acknowledge in clear words that they believe that the Holy Spirit, like the Son, has τὴν ὕπαρξιν [its existence], its *subsistentiam* [subsistence], from the Father, and that the Son does not have τὴν ὕπαρξιν [the existence], the subsistence, of the Holy Spirit. That is, as they themselves explain at the Council of Florence, the Son does not have the τὴν προκαταρκτικὴν

---

67. [Jn. 8:44.]
68. *Aug. lib: 1 de Baptis. c. 9* [St. Augustine, *On Baptism: Against the Donatists,* bk. 1, chap. 9; *PL* 43:116; *NPNF1* 4:417].
†   A grave consideration of why schismatic Rus' are *vere* [truly] schismatics.
‡   That the Romans do not have the Manichaean heresy.

αἰτίαν, the *primordialem [causam],* the primordial cause of the Holy Spirit, since the Father Himself is such a cause.[69] Where in their so Orthodox confession is the Manichaean *haeresis* [heresy]?

†The Romans believe and confess that the Father is one divine person, the Son another, and the Holy Spirit another, each separate from the other in number and in innate causal order; and that one is not called by the name of the other, not the Son by the name of the Father, nor the Father by that of the Son, nor the Holy Spirit by that of the Father or the Son, nor yet the Father and the Son by that of the Holy Spirit. Where in their so Catholic confession is the Sabellian *haeresis* [heresy]?

If the Manichaean two causes are supposed to derive from the same reason as the Sabellian fusing in one of the two persons (those of the Father and the Son), namely that the Father and the Son are two persons separate from each other, from which the Holy Spirit is believed to proceed, then you derive both improperly. There are three persons, the Father, Son, and Holy Spirit, but one God, one Creator, one Omnipotent; and that is because there is one divinity of all three divine persons, one omnipotence, and one power of creation. And since the Father and the Son have one power of the spiration of the Holy Spirit, therefore those two persons are one beginning of the Holy Spirit. Thus argues St. Augustine.[70] Basil the Great says whoever introduces two beginnings tells of two Gods; and he tells of two Gods who confesses two essences. Whence it follows that whoever confesses one essence in three divine persons confesses not two, nor three, but one God. Likewise, whoever confesses that the Father and the Son have one power of the spiration of the Holy Spirit confesses one beginning. Since, for the establishment of two different beginnings, it is necessary to have not only two different persons, but also two different natures and thus also two different forces, as one learns from the teaching of Basil the Great.[71] Thus, as the three separate divine persons, through the unity of the power of creation, are

---

69.   Session 25 [Mansi 31/1:971–2].

†   That the Romans do not have the Sabellian heresy.

70.   *Lib. 5 de S. Trinit.* [St. Augustine, *On the Trinity,* bk. 5, chap. 14; *PL* 42:921; *NPNF1* 3:94–5].

71.   *Hom. 27 in Arrium et Sabellianos etc.* [St. Basil the Great, *Against the Sabellians, Arius, and the Anomoeans, Homily 27* (actually *Homily 24*); *PG* 31:606].

one beginning of creation and not three, likewise also the two persons, the Father and the Son, through the unity of the power of the spiration of the Holy Spirit, are one beginning and not two. And whatever there is in the former case that is different *ad extra* [externally] for all three divine persons, there is *commune* [in common] in the latter case for two divine persons *ad intra* [internally]. And as the Son and the Holy Spirit have community in their personal properties without the fusion of their persons, inasmuch as they are *from* the beginning, so the Father and the Son, without the fusion of their persons, have community in their personal property since they *are* the beginning. Moreover, the Romans divide the Father from the Son through fatherhood, and the Son from the Father through sonhood, that is, through the properties that establish them. So where do we find here in their so genuine Catholic confession either the Manichaean two beginnings or the Sabellian fusion of two persons? Indeed, this is not the heresy of the Roman faith, but of your Orthologue, or even the inventions and calumnies of someone else before him, on which you depended, with great offense to God's majesty and to your conscience; and thus you and yours cry out without any just reason against the Romans that they are Manichaeans, that they are Sabellians.

†Moreover, what does the Roman Orthodox confession about God, the One in the Trinity, have to do with Macedonius the heretic, who considered the Holy Spirit the creature of the Son? Where did you read or hear even one iota about this in Roman writings from their pulpits? For the one who accuses them of all three is your Orthologue. The Romans believe and confess that God the Holy Spirit is from God the Father and the Son, that is, He is of one and the same essence with God the Father and the Son, of the same divinity.

‡What do the Romans have to do with the Apollinarian *haeresis* [heresy] such that your writers slander them as Apollinarians? Do the Romans have any communion with Apollinarius in their confession about the incarnation of the Son of God? Do they believe and confess that the Son of God received a phantasm, and not a true body, for His divine aspect from the Most Holy Virgin? Do they ascribe divinity rather than a soul to the Son of God as man? Do they believe that the human nature

---

†   That the Romans do not have the Macedonian heresy.
‡   That the Romans do not have the Apollinarian heresy.

is consumed by the divine in Christ the Lord? The accursed heretic Apollinarius believed and blasphemed these three things (and not just any one of them) about the Son of God and the man, Lord Jesus Christ. You say that they are Apollinarians because they receive the mystery of the Eucharist in unleavened bread; and since that bread is without a soul, it has something in common with that heresy. But what does this have to do with the matter at hand? Perhaps these writers adhered, and all of you who accuse the Romans of this heresy adhere to this confession of faith concerning the transubstantiation of the bread into the body: that it is not the essence of the bread, nor the essence alone, but also the *accidentia* [accidents] with it that are transformed into the Lord's body? But the eyes and the *palatum* [palate] are trustworthy censors and judges of this since they judge *evidenter et palpabiter* [evidently and palpably] about the accidents *quantitatis* [of quantity] and *qualitatis* [quality] that remain in the transubstantiated bread. For taste (that is, leavenedness and unleavenedness), as also whiteness or blackness, smallness and greatness, quadrangularity and roundness, are *accidentia* [accidents] and not essence.

If only none of your writers believed, or even now believes, so stupidly that the essence of the bread is transformed into the essence of the body, and the leaven of the bread, the *accidens* [accident], is transformed into the soul; for you call unleavened bread soulless bread and, forgive me, you blaspheme in saying that the Romans have a soulless body in the mystery of the Eucharist. But as one can see, this is for no other reason but the fact that few among you know what ἀλληλουχία is, that is *concomitantia* [concomitance]. Once it is thus established in Catholic fashion, so *Orthodoxe* [Orthodoxly], that the *accidentia* [accidents] of the bread in the consecrated and transubstantiated bread remain unchanged in their property, and only the essence of the bread is transformed into the essence of the body, then it is clear that the *accidens* [accident] of our leaven is just as necessary and beneficial to us as is necessary and beneficial to the Romans their *accidens* [accident]. The unleavenedness of the essence of both wheaten breads remains one and the same in both sorts of bread and is subject equally and identically to one and the same transubstantiation. To conduct a disputation about which (except to discuss in love in which of these two breads Christ the Lord gave that sacrament) is to litigate about a shadow and not about the thing itself that casts that shadow.

†Your writers also charge the Romans with the *haeresis Origenis* [heresy of Origen], with regard to which they allege that they leave only the infidels in hell and send to heaven through the fire of purgatory even those among the faithful who lived most impiously and departed this life in mortal sins without repentance, and they place them in eternal life, and that through their purgatory they render hell empty. But this is the pure calumny of shameless people against the Romans and against their doctrine of purgatory. *Origenes* [Origen] teaches that not only any and all malefactors from among the faithful, but also all the infidels and idolaters and even the demons themselves will receive God's mercy at the appropriate time and will be liberated from infernal tortures, whereby he rendered eternal tortures temporal and hell empty. But what does this heretical blasphemy of Origen have to do with the Roman purgatory? The Roman purgatory does not remove hell and eternal tortures, and it does not render it empty. The Romans, as well, teach and believe that the place of eternal tortures that is called hell, tartaris, or *gehenna* is one thing, and the place of the temporal, purgatorial tortures is another. And the Romans teach and believe that the tortures of hell are eternal and that once anyone enters hell he will never leave it for all time and will never experience God's mercy. And they place in it all infidels, idolaters, heretics, schismatics, and all the faithful and Catholics who depart this world in mortal sins without repentance. But in purgatory they place only faithful Catholics who departed this world in venial sins, or also in mortal sins that have been confessed, but for which they had not made penance; and the loved ones who remain behind beg the Lord God with Church benefactions, and they ask for an alleviation of their tortures and for a speedy liberation from them. But they do not pray for those who have gone to hell; rather they leave them in their oblivion as forgotten by God.

Those are the five heresies that are commonly found on the lips of the priests of your side against the Roman Church; and you will see how appropriate they are to the Romans and how justly they are charged against them. A wise and God-fearing man can clearly see that all five are ascribed by them to the Romans *calumniose* [calumniously] and

---

†   That the Romans do not have the Origenist heresy.

that they are alleged[72] by you out of some innate hatred, which harms you yourselves, both with God and with man, more than it does them.

[†]The Romans are accused of the Manichaean *haeresis* [heresy] by your side also because they receive the sacrament of the Eucharist under one species. For the Manichaeans had the custom of receiving it under the species of the bread alone because, by some sort of error, they did not allow anyone ever—not even in the sacrament—to drink wine, which they considered to be snake venom. We do not find anywhere that receiving the sacrament of the Eucharist under the species of bread alone or the nonreceiving under the species of wine was ever charged and recognized as a heresy by Catholics against the Manichaeans. St. Epiphanius and St. Augustine *ex professo* [openly] and broadly, describe and refute the Manichaean errors and heresies, but not one of those doctors of the Church directed even one word against receiving the sacrament of the Eucharist under one species, nor did they charge them with that as a heresy. They would certainly not have kept silent about it if receiving the sacrament of the Eucharist under one species were a *haeresis* [heresy]; rather, they would have placed it among their foremost heresies and refuted it. And since they did not do this, they made it thereby abundantly clear that they did not consider receiving the sacrament of the Eucharist under one species a heresy since it was common *passim* [everywhere] in the Western and the Eastern Church. And that was for no other reason than the fact that those first holy centuries and the apostolic times themselves believed that no greater spiritual benefit is received from the two species than from one and no less from any one of them than from the two, since whether the sacrament is received under any one species or under two, Christ is eaten in it entire and living with all the spiritual effects, benefits, and fruits inherently proper to that sacrament.

The custom of receiving this mystery in the Eastern Church under one species is customarily called *napoienie* [Slavonic: tincture, soaking], but it is not a man of Catholic understanding, rather a Capernaite,[73] or

---

72.   [The reading here is *żądaią* ('they demand'). This is likely a mistake for *zadaią* ('they ascribe, allege').]

†   That the Romans do not have heresy on account of receiving the sacrament of the Eucharist under one species.

73.   [Cf. Jn. 6:52.]

one who believes that the dead body and not the living Christ the Lord is eaten in that mystery, who can be satisfied with the name they give it. For to soak and dry and then to believe that what is usually believed to be under the species of the wine is found under the species of the bread, not by force of concomitance but by force of intinction, where *nulla accidentia* [no accidents] or any *quantitas* [quantity] or *qualitas* [quality] is either seen or felt—this is improper faith, that is, to believe in the existence of what is not. There is no dampness of the consecrated wine, there is none of its taste and color; and nonetheless, those who defend their position by means of intinction—who argue that one should believe that what is usually found in the accidents after consecration remains without the accidents and that one should have such a faith on account of intinction—incorrectly teach that where the body is, there is also the blood, as we are accustomed to teach piously, but only with regard to concomitance.

This alone demonstrates how recently the Greeks and Rus' have alleged that heresy against the Romans: the fact that they do not know how these words of Christ the Lord are to be understood—"he that eateth me, shall live by me,"[74] and "I am the bread which came down from heaven: if any man eat of this bread, he shall live for ever, etc."[75] Although they believe that they eat the entire and living Christ the Lord in this mystery in each and every smallest crumb of consecrated bread and in each and every smallest drop of consecrated wine, under each species separately, they do not know that they must also of necessity believe and confess that where the body is, there is also the blood, *alias* [otherwise] they would eat the dead body, which is against their own faith. For as the blessed apostle Paul teaches, Christ dies no more,[76] and as the blessed apostle John teaches, every spirit that dissolves Jesus is not of God.[77] Wherefore, since Christ the Lord is already in heaven and cannot die and be separated in His innate parts, we Orthodox all believe that in the mystery of the Eucharist we eat Christ the Lord entire and living, the only-begotten Son of God, who sits at the right hand of God

74.   [Jn. 6:57.]
75.   [Jn. 6:51.]
76.   Rom. 6[:9].
77.   1 Jn. 4[:3].

the Father.[78] For if we did not believe this, then even under both species of the entire Christ the Lord we would not receive Him living; for in the body that we take under the species of the bread and in the blood that we receive under the species of the wine, we would be lacking the soul of Christ the Lord and His divinity, without which parts, both as well as one, not only is Christ the Lord not living and whole, but that sort of body is not Christ. Whence it is clear that if the Romans fall into the Manichaean heresy from receiving that holy mystery under one species, then the Eastern Church does so no less through its daily custom of giving communion to sick people under the species of the bread alone and sometimes of the wine alone (not to mention its other customs of receiving that sacrament under one species).

†These, then, are the six heresies on account of which the Eastern Church separates itself from the Western and avoids communion with it. And since you are in it, you do the same thing with it, whereby we Rus′ curse each other. We abuse and dishonor each other: fathers sons, brothers brothers, sons fathers. We are disgusted, one by the other, as if we were some sort of pagans; we persecute each other even unto death, as if we were each other's main enemies. But the matter itself tells how properly you do that on your side, since the Roman Church does not have them, but rather you invent them falsely against it and charge them with it *calumniose* [calumniously] just so that you might lend credence to the pretext that you avoid it on account of heresies, knowing for certain that if you did not charge the Roman Church with heresies, you would have to recognize that you are in schism because of your variance from it, since you are unable to hide your schism any other way. And it is clear that you do this to your detriment out of some sort of ancient hatred toward the Roman Church, which you have not treated honestly for a long time now; rather, you revile it in every way possible, and you are disgusted by its superiors, its rites, and its faith.

---

78.   *Chrysost. Hom. 24. in 1 Epist. ad Corin.* [St. John Chrysostom, *Sermon 24 on 1 Cor. 10:13; PG* 61:200–1, 205; *NPNF1* 12:139–40, 143] *et lib. 3 de Sacerdotio* [and St. John Chrysostom, *On the Priesthood,* bk. 3, chaps. 4 and 5; *PG* 48:642; *NPNF1* 9:46].

†   That schismatic Rus′ never proceeds in an honest manner in its writings against the Catholics; rather it wrests Holy Scripture [cf. 2 Pet. 3:16] and the doctrine of the Church as it sees fit.

And you do all this against your conscience. First, by inventing unfitting things against it, as when, with Orthologue, you title it the Babylonian harlot[79] and the pope the Antichrist. Again, by adding to the holy writ of the holy fathers what is not found in them only because you believe it convenient to you in your struggle against it, as, for example, the passage from Zizanij, "There is the unleavened bread, and here bread."[80] Again, by purposefully suppressing the proper sense in the Fathers, as, for example, Zizanij also does in the passage about the mysterious Most Holy Trinity of one cause in the appearance of the dove during Christ's baptism. Again, by deleting from the text of the works of those same saints what you consider not to your taste in them, as, for example, that passage in the Ostroh *Book of Needs:* "and that through the unity of essence and because it proceeds thence."[81] Again, by citing the writings of those same holy fathers in a perverted manner, as, for example, in the passage in Azarius from St. Gregory the Theologian: "I will declare either the cause of the Son from the Father or the essence of the Spirit from the Son." Again, by slandering, as also in Azarius, where he says that the Romans cleanse through purgatory the mortal sins (even when unconfessed) of murder, thievery, adultery, prostitution, black magic, and similar things.[82] Again, by interpreting Holy Scripture incorrectly, as in that passage of the Clerk from the blessed apostle James: "Every good gift, etc., that cometh down from the Father of lights,"[83] that is through the Son; therefore, the Holy Spirit does not proceed from the Son. Again, by negating obvious and clear things that are common to the Eastern Church in its daily hymns and are articles of faith, as, for example: the primacy of Peter, the placing of holy spirits in heaven and their perfect blessing, and the establishment of sinful souls in hell and their perfect torture, particular judgment, a

---

79. [Rev. 17:5.]

80. [See above, p. 422.]

81. [By Ostroh *Trĕbnik,* or *Book of Needs,* perhaps Smotryc'kyj meant the *Molytovnyk ymĕja v sebĕ cerkovnaja poslĕdovanija,* the Slavonic liturgical book published in 1606 in Ostroh with a preface signed by Dem'jan Nalyvajko. See Zapasko and Isajevyč 1981, 34.]

82. [Azarius (or, as Smotryc'kyj has it, Azariasz), is the way Zaxarija Kopystens'kyj signed his *Knyha o viri jedynoj* (*Book on the One Faith,* Kyiv, 1620). See Zapasko and Isajevyč 1981, 40–1.]

83. [Jas. 1:17.]

third place for the souls for whom the Church makes festivals for the dead.

As far as the primacy of the pope and similar things are concerned—angry at the primacy of the pope, you remove primacy from the blessed apostle Peter. Not accepting the procession of the Holy Spirit "and from the Son," you add the word "alone,"[84] and you incorrectly interpret the words "through the Son." Not wishing to grant perfect blessedness to the holy spirits, you do not admit them into heaven; rather you place them in an earthly paradise. Criticizing purgatory, you do not grant a third place to those souls that depart this world in venial sins. Not accepting that the sinners are tortured in what we call *ad,* that is in the inferno, you deny that *ad* is hell. Criticizing the receiving of the mystery of the Eucharist under one species, you deny that communion of infants is a sacrament. Disgusted by unleavened bread, you deny that unleavened bread should be called bread, and so on, and so forth. All of this is ordered and denied by you and yours against the manifest, clear, and express doctrine of Holy Scripture and of the writings of the holy doctors, just so that you would not seem to be in agreement in anything with the Romans; for the further you set yourselves apart from them in the confession of the dogmas of the faith, the more Orthodox you think you are.

†But you should know that this is the Church with which, through its and the entire Universal Church's universal pastor, every man of true faith, if he wishes to avoid schism, ought to be in communion, in faith and in love, since, as there is one fold, so there is one shepherd,[85] the invisible Christ the Lord and the visible St. Peter and his successors, the bishops of Rome. Thus do the doctors of the Church teach about this, says St. John Chrysostom, that Christ the Lord poured out His blood in order to redeem the sheep, the care of which He entrusted to Peter and his successors.[86] With which pastor, St. Jerome says, "Whoever does not gather, disperses," about which I have written at length and conclusively in my *Apology.* Since I have desired communion with

---

84. [That is, "from the Father alone."]

† The authority of the Holy Western Church and its pastor.

85. [Jn. 10:16.]

86. *Lib. 2 de Sacerdotio* [St. John Chrysostom, *On the Priesthood,* bk. 2, chap. 1; *PG* 48:632; *NPNF1* 9:39].

that Church for several years now, looking upon the lamentable split in the Ruthenian nation and seeing that it is bringing about its ultimate demise, I advised my brethren more than once, for my part, to stop that unfortunate sundering before we come to a complete dissolution. They had ordered the recent council for that very reason, so that we might discuss this and not allow this evil to spread any further. But the envier of the salvation of human souls, the eternal enemy of brotherly love, and the hater of Church integrity—by means of him who declared, "Why should we Orthodox unite in faith with heretics?"—quickly sought to put a stop to it so that at the council we might not discuss or take counsel about that matter.

That is precisely what happened, since we depended on those who, at that first consultation, cry out, "Let everything be according to the old usage." †As if it were according to old usage to become entangled in new heresies and to abandon the old dogmas of Orthodox faith, to adorn oneself with the torn cloak of Christ the Lord and to despise its entirety! For them, Zizanij, Philalethes, Orthologue, the Clerk, and others like them, with their errors and heresies, are of antiquity, and holy Church unity is an innovation. I am truly of the opinion that if those people who call out "Let everything be according to the old usage" could grasp and understand what is antiquity, if they could understand that your Zizanijs, Philaletheses, Orthologues, Clerks, and others like them have introduced into the Ruthenian Church errors and heresies that are new and unknown to the holy antiquity for which those people declare themselves ready to lay down their lives, I am certain that they would treat their guardians of that antiquity in the same manner that the prophet of God, Elijah, treated the ministers of Baal[87] and that they themselves would enter into that holy antiquity, that is, into holy Church unity. Antiquity is antiquity; but they are up to their necks in modernity. Give us, Lord God, antiquity (we too constantly ask the Lord our God for that), but antiquity in deed and not in words, in essence and not in opinion (and a mistaken one at that). Is Church unity not of antiquity? What is older in Christendom than that? What did our holy fathers throughout all the past local and universal councils seek most of all if not that salvatory antiquity? They

---

†   What is holy antiquity?
87.   [1 Kings 18:20–40.]

judged the sundering of the Church to be modernity and unity of the Church to be antiquity.

†But bypassing those centuries of the first thousand years in which holy antiquity reigned in the Church of Christ the Lord in the East and the West, let us examine that holy antiquity, that is, Church unity, in our Ruthenian and the Roman Churches. Without a doubt we find it six hundred years older than the Zizanijs and your accursed schism. There was holy unity of the Eastern and the Western Churches when Galician Rus′ was first baptised around the year of our Lord 872, during the time of the patriarch of Constantinople, St. Ignatius, who lived in holy Church unity with Nicholas I and Hadrian II, popes of Rome, as well as later, when Kyivan Rus′ was baptised, around the year of our Lord 980, during the time of the patriarch of Constantinople, Nicholas Chrysoberges, who lived in holy Church unity with the popes of that time. There was holy unity of the Ruthenian Church with the Roman when, around the year of our Lord 1096, the feast of the translation of the holy relics of St. Nicholas of Myra in Lycia to the Italian city of Bari, approved by Pope Urban II, was received by the Ruthenian metropolitan Ephrem, and he adorned that holy day with hymns; and even today we celebrate this feast throughout the entire Ruthenian land on 9 May. There was holy unity of the Ruthenian Church with the Roman around the year of our Lord 1283, when the Ruthenian Church was governed by Metropolitan Maximus, who had been consecrated by the Patriarch of Constantinople, John XI Beccus, a pious Uniate. There was holy unity of the Ruthenian Church with the Roman also around the year of our Lord 1411, when the Ruthenian Metropolitan Grigorij Camblak was sent to Rome by the Lithuanian and Ruthenian Prince Oleksander Vytautas for confirmation of the unity of the Ruthenian Church with the Roman. There was unity of the Ruthenian Church with the Roman also in the year 1439, when it accepted the Council of Florence. There was unity of the Ruthenian Church with the Roman also in the year 1442, when Gregorius, abbot of Constantinople, who was consecrated by Pope Pius II, occupied the metropolitanate of Kyiv. There was unity of the Ruthenian Church with the Roman also in the year of our Lord 1476, when the entire Ruthenian nation, with its Metropolitan Mysajil,

---

† That the holy unity of the Ruthenian Church with the Western Church is as ancient as its very baptism.

wrote collectively to Pope Sixtus IV and sent its ambassadors to him.[88]
There was holy unity of the Ruthenian Church with the Roman also in
the year of our Lord 1490, when Makarij [I] occupied the see of the
metropolitanate of Kyiv and when he, as the archimandrite of Vilnius,
signed the letter written by Rus' to Pope Sixtus [IV]. (Whose body
lies entire in the Church of St. Sophia in Kyiv as a good witness for
Holy Union and as shame for the Non-Union). There was holy unity
of the Ruthenian Church with the Roman also when, after receiving
information by letter from Patriarch of Constantinople Nephon [II]
that the Council of Florence had been completed in harmony and love,
Metropolitan of Rus' Josyf [II] Soltan maintained holy unity. It is also
clear from certain weighty conjectures that these metropolitans of Rus',
following pious patriarchs of Constantinople who were in holy unity
with the popes, themselves maintained holy unity: Klimentij, who lived
around the year of our Lord 1146; John, who lived around the year of
our Lord 1176; St. Aleksij, who lived around the year of our Lord 1364;
and Jona Hlezna, who lived around the year of our Lord 1482. All of
Rus', considering the former and the latter[89] as its pastors, was obedient
to them in everything and considered holy unity to be the holy antiquity
in which it was reborn through water and the Spirit.[90]

There has been holy unity of the Ruthenian Church with the Roman
also now for thirty-some years, and already the third metropolitan of
Rus', by the grace of God, promotes and strengthens it in good fortune.
We do not see here even the least change or innovation in anything,
with the single exception that nowadays the Uniate metropolitan
commemorates *in primis*—that is, *wo Perwych* [Slavonic: in the first
place]—the Catholic Pope Urban, and the non-Uniate commemorates
in the first place Patriarch Cyril, the heretic. Alas for God's punishment,
alack for the blindness of these people. †Let us ask ourselves on this
occasion: what thing of spiritual value on which we establish our
salvation does that holy unity take away from us? What does it change
in our rite? What does it disturb in the Church customs, ceremonies,

---

88.   [See above, p. 462, n. 287.]
89.   [I.e., hierarchs from before and after the schism of 1054.]
90.   [Cf. Jn. 3:5.]
†   That holy unity does not cause any change for us Rus' in either Orthodox
faith, ceremonies, or Church festivals.

and rites? It leaves our rite entire, the Constantinopolitan *symbolum* [creed] entire, and entire the consecration and eating of the mystery of the Eucharist in leavened bread and under two species. It does not force us to believe in the fire of purgatory, for even the Western Church does not impose an obligation upon itself in this matter. Nor does it intend to marry its priests to the wives of our *pop*s, and it leaves entire everything else that is of the Eastern Church. †You say: "We will have to leave the old calendar in time." But we know well, first, that this is not an article of faith. St. John Chrysostom argues against those who in his day, in one and the same Eastern Church, on one and the same day, celebrated two holidays—the birth of Christ the Lord and Theophany—that they do this in disorderly fashion; to his own people, however, who, along with him, celebrated those holidays differently from the way we do now, he says: "Let us not condemn their belief, but let us follow our own doctrine; let us allow each to retain his own opinion. Certainly the Lord will reveal this to each one. Both those who say that Christ was born then, and we who say that he was born today, all praise one Lord, receive one child."

Let us say the same thing about this holiday, about our day of Easter and about the Roman day of Easter: that we and they both praise one Lord and receive one resurrected Son of God. Once upon a time there were given in some places certain miraculous signs for this most important holiday, such as the water that rises out of the ground in Sicily on that day and the fire that descends in Jerusalem onto the grave of the Lord; but they have both now ceased on account of our sins. Further, we also know that Easterners, seeing that the calendar had strayed far from its normal order, wished to correct it several hundred years before the pope corrected it. The Greek historian Nicephorus Gregoras makes this clear with express words in book 8, chapter 18 of his *History of the Church,* where he demonstrated its defect and described the method of correction; and he says that this good undertaking did not obtain its result on account of the domestic unrest during a time of war.[91] Third, we know that for a long time now even we have not been celebrating our Easter according to the decision of the Council of Nicaea. But since

---

†   Concerning the change of the calendar.

91.   [Nicephorus Gregoras, *Byzantine History*. There is no chapter 18 in book 8 in the edition in *PG* 148.]

this is a *variabilis* [changeable] matter and subject to correction, it is a pity to conduct an argument about this; let us rather correct it and show what we have; I promise that the Romans will not despise our correction.

†You also say, and you fear most of all that through this union of the entire Ruthenian nation we will lose the metropolitanate and the bishoprics, since the Church canons do not allow two metropolitans or two bishops in one diocese. But also this fear is unreasonable, for you are unwilling to see that *ob rituum et caeremoniarum a se invicem independentium* [on account of rites and ceremonies mutually independent of each other] there can be two bishops *a se invicem independentes* [who are mutually independent of each other] in one and the same diocese or in one and the same city and that the Ruthenian Church together with the Roman, which are separated by a *ritus diversus* [different rite] and which are two *partiales* [partial] Churches and one *totalis* [total], do not make *unitatem* [unity], but *unionem* [union]: they are not fused in one patriarchal Church but are joined in one Church of Christ the Lord.

In my *Apology* I provided the example of the union of the Grand Duchy of Lithuania with the Polish Crown, both of which have their *unitatem* [unity] in one superior authority, but their *unionem* [union] in the laws, freedoms, and liberties that pertain to each domain individually and to it alone. For the Union does not turn us into the Western Church; rather it unites us with it, and yet it leaves us with the Church and in the Eastern Church [*cerkiew*]; and it considers us the Eastern Church and not the Western; and the Roman Church [*kościół*] considers our rite Eastern and not Western; likewise it considers our Ruthenian metropolitan and his fellow bishops as the metropolitan *incorporated* into the Holy Eastern Church, with which he has *unitatem* [unity]; but it considers him *united* with itself [i.e., the Roman Church], with which he has *unionem* [union]. For the Uniate spiritual authorities accept, know, and acknowledge the pope as their elder, not to the extent that the pope is the bishop of Rome, but to the extent that he is the pastor of the Universal Church. And in this manner the pope is known

---

†   The method is shown whereby the Ruthenian Church could join with the Western Church and that through such a uniting, by the force of conciliar canons, we cannot lose the metropolitan and episcopal sees.

as their elder—not as the elder of his own diocesans, but as the elder of part of the sheep of Christ the Lord whom Christ the Lord entrusted to him through St. Peter for shepherding. Therefore, it does not follow from the Church canons that we should lose the metropolitanate and the bishoprics on account of the Union, since they allow and order Churches *diversi ritus* [of different rite] in one and the same diocese to maintain entire their laws, prerogatives, customs, and higher and lower prelatures without any *ad invicem* [mutual] dependence *rituum et caeremoniarum* [of rites and ceremonies] and therefore *praelatorum, episcoporum, et archiepiscoporum* [of prelates, bishops, and archbishops].

Thus no pope ever demanded of the Greeks, and does not now demand, that they renounce the Eastern Church or that they forsake the statutes, laws, and rite of the holy Eastern fathers. But he desired and desires that the Eastern Church be joined with the Western Church, maintaining the integrity of its rite and its synodal laws. This is what he also now desires of our Ruthenian Church, for whom Clement VIII confirms its customary rites, laws, and the ancient enjoyment of all its customary spiritual liberties, *non obstantibus contrariis quibusvis de hac re Constitutionibus, et definitionibus* [contrary statutes and definitions about this matter notwithstanding], and to whose metropolitan he gives power to consecrate Ruthenian bishops *independenter a Curia Romana* [independently of the Roman Curia], to say nothing of dependent *ab Episcopis ritus Latini* [upon the bishops of the Latin rite]. Therefore the bishops are not sent to Rome for papal confirmation, only the metropolitan.

All this offers indubitable confirmation that you cannot rightly fear what you fear; to the contrary, what you fear will sooner meet our nation without the Union than with the Union. The Union can maintain all our spiritual and secular laws, freedoms, and liberties, which, now newly renewed by constitutions (as those that pertain to the Union and not to the Non-Union) and guaranteed, will be confirmed by the oath of succeeding Polish kings. But without the Union all that will easily be lost to us because your Non-Union will certainly and quickly draw our gentry away from us. Through whose departure from our side, every prince, lord, and nobleman of the Roman religion will do whatever he should wish to do with the churches and our rite among his subjects on his estates, with a clear conscience, for the increase of the Roman Church. The highest authority will do the same thing in the cities belonging to him, not only not restrained by any human law from doing that, but rather obliged by God's law to do it for the sake of the salvation of his soul.

And if we are not able to convince ourselves in this manner of the maintenance of the metropolitanate and bishoprics, let us be convinced by the very brink, lest we drown in this apparent whirlpool. Let us transfer the patriarchate of Constantinople to the Ruthenian land, for which we have the proper time, climate, and reason, and all three according to God and His truth. The time is proper for it because nowadays, by God's grace, we are repenting of our mad transgression from the true faith. The climate is proper in that, as I see it, we will find the patriarch of patriarchs and His Majesty the King, Our Gracious Lord, helpful to us in this. We have a proper reason for this since the patriarch is a heretic. This is indeed a new means to Church peace, but one highly honorable to our Ruthenian nation and most salvatory for the souls of the entire Eastern Church (for remaining in its present determination, it can never leave the schism or take care for the salvation of its own): for the head of the Eastern Church, rescued from cruel pagan power, will be established and founded in a Catholic state of Christian freedom.

[†]Having offered to your consideration all this, which has been well considered by me, I answer your question, most worthy Vilnius Brotherhood, in this manner: that, after rejecting your Zizanijs, Philaletheses, and Orthologues as hypocritical and heretical and with-drawing my credence from the accounts of the Clerk, on the grounds that they are false and calumnious, I no longer wish to remain with those brethren who curse God's truth, cast it under their feet, and trample it,[92] and who now are not only in the schism, but also in heresies; nor do I wish to remain with their heretical patriarch; rather, by means of the holy universal Council of Florence and here in our fatherland by means of the Council of Brest, I unite with those brethren who kiss that salvatory truth and bear it on their heads; and through it, I unite myself with the holy Roman Church. Thereby I not only do not divide one Rus′ into three (which you fear from me), but in my person I also join the Rus′ that was divided into two, asking the Lord God that I might live

---

†   The author's answer to the question of the Vilnius Brotherhood.
92. [Mt. 7:6.]

to see you in this holy unity along with the entire Ruthenian nation of your side.

†And at the conclusion of my letter, on account of my devoted love for you, most worthy Brotherhood, I announce as certain that even if you or anyone else, whether for a long time or a short time, were to oppose it in every way possible, the Ruthenian nation will be in that holy unity. For it is clear that this matter is of God, and day by day it makes significant progress. Therefore, I ask you, be alert and understand what you must do. Remember Gamaliel's advice: you cannot overthrow it; therefore cease opposing it.[93] What is more, in struggling against it, you struggle against the Lord God, who easily crushes and effortlessly destroys His every enemy. Do not think that by your sharp attack against it (for all the courts, dietines, and Sejms are full of your challenge against this cause) you could destroy it or that you could cause any opposition. Not at all. To the contrary, with your action you make it all the more magnificent, and you suppress yourself; you exalt it, and you humiliate yourself; you multiply it, and you destroy yourself.

Just let your eyes and ears pass over the houses of the princes, lords, and noblemen, nay even the burghers, and you will hear, and you will see, how much you have gained in the years since this matter has been raised. How many people, I say, of other religions have been converted in those thirty-some years to the people of your religion? As we see, there are thousands fewer in it now than there were previously. This is no mean progress: today there are few of you, tomorrow fewer, on the third day fewer still. So then, what are you to expect from day to day? Once one looked upon entire houses of princes, lords, gentry, upon palatines, castellans, *starostas*, thanes, and other holders of court and land dignities and authorities in the Church of your rite. Perhaps you did not even think of the sort of diminution, not to say destruction, upon which you now look. Now many noble families on your side are not to be seen at all; many you see humbled, many divided. The parents are yet of Rus′ of your side's rite, but the sons and daughters are Catholics. After the departure of their parents, what do you think of your chances for increase? The parents, who are of Rus′ of your rite, gave birth to

†   A warning and admonition to the Rus′ of the Non-Uniates to incline to holy unity of their own free will before they are forced to do so involuntarily.
93.   [Acts 5:39.]

their descendants for the increase of that same rite. Do you expect from their descendants, who are Catholics, descendants born for the increase of the Rus' of your rite? I do not think so. It is already too late for that. For if even that is not mine for certain in the disposition of matters where I am at home, what can be mine in someone else's sphere, where I have no right and access?

Just look, most worthy Brotherhood: not so many years ago, when the nation of our rite was fattened with noble families and high offices, it was fleshy and fat and adorned in a most costly manner; it wore the belt of the laws, freedoms, and liberties of this most excellent Crown, and the belt lay on it beautifully and fittingly, and it was of great girth. In this age of ours, however, when quite a little of it has fallen away, it has become so weakened that the belt seems hardly to fit it. And if this was the case in these thirty years, what sort of body do you—whoever of you should live to see it (for the sake of argument)—expect it to have in another thirty years? Certainly it will be so emaciated that the belt will not stay up on it but will fall of its own accord from its thin hips. For the belt always remains the same size; but the body of your nation, as far as those are concerned who properly adorn themselves with the belt, is becoming so thin and emaciated that it will not be able to maintain on itself such an ample and exquisite belt. And although no one will remove the belt from it once it has lost fatness and strength, it will lose it of its own accord. Once you have lost it, you will have no cause to go before the Sejms and the tribunals. The city bench will be your only refuge, and beginning today they will unseat you and many others in that time. And thus it will become necessary for the Ruthenian nation of your side to do unbelted,[94] even against its will, what it could now do wearing the belt and of its own free will. And what it can do today (so long as the belt holds on it more or less) with the honorable maintenance and fortification of that belt, once it has lost it, it will have to do without any hope of acquiring the belt. And the memorable words of a certain pious man will be fulfilled upon it, who said, among his other speeches, to a sizable gathering of the nobility of his Ruthenian nation: "Our Ruthenian nation will join the Union when it has become

94. [Smotryc'kyj puns here in calling the Ruthenian nation *rozpasany,* that is, "de-belted," or without the belt (*pas*) of laws, freedoms and liberties, but also "unbridled" or "licentious."]

nothing but peasants," as if he had said, when it has no more nobility, when the liberties will no longer suit it, toward which matters are quite clearly and quickly tending. For if at the beginning of the Union it was difficult to count the noble houses of the Ruthenian religion in one palatinate, now, in all the areas of the Ruthenian land, they can almost be counted on the fingers of one hand. And so, if we buy holy unity at that time, we will not buy it cheaply, since we now despise it together with its price of purchase.

†Let us now examine, most worthy Brotherhood, what sort of end there is for the case you have brought against the case initiated by God. You can easily see it. You will say: "And what about the Lord God?" And the answer will be: "And what about those to whom you appeal with your obedience?" Unto that nation in which you are now free, since you wear the belt, He will deliver you, unbelted, unto the sort of freedom that the peasants in the villages and the communes in the cities have. The Lord God will punish you for your destruction-bent stubbornness in that the *lex populi* [law of the people], as we hear there, will be called by the names of your Palaeologi, Comneni, Cantacuzeni, etc. And you will have no one else to blame but yourselves, the Ruthenian nation of your side. Thus while you still have the climate for it (and you truly have the most appropriate climate now, while you are subject to your superior pastor, the heretic), kindle in the Ruthenian nation of your side the One that has grown dim, that Christ the Lord inflamed among His disciples. Cease your unrest, cleanse your faith, bring unanimity to the Ruthenian Church. In this salvatory matter look not to Moldavia, nor to Wallachia, nor to the Greeks, nor to Moscow: tyranny reigns there everywhere. For those who are under the Turk, unity is conspiracy; and for those who are under the Muscovite, it is perjury. For as the Turkish ruler does not allow the Greeks to say even a word about unity with the Romans, so the clergy, during their consecration, take an oath to the Muscovite ruler that they will not receive bishops or metropolitans consecrated and sent to them by either the Roman pope or the patriarch of Constantinople and to whom they would be subject.[95]

† The effects of the abominable schism.
95. Maksim Grek, *Ser. 38.* [Sermon 38. Perhaps Smotryc'kyj refers here to the sermon listed by Ivanov under no. 225 (1969, 154). In this work Maksim Grek opposes those who refused to receive not only bishops consecrated by the

So do what you see as belonging to your soul-saving benefit: let us confer with the brethren about an agreement; let us look for and discuss a means for the unification of divided Rus', and thereby let us return holy unity to the Ruthenian Church; and once it has been returned, let us transfer the patriarchate, which has now become heretic, to our Ruthenian Catholic nation. The patriarch of Alexandria resides nowadays in Cairo, and yet he is still patriarch of Alexandria. And if it is true that *ibi Roma, ubi Papa* [where the pope is, there is Rome], this, too, will become true that *ibi Constantinopolis, ubi oecumenicus Patriarcha* [where the ecumenical patriarch is, there is Constantinople]. And God will bless us. So long as you served disharmony and variance, the Lord God punished you terribly through the errors and heresies of your Zizanijs; but as soon as you turn to the service of God with all the strength of your soul, the Lord God will immediately teach you the true dogmas of the Orthodox faith.

But when it is said to you that you lost faith through your Zizanijs, you answer with the words of Christ the Lord: "Nevertheless when the Son of man cometh, shall he find faith on the earth?"[96] †If in your answer you boast of the fact that you lost faith in order that, when the Son of man comes, He should not find it with you, then He will reward you as infidels. If you say this in order to boast of the small numbers of confessors of your faith, that boast will also be in vain. For that same Christ the Lord says: "And this Gospel of the kingdom shall be preached in all the world for a witness unto all nations; and then shall the end come when the Son of man also comes."[97] Therefore, you should argue thus: since the Western Roman Church preaches the Gospel of the kingdom in those nations that it had not yet reached in witness (testimony to this is America, the New—as it is commonly called—World), when Christ the Lord has come to the earth, He will look for the faith in the Church that preaches that Gospel, that is, His faith, unto the ends of the world, that is to say, in the Western Roman Church and not in the Greek Eastern Church, which, from the time of its separation from the Western

---

pope, but also those clergy who had received their consecration from Greek patriarchs.]

96. Lk. 18[:8].

†   The vain boast of schismatic Rus' is suppressed.

97. Mt. 24[:14].

Church, has grown hard, no longer giving birth or nourishing; and thus with your boast you bring your demise upon you. Moreover, you should also know that Christ the Lord will find living, not dead, faith; but faith without love, that is, without holy Church unity, is dead, as it is in the filthy schism.

Therefore, I admonish and I ask you: boast neither that you have lost faith through your Zizanijs, nor that when Christ the Lord comes He should find your faith on earth. If you do not first find your lost faith through holy unity (for otherwise you will not find it living), neither will Christ the Lord find it with you. Likewise, neither wish nor desire that holy unity should not take root in the Ruthenian nation, for you cannot wish or desire that without losing your souls. Neither believe that Non-Union should ever overcome the Union in our fatherland. Those are the dreams that are whispered into your ears by the enemy of brotherly love and unity. [†]For having established indubitably that Christ the Lord, as the one who commended and gave holy unity to His disciples, is its ever present Defender and the One who maintains and strengthens it, holy unity also has a defender and protector in the pope, the Father of Fathers, the universal pastor of the Universal Church; it has his most reverend *consistorium* [consistory]; it has *vigilantissimam ejusdem de propaganda fide Catholica, gravissimorum Patrum S. Congregationem* [his same most vigilant Holy Congregation of the most eminent fathers for the Propagation of the Catholic Faith]; and it has the *Nuncium Apostolicum* [apostolic nuncio], to whom is especially entrusted in this state the defense of holy unity as an ecclesiastical and godly matter. It has a defender and protector in God's anointed, His Majesty the King, Our Gracious Lord. It has the most excellent senate of both estates and all the Catholics of the clerical and lay estates here in the most noble Crown and in the Grand Duchy of Lithuania. Certainly holy unity confidently expects no lesser defense and protection from the most illustrious descendants of His Royal Majesty than it experiences from His Majesty the King himself (although you imagine something to your liking, fascinated by wretched whisperers), who will certainly increase the Church of God in this state and not destroy it so that they

---

[†] What a most weighty and certain defense the holy unity of united Rus' has.

might thereby earn God's grace and blessing and give rise to the love of God's faithful praisers.

For it is not the custom of Catholic kings, nor of their pious progeny to be lenient toward, or to spread, the schism or heresy. Examples are those pious emperors, the Constantines, Constanses, Theodosiuses, Gratians, Marcians, Honoriuses, Justinians, and others. Furthermore, holy unity has as its defenders and protectors the *legitimos episcopos* [legitimate bishops] of the Ruthenian Church: the metropolitan, archbishops, and bishops, most pious men and highly learned, diligently watchful in their vocation, as well as their other followers in every estate. And above all, as I said, it has a defender and protector in the Lord God Himself. It has thus reached the point that He should say, through the highest Church authority, at the time that He himself should establish, "Let it be," and immediately the word will become deed.

†And what do you have for the defense of your Non-Union? Stubbornness. And for its protection? Errors and heresies. You say: "We, with God alone, against all our enemies," as if you had said, "We, with the Lord God, will suppress the Lord God." But this makes no sense. Who does not know that the Lord God is with His own and not with the others; with the Catholics and not with the heretics or with the schismatics? For as the Lord God does not increase the heresies, likewise He does not help the schism. He holds both in enmity; He suppresses both; He punishes through eternal fire the authors as well as the protectors of both.

‡Finally, holy unity also has, in addition to all of these, many defenders and protectors in those of us from your side, who are, by the grace of God, no longer from your side, who ask the Lord God with all our soul in all our prayers, day and night, that He save you and us, whether willing or unwilling, voluntarily or involuntarily; and that He compel us to come in to His costly supper[98] by whatever judgments He himself knows; and that He might deign to give us the easiest means He himself knows to reach the heart of His anointed, His Majesty the King,

---

†   What sort of defense does the accursed schism have?
‡   That the words of Christ the Lord *compelle intrare* [compel to come in (Lk. 14:23)] used against heretics and schismatics are most beneficial and salvatory.
98.   [Lk. 14:23.]

Our Gracious Lord, and that of his most excellent senate of both estates so that, with regard to their salvation, out of the love they have for the Lord God, being obliged to have it also for their neighbor, following the example of that merciful Samaritan, they might have pity upon us, the Ruthenian nation, their neighbors, who have fallen among thieves, the heretics; and that, wounded by them through the many wounds of errors and heresies and already half-dead, they might take us on their beast (that is, on their industry) and lead us to the innkeeper of a Samaritan inn and that they might entrust us and give us up to him that he take us into his care.[99]

For since, by God's command, they are supposed to love their neighbor as they love themselves (and if they do not do this, they will be subject to the entire law), therefore, wishing for themselves eternal life with the Lord God, let them wish it for us as well, not only in words, but also in deed, mindful of the Savior's words *compelle intrare,* "compel them to come in," so that He might convince us to go with Him along whatever that one royal road might be that leads to eternal life, and along which they themselves go; for we have wandered too much along the crossroads and the side roads of errors and heresies.[100] To be lenient toward us in this is not to show us love or mercy; rather it is to envy us the good that they expect, certain in God's grace. For even after we reject your new errors and heresies, when they see our Eastern Church pure, well established in true faith, will they recognize it as the Church of Christ the Lord, or will they recognize their Western one as such? If the Eastern, then out of necessity for their salvation they will be obliged to unite with it. If they recognize their own as that of Christ the Lord, out of necessity for our salvation they will have to unite us with themselves, since outside of the Church of Christ the Lord no one can be saved.[101]

Once that holy deed has been done unto our entire nation throughout all the cities, it will not and cannot properly be judged as force and violence either by those who are dear to God or by the Lord God Himself. A doctor does not inflict violence when, with no small pain to the patient, he pulls on an arm or a leg that has become

99.   [Lk. 10:30–7.]
100. [Lk. 14:23.]
101. [Acts 4:12.]

dislocated from the joint. The same thing will happen to us. For if you do not acknowledge that you have become dislocated from the Church of Christ the Lord (that is, on account of the schism), the swellings and scabs (that is, the errors and heresies) that have settled on the joint must certainly cause you to believe and assure you of this, although you have not acknowledged them to yourselves for the twenty-eight years that have passed since they began to swell. But you must acknowledge them now whether you like it or not, when you no longer see them yourselves nor can hide them from others in any manner, since they are on the surface of the body: for they have been published in print for the entire world to see.

St. Augustine was of the opinion that no one should be compelled to the unity of the Church of Christ the Lord, but that this should be brought about through words, proved through disputations, and be victorious through rational arguments so that we not create, as he says, imaginary Catholics out of those whom we knew as overt heretics. Nonetheless, that holy doctor changed his opinion and said: "My opinion had to give way not to the words of those who opposed me in this, but to the very examples demonstrated in actual fact. For first, my own town was cited against me, which, having been of the Donatist party, was converted to Catholic unity through fear of the imperial laws; but now we see it so disgusted by the greatness of the demise of the Donatists that no one wishes to believe that it was ever in that error of perdition. In this same manner other cities were also mentioned to me by name so that I might understand from the facts themselves that to this matter as well one might properly apply what was written: *Da sapienti occasionem, et addetur ei sapientia;* 'give opportunity to a wise man, and wisdom will be granted to him.'"[102]

Deign to bring it about, Lord Jesus Christ, that the honorable, holy, and soul-saving opinion of that doctor, who was great in the Church of God, be realized upon our Ruthenian nation by that power, unto whose government, industry, care, and defense the Lord God entrusted us [i.e., the Polish king], so that it [St. Augustine's opinion] be praised through the very progress of the matter; and with this reason: that you, too, after acquiring the wisdom thus granted to you, might be wise

---

102. [St. Augustine, *Epistle 93,* chap. 5, sections 16 and 17, *To Brother Vincentius, PL* 33:329–30; *NPNF1* 1:388. Prov. 9:9.]

and might come to the knowledge of the truth;[103] and that our highest power, through the grace of the Righteous Judge, might be worthy of his reward on that day for his pious industry on our behalf, along with those pious emperors and kings who, piously and wisely bringing to effect that salvatory *compelle intrare* among heretics and schismatics, gained countless numbers of heretics and schismatics for the Lord God. Cause this to happen to us in our days, Lord Jesus Christ, whose love and the blessing of my humility be with you. Amen. Derman', the year of our Lord 1628.

And what follows I wrote with my own hand.

I send you, brethren, the peace of Christ the Lord, which, if you receive it, will remain with you. If you do not receive it, it will return to me, and know then that you were not worthy of it. And I, leaving your house, will shake the dust from my feet as a testimony against you on the day of God's terrible judgment.[104]

> Your well-disposed brother in Christ the Lord,
> and Father in spirit, wishes Your Graces
> all good things,
> Meletij Smotryc'kyj, Archbishop of Polack,
> etc., Archimandrite of Vilnius and
> Derman'.

In addition I also send for Your Graces to read a copy of the letter I wrote to His Grace, Father Cyril, the present patriarch of Constantinople, which I sent last year, 1627, the 23rd day of the month of August, with Mr. Andrzej Krasowski, burgher and merchant of Lviv. It certainly reached his hands within six weeks of the date; but to this day I have not had, and do not have, an answer. Therefore (*salvo ejus honore* [saving his honor)] I do what was and is fitting for one troubled in conscience unto the salvation of my soul and of those who would look to me in this matter.

---

103. [1 Tim. 2:4.]
104. [Mt. 10:14; Mk. 6:11.]

A copy of the letter[105]
Written by the reverend in God
Meletij
Smotryc'kyj,
Called Archbishop of Polack, etc.,
Archimandrite of Vilnius and
Derman',
to His Grace,
Father Cyril,
Patriarch of Constantinople,
Which, translated from Latin into the Polish language,
Reads as follows.

Most Reverend Father,
after rendering the requisite greeting to your pastorly dignity
and after humbly kissing Your Reverence's feet:

Since the time when, through my departure from Constantinople, I have removed myself from Your Reverence, I have not had, nor do I have, one day, not to say one hour, in which I have not lamented of my misfortune and sighed at my grief; and this is because, at my advanced age and to no small detriment of my belabored health, after undertaking so many labors, dangers, and hardships in travel on land and at sea,[106] I did not manage to remove there the burden that had weighed me down here at home, to accomplish there what I had set out to do: to free my conscience, I say, through Your Reverence's help, from that by which it was so very enslaved. There, in the presence of Your Reverence, where there was the place and occasion for it, especially since I set off for that country with no other intention but, through the healthy advice and living doctrine from the mouth of Your Reverence, to cleanse, lighten, and heal my soul, which had been troubled by many doubts, and my thoughts, which had been eaten away as if by some gnawing worm by entanglements of various opinions. But what came of it? I accomplished nothing there; and here, when I returned to the fatherland, I was all but

105. [A Latin version of the letter was sent to the *Congregatio de Propaganda Fide* and placed on record there. See above, p. lvi.]
106. [2 Cor. 11:26.]

crucified by envious ingrates. For as soon as I appeared, immediately and without any proper reason, ugly envy together with sordid ignorance, which have no regard for anything beneficial, either for the body or for the soul, were hurled upon me with such ardor that, if my innocence and the righteousness of my conscience in this situation had not preserved me, by the help of God's special grace, through internal consolations, I had thought to abandon my nation, which had fallen wretchedly but which I love with all my heart, and to return again to Your Reverence or to the holy places of Palestine, which are as dear to me as my soul because our Savior lived in them; and there, following the example of the pious men, our holy fathers, to lament my grievous sins so long as God, who created me, should allow my soul to remain in my body.

But love for my neighbor would in no manner permit or allow me to do that, as it showed me indeed that the demise of my neighbors, abandoned in such a dire situation and in mortal danger, was my own demise and perdition. For my God deigned to place me, however unworthy, at this post that I might watch over His holy flock, His sheep, which He redeemed with His most precious, sacred blood; and He entrusted large numbers of them to me (after others) to pasture, in the knowledge that any fall that should occur to them through my lack of watchfulness would be my own fall, and their salvation, my salvation. Wherefore, if I do not return to Your Reverence in my body, I return nonetheless; for this is for me the ultimate thing: that I cannot live in a state of salvation without enjoying your counsel about this matter. Thus I do from a distance with my pen what I could not do in your presence with my mouth; and falling to Your Reverence's feet, I do not intend to rise and depart from them until Your Reverence's love and pity moves me from them with consolation.

I have no one else to whom to turn. Our fatherland is devoid of learned men on our side; you cannot [find such a man], as they say, even with a candle.[107] And although we are all unlearned, nonetheless none of us wishes to acknowledge, nor does acknowledge, that anyone is wiser than ourselves. And although in matters of salvation (alas for our great poverty) for every head there is a different opinion; nonetheless we wish to be known for our unanimity. Whenever there are ten of us not from the common rabble *sed ex iis qui videntur aliquid esse*

107. [*NKPP* 3:416–17, "Szukać," 20. Cf. *NKPP* 1:437, "Diogenes," 2.]

[but from those who appear to be of some importance], there are just as many opinions about one and the same article of faith. The Lord God has confused our minds more than the languages of those stupid giants at the Tower of Babel and in such a matter in which, if anyone is stupid, he insists that he is in no way stupid. We have hungered and starved so that some of us through weakness have lost consciousness, while others hardly move. But we suffer the hunger that weakens a man not in the body, but in the soul: we suffer hunger for the word of God, and it is so severe and unbearable that on account of it, there are fewer of us every day, every hour. For some of us go to the Romans, the Uniates, and others to the Protestants. There are many who even toy with Arianism. Thus there are fewer every day, so that if Your Reverence should have the opportunity to look upon the countenance of the Ruthenian Church now (upon which you looked twenty-some years ago), astounded and not without bitter lamentation, you would say in amazement: *O quantum ab illa! Mira enim est ejus, Pater Beatissime, metamorphosis* ["Oh, how much is changed!"[108] For astonishing is the transformation, Most Blessed Father], that threatens it every day, every hour with mortal ruin. For whenever something makes gains or remains the same size day after day, there is hope for constancy and endurance; but when it loses something every day, every hour, it must certainly lose all this in time, and one must fear the certain demise and destruction of this matter. And one has such a fear for us, for our Ruthenian Church, which neither gains nor remains the same size, but every day loses great numbers so sorely and unrestrainedly that only he does not see its near demise and destruction who does not know that night follows after the setting of the sun.

What are we to do in that case? I found no other remedy than the one I had employed. But it is no secret to Your Reverence how successfully I fared in it. For since I came to know for certain that Your Reverence had in your possession the *Lucubrationes piae memoriae Gennadii Scholarii, Patriarchae Constantinopolitani, contra quinque dissensiones ad Latinos; Meletii Alexandrini Libri 4 de Dogmatibus* [lucubrations of Gennadios Scholarios of blessed memory, Patriarch of Constantinople, against five disagreements against the Latins; Meletius of Alexandria's four books on dogmas], as well as Your Reverence's

108. [Cf. Augustine, *City of God,* 22.29.2; *PL* 41:798.]

own *Catechesis Orthodoxae Fidei* [*Catechism of the Orthodox Faith*], the first three counseled me to have hopeful recourse to Your Reverence concerning the fourth thing: that I should confer about everything found in those writings with Your Reverence face to face and, well informed in all this by Your Reverence, return to my people and inform them from Your Reverence's mouth, as it were. But I do not declare to Your Reverence how successful I was (that I say it again), since you are well aware of this; I only declare and say this: Grant, Lord God, that my greeting Your Reverence by letter rather than in person might compensate for what was omitted during my stay in your presence, of which I am indubitably certain from Your Reverence, whose special grace toward me and innate and truly paternal love toward our Ruthenian nation does not allow me to doubt. For if in my recourse to Your Reverence I should receive a rejection, it is for Your Reverence to show me where I should turn. But I do not suppose that Your Reverence would send me to look for counsel in this matter from anyone beside yourself, especially since, as a student of Your Reverence's in my youth, it was in great measure on account of Your Reverence's writings that I arrived at such a confusion of thoughts and a muddle of opinions.

My lamentatious work testifies to what I was previously, before there came to my attention the letter Your Reverence left in Lviv on the twenty-fourth day of January in the year 1601 with Father Dymitr Solikowski, the archbishop of Lviv of blessed memory (at whose residence I once happened to be present together with Your Reverence), which Your Reverence knew and was aware of, since it was sent to Your Reverence. And what Your Reverence's letter made of me, once it was brought to my attention, Your Reverence can easily conjecture; for my lamentatious writings *in toto fere redolent Luteranismum et Calvinismum, passim* [are redolent almost totally of Lutheranism and Calvinism throughout] in all the chapters, but especially *in catechesi pro colophone addita* [in the catechism added as a colophon] in that work. But Your Reverence's letter *romanae professioni in tantum favet* [is favorable toward the Roman profession to the degree] that it shows the real unanimity of the Eastern Church with the Western in all the articles of the faith. In it Your Reverence said so *libere* [frankly] about the confession of the Protestants: "I know well, and my patriarchs know, that the doctrines and the actions of the Protestants not only give rise to detriment and confusion in the Eastern and Western Churches, as they do now in Germany, France, England, and elsewhere, but they also bring a significant loss of good morals to the Christian kingdoms." And further: "And although heretics from Europe, out of hatred toward the Roman Church and the see of Peter, sought agreement with the Easterners, they were never accepted, for they agree with us only in that in which the Jews and the Mohamedans do: that God is the One Creator and Ruler of the world, righteous and good, who punishes the evil and rewards the good and in other such points of confession. But they do not agree with us on the foremost articles of the Christian faith: they do not have concord with us on the antiquity of Church orders, apostolic traditions, the authority of the holy fathers and doctors of both Churches, whom either all or some of their sects reject, on the number and canon of the books of Holy Scripture, Church customs, justification, the holy liturgy, veneration and the holy relics, the Mother of God, and the most holy Trinity, and they wrench from their heads new interpretations of Holy Scripture. Experience itself testifies that this matter holds great danger. Since they are planted so far away from us, they cannot grow together with us."

Having declared this about the Protestants in your letter, Your Reverence goes on to say the following about the Eastern and Western Churches: "And what is a matter of controversy between the Eastern and the Western Churches may repulse the unlearned and the simple, but the learned easily derive one understanding in the love of Christ. We do not abhor the See of St. Peter; rather we render it the appropriate honor and respect, and we acknowledge it as the first, the mother. We have one and the same faith, one baptism with God the Father, and the Son, and the Holy Spirit, one nature, one omnipotence, one divinity, one hope of vocation, one love, the same prayers and supplications for kings, rulers, and magistrates, the same sacraments, the same holy orders and lesser and greater Church consecrations, one Gospel, the same prophetic and apostolic Scriptures, one authority of the holy Orthodox fathers of the Church, both Greek and Latin. What are we supposed to have in common with other sects, which the one Church considered heretics, and which the other also still considers as such and which it condemns and anathematizes? Both Churches, or rather the one Church of two rites, held the first councils in common, such that there was no contradiction between them in the foundations of Christian doctrine;

there was only variance or diversity and separate ceremonies between the Greek and the Latin nations."

Thus I say: Your Reverence's letter, or rather Your Reverence himself, having shown and confessed that the Protestants, whom you call heretics, are far from the communion and unanimity of the Church, shows and confesses that the Romans are in unanimity with the Greeks. And hearing this from Your Reverence's lips through that letter (from your lips, I say, for I am permitted to see it with my eyes and to read it even now on a daily basis), and being well aware of Your Reverence's handwriting, I received and considered it as if it were being spoken from Your Reverence's lips, and spoken to me, as well, among others. And therefore, after examining my lamentatious work and finding it contrary to Your Reverence's words, as is darkness to light and untruth to truth, I concluded that if Your Reverence's letter had come to my attention before I had published my *Lament,* either I would certainly not have published it, or if I had published it, I would have published it *consonum* [in harmony] with Your Reverence's letter. But since it was only in answer to my *Lament* that the author who responded to me cited it *specifice* [specifically], word-for-word in his work and thus brought it to the attention of all of us,[109] therefore, unaware of the matter, I published my lamentatious work so very much *dissonans* [in disagreement] with Your Reverence's letter.

Thus having acquired from both those writings future struggles in my thoughts and muddles in my opinions and having sorely troubled my conscience, I sought the first occasion when I might have recourse to Your Reverence for the lightening and the deposition of such a heavy burden from the shoulders of my soul. For I often remembered both the words cited in Your Reverence's letter and the other things said there in Your Reverence's name: "As for me, admonished by the majesty of His Majesty the King, I obediently leave this kingdom and return to my people; and I declare that I did not wish to seek anything else in this land but that some peace and harmony might be established between those who wish unity and have already entered into it and those who

---

109. [Smotryc'kyj refers here to Piotr Skarga's *Na Treny y Lament Theophila Orthologa, Do Rusi Greckiego Nabożeństwa, Przestroga (A Warning to Rus' of the Greek Rite against the Threnodies and Lament of Theopil Ortholog,* Cracow, 1610), which published the letter on pp. 108–13.]

are not in it, but suppose that they do so piously and, deferring to their foremost authorities, do not even agree among themselves, but agree in heretical errors."[110]

Recalling, I say, those first and those second words of Your Reverence, I struggled internally with my thoughts; and I could not be calmed in any way until I had informed myself from Your Reverence's lips and calmed my thoughts from the works of the aforementioned patriarchs—Gennadius, Meletius, and Your Reverence. But when I was informed by Your Reverence's oral announcement that the writings of Gennadius were not to be found, with the exception of the treatise *De Processione Spiritus S. adversus Latinos [On the Procession of the Holy Spirit, against the Latins]*,[111] and even that thoroughly excerpted by his descendants and successors, and that also *Meletii quatuor de Dogmatibus libri* [Meletius's four books on dogmas] were burned by Your Reverence at the hour of his death according to his own sworn order—sincerely anxious over Your Reverence's writings, I asked whether there were any writings on that matter, and Your Reverence gave me to read an explication *Symboli Nicoeno-constantinopolitani* [of the Nicene-Constantinopolitan creed] written in the form of a dialogue.

Reading it diligently and eagerly, against my expectations and to my great amazement I found and read things contrary to the letter of Your Reverence that I mentioned earlier. For now Your Reverence establishes and asserts that there are no more than two sacraments and judges that prayers for the dead are unnecessary and not beneficial to the dead. In addition to these two things, you also do away with *judicium particulare* [particular judgment], which is common in the confession of our holy fathers, and especially that of St. John of Damascus. Your Reverence also removes there purgatory, which you state is a cause of our evil life. But elsewhere, that is, in answer to the questions of one of our countrymen drawn from my *Lament* and sent along with it to Your Reverence several years ago, namely, in answer to point four, which reads "man is forgiven his sins by grace, freely, without merits," Your Reverence answers thus: "It was correctly noted on the sheet that this

---

110. [Skarga 1610, 123.]
111. [Gennadius wrote a work in two volumes against the Latins on the procession of the Holy Spirit. The second volume is in *PG* 160:665–714.]

point is Lutheran; for although the mercy of God toward man is great, nonetheless woe to those who think that they can be saved without good works. And thus I do not pause at length on this, for a complete witness on our behalf is Holy Scripture, a complete witness the writings of the holy fathers. And if perhaps Orthologue said that in order to do away with the Roman purgatory, I do not praise him. In this article of faith, the belief of our Church is not in agreement with Luther; rather it agrees with the Romans, with the exception of the material fire of purgatory." These are Your Reverence's words, who certainly knows that even for the Romans it is not an article of faith to establish material fire in purgatory. In addition, I also cite these two things spoken to me by Your Reverence's lips and heard by my ears. First: "I wish to strive in every manner that private confession, which is performed with the enumeration of each sin, be abandoned in the Eastern Church and cast out from it." Second: "The difference that exists between the Eastern and the Western Churches on the procession of the Holy Spirit is such that it can most easily be brought into agreement."

Thus when I brought to mind and considered these things from the letter and from the catechism, along with those things declared orally, and when I pondered them in my mind, I became troubled; and since they were great matters (for what can be a greater thing for a man than the dogmas of the faith?), I did not lightly enter into conversation with Your Reverence about them. Then later, for my sins, I was taken sick there through God's dispensation, on account of which and Your Reverence's great difficulties at that time, I was unable to have a serious discussion about this with Your Reverence; but at Your Reverence's advice, even though I was not thoroughly restored to health, I set out for Palestine, having postponed the things that I had designated for discussion with Your Reverence until my return, God granting, from Palestine.

But since, according to the common saying, *Homo proponit, Deus disponit* [man proposes, God disposes],[112] almighty God changed what I had proposed so that it was different from what I wished and thought; and He ordained that my arrival in Constantinople from Palestine be during a terrible plague, because of which I was unable to enter in any way into those conversations with Your Reverence that I had undertaken and proposed; and I had to leave empty-handed after seeing

112. [Arthaber 403.]

Your Reverence a few times in passing, as it were. Wherefore, now distracted even more by various thoughts and opinions, having become more thoroughly confused after my departure from Constantinople than I was distracted and confused before my arrival before Your Reverence and not finding the means here at home for disentangling myself from these webs and for calming my thoughts, I turn again to Your Reverence, not with an oral conversation, as I said, but with this epistolary question, begging Your Reverence humbly and submissively, as a son does his father, and asking diligently, as a student a teacher, that Your Reverence lead me out of this tangled labyrinth with your wise counsel and salvatory doctrine, teaching me to what I must adhere and what I must think not only about the articles of faith I mentioned earlier, but also about others such as these: *De arbitrio servum, ne illud sit an liberum: de peccato, tum originali, tum actuali; de gratia, de fide, de justificatione, de bonorum operum justitia, de providentia, de praescientia, de praedestinatione, de Ecclesia, de Sacramentis, de Scriptura Sacra, de traditionibus, et de statu animarum, etc. etc.* [about the will, whether it is subject or free; about sin, both original and actual; about grace; about faith; about justification; about the justice of good works; about providence; about prescience; about predestination; about the Church; about the sacraments; about Holy Scripture; about traditions; about the state of souls (that have departed hence),[113] etc. etc.].

Should I follow the decree of the Council of Trent on these divine matters or the side against which the Council had worked in those articles of faith? I wish gladly, aware that my salvation is at stake, to learn this from Your Reverence, as from a pastor and a teacher. And it is not without reason that I seek instruction in all this and in other things; rather, mindful of the custom and order of present times and seeing that, unlike all the other Christian sects that are in our fatherland, only our Ruthenian Church of the Eastern obedience has not had, and does not have, a proper confession of faith described in the manner of a catechism, therefore, although I saw that this matter was beyond my strength, placing my trust in Him, who makes even blind men wise

---

113. [The words in parentheses have been added for clarity on the basis of the Latin version of the letter (p. 136): *"de statu hinc exeuntium animarum."*]

and causes asses to speak,[114] I made bold to write a catechism in the Ruthenian language, which I had with me in Constantinople, although I did not present myself with it to Your Reverence, since that was to be a labor of more than one day.

Thus I postponed that for a time when Your Reverence and I would be free, which did not occur for the reasons I mentioned earlier. And so now, urged both by myself and by clerical and lay brothers who are aware of my work, I turn to Your Reverence concerning the things in which I am insufficient, and I ask for counsel and instruction. Deign to inform me: in all the above-mentioned articles of faith, are we in agreement with the Romans or with the Protestants, or do we adhere to and confess some third, middle thing? Moreover, I also ask for advice in the differences of faith that have long existed between the Eastern and the Western Churches, such as about the procession of the Holy Spirit, purgatory, unleavened bread, the state of blessed and sinful souls, and that which only in our age has come to be charged against them as a difference: *de communione sub una specie* [about communion under one species].[115]

For if the first of these points (as I heard from Your Reverence's lips) is *conciliabilis* [subject to establishment by a council]; and the second, as Your Reverence writes to one of our countrymen, is entirely in agreement with them *salvo igne materiali* [with the exception of the material fire]; the third, as Peter, patriarch of Antioch, believes, is of antiquity in the Western Church;[116] the fourth is essentially in harmony with our Church hymns; and the fifth is not without concomitance, as Meletius acknowledges in his letter to Potij;[117] then I ask and I beg Your Reverence: are not all these points *conciliabilia* [subject to establishment by a council] in one and the same fashion? And is it therefore not rather a debate that exists between us and them, and not a contradiction, according to Your Reverence's words cited above, since in the foundations of Christian doctrine there is no contradiction

114. [Jn. 9:39–41; Num. 22:28–30.]
115. [Of the six differences between the two Churches mentioned elsewhere by Smotryc'kyj, note that he omitted one here in his interrogation of the patriarch: the primacy of the bishop of Rome.]
116. [See above, p. 520.]
117. [Dated from Egypt, 15 October 1599, printed in Derman', 1605.]

between them, but only some sort of variance or diversity and the separate ceremonies of the Greek and Latin nations?

Let us not, then, by missing the mark, remain in the twofold shame Your Reverence described in that same letter. First, where Your Reverence says that *quae inter orientalem et occidentalem ecclesiam aliquam disceptationem retinere videntur, indoctiorum quidem illusio esse videtur; doctiores vero facile eundem, aut proximum sensum in dilectione Christi eliciunt* [the things that seem to maintain some debate between the Eastern and the Western Churches seem to be, however, the illusion of the unlearned; learned men can certainly elicit the same, or nearly the same, sense in the love of Christ]. Second, where Your Reverence says in your own name: *Profiteor, me nihil his in locis nec agere, nec conari voluisse, quam ut inter eos, qui unitatem cupiunt ac profitentur, atque illos qui in ea non sunt, et pie se facere credunt, et summa illa capita sua respicientes, nec inter se ipsos conveniunt; et potius haereticis erroribus consentiunt, pax aliqua et* συμφωνία *institui potuisset* [I confess that I did not wish to do or to attempt anything in these parts, but that some peace and harmony might be established between those who wish and confess unity and those who are not in it and believe that they do that piously and, looking to their foremost authorities, do not agree among themselves and agree rather in heretical errors].

Lest, I say, we suffer that twofold shame described by Your Reverence: *Pati enim illusionem, et pie se facere credere, hoc in sensu, illudi est, atque errare* [For to suffer an illusion and to believe that one acts piously, in this sense, is to be mocked and to err]; lest through our intense opposition to the Union that is making significant progress in our Church from day to day, with no small daily loss to our side, we receive ignorance and error even from Your Reverence, we humbly ask Your Reverence: deign to describe to us, even in a few words, to what we are to adhere, since not only I, but all of us from Rus' are strangers in all this. May Your Reverence deign to take into account the *difficultatem rei* [difficulty of the matter] and to consider the *distantiam loci* [distance of the place], since it is not given to all of us to go or to write and to send to Your Reverence. All this is very difficult for us, and for many it is even impossible.

Show therefore, Your Reverence, your paternal love for us, and save us lest we seek other teachers. Cause us to agree among ourselves and with Your Reverence in the articles of faith upon which the salvation of our souls depends. Send us, Your Reverence, your catechism, and by it and by your epistolary advice give unanimity to our hearts and to our lips about everything in question so that we might confess with our lips unto salvation what we believed in our hearts unto righteousness.[118] Do not think, Your Reverence, that it is I alone who write to Your Reverence. I am one indeed, but such a one whose archiepiscopal diocese is so rich in Christians, by God's grace, as are not to be found in those lands under even ten metropolitans. There are also many from other dioceses, clerics and lay people, who look to me and who seek their faith from my lips, and whom, because they are ignorant, I, who am also ignorant, can both destroy and save by my example. I will certainly not be lying if I also say that the entire Ruthenian Church looks upon me to no small degree. I do not say this in pride or in haughtiness (God forfend); rather I say this according to the old saying: *Inter caecos, et monoculos Rex* [Among blind men even the one-eyed is king].[119] Wherefore, if I should be neglected by Your Reverence in my request and thrust away empty-handed, taking God as my witness, the Creator, who examines the hearts and minds of man,[120] then, *salvo tuo Paterno honore* [saving your paternal honor], I would have to do what I perceived as bringing salvation to my soul through the grace and help of my God, who does not desire the death of the sinner and who grants conversion to man.[121] Thus I await from Your Reverence paternal, pastorly, and magisterial consolation, advice, and instruction; and may almighty God deign to preserve you for many years to come, thoroughly healthy and safe, for the true preaching of the word of His truth and the service of uniting the wretchedly sundered Church of God.

And I would have ended with this, but at the very conclusion of my letter it occurred to me that God knows whether I will ever have another such occasion to write to Your Reverence; therefore, begging Your Reverence's forgiveness for the length of my letter, I add to all this a few more of the worms of my conscience. They are small indeed, as they seem, but they gnaw; and they attacked my soul during my

---

118. [Rom. 10:9–10.]
119. [Erasmus *Ad.* 3.4.96; Arthaber 271.]
120. [Ps. 7:9, 26:2; Jer. 11:20, 20:12.]
121. [2 Pet. 3:9.]

presence in those Eastern lands, and they remain in it even until today, constantly biting at it. There are four of them: first, the burning of the books *de Dogmatibus [On Dogmas]* of Father Meletius, patriarch of Alexandria of blessed memory; second, the burning of the writings of Matthew, metropolitan of Myra; third, the confession of Gabriel, archbishop of Philadelphia, made at the time of his departure from this world in the presence of a monk of the Roman religion; fourth, the fire that appears on Holy Saturday in Jerusalem. These four worms, then, which, *primo intuitu* [at first glance], will seem to be small and not biting, when considered and examined are nonetheless great and very gnawing. I rub at them before Your Reverence, along with the other gnawings at my conscience that I have presented, and I humbly desire and submissively ask that they be removed from my soul through Your Reverence's healthy advice.

For when I consider these first two worms, those words of Ovid come to my mind: *Conscia mens ut cuique sua est, ita concipit intra pectora pro facto, spemque metumque suo* [According to the state of a person's conscience, so do hope and fear on account of his deeds arise in his mind].[122] For my conscience tells me that the burning of both those books took place through one and the same cause and to one and the same end: through the cause of God Himself, who does not desire the death of the sinner,[123] and to the end of God's mercy, which is infinite and exceeds all our iniquities. I first heard it in Constantinople, in the presence of many honorable metropolitans, from the lips of Father Theodosius, metropolitan of Sozopolis, who is well known to Your Reverence and a student of the metropolitan of Myra, and then I heard the same thing in Jerusalem from the lips of Father Lord Theophanes, patriarch of Jerusalem, whom the metropolitan of Myra himself, when he had arrived in the Moldavian land from our Ruthenian land, informed orally why he had burned his writings, in which he was vexatious *usque ad nauseam* [unto nausea] toward the Western Church and the Roman religion regarding the differences between the Eastern and Western Churches. For St. Peter appeared to him there three times at noon, whether in a dream or through *exstasis* [ecstasy] he himself could not discover, and he said to him the first

122. [Ovid, *Fasti* 1.485.]
123. [2 Pet. 3:9.]

and second times: "Matthew, how did my see so offend you that you inveigh against it so shamelessly? I admonish you, desist from this." And when he had said this, he disappeared. And on the third occasion he added the following to those first words: "If you do not desist from this, I will summon you to the terrible divine judgment; there you will give account for this before the impartial judge." Frightened by this, the metropolitan came to his senses and cursed his work, for which he would have suffered God's terrible judgment, and he burned it in the presence of his people.

When I heard this said, and when I considered what I heard, a gnawing worm was born in my conscience and began to drill my heart penetratingly, showing me (since I too had written such works) that it was for no other reason (about which I asked Your Reverence, but I was given to understand that that was kept secret even from Your Reverence) and to no other end, that Meletius, patriarch of Alexandria, Your Reverence's predecessor in that see, ordered under oath at the time of his death that his four books *de dogmatibus orthodoxae fidei* [on the dogmas of the Orthodox faith] be burned; and his letter to Ipatij Potij, written in Alexandria at the time when Potij was bishop of Volodymer, in the year 7108 from the creation of the world [AD 1600], shows splendidly what sort of person he would turn out to be with respect to the Roman religion and the pope. But since, as they say, βροτοῖς ἅπασιν ἡ συνείδησις θεός [for all mortals God is conscience],[124] that pious man probably preferred, through the working of God's grace in his conscience, to feed the temporal fire with his works than to offer himself as food to the eternal fire because of them.

I also cited the confession made by [Gabriel] the archbishop of Philadelphia before a monk of the Roman religion as the third worm, since I heard from honorable Greek monks in Jerusalem and in Constantinople that that man left the λείψανον [remains] of his body; but even in the time of greatest need, our people avoid, as they would hell itself, making a confession before Roman priests and do not grant them the power to bind and to loose.[125]

---

124. [A Gnomic saying attributed to Menander (*Monostixoi* 107), but likely that of a later compiler of late antiquity or the Byzantine period. See Jaekel 1964, 39.]
125. [Mt. 16:19; Mt. 18:18.]

Finally, the Easter Saturday fire at the grave of God is the fourth worm of my soul. And I am certain Your Reverence well remembers the reason: when I asked Your Reverence what it meant that, when Meletius, Your Reverence's *antecessor* [predecessor], wrote against the new Roman calendar, he cited the many miraculous events that no longer happen in these times in order to show that the old calendar is better than the new, but he overlooked such a celebrated annual miracle, the mere mention of which would certainly have been detrimental to the new calendar in comparison with the old. Your Reverence answered me in the presence of two worthy men of your court, the protosyncellus, hieromonk Leontius, and the archdeacon of the father patriarch of Alexandria,[126] that if that miracle were happening in these times, all the Turks would long ago have come to believe in Christ the Lord. But I also heard something even more convincing about that fire from the father patriarch of Jerusalem himself, who receives it at that time, bears it forth, and distributes it; and this caused a rather large worm to attach itself to my soul: namely, that our Orthodox prefer in this matter, which once was, but now, on account of our sins, has ceased to be, to remain rather with the heretics—the Eutychians, Dioscorites, and Jacobites, who lack God's grace—than with the Romans, who, for fitting reasons and on account of the manifest deeds being done there at this time by the heretics, the Abyssinians, do not accept that fire.

For these reasons, then, these four great and harmful worms came to rule over my soul in those Eastern lands; and they do not cease even today to gnaw relentlessly at my soul. For striking me in the head as if with a hammer, especially the first two, they do not cease to speak to me every hour: "You too, following the example of those great men—if you wish at the time of your death to have a peaceful parting of soul and body and to find God's grace after their parting—burn the writings that you wrote against the Roman Church because of the same differences between the Eastern and Western Churches. For who from your Ruthenian nation was ever as vexatious and abusive toward the Roman Church and the Roman religion and the pope and his followers as you were through your writings?" That is what the first two worms seem to whisper to my heart every day, every hour, wherefore they are a millstone on my soul, which oppresses my soul more than all the others

126. [From 1620 to 1636 the patriarch of Alexandria was Gerasimus I.]

to the extent that I am more guilty in this labor than are they. For they suppressed the brood they conceived against the Roman Church while it was yet in their wombs and without any harm to their neighbors; but mine, which were born and sent into the world, were able to delude many. Wherefore in addition to this one fire, they were also deserving of another by Your Reverence's sentence, since, having in your hands the judgment of such things, you decreed in your letter to the Vilnius Brotherhood in the year 1620 such a sentence against the writings of Stefan Zizanij; certainly the works of other writers of our side would not have escaped similar sentence if they had reached Your Reverence's hands, since in them it is not the faith of our holy fathers that is described; rather it is some new and unheard-of faithlet that is created.

In order to demonstrate which, I remind Your Reverence of a few of their erroneous opinions instead of citing the many. At the forefront is Stefan Zizanij: among his other errors, he divested Christ the Lord of His mediatory dignity and cast God's saints down from heaven.[127] Next, Christopher Philalethes, whose works many from our side venerate with admiration, as if he were some sort of witness, although they know well that he was a heretic: in his work entitled *Apokrisis,* he makes fun of transubstantiation; he declares that the office of presbyter and bishop are one and the same; he does not grant that Moses, the seer of God, is a priest, and he asserts rather that he is a layman; he confuses spiritual priesthood with sacramental priesthood, and he does not acknowledge the latter; he says that laymen have the power *suffragii decisivi* [of decision by vote] to make determination about faith; he claims for laymen, *jure divino* [by divine right], the power of selection to the priestly estate; he affirms[128] that bishops are greater in their dignity than priests *non jure divino* [not by divine right], but by human custom; he does not acknowledge that St. Peter was established by Christ the Lord as the pastor of the Universal Church; he does not acknowledge that Christ

127. [See above, pp. 422–4, 410–17.]
128. [This reading is corrected from the Latin version of the letter to Lukaris, which has the third person: *Episcopos presbiteris non jure divino, sed consuetudine humana majores esse dicit* (see Velykyj 1972, 142). The Polish, which has the first person—*Ia affirmuię* [I affirm], *że Biskupowie nad Kapłany w dostoieństwie swym większymi są,* non Iure Diuino, *ale ze zwyczaiu ludzkiego*—is surely in error.]

the Lord called St. Peter "the rock,"[129] nor does he acknowledge that
Christ the Lord built His Church on Peter; he does not acknowledge that
two sorts of keys were given to the holy apostles by Christ the Lord,
that is, *ordinis et jurisdictionis* [of order and of jurisdiction]; he does
not acknowledge that in saying the words "Feed my sheep" to Peter,[130]
He entrusted all His sheep to him for feeding; he does not acknowledge
that according to ancient custom and the decree of Church laws, appeal
properly belonged to the bishop of Rome; he asserts that in spiritual
matters, bishops properly made their appeals to the emperors; he does
not acknowledge that the bishops of Rome occupied the first places in
the universal councils.[131] After Philalethes, a certain anonymous Clerk
of Ostroh does the same thing, who is fuller of blasphemies against
the eternal existence of the Son of God and of falsehoods about the
Council of Florence than he is of doctrine and truth.[132] Thereafter the
author of a work entitled *Antigraphē* does the same thing, who (*alias
homo pientissimus* [otherwise, a most pious man]) in addition to other
inconsistencies considers it *haeresis* [heresy] to confess that the Holy
Spirit also proceeds from the Son. He praises and accepts the works of
the Clerk and Philalethes and acknowledges them as the writers for his
side.[133] Thereupon I do the same thing in my lamentatious work, which
totus fere Calvinizat [almost totally calvinizes].

Thus, bitten by such gnawing worms and greatly weakened in
the strength of my heart, as well as troubled and sore in my soul by
those muddles of various opinions and by many doubts, I fall to Your
Reverence's feet and ask humbly and submissively in the bitterness of
my heart: deign to take me into your care, along with the entire Ruthenian
nation, since we are nearer to falling than to rising, if, lacking divine
mercy, Your Reverence's industry, strengthened by God, will not rescue
and succor us. For, by God's grace you are *tanti* [of such importance]
on account of the authority, wisdom, dignity, and the apostolic throne
of the highest patriarchate in the East, toward which we all hold our
eyes turned; and we await our rescue from it as *ex caelesti aliquo divino*

129. [Mt. 16:18.]
130. [Jn. 21:16.]
131. [See above, pp. 427–39.]
132. [See above, pp. 456–65.]
133. [*Antigraphē* 1608, 1158/A2v and 1185–1213/14r–31r.]

oraculo [from some heavenly divine oracle] for a divine injunction in our matter. And we see clearly (those of us who see) that it is in Your Reverence's hands to allow us to fall and to grant us to stand. To fall, if you will not wish to take us under your protection; to stand, if you will show the proper pastoral solicitude for us. When I say to fall, I mean that Your Reverence will lose us, Rus', from your obedience *etiam invitus* [even against your will]; and in the person of Your Reverence I also understand Your Reverence's successors, if this will continue as long as it has seemed likely to do so.

If Your Reverence does not believe my words, deign to ask your people who spend time here among us; deign also to ask those of our people who travel there how many there are under Your Reverence's obedience who enjoy the laws, freedoms, and liberties of this most noble kingdom. It will be to the common people that it will be said *compelle intrare* [compel (them) to come in],[134] and this will occur almost deservedly. If in that case Your Reverence should abandon us disorderly people, the gates of the Kingdom will be closed for your people to come to us, and for us to go there, especially for monks and priestly authorities who, lightening their want and poverty, travel from there both here and to Moscow through these domains. The Muscovite Tsar did this, who, along with his entire nation, was under the obedience of the see that Your Reverence now occupies: he forbade all his subjects—clerics and laymen—passage to Greece, and he withdrew the local Muscovite Church from the obedience of the patriarchs of Constantinople and did with it what he was pleased to do in his domain. Who will forbid the Polish King to do the same thing in his domain, especially in view of the great enmity in these times toward this most noble kingdom on the part of that ruler, by whose tyranny Greece is oppressed?

Deign, therefore, Your Reverence, to consider what I say: God, before whom I say this, is witness unto my soul that I say this out of humble good will toward Your Reverence and out of sincere love for my nation; and I said this face to face in Your Reverence's presence in Constantinople: if Your Reverence will not be solicitous toward us, you will quickly lose us from your obedience. This is because the foremost nobility of our Ruthenian religion either go directly to the Romans, or they go to the Uniates, and few remain with us; and thus the parents

134. [Lk. 14:23.]

are with us, but their sons and daughters are either with the Uniates or with the Romans. So there is already poor hope here that we will remain standing; it must of necessity come to the sort of fall I mentioned. But Your Reverence, if you will so desire, can quickly and successfully prevent this from happening in the same honorable and holy manner for which you were sent here not long ago as a legate from the patriarchs of the two foremost sees, those of Constantinople and Alexandria, as Your Reverence yourself makes known in the letter I mentioned earlier that was left with the archbishop of Lviv (that I say it for the third time, with proper reason, in Your Reverence's words): "As for me, admonished by the majesty of His Majesty the King, I obediently leave this kingdom and return to my people; and I declare that I did not wish to seek anything else in this land but that some peace and harmony might be established between those who wish unity and have already entered into it and those who are not in it, but suppose that they do so piously and, deferring to their foremost authorities, do not even agree among themselves and agree in heretical errors."[135]

Your Reverence is thus now for us that foremost authority to whom we look and suppose that we are acting piously when we are not in unity; and thus we do not agree with ourselves, and we agree in heretical errors. Deign therefore, Your Reverence, Father, to strive and to cause that you might effect peace and unanimity between those who have entered into unity and those who are not in it, and that you establish that we no longer disagree with one another and that we not agree in heretical errors. The apostle St. Paul teaches us that the word of God is not bound, although he himself was bound.[136] Therefore, Your Reverence can effect that unanimity for us, a nation that is free, by the grace of God, and lives under a Catholic king, and you can do it successfully; and thereby, you will not only very easily rescue it from the fall that hangs over it, but you will also establish it in its original freedom: you will open for the noble estate the doors to land offices and to senatorial dignities; you will make access for the burghers to hold city town hall offices; you will build us schools; you will adorn churches; you will equip monasteries; you will free presbyters from tribute; you will win fraternal love for Poles, Lithuania, and Rus'; and finally, you

135. [See above, pp. 669–70.]
136. [2 Tim. 2:9.]

will wipe the daily tears from the eyes of the entire Ruthenian nation that is miserably afflicted for this very reason. You will cause it to enjoy that heavenly peace while still on earth, and you will grant it countless other goods in God's eyes. You yourself will cause it to be ascribed to you as your eternal monument that you will be known as the *restitutor* [restorer] of peace in the Church of Christ the Lord, which He has in this most noble Polish kingdom, and as the *restaurator* [renovator] of the freedom that is already almost lost in the Ruthenian nation. You will cause happiness on earth and in heaven, and you will leave your name to be revered in future ages. For you will do God's work when you fill in and even out the abyss of the accursed schism with the love and the harmony of the brethren and establish that Rus´, the Poles, and Lithuania praise and revere the name of God their Creator, all as if with one mouth and one heart. For as a wise and sagacious man, Your Reverence must consider wisely that it is an impossibility, as it were, among men that our Ruthenian nation should elude Church unity. Since it will soon have to accept it, even if involuntarily, it behooves it to choose in time: is it to accept it voluntarily now, when it still has freedom, or then, when it will have lost that liberty? Whichever of these two it should suffer it will ascribe to you as the author. I say, and I say honestly, what we already see with our eyes and touch with our hands. May almighty God cause this for us in our days through you, Most Blessed Father; and to the completion of this holy service, may he give you the will and grant you strength. Amen.

Wherefore I commend myself and my submissive obedience, with a humble kissing of Your Reverence's feet, to your paternal grace and pastoral benediction. Given in Derman´, *Anno 1627. Augusti 21.*

This is what I wrote to the father patriarch; and when the aforementioned Mr. Andrzej Krasowki asked several times for an answer to my epistle, he received the reply that it is necessary to answer this with due consideration. And he has already been considering for more than a year now, whence I understand that it will either be that parturiunt montes ["the mountains labor"],[137] *or that answer will be* ad Kalendas, *as they say,* Graecas ["at the Greek calends"].[138]

To the honor of the Triune God and the soul-saving benefit of the Ruthenian nation.

137. [This is the first half of a saying: *"Parturiunt montes, nascetur ridiculus mus"* ("The mountains labor; a ridiculous mouse is born"). Arthaber 1360; Horace *Ars poet.* 139.]

138. [I.e., never. See Erasmus *Ad.* 1.5.84; Arthaber 198. It is, of course, not for nothing that Smotryc'kyj chooses an anti-Greek proverb to make his point in deriding the Greek patriarch.]

Exaethesis

(1629)

Exaethesis,

or,
Expostulation,

That Is,

a Debate
Between *Apology* and *Antidote* Concerning the Remainder
of the Errors, Heresies, and Lies of Zizanij, Philalethes,
Orthologue, and the Clerk,

Made
by the Reverend in God,
Meletij Smotryc'kyj,

Called Archbishop of Polack, Bishop of Vicebsk and Mscislaŭ,
Archimandrite of Vilnius and Derman',

to Both Sides of the Ruthenian Nation.

Anno Domini 1629, Aprilis 3.

In the Monastery of Derman'

Cum Licentia Superiorum.
[With the Permission of the Superiors.]

My Life's One Hope Christ JEsuS

In Lviv, at the Printing House of Jan Szeliga,
Typographer to His Grace the Father Archbishop.

[. . .]¹

For the Illustrious Prince,
His Grace, Prince
Aleksander Zasławski,
Palatine of Kyiv, etc.,
Merciful Lord and Benefactor,
Meletij Smotryc'kyj,
Nuncupate Archbishop of Polack,
Bishop of Vicebsk and Mscislaŭ,
Archimandrite of Vilnius and Derman',
with his humble bow, wishes and desires
the Grace of almighty God.

I WOULD NOT WISH THAT ANY DAY *transiret sine linea* [should pass without a line]² concerning the matter of holy unity, upon which the salvation of human souls has come to depend, partially in order that I not be lacking toward myself, upon whom *impendet* [it is incumbent] to repay the Church of God with a defense of the true faith to the extent that I had harmed it with my glorying in errors and heresies, *tanto enim majora querenda sunt mihi lucra per penitentiam, quanto graviora intuli damna per culpam* [for I ought to have sought gains all the more through penitence, the more serious the losses I inflicted through my sin],³ partially so that I not be lacking toward my brethren as well, to whom in both these things I am as owing and obliged as much as I am to myself, believing that through our frequent sighing to the Lord God and through the incessant admonition of our misled brethren, He will give us *unica hora, quod denegaverat totus annus* [in a single hour what an entire year has denied]. For it is well known that *etiam minima guttula saepe cadendo, excavat lapidem* [even the tiniest droplet, by falling often, can hollow out a stone].⁴ If not all at once, but only by one or two, even so, God willing, there will be much good. Each carrying one

1.   [The coat of arms of the Zasławski family has been omitted; Smotryc'kyj 1629b,)(1v/696.]
2.   [Arthaber 581; Pliny, *Nat. Hist.*, 35.36.10.]
3.   [Cf. commentaries to Lk. 3:8 ("Bring forth therefore fruits worthy of repentance"), e.g., Bede, *PL* 92:353C.]
4.   [Arthaber 601; Ovid, *Ex Ponto*, 4.10.5.]

stone, one log, we raise and we build great machines and bring them to perfection. We also know that there is great joy in heaven over one sinner who repents,[5] and he who converts one sinner from the error of his way hides a multitude of his sins and of his own.[6]

Your Illustrious Prince, my Merciful Lord and Benefactor, is pleased to know why I published to my Ruthenian nation last year under Your Merciful Grace's name an *Apology,* and then immediately a *Paraenesis,* the goal and end of which was none other than that I might demonstrate that it was through righteous divine judgment that the harsh divine punishment had fallen upon the entire Eastern Church and, within it, also upon the Ruthenian Church that is opposed to us; and thus its abandonment by the Lord God and the removal of His grace from it was also a matter of divine judgment. For, first of all, the accursed schism for several hundreds of years deprived it of its external goods and adornments to the point that finally, deprived of *imperium* [power], it gave it over into the servitude of that blasphemer who wrenches from our Lord and Savior Jesus Christ His eternal glory and divine splendor. Which happened to it for no other reason but that it did not wish to be obedient to him who knows, believes, and confesses that Jesus Christ our Lord and Savior is true God and true man and glories and praises Him as such and who is by Him Himself given and established pastor of His Holy Church. And in these times, in our age, it [the schism] has already begun to deprive it so clearly of even its internal good, that is, of its Orthodox Catholic faith, that if God's mercy and the industry of divine men will not oppose it, *actum est* [it is done], it will soon be no more; and it will not even notice when a servitude incomparably heavier than is this one will fall upon it.

I was in Constantinople five years ago. I saw the present patrirach, Cyril. I lived with him for fifteen weeks or so. I often entered into conversation with him. I read the catechism written by him. I came to understand completely, both from this writing of his and from frequent conversations, that he is a heretic. I saw there catechisms published in the vulgar Greek tongue that were full of Lutheran and Calvinistic heresies. I heard the great preacher of the great Church of Constantinople teach heresies *publice* [publicly] from the pulpit. A few pious hieromonks

5.   Lk. 15[:7].
6.   Jas. 5[:20].

who entered into conversations with me complained about this, but they could not undertake anything. At a council, I wished to communicate all of this to those in the schism who ought to know about this; but on account of their stubborn resentment toward the matters of salvation, I could not properly come to this so that for two whole years after my return from the Eastern lands they did not wish to gather in one place. During the third year, when at the insistence of my conscience I could not remain silent about this any longer, since it was a matter most harmful to the Orthodox faith and contagious to human souls, I published it partially through my work called *Apology* and partially through a letter I wrote to him.[7] This moved the wise, by the grace of God, to take care for themselves, and it cast the stubborn into even greater carelessness. For they are so blind and deaf in both those senses that they wish neither to see this nor to hear of it, even though these things are already both palpable and trumpeted to the entire world. And they are so shameless that they are not ashamed to oppose this truth with pure lies, calumny, and heretical hypocrisies. For even in these days they published against my *Apology* a work full of the venom of schismatic and heretical poison and, sugaring it for their followers, entitled it *Antidote*,[8] knowing that Satan does not catch people with evil, but only *sub specie boni* [under the appearance of the good], under the mask of something that purports to be beneficial. He promised the first pair of people that they would be gods, but in paradise that liar for all time and homicide prescribed in the *Antidote* the apples, the poison of eternal death.[9]

Since it concerned me, especially with respect to the remainder of those errors, heresies, and lies that I had suppressed through my *Apology* in Zizanij, Philalethes, Orthologue, the Clerk, and other schismatic writers similar to them (having left the *diacrisis* [determination] of this matter to the coming—God grant it—council of both sides), with the permission of the elders I publish this my *Exaethesis* for this very reason: that I might treat the remainder of those heretical errors which that schismatic side left for itself from the above-mentioned writers

---

7.   [This is the letter that Smotryc'kyj published in a Polish version at the end of his *Paraenesis* of 1628. A Latin version of the letter is preserved in the Vatican archives and published in Velykyj 1972, 130–45. See above, p. lvi.]

8.   [Mužylovs'kyj 1629.]

9.   Gen. 2[:4–5].

unto the perdition of its souls, whereby also at the coming (God grant it) council there might be less difficulty concerning them. And although, to be sure, that *Antidote* was not worthy of response, as something that is composed entirely of hypocrisy, sarcasm, *scommata* [jeers], lies, calumnies, and blasphemies so manifest that every person who has attentive and healthy spiritual sight can easily see them, nonetheless, so that this scoffer, calumniator, and blasphemer not suppose that what he speaks is the truth and that no one fall upon that poison through carelessness, I judged it fitting, with God's help, to write this as a warning and in opposition to that soul-killing *pharmacop[ol]ae* [drug-seller, quack]. And for greater authority among Catholic people I release it to the world under the most noble name of Your Princely Grace for the same salvatory goal and end for which I also released the two above-mentioned writings of mine: that I might demonstrate to my brethren who are perishing in the schism that they are in such mortal danger that if they do not save themselves today, tomorrow will already be too late.

Arius was one man, but he had infected almost the entire world with his heresy. One man was Eutyches, and even today countless nations perish, Abyssinians or Ethiopians, Assyrians, Babylonians, Chaldeans, Pentapolitans, Mesopotamians, Maronites, Karamites, Armenians, and others infected with his heresy. One man was Luther, but how many European kingdoms did he draw unto perdition with his teaching, which is contrary to God and to His holy truth? One man was Cyril, who is solely intent upon introducing the heretics Luther and Calvin into the Eastern schismatic Church, who are until this day barely known in it.

Let us understand this: if through divine dispensation, these above-mentioned heresiarchs, who were only presbyters, should be successful in this impious matter, what will that one, who has the episcopal dignity and occupies the see of the first patriarchate in the East, be able to effect and to prove, especially over those nations who have experienced an angered Lord God against them for many hundreds of years on account of the curse made against them by the highest pastor of the Church of God? Since it concerns all of us Orthodox and Catholics that this horrible schism not introduce the heretical infection here among our schismatics more harmfully than it was introduced by the Zizanijs, it befits us to announce this, to report to people's knowledge, and to summon the Lord God and the people of God for help. For, through the grace of God, many worthy people of the gentry and burgher estate of both sides, having perceived this evil, asked of God's anointed, the King, Our Gracious Lord, at the recent Sejm[10] for the creation of a mutual council of both sides at which the discords that had arisen between them might be erased, peace, harmony, and love might be discussed among the brethren, and holy unity with the Roman Church might be concluded and that efforts might be made so that that man might be knocked from the path he has undertaken before those impious plans of his come to the sort of fruition which it would not be easy later on to avoid: *Saepe enim parva scintilla contempta, magnum excitavit incendium* [For often a little spark that was disparaged has brought forth a great fire].[11] The King, His Grace, Our Gracious Lord, was pleased to give his permission for this: to order separate councils of each side and then a mutual council of both sides in Lviv. *Quod felix faustum fortunatumque sit* [May it be fruitful, prosperous, and fortunate][12] to the honor and glory of the name of almighty God, the increase of His holy Church, the immortal glory of the King, His Grace, Our Gracious Lord, the internal peace of this most noble kingdom, and the salvatory benefit of the souls led astray by the schism.

That Your Princely Grace might be made moderator at it and be asked by both of our sides to be mediator, I desire with all my soul, and I ask the Lord my God that he might be pleased to direct toward this the heart of His anointed, Our Gracious Lord. You are the most noble blood of most noble Ruthenian princes; you love your Ruthenian nation; you consider its glory your own glory; you are saddened at its fall as at your own. You wish for it, as for yourself, the grace and love of God, salvation, and His holy blessing. You delight in the pure faith of your holy ancestors who were in holy unity; you love the rites of the Holy Eastern Church, the hymnologies, the doxologies, and all its ceremonies full of the honor of God, as you do your own soul. You are often piously present at its ceremonies; you mention them piously; you speak of them gravely. I fear lest some Catholics today be found

10.   [Which met in Warsaw, 9 January to 20 February 1629.]
11.   [Arthaber 1243; Quintus Curtius, *History of Alexander,* 6.3.11.]
12.   [A commonly used turn of phrase. Cf. Cicero, *On Divination,* 1.45.102.]

who are so stiff that they have more of a taste for seized [Orthodox/ Uniate] Church property or the [Orthodox/Uniate] priests' rents, wages, and conveyances than for holy unity. For thereby they oppress with words and deeds rather than promote holy unity; they criticize it to their subjects rather than praise it, not wishing to know that it is useless to make jokes with the Lord God and with His holy truth, that *vae homini illi, per quem scandalum venit* [Woe to that man by whom the offense cometh],[13] that his soul will be tormented for the soul of his offended subject. Whenever Your Princely Grace mentions holy unity, you pour forth the tears of most ardent love toward it from your pious heart, and you prefer, assess, and value it above all your goods and above your very health, praise and promote it in deed and word. Wherefore, if they will be grateful for that divine grace and worthy of Your Princely Grace's service, you will be able to achieve much with these people through your princely and senatorial dignity.

Let almighty God cause this for Your Princely Grace: that He not close your eyes until you see the desired comfort of your nation, for which we too moan in our hearts troubled by the demise of our brethren, so that, *solerti prudentia mediante* [with skilled prudence mediating], before Your Princely Grace's eyes, through God's grace toward Your Princely Grace, having left all their enmity toward us, our brethren might return to us their love and might, thereby, crown holy unity with the Holy Roman Church by our example, unto the eternal reward in heaven and the immortal glory on earth of Your Princely Grace, whom I zealously submit to merciful grace with my humble services in my daily priestly prayers. From the Monastery of Derman', *Anno 1629, Aprilis 3.*

Preface
to the Orthodox Reader
of the Ruthenian Nation

If, O Orthodox reader of the Ruthenian nation, the salvatory opinion expressed through the Holy Spirit by the prophet Isaiah and announced to the world in divine writ—that *vexatio dat intellectum* [vexation gives

---

13.   [Mt. 18:7.]

understanding][14]—should have its effect at any time and place, then it ought to do so in these times in the opposing side, and it ought to be verified in it through experience itself, as it came to pass in many other nations. For already now for almost forty years the Ruthenian nation has been in that daily agitation which it itself makes for itself in distinguishing truth from untruth, the way of salvation from the way of perdition, and the true faith from heretical errors; and yet, through such a long and arduous vexation, it has not only not managed an *intellectum* [understanding] of the things of salvation, but it has forced itself into incomparably deeper and cruder darknesses of understanding such that it neither knows what it says, nor sees what it seeks, nor understands by what it stands and what it defends. Which befalls it because it plays at matters of salvation; it jokes in divine affairs; it does not perform them *serio* [seriously], rather it conducts everything hastily. It does everything through vassals, through a hireling, through the untaught or the half-taught, sometimes even through heretics.

It conducted that salvatory matter hastily through Philalethes, hastily through [the author of] *Antigraphē,* and it also conducts it hastily through this Antidotist. Whence what ought to be for it *immutabile et perpetuum* [unchangeable and constant], it jerks, wrenches, tears, and renders *mutabile et ephemeron* [changeable and short lived]. This one teaches this today, another something else tomorrow, a third something different from both of these yesterday. What they write, to what they respond *non volvunt, non revolvunt* [they do not consider, they do not reconsider]; rather, they both speak and narrate *transitorie* [cursorily]. Wherefore they say whatever the *spiritus vertiginis* [perverse spirit][15] brings to their minds and, in answering, whatever their venomous saliva brings to the unrestrained tongue of their unparched mouth.[16] They revile and disgrace honorable and pious people, calumniating their innocence. They exchange Orthodox dogmas for heretical errors. They support their alleged salvatory matters with lies such that when those four things are erased from their writings *censoria veritatis spongia* [with the censorial eraser of the truth], nothing remains but empty words and bare paper. Which every person of whole understanding can

14. Is. 28[:19].
15. [Is. 19:14.]
16. [Cf. *NKPP* 3:435–6, "Ślina," 1.]

easily see as soon as he compares non-Uniate writings with Uniate, the *Apokrisis* with the *Antirresis,* the *Lament* with the *Parēgoria* or with the *Warning,* the Clerk with the defense of the Council of Florence, *Elenchus* with *Antelenchus,* and the present *Antidote* with the *Apology.*

For these people do not have censors for their writings; they all write and submit to print whatever they feel like. Having ascribed to someone something all too wise, even though he be a *faeticus hircus* [stinking goat], they forget their understanding and follow him blindly, not knowing or asking what spirit speaks to and from them: is it Satan or an angel, a man or some beast who stammers; for they ought to have remembered that apostolic saying: *nolite omni spiritui credere, sed probate spiritus, si ex Deo sint* [believe not every spirit, but test the spirits whether they are of God].[17] This apostolic *spirituum probatio* [testing of the spirits] is that prophetic *vexatio* [vexation], which gives the *intellectum* [understanding], and it gives *intellectum auditui* [understanding through the sense of hearing]; not simply *intellectum vexatio* [does vexation give understanding], but *auditui* [through the sense of hearing]. He who wishes to acquire understanding from vexation must listen, test the spirit of him who speaks to him or in his name, and distinguish truth from untruth; and he must listen according to the teaching of Christ the Lord, who says, *qui habet aures audiendi, audiat* [he that hath ears to hear, let him hear].[18] [He must] not listen such that he would not feel that he had *aures audiendi* [ears to hear], but *audire et intelligere* [to hear and understand]: listen, hear, and understand. But hearing they do not hear,[19] and understanding they do not understand. Their hearts are petrified unto the recognition of the truth, which can also be seen manifestly from their newly published work entitled *Antidote,* in which, as usual, there are nothing but errors and heresies, old and new, nothing but blasphemies, nothing but calumnies, nothing but lies, nothing but sarcasms, *scommata* [jeers], words of abuse, ignominies, and similar acts of shamefulness. All of which has been cleverly seasoned and *venenate* [venomously] prepared for no other end but for the infection and perdition of human souls.

Wherefore, so that the manifest poison of this most disgusting

17. 1 Jn. 4[:1].
18. Mt. 11[:15; 13:9; Mk. 4:23].
19. [Ez. 12:2; Jer. 5:21; Is. 6:9–10; Mt. 13:14–15; Mk. 8:18.]

doctor, most harmful to human souls—published and released to the world under the name *Antidote*—might be recognized and avoided, I release to the world after this *Antidote* this *Exaethesis* for the distinguishing in it *panacis a conio, panchresti ab aconitu* [of panacea from hemlock, of universal remedy from wolfsbane], that is, of medicine from poison and for the warning and defense of the health of the souls of faithful people. Through it I clearly demonstrate all his poisons and venomous seasonings, and I express under these names the falsehood, calumny, lie, hypocrisy, blasphemy, heretical error, schismatic deceit, and other similar things, such that everyone can easily see, recognize, and understand, guard, and beware of them and consider this doctor *pro venefico et voluntario homicida* [as a poisoner and a willful murderer], as the one who, now filling his coffers *in praxi* [in business] for the first time, *ob rei medicae imperitiam, loco praesentissimi medicamenti* [on account of ignorance of the art of medicine, in place of the most outstanding medicine], unwisely published and released to the world *praesentissimum venenum* [the most outstanding poison] for the infection and poisoning of innocent souls. Although it was also my place, with regard to the *scommata* [jeers] and calumnies cast upon me, partially to answer here this calumniator of shameless tongue according to his folly, nonetheless, for the time being I will listen to the wise man, who says *noli respondere stulto juxta stultitiam suam, ne efficiaris illis similis* [answer not a fool according to his folly, lest thou also be like unto him].[20] However, if his gang will be so stupid, with whom (after himself) he threatens me, or if he himself should be so in the broader place which he prepares, having taken the counsel of that same wise man—*responde stulto juxta stultitiam suam, ne sibi sapiens esse videatur* [answer a fool according to his folly, lest he be wise in his own conceit][21]—I will answer both these stupid ones. Nonetheless, I will do so in patience and in humility, knowing from experience itself that people of that side are not able to establish, adorn, and defend their matters of salvation any other way but through abuse, calumny, and lying. Witness to this are their above-mentioned writings and this *Antidote,* in the preface of which they calumniate me, alleging that in certain places I desecrated the authority of Holy Writ and the doctors of

20.   Prov. 26[:4].
21.   Prov. 26[:5].

the Church so that I might be able thereby to gain favor with the Roman Church (as if the Roman Church established the truth of its faith by desecrating Holy Writ and the writings of the doctors of the Church). But he did not prove this against me truly in his entire work. I will demonstrate to him clearly, God granting, in my *Expostulation,* that he does nothing else in his entire *Antidote* but lie, calumniate, blaspheme, assert old heretical errors, and introduce new ones, in the demonstration of which I will be rather brief, since my *Paraenesis* sufficiently removed his other objections. Farewell, Orthodox Reader.

To Rus' of the Greek Rite,
against Chapter 1 of the Schismatic Antidote,
in which the Antidotist Treats
of the Deceits of the Apostates
from the Church of Christ:

Expostulation 1,
in Which Are Treated the Deceits of the Schismatic Antidotist

†It is common among people poor in virtue that, when they do not have an ornament from their actions, they snatch that of others in order to adorn themselves. But it suits them as much as gold rings in the snout of that swine, according to Solomon's account.[22] Even the most genuine malefactor, as long as he hides his works of malice from the unknowing people, seems to be good, and when he ascribes virtues to himself he passes for a saint. When a heretic calls himself a Catholic among strangers he is understood to be such, and when he also speaks in a Catholic manner, he is even taken for a Catholic. Likewise when a schismatic praises holy unity, he avoids the suspicion of schism, and when he declares that he is in unity, he is counted as Orthodox. But this is commonly done by people of such character *in hypocrysi* [in feigning], for otherwise they are unable to make themselves worthy of esteem among their own people and among *e diametro oppositis* [those diametrically opposed to them]. But when each of them individually is

---

†   The heretical and schismatic deceits.
22.   Prov. 11[:22].

divested of the fictitious garment that does not belong to him, a mark appears upon him according to which we can easily recognize who is what. A good person recognizes the malefactor by his evil attributes; the Catholic recognizes the schismatic in the rending of Church unity and the heretic by his sundering of the one true faith. Then they themselves, having been revealed not to have that unity of faith, that unity of Church, must willy-nilly acknowledge how they came upon what they appropriated for themselves and in what they conceived the plan to adorn themselves. Complaining about such satanical hypocrites, the blessed apostle Paul says that such false apostles are deceitful workers who transform themselves into the apostles of Christ and pretend that they are ministers of righteousness.[23]

†This Antidotist is just such a person in his entire work, for, considering himself a Catholic and his schism the Universal Church, he appropriates for himself and adorns himself with what is proper to the Church of Christ the Lord, and only to Catholics. Even though he is a schismatic and a heretic, he appropriates for himself what the Holy Writ says about the Church of Christ the Lord and the confessors of the true faith. For as long as these people are in all these errors and heresies, or even in one of those that my *Apology* charges and proves against them, that which applies to Catholics alone cannot apply to them, as schismatics and heretics. And the chapters written by that Antidotist clearly declare that not only the schismatic, but also the heretical mark remains upon them. Wherefore, whenever in his entire work he accuses us Catholics of being heretics, he accuses himself and the fathers and brethren of his ilk. He calls himself, and them, heresiarchs, false prophets, apostates, predatory wolves, and similar names. He spreads their fame with these titles according to their deeds.

Arius did this with his sectarians; Eunomius did it, Nestorius did it, and Eutyches, and Dioscorus; even now their descendants who have remained until today do this—the Arians, the Nestorites, the Dioscorites, and others, of which the Eastern lands are full. Here in Europe too the Anabaptists, the Hussites, the Lutherans, the Calvinists, and others do this, of which the Western lands are full. For having put on the cloak

23.   2 Cor. 11[:13–15].
†   The deceit and the hypocrisy of the Antidotist schismatic, who pretends that he is a Catholic and that his schism is the Church of Christ the Lord.

of Catholicism, they establish themselves in the Church of Christ the Lord, and they speak and write about themselves as if they were true Catholics, and as if they were fellows of Christ the Lord, enjoying the properties that belong only to the Church of Christ the Lord alone and to His elect. But they are that very one of the infernal regions who did not stand in the truth from ages,[24] and they are inhabitants of the infernal synagogue and not of the Church of God. They are those who transform themselves and show themselves as if they were ministers of righteousness, but they are ministers of Satan, workers of every impiety against the Church of Christ the Lord.[25] For among them love is similar to themselves, and hatred is everywhere and toward all things of God. For they are ever learning, but they never come to the recognition of the truth.[26]

†Nor did this Antidotist step forth in order to learn something, that he might recognize the truth, that he might seek faith and truth, but so that he might boast of being that which he is not, and so that he might lead astray the sons of perdition[27] with that which is not his, having the good hope that even among the sons of God his false accounts and heretical teaching might achieve results according to his intent. But which of the sons of God will wish to be so senseless with regard to his salvation that, given the taunts of apostasy and of heresy against our Orthodox side, he would not seek proofs of this in his work and proper arguments against those we raised against them in the *Apology*? Not having found which, he will charge him with schismatic frivolity and heretical hypocrisy. And he himself will do what his good conscience (aided by the grace of God) will counsel.

He ironizes, vociferates, reviles, abuses, (taunts), calls to witness; and he supposes thereby that he will place his untruth on its feet. But the truth is content with nothing other than the straight and genuine account. It does not need falsehood, calumny, interpolations of *scommata* [jeers].

---

24.   [Jn. 8:44.]
25.   2 Cor. 11[:14–15].
26.   2 Tim. 3[:7].
†   The second deceit of the Antidotist, who both strikes and cries. [Based on a Polish saying that means that the aggressor pretends to be the victim. Cf. *NKPP* 1:87, "Bić," 29.]
27.   [Jn. 17:12; 2 Th. 2:3.]

But about what does he vociferate? Why does he revile? Of what does he complain? And against whom? You, Apologist (he says), reviled our Church and the Greek one, and in them the entire Eastern Church. You stained and disfigured it.[28] †I ask with what? He answers: You charged it with errors and heresies. I say: If they are in it, then why do you revile me? If they are not, why do you acknowledge them? He answers that: having erred in the dogmas of the faith, some writers erred on their own account. I accept this; let us agree that it was on their own account, but where was this? Zizanij, Philalethes, and Orthologue in your schismatic Church, and Gerganos and someone else in the Greek Church erred, he says, but on their own, not in the name of the Church.

Do, et concedo [I grant, and I concede] that these are not the errors and heresies of your schismatic Church nor of the Greek, but of those individuals who placed them in your Church and the Greek Church. The Church is in itself pure, but it has become unclean through the placing in it of those errors and heresies. For example, someone gives to a presbyter a physical church newly erected, adorned and pure in every respect. People will be in it once or twice, and they will dirty it. That dirt is not of the church, nor is it from the church, but of those who brought it into the church from outside. Still, it is in the church, inasmuch as it was left in the church. Wherefore, whosesoever it is, it is in the church. And if the church does not place value upon it, it does not belong to it. But if to the contrary, then it is both in it and of it. But who values dirt? Is that parishioner at fault, who, even if it is without the knowledge of the priest, sweeps up the dirt and throws it out of it? This you will not say.

Why then do you vociferate against me for this and revile me? Because I have swept up the dirt in your Church and the Greek Church that has fallen from someone's feet brought in from outside, but which is not of your schismatic Church or of the Greek Church, and because I have cast it out of both the Greek Church and yours? You say: Along with the dirt you also sweep up the proper internal ornament of our Church and of the Greek Church, and thereby of the entire Eastern Church, and you cast it from it. Here, Antidotist, I must take up my stand. And I contend with you that whatever I signified in my *Apology* as dirt in your

---

28.   [Mužylovs'kyj 1629, A2r.]
†   The errors and heresies of the schismatic writers are in their Church.

Church and in the Greek—that is, as error or as heresy—I call, assert, and publish every last example of them as such. If according to you I have not included everything, that forum upon which you stepped forth with this *Antidote* or, God willing, an even wider one at the coming council of both sides of our nation (if my God will lend me both life and health for so long) will demonstrate this and decide among us.

†You allege of me that I came to love the world, that I fell in love with it, and that I gave myself up to its servitude,[29] all three of which, by the grace of God, are as far from me as evil is far from good. I knew that I would be the last on my present side, I, who was almost the first among you. Do you call this loving the world? This could more properly have been ascribed to me had I remained with you: thus would I—who knew no economic burden or care and boasted and delighted in the fact that I was an archbishop, the first after the metropolitan in the Church, an archiereus of your side—thus would I have fallen in love with this world and with myself. At that council of yours in Kyiv you offered me three thousand *złoty*s in ready money on an annual basis from certain places and certain and noble persons from among you, along with the appropriate maintenance of eight persons—clerical and lay—to attend to me, and with a dwelling place in the Monastery of the Caves. Having this from your side as if in my hands—if I were chasing after this world and had come to love this present age—I would have settled upon that and vainly would have unfurled my banners wider there than here, especially since I already had the good earnest of glory that was caused by my writings, both with my own people and among foreigners, as a material for falling in love with myself. But not wishing to be suffocated by the accursed schism, not wishing further to sow and to multiply the heretical errors, or to defend them, not wishing, finally, to be Cain, which you mendaciously allege against our side, so that I might kill my brother Abel,[30] or Esau, that I might persecute Jacob,[31]

---

† The Antidotist's calumny.
29. [Mužylovskyj 1629, A1r–2r.]
30. [Gen. 4.]
31. [Gen. 25–7.]

or the brethren of Joseph, that I might sell him,[32] which I would have to do, if I were to join up with you.[33]

[†]Does not the innocent blood of our brother Abel—Josafat, archbishop of Polack, of blessed memory—nay even of those who were punished for that *parricidium* [parricide]—cry out against your Cains? Does not that of our second brother, the hieromonk Antonij Hrekovyč?[34] Does not that of the two priests, the one in Šarohrod, the other in Kyiv, both cruelly murdered? Does not also that of the honest man, Fedor Xodyka, the *wójt* of Kyiv?[35] And the blood that in recent years flowed in rivers—does it not cry out against you? For they believed that they were dying for the faith at the instigation of you Cains. Nor do I mention the innocent blood of Father Ipatij Potij, metropolitan of Kyiv of blessed memory, that cries out against you, poured out in the middle of the market square of Vilnius.[36] Those three monks from the Holy Trinity that had come to Kyiv from Vilnius in the year 1622: if I had not hindered them from acquiring the crown of martyrdom, would not your Cains have sent them after their other brethren? Even your father[37] will acknowledge this, for together with him I barely managed to win this from one of the Cains, begging upon the living God.

Are we, then, the Esaus? We, the Cains? We, the brothers of Joseph? I ask you, Antidotist, before God and man: who committed these homicides, who committed these fratricides, who committed these patricides? Was it the Uniates who did this to you? It was you merciless Cains who did this to the Uniates, brethren of your own blood. If he is a Uniate, then under the ice with him, then under the knife with him, then under the axes with him. O merciless patri- and fratricides, more cruel than Esau and more merciless than the brothers of Joseph, for

---

32. [Gen. 37.]
33. [Mužylovs'kyj 1629, 1r.]
[†] Schismatic crimes against the Uniates.
34. [On these events, see Hruševs'kyj 1999, 307–12.]
35. [On the murder of Xodyka, see Hruševs'kyj 1999, 415–16, and Kempa 2003.]
36. [In 1609 Potij was attacked in the Vilnius market square by a sword-wielding servant of a certain Tupeka, a city councilor. Potij raised his hand to protect his head, and the sword cut off two fingers on his left hand.]
37. [Metropolitan Jov Borec'kyj.]

they showed some sort of mercy over their brethren. If you could do as your greed for that evil dictates to you, you would eat alive absolutely all the Uniates, just as your ancestors did to St. Proterius, bishop of Alexandria; pulling their reins from them, you would eat them, which those who exerted their cruelty upon the above-mentioned sainted archbishop almost did. And what if we were to pay you in return for your down payment—that if he is a non-Uniate, then under the ice with him, under the sword, under the battle-axe? But I assure you, have no fear, you are not worthy of it. You are brethren of that Sapricius. You are ready to kill, but not to allow yourselves to be killed. The schism does not have the grace of God that it might give birth to martyrs. It gives birth to fratricides, parricides, and similar torches of the infernal abyss.

†Just take account of your conscience now, Antidotist: whom are you taunting with this Cain, Esau, and the brothers of Joseph? To whom do you ascribe persecution? Whom do you abuse with the name Dymas?[38] Whom do you call sons of the world? Whom do you slander as apostates? Those who take care to teach you and your fathers not to kill and murder. Those who lay down their lives for your lives so that they might save you from the accursed schism. Those who strive night and day before God and before man to free you from the soul-killing, heretical errors and to establish you in the true confession of the Catholic faith. Who seek to keep, secure, and maintain for all times the Holy Eastern Church, its faith, rites, ceremonies in the Ruthenian nation. They are the ones whom you, ingrates, persecute; them you strike, slash, kill, drown, and murder. The blood of the brethren you have killed is still flowing from your hands, and yet you are not ashamed to call yourselves SS. Abels, Jacobs, and Josephs. You do an unbearable wrong to those holy men, appropriating for yourselves their holy names, for you surpassed Esau and the brothers of Joseph with your deeds, and you drew equal with Cain the fratricide and with Judas the parricide. The entire most noble Crown and the Grand Duchy of Lithuania are well aware that I speak the truth against you, for this is taking place within their borders. And even if you should wish to excuse yourself on the grounds that it was not you, but someone from among you, know, you Pharisee, that if

---

† The pious concern of the Uniates for the schismatics.

38. [Mužylovs'kyj 1629, 1r.]

it were not for you, that SOMEONE would never have dared this, and
he would not have had the heart for it. You teach people to die for your
schismatic Church and for your heretical errors through your *Antidotes,
Elenchuses, Apocrisises, Laments, Antigraphēs,* Azariuses, and other
similar incitements to shed the blood of your brethren.

Just throw down, O schismatic, the club with which you ride
forth against me from one hundred miles away; fight hand to hand (as
you promise), and you will come to know what the truth has over the
untruth with which you attack me from behind. You call us heretics?
But why? Because we entered into holy unity with the Roman Church?
For no other reason. For without it we would not be different from
you in any way. [†]But just listen. Who of you or of your schismatic
or heretic ancestors ever righteously proved this against the Roman
Church, even though many of you attacked it many times with this?
Never, no one. For this is the stone against both the schismatics and
against the heretics, falling against which they shall be broken.[39] But
through my *Apology* I showed manifestly, clearly, and thoroughly
that you, Antidotist, together with your fathers and brethren, are both
schismatic and heretic; and every wise person can easily see how well
you will explain yourself concerning this in your *Antidote.* You dressed
in the garment that you had lost long ago through heretical errors; you
took up residence in the palace from which you had long ago fallen out
due to the schism. As long as both these things are in you, you cannot
appropriate for yourself the true faith and the palace of the Catholic
Church, even if you were to boast a thousand times that you have both
those things and claim them as yours. For schismatics and heretics do
not have the inheritance of those two things, even though they violently
intrude and force themselves upon both of them.

[‡]You allege in your *Antidote* that Christ the Lord gave your faith,
the apostles preached it, the world received it, the holy fathers wrote it
down, the councils confirmed it, and our Ruthenian nation, in its holy
ancestors, received it from the East during the schism,[40] in which truly

†   That the schismatics have never proved any heresy against the Roman
Church.

39.   [Mt. 21:44; Lk. 20:18.]

‡   That the schismatics lost the faith of their ancestors.

40.   [Mužylovs'kyj 1629, 3r, 4r.]

et falleris et fallis [you are both deceived, and you deceive]. There was holy unity of the Eastern Church with the Western when the Ruthenian Church was baptized and flourished with saints. The accursed schism does not have the grace of God that it might gain for the faith of Christ the Lord new nations or that it be glorified with saints or miracles. It was also the case, it is true, that schismatic metropolitans often intruded upon the Ruthenian metropolitanate, but there were certainly more who ended their pious lives in holy unity. As can be seen manifestly and clearly from the Ruthenian and Muscovite chroniclers, and as I thoroughly demonstrated to you in my *Paraenesis*. But that Christ the Lord gave your present-day heretical faith and that the apostles taught it, this is the most impious lie of all your lies. Nonetheless, you must renounce before God and man your Zizanijs, Philaletheses, Clerks, Orthologues, and similar, right down to the last jot that I censured as heretical in the *Apology,* and you must confess right down to the least tittle according to the true faith that is described in the *Apology* if you wish to be confessors of the faith that Christ the Lord taught, the apostles preached, the world of God's elect received, the holy fathers described, the councils approved, and we, Rus', received from the East in our ancestors. May the Holy Spirit cause this to be for you in our days.

Against Chapter 2 of the Schismatic Antidote, *in Which the Antidotist Treats of the Improper Intent of the Apologist in His Pilgrimage to the Holy Land*

Expostulation 2: In Which the Apologist's Peregrination to the Holy Land Is Freed of the Schismatic Antidotist's Calumny

[†]Having asserted in the first chapter of his *Antidote* as a thing certain in itself—that he and his fathers and brethren are Catholics and that they are the Church of Christ the Lord, but that we Uniates with our fathers and with our brethren the Romans are heretics and outside of

---

†   The schismatic hypocrisy.

the Church of Christ the Lord—[†]in the second chapter the Antidotist charged blindly against me and against my peregrination to the Holy Land.[41] He criticizes, reviles, distorts, dishonors it together with me however he sees fit; but I, God willing, will put a bit on him, and I will demonstrate to him that he dissolutely engages in skirmishing over the salvatory intention of my pious pilgrimage. For a person has no nearer and more righteous witness and judge in all his deeds than his own conscience. To whomever this should cause reproach—even if the soul's foe, or even that of the body, should cast upon him thousands of slanders—it is a trifle, they are words, nothing more. I was, with the help of my God, in the Holy Land, in Jerusalem; and not only was I there, but I even lived there well, by God's grace. And I live here as I lived in Jerusalem. If I lived and live badly, Antidotist, give proof of the evil. But if I lived as I should, why, malefactor, do you revile me? You do not need to run off with a copy of what I wrote to the father patriarch: I published it *in publicum* [to the people]. For this was pleasing to my fathers and lords in the spirit, and it does not befit me to regret what gives birth to consolation in my heart.

[‡]You say of yourself: "Do we not have pastors? Do we not have preachers? Wise and worthy people?"[42] I know well even without your boast, Antidotist, that you have even too many wise people, learned preachers, watchful pastors, at whose watchfulness, learning, and wisdom, the nation of your side has grown so fat on the bread of the word of God that now some in their vigor can barely move on account of the sunken sides of their souls. O unfortunate watchful pastor, wise teacher: what traces do you have of your wisdom now and of that of your schismatic ancestors those many years ago? Of what do you boast? By what are you exalted? These are your most wise preachers who gave birth to those heretical errors.

Were it not for Roman postils, you would not hurry, O orator, to the pulpit; and you, O wise one, would not know how to open your mouth. Kiss Besseus, who teaches you to speak from the pulpit, of which fact I

---

†   The Antidotist dishonors the author's pious peregrination to the Holy Land.

41.   [Mužylovs'kyj 1629, 4v–8v.]

‡   The vain schismatic boast.

42.   [Mužylovs'kyj 1629, 4v.]

am well aware. For without him your wheels creak, as those of a carter without a grease barrel. But you are wise, as are all of your people. One takes a hint from Osorius, another from Fabricius, another from Skarga, others from other preachers of the Roman Church, without whom you do not even take a breath. And yet, you hold as heretics these your masters and teachers, and you, who without them cannot have your sermons (except for the heretical ones), are Catholics? You are hypocrites, with your wisdom and that of your ancestors, through whose watchfulness all of Rus' has been dispersed among the various rites—and what is worse, even among the heretical ones, which you can clearly see throughout all the corners of the Ruthenian land. And today, through your great wisdom, the starved nation of your side is barely still sensible on account of hunger for the word of God, although it has, as you boast, countless of your most wise preachers.

†Show me one learned man from your schismatic ancestors whose wisdom is attested by his writings. But we point to our Uniate ancestors, metropolitans of Rus': Grigorij Camblak, who lived around the year of our Lord 1415; and a second Gregory, hegumen of Constantinople, who occupied the metropolitanate of Kyiv around the year of our Lord 1442, men both pious and highly learned, by both of whom both you and we in the Ruthenian Church have sermons for various high holy days (which we commonly call *slova* [Ruthenian: homilies]) in our anthologies. Will you still boast of your most wise preachers? You will do that when you again give birth to them. But now both you, prevaricator, and all the others are hired laborers and not pastors,[43] who disfigure God's teaching rather than explicate it when you deliver your sermons. Do not revile me. I am satisfied with the little measure given me by the Lord God. In whatever I am capable, by His holy grace, in that I progress; in whatever I am incapable, from that I desist. And my God will not require from me what He did not give me. On your side, as we see, there is more boast than deed. In the entire Ruthenian land so broad, you do not have three preachers, and yet you boast vociferously that you have thousands of them, as if you lived in another world. The

---

† Throughout all its centuries schismatic Rus' did not have a wise man and does not now have, but the Uniates had and do have.

43. [Jn. 10:12–13.]

neighbors know, schimsatic, how things are with you.[44] We see your spiritual abundances.

†You attack the peregrination that I made to the Holy Land. But, like a hoop, before you even notice it, it will sock you in the nose.[45] For it is, by the grace of God, both pious and salvatory and beneficial to me, and in many regards, to the entire Ruthenian nation. If I had brought from there nothing more than that ONE, which worthless people submit to the nation as something to wonder about, ‡it would have received enough from me so that it not become hardened in its schism on account of the miracle that does not occur. You wonder that I went to seek and to test our Ruthenian faith in those parts whence it had come to us and which had been pure and undisturbed up to our very times. Knock that wonder out of your head. For when I acknowledge that the faith that came to our ancestors from the East is pure and immaculate, I say this *ex praesuppositione cognitionis ejus generalis* [from a presupposition of general knowledge about it]. *But when I say that I did not know about my own faith and I did not know what I believed, I say this *ex consideratione cognitionis ejus specialis* [from a consideration of special knowledge about it]. For I knew this for certain even at the time when I was reading the newly published works of our writers and publishing my lamentatious writing; however, when I read Zizanij, Philalethes, and others, and when I wrote my *Lament,* I understood that the faith described by them and by me was the one that had come to our nation *in primordiis fidei* [at the beginning of the faith]. But when, later on, replies to our works were published by the Uniate side, which, as a matter of course, I had to read and to consider and which showed us that the faith we described in our writings was not the faith that our

---

44.   [*NKPP* 3:152, "Sąsiad," 37.]

†   The author gravely defends his peregrination to the Holy Land.

45.   [From a saying referring to the habit of barrel hoops lying on the ground to flip up and strike the person on the nose who happens to step on them. Cf. *NKPP* 2:674, "Obręcz," 1.]

‡   The author speaks of the miracle of the descent of fire from heaven to the grave of the Lord, which does not occur these days.

*   The author does not doubt that the faith of the Holy Eastern Church that came to Rus' at the beginning is Orthodox. Rather he doubts only about the one that the new writers describe and preach nowadays.

nation received at the beginning of its Christianity, but rather a new faith unknown to the Holy Eastern Church, a heretical faith; and they said that our faith that had come to our nation at the time of its baptism was the one that they explained to us in their writings, then the certainty of my knowledge of the faith necessarily became confused here.

For I did not know *cognitione speciali* [with a special knowledge] which faith was that pure and immaculate faith: the one that I and our writers before me had described or the one that the Uniate responses indicated to us or even some other, third one. I did not have that sort of knowledge of the faith. Having divided the knowledge and ignorance of my faith in this same manner, you too, *fraudulente sophista* [deceitful sophist], restrain *linguam tuam dolosam* [your cunning tongue], and cease *cavillis perstringere* [to reprove with jeering] the profound reason for my peregrination, *alieno malo sapere edoctus* [taught to be wise through another's harm]. For I did not conduct it frivolously, as you frivolously allege against me, but with the knowledge, permission, and blessing of him who was at that time my elder,[46] who was supposed to know of this, and with the knowledge of the archimandrite of the Caves Monastery at that time[47] and of his chapter. And I had letters of introduction from both these individuals and from the former even to the father patriarch. In this and in other matters I render account not for your sake, calumniator, but for the sake of those before whom through your mendacious work you represent my good deeds as evil.

[†]You boast in this chapter as in the preceding one of the faith of Christ the Lord, of the blessed apostles, and of the holy fathers of the Holy Eastern Church. You must know, heretic, that your present faith was not known either to the holy fathers or to the blessed apostles or to Christ the Lord. Zizanij, he who did not abide in the truth from of old,[48] sowed these tares among the pure grain of Christ the Lord[49] with which you fatten yourselves today.

---

46.   [I.e., Jov Borec'kyj.]
47.   [I.e., Zaxarija Kopystens'kyj.]
†   The schismatic's vain boast of the Orthodox faith.
48.   [Jn. 8:44.]
49.   [Mt. 13:25–40.]

†As to my catechism and the letter I brought from the father patriarch: the latter was beneficial to our Ruthenian nation; it did not exalt me in the least either personally or with respect to my dignity. Your exarchs, of whom there were two in Kyiv, a third in Stepan', a fourth in Lviv (you ought, anarchist, to have criticized that four-headed monster for their anarchy and ambition)—the fact that that letter removed them and ordered that an exarch be chosen by the entire Ruthenian Church, touched a wound, especially for those in Kyiv. They sent out messengers throughout the entire land of Rus', asserting to the people as certain things of which not one jot was to be found in this letter. Through their greediness they submitted this letter to suspicion and disregard; and you do not cease even until today to calumniate me on account of it. You would have spewed it forth, you malicious calumniator, if you had read there even one tittle to my dishonor. As to the catechism: since I had come to the realization that the patriarch was a heretic through my frequent conversations with him when I lived for fifteen weeks or so in Constantinople, I did not much trust him. And therefore I did not bother him with my catechism, fearing that he might reform it into something like that of Gerganos, which is in use there today, whose heresies you will find specified by me in the *Apology;*[50] or into something like the one which he himself wrote and gave me to read. What sort of heresies he raises and introduces into his Church, you will find specified by me in the letter I wrote to him and published in print.

‡In response to the words that you speak against me, saying that "it was not Rus' you found there, but those who understand matters," I will tell you something strange. In those days when I was in Constantinople there were in the patriarchate two teachers, Matthew, a hieromonk from Athens, and Nicholas, an unmarried presbyter from Crete. The first knew Greek and Latin; the second did not know Latin. They had to leave Constantinople for the following reasons. In the presence of many metropolitans Nicholas rebuked the patriarch on the grounds that he taught, and allowed to be taught, such dogmas of the faith that had

---

†   The author offers a grave account of the letter brought from the patriarch and of his catechism.

50.   [See above, pp. 491–2.]

‡   What sort of wisdom there is today among the clergy of the Greek schismatics.

never been heard of in the Eastern Church. For this he was immediately ordered to leave the patriarchate. In the presence of many metropolitans, Matthew also complained about the evil customs of the unhappy see of Constantinople and about its superiors—that they do not exercise choice and care to see that men trained in God's law and learned in the disciplines be placed upon the episcopal sees and metropolitanates, for they are held here in disrespect and hatred: so long as he has a beard and a purse, he is immediately a bishop and a metropolitan. †For which the metropolitans so attacked him in defense of their beards and purses that he had to make his way out of the patriarchate following the first one. I met up with both of them in Iași on my return trip.

Having presented this, I acknowledge that it was not Rus′ I found there. For in Rus′ of our side, by the grace of God, the sun of truth shines; and from your side we still have some hopes for good. You imagine that you would find something there as in the time of those Constantines, Theodosiuses, Justinians, Marcians, and others like them, but you do not even recall that you will find there now the unbearable *jugum othomanicum* [Ottoman yoke], the heavy Mohammedan servitude. In the letter that I had brought here from the father patriarch there were three metropolitans whose name and hand others were asked to sign, since they themselves did not know how to write. Just listen. ‡I will tell you an even stranger thing (the Lord God is my witness that I do not lie in all this): I also saw there that he who was today a fool became on the morrow the metropolitan of Serrhae. Know, blind schismatic, that I found there those who do not know anything about matters of salvation and are not able to see that the patriarch is a Calvinist heretic. For they do not have any acquaintance with their own or with other faiths. And although this was even mentioned to several of them, they did not dare to open their mouths, for there they give a signal from the cannon announcing whom the Turk drowns; and the one whom you revere so highly does the same thing to the metropolitans without a signal.

Unhappy schismatic Rus′: are you waiting for your patriarch to turn Mussulman (to which he is already nearer rather than far)? In the same year in which I too wrote, one of our neighboring bishops[51] expressed

---

†   There is great simony among the schismatics.

‡   The schismatic *monstrum* [monstrosity].

51.   Bishop John of Mukačevo [Mukaczów, Munkács].

it well in a letter sent to him: *Ambigitur, utrum patriarcha noster sit Christianus* [It is uncertain whether our patriarch is a Christian]. And I, God willing, will prove this to you in my *Expostulation* so that you will be ashamed of your highest pastor, with whom you soar so high. And for my part, I will make my case, God willing, such that either he will renounce his heresies, or you will depose him with his heresies and will not wish to recognize him. So I did not find Rus′ there? *Bona verba quaeso* [I seek good words]. You have no reason to rejoice in that either, schismatic. I sooner expect something good in the Eastern Church from our Ruthenian nation, God granting, than from those whom you hold so highly.

†That I celebrated the Holy Liturgy on Easter Saturday in the Slavonic language at holy Golgotha—make an appeal to your own conscience, schismatic, not to mine. There were there at that time the two Josephs, both of whom are with you. I am certain that both of them will condemn you of lying for your appeal. And on other holy days in other holy places. About which I never spoke otherwise with anyone.

‡The words that my predecessor, the archimandrite of Vilnius,[52] spoke when, during the presence of the patriarch of Jerusalem, he sent me to Kyiv, testify to his attitude toward me during all the time of my residing with him.[53] For, informing me of his severe illness (he took leave of this world in that sickness) and, pointing to the need for a successor, he exhorted and begged me that I not return to Vilnius until I had been made a presbyter. When I refused him this, he, covered with tears, falling upon my neck, begged this of me before the brethren. Where is the place here, shameless liar, for your lies? For you collect these calumnies for no other reason but to submit me to the disgust of your side. But in this matter believe me: the one who will believe you is either he who does not know you or me or he who does not know how to distinguish truth from falsehood.

I do not commend the holy city of Jerusalem in order to lead you

---

† The author answers the lies of the Antidotist.
‡ He answers the calumny of the same.
52. [Leontij Karpovyč.]
53. [Mužylovs′kyj (1629, 6v) alleged that Karpovyč had not wished to receive Smotryc′kyj in the monastery, "knowing that [he] would cause great disturbances in the Church of God."]

away from it, as you wrongly allege of me, but rather so that I might make it even sweeter to you and cause your souls to remain with it in your thoughts.[54] Nor do I commend it to you so that I might lead you somewhere else, away from the East: for since I myself remain in the Holy Eastern Church, not only do I not think to lead anyone away from it, but I desire, yearn, strive, and take care to lead those to it who are neither in it nor in the Western Church. But even if, as you believe, I were to draw you to the Holy Western Church with which we have unity in our Holy Eastern Church, what would you lose thereby of Jerusalem? Do you think that you would abandon those holy places in which the mystery of our salvation is celebrated? This is how you believe, as you make known about yourself. But you err in this greatly. Not only would you not lose them, but you would gain them. [†]Who maintains that holy place in Nazareth in which the glad tidings came to pass? The Romans. Who maintains the holy grotto in Bethlehem where Christ the Lord was born and the manger in which he was laid down? The Romans. Who maintains the life-giving grave of Christ the Lord in Jerusalem? Thus would you not only not lose the East and the holy places of Jerusalem, but you would find them nearer than you have them. And therefore, do not lead yourself astray through this careless belief, nor cause the unknowing who might listen to you to stray. I remain in the Holy Eastern Church. I desire that you too might remain in it, and I ask the Lord God for this.

[‡]You revile me, perfidious soul, for asking the Lord God in those holy places for holy unity for my schismatic nation, and you play stupidly with that word unity.[55] I asked for the sort of unity for my nation through which it would rid itself of the accursed schism and not for the sort that would suffocate it with the schism. But you know, if you know, that even if not only your Church, but all of the Eastern Church, were to rid itself of all the errors newly sown in it, without unity with the Western Church it can in no manner rid itself of the schism. In such holy unity lived those Athanasiuses, Basils, Gregorys, Cyrils, Johns, and the rest of our holy Eastern fathers together with the holy Western fathers,

54. [Mužylovs'kyj 1629, 7r.]
†   The Romans hold the foremost holy places in Palestine.
‡   The ancient unity of the Eastern with the Western Church.
55. [Mužylovs'kyj 1629, 7r–v.]

the Sylvesters, Juliuses, Leos, Martins, Cyprians, Jeromes, Ambroses, Augustines, and others. They had one faith and one love in precisely the same degree of difference as exists today between the Eastern and the Western Churches. At that time those holy Western fathers still wrote and taught that the Holy Spirit proceeds "from the Father and from the Son," and the Eastern fathers wrote "through the Son," but they did not enter into schism on account of that difference in words, but unity in understanding.[56] At that time the Western Church still received the Eucharist in unleavened bread, the Eastern in leavened, and yet they did not make a schism among themselves on account of that difference. Communion under one species was still in daily use in both Churches at that time, but they did not seek either difference or schism. In those first holy centuries the Asiatic Churches used one calendar in celebrating Easter, the Western and Egyptian Churches another, and yet on account of that difference they did not start a schism.[57] [†]This is the sort of holy unity that I wish for my Ruthenian nation, and it was for this sort that I begged the Lord God in those holy places. So what do you say to this? Our Ruthenian nation, you say, did not need, and does not need, such an agreement. *Muta fiant labia tua schismatica, mendatia* [*sic*] *et dolosa* [Let your schismatic, lying, and deceitful lips be put to silence].[58] It needed it and had received it from the Council of Florence, and then around the year 1476, sending a letter to the holy father, Pope Sixtus IV, it renewed it. In our nation it is clearer than the sun that it needs it. For we strive for it day and night, and without it, if the nation wishes to maintain the integrity of its faith, and desires to be sure of its salvation, it cannot make do in any manner.

[‡]You refer the matter of holy unity to the father patriarch together

56.   *S. Maximus Epist. ad Marinum Cypri praesbyterum* [*Letter of St. Maximus to Marinus, Presbyter of Cyprus, on the Procession of the Holy Spirit; PL* 129:577AB–578AB, 568].
57.   *Socrat. lib. 1, cap. 8 et lib. 5, cap. 22* [Socrates Scholasticus, *Church History,* bk. 1, chap. 8 and bk. 5, chap. 22; *PG* 67:59D–62A, 625–46; *NPNF2* 2:8, 130–4]. *Sozom. lib. 7, cap. 19* [Sozomenus Hermias Salaminus, *Church History,* bk. 7, chap. 19; *PG* 67:1473–80; *NPNF2* 2:390].
†   The Antidotist lies.
58.   [Cf. Ps. 31:18.]
‡   Public unity of the Eastern Church with the Western cannot come to pass on the part of the patriarch of Constantinople.

with the holy father.[59] If the Turk would allow this to be, it would long ago have come to pass. But you must know that the Turk considers the unification of the Christians to be his own demise, wherefore he will not permit holy unity for the Christians who are under his rule, nor will he permit the patriarch to confer with the pope in this matter. Moreover, you must know for certain that your present patriarch is a manifest heretic (which, God willing, I will show to you clearly in the *Expostulation* in refutation of your chapter 8), who prefers to have unity with heretics than with Catholics.

[†]You, crafty one, hypocritically play the part of the disturbers in this matter of holy unity, which is felicitously promoted by pious men. I call you and those like you the instrument of the devil, who disturb the matter of holy unity and attempt to destroy it. What did you read about this in the *Desiderosus*? That I went to the father patriarch for the pacification of a sundered Rus' and for the unification of a rent Church: this is what you call a disturbance?[60] And those who strive for this with all their hearts you call disturbers? That is what the Infernal One thinks, whose name is murderer, liar, and disturber of the peace among the brethren.[61] Live with him, wretched schismatic, if the sort of peace you find with him now pleases you. We seek holy unity with our brethren, and we are obliged to lay down our lives for it, trusting in the Lord our God that He will console us His sinful servants in this without delay through the judgments He alone knows. He will not close our eyes until we delight in that sight desired by angels and men.

[‡]Ending your chapter you say: we had begun to tend toward the good in our nation.[62] I ask you, toward what good? Perhaps you consider this good to be your newly established hierarchy, which you would wish

---

59.   [Mužylovs'kyj 1629, 8r.]

[†]   The Antidotist is the disturber of holy unity.

60.   [Kasijan Sakovyč wrote in his introduction to Kasper Wilkowski's translation of *Desiderosus* (Cracow, 1625) that Smotryc'kyj would answer allegations about his trip to the Holy Lands upon his return. See Golubev 1883a, 123 and Sakovyč's preface to Wilkowski 1626,)( )(1r–v.]

61.   [Jn. 8:44.]

[‡]   That so long as the schismatics are in the schism they are unable to come to internal spiritual good.

62.   [Mužylovs'kyj 1629, 8r.]

to direct to the defense of your most miserable schism. But I believe that the Lord God permitted this hierarchy to come into existence so that the hierarchy of both sides of the sundered Ruthenian nation might stand at the service of holy unity and conclude it with its authority. But if the hierarchy that is on your side does not do this, let it know that as an opponent of the will of God even its memory will quickly be gone with the wind[63] from this Catholic kingdom. If, moreover, you believe this good to be schools, monasteries, churches—know that these three things cannot stand in their natural order so long as the unhappy schism knocks them from its proper state and does not allow them to stand in its place. Not only can you not show this, but neither will your descendants be able to do so, since your ancestors, the princes, lords, monarchs, did not show this earlier. And why was this? The reason is clear: on account of the accursed schism. For which reason the Lord God takes no delight in anything of yours, nor does He bless even one of your affairs.

Consider what good thing came into being here in the Ruthenian land under the rule of those lords and princes of your nation and faith? Nothing. They passed away, and their memory followed them. Look what good came to pass under your newly established hierarchy. Nothing. Everything is everywhere as it was before: neither schools nor order in churches or monasteries. What spiritual good does the Muscovite monarch have in his state, even though he has provided his entire hierarchy with bishops, metropolitans, and a patriarch? Not a one. Can he not afford it? Quite to the contrary. But the Lord God does not allow, and does not permit, him to establish anything good in the Church on account of the terrible schism, which deprives every Church of fruit and nourishment. It renders its womb hardened and its breasts withered so that it cannot give birth or nourish. Is this the sort of good toward which the Ruthenian nation of your side had begun to tend? This is certainly a paltry good. The good I have in mind will come to pass in our Ruthenian nation when the Lord God takes mercy upon it, and He will grant it harmony and love in itself, and He will crown it with holy Church unity. May He be pleased to cause this to be in our days.

63. [Ps. 103:16.]

Against Chapter 3 of the Schismatic Antidote,
*in Which the Antidotist Treats of the Improper
Allegation of the Apologist against the Ruthenian
Orthodox Church,
That It Does Not Know What It Believe.*

*Expostulation 3:
in Which It Is Shown and Proved That
Schismatic Rus' Does Not Know What It Believes*

†Having put on the cloak of Catholicism and established himself in the Universal Church, the Antidotist *insolescit* [grows haughty], supposing that no one would notice that he is both a schismatic and a heretic. And if nothing else would give him away, his unbridled tongue itself in this work gives it away that he is such. For in all these twelve chapters he does nothing but revile me, and he believes that when he abuses me, he also immediately achieves victory. But the Lord God Himself *illusores deludet* [scorneth the scoffers].[64] I will conquer his sarcasms with my humility and his untruth with the truth of God. *Rumparis Schismatice* [May you burst, O schismatic], I am not concerned with your sarcasms. For I lived among you, by the grace of God, and I live today such that *anteactae vitae nec paenitet, nec pudet* [I do not regret my past life, nor am I ashamed of it]. You lascivious mug: if you did not fear the Lord God (but what heretic has the fear of God?), then you ought to have been ashamed before people to spit forth such dishonorable words from your priestly lips so shamelessly, if you are a priest. Know, hypocrite, that almighty God, the *scrutator justissimus* [most just beholder] of your heart and mine,[65] will judge between you and me here in this world the sarcasms cast by you upon my piety and honor. *Parata enim sunt derisoribus judicia, et mallet percutientes stultorum corporibus* [Judgments are prepared for scorners, and stripes for the backs of fools].[66]

---

† How the Antidotist treats holy truth and the author in his *Antidote*.
64. Prov. 3[:34].
65. [Wis. 1:6.]
66. Prov. 19[:29].

†You are angry with me because I said in my *Apology* that as long
as I was on your schismatic side I did not know what I believed.[67] I call
upon you yourself to convince you of my truth. For having acknowledged
Orthologue's errors and heresies in your tenth chapter, you say of his
lamentatious writing that he disturbs many Church dogmas in it.[68] In
believing errors and heresies and disturbing Orthodox dogmas, did
I thus know what I believed? I do not think so. To the contrary: the
very ignorance of my faith caused me to write that which disturbed its
dogmas; and as I believed, so did I write. Wherefore, it follows that
I did not know what I believed, since a heretic does not know what
he believes even if it seems to him that he knows. He who believes
correctly knows what he believes. He knows God who knows Him the
way He taught that He is to be known. The pagans knew God, but since
they did not praise Him as He Himself wished and taught that He was
to be praised, they neither praised Him nor knew Him. Even the heretics
believe, but since they do not believe as God wishes and teaches, their
faith is unfaith, and they do not know what they believe. They walk in
darkness.[69]

Why, then, do you rage so ferociously against me and against my
truth? ‡Perhaps you are ashamed that it concerns you and your fathers
and brethren, who know just as much about what you believe as I knew
when I was with you in the schism. Nonetheless, even were you to be as
angry as you wished, I demonstrate and prove what I say against you;
you will not escape. For you have a mark on your forehead and a brand
on your neck[70]—not only the old errors and heresies that I revealed,
expressed, and refuted in the *Apology*, but new ones now that you
have introduced from infernal heretical opinions in this present work.
God granting, I will truly show this later throughout all the following
chapters, even without the horde of my followers. These two things
then follow: first, that the bride of Christ the Lord is not stained,[71] but

†   As long as the author was in the schism, he did not know what he
believed.
67.   [Mužylovs'kyj 1629, 8v.]
68.   [Mužylovs'kyj 1629, 30v–32v.]
69.   [Ps. 82:5; Prov. 2:13; Is. 59:9; Jn. 8:12, 12:35; Eph. 5:8.]
‡   Schismatics do not know what they believe.
70.   [Rev. 13:16, 14:9; Gen. 4:15.]
71.   [Eph. 5:27; S. of S. 4:7.]

your schismatic mistress is only too much so; second, that, according to your own words, you are so blind and lacking in understanding that you do not recognize the truth, and you cannot see that an archbishop in the Ruthenian schismatic Church does not know what he believes.

†And as to your proof that you and I had knowledge of the faith from reading and listening to the Holy Gospel and other religious writings:[72] Luther and Calvin and Münzer do not prove their knowledge of the faith in any other fashion, but you, I suppose, would not wish to acknowledge that they know what they believe. For from that reading and listening to the Holy Gospel and other religious writings, each of them has his own faith. And if they knew what they believe from religious teaching, then without a doubt they would agree on one faith. ‡You err when you say that from the recitation of the symbol of faith [i.e., creed] comes the knowledge and rectitude of faith. Eutychites and Dioscorites, of which the East is full, recite the same Constantinopolitan symbol. Yet even with the same symbol, Gospel, and monastic writings, they are heretics. Likewise you too, who have all those things, are not only ones of little faith,[73] which you charge against me without any proof and reason, but also ones of wrong faith. But I have already shown and proved this against you in my *Apology,* to swallow which you have opened your muzzle wide; and in this work, God willing, I will show and prove this, and I will defend my *Apology* against the gullet you have opened wide for it.

*You say against me that I disturb the Christian people and bring the Eastern Church into dissent with the Western.[74] It is not I who do this, but you and your fathers, who always oppose the Holy Spirit in this salvatory matter. I and my *Apology* came to you in peace and not to disturb; with love toward the Holy Western Church together with the Holy Eastern Church, and not with dissent. Having insulted, at your conventicle in Kyiv, both me as well as the peace and love and harmony

---

† The paltry proof of knowledge of the schismatic faith.
72. [Mužylovs'kyj 1629, 9v.]
‡ Second proof just the same.
73. [Mt. 6:30, 8:26, 14:31, 16:8, 17:20; Lk. 12:28.]
* That the schismatics disturb the Holy Eastern Church and bring themselves into dissent with the Roman Church.
74. [Mužylovs'kyj 1629, 10v–11r.]

and holy unity with which I had come to you, you both disturbed the Christian people and you brought the Eastern Church into even greater dissent with the Western Church, having cursed its Orthodox confession of faith. Whence there were multiplied such theologians as you, Antidotist, not from the little children,[75] nor from the fishermen,[76] but from chaff,[77] and from beasts, from goats,[78] and from tares,[79] and from similar spots.[80] For you do not say or write anything to the point. And if I were not to yield to the demands of precious time and take into consideration my other more beneficial Church occupations, I would show clearly in your work, not only in its every period or line, but in every word, that you do not say anything to the point with respect to my *Apology*. Whatever you do say is either heretical hypocrisy or falsehood or calumny. And that comes from nothing else but from the fact that you do not know what you believe, wherefore you also do not know what you say about your faith. And your knowledge of the dogmas of your faith is just the same as that of all your fathers and brethren and consequently, in precisely the same fashion, of all your schismatic Church. Thus what I said in my *Apology* is the truth, that schismatic Rus' does not know what it believes. Which I will also show in this work, God willing, more clearly than the sun.

[†]You ask why the Eastern Church gave birth to me, joined me with God through baptism, gave me the body and blood of Christ the Lord for the cleansing of soul and body? Why it wished to have me in the choir of the monks, gave me priesthood, and desired to have me as a pastor?[81] I respond to this now through God's mercy and through His holy help. The Holy Eastern Church gave birth to me, bestowed upon me and adorned me with its above-mentioned goods so that I might be in it in its pure and immaculate state; that I might defend it from schism and heresy; that, as my strength allows, I might not allow its sanctity

75.   [Mt. 18:4; Mk. 10:14; Lk. 18:16.]
76.   [Mt. 4:19; Mk. 1:17.]
77.   [Mt. 3:12; Lk. 3:17.]
78.   [Mt. 25:32–3.]
79.   [Mt. 13:25–40.]
80.   [2 Pet. 2:13.]
†   The author's pious work.
81.   [Mužylovs'kyj 1629, 11v.]

to be profaned; that for my part I might maintain monastic humility in its order; that I might perform the priestly dignity appropriately; that I might shepherd the sheep of Christ the Lord that were allotted to me: this was why the Eastern Church, though schismatic, nonetheless through the effort of the Eastern Church that is claimed and loved by holy Church unity, which today *in gremio suo materno fovet* [cherishes (me) in its maternal bosom], bestowed upon me these excellent gifts. Being watchful in all this and especially in that last pastorly gift, I strive that the schism grow together with holy unity in my fathers; I strive to root out in my brethren the heresies that arose and arise in it so that what is written about it might properly in all respects be verified in it: *Tota pulchra es amica mea, et macula non est in te* [Thou art all fair, my love; there is no spot in thee].[82] So that I might work more successfully toward progress in this, God's very mercy upon me transplanted me from its dead offshoot to the living vine,[83] to the true Holy Eastern Church and faith so that you, schismatics, cannot now be offended by me, but can build through me, those of you whose name is written into the books of life.

†You say that your schismatic Church will take all this away from me. But know that, as your schismatic Church, without directing itself toward the Universal Church, could not give to me what it gave me, neither can it take it away from me without the effort of that same Holy Church. I—becoming in the Holy Eastern Church not a dead member on account of the schism, but a living member on account of that holy unity—do not take this into consideration. For Holy Scripture says *maledicent illi, et tu benedices* [let them curse, but bless thou].[84] Whomever a godless one—a schismatic, I say, or a heretic—curses, him the Lord God blesses; the curses of such turn back upon their own pates.[85] I am grateful for this grace of God over me and for all the others. Whence I declare before His omniscient divine majesty that I never departed from that Holy Eastern Church and its salvatory faith,

---

82.   Prov. 6 [S. of S. 4:7].
83.   [Jn. 15:1, 4, 5.]
†   Unless it directs itself toward the Universal Church, the schismatic Church cannot give to anyone, or take away, any salvatory good.
84.   Ps. 108 [109:28].
85.   Ps. 7[:16].

and I will not depart from it either in this age or the next, at the risk of the salvation of my soul.

[†]At the conclusion of this third chapter you cite three signs that I was to depart from you schismatics and to disturb your schismatic Church.[86] No matter how many signs of this there were, they ought to move you all the more to holy unity from this accursed schism. Hope for which is the Lord God, the lover of the salvation of people led astray. I am aware that when I had come to Vilnius, to the Monastery of the Brotherhood of the Holy Spirit, with the intention of entering the monastic order, I had written and submitted among the monks a treatise on the procession of the Holy Spirit, wishing to confer about this with the elder and with the younger ones who were *capaces* [capable] of this matter, for the lamentatious blasphemies cast against the majesty of God in the treatise on the procession of the Holy Spirit[87] had already seized me by the soul. But I dropped this when I saw that a greater uproar, rather than the benefit I sought, would come out of this. And having written propositions from my treatise, I sent them to my present most illustrious father and lord in the spirit, most reverend in God,[88] to the Vilnius Monastery of the Holy Trinity, which, *perpolitae* [thoroughly polished], are published in print in the *Defense of Holy Unity*.[89] And then, living in this monastery for more than a year as a layman, I was often solicited and asked by both the entire brotherhood and especially by my now deceased predecessor in this archimandritehood to take the monastic habit. Varlaam, the former Vasily, a brotherhood priest, is well aware of this, and I know that he will not say otherwise. At whose request and persuasion, as my spiritual father at that time, I made the promise and named the day that I would enter the order. Even you are well aware, *iniquissime obtrectator* [most wicked detractor], with what joy, gladness, and rejoicing of the entire brotherhood, clerical and lay, I was led into the Church and from the Church, saluted, celebrated, and honored with a feast for that act. And yet, angered at me on account

---

† The author renders account of his entry into the monastic order, which was calumniated by the Antidotist.

86. [Mužylovs'kyj 1629, 11v–12r.]

87. [I.e., in Smotryc'kyj's *Thrēnos* of 1610, chapter 5 (91v–130r/108–46).]

88. [I.e., Ruts'kyj.]

89. [*HLEUL* 3:62–6; *HLEULT* 3:149–56.]

of the errors and the heresies of your Zizanijs, you shamelessly lie, and *Theonino* [with a Theonine, i.e., Theon's], not to say *canonino dente proscindis* [with a canine tooth, you cut to pieces][90] the grave act whereby I entered into the order.

†I also remember that at the time of my consecration to the priesthood you (like that loathsome creature, who, as they say, also lifts its own paw for shoeing when they are shoeing horses[91] and latches on where you are not summoned) snatched away the priestly garment that had been prepared for me and put it on yourself. But when, during the laying on of hands, the need arose for me to put on over the deacon's sticharion the priestly chasuble, that which belonged to me and not to you was pulled from your back and placed on me. And so you must correct that *praesagium* [foreboding], together with the exaggeration that you make, that is to your own and not to my shame. For divested of the priestly garment from that time on, you were shown to be *divino nutu* [by divine command] unworthy of the service of the altar. As long as I was a deacon, I had the wedding garment of the deacon; and when I became a presbyter, I was dressed in the wedding garment of the presbyter such that I was not at any point without the wedding garment that belonged to me. But you stood there like a ragged servant just when the king was arriving. Even in the sanctuary you were discovered and divested of what did not belong to you. Wherefore, you could have sung for yourself at that time what you sing for me today, having heard the King who celebrated that wedding saying to you: "Friend, how camest thou in not having a wedding garment?"[92] For precisely at that very time when the King was coming to look at those seated, you had lost the wedding garment since it did not belong to you, and at the time of His arrival you did not have it, and He saw you there, a man not dressed in the wedding garment. You see, hypocrite, how you are a Lynceus[93]

90. [Cf. Horace, *Ep.* 1.18.82.]

†   The Antidotist divested of priestly dignity when the author received the laying on of hands to become a presbyter.

91. [The "loathsome creature" of Polish proverbs who lifts his paw for attention, when it is horses that are being shod, is the frog. *NKPP* 2:124, "Koń," 81.]

92. Mt. 22[:12].

93. [One of the Argonauts, famed for the sharpness of his sight.]

when it comes to the integrity of your neighbor and a *talpa* [mole] when it comes to own your shame.

†The Lord God alone knows whether the pillar you mention fell *fortuito an prodigiose* [by chance or in a miraculous manner]. And yet, as you acknowledge, you lost a pillar of your schismatic Church: that is, not the least author, defender, and promoter of your errors and heresies. For if you acknowledge errors in my lamentatious teaching and the fact that in my work I violated many Church dogmas,[94] then you were to lose the author of those errors and the violator of your dogmas, and you lost him such that you remained by his errors and violated dogmas, and he, since he was unable to bring you—through all the many means [he employed] or through his *Apology,* which you cursed—to renounce along with him his errors and the dogmas of the faith against which he had transgressed, *ultimum vale dixit* [said his last farewell] to you and to his and your errors and violated dogmas. If, as you say, through taking leave of his errors and heresies, many people are coming to their senses and, despising your schism, are going to holy Church unity—may God Almighty be praised for this, who does not wish the death of man.[95] May the Lord Jesus Christ cause it to happen that you come to your senses, if only through these prodigies, and, having taken leave of your schism with its errors and heresies, join up with holy unity. For the Lord God Himself will judge and decree clearly and miraculously between you and me in this matter: who of us is right and who is wrong.

‡I will cite a fresh and new thing, worthy of wonder and consideration—not for you, who know about this well, but for those who do not yet know about this—which happened on the first holy Sunday of Lent in the current year 1629[96] at the cathedral church of the city of Kyiv dedicated to the Most Holy Virgin. For when your priests gathered together with your elder on that day in order to curse us, the archierei who are in holy unity, *and after the celebration of the divine service

---

†   The *praesagium* that the author was to abandon the schism and enter into holy unity.

94.   13r, 15r.

95.   [2 Pet. 3:9.]

‡   A divine miracle worthy of consideration.

96.   [An old-style date: 22 February/4 March 1629.]

*   The name of that calumniator who was sent to the pulpit was Taras in Greek, and *Turbator* [Disturber] in Latin: according to his name were his

they had prepared themselves for their accursed act, they sent one from among them to the pulpit so that he might make known, concerning the matter that was to follow, to the nation gathered for this *spectaculum* [show] from the entire city and the neighboring gentry and that he might make them more eager for the scene; when, among his other invectives against us, he spoke *specialiter* [especially] of me and, having likened me to that persecutor of the Jewish people, Haman, he called me the persecutor of the Ruthenian nation and the apostate from the Holy Eastern Church and faith, after his words (oh, the new, miraculous matter of God, worthy of consideration), from among that great group of people, a boy called out to them in a great voice: [†]"Stop, you speak untruth, you lie." [‡]The Lord God immediately closed the mouth of that liar and calumniator, the shameless scoffer at God's priests, so that he had to abandon his story and descend from the pulpit as if dumb. Whereupon there arose such an uproar in the people: look, ask, who said that, and how did that come to him? The child steps forward, and he says *intrepide* [undauntedly], "I said this, but how this came to me I do not know." They ask: "Whose child?" Father Borec'kyj answers: "Mine." They all said that it was as if he lacked half his soul.[97]

So here you have *prodigia* [prophetic signs]; and here are miracles; here, schismatics, you have Daniel declaring Susanna's innocence.[98] Here you have the significance of your fallen pillar. God Himself judged between you and me in the cathedral metropolitan church, in that place where all the salvatory Church matters of the Ruthenian Church have, since of old, always been discussed, judged, and concluded. He Himself judged and decreed that you speak untruth against me as far as concerns the apostasy from the Holy Eastern Church and from its Orthodox faith, with which you charge me. Thus whatever, Antidotist, you crammed into your *Antidote* about me in order to abuse me—as far

---

deeds. *Conveniunt enim rebus nomina saepe suis* [For names often coincide with their things]. [Smotryc'kyj derives the name from Greek ταράσσω, 'to stir up, to trouble.']

† [There is a pointing hand in the margin at this point.]

‡ A dumb Taras descended from the pulpit.

97. [Smotryc'kyj wrote of this miracle in a report to *Propaganda fide*. See Velykyj 1972, 224–5.]

98. [Sus. 1:45–64.]

as my alleged apostasy from the Holy Eastern Church and its Orthodox faith is concerned—in all of this you speak untruth like your colleague who became dumb in the pulpit, whose deeds are according to his name. May the Lord God grant you repentance in this, as also to him, so that you might become a sheep from a goat,[99] and he a lover of peace from a disturber. You schismatics ought to know from this work of mine, on this topic, that although I, with the leading *legitimi* [legitimate] archierei of the Ruthenian Church who precede me, confess with a pure heart both that the faith in the Holy Western Church is salvatory and all its *ritus* [rites] and ceremonies are full of God's honor; we are, nonetheless, so devoted to the Holy Eastern Church, in which, as in the Western, there is one and the same faith, and to its rites and ceremonies full of the honor of God, that we are ready to lay down our lives and to pour out our blood rather than to allow anything to be changed that was given and established in it from of old by the holy Eastern fathers. Every Ruthenian metropolitan swears to this. You listen on this point to the heretics who allege to you that with time all that is Eastern would be changed to Western, whereby they use you as a shield for their heretical error. Not granting credence to them in this matter, as the main enemies of both our sides, make your way toward peace, and crown holy Church unity with us in unity of faith and love as a heavenly crown. Grant this, Lord God, in our days.

[. . .][100]

Against Chapter 12 of the Schismatic Antidote, in Which the Antidotist Discourses against the Council of Florence

99. [Mt. 25:32–3.]
100. [Expostulations 4–11 are omitted here; Smotryc̆kyj 1629b, 17v–89v/718–92.]

Expostulation 12:
in Which It Is Demonstrated
and Proved That the Council of Florence
Ran Its Course in Peace and That Holy Unity
for the Eastern Church with the Western Was Concluded at It

†Having blasphemed to his heart's content against the Lord God in the previous chapter, *multarum machinationum versipellis artifex antidotista* [the dissimulating ingenious Antidotist of many tricks] makes an easy jump *de techna ad technam* [from one subterfuge to another], from blasphemy to mendacity, and he lies three times right in the third line of that chapter: the first time when he says that "the Greeks did not accept the Council of Florence"; the second time when he says that "at it a thing contrary to the dogmas of the Eastern Church was established"; and a third time when he says that "they were not permitted to discuss as it would have been warranted."[101]

The clear proofs concerning this cited in the *Apology*—that the Council of Florence ran its course—prove the first lie against him, for he does not destroy them with even one proper word, and that is because he has now grown dumb before the manifest truth.[102] The *acta* of this Council prove the second lie against him, where we read that the Greeks gave their consent to purgatory—if not in the material fire, then in some sort of abyss for the cleansing of souls. They gave their consent to the perfect blessing of holy souls. They gave their consent to the primacy of the pope. They also gave their consent to the confession of the Holy Ghost "and from the Son," but in such a way that this addition to the Constantinopolitan Creed not be inserted into their texts. Both the *acta* of that same Council and the historians mentioned in the *Apology* who wrote about that Council prove the third lie against him, for from them it is made known that both Greeks and Latins were permitted to speak and to dispute, and no obstacle was ever made in this; to the contrary, they were summoned in peace, love, and paternal and fraternal respect to conversations and to disputations more frequently than they themselves had the desire for them.

† The Antidotist lies three times at the beginning of his twelfth chapter.
101. [Mužylovs'kyj 1629, 38r.]
102. [See above, pp. 460–5.]

Proceeding several lines from here, he rebukes the Apologist concerning the Clerk of Ostroh, on the grounds that he improperly criticized him for the nonsense he wrote about the Council of Florence. And he proves this impropriety with the testimony of Mark of Ephesus, "whom," he says, "the Clerk has on his side."[103] †This is no mean witness. Nonetheless, this witness never wrote what that Clerk wrote, for he could not have mustered such shamelessness as to allege so contrarily concerning such a recent matter, which was still present in the ears and before the eyes of the entire world. But the fact that Mark of Ephesus wrote against the Council of Florence is not only not a valid reason to suppose that it did not run its course, but one that points rather to the conclusion of that council. For when Mark protests against that council in his circular letter sent to the Greek islands, he places blame upon the clergy that was at that council and on the emperor for his union with the Latins; and he ascribes Latin errors and heresies to them.[104] In this very manner he makes known and he acknowledges that this council ran its course. Otherwise he would not have had any proper reason for protesting against the council, complaining against his fellow representatives at the council, and rebuking them for Latin errors.

‡But the fact that Mark did not remain for the decree of that council concerning Church unity does not derogate in the least from the authority of this council. There was no Universal Council that did not have its vociferous objectors. The first council had its opponent in Arius. The second in Macedonius. The third in Nestorius. The fourth in Dioscorus. And the others in others, together with their followers. And still the councils were councils, and their opponents and objectors were heretics and outcasts from the Church of God. Understand the same

103. [Mužylovs'kyj 1629, 38r.]

†   Mark of Ephesus, the main enemy of the Council of Florence, did not attempt to allege such false things about it as the nonsense this schismatic, an anonymous Clerk of Ostroh, invented concerning it.

104. [The *Response* of Hieromonk Gregory, the Great Protosyncellus, to Mark of Ephesus's *To All the Orthodox Christians, Wherever They Are on Land and Islands,* together with extracts from the text of Mark's letter, is to be found in *PG* 160:112–204; *MarEph* 141–51.]

‡   Every universal council had its opponents, heretics. It is no wonder that the Universal Council of Florence also had its opponent in Mark of Ephesus, a schismatic.

about your witness, the vociferous objector to the Council of Florence, for in giving credence to him in this, you and the Clerk have departed far from the truth. And you are all the more guilty than he, since your cleric made up fables about things that Mark never dreamed of, and you gave credence and defense to his deceit, although you heard, if you did not also see, that this fairy tale was invented. Wherefore you ought rather to believe me in this matter, who faithfully cites for you the certainty of this matter in my *Apology,* not from some sort of obscure interpolations, but from trustworthy histories, and not that anonymous cleric or Mark, the disturber of Church peace and the sunderer of holy unity.

†You say that you "come to listen and to consider in orderly fashion" my reasons concerning this council.[105] And I come with you in order that I not allow you to fall from the way of truth. If you should nonetheless fall, I will bring you back. As far, then, as the proofs from Rus′ about this are concerned—that this council ran its course in peace and in the harmony of both sides—they remain in their authority. There is no description of your schism from even one Ruthenian—when and for what reason it crept into the Ruthenian Church—and yet, although *a testimonio humano* [from a human testimony], as you say, *negative non valet consequentia* [a deduction is not valid negatively], you believe it as if a thousand Ruthenians had described it. Rus′ described that council well when it entered into the Church books the decree of that council concerning the conclusion of holy unity. It also confirmed it well through the seven Ruthenian metropolitans who followed one after the other: Isidore, Grigorij [Camblak], Mysajil, Symeon, Jona [Hlezna], Makarij, Josyf [II] Soltan, all of whom lived in the holy unity that was discussed and accepted at the Council of Florence, and together with all of Rus′ for more than seventy years. And if that infernal witch, that is, the accursed schism, had not entered into our Ruthenian lands together with Queen Helena from Moscow, the holy unity of the Council of Florence would have remained in the Church of our Ruthenian nation until our days. Having founded a monastery in Minsk in Lithuania and placed Jona, a schismatic similar to herself, as archimandrite over it, that lady was then the cause that, after the death of Metropolitan Josyf

---

†　The Council of Florence remains in its authority with respect to the testimonies from Rus′ described in the *Apology.*

105. [Mužylovs′kyj 1629, 38v.]

[II] Soltan, he was raised to the metropolitanate of Rus'. And with him too, the schism was introduced into the Ruthenian Church.[106] Which, on your side, sits even until today on your necks, but on our side, cast under the feet of holy unity, it has been ignominiously dead for the last forty years now. May the Lord God grant that that soul-destroying monster might meet with the same from you as well.

You say: "It is a great wonder that the Apologist could barely come up with one book in all of Rus' in which that decree of the Council of Florence was written."[107] Nay, it is rather a great wonder, Antidotist, that through so many decades that fat sheep survived among the hungry wolves; that, I say, this decree of universal resolution was not ripped out of all the books throughout all Rus' by you schismatics. The Lord God caused this to be so for your shame and for our joy. Marvel rather at your own simplicity, Antidotist, and at your carelessness in writing vain things and not at such a significant and excellent matter. Why, just across the street from you, the fathers of the Monastery of the Holy Trinity in Vilnius will point out to you three books in which that decree has been written of old. Come visit me, and I too will show it to you in my monastery. You will find this in countless examples in other monasteries as well. Even if it were in the books of your library, you would give it up to destruction at your hands in good Zizanij style.[108]

That was one wondrous thing you said. But you say something even more miraculous: "If," you say, "Rus' had accepted the Council of Florence, that phrase 'and from the Son' would have to be in the confession of faith by now."[109] O wretched historian. But it is no wonder. It is most difficult to fall the first time from the way of truth. Thereupon, the farther you go, the farther afield. Blind schismatic: did they not agree at the Council of Florence that our Eastern Church might use the Constantinopolitan Creed without that addition? Are you so well prepared for the strengthening of your schism and for the destruction of holy unity that if you do not lie you have nothing to say?

106. [Helena (fl. 1495–1513) was the daughter of Grand Prince Ivan III Vasil'evič of Muscovy, wife of King Aleksander Jagielloñczyk of Poland. Metropolitan Josyf II Soltan (1507–1521) was *preceded* by Jona II (1502–1507).]
107. [Mužylovs'kyj 1629, 38v.]
108. [See above, p. 422.]
109. [Mužylovs'kyj 1629, 38v.]

"I will add," you say, "yet another thing: if the Council of Florence had run its course in peace and if it had been accepted by the Eastern Church, Rus' would have remained under the obedience of the patriarch of Constantinople."[110] You added it, but it is no less a wondrous lie than the first two. Do you not remain even until this very day under the obedience of that very patriarch? Did the Ruthenian Church not remain so during the lifetimes of the metropolitans I mentioned just a little above? For even the patriarchs of Constantinople, punished by their evil, did not contradict this, as is made clearly known from the letters written to Rus' by the Patriarchs of Constantinople, Dionysius [I] and Nephon [II]. And if the patriarch of Constantinople would give his consent to holy unity, the present-day metropolitan of Rus' would also remain under the patriarchal obedience, consider him his father, and consider the pope the father of his father. Not devoting more attention to this matter, cause your present-day patriarch to give his consent to holy unity, to announce his consent and assent according to the custom of Church laws, and to transmit the maintenance of holy unity under pain of anathema to his descendants the patriarchs. You will see that the metropolitan of Rus' will return to his obedience *favore summi pastoris* [with the approbation of the highest pastor]. But your patriarch prefers to unite, as we already hear and see, with heretics, not with Catholics, and to lead you to that same agreement; whereas our metropolitan prefers to sit for the time being with the father of fathers, to offer his humility to him, and to take care for holy unity in the Church of his Ruthenian nation with his fellow bishops.

†As far as the letter written from all of Rus' to Pope Sixtus IV is concerned, you say that "it was some Muscovite who wrote it to Metropolitan of Moscow Makarij and not Rus' to the Pope."[111] You stupid fool. In your opinion are the pope of Rome and the metropolitan of Rus' one and the same? Sixtus and Makarij? Some anonymous Muscovite and Mysajil, metropolitan of Kyiv, and with him the rest of the honorable clergy and the princes and lords who signed their names

110. [Mužylovs'kyj 1629, 38v.]
†   That the letter to Pope Sixtus IV written by Rus' is genuine, not invented.
111. [Mužylovs'kyj 1629, 39r.]

to that letter? †Why would that Muscovite have praised the Council of Florence and accepted the unity resolved at it? Does that Muscovite ascribe to the metropolitan of Rus' primacy, power, and pastorhood over the four patriarchs of the Eastern Church? Is it the metropolitan of Rus' who sits upon the cathedra of the foremost holy apostles, placed there by Christ the Lord? Madness has overcome you, schismatic, and in fine fashion. For blasphemies and falsehoods repay their sowers and defenders in this way. "Rus'," you say, "was never so careless as to write so incautiously, ascribing great things to man that are usually ascribed only to God alone." What will you say, wretched Antidotist, about the man who writes in this way to the pope: "Well, let us search still more diligently for what you are, what aspect you bear in the Church of God. What are you? You are the great priest, the highest pope. You are the prince of bishops, you the heir of the apostles. You are Abel in primacy, Noah in order, Abraham in patriarchate, Melchizedek in deed, Aaron in dignity, Moses in authority, Samuel in judgment, Peter in power, Christ in anointment. You are the one to whom the keys have been given, to whom the sheep have been entrusted. There are indeed other doorkeepers of heaven, and thus other pastors, but you inherited both those names all the more properly than the others to the extent that you did so more variously. They have flocks that have been entrusted to them, one each, but to you have been entrusted all these flocks, to you alone one flock out of all these flocks. Thus according to your rights, the other pastors are summoned to the part of care, but you are summoned to the entirety of power. The power of others is limited by certain borders; but your power extends even to those very ones who had taken power over others."[112] What will you say about this man, I say, who wrote thus to the pope and about the pope? Is he careless? And does he write this incautiously? This you cannot say. For the Church of God bears witness that he is holy. Even your *Antigraphē* bears witness for you.[113]

You will say: "This was a Roman, what wonder that he wrote so favorably about his Roman pope." It is true that he was a Roman,

---

†   The genuine schismatic deceit.

112.   *S. Bernardus, lib. 2. de Consideratione* [St. Bernard of Clairvaux, *On Contemplation,* chap. 8; *PL* 182:751C–D].

113.   Fol. 60 [*Antigraphē* 1609, 60v; *RIB* 19:1260].

but he was also a saint: he could not write untruth. But I grant you that he is a Roman. †Listen, schismatic, to a Greek, and not just any Greek, but to him whose memory the Holy Eastern Church, nay even your schismatic Church, celebrates with its annual glorification in the month of November, the eleventh day. He gives the pope such titles in the letter he wrote to him: "Most holy, highest father of fathers, equal to the apostles, most blessed, apostolic pope, divine head above all heads, pastor of Christ's sheep ordered by God, holder of the keys to the heavenly kingdom, summit of blessing, lamp of the entire world, source of Orthodox faith, pure and immaculate apostolic head, supreme father, first prince of priests, rock of faith upon which the Universal Church is built: preserve us, archpastor of the Church that is under heaven, for we perish. Imitate in this Christ the teacher, and give the hand of help to our Church."[114] Thus a Greek to the pope.

‡What do you say to this, Antidotist? According to you, is this holy man also careless, who writes so exaltedly to the pope? Does he sing a doxology, or, as you say, a *slavoslovie,* incautiously to him? Does he thereby blaspheme against God's majesty? Did he deviate from the way of truth? Not at all. Judge the same, Antidotist, about the letter from our ancestors as well, holy and highly honorable men, spiritual and secular, which was written carefully and gravely to Pope Sixtus IV. From this holy man, as well as from other Greek teachers, our Ruthenian Church learned to write so highly about the pope to the pope. Go ahead and ascribe this letter, you prisoner of the father of lying,[115] to a prisoner of the tsar of Muscovy; but we ascribe it to our holy ancestors, the Ruthenian nation. That letter of yours, snatched from under the bench, lies even today under the bench;[116] but ours, found in the Church of Krevo in the house of God among the Church books, has been released illustriously to the world in print.

*And not being able to oppose the manifest truth of holy unity

---

†   How the Orthodox Greeks write to the pope.
114. *S. Theodorus Studita in Epist. [33] ad Leonem III. PP.* [Theodore the Studite, *Letters,* bk. 1, letter 33, "To Pope Leo III"; *PG* 99:1017B–1020C].
‡   Now is the time to shut the mug of the schismatic Antidotist.
115. [Jn. 8:44.]
116. [*NKPP* 2:338, "Ława," 1.]
*   The Antidotist *rodit* [disparages] the privilege given by Władysław [III],

attested, among other proofs from Rus', by the privilege given by
Władysław [III], King of Poland and Hungary, to the Rus' that was
united at the Council of Florence, you annihilate that privilege
schismatica tua praesumptiosa arrogantia [with your presumptuous
schismatic arrogance] on the grounds that for one hundred years it was
not shown or seen by anyone.[117] It would be a lot for you, Antidotist,
to deprive each one of his right who did not show you the privilege
given to him for some thing over the last hundred years. All rights and
privileges are produced and shown when necessity indicates; without
necessity they lie in a place of safekeeping. As long as you schismatics
did not appropriate for yourselves the rights and freedoms that do not
belong to you, those rights lay in silence. But as soon as the necessity
occurred for you to be deprived of the cloak with which you have begun
to adorn yourselves improperly, this privilege was also produced and
demonstrated in addition to other rights. When you call it a forgery,
beware, schismatic: it is still the most noble descendants of Jagiełło
and Władysław who are happily ruling over us. You will sooner lose,
deceiver, what you so desire than you will destroy it. For your further,
more complete information about this privilege, I send you, schismatic,
to the book published by Ipatij Potij, Ruthenian metropolitan of blessed
memory,[118] about the privileges granted to the Ruthenian nation that is
in holy unity. And this is the authority of the proofs from Rus'—that the
Council of Florence ran its course, and that it ran its course in peace, in
harmony, and in love.

   You do not make any answer, Antidotist, to the proofs from the
Greeks, wherefore, remaining in their complete authority, they prove
against you that the Council of Florence was concluded in peace,
harmony, and love. For inasmuch as you describe as deserters[119] the
grave, honorable, and pious men, who, as history says *immanitatem
thurcicam pertimenscentes, et instans excidum Graeciae praesagientes,*

King of Poland and Hungary, to the Ruthenian nation that is in holy unity.
[Władysław III, king of Poland and Hungary, *Charter for Ruthenian Clergy,*
Buda, 22 March 1443; *AJuZR* 1:1:442–4; *AJuZR* 1:10:419–21; Harasiewicz
1862, 78–81; Papée 1927, 391–3; *MUH* 1:3–5.]
117. [Mužylovs'kyj 1629, 39r.]
118. [Perhaps Potij 1605.]
119. [Mužylovs'kyj 1629, 39r.]

Italiam petiuere [greatly fearing the Turkish savageness, and foreseeing the impending destruction of Greece, sought out Italy], you do them the sort of wrong that is the usual underhand reward *a detractoribus bonae famae* [from detractors of good reputation]. Likewise, when, in subjecting the letter of Patriarch Nephon [II] of Constantinople to suspicion, you say that "we cannot bring ourselves to believe that Nephon praised the Council of Florence since the Greeks did not accept this Council," you do not speak to the point. Their own harm taught the Greeks to be wiser, since they did not wish to be corrected by that of someone else.[120] As a sign of which, we show the two letters of two patriarchs of Constantinople, Dionysius [I] and Nephon [II], and the third letter of the present patriarch, Cyril, who wrote when he was Catholic in understanding. We show as the fourth sign of this same thing the burning of his books by Patriarch Meletius of Alexandria, whose conscience did not allow him to publish the writings he wrote against the Roman Church and against its truth. And what do you say against this? Nothing, except that you cannot bring yourselves to believe it. There were pious men in Greece, and wise, trained in divine and human arts, who, both before the capture of Constantinople and after its capture by the Turk, saw the necessity of the unification of the sundered Church of Christ the Lord. And to the extent they could, so long as they were in freedom, they helped with pen and letters; once they had become captives, lamenting their misery, they pointed the way to this holy unity to others. Which we see and read in them today, and having given them credence, we find ourselves in holy unity.

What do you think, Antidotist? How many such pious and wise people, spiritual and lay, are there now also among us in Rus′ who, seeing the so manifest demise of their Ruthenian nation and looking upon its daily destruction, are sick in soul and sigh at heart? But they cannot undertake anything for its restoration or for the prevention of its demise. Although for some reasons they waste away in the schism, nonetheless, when asked about the union they give it a good word. The commonality has taken control: today the priests must dance as the peasants play for them. †Do you not wish to do so?—they will show you their weapons, they will frighten you with dangers, they will threaten

---

120. [Cf. *NKPP* 3:397, "Szkoda," 2; Arthaber 629.]
†   The schismatic slogan for the maintenance of their schism.

death. The priests, poor things, who serve them for bread—although they know well that Church unity is a holy and salvatory thing—must remain silent. But when necessity demands it, many of them offer good testimony about it. You should understand the same thing about those patriarchs who, being oppressed in conscience and servitude, when asked about the Council of Florence and about the unity concluded at it, offered good testimony about both these things according to the essence of the matter.

Thus not having answered anything to the point concerning the grave proofs of the Greeks cited by the Apologist, to the effect that the Council of Florence ran its course in peace, harmony, and love, you also did not answer those cited from the foreigners and from the heretics. Wherefore you lost this argument, since you were unable to oppose holy truth. And yet, whoever, having been conquered by the truth, humbles himself before it, wins and does not lose. Which I counsel you to do, as well. You command me to be ashamed of that holy truth, but it does not have this property. Falsehood, lying, calumny, blasphemy, all of which are throughout your *Antidote,* give birth to shame, and they, even should you not will it, will cause you, God willing, *erubescere, ut salva res sit* [to blush with shame, so that all might be well],[121] as a defender of errors and heresies. You commend the decree of your Kyivan council: that it was forbidden there that books about the faith be issued without a censor and that there no longer happen on your side what happened before—that whatever anyone wished to write, he wrote. That decree is, as I see, very much in esteem with you, for you acknowledge that you publish that pasquil of yours without a censor, wherefore you filled it with the sort of errors that were not found either in Zizanij, or in Philalethes, or in Orthologue, or in the Clerk. Your elders certainly do have something to be thankful for, but it will be with a lash. You maintain your obedience only as long as the command of your elder pleases you, and then only to the doorway. Beyond the doorway you do what you feel like, not what the elder wished. However, *de iis qui foris sunt, mihi judicare non est* [it is not for me to judge them that are without].[122] With your conclusion, I too conclude, since I have already

---

121. [Terence, *Adelphoe* 643.]
122. 1 Cor. 5[:12].

given sufficient answer to your orations against my letters and to your summonses through my *Protestation* and *Paraenesis.*

Expostulation 13:
in Which the Apologist Discourses with the Antidotist
Concerning the Improper and Mendacious Defense of the
Errors, and Heresies, and Lies of Zizanij, Philalethes,
Orthologue, and the Clerk

Concluding this my debate with you, Antidotist, whoever you are,[123] I remind you of these words of the wise man: *Non contradicas verbo veritatis ullo modo, et de mendacio [in]eruditionis tuae confundere.* "In no wise speak against the true word, and be abashed of the error of thine ignorance."[124] In the matter of the defense of the remainder of the errors and heresies, which you carried out in your *Antidote,* if you had remembered the words of the wise man and this other thing, that *verbum legis consummabitur sine mendatio,* without lies the word of the law shall be found perfect, and wisdom will be made equal in the mouth of the just[125]—you yourself be the judge: for whatever you said in your *Antidote,* you opposed the righteous word in a multitude of manners, with lying, hypocrisy, blasphemy, and calumny, as if you thought that the word of the law is both fulfilled with these pieces of evil and defended.

†I do not care about the sarcasms and the *scommata* [jeers] cast upon me by you, for I did the same thing to my fathers and brethren when, together with you, I advocated the accursed schism. That same measure, full and overfilled, is now rightfully repaid to me by you.[126] But my patience will either be turned back upon the pain of your head or upon the sort of recognition of the truth (may God grant it), which, by the grace of God, happened to me too. Nor do I care about the taunting concerning Derman', for I live in it before people and with people such

---

123. [A strange statement, since the work was not anonymous, and Mužylovs'kyj's name appears on the title page.]
124. Sir. 4[:30 (in the Vulgate); verse 25 in English versions].
125. Sir. 34[:8].
† What the author forgives the Antidotist.
126. [Mt. 7:2; Mk. 4:24; Lk. 6:38.]

that, to the degree that living previously in your various monasteries I propagated the infernal fury (whom you also serve), planted errors and heresies, infected human souls with blasphemies, with body and soul served discords in my nation, disharmony and enmity, to the same degree now, living in Derman', I propagate, with the help of God, as far as I am able, the Church of God, defend the dogmas of the Orthodox faith in it, show misled souls the true praise of God, serve with my body and my soul, day and night, peace in my Ruthenian nation, unity, and love. I do not care, I say, about those two things you have cast upon me.

†But that you call me an apostate, a deserter—about that I care, and very much so. And I wish to have a debate with you about this very thing (God grant it), if the Lord God will lend me life and health to that time, at the coming Lviv council, which was ordered for us by God's anointed, His Grace, Our Merciful Lord. It is the custom of all Christian sects to call apostates or renegades those who, having abandoned their sect, join another one; and Jews, as well, call apostates those who leave their midst and, through baptism, enter into communion with Christians. But we are not concerned only with the bare word "apostate," but with those whom the Holy Universal Church is accustomed to call *desertores,* apostates from the Orthodox faith, and is accustomed to consider as such; as was that wicked Julian, or also those heretics, Arius, Macedonius, Eunomius, Nestorius, Apollinarius, and others; as you consider me to be when you compare me with them and when you taunt me with being such an apostate from the Orthodox faith, and through your work you allege to people that I am such. About such an apostate I do care. I challenge and summon you concerning such an apostate at this coming (God grant it) council, to show and prove what you charge me with, trusting in God's truth that, not having proved this against me, you yourself, as a heretic, will be censured with the mark of apostasy. And forfend that from the quarrel and disagreement of us two people the entire Ruthenian nation suffer such harm that could not easily be made good, either with the Lord God or with Catholic people.

All of what I wrote in my *Apology,* I defend with the permission of my elders, who acknowledge as Orthodox and accept my work and the dogmas of the faith described in it. Whom you will have as the follower and defender of your errors, that place will show, God willing. And so

---

†   What concerns the author in the *Antidote.*

that you might know about what the debate will be there, God willing, I remind you, together with your errors, so that both you yourself and everyone who loves his salvation might see that you opposed my *Apology* only so that, with lying, calumny, hypocrisy, and blasphemies, you might scratch your tongue, which itches[127] against the truth and might make it pleasant to the schism; so that you might revile the dogmas of the true faith, to the extent you could, and so that you might display the heretical errors newly raised by your sowers of heresies, the Zizanijs, for whom an *exitialis ruina* [fatal fall], with God's help, waits without delay here in Rus'.

[†]First, we will be concerned with particular judgment, which I acknowledge, and you do not acknowledge. And yet you place the souls that are departing hence in three places: in one place the holy souls, who do not need our prayers for them, but who pray for us; in a second place the damned souls, whom prayers can no longer help in any way and for whom the Church does not pray; and in a third place the middling souls, who need our prayers for them and for whom the Church of God prays. And you say that souls are brought to these certain places through divine dispensation. But I term this divine dispensation God's particular judgment. Having established this from your own admission and confession, I say first that the souls are brought to these various places either all *indifferenter* [indiscriminately] by the angels or all by the devils. But as a pure angel does not touch an impure soul, so an impure spirit does not touch a pure soul. It must happen, according to the Orthodox confession of the Church, that an angel brings the holy and the middling soul to their places, while Satan brings a sinful soul to its place.

I say again that this divine dispensation is either the one that occurred before the ages in God, who knows *in praesenti* [in the present] which soul is worthy of which place, or the one that occurs at the departure of every soul from the body. It is not the first, for about such a divine dispensation neither the devils nor the angels know, wherefore neither would they know which soul merits which place or should be delivered to which of their hands. It must be the second, which happens

127. [*NKPP* 1:866, "Język," 17.]

[†]   The author wishes to have a debate with the Antidotist about these dogmas at the coming (God willing) council. Dogma 1.

by divine decree, so that the angel might take the one soul and bring it to this or to that place and so that the devil might take the other soul and bring it to its place. This divine decree occurs only by God's judgment, who judges according to the deeds of our soul which soul is worthy of which place and orders the angel to take and bring the holy soul, and He allows Satan to take and lead away the sinful soul. We call this judgment of God particular judgment. And although we do not know for certain in what manner Christ the Judge carries out this judgment, since He can have thousands of means for this, nonetheless we do know for certain, and we believe that without divine dispensation, that is, without God's judgment and decree, no soul attains the place that it has merited. Having understood from me both your own opinion and mine, Antidotist, see how you will make me an apostate on the basis of this my Orthodox article of faith.

†Second, we will be concerned with the existence of the holy souls in heaven and with their perfect blessing, both of which I acknowledge, but you do not acknowledge any one of them. You acknowledge that the holy fathers confess that the holy souls are in heaven and that they are with Christ the Lord and see Him face to face, whence they also enjoy the complete happiness of perfect blessing. But you say that they say this *figuratim*, figuratively, that is, that they do not say what is, but what is to be. Thus we are in agreement in this confession, but we differ in its understanding on account of the figures you have invented. But St. Theophylactus criticized them in this article of faith, when they are used in the manner in which you use them (consider this well), in the works of perfidious prevaricators such as you, and he destroyed them as wretched and stupid. Thus, as I see, you cannot continue to maintain them in the face of the testimony of this saint. Furthermore, know too that in Holy Scripture heaven is called *figuraliter* [figuratively] paradise, but earthly paradise is nowhere called heaven. Wherefore, see, Antidotist, how you make me an apostate on the basis of my Orthodox article of faith.

‡Third, we will be concerned with purgatory, which I confess, but you do not acknowledge. And yet you acknowledge with clear words that those souls for which the Church offerings are helpful are kept somewhere. Not in paradise, for these souls do not need prayers. Not in

†   Dogma 2.
‡   Dogma 3.

the lowest hell, for prayers do not help them. It follows from your own confession to acknowledge for them a special third place, which place, according to us, the holy teachers understand to be in *ad* [Slavonic: hell] above gehenna. In this then we are in agreement. We differ in that I acknowledge punishment for the souls that are in this third place; you do not acknowledge this. I have on my side the manifest and clear proof that the *damni* [damned] suffer *poenam* [punishment], for being in this place they do not see God. Whence the Holy Church, in praying for them, asks that the Lord God might transfer them from that place to the other place among the saints, where the brightness of God's countenance covers them, which you can in no manner piously deny. And that they also suffer the *poenam sensus* [punishment of sensation], I prove as well *demonstrative* [demonstratively], partially by the location of that place in which there is darkness, wickedness, unease, and some sort of external burning; and partially by the very internal pain of the soul, lament, sorrow, and sighing, which are heavier for a soul that is without a body than for one that was in the body, both as far as its understanding and its will are concerned. Both of which are in the daily confession of the Holy Eastern Church. Since I have this on my side from Church doctrine and from your admission, look, Antidotist, how you make me an apostate from Orthodox faith on the basis of my Orthodox article of faith.

†Fourth, we will be concerned with the primacy of the bishop of Rome, whom I confess to be the bishop of Rome and the pastor of the entire Universal Church, and you acknowledge to him the Roman bishopric, but you do not acknowledge the pastorate over the entire Church of Christ the Lord. Nonetheless, when you are convinced by the doctrine of the holy doctors of the Church, you will have to acknowledge that Christ the Lord, building His Church on St. Peter, made him the foundation of His Church, that is the governor and ruler, teacher and pastor of the entire Christian people everywhere, having acknowledged that the Church is built either upon him or on his faith. Likewise you will have to acknowledge that when he ordered St. Peter to feed His sheep, He thereby commended and entrusted to him oversight, care, rule, and governance of all His sheep, not excluding anyone who considered himself a sheep of Christ the Lord. You will

† Dogma 4.

also acknowledge that all this devolved from St. Peter upon the bishop of Rome and that it remained upon him when you see these words ascribed to Him by the holy fathers, that the Church of Christ the Lord is also built upon him, that Christ also entrusted to him the feeding of His sheep in this same excellent manner that He entrusted them to St. Peter. Whence these same holy fathers acknowledge that he is the father of fathers, pastor of pastors, that Christ the Lord charged him with watching over His vineyard, that he is the first prince of priests, that he is not only the bishop of Rome, but also the archbishop of the entire world. The pastor not only of the Western Church, but of the entire Church which is under one archpastor. And all those *encomia* [eulogies] and *elogia* [maxims] about the pope of Rome are acknowledged to him by our holy fathers, and through their writings they are given to us for its eternal memory, teaching, use, and maintenance. Being defined and guaranteed by them through divine law, the bishop of Rome, not having any human law for this either from the holy fathers or from the Christian emperors, uses it in lordly fashion when he casts some patriarchs (*nemine contradicente* [with no one arguing the opposite]) down from their sees, returns others to their sees, separates some from communion, curses some; some he judges himself, others through his legates. And in all their dioceses he supervises their rule of the Church and judgments upon appeals. He orders the accused to come to him to render account; he judges, decrees, and brings his decrees to execution. When, I say, you see all this indicated to you, you will consider and understand, you will acknowledge in all this that the power belongs to him by divine law; and therefore, you will ascribe to him *pleno ore* [heartily] what you do not wish now to know. But if you do not do this, you will see how you will discover me to be an apostate on the basis of my Orthodox article of faith.

†Fifth and finally from that writing of yours, we will be concerned with the procession of the Holy Spirit, which I confess from the Father through the Son, according to the teaching of the holy Greek fathers, and from the Father and the Son, according to the teaching of the holy Latin fathers. But you confess from the Father alone; and yet you acknowledge two forces in the Father. You also acknowledge that first the Father gives birth, then he brings forth, whence you say that the Son

†   Dogma 5.

is second and the Holy Spirit third. If that first fatherly force is the first in such a way that it can in no manner according to natural order be second, as also the second cannot be the first, then it must of necessity follow that in giving birth to the Son first, He lends to Him through birth His essence (for that is what it is to give birth); He brings forth the Holy Spirit after the begotten Son, and He lends to Him that same essence already lent to the Son, which, if the Son does not also lend it together with the Father, one and the same essence is rent between the Father and the Son such that the filial essence suffers a change from the fatherly essence. Both of which things are *impium* [impious]. If these powers will vary *sine respectu originis* [without regard for the origin], then the persons of the Son and the Holy Spirit must suffer the same variation such that it will not always necessarily remain the case for the Son that He remain without change the second divine person, nor for the Holy Spirit that He always remain the third person. Which is also *impium* [impious]. One can say piously without regard for the originary order that the Holy Spirit is the first divine person, the Son the second, and the Father the third. But with regard to *originem* [origin] one cannot say this *nisi impie* [unless it be impiously]. Likewise one can say piously without that regard for the *originem* that to beget is the second fatherly power and to bring forth the first; but with regard to the originary order one cannot say this piously. Whence it follows that having lent His own essence to the Son through begetting, the Father lends one and the same essence to the Holy Spirit together with the Son. Having had to acknowledge this of necessity in order to avoid these impieties, you will confess in Orthodox fashion that the Holy Spirit proceeds from the Father and from the Son, as from one origin, through unity of release of the force that is the same one that was lent to the Son by the Father. But if not, you must see how you make me an apostate on the basis of my Orthodox article of the faith.

This is the recollection of your errors. You do not mention more differences between the Eastern and the Western Churches, nor do I seek them in you. For these too are more from opinion, and from some sort of contrary persuasion from of old, and from a suspicion inculcated in human hearts through the schism, than they are differences in actual fact. Which everyone who is wise and loves God and the unity of faith and love can easily see.

†Having presented this in this manner, I, for my part, ask both you, Antidotist, and all your elders and peers, before whom, through this work of mine, I present myself with my bow, and I ask in the name of the Lord, who created, redeemed, and sanctified us, that, having cast behind you private rancors toward the persons who are in holy unity, you might wish to take care for the matter of the unification of the Eastern Church, which has been rent from the Western, through the means of the unity of the Ruthenian Church, in the love of your salvation and of the people that follow you; and to take counsel that, through those whom the Lord God wished to have for the raising, through holy unity, of the Holy Eastern Church from the fall of the schism, this holy and salvatory deed, desired by all of God's Church for many ages, might receive its happy effect, ‡not looking upon the antiquity of the schism, but considering the reasons for its rise, progress, and consolidation, and how the Lord God severely punished it with servitude, anarchy, infertility, and hunger for the word of God, how He does not bless it in any manner anywhere, either in freedom or in servitude, and does not take delight in it in any manner. For it suffers this same fall of the entire spiritual good in the Muscovite freedom that it suffers in the Turkish servitude: everywhere in it the spiritual consolations have fallen; everywhere the salvatory Church matters have grown cold; everywhere the celebration of salvatory things and matters is as by contract and compulsion, just so that it be, just so that it be performed. The monasteries have everywhere turned Sarabite.[128] Monastic obedience has grown stiff, the caretaking of the elders has frozen. You will not find a spiritual man among the monks with a candle;[129] and do not even look among the laity. The schools have fallen. Church singing is growing weak. Tachygraphy is failing us (which is very important for us for the Lithuanian and Ruthenian laws).

---

†   The fraternal admonition from the author to the schismatics.
‡   The effects of the accursed schism.
128. [Sarabite: "A name, of doubtful derivation, given in the early Church to a class of ascetics who dwelt either in their own houses or in small groups near cities and acknowledged no monastic superior. Their mode of life seems to have been regarded with disfavor, notably by St. Benedict, who refers to them adversely in the first chapter of his rule" (Cross 1958, 1215).]
129. [*NKPP* 3:416–17, "Szukać," 20.]

It is difficult to find a good deacon, more difficult to find a learned priest; do not even ask about a wise preacher.

Those Christian nations that are in the Turkish servitude have already for the most part become turkified; and the Roman Church has taken no little part of our nation; no little part has been taken by the heresies, Calvinism, Arianism, nay, even Mohammedanism. We have lost princely houses. There is little of the gentry. Fewer of the lords. The higher and lower clergy have come to disrespect among their own people. In Moscow the boyars beat them with the knout if they do not follow their ideas in spiritual matters. And it is not the pastors that tend the flock, but the flock that tends the pastors. And whence comes the punishment for such debasement? Certainly from nowhere else but from the fact that they hold the father of fathers in disregard, for which reason the Lord God submitted them to the disregard of secular people. Unto you was born that infernal fury of new errors and heresies, of new interpretations of Holy Scripture and the writings of the holy doctors of the Church. †That accursed schism has whelped schismlets for you. Every more excellent city in the bishoprics has in it the schismlet of the *stauropegium,* where the bishop must indulge his little sheep. And they respect him when they will. All of which occurs not by any happenstance or any ordinary course among people, but by God's manifest anger, by His harsh punishment.

There used to be riches in our Ruthenian nation; there are even now in the Muscovite nation. The Lord God, however, did not allow schools to be raised either here among us or there in Muscovy. And wherever anything is undertaken toward raising them, it only smokes but does not burn. The children in them receive only the benefit that they grow up from calves into oxen. Schools are the granaries of the Church. They enrich the cities, towns, and villages in wise people, trained deacons, judicious priests, learned preachers. Without schools the Church is like a body without a soul. And it is certainly for no other reason than on account of the schism that is disgusting to His majesty that the Lord God does not allow you to have this good throughout your entire Eastern schismatic Church. And no matter how hard you were to strive and apply your care day and night with your greatest expenses, the Lord God will not give you this good without holy unity. He allows

† The *stauropegia* are the degenerate offspring of the accursed schism.

this good to heretics, as He previously allowed it to the pagans—unto the deceivableness of unrighteousness in them that perish, because they received not the love of the truth, that they might be saved.[130] He does not allow it to the schismatics so that they, who have one and the same faith with the Universal Church, might also learn from it one and the same love. Which may the Lord God grant also you.

You cry out: "O evil Union, evil Union." It is not long since you likewise cried out: "O evil sermon, O evil figural singing, O evil," to go with the little bell before the sacrament—this is all Polish. But now this is all in use, it is all good. With the same understanding you cry out against holy unity as you not long ago cried out against all this, and as you today cry out against the correction of the *heirmologia,* both text and notes, and against the correction of the scribal errors and the incorrect translation in the Church books. All of this you consider Latin heresy. But when you examine these matters for yourselves, then that which you criticized yesterday, today you praise. What was evil yesterday is already good today. The same thing will happen with holy unity as well, which you now consider evil, but as soon as you receive it (God grant it), you will consider it good. [†]For it does not change anything of yours from the pure Eastern faith or from the rite; it leaves everything as it was before. And in addition to this, in whatever you now experience God's unblessing on account of His righteous anger toward you, it will be changed for you into blessing. Schools will arise, seminaries will arise, and the Ruthenian Church will arise such that from the abundance of its internal and external goods, other nations of the Eastern rite will enrich themselves bounteously. Just a catechism edited by our Ruthenian Church in various languages and released to the nations of the Eastern rite will work an inestimable benefit in people's souls. And what about postils, what about lives of the saints, and other similar Church goods? Even you yourselves see this well.

Nonetheless, the wretched schism allows you to disregard this. But you must know, brethren, that if you should continue to blaspheme both the Lord God and His saints in this Catholic kingdom before the entire world through such *Antidotes,* and if you should not wish, through your very stubborn obstinacy, to pay heed to these many and

---

130. 2 Th. 2[:10].

† The benefits of holy unity.

frequent cries of us your brethren and to mend your ways, having called to testimony the Lord God and His Holy Church, you will become for us, all the Catholics, *sicut aethnici et publicani* [as heathen men and tax collectors].[131] Are these really jokes for you: to cast through your pasquils, *sub titulo specioso* [under well-sounding pretense], such blasphemies against God's majesty, such lies against Church laws, such calumnies against Catholics, such *scommata* [jeers] against honorable people? In a Catholic kingdom can *blasphemi, calumniatores, internae et externae pacis turbatores, extra Ecclesiam Dei positi schismatici* [blasphemers, calumniators, disturbers of the internal and external peace, schismatics who have been set outside the Church of God] do this *impune* [without fear of punishment]? For wherever the schism is, there is not the Church of God. Nor is there the priesthood. Nor is there the inheritance of the Kingdom of Heaven. The schism takes away from a man the divine sonhood, removes him from among the members of the body of Christ the Lord. It brings the entire spiritual good to its fall. A schismatic can be killed, but he cannot be crowned from that death.[132] For such a person always calls out with that lascivious voice: "Divide it; let it be neither mine nor thine."[133] There is nothing left of the harmony of born brethren. They have nothing left of the love commanded by Christ the Lord, nothing of Church unity. But my fathers in the spirit, and I with them—we all summon the brethren to harmony, love, peace, holy unity. For Christ the Lord commanded us to maintain all this, and without these four things no one was ever saved, nor can he be saved.

†You say: "We want everything according to old usage." We say the same thing as you do. And we struggle for that old usage. But since you appropriate it for yourselves, and we indicate that it is with us, one side does not grant the other credence in this matter; but now, through God's grace and help, we will dispute about this old usage amicably in peace at the coming council of Lviv. And we will crown holy Church

---

131. [Mt. 18:17.]

132. *Cypr. de simplicit. praelat.* [St. Cyprian, *On the Simplicity of Prelates (On the Unity of the Church); PL* 4:493–520, especially 510; *ANF* 5:421–9, especially 425–6].

133. 1 Kg. 3[:26].

† This is the matter that is to be discussed between the Uniates and the schismatics at the coming (God grant it) council in Lviv.

unity in mutual love. *Contremiscant in vobis viscera misericordiae* [may your bowels of compassion be moved], that I speak with St. Augustine to you in this salvatory matter.[134] May your bowels of compassion be moved so that you might finally wish to discuss this matter, ardently praying to the Lord God and conferring among yourselves in peace so that the wretched commonality, which depends upon your honor, might not oppress you by its obedience at God's judgment, but rather, turned away from errors and disagreements by your unfeigned love, might be led with us unto the way of truth and peace. Deign, Lord Jesus Christ, Granter of peace and love, harmony and unity, to cause this to come to pass for both our sides at the coming council, which is to gather in Your holy name. To which let us all, both you and us, and every Orthodox person, say amen, amen, grant it, Lord God.

Unto the honor of God, the One in the Trinity, and unto
the Soul-Saving Benefit
of the Ruthenian Nation.
Meae vitae unica spes IEsus ChristuS.
[My life's one hope, Christ JEsuS.][135]

---

134. *Epist.* 147. [St. Augustine, *Letter* 147 (alternate numeration, 2nd division, letter 33); *PL* 33:131; *NPNF1* 1:262. Cf. 1 Macc. 2:24; Lk. 1:78; Col. 3:12.]
135. [See above, p. 231.]

A Final Letter
(1630)

[Letter to Pope Urban VIII, Derman', 16 February 1630.]

M OST HOLY AND MOST BLESSED FATHER.
To Peter, who asked, "Lord, how oft shall my brother sin against me, and I forgive him? till seven times?" Jesus responded, "I say not unto thee, Until seven times: but, Until seventy times seven."[1] What then is it, if I should have sinned against You, my brother, many more times than seventy times seven? But why do I say lightly: "brother?" Rather against the father, to whom, over all fathers from sea to sea and from river until the ends of the world, rule, care, power is submitted, entrusted, committed by Him, to [dis]obey Whom is to say in one's heart: there is no God.[2]

Against You, therefore, my most devout father, and not against You alone, but also against my mother, the most chaste bride of my Lord Jesus Christ; not only against You, such and so great a father, and against such and so great a mother, but against God Himself (oh, the crime!), against my one Creator, Redeemer, Consoler Himself, if I, most shameless and blasphemer, both schismatic and heretic, should have sinned most gravely, many more than seven times seven, You, who are to me more than a brother (even if You called me a brother, and a venerable one, in the most greatly pleasing breve that You granted to me, Your unworthy son, indeed Your useless servant) will forgive me all that I have sinned. Nor will You forgive only paternally, but also You will bestow abundantly Your apostolic benediction. Wherefore, I say, is this? Is it that You are greater than our father Jacob? Is it that You are greater than Peter, to whom it was given to forgive one who sinned seventy times seven? You have forgiven ἁμαρτήσαντα [him that had sinned] more than seven hundred times seventy times seven. You are greater indeed, greater to the extent that, with my sins, I have surpassed all sinners, the sins of each of whom Peter forgave individually, not to mention all together. You are greater, and greater to the extent that my sins had extended themselves more broadly and more deeply than those of them whom Peter was commanded to forgive. If they sinned against Peter, Peter was then permitted the power to forgive seventy times seven; and if I had sinned not only against quite innumerable ones of my

1.   [Mt. 18:21–2.]
2.   [Ps. 53:1.]

brothers and fathers, against You, the high father of the highest fathers, who are Peter to me and to all of them, and against my mother, but, as I said, even against my God Himself, You have forgiven more than seven hundred times seventy times seven. For however many words there are in my schismatic writings, which are nearly innumerable, so many are the horrible sins. Would that no eye had ever seen them, no ear had ever heard! Nay rather, would that they had never existed, conceived within my heart! It would have been more bearable for me, a schismatic, on the day of judgment than for the land of Sodom and Gomorrah.[3] Now, however, since so many ears will have heard and hear, so many eyes will have seen and see, it would be clearly more bearable in the day of judgment for the land of Sodom and Gomorrah than for me, a schismatic and a heretic, if You had not come to my succor and kept me safe, such and so great a sinner, from this unbearable punishment through Your more than human authority. Wherefore, by my reckoning, You have stood forth all the more to the extent that You have forgiven more than it was granted, in Peter, to forgive.

On account of which, what should I offer that would be worthy in response to such an act of kindness? What should I repay to You, my so great benefactor? This: it is necessary that I love You more than the others (since You have given more to me than to the others), and if conscience is the witness of those things that take place within a man, I make an offering by that very Witness, Who examines hearts and reins,[4] of the fact that I love You, that I do not yield to anyone in loving You. May I die for the sake of Your honor, for the sake of Your authority, which You hold as the highest vicar of Christ my Lord in His Church. Moreover, no one has greater love than this, as Christ the Lord Himself is my witness that I do not know how to lie, that he lay down his life for him, whom he loves.[5]

Come now, Most Holy Father, and have me who loves You so among those most devoted to You, and thus use me, ordered by You Yourself, for whatever it pleases and seems good according to God and according to my strength. For I have already produced, by God's grace, a private account of my entire previous life for him, for whom, according

3.   [Mt. 10:15; Mk. 6:11.]
4.   [Ps. 7:9; 26:2; Jer. 11:20; 20:12.]
5.   [Jn. 15:13.]

to the rules and the standard of the Catholic Church, I was supposed so to do;[6] and, having abjured the schism, condemned the heresies, I carried out, completed, consummated faithfully, fully, intimately, an incorporation into the body of Christ, which is His Church, and a public confession, in the ear of the entire Church of Christ that is in this most populous Kingdom of Poland, of all the public sins I have committed—conceived, expressed, said, done, and carried out against the matter of the holy union, striving against it with might and main, with sails (as they say) and oars,[7] evilly, perversely, scandalously, impiously, blasphemously, sacrilegiously, and of that impetus, to which, not through love of life or fear of death, but through hope and desire for greater profit in acquiring the schismatic souls of the Church of God, I yielded for a time.[8] And I opposed to the two blasphemous works of the schismatics, which are recently published against my Orthodox *Apology,* my two Catholic works; and I explained the pious sense of the dogmas in which the Eastern Church seems to differ from the Western one. Now, what seems to me to be lacking (lest I be lacking in this part either for myself or for my people, for, I say, my brethren), I eagerly fulfill by this my unworthy letter unto the hands of Your Holiness.

And first of all, I most humbly entreat indulgence for my audacious deed, hoping it not be rashness that I so presume with Your Holiness in suggesting a difficult thing: for since it is beyond me, it ought not to concern me at all. Then I offer the required thanks to Your Holiness that, with Your breve, which I must revere in the highest degree, beyond my expectation, You should deign in it to honor me and to bestow upon me Your benediction. Because even if it does not have the subscription (as, perhaps, custom has it) of Your honored hand, nonetheless Your name, which I especially revere, offers itself to me to be kissed. Then I ask Your Holiness humbly that You might paternally, in Your pastoral heart, help and love me, the son newly added to the flock and received in the bosom of holy mother Church under Your most fortunate pontificate and that You might console me with salutary warnings. Further, what

6.   [I.e., Uniate Metropolitan of Kyiv Ruts´kyj.]

7.   [Cf. Cicero, *Tusc.* 3.11.25.]

8.   [A reference to Smotryc´kyj's behavior at the Kyiv Council of August 1628, where, in his representation of events, he chose temporary compromise rather than a martyr's crown. See above, pp. 587–99.]

I said is beyond me, what I considered necessary to fulfill by reason of the necessity of helping the brethren entangled by the schism, I suggest as attentively as can be to Your Holiness, whom this concerns as greatly as possible; and I reveal as faithfully as possible the cause of the tardiness and the hardness that keeps those men from entering into holy union (although they have been proved evidently mistaken in their errors by Uniate Catholics for a long time now). For in what I have myself experienced and put to the test, I am capable of showing clearly the experience and the trials of those who are being put to the test.

It does not seem to be a wonder, Most Holy Father, that this people (as also all the others separated from the union of the Western Church and puffed up with the name of the Eastern Church), seized by crass ignorance of divine things, by and of themselves should not be able either to know or to understand anything of the divine. For where the light of the liberal sciences is always setting and never rising, it is necessary that there be darkness. However, if one seized with darkness trembles, it is not a wonder. Nor is it a wonder if someone deprived of bright light for his sight either strikes his forehead against walls or stumbles with his feet against rocks, falters, falls, and does not know which way to turn. But it is a wonder if someone prefers to undergo for hours, even for moments, so many difficulties, so many perils to life of this sort, than to be led by the hand safely and correctly by someone who sees. Of which sort certainly are all the men blinded by the abominable schism, who freely, in no way different from those forsaken by reason, rush to their own fall. They themselves see nothing at all in matters of salvation, in, I say, the dogmas of the faith, and yet they do not suffer themselves to be led by the hand. What, then, to do with such people? Indeed, thoroughly instructed by the teacher, experience itself, I do not find another means than the one most efficient one pointed out by the Savior, to which I now refer. For where reason is given to reason, neither is disagreement obstinate nor agreement slow; but where one proceeds according to opinion, there one vainly opposes reasoning.

For what else is "compel them to come in"[9] than not to allow the opinionated and obstinate to perish? If therefore they undertake to perish, and he who is able to help despises to do so, we will certainly be obliged to help them, lest we commit the crime of homicide through our

9.   [Lk. 14:23.]

voluntary contempt. To help them, however, not as sane but as insane. Indeed, the obstinate differs little from the insane; because the insane does not desist from doing wrong unless he is proved mistaken, so also the obstinate does not do anything good unless he is forced to do so. Wherefore, each is to be brought back, willy-nilly, to a more healthy mind by one and the same means: just as the insane is to be bound, lest he do evil things, so also the obstinate is to be forced so that he do good things. Clearly nothing ought to be granted to their judgment, since it is manifestly blind. For what is lacking that in our Rus', for the recovering of the schismatics to a more healthful state of mind, Uniate Catholics have not tried for more than thirty continuous years, have not pursued through sermons, disputations, daily colloquies, admonitions, writings—private and public—and, according to the apostle, in season, out of season, reproving, rebuking, exhorting with all long suffering and doctrine?[10] By all of this, however, they have brought about not more with those obstinate men than if they were to tell a story (as the proverb has it) to the deaf.[11] But in fact the means I mentioned above, given by Christ the Lord to His Church for inviting disobedient guests to the banquet in such a manner, and brought to bear by some faithful servants of their lord in his domains, caused many in a short time to enter into the house of the lord from the highways and the hedges.[12] And if this were brought to bear by all Catholics, surely the house of the Lord will be filled more quickly than was supposed. Certainly there would remain outside of the house no one except the son of perdition,[13] a wandering and perfidious man unworthy of the common life.

But what then? Since this matter is conducted in this way, should I blame the inflexible obstinacy of the schismatics toward Your Holiness, or the negligent folly of certain of the Catholics in this kingdom? I know not at all; let me inquire nonetheless. The Lord says: that servant which knew his lord's will, and prepared not himself, neither did according to his will, shall be beaten with many stripes.[14] One servant is schismatic, another servant is Catholic. But the schismatic knew not the will of his

10. [2 Tim. 4:2.]
11. [Erasmus *Ad.* 1.4.87; Arthaber 1111.]
12. [Lk. 14:23.]
13. [Jn. 17:12.]
14. [Lk. 12:47.]

Lord, whereas the Catholic knew it. And so, if each of these servants did not do the will of his Lord, each will be beaten; but the latter more, the former less. Therefore, those servants are properly to be blamed who will be beaten with many stripes: those who knew the will of their Lord and prepared not themselves, neither did according to His will. Catholics are rightly to be blamed, who knew this will of their Lord, that He wishes that all men be made saved and to come unto the knowledge of the truth,[15] but prepared not themselves, neither did according to His will. They prepared not themselves in that they permitted their subjects to be possessed by the abominable schism and to be buried by the filth of heresies. They did not do according to His will in that they did not compel their servants to enter into the house of their Lord. These are the sorts of servants that are to be blamed. These servants, in my meager opinion, are not dissimilar to those pastors in the prophet Ezekiel. For just as they, enveloped and fattened with the wool, milk, and meat of their sheep, did not feed the sheep,[16] so also these, placed in the daily labors of their subjects, are made rich from their properties and taxes, clothed in purple and fine linen, and feast daily, but they have no care at all for the health of their souls. And what is more execrable, many of them (oh, immortal God!) entirely purposefully take pains that their subjects not come unto the knowledge of the truth and be saved, while they suffer them not only to remain in the schism full of blasphemies, heretical errors, but even exhort them to remain (always calling that stubbornness of theirs constancy): they permit usurper-bishops to consecrate their *pop*s and urge them to maintain obedience. They undertake to esteem in words the Uniate bishops, their legitimate pastors, but in actual fact they despise them excessively, while they do not allow them rightly to exercise due jurisdiction over those *pop*s of theirs, and if requested to do so, they would refuse.

Oh, those servants who will be beaten with many stripes! Oh, evil lords, not good Catholics! They, they are the ones, Most Holy Father, whom I would fault before Your Holiness. These cold Catholics are the cause why this spark of the salvatory holy union in our fatherland, long maintained by the wise diligence of many (which still now is incessantly maintained) has not kindled, nor kindles, the desired fire,

15.   [1 Tim. 2:4.]
16.   [Ez. 34.]

since they extinguish it with their abominable coldness among the most fiery tinder of the Uniates, and they keep it from being highly inflamed. Such are the Catholics who foster, maintain, and promote the schism in our Rus'. It is they who supply usurper-bishops with monasteries of their patronage for their dwelling; it is they who feed them, they who defend them. And they, relying on their patronage, running about hither and thither throughout all Rus', simonize their *pop*s, men of crass ignorance, make the schism into the Church, make heresies into Orthodoxy; and thus they lay up for themselves, their followers, and those patrons— with a great scandal of the little ones and with a great harm to the holy union—wrath on the day of wrath and revelation of God, the just Judge. It is Your task, Most Holy Father, to oppose this evil and to cause that in one and the same body all the members exercise the office that is employed for them by the judgment of the head and not what seems fit to them themselves, lest this fault of theirs be turned upon that very head by whose power these things are kept to be ruled. You, the head, for the sake of the salvation of the perishing souls nearly exhaust Yourself through daily solicitude so that, by pious means, You might draw, pull, attract the Ruthenian nation to Your holy union, without which there is perdition for it; the members, however, seem, on the contrary, to exercise something quite different, contrary to Your will.

Since, then, the affairs of the accursed schism stand thus, do You wish, O Most Blessed Father (who, imitating the will of Your Lord, as the matter proclaims, wishes nothing other than the salvation of souls), to see that all Ruthenians in our Rus' enter entirely into the holy union that was long ago desired and advanced by many of Your antecessors? Behold, I offer to Your Beatitude a means, both plain and pious, most easy and most effective. By Your authority, in which You are strong by the design of God, delaying nothing, let You, the head, say to Your arms, which You have in this most illustrious Kingdom of Poland, the one spiritual, the other secular: let there be Union in the Kingdom of Poland; and, as soon as it is said, the deed will be seen. For what are You not able to do, who have as Your Co-Laborer the Omnipotent, since You are His faithful servant and skilled steward, established over His family that You give them food in the proper time and strive to bring all together in one? If these arms would receive that "Let it be" of Yours with unanimous agreement and were unanimously to carry it out, You would see, the Lord God aiding, what You long for there to be done in our Rus', and You will delight most happily, witnessing the desired end of Your solicitude. But if these arms are in discord with each other such that the one of them raises something up, and the other presses down the thing raised up, we strive in vain, we hope in vain, we await in vain. Yes indeed, this contest will be a more than childish plaything, such that what the one today has brought forward, the other tomorrow would destroy. As it almost seems to be done now among us.

You have, Most Holy Father, Your beloved son in the Lord, our most illustrious king (may the Lord God preserve him for us safe, sound, and uninjured for many years), the secular arm, most fervent and vigilant in the execution of this salvatory office, whose sincerity in maintaining and advancing the holy union has become most well known to all Catholics, as well as to the schismatics.

You also have Your spiritual arm, not less suitable for executing this office, the most illustrious and most reverend archbishops and bishops, the first senators of this kingdom; further, You have the most illustrious and most reverend nuncio from Your side.

What now is missing? These two things: first, if by the commission and the order of the spiritual arm the priests, both secular and regular, and especially the fathers of the Society of Jesus, who have—throughout the individual Ruthenian provinces—parishes, convents, and colleges; if, I say, they would faithfully undertake to carry out that aforementioned "Let it be" of Yours, immediately that aforementioned "It will be done" would be done, and in this manner. Let it be given in charge under the conscience of holy obedience to each individually who hear confession that they absolve no one nor admit to the communion of the sacrament of the holy altar any of those who either in word or in deed oppress the union and promote the schism. Of which sort are those voluntary patrons of the schismatic intruders, the supporters, defenders, and, in like manner, the favorers of the accursed schism and its promoters, to the extent they are able. For they are deserving of ecclesiastical censure for this their auxiliary evil-doing not less than are those themselves, the workers of this malice. Moreover, as a part of penitential satisfaction let it be enjoined upon all such people that they oppress the schism and promote the union. Henceforth let them cast out the schismatic bishops from their monasteries, let them take away their sustenance, let them decline them favor, let them deny them protection, if they will not allow Uniate priests for their subjects; let them permit the monasteries, with their right of patronage intact, to be subject to the jurisdiction of Uniate bishops: and right there Your Holiness's word will become deed. For once the columns have been moved away, it will be necessary that the entire edifice built upon them will collapse. Right away we will see that those schismatic invaders, who now ride about on the arms of the Catholics, either will wander out beyond the borders of the Kingdom or will willingly seek holy union, after they have come to know by the thing itself that they would be frustrated of hope of the long-standing favor and patronage of their patrons. For they which sought the young child's life are dead;[17] the persecutors, I say, of the holy union, have vanished, the magnates, princes, who maintained for themselves and their subjects the foreigner bishops and those ἐπιβάντας [intruders], sustained and defended them. Nor is the schism able any more to provide for itself such protectors and nourishers. This is one thing we desire.

I offer the second thing. That the youth of the Ruthenian nation, noble and plebeian, devoted to the schism, who zealously study letters in the colleges of the fathers of the Society of Jesus, not be constrained to change their rite. Nay rather, even if they should wish it, let it not be allowed; rather, brought to the holy union by pious admonitions, let them be made firm, let them remain constant in their own rite. For thus will be furnished in abundance laborers to that harvest[18] of the Lord, to the urging, I say, and the promoting of the Holy Union. And for persuading this upon their students, in addition to six hundred others, there is for these teachers also this most evident and firm reason at hand, that of the apostle who said: But if any provide not for his own, and specially for his own house, he hath denied the faith, and is worse than an infidel.[19] For even if they would wish to oppose, they can easily be constrained. For they cannot truly assert with equal reason that they are more able to help the afflicted mother Eastern Church once they have changed their rite, than if they were to continue steadfastly in the rite. For he offers greater help to him who is in danger of losing his life, who helps with living voice with laid-on hand, than he who helps from far away only by shouting. By the former method, those who remain in their Greek rite are considered to help their mother, the Eastern Church; by the latter,

17.   [Mt. 2:20.]
18.   [Mt. 9:37; Lk. 10:2.]
19.   [1 Tim. 5:8.]

those who change their rite. And they [help], the more firmly, the more effectively, who themselves likewise maintain and follow what they recommend to their mother and brothers as good and salutary, than do they who are themselves presumed to have despised as evil or as less good what they recommend to their mother and brothers.

If You would cause these two things, Most Holy Father, by Your vigorous pastoral authority in all, behold, You will have the desired union in our Rus' at Your hands. Having become master of which, expect that You, through Your Ruthenians, in the succession of brief time, will have obtained it in all the nations which, in the name of the Eastern Church, boast that they are in the schism. Liberty raises up the arrogance of the schism, servitude presses it down. As soon as that κακοδαίμων [evil spirit] has been cast out from our free nation, it will be driven off more quickly than had been supposed from the nations oppressed by tyranny. God Himself will provide the means. Wherefore, if it is reasonable, Most Blessed Father, show favor to this my suggestion through action, and do not delay; for the favorable moment must be anticipated, since at this time among us the most unbending schismatics, inflamed by the constant exertion of the Uniates, are becoming warm and soft; and through weariness of the schism, which in some means has been made most hateful to themselves, they fight mutually for the union, and they exert themselves far and wide for its foreseen good. Today (for tomorrow it will be less fitting), as a strong David cast down the Philistine triumphing over that powerful people of God, devote all care to gain Your Ruthenians, having convinced Yourself, by the grace of God, that through them You will soon achieve the desired effect of Your wish in the entire Eastern schismatic Church.

Meanwhile, I, Your useless servant, cast myself most humbly at the feet of Your Holiness, and I kiss them reverently. I earnestly entreat the forgiveness for my sins, and I desire to take comfort in the pastoral benediction of Your holiness. May the Lord God preserve Your Holiness for many years, through His divine grace, for the rule of His holy Church unto the peace of the entire Christian world.

Given in Volhynia, province of the Principality of Rus', incorporated into the Kingdom of Poland, in the monastery called Derman', patrimony of the Most Illustrious princes of Ostroh, in the year of our Lord 1630, the month of February, the 16th day.

Your Beatitude's unworthy son and daily
    suppliant of God,
    Meletij Smotryc'kyj,
    called Archbishop of Polack,
    Archimandrite of Vilnius and Derman'.

Plate 9. Jerusalem, from Stefano Du Perac, *Hierusalem* (Rome, 1570?). Courtesy of Historic Cities Research Project, Hebrew University of Jerusalem, The Jewish National and University Library (historic-cities.huji.ac.il).

Glossary

Anabaptism. A general designation for the Protestant Christian groups who, in the sixteenth century, rejected infant baptism and, in their belief, reinstituted the baptism of adult believers.

Arian heresy. The principle heresy that denied the divinity of Christ. Named for its author, Arius (d. ca. 336). This teaching held that the Son of God was not eternal but created by the Father, thus not God but changeable creation.

Belial. A Hebrew word of unknown etymology meaning "worthlessness," "wickedness," "destruction," usually used in constructions such as "sons of Belial," although St. Paul used the word as a name for Satan; see 2 Cor. 6:15.

bench. Here, the court of the burghers' magistracy.

benefice. Revenues awarded for the discharge of the prescribed duties of a particular ecclesiastical office.

Cerinthianism. A heresy that taught that the world was the creation not of the supreme God (who transcended the universe completely), but either by a Demiurge or by angels, who had produced it out of formless matter. Jesus began His earthly life as a mere man, though at His baptism "the Christ" descended upon him; it then departed from him before the crucifixion. Named for its author Cerinthus (fl. ca. 100).

chorepiscopus. A rural bishop.

circular letter. In Polish-Lithuanian practice, a "universal [letter]" issued by the king, primate, palatine, or other important individual or body (such as a Sejm) that was intended for public reading.

Donatism. A schismatic movement in the African Church that became divided from the Catholics through its refusal to accept Caecilian, bishop of Carthage (consecrated 311). The Numidian bishops, supporting the schismatics, consecrated Majorinus as a rival to Caecilian, and he was soon succeeded by Donatus, who gave his name to the movement.

Ebionites. "Poor men." A sect of Jewish Christians of the early centuries of the Christian era. The sect flourished on the east of the Jordan. It had two main doctrines: (1) Jesus was the human son of Joseph and Mary, (2) emphasis on the binding nature of Mosaic law.

Eutychianism (Monophysitism). Named for Eutyches who taught "one nature," the teaching that in the incarnate Christ there was one nature, the divine one, and not the teaching of a double nature, first divine, then human after the incarnation.

Lateran Councils. A series of councils that took place in the Lateran Palace at Rome from the 7th to the 18th centuries. The Roman Church considers five of them ecumenical.

Macedonianism (Pneumatomachian heresy). A fourth-century heresy that denied the full personality and divinity of the Holy Spirit. This teaching made the Holy Spirit the creature of the Son and thus subordinate to the Father and the Son.

Manicheanism. A non-Christian religion derived in part from Gnostic doctrines with origins in Christian heresy. A strong competitor for the Christian Church in the fourth century, it was based on a dualistic belief in a primeval conflict in the world between light and darkness.

Monophysitism. "One nature." The teaching that in the incarnate Christ there was one nature, the divine one, and not the teaching of a double nature, first divine, then human after the incarnation.

Monothelitism. "One will." A seventh-century heresy confessing only one will in the God-man. The Council of Constantinople (680) reasserted the orthodox doctine of two wills in Christ, divine and human, as the accepted teaching of the universal Church.

Nalyvajko. A term of derision for Orthodox Ruthenians in the Polish-Lithuanian Commonwealth. It derives from Severyn Nalyvajko, a Cossack leader who headed an uprising of burghers and peasants against the Polish-Lithuanian state in 1594–1596. It thus identifies the Orthodox with non-nobles and with treason.

Nestorianism. The doctrine that there were two separate Persons in the Incarnate Christ, the one divine and the other human, as opposed to the orthodox doctrine that the Incarnate Christ was a single Person, at once God and man. It was characterized by its rejection of the term Theotokos ("God-bearer") as a title for Mary, who, according to the teaching, had given birth only to the human person of Christ. Named for its founder Nestorius (d. ca. 451).

pallium. The piece of ecclesiastical garment granted to archbishops by the pope and to metropolitans by patriarchs, symbolizing the participation in papal and patriarchal authority. The Eastern term is ὠμοφόριον.

Photinianism. Named for fourth-century heretic, Photinus, bishop of Sirmium ca. 344, who taught a kind of Sabellianism. According to St. Augustine, Photinus denied the pre-existence of Christ.

pop. Orthodox priest. Often used in Polish derogatorily.

protothronos. Occupant of the chief throne. Honorofic title given to certain ecclesiastical hierarchs.

Sabellianism. Sabellius was probably an early third-century theologian of Roman origin. The heresy that was identified with him taught that the three Persons of the Trinity are three modes of God, in the same sense that the sun is bright, hot, and round.

Sacra Congregatio de Propaganda fide. The Sacred Congregation for the Propagation of the Faith. The Roman Catholic office charged with missions to non-Christian lands and the administration of territories lacking established ecclesiastical hierarchies. Established in the second half of the sixteenth century, it soon became a tool of the Counter-Reformation, directing its attention not only to missions to the heathens, but also to heretics and schismatics.

Samosatenism. Named for Paul of Samosata, a third-century heretical bishop of Antioch and precursor of Nestorius who taught that from the Incarnation the Word rested upon the human Jesus as one person upon another, and that the Incarnate Christ differed from the Prophets only in degree.

Sejm. The Polish-Lithuanian Diet.

starosta. The administrator of a castle with juridical and police powers in royal demesnes in the Polish-Lithuanian Commonwealth.

szlachta. The nobility of the Polish-Lithuanian Commonwealth.

Union of Florence. The reunion of the Greek and Roman Churches concluded at the Council of Ferrara-Florence in 1439.

wójt. The chief juridical authority of a Polish-Lithuanian town or group of villages. In some he was named by the king or owner of the town, in others he was elected by the magistracy.

złoty. Unit of currency in the Polish-Lithuanian Commonwealth equal to thirty
   Polish groschen.

Works Cited

Andrusiak, Mikola. 1934. "Sprawa patriarchatu kijowskiego za Władysława IV." *Prace historyczne w 30-lecie działalności profesorskiej Stanisława Zakrzewskiego,* pp. 269–85. Lviv.

Antelechus, To iest odpis na skrypt vszczypliwy zakonników Cerkwie odstępney Ś. Ducha, Elenchus nazwany. 1622. Vilnius. [Reprint: *AJuZR* 1:8:674–731. The edition I consulted had a pagination different from the one used by the editors of *AJuZR.* Apparently there was more than one edition of the work that bore the date 1622.]

Antigraphē, albo Odpowiedź na skrypt uszczypliwy. 1608. Vilnius. [Reprint: *RIB* 19:1149–1300.]

Anuškin, A. I. 1970. *Na zare knigopečatanija v Litve.* Vilnius.

Apolleia Apolohii Knyžky. 1628. Kyiv. [Reprint: Golubev 1883b, 302–17.]

Bardach, Juliusz. 1964. *Historia państwa i prawa Polski.* Vol. 1, *Do połowy XV wieku.* Warsaw.

Broniewski, Marcin. 1994. *Apokrisis, abo odpowiedź na książki o synodzie brzeskim 1596, imieniem ludzi starożytnej religiej greckiej przez Chrystophora Philaletha.* Eds. Józef Długosz and Janusz Byliński. Wrocław.

Brückner, Aleksander. 1990. *Encyklopedia staropolska.* Vol. 1. Reprint of 1939 edition. Warsaw.

Budny, Szymon, trans. 1574. *Nowy Testament znowu przełożony.* Losk.

Calvin, John. 1950. *Commentaries on the Book of the Prophet Jeremiah and the Lamentations.* Vol. 3. Ed. John Owen. Grand Rapids, Mich.

Cassander, Georg. 1616. *Opera quae reperiri poterunt omnia.* Paris.

Chodynicki, Kazimierz. 1931. "T. z. prawo 'podawania' w Cerkwi prawosławnej na ziemiach Rzeczypospolitej w XV i XVI w." *Sprawozdania Poznańskiego Towarzystwa Przyjaciół Nauk* 5:44–8.

Clerk of Ostroh. 1598. *Otpys na lyst v bože velebnoho otca Ypatija volodymerskoho i berestejskoho episkopa.* Ostroh.

Cross, F. L., ed. 1958. *The Oxford Dictionary of the Christian Church.* London.

Curtius, Ernst Robert. 1973. *European Literature and the Latin Middle Ages.* Trans. Willard R. Trask. Bollingen Series 36. Princeton.

Czerniatowicz, Janina, ed. 1991. *Corpusculum poesis polono-graecae saeculorum XVI–XVII (1531–1648).* Polska Akademia Nauk Oddział w Krakowie, Prace Komisji filologii klasycznej 22. Wrocław.

De Dominis, Marcantonio. 1618. *De Respublica Ecclesiastica.* Pt. 1, bks. 1, 2, and 3. Heidelberg.

Długosz, Jan. 1962. *Roczniki czyli kroniki sławnego Królestwa Polskiego.* Vols. 1, 2. Warsaw.

Dubiński, Piotr. 1788. *Zbiór Praw i Przywilejów Miastu Stołecznemu W.X.L. Wilnowi nadanych. Na żądaniu wielu Miast Koronnych, jako też Wielkiego Księstwa Litewskiego ułożony i wydany.* Vilnius.

Examen Obrony, To iest Odpis na Script Obrony Werificatij nazwany. 1621. Vilnius. [Reprint: *AJuZR* 1:8:562–96.]

Florja, Boris Nikolaevič. 1992. *Otnošenija gosudarstva i cerkvi u vostočnyx i zapadnyx slavian. (Ėpoxa srednevekov'ja.)* Moscow.

Frick, David A. 1985. "Meletij Smotryc′kyj and the Ruthenian Language Question." *Harvard Ukrainian Studies* 9:25–52.

———. 1987. "Meletij Smotryc′kyj's *Threnos* of 1610 and Its Rhetorical Models." *Harvard Ukrainian Studies* 11:462–86.

———. 1988. "Petro Mohyla's Revised Version of Meletij Smotryc′kyj's Ruthenian Homiliary Gospel." In *American Contributions to the Tenth International Congress of Slavists.* Vol. 1, Linguistics, ed. Alexander M. Schenker, pp. 107–20. Columbus.

———. 1994. "'Foolish Rus′': On Polish Civilization, Ruthenian Self-Hatred, and Kasijan Sakovyč." *Harvard Ukrainian Studies* 18:210–48.

———. 1995. *Meletij Smotryc′kyj.* Cambridge, Mass.

———. 2002. "*Słowa uszczypliwe, słowa nieuczciwe:* The Language of Litigation and the Ruthenian Polemic." In "Χρυσαῖ Πύλαι, Златаіа Врата: Essays Presented to Ihor Ševčenko on His Eightieth Birthday by His Colleagues and Students." Ed. Peter Schreiner and Olga Strakhov. *Palaeoslavica* 10(1):122–38.

Golubev, Stefan Timofeevič. 1883a. *Kievskij Mitropolit Petr Mogila i ego spodvižniki. (Opyt istoričeskogo issledovanija.)* Vol. 1. Kyiv.

———. 1883b. *Kievskij Mitropolit Petr Mogila i ego spodvižniki. (Opyt istoričeskogo issledovanija.)* Vol. 1, *Priloženija (=Materialy dlja istorii Zapadnorusskoj cerkvi).* Kyiv.

Gonis, Dimitrios. 1982. "Carigradskijat patriarx Kalist I i 'Učitelnoe evangelie.'" *Palaeobulgarica* 6:41–55.

Gregory, St., Pope. 1608. *The Dialogues of St. Gregorie*. Paris. Reprinted in D. M. Rogers, ed. 1975. *English Recusant Literature, 1558–1640*. Vol. 240. London.)

Gudziak, Borys. 1998. *Crisis and Reform: The Kyivan Metropolitanate, the Patriarchate of Constantinople, and the Genesis of the Union of Brest*. Cambridge, Mass.

Gwagnin, Aleksander. 1584. *Rerum polonicarum tomi tres*. Vol. 2. Frankfurt.

Harasiewicz, M. 1862. *Annales Ecclesiae Ruthenae*. Lviv.

Hruševs'kyj, Myxajlo [Hrushevsky, Mykhailo]. 1999. *History of Ukraine-Rus'*. Vol. 7, *The Cossack Age to 1625*. Edmonton and Toronto.

———. 2002. *History of Ukraine-Rus'*. Volume 8, *The Cossack Age, 1626–1650*. Edmonton and Toronto.

Ivanov, A. I. 1969. *Literaturnoe nasledie Maksima Greka*. Leningrad.

Jaekel, Siegfried, ed. 1964. *Menandri sententiae*. Leipzig.

Kaczmarczyk, Zdzisław, and Bogusław Leśnodorski. 1966. *Historia państwa i prawa Polski*. Vol. 2, *Od połowy XV wieku do r. 1795*. Warsaw.

Kempa, Tomasz. 2003. "Sprawa zabójstwa wójta kijowskiego Teodora Chodyki przez Kozaków. Przyczynek do wyjaśnienia sytuacji na Kijowszczyźnie w przedeniu powstania kozackiego 1625 r." In *Między Zachodem a Wschodem*. Vol. 2, *Studia ku czci profesora Jacka Staszewskiego,* ed. J.Dumanowski, B. Dybaś, K. Mikulskiego, J. Poraziński, and S. Roszak, 298–300. Toruń.

———. 2004. "Nieznany list Melecjusza Smotryckiego (do Adama Chreptowicza)." *Nasza Przeszłość* 102:427–48.

Kojalovič, M. 1861. *Litovskaja cerkovnaja unija*. Vol. 2. St. Petersburg.

Kortycki, Wojciech. 1634. *Widok potyczki wygraney, zawodu dopędzonego, wiary dotrzymaney, od przewielebnego w Chrystusie Jego Mości Oyca Meletiusa Smotryskiego, Archiepiskopa Hierapolitańskiego, Arhimandryty Dermańskiego, na jegoż pogrzebie*. Vilnius.

Kosov, Sylvestr. 1635. *Paterikon, abo żywoty śś. Ojców Pieczerskich*. Kyiv.

Krajcar, J. 1964. "The Ruthenian Patriarchate. Some Remarks on the Project for Its Establishment in the 17th Century." *Orientalia Christiana Periodica* 30:65–84.

Krevza, Lev. 1617. *Obrona jedności cerkiewnej, abo dowody którymi się pokazuje, iż grecka cerkiew z łacińską ma być zjednoczona*. Vilnius.

Kromer, Marcin. 1558. *De origine et rebus gestis Polonorum libri XXX.* Basel.

———. 1568. *Polonia, sive de origine et rebus gestis Polonorum libri XXX.* Basel.

———. 1611. *O sprawach, dziejach i wszytkich inszych potocznościach koronnych polskich, ksiąg XXX.* Trans. Marcin Błazowski z Błazowa. Cracow.

Kryp'jakevyč, Ivan. 1913. "Kozaččyna v polityčnyx kombinacijax 1620–1630 rr." *Zapysky Naukovoho tovarystva imeny Ševčenka* 117/118:65–114.

Kutrzeba, Stanisław, and Władysław Semkowicz, eds. 1932. *Akta unji Polski z Litwą, 1385–1791.* Cracow.

Leunclavius, Joannes. 1596. *Juris Graeco-Romani tam canonici quam civilis tomi duo.* Frankfurt.

Lipiński, Wacław, ed. 1912. *Z dziejów Ukrainy, Księga pamiątkowa ku czci Włodzimierza Antonowicza, Paulina Święcickiego i Tadeusza Rylskiego.* Kyiv.

Lipsius, Justus. 1589. *Politicorum, sive civilis doctrinae libri sex.* Louvain.

———. 1610. *Politicorum, sive civilis doctrinae libri sex.* Antwerp.

List do zakonników monastera cerkwie ś. Ducha Wileńskiego, na ich przedmowę, w Werificatiey iakoby niewinności ich powtóre wydaney położoną, odpisany. 1621. Reprint: *AJuZR* 1:8:732–61. [I cite from the reprint.]

Litwin, Henryk. 1987. "Catholicization Among the Ruthenian Nobility and Assimilation Processes in the Ukraine During the Years 1569–1648." *Acta Poloniae historica* 55:57–83.

Malcolm, Noel. 1984. *De Dominis (1560–1624): Venetian, Anglican, Ecumenist and Relapsed Heretic.* London.

Maslov, S. 1908. "Kazan'e M. Smotrickogo na čestnyj pogreb o. Leontija Karpoviča." *Čtenija v Istoričeskom obščestve Nestora-letopisca* 20 (3), pts. 2–3:101–55.

Miechowita, Maciej. 1521. *Chronica Polonorum.* Cracow.

Moroxovs'kyj, Illja [Morochowski, Heliasz]. 1612. *ΠΑΡΗΓΟΡΙΑ Albo Utulenie uszczypliwego Lamentu mniemaney Cerkwie Świę wschodniey zmyślonego Theophila Orthologa.* Vilnius.

Mužylovs'kyj, Andrij [Mużyłowski, Andrzej]. 1629. *Antidotum, Przezacnemu narodowi ruskiemu. Albo Warunek przeciw Apologiey jadem napełnionej, którą wydał Melety Smotrzyski niesłusznie Cerkiew ruską prawosławną w niej pomawiając haeresią i Schismą dla niektórych scribentów, w porywczą przygotowany i podany.* Vilnius.

Myc'ko, I. Z. 1990. *Ostroz'ka slov'jano-hreko-latyns'ka akademija (1576–1636)*. Kyiv.

Mycyk, Jurij A. 1993. "Iz lystuvannja ukrajins'kyx pys'mennykiv-polemistiv 1621–1624 rokiv." *Zapysky Naukovoho tovarystva imeny Ševčenka* 225:310–47.

———. 1997. "Z novyx dokumentiv do istoriji mižkonfesijnyx vidnosyn v Ukrajini XVII–XVIII st." In *Dnipropetrovs'kyj istoryko-arxeohrafičnyj zbirnyk*, no. 1, *Na pošanu profesora Mykoly Pavlovyča Koval's'koho*, pp. 134–45. Dnipropetrovs'k.

Nimčuk, V. V., ed. 1979. *Hramatyka M. Smotryc'koho*. Kyiv.

Orzechowski, Stanisław. 1548. *Diatriba Stanislai Orichovii Ruteni contra calumniam, Ad Andream Miekicium Tribunum, ac Equitem Rutenum*. Cracow.

Otwinowska, Barbara. 1974. *Język—Naród—Kultura. Antecedencje i motywy renesansowej myśli o języku*. Studia staropolskie 44. Wrocław.

Papée, F. 1927. *Acta Alexandri regis*. Cracow.

Plokhy, Serhii. 2001. *The Cossacks and Religion in Early Modern Ukraine*. Oxford.

Podskalsky, Gerhard. 1982. *Christentum und theologische literatur in der Kiever Rus' (988–1237)*. Munich.

———. 1988. *Griechische Theologie in der Zeit der Türkenherrschaft (1453–1821). Die Orthodoxie im Spannungsfeld der nachreformatorischen Konfessionen des Westens*. Munich.

Potij, Ipatij (?). 1595. *Unija albo vyklad prednejšix artikulov ku zodnočeniju Hrekov z kostelem rimskim naležaščix*. Vilnius.

——— (?). 1603. *Rozmova berestjanina s bratčikom*. Vilnius.

———. 1605 (?). *O przywilejach nadanych od najaśniejszych królów polskich i przedniejszych niektórych dowodach, które świętą unią wielce zalecają i potwierdzają*. Vilnius (?).

——— (?). 1607. *Zmartwychwstały Nalewajko*. Vilnius (?).

———. 1608. *Harmonia abo konkordancja cerkwi ś., orientalnej z kościołem ś. rzymskim*. Vilnius.

Sakovyč, Kasijan. 1642. *ΕΠΑΝΟΡΘΩΣΙΣ abo Perspektiwa, y obiaśnienie Błędow, Herezyey, y Zabobonow, w Grekoruskiey Cerkwi Disunitskiey tak w Artykulach Wiary, iako w Administrowaniu Sakramentow, y w inszych Obrządkach y Ceremoniach znayduiących sie*. Cracow.

Šeptyc'kyj, A., ed. 1971. *Monumenta Ucrainae historica*. Vols. 9–10. Rome.

Skarga, Piotr. 1577. *O jedności Kościoła Bożego pod jednym Pasterzem i o greckim od tej jedności odstąpieniu.* Vilnius.

—————. 1610. *Na Treny i Lament Theophila Ortologa, Do Rusi greckiego nabożeństwa przestroga.* Cracow.

Smotryc´kyj, Meletij. 1610. *ΘΡΗΝΟΣ To iest Lament iedyney ś. Powszechney Apostolskiey Wschodniey Cerkwie.* Vilnius. [Facsimile edition: *HLEULT* 1:1–235.]

—————. 1616. *Jevanhelije učytel'noje.* Vievis. [Facsimile edition: *HLEULT* 2.]

—————. 1618–1619. *ΓΡΑΜΜΑΤΙΚΗ Slavenskię pravilnoje Syntahma.* Vievis. [Facsimile edition: Nimčuk 1979].

—————. 1620. *Kazan'e: Na čestnyj pohreb prečestnoho i prevelebnoho Muža Hospodyna i Otca: Hospodyna Otca Leontię Karpovyča.* Vilnius. [Reprint: Maslov 1908.]

—————. 1621a. *Kazanie: Na znamienity Pogrzeb przezacnego y przewielebnego Męża, Pana y Oyca: Leontego Karpowicza.* Vilnius. [Facsimile edition: *HLEULT* 1:236–64.]

—————. 1621b. *Verificatia niewinności.* Vilnius. [Facsimile edition: *HLEULT* 1:313–98.]

—————. 1621c. *Obrona verificaciey.* Vilnius. [Facsimile edition: *HLEULT* 1:399–462.]

—————. 1622. *Elenchus pism uszczypliwych.* Vilnius. [Facsimile edition: *HLEULT* 1:463–513.]

—————. 1623. *Iustificacia niewinności.* Vilnius (?). [Reprint: *AJuZR* 1:7:511–32; I have cited and translated from the reprint, as the original was unavailable to me.]

—————. 1628a. *Apologia peregrinatiey do Kraiow Wschodnych.* Lviv. [Facsimile edition: *HLEULT* 1:514–625.]

—————. 1628b. *Protestatia przeciwo Soborowi w tym Roku 1628 we dnie August Miesiąca, w Kiiowie Monasteru Pieczerskim obchodzonemu, uczyniona przez ukrzywdzonego na nim.* Lviv. [Facsimile edition: *HLEULT* 1:627–42.]

—————. 1629a. *Paraenesis abo Napomnienie.* Cracow. [Facsimile edition: *HLEULT* 1:643–94.]

—————. 1629b. *Exęthesis abo Expostulatia.* Lviv. [Facsimile edition: *HLEULT* 1:695–805.]

Šmurlo, E. 1928. *Le Saint-Siège et l'Orient orthodoxe Russe 1609–1654.* Prague.

———. 1932. "Meletij Smotrickij v ego snošenijax s Rimom." In *Trudy V-go S˝ezda russkix akademičeskix organizacij za granicej v Sofii 14–21 sentjabrja 1930 goda.* Part 1, pp. 501–29. Sofia.

Sowita Wina. To iest Odpis na script, Maiestat Krola Iego Mości honor y reputatią Ludzi Zacnych Duchownych y Świeckich obrażaiący, nazwany, Verificatia Niewinności. 1621. [Reprint: *AJuZR* 1:7:443–510.]

Stryjkowski, Maciej. 1582. *Która przedtem nigdy światła nie widziała, Kronika polska, litewska, żmódzka i wszystkiej Rusi.* Königsberg.

———. 1846. *Kronika polska, litewska, żmódzka i wszystkiej Rusi.* 2 vols. Warsaw.

Studyns´kyj, Kyrylo. 1906. *Pam'jatky polemičnoho pys'menstva kincja XVI i poč. XVII v.* Vol. 1, *Pam'jatky ukrajins'ko-rus'koji movy i literatury.* Arxeohrafična komisija Naukovoho Tovarystva im. Ševčenka 5. Lviv.

———. 1925. "Ἀντιγραφή polemičnyj tvir Maksyma (Meletija) Smotryc´koho z 1608 r." *Zapysky Naukovoho tovarystva imeny Ševčenka* 141–43:1–40.

Suarez, Francisco. 1859. *Opera omnia.* Vol. 14. Paris.

Suša, Jakiv [Susza, Jakub]. 1666. *Saulus et Paulus Ruthenae unionis sanguine B. Josaphat transformatus. Sive Meletius Smotriscius archiepiscopus polocensis.* Rome.

Symanowicz, Tymoteusz. 1621. *Proba Verificatiey Omylnej. Y Dowod swowoleństwa małosłychanego Czerńcow, y Iednomyślnych Bratctwa Wileńskiego, Chrześciańskiem Katholickiem uważeniem.* Zamość.

Sysyn, Frank E. 1979–1980. "Adam Kysil and the Synods of 1629: An Attempt at Orthodox-Uniate Accommodation in the Reign of Sigismund III." *Harvard Ukrainian Studies* 3–4:826–45.

———. 1985. *Between Poland and the Ukraine: The Dilemma of Adam Kysil, 1600–1653.* Cambridge, Mass.

Tanczuk, D. 1949. "Quaestio patriarchatus Kioviensis tempore conaminum Unionis Ruthenorum (1582–1632)." *Analecta Ordinis Sancti Basilii Magni* 1 [7]:128–46.

Theiner, Augustin. 1863. *Vetera monumenta Poloniae et Lithuaniae gentiumque finitimarum historiam illustrantia maximam partem nondum edita ex tabulariis vaticanis deprompta collecta ac serie chronologica disposita.* Vol. 3, *A Sixto Pp. V. usque ad Innocentium Pp. XII. 1585–1696.* Rome.

Thomas Aquinas, St. 1897. *Opera omnia.* Vol. 9, *Secunda secundae Summae Theologiae, A questione LVII ad questionem CXXII.* Rome.

Thomson, Francis. 1998. "Meletij Smotrickij i unija s Rimom: religioznaja dilemma v Rutenii XVII veka." *400 let Brestskoj cerkovnoj unii 1596–1996, kritičeskaja pereocenka: Sbornik materialov meždunarodnogo simpoziuma, Nejmegen, Gollandija,* pp. 177–217. [Moscow.]

Velykyj, Athanasius, ed. 1953. *Documenta Pontificum Romanorum historiam Ucrainae illustrantia (1075–1953).* Vol. 1, *1075–1700.* Analecta Ordinis Sancti Basilii Magni, Series II, Sectio III, Documenta Romana Ecclesiae Catholicae in Terris Ucrainae et Bielarusjae. Rome.

————, ed. 1956. *Epistolae Josephi Velamin Rutskyj Metropolitae Kioviensis Catholici (1613–1637).* Analecta Ordinis Sancti Basilii Magni, Series II, Section III, Documenta Romana Ecclesiae Catholicae in Terris Ucrainae et Bielarusjae. Rome.

————, ed. 1960. *Litterae nuntiorum apostolicorum historiam Ucrainae illustrantes (1550–1850).* Vol. 4, *1621–1628.* Analecta Ordinis Sancti Basilii Magni, Series II, Section III, Documenta Romana Ecclesiae Catholicae in Terris Ucrainae et Bielarusjae. Rome.

————, ed. 1972. *Litterae episcoporum historiam Ucrainae illustrantes (1600–1900).* Vol. 1, *1600–1640.* Analecta Ordinis Sancti Basilii Magni, Series II, Sectio III, Documenta Romana Ecclesiae Catholicae in Terris Ucrainae et Bielarusjae. Rome.

Vladimirskij-Budanov, M. F. 1907. "Cerkovnye imuščestva v Jugo-Zapadnoj Rossii XVI veka." *AJuZR* 8:4:3–224.

Wilkowski, Kasper, trans. 1625. *Desiderosus abo ścieżka do miłości Bożej i do doskonałości żywota chrześcijańskiego.* Cracow.

Wolff, Józef. 1885. *Senatorowie i dygnitarze Wielkiego Księstwa Litewskiego, 1386–1795.* Cracow.

Zapasko, Jakym, and Jaroslav Isajevyč. 1981. *Pamjatky knyžkovoho mystectva. Kataloh starodrukiv, vydanyx na Ukrajini. Knyha perša (1574–1700).* Kyiv.

Zbiór dawnych dyplomatów i aktów miast: Wilna, Kowna, Trok, prawosławnych monasterów, cerkwi i w różnych sprawach. 1843. Vilnius.

Žukovič, P. N. 1911. "L'vovskij sobor 1629 goda v svjazi s političeskimi obstajateľstvami vremeni." *Xrestianskoe čtenija* 235 (pt. 2):661–84.

Index of Biblical References

Book	Chapter	Page	Book	Chapter	Page
Gen.	1:22	5		32	618
	1:28	5			
	2:4–5	690	Lev.	18:7	45
	2:7	446		19:11	188
	3	227		19:13	114, 127
	4	613, 701		19:16	114, 207
	4:15	718		24:5–9	152
	5:3	47		24:19–22	116
	8:17	5			
	9:1, 7	5	Num.	11:5	27
	9:22–3	425, 427		16:31–3	17
	18:1	6		16:32–3	63
	18:1–15	105		22:21–33	304
	19:24	63		22:28–30	673
	21	105			
	24:2	454	Dt.	2:30	231
	25–7	701		11:26–8	497
	27:1–29	152		11:28	497
	32	312		13:2	497
	37	702		13:6	497
	41:40–5	310		13:13	497
				19:16–21	116
Ex.	4:25	227		22:1	39
	7:11	544		23:10	485
	10	213		24:8	485
	12:5–6	522		27:19	168
	12:8	523		27:26	523
	12:15	425		28:64	497
	12:18–19	522		29:4	392, 428
	13:6	425		32:35	214, 319
	14	231		32:41	214
	14:8	231, 497		32:43	214
	21:15	537		32:44–52	385
	21:24	116			
	22:1	485	1 Sam.	16:7	409, 577, 625
	23:1	188		21:6	152

Book	Chapter	Page	Book	Chapter	Page
2 Sam.	11	491		31:17	418
	12:6	485		31:18	459, 714
	12:13	353		31:19	11
	15–17	584		32:9	304
	17:1–23	207		33:13	628
				37:1	213
1 Kg.	3:26	207, 747		37:6	17
	18:20–40	648		37:15	17
	19:16	206		38:11	23
	22	478		43:1	144
	22:11	467		44:21	334
				45:11	23
2 Kg.	11:18	27		45:13	9
				51:5	47
2 Ch.	18	478		53:1	751
	18:10	467		54:13–15	584
	18:23	467		63:11	195
				64	144
Neh.	2–6	118		64:3	17, 50, 52
	9:11	231		69:11	24
				70:1–2	52
Esther	7:9–10	207		72:1–2	145
				74:13	231
Job	10:9	56		79:1	459
	13:4	188		82:5	718
				84:1–2	389
Ps.	5:5–6	17, 188		84:10	6
	6:10	195		89:32–3	53
	7:9	334, 625, 675, 752		99:6	430
				102:3–5	24
	7:14–16	18		103:4–5	327
	7:15–16	168		103:16	716
	7:16	584, 721		106:17	17
	9:17	418		109:28	721
	10:7	17		110:4	422
	10:7–8	144		112:6	106
	11:7	17		115:17	418
	14:1	25		119:137	238
	17:3	577		120:4	17
	19:14	524		128:5	196
	26:2	157, 334, 577, 625, 675, 752		133:1	371
				135:6	106
	28:4	227		137:1	55

Book	Chapter	Page	Book	Chapter	Page
Ps. (cont'd.)	139:22	227		30:17	212
	140:2–3	145			
	140:3	17, 25, 50	Eccl.	4	125, 126
	149:1	195		10:8	630
				12:7	446
Prov.	1:28	50			
	2:13	718	S. of S.	1:3	23
	3:13–14	46		1:5	9
	3:13–15	55		2:2	23
	3:34	717		4:7	396, 718, 721
	4:7	56		4:15	23
	6:12–14	290		6:4	23
	6:15	291		6:10	525
	9:4–6	47		7	23
	9:7	51			
	9:9	662	Is.	5:2	58
	10:1	25		5:20	293, 425, 576,
	10:13	607			623
	10:23	607		6:1	7
	11:14	485		6:9–10	36, 695
	11:22	697		6:10	26, 392, 428
	14:33	607		8:14	373, 630
	15:14	607		11:6	121
	16:22	607		19:14	694
	16:23	524		28:19	208, 694
	17:15	168		29:13	398
	17:24	607		32:3	392, 428
	18:23	283		33:15	428
	19:25	607		40:12–13	105
	19:29	717		46:10	287
	20:12	392		56:10–11	24
	22:22	127		59:9	718
	24	336		60:16	159
	24:6	485		64:4	416
	25:21	90		64:8	56
	26:4	696		65:25	121
	26:5	696		66:16	254
	26:5–6	300			
	26:27	630	Jer.	2:21	58
	26:28	213		5:21	26, 37, 392,
	27:2	287			428, 695
	28:10	630		7:9	26
	29:19	53		7:27	50

Book	Chapter	Page	Book	Chapter	Page
Jer. (cont'd.)	9:1	10		3:10	201
	9:8	17		3:12	199
	9:14	26		3:15	199
	11:20	334, 577, 625, 675, 752		3:22	201
				3:24	201
	14:7	25		3:25–6	201
	17–18	29		3:32	201
	17:10	334		3:44	201
	18:6	56		3:46	199
	19:4	497		3:46–7	201
	20:12	334, 625, 675, 752		3:52	201
				3:53	201
	22:3	114, 168		3:56	201
	23:1–2	39		3:57	202
	23:1–4	24		3:58	202
	31:15	55		3:59	202
	33:8	25		3:60	202
	48:10	553		3:61	202
				3:63–4	202
Lam.	1:2	23, 199		5:2	200
	1:3	199		5:4	200
	1:4	199			
	1:6	199	Ez.	3:18	35, 271, 484, 554, 576
	1:8	22			
	1:9	199		3:20	35, 271, 484, 554, 576
	1:12	199			
	1:14	22, 199		4	118
	1:17	23, 199		12:2	392, 428, 695
	1:18	200		18:7	127
	1:18–19	24		33:6	35, 271, 484, 554, 576
	1:20	24, 199			
	1:21	23, 199		33:7–8	40
	1:22	199		33:8	35, 271, 484, 554, 576
	2:1	199			
	2:3–4	199		34	756
	2:11	24		34:1–10	24, 45
	2:15	199		34:2–3	40
	2:16	24, 199		34:5	39
	2:16–17	200		34:5–6	40
	2:18	23, 200		34:10	35, 271, 484, 554, 576
	2:19	200			
	2:20	200		34:23	307
	3:5	200		37:24	307

Book	Chapter	Page	Book	Chapter	Page
Hos.	4:14	24		42–60	18
	6:6	354			
	14:2	432	Tob.	4:7	116
				4:15	226
Joel	2:28–9	504, 507			
			Wis.	1:6	717
Mic.	6:12	212		1:11	456
				9:13	105, 106
Zech.	2:8	214, 554		9:13–17	287
	7:10	127		9:17	105
	8:16–17	207			
	12:1	446	Mt.	2:20	759
				3:8	33, 61, 234
Mal.	2:6–7	431		3:10	33
				3:12	33, 408, 440, 720
1 Esdr.	4:47–61	118		4:19	720
				5:11	xxvii, 16
2 Esdr.	2:3	55		5:11–12	21
	5:23–7	52		5:13	39, 441
	8:21–3	51		5:13–14	34
				5:13–16	58
1 Macc.	2:24	748		5:16	25
				5:17	523
Sir.	2:7–17	56		5:19	523
	2:17	56		5:23–4	117
	3:9	55		5:38	116
	4:25	737		5:38–48	117
	4:30	737		6:24	27
	5:3–7	51		6:30	719
	6:36	385		7:1–5	116
	19:4	459		7:2	227, 291, 513, 737
	22:15	46			
	22:19	46, 286		7:3–5	297
	23:18–19	34		7:6	654
	27:11	213		7:7	390
	27:13	213		7:7–8	499
	27:14	213		7:9–10	470
	27:23	213		7:13	10
	34:8	737		7:13–14	53
	51:6	127, 142, 212, 336		7:15	13
				7:16–20	32
				7:17, 18	90
Sus.	1:45–64	725		7:24–7	4

Book	Chapter	Page	Book	Chapter	Page
Mt. (cont'd.)	7:25	81		17:20	719
	7:26–7	5		18:4	720
	7:27	81		18:7	425, 614, 693
	8:12	50		18:17	399, 747
	8:26	719		18:18	34, 38, 677
	8:29	420		18:20	499
	8:31	421		18:21–2	751
	9:13	354		18:33–4	34
	9:37	759		20:1–16	13, 46, 479
	10:14	66, 663		21:40–1	44
	10:15	40, 397, 752		21:41	32, 51
	10:16	469		21:33	58
	11:15	695		21:44	393, 426, 704
	11:19	486		22:12	lxiii, 723
	11:24	397		22:13	44, 50
	11:28–30	26		22:16	59
	11:30	157, 165, 286		22:21	35
	12:4	152		23:2	39
	12:7	354		23:4	38
	12:25	279, 383, 440, 476, 499, 618		23:5	39
				23:13	39
	12:32	631		23:16	42
	12:33	90		23:24	39, 42, 630
	12:36	188		23:33	26
	13:9	695		24:2	193
	13:13	63		24:10–13	13
	13:13–15	392		24:11	6
	13:14–15	695		24:12	6
	13:15	428		24:14	658
	13:24–40	28		24:16	14
	13:25	440		24:24	7
	13:25–30	460, 598		25:14–30	59
	13:25–40	709, 720		25:18	58
	13:40	440		25:26–30	39, 41, 379
	14:31	719		25:30	50
	15:14	39, 42, 428, 630		25:32–3	720, 726
	16:8	719		26:3–4	206
	16:18	11, 52, 310, 433, 477, 501, 526, 536, 560, 562, 680		26:24	409
				26:26–7	77
				26:26–8	30
				26:75	573
	16:19	34, 38, 78, 677		28:20	477
	16:26	12, 386			

Book	Chapter	Page	Book	Chapter	Page
Mk.	1:17	720		8:31	421
	2:26	152		9	445
	3:24–5	440, 618		9:5	66
	3:25	476, 499		9:25	386
	4:12	63		10:2	759
	4:23	695		10:30–7	90, 583, 661
	4:24	227, 513, 737		10:34	27
	5:8	421		11:9–10	499
	5:10	421		11:17	476, 499, 618
	6:11	66, 663, 752		11:52	495
	8:18	392, 428, 695		12:28	719
	8:35	387		12:32	558
	8:36	386		12:42–8	445
	9:50	441		12:47	40, 755
	10:14	720		13:6–9	513
	12:1	58		14:15	391
	12:9	51		14:18–20	391
	12:14	59		14:23	lxv, 391, 563,
	13:2	193			660, 661, 681,
	14:11	206			754, 755
	14:22	539		14:34	441
	14:22–4	77		15:7	53, 689
	14:24	539		15:8–9	390
	14:58	11, 17, 414		15:18–19	353
				16:13	27
Lk.	1:24–5	105		16:22–3	419
	1:58	106		16:23	417
	1:78	748		16:25	419
	3:2	7		18:8	658
	3:8	688		18:16	720
	3:14	127		19:12–27	41, 59
	3:17	408, 440, 720		19:40	167, 397, 425,
	4:23	57			482
	6:4	152		19:44	193
	6:31	116, 226		20:9	58
	6:38	227, 513, 737		20:16	51
	6:39	39, 630		20:18	426, 704
	6:43–4	90		20:25	348
	6:43–5	32		22:2	206
	6:48–9	4		22:19	535
	7:34	486		22:19–20	77
	8:10	63		22:32	560
	8:29	421		23:2	17

Book	Chapter	Page	Book	Chapter	Page
Lk. (cont'd.)	23:18	620		15:20	206
	23:43	409, 414		15:26	299, 455
	24:30	425, 518		16:23	390
	24:35	425, 519		17:11	371, 388, 391
				17:12	205, 254, 320,
Jn.	3:5	5, 48, 154, 225,			617, 699, 755
		583, 650		17:21	388, 391, 545
	3:29	105		17:22	586
	5:19	452		18:24	7
	6:51	536, 644		20:21	431, 436
	6:52	643		20:22	506
	6:53	537, 538		20:23	436
	6:53–4	536		21:15	526
	6:53–8	29		21:15–17	432, 435, 436
	6:54–5	537		21:16	434, 436, 680
	6:56	536		21:17	403, 478, 526,
	6:57	644			527
	6:57–8	537			
	7:24	513	Acts	1:1	28
	8:12	718		1:5	154
	8:33–44	621		1:24	409
	8:36	333		2:17–18	504
	8:44	16, 20, 44, 63,		4	311
		125, 144, 399,		4:12	661
		420, 426, 464,		5:39	655
		562, 638, 699,		6:2–3	42
		709, 715, 733		7:48	414
	8:48	17, 206, 486		7:59	415
	9:39–41	673		8:18–20	296
	10:2–3	209		8:18–24	43
	10:12	58		9:5	392, 466
	10:12–13	56, 396,		11:16	154
		427, 484, 707		17:24	414
	10:14	307		20:28	34, 159
	10:16	307, 647		20:28–35	431
	10:30	514		26:14	392, 466
	12:35	718		28:26	63
	14:3	416		28:27	392
	15:1	5, 90, 721			
	15:4	27	Rom.	1:8	559
	15:5	721		3:8	188, 276, 426
	15:13	752		6:3–6	49
	15:15	206		6:9	644

Book	Chapter	Page	Book	Chapter	Page
Rom.	6:12–13	49		11:24–5	30, 77
(cont'd.)	6:13	333		11:25	536
	6:14	48		11:27	537
	6:22	333		11:28–9	538
	8:18	81		12:12–27	223
	8:31	193		12:21	526
	8:38–9	27		13:2	406
	9:32–3	373		13:3	546
	9:33	581		13:5–7	200
	10:9	524		13:12	411
	10:9–10	390		13:13	9, 394
	10:10	81, 615		14:19	xxxi, 92
	11:2–3	206		15:9	224
	11:8	392, 428		15:22	48
	11:33	105, 346		15:44	416
	11:33–4	287			
	11:33–5	106	2 Cor.	1:12	203
	12:4–6	223		5:1	414
	12:19	214		5:1–4	11
	13:1–4	328		5:6–8	414
	13:3–4	35		3:13–18	25, 26
	13:4	343		3:17	333
	13:7	348		6:14	623
	13:7–8	35		6:14–15	144
	14:4	573		6:15	408, 455, 470
				11:13–15	698
1 Cor.	1:10	224		11:14–15	399, 699
	1:20	46		11:20	323
	2:9	416		11:26	22, 664
	2:16	105		12:9	365
	3:11	5		13:1	443
	3:12	89			
	4:15	106	Gal.	1:13–14	479
	5:6–8	521		2:16	507
	5:12	736		2:19	332
	7	334		3:1	406
	7:21	333		3:3	406
	7:22	333		3:10	523
	9	127		4:2	26
	9:13–18	296		5:24	191
	9:15	203, 331		5:24–5	49
	10:13	645		6:2	194
	11:24	535		6:14	191

Book	Chapter	Page	Book	Chapter	Page
Eph.	1:18	56		2:4	663, 756
	2:1–6	48		3:2	394
	2:20	5		3:2–4	34
	4:2–3	223		3:2–10	43
	4:4	546		4:1–2	445
	4:17–24	48		5:8	759
	4:25	207		5:19	430
	5:8	718		5:22	43
	5:9–11	49		6:8	285
	5:23–7	24			
	5:25–7	48, 396	2 Tim.	2:5	621
	5:27	23, 718		2:9	257, 682
	6:9	34		2:14–15	293
	6:17	29		2:23	293
				3:7	699
Phil.	1:21–2	415		3:8	544, 559
	1:22–6	415		3:16	27
	1:23	415		4:2	34, 382, 755
				4:3–4	41
Col.	1:11	223		4:7–8	468
	1:18	528			
	3:3–4	81	Tit.	1:5	430
	3:4	416		1:5–9	43
	3:11	27		1:10	30
	3:12	748		3:10	399
	4:1	34			
			Heb.	4:12	380, 545, 559
1 Th.	1:3	223, 394		6:4–6	400
	5:3	558		9:11	414
	5:5	559		9:24	414
	5:8	394		10:26–7	50
	5:13	35		10:26–31	398
	5:14	34		10:31	17, 32
	5:21	406		11:6	394
	5:22	188		11:13	417
				11:39–40	416
2 Th.	2:3	617, 699		12:9	446
	2:3–4	29		13:17	35
	2:10	6, 13, 746			
	2:10–11	427	Jas.	1:8	391
				1:12	5, 6, 33
1 Tim.	1	42		1:17	88, 107, 646
	2:1–2	xx, 18		2:10	397

Book	Chapter	Page	Book	Chapter	Page
Jas. (cont'd.)	2:12	333		3:16	645
	5:19–20	374			
	5:20	689	1 Jn.	1:9	49
				2:16	333
1 Pet.	2:8	428, 442, 581, 630		2:16–17	191
				3:19–21	347
	2:9	27, 61, 432		4:1	695
	2:12	25		4:3	539, 644
	2:14	334			
	2:15–16	334	Rev.	2:7	13
	2:15–22	35		2:10	5, 6, 13, 33
	2:17	195		2:23	334
	2:20	621		3:5	13
	2:25	159		3:20	390, 499
	3:9	33		6:9	414
	3:10	167		6:11	414
	5:1–4	34		7:9	415
	5:4	307		7:9–17	417
				7:14–15	415
2 Pet.	1:3	33		13:16	718
	2:1–3	611		13:18	607
	2:9	18, 419		14:9	718
	2:13	720		17:5	646
	2:15	26		18:7	387
	3:9	479, 675, 676, 724		21:6	13

Index

Aaron (brother of Moses), 430, 431–2, 732

Abel (son of Adam and Eve), 409, 416, 453, 701, 732

Abiram (a son of Eliab, a Reubenite, who conspired with his brother Dathan against Moses and Aaron in the wilderness and perished), 17

Abraham (progenitor of the Hebrews, Old Testament patriarch), 86, 105, 416, 418–19, 621, 732

Adam (first man of the Old Testament), 453

Aetherianus, Hugo [Eteriano, Hugo] (d. 1182; Tuscan lay theologian and author, employed at the court of Constantinople under Emperor Manuel I Comnenus), 509

Agatho (d. 681; pope), 439, 560

Ahithophel (privy counselor to David who joined Absalom and then hanged himself), 207, 584

Aleksander Jagiellończyk (d. 1506; grand duke of Lithuania, king of Poland), 730n106

Aleksij (d. 1378; metropolitan of Kyiv residing in Moscow), 650

Alexander I (d. ca. 115; pope), 519

Alexandria, see of, 311

Alexis, Saint (d. 417 according to legend), lxv, 475

Algirdas [Olgierd] (d. 1377; grand duke of Lithuania), 259–60

Ambrose (d. 397; bishop of Milan), 28, 263, 404, 433
  Commentaries on the First Epistle to the Thessalonicans, 413

Ammon, Saint (d. ca. 350; Egyptian hermit), 413, 444

Anabaptists, xxiv, 28, 68, 205n178, 303, 472, 558, 698

Anastasius [Flavius Anastasius I] (d. 518; emperor of Byzantium), 532

Anastasius of Sinai, Saint (d. after 700; theologian and abbot of the monastery of St. Catherine on Mount Sinai), 475n308, 516, 521

Andrew (d. 740; archbishop of Gortyna in Crete, poet and ecclesiastical orator), 417

Andrij (monk, brother of Jov Borec'kyj), 582

Andronicus II Palaeologus (d. 1332; emperor of Byzantium), 508

Anicetus (d. ca. 168; pope), 555

Annas (fl. ca. 7–15; Jewish high priest), 7, 191

Anthimus II (fl. 1623; metropolitan of Adrianople, patriarch of Constantinople), 637n66

Anthony, Saint (d. 356; hermit), 444

Antidote for the Most Noble Ruthenian Nation . . . , lxii–lxiv, 687, 690–1, 694–7
  Smotryc'kyj's response to, 698–709, 717–22, 725, 727–44

Antigraphē, xix, 205, 441, 467, 519, 680, 694, 704, 732

Antioch, see of, 311

Apolleia. See Destruction of the Book "Apology"

Apollinarian heresy, 378, 489, 519, 543, 585, 595, 638, 640–1, 738

Aquinas, Thomas, Saint (d. 1274; theologian and philosopher, doctor of the Church), 188n105, 360

Arian heresy, xxiv, 20, 28, 407, 423, 472, 478, 666, 698, 745

Arius (d. ca. 336; heresiarch), 7, 28, 68,
    312, 401, 430, 691, 698, 728, 738
Armenia, 632
Arsenius (clerk of St. Athanasius), 20
Arsenius (exarch to Rus' from Patriarch
    Timothy II of Constantinople in 1620,
    archimandrite of the Great Church in
    Constantinople), 130
Athanasius, Saint (d. 373; archbishop
    of Alexandria, theologian and
    philosopher), 7, 20–1, 28, 311, 424,
    436, 453–4, 506, 532, 555, 561, 630
    Defense before Emperor Constantinus,
        125
    Epistles to Serapion, 451, 454
    Four Discourses against the Arians, 506
    Life of Saint Anthony, 413, 444
    Questions to Antioch, 444
Athos, Mount, 365, 459
Augustine, Saint (d. 430; bishop of
    Hippo Regius, a doctor of the
    Church), xxviii, 10, 28, 72, 75, 309,
    404, 413, 433, 643
    *Contra Faustum Manichaeum [Against
        Faustus Manichaeus]*, 606
    *Contra Maximinum [Against the
        Heretic Maximus]*, 506
    *De anima et ejus origine [On the Soul
        and Its Origin]*, 409, 447
    De baptismo [On Baptism], 546
    De civitate Dei [City of God], 666n
    De trinitate [On the Trinity], 424, 506,
        511, 528, 639
    Epistle 93, 662
    Epistle 147, 748
autocephalous churches, 278, 633–7
    Cypriot, 634
    Georgian, 634
    Illyrian, 634
    Russian, 633–4, 681
    Serbian, 634
Aventinus. *See* Thurmair, Johannes
Azarij/Azarius. *See* Kopystens'kyj,
    Zaxarija

Balaam (Midianite prophet), 26, 304
Balaban, Hedeon (d. 1607; Orthodox
    bishop of Lviv), xxxiv, 232
Balsamon, Theodore (d. after 1195;
    Byzantine canonist), 256, 305,
    407n79, 549n483, 550n487, 634n62
Bandini, Ottavio (d. 1629; archbishop
    of Fermo, cardinal, deacon of the
    College of Cardinals of the Roman
    Catholic Church), liv. *See also*
    Smotryc'kyj, Meletij, letter to Bandini
baptism, 266
Baradeus, Jacob (d. 578; bishop of
    Edessa, defender of Monophysitism),
    478
Baranowicz, Wasyly (fl. 1621, imprisoned
    Orthodox citizen of Vilnius), 191n113
Baronius, Cesare (d. 1607; cardinal,
    librarian of the Vatican, ecclesiastical
    historian)
    Annales ecclesiastici, 209n187,
        264nn50–1, 294n33, 315n84, 319n93
Basil the Great (d. 379; bishop of
    Caesarea, Cappadocian Father), xl,
    28, 71, 72, 77, 413, 469, 549, 550,
    561
    Against Eunomius, 448, 452–4
    *Homily against Sabellians, Arius, and
        Anomeoans*, 473, 639
    Letter 52, 449, 452
    Letter 63, 126
    Letter 80, 7
    Sermon 19 on the Holy Forty Martyrs,
        412–13
Bede, the Venerable (d. 735; biblical
    scholar), 309
Belial, 408, 455, 470
Benedict (fl. 1625; hieromonk of the
    Great Church in Constantinople),
    426n156, 494
Berdyczów (town), 290
Bernardine church in Vilnius, 302
Bernard, Saint (d. 1153; abbot of
    Clairvaux), 74, 320n98, 732n112

Bessarion, John (d. 1472; archbishop of Nicaea, cardinal, Greek scholar and statesman), 463, 509

Besseus, Petrus [Pierre de Besse] (d. 1639; French postillographer, court preacher to Louis XIII, author of *Conciones, siue Conceptus theologici ac praedicabiles* [Cologne, 1613]), 706–7

Beza, Theodore (d. 1605; Calvinist theologian), xxvii

Bielica (town), 290

Bielski, Marcin (d. 1575; Polish poet, translator, chronicler, Catholic with Protestant sympathies), 246

Blastares, Matthew (d. after 1346; monk of Thessalonica, canonist and theologian), 550n485

Błażewski, Marcin (d. ca. 1628; Polish poet and translator), 345n

Blemmydes [Blemmida], Nicephorus (d. 1269; Byzantine teacher and writer in the empire of Nicaea), 509

Bobryc'kyj [Bobrykovyč], Josyf (d. 1635; Smotryc'kyj's deputy, later successor as archimandrite of the Orthodox Holy Spirit monastery in Vilnius, bishop of Mscislaŭ from 1633), lx, 591, 607

Bogomil, Basil (fl. 10th c.; priest and presumed heresiarch), 468

Bojarski, Lord, 362

Boleslav II the Pious (d. 999; duke of Bohemia, brother of Dubravka), 258

Bolesław IV the Curly (d. 1173; Piast prince of Mazovia), 245

Bolharynovyč, Josyf. *See* Josyf I Bolharynovyč

Bologudes [Bolosudes, Bulcsu] (fl. 950; Hungarian duke), 259

Borec'kyj, Jov (d. 1631; metropolitan of Kyiv and all Rus'), xxxiv, xxxv–xxxvi, xlix, lvii–lviii, lix, lxi, lxii, 104, 106n13, 127, 140, 143–4, 156, 208, 267, 269, 337–8, 348n34, 349,

Borec'kyj, Jov (*continued*) 359, 362–3, 493, 569n, 574–6, 580, 584–7, 591, 593, 612n10, 613n15, 702n37, 709, 725

Boris, Saint (d. 1015; son of Prince of Kyiv Volodimer I, martyred by elder half brother [or cousin] Svjatopolk), 419

Bořivoj I (d. 888/889; duke of Bohemia), 258

Boryskovyč, Isakij (d. 1633; bishop of Luc'k and Ostroh), lvii, 575, 591, 592

Borysowicz, Bogdan (fl. 1621; imprisoned Orthodox citizen of Vilnius), 191n113

Boskołoboski Monastery, 363

Braclav (town), 177n97, 337

Braslav (town), 337n

bread, leavened and unleavened, 222, 234, 266, 292, 402, 407, 424–5, 474–5, 489, 502, 518–23, 562, 641, 646–7, 651, 673, 714

Brest, 290. *See also* Council of Brest; Union of Brest

Brolnyc'kyj, Hedeon (d. 1618; archbishop of Polack), 270

Broniewski, Marcin (d. 1624; Polish political and religious activist, Protestant, possible author behind the pseudonym "Christopher Philalethes"), 372n3. *See also* Philalethes, Christopher

Budny, Szymon (d. 1593; Polish Antitrinitarian theologian, polemicist, and biblical translator), xxix, 366n17

Busko (town), 290

Bychow (town), 290

Cabasilas, Constantine (fl. ca. 1260; archbishop of Ohrid), 520

Caiaphas (Jewish high priest at Christ's trial), 7, 191

Cain (son of Adam and Eve), 409, 453, 703

Caleca [Calecas], Manuel (d. 1410 on Lesbos; Greek theologian, convert to Catholicism, translator of St. Thomas Aquinas, friend of Cynodius [Cydones]), 509

Callistus I (d. 1363; patriarch of Constantinople, to whom Orthodox Slavs ascribed authorship of a homiliary gospel translated into Slavonic and Ruthenian), xxviii, 85, 91, 94

calumny, 124–6, 144

Calvin, John, and Calvinism, xvii, xxiv, xxvii, xxix, 29n113, 302–3, 427, 464, 468, 472, 558, 596, 609, 619, 620–1, 667, 680, 689, 691, 698, 711, 719, 745

Camblak, Grigorij (d. 1419; metropolitan of Kyiv from a noble Bulgarian family of Byzantine origin, writer), 634, 649, 707, 729

Cantacuzeni (Greek merchant aristocractic family claiming origins from Byzantine emperor John VI Cantacuzenus [d. 1383]), 657

Carleton, Sir Dudley (d. 1632; viscount of Dorchester and English legate in Venice), xliv

Cassander, Georg (d. 1566; eirenic Catholic theologian)
Consultatio de Articulis Religionis . . . , 11

Cassiodorus, Flavius Magnus Aurelius (d. ca. 580; Roman author and monk), 288, 532

Cathedral Church of the Most Pure Virgin in Vilnius, 302, 724

Cedrenus, Georgius (fl. 12th c.; Byzantine historian), 468

Celestine I (d. 432; pope), 402, 407, 426, 439, 475n309, 555

Cerdo (fl. ca. 140; Syrian Gnostic who taught in Rome), 68

Cerinthus (fl. ca. 100; Gnostic heretic), 29, 68

Cerularius, Michael (d. 1058; patriarch of Constantinople), 510, 519–20, 533n†, 534, 557, 634

Chalcocondylas, Demetrius (d. 1511; teacher of Greek letters and philosophy in Italy, brother of Laonicus), 509

Chalcocondylas, Laonicus (d. ca. 1490; Byzantine historian, brother of Demetrius), 462, 508

Chalecki, Lord, 163

Chociejewicz, Jerzy (fl. 1621; Vilnius city councilor), 191–2

Chodkiewicz, Jan Karol (d. 1621; grand hetman of Lithuania, palatine of Vilnius), 218n202

Chomatenos, Demetrios (d. ca. 1236; archbishop of Ohrid), 520

Choniates, Nicetas (d. 1217; Byzantine statesman, historian, and theologian), 550n488
Thesaurus of the Orthodox Faith, 545n477

Chreptowicz [Xrebtovyč], Adam Iwanowicz Littawor (d. after 1627; chamberlain of Naŭharadok), xl, 1n92, 115

Chrysoloras, Manuel (d. 1415; Greek teacher in Renaissance Italy), 509

Chrysostom, John. *See* John Chrysostom, Saint

Church of St. Sophia in Kyiv, 650

Church of the Dormition of the Most Holy Virgin in Kyiv, 132

Chytraeus, David (d. 1600; Lutheran theologian, Church historian, educator, professor at Rostock), 61, 62n237

Cicero, Marcus Tullius (d. 43 BC; Roman statesman and orator), 289n18
De Divinatione [On Divination], 692n12
De Officiis [On Duties], 120
Tusculanae disputationes [Tusculan disputations], 753n7

Clement I, Saint, of Rome (fl. ca. 96; pope), 313n80

Clement VIII (d. 1605; pope), 653

Clement of Alexandria, Saint (d. ca. 215; head of the Catechetical School at Alexandria), 311

clergy
benefices of, 140, 145–51, 159–60, 180
consecration of, 154–5, 161
dignities of, 145–56, 401, 430, 679
presentation of, 148–9, 152–3, 159–60, 301, 344–7
twice- and thrice-married, 58, 79, 204

Clerk of Ostroh (pseudonym), xix, lxi, lxii, 205, 441–2, 456–60, 462–5, 467–70, 472, 479, 482, 543, 554–5, 592, 609–11, 618–19, 624–5, 629–31, 646, 680, 687, 690, 695, 705, 728–9, 736

Codinus, Georgius (d. after 1453; compiler of Greek history), 468

Codrus (fl. ca. 1068 BC; last of legendary kings of Athens), 86

College of St. Athanasius in Rome, 380n13

communion under two species, 76–7, 222, 266, 292, 475, 489, 502, 534–41, 550, 643–5, 647, 651, 673, 714

Comneni (dynasty of Byzantine emperors who ruled from 1057–1185), 657

compelle intrare, lxv, 391n35, 660–3, 681, 754–5

Congregation for the Propagation of the Faith [Congregatio de Propaganda fide], liv, lv–lvi, 664n105

Constans II (d. 668; emperor of Byzantium), 660

Constantine (fl. 1167–1177; metropolitan of Kyiv of Greek origin), 245

Constantine VII Porphyrogenitus (d. 959; emperor of Byzantium), 259

Constantine XI Palaeologus (d. 1453; emperor of Byzantium, brother of John VIII Palaeologus), 513

Constantine [Cyril], Saint (d. 869; apostle of the Slavs, brother of Methodius), xlviii, 258–9

Constantinople, l, 735
as new Rome, 297–9
see of, 311

constitution of 1607, xxxvii, xli, 131, 159, 176–9, 180, 189, 243–4, 248, 273, 289, 346n30

constitution of 1609, 179–81

constitution of 1618, 180

constitution of 1620, 131, 180–2, 346n30

Cosmas Melodus [of Jerusalem] (b. ca. 700; Greek liturgical hymnographer, adopted by the father of St. John of Damascus), 417

Cossacks, xlii, xlix, lix, lxvii, 16n43, 163, 284, 582, 584–5, 588

Council of Bari, 507

Council of Brest, 654. See also Union of Brest

Council of Kyiv (1628), liv, lvii, lviii–lix, lx–lxi, lxii, lxiv, 573–4, 579–80, 588, 591, 596, 611n9, 613–14, 617, 619, 626, 629, 631–2, 719–20, 753n8

Council of Lviv (1629), lxiv, 690–2, 701, 738, 747–8

Council of Sardica, 436

Councils, Ecumenical
Chalcedon (451; Fourth), 11–12, 146n45, 170, 256–7, 260, 297–8, 320n98, 373, 433–4, 437, 438n213, 439, 448, 512–13, 531–3
Constance (1414–1418; Sixteenth), 541
Constantinople I (381; Second), 169, 297, 439, 510–11, 634n62
Constantinople II (553; Fifth), 439
Constantinople III (680–681; Sixth), 298–9, 439, 474, 504, 550
Constantinople IV (869–870; Eighth), 304–7
Ephesus (431; Third), 146n46, 169–70, 407, 439, 511–12, 634n61
Florence (1438–1439; Seventeenth), lxiv, 221–2, 232, 234, 380, 456–64,

Councils, Ecumenical (*continued*)
  Florence (*continued*)
    474, 487, 507–10, 513, 541, 561–2,
    609, 624, 633n59, 638, 649, 650, 654,
    680, 695, 714, 726–37
  Lateran IV (1215; Twelfth), 507
  Lyons II (1274; Fourteenth), 507–8,
    561
  Nicaea I (325; First), 169, 299n43,
    314n81, 437n211, 439, 473, 520, 651
  Nicaea II (787; Seventh), 431,
    437n211, 439, 474, 504
  Trent (1545–1563; Nineteenth), 235,
    236, 562–3, 672
  Trullan (692; Quinisext, in
    Constantinople), 634n61
Counter-Reformation, xvii, xxiv, lxvii
Counter-Refutation [Antelenchus],
  xlviii–xlix, 695
Craterus (d. 321 BC; Macedonian
  general under Alexander the Great),
  330
Crusades, 364n14
Curopalates, Georgius Codinus. *See*
  Codinus, Georgius
Curtius, Quintus (fl. 1st or 2nd c.; Roman
  historical writer), 692n11
Cydones, Demetrius (d. ca. 1398 in
  Venetian Creta; Greek theologian,
  convert to Catholicism, translator
  of St. Thomas Aquinas, friend of
  Calecas), 509
Cynodius, Demetrius. *See* Cydones,
  Demetrius
Cyprian, Saint (d. 258; bishop of
  Carthage), 28
  Book on the Unity of the Church, 546,
    627, 747n132
  Letter to Antonianus, 529
Cyril (fl. 1626; patriarch of Antioch
  according to Smotryc'kyj), 547
Cyril Lukaris (d. 1638; patriarch
  of Alexandria, patriarch of
  Constaninople, author of a

Calvinizing confession of the
  Orthodox faith), xv, xviii, xxv–xxvi,
  l, li, liv–lv, 210, 295n35, 356, 387–8,
  426n155, 481, 495n360, 510, 513,
  547, 552–3, 637, 650, 654, 689–91,
  710–12, 715, 731, 735
  Catechesis Orthodoxae Fidei
    [Catechism of the Orthodox Faith],
    667
Cyril of Jerusalem, Saint (d. 386; bishop
  of Jerusalem), 555, 561
  Catechetical Lectures, 413, 540n
Cyril, Saint (d. 444; patriarch of
  Alexandria, theologian), 28, 170, 311,
  407, 503–4, 555, 561
  Commentary on the Prophet Joel,
    504n368
  Letter to the Monks of Egypt, 446
  On the Gospel of Saint John, 413, 506
  Thesaurus on the Holy and
    Consubstantial Trinity, 473n305

Dąbrowna (town), 290
Damascene, John. *See* John of Damascus
Damasus (d. 384; pope), 439
Daniel (fourth of the so-called greater
  prophets), 87, 207, 725
Dathan (son of Eliab, a Reubenite, who
  conspired with his brother Abiram
  against Moses and Aaron in the
  wilderness and perished), 17
David (Old Testament king and prophet),
  106, 152, 188, 207, 418, 430
Decius, Gaius Messius Quintus Trajanus
  (d. 251; Roman emperor), 86
De Dominis, Marcantonio (d. 1624;
  archbishop of Spalato, eirenicist and
  defender of national churches, convert
  to the Church of England, reconvert
  to Roman Catholicism), xliii–xliv,
  xlvii, xlix, lv, 226n213, 252n21
  De Republica Ecclesiastica, xliii, xlvii
Demetrius of Phalerum (d. ca. 280 BC;
  Athenian statesman and philosopher),
  273

Demetrius Palaeologus (d. 1470; emperor of Byzantium, despot of Morea, brother of John VIII Palaeologus), 508

Derman' Monastery, liv, lix

Destruction of the Book "Apology" [Apolleia Apolohii Knyżky], lix, lx–lxi, lxii, 611–13, 615n17, 617n21, 619

Diogenes Laertius (fl. ca. 250; Greek biographer), 194n121

Diogenes of Sinope (fl. ca. 4th c. BC; Cynic philosopher), 193–4, 330

Dionysius I (d. 1491; patriarch of Constantinople), 731, 735

Dionysius the Great (d. ca. 264; bishop of Alexandria), 404

Dioscorus (d. 454; patriarch of Alexandria, supporter of Monophysite monk Eutyches), 373, 436, 438, 478, 531, 678, 698, 728

Divočka, Onysyfor. *See* Onysyfor Divočka

Długosz, Jan (d. 1480; Polish historian), 246, 258

  Historia Polonica [History of Poland], 195n123

Dobrovský, Josef (d. 1829; Czech Jesuit and "father of Slavic philology"), xxxi

Drevyns′kyj, Lavrentij (d. 1640; Orthodox patron from the middling nobility), lx

Drucki-Sokoliński, Michał, Prince (d. 1621; palatine of Polack), 219n†, 271

Druhowina, Wasyly (fl. 1621; imprisoned Orthodox citizen of Vilnius), 191n113

Dubno Monastery, lvii

Dubovyč, Ivan (d. 1640; from the early 1620s, vicar general of the Vilnius Basilian [Uniate] monks; from 1633, Smotryc′kyj's successor as archimandrite of the Derman′ monastery), 359–60

Dubravka (d. 977; wife of Mieszko I, daughter of duke of Bohemia Boleslav I), 258–9

Dušan, Stefan (d. 1355; king of Serbia), 634n63

Easter service, 314–16, 651–2

Ebion (legendary founder of the Ebionite heresy, which flourished in the early centuries of the Christian era), 68

Elenchus. See Smotryc′kyj, Meletij, *Refutation of Acrimonious Writings*

Elijah (Old Testament prophet), 87, 206, 648

Elizabeth (mother of John the Baptist), 105, 446

Ephrem (fl. 1088–1097; metropolitan of Kyiv), 245, 649

Ephrem, Saint (d. 373; Syrian biblical exegete, ecclesiastical writer, and hymnographer), 413, 512

  Homily on the Transfiguration of the Lord, 434

Epiphanius of Constantia, Saint (d. 403; bishop of Constantia [Salamis]), 454, 506, 643

  Adversus Haereses [Against Heresies], 413

  Ancoratus [The Well-Anchored], 433, 448, 473n305, 507n378

Erasmus, Desiderius (d. 1536; Augustinian canon, scholar, editor of Church Fathers and biblical texts, Christian humanist)

  Adagia, 46n181, 120n10, 158n, 204n175, 270n71, 279n87, 289n16, 300n45, 302n48, 320n95, 402n56, 589n27, 589n29, 608n6, 675n119, 684n138, 755n11

Esau (eldest son of Isaac, twin brother of Jacob), 311, 701–3

Etna, Mount, 418–19

Eucharist. *See* communion

Eulogius I (d. 607; patriarch of Alexandria), 512

Eunomian heresy, 448, 505

Eunomius (d. ca. 394; Arian bishop of Cyzicus in Mysia), 401, 698, 738

Eutyches (d. 454; monk and archimandrite of a suburban Constantinopolitan monastery, heresiarch), 69, 312, 373, 401, 478, 678, 691, 698

Evagrius "Scholasticus" (d. after 594; Byzantine Church historian), 531–2

Examination of the "Defense" [Examen Obrony], xliv–xlviii, 300–23

Ezekiel (Old Testament prophet), 307, 310

Fabius (a general reference to Roman army leaders, perhaps to Fabius Maximus Quintus, either Rullus or "Cunctator," both of whom fl. in the 3rd c. BC), 86

Fabricius (Roman Catholic homileticist), 707

faith
  excesses and defects of, xliii, xlvii– xlviii, xlix, 252, 263, 308, 310, 311–12
  loss of, 445, 623

Felix of Africa, 436

Filaret. *See* Romanov, Fedor Nikityč

filioque, 30n120, 266, 305–6, 426, 472–3, 487–8, 502–15, 562, 622, 638, 647, 673, 680, 714, 730. *See also* Holy Spirit, nature of; Niceno-Constantinopolitan creed

Flavian I (d. 404; bishop of Antioch), 530

Flavian, Saint (d. 449; patriarch of Constantinople), 436

Fortunatus (perhaps St. Fortunatus, martyred ca. 212), 436

Functius, Johannes (chronicler of Nuremberg whose work was placed on the *Index librorum prohibitorum* in 1559), 463

Gabriel (archbishop of Philadelphia), 443, 676–7

Galata (settlement), 380n14

Gamaliel (Pharisee and rabbi, grandson of Hillel the elder, teacher of St. Paul), 655

Garamantian Empire, 228n

Gazes, Theodore (d. 1475/1476; Greek émigré teacher and translator in Italy), 509

Gdańsk Bible, xxix

Gelasius (d. 496; pope), 29, 76
  On Distinction of Consecration, 30n118

Gembicki, Piotr (d. 1657; regent of the Great Chancery, future crown chancellor and bishop of Cracow), 137

Gennadius II Scholarius (d. ca. 1472; patriarch of Constantinople, theologian), 463, 508–9, 521n406, 557, 666, 670

Gentile, Giovanni Valentine (d. 1566; Italian Antitrinitarian), 468

George (fl. ca. 1072; metropolitan of Kyiv of Greek origin), 245

George of Trebizond (d. 1486; Greek scholar, teacher of Greek, philosophy, and rhetoric in Italy), 463, 509

Gerasimus I (fl. 1620–1636; patriarch of Alexandria), 678n

Gerganos, Zacharias (d. after 1626; Greek student in Wittenberg ca. 1619–1621, active thereafter in Constantinople, author of Greek catechism with Calvinist elements), 481, 491–2, 494, 548, 551, 592, 700, 710

Glagolitic, xxxi

Gleb, Saint (d. 1015; son of Volodimer I, martyred by elder half brother [or cousin] Svjatopolk), 419

Godfrey of Winchester, "Pseudo-Martial" (d. 1107; epigrammatist), 287n11

Goliński, Grzegorz (d. 1631; Cracow professor of rhetoric, author of Latin encomiastic poetry), 604n

Gratian (d. 383; emperor of Rome), 660

Gregoras, Nicephorus (d. between 1358 and 1361; Byzantine historian and theologian), 651

Gregorius (fl. before 1464; abbot of Constantinople, metropolitan of Kyiv), 635, 649, 707

Gregory (fl. after 1445; hieromonk and protosyncellus of Constantinople), 463, 728

Gregory I the Great, Saint (d. 604; pope), 171, 292–3, 404, 475, 515–16, 521

Exposition on the Book of Job, 420

Gregory III Mammas (d. 1450; patriarch of Constantinople), 509

Gregory IV of Amosea (fl. 1620–1623; patriarch of Constantinople), 637n66

Gregory XIII (d. 1585; pope), 380n13

Gregory of Nazianzus, Saint (d. ca. 390; Cappadocian Father, bishop of Constantinople, bishop of Nazianzus), 28, 311, 490, 561, 646

On the Need to Maintain Moderation in Disputations, 433

Oration in Praise of Basil the Great, 413

Gregory of Nyssa, Saint (d. after 394; bishop of Nyssa, Cappadocian Father), 73, 404, 515–16, 561

Life of Our Holy Father Ephrem of Syria, 413

Sermon on the Dead, 516

Grigorij (hegumen of Constantinople), 246

Grodek Dawidowy (town), 290

Grodno (town), 290

Guagninus [Gwagnin], Aleksander (d. 1614; Italian chronicler of Polish-Lithuanian history), 246

Rerum Polonicarum [History of Poland], 155n

Gylas [Geula] (fl. 10th c.; Magyar chief mentioned in early chronicles as a convert to Christianity), 259

Hadrian I (d. 795; pope), 439

Hadrian II (d. 872; pope), 305, 533, 649

Hájek, Venceslas [Václav Hájek z Libočan] (d. 1553; Czech chronicler), 258

Haman (fl. 510 BC; chief vizier of Xerxes), 725

Haraburda, Petro (castellan of Minsk according to Smotryc'kyj, but there was no such person; perhaps he meant Michał Bohdanowicz Haraburda, who held that office in 1585–1586 during the reign of Stefan Batory), 123

Helena (fl. 1495–1513; daughter of Ivan III), 729, 730n106

hell, 221, 235, 266, 402, 407, 417–18 torments in, 418–21, 642, 646

Henryk (d. 1166; prince of Sandomierz, brother of Prince of Mazovia Bolesław IV the Curly), 245

Herberstein, Sigmund Freiherr von (d. 1566; ambassador of the Holy Roman Empire who made two trips to Russia), 246

Herburt, Jan Szczęzny (d. 1616; polemicist, publisher of Polish historians), xvi, 203n174, 246

heresy, nature of, 397–401. See also faith, excesses and defects of

Herod (d. 2; procurator of Judea under Julius Caesar and king under Augustus), 555

Hilarius (perhaps Pope Hilarius, Saint, d. 468), 69

Commentaries on Matthew, 433

Hlezna, Jona. See Jona Hlezna

Hohol', Jona (bishop of Pinsk and Turov), 232

Holšans'kyj-Dubrovyc'kyj, Ivan, Lord (d. 1549; palatine of Kyiv, palatine of Trakai), 123

Holy Spirit, nature of, 66–7, 404, 447–55, 476, 480, 742–3

Holy Trinity Monastery in Vilnius, xxxvi, xxxvii, xliv, xlviii, 176n93, 181, 272, 462, 702, 730

Honorius (Orthodox emperor), 468, 660
Honorius I (d. 638; pope, formally
    anathematized at the Council of
    Constantinople in 681 for his
    Monothelite formulation of "one will
    in Christ"), 560
Horace [Quintus Haratius Flaccus] (d.
    8 BC; Latin poet), 267n60, 335n21,
    383n16, 684n137, 723n90
Horodok (town), 575, 579, 590, 612, 614
Hrekovyč, Antonij (d. 1618; martyred
    Uniate hieromonk, vicar of Ipatij Potij
    in Kyiv), 702
Hungary, Christianity in, 259
Hus, Jan (d. 1415; Czech theologian and
    reformer), 468, 541, 698

Iași (city), 711
Ignatius I (d. 877; patriarch of
    Constantinople), 304–5, 306n57, 545,
    649, 556, 561
Ignatius III Attiyah (d. after 1631; Greek
    patriarch of Antioch), 547
Ilarion (d. before 1054; metropolitan of
    Kyiv), 244, 245, 634
Ilija Kuča (fl. 1577–1579; metropolitan
    of Kyiv residing in Naŭharadok), 249
Ilkowski, Heliasz (subordinate of
    Smotryc'kyj at the Derman' monastery
    in 1628), 361
indulgences, 236
Innocent I, Saint (d. 417; pope), 555
Ippolytovyč, Pajisij (d. 1632; Orthodox
    bishop of Chełm and Belz), lvii, 575,
    592
Irenaeus, Saint (d. ca. 200; bishop of
    Lyons), 404
    Against Heresies, 529n426
Isaiah (Old Testament prophet), 693
Isaja (Smotryc'kyj's deacon at the
    Derman' monastery in 1628), 582
Isidore (d. 1463; matropolitan of Kyiv,
    cardinal), 246, 729
Isidore of Seville, Saint (d. 636), 299n43
Islam, 478, 551, 668, 745

Ivan III Vasil'evič (d. 1505; grand prince
    of Moscow), 730n106
Iwanowicz, Semen (fl. 1621; imprisoned
    Orthodox citizen of Vilnius), 191n113
Izjaslav (prince of Kyiv), 245

Jacob (second son of Isaac and Rebekah,
    twin brother of Esau), 152, 312, 701,
    751
Jakub of Sienno (d. 1463; Roman
    Catholic bishop of Cracow), 317–19
James (apostle, brother of Christ), 77, 80,
    130, 213, 397, 435, 550, 646
Jaroslav I (d. 1054; prince of Kyiv, son
    of Volodimer I), 248
Jarosław (town), 290
Jelec, Fedor (d. after 1648; vice-palatine
    of Kyiv), 582
Jełowicki, Zachariasz (d. 1629; royal
    secretary to Sigismund III, esquire
    carver of Kyiv), 179
Jeremiah (Old Testament prophet), 528
Jeremiah II Tranos (d. 1595; patriarch
    of Constantinople), 153–4, 175, 197,
    210, 245, 251, 278, 295n35, 339, 344,
    443
Jerome, Saint (d. 420; biblical scholar
    and translator), 28, 647
    Apology against the Books of Rufinus,
        529n427
    Book 3 on Jer. 16, 433
    On Ecclesiastes, 447
    Letter 15, 529
    Letter 23, 413
Jerusalem, 1, 388
    see of, 311
Jesuits
    academy in Vilnius of, xviii, xxxiv
    school in Galata of, 380, 547
Jesus Christ
    divine status of, 67–8
    as head of Church, 307, 402, 426,
        527–8
    priestly status of, 400–1, 402, 422–4,
        621

Jevanhelije učytelnoje. See Smotryc′kyj, Meletij, *Homiliary Gospel*

Joachim V (d. ca. 1592; Greek patriarch of Antioch), 210, 295n35

Joannes Sacranus (d. 1527; theologian, rector of the Cracow Academy), 61–2

John (bishop of Mukačevo), 711

John (fl. 1164–1166; metropolitan of Kyiv of Greek origin), 650

John II the Good ["Christopodromos"] (fl. 1077–1089; metropolitan of Kyiv of Greek origin), 245

John III the Castrate (fl. 1089–1090; metropolitan of Kyiv of Greek origin), 245

John VIII (d. 882; pope), 305

John VIII Palaeologus (d. 1448; emperor of Byzantium, brother of Demetrius Palaeologus), 364, 458, 508, 513

John XI Beccus (d. 1297; patriarch of Constantinople), 364, 508–9, 561, 649

John Chrysostom, Saint (d. 407; bishop of Constantinople, doctor of the Church), 6–7, 14–15, 28, 72–3, 74, 77, 125, 311, 407, 412, 416, 419, 421, 422, 426, 436, 454, 469–70, 490, 549, 550, 555, 561, 610, 651

Book on the Priesthood, 527, 645n78, 647

Homily 11 on Eph. 4, 171, 173–4, 196, 224, 546

Homily 12 on John, 125n21

Homily 25 on Matthew, 446

Homily 38 on 1 Cor., 130n28, 213n193

Homily 42 on Matthew, 114, 125n21

Homily 54 on Matthew, 432, 434

Homily 80 to the People of Antioch, 526n421

Homily on Matthew, 14

Homily on the Feast of the Exaltation of the Cross, 433, 526

On the Words of the Prophet Isaiah, 7

Sermon 4 on Phil. 1:22–6, 415

Sermon 24 on 1 Cor 10:13, 645n78

Sermon 34 on Matthew, 420n133

John Chrysostom, Saint (*continued*)

Sermon 55 on Mt. 16, 526n421, 528

Sermon 88 on John 21, 435, 436, 526n421

John of Damascus [Damascene], Saint (d. ca. 749; Greek theologian and doctor of the Church), 30, 70, 409–10, 413, 417, 423n143, 469, 510, 516–17, 560, 561, 670

Book on Heresies, 430n172

Exposition of the Orthodox Faith, 429, 452, 504–5, 550n488

Oktoechos, 213n194

John the Baptist, 446

John the Evangelist (apostle), 71, 406, 414–15, 616, 644

Jona II (d. 1507; metropolitan of Kyiv), 730n106

Jona III Protasovyč (d. 1577; metropolitan of Kyiv and all Rus′ residing in Naŭharadok), 249, 276

Jona Hlezna (d. 1494; metropolitan of Kyiv), 650, 729

Jornandes [Jordanis] (fl. mid-6th c.; historian of the Goths living in the Eastern Roman Empire)

De Getarum sive Gotharum Origine [History of the Goths] . . . , 209n187

Joseph (d. 1635 BC; eleventh son of Jacob and first of Rachel), 86, 702–4

Joseph (fl. 1237–1240; metropolitan of Kyiv of Greek origin), 245

Joseph (fl. after 1445; bishop of Methone), 463, 509

Joseph II of Ephesus (d. 1439; patriarch of Constantinople), 237, 246, 364, 458, 508–9, 561

Joseph of Studios (fl. ca. 800; brother of Theodore of Studios), 417

Joseph the Hymnographer, Saint (d. ca. 886; monk), 417

Josyf I Bolharynovyč (d. 1501; metropolitan of Kyiv), 462n290, 510

Josyf II Soltan (d. 1521; metropolitan of Kyiv and all Rus′), 462, 650, 729–30

Judas (apostle who betrayed Christ), 191, 193, 304, 409

Julian the Apostate (d. 363; Roman emperor), 738

Julius I, Saint (d. 352; pope), 531, 532–3, 555, 630

Juretus, François (d. 1626; French scholar and editor)
Observations on the Letters of Ivo of Chartres, 131n, 132n, 147n47, 148n51

Justinian (d. 565; Eastern Roman emperor), 209, 660

Juvenal (fl. 98–128; Roman satirist), 289n15

Kadłubek, Wincenty (d. 1223; Polish chronicler), 246

Karpovyč, Leontij (d. 1620; archimandrite of the Vilnius Orthodox Holy Spirit Monastery), xxiii, xxxiv–xxxv, xlvi, 97, 103, 106, 139, 262, 609n, 712
Kazan'e dvoe [Two Sermons], 107n15

Kazimierz IV Jagiellończyk (d. 1492; king of Poland, grand duke of Lithuania), 318–19

keys given to the apostles, 435–6, 622, 680

Kirill the Clerk (fl. 1240–1281; metropolitan of Kyiv), 245

Kleck (town), 290

Klimentij [Klim Smoljatič] (fl. 1150; metropolitan of Kyiv), 245, 634, 650

Kmita, Fylon Semenowicz (d. 1587; palatine of Smolensk), 123

Kocel (d. ca. 873; prince of Pannonia), 259

Kopyns'kyj, Isaija (d. 1633; archbishop of Smolensk and Černihiv), 362, 467n294, 478n316, 592

Kopystens'kyj, Mixajil (d. 1610; Orthodox bishop of Przemyśl and Samborz), xxxiv, 232

Kopystens'kyj, Zaxarija (d. 1627; archimandrite of the Kyiv Caves

Monastery; pseud. Azarius), 203n174, 467–8, 488n‡, 519, 544n†, 579, 646, 704, 709

Korec'kyj family, 150

Korsakivna, Eva. *See* Solomerec'ka, Eva

Korsak, Rafajil (d. 1637; bishop of Pinsk and Halyč), 364n13

Kortycki, Wojciech (d. after 1633; Jesuit confessor to Smotryc'kyj), lii, lxv
View of the Fight Well Fought . . . , A [Widok potyczki wygraney . . .], lxv

Korybut, Mixajil. *See* Vyšnevec'kyj, Mixajil Korybut

Kotowicz, Jan (fl. 1621; imprisoned Orthodox citizen of Vilnius), 191n113

Krasnystav (town), 290

Krasowski, Andrzej (fl. ca. 1627; burgher of Lviv), 663, 683

Krasowski, Semen (fl. 1621; imprisoned Orthodox citizen of Vilnius), 191n114

Kreva (town), 461

Krevza, Lev (d. 1639; Uniate archimandrite of the Holy Trinity Monastery), xxxvi, 245, 246, 262
Obrona iednosci cerkiewney [Defense of Church Unity], 722

Kromer, Marcin (d. 1589; Polish historian, bishop of Warmia [Ermland], 245, 246, 258, 260, 317, 345n
History of Poland, 155n

Krupec'kyj, Oleksandr [Atanazy] (d. 1652; Uniate bishop of Przemyśl), xxxiv

Kułakowski, Wasyly (fl. 1621; imprisoned Orthodox citizen of Vilnius), 191n113

Kunaševyč-Sahajdačnyj, Petro (d. 1622; hetman of Zaporozhian army), 166, 210–11

Kuncevyč, Josafat (d. 1623; Uniate archbishop of Polack), xviii, xxxvi, xlii, li–liii, lvi, 157n57, 262, 269, 271, 274, 702

Kurcevyč, Josyf (bishop of Volodymer and Brest), 337–8, 342, 346

Kuszelicz, Fedor (fl. 1621; imprisoned Orthodox citizen of Vilnius), 191n113
Kyivan Caves Monastery, lvii, 132, 195, 362, 569, 579, 589, 598, 612
Kyiv Council of 1628. *See* Council of Kyiv

Labetus, 121n13
Lament. See Smotryc'kyj, Meletij, *Thrēnos*
Lascaris, Constantine (d. 1501; Greek scholar and grammarian teaching in Italy), 509
Latin language, 21
Lazarus (beggar in biblical parable), 418–19
Leo (d. 1056; archbishop of Ohrid), 519
Leo I the Great (d. 461; pope), 29, 439, 531, 533, 555–6
Letter 92, 171
Sermon 42, On Lent IV, 30
Leo V the Armenian (d. 820; emperor of Byzantium), 263
Leo VI the Wise (d. 912; emperor of Byzantium), 259, 550n484
Leo IX (d. 1054; pope), 534
Letter 5, 519–20
Leontievyč, Feodor (fl. ca. 1628; protopope of Dubno), 582, 585
Leontij (fl. 991–1004; metropolitan of Kyiv), 425
Leontius (hieromonk, protosyncellus of Constantinople in 1626), 678
Letter to the Monks . . . [List do zakonników . . .], xxxix–xlii, xlviii
lex talionis, 19n
Liberatus (d. after 555; archdeacon of Carthage)
Breviarium [Breviary] causae Nestorianorum et Eutychianorum, 209n188
Liberius (d. 366; pope, forced and temporary adherent of Arianism), 294, 560

Lipsius, Justus (d. 1606; Flemish philologian and humanist), 113
Lipski, Andrzej (d. 1631; crown chancellor, bishop of Kujawy, bishop of Cracow), 129, 137
Lithuania, Christianity in, 259–60
Lityns'kyj, Lord, 588
Lot (nephew of Abraham), 86, 409
Lucifer, 74
Luc'k (town), 290
Ludmila, Saint (d. 921; wife of Bořivoj I, Roman Catholic martyr; Smotryc'kyj speaks of two Ludmilas, the second called saint and wife of Moravian "king" Svjatopolk), 258, 259
Ludwik, Jan. *See* Vives, Juan Luis
Lukaris, Cyril. *See* Cyril Lukaris
Luke, Saint (evangelist), 28, 295, 421, 424–5
Lutheranism, xxiv, xxix, 596, 609, 620–1, 667, 689, 698
Luther, Martin (d. 1546; Augustinian monk, founder of the German Reformation), xix, xxvii, 464, 472, 498n, 558, 691, 719
Lycurgus (perhaps Smotryc'kyj meant the legendary legislator of Sparta who fl. ca. 600 BC), 86
Lynceus (Argonaut of Greek mythology), 723
Lyranus. *See* Nicholas of Lyra

Maccabees, 87
Macedonian heresy, 378, 543, 595, 638, 640
Macedonius (d. ca. 362; bishop of Constantinople, exiled from Constantinople by the Arians, regarded, probably falsely, as the founder of the Pneumatomachi, thus giving them the name "Macedonians"), 28, 29, 728, 738
Macedonius II, Saint (d. 517; patriarch of Constantinople), 532

Mahilëŭ (city), 108, 247, 270, 273, 290
Makarij (d. 1563; metropolitan of
    Moscow), 731
Makarij I (d. 1497; metropolitan of Kyiv
    residing in Naŭharadok), 650, 729
Maksim Grek [Maximus the Greek] (d.
    1556; Greek Orthodox monk and
    philologian active in Muscovy), 418,
    657n95
Mani (d. 274 or 277; religious leader,
    heresiarch), 68
Manichaean heresy, 30, 378, 468, 487,
    489, 511, 543, 585, 595, 638–9,
    643–5
Marcellinus (d. 304; pope), 294, 560
Marcian (d. 457; emperor of Byzantium),
    660
Marcion of Pontus (d. ca. 160;
    heresiarch), 68, 436
Maria of Tver' (actually Juliana/
    Uliana, daughter of Prince of Tver'
    Aleksander, 2nd wife of Grand Duke
    of Lithuania Algirdas [Olgierd]; d.
    1392), 260
Marinus (fl. ca. 650; presbyter of
    Cyprus), 474
Mark, Saint (evangelist), 421, 550
Mark of Ephesus (d. 1452; bishop of
    Ephesus famous for his defense
    of Orthodoxy at the Council of
    Florence), 30, 462, 508, 510, 534,
    728–9
Martial [Marcus Valerius Martialis] (d.
    104; Roman poet and epigrammatist),
    287n11
Martin I, Saint (d. 655; pope), 555
Marullus, Michael (d. 1500; Greek exile
    in Italy, author of Latin poetry), 509
Matthew (fl. 1210–1220; metropolitan of
    Kyiv of Greek origin), 245
Matthew (fl. 1626; hieromonk from
    Athens), 710–11
Matthew (metropolitan of Myra), 676–7
Matthew II (d. after 1603; patriarch of
    Constantinople), 387, 551

Matthew, Saint (apostle), 421
Maximus (fl. 1283–1305), metropolitan
    of Kyiv of Greek origin, 649
Maximus the Confessor, Saint (d.
    662; Greek theologian and ascetic
    writer, abbot of the monastery at
    Chrysopolis), 30, 474, 511–12, 555,
    560, 561
Letter to Marinus, 504, 714n56
Melchizedek (priest and king of Salem
    who met Abraham and blessed him),
    422, 732
Meletius I Pegas (d. 1601; patriarch of
    Alexandria), 180, 210, 387, 481, 551,
    666, 670, 673, 676–7, 735
Menander (d. 292 BC; Attic poet, most
    famous author of New Comedy),
    677n124
Methodius I (d. after 843; patriarch of
    Constantinople), 258–9
Methodius, Saint (d. 885; apostle of the
    Slavs, brother of Constantine/Cyril),
    xlviii, 258–9
Methodius, Saint (bishop of Pamphylia),
    447, 561
Metrophanes III (d. 1580; patriarch of
    Constantinople), 249, 276
Michael (fl. 1130–1145; metropolitan of
    Kyiv of Greek origin), 245
Michael III the Drunkard (d. 867;
    emperor of Byzantium), 264
Michael IX Palaeologus (d. 1320;
    emperor of Byzantium, father of
    Andronicus), 364, 507–8
Miechowita [Maciej z Miechowa] (d.
    1523; Polish historian, geographer,
    245, 246
Mieleszko [Meleško], Jerzy (d. ca. 1635;
    standard-bearer of Slonim), xl, 115,
    363
Mieszko I (d. 992; duke of Poland),
    258–9
Minsk (city), 204, 729
Mohammedans. See Islam

Mohyla, Peter (d. 1646; Orthodox metropolitan of Kyiv), xxviii–xxix, lv, lvii–lviii, lix, lxi, lxii, lxvii, 362–3, 574–5, 579, 590–1, 593, 612n10, 613n15

Molytovnyk yměja v sebě cerkovnaja poslědovanija, 646n81

Monastery of St. Michael the Archangel in Kyiv, 349, 589

Monophysite heresy, 69

Monothelite heresy, 69, 478, 560

Moravia, Christianity in, 258–9

Mordecai (biblical figure), 207

Moroxovs'kyj, Illja (d. 1631; Uniate bishop of Volodymyr and Brest), xxvi–xxviii, xlvi

Moschopulus, Manuel (fl. 1300; Byzantine commentator and grammarian), 509

Moschos, John "Eukratas," Saint (d. 619; Greek spiritual writer), 517n398

Moses (lawgiver who led the Israelites out of Egypt), 70, 86, 403, 430, 431, 732

Münzer, Thomas (d. 1525; German Anabaptist, leader of the Peasants' Revolt), 719

Musurus, Marcus (d. 1517; Greek scholar and humanist active as a teacher in Italy), 509

Mužylovs'kyj, Andrij (d. after 1629; protopope of Sluck), 1n92, lxii–lxiii, 579–80, 587–8, 591, 593, 737n123. See also *Antidote for the Most Noble Ruthenian Nation . . .*

Mysajil (fl. 1445–1480; metropolitan of Kyiv residing in Naŭharadok), 462n287, 649, 729, 731

Nalyvajko (epithet), xxiv, 188–90

Nalyvajko, Dem'jan (d. 1627; Orthodox priest, brother of Severyn), xxi, 610n†, 646n81

Nalyvajko Resurrected [Zmartwychwstały Nalewayko], 16n43, 205, 219, 480

Nalyvajko, Severyn (d. 1597; leader of a 1594–1596 Cossack uprising), xxi, xxiv n24, 16n43

Naŭharadok (city), 205, 303

Nehemiah (biblical figure credited with repairing a portion of the wall of Jerusalem in 445 BC), 118

Nephon II (d. 1502; patriarch of Constantinople), 462, 510, 650, 731, 735

Nestorius (d. after 451; heresiarch, patriarch of Constantinople), 28, 69, 312, 401, 407, 503–4, 698, 728, 738

Niceno-Constantinopolitan creed, 221–2, 235, 292, 306, 473, 511, 670. See also *filioque*

Nicephorus I (d. 1121; metropolitan of Kyiv of Greek origin), 245

Nicephorus II (fl. 1182–1198; metropolitan of Kyiv of Greek origin), 245

Nicephorus Callistus Xanthopulus (d. ca. 1335; Byzantine writer, Church historian, priest at Hagia Sophia), 264n50, 319n93, 408n79, 438n212, 510, 532–3

Nicetas (fl. 1122–1127; metropolitan of Kyiv of Greek origin), 245

Nicholas (fl. 1097–1101; metropolitan of Kyiv of Greek origin), 245

Nicholas (fl. ca. 1626; presbyter from Crete), 710–11

Nicholas I (d. 867; pope), 314n82, 649

Nicholas V (d. 1455; pope), 513

Nicholas Chrysoberges (d. 996; patriarch of Constantinople), 649

Nicholas of Lyra [Lyranus] (d. 1340; Franciscan biblical scholar), 310–11

Nicholas of Myra in Lycia, Saint (d. 345 or 352), 649

Nikon, Saint, 510, 516–17

Nilus Cabasilas (fl. 14th c.; metropolitan of Thessalonica), 30

Noah (biblical figure), 416, 732

Novatian (d. ca. 257; schismatic), 28

Nuceryn, Sebastian (d. 1635; Roman Catholic theologian, preacher, writer, translator), 605

Obałkowski, Bartłomiej (envoy from Sigismund III), 162, 164
Ohins'kyj, Bohdan (d. 1625; chamberlain of Trakai, Orthodox patron), xxviii, xxxi, xxxvi, 85, 86, 98n1, 133, 138–9
Ohrid (town), 634n64
Olesk (town), 290
Ołyca (town), 290
Onysyfor Divočka (fl. 1585; metropolitan of Kyiv), 197n, 246
Origenist heresy, 378, 488, 489, 517, 543, 595, 638, 642
Order of St. Basil the Great, 381
Orša (town), 108, 247, 273, 290, 363
Orthodox and Roman Churches differences between, 313–17, 501–2 similarities between, 668–9
Orthodox Brotherhood Monastery of the Descent of the Holy Spirit in Vilnius, xix, xxiii, xxviii, xxxiii–xxxiv, xxxiv, xxxvi, xlvi, lii, lx, lxi, 119, 150, 176, 219, 261–2, 269, 272, 321–3, 461, 480, 603, 607, 616, 679, 722
Orthologue, Theophil (pseud. for Meletij Smotryc'kyj for *Thrēnos*), xix, lxi, lxii, 374–5, 404–5, 440–4, 447–55, 459, 467–70, 472–4, 479, 482, 498, 543, 554, 592, 595, 609, 613–15, 618–19, 621–5, 629–31, 640, 646, 671, 687, 690, 700, 705, 718, 736. *See also* Smotryc'kyj, Meletij, *Thrēnos*
Orzechowski, Stanisław (d. 1566; canon of Przemyśl, Polish and Latin political writer and confessional polemicist, historian, orator), 310, 311 *Diatriba . . . contra calumniam [Diatribe against Calumny]*, 310n71
Osorius, Hieronymus [Osório, Jerónymo] (d. 1580; bishop of Silves, professor at the University of Coimbra, "the Portuguese Cicero," postillographer), 707
Ostroh (town), xviii, 461
Ostroh Bible, xvi, 265n55
Ostroz'ka, Eufrozyna (d. 1628; wife of Aleksander Zasławski, granddaughter of Kostjantyn Ostroz'kyj), liii, 376n
Ostroz'ka, Katarzyna (d. 1642; wife of Tomasz Zamoyski), 375n8
Ostroz'kyj, Aleksander (d. 1603; palatine of Volhynia), 123
Ostroz'kyj, Kostjantyn Ivanovyč (d. 1530; palatine of Trakai, grand hetman of Lithuania), 123
Ostroz'kyj, Kostjantyn Vasyl' (d. 1608; palatine of Kyiv), xvi, xviii, liii, 123, 150, 265n54, 376n, 610n8
Ottoman Empire. *See* Turks
Ovid, xxxiii, 676, 688n4

Pac, Mikołaj (d. 1585; Roman Catholic bishop-elect of Kyiv who held Protestant views, castellan of Smolensk), 226n212
Paczanowski, Lord (courtier to Sigismund III), 133–4, 135, 136, 137, 143
paradise, earthly versus heavenly, 402, 405, 407, 410–17, 443–4, 476, 524–5, 562, 622, 647, 740
Parēgoria, xxvi–xxviii, 205, 695
particular judgment, 401, 402, 405, 407, 408–10, 445, 476, 622, 646, 739–40
Paterik of the Kyivan Caves Monastery, 244
Paul I (d. ca. 351; patriarch of Constantinople), 532, 630
Paul, Saint (apostle), xx, 5, 17, 18, 72, 75, 79, 188, 195, 203, 223, 224, 276, 296, 328, 331, 333, 394, 397, 399, 405–6, 407, 410–11, 414–16, 434n199, 492, 507, 521, 535–6, 538, 546, 558, 644, 682, 698
Paul the Deacon (d. ca. 800; chronicler), 209n187

Paul the Samosatene [Paul of Samosata] (fl. ca. 260; bishop of Antioch, heresiarch), 69

Pelagius (fl. ca 400; heresiarch), 28

Peter III (d. 1051; Greek patriarch of Antioch), 520, 556, 673

Peter, Saint (apostle), 18, 296, 307, 409, 525, 549, 555, 559, 560, 676–7, 732, 751–2

   as head of Church, 401, 403, 432–5, 476, 492, 526–9, 622–3, 646, 647, 679–80, 741

Phalereus. *See* Demetrius of Phalerum

Philalethes, Christopher (pseud. for Marcin Broniewski), lxi, lxii, 372–5, 402–4, 427–9, 431–2, 434, 437, 439–42, 450, 455, 459, 465, 467–70, 472, 479, 482, 498, 543, 554, 592, 595, 609–10, 613–15, 618–19, 621–5, 629–31, 679–80, 687, 690, 694, 700, 705, 708, 736

   Apokrisis, 373, 402, 427, 679, 695, 704

Philelphus, Franciscus [Filelfo, Francesco] (d. 1481; Italian poet and humanist who spent several years in Constantinople and married the daughter of his Greek teacher, Johannes Chrysoloras), 509

Philip of Macedonia (d. 336 BC; king of Macedonia), 330–1

Philip, Saint (apostle), 549

Photinus (fl. ca 350), bishop of Sirmium, heresiarch, 68

Photius (d. 893; patriarch of Constantinople, scholar and politician), 305, 306n57, 510, 533–4, 556

Pinsk (town), 290

Piotrkowczyk II, Andrzej (d. 1645; Polish printer), 603

Pius II (d. 1464; pope), 246, 635, 649

Platina, Bartolomeo (d. 1481; Italian humanist), 519

Pliny the Elder (d. 79; Roman scholar) *Naturalis historia [Natural History],* 158n, 688n2

Plutarch (d. ca. 120; Greek biographer and moral philosopher), 331

Polack (town), 268–71, 273, 290

Polish language, xix–xx, 8, 21, 287, 480, 569

Polycarp, Saint (d. ca. 155; bishop of Smyrna), 555

pope

   as head of Church, 235, 292, 474, 475, 489, 492, 502, 525–34, 647, 652–3, 673n115, 741–2

   spiritual appeals to, 436–7

   as successor of St. Peter, 235, 236

   universal councils and, 437–40, 623, 680

Porfirij (fl. ca. 1626; deacon, brother of Jov Borec'kyj), 580, 581

Potij, Ipatij (d. 1613; bishop of Volodymyr and Brest), xix, xxii, 16n43, 54n, 108n18, 118n8, 160, 180–1, 232, 236–7, 302, 462n287, 673, 677, 702, 734

   Rozmova berestjanina s bratčikom [Conversation of the Adherent of Brest and a Member of the Brotherhood], 480

   Unija [Union], 480

Probus (d. 282; Roman emperor), 7

Prons'kyj, Semen Hlebovyč (d. 1555; Orthodox palatine of Kyiv), 123

Proof of the Unheard-of Audacity . . . , xlii, xlviii

Protasovyč, Jona. *See* Jona III Protasovyč

Proterius (d. 457; archpriest of Alexandria, adherent of the Council of Chalcedon, named to replace Dioscorus I as patriarch), 703

protopope, 181n

Przemyśl (town), 290

punishment in kind. See *lex talionis*

purgatory, 80, 221, 234, 236, 402, 404, 426, 474, 488, 502, 515–18, 562, 642, 647, 651, 671, 673, 740–1

Putjatycki, Aleksander, 461

Puzyna, Jurij (Orthodox nobleman), xviii

querela, xxi–xxii

Rahoza, Myxajil (d. 1599; Orthodox,
  then Uniate, metropolitan of Kyiv),
  155, 197n, 232, 246, 249, 256, 344
Rastislav (d. after 870; prince of Great
  Moravia), 259
Reformation, xvii, lxvii
Rej, Mikołaj z Nagłowic (d. 1569;
  Calvinist poet, writer, and translator),
  xxix
*Report and a Consideration . . . [Relacja
  i uważenie . . .],* 16n43
Rivno (town), 290
Roman Catholic Church, as free from
  heresy, 490–1
Romanov, Fedor Nikityč (d. 1633;
  Muscovite patriarch Filaret), xxxiv
Rus'
  as equal member of Polish-Lithuanian
    Commonwealth, xv–xvi, xxxvii, lxvii,
    330
  free status of, 331–2, 339
  as an identity, 217–19
  spiritual freedom of, 248–50
Ruthenian language, xxx, xxxi, 91–2,
  287, 378
Ruthenian noble houses, 44–5, 119–20
Ruthenian Orthodox Church
  heresies in, 470–7, 618, 623–4, 700
  quality of clergy in, 41–4
  response to Reformation, xvii, xxix,
    xxxiii
  subject to patriarch of Constantinople,
    244–8, 250, 339–41
  vacant sees of, xxxiv–xxxv, 108, 182–
    5, 214, 255–60
Ruts'kyj, Josyf (d. 1637; Uniate
  metropolitan of Kyiv and all Rus'),
  xxxvi, xxxvii, liii–lv, lvi, lxiv, lxvi,
  122, 156, 255n26, 262, 302, 353n3,
  355, 359, 597n43, 605, 633n58, 722,
  753n6. *See also* Smotryc'kyj, Meletij,
  letter to Ruts'kyj

Sabellian heresy, 30, 378, 487, 489, 543,
  585, 595, 638–40
Sabellius (fl. early 3rd c.; heresiarch), 401
sacraments, 235, 312, 401, 405, 622
Sahajdačnyj, Petro Kunaševyč. *See*
  Kunaševyč-Sahajdačnyj, Petro
Sakovyč, Kasijan (d. 1647; theologian,
  polemicist, convert from Orthodoxy
  to the Uniate Church and eventually
  [1641] to Roman Catholicism), xxix,
  lvii, lix, 564n511, 565n, 566n, 569,
  589, 591, 592, 715n60
Sallust [Gaius Sallustius Crispus] (d. 35
  BC; Roman historian and politician)
  *De conjuratione Catilinae [The War
    with Catiline],* 329
Samuel (fl. 11th c. BC; Hebrew judge
  and prophet), 87, 732
Sanhuško [Sanguszko], Roman, Prince
  (d. 1571; palatine of Braclav, field
  hetman of the Grand Duchy of
  Lithuania), 123
Sapieha, Bogdan Pawlowicz [Sapiha,
  Bohdan] (d. 1593; palatine of Minsk),
  123
Sapieha, Lew Iwanowicz [Sapiha, Lev]
  (d. 1633; palatine of Vilnius, grand
  hetman of Lithuania), 218n202, 272,
  275n79
Sapiha, Ivan (palatine of Vicebsk, either
  Ivan Semenovyč [d. 1517] or Ivan
  Bohdanovyč [d. 1546]), 123
Sapricius, 703
Sarah (wife of Abraham), 105
Sarmatism, xxxiii
Satan, 399
Schedel, Hartman (d. 1514; chronicler of
  Nuremberg), 463, 519
Scholarius, George. *See* Gennadius II
Sejm of 1575, 147n49
Sejm of 1607, 131, 132, 140, 176–9, 230
Sejm of 1620, 131, 132, 140, 151, 184,
  212, 230, 243, 268
Sejm of 1621, 342

Sejm of 1623, xlix, 343
Sejm of 1627, 612
Sejm of 1629, 692
Seljava, Antonij (d. 1655; archimandrite of the Uniate Holy Trinity Monastery, Uniate archbishop of Polack, metropolitan of Rus'), xlviii–xlix, lvi
Seneca, Lucius Annaeus (d. 65; Roman philosopher, politician, tragedian), 4
Sergius, 556
Servetus, Michael (d. 1553; physician and heretic who held Antitrinitarian views; burned at the stake by John Calvin), 68, 468
Seth (son of Adam and Eve), 453
Sienczyłowicz, Filip (fl. ca. 1620; Orthodox Vilnius city councilor), 192
Sienieński, Jakub. See Jakub of Sienno
Sigismund I the Old (d. 1548; king of Poland, grand duke of Lithuania), 249, 276n83, 277n84
Sigismund II August (d. 1572; king of Poland, grand duke of Lithuania), 147n48, 249n, 276n83, 331, 332n7, 340
Sigismund III Vasa (d. 1632; king of Poland, grand duke of Lithuania), xx–xxi, xxxvi, xxxvii, xlix, 116, 119, 127, 129–30, 134–7, 140–1, 142, 162, 167, 175–6, 177–9, 224–5, 230–1, 244, 250–4, 263, 272, 328, 342, 348–9, 579, 596, 633n58, 692
campaign against Moscow of, xx, 125
Silverius (fl. 536; pope), 209, 294
Simeon Metaphrastes, Saint (fl. ca. 960; Byzantine hagiographer), 438n214
Simon Magus (fl. 1st c. BC; Samaritan sorcerer, convert to Christianity), 295–6
simony, 295–7
sin, punishment of, 444–5
Sixtus IV (d. 1484; pope), 461, 510, 650, 714, 731, 733
Skarga, Piotr (d. 1612; Polish Jesuit, homileticist, hagiographer,

confessional polemicist), xxiii–xxvii, xxxii, 20, 61–2, 310, 311, 553n489, 707
Kazania przygodne, 238n
Na Treny i Lament Theophila Orthologa, Do Rusi greckiego nabożeństwa przestroga [A Warning to Rus'], xxiv–xxv, 310, 510, 561n506, 669n, 695
O jedności kościoła Bożego [On the Unity of God's Church] . . . , xxiii, xxxii, 62n237
Skumin, Fedor [Teodor Skuminowicz Tyszkiewicz] (d. 1618; palatine of Naŭharadok), 123
Skumin Tyszkiewicz, Janusz. See Tyszkiewicz [Tyškevyč], Janusz Skumin
Slavonic language, xix, xxviii, xxx, xxxi–xxxii, 21, 91–2, 98–9, 287, 378, 381, 389, 559, 712
Smotryc'kyj, Herasym Danyjilovyč (fl. 1576–1594; Ruthenian man of letters, educator, translator, father of Meletij), xvi, xviii, 265
Smotryc'kyj, Meletij
advocacy of union between Orthodox and Uniate Churches of, xv, xxxix, xlvi, liv–lv, lvi–lviii, lxv, 357, 376–9, 381–2, 493–5, 548–63, 575, 607–9, 627–9, 632–3, 635–6, 638, 647–55, 658–61, 693, 713–16, 721, 746
Apology . . . for the Peregrination to the Eastern Lands, lvi–lviii, lxiii, lxiv, 361, 526, 569, 576, 579–80, 584, 585, 587, 596, 599, 608, 611–14, 616–20, 621–4, 630–2, 647, 652, 687, 689–90, 695, 698–700, 704–5, 710, 718–20, 727–9, 738–9, 753; anathematization of, lix, 574, 591–5; revocation of, 588–90, 597n42. See also Smotryc'kyj, Meletij, Revocation
as archimandrite, xxxiv, 356
attacks against, xl–xli, xliv–xlv, xlviii–xlix, 261, 268–9, 271, 321, 337–8,

Smotryc'kyj, Meletij (*continued*)
attacks against (*continued*)
587, 595–6, 620, 665, 725, 737–8
catechism of, li, liv, 361, 366, 481–2,
574–5, 673, 710
Church Slavonic Grammar, xxviii,
xxxi–xxxiii, xxxvi
"Considerations . . . ," liv, lv, lvii, lviii,
357, 361, 366, 381, 383–4, 482, 489,
549, 575, 616
conversion to Uniatism of, xvii, xxv,
xxix, xxxviii–xxix, xlvi–xlvii, li–liv,
lxiv, lxvi; hiding of, liv–lvi, 356–8,
361
death of, lxv
Defense of the "Verification," xxxv,
xxxviii, xlii–xliv, 300–1, 304, 307–9,
312–13, 316–17, 480, 626
early life of, xvi–xix, 261
Exaethesis [Expostulation], lxii–lxiv
excommunication of, xxxvi
Funeral Sermon, xxiii, xxxiii–xxxvi
*Homiliary Gospel [Jevanhelije
učytelnoje],* xxviii–xxxi, xxxiii,
xxxiv, xxxvi
Justification of Innocence, xxxv, xlviii–
l, 480, 626
letter to Bandini, liv, 354–5
letter 1 to Borec'kyj, 576–7
letter 2 to Borec'kyj, 581, 589
letter 3 to Borec'kyj, 582–3
letter to Holy Office of the Inquisition,
liv–lv, lx, 355–8
letter to Lukaris (1627), liv–lv, lvi, lx,
366, 590, 663–84, 690
letter to Mohyla, 577–8
letter to Orthodox Brotherhood
Monastery, liv, 358–60
letter to Ruts'kyj, liv–lv, 360–
letter to Urban VIII (1627), liv, 353–4
letter to Urban VIII (1630), lxiv–lxv,
751–61
ordination of, xxxiii–xxxiv, lii, lxiii,
lxiv, 723

Smotryc'kyj, Meletij (*continued*)
Paraenesis [Admonition], lvi, lix–lxi,
lxiii, 590n, 689, 690n7, 697, 705, 737
pilgrimage to the East of, l–liii, lxiv,
356, 385–95, 397, 425, 455–6, 466–7,
481, 611, 625, 671, 689, 705–6, 708,
710–11
Protestation . . . , lvii, lviii–lix, lxii,
611, 737
*Refutation of Acrimonious Writings
[Elenchus],* xxxv, xliv–xlviii, 467–8,
480, 586, 626, 695, 704
renouncement of Orthodoxy of, 628–31
Revocation, lviii–lix, lxiv, 588, 597n42
Saul-Paul metaphor and, li–liii, liv
Thrēnos, xix–xxviii, xxxiv, xxxv, xlv,
lxi, 205, 465, 481, 510, 586, 596n40,
618, 626, 628, 667, 669–70, 680, 695,
704, 708, 718, 722–3; authorship
of, xxiii, xxvi, xlii, 321; response to,
xxiii, xlv–xlvi; structure of, xxi–xxii;
as treason, xx, xxiv–xxv, 618
Uniate propaganda about, li–lii
Verification of Innocence, xxxv,
xxxvii–xlii, xl, xlviii, 242, 300–1,
480, 626
Sobol, Łukasz (fl. 1621; imprisoned
Orthodox citizen of Vilnius), 192
Socrates "Scholasticus" (d. 450; Greek
Church historian), 21n67, 437n212,
530, 630n54, 714n57
Sokal (town), 290
Solenyk (Kyivan Cossack), 584
Solikowski, Jan Dymitr (d. 1603; Roman
Catholic archbishop of Lviv, writer,
polemicist, poet), xxv, 510, 551, 667
Solomerec'ka, Eva Borkolabivna (d.
between 1618 and 1626; wife of
Bohdan Ivanovyc Solomerec'kyj,
mother of Bohdan Bohdanovyč
Solomerec'kyj), 93
Solomerec'kyj, Bohdan Bohdanovyč
(d. ca. 1630; Orthodox nobleman),
xviii–xix, xxviii, xxxi, 93

Solomerec'kyj, Ivan, Prince (d. 1586;
   castellan of Mscislaŭ), 123
Solomon (Old Testament king), 213, 269
Solomon (fl. ca. 1600; protopope of
   Polack), 269
Sophocles (d. 404 BC; Greek tragedian),
   120n12
Sophronius (d. 638; patriarch of
   Jerusalem), 517
souls
   creation of, 445–7, 476
   disposition of, 474–5, 489, 502, 673
Sowita Wina. See *Twofold Guilt*
Sozomenus, Hermias Salaminus (d. ca.
   450; Greek Church historian from
   Palestine), 437n212, 530–1, 630n54,
   714
spiritual servitude, 332–3
Stahons'kyj, Avramij (bishop of Pinsk
   and Turov), 592
Stephen Batory (d. 1586; king of Poland,
   grand duke of Lithuania), 172n, 175
Stephen, Saint (d. ca. 33; protomartyr),
   415, 438
Stetkevyč, Ivan, 588
Stryjkowski, Maciej (d. before 1593;
   Polish poet and historian), 245, 246,
   258, 260
   Kronika, xxxiii, 155n, 195n123
suffrage, 403, 431–2, 622, 679
Süleyman the Magnificent (d. 1566;
   sultan of the Ottoman Empire), 310
Suraz'kyj, Vasyl' (d. ca. 1598; Ruthenian
   polemicist), 467, 519
Suša, Jakiv (d. 1687; Uniate bishop of
   Chełm, biographer of Smotryc'kyj),
   xviii, liii
Susanna (captive in Babylon falsely
   accused of adultery and saved from
   death by Daniel), 18, 725
Svjatopolk I [Świątopołk] (d. 894; king
   of Moravia), 258–9
Sylvester I, Saint (d. 335; pope), 439, 475
Symanowicz, Tymoteusz (d. after 1621;
   Uniate polemicist), xlii, xlviii, 290n20

Symeon (d. 1488; metropolitan of Kyiv),
   729
Symonowicz, Bogdan (fl. 1621;
   imprisoned Orthodox citizen of
   Vilnius), 191n114
Szeliga, Jan (d. ca. 1637; printer in
   Cracow, Dobromil, Lviv, Jaworów,
   and Jarosław), 573, 687
Szklow (town), 290
Szyszkowski, Marcin (d. 1630; bishop of
   Cracow), 143, 163–4, 167

Tacitus, Publius Cornelius (fl. ca. 100;
   Roman historian and orator)
   Historiae [Histories], 304n51
Tarasius (d. 806; patriarch of
   Constantinople), 561
Tarnowski, Jan (d. 1561; memoirist,
   military writer, orator, grand crown
   hetman, castellan of Cracow), 246
Terence [Publius Terentius Afer] (d. 159
   BC; Roman author of comedies),
   267n60, 275
   Adelphoe, 736
   Andria, 120
Terlec'kyj, Lord Kyryl (d. 1607; exarch,
   Uniate bishop of Luc'k and Ostroh),
   233, 237
Tertullian, Quintus, Septimus Florens (d.
   ca. 220; African Church Father), 20
Themistocles (d. 459 BC; Athenian
   statesman and commander), 86
Theodora (wife of Honorius), 468
Theodore (fl. 1160–1163; metropolitan of
   Kyiv of Greek origin), 245
Theodore Anagnosta [Theodore the
   Lector] (fl. early 6th c.; Byzantine
   Church historian), 532
Theodore of Studios [Studite], Saint
   (d. 826; monastic reformer and
   theologian), 264, 320n96, 417, 475,
   555, 561, 733n114
Theodoretus (d. ca. 466; bishop of
   Cyrrhus, follower of Nestorius until
   ca. 451), 436, 503–4, 530, 555

Theodosius (fl. ca. 1626; metropolitan of Sozopolis), 676

Theodosius I the Great (d. 395; emperor of Byzantium), 530, 660

Theon's tooth, 335, 383, 723

Theophanes III (d. 1644; patriarch of Jerusalem), xxxiv, xxxv–xxxvi, xxxvii, l, lxiii, 105n1, 106n13, 116, 127–33, 134–8, 141–4, 162–7, 210, 212–14, 270, 274, 290, 295n35, 297, 336–7, 338–9, 347, 569, 676
ordination of Ruthenian Orthodox clergy of, 131–2, 336, 341

Theophanes the Stigmatized (d. 845; Byzantine hymnographer, iconodule), 417

Theophano (d. 895 or 896; empress of Byzantium, wife of Leo VI), 550n484

Theophilus (d. 842; emperor of Byzantium), 304

Theophilus I (d. 412; Nicene patriarch of Alexandria), 436, 530

Theophylactus (d. 1126; archbishop of Ohrid, Byzantine exegete), 30, 259, 415–16, 436, 506–7, 520, 634n64, 740
Exposition on the Gospel of Luke, 413–14
Sermon on John 21, 435
Sermon on Matthew 16, 434

Thraso, character in Terence's *The Eunuch,* 275

Thurmair, Johannes [Aventinus] (d. 1534; Bavarian historian)
Annales Boiorum, 65n243

Timothy II (d. 1620; patriarch of Constantinople), 97, 130, 133, 141–2, 212, 547, 632

Timothy, Saint (St. Paul's companion on his 2nd missionary journey and addressee of two Pauline epistles), 430

Titus, Saint (disciple of St. Paul and addressee of one Pauline epistle), 430

transubstantiation, 236, 401, 403, 429–30, 475–6, 621, 679

treason, accusations of, xxxv–xxxvi, xlii, xlix, 16, 107, 126–8, 133, 143, 156, 160, 161–2, 167, 185–90, 208, 219, 336–8, 346. *See also* Smotryc'kyj, Meletij, *Thrēnos,* as treason

Tri-Lingual Academy of Ostroh, xviii

Tryzna, Mikołaj (d. 1640; chamberlain of Slonim), xl, 115

Turks, xxv, xxvii, xxxvi, 127, 209, 212, 296, 315, 364, 366, 458, 490, 491n†, 509, 513, 545, 556, 557–8, 618–19, 633n59, 636n, 657, 711, 715, 735, 744–5

Ţuţora (battle), xxxv, 129n

Twofold Guilt [Sowita Wina], xxxvii–xxxix, xlii, xlv, 241, 243n4, 301

Tysarivs'kyj, Jarema (d. 1641; Orthodox bishop of Lviv after Balaban), xxxiv, 141, 285n4

Tyškevyč, Martyn [Tyszkiewicz, Marcin] (d. after 1595; marshal of the court of the Grand Duchy of Lithuania, son of palatine of Brest, Jurij Wasilewicz Tyszkiewicz), 123

Tyškevyč, Vasyl [Tyszkiewicz, Wasyl] (d. 1571; palatine of Smolensk), 123

Tyszkiewicz [Tyškevyč], Janusz Skumin (d. 1626; notary of the Grand Duchy of Lithuania, *starosta* of Braslav), xl, 115

Uliana of Vicebsk (actually Maria, daughter of Prince of Vicebsk Jaroslav, first wife of Grand Duke of Lithuania Algirdas [Olgierd]; d. 1346), 260

Uniate Church, xv
as apostasy, 155–6, 168–74, 185–90, 197, 208, 215–17, 267, 285–92, 301–4

Union of Brest, xvii, xxii, xxxiv, xxxvii, 108n18, 122, 197n, 237–8
impact on Rus' after, 126, 203–5, 222–3, 225–31, 253–4, 290–1, 652–4, 656–7, 694

Union of Florence, 220–1, 237. *See also* Councils, Ecumenical, Florence

Union of Lublin, 249n, 652

Urban II (d. 1099; pope), 649

Urban VIII (d. 1644; pope), liv, lvi, 381, 650. *See also* Smotryc'kyj, Meletij, letters to Urban VIII

Vaclav I (d. 935 or 929; duke of Bohemia, actually uncle of Boleslav II and Dubravka, martyred by partisans of his brother Boleslav I the Cruel), 258–9

Valentinus (fl. 150; heresiarch), 68

Valerius Maximus (fl. ca. 14–26; Latin writer), 616n

Vicebsk (city), 290

Vievis [Jewie] (town), xxviii

View of the Fight Well Fought . . . , A. See Kortycki, Wojciech

Vigilius (fl. ca. 500; bishop of Thapsus, author of writings against Monophysitism and Arianism), 8n

Vigilius (d. 555; pope), 439

Vilnius, 204, 290
imprisonment of citizens of, 126, 156, 190–4

Virgil (d. 19 BC; poet)
Aeneid, 477n313

Vives, Juan Luis [Joannes Lodovicus Vivis Valentinus] (d. 1540; Spanish humanist and philosopher), 418

Vjaževyč, Hleb (palatine of Smolensk according to Smotryc'kyj, who likely got this false information from Stryjkowski; see Wolff 1885, 55), 123

Vojna, Symeon [Wojna, Szymon Matwiejewicz] (d. 1599; castellan of Brest according to Smotryc'kyj, actually castellan of Mscislaŭ), 123

Volodimer I (d. 1015; prince of Kyiv), 174, 195, 248

Volovyčivna, Rajina (d. 1637; wife of Bohdan Ohins'kyj), xxxi, 85, 86

Vyšnevec'kyj, Mixajil Korybut (d. 1616; *starosta* of Ovruč), xxviii, 4, 150, 362

Vytautas, Oleksander [Witold, Aleksander] (d. 1430; grand duke of Lithuania), 649

Wapowski, Bernard (d. 1535; Polish historian, cartographer, orator), 246

Warning to Rus', A. See Skarga, Piotr, *Na Treny i Lament Theophila Orthologa*

Wasylewicz, Krzysztof (imprisoned citizen of Vilnius), 191n113

Wielbojno (village), 461

Władysław III of Varna (d. 1444; king of Poland and Hungary), 462, 733n*, 734

Władysław IV Vasa (d. 1648; king of Poland, grand duke of Lithuania), lxvii

Wojna, Benedykt (d. 1615; bishop of Vilnius), xxiv

Wołkowicz, Izaak (fl. 1621; imprisoned Orthodox citizen of Vilnius), 191n114, 362

Wujek, Jakub (d. 1597; Polish Jesuit, postillographer, biblical translator), xxix

Xanthopulus, Nicephorus Callistus. *See* Nicephorus Callistus Xanthopulus

Xmel'nyc'kyj Uprising, xxii

Xodkevyč, Hryhorij Oleksandrovyč [Chodkiewicz, Hrehory Aleksandrowicz] (d. 1572 or 1573; Lithuanian hetman, *starosta* of Hrodna and Mahilëŭ, castellan of Vilnius), xxviii, 123

Xodyka, Fedor (d. 1625; *wójt* of Kyiv), 702

Xrebtovyč, Hryhorij (d. 1600; Uniate archbishop of Polack and Vicebsk), 232, 269n69

Zahorski, Stefan (imprisoned citizen of
    Vilnius), 191n113
Zamoyski, Jan (d. 1605; father of
    Tomasz; chancellor and grand
    hetman), lviii, 372
Zamoyski, Tomasz (d. 1638; son of
    Jan; palatine of Kiev until 1628,
    then crown vice chancellor, later
    chancellor), lviii, 372, 375n8
Zaporozhian army, 162, 164–6, 196, 210,
    338, 342
Zasławski, Aleksander (d. 1629; palatine
    of Braclav), lii–liii, lviii, lix, lxiv,
    354, 360, 376, 604, 688
Zbaraski, Krzysztof (d. 1627; *starosta* of
    Pinsk, crown equerry), 129, 138, 143
Zbirujs'kyj, Dionisij (d. 1604; Orthodox,
    then Uniate, bishop of Chełm), 232
Zebrzydowski Rebellion of 1606–1607,
    xxii
Zedekiah (false prophet of the Old
    Testament), 467, 478
Zeno (d. 491; emperor of Byzantium),
    532
Zizanij, Lavrentij (d. after 1634;
    Ruthenian grammarian and polemicst,
    protopope of Korec, brother of
    Stefan), 591, 593

Zizanij, Stefan (d. before 1621;
    Ruthenian author of theological
    and polemical works, brother of
    Lavrentij), lxi, lxii, 374–5, 402,
    406–12, 414–15, 417–27, 428, 440,
    442, 443–5, 450, 455, 460–1, 465,
    467–8, 472, 479, 482, 484, 498, 519,
    524, 543, 548, 551, 554, 592–3, 595,
    598, 609–10, 613–15, 618–19, 621–5,
    629–32, 646, 679, 687, 690, 700, 705,
    708–9, 723, 730, 736
Żółkewski, Stanisław (d. 1620; grand
    hetman and chancellor of the
    Kingdom of Poland), xxxv, 128–9,
    133–4
Zonaras, John (d. after 1159?; Byzantine
    canonist, historian, and theologian,
    high-ranking official at the court of
    Emperor Alexius I), 245
Annales, 195n123, 259
Żórawski, Mikołaj (d. after 1666;
    professor of philosophy at the Cracow
    Academy, author of a neo-Greek
    encomiastic poem at the end of
    Paraenesis dedicated to Smotryc'kyj),
    lxi
Zosimus (d. 418; pope), 170–1